Year	National Income	Corporate Profits with Inventory Valuation and Capital Consumption Adjustments	Net Interest	Contributions for Social Insurance	Wage Accruals Less Disbursements	Government Transfer Payments to Persons	Personal Interest Income	Personal Dividend Income	Business Transfer Payments	Personal Income
		Less:				Plus:				Equals:
1929	84.8	9.0	4.7	0.2	0.0	0.9	6.9	5.8	0.6	85.0
1933	39.9	−1.7	4.1	.3	.0	1.5	5.5	2.0	.7	47.0
1939	71.4	5.3	3.6	2.1	.0	2.5	5.4	3.8	.5	72.4
1940	79.7	8.6	3.3	2.3	.0	2.7	5.3	4.0	.4	77.9
1941	102.7	14.1	3.3	2.8	.0	2.6	5.3	4.4	.5	95.4
1942	135.9	19.3	3.1	3.5	.0	2.7	5.2	4.3	.5	122.6
1943	169.3	23.5	2.7	4.5	.2	2.5	5.1	4.4	.5	150.8
1944	182.1	23.6	2.4	5.2	−.2	3.1	5.2	4.6	.5	164.5
1945	180.7	19.0	2.2	6.1	.0	5.6	5.9	4.6	.5	170.0
1946	178.6	16.6	1.8	6.1	.0	10.8	6.6	5.6	.5	177.6
1947	194.9	22.3	2.3	5.8	.0	11.2	7.6	6.3	.6	190.1
1948	219.9	29.4	2.4	5.4	.0	10.6	8.1	7.0	.7	209.0
1949	213.6	27.1	2.7	5.9	.0	11.7	8.7	7.2	.8	206.4
1950	237.6	33.9	3.0	7.1	.0	14.4	9.7	8.8	.8	227.2
1951	274.1	38.7	3.5	8.5	.1	11.6	10.5	8.5	.9	254.9
1952	287.9	36.1	4.0	9.0	.0	12.1	11.2	8.5	1.0	271.8
1953	302.1	36.3	4.4	9.1	−.1	12.9	12.5	8.8	1.2	287.7
1954	301.1	35.2	5.3	10.1	.0	15.1	13.7	9.1	1.1	289.6
1955	330.5	45.5	5.9	11.5	.0	16.2	14.9	10.3	1.2	310.3
1956	349.4	43.7	6.6	12.9	.0	17.3	16.7	11.1	1.4	332.6
1957	365.2	43.3	7.9	14.9	.0	20.1	18.8	11.5	1.5	351.0
1958	366.9	38.5	9.6	15.2	.0	24.3	20.3	11.3	1.6	361.1
1959	400.8	49.6	10.3	18.0	.0	25.2	22.5	12.2	1.8	384.4
1960	415.7	47.6	11.4	21.1	.0	27.0	25.0	12.9	2.0	402.3
1961	428.8	48.6	13.0	21.9	.0	30.8	26.4	13.3	2.0	417.8
1962	462.0	56.6	14.7	24.3	.0	31.6	29.0	14.4	2.1	443.6
1963	488.5	62.1	16.4	27.3	.0	33.4	32.2	15.5	2.4	466.2
1964	524.9	69.2	18.3	28.7	.0	34.8	35.6	17.3	2.7	499.2
1965	572.4	80.0	21.0	30.0	.0	37.6	39.7	19.1	2.8	540.7
1966	628.1	85.1	24.4	38.8	.0	41.6	44.4	19.4	3.0	588.2
1967	662.2	82.4	27.6	43.4	.0	49.5	48.3	20.2	3.1	630.0
1968	722.5	89.1	30.0	47.9	.0	56.4	53.4	21.9	3.4	690.6
1969	779.3	85.1	34.8	55.0	.0	62.8	61.1	22.4	3.9	754.7
1970	810.7	71.4	41.4	58.6	.0	76.1	69.4	22.2	4.1	811.1
1971	871.5	83.2	46.5	64.6	.6	90.0	74.8	22.6	4.4	868.4
1972	963.6	96.6	51.2	74.2	.0	99.8	80.9	24.1	4.9	951.4
1973	1,086.2	108.3	60.2	92.4	−.1	114.0	93.9	26.5	5.5	1,065.2
1974	1,160.7	94.9	76.1	104.3	−.5	135.4	112.4	29.1	5.8	1,168.6
1975	1,239.4	110.5	84.5	110.9	.0	170.9	123.2	29.9	7.4	1,265.0
1976	1,379.2	138.1	87.2	126.0	.0	186.4	132.5	36.5	7.9	1,391.2
1977	1,546.5	164.7	100.9	140.6	.0	199.3	151.6	38.7	8.2	1,538.0
1978	1,745.4	185.5	115.8	161.8	.2	214.6	173.2	43.1	8.7	1,721.8
1979	1,963.3	196.8	143.4	187.1	−.2	239.9	209.6	48.6	9.4	1,943.8
1980[p]	2,120.5	181.7	179.8	203.7	.0	284.0	256.3	54.4	10.5	2,160.5

ECONOMICS

ECONOMICS

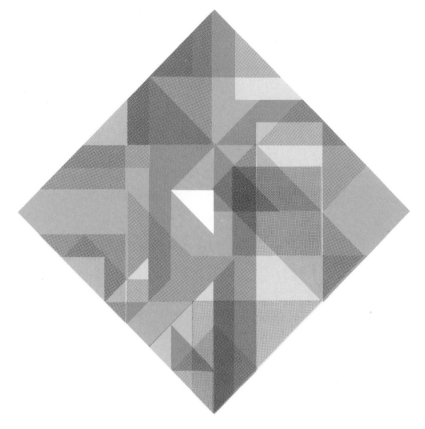

LILA J. TRUETT   DALE B. TRUETT
The University of Texas at San Antonio

WEST PUBLISHING COMPANY

Saint Paul   New York   Los Angeles   San Francisco

Library of Congress Cataloging in Publication Data

Truett, Lila J.
  Economics.

  Includes bibliographical references and index.
  1. Economics. I. Truett, Dale B. II. Title.
HB171.5.F63   330   81-21903
ISBN 0-314-63298-0   AACR2

Copy Editor   Jo-Anne Naples
Artwork   John Foster
Composition   The Clarinda Company

A study guide has been developed to assist you in mastering concepts presented in this text. The study guide reinforces concepts by presenting them in condensed, concise form. Additional illustrations and examples are also included. The study guide is available from your bookstore under the title, *Study Guide to Accompany Economics*, prepared by Kenneth E. Weiher.

PHOTO CREDITS

p. 26 Aristotle—CULVER PICTURES
p. 26 St. Thomas Aquinas—THE GRANGER COLLECTION, New York
p. 27 British East India Headquarters—THE GRANGER COLLECTION, New York
p. 76 Adam Smith—CULVER PICTURES
p. 77 David Ricardo—CULVER PICTURES
p. 78 Thomas Malthus—Historical Pictures Service, Inc., Chicago
p. 78 John Stuart Mill—CULVER PICTURES
p. 79 Millicent Garrett Fawcett—CULVER PICTURES
p. 272 Jean B. Say—Historical Pictures Service, Inc., Chicago
p. 272 Karl Marx—Historical Pictures Service, Inc., Chicago
p. 273 Irving Fisher—CULVER PICTURES
p. 274 John Maynard Keynes—Wide World Photos
p. 516 Jeremy Bentham—Historical Pictures Service, Inc., Chicago
p. 517 William Stanley Jevons—Historical Pictures Service, Inc., Chicago
p. 518 Alfred Marshall—Historical Pictures Service, Inc., Chicago
p. 519 Milton Friedman—Wide World Photos
p. 519 Thorstein Veblen—Historical Pictures Service, Inc., Chicago
p. 520 John Kenneth Galbraith—Wide World Photos

ACKNOWLEDGMENTS

p. 70 Reprinted by permission of *The Wall Street Journal*, © Dow Jones & Company, Inc., 1979. All Rights Reserved.
p. 147 Reprinted by permission of *The New Republic*, © 1980, The New Republic, Inc.

p. 168 Reprinted by permission of *The Wall Street Journal*, © Dow Jones & Company, Inc., 1978. All Rights Reserved.
p. 172 Reprinted by permission of San Antonio Express and News.
p. 221 Reprinted from the March 10, 1980, issue of *Business Week* by special permission, © 1980 by McGraw-Hill, Inc., New York, NY 10020. All rights reserved.
p. 240 Reprinted by permission of *The Wall Street Journal*, © Dow Jones & Company, Inc., 1979. All Rights Reserved.
p. 284 Reprinted by permission of the author and the American Economic Association. Dr. Friedman is Senior Research Fellow, Hoover Institution, and Professor of Economics, University of Chicago.
p. 299 Copyright 1981 Time Inc. All rights reserved. Reprinted by permission from TIME.
p. 304 Reprinted by permission of *The Wall Street Journal*, © Dow Jones & Company, Inc., 1979. All Rights Reserved.
pp. 306–307 Reprinted by permission of AmeriTrust Company, Cleveland, Ohio.
p. 320 Reprinted by permission of *The Wall Street Journal*, © Dow Jones & Company, Inc., 1979. All Rights Reserved.
p. 342 Reprinted from the September 10, 1979, issue of *Business Week* by special permission, © 1979 by McGraw-Hill, Inc., New York, NY 10020. All rights reserved.
p. 365 Reprinted by permission of *The Wall Street Journal*, © Dow Jones & Company, Inc., 1979. All Rights Reserved.
p. 389 Reprinted by permission of the author and the American Economic Association. Dr. Worcester is Professor of Economics, University of Washington.

(Continued on p. 848)

CONTENTS IN BRIEF

CONTENTS

PART TWO

THE ECONOMICS
OF MARKETS:
SUPPLY, DEMAND,
AND PRICES
45

P A R T T H R E E

THE ECONOMICS OF NATIONAL PRODUCT, GOVERNMENT SPENDING, AND TAXATION
97

PART FOUR

◆

THE ECONOMICS
OF MONEY: BANKS,
THE FEDERAL RESERVE,
AND NATIONAL INCOME
203

P A R T F I V E

◆

THE ECONOMICS
OF STAGFLATION,
BUSINESS CYCLES,
AND GROWTH
275

PART SEVEN

◆

THE ECONOMICS OF PRODUCT AND INPUT MARKETS
451

P A R T E I G H T

◆

THE ECONOMICS
OF GOVERNMENT-BUSINESS
RELATIONSHIPS
589

PART NINE

◆

THE ECONOMICS
OF INTERNATIONALISM:
TRADE,
PAYMENTS,
AND GROWTH
653

PART TEN

◆

CONTINUING ECONOMIC PROBLEMS
747

INSTRUCTOR'S PREFACE

Economics is in the limelight today, perhaps more so than at any time since the Great Depression. People are bombarded with economic news and commentary from all sides, and they are acutely aware of the way changes in economic conditions have affected their everyday lives. There is no shortage of confusion and controversy surrounding recent economic developments, and the task of explaining economic change has certainly become more difficult. To introduce a new economics textbook in this setting is no small challenge.

What lies behind our decision to write the present book is a feeling that many instructors have had—that the standard texts can be improved on in ways that will be helpful to both student and faculty users. Specifically, learning can be made more interesting, organization and pedagogy can be improved, and examples that are readily understandable and relevant can be increased. Students can be given a better idea of where chapters are lead-

ing them and where they have been. Finally, it is certainly possible to bridge the gap between textbook economics and the real world by providing students with opportunities to analyze actual economic events and put their newfound economic understanding to work. We hope this preface will show how we have responded to these thoughts and how the book we have produced can improve the principles course and make it a more enjoyable and constructive part of the undergraduate curriculum.

THINGS THAT ARE THE SAME

The content and design of this book respond to surveys of faculty preferences and extensive reviewing by economists from many colleges and universities. Both our own preconceptions about the principles market and subsequent research indicated that the book would have a good deal in common with those that have dominated the field since the early 1960s. For example, there is still a strong preference for a "macro first" form of organization, even though it is mandatory to precede the book's macro chapters with some explanation of markets, demand, and supply. Furthermore, the familiar introductions to the economizing problem and to economic systems and their role in answering the fundamental economic questions of society has become an obligatory part of each book's early chapters.

The sequencing of chapters and topics in the macro and micro sections of this text is similar enough to that of other popular books to allow changing from them to it with only a slight adjustment in class procedures and lecture materials. The book is also available in separate macro and microeconomics paperbacks, making it adaptable to a wide range of programs and academic calendars. Finally, the book offers substantial sections covering the international economy and current economic problems (agriculture, poverty, environmental economics, energy, economic growth, and systems) to allow instructors to specialize in the application of economic principles to specific questions or issues.

THINGS THAT ARE DIFFERENT

We want to make it clear that this text is different from its competitors in a number of important respects. First, we have gone to a great deal of effort to offer a book that is clearer and more readable without being dull. More importantly, it employs a number of innovative pedagogical devices that will help students organize their thoughts about economic analysis and issues.

Front-end Materials

Each chapter is preceded by a brief introductory vignette or narrative called a "Perspec-

tive." The Perspectives use interesting and current economic events to set the stage for the chapter and show how it applies to the real world. They are intended not to provoke a great deal of discussion or analysis but simply to serve as motivational devices suggesting the type of analysis that will be developed in the chapter.

Each Perspective is followed by a list of key topics, entitled "What This Chapter Is About." Important subjects are thus clearly listed at the outset where (1) students will know what to look for as they read the chapter, (2) instructors will easily recognize familiar concepts to be covered, and (3) instructors who prefer to do so can state formal learning objectives related to the items in the list.

Innovations in Coverage and Presentation

Certain chapters of the book either employ new devices or touch on timely materials that will help students understand economic analysis and its current application. For example, the discussion of demand in Chapter 3 clarifies the distinction between a demand function and a demand curve by using a unique set of diagrams which emphasizes the *ceteris paribus* condition while recognizing that quantity purchased depends on factors other than a product's own price. Other innovations in presentation and coverage include the following:

1. A supplementary chapter (Chapter 4) on demand and supply that shows how basic concepts can be used to analyze current market behavior.
2. Treatment of the concept of supply-side economics in the context of the traditional macro chapters.
3. Up-to-date coverage of the Depository Institutions Deregulation and Monetary Control Act of 1980 and the Economic Recovery Tax Act of 1981, as well as discussion of their probable effects.

4. A discussion of international payments, investment, and foreign exchange that emphasizes the role of banks and monetary authorities and can be integrated into the general discussion of domestic monetary economics.

5. Detailed coverage of the economic growth issue, as it affects industrialized nations, less developed countries, and the planet as a whole.

6. A set of chapters on demand and the theory of the firm that clarifies revenue concepts, explicitly treats the connection between production theory and the cost of production, and describes the fundamentals of profit analysis.

7. Two chapters on the microeconomics of public sector decisions that concisely explain both the externalities issue and the steps required to conduct rational analyses of public capital projects.

8. A selection of optional "Special Topics" tailored to allow discretion in depth of coverage of certain theoretical materials and related subjects. Special Topics are found at the end of the related chapter and are printed on alternate color paper.

Not all instructors will choose to use every one of these unique features. Indeed, in a one-semester course such a strategy would not be possible. However, we think that all the features are useful and add to the instructor's flexibility in course design.

Definitions and Cross-referencing System

This book introduces some new design elements specifically intended to enhance students' grasp of basic terms and concepts. Whenever a new term is first defined, it appears in boldface type and is offset from the body of the text along with its definition. The highlighting of terms and concepts is combined with a system of cross-referencing them from one chapter or subsection to another. For example, a student who runs across a reference to "factor of production" on page 34 in Chapter 2 (Economic Systems and Policies) will note that the term is followed by a little box like this: ▫. In the margin, a larger box will contain a reference to page 13, where the original highlighted definition of the concept appears. The book also contains a complete glossary, but the cross-referencing system gives students stronger reinforcement by association of terms with the context in which they are employed. In fact, some cross references are to points in the text where more detailed discussion of a concept appears, rather than just to earlier definitions. Thus, students are encouraged to find out more about the concept once they have been introduced to it.

End-of-chapter Materials

Each chapter concludes with the following learning aids:

1. Summary- A numbered review of the major subjects in the order that they were discussed.

2. Important Terms and Concepts- List of terms and concepts in the order that they were defined in the chapter.

3. Questions and Problems- For student self-testing or assignments, these items frequently test analytical ability rather than memory. Numerical problems related to the chapter's main arguments are provided whenever possible. Answers to odd-numbered questions and problems are supplied at the back of the book, so students can easily check their own progress.

In addition to these learning aids, each chapter has an end-of-chapter reading that appears under the heading "For Discussion." The For Discussion readings have been carefully selected to relate directly to the analysis of the chapter. They are interesting, current, and in some cases just plain fun to read. A set of questions following each of the readings helps students interpret and analyze what they have read and ties the reading back into the chapter.

History of Thought

A brief history of the economists and their ideas is provided as an integral part of this text. To avoid the discontinuities inherent in scattering such materials throughout the chapters on theory, issues, and policies, we have presented them as a four-part essay entitled "Economic Origins." The Economic Origins follow Chapters 1, 3, 12, and 22. This treatment of the history of economic thought allows instructors a degree of choice regarding the use of such material. On the other hand, limiting it to only four parts avoids student confusion about what to read and what to omit.

OTHER TEACHING AIDS

We have attempted in this book to strike a reasonable balance among the verbal, graphical, and numerical methods of description and analysis. Immediately following Chapter 1 is a Special Topic on the use of graphs in economic analysis that serves to acquaint students with coordinate systems, plotting, slopes, and linear versus nonlinear curves. The early chapters also introduce theory construction, marginalism, and both partial and general equilibrium in a way that makes understanding easy. There is a study guide that will reinforce what students learn from the text, and a comprehensive instructor's manual and test bank are available through West Publishing Company.

Study Guide

In collaboration with the authors, Kenneth Weiher has prepared the *Study Guide* to accompany this book. For each chapter of the text, the *Guide* contains a programmed review using a fill-in-the-blank approach. There are also multiple choice questions, true-false questions, and problems which are closely keyed to examples and end-of-chapter problems in the text. Instructors may wish to make the *Study Guide* an optional tool for students, or they may wish to assign specific problems to be handed in for credit. In general, we have found that students who use study guides believe that the guides help them to succeed on exams.

Instructor's Manual and Test Bank

The *Instructor's Manual* to accompany this text is unusually comprehensive. For each chapter, learning objectives are formally stated, and an instructor's guide gives helpful teaching hints and suggestions. The manual includes "capsule" or abbreviated answers to selected end-of-chapter questions and to all numerical end-of-chapter problems. Answers to the questions following the "For Discussion" readings also appear in the *Manual*.

The *Manual* includes an extensive test bank with over 1,400 test items. For each chapter, there are multiple choice questions, true-false questions, and discussion questions. A special feature is the inclusion of "cognate problems." These problems are keyed to specific end-of-chapter problems in the text and provide an efficient means to coordinate test items with work assigned from the book. The primary authors of the *Instructor's Manual* and test bank items are Steven Millsaps and Larry McRae. The cognate problems and answers to end-of-chapter materials were prepared by Ron Ayers. The test bank items are available also on computer tape from the publisher.

ACKNOWLEDGMENTS

A project the magnitude of this book cannot be carried to fruition by authors alone. Scores of people, including survey respondents, reviewers, editors, designers, and typists have contributed to the production process, and all deserve a vote of gratitude. In particular, we are indebted to Clyde Perlee, Editor in Chief, who suggested many of the pedagogical features that appear in the book. His staff and our copy editor, Jo-Anne Naples, did much to refine our work and help us keep up with a very demanding schedule. In addition, our production editor, Bill Stryker, deserves special thanks for his excellent design and his good humored approach to the difficult and tedious task of getting us from a final manuscript to completed book. Also, we especially wish to thank our reviewers, who helped us immeasurably. Their names and academic affiliations follow:

Carl Austermiller, Oakland Community College, Michigan

Charles Berry, University of Cincinnati

Robert Berry, Miami University, Ohio

Ernest M. Buckholz, Santa Monica Community College, California

Robert B. Carson, State University of New York, Oneonta

Ed Cobb, Elgin Community College, Illinois

Brenda Cox, Valdosta State College, Georgia

Robert L. Crouch, University of California, Santa Barbara

Wilford Cummings, Jr., Grossmont College, California

Frank Curtis, Ferris State University, Michigan

John Elliott, University of Southern California

Michael Ellis, North Texas State University

Keith Evans, California State University, Northridge

Richard Evans, Memphis State University

Otis Gilley, University of Texas, Austin

Eric Graber, St. Louis University

Paul F. Haas, Bowling Green State University, Ohio

Kenneth Hise, Valencia Community College, Florida

Minehiro Inouye, El Camino College, California

J. Paul Jewell, Kansas City (Kansas) Community College

Richard Luchessi, American River College, California

Michael Magura, University of Toledo

John G. Marcis, Kansas State University

Sarapage McCorkle, University of Missouri, St. Louis

Gerald S. McDougall, Wichita State University

W. Douglas McMillin, University of Kentucky

Barbara Miller, University of Nebraska, Omaha

Douglas W. Mitchell, Temple University, Pennsylvania

James Nordyke, New Mexico State University

Duane Oyen, University of Wisconsin, Eau Claire

Joseph Pluta, University of Texas, Austin

Earl Purkhiser, Mt. San Antonio College, California

Ron Reddall, Allen Hancock College, California

Bernard Rose, Idaho State University

Richard Rosenberg, University of Wisconsin, Parkside

Robert Ross, Bloomsburg State University, Pennsylvania

Jeff Ryan, McHenry County College, Illinois

Patricia Sanderson, Mississippi State University

Stan Sofas, Santa Barbara City College, California

James Sutton, California State Polytechnic University, Pomona

Tim Tregarthen, University of Colorado

Barbara Vatter, Memphis State University

Joseph Zeigler, University of Arkansas

SUGGESTED CHAPTER LISTS FOR ONE-SEMESTER COURSES

Macro Emphasis*	Micro Emphasis*	Combined Survey
1 2 (Economic Origins I)	1 2 (Economic Origins I)	1 2 (Economic Origins I)
3 (Economic Origins II)	3 (Economic Origins II)	3 (Economic Origins II)
4 (optional)	4	4
5	16	17
6	17	18
7	18	19
8	19	20
9	20	21
10	21	22 24 (Economic Origins IV)
11	22 23 (Economic Origins IV)	5
12 13 (Economic Origins III)	24	6
14	25	7
15	26	8
29	27	9
30	28	10
31	29	11
32	30	12 13 (Economic Origins III)
33	31	14
34	33	15
36	35	
	36	

*International economics, agriculture, and economic systems have been included in both the macro and the micro lists. If students typically take a two-course sequence, a decision will have to be made regarding the distribution of this material.

STUDENT'S PREFACE

Many college and university students complete two or more courses in economics. However, very few people take beginning economics as an elective. It is, instead, a *requirement* for students in business administration and certain social sciences, as well as for economics majors. The latter usually are few in number, and introductory economics classes are thus filled with students whose goal is to become something other than an economist.

Why so much emphasis on economics if only a handful of students will ever get a degree in the field? The reason is simple. In business, government, and everyday life a large share of the most important and frequently asked questions that must be dealt with are fundamentally economic in nature. For example, your choice of a career involves evaluation not only of the purely monetary rewards that the career offers but also the personal satisfaction you get from doing one job rather than another. Both of these are economic questions involving economic choices.

In a very real sense, choices are what economics is all about. As an individual in a free society, your future life will involve thousands and thousands of choices—not just about using your time or choosing your occupation but also about whom to vote for and what kinds of public programs you want or don't want. Economics, in one form or another, will often affect your decision.

In 1981, the Congress of the United States opened its ninety-seventh session with a host of newly elected senators and representatives, many of them Republicans. The Public Broadcasting System checked into their preferences regarding committee assignments. Its report concluded that virtually all of them wanted to be on "money" committees. When asked why, they usually responded that the economy was responsible for getting both them and the rest of their ticket elected—that the state of the economy was *the issue* and that they wanted to serve on a committee where they could do something about it.

No matter where your career may lead, you can bet that it will be filled with economic choices. That is why this book and the course or courses that go with it will be useful to you—not only to fulfill a degree requirement but also to show you how to think about economic events and their consequences. Here is how the book can do you the most good.

TEN HELPFUL HINTS

1. Read all assignments *before* they are discussed in class. If at first you do not understand, read again.

2. Pay attention to the "Perspectives" and the "What This Chapter Is About" lists that appear at the beginning of each chapter. You can use these materials to help orient your thinking about the chapter.

3. Take advantage of the way this book handles terms and definitions. Most important terms are set in boldface type like this: **term.** Definitions are offset into the page margin to make them stand out. In addition, terms are cross referenced from one point in the book to another. When a term is cross referenced, you will see a small white box next to it like this:□. In the margin, you will find a larger box with a page reference. If you go to that page, you will find further information on the term or concept. There is also a glossary of terms at the end of the book.

4. Take your time when you come to numerical examples in the chapters. If you gloss over them, you probably will not get the point.

5. Use the end-of-chapter summaries to review the major points in each chapter. Don't trick yourself into thinking you can read the summaries only and ignore the detailed analyses that appear in the chapter itself.

6. Answer all of the end-of-chapter questions and problems that your instructor assigns. For self-check, answers to odd-numbered questions and problems can be found in the back of the book.

7. A study guide has been prepared to accompany this book. It contains a programmed review of each chapter and many questions and problems that you can use to test your understanding of what you have read or heard in class.

8. To give you a bit of history on the evolution of economic concepts, the text contains a brief history of the economists and their ideas. The history is called "Economic Origins" and appears in four parts (after Chapters 1, 3, 12, and 22). It can help you to understand how the various pieces of economic theory were eventually put together.

9. The "For Discussion" readings that follow each chapter are designed to help you apply the chapter's analysis to an interesting real world problem. These readings come from popular sources and can be fun to analyze. Each reading is followed by a few questions to help you think about its economic content. You can use the readings to test your skills in applying economic analysis.

10. Pay attention to the economic events going on around you. Read the local paper, the *Wall Street Journal*, *Newsweek*, *Time*, *Business Week*, or similar publications. Many of the "Perspectives" and "For Discussion" readings are based on economic news that has appeared in one of these sources. The more you read, the more you will convince yourself of the importance of economic analysis in making personal, business, and social decisions.

A LAST WORD

As textbook writers and professional economists we hope we have given you a product that will make learning economics relatively easy and even, at times, fun. Perhaps you will not take more than one or two economics courses beyond the principles level. At the other extreme, you may find that economics interests you enough to choose it as a major, either in business or in liberal arts. Whatever your choice, we hope you will remember this book and refer back to it frequently as a reference on a broad range of economic questions and issues.

PART ONE

WHAT
IS
ECONOMICS?

CHAPTER 1

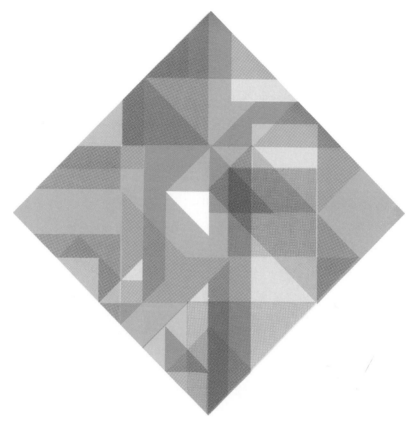

ECONOMIC PROBLEMS AND ECONOMIC DECISIONS

THE
ECONOMICS
AROUND
US

Take a look at the following headlines from a number of recent newspaper articles:

"Exxon Sees Oil Prices Increasing at a Rate 50% Ahead of Inflation"

"Funds for Revenue Sharing Restored on Vote of Senate"

"Measure Creating Superfund to Clean Up Chemical Wastes Is Voted by Senate Panel"

"World Bank Approves Loans to Nine Nations Totaling $726.4 Million"

"South Korea's Trade with U.S. Is Hurt by Protectionism, Growing Competition"

What these headlines have in common is that they are all about economic problems that concern not only national policymakers but also ordinary citizens. Our nation's leaders may find themselves in trouble if inflation hits 20 percent, but their plight may be much less bleak than that of a Florida pensioner who cannot afford a 20 percent increase in living costs or a factory worker who will have to give up the dream of a new home or of college for the kids.

As individuals, we can do two things about the economic events that shape the world. First, we can react to them by adjusting our own decisions in a way that compensates for the changing economic environment. Second, we can try to change that environment directly through our own efforts and through the political process. Either choice requires action based on knowledge and understanding of economic problems. The purpose of this introductory chapter is to take some necessary first steps toward defining economics, identifying economic problems, and developing a framework for analyzing economic events.

C H A P T E R 1

ECONOMIC PROBLEMS AND ECONOMIC DECISIONS

WHAT THIS CHAPTER IS ABOUT

WHAT IS ECONOMICS?
WHY STUDY ECONOMICS?
Social Point of View
Individual Level
SCARCITY AND CHOICE
The Production Possibilities Curve
Principle of Increasing Cost
METHODOLOGY OF ECONOMICS
Observation of Facts
Developing a Theory
Testing the Theory
Applying the Theory
Some Easy Mistakes
SOME FUNDAMENTAL ECONOMIC QUESTIONS
What Is to Be Produced?
How Is This Output to Be Produced?
Distribution : Who Gets What?
Will Future Growth Be Facilitated?
Rules for Choice: The Marginal Approach
Macroeconomic Decisions vs. Microeconomic
 Decisions

The headlines that open this chapter reflect a small fraction of the economic decisions that frequently must be made in the world. How are they made?

One way to make decisions is to throw dice. Another is to pick petals off daisies. This book will offer a third method—economic analysis.

Economics, of course, cannot answer all of the questions that face society; some questions involve ethics and morality, others tradition and law. Nevertheless, economic principles influence all sorts of choices to a greater extent than most people realize. John Maynard Keynes, a famous economist whose writing had a profound effect on national income analysis, put it this way:

The ideas of economists and political philosophers, both when they are right and when they are wrong, are more powerful than is commonly understood. Indeed, the world is ruled by little else. Practical men, who believe themselves to be quite exempt from any intellectual influences, are usually the

5

slaves of some defunct economist. Madmen in authority, who hear voices in the air, are distilling their frenzy from some academic scribbler of a few years back. I am sure that the power of vested interests is vastly exaggerated compared with the gradual encroachment of ideas. Not, indeed, immediately, but after a certain interval; for in the field of economic and political philosophy there are not many who are influenced by new theories after they are twenty-five or thirty years of age, so that the ideas which civil servants and politicians and even agitators apply to current events are not likely to be the newest. But, sooner or later it is ideas, not vested interests, which are dangerous for good or evil.[1]

WHAT IS ECONOMICS?

To most people the word *economizing* probably brings to mind the notions of frugality and efficiency—the opposite of wastefulness. Such people have an idea of what economics is all about—or at least why economics is important.

Economics has been defined informally as the science of common sense and the science of making a living. Certainly, many economic principles discussed later in this book will seem like common sense. Moreover, a knowledge of them may indeed help us earn a living and spend our money so as to get the greatest satisfaction possible. However, economics is much broader than these two definitions indicate.

More formally, *economics* is defined as the study of *how scarce resources are and can be used to satisfy wants and needs.* **Scarce resources** are such things as raw materials, energy, and labor, that can be used to produce goods and services to satisfy human wants and needs. Besides giving businesses and consum-

1. John Maynard Keynes, *The General Theory of Employment, Interest, and Money* (New York: Harcourt, Brace & World; Harbinger, 1964), pp. 383–384.

ers principles that help them achieve their goals, economics also attempts to answer the following kinds of questions:

1. How do we determine what to produce?
2. How can production be carried on with the greatest efficiency of resources and cost?
3. What forces affect how much income each person receives?
4. What alternatives do we have with respect to the use of our scarce resources, and how do our choices affect our future alternatives?
5. Is there any way in which the production and distribution of goods can be changed so that some people will be better off and none will be worse off?

As we will see later, the study of economics can yield answers to such questions for individual consumers, for businesses, for nations, or for the world.

Economics is a science concerned with choosing among alternatives involving scarce resources.

WHY STUDY ECONOMICS?

All societies are faced with a common problem—the need to decide how they will use their scarce resources to satisfy the needs and wants of their people. *Scarcity* refers to the fact that, over a given time period, things (cars, gold, machinery, workers, or love, for example) are limited in number or availability. Many of them occur in amounts too small to satisfy all of people's needs or desires. In other words, *our means are limited, but our wants are unlimited.* Consequently, choices must be made.

Economics includes a description of how such choices are made, but it also goes beyond description. Economic principles yield *decision rules* that tell us how to make choices in order to achieve certain goals. These principles can be stated from both the social point of view and the point of view of an individual economic unit such as a consumer or business firm.

SOCIAL POINT OF VIEW

Many choices involving scarce resources are made from the viewpoint of society as a whole. These choices encompass such issues as:

■ Shall we attempt to reduce unemployment or inflation—or possibly some of both?
■ Shall we raise taxes to finance further production of public goods such as roads and dams, or shall we lower taxes to increase incentives for the production of private goods such as cars and televisions?
■ Shall we use our resources to produce missiles, to construct airports for the rich, or to build low-cost housing for the poor?

In a later section of this chapter, the nature of such choices will be illustrated with a graphical device known as a production possibilities curve.

INDIVIDUAL LEVEL

As indicated above, much of economics is concerned with a description of the alternatives and outcomes of choices from a social point of view. A substantial part of economics, however, is concerned with describing the alternatives available to individuals and business firms. Many of the economic principles that will be discussed later explain how individuals and firms will behave if they wish to achieve certain goals.

This book considers social issues, but it also examines questions such as these:

1. How does a consumer spend his or her income so as to achieve the greatest satisfaction or happiness?
2. How does a business firm determine which combination of resources will allow produc-

tion of a given quantity of output at the lowest possible cost?
3. How does a firm determine what price to charge for its product and what quantity to produce so that it will obtain the greatest amount of profit?

Those who understand economic analysis may increase their chances of material success, but this success is not the only purpose of economic analysis. Like other sciences, economics seeks to *describe* the world and *explain* why it functions the way it does. Practical applications follow from its discoveries, just as space flights follow in part from the discoveries of theoretical physics and astronomy.

SCARCITY
AND
CHOICE

We have emphasized so far the significance of *scarcity*—the limited means to satisfy wants and needs. Because of scarcity, *choices* are necessary. We can illustrate this fact of life through the use of production possibilities curves.

THE PRODUCTION POSSIBILITIES CURVE

A ***production possibilities curve*** *indicates the various combinations of two goods or services that can be produced by a country or other economic entity (an "economy") when, in a technological sense, all of its resources are fully and efficiently utilized.*

Technological efficiency means that resources are combined in the productive process in such a way that none are wasted or used to produce less output than is physically possible.

A production possibilities curve appears in Figure 1–1. Line *AB* shows the various com-

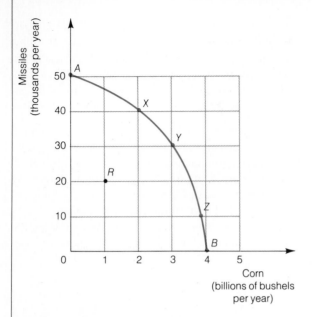

FIGURE 1–1 A Production Possibilities Curve

In this figure we have drawn a hypothetical production possibilities curve for an economy. Points *A, X, Y, Z,* and *B,* respectively, indicate various combinations of missles and corn which the economy could produce if its resources were fully employed. At points inside the curve, such as *R,* resources are not fully and efficiently employed.

TABLE 1–1 **Combinations of Missiles and Corn on the Production Possibilities Curve**

Point	Number of Missiles (per Year)	Bushels of Corn (Billions per Year)
A	50,000	0
X	40,000	2.0
Y	30,000	3.0
Z	10,000	3.8
B	0	4.0

unemployed or inefficiently employed labor. However, since the country's resources must be used as efficiently as possible to produce the combinations of missiles and corn on the production possibilities curve, this country does not have the capacity to produce combinations of missiles and corn to the right of the curve.

PRINCIPLE OF INCREASING COST

*The **principle of increasing cost** states that as an economy produces more and more of one good and less of a second good, the amount of the second good that must be given up in exchange for one more unit of the first good will increase.*

This principle can be illustrated through the use of Figure 1–1 and Table 1–1.

At point *A* in Figure 1–1 the country produces 50,000 missiles and no corn. At point *X* it produces 40,000 missiles and 2 billion bushels of corn. Thus 10,000 missiles are given up for 2 billion bushels of corn (or 5,000 missiles per billion bushels of corn). At point *Y* the country produces 30,000 missiles and 3 billion bushels of corn. Therefore, between points *X* and *Y* it must give up 10,000 missiles for each additional billion bushels of corn, whereas between points *A* and *X* it must give up only 5,000 missiles for each additional billion bushels of corn produced. Thus, as more and more corn is produced, corn becomes increasingly costly in terms of the number of missiles that must be given up

binations of missiles and corn that a country can produce in a given year. If the country produces only missiles, it can make 50,000 of them. If it produces only corn, it can grow 4 billion bushels of it. Other possible full employment combinations of missile and corn production are represented by points *X, Y,* and *Z* in Figure 1–1 and are listed in Table 1–1.[2]

The country can produce any combination of missiles and corn inside the production possibilities curve as well. For example, at point *R,* 20,000 missiles and 1 billion bushels of corn are produced. Here, not all of the country's resources are being used to the fullest possible extent. Consequently, more of both products can be obtained. Such a situation occurs, for example, when a country has

2. Historically, the production possibilities curve has been discussed in terms of the production of guns and butter. See the reading at the end of this chapter.

for another billion bushels of it. (You can verify that between points Y and Z 20,000 missiles must be given up in order to obtain an additional 0.8 billion bushels of corn.)

When we say that corn is becoming increasingly costly in terms of the number of missiles that must be given up for an additional billion bushels of it, we are using the concept of *opportunity cost*. An action (such as producing corn) has an opportunity cost connected with it if it requires giving up the opportunity for something else (such as the production of missiles).

> The **opportunity cost** of doing or choosing one thing over the next best alternative is the forgone benefit that the alternative would have provided.

An opportunity cost does not necessarily involve a money payment; it simply represents an opportunity given up.

The principle of increasing cost holds because resources are not perfectly adaptable between alternative uses. Thus, as resources are shifted out of corn production and into missile production, more and more corn must be given up in order to get a one-unit increase in missile output. For example, at first we may be able to increase missile production by shifting tractor machinists into the job of fabricating missile parts. However, as more and more missiles are built, the opportunities for getting machinists from the corn-producing sector become exhausted. If we are to make more missiles, we must switch farmers, their hired hands, spouses, children, and sheep dogs into missile production. As inputs that are less and less suitable for missile production are switched over to that activity, we must accept greater and greater reductions in farm output in order to get a unit of missile output.

Thus economists would say that the opportunity cost of missiles, in terms of the number of bushels of corn that must be given up to get a one-unit increase in missiles, rises as missile production is increased. In fact, another name for the production possibilities curve is

opportunity cost curve. As long as the principle of increasing cost holds, the production possibilities curve will have the general shape of the one drawn in Figure 1–1. Mathematicians state that the curve is concave toward the origin, or zero point, of the graph.

We know that all of the missile-corn combinations on the production possibilities curve entail a *technologically* efficient use of resources. The question now is: Which combination is *economically* efficient? The pat answer is: the combination of missiles and corn that maximizes the welfare or well-being of society. It is usually impossible, however, to objectively select this combination.

Production possibilities curves involving many other types of goods could be drawn. For example, we could draw such a curve for capital goods□ (machinery, factories) and consumption goods or for national defense goods and capital goods. In either case, the curve would illustrate that the choices which a society makes will affect both its current and its future welfare.

Over time, it is possible for a country's production possibilities curve to shift outward. The increase in productive capacity represented by such a shift may occur because of population growth, the discovery of additional natural resources, advances in technology, or the addition of productive equipment (capital goods). On the other hand, the curve may shift inward if productive resources are destroyed and not replaced.

The principle of increasing cost represents a theory of how substitutable resources can be used to produce various outputs. The next section will briefly examine how economic theories are constructed.

METHODOLOGY OF ECONOMICS
◆

Economic theories are developed in somewhat the same way as theories are developed in the natural science. Economists observe economic events, attempt to find patterns in them, formulate theories about them, test their theories, and finally apply them. Each of these steps is discussed below.

OBSERVATION OF FACTS

As in the natural sciences, the first job of the economic theorist is to observe the events about which a theory is to be constructed. In the natural sciences, such observations may be made easier through the use of controlled experiments. However, in economics, collecting the relevant data or facts is frequently more difficult. (For example, economists would not try to create a depression just so they could better understand its causes and effects.) Still, historical data regarding economic phenomena have been collected by government agencies and are available to researchers. Some data are also available from business firms.

FORMULATING A THEORY

Economists try to find patterns or consistent relationships in the data they collect. They might ask, for example, "Does a decrease in the growth rate of the money supply frequently precede a recession?" Or "Does a decline in the price of a product usually precede an increase in the quantity purchased of that good?"

However, the facts surrounding any single economic event are so numerous that it is virtually impossible to list all of them. For example, we could not analyze all the facts connected with a *single* depression or recession, not to mention those associated with *several* depressions.

Economic theorists try to cope with this situation by first analyzing the facts that they believe are most likely to be relevant to a specific economic event. Next, they look for patterns in the data. For example, they might see that

people's consumption expenditures usually increase when their disposable income increases. From such patterns, economists formulate a theory or model which, if it is to be useful, explains a certain type of economic event.

> An ***economic theory or model*** *is a generalization, based on a variety of facts, about why or how an economic event occurs.*

The theory or model is a generalization because it explains how economic variables generally behave when certain conditions exist. As we will see in the next section, economic theories are usually stated in terms of what will happen in a particular situation *if all other factors remain the same.* Many times, what may at first seem to be an exception to an economic theory occurs because this last condition is not met.

TESTING THE THEORY

Once a theory has been formulated, it must be tested to see if additional data are consistent with (do not contradict) it. The testing process is frequently one of the more difficult aspects of economic theorizing because it is hard to set up controlled experiments. In a *controlled experiment*, all factors other than the ones under study are kept constant. In economics, however, it may be difficult or impossible to maintain such conditions.

The law of demand□ is an example of an economic theory that requires conditions similar to those of a controlled experiment. This theory states that if the price of a product falls, the quantity of it that consumers will buy can be expected to increase, *as long as all other things remain the same.* (Economists frequently say "other things equal" or use the Latin phrase, **ceteris paribus,** to mean that all other things are assumed to remain the same.) But even in the case of a price decrease for a specific product, it is often difficult to keep

52

other things constant. For example, the price of a competing product may also fall. Or personal incomes may fall at the time the price decrease is initiated. In either case, the effect of both changes may actually be a decrease in the quantity purchased of the given product.

Thus, in testing a theory, economists must be aware of the possibility that the *ceteris paribus* condition may not hold. In some cases, they can easily cope with this situation by using statistical procedures. In other instances, however, they face a more difficult dilemma. The problems encountered in the testing of economic theories are responsible for many of the disagreements among economists.

The process of theory construction described above uses *inductive reasoning.* That is, a general economic relationship is induced, or discovered, from a large number of facts.

APPLICATION OF THE THEORY

Once an economic theory has been generally accepted as valid, we can use it to predict the outcomes of specific economic events or to explain these events. In this process we use *deductive reasoning.* With the help of a general rule or theory, we deduce what will happen or why something happened in a particular case.

For example, the *law of demand* states that as the price of a product falls, the quantity demanded of the product rises. We would therefore presume that if the price of shoes falls, *ceteris paribus,* people will buy more shoes. Again, however, it is important to keep in mind the "all other things remaining the same" condition in both applying and testing economic theories. If other relevant factors do not remain the same, we must allow for that fact.

SOME EASY MISTAKES

In the process of inducing an economic theory from the observation of data, we can easily make mistakes in reasoning. Two common errors, the fallacy of composition and the fallacy of drawing false conclusions, are discussed below.

Fallacy of Composition The fallacy of composition can be summarized as: What is good (or bad) for one is necessarily good (or bad) for all.

> *We make the **fallacy of composition** error when we assume that what is true for one person or for part of an economic entity is also necessarily true for society as a whole or for the economic entity as a whole.*

The statements below all involve the fallacy of composition:

1. If an individual saves more out of current income, the person's total savings will increase at a faster rate. Therefore, if all households in the economy increase their saving, the total savings for the economy will necessarily increase at a faster rate.

2. A reduction in a worker's wage rate makes the worker worse off. Therefore, a general reduction in wage rates would necessarily make all workers worse off.

3. If one person stands up at a ball game, that person will have a better view. Therefore, if all the people at a ball game stand up, all will have a better view.

4. If one farmer's fields receive more rain, enabling the farmer to harvest a bumper crop, the farmer will be better off. Therefore, all farmers will necessarily be better off if rains enable all of them to produce bumper crops.

At this point, it may be difficult to see why these statements contain fallacies. However, as some of the topics are covered in more detail later in the book, the fallacies of composition in each case should become clear.

Fallacy of Drawing False Conclusions The fallacy of drawing false conclusions is more formally designated the *post hoc, ergo propter hoc* fallacy. The Latin phrase *post hoc, ergo propter hoc* can be translated as "after this, therefore *necessarily because of this.*"

The ***fallacy of drawing false conclusions*** *refers to the common mistake made when a person observes one thing happening after another and concludes that the first event necessarily caused the second one.*

This mistake can also be designated the fallacy of jumping to conclusions.

We may observe that after we wash our cars, it rains. Does this mean that washing our cars caused the rain? Of course not. In the realm of economics, we may observe that after a certain firm has lowered the price of its product, the firm has gone bankrupt. Was the price decrease necessarily the cause of the bankruptcy? Certainly not. It may have been merely a last-ditch attempt to save the failing business, a move that did not improve the situation enough to prevent bankruptcy.

POSITIVE VERSUS NORMATIVE ECONOMICS

Positive economics *refers to objective economic statements that explain that if certain conditions hold, then certain things can be expected to happen.* ***Normative economics*** *refers to economic statements that involve value judgments or subjective conclusions.*

It is a positive economic statement to say, "Inequality of incomes may be reduced through a system of income taxes." It is a normative economic statement to say, "Consequently, such an income tax system is a good thing." This example does not mean that normative economic statements are bad; it means only that they involve value judgments. Thus they are statements about which intelligent, honest, and compassionate people can disagree.

In general, the chapters that follow this one will be concerned with positive economics. However, often they will analyze the positive economic aspects of issues on which strong normative economic opinions are held, such as unionism and poverty.

SOME FUNDAMENTAL ECONOMIC QUESTIONS

Every society must resolve some fundamental economic issues. Among them are:

1. What is to be produced?
2. How is this output to be produced?
3. To whom is the output to be distributed?
4. What measures, if any, are to be taken now to facilitate future growth?

Each of these issues is discussed briefly below.

WHAT IS TO BE PRODUCED?

Every society must determine in some manner how much of each possible product is to be produced during each period of time. It must decide on how many missiles, how much corn, how many automobiles, how many drill presses, how many computers, and how much of every other possible item to produce. Of course, the amounts decided on must not exceed the ability of the economy to produce the products. In other words, an economy cannot produce output combinations that are outside its production possibilities curve. What is to be produced is an important question because resources are limited or scarce. The society cannot produce as much as it wishes of all goods. Consequently, it must make choices.

HOW IS THIS OUTPUT TO BE PRODUCED?

Once the total quantity of each item to be produced is determined, decisions on how it is to be produced must be made. There are many types of factors of production, or inputs into the productive process.

A *factor of production* is something that can be used in the production of a commodity or service.

Economists usually classify factors of production into four general categories: labor, land, capital, and entrepreneurship.

Labor is a general term for the services of all human beings except for those of entrepreneurs.

Land includes all types of natural resources.

Capital refers to items such as tools, machines, and buildings, used in the productive process.

Entrepreneurship denotes the business owner's innovative ability, farsightedness, and willingness to take risks.

Usually a business firm can use many different combinations of these four factors to produce its product. Each firm must decide on the particular combination of inputs to be used. To do so, it might ask how labor intensive its production methods will be (how much labor will be used relative to machines). It might also ask what type of materials, such as aluminum, steel, or fiberglass, it will use. Also, which business firms will produce particular goods and services and the level of output to be produced by each firm must be established.

DISTRIBUTION: WHO GETS WHAT?

Probably no other basic economic issue causes as much social unrest as that of the distribution of the output of an economy. Somehow, the returns to each type of productive input—labor, land, capital, and entrepreneurship (firm ownership)—must be determined. These returns are classified as wages and salaries, interest, rent, and profit, respectively. They are discussed in more detail in Chapter 24.

Wages and salaries are payments made for the services of labor.

Rent is the payment made for the use of land and other natural resources.

Interest is the payment made for the use of capital.

Profit is the return to owners of business firms for their innovative skills and risk taking.

Other questions concerning the distribution of output must also be resolved. Some of them are: How much assistance should the poor and nonproductive members of society receive? Should taxes be levied? If so, how should the tax burden be distributed? What should be the level of taxes?

WILL FUTURE GROWTH BE FACILITATED?

The answers that a society gives to the questions about distribution will at least partly determine the answer to the last basic question: How will growth be facilitated? Each society must decide at what rate it will use up its natural resources and whether it will attempt to replenish or develop substitutes for those resources.

In addition, the decisions a society makes regarding the *composition*, or mix, of current output—capital goods versus national defense goods versus consumer goods and services—will affect its future production possibilities. Finally, a society must consider the extent to which the quality of the environment is to be preserved and, perhaps at the same time,

long life as it is now known will be able
xist.

Most of these decisions will be discussed in greater detail in the chapters that follow. This chapter closes with a discussion of *marginalism*, an approach to economic decision making that will be used frequently throughout the book. In addition, the difference between microeconomic decisions and macroeconomic decisions will be explained.

RULES FOR CHOICE: THE MARGINAL APPROACH

◆

In most of this book, individuals and firms will be assumed to be making the economic choices under discussion. Nevertheless, in many cases economic decision making by the government will also be considered. In either case, optimal decisions (those that facilitate the achievement of consumer, producer, and social goals) on the part of both the private sector and the public sector involve marginal analysis.

Marginal analysis is the analysis of the incremental or additional benefits and costs associated with a particular activity.

A firm that wishes to maximize its profit will attempt to determine if the production of one more unit of output will add more to its sales revenues than to its costs. Likewise, a government that wishes to maximize social welfare will produce a public good or service until the incremental, or marginal, social benefit of another unit of that good or service is equal to its additional social cost.

MICROECONOMIC DECISIONS VERSUS MACROECONOMIC DECISIONS

◆

Chapters 5 through 15 of this book are concerned with macroeconomic decisions—decisions involving the national economy or aggregate economic variables such as gross national product, government spending, the level of taxes, inflation, and unemployment. *Macroeconomics* deals primarily with explanations of a country's overall level of economic activity. Thus, decisions about the total amount of government spending, new investment, or taxes during a given year are macroeconomic decisions.

Much of the rest of this book (especially chapters 16 through 25), is concerned with microeconomics. *Microeconomics* analyses the objectives and decisions of individual economic units—consumers, firms, government agencies, or specific projects, for example. A consumer's choice about what goods and services to buy is a microeconomic decision. So is a firm's determination of how much output to produce. A government agency's decision about how much to spend on a specific project is a microeconomic decision, but the total amount of the federal budget approved by Congress is a macroeconomic decision.

Before we consider macroeconomic and microeconomic decision making in the context of an economic system like that of the United States, it is important to recognize the existence of other types of economic systems. Thus in Chapter 2 we will analyze how different economic systems find answers to the fundamental economic questions.

SUMMARY

1. Economics is the science of how scarce resources are and can be used to satisfy wants and needs. Because our means of production are limited and our wants are unlimited, we must make choices. Economic principles can explain both how such choices are made and how they should be made if certain goals are to be achieved. Thus a knowledge of economics can help individuals, business firms, and society make choices.

2. Production possibilities curves indicate the various combinations of two goods or services that can be produced by an economy when, in a technological sense, all of its resources are fully and efficiently utilized. Thus all combinations of goods along a production possibilities curve represent an efficient utilization of resources, but all points inside it do not. Choosing the socially optimal combination of goods from the production possibilities curve is difficult.

3. Production possibilities curves usually reflect the principle of increasing cost, which states that as an economy produces more and more of one good and less of a second good, the amount of the second good that must be given up in exchange for one more unit of the first good will increase. The principle of increasing cost holds because resources are not perfectly adaptable between alternative uses.

4. Economists develop theories in the following steps. First, they observe economic events. Then, they attempt to find patterns in these events and to formulate a theory about them. Next, they test their theories. Finally, they apply the theories.

5. Two easy mistakes that can be made when theories are being developed are the fallacy of composition and the fallacy of drawing false conclusions. The fallacy of composition can be summarized as the belief that what is good (or bad) for one is necessarily good (or bad) for all. The fallacy of drawing false conclusions, or the *post hoc, ergo propter hoc* fallacy, refers to the tendency for a person, upon observing one thing happen after something else, to conclude that the first event necessarily caused the second one.

6. Positive economics refers to objective economic statements that explain that if certain conditions exist, then certain things can be expected to happen. Normative economics refers to economic statements that involve value judgments or subjective conclusions.

7. Some fundamental economic questions that every society must answer are:
■ What is to be produced?

■ How is this output to be produced?
■ Who gets what?
■ Will future growth be facilitated?

8. Optimal decisions (those that facilitate the achievement of consumer, producer, and social goals) involve the use of incremental, or marginal, analysis—for example, the effect of buying or producing one more unit of a good or service.

9. *Macroeconomics* is the economics of aggregate variables like inflation, gross national product, and unemployment. *Microeconomics* is the economics of individual economic units such as firms, consumers, and specific projects.

IMPORTANT TERMS AND CONCEPTS

Economics	Factor of production
Scarce resources	Labor
Production possibilities curve	Land
	Capital
Principle of increasing cost	Entrepreneurship
	Wages and salaries
Opportunity cost	Rent
Economic theory or model	Interest
	Profit
Fallacy of composition	Marginal analysis
	Macroeconomics
Fallacy of drawing false conclusions	Microeconomics
Positive economics	
Normative economics	
Fundamental economic questions	

QUESTIONS AND PROBLEMS

1. How would you go about developing a theory to explain the quantity demanded of subcompact cars over some specific time period?

2. Explain what you think economics is.

3. In what ways is a knowledge of economics useful?

4. What is the fallacy of composition? Give an example.

What is a production possibilities curve?

Explain the principle of increasing cost. Give an example.

7. What is the difference between positive and normative economics?

8. Explain the *post hoc, ergo propter hoc* fallacy by using an example.

9. Suppose an economy can produce the following combinations of consumer goods and capital goods when its resources are fully and efficiently employed.

Combination	Consumer Goods (Million Units)	Capital Goods (Million Units)
A	0	38
B	10	36
C	20	32
D	30	27
E	40	20
F	50	0

a. Sketch a production possibilities curve for the economy. (Put consumer goods on the horizontal axis.)

b. If there is unemployment, where will the economy operate? Indicate such a point on the diagram, and label it point *U*.

c. Indicate a point that the economy cannot reach, and label it point *I*.

d. Briefly explain the reason for the shape of the production possibilities curve you have drawn.

TILTING AT REAGAN'S BUDGET

It may not have aided his recovery, but the news must certainly have boosted his morale. The Republican-dominated Senate voted to approve almost all of Ronald Reagan's spending cuts for fiscal 1982 and threw in another $3 billion in budget reductions for good measure. With the President's popularity soaring in the public-opinion polls, draconian cuts in the Federal budget were suddenly a foregone conclusion. The best House Democratic leaders could hope to accomplish was to color the reductions with the more liberal values of their own party—and last week they were attempting to do just that.

Democrats on the House Budget Committee were crafting a spending plan that would restore more than $7 billion to social programs and still cut Reagan's Federal spending proposal by $4 billion. But to pull off that trick, the committee used a familiar tactic: it changed the underlying economic assumptions. Assuming higher levels of inflation and interest rates, committee staffers calculated that the Reagan package would actually yield spending of $720 billion, compared with the $695.5 billion projected by the Administration. The committee then used the higher figure as its target—and produced an alternative budget proposal of $716 billion.

UNHOLY TRINITY

On the surface, there is much in the Democratic package that is politically appealing. Working closely with a group of moderate Democrats known as the "gang of four," House Budget Committee chairman Jim Jones proposed, for example, to restore $1 billion of the $1.8 billion Reagan wants to cut from the food-stamp program. Waste, fraud and mismanagement—Washington's new unholy Trinity—also get attention: according to the committee, $4 billion can be saved. . . .

Nevertheless, the new Budget Committee proposals represent a challenge to Administration priorities and are certain to provide a rallying point for some Democrats. Besides seeking to bolster the food-stamp program, the Budget Committee also wants to restore $1 billion cut out of child-nutrition programs, including school lunches, under the Reagan

©1980 Gamble—Nashville Banner

budget and about half the $1.2 billion taken out of Medicaid. The Democratic proposal would also add money for student loans, economic development, pollution contol, energy conservation and the post office.

On the reduction side, the biggest bite would come out of the Pentagon, with a proposed cut of $4 billion in "nonessential" military outlays, including a scaling back of scheduled pay increases. The Democrats figure they can also save $1.5 billion by partially financing the strategic petroleum reserve by selling "oil-backed bonds" to private investors (NEWSWEEK, March 30). The Budget Committee estimates that as much as $4 billion in spending cuts and revenue gains can be achieved with improved debt and tax collection, reduced paperwork and better procurement policies.

To a large extent, Jones's "markup" reflects the growing influence of the gang of four— Norman Mineta and Leon Panetta of California, Richard Gephardt of Missouri and Timothy Wirth of Colorado. All in their 40s with moderate voting records, they grew into mutual respect while serving on the Budget Committee during the last session. Convinced that the committee had lost control of the budget process, the four began to explore ways to cut spending—and last spring, when Jimmy Carter embarked on his ill-fated quest to balance the 1981 budget, they were suddenly in the limelight. "They knew everything line by line," says one key House staffer. When White House and Congressional leaders emerged from their closed-door sessions with what seemed to be a balanced budget, the four men supported the package. But after a House-Senate conference committee came up with a $5.8 billion increase in military spending, the four led a floor fight that resulted in House defeat of the compromise budget—and earned the men their nickname.

This year, when budget-cutting again became the top Congressional priority, the gang decided to help draft the Democratic position. This time the party was in disarray, and the first task, says Mineta, was "to see how we could help put Humpty Dumpty back together." After sounding out House Democrats, the gang drafted a "statement of principles," chunks of which were translated into the Jones budget markup last week. Skepticism about the Administration's rosy economic projections forced the group to cut more deeply than they had expected, but there was never any question of acquiescing to a deficit larger than the one proposed by the President. "The bottom line is that you don't have a credible alternative unless you're close to Reagan's numbers," Panetta says. "Otherwise it would be an effort in self-flagellation. . . ."

QUESTIONS

1. Does this article involve primarily microeconomics or macroeconomics? Explain.
2. According to the article, what kinds of budget changes were found in the committee proposals endorsed by the "gang of four"?
3. What do the proposed budget changes have to do with the concept of the production possibilities curve discussed in this chapter?

WORKING
WITH
GRAPHS

Graphs are commonly used by professors, students, businesses, government officials, and the news media to illustrate economic relationships. Two graphs depicting some everyday relationships appear in Figure A–1.

Since graphs are frequently used in both the academic and the nonacademic world to depict many types of relationships, the ability to read them—to understand their language—and to draw them is useful. Although graphs may be intimidating at first, their language can be quickly and easily mastered.

FIGURE A–1   Two Examples of Graphs

U.S. Mineral Production as Percent of World Total: 1977

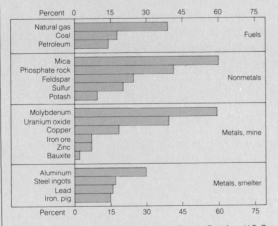

Sources: Chart prepared by U.S. Bureau of the Census. Data from U.S. Bureau of Mines.

National Health Expenditures: 1960 to 1978

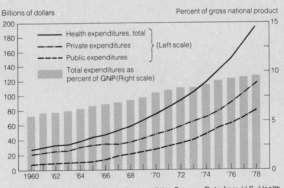

Sources: Chart prepared by U.S. Bureau of the Census. Data from U.S. Health Care Financing Administration.

THE COORDINATE PLANE

In economics, most graphs are drawn in two-dimensional space, or, as a mathematician would put it, in the **coordinate plane.** Two-dimensional space is called a coordinate plane because any point in such a space can be defined by a set of numbers, called coordinates.

Figure A−2 shows two straight lines that intersect each other at right (90-degree) angles. The numbers on the vertical line, labeled Y, decrease in size from top to bottom. The numbers on the horizontal line, labeled X, decrease from right to left. The two lines intersect at zero, which is called the **origin** of the graph.

Any point in two-dimensional space (the coordinate plane, or the XY plane) can be described through the use of these two lines. The coordinate plane is divided into four quadrants—labeled I, II, III, and IV—by the two lines. We can define any point in each of these quadrants by specifying its position with respect to the X and Y lines, which are called **axes.** Thus point A in Figure A−2 can be de-fined as being four units to the right of the origin along the horizontal, or X, axis and three units above the origin along the vertical, or Y, axis.

It is customary to denote these values of X and Y by enclosing them with parentheses and separating them with a comma as (X_i,Y_i), where X_i is the value of the variable on the X axis and Y_i is the value of the variable on the Y axis. The value of the variable on the horizontal, or X, axis is always given first. Therefore, point A in Figure A−2 is given as (4,3). The numbers that define a point in two-dimensional space, such as (4,3), are called **coordinates.** It is essential that the coordinates of a point be listed in the proper order. For example, can you explain why the point defined by the coordinates (4,3) is not the same as the point defined by the coordinates (3,4)? In a similar fashion, point B in quadrant II is defined by $(-2,6)$, and point C in quadrant III is defined by $(-5,-3)$. Can you define point D in quadrant IV?

Since most of the economic variables we are concerned with usually have positive values, we will generally use graphs drawn in quadrant I. Consequently, we will not even draw the other three quadrants in most cases.

DIRECT AND INVERSE RELATIONSHIPS

The coordinate plane can be used to depict any numerical relationship between two variables. In Figure A−3 the straight-line relationship defined by the function $Y = 2X + 1$ is graphed. We can plot this line by picking values for X at random, substituting them into the function, and finding the corresponding values for Y. If we select X values of 0, 1, 2, and 3, we can find the corresponding values for Y and complete this table:

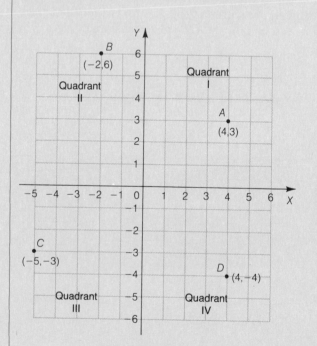

FIGURE A−2 The Coordinate Plane

X	Y
0	1
1	3
2	5
3	7

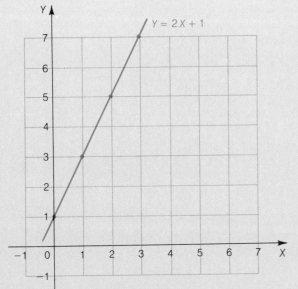

FIGURE A–3 **Graph of Y = 2X + 1**

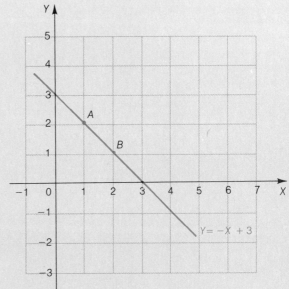

FIGURE A–4 **Graph of Y = –X + 3**

Next, we can plot each (X_i, Y_i) pair of numbers on a graph with the two axes labeled as in Figure A–3. Finally, we can complete the graph by drawing a straight line through the plotted points.

In Figure A–3, the variables X and Y are said to be directly related. Two variables are *directly related* when one increases if the other increases and decreases if the other decreases. In other words, they are directly related if they vary in the *same* direction. A graph of two variables that are directly related slopes upward from left to right.

An inverse relationship between two variables is shown in Figure A–4, which is a graph of the function Y = –X + 3. Two variables are *inversely related* when one decreases if the other increases and increases if the other decreases. A graph of two variables that are inversely related slopes downward from left to right.

Some economic variables are inversely related. For example, the quantities purchased of most products are expected to fall as the prices of the products rise, *everything else remaining constant*. Other economic variables are directly related. For example, consumers'

expenditures are generally expected to rise when their incomes increase, and business firms are generally willing to supply a larger quantity of output at higher prices than at lower prices.

SLOPE

The slope of the graph of a straight-line function, Y = aX + b, is found by dividing the change in variable Y by the change in variable X between any two points on the graph. The change in Y divided by the change in X is written as $\frac{\Delta Y}{\Delta X}$. The Greek letter "Δ" means "change in."

For example, the function Y = 2X + 1 is redrawn in Figure 1A–5. At point A, X is equal to 1 unit and Y is equal to 3 units. At point B, X is equal to 2 units and Y is equal to 5 units. Between points A and B, the change in X is equal to 2 minus 1, or 1 unit. The change in Y is equal to 5 minus 3, or 2 units. Therefore, $\frac{\Delta Y}{\Delta X}$ is equal to $\frac{2}{1}$, or 2.

21

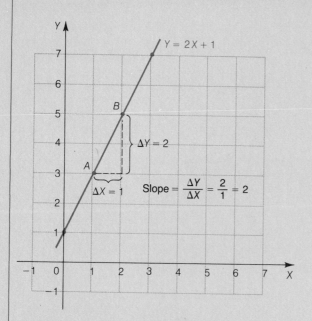

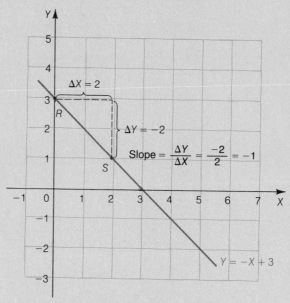

FIGURE A–5 Finding the Slope of $Y = 2X + 1$

FIGURE A–6 Finding the Slope of $Y = -X + 3$

We find the change in a variable by subtracting its old (original) value from its new value. Thus ΔX is equal to $X_{new} - X_{old}$. This expression is often written as $X_2 - X_1$. (In the example above, we would have found the same answer for the slope if we had gone from point B to point A: $\dfrac{\Delta Y}{\Delta X} = \dfrac{-2}{-1} = 2$.)

The graph of the function $Y = -X + 3$ is redrawn in Figure A–6. At point R, X is equal to 0 units and Y is equal to 3 units. At point S, X is equal to 2 units and Y is equal to 1 unit. Between points R and S, $\dfrac{\Delta Y}{\Delta X} = \dfrac{1 - 3}{2 - 0} = \dfrac{-2}{2} = -1$. As the two examples above indicate, the graphs of two variables that are directly related have positive slopes, whereas the graphs of two variables that are inversely related have negative slopes. A slope of 2 in Figure 1A–5 means that Y increases (or decreases) twice as rapidly as X increases (or decreases). A slope of -1 in Figure A–6 means the Y increases (or decreases) by 1 unit for every 1-unit decrease (or increase) in X.

The slope of a *nonlinear function*—one that

cannot be graphed as a straight line—varies from point to point on the function, since its graph is a curve. Nonetheless, a line that is tangent to such a curve can be used to estimate the slope at a given point on the curve.[1] A line is tangent to a curve at a point (such as point A in Figure A–7) if it just touches the curve but does not intersect it at that point. A tangent line can be used to estimate the slope because the curve and its tangent have the same slope and location at the point of tangency. Furthermore, since the tangent is a straight line, its slope can be found by calculating $\dfrac{\Delta Y}{\Delta X}$ *between any two points lying on it.*

For example, in Figure A–7, the slope of the curve OR at point A is the same as the slope of the line drawn tangent to the curve at that point. Between A and A' or any other point on the tangent line the slope of the tangent is calculated as $\dfrac{\Delta Y}{\Delta X} = +2$. This slope is

---

1. The slope of a function that cannot be graphed as a straight line can be found precisely through the use of calculus techniques. It can also be found precisely if the exact slope of the relevant tangent line is known.

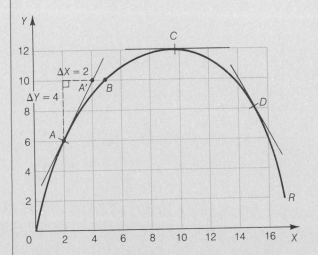

FIGURE A–7 **Use of Tangents to Estimate Slope of Curve**

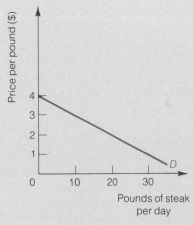

(a) Demand Curve

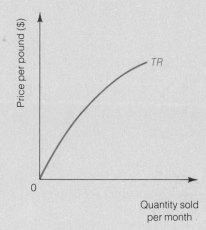

(b) Total Revenue Curve

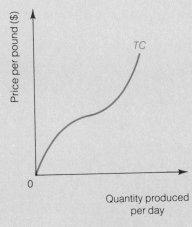

(c) Total Cost Curve

FIGURE A–8 **Three Common Economic Relationships**

also the slope of curve OR at Point A. However, the slope of the curve at point B is not equal to 2, since a line that is less steeply sloped will be tangent to curve OR at point B. Similarly, the slope of curve OR at point C is zero (neither positive nor negative) or $\frac{\Delta Y}{\Delta X} = \frac{0}{\Delta X} = 0$. At point D in Figure A–7, the slope of curve OR is negative, since ΔY is negative when ΔX is positive.

In economics, the concept of slope of a line or curve is frequently used to describe the rate of change of a dependent variable with respect to an independent variable. Usually this rate of change is called the **marginal value** of the dependent variable.

The graphs of three functions typically found in economic analysis are sketched in Figure A–8. Panel (a) shows a demand curve that depicts the relationship between the quantity of a good (steak) that people are willing and able to buy over some specific period of time and its price. In this case the demand curve is drawn as a straight line, though all demand curves may not be straight lines. Usually, however, demand curves slope downward to the right, indicating that price and quantity purchased are inversely related.

Panel (b) shows the total revenue curve for

a firm. A total revenue curve depicts the relationship between the quantity sold of a product and the total sales revenue of a firm. In this case, the total revenue of the firm increases as the quantity sold increases, but at a decreasing rate. Since the slope of this function is not constant, it is nonlinear.

Panel (c) shows the total cost curve for a firm. Although this firm's total cost always increases as the quantity produced increases, it does so at first at a decreasing rate and then at an increasing rate. Thus panel (c) is another example of a nonlinear relationship.

QUESTIONS

1. Graph the function $Y = X + 5$. What is its slope? Are X and Y directly or inversely related?
2. Graph the function $Y = -2X + 3$. What is its slope? Are X and Y directly or inversely related?
3. Graph the function $Y = X^2 + 1$. Is it linear or nonlinear? Explain.
4. Draw a graph depicting an economic relationship.

EARLY IDEAS
ABOUT
ECONOMICS

In ancient times, there were philosophers, monks, and merchants. There was writing about economic matters important to specific societies or nation-states, but there was no formal discipline of economics. No one was called "economist." Thus we must begin our search for the origins of modern economics by looking for ideas and for those who wrote about them. The starting point for our study is ancient Greece, where the two best-known philosophers, Plato (427–347 B.C.) and Aristotle (384–322 B.C.), contemplated how citizens might achieve happiness and the good life in a just society.

Plato and Aristotle discussed economic matters only incidentally; their primary concern was the nature or form of an ideal society and the type of government that would go with it. Yet we owe the modern term *economics* to their culture and language. In ancient Greece, *oikonomia* referred to the management of the household, which might be an estate involving an extended family, artisans, freemen, and slaves. The Greeks, however, generally restricted the use of the term to the household setting; they did not carry it over to policy prescriptions for the state.

What was the ideal state? For both Plato and Aristotle it was a state in which citizens could be free to devote leisure time to self-improvement, that is, improvement of the mind. It was also a state with a rigid class system; in it most physical work was considered degrading for citizens and was therefore left to slaves. Neverthless, Plato noted that specialization, or what Adam Smith would in the eighteenth century call "division of labor," led to increases in productivity and in quality of output. However, Plato believed that the upper classes of society (rulers and warriors) should be unconcerned about profit and should not own private property. In the ideal state, these people would look after truth, justice, and defense while the lower classes pursued economic goals, providing for both themselves and the upper classes.

In Aristotle's view, citizens should accumulate property, including slaves. It would be appropriate in the ideal state to have some people of great wealth and benevolence. To Aristotle, money was not

Aristotle

maxims of management for large, profit-oriented commercial farms that used both slave and free labor. The early Christians (to 600 A.D.) "preached against wanton luxury and irresponsible wealth, they enjoined charity and restraint in the use of worldly goods, but they did not analyze at all."[1] Not even under the great emperor Charlemagne (742–814 A.D.) did any significant economic ideas develop. These ideas awaited the attention of the Roman Catholic Church's finest scholars during the eleventh century and later.

St. Thomas Aquinas (1225–1276 A.D.) was one of many scholastic monks, known as Schoolmen, who wrote about the application of Church doctrine to everyday life. Indeed, the Schoolmen were the teachers and university professors of the Middle Ages, and virtually all intellectual activity centered around their studies. St. Thomas's great work, the *Summa Theologica,* was meant to be a textbook of both philosophy and sacred doctrine.

Aquinas was much less interested in economic than in spiritual matters. Nonetheless, he was compelled to devote certain parts of his text to two issues, just price and interest. On both of these issues he was completely Aristotelian. It would be wrong to charge more than a just price for a good or service, and it would be wrong to collect interest for lending money.

1. Joseph A. Schumpeter, *History of Economic Analysis* (New York: Oxford University Press, 1954), p. 71.

wealth. Wealth was real property—instruments—things clearly useful to the household and the state. In Aristotle's ideal state, useful things also would have exchange value and could thus be traded for other items, but that would not be their main purpose. Further, it would be improper to get wealth through trading, as opposed to artisanry or agriculture. The most improper way to get wealth would be through usury. Money would be used properly as a medium of exchange, a unit of account, and a store of value; but to loan money at interest would be to take advantage of someone else's misfortune.

According to modern scholars in the field of economic thought, very little was added to the economic ideas of the Greek philosophers by either the Romans or the early Christians. The Romans echoed the Greek philosopher's appraisal of the demeaning nature of physical work, but they did prescribe simple

St. Thomas Aquinas—fresco by Fra Angelico.

To Aquinas *just price* meant the price commonly paid for something—a notion similar to that of competitive market price. Other Schoolmen defined *just price* as the cost of production, including risk—an idea that is compatible with long-run price under the modern theory of perfect competition. Despite Aquinas's condemnation of usury, later Schoolmen struggled to liberalize doctrinal views on interest (both the Church and the nobility often charged interest) by defining loopholes and by calling interest by various other names. In the fifteenth century St. Antonio argued that one who lent money could rightfully be compensated for a loss incurred or a gain foregone; today this notion is known as the opportunity cost principle.

The Middle Ages constituted a period of slow but important progress in Europe. Advancements in technology, the emergence of new goods, and the growth of towns led to flourishing trade. Voyages of discovery further stimulated commerce. There arose a class of lay scholars, whose ideas would eventually compete with those of the Schoolmen, and a merchant class that would continue to grow in size and influence. Our discussion now turns to the latter group.

The headquarters of the British East India Company in London—Dutch line engraving, seventeenth century.

Mercantilism is the name attached to a system of government regulation of economic life that became entrenched in Eurpoe during the sixteenth through the eighteenth centuries. It appeared at a time when international trade had grown to be an especially important economic concern and when the new nation-states of Europe, particularly England, France, and Spain, were frequently engaged in wars. Merchants were an important and influential group, because their activities provided both the materials and the wealth that warring monarchs needed to counter their adversaries.

To the mercantilists, who were for the most part either merchants or government administrators, gold was wealth, or at least the most desirable form of wealth for a nation or sovereign to accumulate. Increasing a country's gold stock increased its wealth, and a country without gold mines could get more gold only through international trade. Thus the mercantilists argued for an export balance of trade, a form of trade under which a nation exports more to foreigners than it imports from them, in terms of the value of the goods traded. In the context of the times the excess of exports would be paid for in gold by the foreigners. An export balance of trade would therefore add to a nation's wealth.

Thomas Mun, an official of the British East India Company, wrote a tract in the mid seventeenth century that put the principle as follows:

Although a Kingdom may be enriched by gifts received, or by purchases taken from some other Nations, yet these things are uncertain and of small consideration when they happen. The ordinary means therefore to increase our wealth and treasure is by Forraign Trade, where wee must ever observe this rule; to sell more to strangers yearly than wee consume of theirs in value.[2]

2. Thomas Mun, *England's Treasure by Forraign Trade (1664),* as quoted in Robert Lekachman, *A History of Economic Ideas* (New York: McGraw-Hill, 1976), p. 33.

Typical mercantilist policies in international trade were import tariffs (taxes) on foreign goods, laws prohibiting the export of gold, and navigation acts regulating ocean shipping. (England's Navigation Acts, which penalized colonial shipping and ship-building, were one of the underlying causes of the American Revolution.) As the merchant and administrator classes grew more powerful, their regulations became more widespread and oppressive. Even domestic commerce became highly regulated.

Some of the later British mercantilists, including Mun, fought against certain government regulations, particularly those prohibiting the export of gold. Its export, they argued, was necessary to facilitate the very commerce that would assure England of an export balance of trade. Indeed, some contemporaries of the mercantilists, such as the philosopher David Hume (1711–1776), believed that free trade was the natural order of things and was of mutual benefit to all. Hume noted also that an export balance of trade would be self-correcting, since an inflow of gold would cause prices to rise, making domestically produced goods expensive and imports cheap. However, the free trade doctrine that would capture people's minds was not to appear until the year of Hume's death, when a Scottish philosophy professor, Adam Smith, published *The Wealth of Nations.*

C H A P T E R 2

ECONOMIC
SYSTEMS
AND
POLICIES

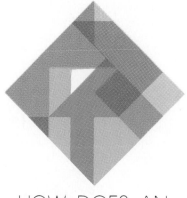

HOW DOES AN ECONOMIC SYSTEM SOLVE ITS PROBLEMS?

What is a "flying squad"? In Warsaw, Poland, it is a band of marauding housewives who swoop down on stores and buy on sight any rice, potatoes, or bread that appears on the shelves. Flying squads have become a way of life in Warsaw because the Polish economy has been failing to perform the tasks of every economic system. Chaos exists in Poland because the questions of what to produce and how and those of distribution and growth cannot be answered by the system of state controlled economic activity in its present condition.

The Polish crisis is attracting worldwide attention, not only because of the country's domination by the Soviet Union but also because the solution to Poland's economic woes will undoubtedly involve a move toward either more freedom of economic activity (as in Western Europe) or stricter state control of the economy (as in Russia). The question really is whether Poland will begin to rely more on markets and on individual responses to economic incentives to organize its national economic life or whether it will move toward a more disciplined type of state control. How Poland answers this question will have a lot to do with both East-West relations and the economic evolution of the Eastern bloc countries.

This chapter considers the nature of an economic system and the alternative forms of economic organization that can shape a society's economic life. The issue of individual freedom of action versus group control of economic activity is important in defining the differences between the various types of economic systems.

C H A P T E R   2

ECONOMIC
SYSTEMS
AND
POLICIES

WHAT THIS CHAPTER IS ABOUT

THE TRADITIONAL ECONOMY
CAPITALISM
Characteristics of Capitalism
Capitalistic Answers to the Fundamental Economic
  Questions
The Circular Flow of Income
Potential Problems under Capitalism
COMMAND ECONOMIC SYSTEMS
MIXED ECONOMIC SYSTEMS

This chapter discusses how the fundamental economic questions are answered under different types of economic systems.

Economic system *refers to the means by which decisions involving economic variables are made in a society.*

Thus a society's economic system determines how the society answers the fundamental economic questions of what is to be produced, how the output is to be produced, who is to get this output, and how future growth will be facilitated, if at all.

Economic systems come in many varieties. Their essential differences lie in the extent to which economic decisions are made by individuals as opposed to governmental bodies or other collective groups, and in whether the means of production are publicly or privately owned. This chapter will discuss four general types of economic systems: the traditional economy, pure capitalism, the command economy, and mixed economic systems.

Throughout this book, references to capitalistic systems will frequently use the terms *market, industry, firm,* and *plant.*

*A **market** consists of all of the potential buyers and sellers of a particular good or service.*

*The seller group is frequently identified as the **industry** that produces the good or service.*

*An individual business organization that produces the good or service is called a **firm.***

*A firm may have many **plants,** or sets of production facilities. For example, General Motors is a firm with plants in Detroit, Flint, Mexico City, and elsewhere.*

31

THE TRADITIONAL ECONOMY

In the **traditional economy,** *economic matters are largely determined by social or religious customs and traditions.*

Frequently, a caste system is present, and movement from one socioeconomic class to another is usually difficult, if not impossible. Traditional economic systems are often found in less developed countries, where they may be an impediment to economic progress.

Tradition may help a society function, but it may also inhibit change. For example, in Africa the Masai tribes have a traditional economy, based on cattle raising, that has functioned for centuries. Everyone's role is defined in relation to the ownership and tending of cattle. Since cattle are the chief form of wealth, families strive to maximize the size of herds. Thus, as the tribes have grown, so have the herds. Pastures are becoming deserts, however, and the Masai are in danger of grazing themselves out of existence. Still, they cling to their rigid traditions, making no adjustments for their changing economic environment.

The recent turmoil in Iran is an example of the conflict that can ensue when pressures to develop economically occur in a traditional economy. Despite any possible failings of his regime, Shah Mohammad Reza Pahlavi made efforts to hasten the economic progress of Iran. In so doing, he aroused the animosity of the Shi'ite Muslims, who wanted the country to be governed according to Islamic laws. The shah's breaches of tradition contributed to his downfall, but a return to tradition as a dominant force in Iranian economic life may well prove the undoing of much of the country's economic progress.

Finally, tradition has left its mark on even the most modern economies. It is why most presidents of U.S. corporations and members of the Soviet Politbureau (ruling committee)

are men, and it is why England still supports a royal family. Such things will change over time, but probably very slowly.

PURE CAPITALISM

Much of this chapter will be devoted to discussions of mixed capitalism and pure capitalism. The reason for this emphasis is that mixed capitalism best characterizes the economic structure of the United States. Moreover, an understanding of how a purely capitalistic economic system operates is helpful in seeing why a system of mixed capitalism has evolved in this country. We will begin by examining the nature of a purely capitalistic economic system.

CHARACTERISTICS OF PURE CAPITALISM

Purely capitalistic economic systems *are based on private ownership and the freedom of individuals to conduct their economic affairs without interference from government bodies or other groups.*

Thus under capitalism we find freedom of choice and enterprise as well as private ownership of the means of production. Although it is not always present, we also expect to find some measure of competition among the various economic entities for jobs or markets.

Freedom of Choice and Enterprise   Under a purely capitalistic system, individuals are free to engage in any type of economic activity they wish, as long as they have the means of doing so. In other words, if they have the necessary ability or financing, and if there is a demand for their services, individuals can choose to be merchants, bankers, bricklayers, teachers, doctors, plumbers, or assembly-line workers, for example. Moreover, they can choose what they wish to do with their income and accumulated wealth—buy new cars, invest in businesses, gamble, or donate to charities, among many other possibilities.

Freedom of enterprise means that people are free to engage in any type of business, so long as they have the required ability and financial capital. No one will insist that John Doe must own a shoe store if he would really rather have a restaurant, as long as he has sufficient ability and financial resources for owning a restaurant. Similarly, Jane Smith is not forced to own a beauty parlor if she would rather have an electrical shop.

Private Ownership *Private ownership* means that individuals own the goods and the means of production in an economy. That is, they own not only the cars, stereos, and houses produced by the capitalistic system but also the factories, land, and their own labor. Private ownership is either less extensive or nonexistent in other types of economic systems.

Competition In a free enterprise system we expect to see many firms and individuals competing with one another. The firms compete for markets and for the consumer's dollar, whereas individuals compete for goods and services that they are willing and able to buy. Prices are kept at levels that reflect the costs of doing business, which include making a profit.

CAPITALISTIC ANSWERS TO THE FUNDAMENTAL ECONOMIC QUESTIONS

Chapter 1 presented four fundamental questions that every economic system must answer in some fashion:

1. What is to be produced?
2. How is it to be produced?
3. Who gets what?
4. Will future growth be facilitated?

We will now examine the capitalistic solutions to these questions.

What Is to Be Produced? Under a capitalistic system what is to be produced is determined by the votes which consumers express in the marketplace through offers to purchase goods and services at various prices, and by the available means of production and their costs. Thus, when consumers wish to purchase video recorders at a price sufficient to cover the production costs, including a reasonable profit, video recorders will be produced if the means of production are available. The same relationship holds for small cars, big cars, hot dogs, pet rocks, prunes, and whiskey.

It is through this system of prices that order is maintained in the marketplace and production of the goods and services that a society wants is stimulated. According to Adam Smith,□ the father of modern economic theory, in a market economy it appears as if an **invisible hand** is guiding economic activity so that the wishes of society are fulfilled, even as individuals work to further their own gain:

> As every individual, therefore, endeavours as much as he can both to employ his capital in the support of domestic industry, and so to direct that industry that its produce may be of the greatest value; every individual necessarily labours to render the annual revenue of the society as great as he can. He generally, indeed, neither intends to promote the public interest, nor knows how much he is promoting it. . . . he intends only his own security; and by directing that industry in such a manner as its produce may be of the greatest value, he intends only his own gain, and he is in this, as in many other cases, led by an invisible hand to promote an end which was no part of his intention. . . . *By pursuing his own interest he frequently promotes that of the society more effectually than when he really intends to promote it.*[1] (Emphasis added.)

How Will the Output Be Produced? Under a capitalistic system, competition presumably

----

1. Adam Smith, *The Wealth of Nations* (1776; New York: Random House, Modern Library, 1937), p. 423.

forces firms to produce their goods and services at the lowest possible cost. Thus, how a good is produced will depend on the available technology, natural resources, capital equipment, and labor—and on the relative costs of these items. For example, if it is cheaper to use a machine than to use human labor to pick tomatoes, free enterprise firms will use the machine. Competition among workers for jobs and among producers of equipment for sales will help determine the costs of labor and machines.

Moreover, the same competitive forces and our own self-interest encourage specialization of labor. As Adam Smith put it:

The greatest improvement in the productive powers of labour, and the greater part of the skill, dexterity, and judgment with which it is anywhere directed, or applied, seem to have been the effects of the division of labour.[2]

As it is by treaty, by barter, and by purchase, that we obtain from one another the greater part of those mutual good offices from which we stand in need of, so it is this same trucking disposition which originally gives occasion to the division of labour. In a tribe of hunters or shepherds a particular person makes bows and arrows, for example, with more readiness and dexterity than any other. He frequently exchanges them for cattle or for venison with his companions; and he finds at last that he can in this manner get more cattle and venison, than if he himself went to the field to catch them. From a regard to his own interest, therefore, the making of bows and arrows grows to be his chief business, and he becomes a sort of armourer. Another excels in making the frames and covers of their little huts or moveable houses. . . . And thus the certainty of being able to exchange all that surplus part of the produce of his own labour, which is over and above his own consumption, for such parts of the produce of other men's labour as he may have occasion for, encourages every man to apply himself to a particular occupation, and to cultivate and bring to perfection whatever talent or genius he may possess for that particular species of business.[3]

_____

2. Ibid., p. 3.

3. Ibid., p. 15.

In a similar manner, we find that it is often advantageous to use roundabout methods of production involving capital equipment.

*The use of capital machinery is termed a **roundabout method of production** because such equipment is made before consumer goods are produced.*

A large tree can be cut down far more quickly with a chain saw than with an ax, and even the ax is a form of capital equipment. An automobile can be made much faster with assembly-line machinery than with hand tools. Thus capital equipment often becomes profitable because the gains in output from its use more than offset its cost.

Who Gets What Output?   In a capitalistic system, who gets the goods and services which are produced is also determined in the marketplace. The people who receive them are those who are *willing and able to buy them*. Therefore, those who desire certain goods or services and have the income or wealth to make their wants known in the marketplace through offers to purchase at the going prices will end up with them. Economists say that these people are expressing an *effective demand*□ for the goods and services.

Of course, the outcomes of these transactions reflect the distribution of income and wealth. In a free enterprise economy the distribution of income and wealth depends on the distribution of talents and abilities and the ownership of other factors of production□ by individuals. The ownership of factors of production can also be determined by environmental factors or circumstances of birth. However, the *worth* of these factors in terms of their ability to generate income is determined by market forces as well.

Will Future Growth Be Facilitated?   In a purely capitalistic system, future growth is determined by individuals as consumers, workers, parents, and owners and managers of firms. In this book it is assumed that the goal of *individuals* is to achieve the greatest level of satisfaction possible (that people want to maximize their *utility*)□ and that the goal of *firms* is to obtain the greatest amount of profit possible. Whether individuals and firms take into account the long-term implications of their current decisions is open to question.

THE CIRCULAR FLOW OF INCOME

Figure 2–1 illustrates the process through which the fundamental economic questions are answered in a purely capitalistic economic system. The system is made up of two basic types of economic decision-making units—households and business firms. Transactions between households and firms take place in two types of markets—factor markets and product markets. In the **factor markets,** households are the suppliers of resources, and businesses are the resource buyers. Businesses purchase the services and resources of individuals, paying them wages, rent, interest,

and profit. Then, the businesses use the productive services and resources they have purchased to produce goods and services, which are then sold to individuals or households. The sales transactions for goods and services take place in **product markets.**

Product prices are established by the activities of independent buyers and sellers in the product markets, and factor prices are established in the factor markets. Thus income moves in a circular flow—from businesses to households and then back to businesses.

Even for a purely capitalistic system, however, Figure 2–1 presents a simplified picture of the economic transactions that occur. For example, some businesses manufacture equipment that they then sell to other firms. Individuals also sell their productive services to other individuals. In addition, Figure 2–1 leaves out the role of money and the financial system in facilitating payments and exchange and borrowing and lending. Nevertheless, the figure captures the general nature of the transactions in a pure market economy.

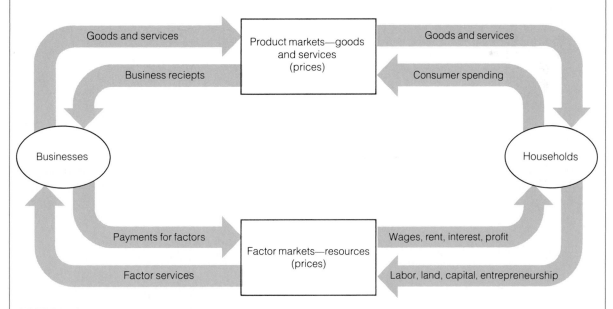

FIGURE 2–1   **The Circular Flow of Income**

In this simplified model of an economy there are two types of markets—markets for goods and services and markets for factors of production. There are also two basic sets of participants in these markets—households and businesses. Prices are determined by the interaction of these participants as buyers and sellers in the two markets.

POTENTIAL
PROBLEMS UNDER CAPITALISM

Although a purely capitalistic economic system allows for free choice and free enterprise, several problems may still arise. These possible trouble spots include a discrepancy between social and private benefits and costs, monopolization, distribution of income, and alienation of workers. Each of these issues will be discussed below.

Social versus Private Costs and Benefits

The **social benefit** of a good or service is the benefit its production brings to a society as a whole.

The **social cost** of a good or service is the cost that society as a whole incurs as a result of the production of the good or service.

Social costs and benefits may or may not be equal to the private costs and benefits connected with the production and consumption of a good or service.

For example, if someone buys a video recorder and neither shares it with the neighbors nor disrupts their lives with it, the private benefit accruing to the owner of the recorder may reflect the total social benefit of the recorder. Moreover, if the cost of production to the manufacturer reflects the cost of all productive resources used in making the recorder, then the social cost of the recorder will be equal to its private cost.

In many cases, however, private benefits and costs do not reflect all the social benefits and costs. For example, if children go to school, the education they obtain will benefit them. An educated citizenry will also benefit society as a whole. Consequently, the social benefits of education, at least up to some point, are greater than the private benefits. If one of our neighbors has a lovely and safe fireworks display, which we have the pleasure of watching, the social benefits of this display are greater than the private benefits. On the other hand, if, in the process of producing a good or service, a firm pollutes the surrounding air and water and does not have to incur the cost of cleaning them up, then the firm's private cost of production is less than the social cost of production.

The problem with a disparity between private and social costs and benefits in a free enterprise system is that firms and consumers make their decisions on the basis of private benefits and costs. They may ignore the total social benefits and costs. Consequently, in a purely capitalistic economy, pollution might be rampant and few people might receive a good education.

Monopolization As indicated earlier, Adam Smith believed that, in a capitalistic economy, people acting to further their own self-interests will promote economic efficiency and the interests of society as a whole. Aside from the other problems discussed in this section, Chapter 20 will show that, under a perfectly competitive industry structure, self-interest *does* promote economic efficiency and the welfare of society.

Perfect competition *exists only when each firm or business is so small, relative to the entire market for a product, that it cannot affect the market price.*

However, nothing inherent in a capitalistic system prevents the formation of monopolies or the achievement of monopoly power such as that obtained by big business or big labor.

Monopoly power *is the ability of a firm or group of firms to determine market price by restricting the quantity of output produced. It generally results in higher prices than would otherwise exist.*

The holders of monopoly power may act to promote their own interests at the expense of the interests of society as a whole. (See Chapters 21 and 22 for more discussion on this subject.)

Distribution of Income   Under a capitalistic economic system the income that individuals receive depends on the productive resources which they own and on how these resources are used. To a large extent, economists believe that this system of income distribution is beneficial to a society because individuals are given an incentive to work, to develop their talents and abilities, and to invent new things.

However, we are not all born with the same level of intelligence or the same capacity to develop musical, athletic, or other talents. Nor are we all born with the same qualities that affect our ability to earn a living. Moreover, environmental factors or other circumstances of birth (such as wealthy parents) may also be relevant in determining income-earning ability.

A purely capitalistic system would imply that individuals who own no productive resources of value in the marketplace should receive no income. However, is such harsh treatment ethical? Most of us would agree that it is not. Nevertheless, what does constitute a just or ethical distribution of income is one of the most divisive questions in any society.

Specialization and Alienation   In a free enterprise system the incentives of the marketplace encourage specialization of labor and capitalization, or roundabout methods of production. However, such methods may also involve monotonous and repetitive jobs and may therefore result in worker alienation and dissatisfaction. These feelings, in turn, may reduce worker efficiency and carefulness. Of course, such problems can occur under any economic system with specialization of labor and capitalization.

Many large firms are now seeking ways to prevent or reduce such problems. For some, the achievement of that goal may mean a modification of assembly line procedures.

COMMAND ECONOMIC SYSTEMS

A command economy is the antithesis of a purely capitalistic economy.

> In a **command economic system,** all of the what, how, and for whom decisions are made on a collective or group basis. Moreover, there is collective ownership of the factors of production.

The group that makes the decisions or owns the factors of production may be some government body or other quasi-governmental group. Economists usually characterize command economies as having *centralized planning.*☐

811

Under such a system the incentives of the market are replaced by decisions made and directives issued by the collective body. The occupations of workers, the quantities of each type of good or service produced, and the distribution of income are determined by the central planners. These planners also decide what provisions, if any, will be made for future economic growth. In the USSR and many other nations with communistic economic systems, the collective body that does the planning is usually the government.

MIXED ECONOMIC SYSTEMS

Most economic systems in existence are neither purely capitalistic nor command. In general, they are a mixture of both. This section will discuss mixed capitalism, which is the system in the United States, and other types of mixed economic systems.

MIXED CAPITALISM

A **mixed capitalistic economic system** exhibits the characteristics of a free enterprise economy in much of its economic activity. However, it also makes some economic decisions on a collective level. Moreover, some of the productive resources or goods typically are owned by a group. Frequently the group involved is some governmental body.

Economic Goals of Mixed Capitalistic Systems   Most mixed capitalistic economic systems share the following economic goals:

1. Economic freedom.
2. Equitable distribution of income.
3. Full employment with price stability.
4. Economic growth.

Citizens of the United States and other mixed capitalistic countries generally wish to live in a society where businesses and consumers have a great deal of freedom to pursue their economic goals. In such a society, businesses can for the most part produce what they want to produce in any way they choose to produce it. Also, individuals are generally free to choose their careers and consumers to purchase the goods and services which they desire, as long as they have the means of doing so.

Most mixed capitalistic systems make efforts to provide an equitable distribution of income among individuals. Although there is much disagreement about what constitutes a fair distribution of income, mixed capitalistic countries generally have some mechanism for assuring at least a minimum level of income for their citizens.

Third, most countries with mixed capitalistic systems want to achieve full employment and price stability. *Full employment* means basically that every person who wishes to work can find a job. These days *price stability* usually refers to the avoidance of large swings in prices, particularly high rates of inflation (general price increases in an economy).

Finally, the goal of economic growth means that the general well-being of individuals should increase over time. This goal is often stated in terms of an increase in income per person.

The Role of Government   What is the role of government in achieving the four general economic goals of mixed capitalism? The responsibilities of government usually include the following:

1. Provision of a legal framework consistent with economic freedom but prohibiting abuses of economic power.
2. Development of policies that adjust for third-party costs and benefits and ensure adequate production of public goods.
3. Promotion of economic stability and growth.
4. Promotion of an equitable distribution of income.

Government in a mixed capitalistic economic system is responsible for providing a legal framework in which all citizens can exercise their economic freedom in the marketplace. For example, governments try to limit the practice of monopolization. As discussed earlier, monopolization occurs when one firm or a few firms acting together restrict the quantity of a product offered for sale, usually for the purpose of maintaining a higher price than would be present in a more competitive environment. This practice typically is limited by antitrust laws□ and various types of business regulations.

In some cases the production or consumption of a good or service is accompanied by externalities.

> *A good or service has an **externality** associated with it if its production or consumption imposes costs on or provides benefits to third parties not directly involved in either the production or the purchase of the product.*

For example, if the production of steel results in air pollution that neither producers nor buyers of steel have to clean up, the pollution

593

is an *external cost* to those who breathe the polluted air. On the other hand, the benefits of an educated citizenry that are obtained by society as a whole are an *external benefit* of the education.

For goods with external costs, government either limits the extent of the production of such goods or it more directly limits the extent of the external cost itself. For example, the U.S. government bans the production and sale of certain drugs (such as narcotics) except under carefully regulated circumstances. It also restricts the amounts of various pollutants that a business can discharge, and it requires certain safety features for automobiles and other products.

The production of public goods generally involves externalities.

A ***public good*** is a good whose benefits cannot be limited to those who directly pay for it.

As mentioned above, education is one example of a good whose benefits accrue at least partly to society as a whole as well as to the individuals who obtain the education. National defense is another example of a public good; it is impossible to restrict its benefits to those who pay federal income taxes. Because of the existence of external benefits, government in most mixed economic systems is involved in the production of such public goods as national defense, education, flood control, and fire and police protection.

Many people in countries characterized by a mixed capitalistic economic system perceive a third function of government to be the maintenance of economic stability and growth. The term *economic stability* generally refers to a situation in which full employment and price stability are both present. Although they disagree on this issue, many economists believe that government, through its spending, taxing, or monetary policies, can and should promote economic growth and stability.

Finally, many people believe that it is the responsibility of government to promote an eq-

uitable distribution of income. In order to do so, a government may transfer income from one group in society to another. For example, it may heavily tax people who earn high incomes and pay benefits to those who cannot work. It may also pass laws to provide job security for workers, prohibit discrimination in employment, and supply pensions for the elderly.

The role of government in formulating and implementing policies consistent with the goals of a mixed capitalistic economic system is a subject that will reappear frequently in this book. The present section has simply outlined the areas where government can be expected to develop policies designed to achieve society's overall economic objectives. More specific discussions of policy alternatives will appear in many of the chapters ahead.

As noted earlier, the economy of the United States is characterized by mixed capitalism. Some goods—national defense, police protection, roads, and dams, for example—are produced by the public sector (government). Some decisions involving what, how, and for whom are also made by one or more government bodies through laws and taxing and spending policies.

In Great Britain, some firms in some major industries (including coal, steel, gas, transportation, and communications) are owned by the government. The government also intervenes in the economy through various policies, such as the imposition of strict anti-inflation measures. However, many sectors of the British economy still exhibit the characteristics of capitalism.

Ideally, a system of mixed capitalism would incorporate all the benefits of a free enterprise economy as well as alleviating the problems that can occur under pure capitalism. Consequently, production would reflect social benefits and costs, and an equitable distribution of income would be maintained. Of course, anyone who reads the newspapers knows that there is a great deal of disagreement about whether the various levels of government in the United States, Great Britain, and other countries with mixed capitalism are performing their economic functions satisfactorily.

OTHER ECONOMIC SYSTEMS

In general, countries with a communistic approach to social and economic organization rely much more on command than market systems to answer the fundamental questions of production, distribution, and growth. As a result, countries such as the Soviet Union, Bulgaria, Poland, and China have found it difficult to coordinate the production of goods and services with consumer demand for output. In addition, their central planners frequently have had trouble maintaining production incentives because rewards (profits) are not always related to the market value of what is produced.

In some cases these countries have used market techniques as a last resort. For example, even though tobacco, the principal crop in the tiny Bulgarian village of Gorna Sushita, is produced, by government decree, on collectively owned farms, families are allowed to grow their own grapes. From these grapes they can make wine, which they can then sell for private profit. One family earned $1,000 in this manner.[4]

Yugoslavia is another country characterized by much collective ownership of the means of production. However, as a result of difficulties with state centralized planning, many firm-level decisions are made by worker committees. Moreover, the workers may receive a share of the profits earned. A system of prices is allowed to operate in a limited fashion.

According to one source, in 1980 the citizens of the Soviet Union did not have sufficient work incentives because of a lack of consumer goods. Consequently, the Communist Party newspaper, *Pravda*, published a proposal that, instead of distributing goods and services "democratically," premium products should be made available to those who want to pay for them. The proposal also suggested that waiting times for certain services be reduced for those willing and able to pay higher prices.[5]

China is also attempting to build an economic system that combines central planning with market incentives. For example, the managements of some factories have been authorized to retain a portion of their plants' profits to invest as they see fit. Moreover, these plants are now permitted to sell some of their output directly rather than turn it all over to the state.[6]

Centralized planning is not necessarily accompanied by public ownership of the means of production. Under fascism, in Hitler's Germany, property was privately owned, but many economic decisions were controlled by the government.

Whatever the economic system of a country, it probably will not be perceived as completely satisfactory by all of the nation's citizens. However, for the most part, the U.S. system of mixed capitalism has worked reasonably well. As a result, and because it is the U.S. economic system, most of the rest of this text will be devoted to a discussion of economic decisions and events within the framework of a mixed capitalistic system. In Chapter 36, however, alternative types of economic systems will be more thoroughly discussed.

Before moving on to macroeconomics, the text examines in greater detail the prime mover in a free enterprise economy—*the market*. Chapters 3 and 4 analyze the roles of supply, demand, and prices in promoting or discouraging economic activity. These tools will be used again and again throughout the book.

---

4. Boyd Gibbons, "The Bulgarians," *National Geographic*, July 1980, p. 97.

5. "A Touch of Capitalism to Spur Soviet Spending," *Business Week*, June 23, 1980, p. 19.

6. "China's Slow Turn toward a Free-Market System," *Business Week*, May 19, 1980, pp. 46–62.

SUMMARY

1. This chapter has discussed four broad types of economic systems—the traditional economy, pure capitalism, command economic systems, and mixed economic systems. In a *purely capitalistic economic system* individuals are free to buy and sell what they wish, so long as they have the financial means of doing so. This system is said to allow freedom of choice and enterprise. Pure capitalism is also characterized by private ownership of the factors of production and of goods and services and by competition in the marketplace.

2. Under pure capitalism, the questions of what, how, and for whom goods and services are to be produced and the issue of future growth are settled in the marketplace through a system of prices. These prices determine the production and sale not only of goods and services but also of factors of production. The system of prices is Adam Smith's "invisible hand" ensuring, at least in the presence of perfect competition, that economic activity is carried on efficiently and in the best interests of society.

3. Several problems may arise under an economic system of pure capitalism. For example, there may be a disparity between social benefits and costs and private benefits and costs. However, participants in a market economy act on the basis of private benefits and costs. Second, nothing inherent in capitalism prevents the formation of monopolies or at least the achievement of some degree of *monopoly power* (reduction of competition). As Chapter 21 will show, market incentives encourage monopoly firms not to act in the best interests of society. Third, in a purely capitalistic economic system the distribution of income is based on individual ownership of factors of production and the value the market places on those inputs. Anyone who cannot contribute to the productive process is not entitled to any income. Although market incentives generally do promote economic efficiency and output, most of us would agree that the distribution of income strictly according to the dictates of a free enterprise system is unjust. Finally, market incentives that encourage specialization of labor and capitalization may result in worker alienation.

4. In a *command economy* all production of goods and services and all ownership is on a collective basis. The nations that have predominantly communistic economic systems have found that it is difficult to achieve their economic goals without market incentives to encourage productive activity.

5. The U.S. economic system of mixed capitalism has been developed at least partly in response to some of the potential problems of pure capitalism. Under a system of *mixed capitalism*, some of the answers to the fundamental economic questions are determined on a collective or group basis. There is usually also some collective ownership of the means of production and perhaps of final goods and services. Ideally, an economic system of mixed capitalism would have all of the advantages of pure capitalism and none of its disadvantages. However, the achievement of this ideal remains elusive. Other mixed economic systems resemble command economies more than capitalistic ones.

IMPORTANT TERMS AND CONCEPTS

Economic system	Roundabout method
Pure capitalism	of production
Command economy	Factor market
Traditional economy	Product market
Mixed capitalism	Social benefit
Market	Social cost
Industry	Perfect competition
Firm	Monopoly power
Plants	Externality
Invisible hand	Public good

QUESTIONS AND PROBLEMS

1. Compare the economic systems of pure capitalism, mixed capitalism, and a command economy. How are the fundamental economic questions answered under each type of system?

2. What are some potential problems that may occur under pure capitalism? In a pure command economy? Explain.

3. In what ways could the economic system of the United States be improved? Explain.

4. What did Adam Smith mean when he spoke of the "invisible hand"?

5. How may striving to promote one's self-interests also further the interests of society?

6. How does a market economy produce incentives for specialization of labor? Give an example.

SOVIET UNION:
A CRITICAL SHORTAGE
OF FOOD

Day after day, the reports surfaced in Moscow. First came the report of two walkouts in the giant automotive-manufacturing complexes at Gorki and Togliatti in the Volga Basin. Then, there was a work stoppage at a tractor factory in the Ural Mountains city of Chelyabinsk. And next, a four-hour shutdown of the giant Kama River truck plant in Naberezhniye Chelny. In every case, the cause was said to be the same: workers' anger over critically short supplies of food.

They are extraordinary—if not unbelievable—stories. Labor

protests are not only rare in the Soviet Union but, in theory, are unthinkable in a system in which the interests of the leadership and the proletariat are presumed to be identical. Diplomats in Moscow concede they cannot confirm the accounts, though they say the reports come from reliable dissident sources and Western businessmen. But Kremlin leaders have moved promptly, and pointedly, to deny the stories—which have gained wide circulation as the result of Western radio broadcasts—and have described them as slander fabricated by the Central Intelligence Agency. Clearly, the stories have touched a sensitive nerve within the Soviet power structure.

. . . The Kremlin is facing

critical problems in providing millions of its people with reliable supplies of milk, meat and other basic foodstuffs. In Tyumen, the Western Siberian city where the Soviets have funneled millions of dollars to develop critical oil and energy reserves, milk, butter, cheese and meat have been in chronically short supply. In Arkhangelsk, in northern Russia, diplomatic sources say milk is sometimes sold only by doctor's prescription or to nursing mothers. Even officially sanctioned Soviet press reports acknowledge that dairy production in the Volga basin is running 45 per cent below planned levels this year. And in Magnitogorsk, in the southern Urals, some families are requesting food parcels from relatives in Moscow, which is traditionally better provisioned than other Soviet cities. But even in the capital, food stocks are lower than usual. Cabbage, which is usually available, disappeared from the market for most of the spring and, for the first time in memory, shops are running out of milk.

PROBLEMS

Food shortages are not a new phenomenon in the Soviet Union. But, as the reports of worker protest suggest, the problem this spring has been especially trying. Some have blamed it on government stockpiling to guarantee a bounty of goods for the Moscow Olympics. Others say that the U.S. embargo has cut into stocks of high-quality feed grains—especially soy and corn— for beef and dairy herds. There has been some distress slaughtering, and a cold spring damaged fruit and vegetable production. But it is more than that: the root causes are the general inefficiency of Soviet agriculture and an erratic food-distribution system. A disastrous harvest in 1975 was compounded by another poor grain yield last year, while the urban population has grown at three times the rate of food production over the past decade. The system simply cannot keep pace.

All this presents the aging Kremlin leadership with increasingly difficult choices. "No one, even those workers in cities like Tyumen or Togliatti, is much

inspired these days by Communist ideology," a Western diplomat told me. "But they do believe that standards of living are getting better. If that belief is eroded or undermined, it would destroy the one thing people believe in. And that, in turn, would remove what is perhaps the government's most important source of legitimacy."

It is true that Soviet workers own more cars and color television sets these days, make more money and wear better clothes than ever before. But when it comes to food consumption, particularly among people living in the rapidly expanding urban centers of central Russia, the Urals and Western Siberia, they are not only finding less food on the shelves than they expect, but in many cases less than was there even a year ago. The Soviet diet is still based on starchy staples such as potatoes and bread. Per capita consumption of milk, meat, fruits and vegetables is no better than it was in 1975—and is substantially below the standards set by Soviet nutritionists.

"DISCONTENT"

Western analysts in Moscow see the pervasive reports of labor trouble as a logical consequence of the dismal food supply situation. Even workers in high-priorty jobs are finding the system is not delivering the goods. "No one is predicting a revolution, and there is not widespread unrest," said a diplomat here. "But I think we are

seeing the beginning of some real unhappiness and discontent."

So far, the reports in Moscow suggest that Soviet authorities have responded to worker protests by moving quickly and quietly to improve supplies of food products. Western diplomats note that two of the cities where protests were said to have taken place, Naberzhniye Chelny and Chelyabinsk, were visited recently by ranking Politburo members. The speculation is that Kremlin leaders—aware that labor productivity is the key to increasing economic growth—see more to be gained by giving in than cracking down.

Given the sluggish Soviet economy and the potential drain of a prolonged military involvement in Afghanistan, the Kremlin's dilemma will not get any easier. Its resources are not limitless. A decision to make more guns quite literally means producing less butter. Unless there is a thaw in the chilly international climate, Soviet workers may find they will have no choice but to keep tightening a belt that already has very little slack.

QUESTIONS

1. What problems in the Soviet economic system does this article mention?
2. What solutions are proposed?
3. How are these problems different from and similar to those that might be found in a capitalistic economy?

PART TWO

THE
ECONOMICS OF
MARKETS:
SUPPLY, DEMAND,
AND PRICES

CHAPTER 3

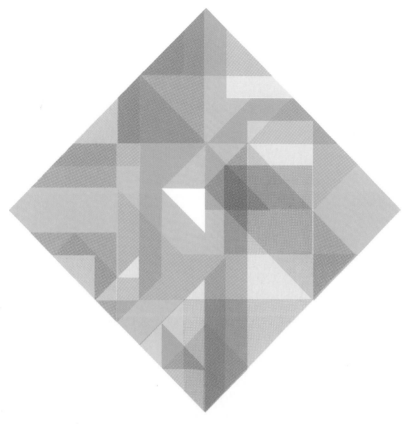

DEMAND
AND
SUPPLY

DEMAND AND SUPPLY DURING DOG DAYS

The summer of 1980 was a scorcher, and the weather had far-reaching economic effects. For example, in Texas, where many cities had thirty or more consecutive days of 100-degree-plus temperatures, shops began to sell "I Survived the Great Texas Heat Wave" T-shirts, complete with a map of the Lone Star State and a bulging, sweating thermometer. Whether the soaring temperatures also created a demand for such apparel is for the income statements of the sellers to say, but we can certainly attribute the supply of the product to the weather. (Can you imaging anyone producing the shirts if there hadn't been a heat wave?)

The hot, dry summer had many other effects on the supply of and demand for various kinds of products. In fact, in late July, the Wall Street Journal reported:

1. Heat damage was reducing supplies of farm products, including corn, sorghum, cotton, soybeans, and livestock.
2. The hot weather was causing significant increases in the demand for beer and ice cream.
3. Demand for residential water had increased so much that city water companies could not function without rationing.
4. Demand had decreased at amusement parks, zoos, and baseball games.

5. Demand for servicing of television sets and air conditioning units had increased substantially.[1]

On the basis of this list of changes in supply and demand, what predictions can be made about the prices of corn, beef, beer, or amusement park tickets? The answers are fairly obvious and will become more so once you are familiar with the tools of demand and supply analysis presented in this chapter.

1. "Heat, Drought Hurt Many Farmers, Firms; But Others Are Helped," *Wall Street Journal,* July 29, 1980, pp. 1, 10.

C H A P T E R   3

DEMAND
AND
SUPPLY

WHAT THIS CHAPTER IS ABOUT

DEMAND CONCEPTS
Demand Function
Demand Schedule and Demand Curve
Change in Quantity Demanded
Change in Demand
SUPPLY CONCEPTS
Supply Schedule and Supply Curve
Law of Supply
MARKET EQUILIBRIUM
PARTIAL versus GENERAL EQUILIBRIUM

In the preceding two chapters we have seen that a capitalistic system, whether pure or mixed, relies greatly on markets and on the free interaction of buyers and sellers to answer the what, how, and for whom questions that every society must resolve. In such a system, prices are the guide to what gets produced, how it is made, and who gets the output. And prices depend on supply and demand.

We know that supply and demand help explain such phenomena as:

■ Why a gallon of gasoline costs more than a gallon of water.
■ Why the price of gold fluctuates widely.
■ Why a professional football star makes more than the average plumber.
■ Why the average plumber makes more than the average schoolteacher.

In short, we know that supply and demand work. The questions is *how* they work. In order to put together a picture of the interaction of supply and demand in a market system, it is first necessary to define a number of concepts related to the amount of any good, service, or resource that people will buy or sell during a given period of time. The first few sections of this chapter define and explain some important demand and supply concepts. Later ones discuss the determination of market prices and the way such prices fit into an overall view of the economic system.

THE DEMAND FUNCTION

Economists recognize that at any point in time the amount of a given product (good or service) that consumers will purchase depends on a number of key variables. For example, the quantity of cantaloupes people will buy in a given market area during a midsummer week may depend on the price of cantaloupes, the prices of cantaloupe substitutes (honeydews and other melons), the incomes of consumers, and the weather. All of these variables play a role in what is called the demand function for cantaloupes.

> A **demand function** is a statement telling how each of a number of relevant variables affects the quantity of a product that consumers will buy during some time period.

In the case of cantaloupes, it would be reasonable to expect the demand function to show that the quantity purchased per week will be greater the lower the price of cantaloupes, the higher the price of cantaloupe substitutes (other kinds of melons), and the higher the incomes of consumers.

Figure 3–1 shows a demand function in diagram form. The sign (+ or −) alongside each variable indicates whether the relationship between a change in that variable and quantity purchased is direct (+) or inverse (−).□ Of the three variables included in the cantaloupe demand function, only the price of cantaloupes is inversely related to the quantity purchased. That is, if the price of cantaloupes rises, the increase will tend to cause the quantity purchased to fall. However, an increase in any of the other two variables will tend to cause the quantity purchased to rise (a direct relationship).

We can conceive of a demand function for virtually any good or service, and the list of variables that have an impact on the quantity consumers will buy may differ from one prod-

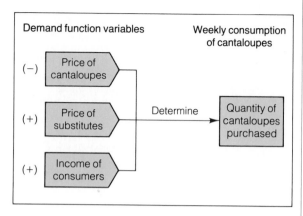

FIGURE 3–1   A Demand Function in Diagram Form

The quantity of cantaloupes consumers are willing and able to purchase per week depends not only on the price per cantaloupe but also on consumer incomes and the price of honeydews (cantaloupe substitutes).

A demand function is usually represented by an equation. An example of a demand function in the form of an equation appears in this chapter's special topic.

uct to another. Usually, the product's own price, the price of substitute goods, and the income of consumers are key variables in the demand function for just about any good or service. However, in a demand function for new houses or automobiles, credit terms or consumers' expectations about future prices may also be important variables. This occurs because the decision to make a purchase can well depend on whether a satisfactory loan is available or on how much higher a price consumers think they will have to pay at a later date if the purchase is put off. Finally, consumer tastes and the number of buyers in the market generally affect the amount of a product people will buy. These variables explain both the birth and death of fads such as designer jeans and citizens' band radios.

DEFINITION OF DEMAND

Generally, a product's own price is among the most important variables in its demand function. Thus, when economists speak of demand, they mean the specific relationship between possible values of this price and the quantities of the product consumers will buy. To define this relationship apart from those between quantity purchased and the other variables in the demand function, the other variables must not be allowed to change. As indicated in Chapter 1, such a situation or assumption is usually described by the phrase *others things equal.* (Sometimes the Latin phrase *ceteris paribus*□ is used instead.) *Equal* in this case means constant.

| **Demand** is the relationship between the various possible prices of a product and the amounts of it that consumers are willing and able to buy during some period of time, other things equal.

Figure 3–2 shows the demand for cantaloupes in diagram form. Here, the quantity of cantaloupes purchased still depends on all three demand function variables, but two of the variables are not allowed to change. Thus only changes in the price of cantaloupes lead to changes in the quantity purchased, even though the other variables can have an effect on purchases if they do change. The point is that when we speak of the demand for a product during some time period, we mean the relationship between its own price and the quantity purchased; we assume that no other demand function variables change.

Finally, it is important to view demand as a "willing and able" concept—something different from consumers' wants or needs. Adam Smith noted in 1776 that a consumer's willingness to purchase something has no impact on demand if the consumer does not have sufficient purchasing power to buy it. "If wishes were horses, beggars would ride," goes the old adage. What beggars lack is the means to make their latent demand effective. In this book the word *demand* will always mean both willingness and ability to buy; the concept is also known as **effective demand**.

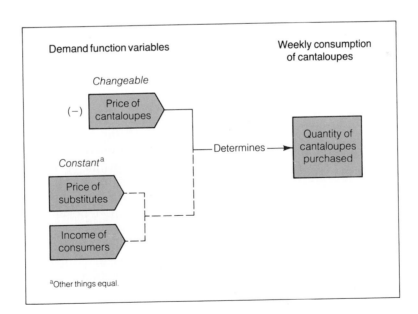

FIGURE 3–2   Demand for Cantaloupes, Other Things Equal

The demand for cantaloupes, "other things equal," is the relation between their price and the quantity consumers are willing and able to purchase, assuming other demand function variables remain constant.

DEMAND SCHEDULE
AND THE LAW OF DEMAND

Returning to the example of cantaloupes, weekly demand for cantaloupes in the local market area is defined as, other things equal, the relationship between the various possible prices of cantaloupes and the amounts that consumers will purchase per week. So defined, the demand for this product is easily represented by means of a table, known as a demand schedule.

*A **demand schedule** is a table showing the relationship between the various possible prices of a good or service and the quantity purchased of that good or service over some period of time.*

Table 3–1 shows the demand schedule for cantaloupes. As the second table heading suggests, it is customary to refer to the amount consumers will buy at each possible price as the **quantity demanded** by consumers. The data in Table 3–1 are inversely related. That is, the quantity demanded of cantaloupes rises as the price of cantaloupes falls. This relationship is in keeping with the law of demand, which was introduced briefly in Chapter 1.

*The **law of demand** states that, other things equal, the amount of a product that consumers are willing and able to purchase during some period of time varies inversely with the price of that product.*

The law of demand has been around a long while. The early British economists Adam Smith,□ David Ricardo,□ and John Stuart Mill□ all struggled with various explanations of demand and price behavior that implied a demand law. However, the first concise statement of the law is attributed to a French economist, Augustin Cournot□ (1838). Cournot's work was not well known in its time, and

TABLE 3–1 Demand Schedule for Cantaloupes

Price per Cantaloupe (P)	Quantity Demanded per Week (Q_d)
$2.00	40,000
1.75	60,000
1.50	80,000
1.25	100,000
1.00	120,000
0.75	140,000
0.50	160,000
0.25	180,000

it was left to Alfred Marshall,□ the great English neoclassical economist, to popularize the law of demand in the late nineteenth century.

On its surface, the law of demand seems a reasonable enough proposition. If the price of something falls, people are likely to buy more of it, especially if no other relevant variables change. Wouldn't anyone buy more Cokes per week at 15 cents per can than at 45 or 60 cents per can? Businesses have sales and publicize them widely because they believe consumers will respond by buying more at lower prices. Certainly, U.S. automobile manufacturers believe in the law of demand, for almost every year they clear out inventory by offering re-*bates*, which are nothing more than price cuts.

Validity of the Law of Demand   There are three good reasons for expecting the law of demand generally to be valid. First, consumers tend to substitute relatively cheaper products for those that are relatively more expensive. Thus, if the price of cantaloupes rises, but the price of honeydews does not, consumers will substitute some honeydews, which are now relatively cheaper than before, for cantaloupes. The tendency to substitute relatively cheaper things for those that become relatively more expensive when a price change takes place is called the *substitution effect.*□ For a price change in a single product, the substitution effect on quantity demanded is always in the opposite direction of the price change. Thus the substitution effect is one reason the law of demand can be expected to hold.

A price change also has an *income effect*□ that tends usually to reinforce the substitution effect. This is understandable if we realize that a change in the price of anything a consumer normally purchases has an impact on the consumer's purchasing power. For example, if the price of gasoline doubles next week, you will probably feel a lot poorer in comparison with this week, especially if your weekly money income remains constant (*ceteris paribus* again). You will most likely purchase less gasoline and less of other goods too, because your purchasing power will have fallen. The reverse would happen if the price of gasoline decreased. Since consumers tend to increase their purchases of most goods when their purchasing power rises and decrease them when their purchasing power falls, the income effect of a price change will usually reinforce the substitution effect and, therefore, the law of demand.

Finally, the law of demand is reinforced by the tendency of individual consumers to become saturated with a particular good. For example, if you are already buying two cantaloupes per week, it is unlikely that you will be willing to increase your consumption to three per week, unless the price falls significantly. Why? Because you already have plenty of cantaloupes for one stomach, and additional cantaloupes will become less and less attractive to you the more of them you have. This phenomenon is known in economics as the *principle of diminishing marginal utility,*□ its name reflecting the idea that additional units of any product become less and less useful or satisfying to a consumer as the person consumes more and more of the product.

To summarize, other things equal, there are three reasons to expect an inverse relationship between the price of a product and the amount of it that consumers will purchase during some period of time: the substitution effect, the income effect, and the principle of diminishing utility.

*The **substitution effect** is a tendency to substitute relatively cheaper products for those that are relatively more expensive.*

*The **income effect** for most products is a tendency to purchase more as purchasing power increases and less as it falls.*

*The **principle of diminishing marginal utility** states that consumers find additional units of a product less and less attractive the more of it they consume.*

The law of demand is reinforced by these propositions, and it can thus be expected to hold for most products. (Exceptions are discussed in Chapter 16 and its special topic.) However, this is likely to be true for any specific product only at a particular point in time or over some short period of time. The reason for such qualification is the "other things equal" assumption. The longer the period of time under study, the more likely it is that some variable other than the price of the product in question will change, thereby affecting the quantity people buy.

THE DEMAND CURVE

If the data of Table 3–1 are plotted in a coordinate system (graph),□ they will trace out the demand curve for cantaloupes.

*A **demand curve** is a graphical representation of a demand schedule.*

Figure 3–3 plots the demand curve for cantaloupes from the data of Table 3–1. That curve is the line D_c. Point A in the figure represents the first entry in the demand schedule: $P =$ $2.00; $Q =$ 40,000 cantaloupes per week. Point C corresponds to a price of $1.00 and a quantity demanded of 120,000 cantaloupes per week. The other (unlabeled) points along demand curve D_c correspond to the remaining price and quantity combinations in Table 3–1.

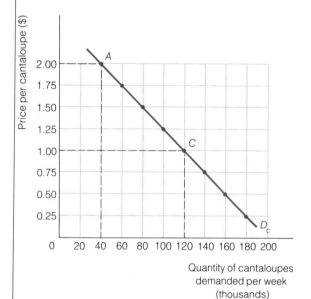

FIGURE 3–3   Demand Curve for Cantaloupes

In keeping with the law of demand, this demand curve slopes downward and to the right. The points marked on the curve correspond to the combinations of P and Q_d shown in Table 3–1. When P = $2.00, quantity demanded is 40,-000 cantaloupes per week; when P = $1.00, quantity demanded is 120,000 cantaloupes per week.

The cantaloupe demand curve in Figure 3–3 is a straight line, sloping downward to the right. Such a line is a convenient way to describe the inverse relationship between price and quantity demanded that corresponds to the law of demand. However, there is no reason to believe that demand curves will always be straight lines (hence the name "curve," rather than "line"). A demand curve could easily bend one way or another, as in Figure 3–4.

For some given product, we might even find a demand curve with a kink in it. The shape of the curve will depend on the data found for the product or on what investigators (economists, statisticians, market researchers) are willing to assume about the data. Some special demand curves will be introduced in later chapters, but for the time being a straight-line demand curve such as that in Fig-

ure 3–3 will serve to explain the basics of demand.

CHANGE IN QUANTITY DEMANDED

The amount of a product consumers are willing and able to purchase at each price in the demand schedule has already been identified as the quantity demanded. Thus a change in the price of a product, other things equal, results in a change in the quantity demanded of that product. Such a change is represented by a movement along the demand curve for the product. For example, in Figure 3–3 a change in the price of cantaloupes from $2.00 apiece to $1.00 apiece will cause a movement along the demand curve from point A to point C, and quantity demanded will increase from 40,000 cantaloupes per week to 120,000 cantaloupes per week.

When a change occurs in the quantity demanded, nothing happens to the demand curve. There is only a movement from one combination of price and quantity to another combination on the same curve. Thus the phrase **change in quantity demanded** is reserved for describing what happens to the amount consumers are willing and able to purchase when a change in a product's own price takes place, other things equal.

CHANGE IN DEMAND

The phrase **change in demand** is used to describe a change in the entire set of relations for a given product's price and quantity demanded. A change in demand will occur when some demand function variable other than the product's own price is changed. In other words, one of the "other things equal" must change in order for a change in demand to occur.

A change in demand will result in a shift of the demand curve for a given product, since every possible price will thereafter correspond to a new quantity demanded. Figure 3–5 illus-

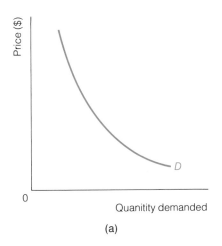

(a)

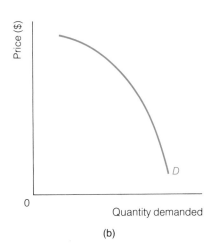

(b)

FIGURE 3–4 Demand Curves That Are Not Straight Lines

Demand curves may or may not be straight lines. Although we recognize that they may curve or bend, we frequently use straight-line demand curves such as that in Figure 3–3 for illustrative purposes.

trates a change in demand for cantaloupes. Suppose that the price of honeydews falls. Since honeydews are one of the goods identified as a cantaloupe substitute in the original

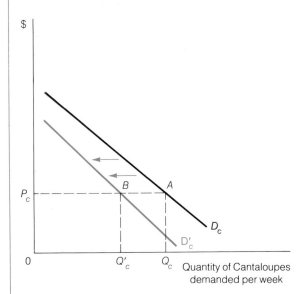

FIGURE 3–5 Change in Demand (Decrease in Demand for Cantaloupes)

A change in demand for a good occurs when a demand function variable other than the good's own price is changed. A fall in the price of honeydew melons causes a decrease in demand for cantaloupes and shifts D_c inward.

demand function for cantaloupes, we can expect people to increase their purchases of honeydews and decrease their purchases of cantaloupes. Thus, at every possible price of cantaloupes, consumers will purchase a smaller amount (quantity demanded will be less). The demand curve will shift inward (sometimes referred to as to the left or downward), indicating that a decrease in demand has occurred.

In Figure 3–5, if the price of cantaloupes remains unchanged at P_c and D_c is the original demand curve for cantaloupes, consumers will purchase Q_c of cantaloupes per week (point A). If the price of honeydews falls, the demand curve for cantaloupes will shift to D_c', where consumers, at point B, will purchase only Q_c' of cantaloupes per week. Furthermore, at every possible price of cantaloupes, the decrease in demand from D_c to D_c' indicates that consumers will reduce their purchases of cantaloupes. Finally, if consumers' demand is initially represented by the demand curve D_c', and the price of honeydews rises rather than falls, the preceding statement will be reversed. Demand will increase, and the demand curve will shift outward (sometimes referred to as to the right or upward). Consumers will thereafter be willing and able to purchase larger quantities of cantaloupes at every possible price.

Every demand function variable other than a product's own price can cause a change in demand. In the preceding example, the demand for cantaloupes changed when the price of a related good was altered. Changes in income, tastes, credit terms, the number of buyers in the market, consumers' expectations about the future, and even advertising can cause changes in demand and can shift the demand curve.

In many cases, it is reasonable to expect that a change in one of the demand function variables will lead to a particular direction of change in demand. For example, the change in the price of a substitute illustrated by the honeydew-cantaloupe case suggests that an increase in the price of a substitute will increase the demand for a given product, whereas a decrease in the price of a substitute will do the reverse. Likewise, for most goods, increases in income will cause demand to increase, whereas decreases in income will cause demand to decrease. Table 3–2 summarizes the expected relationships of changes in a number of frequently cited demand function variables

to changes in demand. The following sections explain these relationships in some detail.

Income Changes and Demand Although it is reasonable to expect an increase in consumers' incomes to cause an outward shift in the demand curve for a particular item, this is not always the case. Economists say that a good is "normal" with respect to income if its demand curve shifts outward when incomes increase and inward when incomes decrease, other things equal. However, they have also identified some goods and services that have the opposite relationship to changes in income. They have called them inferior goods and services.

*If a good or service is **normal,** consumers will buy more of it when their incomes rise and less of it when their incomes fall. For **inferior goods** or services the opposite occurs.*

It has been argued that hamburger is an inferior good for some consumers, since when their incomes go up, they reduce their hamburger consumption and switch to higher quality beef, such as steaks and roasts. Black-and-white television sets can also be viewed

---

TABLE 3–2 Expected Relationships of Selected Variables to Changes in Demand

Variable	Change in Variable	Change in Demand	Shift in Demand Curve
Income (usual or "normal" good" case)	Increase	Increase	Outward
	Decrease	Decrease	Inward
Price of related good or service			
(a) Substitute (used instead of good or service in question)	Increase	Increase	Outward
	Decrease	Decrease	Inward
(b) Complement (used with good or service in question)	Increase	Decrease	Inward
	Decrease	Increase	Outward
Credit terms	Improvement	Increase	Outward
	Worsening	Decrease	Inward
Number of buyers	Increase	Increase	Outward
	Decrease	Decrease	Inward
Advertising	Increase	Increase	Outward
	Decrease	Decrease	Inward

as an inferior good, since rising incomes may well be accompanied by falling purchases of such sets and rising purchases of more expensive color televisions. Thus the relationships of income to shifts in the demand curve that are listed in Table 3–2 are not hard and fast; they are just the ones expected for so-called normal goods.

Substitutes and Complements

Two goods or services are **substitutes** *if one can be used in place of the other.*

The cantaloupe example of Figures 3–3 and 3–5 noted that some consumers would view honeydews as substitutes for cantaloupes— that when the price of honeydews increased, the quantity of cantaloupes bought also would increase. This is so because some potential purchasers of honeydews would switch to cantaloupes when the price of the competing fruit rose. Likewise, a fall in the price of honeydews would reduce the quantity of cantaloupes bought, since some buyers would switch to the substitutes.

As Table 3–2 shows, an increase in the price of a substitute will shift the demand curve for a given good or service outward, but a decrease in the price of a substitute will shift the demand curve for a related good or service inward. Some additional examples of substitutes are coffee and tea, margarine and butter, Fords and Chevys, movies and television. Obviously, the degree to which a change in the price of one of these items will affect the quantity bought or sold of its particular substitute varies from good to good, but each pair of goods in this list can be expected to have a substitute-type relationship.

Complements *are goods that are used with one another.*

As Table 3–2 also shows, we can expect the quantity of a good to adjust in a direction opposite to that of a price change in another good that is its complement. We should expect this result because the good whose price has changed will most likely obey the law of demand.

For example, coffee and cream are complements. If the price of coffee increases, people will probably buy less coffee. Because many people drink their coffee with cream, a reduction in the quantity of coffee bought will reduce the demand for cream. The demand curve for cream will therefore shift inward. The reverse would happen if the price of coffee were to fall. Other examples of goods that are complements are cameras and film, records and record players, automobiles and gasoline, and bread and butter.

CREDIT TERMS, NUMBER OF BUYERS, AND ADVERTISING

In general, if credit terms improve, people's ability to buy will be enhanced, and demand will increase. Worsening credit terms will decrease demand. Credit terms have a lot to do with the demand for relatively expensive goods that last a long time (known as *durable goods*), such as cars, major appliances, and houses. Demand for all of these goods tends to decrease when interest rates are high and loans are hard to get and to increase when the reverse occurs.

When the number of buyers in the market for a given product increases, demand for that product will increase. This often happens with new products, since it takes a while for consumers to find out about them. If the product catches on, demand increases dramatically. In the case of fads (recall the citizens' band radio example) it may decrease just as dramatically some time later. Migration of consumers into a market area will also increase market demand for specific products. For example, the demand for housing has increased in the southern United States because of the "sunbelt effect," a popular term for a host of factors causing people to move south.

Finally, advertising, if it does what its sponsors hope it will do, should increase demand when its use is increased and decrease demand when its use is reduced. However, many economists hold that when rival firms engage in advertising campaigns, they simply cancel each other out. If these economists are right, all the advertising for Coke, Pepsi, and RC has no effect on the general level of demand for cola. However, the effects of advertising are still being debated.

AN INDIVIDUAL'S DEMAND VERSUS MARKET DEMAND

Up to now, our examples of demand have dealt with the market demand curve of a group of consumers. However, it is useful to relate the demand of a single individual to market demand, since the latter depends on how each single person changes his or her quantity demanded as the price of a given product changes. To begin, suppose that each person's behavior is governed by the income and substitution effects and the principle of diminishing utility, as described earlier. Each single consumer will then have, for any given product, an individual demand curve that obeys

the law of demand. For example, if there are only two people in the local cantaloupe market, you and me, each of us will have a demand curve for cantaloupes. Furthermore, the market demand curve will be related in a very specific way to your demand curve and to my demand curve, because the demand of the two of us is the market demand.

To get the market demand curve for our hypothetical, two-person cantaloupe market, we must add my quantity demanded to your quantity demanded for each possible price of cantaloupes. This is done in Figure 3–6, where the aggregate of your demand curve and my demand curve is the market demand curve. Again, what we have done is to add the quantity you will buy at P_c (quantity Q_{y1}) to the quantity I will buy at P_c (quantity Q_{m1}) to obtain the market quantity demanded at P_c—quantity Q_1^*. At price P'_c, we add Q_{y2} and Q_{m2} and get market quantity Q_2^*. This process is known as *calculating a horizontal sum*. The reason for this phrase is that we have summed horizontally the values on the Q axes of the two individuals' diagrams to get the market value for a given P coordinate on the vertical axis.

The conclusion to draw from Figure 3–6 and the described process is the following.

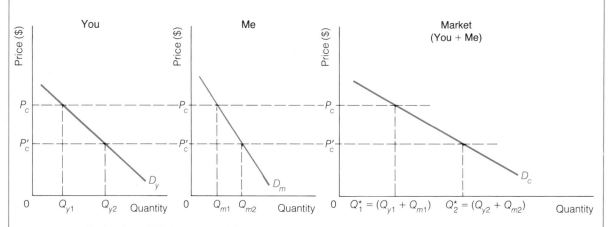

FIGURE 3–6 Derivation of Market Demand Curve

If you and I are the only people in this market, market demand *(D_c)* can be found by summing your quantity demanded plus my quantity demanded at each possible price. This is known as finding a *horizontal sum*.

*The **market demand curve** for a product is the horizontal sum of the demand curves of the individual consumers in the market.*

The market demand curve will slope downward to the right because the curves of the individual consumers slope that way. Furthermore, any change in the number of consumers will shift the demand curve. As stated above, if the number of consumers increases, the market demand curve will shift outward. If the number of consumers decreases, the reverse will occur. Anything that will shift the demand curve of an individual consumer in the market (such as changes in income or prices of related goods) will also shift the market demand curve.

In Chapter 16 the relationship between individual consumer behavior and market demand will be more thoroughly examined. At this point, however, we change our focus from the nature of demand to the nature of supply. In the last two sections of this chapter demand will again enter the picture, when the determination of market price and a general equilibrium are discussed.

SUPPLY
CONCEPTS

In this section we introduce the supply side of markets. First, a supply function is defined, and then the nature of a supply curve and the law of supply are explained.

SUPPLY FUNCTIONS

*A **supply function** describes the relationship between the quantity of a product supplied and a set of variables that determine it.*

Quantity supplied means the amount of a good or service that producers will make available for sale during a particular period of time. Usually, this amount depends primarily on the price of the good or service being sold, but a number of other variables may also be important. For example, the prices of inputs that businesses must buy in order to manufacture or distribute their product certainly affect the amount of output they will be willing to produce and sell at any given price. Other variables that often affect the amount that suppliers will offer for sale are technology, the prices of related goods, expectations about future market conditions, the number of suppliers in the market, and motives or objectives regarding profit and other producer goals.

SUPPLY SCHEDULES AND SUPPLY CURVES

When all the variables of the supply function other than the price of the good or service itself are constant, we can define the *supply schedule*, which relates the price of a good to the quantity supplied. If we return to the cantaloupe example, we can examine a case using the concepts of supply function, supply schedule, and supply curve.

Suppose the quantity of cantaloupes that farmers will harvest and offer for sale during any given week in the summer depends on their price, the number of acres previously planted in cantaloupes, the hourly wage of farm laborers, the price of fuel for farm machinery and transportation, and the weather. The supply function for cantaloupes will relate all these variables to the quantity of cantaloupes that farms are willing and able to bring to market during the week. It is likely that the quantity brought to market will be larger the higher the price of cantaloupes, the more acreage planted, the lower the hourly wages of farm laborers, the lower the price of fuel, and the hotter the weather.

If all the variables other than the price of cantaloupes remain constant, a supply schedule for cantaloupes can be defined. Other things equal, it is the relationship between the price of cantaloupes and the amount farmers are willing and able to sell. For any given price, the amount offered for sale is the *quantity supplied*. A supply schedule for cantaloupes is shown in Table 3–3. Figure 3–7 plots the data from Table 3–3 as a *supply curve* for cantaloupes. Both the supply schedule and the supply curve show that as the price of cantaloupes rises, the quantity that farmers will offer for sale increases. The term *supply* refers to the entire supply schedule or curve. A change in supply or a shift of the supply curve will occur if any supply function variable other than price of cantaloupes changes.

> A **supply schedule** is a table that relates the quantity supplied of a good or service during some time period to the various possible prices of that good or service.

> A **supply curve** is a graphical representation of a supply schedule.

LAW OF SUPPLY

In Table 3–3 and Figure 3–7 the direct relationship between the price of cantaloupes and the quantity that producers will offer for sale conforms to what is known as the *law of supply*.

> The **law of supply** states that, other things equal, sellers will increase the quantity of a product they are willing and able to offer for sale as the price of that product is increased.

In short periods of time, when the supply function variables other than a product's own price remain constant, we can expect the law of supply to hold—for two principal reasons. First, production will be subject to what is known as *diminishing returns.*□ That is, suppliers will find that they can squeeze more output from their productive facilities (plant, equipment, land) only at higher and higher cost per additional unit of product. They will

TABLE 3–3   Supply Schedule for Cantaloupes

Price per Cantaloupe	Quantity Supplied per week
$2.00	190,000
1.75	180,000
1.50	170,000
1.25	160,000
1.00	150,000
0.75	140,000
0.50	130,000
0.25	120,000

require higher prices to induce them to incur these increases in cost. Second, increasing the quantity supplied of some particular good may entail reducing the output of other goods. If suppliers at some point in time are already producing the level of output of each good that is best for them in terms of profit, they will be willing to increase their production of a particular good only if it becomes profitable to shift resources from the production of other goods to the production of that good. In general, this

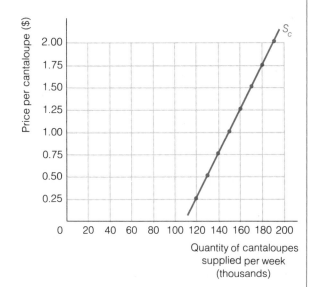

FIGURE 3–7   Supply Curve for Cantaloupes

In keeping with the law of supply, this supply curve slopes upward to the right. The points marked on the curve correspond to the combinations of price and quantity shown in Table 3–3.

will require an increase in the price of the good.

Normally, then, we expect to find a direct relationship between price and quantity supplied, especially when the time period is relatively short and variables such as input prices or technology are unlikely to change. However, over longer time periods, suppliers sometimes offer more output at lower prices, because modern industry is frequently successful at introducing changes that reduce production costs. Recent examples of products whose cost and price reductions are associated in part with technological change are electronic calculators, digital watches, smoke detectors, and citizens' band radios. However, each of these markets has also been affected by increases in the number of sellers (outward shift of the supply curve) and slower growth of demand as the novelty of owning the product wears off.[1] Indeed, shifts in both the supply curve and the demand curve could lead to falling prices over longer time periods, as will be shown in the following section. (The supply curve of a firm□ and of the industry for a given product will be more fully examined in Chapter 20.)

| 31 |

MARKET EQUILIBRIUM
◆

A competitive market is characterized by the presence of many independently acting buyers and sellers and the absence of any interference by government or extraordinarily powerful business firms. A market that is also characterized by a standardized product, the freedom of producers to enter and leave, and widespread knowledge of changing conditions qualifies as a *perfectly competitive market.*

---

1. See "Angry Because You Think Prices Only Go Up, Not Down?" *Wall Street Journal,* January 17, 1979, pp. 1, 30.

Perfect competition is an ideal situation that seldom exists in the real world. Economists have likened the Chicago commodities market and the New York cotton exchange to the ideal of perfect competition, where price is determined by the "invisible hand" □ of buyers' and sellers' independent activities. Our local cantaloupe market is unlikely to qualify as perfectly competitive. However, it may well be competitive enough to approximate the perfectly competitive ideal. For purposes of illustration, we will assume that it is.

| 33 |

EQUILIBRIUM PRICE AND QUANTITY

In a competitive market, where there are many buyers and many sellers of a particular good or service, it is relatively easy to explain the establishment of a market price that will be maintained as long as other variables of the supply and demand functions do not change. Such a price is called an *equilibrium price,* because the market will tend to move toward it if, for any reason, some other price temporarily exists.

Once the equilibrium price is established, there will also be an equilibrium quantity that is the same for both buyers and sellers. At this point the market is "in equilibrium." This phrase is a way of saying that no further adjustments will be made in price or quantity traded, because suppliers are willing to bring to the market exactly the same quantity as buyers demand at the going market price.

An **equilibrium price or quantity** is a price or quantity that will tend to be maintained naturally by market forces.

Figure 3–8 shows the cantaloupe supply and demand curves in the same price-quantity quadrant. Where the two curves intersect, at $P_e = \$0.75$ and $Q_e = 140,000$ cantaloupes per week bought and sold, are the equilibrium price and the equilibrium quantity. Price P_e is

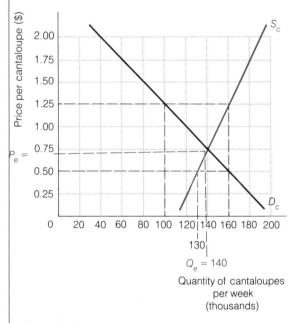

FIGURE 3–8 Equilibrium in the Market for Cantaloupes

At the market equilibrium price of $0.75 per cantaloupe, quantity supplied and quantity demanded are both 140,000 cantaloupes per week. No other price will equate quantity supplied with quantity demanded.

the equilibrium price because no other price will equate the quantity that buyers are willing and able to purchase with the quantity that sellers are willing and able to offer for sale. Any price other than $0.75 will not be an equilibrium price and will not be maintainable, since there are built-in market forces that will cause the price to change.

MAINTENANCE OF EQUILIBRIUM

The notion of equilibrium is borrowed from the natural sciences and refers to a state or circumstance that will be automatically maintained unless it is disturbed. Where markets with large numbers of buyers and sellers are free from government interference or monopolization, it is said that an equilibrium price

will be generated. Perhaps the best way to explain why the price of $0.75 in Figure 3–8 tends to hold is to ask what would happen if some other price were momentarily in effect.

For example, suppose the price were $1.25. What does Figure 3–8 tell us? It says that sellers would bring 160,000 cantaloupes to market, but buyers would purchase only 100,000 of them. There would be a surplus of cantaloupes. Some sellers would be stuck with unsold cantaloupes, and harvesting activities might have to taper off. In order to sell the cantaloupes rather than have them rot in the fields, the sellers would cut their price. Since the quantity demanded by buyers is greater at lower prices, the price cutting would alleviate the inventory problem. In addition, sellers would bring fewer cantaloupes to the market at lower prices, since the price might get so low that some suppliers could not cover their harvesting and transportaion costs. The surplus would disappear when the price fell to $0.75 and the quantity supplied was 140,000 cantaloupes per week.

If the price were at first below $0.75 instead of above it, we would again find forces that would move the market toward equilibrium at the $0.75 price. For example, if the price were momentarily at $0.50, the number of cantaloupes brought to market would be 130,000, but buyers would want to purchase 160,000 of them. There would be a shortage of cantaloupes. Some sellers would run out of cantaloupes, and some buyers would be unable to find a cantaloupe.

Of course, some sellers would figure they could charge a higher price and still sell all their cantaloupes, while others would try to bring more cantaloupes to market, thereby incurring greater harvesting expenses. Some buyers would be willing to pay more for a cantaloupe when they became aware of the shortage. All these actions would move the price upward and close the gap between quantity demanded (160,000) and quantity supplied (130,000). The price would rise until the $0.75 level is reached. At this point the quantities demanded and supplied would be the

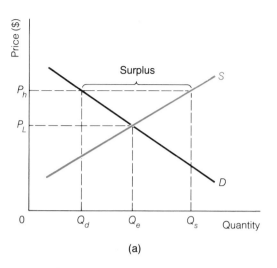

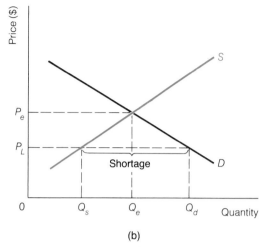

(a)   (b)

FIGURE 3–9 **Disequilibrium Prices and Their Effects**

A price that is higher than the equilibrium one will result in a surplus or excess of quantity supplied over quantity demanded. A price that is lower than equilibrium will result in a shortage or excess of quantity demanded over quantity supplied. Market forces will move the price toward P_e in either case.

same, and the market would be in equilibrium. Thus the equilibrium price would be $0.75, and the equilibrium quantity would be 140,000 cantaloupes per week.[2]

This equilibrium discussion can be graphically summarized with the help of Figure 3–9. In panel (a), P_h is a higher-than-equilibrium price, and it leads to a surplus equal to (Q_s − Q_d). The price will fall as producers attempt to get rid of inventories. In panel (b), P_L is a lower-then-equilibrium price, and it leads to a shortage equal to (Q_d − Q_s). The price will rise, because consumers will bid it up while producers will increase the amount they bring

to market. Thus, in either case, the price will tend to settle at P_e and the quantity at Q_e.

CHANGE IN EQUILIBRIUM

The equilibrium market price and quantity traded of a good or service will not change as long as both the demand and the supply curve for the item do not shift. However, a shift in one or both of these curves will lead to the establishment of a new equilibrium position. This point can be illustrated with some additional diagrams.

Figure 3–10 contains several panels that summarize how shifts in demand and supply can affect equilibrium price and quantity. In panel (a), the price rises because demand has increased (shifted outward) with no change in supply. The price-quantity combination at point A will not be maintained after the shift from D to D', since at price P there will be a shortage. In the cantaloupe example, an increase in the price of honeydews might cause such an adjustment, because some consumers would substitute cantaloupes for the more expensive honeydews. Note that in this case the

2. Note that in our example this is not the quantity that maximizes the sales revenue of the sellers. As a group, they would be better off with P = $1.25 and Q_d = 100,-000 cantaloupes per week, which would yield a total sales revenue of $125,000 per week, or $20,000 more than they get at the $0.75 price. However, unless they form an organization to restrict cantaloupe supply, it will be impossible to maintain the price at a level above $0.75. Many farm product markets generate this kind of result, and that is why farmers try to form organizations or turn to the government for help in maintaining their incomes (see the discussion of this subject in Chapter 33).

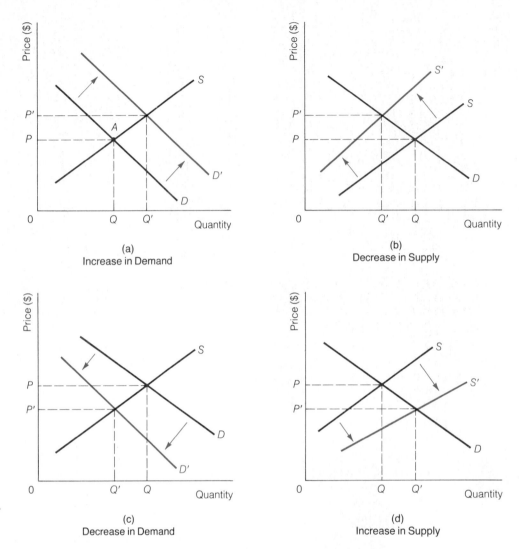

FIGURE 3–10 Shifts in Demand and Supply

Price will rise if demand increases and supply remains unchanged, or if supply decreases and demand remains unchanged. Price will fall if demand decreases and supply remains unchanged, or if supply increases and demand remains unchanged.

quantity traded increases to Q', even though the price has risen to P'.

In panel (b), the price also rises, but this time Q falls, or Q' is less than Q. This will always be the result when supply decreases (shifts inward) but demand does not change. In the cantaloupe example, an increase in the wages of farm laborers or in the price of fuel would produce such an adjustment.

Panels (c) and (d) show shifts in demand and supply that result in a lowering of the equilibrium price. In panel (c) demand decreases and supply remains unchanged. Thus both the equilibrium price and the equilibrium quantity fall. Panel (d) gives the same price result, but the quantity increases because the supply curve has shifted outward along an unchanging demand curve. In the cantaloupe ex-

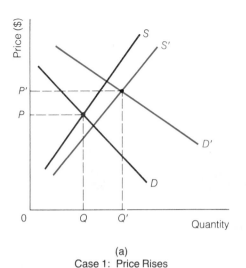

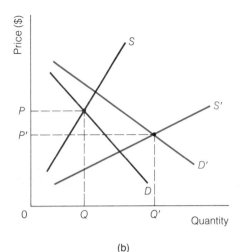

(a)
Case 1: Price Rises

(b)
Case 2: Price Falls

FIGURE 3–11   Growth: Demand and Supply Both Increase

When growth occurs, increasing both the number of consumers and the number of producers in a market, price may either rise, fall, or remain the same, depending on exactly how the supply and demand curves have shifted.

ample, an abundant supply of the substitute honeydews could cause a shift such as that in panel (c), whereas a prior decision of many farmers to plant cantaloupes could lead to a supply increase such as that shown in panel (d).

Finally, Figure 3–11 illustrates two possible results when both supply and demand for a particular good or service increase. In panel (a), the price rises because growth in demand has been large relative to growth in supply. However, in panel (b), the price falls because the outward shift of the supply curve is large relative to the outward shift of the demand curve. Of course, a third possibility also exists. The price may remain the same even though both curves shift outward. In this case, intersection B will be directly to the right of the initial equilibrium point at interesection A. (You might want to draw this case to make sure you understand.) In all three cases the quantity traded increases. Such shifts help explain why, when economic growth takes place and the quantity of output in the market increases, some prices remain unchanged while others rise or fall.

PARTIAL EQUILIBRIUM, GENERAL EQUILIBRIUM, AND THE INTERRELATEDNESS OF MARKETS

An economy's markets are interrelated. For example, we saw in the preceding section that the demand for a given product will change if the price of a substitute for that product changes. Thus the equilibrium price for the first product depends on the equilibrium price for the second, and vice versa. We know that the market price for cantaloupes will depend on the market price for honeydews. A change in the price of one of the two products will very likely result in a change in the price of the other.

PARTIAL EQUILIBRIUM ANALYSIS

The kind of market equilibrium we describe when we consider the price of a given product, other things equal, is known as *partial equilibrium.*□

518

Partial equilibrium analysis *focuses attention on a part of an economic system under the assumption that changes in related elements of the system either will not occur or will not be significant.*

The partial equilibrium approach is extremely useful in economics, because it allows us to examine a specific problem, such as the establishment of price in a given market, and ignore interrelationships that may complicate the problem unduly.

Partial equilibrium analysis plays a role in economics similar to that of a controlled experiment in physics. In physics we can show that if we create a vacuum, so there is no air resistance, two falling objects of different sizes will accelerate toward the earth at the same rate. In economics we can show that if consumers' incomes, the price of substitutes and complements, tastes, and other demand-related variables remain constant, an increase in the supply of a given product will cause its equilibrium price to fall and its quantity demanded to rise. (See Figure 3–10, panel [d].) Partial equilibrium analysis, then, is the type of analysis used extensively in this chapter, and it will be the main approach to economic problem solving throughout this book.

GENERAL EQUILIBRIUM ANALYSIS

517

A branch of economic analysis, *general equilibrium analysis,*□ deals specifically with the interrelationships of the various microeconomic elements of a market economy, examining and describing how a systemwide equilibrium of markets can take place. This equilibrium requires all the market interrelationships of substitute and complementary goods and of product markets and the markets for factors of production to move simultaneously toward a particular set of prices and quantities purchased or sold.

General equilibrium analysis *is a systemwide examination of prices and markets, focusing specifically on the interactions between the system's many product and resource markets.*

Because of the many potential interactions among the markets for all the various products and resources in an economic system, general equilibrium analysis is necessarily complex. We can learn about the nature of a general equilibrium situation with the help of Figure 3–12, which shows several interrelated markets.

In panel (a), the supply of gasoline decreases because of the actions of the oil-producing nations. The price of gasoline rises to P'. Because of higher gasoline prices, consumers drive less and try to make their old cars last longer. Thus demand for autos declines from D to D', and automobile prices fall as manufacturers are forced to resort to rebates in order to sell cars. In panel (c), the demand for auto workers declines because of the decrease in the demand for cars. (This is a case of *derived demand*. That is, the demand for auto workers depends on, or is derived from, the demand for automobiles. In general, the demand for any factor of production is a derived demand.)

Continuing in Figure 3–12, we find that the auto workers who lose their jobs in panel (c) will seek other employment. This process may increase the supply of taxi drivers, thereby reducing the wage rate of taxi drivers, as in panel (d). If there is reduced income for both auto workers and taxi drivers, the demand for steak, seen in panel (e), may fall. Both groups may have to eat more beans and less meat, which will lead to an increase in both the demand for and the price of beans.

Now, what about tin cans? Beans come in tin cans, so there must be some effect on the tin can market. Finally, if all these other markets are affected, won't this affect the demand for gasoline (used to ship products and power taxis) back in panel (a)? It appears at this point that we are getting nowhere fast (or, perhaps,

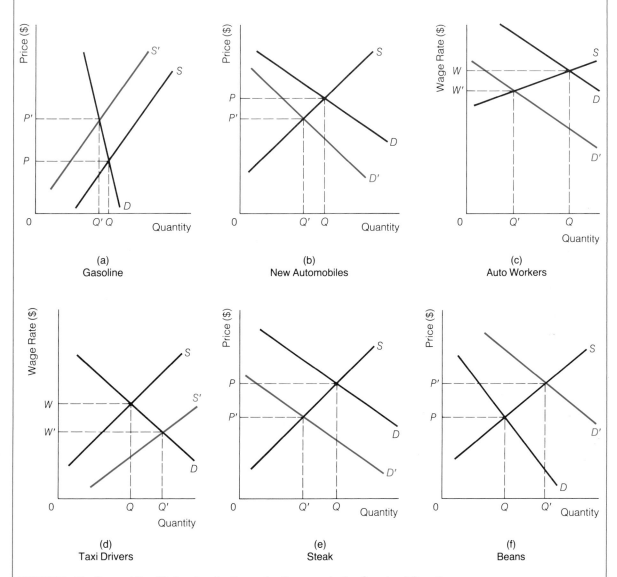

FIGURE 3–12 General Equilibrium Implications of a Decrease in the Supply of Gasoline

If the supply of gasoline decreases to S', the demand for new autos decreases, the demand for auto workers decreases, the supply of taxi drivers increases, the demand for steak decreases, and the demand for beans increases. All of these resultant changes have price and quantity effects.

somewhere very slowly). In fact, the example of Figure 3–12 can be employed to illustrate both the nature of general equilibrium in a system of markets and the usefulness of partial equilibrium as a problem-solving approach.

General Equilibrium and the Economic System General equilibrium analysis shows us

that a market system is in a constant state of flux—that because of the vast network of interrelated economic events in the system, adjustments in prices and production are taking place all the time. It tells us, then, that a complete model of a market economy must in some way take into account the general equilibrium nature of the system.

In terms of the circular flow□ model of Chapter 2, the product and factor market boxes can be viewed as containing innumerable supply and demand curves for all the interacting markets of the economy. We may examine the macroeconomic workings of the economy by looking at the behavior of the flows between households and business firms or between either of them and the government. When we do so, we usually assume that all the markets in the economy are tending toward a state of general equilibrium and that the what, how, and for whom questions are being answered by the actions of all the individual buyers and sellers in the markets.

Usefulness of Partial Equilibrium Analysis The partial equilibrium approach recognizes that it is not necessary to look at the entire system of economic interrelationships in order to analyze one or a few of its parts. In the context of the gasoline to beans example of Figure 3–12, we might wish to know only the impact of a decrease in the supply of gasoline on the market for new cars. We could reasonably examine this effect by ignoring the further impacts of the change in gasoline supply on auto workers, taxi drivers, or suppliers of steak and beans.

In short, partial equilibrium analysis allows us to look at economic problems in a manageable fashion by isolating the aspects of the problem that we think are the most important. It is an approach that will prove useful throughout our study of both macro- and microeconomics.

SUMMARY

1. A *demand function* relates the amount of some good or service that consumers are willing and able to purchase at some point in time or over some time period to a number of key variables that might affect such purchases. A good's own price, the prices of related goods, consumers' income, and consumers' expectations and tastes are some important demand function variables.

2. The demand for a good or service can be repre-sented by a *demand schedule* (table) or by a *demand curve* (graph). *Demand* is the set of possible prices and related quantities that consumers will purchase. It is depicted by the schedule or curve, under the assumption that other demand function variables are constant (other things equal).

3. The *law of demand* states that when only the price of a given good or service changes, while all other demand function variables remain constant, the quantity demanded will change in a direction inverse to that of the price change. In other words, consumers will buy less of a product when its price rises and more of it when its price falls, other things equal. Income and substitution effects and the principle of diminishing utility provide support for the law of demand.

4. The demand curve for a particular good will shift whenever a demand function variable other than the good's own price is changed. For example, income changes or changes in the prices of related goods will shift the demand curve for a given good. A shift in a demand curve is called a change in demand. However, a movement along a given demand curve in response to a change in a good's own price is called a change in the quantity demanded.

5. Changes in income will have different effects on the demand curve, depending on whether the good or service in question is normal or inferior. Likewise, the effect on demand of a change in the price of a related good depends on whether that good is a substitute for or a complement to the good in question.

6. The *supply function* for a given good or service relates the quantity that sellers will make available for sale at some point in time or during some time period to a number of key variables that determine the quantity. Besides the price of the good or service in question, supply function variables include the prices of productive inputs, the prices of related goods, businesses' goals and expectations, and technology.

7. Both the *supply schedule* and the *supply curve* for a good or service depict the relationship between a good's own price and the quantity supplied, other things equal. Generally, they obey the *law of supply*, which states that price and quantity supplied are directly related. In other words, in most cases producers will increase the quantity of a good supplied when its price rises and decrease the quantity when its price falls.

8. In a competitive market—one with many inde-

pendently acting buyers and sellers—the interaction of buyers and sellers is expected to generate an *equilibrium price* for the good or service traded. This price will tend to be maintained as long as supply and demand for the item do not change. Shifts in the demand curve or the supply curve will lead to changes in the equilibrium price and the quantity consumed.

9. *General equilibrium analysis* deals with the conditions for a simultaneous equilibrium of all product and factor markets in an economic system and focuses on the interrelationships of the various prices and markets. *Partial equilibrium analysis* is extensively used in economic theory because it allows the analyst to single out specific interrelationships for study without always having to take a systemwide view of each economic problem.

IMPORTANT TERMS AND CONCEPTS

Demand function	Complementary good
Demand	Market demand curve
Demand schedule	Supply function
Quantity demanded	Quantity supplied
Law of demand	Supply schedule
Substitution effect	Supply curve
Income effect	Law of supply
Principle of	Perfect competition
diminishing utility	Equilibrium price
Demand curve	Equilibrium quantity
Change in demand	Partial equilibrium
Normal good	analysis
Inferior good	General equilibrium
Substitute good	analysis

QUESTIONS AND PROBLEMS

1. Define the following:
   a. demand function
   b. demand schedule
   c. demand curve

2. Discuss the difference between a change in demand and a change in quantity demanded.

3. What is the law of demand? Why does it generally hold?

4. What would you expect to happen to the demand curve for:
   a. automobiles, if consumer income decreased
   b. cream, if coffee prices increased 400 percent
   c. mopeds, if the price of gasoline tripled

d. home movie projectors, if the price of video tape decks fell 50 percent

5. List some of the variables that you think should be included in the supply function for:
   a. automobiles   c. medical doctors
   b. oranges   d. T-shirts

6. Discuss the forces that cause a competitive market to adjust toward an equilibrium price if, for some reason, the price is temporarily above or below equilibrium.

7. Given:

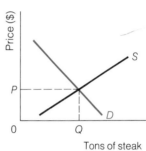

Suppose consumers' incomes increase. Explain what will happen in the diagram, assuming no change in the supply of steak.

8. The prices of many high-technology goods have fallen over recent years, even though prices in general have increased. Explain why this has happened, and cite examples of such goods.

9. Suppose the following data describe the demand and supply for apples in a given competitive market:

Price of Apples (per Bushel)	Quantity Demanded (Bushels per Week)	Quantity Supplied (Bushels per Week)
$50	1,000	7,000
45	2,000	6,000
40	3,000	5,000
35	4,000	4,000
30	5,000	3,000
25	6,000	2,000
20	7,000	1,000
15	8,000	0

a. What is the equilibrium price of apples? How do you know?
b. Sketch the demand and supply curves for apples in a single quadrant, and indicate the equilibrium price and quantity.
c. Why would it be impossible for a price of $25 per bushel to be maintained in the apple market?

THE TRAUMATIC TRUFFLE MARKET

"It is one of the worst years in memory," says Gerard de Trobriand, secretary general of the Federation of Truffle Producers. From a peak harvest of 2,000 tons a year at the turn of the century, when French turkeys sometimes were stuffed with handfuls of truffles, the nation's production has declined to less than 100 tons in a good year. A major factor has been the huge drop in France's agricultural population. Nowadays, a mere truffle sliver may garnish a *pate de foie gras,* hardly enough to lend a whiff of its distinctive aroma. This winter, after an abnormally dry summer, truffle markets in Perigord, the prime

Source: Adapted from "At Last, Good News for Long-Suffering Fanciers of Truffles," *Wall Street Journal,* February 12, 1979, pp. 1, 16.

truffle region, are almost empty, and France's total output won't reach 25 tons.

High cost and lack of supplies have forced many Paris restaurants to drop truffle specialties. Even in the heart of truffle country, at nearby Cahors, La Taverne restaurant's owner-chef, Pierre Escorbiac, says that his fabled *truffes en croustade,* a delectable truffles-and-duck-liver puff pastry concoction, may have to be deleted from his culinary repertoire. Even at the present $25 a plate, he is losing money, he says, and anyway, there aren't any truffles around.

PROTECTED CROP

Yet salvation may be at hand. . . . Truffle cultivation in a nursery is

possible because of techniques developed at the French National Institute of Agronomic Research in Clermont-Ferrand. Agronomist Jean Grente obtained pure truffle cultures, grafted the germinating seeds to the roots of oak and hazelnut seedlings, planted the saplings in chalky soil—and let nature take its course. The first Grente-made truffle emerged in 1977, a replica of nature's own.

"It's only the beginning," declares Mr. Grente, predicting that production of cultivated truffles will overtake the crop of natural truffles in five to ten years. . . .

The Lalanne nursery's greenhouses shelter 100,000 young oak and hazelnut saplings, all guaranteed to be nurturing embryonic truffles among their roots. When these have been replanted in areas where the soil and climate are suitably receptive, says Mr. Grente, the mature trees should begin yielding an annual truffle harvest of 250 tons—or five to ten times France's recent output. . . .

"The truffle is a mystery," insists a Cahors truffle canner. "If there are too many, what will their attraction be?" . . .

QUESTIONS

1. What accounts for the recent high cost of truffles?
2. What variables would you include in a supply function for natural truffles? For truffles in general?

3. Italy also produces truffles, but of a lower quality than those found in France. Economically speaking, what kind of relationship do you expect between Italian truffles and French truffles? How are Italian truffles related to the demand for French truffles?
4. Given the information in the article, what would you predict about the behavior of truffle prices in the future?

SPECIAL TOPIC B

THE DEMAND FUNCTION AND THE DEMAND CURVE IN EQUATION FORM

This text does not emphasize the mathematical side of economics. Most of what it discusses is presented in verbal and graphical form. However, mathematics, particularly algebra, is a convenient shorthand method for stating economic concepts that can actually make them easier to understand. This possibility was recognized early in the development of economic theory. In fact, Augustin Cournot□, the Frenchman who first stated the law of demand, wrote in 1838: "Anyone who understands algebraic notation, reads at a glance in an equation results reached arithmetically only with great labor and pains."[1]

Cournot was right. Algebra can help people understand economic analysis. Thus, even though Chapter 3 does not rely on algebra, this section supplies the equations for the demand function and the demand curve, so that those who wish to see the algebraic shorthand will have it available.

_____
1. Augustin Cournot, *Researches into the Mathematical Principles of the Theory of Wealth* (1838; New York: Augustus M. Kelley, 1960), p. 4.

THE DEMAND FUNCTION

A *demand function* can be expressed as an equation relating the quantity purchased of some good or service to the independent variables which affect that quantity. For most goods and services, their own price is an important independent variable in the demand function. Other variables that are likely to be important in terms of their effect on quantity bought are the prices of related goods or services, consumers' income, credit terms, tastes, advertising, the number of consumers in the market, consumers' expectations about the future, and even the weather.

If we use the example of the demand function for cantaloupes that was introduced in the chapter, we will expect the amount of cantaloupes bought per week to depend on the price of cantaloupes, the price of honeydews, and the incomes of consumers. An *unspecified demand function* for cantaloupes can be written in equation form as follows:

$$Q_d = f(P, P_h, I), \qquad \text{(B--1)}$$

where Q_d is the quantity of cantaloupes bought per week, P is the price per cantaloupe, P_h is the price per honeydew, and I is the income of consumers.

Equation B–1 is called an unspecified function because it states what Q_d depends on but not how Q_d depends on the independent variables P, P_h, and I. A *specified demand function* might look something like this:

$$Q_d = 183,000 \ - 80,000 \ P$$
$$+ \ 10,000 \ P_h \ + 0.10 \ I. \qquad \text{(B–2)}$$

All the constants in Equation B–2—the numbers 183,000, 80,000, 10,000, and 0.10—could be obtained by using a computer to fit the equation to data on the independent variables and Q_d.

QUANTITY DEMANDED

The discussion that follows will assume that Equation B–2 describes cantaloupe demand in central Texas during the summer months. When the long, hot summer arrives, the local market for cantaloupes becomes highly competitive. Hundreds, perhaps even thousands, of small farmers plant and harvest cantaloupes each year, and hundreds of thousands of consumers buy them from pickup truck vendors and roadside stands. Honeydews and other substitutes for cantaloupes also come in season at about the same time.

Let us suppose that Equation B–2 pertains to demand for cantaloupes and that the variables are explicitly defined as follows:

Q_d = quantity of cantaloupes bought by consumers per week,

P = price per cantaloupe,

I = average annual income of a family of four persons in the market area, and

P_h = price per honeydew.

If, for a given midsummer week, the data for the three independent variables are:

$$P = \$1.00,$$
$$P_h = \$1.50, \text{ and}$$
$$I = \$20,000,$$

then we will have:

$$Q_d = 183,000 \ - 80,000(1.00)$$
$$+ \ 10,000(1.50) \ + 0.10(20,000) \qquad \text{(B–3)}$$
$$= 120,000$$

cantaloupes per week. In relation to the independent variable P, the amount Q_d is called the quantity demanded. Thus, at a price of \$1.00 per cantaloupe, the quantity demanded is 120,000 cantaloupes per week, the values of the other variables remaining the same. If P changed but the other independent variables did not, a change in quantity demanded would occur.

DEMAND SCHEDULE AND DEMAND CURVE

As defined in Chapter 3, a demand schedule is a table showing the relationship between the quantity demanded of some good or service and the price of that good or service, when all other variables in the demand function remain constant. If we now employ the data on the independent variables from the cantaloupe demand function and vary P over the range of prices from $P = \$2.00$ to $P = \$0.25$, holding all other independent variables at their initial values, we can construct a demand schedule for cantaloupes.

The demand schedule of Table 3–1 shows what will happen to the quantity demanded of cantaloupes as the price is varied in 25 cent increments over the range $P = \$2.00$ to $P = \$0.25$. The quantities shown for each price are found by plugging the above-mentioned values of P_h and I into Equation B–2 and substituting for P the values of \$2.00, \$1.75, \$1.50, . . . , \$0.25. Since all of the independent variables but P will be constant as the demand schedule is developed, using Equation B–3 we can write an expression for the price-quantity relationship in Table 3–1 as follows:

$Q_d = 183,000 \quad - 80,000 \ P$

$$+ \ 15,000 \ + 2,000, \quad \text{(B-4)}$$

or

$$Q_d = 200,000 - 80,000 \ P. \quad \text{(B-4a)}$$

Equation B–4a is that of the demand curve for cantaloupes. It could also be written as:

$$80,000 \ P = 200,000 \quad - Q_d, \quad \text{(B-5)}$$

or

$$P = 2.5 \ - \frac{Q_d}{80,000}. \quad \text{(B-5a)}$$

If either Equation B–4a or B–5a is plotted in a quadrant with price, P, on the vertical axis and quantity demanded, Q_d, on the horizontal axis, the result will be a graph showing the demand curve for cantaloupes. The plot will be exactly the same as in Figure 3–3. Finally, for those who wish to go a bit farther,

the supply curve of Figure 3–7 (created from data in Table 3–3) conforms to the equation $Q_s = 110,000 + 40,000P$. Solving for $Q_s = Q_d$, we have:

$$110,000 + 40,000P = 200,000 - 80,000P$$
$$120,000P = 90,000$$
$$P = 0.75,$$

which is the equilibrium price shown in Figure 3–8. Figure B–1 is a reconstruction of Figure 3–8 and shows how the above demand and supply curve equations are plotted as straight lines. Equilibrium occurs at a price of $0.75, where quantity demanded and quantity supplied are both 140,000 cantaloupes per week.

PROBLEM

Suppose the demand function for product x has been estimated to be:

$$Q_x = 3,848 \ - \ 2P_x + 0.004I + 3P_y,$$

where Q_x is the quantity of product x sold per month, P_x is its price per unit, I is median family income, and P_y is the price of a related good.

a. Develop a demand schedule (table) for product x over the price range $P_x = \$800$ to $P_x = \$400$, if $I = \$12,000$ and $P_y = \$600$. (Use $50 changes in P_x over the range.)

b. Assuming the above values for I and P_y, write an equation for the demand curve for product x.

c. Draw the demand curve on a piece of graph paper.

d. Explain how the demand curve would shift if median family income were to increase.

e. Discuss the nature of the economic relationship between product x and product y.

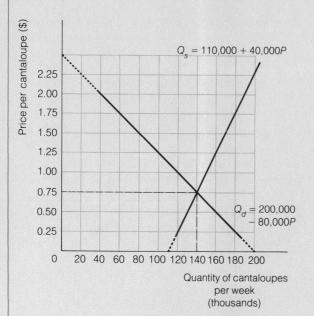

FIGURE B–1 Plots of Demand and Supply Equations Showing Equilibrium in the Market for Cantaloupes

The equations for Q_s and Q_d plot as two straight lines that intersect at the equilibrium price, $0.75. Note that the constant term in each equation is the Q-axis intercept of the line.

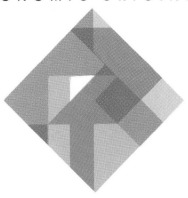

ADAM SMITH
AND THE
CLASSICAL SCHOOL

Adam Smith (1723–1790) is the recognized founder of the modern discipline of economics, or, as it was known during the eighteenth and nineteenth centuries, political economy. Smith, like Hume, came to economics through philosophy. His major philosophical work, *The Theory of Moral Sentiments*, was published in 1759. In this work, Smith firmly established his belief in the principle that an individual's actions are governed by self-interest. However, he argued on a moral plane that people tempered their behavior to conform with enlightened reason and the opinion of others. They acted as though their deeds were being viewed by an impartial spectator, an enlightened and reasonable person whose approval they valued. Smith concluded that ethical systems developed naturally on the basis of such restrained self-interest.

Smith's concept of a naturally evolving system of ethics was easily accepted by the intellectuals of his day, because his work was preceded by that of a number of seventeenth and eighteenth century philosophers (Hobbes, Locke, and Rousseau, for example) who had popularized the idea that natural law— the immutable laws of nature and of human existence, conditioned not only science but ethics, law, and political organization. In addition, the remarkable advancement of science in the seventeenth and eighteenth centuries (through the work of Galileo, Descartes, Newton, Lavoisier, and many others) further convinced the intellectuals that natural laws did exist and could be proved. Finally, the idea that self-interest was the prime mover in human behavior was fostered by many of the philosophers who preceded Smith (Hobbes, Locke, and Hume, for example), even when they disagreed about how to control people's selfish nature.

Smith traveled in France as a private tutor. There he encountered a group of economic thinkers known as physiocrats. The physiocrats, led by a physician named François Quesnay, formed the first group of intellectuals that can be identified with a "school" of economic thought. Moreover, their efforts were the first to produce a view of the economy as a system,

Adam Smith

and their attempt to quantify the output of the sytem resulted in an economic model based on rudimentary national income accounting.

The **physiocrats** believed that all wealth originated in agriculture. Their model, which found its highest expression in Quesnay's *Tableau Economique* (Economic Table), traced the circular flow of income from agriculture to landowners and the nonagricultural class and back again to agriculture. The physiocrats held that their system described the natural workings of the economy, and, like Smith, they believed that the prime mover of human behavior was self-interest. They argued that the system would function best if individuals were left to pursue their own interests with a minimum of government interference. It is from the French of this period that we get the phrase *laissez-faire, laissez-passer* (free enterprise, free trade).

The physoicrats' ideas meshed well with Smith's philosophy and beliefs about economics, and it was in France that Smith began work on *The Wealth of Nations (1776)* "to pass away the time," as he put it in a letter to Hume. Smith spent more than ten years on this great work, and when he was finished, he had firmly laid the foundations for both the nineteenth

century classical school of economics and the modern economics that was to follow. Smith's ideas about human behavior, free trade, and the market mechanism would continue to occupy center stage in economic literature for generations to come.

What did Smith argue in *The Wealth of Nations*? The book is lengthy and complex, filled with casual observations and commentaries on the times. However, we will attempt to summarize its main arguments in the following list:

1. People are born equal; the differences in them as adults stem for the most part from habit, custom, and education.

2. A principal trait of human nature is "the propensity to truck, barter, and exchange one thing for another."

3. The propensity to truck, barter, and exchange gives rise, slowly and gradually, to specialization, or the division of labor.

4. Division of labor leads to gains from trade and is the primary source of economic growth or progress. It is limited by the extent (size) of the market.

5. The force of competition in free markets will automatically determine the natural, or equilibrium, price of both products and resources. The market mechanism, like an "Invisible Hand," will determine how to best allocate resources, given the self-interests of consumers and producers.

6. Economic progress depends also on saving, which provides the entrepreneur with a fund to invest in the employment of more labor and the production of greater output.

7. Government intervention in economic life is unnecessary and, in many cases, harmful. Therefore, government activities should be limited for the most part to national defense, public safety, and the protection of individual liberty.

All of the above arguments are still heard today, and some of them are considered to be broadly accurate, with very little qualification. Smith succeeded in describing an orderly economic system based on individualism and freedom, and he supplied an adequate description of how such a system functioned. His was far from the last word on many of the economic propositions he advanced, and on certain issues his writing was obscure or inconclusive. However, his description of the self-regulating market mechanism constituted an important first word that

David Ricardo

Thomas R. Malthus

would be the point of departure for much subsequent economic analysis.

David Ricardo (1772–1823) was perhaps the most important contributor to classical economics in the half century following the publication of *The Wealth of Nations*. Ricardo was a self-made millionaire, a stockbroker, and the son of Jewish parents who disowned him when he married a Quaker in 1793. He later bought a seat in Parliament, where he became known as a reform-minded radical. Ricardo's thinking was strongly influenced by several of his contemporaries as well as by the work of Smith. In particular, he accepted a theory of population advanced by **Thomas R. Malthus** (1766–1834) and a theory of aggregate demand formulated by French economist **Jean-Baptiste Say** (1767–1832).

Malthus's first *Essay on Population* appeared in 1798; and although Malthus published a much enlarged edition in 1803, his argument remained basically the same. He believed that there was a natural tendency for population to increase faster than the supply of food. Thus economic progress could not continue indefinitely, because there simply would not

be enough food available to support the population. If population growth continued unchecked by either moral restraint or such "positive checks" as war, plagues, or epidemics, famine would eventually halt it. Worse yet, the lower classes could hardly be expected to practice moral restraint, and there would always be a tendency for their number to increase when, because of economic progress, wages rose above the subsistence level.[1] Malthus therefore advised against systems of poor relief (welfare), because they would only cause the poor to multiply.

Say was concerned with a much different issue, namely, whether aggregate demand could ever be insufficient to generally clear the market of goods. Say argued that such a deficiency of demand, a general glut of goods, was impossible, because production of the goods would create sufficient aggregate demand to ensure that they would be purchased. According to Say, people produced output either for their own consumption or to exchange it for goods produced by others. Therefore, the fact of production

1. Malthus's population argument is discussed further in Chapters 15 and 32 of this text.

itself implied a demand for all of the output. Although a glut might be possible for a particular good or industry, such excess supply would lead to a fall in market price and an eventual clearing of the market. The notion that "supply creates its own demand" became known as **Say's law of markets.**

Ricardo's major work, *Principles of Political Economy and Taxation*, appeared in 1817. In it, Ricardo synthesized the ideas of Smith with those of Malthus, Say, and several of their contemporaries and provided cogent theories of rent, profit, and international trade.[2] Ricardo presented a tightly knit economic system wherein maximum economic progress was achieved under free trade and self-regulating markets. The engine of progress was accumulation of capital funds by business owners, a phenomenon that would lead to increases in employment and output.

In Ricardo's system, rent accrued to landowners in increasing amounts as growth required the use of poorer and poorer grades of cropland. Prices would just cover the cost of production on the least productive land in use, and the owners of more productive land would receive the rents. Wages would increase as the economy grew, because employers would bid up the price of labor. However, in tune with Malthus's doctrine, population would expand, causing wages to fall back to a subsistence level. Profits would fall as rents rose. When the economy reached its maximum level of growth or was supporting the largest population possible, a stationary state would be reached, one with subsistence wages, higher rents, and profits sufficient only for capital replacement.

For Ricardo, all of these events would take place automatically in a system characterized by private property, individual liberty, and free trade. Such a system would produce the greatest good for the greatest number, as Ricardo's friend Jeremy Bentham, the utilitarian philosopher and economist, might have put it. Others saw it differently; to them it was obvious that the system enriched landlords and resulted in a tug-of-war between labor and business owners (capitalists) for the remainder of society's output. Parts of Ricardo's analysis would come to be accepted by nineteenth century socialists and by Karl Marx, but their ideas about the good society would differ radically from those of the classical economists.

In the eighteenth and nineteenth centuries economists frequently took the position that labor cost was the appropriate measure of the value of goods. Ricardo recognized that value depended also on utility—the ability to satisfy human wants—and scarcity. Nevertheless, he vehemently argued that for the general run of goods a society regularly produces, labor content was the best measure of relative values. This labor theory of value was perhaps overemphasized by the classical school and produced many errors in economic reasoning during its time. The theory was appropriated by Marx and played an important part in his attacks on capitalism.

Despite some of the confusions in his book, Ricardo had many admirers and disciples. His views were popularized during the balance of the nineteenth century by several important textbooks on economics, the most sophisticated being John Stuart Mill's *Principles of Political Economy* (1848).

John Stuart Mill

2. For more on Ricardo's theory of international trade, see Chapter 29 of this text.

John Stuart Mill (1806–1873) was the son of one of Ricardo's fellow classicists, James Mill. The younger Mill was subjected to a severe intellectual upbringing by his father and Jeremy Bentham. He began to learn Greek at the age of three and Latin at eight. By the time he was seventeen, he had a thorough knowledge of chemistry, psychology, philosophy, botany, law, and, of course, economics. The strain of his upbringing no doubt contributed to a mental crisis that almost destroyed him in his early manhood.

Although Mill's training in economics was Ricardian, he was a reform-minded romantic who knew the Utopians and other socialists well. He viewed the stationary state as a situation perhaps superior to the growing economy characterized by incessant struggling to advance, and in his *Principles* he was sympathetic to the poor and prescribed social policies such as universal education, limitation of population, and profit sharing. However, in most instances he bowed to his predecessors and their traditional suspicion of government intervention. Laissez-faire, he said, "should be the general practice; every departure from it, unless required by some great good, is a certain evil."[3]

Mill's book had a number of surrogates, some of which were more easily understood and widely read. Three such books were written by Jane Marcet (1769–1858), Harriet Martineau (1802–1876), and Millicent Garrett Fawcett (1847–1929). The works of Marcet and Martineau preceded Mill's *Principles* and were written in dialogue and narrative forms, respectively. Fawcett's *Political Economy for Beginners* (1870) was a text based on Mill's book. Fawcett's text remained popular for forty years, and ten editions were published.

In the latter half of the nineteenth century, classical economics had triumphed in British thought and policy. Only vestiges of the mercantilist impediments to free trade remained, and government reforms had extended suffrage and overhauled the system of poor relief. Britain prospered, but in the process of growth it had developed an industrial working class that would eventually demand a larger role for government than that prescribed by the classical economists. Economic thought would continue for some time to expand along classical lines, but the discipline would begin to define two distinct, yet related, areas of inquiry. One, eventually to be labeled *macroeconomics*, would focus on the issues of aggregate economic activity and growth. The other, *microeconomics*, would seize upon the rational self-interest approach of the classical economists to develop a theory of consumer and business behavior.

Millicent Garrett Fawcett

3. John Stuart Mill, *Principles of Political Economy* (1848; London: Longmans, Green, 1920), p. 950.

CHAPTER 4

SOME
EXPERIENCES
WITH THE
MARKET
MECHANISM

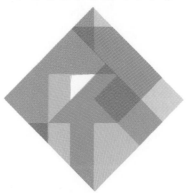

THE
DECAYING
MARKET
FOR
DENTISTS

Picture a waiting room full of dental patients who are sipping wine or coffee while they fill out raffle coupons for the turkey that one of the dentist's lucky clients will win and sign up to use the good doctor's hot tub after their appointments. Meanwhile, the doctor is slipping into his Plaque Vader outfit to work on one of his child patients, who had her choice of Plaque, Uncle Sam, or Santa Claus.

Why is an otherwise normal dentist going to such lengths to attract and keep patients? The plain fact is that the demand for dentists is not what it used to be. Why? Well, first of all there is fluoride. People, especially children, do not get as many cavities as they did ten or fifteen years ago. And there are fewer children these days. In fact, the number of U.S. youngsters in the five-to-seventeen age group has fallen by 3 million in the last ten years.[1] Finally, we all are brushing and flossing more than ever because the dental profession itself has been successful at promoting oral hygiene. All these changes have shifted the demand curve for dentistry inward.

While the demand for dental services has been slowly decreasing, the output of new dentists from dental schools has been grow-

1. "Dentists Ponder Case of the Missing Patients as Appointments Lag," *Wall Street Journal*, October 10, 1980, pp. 1, 4.

ing. During the decade of the 1970s the U.S. population grew 8.8 percent, but the number of active dentists in the country jumped 21 percent.[2] The combined effect of the increase in the supply of dentists and the decline in demand for what they do is taking a bite out of the average dentist's earnings and is turning some dentists into marketing experts. However, there are recent signs that the dentists' problems may be alleviated by an increase in demand caused by the inclusion of dental coverage in many employee insurance programs and a decline in enrollment at dental schools. Both factors should shift the demand and supply curves in a way that will improve dentists' smiles.

This chapter will apply the demand and supply tools explained in Chapter 3 to a number of market situations that frequently attract the attention of the news media.

2. Ibid.

C H A P T E R 4

SOME EXPERIENCES WITH THE MARKET MECHANISM

WHAT THIS CHAPTER IS ABOUT

The purpose of this chapter is to examine the recent behavior of four markets—the markets for gasoline, air-travel, gold, and engineers—that receive a good deal of attention from the news media. The news media, of course, seldom use supply and demand curves to analyze what takes place in these markets. With a little help from the demand and supply concepts discussed in Chapter 3, it is possible to make some meaningful statements about the behavior of prices and quantities in these and many other markets. The statements will apply to all the markets discussed even though the structures of these markets vary greatly.

MARKET STRUCTURE AND COMPETITION

Market structure means, fundamentally, the nature and extent of competition existing in each market. Economists characterize a market as *competitive* when it is made up of a large number of independently acting buyers and sellers. The ultimate competitive market structure is *perfect competition* □ (which is discussed in Chapter 20). In this case all the sellers supply exactly the same product, and none of them believes it is either possible to charge a price higher than the going (equilibrium) market price or necessary to accept a price lower than the going price. Furthermore, there is no government interference, nothing stops firms from entering or leaving the market at will, and all market participants (buyers and sellers) have perfect knowledge of all data.

Many markets are competitive, but few are perfectly competitive. In fact, a situation common in many product and service markets in the United States is that the buyers' side of the market, consisting of all people whose desires and abilities to purchase underlie the demand curve, is made up of a large number of independently acting participants. Literally millions of consumers are involved as buyers in a large number of markets. However, the sellers', or supply side of many U.S. markets is a different story altogether. For example, the United States has only four domestic automobile producers, and the number of makes of autos in the entire world is only about thirty. Only two major interstate buslines and nine transcontinental air carriers exist in the United States Fewer than a half-dozen firms supply our entire output of light bulbs.

Part 7 of this book, the economics of various market structures will be examined in detail. This analysis will show that it is relatively easy to define the supply curve of a perfectly competitive industry but next to impossible to define it logically or theoretically for a market where the number of sellers is at all limited. Nevertheless, industry supply curves will be drawn in the present chapter, because they do help us interpret changes in market data and understand the forces leading to adjustments in market prices. The point is that even if it is impossible to construct an industry supply curve from data on the individual firms in the industry, the notion of a market equilibrium price that will equate the quantities demanded and supplied remains useful.

GASOLINE: FROM ABUNDANCE TO CRISIS

During the 1950s and 1960s gas wars were commonplace. Service stations often engaged in drastic price cutting to attract customers from nearby rivals. The international oil companies had succeeded in tapping vast and seemingly unlimited supplies of oil in countries whose govenments appeared willing to accept whatever prices were offered. At home in the United States, the companies often competed fiercely for retail trade in local markets, especially in Texas, where independent refiners and distributors could capture significant market shares. In Temple, Texas, the 1963 low for Gulftane was 18.9 cents a gallon at the retail pump, and an attendant at the station would not only run the pump but wash windshield as well.

The key to the ability of U.S. gasoline refiners and distributors to supply ever-increasing amounts of motor fuel at relatively stable, and sometimes declining, prices was a ready source of cheap, foreign crude oil.[1] Most of the foreign oil for U.S. refineries came either from the Arab nations of the Persian Gulf or from Venezuela. In 1960 these countries formed the Organization of Petroleum Exporting Countries (OPEC). Their move was a response to the lowering of posted crude oil prices forced on them by the international oil companies. After many years of negotiations

---

1. The historical background is discussed briefly in Jai-Hoon Yang, "The Nature and Origins of the U.S. Energy Crisis," *Federal Reserve Bank of St. Louis Review*, July 1977, pp. 2–12.

among the members of OPEC and a gradual nationalization of crude oil production facilities in the OPEC countries, the stage was set during the early 1970s for a substantial upward movement in crude oil prices.

CRUDE OIL AND
THE SUPPLY OF GASOLINE

OPEC molded itself into a successful cartel□; and after the Arab exporting countries placed an embargo on sales to the United States in 1973, they raised the price of foreign crude oil by approximately 400 percent.[2] Throughout the remainder of the 1970s, OPEC continued to raise the price each year. Because the cartel controlled a large share of the world's supply of crude oil, it was able to make its prices stick.

Chapter 21 deals with the operation of cartels. However, in the context of the gasoline problem in the United States, all we need to know now is that the price of the refiners' key input, crude oil, rose repeatedly after 1972. As discussed in Chapter 3, the supply curve□ of any product is likely to be affected by a change in input prices. Specifically, we can expect the supply curve for gasoline to shift upward when the price of crude oil rises. This is so because refiners will have to receive a higher price for each possible quantity of gasoline sold in order to cover the increased cost of the crude.

DEMAND, SUPPLY, AND MARKET PRICE

During the second half of the 1970s the demand curve□ for gasoline shifted outward significantly as growth occurred in the U.S. econ-

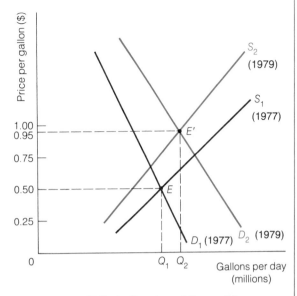

FIGURE 4–1 Shifts in Supply and Demand for Gasoline, 1977 to 1979

An increase in demand and a decrease in supply combined to raise gasoline prices dramatically from 1977 (D_1 and S_1) to 1979 (D_2 and S_2).

omy.[3] However, sharp gasoline price rises, caused in part by increases in the price of crude oil, appeared to have little effect on the quantity of gasoline demanded by consumers. Thus the supply curve for gasoline shifted upward, while the rather steep demand curve shifted outward. The result was tremendous upward pressure on the price.

Figure 4–1 diagrams this situation. Curves D_1 and S_1 are the demand and supply curves for gasoline in 1977, when market equilibrium price was 50 cents per gallon. By 1979 the demand curve had shifted to D_2, but the supply curve had also shifted, to S_2. As a result of the two shifts, the price almost doubled, although the quantity consumed rose only slightly, from Q_1 to Q_2. It became evident that barring any general reduction in con-

---

2. The actual price increase in crude oil was from $2.59 per barrel to $11.65 per barrel during late 1973. See Charles P. Kindleberger and Peter H. Lindert, *International Economics*, 6th ed. (Homewood, Ill.: Irwin, 1978), pp. 4–6.

---

3. By 1978 American consumption reached 8 million barrels of gasoline per day during the peak summer vacation months. See "A Surging Thirst for Gasoline," *Business Week*, September 4, 1978, pp. 69–72.

sumer demand, price would remain at its new, higher level. In addition, new increases in the price of crude oil would shift the supply curve further upward, pushing the market price of gasoline still higher.

PRICE CONTROL AND SHORTAGES

You may remember that 1978 and 1979 were not only years of rising gasoline prices but also years when the summers were characterized by gasoline *shortages*. Some filling stations closed altogether; others cut back their hours of operation. Consumers in certain markets had to put up with long lines at the pumps or odd-even rationing. (The latter used odd and even license plate numbers to restrict a consumer's purchases to certain days of the week.) Many economists believe that the shortages were caused by government price controls, which created a gap between quantity demanded and quantity supplied in the retail gasoline market.

Such a situation is illustrated in Figure 4–2.

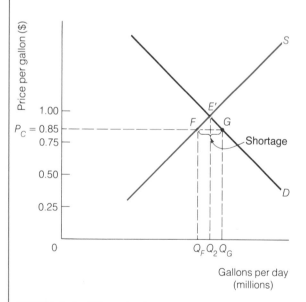

FIGURE 4–2 **Effect of a Ceiling Price on the Gasoline Market**

A price ceiling set by government at P_C results in a shortage of gasoline equal to $(Q_G - Q_F)$.

Here, the new demand and supply curves, D_2 and S_2 from Figure 4–1, are redrawn, but the government imposes a *price ceiling* of 85 cents per gallon instead of allowing the price to rise to the market equilibrium of 95 cents per gallon. The result is a gasoline shortage equal to $(Q_G - Q_F)$. The shortage will persist unless the government removes the price ceiling or changes in demand or supply lead to an equilibrium price that is equal to or lower than the government's ceiling.

In both 1978 and 1979 the shortages disappeared by late fall, due to a seasonal reduction in demand (fewer vacation trips) and an upward movement of the government's ceiling price. The main lesson to be learned here is that insisting on a ceiling price that is below the market equilibrium price is tantamount to insisting on lines at the pump, rationing, or both. In 1980 and 1981, price controls were relaxed, and gasoline shortages no longer occurred.

AIRLINES: REGULATION OR COMPETITION?

During the late 1960s and early 1970s a frequent complaint of economists and government officials was that airlines in general, and U.S. airlines in particular, had a good deal of excess capacity. That is, many flights left the ground with few passengers in comparison to the number of seats on the aircraft. The conventional wisdom was that the carriers had talked themselves into buying newer and larger planes in order to defend themselves from each other (no one wants to fly on an outdated plane) but that the passenger demand simply was not there.

AIRLINE REGULATION

Interstate airline service and fares in the United States have been regulated by the Civil

Aeronautics Board (CAB). Historically, the CAB has not tried to promote competition among the various airlines. Instead it has attempted to ensure that all areas of the country receive adequate service and that the airlines are permitted to charge fares that will generate reasonable profits, even if they must cover certain specific routes at a loss.

Until the second half of the 1970s neither the airlines nor the CAB paid much attention to price (fares) as a determinant of the quantity of passengers carried. Both seemed to view the demand curve as fairly steep but shifting inward and outward in response to general economic conditions. To cope with the low profits that accompanied the excess capacity of the late 1960s and early 1970s the CAB prescribed fare increases. People in the industry seemed to think that the higher fares would affect traffic very little and would increase the revenues of the carriers.[4]

A NEW LEAF

During the late 1970s, when the price of aviation fuel skyrocketed, a peculiar thing happened. Airline fares actually fell for a while during 1977–1979, and traffic increased tremendously. Airline profits took off like jets during 1978, even though it appeared that a dog-eat-dog price war was going on among the various lines.[5] Indeed, the CAB did an abrupt about-face and approved fare cuts and special discount plans almost as quickly as they were proposed.

The events of 1978 were set off by some changes in thought about the relationship between fares and people's willingness to travel. The issue was forced on the airlines by an innovation in charter service that was the brainchild of a British entrepreneur, Sir Freddie

Laker. Laker believed that at transatlantic fares significantly below those charged by the major airlines the quantity demanded of tickets for flights between the United States and Europe would expand tremendously. Laker proved his point with his highly successful Skytrain operation in the summer of 1977, and later that year "discount mania" hit the airlines.[6]

Meanwhile, as luck would have it, President Jimmy Carter's appointee to the chairmanship of the CAB turned out to be a person who believed that more competition was the right prescription for breathing some vitality into the U.S. airlines. This man, economist Alfred E. Kahn, was an expert on regulated industries. Best of all, he must have recognized that what his predecessors and the airlines had long thought about passengers' demand for service at low prices was simply wrong.

ECONOMIC ANALYSIS AND AIR FARES

We can use the basic tools of demand and supply analysis from Chapter 3 to see what happened. Figure 4–3 shows the industry supply curve for U.S. transcontinental economy flights (all carriers combined) from New York to Los Angeles, along with two demand curves. Demand curve D_1 is the demand curve portrayed by the CAB and the airlines prior to the advent of discount mania. D_2 is the actual demand curve. Before the discounting began, the round-trip price set by the CAB was $400. At that price, quantity Q_1 of passengers would buy tickets, while the airlines would have seats available (point B) for up to Q_4 passengers. The surplus ($Q_4 - Q_1$) resulting from this higher-than-equilibrium price constituted excess capacity. The CAB and the airlines thought that cutting the price to, say, $270 would move the industry along D_1 from point A to point C. Very little increase in ticket sales would occur, and the quantity of service supplied would drop (point F) as fewer planes

4. The CAB's traditional stance is discussed in John M. Blair, *Economic Concentration: Structure, Behavior, and Public Policy* (New York: Harcourt Brace Jovanovich, 1972), pp. 659–660.

5. See "Airline Profits Are Taking Wing," *Business Week*, June 26, 1978, p. 39.

6. "Discount Mania Hits the Airlines," *Business Week*, August 8, 1977, p. 26.

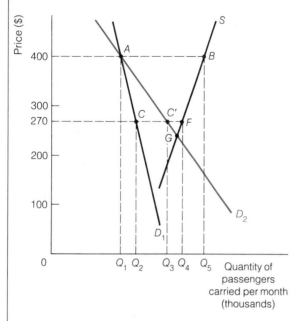

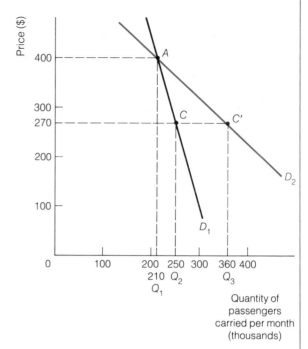

FIGURE 4–3   Effect on Price Reductions on Transcontinental Air Passenger Traffic

At the high ticket price of $400, the airlines had excess capacity of ($Q_4 - Q_1$). They thought a $270 price would move them to point C on D_1, but instead, the demand curve was D_2 and they would sell Q_3 at point C'. Without regulation, point G would be equilibrium.

FIGURE 4–4   Effect of a Price Decrease on Airline Revenues

A reduction in fares from $400 to $270 results in decreased revenue if the demand curve is D_1, but increased revenue if the demand curve is D_2. (Compare $400 × 210,000 to $270 × 360,000.)

were kept on the route. However, the actual demand curve, D_2, tells us that at a fare of $270, quantity Q_3 of tickets would be sold, and little excess capacity would exist. If regulation of fares were dropped altogether, the ticket price would fall below $270, where excess capacity would be eliminated (point G).

DEMAND, REVENUE, AND PROFITS

In Figure 4–4, the two demand curves are redrawn using some likely, but not real, numbers to help illustrate what happened. Suppose Q_1 = 210,000 passengers per month, Q_2 = 250,000 passengers per month, and Q_3 = 360,000 passengers per month. Given the demand curve that the airlines believe in (D_1), a fare cut from $400 to $270 would increase

the quantity of tickets sold by 40,000 per month, or by about 14.3 percent. However, the actual demand curve (D_2) shows that the quantity sold would increase by 150,000, to 360,000. This would be an increase of about 71.4 percent.

The difference in the responsiveness of consumers to the price cut along the two demand curves is significant. If we calculate the effect on airline revenues from ticket sales, we get the following results:

	Passengers per Month (Q)	Fare (P)	Airline Revenues (P × Q)
Point A	210,000	$400	$84,000,000
Point C	250,000	270	67,500,000
Point C'	360,000	270	97,200,000

From these figures we see that with demand curve D_2, airline revenues from ticket sales actually increase from $84 million per month to $97 million per month when the fare is cut from $400 to $270. There is a big difference between what happens along demand curve D_1 and what happens along curve D_2 in the price range $400 to $270. Economists would say that D_2 is elastic over this range and D_1 is inelastic.

In Chapter 17 the concept of elasticity of demand □ will be explained in greater detail. For the time being, it is sufficient to know that when *demand is elastic*, the response of consumers to a price change is relatively large; and when *demand is inelastic,* the response is relatively small. A fare increase from $270 to $400 would therefore cause airline revenues to fall along the elastic demand curve D_2 and to rise along the inelastic curve D_1. Thus, if D_1 were the actual demand curve, the CAB and the airlines would have been able to achieve an increase in revenues by raising fares.

During 1978 the airlines found that consumer demand for tickets on many routes was more like D_2 than D_1. Thus the discount mania resulted in a boom in traffic and airline revenues. Profits soared for a while; but in 1979 demand waned, fuel prices rose, and the industry was disrupted by a major strike and a disastrous accident. Fares moved upward, but it was clear that in the future neither the industry nor the CAB would be as naive about passenger responsiveness to fares as it has been in the past.

GOLD:
MONEY
OR METAL?

Suppose someone owed you $1,000. On the due date the person offered to pay you with a piece of plain, unmarked gold about the size of a dime. Would you take the gold in payment? Probably not. However, your decision would most likely depend on two things: how much you trusted your debtor and how much you knew about gold and its market value. Certainly the gold would not be the same thing as money to you. The main reason is that money, whether U.S. dollars, German marks, or Mexican pesos, comes in clearly marked denominations so that you are sure how much, in terms of purchasing power, you are getting when you receive it.

Even if your debtor had offered you German marks, you could easily establish their dollar value by checking the financial pages of a newspaper or phoning a bank. Indeed, both the newspaper and the bank could also tell you the current dollar value of an ounce of gold, but this would not solve your dilemma unless you knew the weight of the gold and its purity. In fact, you might have to go to a lot of trouble and expense to establish the monetary value of the unmarked piece of gold.

We can conclude from this situation that gold is not money (although it has been, when it was coined in times past) but is a money substitute. Fundamentally, its market value is determined by supply and demand. Today's most popular gold coin, the South African Krugerrand, does not have any nominal value imprinted on its face. It bears a variable, market determined value in respect to the rand, South Africa's unit of currency. Each Krugerrand contains exactly one troy ounce of pure gold, so it is the precious metal that accounts for the coin's value, not the purchasing power of the rand. Buying a Krugerrand is, in fact, purchasing a scarce metal, not exchanging one kind of money for another.

GOLD'S SCARCITY

Like many other precious metals and minerals, one of the major economic characteristics of gold is that it is scarce. In fact, the Gold Information Center, which specializes in promoting the sale of gold, runs full-page ads in magazines like *Newsweek* just to tell us how

381

little gold there really is.[7] The total amount that has thus far been recovered from the earth is about 80,000 metric tons. According to the Gold Information Center, this amount is enough to form a cube of gold eighteen yards on each side, or something about one-tenth the size of the Washington Monument.

Furthermore, the annual addition of new gold to the world's total stock of it was estimated in 1979 to be about 1,400 tons per year, or a total supply increase of about 1.7 percent annually, regardless of market price. Finally, current estimates of gold reserves yet to be mined suggest that the upper limit for the world's gold stock is about 120,000 tons. This compares with the following reserve estimates for other common metals: silver, 943,000 tons; copper, 2,050,000,000 tons; tin, 41,477,000 tons; and zinc, 270,000,000 tons.[8]

DEMAND FOR GOLD

Apparently, King Tut was fond of gold. Today, lots of rich folks like it too (although perhaps not as much as they like diamonds). For thousands of years, one of the primary sources of demand for gold has been people's fascination with its unique ornamental qualities. In addition, gold has industrial uses, is a mainstay of the dental profession, and has served as both money and money substitute.

Fundamentally, people who are interested in gold as a money substitute are betting that the purchasing power of money will fall, while the price of gold will rise. Of course, when the purchasing power of money falls, the prices of many things other than gold rise. However, gold's price rise may outstrip that of other goods and services because an important force in the market for gold is *speculation.*□

Speculation occurs when someone who purchases or sells an item does so in anticipation of profiting from a change in its price. When gold speculators start to drive up the price of gold, they are doing so because they think others will enter the market and drive the price up still farther, netting the early arrivals a fine profit. Of course, when speculators start to unload their holdings of gold, the price may drop precipitously as everyone tries to sell before a further decline occurs. Thus the gold market is volatile (characterized by wide fluctuations in price), because demand can change sharply as the expectations of speculators and others are revised.

ANALYSIS OF PRICE BEHAVIOR

We have characterized the supply of gold as being virtually fixed for any given short period of time. Increasing the price of gold may bring some of it out of people's private hoards, but by and large the gold that is traded on the world's markets each day represents the same stock turning over again and again. For a short period of time (say one year or less), we can expect the supply curve for gold to be just about vertical and the demand curve downward sloping and subject to sudden shifts outward or inward. Figure 4–5 illustrates such a situation. Curve S_1 is the actual supply curve for gold, and curve D_1 is current demand curve. If speculators' activities shift the demand curve out to D_2, the price of gold will rise sharply, since the quantity supplied is not much affected by price. Something like this happened in late 1979 and early 1980, when gold skyrocketed from $250 per ounce to over $800 per ounce.[9]

The lack of responsiveness in quantity supplied (economists call this *inelasticity of supply*□) that goes with the nearly vertical supply curve for gold combines with the volatile, shifting demand curve to cause great changes

7. For an example of gold promotion, see the ad placed by the Gold Information Center in *Newsweek*, July 9, 1979, p. 69.

8. U.S. Bureau of Mines, *Mineral Facts and Problems* (Washington, D.C.: Government Printing Office, 1976), pp. 298, 1005, 1131, 1228.

9. See "The Gold Rush of '79," *Newsweek*, October 1, 1979, pp. 48–54; and "A New Gold Standard," *Newsweek*, January 28, 1980, pp. 66–67.

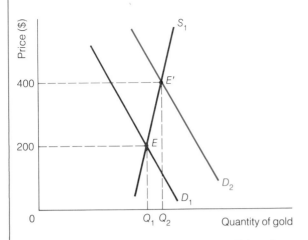

FIGURE 4–5 Effect of Demand Increase on Price of Gold

An increase in the demand for gold has a marked upward effect on its price, since the quantity supplied of gold is not very responsive to short-term price changes (supply is *inelastic*).

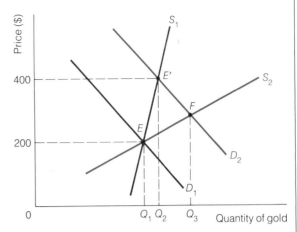

FIGURE 4–6 Comparison of Gold Price Increase with Different Elasticities of Supply

If the supply curve for gold were S_2 instead of S_1, an increase in demand from D_1 to D_2 would result in an equilibrium at point F, where price is less than at E' on S_1.

in price. Figure 4–6 introduces a more elastic (less steep in the neighborhood of point E) supply curve, S_2. If the supply curve for gold were more like S_2 than S_1, the quantity of gold supplied to the market would increase to Q_3, and the price would not rise so sharply when D_1 shifted to D_2. (See point F in Figure 4–6.) However, because the quantity of gold supplied to the market does not respond very much to increases in price, demand shifts do indeed cause wide fluctuations in price. Thus one who buys gold as an investment should keep in mind that its price can fall as quickly as it rises. Even a gold speculator who believes that the long-run trend in the price of gold is upward will need staying power and, perhaps, a strong cardiovascular system.

LABOR: ENGINEERS
PUMPING GAS?

◆

The year 1971 found many highly trained engineers working in the oil industry. Unfortunately for a large number of them, the job they held was one that most of us would associate with the title "gas pump jockey." Some less fortunate but equally qualified engineers were just plain out of work. The *Wall Street Journal* lamented their situation in an article headlined "The Breaking Point: As Jobs Stay Scarce, Unemployed Engineers Face Family Crises . . . Broken Marriages and Suicides."[10] The profession was stunned. During the 1960s the demand for engineers of all specializations had soared, and the typical college graduate could pick and choose among several attractive job offers. How could the situation have turned around so quickly at the beginning of the 1970s?

SUPPLY OF AND
DEMAND FOR ENGINEERS

By using the tools developed in Chapter 3 to analyze what happened to engineers in the

10. "The Breaking Point: As Jobs Stay Scarce, Unemployed Engineers Face Family Crises-Months Without Work Bring Emotional Strain; Dearth of Money Becomes Acute-Broken Marriages and Suicides," *Wall Street Journal*, November 30, 1971, p. 1.

early 1970s, we can easily understand the turnaround. First, the supply of engineers is relatively fixed, even over a period of several years, since the typical engineering student takes four or five years to complete a bachelor's degree. Although high prices for engineers can lure some students away from the pure sciences and mathematics in midstream, a decision to change majors is often a difficult one for college sophomores or juniors. In addition, the total market for engineers is segmented into specialties (such as mechanical, electronic, civil, and chemical), and "retooling" within the general field calls for significant effort, time, and expense.

On the demand side, the market for engineers is more volatile. Although the short-run demand curve for engineers is steep (firms that need a specific type of engineer will not reduce hiring even if salaries rise substantially), from year to year it may shift markedly inward or outward. The major factors that cause such shifting are industrial expansion and contraction, technological change, and government programs related to the aerospace industry and to university research.

ANATOMY OF A CRISIS

The job crisis for engineers during 1969–1972 was a case of an inward shift of the demand curve along the fairly steep supply curve of engineers. As Figure 4–7 shows, such a shift resulted in lower salary offers (P_2) and lower employment (Q_{d2}). (In Figure 4–7, P_1 and Q_1 represent the original salary and level of employment.) The wage rate did not fall far enough to establish a new equilibrium, so the result was unemployment equal to (Q_{s2} – Q_{d2}). This lack of flexibility in salaries, at least in the short run, is typical of many labor markets and occurs because there is much resistance to lowering pay scales once they are established at a given level. Neither of these changes is shown as being large in comparison to the total number of engineers employed in 1968–1969. The reason for this approach is

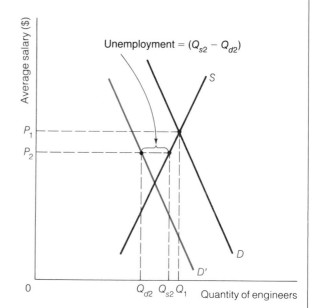

FIGURE 4–7 Unemployment in the Market for Engineers

A decrease in the demand for engineers causes unemployment equal to (Q_{s2} – Q_{d2}), since price is not sufficiently flexible to fall to the level where D' interesects S.

that even though the unemployment rate of engineers was widely described as having attained a crisis level by 1971–72, the proportion of engineers out of work and actively seeking employment never reached 3 percent.[11] Why, then, was the situation termed a crisis?

The answer, of course, is that even 2 or 3 percent unemployment of engineers was unheard of in the 1960s. Layoffs of experienced engineers and joblessness among new engineering graduates came as a shock to a profession that had been riding high. A significant number of engineers had found out the hard way that cutbacks in government spending on research and aerospace programs could have a noteworthy effect on the market.

However, it quickly became clear also that a leveling or slight decline in the output of new engineers by colleges and universities,

11. See "An Engineer Shortage Hits Industry Again," *Business Week,* July 3, 1978, p. 18.

along with some exodus of experienced engineers into management (many retooled by obtaining MBA degrees), would be more than sufficient to set the stage for great improvement in the fortunes of the profession during the second half of the 1970s. When demand again shifted outward in response to increased government spending and industry's heightened emphasis on energy and transportation technologies, a new shortage of engineers developed. *Business Week* reported in mid 1978 that some experts were predicting a glut of engineers before too long, because student enrollment in the field was moving upward at many colleges and universities.[12] However, the shortage persisted into the 1980s.

SUMMARY

1. The supply and demand curve analysis of Chapter 3 was used in this chapter to examine the recent behavior of some specific markets. Although market structure, or degree of competition, varies from one market to another, the idea that price tends toward an equilibrium level that will equate quantity supplied with quantity demanded remains a useful concept.

2. The analysis of supply and demand in the gasoline market suggests that after 1972 the supply curve of refiners shifted upward in response to increases in the price of crude oil. Since consumer demand for gasoline proved unresponsive to price changes (the demand curve was almost vertical), the price of gasoline almost doubled from 1977 to 1979, while the quantity demanded increased. The latter is explained by an outward shift of the demand curve as the supply curve shifted upward. Finally, government regulation of the price contributed to gasoline shortages that occurred during the summers of 1978 and 1979.

3. In the case of the market for air travel, both the airlines and the Civil Aeronautics Board tended to underestimate consumer response to fare reductions in the late 1970s. In fact, the demand for tickets proved to be elastic on many routes; thus the quantity of tickets sold increased greatly when fares

were cut. The result was a great increase in revenues and profits for the airlines. Later, profits fell as fuel costs increased.

4. Two characteristics of the market for gold contribute to its volatile behavior. They are relatively fixed supply and dramatic shifts in speculators' demand. Although the price of gold has been in a general uptrend for many years, it is subject to marked fluctuations. Thus a strong constitution and a good deal of staying power are prerequisites for successful speculation in gold.

5. The engineering profession periodically goes through hard times, because the demand for engineers drops if government expenditures on aerospace programs or research are cut back. The inward shift of the demand curve causes some layoffs and reduces average salaries, but its major effect is on new engineering graduates attempting to find jobs. Furthermore, since the supply of engineers cannot be increased quickly, when demand increases (shifts outward), salaries rise sharply. Thus the characteristics of the market for engineers suggest that it will continue to go through periodic booms and crises.

IMPORTANT TERMS AND CONCEPTS

Market structure	Elastic demand
Shortages	Inelastic demand
Price ceiling	Speculation
Revenues	Inelastic supply

QUESTIONS AND PROBLEMS

1. What is the relationship between crude oil prices and shifts in the supply curve of gasoline produced by refiners and distributors in the United States?

2. Why were there shortages of gasoline in the United States during the summers of 1978 and 1979? Is it likely that these shortages could have been avoided without increasing the price of gasoline? Explain.

3. Before 1977, what was the attitude of the Civil Aeronautics Board regarding consumer demand for air transportation? Why did the CAB believe that price increases would improve the airlines' profits in the early 1970s?

---

12. Ibid.

4. What was the result of the airlines' discount mania during 1977–78? Relate this result to the economist's notion of elasticity of demand.

5. If fuel prices increase significantly, what will happen to the supply curve of airline services on the transcontinental route? What will happen to fares, assuming no change in consumer demand?

6. Which of the following supply curves best represents the supply of gold over a fairly short period of time? Explain.

7. If the industrial, dental, and ornamental demand for gold does not fluctuate much over the course of a year, why do gold prices sometimes fluctuate widely over relatively short periods of time?

8. Employ a set of hypothetical supply and demand curves to explain how a change in speculators' demand for gold could cause its price to fall drastically.

9. What major determinants of the demand for engineers accounted for the crisis in the engineering job market during the early 1970s?

10. To some extent, the engineering job market appears to go through cycles of feast and famine for those in the profession. What characteristics of the supply and demand sides of the market contribute to this result?

THE MARKET FOR KEEPING YOU COOL AND STAYING WARM

Of the dozens of proposals in Jimmy Carter's ambitious energy plan, none seemed more straightforward and less controversial than the incentives for home insulation. By offering homeowners a chance to recoup part of their investment in better insulation, Administration energy planners hoped to spark an insulating boom that would reduce fuel consumption in the home and help restrain the nation's growing appetite for imported oil. But now energy officials are wondering whether their strategy can pay off any time soon. For even though

the consumer demand is there, the insulation clearly is not. And the reason, says an executive of one company that manufactures the stuff, is "the most monstrous insulation shortage facing us that I have ever seen."

As passed by the House last week, the National Energy Act will provide a tax credit of up to $400 and a subsidy for low-interest loans to encourage home insulation. It also requires utilities to advise customers on their insulation needs and, in some cases, even to do the actual installation and handle the financing. But there is a growing concern that the legislation may offer too much, too soon. In addition to worsening an existing shortage, the growing demand is also reviving old questions about

the safety of insulation materials. Later this month the Consumer Product Safety Commission will hold hearings to examine the risks, including the charge that fiber-glass particles cause cancer—an alegation that producers have long denied. And shoddy installation may also prove toublesome, with the legislative boost to insulation serving as a "virtual invitation to unscrupulous, marginal home-improvement contractors," says Federal Trade Commission staffer Robert B. Reich.

Even without the added stimulus from Carter's bill, insulation is in short supply. For instance, cellulosic insulation, a product made principally from shredded paper, obviously requires treatment with a flame retardant before it is installed-- and

95

production of boric acid, the retardant used, cannot be expanded fast enough to keep up with demand. Fiber-glass insulation manufacturers are in a similar bind; their plants now operate near full capacity and they are already rationing supplies to customers. Major plant-expansion programs are in the works, but industry officials say they will take years to complete. Meanwhile, "the whole industry is backlogged," says an executive of Certain-Teed Corp., one major producer. "Right now we're capacity-limited and all those people who want insulation are going to have to wait."

As a result, prices are already rising. . . . But the main problems attending a surge in demand will probably be on the local level. Soaring heating bills have already proved a boon to insulation installers; in Massachusetts, for example, the number of insulating firms doubled in the past year, and in Wisconsin, says a state official, new companies are "sprouting like mushrooms." So are the customer complaints, and consumer-protection officials worry that a government-fed surge in home insulation will only make matters worse. . . .

QUESTIONS

1. Use a demand and supply curve diagram to explain the immediate effect of the energy tax credit on the market for insulation.

2. According to this reading, what is the relationship between boric acid and insulation? How would you expect rising prices for insulation to affect the demand curve for boric acid?

3. If energy prices continue to rise, what should happen to the supply curve for insulation? Is there any indication in the reading that what you predict will take place? Explain.

4. With both supply of and demand for insulation increasing, can you say anything concrete about the future price of this product? Explain.

PART THREE

THE
ECONOMICS OF
NATIONAL PRODUCT,
GOVERNMENT SPENDING,
AND TAXATION

C H A P T E R 5

MEASURING
NATIONAL PRODUCT
AND
INCOME

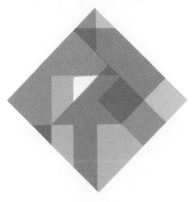

THE
BIG AND SMALL
OF
NATIONAL OUTPUT

Toward the end of Robinson Crusoe's stay on his famous Island of Despair he found himself accompanied not only by the native called Friday but also by some shipwrecked Spaniards, and he realized that they too would have to be provided for by the island's economy. He increased his work and that of the others and reported:

I contrived to increase my little flock of tame goats as much as I could; and to this purpose I made Friday and the Spaniard go out one day, and myself with Friday the next day, for we took our turns, and by this means we got above twenty young kids to breed up with the rest. . . .

It was now harvest, and our crop in good order; it was not the most plentiful increase I had seen in the island, but, however, it was enough to answer our end; for from our twenty-two bushels of barley we brought in and thrashed out above 220 bushels; and the like in proportion of the rice, which was store enough for our food to the next harvest, though all the sixteen Spaniards had been on shore with me; or if we had been ready for a voyage, it would very plentifully have victualed our ship, to have carried us to any part of the world, that is to say, of America.[1]

Crusoe's island was not much of a country, but the output of his miniature economy was a deadly serious issue to him. So it is with nations and with certain trans-nations that we now call multinational corporations. After all, how do they know how big they are or whether they are getting better off or worse off if they fail to do some accounting or record keeping?

The gross national product (GNP) has become one widely accepted measure of an economy's total output. It is a monetary measure and thus must be adjusted for inflation. After all, a country that for a given year has a 10 percent increase in money GNP and 10 percent inflation will end up with a zero increase in real GNP. Crusoe did not have this problem, because he did not have money and prices to contend with--just numbers of goats and bushels of grain. The more of these, the greater the island's GNP.

Today's GNP figures reveal some interesting facts about the meaning of the word big. For example, the United States is really big because its GNP (over $2,500 billion) is more than four times that of West Germany and nine times that of Canada. General Motors (GM) is not a country, but its gross output (sales) is larger than the GNP of many countries. For example, in 1978 GM's $63.2 billion in sales made it the world's largest corporation, and only 22 of the 150 or so countries in the world had GNPs greater than its total sales. This makes GM bigger than such countries as Austria, Argentina, Greece, Hungary, Indonesia, Korea, Turkey, and Venezuela. In fact, a 1980 report showed that 40 percent of the top economic units in the world were firms, not nations.[2]

Still, each nation's planners are vitally interested in how the GNP is behaving. For example, one day in January 1981, on two adjacent pages, the Wall Street Journal reported that (1) South Korea suffered a slump of 5.7 percent in GNP for 1980, its worst drop in output in more than twenty years; (2) Taiwan was expecting 6 to 7 percent real growth in GNP for 1981 despite a worldwide recession; (3) Denmark, while making some economic progress, forecast declines in real income for the next five years; and (4) Poland's GNP would slide downward for about two or three years but might turn around by 1985 or 1986.[3]

Of course, our major concern is with the United States and how well it does from year to year. In order to evaluate this and other questions, we need to study the system of national income accounting used by the U.S. government. This chapter does just that, and in considerable detail.

1. Daniel Defoe, *Robinson Crusoe*(New York: Walter J. Black, 1941), p. 239.

2. "40% of World's Top Economic Units Are Firms, Not Nations," *Los Angeles Times*, April 7, 1980.

3. *Wall Street Journal*, December 31, 1980, pp. 10–11.

CHAPTER 5

MEASURING
NATIONAL PRODUCT
AND
INCOME

WHAT THIS CHAPTER IS ABOUT

It is hard to imagine a household that would not keep track of its income and expenditures. It is even harder to imagine a business that would not keep an account of its revenues and expenses, even if the record keeping were not required by the Internal Revenue Service. Similarly, it is difficult to imagine that a nation would not keep track of the output produced within its borders and the income generated by and for its people.

Of course, the goals of a business are somewhat different from those of a nation. Economists generally assume that the primary aim of a firm is to maximize its profit□. A country is presumably more interested in the well-being of its citizens. Nevertheless, both firm and nation wish to be aware of the progress being made toward achieving their respective goals.

GROSS NATIONAL PRODUCT

The gross national product is one measure of the well-being of a nation's citizens. (As we will see later, it is not a perfect measure.)

> The ***gross national product (GNP)*** *for a country is the market value of all final goods and services produced during some particular time period, such as a year.*

This definition contains several key words, each of which will be discussed.

MARKET VALUE

The output of the U.S. economy is valued at current market prices. This way of valuing output offers a common unit of account in order to measure the total production of unlike things.

For example, suppose that one year the United States produced three Chevrolet Impalas and sixteen thousand bushels of wheat; and the next year it produced two Chevrolet Impalas, fourteen thousand bushels of wheat, and twenty-five dirt bikes. How can we compare the output in the two years without listing each item separately? We can do it by computing the *market value* of each of the products.

In Table 5–1 the market value of the output produced during each of the two years is computed. It is assumed that the price of an Impala is $8,000, the price of a bushel of wheat is $4, and the price of a dirt bike is $850. In this case, GNP was higher in the second year.

At this point, some additional questions arise. One might ask, for example, "How can we say the economy is doing better by producing two Impalas, fourteen thousand bushels of wheat, and twenty-five dirt bikes than by producing three Impalas and sixteen thousand bushels of wheat?" (Certainly, there are those who would argue that anyone who has ever listened to dirt bikes knows the nation was much better off without them.)

The question can be answered with two comments. First, GNP is not a perfect measure of a nation's welfare. Second, the market value of an item is an indication of its worth to someone, so there must be at least one person or one group of people to whom dirt bikes are worth $850.

Another question that arises is: What happens when prices change from year to year? Could the change affect the value of GNP even if physical output remains the same? The answer, of course, is yes. To alleviate this problem the government has developed price indexes to adjust GNP for changes in the general

level of prices. The methodology of using price indexes to adjust GNP data will be discussed in a later section of the chapter.

GOODS AND SERVICES PRODUCED

The word *produced* refers to goods and services actually manufactured, constructed, or otherwise created during the time period under consideration. In other words, it excludes secondhand products. The reason is that the measurement is of new output only.

GNP attempts to record the value of new production whether or not the output is actually sold during the relevant accounting period. Any disparity between the value of production and the value of sales is resolved by changes in the market value of inventories. If more of an item is produced than is sold, the market value of it's inventories will rise, and this increase in inventory value will be added to GNP. If less of an item is produced than is sold, the market value of it's inventories will fall, and this decrease in inventory value will be subtracted from GNP.

FINAL GOODS AND SERVICES

The specification of *final goods and services* is an explicit effort to avoid the double counting of production. Possible confusion arises because many goods go through various stages of production in different firms before they are ready for marketing to the final customer.

To illustrate this problem, we can consider the production of a can of green beans that has a supermarket price of 39 cents. The steps involved in getting the can of beans to the public may include the following: a truck farmer grows the beans and sells them to a cannery, the cannery cans them and sells them to a wholesaler, the wholesaler sells them to a supermarket, and the supermarket sells them to the final customer.

Table 5–2 shows the value of the beans at each stage of the production and selling pro-

TABLE 5–1   Computing the Market Value of GNP

Year 1

3 Impalas × $8,000	$24,000
16,000 bushels of wheat × $4	64,000
Total = GNP	$88,000

Year 2

2 Impalas × $8,000	$16,000
14,000 bushels of wheat × $4	56,000
25 dirt bikes × $850	21,250
Total = GNP	$93,250

TABLE 5–2 The Value-Added Method of Computing Production

	Value at Each Stage of Production	Value Added
Value of beans from the farmer	$0.05	$0.05
Value of beans from the cannery	0.23	0.18
Value of beans from the wholesaler	0.30	0.07
Final value of beans at the supermarket	0.39	0.09
Total value added		$0.39

cess. If we add up all of these amounts, we will get a total production value of 97 cents. But this is nonsense. We know that the final market value of the beans is only 39 cents.

From the values given in Table 5–2, we see that this problem has two solutions. One is to count the value of goods and services as they are offered for sale to the *final customer*. The other is to compute the *value added* at each stage of the production process. Using either method, we obtain a final market value of 39 cents. However, it is simpler for us to add the market values of all goods and services at their point of final sale.

Of course, some items will not have reached the final stages of production by the time the accounting period ends. This problem can be resolved by adding to GNP any increases (or subtracting any decreases) in the inventory levels of intermediate, or unfinished, products.

FINANCIAL TRANSACTIONS

Besides the sale of secondhand items, some other transactions that take place are also purely financial in nature and do not reflect productive activity. Transfer payments, one example of these transactions, often have the nature of a gift. They can occur between governments, between governments and individuals, between businesses and individuals or other recipients, and between individuals. Welfare payments and foreign aid are examples of government transfer payments. A contribution by a business firm to a college or university is a business transfer payment. A gift of $100 from Sherry Brown to Richard Dane is a transfer payment from one individual to another. This kind of financial transaction does not represent direct payment for goods or services currently produced.

Financial transactions also include the purchase and sale of stocks and bonds. Although interest payments are generally included in GNP because they represent payment for services rendered, the sale of stocks and bonds is not included because it represents only a transfer of funds from one economic entity to another.

PRICE INDEXES AND REAL GNP
◆

We have already found that GNP may increase merely because of a general rise in prices, while output remains constant. For example, suppose that total output for each of the last two years has consisted of ten Chevrolet Impalas. Furthermore, assume that last year the price of one Impala was $8,000 and that this year it is $10,000. Table 5–3 shows that GNP rose by $20,000 this year because of the price increase, while physical output did not change.

How can we adjust our measure of GNP to reflect only changes in physical output? One way of doing so is through the use of a price index.

*A **price index** gives an indication of the level of prices in a current year relative to the level of prices in some base year.*

We can compute a price index for our example as follows.

TABLE 5–3   Variations in the Value of GNP Because of Price Changes

Year 1
GNP = 10 Impalas × $8,000 = $80,000.
Year 2
GNP = 10 Impalas × $10,000 = $100,000.

TABLE 5–4   GNP Adjusted for Price Changes

Year 1	
GNP at market prices	$80,000
Price index	100
GNP at base prices	
$= \text{GNP at market prices} \div \dfrac{\text{Price index}_{\text{current year}}}{\text{Price index}_{\text{base year}}}$	
$= \$80,000 \div 1.00 = \$80,000$	
Year 2	
GNP at market prices	$100,000
Price index	125
GNP at base prices	
$= \text{GNP at market prices} \div \dfrac{\text{Price index}_{\text{current year}}}{\text{Price index}_{\text{base year}}}$	
$= \$100,000 \div 1.25 = \$80,000$	

First, let us take year 1 as the base year. Our price index for this year will be 100, which means that prices in year 1 were equal to 100 percent of the base year prices. We calculate the price index for year 2 in the following manner. We assume that the price of an Impala in year 1 was $8,000 and that it rose to $10,000 in year 2. Thus the ratio of the price in year 2 to the price in year 1 is $\text{Price}_2/\text{Price}_1 = \$10,000/\$8,000 = 1.25$, or 125 percent. Consequently, our price index for year 2 will be 125, which indicates that prices in year 2 are equal to 125 percent of the prices prevailing in the base year.

We obtain the value of GNP at base year prices by dividing the value of GNP at current prices by the ratio of the price index for the current year to the price index for the base year. In year 1 the ratio of the current year price index to the base year price index is $100/100 = 1.00$. For year 2 the ratio is $125/100 = 1.25$. We can see from Table 5–4 that the adjusted values for GNP are the same in year 1 and year 2.

Therefore

$$\text{Real GNP}_2 = \frac{\text{GNP}_2}{P_2/P_1}$$

where the subscripts 1 and 2 refer to years 1 and 2 and P_1 and P_2 are price indexes for years 1 and 2. If we invert the denominator of the above expression and multiply, we obtain

$$\text{Real GNP}_2 = \text{GNP}_2 \times \frac{P_1}{P_2}$$

In general, the value of GNP in the current year according to prices in some base year can be computed as follows:

$\text{Real GNP}_{\text{current year}}$

$$= \text{GNP}_{\text{current year}} \div \frac{\text{Price index}_{\text{current year}}}{\text{Price index}_{\text{base year}}}$$

$$= \text{GNP}_{\text{current year}} \times \frac{\text{Price index}_{\text{base year}}}{\text{Price index}_{\text{current year}}}.$$

This expression is approximately equivalent to stating that

$$\text{Output}_{\text{current year}} \times \text{Price}_{\text{current year}}$$

$$\times \frac{\text{Price}_{\text{base year}}}{\text{Price}_{\text{current year}}}$$

$$= \text{Output}_{\text{current year}} \times \text{Price}_{\text{base year}}.$$

The last expression is obviously true because the $\text{Price}_{\text{current year}}$ terms cancel. This adjusted value of GNP is often called *real GNP*, because it attempts to more closely reflect actual production of physical goods and services.

Real gross national product *is GNP valued by using the prices of some base period.*

As already indicated, adjusting GNP through the use of price indexes is approximately equivalent to actually figuring the value of current year output at base year prices. The result is an approximate value be- cause a variety of goods and services are pro-

TABLE 5–5   GNP and Real GNP for the United States, 1929–1980 (in Billions of Dollars)

Year	GNP (Current Prices)	Price Index (1972 Base Year)	Real GNP (1972 Prices)
1929	$ 103.4	32.76	$ 315.7 (= $103.4 × $\frac{100}{32.76}$)
1933	55.8	25.13	222.1
1940	100.0	29.06	344.1
1945	212.4	37.91	560.4
1950	286.5	53.56	534.8
1955	400.0	60.84	657.5
1960	506.5	68.70	737.2
1965	691.1	74.36	929.3
1970	992.7	91.45	1,085.6
1972	1,186.9	100.00	1,185.9
1975	1,549.2	125.56	1,233.9
1976	1,718.0	132.11	1.300.4
1977	1,918.0	139.83	1,371.7
1978	2,156.1	150.05	1,436.9
1979	2,413.9	162.77	1,483.0
1980	2,627.4	177.45	1,480.7

Source: "Table B–1: Gross National Product, 1929–80";"Table B–2: Gross National Product in 1972 Dollars, 1929–80"; and "Table B–3: Implicit Price Deflators for Gross National Product, 1929–80," *Economic Report of the President* (Washington, D.C.: Government Printing Office, 1981), pp. 233–237.

duced within the economy and the price of each is likely to change by a different percentage from one year to the next. Several price indexes computed by the federal government are discussed below.

GNP IMPLICIT PRICE DEFLATOR

The GNP *implicit price deflator*, the price index most frequently used for computing real GNP, is obtained by finding a weighted average of the price indexes for the goods and services that make up GNP. Roughly speaking, the weights correspond to the percentage of total production accounted for by the production of a specific category of goods and services.

In Table 5–5 the GNP implicit price deflator measures the price change of a particular group of commodities, or market basket of goods, since the base year of 1972. The market basket is supposed to represent the composition of GNP. However, because the fraction of GNP accounted for by each type of product may change over time, the market basket chosen for years other than the base year may

change from year to year. Thus the GNP implicit price deflator may change from one year to the next because of changes in the market basket of goods chosen to reflect the *composition* of GNP as well as because of changes in prices.

Table 5–5 presents values for GNP, the GNP implicit price deflator, and real GNP, valued at 1972 prices, for selected years from 1929 to 1978. As is readily apparent, the variations in current value, or nominal GNP,

"Sure, you're raising my allowance. But am I actually gaining any purchasing power?"

Reprinted by permission of the Wall Street Journal

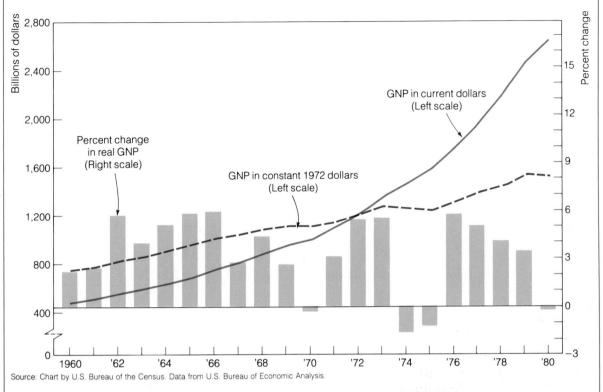

Source: Chart by U.S. Bureau of the Census. Data from U.S. Bureau of Economic Analysis.

FIGURE 5–1   Gross National Product in Current and Constant 1972 Dollars: 1960 to 1980

for year to year were far greater than those of real GNP. The relationship between GNP and real GNP is also depicted in Figure 5–1.

OTHER PRICE INDEXES

Various agencies of the federal government compute other price indexes, such as the producer price index (formerly the wholesale price index) and the consumer price index (CPI). The CPI, which is probably of greatest interest to the general public, attempts to measure the increase in retail prices of a specific market basket of goods purchased by all urban consumers. (Another version of the CPI measures price changes of a market basket of goods purchased by urban wage earners and clerical workers.)

The CPI has some discrepancies in its measure of general purchasing power because the market basket of goods used to compute the index changes only about once every ten years. Consumer buying patterns change more often, especially as new products become available. Also, not all families purchase the same market basket of goods. Still, the CPI constitutes an adequate approximation to changes in consumer buying power for many purposes.

NET
NATIONAL
PRODUCT

Net national product (NNP) *is a measure of the final market value of newly produced goods and services, minus the value of plant and equipment and natural resources used up during the production process and as a result of "acts of God" and obsolescence.*

Net national product is equal to GNP less a capital consumption allowance.

CAPITAL CONSUMPTION ALLOWANCE

*The **capital consumption allowance** is a measure of the productive capacity of capital goods—plant and equipment—used up or destroyed during the current accounting period. It also includes an estimate of the natural resources depleted during that time period.*

The *depreciation expenses* of businesses are the basis for computing the capital consumption allowance. Depreciation expenses are figured in the following way. Suppose a firm purchases a machine for $10,000 at the beginning of an accounting year and that the machine is supposed to last ten years. Because of its long life, it is unreasonable to consider the entire cost of the machine an expense in the year of purchase. Therefore, the depreciation expense for this machine for the first year and each year for the next nine years is approximately equal to $10,0000/10 = $1,000 per year.[1] The individual firm depreciation expense figures are summed to calculate the capital consumption allowance. Losses of capital equipment as the result of catastrophes such as fires or floods and of obsolescence are also included.

GROSS INVESTMENT
VERSUS NET INVESTMENT

The capital consumption allowance is also equal to the difference between *gross investment* expenditures and *net investment expenditures*. If a firm purchases a new maching for $10,000 and in the same year has total depre-

---

1. There are various accounting methods for computing depreciation, each of which gives a somewhat different result. We used the straight-line method. There are also methods for computing depreciation expense when a machine is held only part of a year.

ciation expenses equal to $6,000 for its entire plant and equipment, then its net investment is equal to $10,000 - $6,000 = $4,000.

***Net investment** in the GNP accounts is a measure of the net addition to the nation's capital stock—plant and equipment—during a particular accounting period.*

Therefore, **gross investment** is equal to net investment plus the capital consumption allowance. In the example cited above, gross investment is equal to $10,000.

GROSS NATIONAL PRODUCT AND NATIONAL INCOME

When we attempt to break GNP down into its component parts, we recognize that every newly produced good can be viewed in two ways. First, it is an expenditure item for a government agency, business, or consumer in the country or a purchaser from a foreign country. Second, its value represents income in the form of wages, rent, interest, and profit paid to those who produced it.

In Figure 5–2 the circular flow □ of goods, services, and expenditures in a four-sector economy consisting of business, household, government, and foreign sectors is sketched. *Businesses* purchase the services of factors of production and supply goods and services. They receive payments for these goods and services and make income payments for the factors of production. *Households* supply factors of production, receive income payments, and purchase the goods and services produced by businesses. *Government* purchases some of the goods and services produced by businesses and supplies some goods and services, such as electricity from the Tennessee Valley Authority and fertilizer. In the process of pro-

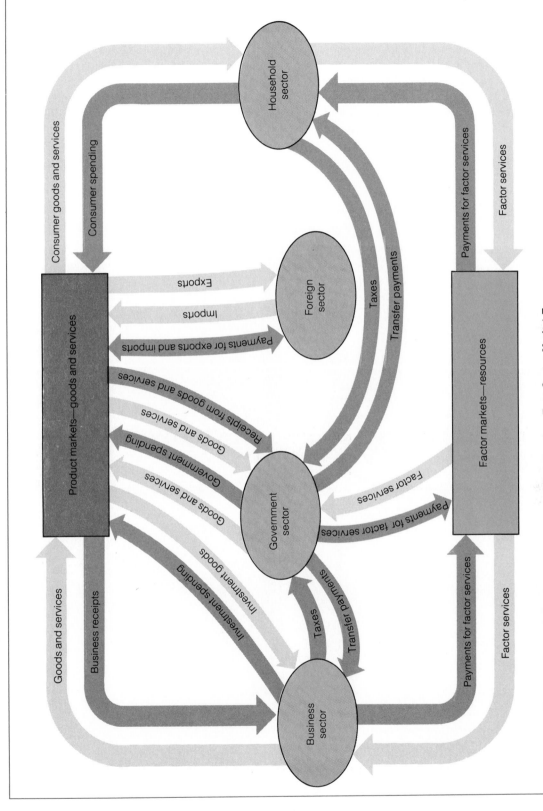

FIGURE 5–2 Flows of Expenditures, Income , Goods, and Services in a Four-Sector Market Economy

This circular flow diagram is an expanded version of the simple model of a market economy that was introduced in Figure 2–1 of Chapter 2. Note that real flows of goods and services between the four sectors of the economy are matched by flows of income and expenditure. A given sector's income is composed of expenditure flows from other sectors of the economy.

ducing these services, government uses the services of some productive inputs. Foreigners purchase the country's exports of goods and services, while imports are bought *from* foreigners. Net exports, equal to exports minus imports, may be positive or negative depending on the relative sizes of export and import flows.

Although such payments represent purely financial transactions, businesses and households pay taxes to the government, and the government gives them transfer payments. (Transfer payments by the government are subsidies to businesses and households that do not represent payments for goods and services received from them.)

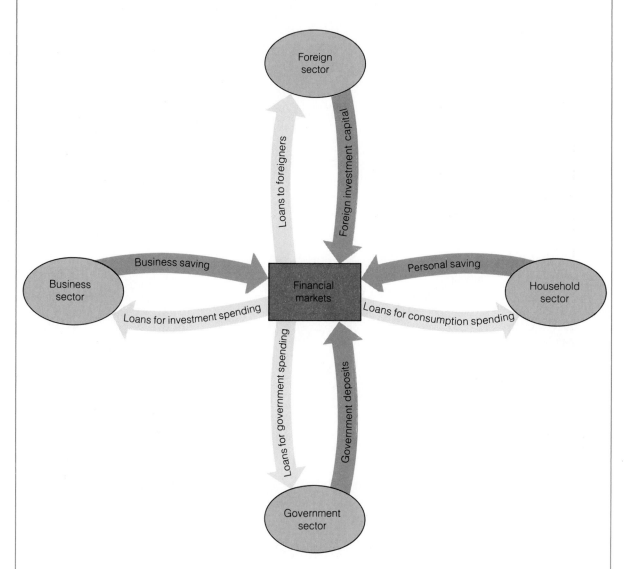

FIGURE 5–3 Financial Flows in a Four-Sector Market Economy

Financial markets facilitate the transfer of purchasing power, by means of loans from savers to borrowers. Purchasing power may be transferred both within and between sectors.

Many of the transactions illustrated in Figure 5–2 are carried out with the aid of financial institutions, such as commercial banks, and a third set of markets, the financial markets, as illustrated in Figure 5–3. Businesses, households, government, and foreigners all supply funds to the financial markets. All four sectors also receive funds from the financial markets in the form of loans. (The operations of the financial markets will be discussed more thoroughly in Chapters 10, 11, and 12.)

Since a newly produced good represents both an expenditure item and an income item, we have two ways of counting up, or valuing, GNP: (1) by adding together all expenditures for newly produced goods and services during the year and (2) by adding together all of the income generated by the producton of goods and services during the year. By using both methods the government can check its figures. Each of these ways of computing GNP will be explained in the following sections.

EXPENDITURE APPROACH

There are four main categories of expenditures for newly produced goods and services: personal consumption expenditures, gross private domestic investment, government expenditures for goods and services, and net exports. Table 5–6 indicates the amounts of these expenditures for 1980. Each of these expenditure categories will now be examined.

Personal Consumption Expenditures According to the government publication, Historical Statistics of the United States:

> ***Personal consumption expenditures*** *represent the market value of purchases of goods and services by individuals and nonprofit institutions and the value of food, clothing, housing, and financial services received by them as income in kind. It includes the rental*

TABLE 5–6   U.S. Expenditures on GNP for 1980 (in Billions of Dollars)

Expenditure Item		Total Amount	Percent of GNP
Personal consumption expenditures			
Durable goods	$210.2		
Nondurable goods	674.4		
Services	785.5		
		$1,670.1	63.6
Gross private domestic investment			
Nonresidential	295.0		
Residential	104.0		
Change in business inventories	−3.9		
		395.1	15.0
Government purchases of goods and services			
Federal	198.9		
State and local	335.9		
		534.8	20.4
Net exports		27.5	1.0
Gross national product		$2,627.4	100.0

Source: "Table B–1: Gross National Product, 1929–80"; "Table B–13: Personal Consumption Expenditures, 1929–80"; and "Table B–14: Gross Private Domestic Investment, 1929–80," *Economic Report of the President* (Washington, D.C.: Government Printing Office, 1981), pp. 233, 248, 249.

value of owner-occupied houses but does not include purchases of dwellings, which are classified as capital goods.[2]

In 1980 personal consumption expenditures accounted for 63.6 percent of GNP. As Table 5–6 shows, consumption expenditures are divided into three categories: durable goods, nondurable goods, and services. Durable goods are consumer products, such as stereo phonographs and television sets, with an average life of at least three years.[3] Nondurable goods are items such as clothes and food. Services include the services of doctors, lawyers, mechanics, maids, and shoeshiners, among others.

Gross Private Domestic Investment

***Gross private domestic investment** is all purchases of capital goods, including buildings and equipment, by private businesses and nonprofit institutions.*

Capital equipment is restricted to equipment with an average life of at least one year.

Gross private domestic investment also includes all expenditures for residential housing, whether rental or owner occupied. The reason that owner-occupied housing is included is that the owner could rent it and thereby receive income. Moreover, more and more people explicitly consider the purchase of a house to be an investment even if they intend to live in it.

Finally, the change in business inventories is also part of investment expenditures. As already indicated, an *increase* in business inventories must be *added* to GNP. Likewise, a *decrease* in business inventories is *subtracted* from GNP.

It should be emphasized that gross private domestic investment includes purchases of

capital goods produced only in the country involved, for us the United States. Also, investment expenditures include only purchases of new buildings and equipment; secondhand sales are omitted because they do not represent new production. Stock and bond purchases constitute purely financial transactions and are not included in investment expenditures. In 1980, gross private domestic investment was 15.0 percent of GNP, far less than consumption spending.

Government Purchases of Goods and Services

***Government purchases of goods and services** represent the expenditures for newly produced goods and services, including government investment expenditures, by all levels of government.*

Such items as compensation of government employees, purchases of equipment, and construction expenditures for schools, highways, and dams are considered government expenditures.

Government transfer payments, however, are not included in government expenditures.

*In general **transfer payments** are payments between sectors of an economy for which no productive services are received in return.*

Thus transfer payments such as welfare, social security, and unemployment benefits are excluded because they do not represent payment for current services received. In other words, even though people receiving social security payments may have earned or partly earned these benefits by working in previous years, they are not currently giving the government any services in exchange for the payments. The same principle holds for welfare, unemployment insurance, government subsidies, and simiar payments.[4]

Total government expenditures accounted

---

2. U.S. Department of Commerce, Bureau of the Census, *Historical Statistics of the United States: Colonial Times to 1970* (Washington, D.C.: Government Printing Office, 1975), p. 218.
3. Ibid.

---

4. Ibid. Government interst payments are also excluded, but the reason is somewhat less clear. This matter is further discussed in chapter 8.

for 20.4 percent of GNP in 1980. Federal government expenditures, which accounted for about 37 percent of total government expenditures, amounted to 198.9 billion; state and local government expenditures amounted to $335.9 billion.

Net Exports

For **net exports** the GNP accounts are adjusted to reflect the purchases of new goods and services produced in the country (for us, the United States) by foreigners, less the purchases of new foreign-produced goods by the country's residents.

Foreign purchases of U.S. goods represent U.S. production, while foreign goods purchased by U.S. citizens represent the productive efforts of foreign countries.

In 1980 U.S. exports of goods and services to other countries totaled $341.2 billion, whereas U.S. imports amounted to $313.7 billion. Thus net exports for the United States in 1980 were equal to $341.2 billion minus $313.7 billion, or $27.5 billion. This figure means that U.S. residents purchased $27.5 billion less of foreign goods and services than citizens of foreign countries purchased from the United States. It is possible, of course, for the value of net exports to be either positive or negative.

The sum of all these expenditure items must be equal to GNP. We can write this equation in mathematical form as

$$C + I_g + G + X_n \equiv GNP,$$

where:

  C = private consumption expenditures,
  I_g = gross private domestic investment,
  G = government expenditures, and
  X_n = net exports.

The $\equiv$ sign means that the sum of these expenditures must be *identical* to GNP.

The next section will examine the components of gross national product using the income approach.

INCOME APPROACH

Each good or service produced can be regarded either as an item of expenditure (for households, businesses, the government, or foreigners) or as an item that generates income for those involved with its production and related selling activities. This section analyzes the relationship between GNP and the various types of income generated through the nation's productive activities.

Nonincome Items in GNP Certain items in gross national product do not represent income to a factor of production. The first of these is the capital consumption allowance, □ an estimate of the nation's capital (plant and equipment) that has been consumed, or used up, as a result of the production of output during the current accounting period. Since this figure merely indicates the amount of production needed to maintain the original level of capital stock, it does not represent an addition to income. As defined here and as shown in Table 5–7, gross national product less the capital consumption allowance equals net national product (NNP).

Two other items that must be subtracted from NNP to obtain national income are indirect business taxes and business transfer payments. *Indirect business taxes* are taxes that have no direct relationship to business profit. They include license fees, sales and excise taxes, property taxes, and other similar fees levied on businesses. These taxes are excluded from national income because they are not directly based on the level of income for a firm. *Corporate profit taxes*, on the other hand, are included because they are directly related to the level of firms' profits.

Business transfer payments include such things as theft losses incurred by firms and business gifts to individuals and charitable organizations. These payments are excluded from national income because they do not represent payments for productive activity (maybe a thief would disagree!) However, both indirect business taxes and business

TABLE 5–7   Gross National Product in the United States: The Income Approach, 1980 (in Billions of Dollars)

Gross national product		$2,627.4
Less:		
Capital consumption allowance		287.8
Net national product		$2,339.6
Plus:		
Subsidies less current surpluses of government enterprises	$4.7	
Less:		
Indirect business taxes	211.7	
Business transfer payments	10.5	
Statistical discrepancy	1.6	−219.2
National income		$2,120.5
Including:		
Compensation of employees	1,596.5	
Rental income	31.9	
Net interest	179.8	
Proprietors' income	130.6	
Corporate profits	181.7	
	$2,120.5	

Source: "Table B–17: Relation of Gross National Product and National Income, 1928–80"; "Table B–19: National Income by Type of Income, 1929–80," *Economic Report of the President* (Washington, D.C.: Government Printing Office, 1981), pp. 252, 254–255.

transfer payments *are included* in GNP, since these costs are reflected in the market values (prices) of the goods and services produced.

Government Subsidies   Finally, the net subsidies of government enterprises or subsidies by government to private enterprises must be *added* because they represent payments to factors of production for their services. However, since these payments are not given in exchange for the goods themselves, they are not included in the market value of the products or in GNP.

For example, suppose that Amtrak has $4 billion in revenues from ticket sales for one year. Furthermore, assume that the federal government pays Amtrak a subsidy of $800 million. The market value of Amtrak's services is still only $4 billion. However, presumably the production costs totaled $4.8 billion or the government subsidy would have been unnecessary. Thus the whole $4.8 billion is included in national income.

The statistical discrepancy is merely a balancing item that the government adds or sub-

tracts to make GNP calculated with the income approach equal to GNP calculated by totaling expenditures on newly produced goods and services. Although these values must be identically equal by definition, the government's data are imprecise and discrepancies do arise. After making these adjustments to gross national product, we arrive at national income, which is discussed in the next section.

NATIONAL INCOME

National income represents the earnings of factors of production for their services during the current accounting period.

As we can guess, national income is made up of the compensation of employees, rental income, interest, and profit. Although we know intuitively what they mean, each of these types of income will be briefly described below in terms of its national income definition.

Compensation of Employees

Compensation of employees *consists of wages and salaries, including payments in kind, and supplemental benefits.*

Payments in kind can be such things as employer supplied housing and food. Supplemental benefits include the employer's share of social security payments; unemployment insurance payments; employer contributions to private health, pension, unemployment, and welfare funds; and compensation for injuries. Compensation of employees accounted for 75.3 percent of U.S. national income in 1980, by far the largest payment to a particular type of productive input.

Rental Income

Rental income *consists of the monetary earnings from the rental of real property, including the estimated net rental returns to owner-occupied nonfarm dwellings.*

The earnings of people involved primarily in the real estate business are exluded from rental income, but they are included in proprietors' incomes and corporate profits (defined below). These earnings appear in the latter two categories because they represent the profits of businesses. However, the royalties received by individuals from patents, copyrights, and rights to natural resources are included in rental income. In 1980 rental income made up only about 1.5 percent of U.S. national income.

Net Interest

Net interest *is equal to the interest payments minus the interest receipts of domestic business, plus net interest payments received from foreign sources.*

Net interest also includes imputed interest income from certain activities of financial intermediaries, such as checking account services. However, government interest payments are excluded because they are not considered expenditures for productive factors.

The reasoning behind this exclusion is that a significant portion of the government's debt was incurred as a result of wars and government transfer payments, neither of which is considered to be payment for productive activity in the sense that the assets of society are increased. (No offense to the military or the poor is intended!) Interest payments by consumers are also excluded from national income for similar reasons. In 1980 net interest accounted for approximately 8.5 percent of U.S. national income.

Proprietors' Income

Proprietors' income *includes the monetary earnings and payments in kind of sole proprietorships, partnerships, and producers' cooperatives from current business operations.*

Proprietors' income was 6.1 percent of U.S. national income in 1980.

Corporate Profits   The second-largest component of national income is corporate profits.

Corporate profits *are the before-tax earnings of corporations, excluding nonprofit corporations, that accrue to residents of the United States.*

Corporate profits include the net receipts of dividends and branch profits from abroad as well as profits of domestic operations. Corporate profits made up 8.6 percent of U.S. national income in 1980.

The next section examines national income from another perspective--the income that is received by individuals and what they do with it.

NATIONAL INCOME
VERSUS
PERSONAL INCOME

◆

As stated above, National income is a measure of the earnings of productive inputs for their services during the current accounting period.

> **Personal income** is a measure of the income that individuals actually receive during the current accounting period, whether or not it is payment for productive services.

PERSONAL INCOME

Table 5–8 shows how to compute personal income from national income data. First, corporate profits, net interest, and contributions for social insurance are *subtracted* from national income. Corporate profits are subtracted because only the dividends paid represent earnings actually received by individuals. Dividends are added in below. Net interest is subtracted because, again, not all of these payments go to individuals. Finally, contributions for social insurance are also subtracted, because they are not received by individuals during the period in which they are earned.

TABLE 5–8 The Relationship between National Income in the United States, and Personal Income (in Billions of Dollars)

National income		$2,120.5
Less:		
Corporate profits	$181.7	
Net interest	179.8	
Contributions for social insurance	203.7	
Plus:		−565.2
Government transfer payments to persons	$284.0	
Personal interest income	256.3	
Dividends	54.4	
Business transfer payments	10.5	
		+605.2
Personal income		$2,160.5

Source: "Table B–18, Relation of National Income and Personal Income, 1929–80," *Economic Report of the President* (Washington, D.C.: Government Printing Office, 1981), p. 253.

Now government transfer payments to individuals are added to personal interest income, dividends, and business transfer payments. □ Although not all of them represent payment for current productive services, they are received as income by individuals. The net result of these calculations is personal income.

 112

As shown in Table 5–8, personal income was larger than national income in 1980. This phenomenon was due in large part to government transfer payments such as social security, unemployment and welfare payments, and veterans' benefits.

The net interest figure, which represents income payments considered to be part of national income, is much smaller than personal interest income. Although some interest income does not accrue to individuals, the discrepancy occurs mainly because government interest payments are not considered to be expenditures for productive services.

Business transfer payments are also a part of personal income that does not repesent a payment for productive services. The payments include charitable gifts by firms and business losses due to theft.

DISPOSABLE PERSONAL INCOME

Disposable personal income is the income figure that interests people the most. As shown in Table 5–9:

> **Disposable personal income** is the income paid to individuals which remains after personal income, property, excise, gift, and inheritance taxes are subtracted from personal income.

Personal income taxes account for over 80 percent of personal taxes, by far the largest portion.[5]

5. See "Table B–70: Federal Budget Receipts, Outlays, and Debt, Fiscal Years 1970–82"; and "Table B–75: State and Local Government Receipts and Expenditures, Selected Fiscal Years, 1927–79," *Economic Report of the President* (Washington, D.C.: Government Printing Office, 1981), pp. 315, 321.

PERSONAL OUTLAYS

Personal outlays consist of personal consumption expenditures, interest paid by consumers to businesses, and net personal transfer payments (gifts) to foreigners. Nearly all of these outlays are consumption expenditures.

PERSONAL SAVING

Personal saving is the portion of personal income that is not spent.

Personal saving was 4.8 percent of personal income in 1980 (see Table 5–9). Personal saving and personal consumption expenditures, the factors that determine them, and their impact on gross national product are further discussed in Chapter 6.

GNP: A RECAP

We have examined gross national product from three perspectives--the expenditure approach, the national income approach, and the personal income approach. These approaches are summarized in Table 5–10. The final section of this chapter considers GNP as a measure of social welfare.

TABLE 5–9   The Disposition of Personal Income in the United States, 1980 (in Billions of Dollars)

Personal income		$2,160.5
Less:		
Personal taxes		338.8
Disposable personal income		$1,821.7
Less:		
Personal consumption expenditures	$1,670.1	
Interest paid by consumers to business	46.4	
Net personal transfer payments to foreigners	1.0	
		1,717.5
Personal saving		$ 104.2

Source: "Table B–21: Dispositon of Personal Income, 1929–80," *Economic Report of the President* (Washington, D.C.: Government Printing Office, 1981), p. 258.

GNP: A MEASURE OF SOCIAL WELFARE?

We know that GNP is a measure of the current market value of final goods and services produced in a country during a specific accounting period. It is often assumed that the greater a nation's GNP, the better off its citizens are.

However, GNP, *by itself* may not be an adequate yardstick by which to measure social welfare. We have already discussed the misleading effects of price increases on GNP. In the following section we will examine other qualifications in using GNP as a measure of social well-being.

UNRECORDED SOCIAL COSTS

Certain costs that are external to the market system may not be reflected in GNP data. For example, if a steel mill pollutes the air and thereby imposes a social cost ▫ on society, this fact will not be reflected in GNP unless the steel mill is subsequently required to install pollution control equipment. When such equipment is installed, it represents an increase in GNP.

The national income and product accounts frequently ignore other, similar by-products of economic growth, such as congestion and various forms of pollution, including noise. Later, as resources are used to clean up the pollution, GNP is increased even more. (Social benefits and costs are discussed at greater length in Chapter 27).

NATURE OF THE OUTPUT

As long as the output produced represents legal market activities, it is valued at its current market value. Thus, if two countries have the same level of GNP, we cannot determine the welfare of each country's citizens using this

TABLE 5–10 Summary of the National Income and Product Accounts

Expenditure Approach	National Income Approach	Personal Income Approach
GNP ≡	GNP	GNP
Personal consumption expenditure	− Capital consumption allowance	− Capital consumption allowance
+	≡ Net national product	≡ Net national product
Gross private domestic investment	− Indirect business taxes	− Indirect business taxes
+	− Business transfer payments	− Business transfer payments
Government expenditures	+ Net government subsidies	+ Net government subsidies
+	≡ National income ≡	≡ National income
Net exports	Compensation of employees	− Corporate profits
	+	− Net interest
	Rental income	− Contributions for social insurance
	+	+ Government transfer payments
	Net interest	+ Personal interest income
	+	+ Dividends
	Proprietors' income	+ Business transfer payments
	+	≡ Personal income
	Corporate profits	− Personal taxes
		≡ Disposable personal income
		− Personal consumption expenditures
		≡ Personal saving

measure. However, suppose that one country is producing primarily defense and consumption goods while the other is producing primarily capital goods such as factories, dams, and schools.

Can we assume that the citizens of the two countries are equally well off, or should we consider differences in the types of goods produced? Many people contend that the composition as well as the level of GNP is important.

PER CAPITA OUTPUT

In measuring social welfare, total output, or GNP, matters less than *output per capita,* or per person. A country may have a rising real GNP; but if its population is growing at an even faster rate, the well-being of its citizens may actually be declining.

DISTRIBUTION OF INCOME

The value of GNP does not take into account changes in the *distribution* of income. However, many people argue that at least some

changes in the distribution of income in favor of greater equality would improve the welfare of a society. (Others, of course, disagree.)

QUALITY CHANGES

As the value of GNP is calculated at the present time, we do not have a very accurate measure of the quality changes that occur in goods and services produced from year to year. While the U.S. Bureau of Labor Statistics does make some estimates of such changes in automobiles, little official information exists on quality changes for other products. Sometimes these changes are reflected in price increases, but often they are not.

NONMARKET ACTIVITIES

Many nonmarket activities that add to the well-being of society are not counted in GNP. For example, a woman who cleans, cooks, and cares for her children, among other tasks for which she is not paid, adds nothing to GNP. Such activities as repairing one's own house or entertaining one's friends by playing the guitar are likewise only partly or not at all reflected in GNP. (They are reflected only to the extent that materials or tools are purchased in the marketplace.)

Of course, as more and more women work outside the home and as the economy grows, more and more of these nonmarket activities are becoming market activities and therefore are being counted in GNP. Does this fact mean that the welfare of the nation is necessarily increasing? Because of increases in income tax rates, a recent trend has been for people to do more jobs for themselves and each other outside the market system. Does this trend imply a decrease in social welfare?

ILLEGAL ACTIVITIES

Another touchy issue is the question of illegal activities. The value of these activities is, of course, not included in GNP, even if they are market activities. Most of us would probably agree that many illegal goods and services do not add to social welfare. But what about liquor? And gambling? In some places it is illegal to sell liquor by the drink. Gambling is illegal in even more places.

For many situations, even economists do not agree on the social welfare implications. In cases where they agree on the nature of the effect on social welfare (positive, negative, or neutral), measurement of the size of the effect often presents substantial problems.

Perhaps the most that can be said is that GNP is an estimate of the productive activity of a nation and one indication of social welfare. It is not a perfect measure of either the goods and services produced or of social welfare. Nevertheless, it is a useful approximation in many cases.

SUMMARY

1. This chapter examined the concept of gross national product--the current market value of all final goods and services produced within a country during the current accounting period, excluding the sale of secondhand items and purely financial transactions.

2. GNP may increase merely because the general price level has increased. For this reason, price indexes and the concept of real GNP have been developed. Real GNP is current period GNP measured in the prices of some base period.

3. The composition of GNP can be measured from three perspectives—the expenditure approach, the national income approach, and the personal income approach. The four types of expenditures that make up GNP are personal consumption expenditures, gross private domestic investment, government expenditures, and net exports.

4. The difference between gross investment and net investment is the capital consumption allowance, which is a measure of the capital stock used up in the production of GNP during the current period. Thus net investment is the net addition to the nation's capital stock.

5. Using the net income method of looking at the composition of GNP, we find that GNP less the capital consumption allowance is equal to net national product. Net national product minus indirect business taxes and business transfer payments plus net subsidies to government enterprises equals national income. National income consists of payments to productive inputs for their services during the current period. These payments can be divided into five types: compensation of employees, rental income, net interest, proprietors' income, and corporate profits.

6. We can also look at national income from the perspective of income received by individuals, or personal income. First, corporate profits, net interest, and contributions for social insurance are subtracted from national income. Next, government and business transfer payments, personal interest income, and dividends are added to the resulting figure to obtain personal income. Personal income less personal taxes is disposable personal income. Disposable personal income minus personal consumption expenditures is personal saving.

7. It is frequently argued that GNP is not an adequate measure of social welfare because certain social costs are not taken into account and composition of output, distribution of income, quality changes, nonmarket activities, and illegal activities are not considered. Also, it is argued that per capita output is a more relevant indicator of social welfare than is GNP.

IMPORTANT TERMS AND CONCEPTS

Gross national
  product
Transfer payments
Price index
Real gross national
  product
Net national product
Gross investment
Capital consumption
  allowance
Net investment
Personal consumption
  expenditures
Government
  purchases of goods
  and services

Net exports
National income
Compensation of
  empolyees
Rental income
Net interest
Proprietors' income
Corporate profits
Personal income
Disposable personal
  income
Personal saving

QUESTIONS AND PROBLEMS

1. What is GNP?

2. Given the following data, find personal consumption expenditures:

Gross private domestic investment	$ 16 billion
Net exports	7 billion
GNP	113 billion
Government expenditures	11 billion

3. What is the difference between GNP and real GNP?

4. What is the capital consumption allowance? If the capital consumption allowance is $6 billion and net investment is $8 billion, what is gross investment?

5. Given the data in the table below, find real GNP in terms of 1972 prices (all in billions of dollars):

Year	GNP (Current Prices)	Price Index (1972 = 100)	Real GNP (1972 Prices)
1941	$ 124.9	31.34	_____
1951	330.2	57.27	_____
1961	523.3	69.28	_____
1971	1,063.4	96.02	_____
1972	1,171.1	100.00	_____
1973	1,306.6	105.80	_____

6. Given the following data (all figures in billions of dollars), find the capital consumption allow-

ance, net national product, corporate profits, and government expenditures:

Gross national product	$621
National income	547
Rental income	14
Compensation of employees	435
Personal consumption expenditures	478
Net interest	7
Gross private domestic investment	47
Proprietors' income	23
Business transfer payments	2
Indirect business taxes	17
Net exports	24
Net government subsidies	8

7. Is it possible for GNP to increase without an increase in physical output? Explain.

8. Whay has the use of GNP as a measure of social welfare been criticized?

9. Which of the following items were included in GNP in 1980?

Sale of a 1976 car
Welfare payments
Wages paid to a cook
Purchase of a bond issued by IBM
Money saved by a professor when fixing the plumbing in the family home
Increase in business inventories
Purchase of a piece of antique jewelry
Rental value of an owner-occupied house
Value of a parent's time spent caring for the children
Income of the owner of a jewelry store

10. What is meant by *net exports*? Give an example.

11. What is national income? What is personal income? How can we obtain personal income from data for national income?

12. How would government statisticians use the value-added approach to determine GNP? Give an example.

13. How would a $3 billion increase in business inventories affect GNP?

14. Define *personal saving*, *disposable personal income*, and *personal consumption expenditures*.

15. Complete the table below (figures in billions of dollars):

Personal consumption expenditures	$363
Personal income	498
Disposable personal income	_____
Personal taxes	$85
Personal saving	_____

THE UNDERGROUND ECONOMY

In the government's books, 29-year-old Carl C. of Hollywood, Calif., appears as a part-time actor who supplemented his 1977 unemployment insurance by taking handyman jobs worth $2,700. In fact, Carl made $12,000 building sundecks, laying patios and painting garages; he received most of his payments in cash and simply did not report the income. Solomon A. of Chicago, Ill., works in his son's liquor store for about $10,000 a year in cash. Neither he nor his son ever mentions the arrangement to the government. That off-the-books salary, added to his monthly social-security checks, enables the 70-year-old

grandfather to live in comfortable style, complete with a three-month vacation in Florida every winter. Jack D. is an antiques dealer in New York City. Customers who are willing to pay him in cash get significant discounts on his merchandise, and Jack records on his books only part of what they actually pay. The result: lower income taxes plus a safety-deposit box chock-full of ready cash.

Carl, Solomon and Jack have slid into the "underground economy"--the vast and murky nether world of jobs, services and business transactions that never show up in official records. Some of their colleagues there are prostitutes, drug dealers, bank robbers and illegal aliens who do not want their activities publicly recorded for obvious reasons. But many more are otherwise law-abiding Americans who simply want to avoid paying taxes, and

either deliberately understate the amount of their incomes or fail to report them at all.

Some experts think that the underground economy may be growing even faster than the "legal" one. Resentful of high taxes and wrung by inflation, more and more Americans may be looking for--and finding--ingenious ways to beat the system. "Once that voluntary compliance breaks down," warns Mort Levy, head of San Francisco's Accountants for the Public Interest, "it's the beginning of the end."

SUBTERRANEAN BLUES

By definition, the real dimensions of the subterranean economy are immeasurable. But one economist at the City University of New York has reached an alarming estimate that has caused wide-spread controversy. Prof, Peter Gutmann of Baruch College calculates that the income generated by the underground economy in 1977 added up to $195 billion--about 10 percent of the acknowledged gross national product. Had taxes been collected on that sum, Gutmann estimates, they might nearly have eradicated the $48 billion U.S. budget deficit. If hidden employment could have been tabulated in official labor statistics, he suggests, the nation's 6.4 per cent unemployment rate would surely have been reduced. And since much of the subterranean economy flourishes in the poor urban ghettos, says Gutmann, there are probably fewer American families living in poverty than the official statistics indicate.

CASH AND CARRY

. . . In January, readers of *The Chicago Sun-Times* had a rare chance to see just how pervasive the underground economy can be. The newspaper, in collaboration with the Chicago Better Government Association, bought a Near North Side bar, which they named the Mirage. The owner of record and the the bartenders were all employees of the sponsoring organizations, and in the guise of ordinary entrepreneurs, they set out to document corrupt Chicago business practices.

CHEATING LESSONS

An accountant told them that he kept tax accounts for 700 local businesses, and that all but four cheated on their returns. He taught them to pay off city inspectors, police and firemen, and to skim 40 per cent off the top of their receipts, keeping special books for the tax man. They were not to keep cash-register tapes, which might give them away. They were not to list the bar's four part-time employees on the payroll, so that they could avoid paying social-security and workmen's compensation taxes for them. The Mirage team contacted ten other local accountants to see what they would advise; eight told them to cheat.

At higher levels, a growing number of executives are rediscovering a grand old way to avoid taxes: the barter system. Some use it to avoid capital-gains taxes by claiming that the property they trade away is equal in value to what they get in return--with no profit on either side of the transaction. "I know a man who recently exchanged six city blocks for a hotel, two Cadillacs and an option on some oil-drilling rights," reports Roy Herberger, Jr., associate dean of the University of Southern California's business school.

Some local businessmen have so refined the barter system that it nearly replaces other forms of currency. One Denver club uses credits as its sole medium of exchange. A carpenter who makes six cabinets, for example, earns twelve credits that he might use to pay a member lawyer for a divorce. "Since there's no cash and no W–2 forms," says Denver CPA Jack Anderson, "people feel they don't have to count it as income." . . .

"DO IN MODERATION"

Such barter arrangements have not been thoroughly tested in court. And like most other aspects of the underground economy, they are not easy for the tax collectors to ferret out for a challenge. "If you do it in moderation, they'll probably never get you," says Herb Kuschner, a New York tax attorney.

Some experts worry that growth in the underground economy is a serious sign that the American system of voluntary tax compliance is in trouble. Few think there is real danger that tax evasion will become a national sport, as it has in France and Italy. Buy they do point to flourishing hidden economies in Germany, where thousands of *Schwarzarbeiter* (illicit workers) never report their incomes; in Sweden, where professionals use an unreported barter system almost as a matter of course, and in the United Kingdom, where "the fiddle" with the tax rules is now epidemic. Like the United States, all three nations were once models of taxpayer compliance.

QUESTIONS

1. What is meant by *underground economy*?
2. How significant is the underground economy? Explain.
3. Why does Gutmann believe that the size of the underground economy is increasing?
4. What are the most serious areas of noncompliance with the tax system?

CHAPTER 6

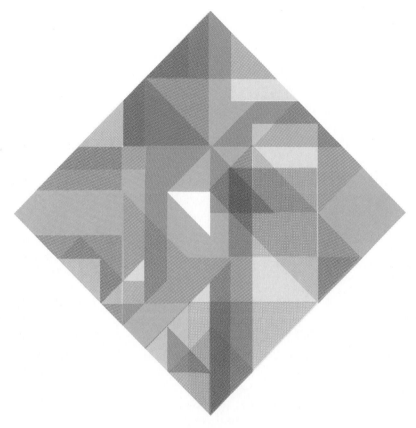

A KEYNESIAN
EXPLANATION
OF
NATIONAL INCOME
DETERMINATION

ANATOMY
OF A
RECESSION

Detroit, September 15, 1981

The phone rings at Bob Farnsworth's house. "Hello, Bob. This is Bill Brickson, the contractor. When do you want me to get started on that new country home of yours?"

"Nothing doing, Bill. I just can't swing it right now."

"But, Bob, I thought you said my bid was right in the ballpark. I felt sure you would want to go ahead with the job."

"Sorry, Bill. Everyone at the plant has the jitters. What with interest rates and buyer resistance, those new compact cars just aren't selling. We might have to shut down some lines, and a few of us supervisors could get axed."

As soon as Brickson hangs up, he calls Jill Coachman, the Cadillac dealer. "Jill, when those Eldorados come in, don't bother to save one for me. Fransworth just backed out on that country home he was going to build, and at the prices you've got on those new babies, we'll just have to make our '79 last a bit longer."

Coachman bids farewell to Brickson and calls her banker, Grosswald. "Greg," I'm going to have to ask you for an extension on that inventory note. The Eldorado shipment is on its way, but I think I'm going to be stuck with a few of the cars for a while."

Grosswald grants the extension, but later that day he refuses to give a loan to Albertson, who is planning to build a new restau-

Source: This parable was inspired by a similar piece written by columnist Art Buchwald to describe the onset of a recession in 1975. See Art Buchwald, "You Gotta Patronize Peter If You Wanna Pay Paul," *Washington Post*, February 20, 1975, p. C–1.

rant. Albertson then notifies his contractor, Brickson, that the restaurant will not be constructed because he cannot get a loan. Albertson also calls Hernandez, his restaurant equipment supplier, to tell him that no equipment will be bought. Hernandez promptly calls Brickson to let him know that because of a drop in equipment sales, the planned addition to the Hernandez house will have to be canceled.

Later that day, Coachman finds out from the General Motors distribution office that dealer rebates will be given on sales of Eldorados. She happily calls Brickson. "Bill, I have good news. GM is rebating the Eldorados, so I can give you a price that will make it possible to get that car!

Brickson replies, "No way, Jill. After Farnsworth backed out on the country home, Albertson told me he wasn't going to build his new restaurant. To make matters worse, I had a good-sized home addition job lined up for Hernandez, the wholesaler, and he backed out too. Business is getting lousy."

"Oh no!" groaned Coachman. "I was planning on selling cars to Albertson and Hernandez too."

The point of this hypothetical dialogue is that one person's spending is another person's income. An unexpected drop in spending, particularly on durable goods or investment goods, can result in economic disaster through a chain-reaction known as the multiplier effect, the major topic of this chapter.

CHAPTER 6

A KEYNESIAN EXPLANATION OF NATIONAL INCOME DETERMINATION

WHAT THIS CHAPTER IS ABOUT

AGGREGATE DEMAND AND AGGREGATE
  SUPPLY
PLANNED SAVING AND INVESTMENT
THE "FUNDAMENTAL LAW" OF
  CONSUMPTION
The Consumption Function
Nonincome Determinants of Consumption
THE EQUILIBRIUM LEVEL OF INCOME
THE MULTIPLIER
THE PARADOX OF THRIFT
SAVING: ANOTHER POINT OF VIEW

This chapter begins with an analysis of the variables that affect the level of national income and employment and the rate of economic growth. As explained in Chapter 1, *macroeconomic analysis* is the branch of economic thought that deals with a country's aggregate economic variables, such as levels of income, consumption, investment, and employment in a country.

Industrialized, capitalistic economies continually experience fluctuations in the levels of national income□ and employment. *Depressions and recessions* are reductions in the

114

level of economic activity (national income and employment). They are frequently characterized by a significant amount of *unemployment*. When *unemployment* exists, there are people who are willing and able to work but cannot find jobs. When economists state that the *unemployment rate* is 6 percent, they mean that 6 percent of those who are willing and able to work—who are in the labor force—cannot find jobs. (A more technical definition of unemployment is given in Chapter 13.)

Periods of recession are frequently followed by *boom periods*, when national income increases. During such periods the general level of prices may also rise. When prices rise in the economy as a whole, *inflation* is said to exist.

In general, governments wish to avoid both excessive amounts of unemployment and high rates of inflation, since these factors may reduce the well-being of society as a whole. Thus it is easy to understand why a country's government officials and economists want explanations for variations in the general level of economic activity. However, many other people are also concerned with this topic. Why?

For one thing, most people living in industrialized countries share the goal of wanting to get ahead. They want to advance in their jobs and attain higher and higher levels of real income.

Although the belief that hard work brings success need not be entirely disregarded, most of us realize that life is not so simple. The Great Depression of the 1930s, with unemployment rates as high as 25 percent in the United States, was sufficient to obliterate this optimistic point of view for many people. In addition, most of us have faced the disappointment of being turned down for a job. We came with high anticipation, *knowing* we could do the work, and believing that it must be obvious to our prospective employer what a good job we would do. Unfortunately, it later turned out that someone else got the job, and there were just not enough jobs to go around. It is difficult to get ahead without a job.

Economists have spent many years wrestling with the causes of and potential cures for unemployment. However, in recent years their attention has been directed increasingly to another ogre—inflation. This chapter and Chapter 7 will examine some of their explanations of how the level of national income for a country is determined and why unemployment and inflation exist.

This chapter will also describe the theory of national income determination that evolved from the 1930s work of the English economist John Maynard Keynes,□ a leading economic thinker whose career spanned most of the first half of the twentieth century. Since the Great Depression, Keynes' analysis of the forces that determine the level of national income has become an important influence on the economic policies of countries with capitalistic economies.

The key variables in this chapter are consumption, saving, investment, and the level of national income. As explained in the pages which follow, in a simplified Keynesian model the levels of the first three variables interact in a specific way to determine the equilibrium level of national income. The chapter will explain the Keynesian view of how fluctuations in the levels of consumption and investment may cause national income to rise or fall.

AGGREGATE DEMAND AND AGGREGATE SUPPLY
◆

Chapter 5 discussed how the government measures the levels of national output and income. The national income accounts tell us what quantities of goods and services the country actually produced during a particular year. Thus they indicate the aggregate quantity supplied.

The **aggregate quantity supplied** is the total quantity of goods and services a country produced during a particular year.

274

The word *aggregate* is used to mean the total quantity for the entire country. Each item produced represents an income flow to some sector—household, business, government, or foreign. Thus the aggregate quantity supplied and gross national income are identical. Using the figures for consumption expenditures, government purchases of goods and services, net exports, and business investment, the national income accounts also give us some idea of what happened to the goods and services during a given year.

While the national income accounts present a picture of what actually *did* happen to the goods and services produced during a given year, they do not, however, tell us how much consumers, government, businesses, and foreigners were *willing and able to spend* on newly produced goods and services during the year. The next section will explain why. The amounts these groups were willing and able to spend are important because their total represents aggregate demand.

The aggregate quantity demanded *is the expenditures that all potential purchasers (consumers, business, government, and foreigners) of a country's output are willing and able to make, given a particular level of gross national product.*

We will see that aggregate demand occupies center stage in the Keynesian explanation of the forces that determine the level of GNP.

On the basis of Chapters 3 and 4, it is tempting to depict aggregate demand and aggregate supply as shown in Figure 6–1. The overall price level prevailing in the economy is indicated by the price index □ along the vertical axis. An index of the physical output of goods and services is on the horizontal axis. The aggregate demand curve is shown as a downward-sloping line, which indicates that the quantity demanded will increase as the price level falls. The aggregate supply curve is upward sloping, which indicates that the quantity supplied will increase when prices rise.

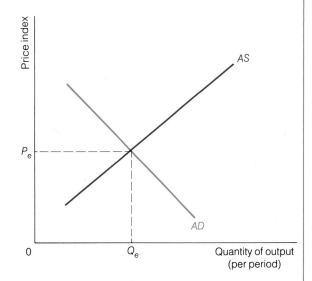

FIGURE 6–1   One Possible View of Aggregate Supply and Demand

In this case the aggregate supply curve is depicted as an upward-sloping line, which indicates that the aggregate quantity supplied is greater at higher prices than at lower prices. The aggregate demand curve is downward-sloping, indicating that a greater quantity of goods and services will be demanded at lower prices than at higher prices.

Given Figure 6–1 and the analysis in Chapters 3 and 4, it would be easy to conclude that if the aggregate quantity of goods and services demanded were not equal to the aggregate quantity supplied, prices and quantity produced would adjust so the economy would reach an equilibrium at P_e and Q_e. As in the earlier chapters, **equilibrium** □ means that the quantity demanded is equal to the quantity supplied. The only difference is that here we are referring to aggregate, or total, quantities demanded and supplied of all newly produced goods and services in the entire national economy, rather than of a single good or service. Thus, in the context of Figure 6–1, the achievement of an equilibrium level of national income that would also include an equilibrium in the market for labor seems simple enough.

Until the 1930s most economists did not consider unemployment a potentially serious difficulty. A simplified version of classical economic thought on this issue is depicted in

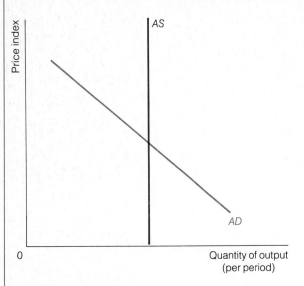

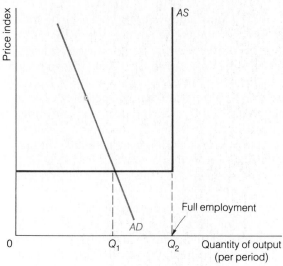

FIGURE 6-2 The Classical View of Aggregate Supply and Demand

The classical economists thought that the aggregate quantity supplied of goods and services was fixed in the short run. Accordingly, the aggregate supply curve is drawn as a vertical line. The aggregate demand curve is still drawn as a downward sloping line. The intersection of the aggregate demand and supply curves determines the overall price level in the economy.

FIGURE 6-3 The Keynesian View of Aggregate Supply and Demand

Keynesian economists view the aggregate supply curve as being a horizontal line until full employment is reached, at Q_2. In this case, the intersection of the aggregate demand and supply curves determines the aggregate quantity of goods and services produced and the level of employment as well as the general price level.

Figure 6-2. Classical economists□ believed that the aggregate quantity of goods and services that could be supplied at a given point in time was fixed—that it was a function of the available labor force, the existing capital stock (plant and equipment), and the available technology. Thus the aggregate supply curve in Figure 6-2 is depicted as a vertical line, *AS*, representing production of goods and services with full employment of labor. The aggregate demand curve, *AD*, is downward sloping, as it was in Figure 6-1. The economists believed that prices would adjust so an equilibrium level of income with full employment could be attained.

After Keynes' landmark work, *The General Theory of Employment, Interest, and Money* was published in 1936, economists who accepted Keynes' explanation of national income determination were no longer willing to accept the economic theory depicted in Figure 6-2.

A simplified version of the Keynesian view

is shown in Figure 6-3. In this figure the aggregate supply curve for goods and services is drawn as a horizontal line for some range of output and then as a vertical line. The vertical portion of the curve corresponds to the classical aggregate supply curve at full employment. The horizontal portion reflects the presence of unemployment and of inflexible wage rates and prices. Keynes believed that this portion of the aggregate supply curve for goods and services could exist because while wage rates and prices would rise in response to excess demand, they would be rigid or inflexible in a downward direction in response to decreased demand. Thus the market for newly produced goods and services, accompanied by unemployment, could reach an equilibrium at a point such as Q_1; and no economic forces would automatically cause the equilibrium to move to the full employment level of output, Q_2.

Many factors may be responsible for wage

rate rigidities. Among them are union agreements, minimum wage laws, and other set pay scales, such as teachers' and administrators' salaries. Unemployment may also occur because of lack of information on the part of labor and business. Workers may not know of available jobs, and businesses may be unable to locate people willing to work. Likewise, the prices of goods and services may not fall in the presence of excess supply because of the pricing policies of businesses.

In Figure 6–3 aggregate demand plays a critical role in determining the equilibrium level of national output and income. This chapter and Chapter 7 will assume, in keeping with the simplified Keynesian view of the national economy, that the equilibrium level of output is less than Q_2, as shown in the figure. Thus, even if the market for newly produced goods and services is in equilibrium, if the labor market is not, unemployment will exist.

*As the term is used here and in the next two chapters, **equilibrium level of income** means that the aggregate quantity demanded of newly produced goods and services is equal to the aggregate quantity supplied. However, disequilibrium in the labor market, especially unemployment, may be present.*

Since a country's annual output consists of many different types of products (not only apples and oranges but also roller skates, automobiles, and Silly Putty, for example), we must value the total amount produced in dollar terms. However, it is generally assumed in this chapter and Chapter 7 that the prices of these goods and services are constant. Thus changes in expenditures for goods and services and changes in income represent changes in the actual quantities of goods and services purchased and supplied.

Economists who believe, as Keynes did, that unemployment may be a serious problem are concerned with how the aggregate market for goods and services reaches an equilibrium. The reason for their interest is that they be-

lieve that government can reduce unemployment through taxing and spending policies which affect the aggregate demand and supply of goods and services. They also believe that such policies can be used to combat inflation caused by excess aggregate demand.

This chapter's description of the operation of the aggregate market for newly produced goods and services uses a simple economy that consists of only business and household sectors. Chapter 7 will explain how government spending and taxing policies influence aggregate demand and supply. The simple economic system is introduced first in order to make the interaction of aggregate demand and supply easier to grasp. Once this basic model is understood, the effects of government policies in a more advanced model will be easily comprehended.

This section of the chapter explains the significance of the levels of planned or desired saving and investment in achieving an equilibrium level of income. We shall see that since saving depends primarily on the level of national income, whereas investment does not, it would be a lucky break if the equilibrium level of output of newly produced goods and services occurred at the full employment level of output. As stated above, the simplified version of the Keynesian theory which follows will ignore the economic impact of government purchases of goods and services, taxes, and foreign trade. It will also assume that corporations do not retain earnings; thus all profits are received by individuals as income.

PLANNED SAVING
AND
INVESTMENT
◆

Chapter 5 showed that gross national expenditure must always be equal to gross national income as measured by the national income and product accounts◻. These accounts, however, measure the actual levels of saving and investment. When we speak of the *equilibrium*, or *sustainable*, level of output and income, we are concerned with the *desired* or *planned* levels of investment and saving. **Planned levels of saving and investment** are important because the expectations of all participants in the market for newly produced goods and services must be met if equilibrium is to occur. The aggregate quantity of these items demanded must equal the aggregate quantity supplied.

Thus *when the economy is at an equilibrium level of income, planned saving and investment must be equal to actual saving and investment.* Otherwise, the aggregate quantity demanded (measured in dollar terms) will not be equal to the aggregate quantity supplied, and actions taken by consumers or businesses will tend to cause the current level of income to change. We will see why next.

In our simple model, expenditures for newly produced goods and services can come from two sources: the consumption expenditures of individuals and the investment spending of businesses (assuming, still, that there are no taxes, transfer payments, or undistributed corporate profits; that all investment is net investment; and that there is no depreciation). Therefore, all income earned by factors of production is personal disposable income, and this income is equal to the aggregate quantity of goods and services supplied, or GNP.

Individuals can do two things with their income—save it or spend it on consumption goods. (The assumption here is that only businesses make investment expenditures for plant and equipment. Individuals may buy the stocks and bonds of businesses, but such actions do not represent investment expenditures in the sense that the term is used here.) Thus for the aggregate quantity supplied to equal the aggregate quantity demanded, planned investment expenditures must make up for the portion of income that individuals save.

For example, if *planned* investment expenditures are less than the amount which individuals wish to save, aggregate quantity demanded will be less than aggregate quantity supplied. In this case, businesses will not sell as much of their product as they expected, and they or their suppliers will have a greater amount of inventory on hand than they wish to have. Such *excess*, or *unplanned*, investment in inventories will usually cause firms to cut back on the production of their products or on orders for materials and other inputs. If suppliers are affected, they in turn will usually cut back their production quotas or their orders from other suppliers. Thus production will be reduced, and national product and income will fall. As we will see later, national income will in fact fall by more than the original cutback in output. This will occur because as production declines, so do consumers' incomes and, consequently, consumers' demand for goods and services.

On the other hand, if planned investment expenditures are greater than planned saving, the aggregate quantity demanded will be greater than the aggregate quantity supplied and the inventories of some firms will be decreased to undesirably low levels. In this case, businesses will have invested less than they desired in inventories. Consequently, they will probably increase their output or their orders from suppliers, which will result in an increase in national income. This increase in national income will in turn cause consumer demand for goods and services to increase. How long this process continues will be discussed later in the chapter.

Similar reactions will occur if consumers or businesses save more than they planned to because the goods and services they wish to purchase are not available in sufficient quantities. Of course, if the economy is at full employment, prices will have to rise enough to eliminate the excess demand.

Thus national income is at an equilibrium level only when both savers and investors *actually* save and invest, respectively, as much as they *planned* to save and invest. Otherwise, these groups will take actions that will cause national income to rise or fall. This point will be discussed in greater detail later in the chapter. The next section of the chapter explains the Keynesian view of which economic variable is most important in determining the level of planned consumption expenditures and, therefore, the level of planned saving.

THE FUNDAMENTAL
LAW OF
CONSUMPTION

◆

In *The General Theory* Keynes stressed the importance of the propensity to consume—the relationship between income and consumption.

According to Keynes, the **fundamental psychological law of consumption** is that "men are disposed, as a rule and on the average, to increase their consumption as their income increases, but not by as much as the increase in their income."[1]

In other words, consumers as a group do not spend every penny of an additional dollar of income.

MARGINAL AND AVERAGE
PROPENSITIES TO CONSUME

Before the discussion of Keynes' "law" goes any further, two terms must be defined: average propensity to consume and marginal propensity to consume.

The **average propensity to consume** is given by total consumption expenditures divided by disposable income, or the fraction of each dollar of income, on the average, that is spent on consumption goods.

Thus the average propensity to consume (APC) is shown as $\frac{C}{Y_d}$, where C is consumption expenditures and Y_d is disposable income.

The **marginal propensity to consume** is given by the change in consumption expenditures resulting from a change in disposable income divided by the change in income.

The marginal propensity to consume (MPC) is expressed as $\frac{\Delta C}{\Delta Y_d}$, where Δ (the Greek letter delta) means "change in."

Thus a family with an annual income of $10,000 that spent $9,500 would have an average propensity to consume of $\frac{C}{Y_d} = \frac{\$9,500}{\$10,000} = 0.95$. If it spent $900 out of an additional $1,000 in disposable income, its marginal propensity to consume would be:

$$\frac{\text{change in consumption spending}}{\text{change in disposable income}} = \frac{\$900}{\$1,000} = 0.9.$$

Keynes argued that, as a group, people in developed countries do not spend all their current income on current consumption. They save for various reasons: to make a future purchase, for a rainy day, or out of thriftiness. Moreover, it seems reasonable to argue, as Keynes suggested, that the proportion of total disposable income spent on consumption items declines as income rises.[2]

For example, a family with a low level of disposable income, say $4,500 per year, may have to spend all its income, or perhaps even more, just to stay alive. On the other hand, a family with a high level of disposable income, say $200,000 per year, may prefer to save a substantial percentage of the income since it can live comfortably on a much smaller amount. However, a family's marginal pro-

---

1. John Maynard Keynes, *The General Theory of Employment, Interest, and Money* (New York: Harcourt, Brace, and World, 1964), p. 96.

2. Ibid., pp. 97–98.

pensity to consume does not necessarily fall as its income rises. For the United States as a whole, the MPC is between 0 and 1.

For the sake of simplicity the marginal propensity to consume is assumed to be constant in this book, whereas the average propensity to consume is not necessarily so. The APC will not be constant if people with low levels of income spend more than their disposable income (temporarily, of course). See Table 6–1 for examples of a constant APC and a declining APC (but a constant MPC in both cases).

THE CONSUMPTION FUNCTION

The **consumption function** expresses the relationship between consumption and disposable income.

If we assume that the MPC is constant, we can represent the consumption function graphically by a straight line. Suppose the consumption function for a family is given by $C = 500 + 0.9Y_d$. In this case, 0.9 is the marginal propensity to consume; it is the slope of the line representing consumption in Figure 6–4. The $500 is the amount the family would spend, at least temporarily, if its disposable income were $0, given its level of wealth, its tastes and preferences, and the amount of spending necessary for its members to stay alive.

Because of this $500 amount, the average propensity to consume will be greater than the marginal propensity to consume. For example, if disposable income is $5,000, consumption expenditures by the family will be $500 + 0.9 ($5,000) = $500 + $4,500 = $5,000. Thus APC = C/Y_d = $5,000/$5,000 = 1. However, at an income level of $10,000, consumption expenditures total $500 + 0.9 ($10,000) = $9,500, and APC = $9,500/$10,000 = 0.95. In this case and for all similar consumption functions where consumption spending is positive at a zero level of income, the average propensity to consume decreases and approaches the value of the marginal propensity to consume as income rises. In the

TABLE 6–1 Consumption, Disposable Income, Average Propensity to Consume, and the Marginal Propensity to Consume

(a) Constant APC: $C = 0.9Y_d$

Y_d	C	APC	$MPC = \dfrac{\Delta C}{\Delta Y_d}$
$ 0	$ 0	Undefined	
			0.9
2,000	1,800	0.9	
			0.9
4,000	3,600	0.9	
			0.9
6,000	5,400	0.9	
			0.9
8,000	7,200	0.9	
			0.9
10,000	9,000	0.9	
			0.9
12,000	10,800	0.9	
			0.9
14,000	12,600	0.9	

(b) Decreasing APC: $C = 500 + 0.9Y_d$

Y_d	C	APC	MPC
$ 0	$ 500	Undefined	
			0.9
2,000	2,300	1.15	
			0.9
4,000	4,100	1.02	
			0.9
6,000	5,900	0.98	
			0.9
8,000	7,700	0.96	
			0.9
10,000	9,500	0.95	
			0.9
12,000	11,300	0.94	
			0.9
14,000	13,100	0.94	

case above, the average propensity to consume would approach 0.9.

By examining the triangle *ABD* in Figure 6–4, we can see that the marginal propensity to consume is the slope of the consumption function. The distance *AB* represents a change in disposable income of $5,000. The distance *BD* represents the corresponding change in consumption expenditures, or $4,500. Thus:

Change in consumption spending

  Change in disposable income

$$= \frac{\$4,500}{\$5,000} = 0.9,$$

which is the marginal propensity to consume and the slope of the consumption line. This

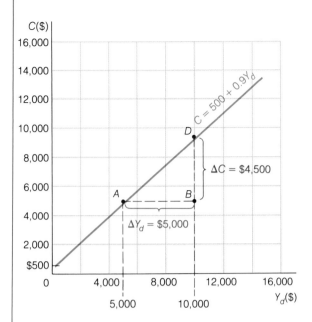

FIGURE 6–4 The Consumption Function $C = 500 + 0.9Y_d$

The consumption function $C = 500 + .9Y_d$ is drawn in this graph. Note that the marginal propensity to consume, given by $\frac{\Delta C}{\Delta Y_d}$, is equal to $\frac{\$4,500}{\$5,000}$ or 0.9. As incomes rise, consumers spend $.90 of each additional dollar of income recieved.

relationship holds because the slope of the consumption line measures the rate of change in consumption expenditures with respect to a change in income.

MARGINAL AND AVERAGE PROPENSITIES TO SAVE

Two terms that are used frequently in discussions of the average propensity to consume and the marginal propensity to consume are *average propensity to save (APS)* and *marginal propensity to save (MPS)*.

The **average propensity to save** out of disposable income is the amount saved out of disposable income divided by the total amount of disposable income, or APS = $\frac{Saving}{Disposable\ income}$.

Since this chapter considers disposable income to be either saved or spent on consumption goods,[3]

$$\frac{Consumption\ expenditures}{Disposable\ income} + \frac{Saving}{Disposable\ income} = 1.$$

Therefore, the average propensity to consume plus the average propensity to save must equal 1, and APS = 1 − APC.

The **marginal propensity to save** is the change in saving that occurs as a result of a change in disposable income divided by the change in income, or MPS = $\frac{Change\ in\ saving}{Change\ in\ disposable\ income}$.

Again, since a consumer must either spend or save any addition to disposable income:

$$\frac{Change\ in\ consumption\ expenditures}{Change\ in\ disposable\ income} + \frac{Change\ in\ saving}{Change\ in\ disposable\ income} = 1.$$

Thus the marginal propensity to consume plus the marginal propensity to save must be equal to 1, and MPS = 1 − MPC. For example, if the marginal propensity to consume is 0.9, the marginal propensity to save must be 1 − 0.9 = 0.1.

In the example where the consumption function is $C = 500 + 0.9Y_d$, the average propensity to save at an income level of $5,000 is equal to 1 − APC = 1 − 1 = 0. At a $10,000 income level APS = 1 − 0.95 = 0.05. The marginal propensity to save is equal to 0.1 at all income levels.

---

3. This proposition is incorrect, strictly speaking, because, as indicated in Chapter 5, interest paid by consumers to businesses and net personal transfers to foreigners are not considered consumption expenditures. However, because these expenditures are only 2 to 5 percent of disposable income, we can ignore them at this point.

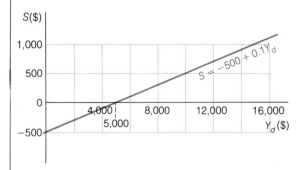

FIGURE 6–5   **The Saving Function $S = -500 + 0.1Y_d$**

The saving function $S = -500 + .1Y_d$ is drawn in this graph. At a level of income equal to \$0, consumers would spend \$500, or saving would be equal to \$ – 500. The marginal propensity to save, or $\dfrac{\Delta S}{\Delta Y_d}$, is equal to .1.

As already indicated, the amount saved out of disposable income is given by disposable income minus consumption spending, Y_d – C. In the example above, at a level of disposable income equal to \$0, \$500 will be spent. Thus saving, S, will be equal to \$0 – \$500 = – \$500. At a \$5,000 income level, saving will be equal to \$0; and at a \$10,000 income level, saving will be \$500.

▌The **saving function** expresses the relationship between saving and disposable income.

We can represent the saving function graphically by noting that the amount saved when disposable income is equal to \$0 is the saving-axis intercept term. Also, the marginal propensity to save is equal to 1 minus the marginal propensity to consume and is the slope of the saving function. (See Figure 6–5.) In this case the saving function is $S = -500 + 0.1Y_d$.

The long-run trend of the average propensity to save disposable income in the United States has been 0.06 to 0.065.[4] In other words, consumers historically have tended to save about

6 to 6.5 percent of their disposable income. Table 6–2 presents data on aggregate consumption expenditures and disposable income in the United States from 1929 to 1980. It shows that the average propensity to consume has ranged from a high of 1.00 during the depression in 1933 to a low of 0.74 during World War II, when goods were rationed by the government. From 1970 through 1980 the average propensity to consume ranged from 0.89 to 0.92. (The average propensity to save plus the average propensity to consume may not be exactly equal to 1 because of the presence of interest paid by consumers to businesses and net personal transfers to foreigners. Neither item is considered a consumption expenditure or saving.)

NONINCOME DETERMINANTS OF CONSUMPTION EXPENDITURES

Most of this book emphasizes the relationship between consumption expenditures and disposable income. However, other factors also affect the level of consumer spending for newly produced goods and services. Among these factors are wealth, expectations, and indebtedness.

Wealth   The wealth that consumers have affects their willingness and ability to purchase goods and services. Other things remaining equal, wealthy consumers can obtain funds (from sales of assets, savings accounts, or loans) for consumption expenditures more easily than can other consumers. On the other hand, wealthy consumers may already own a large stock of consumer goods such as automobiles, television sets, and video cassette recorders, which may somewhat offset the tendency of this group of people to spend more.

Expectations   Consumers' expectations about future prices, future income levels, and the availability of certain goods and services also affect spending patterns. For example, con-

4. "The U.S. Bias against Saving Leads to High Inflation, Weak Dollar, Slow Growth, Declining Productivity," *Business Week*, December 11, 1978, p. 91.

TABLE 6-2 **Personal Disposable Income, Consumption Expenditures, and the APC in the United States, 1929-1980 (in Billions of Dollars)**

Year	Personal Disposable Income	Consumption Expenditures	APC = $\frac{C}{Y_d}$	Year	Personal Disposable Income	Consumption Expenditures	APC = $\frac{C}{Y_d}$
1929	$ 82.4	$ 77.3	0.938	1959	$ 338.4	$ 310.8	0.918
1933	45.6	45.8	1.004	1960	352.0	324.9	0.923
1939	70.0	67.0	0.957	1961	365.8	335.0	0.916
1940	75.3	71.0	0.943	1962	386.8	355.2	0.918
1941	92.2	80.8	0.876	1963	405.9	374.6	0.923
1942	116.6	88.6	0.760	1964	440.6	400.5	0.909
1943	133.0	99.4	0.747	1965	475.8	430.4	0.905
1944	145.6	108.2	0.743	1966	513.7	465.1	0.905
1945	149.1	119.5	0.802	1967	547.9	490.3	0.895
1946	158.9	143.8	0.905	1968	593.4	536.9	0.904
1947	168.7	161.7	0.960	1969	638.9	581.8	0.911
1948	188.0	174.7	0.930	1970	695.3	621.7	0.894
1949	187.9	178.1	0.948	1971	751.8	672.2	0.894
1950	206.6	192.0	0.929	1972	810.3	731.1	0.902
1951	226.0	207.1	0.916	1973	914.5	812.0	0.888
1952	237.7	217.1	0.913	1974	998.3	888.1	0.890
1953	252.2	229.7	0.911	1975	1,096.1	976.4	0.891
1954	257.1	235.8	0.917	1976	1,194.4	1,084.3	0.908
1955	275.0	253.7	0.923	1977	1,311.5	1,205.5	0.919
1956	292.9	266.0	0.908	1978	1,462.9	1,348.7	0.922
1957	308.6	280.4	0.909	1979	1,641.7	1,510.9	0.920
1958	319.0	289.5	0.908	1980	1,821.7	1,670.1	0.917

Source: *Economic Report of the President* (Washington, D.C.: Government Printing Office, 1981), p. 258.

sumers who expect the prices of nonperishable goods such as automobiles to rise in the near future will tend to buy more of them now than they would if they expected prices to fall or to remain constant.

Likewise people who expect their real incomes to rise in the future are usually willing to spend greater amounts now than they would if they expected their incomes to fall. Thus a student nearing graduation might be willing to take out a loan to buy a new car, whereas a construction worker anticipating a layoff would not.

Moreover, consumers who expect limited quantities of a good to be available in the future tend to increase their current expenditures for that product. During the gas crisis many people waited in long lines at service stations to top off their gas tanks because they feared it would be more difficult to purchase gasoline a few days later. Other people purchased gasoline storage tanks. In the last few years we have also lived through so-called shortages of sugar, coffee, peanut butter, and paper products, with corresponding panic buying on the part of consumers.

Consumer Credit The level of consumer indebtedness and the availability of consumer credit also affect consumer spending. For example, during the fall of 1980 the level of consumer debt was fairly high relative to disposable income. As a result, consumers kept their spending at low levels. In the spring of 1980 President Carter placed additional restrictions on the issuance of consumer credit, an action that further limited consumer spending. Consumer attitudes toward debt and thriftiness in general also influence the level of consumption expenditures.

The next section of this chapter explains how consumption and investment expenditures determine the equilibrium level of income in the economy.

THE EQUILIBRIUM LEVEL OF INCOME: AGGREGATE DEMAND AND SUPPLY APPROACH

The level of national income is important to both the economist and the noneconomist because it reflects a country's output of goods and services and level of employment. The *eqilibrium* level of national income is important because it reflects either the current level of economic activity or the direction in which national income and employment will probably head.

The discussion of national income determination in this chapter and in Chapter 7 will continue to assume that no price changes occur, so that all the changes taking place are changes in the *real* values of such variables as consumption, saving, and investment. The discussion will also assume that unemployment exists, so that sufficient resources are available for the economy to expand its level of real output. In this situation aggregate demand plays the dominant role in determining the equilibrium level of income.

For the sake of simplicity the discussion will continue to assume that all investment is net investment (no depreciation), that no government taxes or transfer payments exist, and that no undistributed corporate profits remain. Under these assumptions all income earned by factors of production is also personal disposable income. Therefore, personal disposable income is equal to national income, and both are equal to the aggregate quantity of goods and services supplied (the latter valued in real or constant dollar terms). The letter Y will be used to designate aggregate supply and income. With prices assumed to be constant, even though the aggregate quantity demanded and the aggregate quantity supplied are shown in dollar terms, changes in the quantities as measured in these terms do reflect changes in real, or actual, quantities of goods and services.

Figure 6–6 shows an example of an aggregate consumption function, $C = 50 + 0.8Y$, where all numbers represent billions of dollars. An aggregate consumption function expresses the relationship between consumption spending and the level of disposable income for an entire economy. We can use Y or national income in the consumption function because under the assumption of no taxes or undistributed corporate profits, income and disposable income are equal. The previous consumption function, $C = 500 + 0.9Y_d$, was the consumption function for a single family. The remainder of the chapter will assume for purposes of illustration that the consumption function for the economy as a whole is $C = 50 + 0.8Y$, again in billions of dollars. The lower marginal propensity to consume could be caused by the spending habits of families with high incomes, since these families tend to spend a lower proportion of their incomes than do families with lower incomes.

A line that forms a 45-degree angle with either axis has been added to figure 6–6. Since the same scale is used for both axes of the graph, the 45-degree line has the property that any point on it designates an equal distance from the origin on either the vertical axis or the horizontal axis. This property is quite useful in analyzing aggregate demand and supply and the equilibrium level of income.

If, as in Figure 6–6, the horizontal axis represents both aggregate income and aggregate quantity supplied, and if the total expenditure that makes up aggregate demand is measured on the vertical axis, then aggregate quantity demanded will equal aggregate quantity supplied where a line representing aggregate expenditures crosses the 45-degree line. This result holds because the level of income associated with such a point is equal to the amount of expenditure it represents.[5]

---

5. Some economists prefer to call the 45-degree line the aggregate supply curve. Their reasoning is that businesses would wish to supply an amount equal to the aggregate quantity demanded at any point. Otherwise, the aggregate quantity demanded of goods and services would either exceed or be less than the aggregate quantity supplied. In the

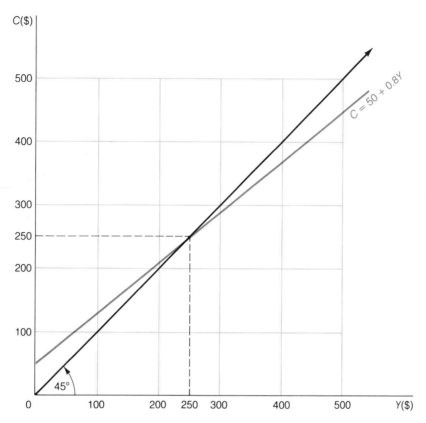

FIGURE 6–6   The Consumption Function and Aggregate Supply (in Billions of Dollars)

The aggregate consumption function $C = 50 + 0.8Y$ (in billions of dollars) is drawn in this graph. The 45° line has the property that any point on it is equidistant from either the horizontal or the vertical axis. Thus, if consumption expenditures were the only component of aggregate demand, the aggregate quantity demanded of goods and services would be equal to the aggregate quantity supplied where the consumption line intersected the 45° line. In this graph, the aggregate quantity demanded of goods and services will equal the aggregate quantity supplied (an equilibrium level of income will be reached) at $250 billion.

If consumption expenditures were the only expenditures for goods and services in the economy, then in Figure 6–6 aggregate quantity demanded would equal aggregate quantity supplied at an income level of $250 billion, where the consumption expenditure line crosses the 45-degree line. At this point both

first case businesses would have excessive inventories; in the second case they would have to give up possible sales. Since each point on the 45-degree line is equidistant from both the expenditure axis and the income axis, we can say that at the point where the aggregate demand curve crosses the the 45-degree line, total expenditure for newly produced goods and services is equal to total quantity supplied, with all values in constant, or real, dollars.

consumption expenditures (aggregate quantity demanded) and national income (aggregate quantity supplied) would be equal to $250 billion.

At other levels of income, aggregate quantities demanded and supplied would not be equal. For example, at an income level of $100 billion, desired consumption expenditures would be $130 billion—$30 billion more than national income or aggregate quantity supplied. The inventories of businesses would fall, firms would increase output, and national income would increase. At an income level of $400 billion, desired consumption expenditures would be $370 billion—$30 billion less than aggregate quantity supplied. Consequently, businesses would sell less than they expected to and would cut back on production, and national income would fall. Therefore, in Figure 6–6, $250 billion is the only equilibrium level of income—in the sense that aggregate quantity demanded is equal to aggregate quantity supplied.

In Figure 6–7 the model is expanded to include investment expenditures. In this chapter and Chapter 7, it is assumed that investment expenditures are exogenously determined. The term *exogenous* refers to variables that are determined by factors not included in, or external to, a model. In other words, these chapters assume that neither current consumption expenditures nor national income, the other two variables, affect investment spending. In

the context of this discussion, *investment spending* means planned purchases of new plants or equipment or net increases in inventory levels by businesses or purchases of new residential housing by consumers. It does not refer to purely financial investments, such as purchases of stocks and bonds. This definition of investment spending is used so the effect of the business component of aggregate demand on the equilibrium level of national income can be analyzed.

In chapters 12 and 14, the simple Keynesian model will be expanded to include some variables that affect the level of investment spending. One of these variables is the interest rate, which represents the cost of funds used to purchase plant and equipment. A second variable is business expectations about future

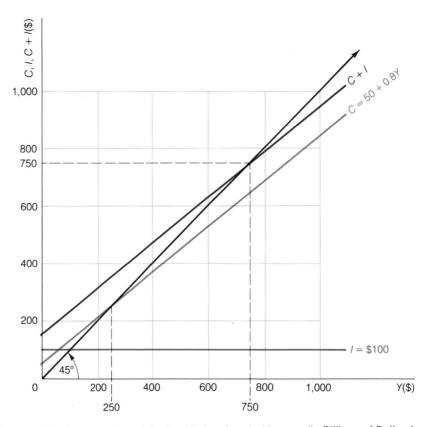

FIGURE 6–7 **Consumption, Investment, and the Equilibrium Level of Income (in Billions of Dollars)**

The original equilibrium level of income was equal to $250 billion. After the addition of $100 billion of investment spending the equilibrium level of income rises to $750 billion.

levels of business activity. Chapter 14 will show that changes in the level of national income may result in changes in the level of investment as firms attempt to adjust the capacity of their plants.

Figure 6–7 assumes that investment spending is equal to $100 billion, as shown by the horizontal line labeled *I*. The increase in investment is assumed to be a permanent increase, not just a one-period increase, in the flow of expenditures on capital goods by businesses. Otherwise, the equilibrium level of income would increase only temporarily. The line labeled *C + I* is consumption and investment expenditures added together. That is, $100 billion of investment spending has been added to consumption spending at each level of income. The *C + I* line consequently represents total expenditures for new goods and services in the economy,or aggregate demand. Again, the equilibrium level of income occurs where the line representing aggregate demand cuts the 45-degree line, in this case at an income level of $750 billion. At this point, *C + I* (aggregate quantity demanded) and *Y* (aggregate quantity supplied) both equal $750 billion.

When investment expenditures of $100 billion are added to total spending, the equilibrium level of income rises by $500 billion, or five times the increase in investment spending.(Compare Figures 6–6 and 6–7.) Why does the equilibrium level of income rise by so much? This question will be answered in the next section, which discusses the multiplier, an important Keynesian concept.

THE
MULTIPLIER

In the last section an increase in investment spending of $100 billion resulted in an increase in the equilibrium level of income of $500 billion, five times the increase in investment. The reason that the equilibrium level of income increased by so much is that when in-

vestment expenditures increased by $100 billion, they generated $100 billion of additional income for people involved in the production of the goods involved.

These individuals will now spend an additional $80 billion on consumption goods and services. This additional spending occurs because the marginal propensity to consume□ is 0.8 when the consumption function is *C =* 50 + 0.8*Y* (in billions of dollars), and 0.8 × $100 billion = $80 billion. This extra $80 billion of spending will generate $80 billion of additional income for people involved in the production of consumption goods and services. These people in turn will spend an additional 0.8 × $80 billion = $64 billion on new consumption goods. The $64 billion of spending will generate in turn $64 billion of new income, and the process will continue, as illustrated in Table 6–3.

The investors of the original $100 billion have started an income generation stream equal to $100 billion + 0.8 ($100 billion) + 0.8 ($80 billion) + 0.8 ($64 billion) + 0.8 ($51.2 billion) + . . ., which is an infinite series. The additions to the stream will become smaller and smaller because during each round of new income generation the income recipients will save a portion of what they receive and will therefore spend somewhat less than the total addition to their income.

Where will it all end? Using fairly simple mathematics, we can prove that the eqilibrium level of income will rise by

TABLE 6–3 The Multiplier Effect (in Billions of Dollars)

Expenditure Rounds	Increase in Income (Y)	Increase in Consumption (0.8 Y)	Increase in Saving (0.2 Y)
1 Increase in investment equal to $100 billion	$100.0	$ 80.0	$ 20.0
2	80.0	64.0	16.0
3	64.0	51.2	12.8
4	51.2	41.0	10.2
From all other rounds	204.8	163.8	41.0
Total	$500.0	$400.0	$100.0

$$\frac{1}{1 - 0.8} \times \$100 \text{ billion} = \frac{1}{0.2} \times \$100 \text{ billion}$$

$$= \frac{1}{(1/5)} \times \$100 \text{ billion}$$

$$= 5 \times \$100 \text{ billion}$$

$$= \$500 \text{ billion.}[6]$$

This figure is the amount we would obtain if we were to sum all of the amounts in the series above. In fact, we could prove that, in general, a change in national income,

_____

6. We can prove this result as follows. We write the series of new expenditures generated by the $100 billion as

$100 billion + 0.8 ($100 billion) + 0.8 (0.8) ($100 billion) + 0.8 (0.8) (0.8) ($100 billion) + . . . + 0.8^n ($100 billion),

where n approaches infinity. We factor out the $100 billion from each term to obtain

$$\Delta Y = \$100 \text{ billion} \times (1 + 0.8 + 0.8^2 + 0.8^3 + . . . 0.8^n). \quad (1)$$

Now we multiply Equation 1 by 0.8, obtaining

$$0.8 \Delta Y = 0.8 (\$100 \text{ billion}) \times (1 + 0.8 + 0.8^2 + 0.8^3 + . . . 0.8^n) \quad (2)$$
$$= \$100 \text{ billion} \times (0.8 + 0.8^2 + 0.8^3 + 0.8^4 + . . . 0.8^{n+1}).$$

By subtracting Equation 2 from Equation 1 we get

$$\Delta Y - 0.8 \Delta Y = \$100 \text{ billion} \times (1 - 0.8^{n+1}), \quad (3)$$

since all other terms drop out. Factoring out ΔY, we find

$$\Delta Y (1 - 0.8) = \$100 \text{ billion} \times (1 - 0.8^{n+1}). \quad (4)$$

To solve for ΔY, we divide Equation 4 by $(1 - 0.8)$, obtaining

$$Y = \$100 \text{ billion} \times \frac{(1 - 0.8^{n+1})}{(1 - 0.8)}. \quad (5)$$

As $n+1$ in Equation 5 gets larger and larger, 0.8^{n+1} gets smaller and smaller. Therefore, we can say that the limit of $(1 - 0.8^{n+1})$ as $n+1$ approaches infinity is $1 - 0$, or simply 1. Thus:

$$\Delta Y = \$100 \text{ billion} \times \frac{1}{1 - 0.8}$$

$$= \$100 \text{ billion} \times \frac{1}{0.2}$$

$$= \$100 \text{ billion} \times 5$$

$$= \$500 \text{ billion.}$$

In a similar manner we could prove that $\Delta Y = \Delta I \times (\frac{1}{1 - MPC})$ for any change in investment spending and any MPC such that $0 \leq MPC < 1$. (See if you can prove that if MPC = 1, the change in Y will be infinite.)

Y, equal to the change in investment $\times \left(\frac{1}{1 - MPC}\right)$ or the change in investment $\times \frac{1}{MPS}$ would be obtained. The graph in Figure 6–7 is redrawn in Figure 6–8. The reader can verify from this graph that the change in national income is equal to five times the change in investment spending and that consumption has increased by $400 at the higher level of income.

*The term $\frac{1}{1 - MPC}$, or $\frac{1}{MPS}$, is called the **multiplier** because it indicates the number by which an increase in investment or other exogenous spending should be multiplied in order to arrive at the change in equilibrium level of income.*

In the case above, the multiplier was 5. If the MPC were 0.9, the multiplier would be

$$\frac{1}{1 - 0.9} = \frac{1}{0.1} = \frac{1}{(1/10)} = 10.$$

If the MPC were 0, the multiplier would be $\frac{1}{1 - 0} = 1$. If the MPC were 1, the multiplier would be $\frac{1}{1 - 1} = \frac{1}{0} = \infty$, and the economy would never reach a new equilibrium level of income. Thus the larger the marginal propensity to consume (or the smaller the marginal propensity to save), the larger the multiplier will be.

In the example of Figure 6–8 the marginal propensity to consume was 0.8 and the multiplier was 5. A $100 billion increase in investment resulted in a $500 billion increase in income. If the marginal propensity to consume had been 0.75, the multiplier would have been $\frac{1}{MPS} = \frac{1}{0.25} = 4$, and income would have increased by only $400 billion. Thus the larger MPC (or the smaller MPS) produces a larger multiplier. This relationship exists because in each round of new expenditure that follows the initial $100 billion increase in in-

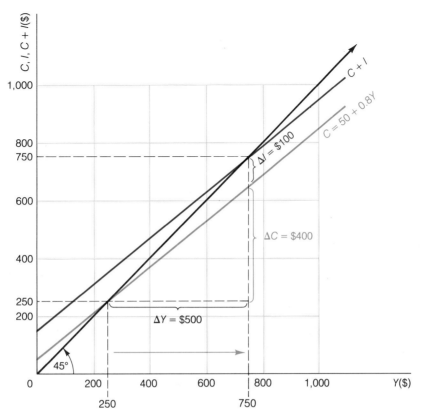

FIGURE 6–8 **The Multiplier (Data in Billions of Dollars)**

The original equilibrium level of income was equal to $250 billion. When $100 billion of investment spending is added, the equilibrium level of income rises by $100 billion times the multiplier ($100 billion × 5) to $750 billion. Consumption spending rises by $400 billion as a result of the new income generated.

vestment, consumers spend more (save less) when the marginal propensity to consume is 0.8 than when it is 0.75. As the successive rounds of new expenditure add up, they result in a greater total change in income with the higher marginal propensity to consume than with the lower one. The multiplier works for both increases and decreases in investment, as shown below.

Suppose that investment spending decreases by $60 billion—from $100 billion to $40 billion—perhaps because businesses are pessimistic about the future. The equilibrium level of income will decrease by $60 billion × 5, or $300 billion, to $450 billion, as shown in Figure 6–9. In this figure, $C + I_0$ is the original aggregate demand curve when investment

spending equals $100 billion. The curve labeled $C + I_1$ is the new aggregate demand curve after investment spending falls to $40 billion. The new equilibrium level of income occurs where the new aggregate demand curve crosses the 45-degree line, at $450 billion.

It is evident from the preceding examples that the multiplier plays an important role in the Keynesian explanation of the determination of national income and employment. Changes in key types of expenditures, such as business investment, can result in greatly magnified changes in the level of aggregate income. Thus the multiplier provides one explanation of why an economy may be characterized by wide swings in income and employment.

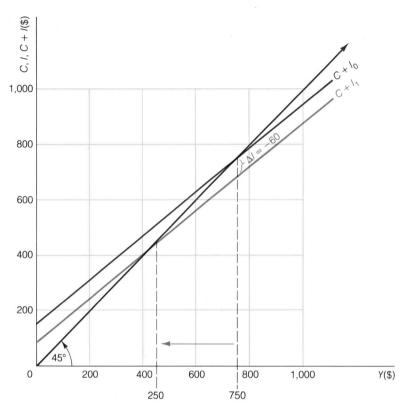

FIGURE 6–9 **Effect of a $60 Billion Decrease in Investment**

The original equilibrium level of income was equal to $750 billion. After a decrease in investment spending of $60 billion, the equilibrium level of income falls by $60 billion × the multiplier ($60 billion × 5) to $450 billion.

THE EQUILIBRIUM LEVEL OF INCOME: SAVING AND INVESTMENT APPROACH

◆

In our simple model, national income, which is aggregate supply, must be either spent on consumption goods and services or saved. On the other hand, aggregate demand consists of consumption expenditures plus investment spending. Therefore, if aggregate quantity demanded is to equal aggregate quantity supplied at a particular level of income, it must be true that

Consumption expenditures + Saving
= Consumption expenditures + Investment.
(6–1)

If we subtract the consumption expenditures from both sides of Equation 6–1, the result is that for an equilibrium level of income to exist:

$$\text{Saving} = \text{Investment.} \qquad (6-2)$$

Remember that it is *planned* saving and investment that we are dealing with here, not merely *actual* levels of saving and investment.

The data in Figure 6–8 will be used now to illustrate the saving-investment approach to finding the equilibrium level of income. The consumption function in Figure 6–8 was given by $C = 50 + 0.8Y$ (in billions of dollars), and investment spending was $I = \$100$ billion. We can obtain the saving function, S, by using the relationship $Y = C + S$, or $Y - C = S$. Therefore, substituting for C in that equation:

142

$$S = Y - 50 - 0.8Y$$
$$= -50 + 0.2Y.$$

In Figure 6–10 the saving function, $S = -50 + 0.2Y$, and the line representing $I = \$100$ billion are drawn. As can be seen from the graph, saving and investment are equal at $750 billion, the equilibrium level of income found in Figure 6–8. If there were no investment expenditures, the equilibrium level of income would occur where saving was equal to $0, or at $250 billion, as shown in Figures 6–8 and 6–10.

If the level of investment spending now falls by $60 billion—from $100 billion to $40 billion—the investment curve will shift downward, as shown in Figure 6–11. According to that graph the new equilibrium level of income will be $450 billion. This amount is consistent with the amount obtained in Figure 6–9. Thus we can use either the aggregate demand–aggregate supply approach or the saving-investment approach to find the equilibrium level of income.

THE PARADOX
OF THRIFT

The **paradox of thrift,** *a seeming contradiction, refers to the fact that while an individual may save more by being thrifty and spending less out of a given level of income, if a nation as a whole decides to save more, national income may fall and total saving may be no greater than before.*

According to popular wisdom, thriftiness is a virtue: "A penny saved is a penny earned." However, while increased thriftiness may benefit an individual, the issue is more complicated for society as a whole. We have seen earlier in the chapter that a change of any size in exogenous investment expenditures can have a larger effect on national income. A change in exogenous saving can also have a larger effect on national income, but in the opposite direction.

For example, previous sections used the consumption function $C = 50 + 0.8Y$ and the corresponding saving function $S = -50 +$

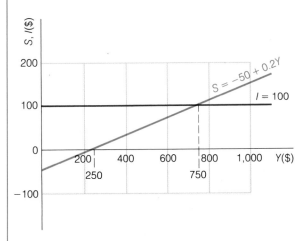

FIGURE 6–10   Saving, Investment, and Equilibrium Income (in Billions of Dollars)

In this simple model, the equilibrium level of income will occur where investment spending is equal to the amount which consumers save from their incomes. In this case, investment spending is equal to $100 billion and the saving function is given by $S = -50 + 0.2Y$. The equilibrium level of income occurs where the saving line intersects the line depicting the level of investment, at $750 billion.

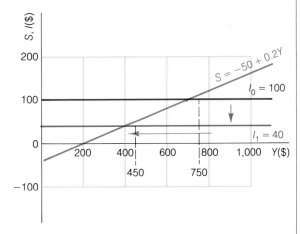

FIGURE 6–11   The Effect of a $60 Billion Decrease in Investment

The original equilibrium level of income was $750 billion. A decrease in investment spending of $60 billion causes the equilibrium level of income to fall by $60 billion × the multiplier ($60 billion × 5) to $450 billion.

0.2 Y (all terms in billions of dollars). The − 50 in the saving function is exogenous saving (or dissaving in this case), because it is not affected by the level of national income. Suppose now that saving rises by $40 billion at all levels of income, so that the saving function becomes $S = -10 + 0.2Y$.

We have already seen that the multiplier, equal to $\dfrac{1}{MPS}$, is 5 in this case. Thus the effect of a $40 billion increase in saving will be a $200 billion decrease in national income, from $750 billion to $550 billion, as shown in Figure 6−12. Why? Because the reduction in consumption expenditures will cause businesses to cut back production, which will cause the incomes of people associated with these businesses to fall. These people in turn will reduce their consumption spending, which will further reduce incomes, and the familiar multiplier process will continue on. In this case the new consumption function will be given by $C = 10 + 0.8Y$. The opposite effect will occur if people decrease their saving.

A change in the MPS can also have a large effect on national income. A previous section pointed out that an increase in MPC from 0.8 to 0.9 or a decrease in MPS from 0.2 to 0.1 will raise the multiplier from 5 to 10.

Moreover, the effect of a change in saving will be even greater if it causes businesses to change their expectations about future prospects and consequently to change their investment spending. As national income begins to fall because of the increase in saving, firms may become pessimistic and reduce their investment expenditures, which will cause a *still greater decrease* in national income. Of course, the opposite effect will probably prevail if saving is reduced.

Figure 6−13 is a graph of an investment function that is slightly upsloping, which indicates that businesses are willing to make greater investment expenditures at higher levels of income and lower investment expenditures at lower levels of income. Once again, the figure also shows the effect of a $40 billion increase in saving, using the same saving

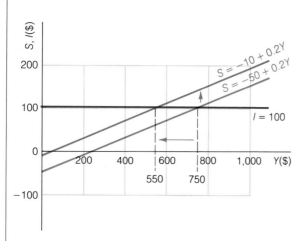

FIGURE 6−12 **The Effect of a $40 Billion Increase in Saving**

The original saving function is $S = -50 + 0.2Y$ (in billions of dollars), and the original equilibrium level of income is $750 billion. When an additional $40 billion is saved at all levels of income, the new saving function becomes $S = -10 + 0.2Y$. The equilibrium level of income falls to $550 billion.

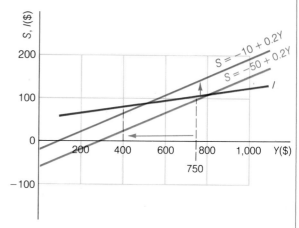

FIGURE 6−13 **The Effect of a $40 Billion Increase in Saving When Investment Varies with Income**

As in Figure 6−7, the original saving function is given by $S = -50 + 0.2Y$ (in billions of dollars), and the original equilibrium level of income is $750 billion. In this case, however, the level of investment spending increases as national income rises and decreases as national income falls. Now, a $40 billion increase in saving will result in a greater decrease in the equilibrium level of income than Figure 6−7, to $400 billion.

functions as in Figure 6–12. The initial equilibrium level of income is also the same as in Figure 6–12: $750 billion. In this case, however, the $40 billion increase in saving causes a decrease in the equilibrium level of income to $400 billion, rather than to the $550 billion in Figure 6–12. In this case too, the actual amount of saving and investment at the new equilibrium level of income has decreased.

SAVING: ANOTHER POINT OF VIEW

◆

Up to this point we have been pretty negative about the idea that increased saving benefits the nation as a whole. However, the picture is not all one-sided. For example, we have assumed that an increase in aggregate demand results in a higher level of real national income and is therefore good for the economy.

However, if the economy is at full employment, the increase in aggregate demand may result in inflation. Moreover, the nations of the world are becoming more and more concerned with conservation of resources and with planning for the future, even at the expense of short-term growth in national income.

Finally, if saving is increased, more funds may be made available to those who wish to do investment spending. If spending is merely transferred from consumption expenditures to investment expenditures, aggregate demand will be unaffected and a larger basis will be built for future growth in the productive capacity of the economy. In fact, some economists argue that the marginal propensity to save in the United States has been too small.[7]

Still, the relationship between saving and investment is not clear-cut. Differing views on the subject were responsible for a major part of

the disagreement between Keynes and the classical economists—and for the disagreements among modern-day economists. The saving-investment connection (or lack thereof) is discussed in greater depth in the next chapter, since economists' views of the roles and effectiveness of fiscal policy are strongly influenced by their beliefs on this issue.

This chapter has shown how consumption and investment spending interact within the framework of a simple Keynesian model to determine the equilibrium level of national income. The level of national income is important because it reflects the output of goods and services and of employment. As demonstrated here, fluctuations in investment spending and saving may have larger (multiplied) effects on national income. Chapter 7 uses the same framework to explain how government spending and taxing policies can affect the level of economic activity. Such policy tools can be instrumental in combating unemployment and inflation.

SUMMARY

1. This chapter has analyzed on a simple level the factors that affect the equilibrium level of national income. It emphasized that for an equilibrium level of income to be obtained, planned saving and planned investment must be equal to actual saving and actual investment.

2. The term *equilibrium level of income* as used in this chapter and in Chapter 7 means that the aggregate quantity supplied and the aggregate quantity demanded of goods and services are equal. It does not imply full employment. In fact, the chapter has assumed that the economy is not at full employment.

3. Keynes' law of consumption states that while people usually increase their consumption expenditures as their incomes increase, the increase in consumption expenditures tends to be less than the increase in income. The meaning and implications of this law can be readily recognized if they are discussed in terms of the marginal and average propensities to consume and save.

4. The average propensity to consume can be found by dividing total consumption expenditures by dis-

---

7. See "The U.S. Bias against Saving Leads to High Inflation, Weak Dollar, Slow Growth, Declining Productivity," pp. 90–98.

posable income, or APC $= \dfrac{C}{Y_d}$. The average propensity to save is equal to total saving divided by disposable income, or APS $= \dfrac{S}{Y_d} = 1 - \text{APC}$.

5. The marginal propensity to consume is the fraction of an additional dollar of disposable income that would be spent on consumption goods and services. In other words,

$$\text{MPC} = \frac{\text{change in consumption spending}}{\text{change in disposable income}}.$$

The marginal propensity to save is the fraction of an additional dollar of disposable income that would be saved. Stated another way,

$$\text{MPS} = \frac{\text{change in saving}}{\text{change in disposable income}}.$$

6. Given an aggregate consumption function and a specified level of investment, the corresponding equilibrium level of income can be found by two methods: (1) a graphical analysis of aggregate demand and aggregate supply and (2) a graphical analysis of saving and investment.

7. A change in exogenous spending may cause national income to change by a much greater amount. Specifically, the value of the multiplier is given by $\dfrac{1}{1 - \text{MPC}} = \dfrac{1}{\text{MPS}}$. The change in national income resulting from a change in exogenous spending is given by the following formula: $\Delta Y =$ the change in exogenous spending times the multiplier.

8. The paradox of thrift refers to the possibility that an increase in saving by people in an economy that is already experiencing unemployment is not necessarily desirable. In fact, such saving may reduce the equilibrium level of income and increase unemployment.

IMPORTANT TERMS AND CONCEPTS

Aggregate supply
Aggregate demand
Equilibrium
Equilibrium level of
  income
Planned saving and
  investment
Marginal propensity
  to consume
Consumption
  function
Average propensity to
  save
Fundamental law of
  consumption
Average propensity to
  consume
Marginal propensity
  to save
Saving function
Multiplier
Paradox of thrift

QUESTIONS AND PROBLEMS

1. What is meant by the term *equilibrium level of income?*

2. Define *average propensity to consume* and *marginal propensity to consume.*

3. Define *average propensity to save* and *marginal propensity to save.* How are they related to the APC and the MPC?

4. What is Keynes's law of consumption? Do you agree with it? Explain.

5. What is the multiplier? How is its value determined?

6. Find the change in the equilibrium level of income that would occur if MPC were equal to 0.5 and exogenous investment spending increased by $75 billion.

7. Find the change in the equilibrium level of income if MPS were equal to $\frac{1}{3}$ and exogenous investment spending decreased by $30 billion.

8. Assume that the aggregate consumption function is given by $C = 40 + 0.5Y$ (in billions of dollars). Graphically illustrate the equilibrium level of income if investment is equal to $200 billion. Use the aggregate demand–aggregate supply approach.

9. Using the saving-investment approach, graphically find the equilibrium level of income in Question 8.

10. Explain how an increase in investment spending may have a much larger effect on the equilibrium level of income.

11. What is the paradox of thrift? Is there any situation in which it may not be valid?

12. Explain the usefulness of a 45-degree line in graphically finding the equilibrium level of income.

13. What factors may prevent the labor market from reaching equilibrium?

FOR DISCUSSION

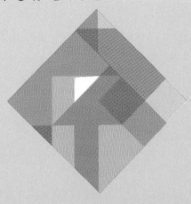

IS
KEYNES
DEAD?

Economic policy in immediate postwar decades was dominated by the writings of John Maynard Keynes. An almost idolatrous adoration surrounded him. This was mainly because the Keynesian prescriptions were politically rather mild. They did not involve direct government intervention or nationalization. This phase petered out some time in the 1960s. With the victorious penetration of monetarism into treasuries and central banks during the 1970s it has become fashionable to denigrate not merely Keynes's

Source: Adapted from Thomas Balogh, "Economists in the Long Run: Is Keynes Dead?" *The New Republic*, 182:23, June 7, 1980, pp. 15–18. (*Lord Balogh* was economic advisor to British prime minister Harold Wilson.)

political stance but his life and professional knowledge. . . .

Yet by all standards the period of Keynesian ascendancy after the war was an unparalleled success. Reconstruction after the most devastating hostility proceeded with unexpected dispatch. By 1949 or so prewar prosperity had been attained or even surpassed in Europe. Unemployment was a fraction of that endured before the war. The Western economies grew faster than they had in earlier periods. This was true even of countries like Britain, which had a relatively inferior postwar record. There were periods of slower progress, but until 1971 they had little in common with the prewar cycles. A more equitable, more compassionate society and

international order seemed to emerge.

There was a snag in this triumphal vindication of the economic policy design based on Keynes. It turned out to be fatal. For more than a generation, the whole world—communist, anti-communist, and uncommitted—has been engaged in a vain struggle to combine internal stability, the avoidance of accelerated price rises, full employment, and sustained material expansion. The whole world has failed. This failure resulted either in the fight against rising prices causing unemployment beyond what was politically acceptable, or in measures to mitigate unemployment, bringing intolerable price explosions.

The liberal Keynesians dismissed the threat of inflation. After years and years of failure, they continued with the effort to achieve a harmonious balance on the tightrope, managing demand so as to have both full employment and price stability. Once investment, consumption, savings, imports, and exports are linked by a rigid equation system, however, policy becomes the hostage plaything of wrong—because inflexibly framed—predictions. Some of the gravest mistakes in policy certainly can be attributed to consistently wrong (and usually far too optimistic) forecasts based on Keynesian models.

The Keynesians failed to detect that new problems would emerge from the conjunction of full employment with the increasing concentration of economic power on both sides of industry. The market *power* of the steadily decreasing number of giants, and no longer the impersonal signals of market *forces* emanating from myriads of units, dominates the price system. Market power

enables employers to shift the burden of increased wages onto prices, and thus decreases employer resistance against wage increases. . . .

The ultimate cause of the failure by most economists (Galbraith was a notable exception) to appreciate how the system was malfunctioning, and to devise policies that deal with it, was that most of the profession—neo-pseudo Keynesian, monetarist, and all—were passionately concerned that any policy should be "conformable" to the price mechanism and neoclassical analysis. To this end, and mainly implicitly, they assumed that effective competition prevailed, and that sensitivity to changes in price was high. The "consensus" case is based not on the real world with its massive concentration of economic power, but on an economic system of fine and smooth adjustments through the price mechanism, a system that existed only in the minds of academe. . . .

In the present structure of the economic system the only peaceful

way of dealing with the mixture of oligopoly and monopoly is by consensus, a new *contrat social*. Such a contract would limit the use of coercive measures, whether originating in strikes or in legislation. It will not be easy. The present power of the labor monopoly is inconsistent with the actual distribution of income. It will take more to achieve domestic peace than a temporary wage freeze. But Austria and lately Norway have shown that it can be done. Keynes, having shed his neoclassical outgrowth, will resurge again.

QUESTIONS

1. How does the writer of this article rate the performance of Keynesian economics after World War II?

2. According to the article, what did Keynesians fail to recognize during the 1960s and 1970s?

3. How is the article related to the difference between Keynesian economics and the views of the classical economists?

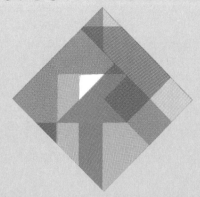

THE
EQUILIBRIUM LEVEL
OF INCOME—
ALGEBRAIC APPROACH

This chapter has noted that the equilibrium level of income occurs where national income, or aggregate quantity supplied, is equal to aggregate quantity demanded, or planned consumption expenditures plus planned investment expenditures in the simple model. We can write this equilibrium condition mathematically as

$$Y = C + I, \qquad \text{(C–1)}$$

where:

Y = level of gross national income,
C = planned consumption expenditures, and
I = planned investment expenditures.

We shall use the same consumption function and level of investment as we used in the immediately preceding sections to show how the equilibrium level of income may be found from Equation C–1. Therefore, $C = 50 + 0.8Y$, and $I = \$100$, all figures in billions of dollars.

Substituting these values in Equation C–1 for C and I, respectively, we obtain

$$Y = 50 + 0.8Y + 100. \qquad \text{(C–2)}$$

We made these substitutions in Equation C–1 in order to obtain an equation with only one unknown, variable Y, and thus solve Equation C–2 for the equilibrium level of income.

If we subtract $0.8Y$ from both sides of Equation C–2, we find that

$$Y - 0.8Y = 150.$$

Factoring out Y from both terms on the left-hand side, we obtain

$$Y(1 - 0.8) = 150.$$

Dividing both sides by $1 - 0.8$, we finally get

$$Y = 150 \left(\frac{1}{1 - 0.8}\right)$$
$$= 150 \left(\frac{1}{0.2}\right)$$
$$= 750.$$

The $750 billion is the same equilibrium level of income as in Figures 6–8 and 6–10. We can check our answer by finding $C = 50 + 0.8 (750) = 50 + 600 = 650$. Then, $C + I = 650 + 100 = 750 = Y$.

We can also use algebra to find the equilibrium level of income in the saving-investment approach. The equilibrium condition using this approach is

$$S = I, \qquad \text{(C–3)}$$

where:

  S = planned saving, and
  I = planned investment spending.

The chapter showed that the saving function corresponding to the above consumption function is $S = -50 + 0.2Y$. If we substitute this function and $I = 100$ into Equation C–3, we get

$$-50 + 0.2Y = 100$$
$$0.2Y = 150, \text{ and}$$
$$Y = 750.$$

The $750 billion figure is the same one we obtained above. We can check our answer by finding

$$S = -50 + 0.2(750)$$
$$= -50 + 150$$
$$= 100$$
$$= I.$$

We can write a general mathematical formula for the equilibrium level of income by using $C = C_0 + bY$ for the general consump-

tion function and $I = I_0$ for planned investment. The term C_0 represents the level of consumption expenditures that is determined exogenously or externally to the model. In other words, it is the part of consumption spending that is not affected by the level of income and that would occur (in the short run) even if income were $0. I_0 indicates investment spending, which is exogenous.

If we substitute these values for C and I into the equilibrium condition $Y = C + I$, we obtain

$$Y = C_0 + bY + I_0. \qquad \text{(C–4)}$$

Subtracting bY from both sides of Equation C–4, we obtain

$$Y - bY = C_0 + I_0 \qquad \text{(C–5)}$$
$$Y(1 - b) = C_0 + I_0.$$

By dividing equation C–5 by $1 - b$, we finally arrive at the general formula for the equilibrium level of income in the model:

$$Y = (C_0 + I_0) \left(\frac{1}{1 - b} \right),$$

where $\dfrac{1}{1 - b}$ is the multiplier.

Thus, in the example above, where $C_0 = 50$, $I_0 = 100$, and $b = 0.8$, the equilibrium level of income was given by $Y = (50 + 100) \left(\dfrac{1}{1 - 0.8} \right) = 750$ (all figures in billions of dollars).

CHAPTER 7

FISCAL
POLICY
AND
NATIONAL
INCOME

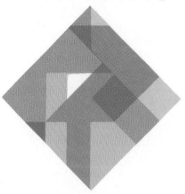

GOVERNMENT SPENDING: MANAGEMENT OF THE INEVITABLE

Remember the old saying "Nothing is as certain as death and taxes"? If you think about it, this saying is only a half-truth—or better yet, a two-thirds truth. It really should be "Nothing is as certain as death, taxes, and government spending." After all, government cannot supply even the most meager array of public services if it does not spend money on its employees and contractors.

How much should government spend? What should it spend money on? When should it increase spending, and when should it reduce spending? Where should it get the money it chooses to spend? For a big country with a big government, these are complicated questions. They are also controversial questions.

In macroeconomic terms the big questions about government spending and taxation are how much and when. (Whether government should support the construction of a given canal or whether it should pay for school lunches are issues in microeconomics. The microeconomics of government policy is discussed in chapters 27 and 28.) This chapter deals with overall spending and taxation at the federal level, a subject known as fiscal policy.

The growth of both government spending and taxation probably had a significant effect on the election of President Reagan in 1980. Paul A. Samuelson, the first American to receive a Nobel Prize in economics, wrote about the mood of voters back in April 1979:

Many American voters are fed up with taxes. . . . The governmental share of the national income seems to them to grow remorselessly. . . .

If the trend of the twentieth century's middle two quarters continues, by the year 2000 the people best educated and most industrious in the arts of commerce and production will be turning over to the rest of the community half the fruits of their effort.[1]

However, Samuelson himself was more afraid of an overzealous backlash against government spending than of faster growth of government. He added:

Nor will historical experience with the politics of social choice bear out the diagnosis that democracy by its nature must produce overlarge public spending . . . . there is as much an inherent tendency for governments to spend *too little* as too much.

Government may also try to tax too much in a misguided effort to force its budget into balance. Samuelson continues:

Only recall 1930–32. Herbert Hoover tried disastrously to raise tax rates in the teeth of a worsening depression in order to balance the budget that inevitably had gone into deficit because of reduced tax collections. Had Roosevelt been forced by the Constitution to do the same, blood would have run in the streets.

In Chapter 6 the investment multiplier—a phenomenon that shows how a new injection of investment spending can have a magnified effect on economic activity or GNP—was introduced. This chapter shows that changes in government expenditures and taxation also have multiplier effects. Once they are explained, it will be easy to see why Samuelson is so concerned about both the timing and the magnitude of changes in government taxation and spending policy.

---

1. Paul A. Samuelson, ''Too Much Democracy,'' *Newsweek*, April 9, 1979, p. 79. Condensed from Newsweek. Copyright, 1981, by Newsweek, Inc. All Rights Reserved. Reprinted by Permission.

FISCAL
POLICY
AND
NATIONAL
INCOME

WHAT THIS CHAPTER IS ABOUT

This chapter will discuss how government fiscal policies work and why many economists consider them necessary.

> The term ***fiscal policy*** *refers to government policies of taxing and spending designed to affect the equilibrium level of national income.*

Since government fiscal policies affect the rate of inflation, the level of unemployment, the taxes we pay, and the environment in which we live, it is important that we understand them. In fact, it is doubtful that there is even one of us whose life has not been significantly touched by one of more of these policies. The Keynesian theory of how our lives are touched by such policies will be explained in this chapter.

127 We first examine the classical belief that inadequate aggregate demand☐ would never be a serious problem in a free enterprise economy and explain why Keynes believed there were flaws in this theory. Next we discuss the Keynesian theory of how government expen-

ditures and taxes affect the equilibrium level of income.☐

129

Some economists do not agree with all the views that will be presented in this chapter. The positions of those with opposing views will be discussed in detail in Chapter 12, when the role of monetary policy is examined.

THE
SAVING-INVESTMENT
CONTROVERSY

Chapter 6 showed that in a simple model with no government taxes or spending and no exports or imports, an equilibrium level of income requires *planned* saving to be equal to *planned* investment spending.☐ If planned saving is greater than planned, or desired, investment, aggregate quantity supplied☐ will be greater than aggregate quantity demanded☐, firms will cut back on production, and national income will fall.

130 126 127

The reverse process will occur if investment spending is greater than saving; national income may rise and/or prices may rise. However, since periods of apparently insufficient aggregate demand and the resulting unemployment sparked the "Keynesian revolution," the possibility of that condition will be discussed first.

THE CLASSICAL VIEW

For the most part, classical economists could not imagine how aggregate quantity demanded would be less than aggregate quantity supplied at a full employment level of national income. According to the French economist Jean Baptiste Say,□ supply implies its own demand. In Say's words, written around 1820:

No person produces but with the intention of consuming or selling the article he produces, and no one sells but with the intention of buying some other production, which may be of immediate use, or contribute to future production.[1]

Thus Say argued that current income would be spent either on consumption goods or on investment goods, and most economists of that time agreed with him. This principle is often called **Say's law.**

John Stuart Mill,□ another prominent nineteenth century economist, stated:

Whoever brings additional quantities to the market brings an additional power of purchase; we now see that he brings also an additional power to consume; since if he had not that desire, he would not have troubled himself to produce. *Neither of the elements of demand, therefore, can be found wanting, when there is additional supply,* though it is perfectly possible that the demand may be for one thing and the supply may unfortunately consist of another.[2] (Emphasis added.)

Later, Mill admitted that with the use of money the act of exchange can be divided into two separate operations that need not occur at the same time. That is, we bring our goods to market, sell them, and receive money in return. In separate transactions, we then buy the goods we desire. Mill also acknowledged that a general wish to sell could occur at the same time there was a general desire to postpone buying. He thought, however, that this state of events would be temporary.[3]

Mill did recognize that a few people produce and accumulate from habit or custom. Still, he maintained that even these people spend what they save on investment goods and that there can be no surplus of production until the working classes have reached the point where they desire no more consumption goods. Even in this case, Mill stated, there can be no excess of goods produced, because no one will be willing to work. He concluded: "Thus in whatever manner the question is looked at, the theory of general over-production implies an absurdity."[4]

Given this optimistic scenario, why did Keynesian economics develop? The economies of the world simply did not realize that depressions of any significant seriousness or length were supposed to be impossible! For example, in 1894 the unemployment rate in the United States was 18.4 percent; in 1933 it was 24.9 percent.[5] Obviously, all was not well.

KEYNES AND THE GENERAL THEORY

Finally, in the midst of the Great Depression of the 1930s, Keynes's *General Theory* was published. It was an event that affected most of the developed countries, including the United States. In his book, Keynes attacked the classical belief that saving and investment are closely related:

Any individual act of abstaining from consumption necessarily leads to, and amounts to the same thing as, causing the labour and commodities thus released from supplying consumption to be invested in the production of capital wealth.

Contemporary thought is still deeply steeped in the notion that if people do not spend their money in one way they will spend it in another.

1. Jean-Baptiste Say, *Letters to Thomas Robert Malthus on Political Economy and Stagnation of Commerce,* (English translation London: George Harding's Bookshop, 1936), p. 7.

2. John Stuart Mill, *Principles of Political Economy,* ed. W.J. Ashley (1848; London: Longmans, Green, 1923), pp. 559–560.

3. John Stuart Mill, *Essays on Some Unsettled Questions of Political Economy,* 3rd ed. (London: Longmans, Green, 1877), pp. 69–70.

4. Mill, *Principles,* p. 560.

5. U.S. Department of Commerce, Bureau of the Census, *Historical Statistics of the United States: Colonial Times to 1970* (Washington, D.C.: Government Printing Office, 1975), p. 135.

Those who think in this way are deceived, nevertheless, by an optical illusion, which makes two essentially different activities appear to be the same. *They are fallaciously supposing that there is a nexus which unites decisions to abstain from present consumption with decisions to provide for future consumption; whereas the motives which determine the latter are not linked in any simple way with the motives of the former.*[6] (Emphasis added.)

Thus was Keynesian economics born.

As we know from Chapter 6, Keynes went on to argue that consumption spending and, consequently, saving were determined by the level of national income. He also believed, however, that investment expenditures were determined by the relationship between the return that businesses believed they would receive from such spending and the market rate of interest.[7] Because saving and investment depended on different variables, there was no reason why the amount of saving would necessarily equal the amount of investment spending at any particular level of national income. Consequently, there was no reason why aggregate quantity demanded would necessarily be equal to aggregate quantity supplied at a sufficiently high level of national income for labor to be fully employed.

Of course, aggregate quantity demanded □ might be either greater or less than aggregate quantity supplied □ at the full employment level of income. However, Keynes believed that deflation (or recession) has inflicted more serious injuries than had inflation.[8] Thus most of his fiscal policy prescriptions in *The General Theory* was formulated from that vantage point.

The next two sections will discuss the Keynesian theory of how government fiscal policy works. The primary emphasis will be

6. John Maynard Keynes, *The General Theory of Employment, Interest, and Money* (New York: Harcourt, Brace, and World, Harbinger, 1964), pp. 19–21.

7. Ibid., pp. 135–137.

8. John Maynard Keynes, *A Tract on Monetary Reform* (London: Macmillan, 1924), p. 4.

on policies that alleviate economic recessions and depressions. Chapter 13 will consider inflation and that troublesome combination, inflationary recessions, in detail.

GOVERNMENT EXPENDITURES AND NATIONAL INCOME

The impact of consumption and investment expenditures on the equilibrium level of national income was discussed in Chapter 6. Now, the way that government spending affects national income will be analyzed. Strictly speaking, government expenditures do not include government transfer payments, such as social security and welfare payments. These payments should therefore be subtracted from tax receipts to obtain net taxes. Government expenditures are direct purchases of goods and services by the government.

AGGREGATE DEMAND–AGGREGATE SUPPLY APPROACH

Three aggregate demand curves are sketched in Figure 7–1: the first with only consumption expenditures, the second with consumption expenditures plus investment spending of $100 billion, and the third with government expenditures of $50 billion added to each level of consumption plus investment (or private) spending. The consumption function □ used in this graph is $C = 50 + 0.75Y$, with all terms in billions of dollars. When aggregate demand consists of only consumption expenditures, the equilibrium level of income is equal to $200 billion. (In Figure 7–1 the consumption line cuts the 45-degree line at $Y = $200 billion.)

When $100 billion of investment spending

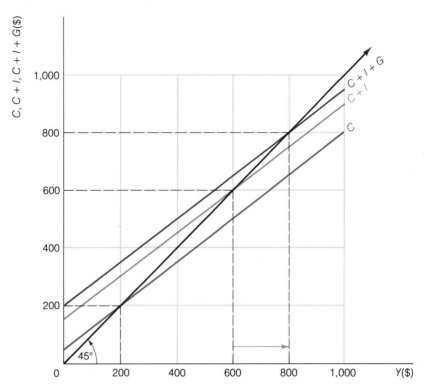

FIGURE 7-1 Effect of Government Expenditures on the Equilibrium Level of Income (in Billions of Dollars)

With only consumption spending making up aggregate demand, the equilibrium level of income is $200 billion. When $100 billion of investment spending is added, the equilibrium level of income rises by $100 billion × the multiplier ($100 billion × 4) to $600 billion. When $50 billion of government spending is added, the equilibrium level of income rises by $200 billion, that is; $50 billion × 4, to $800 billion.

is added, the equilibrium level of income increases to $600 billion (where the C + I line intersects the 45-degree line). Thus an addition of $100 billion in investment spending results in an increase of $400 billion in the equilibrium level of income. The multiplier formula □ derived in Chapter 6 gives the same answer as the graph: the multiplier =

$$\frac{1}{1 - MPC} = \frac{1}{1 - 0.75} = \frac{1}{0.25} = \frac{1}{1/4} = 4;$$ and

the change in investment × 4 = $100 billion × 4 = $400 billion.

When the $50 billion in government expenditures is added, the equilibrium level of income goes up by an additional $200 billion (see Figure 7–1). Thus the multiplier effect for a change in government expenditures is the same as that for a change in investment spending. In this case the change in government spending × the multiplier = $50 billion × 4 = $200 billion.

Therefore, when an economy is at less than full employment,□ an increase in government expenditures will cause the equilibrium level of national income to rise by an amount equal to the change in government expenditures times the multiplier. Of course, if an economy is at full employment, an increase in government expenditures will also increase the equilibrium level of national income. However, since output cannot expand, prices will rise as a result of the excess demand. The reverse will occur if the government decides to cut spending. In this case, the equilibrium level of income will fall by the amount of the cut in government spending times the multiplier.[9]

SAVING-INVESTMENT APPROACH

We can also find the equilibrium level of income by using the saving-investment approach discussed in Chapter 6. As before, the equilibrium level of income occurs where aggregate quantity demanded equals aggregate quantity supplied. Now, however, aggregate demand consists of consumption expenditures plus investment and government spending. Therefore, the equilibrium level of income will occur where

$$Y = C + I + G. \qquad (7\text{--}1)$$

Since income still must be either spent on consumption goods or saved, we can replace Y in Equation 7–1 with $C + S$ to obtain

$$C + S = C + I + G. \qquad (7\text{--}2)$$

Subtracting C from both sides, we find that the equilibrium level of income will occur where

$$S = I + G. \qquad (7\text{--}3)$$

---

9. We can use the algebraic method to find the equilibrium level of income, which occurs where

$$Y = C + I + G. \qquad (1)$$

Substituting $C = 50 + 0.75Y$, $I = 100$, and $G = 50$, into Equation 1 we obtain

$$Y = 50 + 0.75Y + 100 + 50 \qquad (2)$$
$$= 200 + 0.75Y.$$

If we subtract $0.75Y$ from both sides of Equation 2 and factor out Y, we get

$$Y - 0.75Y = 200 \qquad (3)$$
$$Y (1 - 0.75) = 200.$$

Dividing Equation 3 by $1 - 0.75$, we finally arrive at

$$Y = 200 \left(\frac{1}{1 - 0.75}\right)$$
$$= 200 \left(\frac{1}{0.25}\right)$$
$$= 800$$

The $800 billion figure is the same equilibrium level of income as in Figure 7–1.

In Figure 7–2 the saving function corresponding to the consumption function $C = 50 + 0.75Y$, shown in Figure 7–1, is graphed. (We obtained this saving function by finding $Y - C = Y - 50 - 0.75Y$, or $S = -50 + 0.25Y$.) As in Figure 7–1, we assume that government expenditures plus investment spending total \$150 billion. In Figure 7–2 saving equals investment spending plus government expenditures at a level of national income equal to \$800 billion, the same equilibrium level of income as in Figure 7–1.[10] Of course, this result holds only as long as there are no taxes. The model will be expanded to include taxes in the next section.

TAXES AND THE MULTIPLIER

We now turn to a less pleasant aspect of fiscal policy—taxes. Although few of us enjoy pay-

---

10. With the saving-investment solution method, the condition for an equilibrium level of income becomes, as stated in Equation 7–3:

$$S = I + G.$$

If we substitute in the saving function corresponding to the consumption function and $I = 100$ and $G = 50$, we find:

$$-50 + 0.25Y = 100 + 50$$
$$0.25Y = 200$$
$$Y = 800,$$

as we found in footnote 9.

The general solution for this model, with exogenous investment expenditures I_0 and government spending G_0, can be found as follows. First, the condition for an equilibrium level of income is

$$Y = C + I + G$$
$$= C_0 + bY + I_0 + G_0.$$

As in Chapter 6, C_0 represents the amount of consumption spending that would occur even if income were \$0, and b is the marginal propensity to consume. Then:

$$Y - bY = C_0 + I_0 + G_0$$
$$Y(1 - b) = C_0 + I_0 + G_0$$
$$Y = (C_0 + I_0 + G_0) \left(\frac{1}{1 - b}\right).$$

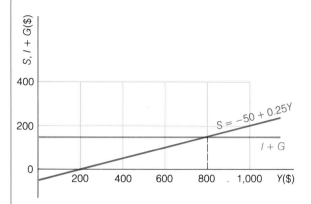

FIGURE 7–2 Government Expenditures and the Saving-Investment Approach (in Billions of Dollars)

When government spending but no taxes are present, the equilibrium level of income will occur where the amount saved out of income is equal to investment plus government spending. In this graph, the saving function is $S = -50 + 0.25Y$ (in billions of dollars). Investment spending plus government spending is equal to $150 billion. The equilibrium level of income is equal to $800 billion, the same amount as in Figure 7–1.

ing taxes, taxes do play an important role in promoting economic stability and maintaining our style of government. Consequently, it is important for us to understand how they affect the economy as well as our own pocketbooks. This book will examine only the most simple model, leaving more complicated models for advanced texts. Of course, the more elaborate models work in much the same manner as the simple ones.

AGGREGATE DEMAND–AGGREGATE SUPPLY APPROACH

Suppose the economy is in the situation depicted in Figure 7–1, with the consumption function given by $C = 50 + 0.75Y$, investment spending, I, equal to $100 billion, and government expenditures, G, equal to $50 billion. Suppose further that the government decides to impose a lump sum tax on consumers which for the whole group will amount to $40 billion. (A **lump sum tax** is a tax that does not depend on income or sales; it is a fixed amount per person, household, or business, etc.)

Chapter 6 argued that consumption spending is a function of consumer disposable income. Before taxes are introduced, consumer disposable income (the income that consumers can decide whether or how to spend) was equal to national income. With taxes, however, consumer disposable income is less than national income by the amount of the taxes. (We cannot legally decide not to pay taxes!) Thus:

$$Y_d = Y - T, \qquad (7-4)$$

where:

Y_d = disposable income,
Y = national income, and
T = the level of taxes.

The consumption of the previous section now becomes $C = 50 + 0.75Y_d = 50 + 0.75(Y - T)$. In figure 7–3 we have sketched the original consumption function, $C = 50 + 0.75Y$, which applied when there were no taxes, as well as a second consumption function, $C' = 50 + 0.75(Y - 40)$, which gives consumption expenditures after a tax of $40 billion is imposed by the government.

When the tax is imposed, consumption expenditures drop by $30 billion at each level of income. This reduction occurs because personal disposable income has fallen by $40 billion, of which consumers would have spent $0.75 \times \$40$ billion = $30 billion. (In this case 0.75 is the marginal propensity to consume.□) Consumers would have saved the remaining $10 billion because the marginal propensity to save□ is equal to $1 - MPC = 0.25$, and $0.25 \times \$40$ billion = $10 billion.

In Figure 7–4 we have redrawn the original aggregate demand $(C + I + G)$ curve with investment spending equal to $100 billion and government expenditures equal to $50 billion, the same levels as in Figures 7–1 and 7–2. After $40 billion in taxes is imposed the aggregate demand curve is $C' + I + G$. From Figure 7–4 we can see that the government's imposition of $40 billion in taxes results in a lower-

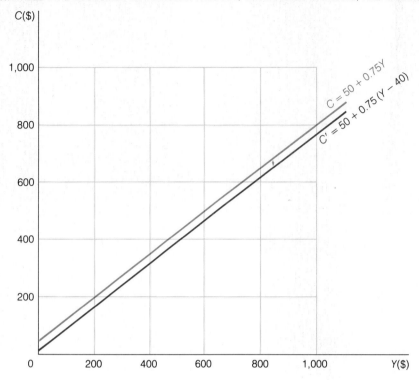

Figure 7–3 Effect of Taxes on Consumption (in Billions of Dollars)

The original consumption function is $C = 50 + 0.75Y$ (in billions of dollars). When $40 billion of taxes is imposed on consumers, the consumption function becomes $C' = 50 + 0.75(Y - 40)$, since consumers must now pay $40 billion in taxes at all levels of income. Their *disposable* income will now be $40 billion less at each level of national income than before. As a result, the consumption function shifts downward, indicating that consumers spend less relative to a given level of national income than before the taxes were imposed.

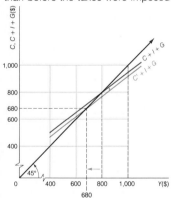

FIGURE 7–4 Effect of Taxes on the Equilibrium Level of Income (in Billions of Dollars)

The original aggregate demand curve is given by $C + I + G$, and the original equilibrium level of income is $800 billion. After $40 billion in taxes is imposed, the aggregate demand curve is $C' + I + G$. The equilibrium level of income changes by $40 billion × the tax multiplier ($40 billion × −3) and falls to $680 billion.

ing of the equilibrium level of income by $120 billion, from $800 billion to $680 billion.

We know that the investment and **government expenditures multiplier** is given by $\dfrac{1}{1 - \text{MPC}} = \dfrac{1}{\text{MPS}}$, which in this case is equal to 4. However, it is obvious that the government expenditures multiplier does not apply to taxes. (If it did, income would have risen by $160 billion.)

We expect the sign of the **tax multiplier** to be *negative* because an *increase* in taxes *decreases* consumer spending and therefore *causes aggregate demand and the equilibrium level of income to fall.* However, it is also apparent that the *absolute size* (not considering the sign) of the tax multiplier is less than for the government expenditure and investment multiplier because an increase in taxes of $40 billion causes a decrease in the equilibrium level of income of $120 billion. This figure is only three times the change in taxes, not four.

Why do taxes have a smaller effect? Because some of the taxes come from income that would have been saved if the taxes had not been imposed. This amount would not have contributed to aggregate demand anyway. In the case above, this amount was $10 billion, which is equal to the marginal propensity to save multiplied by the change in taxes. Therefore, *only the portion of the tax that reduces consumption spending affects the equilibrium level of income.* This amount is given by the marginal propensity to consume times the change in taxes, which is equal to the change in consumption spending. In the example above, the change in consumption spending is equal to $-0.75 \times \$40$ billion, or $-\$30$ billion.

Thus the tax multiplier in this simple model is given by $\dfrac{-\text{MPC}}{1 - \text{MPC}}$. The change in income equals $\dfrac{-\text{MPC}}{1 - \text{MPC}} \times$ the change in taxes,

which is equal to $\dfrac{1}{1 - \text{MPC}} \times$ the change in consumption spending, or the change in consumption spending times the expenditures multiplier. The negative sign in the numerator of the tax multiplier reflects the negative effect taxes have on consumption and therefore on the equilibrium level of income.

SAVING-INVESTMENT APPROACH

We can also use the saving-investment approach to find the equlibrium level of income in this example. As before, when aggregate quantity demanded is equal to aggregate quantity supplied:

$$Y = C + I + G.$$

Now, however, national income can be consumed, saved, or paid to the government as taxes, so that

$$C + S + T = C + I + G. \qquad (7-5)$$

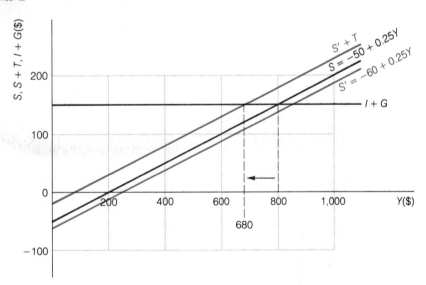

FIGURE 7–5 The Effect of Taxes: Saving-Investment Approach (in Billions of Dollars)

The original saving function is $S = -50 + 0.25Y$ (in billions of dollars). When $40 billion of taxes is imposed, the saving function becomes $S' = -60 + 0.25Y$. The line $S' + T$ depicts the $40 billion of taxes added to each level of saving given by the new saving function. The original equilibrium level of income occurred where the old saving line intersected the $I + G$ line, at $800 billion. With taxes added, the new equilibrium level of income will occur where saving plus taxes is equal to investment spending plus government spending, at $680 billion.

If we subtract consumption spending from both sides of Equation 7–5, we find the new equilibrium condition:

$$S + T = I + G. \qquad (7-6)$$

Economists call saving and taxes **leakages** from the spending stream because they represent the part of national income that is not necessarily reflected in aggregate demand, or, in other words, the part that might not be spent. Only when the leakages from the spending stream equal the injections of investment and government expenditures will aggregate quantity demanded equal aggregate quantity supplied.

In Figure 7–5 we have sketched the saving function used in Figure 7–2 before taxes were imposed: $S = -50 + 0.25Y$, all terms in billions of dollars. As Figure 7–2 showed, the equilibrium level of income in this situation is $800 billion. After the tax of $40 billion is imposed, saving decreases by $10 billion at all levels of income and the saving function shifts downward to $S' = -60 + 0.25Y$. The saving plus tax function, $S' + T$, is found by adding the $40 billion in taxes to the saving function: $S' + T = -60 + 0.25Y + 40$, or $S' + T = -20 + 0.25Y$. As we found in Figure 7–4, the new equilibrium level of income is $680 billion.

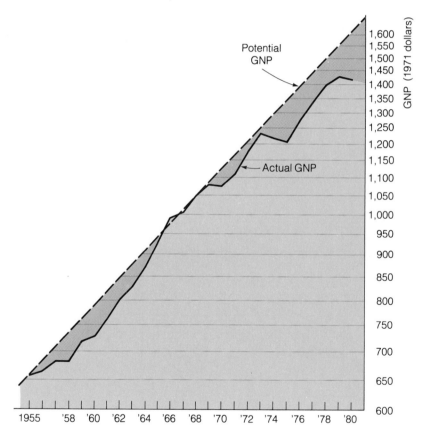

FIGURE 7–6 Actual and Potential Gross National Product

Potential GNP, or the quantity of goods and services which the economy could produce if all members of the labor force were employed, is given by the dashed line. Actual GNP is the quantity of goods and services (measured in 1972 dollars) which the U.S. economy actually produced during each respective year. When equilibrium GNP is less than potential GNP, a deflationary gap is said to exist.

Source: *Business Conditions Digest*

THE GOAL OF GOVERNMENT FISCAL POLICY

◆

The goal of government fiscal policies regarding taxes and government expenditures is assumed to be the maintenance of gross national product at the **full employment level of output**. We could express this objective as keeping the national economy on the production possibilities curve □. This goal and the success (or lack thereof) of the United States in achieving it are illustrated in Figure 7–6. This figure shows both the estimated level of GNP at full employment and the actual level of GNP.

When equilibrium GNP is less than full employment GNP, a **deflationary gap** is said to exist. The deflationary gap is equal to the amount by which the aggregate demand curve would have to shift upward for the equilibrium level of income to coincide with full employment.

Thus the deflationary gap reflects an inadequacy of aggregate demand.

An **inflationary gap** occurs when aggregate demand is so high that the equilibrium level of GNP exceeds the full employment level.

In this case, excess aggregate demand results in inflationary pressures.

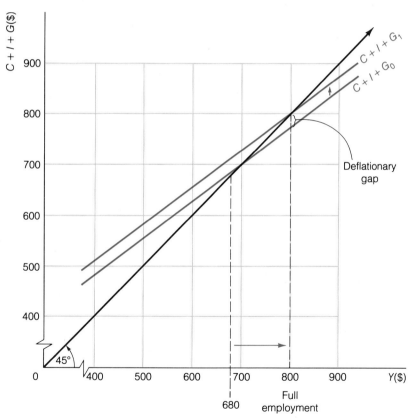

FIGURE 7–7 Elimination of a Deflationary Gap with an Increase in Government Spending (in Billions of Dollars)

In this graph the full employment level of national income is $800 billion. The original aggregate demand curve is given by $C + I + G_0$, and the equilibrium level of income is $680 billion. In this case, a deflationary gap is present. An increase in government spending, depicted by the aggregate demand curve $C + I + G_1$, eliminates the deflationary gap and unemployment.

Ideally, government fiscal policies would eliminate both inflationary and deflationary gaps. Previous sections have discussed how government fiscal policies affect national income. We saw that an increase in government expenditures or a reduction in taxes will cause the equilibrium level of income to rise. We also saw that a reduction in government spending or an increase in taxes will result in a lower equilibrium level of income.

For example, the aggregate demand curve $(C + I + G_0)$ from Figure 7–4 is redrawn in Figure 7–7. In the earlier figure, government expenditures are equal to $50 billion, and taxes are equal to $40 billion. The original equilibrium level of income is $680 billion,

and the full employment level of income is $800 billion. Thus a deflationary gap occurs. If government expenditures are increased by $30 billion, the equilibrium level of income increases by $30 billion × 4 (the multiplier), or $120 billion, to $800 billion and the deflationary gap is eliminated. The new aggregate demand curve in Figure 7–7 is $C + I + G_1$.

We can verify that a decrease in taxes of $40 billion will also eliminate the deflationary gap. Since the tax multiplier is -3, $-\$40$ billion × -3 equals a $120 billion increase in the equilibrium level of income. If we graph the new aggregate demand curve, the new consumption function will be given by $C = 50 + 0.75(Y - T_1)$, or $C = 50 + 0.75(Y - 0)$

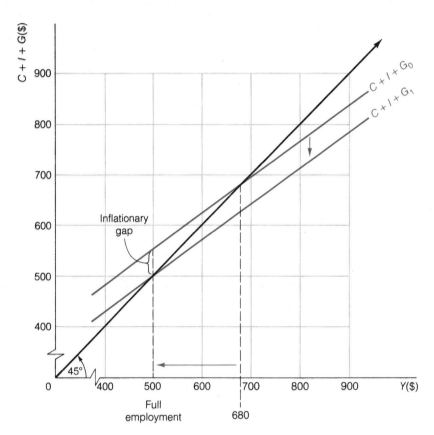

FIGURE 7–8   Elimination of an Inflationary Gap with a Decrease in Government Spending (in Billions of Dollars)

Here, the full employment level of income is $500 billion. The original aggregate demand curve is given by $C + I + G_0$, and the equilibrium level of income is $680 billion. In this case, an inflationary gap is present. A decrease in government spending, depicted by the aggregate demand curve $C + I + G_1$, eliminates the excess demand.

= 50 + 0.75 Y. We add investment expenditures of $100 billion plus government expenditures of $50 billion to the consumption function to obtain the new aggregate demand curve.

In Figure 7–8 the original equilibrium level of income is once again equal to $680 billion. However, in this case the full employment level of income is equal to $500 billion, and an inflationary gap is present. A reduction of $45 billion in government expenditures will decrease the equilibrium level of income by $45 billion × 4, or $180 billion, to $500 billion, which will eliminate the inflationary gap. We can verify that an increase in taxes of $60 billion will also eliminate the inflationary gap, because $60 billion × −3 is equal to a $180 billion decrease in the equilibrium level of income.

Unfortunately, there are some problems connected with the achievement of the goal of eliminating deflationary and inflationary gaps. One problem concerns timing. It usually takes a long time for Congress to pass a government spending or tax bill and an even longer time for the bill to have an impact on the economy. A public expenditures project usually requires a great deal of planning and often contract bidding before it can be implemented.

Another complicating factor centers around balancing the federal budget. This issue is explained in the next section and discussed more fully in Chapter 8.

THE
PROBLEM OF
BALANCING
THE BUDGET
◆

Should the federal government keep its budget balanced, even if a balanced budget means some unemployment? More and more politicians and some economists are answering yes to this question. In fact, by spring of 1981,

thirty states had passed resolutions calling for a constitutional convention in order to draft an amendment to the United States Constitution that would require the federal budget to be balanced except in the case of national emergency.[11]

BALANCED BUDGET MULTIPLIER

Before we discuss this question any further, an explanation is needed for one additional feature of the equilibrium income determination model: the *balanced budget multiplier.* The balanced budget multiplier indicates what effect an equal increase (or decrease) in government expenditures and taxes (hence a balanced budget) will have on the equilibrium level of income.

It was stated in previous sections that the government expenditures and investment multiplier is given by $\frac{1}{1 - MPC}$, and the tax multiplier is given by $\frac{-MPC}{1 - MPC}$. If the marginal propensity to consume is 0.75, the government expenditures multiplier will be $\frac{1}{0.25} = \frac{1}{1/4} = 4$. The tax multiplier will be $\frac{-0.75}{0.25} = -0.75(4) = -3$.

Suppose we have an equal increase, say $50 billion, in taxes and government expenditures. The effect of the increase in government expenditures is a rise in the equilibrium level of national income equal to the change in government expenditures × the government expenditures multiplier = $50 billion × 4 = $200 billion. The effect of the increase in taxes is a fall in the equilibrium level of national income equal to the change in taxes × the tax multiplier = $50 billion × −3 = −$150 billion. The net effect of the $50 billion increase in government spending and taxes is an in-

11. "Balance-the-Budget Boom," *Newsweek*, February 12, 1979, p. 28.

crease of $50 billion in the equilibrium level of national income:

$200 billion = effect of increase
             in government expenditures

− 150 billion = effect of increase
             in taxes

$50 billion = net increase
             in equilibrium level
             of income.

Thus the equilibrium level of income goes up by the same amount as the increase in government spending and taxes. Consequently, in this simple model the balanced budget multiplier is equal to 1, because an equal increase in government expenditures and taxes results in an increase of the same amount in the equilibrium level of national income. If taxes and government expenditures are decreased by an equal amount, the equilibrium level of income falls by the same amount.[12]

Why a Federal Debt? A balanced budget multiplier equal to 1 would seem to be a positive state of affairs. If unemployment existed, the government could increase the equilibrium level of national income by increasing government expenditures and taxes by an equal amount. It could thereby increase aggregate demand and employment and still *maintain a balanced budget*. In an inflationary period the government could reduce aggregate demand by reducing government expenditures and taxes and again keep the budget balanced.

Why, then, was the federal debt approximately $910 billion in November, 1980?[13] And why was the projected deficit in the president's budget for the 1981 fiscal year $55 billion?[14]

---

12. We can prove this result by adding together the government expenditure multiplier and the tax multiplier:

$$\frac{1}{1 - \text{MPC}} + \frac{-\text{MPC}}{1 - \text{MPC}} = \frac{1 - \text{MPC}}{1 - \text{MPC}} = 1.$$

13. Steven A. Seiden, "Interest Is Eating Up The Budget," *Business Week*, February 9, 1981, p. 10.

14. Ibid.

For one thing, many factors not directly related to government fiscal policy affect government spending and taxes. Wars and threats of wars come and go, natural disasters strike, and people demand government services regardless of how government spending affects the economy. Moreover, raising taxes is generally an unpopular policy. Finally, in the real world, where many more factors than are included in the simple model affect the equilibrium level of national income, the balanced budget multiplier is less than 1.

The next chapter will discuss various theories about the federal budget and the effects of the national debt.

SUMMARY

1. This chapter deals with fiscal policy and the role of the federal government. The first section explains the belief of classical economists that lack of aggregate demand could not be a significant problem.

2. In the midst of the Great Depression, John Maynard Keynes argued that saving and investment were unrelated functions. A country could be faced with inadequate aggregate demand at a full employment level of income because the income saved would not necessarily be spent on investment goods. Keynes believed that when such a situation occurs, government intervention in the economy is required to restore full employment within a reasonable length of time.

3. The goal of government fiscal policy is to maintain gross national product at the full employment level. If actual GNP is less than the full employment level, a deflationary gap exists. If actual GNP is greater than the full employment level, an inflationary gap exists.

4. Government fiscal policy actions—taxes and expenditures—affect the economy in a number of ways. In the simple model, the government expenditure multiplier is the same as the investment multiplier, and it is equal to $\frac{1}{1 - \text{MPC}}$

5. The tax multiplier has a sign opposite to that of the government expenditures multiplier because tax increases reduce aggregate demand and government spending increases raise aggregate demand. The absolute size of the tax multiplier is also smaller because some of the taxes come from income that would have been saved; therefore, this portion of the taxes does not lower aggregate demand. The tax multiplier is given by $\dfrac{-MPC}{1 - MPC}$ because MPC represents the fraction of a tax dollar that consumers would have spent.

6. In the simple model the balanced budget multiplier is equal to 1. That is, an equal increase in taxes and government expenditures increases equilibrium income by the same amount. However, in the real world, neither the economics nor the politics of the balanced budget is simple. People demand government services, but they do not like to pay taxes. Consequently, the size of the federal debt stood at about $910 billion in November, 1980.

IMPORTANT TERMS AND CONCEPTS

Say's law	Tax multiplier
Fiscal policy	Leakages
Lump sum tax	Deflationary gap
Government	Inflationary gap
expenditures	Balanced budget
multiplier	multiplier

QUESTIONS AND PROBLEMS

1. Why did the classical economists believe that an excess supply of goods and services would never become a significant problem?

2. Why, according to Keynes, could planned saving and investment not be equal to each other at a full employment level of income?

3. Explain the balanced budget multiplier.

4. Why do we have such a large (approximately $910 billion in November, 1980) federal debt in spite of the balanced budget multiplier?

5. Why is the value of the tax multiplier different from that of the government expenditures multiplier?

6. Given the consumption function $C = 100 + 2/3Y_d$ (all terms in billions of dollars), find the change in the equilibrium level of national income that will occur as a result of a $200 billion increase in government expenditures.

7. Using the consumption function in Problem 6, find the change in equilibrium income that will occur if taxes increase by $200 billion.

8. Using the consumption function in Problem 6, find the change in the equilibrium level of income if both taxes and government expenditures increase by $200 billion.

9. Given the consumption function $C = 200 + 0.5Y_d$ (all terms in billions of dollars), planned investment spending of $500 billion, and government spending of $100 billion, find the equilibrium level of income graphically.

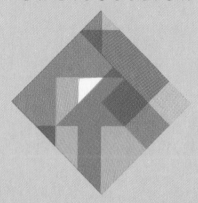

ARTHUR LAFFER'S INFLUENCE
CLIMBS A RISING CURVE,
ALTHOUGH MANY OTHER ECONOMISTS
FLUNK HIS IDEAS

Battling a bulging waistline several years ago, Arthur B. Laffer didn't pussyfoot. He studied, among other things, the body's caloric intake and concluded that a good way to fight fat was to spend long periods in cool water. "The water helped drain off my body heat," he explains, adding, "I lost 50 pounds in 40 days."

The 38-year-old, still-pudgy economist at the University of Southern California here hasn't sparked any controversy in the contentious world of weight reduction, perhaps because he

Source: Alfred J. Malabre, Jr., "Arthur Laffer's Influence Climbs a Rising Curve, Although Many Other Economists Flunk His Ideas," *Wall Street Journal,* December 1, 1978, p. 38.

hasn't published his views. But not so in the contentious world of *tax* reduction—in which Mr. Laffer has taken every opportunity to push his views.

"He is the most controverisal economist in the United States today—as well as one of the most influential," says Robert A. Mundell, an economist at Columbia University. Mr. Mundell adds: "Art is also one of the very best economists around and, I believe, has been treated badly" by his critics.

To many critics, however, Mr. Laffer's proposals for huge tax cuts are all wet. Martin Feldstein, a Harvard University economist who also is president of the National Bureau of Economic Research, a nonprofit organization whose staff

includes many prominent analysts, finds "absolutely no indication that Laffer's ideas will work in the way he suggests."

Ideas about taxes tend, of course, to be controversial. Mr. Laffer's theory holds, in essence, that a large tax cut, far beyond the recent federal legislation, would spur economic growth, increase tax revenues and curb inflation— all without a painful slash in federal spending. In sum, he suggests that if economic incentives are bolstered, there *is* such a thing as the proverbial free lunch.

Many economists refuse to buy that. A steep drop in tax rates, they contend, would depress tax revenues, and, without a cut in spending, federal budget deficits would swell. Ultimately, the huge Treasury borrowings needed to finance the deficits would balloon the money supply, and inflationary pressure would mount further. . . .

Mr. Laffer's basic concept can be glimpsed in the accompanying sketch, a so-called Laffer curve.

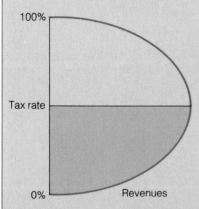

The curve theory states, essentially, that for every dollar of tax revenue collected by the government there exist, except at a single optimal point, two distinct tax rates, one high and one low. When the tax rate is zero, quite obviously, no revenues can be collected. And a 100 percent tax rate also would yield no revenues, according to the theory, because, with all income confiscated, there wouldn't be any incentive to work.

The optimal point, that tax rate producing the most revenue, is at the extreme right edge of the curve, where the shaded and unshaded sections meet. Despite the sketch's appearance, the optimal point isn't necessarily at a 50 percent tax rate. Rather, it represents a rate above which— moving up the curve's unshaded section—further tax increases grow increasingly

counterproductive. As the 100 percent level approaches, incentives and production decline, and tax revenues dwindle toward zero.

Mr. Laffer contends that taxation in America today has moved appreciably above the optimal point on his curve. Further increases in tax rates, he maintains, would only reduce tax revenues. Conversely, he argues that substantial tax cuts would increase incentive, and so production and revenues. Rising production and revenues would help ease inflation, he says, because the supply of things to buy would expand and federal budget deficits would shrink.

The Laffer notion that taxes can be cut so painlessly provides, among other things, an intellectual underpinning for various tax-cut proposals that otherwise might seem illconceived, even reckless. Certainly, the influence of the Laffer curve can be detected in recent legislation trimming federal capital-gains taxes, as well as in the passage of California's Proposition 13, which slashes that state's property taxes.

Unswayed by the political enthusiasm, Harvard's Mr. Feldstein derisively calls the Laffer curve "something a Congressman can digest in about 30 seconds and then talk about for months."

UNPERTURBED BY CRITICISM

However, Mr. Laffer seems generally unperturbed by such comments. "I know there's an element of uncertainty and inflationary risk involved in putting the theory into practice," he

concedes, "but I believe it's well worth the chance."

He stresses the importance of looking at tax rates in terms of their impact at progressively higher income levels. More than a country's overall level of taxation, it is the impact of higher and higher tax rates on higher and higher income levels, he argues, that erodes incentive. He cites, moreover, a widening "wedge" between what an employer pays a worker and what actually is brought home. As evidence that his curve can work, he recalls the U.S. economy's sustained growth—with little inflation and rising tax revenues—after a succession of federal tax cuts in the early 1960s. . . .

There's an obvious temptation to dismiss Mr. Laffer's curve as merely the opportunism of a publicity seeker. However, his credentials are considerable. The son of a wealthy Cleveland businessman, he received his undergraduate training at Yale and his doctorate at Stanford. His dissertation explored international trade and money flows. It was "a very good job," recalls Robert Mundell, an authority in that field.

QUESTIONS

1. What is the Laffer curve?
2. What benefits does Laffer believe a large tax rate reduction would yield?
3. Why does Laffer think a tax rate reduction would result in an increase in taxes?
4. What do the economists who disagree with Laffer argue?

CHAPTER 8

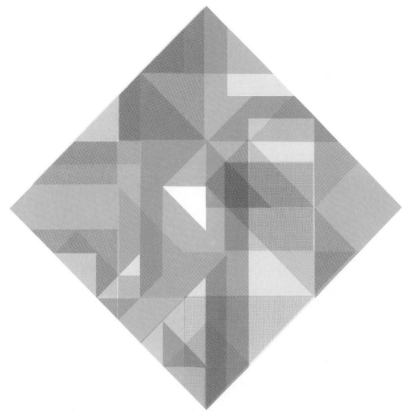

FISCAL POLICY
AND THE
FEDERAL DEBT

PERSPECTIVE

ON DEATH
AND DEBT

It was a marvelous thing the late Lee Hamlin Edwards did in leaving his $1 million estate to the United States to help the government pay off its debt.

Edwards, who lived in Alvin, Tex., joined the Army in San Antonio, served three tours of duty at Fort Sam Houston and is buried in the national cemetery here.

In his will he called having been born in the United States and having "lived a good life under the government of such a country" one of his highest blessings.

Alas, his money did not go to directly paying off and the "retirement"—the word he used—of a single penny of the debt itself.

A spokesman for the Federal Reserve Bank of Dallas says that instead it will go toward paying interest on the debt, not to the debt itself.

The spokesman says that paying the interest will amount to the same thing as paying the debt.

Technically and legally, he probably is right. But using it just to pay interest and not the debt itself misses entirely the symbolism of Edward's gift.

And the $1 million that could have been paid off will go right on costing the taxpayer interest year after year.

Let's put it in simple terms.

Suppose a young man had borrowed several thousand dollars and found himself unable to meet his payments. His father comes to him and says:

"Son, it won't go very far but take this $100 and pay off that much of what you owe."

That father would have been much upset if the son had come to him a few days later and said:

"Dad, I didn't use that $100 to pay off any of my debts. I just used it to pay interest."

In a sense the federal government has done just what the son did.

But maybe it's too much to ask any bureaucrat to even consider the federal government paying off anything it owes.

Besides, it's only a million dollars.[1]

Now for the big question: How many times should Edwards roll over in his grave if he finds out that his million dollars was used just to pay interest instead of to retire debt? If he knew any economics, he will probably be content to just rest in peace.

For a country, as for a person, the question is not how much debt you have but how much debt you can service. To service debt simply means to make the payments on it—sometimes just interest and sometimes principal and interest. If your current income allows you to service your current debt comfortably, the debt is not pauperizing you.

For most middle-income families the biggest chunk of debt service is the home mortgage. These families are perfect examples of deficit spenders. Customarily they will in some given year spend two to three times their annual income on buying a home. About 80 percent of this outlay (now $53,000 or more) will be represented by debt in the form of a mortgage loan. Most of these loans run from twenty-five to forty years in length and require installment payments of more than $500 per month.

A house is a durable capital good. Many houses last longer than their owners do, and many owners never completely retire the debt on their houses, even if they never resell them and reside in them until death.

Business firms buy capital goods through debt financing in much the same way that consumers buy houses and cars; and these assets, much like homeowners' houses, are what back up the decisions of lenders to extend them credit. As an economy grows, both business debt and consumer debt, in the aggregate, grow along with it. More businesses and consumers borrow greater amounts to acquire more capital goods and to add to their wealth. The debt in the aggregate, then, is never paid off.

A government can do much the same thing as its citizens and business firms do in terms of borrowing to acquire capital goods (jet fighters, dams, roads, ports) that will last for long periods of time. Technically, its aggregate debt need never be paid off either. However, there are some differences between government debt and private debt that require us to look into such issues as the timing of government deficits, the types of things on which the money is spent, and the government's methods of borrowing. This chapter will do just that.

1. "$1 Million Gift to National Debt," editorial in *San Antonio Express*, December 31, 1980, p. 14–A.

CHAPTER 8

FISCAL POLICY
AND THE
FEDERAL DEBT

WHAT THIS CHAPTER IS ABOUT

As indicated in Chapter 7, the intervention of the government in the national economy through taxation and government expenditures allows for the possibility that the federal budget may not always, or even ever, be balanced. That is, tax receipts may not equal government expenditures.

This chapter begins with an analysis of three philosophies regarding the importance of a balanced federal budget. It will show that views on this matter depend primarily on opinions about the federal debt—and most of us do have strongly held beliefs on this subject.

The last section of the chapter discusses the question of whether the federal government has become too involved in the economic affairs of the nation. It cites some examples that will cause us to seriously ponder this issue.

THE FEDERAL BUDGET

The **federal budget** is the financial plan for the federal government during a particular twelve-month period, called a fiscal year.

The budget is prepared and executed in four basic steps. First, the Office of Management and Budget, after considering presidential guidelines and requests by individual federal agencies for funds, prepares a proposed budget. This proposal is reviewed by the president. The president then submits a final draft of the proposed budget for the coming fiscal year to Congress each January.

After the budget proposal is presented to Congress, the second step begins. Congress first passes laws authorizing certain programs. Then it passes laws appropriating funds for these programs. The third step in the budgetary process is the execution, or carrying out, of the budget. Finally, The fourth step is an audit by the General Accounting Office to see that funds are obtained and spent in accordance with the law.

At the beginning of the fiscal year the budget of the federal government outlines the government's expected revenues and expenditures for that year. The fiscal year of the federal government currently runs from October 1 of one year through September 30 of the next. Since some of the federal government's revenues and transfer payments vary automatically with changes in the level of national income, the federal budget at the beginning of the fiscal year is only an estimate of what will actually happen during the coming year. Moreover, Congress may exercise its right to pass new laws that alter expenditures or taxes during the year.

Accordingly, we often speak of both the proposed and the actual budget deficit for a particular year. Frequently, for the reasons given here, these two figures differ significantly.

*The federal budget has a **deficit** if expenditures exceed receipts; it has a **surplus** if receipts exceed expenditures.*

At the present time the federal government uses a *unified budget,* a comprehensive budget that includes both regular federal funds and trust funds. *Regular federal funds* are derived primarily from taxes and borrowing, and they are not restricted by law to any specific purpose until Congress passes the appropriations bills. *Trust funds* collect certain taxes and receipts for specific purposes, such as social security and unemployment insurance.

Nevertheless, in recent years some activities of the federal government have been excluded from the budget. Among them are activities of the Federal Financing Bank and the Postal Service and the lending activities of the Rural Electrification Administration. For fiscal year 1980 such off-budget activities were equal to about 3 percent of the unified budget outlays.

The revenues and expenditures of the federal government are discussed in more detail in Chapter 9. In the next section of this chapter three important philosophies about the federal budget will be examined.

THREE
BUDGET
PHILOSOPHIES

We can classify the attitudes of people toward the possibility of a federal deficit or surplus into three broad categories: (1) a belief that the budget should be balanced annually, (2) a belief that the budget should be balanced over the course of the business cycle, and (3) a belief that balancing the budget is not as important as using fiscal policy□ to maintain the economy at a full employment but noninflationary level of income.

ANNUALLY BALANCED BUDGET

*The **annually balanced budget** philosophy is the belief that the federal budget should be balanced each year.*

Although widely held in the past, this point of view was discredited as Keynesian economics grew in popularity. More recently, however, it has once again been gaining converts. (Chapter 7 noted that thirty states had passed resolutions by early 1980 requesting that a constitutional convention be called to draft an amendment to the United States Constitution requiring that the federal budget be balanced each year.) Why do so many people think the budget should be balanced? Some of the most frequently given reasons are (1) debt is evil, (2) debt is a burden, (3) we may be unable to make the required payments, (4) debt represents government use of resources better used by the private sector, and (5) financing the debt disrupts private capital markets and investment.

Debt is Evil In earlier periods people believed that debt in general was bad. Ralph Waldo Emerson admonished:

> Wilt thou seal up the avenues of ill?
> Pay every debt as if God wrote the bill![1]

People believed that the presence of debt indicated wasteful, or at least unwise, spending. Today most people have a less simplistic attitude toward debt. They recognize that it may be a necessary partner to investment.

For example, individuals and families readily incur debt to buy houses. If they waited to purchase a house until they could buy it outright, many families might never own one. A business that never built a plant or purchased a piece of equipment until it could pay for it completely would find its opportunities for

---

1. Ralph Waldo Emerson, "Suum Cuique," *The Complete Writings of Ralph Waldo Emerson* (New York: Wise, 1929), p. 932.

profit severely restricted. Furthermore, many people with savings are pleased to be able to hold the promissory notes of highly regarded corporations and governments and to collect the interest they pay.

Debt Is a Burden Many people still think of debt merely as a burden, and these people view the national debt as a special burden, because it may be handed down from generation to generation. Clearly, an individual or business would be better off if it had a specific amount of assets and *no debt* than it would be if it had the same amount of assets and debt. Its net worth would be greater in the first instance.

However, we cannot categorically say that that same individual or firm would be better off with a smaller amount of assets and no debt than with a larger amount of assets and debt. Housing loans are one instance where people are usually better off with debt. Moreover, successful firms of all types and sizes have found properly managed debt to be a source of financial capital that enables them to make greater profits. Although most debt requires interest payments, as long as the firm's return on the borrowed money is greater than the cost of servicing the debt, the firm will increase its profits by incurring debt.

The burden of debt is somewhat more complicated for a national government, such as the federal government of the United States. To the extent that the national debt requires interest payments to foreigners, U.S. residents must give up goods and services to those holders of the debt—at least when they decide to exchange U.S. interest payment dollars for goods and services produced in the United States.

However, by far the largest portion of the U.S. national debt is owed to U.S. residents, corporations, and other institutions. In other words, we owe it to ourselves.[2] Therefore, the tax revenues that are used to service the debt

merely represent income transfers from one set of U.S. citizens to another. In this case it is difficult to conclude that interest payments on the national debt make the country as a whole worse off. (There may be, of course, a redistribution of income that will make some people worse off and others better off. However, taxes may also have this effect.)

Still, the national debt may represent a burden to future generations if the government spending for which the debt was incurred results in a lower level of capital formation and, therefore, a lower national capacity for production and growth in future years. Economists often speak of the burden of debt from World War II, when resources were used for guns and tanks rather than for plants and capital equipment.

Even in this case, however, the burden to future generations as a whole is the same whether the expenditures are financed by taxes or by debt.[3] Thus it is government spending itself, not how it is financed, that may place a burden on future generations. On the other hand, if the government spending is used to put unemployed individuals to work or to increase the nation's output of capital goods (dams, roads, schools etc.), it increases the productive capacity of the country, which will benefit future generations.

We May Not Be Able to Make the Payments As mentioned above, if the national debt is owed to foreigners, interest and principal payments will have to be made in a manner acceptable to them. In this case a country can conceivably be in default on the loan. However, most U.S. debt is owed to U.S. citizens, and the federal government, through its power to print money and levy taxes, has the means available to make the required pay-

---

2. However, the portion of the federal debt held by investors outside the United States has increased in re-

cent years. See Dan M. Bechter, "Federal Government Spending on Interest, Transfers and Grants," *Monthly Review of the Federal Reserve Bank of Kansas City*, May 1976, p. 15.

3. The effects on the money supply and perhaps on private spending will differ. These matters will be discussed in more detail in later chapters.

ments. This situation is different from that of a business or individual. Neither can legally print money, and neither can usually control its income stream as effectively as can the government.

In Table 8–1 gross national product, the federal debt, and interest payments for selected years between 1916 and 1980 are compared. We can see that the national debt as a percent of GNP remained fairly stable during the 1970s. Moreover, it represented a far higher percentage of GNP between 1935 and 1965 than between 1965 and 1980. Interest payments as a percent of GNP have risen during the 1970s, so that from 1974 to 1980 they represented about 2 percent of GNP. This in-

crease corresponds with rising interest rates during the 1970s.

Nevertheless, given the historical perspective of Table 8–1, it does not seem reasonable to conclude that the federal debt has grown so large that it is unmanageable. Rather, the burden of the debt and of government spending in general depends on the uses made of society's scarce resources. This question is addressed explicitly in the next section.

Debt Represents Government Use of Resources Better Used by the Private Sector The argument about government using resources that would be better used by the private sector should not be taken lightly, although it is really

TABLE 8–1 Gross National Product, Gross Federal Debt, and Interest Payments, 1916–1980 (In Billions of Dollars)

Year	Gross National Product[a]	Gross Federal Debt[b]	Debt as Percent of GNP	Interest Payments[c]	Interest Payments as Percent of GNP
1916	$ 48.3	$ 1.2	2.5	$ 0.02	0.0
1920	91.5	24.3	26.6	1.0	1.1
1925	93.1	20.5	22.0	0.9	1.0
1929	103.4	16.9	16.3	0.7	0.7
1930	90.4	16.2	17.9	0.8	0.9
1933	55.8	22.5	40.3	0.7	1.2
1935	72.2	28.7	39.8	0.8	1.1
1940	100.0	50.7	50.7	1.0	1.0
1945	212.3	260.1	122.5	3.6	1.7
1950	286.2	256.9	89.8	5.7	2.0
1955	399.3	274.4	68.7	6.0	1.5
1960	506.0	290.9	57.5	8.3	1.6
1965	688.1	323.2	47.0	10.4	1.5
1970	982.4	382.6	38.9	18.3	1.9
1971	1,077.6	409.5	38.0	19.6	1.8
1972	1,186.9	437.3	36.8	20.6	1.7
1973	1,326.4	468.4	35.3	22.8	1.7
1974	1,434.2	486.2	33.9	28.1	2.0
1975	1,549.2	544.1	35.1	31.0	2.0
1976	1,718.0	631.9	36.8	34.6	2.0
1977	1,918.0	709.1	37.0	38.0	2.0
1978	2,156.1	780.4	36.2	44.0	2.0
1979	2,413.9	833.8	34.5	52.6	2.2
1980	2,627.4	914.3	34.8	64.5	2.4

[a]Series F1, U.S. Department of Commerce, Bureau of the Census, *Historical Statistics of the United States, Colonial Times to 1970* (Washington, D.C.: Government Printing Office, 1975), p. 224; and "Table B–1: Gross National Product, 1929–1980," *Economic Report of the President* (Washington, D.C.: Government Printing Office, 1981), p. 233.

[b]Series Y 488 and Series Y 493, *Historical Statistics of the United States, Colonial Times to 1970*, pp. 1116, 1117; and "Table B–70: Federal Budget Receipts, Outlays, and Debt, Fiscal Years 1968–1982," *Economic Report of the President*, 1981, pp. 314–315. Data before 1940 came from Series Y 493.

[c]Series Y 470 and Y 485, *Historical Statistics of the United States, Colonial Times to 1970*, pp. 1115, 1116; and "Table B–70: Federal Budget Receipts, Outlays, and Debt, Fiscal Years 1968–1982," *Economic Report of the President*, 1981, pp. 314–315.

an argument against government spending rather than government debt per se. Of course, if government spending results in unproductive national resources becoming productive, it is difficult to see how such action is taking resources away from the private sector.

However, government spending has also been of the type that does take resources away from the private sector. In this case, our attitudes toward such spending are likely to depend on how the resources were used, how we were affected, and what our value systems are. Many people who want government spending reduced believe that it has limited more preferable private spending, particularly investment in capital goods. This question will be discussed in a later section of this chapter and in Chapter 28.

Financing the Debt Disrupts Private Capital Markets The argument that financing the debt disrupts private capital markets also has some validity. A greater demand for loans causes interest rates to rise, which, other things equal, tends to reduce investment spending (purchases of capital goods).

Crowding out refers to the possibility that a reduction in private sector expenditures for capital goods may occur as a result of rising interest rates due to public borrowing.

To what extent financing of the federal debt by Treasury sales of bonds has discouraged private investment is not clear. It is a factor that must be considered along with the question of whether the government spending or any private spending that would be foregone is preferable for the nation as a whole.

In summary, we can say that it is not so much the size of the national debt that matters, especially if we owe it to ourselves. *What is important is how and if the resources required for government expenditures are used to benefit the nation.* This conclusion leads us to consider two other budget philosophies: a cyclically balanced budget and functional finance.

CYCLICALLY BALANCED BUDGET

*The **cyclically balanced budget** philosophy is that the federal budget need not be balanced every year but should be balanced over the course of the business cycle.*

Simply put, a *business cycle* □ within a nation consists of one recessionary period, or trough; an expansion, or boom, period followed by a peak; and then a decline once more in economic activity.

It is expected that when economic activity is at a relatively low level, the federal government will cut taxes or increase government spending in order to stimulate aggregate demand□. During this period the government may well incur a budget deficit. On the other hand, when economic activity is at a relatively high level, the government will raise taxes or decrease government spending in order to reduce aggregate demand and thereby limit the pressures for price increases. People who accept the notion of a cyclically balanced budget argue that while government expenditures are expected to exceed tax receipts in recessionary periods, these deficits will be covered by budget surpluses once the economy has recovered.

The cyclically balanced budget is an appealing hypothesis, but no economic law ensures that the length and magnitude of depressions or recessions will be equal to the length and magnitude of booms. Therefore, there is no reason to believe that the government can keep the economy at a full employment but noninflationary level of income and still balance the budget over the course of the business cycle.

FUNCTIONAL FINANCE

*The philosophy of **functional finance** holds that a balanced budget is of secondary importance to keeping the economy at a full employment but noninflationary level of income through appropriate spending and taxing policies on the part of the federal government.*

People who adhere to this theory believe that the government should use both automatic stabilizers and discretionary fiscal policy to affect the economy.

Automatic Stabilizers

Automatic stabilizers *are mechanisms that act automatically to increase aggregate demand during recessionary periods and to decrease demand during boom periods.*

For example, income tax receipts automatically fall when income falls and rise when income rises. We know from Chapter 7 that an increase in taxes will cause a decrease in aggregate demand and that a decrease in taxes will cause an increase in aggregate demand. Thus, as incomes fall, tax revenues also fall, which reduces the net effect on aggregate demand. The reverse effect occurs when aggregate demand rises. Moreover, the more *progressive* □ the income tax—the more the tax rate rises as income rises—the greater is its effect as an automatic stabilizer.

Certain government expenditures, such as welfare and unemployment insurance payments, increase automatically as national income falls and decrease as income rises. The behavior of these expenditures also tends to have a countercyclical (offsetting the business cycle) effect, moderating the impact of other factors that cause changes in aggregate demand.

Finally, there are also automatic stabilizers in the private economy, such as people's desire to maintain the same standard of living even if their incomes fall. Individuals are reluctant to decrease their consumption expenditures after a decrease in income, especially when they perceive the reduction as temporary.

The present system of automatic stabilizers in the United States only moderates the ups and downs of the business cycles; it does not completely eliminate them. One economist has estimated that these built-in stabilizers have reduced the decline in aggregate income during recessions after World War II by 35 to 50 percent and have reduced increases in income during expansions by 25 to 40 percent.[4]

The countercyclical effect of these stabilizers could be strengthened if the income tax were made more progressive or if unemployment and welfare benefits were increased. However, the impact of any politically feasible tax or government transfer payment policy will still be only to moderate business cycles, not to eliminate them. For this reason, many economists believe that additional government policies to affect aggregate demand are needed.

Discretionary Fiscal Policies

Discretionary fiscal policies *are deliberate actions the government takes to reduce fluctuations in the levels of national income and employment and to promote economic growth.*

Thus discretionary policies involve tax system changes, programs involving transfer payments, and government spending made specifically in response to an actual or expected change in aggregate demand. Because the automatic stabilizers only moderate business cycles, many economists believe that additional spending and taxing policies are necessary in order to stabilize the economy.

The automatic stabilizers do reduce the expansionary impact of government spending policies designed to stimulate aggregate demand. They also decrease the impact of increases in demand for goods and services by the private sector. This phenomenon is called **fiscal drag.**

The United States Congress indicated its willingness to implement discretionary fiscal policies by passing the **Employment Act of 1946**. This act states that it is the policy and responsibility of the federal government to

---

4. Peter Eilbott, "The Effectiveness of the Automatic Stabilizers," *American Economic Review*, Vol. 56 (June 1966): 463.

use all practicable means consistent with its needs and obligations and other essential considerations of national policy, with the assistance and cooperation of industry, agriculture, labor and state and local governments, to coordinate and utilize all of its plans, functions, and resources for the purpose of creating and maintaining, in a manner calculated to foster and promote free competitive enterprise and the general welfare, conditions under which there will be afforded useful employment opportunities, including self-employment, for those able, willing, and seeking to work and to *promote maximum employment, production,* and purchasing power.[5] (Emphasis added.)

More recently, Congress reaffirmed its commitment to promoting full employment with the passage of the Humphrey-Hawkins Act□ in 1978. This act is more formally known as the Full Employment and Balanced Growth Act.

The **Humphrey-Hawkins Act** *states that the opportunity for employment at fair wage rates for all those willing and able to work is a national goal. It also recognizes reasonable price stability as a national goal. Finally, it states that a balanced federal budget is a policy objective, as long as it does not interfere with the other goals.*

The specific provisions of this act are discussed in greater detail in Chapter 13.

Full Employment Budget The interventionist nature of the federal budget with respect to the economy is often described through the concept of the full employment budget surplus or deficit.

The **full employment budget surplus or deficit** *is the surplus or deficit that would result from the budget if the economy were at full employment.*

Full employment means basically that any person who is willing and able to work can find a job. (The official definitions of the *labor force* and *unemployment* are given in Chapter 13.)

We have already seen how the presence of automatic stabilizers alone tends to increase the size of the federal budget deficit or to reduce any surplus when aggregate income falls. Tax revenues fall, and transfer payments rise. Discretionary fiscal policies make the effect on the federal budget even more pronounced. Thus, if government expenditures and transfer payments exceed tax revenues, the corresponding budget deficit may merely reflect the effects of automatic stabilizers and of discretionary policies implemented to reduce a recession. The same principle may hold with respect to a budget surplus during a boom period. Therefore, economists describe the overall nature of federal tax and spending policies by using the full employment budget as a reference point (see Figure 8–1).

A federal budget that results in a deficit in a full employment economy is considered to be *expansionary.* A budget that is balanced is said to be *neutral.* A budget that results in a surplus if the economy is at full employment is considered to be *deflationary.* (However, we know from Chapter 7 that taxes and government expenditures do not have impacts of equal magnitude on the economy. Thus the actual net effect of government taxes and expenditures cannot be determined merely by finding their net effect on the federal budget.)

Given that an unemployment rate of 5.1 percent is considered "full employment," the full employment budget deficit has been calculated to be $31 billion in 1978, $23 billion in 1979, and $8 billion in 1980. The actual deficits for 1978, 1979, and 1980 were $48.8 billion, $27.7 billion and $39.8 billion, respectively.[6]

---

5. "Employment Act of 1946," *U.S. Statutes at Large,* vol. 60, part I (Washington, D.C.: Government Printing Office, 1947), p. 23.

6. "Carter Faces Problems in Achieving His Budget Goals," *Wall Street Journal,* January 23, 1979, p. 4; and Department of Commerce, Bureau of the Census, *Statistical Abstract of the United States: 1980* (Washington, D.C.: Government Printing Office, 1980), p. 258.

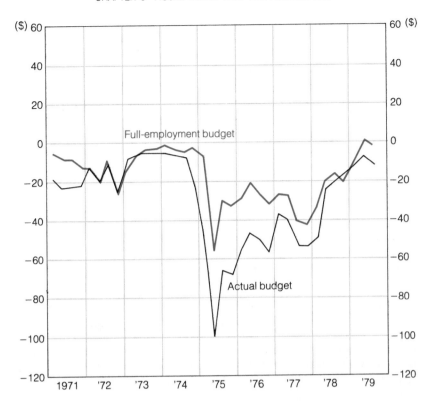

FIGURE 8-1 Full Employment and Actual Budget Deficits (−) or Surpluses (+) (Quarterly Data in Billions of Dollars)
Sources: U.S. Department of Commerce and Federal Reserve Bank of St. Louis.

The difference between the full employment budget deficits and the actual deficits occurs because tax receipts would be greater and certain government expenditures lower if the economy were at full employment.

Although in recent years the federal government has seemed to be committed to the idea of functional finance, many people still question the role of government in the economy. This matter will be briefly discussed in the next section.

IS GOVERNMENT TOO BIG?

A television program in 1979 told the story of a small town, Bordentown, New Jersey, that wanted to run its own welfare program, called "workfare." All unemployed, able-bodied people were supposed to work for the city; those who could not work were given support payments. The state of New Jersey protested this policy because, according to state regulations, all welfare programs throughout the state had to be uniform (in conformance with a set of State regulations). The citizens of Bordentown (both on and off workfare) seemed happy with the program, but that did not satisfy the state.[7]

Is this case an example of too much government, or was the state merely acting to prevent its citizens from being the victims of unscrupulous city welfare programs? Such questions are not easily answered, but they should be carefully considered.

---

7. "Sixty Minutes," CBS Television Network, February 4, 1979.

long-time opponent of big government, argues that the current public dissatisfaction with government and the "tax revolt" occurring in some states are results of government expanding its role too greatly. Friedman points out that government not only supplies the traditional services of national defense, police and fire protection, elementary and secondary education, roads, and the courts but also has ventured into the areas of social security, welfare, Medicare and Medicaid, and other transfer payments and has established many new regulatory agencies. He believes that government expenditures in these nontraditional areas are what "set group against group," because "they involve taking from some to give

to others, or imposing some people's values on other people."[8]

Of course, to some extent, all government spending is of this nature. People do not benefit equally—or do not view themselves as benefiting equally—from most of the traditional services. They do not agree on the desirable amount of defense spending or on the desirable level of police and fire protection. Not all citizens benefit equally from the "free" primary and secondary education or the roads or the courts.

---

8. Milton Friedman, "The Paternal State," *Newsweek*, January 22, 1979, p. 56. Also see Milton Friedman and Rose Friedman, *Free to Choose* (New York: Harcourt Brace Jovanovich, 1980).

TABLE 8–2 Gross National Product and Government Expenditures, 1916–1980 (in Billions of Dollars)

Year	Gross National Product[a]	Federal Government Expenditures[b]	Federal Government Expenditures (Percent of GNP)	Total Government Expenditures (State, Local, and Federal)[c]	Total Government Expenditures (Percent of GNP)
1916	$ 48.3	$ 0.7	1.4	—[d]	—
1920	91.5	6.4	7.0	—	—
1925	93.1	2.9	3.1	—	—
1929	103.4	3.1	3.0	$ 10.3	10.0
1930	90.4	3.3	3.6	—	—
1933	55.8	4.6	8.2	10.7	19.2
1935	72.2	6.5	9.0	—	—
1940	100.0	9.6	9.6	18.4	18.4
1945	212.3	95.2	44.8	92.7	43.7
1950	286.2	43.1	15.1	61.0	21.3
1955	399.3	68.5	17.2	98.0	24.5
1960	506.0	92.2	18.2	136.4	27.0
1965	688.1	118.4	17.2	187.8	27.3
1970	982.4	196.6	20.0	311.9	31.8
1971	1,077.6	211.4	19.6	342.0	31.7
1972	1,186.9	232.0	19.5	371.6	31.3
1973	1,326.4	247.1	18.6	405.3	30.6
1974	1,434.2	269.6	18.8	460.0	32.1
1975	1,549.2	326.1	21.0	534.3	34.5
1976	1,718.0	366.4	21.3	574.9	33.5
1977	1,918.0	402.7	21.0	624.0	32.5
1978	2,156.1	450.8	20.9	681.9	31.6
1979	2,413.9	493.6	20.4	753.2	31.2
1980	2,627.4	579.6	22.1	869.0	33.1

[a]Data from Table 8–1.

[b]Includes some transfer payments. See Series Y 466 and Y 472, U.S. Department of Commerce, Bureau of the Census, *Historical Statistics of the United States, Colonial Times to 1970* (Washington, D.C.: Government Printing Office, 1970), pp. 1115–1116; and "Table B–70: Federal Budget Receipts, Outlays, and Debt, Fiscal Years 1970–1982," *Economic Report of the President* (Washington, D.C.: Government Printing Office, 1981), pp. 314–315.

[c]"Table B–7: Government Precipts and Expenditures, National Income and Product Accounts, 1929–1980," *Economic Report of the President*, 1981, p. 318. The series for federal expenditures used here does not exactly correspond with column 3.

[d]Figures not available.

Still, Friedman asserts:

Our government has been changing from a service state through which we jointly finance activities from which all or most of us benefit to a paternal state that increasingly decides what is good for us and increasingly redistributes income, taking from some and giving to others. Those who pay are understandably unhappy—but so are most of those who receive. They know that their cause is just and that they should get still more.[9]

The last two sentences clearly show the dilemma. Both those who pay and those who receive are unhappy. While many taxpayers agree that government spending is too great, few wish to reduce it in an area where it has benefited them.

Moreover, most people view themselves as beneficiaries of one or more nontraditional programs. For example, in early 1979, farmers demonstrated in Washington, D.C., for higher price supports, and small oil refineries asked the government to intervene in the market for crude oil.[10]

A somewhat different approach is taken by several economists who have been quoted as saying that the federal government, in its desire to maintain full employment and through its tax structure and ceilings on interest rates paid by financial institutions, has seriously discouraged saving □. These people discredit the notion that too much saving causes unemployment and argue that in the long run too little saving will severly limit investment in productive capacity and the future growth of the nation.[11] Moreover, the presence of government borrowing in the financial markets may limit the amount of loans available to businesses for the purchase of capital equipment. In this way, it is argued, government spending crowds out investment spending by businesses.

Table 8–2 shows gross national product, federal government expenditures, and total government expenditures from 1916 to 1980. It also shows the two expenditure figures as a percent of GNP. Except for 1945, while World War II was still being fought, the proportion

---

9. Friedman, "The Paternal State," p. 56.

10. "Oil: The Little Guys," *Newsweek*, February 5, 1979, pp. 88, 91.

11. "The U.S. Bias against Saving Leads to High Inflation, Weak Dollar, Slow Growth, and Declining Productivity," *Business Week*, December 11, 1978, pp. 90–98.

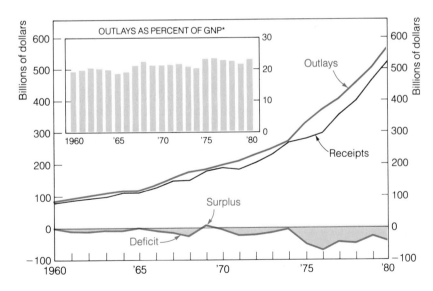

FIGURE 8–2 **Federal Budget Receipts and Outlays: 1960 to 1980**

*Gross National Product.
Source Chart Prepared by U.S. Bureau of the Census.

of GNP that consists of government expenditures has indeed increased. In fact, in 1980 government expenditures accounted for nearly one-third of gross national product. The relationship between federal budget receipts and outlays, and between federal outlays and GNP are further illustrated in Figure 8–2. Clearly, government expenditures are using a significant portion of the nation's resources.

SUMMARY

1. This chapter discussed three philosophies about the federal budget: the annually balanced budget, the cyclically balanced budget, and functional finance. Beliefs concerning the desirability of a balanced budget are determined primarily by opinions about the federal debt.

2. Various reasons are given to support the annually balanced budget (the position that the federal budget should never have a deficit). They include the following: (1) debt is evil, (2) debt is a burden, (3) we may not be able to make the payments, (4) debt represents government use of resources better used by the private sector, and (5) financing the debt disrupts private capital markets. The burden of the federal debt, especially of the portion of the debt owed to ourselves, and of government spending in general depends on how the resources of the nation are used.

3. Under the cyclically balanced budget philosophy the federal budget should be balanced over the business cycle. However, it is unrealistic to expect surpluses and deficits to always equal each other over the course of one cycle. No economic law states that the magnitude and length of booms and recessions will be equal.

4. The philosophy of functional finance is the belief that the federal government should be more concerned with promoting a full employment but noninflationary level of national income than with balancing its budget. Automatic stabilizers are the factors that tend to reduce the decrease in national income during a recession and slow its increase during a boom.

5. The Employment Act of 1946 states that it is the policy and responsiblity of the federal government to promote full employment, production, and maximum purchasing power. The Humphrey-Haw-

kins Act of 1978 reaffirms these goals. To achieve these ends government may well have to use discretionary fiscal policies in addition to automatic stabilizers.

6. The full employment budget surplus or deficit is the surplus or deficit that would result from the federal budget if the economy were at full employment. If the full employment budget has a deficit, the federal budget is said to be expansionary. If the budget is balanced, it is said to be neutral. If the budget has a surplus, it is said to be deflationary.

7. It is not easy to define the proper role of government. Nevertheless, the citizens of a country should be mindful of the fact that resources are scarce and that the use of them in one way will often restrict their use in other ways.

IMPORTANT TERMS AND CONCEPTS

Federal budget	Discretionary fiscal
Budget deficit	policy
Budget surplus	Fiscal drag
Annually balanced	Employment Act
budget	(1946)
Crowding out	Humphrey-Hawkins
Cyclically balanced	Act (1978)
budget	Full Employment
Functional finance	budget surplus or
Automatic stabilizers	deficit

QUESTIONS AND PROBLEMS

1. What are the three basic philosophies about the balancing of the federal budget discussed in this chapter? Briefly explain each position.

2. Explain why some people believe that an annually balanced federal budget is desirable.

3. Why might a cyclically balanced budget policy not work in practice?

4. What are automatic stabilizers? Give some examples.

5. Why do some people believe that the federal government has gotten too big? Is there any evidence to support their opinion? Explain.

6. How has the federal debt as a percentage of GNP varied over the last sixty years?

7. What is the full employment budget?

CAPITALISM
AND THE
GROWTH OF
GOVERNMENT

In the September 29, 1978 *Wall Street Journal* ("Has Capitalism a Future?") Paul Johnson identifies the growth of government as one force likely to have serious consequences for the future of capitalism and the wealth and freedom capitalism generates. This is a common view, of course, having been expressed in different forms by writers tracing their intellectual heritage back to Adam Smith and through the political and economic liberalism of the nineteenth century. The argument usually assumes the following form: (1) capitalism (decentralized decision making) generates material well-being and personal

Source: James J. Lakso, "Capitalism and the Growth of Government," *Collegiate Forum*, Winter 1979, pp. 2, 11. Reprinted with permission of James J. Lakso, Professor of Economics at Juniata College. From the *Collegiate Forum*, published by Dow Jones & Company, Inc. Princeton, NJ, 08540. Copyright 1979—All Rights Reserved.

freedom; (2) the growth of government threatens the development of capitalism; (3) the growth of government therefore threatens material well-being and personal freedom; (4) small government therefore is preferable to big government.

We may better be able to analyze the effects of the growth of government on capitalism if we try to understand the causes of that growth. There are many hypotheses regarding the causes of the growth of government, several of which regard it as inevitable in market societies. I will briefly review three of them and examine their consequences for public policy arguments about the size of government. All three share the view that the growth of government may best be understood as an attempt to trade off personal freedom and efficiency for other important social values.

John Maynard Keynes provides

a theoretical foundation for the growth of government in his *General Theory*. Keynes argues that in a modern, capitalist, money economy long periods of unemployment are likely. Keynes sees the growth of the state as an effort to gain stability in the system. In *The General Theory* he reasons, "It is certain that the world will not much longer tolerate the unemployment which, apart from brief intervals of excitement, is associated—and, in my opinion, inevitably associated—with present day capitalistic individualism. But it may be possible by a right analysis of the problem to cure the disease whilst preserving efficiency and freedom" (p. 381). For Keynes, then, the growth of government is necessary given the instability "inevitably associated" with capitalism. Some loss in personal freedom caused by the enlargement of the functioning of the state is thus necessary to protect as much of existing economic order as possible.

Karl Polanyi's analysis of capitalism in *The Great Transformation* also suggests the inevitability of government growth in a market economy. He asserts it is an elementary point of understanding regarding man and society that individuals must be protected from the whimsical play of market forces. He further states that government is responsible for controlling the rate of social change to protect individuals. Polanyi therefore suggests the necessity of giving up some of the dynamic efficiency resulting from unrestricted market forces in exchange for greater individual security.

John Rawls' *Theory of Justice* also implies the likelihood, if not the inevitability, of larger government. In Rawls' framework the market has an advantage over other economic forms in allowing free occupational choice, but market forces do not produce a "just" distribution of income. The state must function as a redistributive mechanism in a market society, but within limits necessitated by the need for reward differentials to motivate individual output. A trade-off is suggested here between market efficiency and greater equality. Rawls argues that greater equality is desirable until the point is reached where the loss of efficiency caused by greater equality begins to reduce the well-being of those persons least well off.

Keynes, Polanyi and Rawls all suggest that the growth of government involves trade-offs. For

Keynes greater stability is achieved, although some personal freedom may be sacrificed. For Polanyi greater personal security, and for Rawls greater justice is gained through the growth of the state. The growth of government is seen as an attempt to secure particular social values, recognizing that they are not gained freely, but rather are paid for with some losses in efficiency or personal freedom.

The minimal state may indeed lead to maximum personal freedom and maximum output over time (there are many who would deny this), but other values are likely to be sacrificed. Defenders of market societies would have more success in convincing people of the virtues of the market if they argued for the *optimal-sized* state rather than the *minimal* state. This argument would assume the existence of a number of desirable social values such as personal freedom, efficiency, security, stability and justice and would determine the right size of government in terms of trade-offs among these values. Critics of government growth would then need to demonstrate either that particular government programs did not actually produce gains in some values to compensate for the loss in others, or that the marginal value of a further gain in stability, justice or personal security would be less than its marginal cost in reduced efficiency or reduced freedom.

Freedom and efficiency are important values promoted by a liberal, democratic market society. Stability, personal security and distributive justice are also

important, however. The growth of government in recent years is probably best understood as an attempt to make gains in these latter values without paying sufficient attention to the cost in efficiency and personal freedom. On the other hand, arguments for a small government will not be effective if they ignore the gains that have been made in these social values.

The job of public policy analysis is to recognize value trade-offs implicit in providing or failing to provide added government services. The job of government is to provide mechanisms to better resolve these value conflicts so that the public is asked to decide, not between big government and small government, but between more government and less. No economic system can maximize all social values simultaneously. Proponents of the market would be better off defending it on comparative rather than absolute terms.

QUESTIONS

1. What were the positions of Keynes, Polanyi, and Rawls with respect to the growth of government?

2. Summarize the main points of the argument that the growth of government will "have serious consequences for the future of capitalism and the wealth and freedom capitalism generates."

3. What is the main point Lakso is trying to make in this article? Explain.

4. What is your position on the issue of government growth? Explain.

CHAPTER 9

WHO PAYS
THE
TAXES?

ON
TOM'S TAXES
VERSUS
DICK'S TAXES

Dear Reader,

Back in 1973 my neighbor, Tom, was in a foul mood 'long about tax time. Why? Well, he hadn't had such a bad year (made more than $20,000 and wasn't much in debt), but his federal income tax bill came to $4,100. This didn't bother him much either, since it averaged less than 21 percent of his gross income. In lots of countries, middle-class people pay a much higher average tax rate than that.

What was it, then, that roused his temper? Not Tom's taxes but Dick's! Dick who? Richard Nixon, at that time our president. It seems that Mr. Nixon had a pretty good year, too, at least financially. The president apparently grossed over $500,000, but his federal income taxes, $4,300, were hardly any more than Tom's.[1] To pour salt on Tom's wound, he later found out that Mr. Nixon's friend and confidant, Nelson Rockefeller (later to become vice-president under Gerald Ford), typically paid no federal income taxes but as a goodwill gesture donated a couple hundred thousand dollars to the Treasury each year.

Of course, the Democrats don't deserve to miss recognition on this issue, either. By 1977 Tom's wife was working, and their joint income was considerably up from what he had grossed in 1972,

---

1. "Nixon Revealing Financial File, Asks Ruling on Whether He Owes $267,000," *New York Times*, December 9, 1973, p. 62.

but still in the low five figures. Tom paid income taxes of $7,200, which, in fact, was less than 20 percent of what he and his wife had earned, since they now had interest and property tax deductions for a new house. According to the press, President Jimmy Carter did all right too. He made $495,000 and paid federal income taxes of $48,000, or about 9.7 percent of his total income.[2]

What is all of this nonsense anyway? Isn't the United States supposed to have a progressive income tax—one where the rich pay more? In theory, this is certainly the case. In practice? Well, read on!

2. "Returns Show Carter Paid $48,000 in Taxes in '77," *New York Times,* June 16, 1978, p. 16.

C H A P T E R 9

WHO PAYS
THE
TAXES?

WHAT THIS CHAPTER IS ABOUT

TYPES OF TAXES
WHO SHOULD PAY THE TAXES?
The Benefit Argument
The Ability-to-Pay Criterion
CLASSIFICATION OF THE TAX STRUCTURE
SUMMARY OF GOVERNMENT RECEIPTS AND
  EXPENDITURES
Federal
State and Local
THE OVERALL TAX BURDEN

The question of how the tax burden should be distributed has always been a controversial one. This chapter describes the most common taxes in the United States, discusses two basic philosophies of who should pay them, describes a classification system for the tax structure, and briefly examines government receipts and expenditures in the United States.

TYPES OF TAXES

In this section we briefly look at some of the major types of taxes in the United States. As we will see shortly, some of these taxes depend on the level of income of a person or corporation while others do not.

SALES TAXES

Sales and excise taxes are taxes levied on the sale of goods and services.

*As the terms are generally used, a **sales tax** is a tax imposed on the sale of a large number of commodities, whereas an **excise tax** is a tax levied on the sale of a specific item.*

The federal government does not have a general sales tax. However, it does levy excise taxes on certain items, such as gasoline, tires, alcoholic beverages, and tobacco. In contrast, many state and local governments rely heavily on sales taxes for revenues.

PERSONAL INCOME TAXES

Personal income taxes *are taxes levied on the taxable income of individuals.*

Taxable income is computed by subtracting certain expenses and deductions from gross income. Also, each taxpayer is entitled to one or more *exemptions,* which exclude a fixed amount of income from taxable income. The federal government relies heavily on the personal income tax for its revenues. Many states and some local areas also impose a personal income tax.

PAYROLL TAXES

Payroll taxes, *or employment taxes, are based on the payrolls of businesses. They include employer, employee, and self-employed taxes for the federal Old-Age, Survivors, and Disability Insurance (OASDI) system; the federal and state unemployment insurance tax on employers; and the railroad retirement tax on employers and employees.*

Most workers are now covered by Old-Age, Survivors, and Disability Insurance (social security)□. Retired or disabled workers and their families may receive OASDI payments each month. The amount of the payment depends on the past earnings of the covered worker. (Chapter 34 will explain this topic in more detail.)

In 1981 an employee covered by OASDI was required to contribute a tax equal to 6.65 percent of his or her individual income, up to an income limit of $29,700. The employer had to pay a matching sum for each employee. More-

over, the upper limit on these payments is scheduled to be raised in future years.

Unemployment insurance is funded by a federal tax imposed on the taxable payrolls of most employers. Some states also collect an unemployment tax. The portion of the payroll on which the unemployment taxes are levied under federal law and many state laws is the first $8,000 paid each worker during a year. Employers may receive a credit on the unemployment taxes due the federal government equal to a percentage of the contributions paid to the states under state unemployment insurance laws.

CORPORATE INCOME TAXES

Corporate income taxes *are levied on the taxable incomes of corporations.*

A corporation is a form of business organization in which the owners are individuals or other economic entities that have purchased shares of stock issued by the firm. The federal government, many states, and some local governments levy income taxes on corporations.

Because individuals are taxed on the dividends paid them by corporations, the corporate income tax represents a form of double taxation. The corporate income tax rate varies with the level of income, ranging in 1981 from a low of 17 percent to a high of 46 percent on income over $100,000.

ESTATE AND GIFT TAXES

Estate taxes *are taxes levied on the estate of an individual when he or she dies. The federal government imposes an estate tax. Many states also have inheritance taxes, which they levy on individuals who receive bequests of property after the death of another person. A* **gift tax** *is a tax imposed by the federal government and some state governments on the donor of a gift, not the recipient.*

The federal government shares part of its revenues with states that have inheritance or estate taxes. Moreover, state death tax receipts can be used by individuals to obtain a credit against part of the federal estate taxes due.

PROPERTY TAXES

Property taxes *are imposed on owners of property.*

Many state and local governments impose property taxes, most of which apply to *real property*—land and buildings. Some areas also levy taxes on personal property, such as automobiles and furniture.

Each area sets an annual property tax rate, usually expressed as so many dollars per $1,000 of *assessed valuation.* For example, the property tax rate may be $35 per $1,000 of assessed valuation. (The rate can also be expressed as 3.5 percent, or 35 mils.)

Often, the assessed valuation is much less than the actual market value of the property. The assessed value may be lower for two reasons: because the taxing authority states that the assessed valuation will be some fraction, such as two-thirds, of the market value and because the taxing authority has not appraised (estimated the value of) the property recently. In the latter case, inflation often results in appraised values and market values that are far apart.

VALUE-ADDED TAX

In recent years there has been renewed interest in value-added taxes (VATs).

A **value-added tax** *is a tax imposed on the value added to a good at each stage of production.*

Chapter 5 illustrated the concept of value added with the example of a can of green beans and isolated the following stages of production:

1. Growing and harvesting the beans (truck farmer).

2. Canning the beans (cannery).

3. Selling the beans to the supermarket (wholesaler).

4. Selling the beans to the public (supermarket).

If a value-added tax were imposed on the production and distribution of green beans, the truck farmer, cannery, wholesaler, and supermarket would be forced to pay a tax on the value added by their activities at their respective stages of production. The tax would apply only to consumption goods, not investment goods. This type of tax, which is widely used in Europe, is similar to a sales tax and would probably be at least partly reflected in higher prices to consumers.

The impetus toward a value-added tax seems to be occurring for two reasons. First, many business people and some economists believe that the present income tax system penalizes productive activities and investment too heavily. The VAT would be more in the nature of a consumption tax than an income tax. Second, the VAT is, politically speaking, a relatively painless way to raise taxes. The effect of the tax on prices is not very evident because the tax is hidden at the various stages of production.[1]

The next section of this chapter discusses two philosophies about who should bear the tax burden.

WHO
SHOULD
PAY?

The two basic philosophies of how the tax burden should be distributed are the benefit criterion and the ability-to-pay criterion.

1. See "Experience with VAT in Europe Leads Some to Propose It for U.S.," *Wall Street Journal,*February 2, 1979, pp. 1, 26; and "The Renewed Appeal of VAT," *Business Week,* February 12, 1979, pp. 63−64.

The **benefit criterion** holds that those who receive the benefits financed by taxes should pay for them.

The **ability-to-pay criterion** holds that those whose ability to pay is greatest should pay the most taxes.

As we will see, these philosophies sometimes conflict with each other.

BENEFIT ARGUMENT

On first thought it might seem that a pay-in-accordance-with-benefits-received philosophy would be fair. Certainly, the notion of paying for what you get is widely accepted. In some cases this policy might work well. Citizens who take advantage of government subsidies to, say, medical schools or air travel could perhaps be asked to pay extra taxes of one sort or another to compensate the government. We do follow this criterion to some extent, such as by paying camping fees for the use of federal parks and tolls for the use of certain roadways and bridges.

However, if we strictly adhere to such a philosophy, those who receive income subsidy payments will have to reimburse the government for them—an impossibility for some people. For example, a person who gets cancer or some other disease and who benefits from government sponsored medical research would have that cost added to other burdens. Moreover, we would have to find a way of measuring the benefits each of us receives from national defense expenditures, education, police and fire protection, natural resources conservation, roads, and the many other services supported by government funds.

Take education, for example. People generally agree that education benefits those who become educated. Most people also agree that at least up to a point the education of citizens benefits the entire society. How should the relative benefits be determined?

Furthermore, even in the case of medical

school, if medical students are required to bear a greater share of the cost of their education, that cost will probably be reflected in the prices they will later charge for their services. Also, it is possible that the children of rich parents will be the only ones who can afford to go to medical school.

At any rate, it seems obvious that in some cases at least the pay-for-benefits-received principle would cause problems. Unfortunately, the ability-to-pay criterion also causes difficulties.

ABILITY-TO-PAY CRITERION

As already indicated, the ability-to-pay philosophy holds that those who have the greatest ability to pay should do so. Presumably, this statement means that those with greater material wealth or income should pay more taxes.

This interpretation is not precise enough, however, to enable us to begin printing tax schedules. First we have to decide whether wealth, income, or both are to be taxed. Next we have to decide whether "pay more" means more in total dollars or a greater proportion of one's wealth or income. Then we must determine the tax rate or rates.

We also need to consider the effect of each type of tax rate schedule on citizens' incentives to save and to earn income. For example, if wealth is taxed, the incentive is to consume more and save less. If income is taxed, the incentive is to work less. These reactions to the tax structures will affect the economy and everyone's well-being.

Finally, the ability-to-pay principle is based largely on the idea that those who have greater financial resources can pay a larger amount of taxes without any more hardship or sacrifice than paying a smaller amount of tax imposes on those with less income or wealth. If we consider a family that is exhausting its income in order to stay alive versus one that is saving $50,000 a year, the philosophy seems reasonable.

Nevertheless, if we consider cases between

the extremes, the degree of sacrifice required to pay taxes is less obvious. For example, is it less painful to give up $500 from an annual income of $25,000 or from an income of $30,000? It is painful to give up the money in either case; furthermore, as our incomes rise, so do our wants.

What can we conclude? Only that determining how to divide the tax burden so it will have the least negative effect on our economy and still be fair is a difficult problem. One commonly accepted classification system of tax structures will be discussed in the next section.

TAX STRUCTURE CLASSIFICATION

◆

In this section tax structures will be divided into three basic types: progressive, proportional, and regressive. The label attached to each type of structure is not meant to denote the goodness or badness of the system. For example, a progressive tax structure is not necessarily modern or forward-looking, and a regressive tax structure is not necessarily backward.

*A **progressive tax** is a tax whose rate rises as income increases. Thus those with high incomes pay a greater percentage of their incomes as tax than do those with lower incomes.*

*A **regressive tax** is a tax for which the percentage of income paid out in tax falls as income rises. Therefore, those with low incomes pay a proportionately greater share relative to their level of income than do those with high incomes.*

*A **proportional tax** is a tax for which people pay the same percentage of their incomes regardless of their level of income.*

If all people paid the same percentage, say 15 percent, of their incomes in income tax, the tax structure would be proportional. If people with incomes of $10,000 paid an income tax of 10 percent of their incomes while those with incomes of $20,000 paid an income tax of 15 percent of their incomes, the tax structure would be progressive. If people with incomes of $10,000 paid 15 percent of their incomes in taxes while those with incomes of $20,000 paid only 10 percent of their incomes in taxes, the tax structure would be regressive.

Sales taxes, value-added taxes, and the social security tax are all regressive taxes. Sales taxes are regressive because people with low incomes spend a larger percentage of their incomes on consumption goods than do those with higher incomes. Value-added taxes are similar to sales taxes in terms of the portion of income spent on them. (These taxes are discussed at greater length in the special topic for Chapter 22.) Because the social security tax rate is levied as a percent of income up to a set maximum, the tax, taken by itself, is regressive. However, when the benefits received in exchange are considered, the tax is less regressive.

Economists do not agree on whether property taxes are regressive, progressive, or proportional. To the extent that those who have higher incomes own more real property, the tax is progressive. However, the wealthy hold their wealth in many other forms, such as stocks and bonds. Moreover, many elderly people with low incomes own their own homes and therefore pay a relatively high portion of their incomes in property taxes. One economist has concluded that the property tax is roughly proportional.[2]

Estate and gift taxes are usually considered progressive, because those with higher incomes tend to leave larger estates and to give larger gifts. Also, estate and gift taxes are not charged until some minimum dollar limit is

---

2. Henry Aaron, *Who Pays the Property Tax?* (Washington, D.C.: Brookings Institution, 1975).

passed. After that point, the tax rate gets steeper as the amount of the gift or estate increases. The progressive nature of this tax is somewhat offset, however, by the fact that income and wealth can be given to others in a variety of ways that will decrease the total taxes paid (such as through trusts).

The federal income tax on individuals in the United States is, in theory, progressive. The tax rate as a percentage of taxable income rises as taxable income rises. However, as we will see, the tax structure is not as progressive as the rate schedule makes it seem.

GOVERNMENT
RECEIPTS
AND
EXPENDITURES

◆

This section briefly discusses the sources of government income and the manner in which the income is spent. First, it describes the receipts and expenditures of the federal government; then it examines the combined finances of the state and local governments. After looking at these figures, perhaps we can begin to grasp the financial impact of the various levels of government on the economy.

TABLE 9–1 Federal Government Receipts, 1980 (in Billions of Dollars)

Source	Amount	Percent of Total
Individual income taxes	$244.1	47.0
Social insurance taxes and contributions	160.7	30.9
Corporate income taxes	64.6	12.4
Excise taxes	24.3	4.7
Customs duties	7.2	1.4
Estate and gift taxes	6.4	1.2
Miscellaneous	12.7	2.4
Total	$520.0	100.0

Source: "Table B–70: Federal Budget Receipts, Outlays, and Debt, Fiscal Years 1971–82," *Economic Report of the President* (Washington, D.C.: Government Printing Office, 1981), pp. 314–315.

TABLE 9–2 Federal Government Outlays, 1980 (in Billions of Dollars)

Type of Expenditure	Amount	Percent of Total
Income security	$193.1	33.3
National defense	135.8	23.4
Net interest	64.5	11.1
Health	58.2	10.0
Education	30.8	5.3
Commerce and transportation	28.9	5.0
Veterans' benefits	21.2	3.7
Natural resources	20.1	3.5
International affairs	10.7	1.9
Community and regional development	10.1	1.7
Revenue sharing	8.6	1.5
General science, space, technology	5.7	1.0
Agriculture	4.8	0.8
General government	4.5	0.8
Law enforcement, justice	4.5	0.8
Undistributed offsetting receipts	−21.9	−3.8
Total	$579.6	100.0

Source: "Table B–70: Federal Budget Receipts, Outlays, and Debt, Fiscal Years 1971–82," *Economic Report of the President* (Washington, D.C.: Government Printing Office, 1981), pp. 314–315.

FEDERAL GOVERNMENT

In 1980 the federal government had receipts estimated at $520 billion and expenditures estimated at $579.6 billion, leaving a deficit estimated at $59.6 billion. Tables 9–1 and 9–2 and Figure 9–1 summarize the primary sources of federal government receipts and the main categories of federal government outlays.[3]

As we can see from Table 9–1, the greatest single source of federal government revenues was individual income tax payments; they were followed by social insurance taxes and contributions and corporate income taxes. The two largest categories of federal government outlays according to Table 9–2 are income security and national defense.

If we analyze federal income tax payments by individuals, we can get a picture of the tax

3. The term *federal government outlays* is used because the figures include transfer payments as well as expenditures for goods and services.

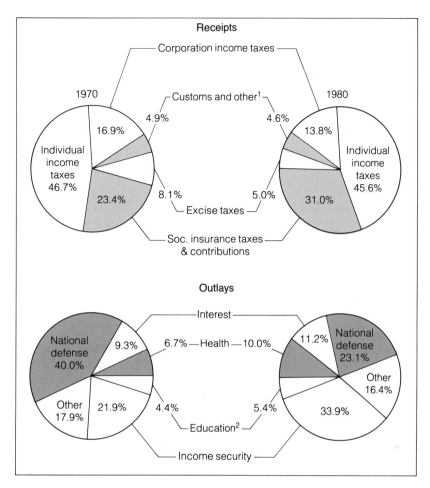

FIGURE 9–1   Federal Budget–Percent Distribution by Function: 1970 and 1980

[1]Other includes gift taxes and other receipts. [2]Includes training, employment, and social services.
Source: Chart prepared by U.S. Bureau of the Census.

burden for the various income classes. First, from Table 9–3, we can see that people with adjusted gross incomes between $10,000 and $49,999 have 72.3 percent of the adjusted gross income and pay 69.6 percent of the individual income taxes.[4] Those in lower income brackets have 10.9 percent of the adjusted gross income and pay 5.0 percent of the taxes. Those in higher income brackets have 12.1 percent of the adjusted gross income and pay 25.4 percent of the income taxes.

Table 9–4 shows the average federal income tax paid by individuals in various adjusted gross income classes and the tax paid as a percentage of taxable income. From these figures, we might conclude that the federal income tax is progressive. People with higher incomes do pay a greater percent of their incomes in tax if we are referring to taxes paid as a percentage of taxable income. The picture changes to some extent, however, if we look at the average federal income tax paid as a percent of adjusted gross income. *Adjusted gross income is*

---

4. Adjusted gross income is income after business expenses but before deductions. Taxable income is income after deductions but before exemptions, such as for number of dependents.

TABLE 9–3 Individual Income Tax Returns by Adjusted Gross Income Class, 1978 (in Billions of Dollars)

Adjusted Gross Income Class	Adjusted Gross Income		Taxable Income		Income Tax	
	Total	Percent	Total	Percent	Total	Percent
Less than $5,000	$ 19.9	1.5	$ 16.6	1.5	$ 0.6	0.3
$5,000–$9,999	122.9	9.4	100.8	9.5	8.8	4.7
$10,000–$14,999	171.9	13.2	142.1	13.4	17.1	9.2
$15,000–$24,999	386.4	29.7	320.4	30.1	48.7	25.9
$25,000–$49,999	383.4	29.4	318.6	30.0	64.5	34.5
$50,000–$99,999	95.3	7.3	78.7	7.4	24.0	12.8
$100,000–$499,999	54.1	4.1	44.6	4.2	19.4	10.4
$500,000–$999,999	4.6	0.4	3.6	0.3	2.0	1.1
$1,000,000 and above	4.2	0.3	3.2	0.3	2.0	1.1
Nontaxable returns	61.8	4.7	34.6	3.3	0.0	0.0
Total	$1,304.2	100.0	$1,063.3	100.0	$187.2	100.0

Some columns do not sum to totals because of rounding.

Source: U.S. Department of Commerce, Bureau of the Census, *Statistical Abstract of the United States, 1980* (Washington, D.C.: Government Printing Office, 1980), p. 271.

an individual's or a couple's income remaining after deductions for certain business expenses are subtracted from gross income. *Taxable income* is adjusted gross income less deductions for such things as interest payments on home mortgages and consumer loans, sales taxes on consumer purchases, medical expenses, and personal exemptions. Official data on these percentages are not available. However, rough approximations to these values can be computed by dividing average taxes paid by the midpoint of each adjusted gross income category. The results are presented in Table 9–5.

A somewhat different picture of the progressiveness of the federal tax structure emerges from these calculations, particularly in the $5,000 to $500,000 range. Although the federal income tax system is still generally progressive, it appears to be less so in this table than in the previous one. The figures in Table 9–5 are only rough approximations, but we can guess that they give a clearer indication of the relative federal income tax burden according to adjusted gross income class than do the figures in Table 9–4.

TABLE 9–4 Average Tax of Individual Income Tax Returns, 1978

Adjusted Gross Income Class	Average Tax	Percent Total Tax of Taxable Income
Less than $5,000	$ 134	4.1
$5,000–$9,999	539	8.7
$10,000–$14,999	1,200	12.1
$15,000–$24,999	2,500	15.2
$25,000–$49,999	5,500	20.3
$50,000–$99,999	16,700	30.9
$100,000–$499,999	57,700	44.5
$500,000–$999,999	308,000	59.2
$1,000,000 and above	998,000	65.4
All income levels	$ 2,741	18.3

Source: U.S. Department of Commerce, Bureau of the Census, *Statistical Abstract of the United States, 1980* (Washington, D.C.: Government Printing Office, 1980), p. 270.

TABLE 9–5 Tax Rates as a Percent of Adjusted Gross Income, 1978

Adjusted Gross Income Class	Percent Total Tax of Adjusted Gross Income[a]
Less than $5,000	5.4
$5,000–$9,999	7.2
$10,000–$14,999	9.6
$15,000–$24,999	12.5
$25,000–$49,000	14.7
$50,000–$99,000	22.3
$100,000–$499,000	19.2
$500,000–$999,999	41.1
$1,000,000 and above	Cannot be computed

[a]Computed by taking average tax paid for each adjusted gross income class, dividing by the midpoint of each class, and transforming these fractions into percentages.

The next section will summarize the combined receipts and expenditures of all state and local governments.

STATE AND LOCAL GOVERNMENTS

Tables 9–6 and 9–7 indicate state and local government receipts and expenditures for 1978. As shown in Table 9–6, the largest source of receipts ($69.6 billion) was the federal government. The second largest source of state and local government receipts is sales and gross receipts taxes, amounting to $67.6 billion. Property tax receipts of $66.4 billion are in third place. Individual income tax receipts were fifth, but at $33.2 billion they were less than half of either of the first two categories. Since the largest sources of state and local government tax revenues are property and sales taxes, the tax structures at these levels of government tend to be more regressive than the tax structure of the federal government. State and local government receipts and expenditures from 1960 to 1979 are illustrated in Figure 9–2.

Turning to Table 9–7, we see that by far the largest single expenditure of state and local governments was $110.8 billion for education. The next two highest expenditure categories were public welfare and utilities and liquor stores, but their combined expenditures amounted to only $64 billion. Most of the other expenditures were of much lower amounts.

THE
OVERALL
TAX BURDEN
◆

Before we can determine the overall burden of taxes, we must consider the effect of government transfer payments□. As Table 9–8 indi-

112

TABLE 9–6 State and Local Government Receipts, 1978 (in Billions of Dollars)

Source	Amount	Percent of Total
Federal government	$69.6	18.7
Public welfare	$20.2	5.4
Education	11.4	3.1
Highways	6.4	1.7
Employment security administration	1.9	0.5
Revenue sharing	6.8	1.8
Other	22.9	6.2
State and local sources	302.0	82.0
Sales and gross receipts taxes	67.6	18.2
Property taxes	66.4	17.9
Insurance trust revenues	35.6	9.6
Individual income taxes	33.2	8.9
Utility and liquor stores revenues	20.0	5.4
Corporation income taxes	10.7	2.9
Charges and miscellaneous	68.5	18.4
Total	$371.6	100.0

Source: U.S. Department of Commerce, Bureau of the Census, *Statistical Abstract of the United States, 1980* (Washington, D.C.: Government Printing Office, 1980), p. 296.

TABLE 9–7 State and Local Government Expenditures, 1978 (in Billions of Dollars)

Type of Expenditure	Amount	Percent of Total
Education	$110.8	32.1
Public welfare	37.7	10.9
Utilities and liquor store expenditures	26.3	7.6
Highways	24.6	7.1
Insurance trust expenditure	23.5	6.8
Hospitals	18.6	5.4
Police protection	12.9	3.7
Interest on general debt	12.0	3.5
Sanitation and sewerage	9.8	2.9
Housing and urban renewal	7.1	2.1
General control	7.0	2.0
Health	6.3	1.8
Financial administration	5.3	1.5
Local parks and recreation	5.3	1.5
Local fire protection	4.8	1.4
Natural resources	4.2	1.2
Other	29.1	15.3
Total	$345.3	100.0

Source: U.S. Department of Commerce, Bureau of the Census, *Statistical Abstract of the United States, 1980* (Washington, D.C.: Government Printing Office, 1980), p. 296.

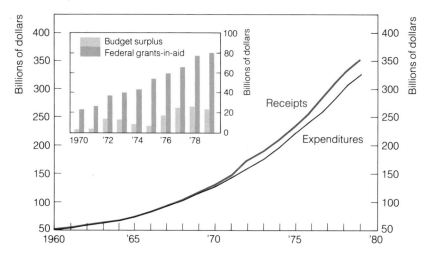

FIGURE 9–2 State and Local Government Finances: 1960 to 1979

Source: Chart prepared by U.S. Bureau of the Census.

cates, people with lower incomes receive a larger proportion of their incomes from transfer payments than do people with higher incomes.

Table 9–8 summarizes the results of one attempt to calculate the total tax burden, including federal taxes, state and local taxes, and transfer payments, by level of income. When all these factors are considered, the total tax burden does appear to be relatively progressive, with the net tax rate ranging from a low of −56.5 percent to a high of 44.7 percent.

SUMMARY

1. This chapter discussed the various types of taxes commonly levied in the United States. They include sales taxes, personal income taxes, payroll taxes, corporate income taxes, estate and gift taxes, and property taxes. In recent years, renewed interest in a value-added tax has been expressed.

2. The two basic philosophies about who should bear the tax burden are the benefit criterion and the ability-to-pay criterion. The first one argues that those who benefit from government expenditures should pay a corresponding portion of the taxes,

TABLE 9–8 Estimated Tax Rate by Level of Income

(1) Family Income	(2) Federal Taxes	(3) State and Local Taxes	(4) All taxes (2) + (3)	(5) Government Transfer Payments	(6) Net Taxes (4) − (5)
Under $2,000	22.7%	27.2%	50.0%	106.5%	−56.5%
$2,000–$4,000	18.7	15.7	34.6	48.5	−13.9
$4,000–$6,000	19.0	12.1	31.0	19.6	11.4
$6,000–$8,000	19.4	10.7	30.1	8.6	
$8,000–$10,000	19.1	10.1	29.2	5.5	23.7
$10,000–$15,000	19.9	9.9	29.8	3.9	25.9
$15,000–$25,000	20.7	9.4	30.0	3.0	27.0
$25,000–$50,000	25.0	7.8	32.8	2.1	30.7
$50,000 and over	38.4	6.7	45.0	0.4	44.7
Total tax on all income	21.7%	9.9%	31.6%	6.9%	24.6%

Source: Adapted from Roger A. Herriot and Herman P. Miller, "The Taxes We Pay," *Conference Board Record*, May 1971, p. 40.

and the second one argues that those who have the greatest ability to pay should do so.

3. Problems are associated with both methods of apportioning the tax burden. For example, it is often difficult to determine the total benefit an individual receives from government expenditures. Moreover, those who receive certain benefits are not always able to pay for them. On the other hand, the ability-to-pay criterion may negatively affect the incentives of citizens to save and work. It is also difficult to measure the relative degree of sacrifice that a given tax will impose on individuals with various levels of income.

4. The overall structure of any particular tax can be categorized as progressive, proportional, or regressive. If the tax structure is progressive, a greater percentage of one's income or wealth is paid in taxes as one's income or wealth increases. If the tax structure is regressive, a smaller proportion of one's income or wealth is paid out in taxes as one's income or wealth rises. If the tax structure is proportional, taxes are a constant percentage of income at all levels of income.

5. The two largest sources of federal government receipts are personal income taxes and social insurance taxes. The two largest sources of income for state and local governments are property taxes and sales taxes. The two largest categories of outlays for the federal government are income security and national defense. The largest categories of expenditures for state and local governments are education and public welfare.

6. It is difficult to classifiy the overall tax structure in the United States as progressive, proportional, or regressive. The federal tax structure tends to be somewhat progressive, whereas the tax structures of state and local governments tend to be regressive.

7. At each level of government, income security payments make up a large portion of government outlays. These transfer payments should be considered when we figure the net tax burden of an individual or family. Moreover, to be accurate, we should probably figure the expenses saved by those who take advantage of various indirect government subsidies, such as those for education.

8. Computing the net tax burden borne by an individual or family is a complicated task. Getting everyone to agree on how it should be apportioned is next to impossible.

IMPORTANT TERMS AND CONCEPTS

Sales tax	Property taxes
Excise tax	Value-added tax
Personal income taxes	Benefit criterion
Payroll taxes	Ability-to-pay
Corporate income	criterion
taxes	Progressive tax
Estate taxes	Regressive tax
Gift tax	Proportional tax

QUESTIONS AND PROBLEMS

1. What is a progressive tax structure? A regressive tax structure? A proportional tax structure?

2. What are the two largest sources of income for the federal government? For state and local governments?

3. What are the two largest types of outlays for state and local governments? For the federal government?

4. Explain the benefits-received criterion for apportioning the tax burden. What are some problems associated with such a system?

5. Discuss the ability-to-pay criterion for apportioning the tax burden. What drawbacks does this method have?

6. Describe what you think is the ideal tax system. Explain why it is the best system.

7. Which taxes tend to be regressive? Which tend to be progressive? Why?

8. What do you think of the value-added tax? Explain.

INFLATION, PROGRESSIVE INCOME TAXES, AND DO-IT-YOURSELF ACTIVITY

According to the results of a Roper Poll cited in the November 30, 1977 issue of *The Wall Street Journal,* do-it-yourself activity has been on the rise in recent years. Growth in the number of tool rental companies, the increase in advertising aimed at promoting the sale of "handyman's" tools, and the casual observation that everybody seems to be doing it themselves provides weaker, but nonetheless persuasive, evidence of this phenomenon. Examples of such activities range from housepainting and car repairs to selling one's house without employing the services of a real

estate broker. The increasing popularity of self-serve filling stations is further testimony to the trend.

Some analysts have suggested that this phenomenon is explained by a worsening "shortage" of qualified repair people. Others have stressed the self-satisfaction derived from successfully completing such projects. Another view maintains that people are simply trying to save money in an inflationary economy, while others claim that people now have more leisure time to devote to do-it-yourself projects.

Each of these explanations is either only superficially plausible or only partly true. The same *Wall Street Journal* article quoted Commerce Department figures showing that the number of companies engaging in house repairs and remodeling has not changed in five years. It is hard to

imagine that this is due to a persistent shortage of workers possessing the skills necessary to work in the industry. If this were true, inflation-adjusted wages earned by home-repair workers would have risen sharply, and the number of job openings would have increased. There is little such evidence. Rather, the absence of growth is more likely due to the declining market demand for such service as people prefer to do it themselves.

The supposed relationship between inflation, the desire to save money, and the increase in do-it-yourself activity is rarely explained in precise terms. It is one of those explanations that sounds plausible but comes up short under close examination. If all wage rates, prices, and taxes were to rise by the same percentage over a period of time, there is no reason to believe that people would want to save more, or work less, or devote more to do-it-yourself activity.

Elementary economics suggests that as something becomes more costly relative to its substitutes, less of that thing will be demanded. For a fairly wide variety of services the consumer is in a position to choose between direct (do-it-yourself) production and indirect production. Indirect production occurs when the individual sells his labor in the marketplace in exchange for money income which is then used to purchase the desired goods and services. As markets become more highly developed and specialized, it behooves the individual to substitute indirect production for direct production. This illustrates the law of comparative advantage, which predicts that members of a society can attain a higher living standard through specialization and trade. How, then, can we explain the fact that people are spending more and more time producing in areas where they possess a comparative disadvantage? The following anecdote suggests an answer.

A physician friend was having a house built and at one point decided to do all of the interior finish work himself. Although this individual was capable of expert carpentry work, paper-hanging, painting, etc., it seemed to me—an economist well-versed in the concept of comparative advantage—that his decision was irrational. After all, by taking on a few additional patients he could easily have earned enough to pay for the services of carpenters, painters, etc., and have had

money left over. Surely, an hour's worth of physician's services are worth more than an hour's worth of carpentry work in the marketplace, and helping the sick has to provide more self-satisfaction than carpentry to a devoted doctor.

Ignoring taxes based on income—that is, in terms of gross wages—there's no question that a physician-hour is more valuable than a carpenter-hour. When income taxes are netted out, however, the difference is less dramatic. For example, if our physician grosses $40 per hour, and the contractor charges $20 per hour for carpentry work (the carpenter, of course, earns less than $20 per hour) as long as the carpenter-physician's marginal income tax rate exceeds 50 percent he can save by doing his own carpentry, if he is an expert carpenter. . . .

Let us assume that all prices and wage rates double. The typical worker earns twice as much income and has to pay prices that are twice as high. It would seem that nothing has changed, but this would be false. With progressive income taxes, the tax rate would rise and tax liability would more than double. This is sufficient to bring about an increase in direct production and a reduction in market work effort. At some point, for some workers, the numbers of hours they have to devote to marketplace work in order to earn the money to, say, have the house painted exceeds the time it would take them to do it themselves. This motivation is reinforced by the fact that, according to Labor Department statistics, the price of home maintenance and repairs

has risen faster, since 1967, than prices in general. . . .

The welfare costs of this phenomenon are fairly obvious: physicians, for example, are encouraged (by taxes) to ignore their patients and paint their own houses. This is surely a case where lower GNP reflects a lower living standard for all—patients, doctors, and house-painters! In addition, should this trend continue, we should not be surprised to see greater efforts aimed at reducing do-it-yourself activity through political means. At the local level, stricter requirements for the issuance of building and repair permits are already being enacted in the name of greater safety.

The real culprit, however, is the combined effect of inflation and progressive income taxes. Slower inflation would reduce the trend and significant cuts in marginal tax rates would probably reverse it.

QUESTIONS

1. Explain why the author of this article believes that the number of house repair and remodeling companies has not changed in five years.
2. Why might a medical doctor wish to paint his or her own house if the doctor's hourly fee is $40 and the painter's hourly fee is $20?
3. Why does the article argue that society may be worse off if professionals engage in do-it-yourself activity?
4. Why do professionals have a greater incentive to engage in do-it-yourself activity when both prices and wages double?

PART FOUR

THE
ECONOMICS OF MONEY:
BANKS,
THE FEDERAL RESERVE,
AND
NATIONAL INCOME

CHAPTER 10

MONEY:
ITS FUNCTIONS
AND ITS
CREATION

MONEY, MONEY, MONEY!

Money, it's a gas.
Grab that cash with both
hands and make a stash.
New car, caviar, four star daydream,
think I'll buy me a football team.[1]

Recognize the words of that song? You can bet they weren't penned by the chairman of the Federal Reserve Board or the secretary of the Treasury. No, they're just the musings of Roger Waters, the lyricist for the rock group Pink Floyd. The song, "Money," dropped off the charts after 1973, but not before it made Waters and his colleagues the stash about which they sang.

Everybody wants money, and it is the government's job to make sure enough of it—but not too much—is around. Too much money is worthless, but the right amount is just fine. Money is strange stuff. It is coins, bills, and, mostly, entries in people's account books. In a book entitled The Paper Economy, *author David Bazelon flatly stated, "Money is not real!"[2] There is a lot to that idea. After all, money is useful only because of what it can do for us.*

This chapter considers the nature and functions of money. More importantly, it discusses how the banking system, a primary element in a modern system of monetary management, creates the money that the economy requires.

WHAT THIS CHAPTER IS ABOUT

Money is a new form of slavery, and distinguishable from the old simply by the fact that it is impersonal—that there is no human relationship between master and slave.[1]

In this quotation the Russian writer Leo Tolstoi takes a dim view of the usefulness of money. However, few modern economists would agree with him. Indeed, most would argue that money is an essential element in the functioning of a market economy and that when it is properly managed by government, it is really useful. Economic transactions are generally much easier to make when money is available than when it is not. Money also has several other functions, among which is its role in determining the levels of national income, employment, and prices.

This chapter examines the characteristics and functions of money and explains how money is created by banks. The relation of money to the level of economic activity and the general level of prices is left to Chapter 12. The discussion begins with the definition of money.

---

1. Leo Tolstoi, *What Is To Be Done?*

WHAT IS MONEY?

Money is anything that is widely accepted in exchange for goods and services and as payment for debt.

In the past, various metals, diamonds, shells, beads, and even slaves have all been used as money. Significantly, the legal definition of money does not limit what is generally used as money. For example, in the United States, from the 1930s on, the term *money* has included coins, paper currency, and demand deposits (checking accounts) held by the nonbank public.[2] Of these items, only paper currency has stamped on it, "This note is legal tender for all debts, public and private," although coins are also legal tender. (*Legal tender* is anything declared by law to be money.)

Nevertheless, checks too are readily accepted in payment of debts or for goods and services, as long as the person being paid believes that the checks are backed by bank deposits. In fact, it would be cumbersome if all debts has to paid with "legal tender." People usually do not wish to carry much cash with them because it is bulky and an easy target for robbers.

---

2. Technically, the traditional definition of money stated that the money supply consisted of demand deposits at commercial banks other than domestic interbank and U.S. government, less cash items in process of collection and Federal Reserve float; foreign demand balances at Federal Reserve Banks; and currency outside the Treasury, Federal Reserve banks, and commercial bank vaults. See *Federal Reserve Bulletin* 65 (May 1979): A14, footnote 1.

Using the "readily acceptable as payment" definition of money, we can say that the average money supply in the United States during December 1979 consisted of the following:

- Coins and paper currency $108 billion
- Bank demand deposits $273 billion[3]

Thus about 72 percent of our money was in the form of checking account balances or simple account-book entries (or computer files) at banks.

The concept of the money supply illustrated by these figures has traditionally been called M_1 by economists. It includes all coin, currency, and demand deposits held by the nonbank public. However, in early 1980 the Federal Reserve□ (discussed in Chapter 11) officially broadened the definition of the money supply. As a result, M_{1A} is now the designation given to the money supply as defined above. In addition, a new official definition of the money supply, represented by M_{1B}, was created. M_{1B} includes all the items in M_{1A} plus such things as negotiable order of withdrawal (NOW) accounts and automated transfer service (ATS) accounts at banks and thrift institutions, credit union share draft accounts, and demand deposits at mutual savings banks. The latter items are included in the money supply because the Federal Reserve recognizes that they have checking-type services available to them. (Negotiable Order of Withdrawal or NOW accounts are similar to checking accounts, but they earn interest.)

An even broader definition of the money supply, called M_2, includes all the items in M_{1B} plus savings deposits held by the nonbank public, cash invested in money market mutual funds, and certain overnight investments of funds.[4] These definitions of the money supply are summarized below.

---

3. "Table 1.21: "Money Stock Measures and Components," *Federal Reserve Bulletin* 66 (February 1980): A14.

4. During December 1979, M_{1B} averaged $387.7 billion, and M_2 was $1,523.9 billion, a much larger figure. See "Table 1.21: Money Stock Measures and Components," p. A14.

M_{1A} *is coin, currency, and demand deposits held by the nonbank public.*

M_{1B} *is* M_{1A} *plus NOW accounts, credit union share draft accounts, and demand deposits at mutual savings banks.*

M_2 *is* M_{1B} *plus savings deposits held by the nonbank public, cash invested in money market mutual funds, and certain overnight investments of funds.*

All these concepts of money are based on the notion of liquidity. An asset (something of value) is said to be *liquid* if it is readily accepted in exchange for goods and services at (or close to) what is generally considered its fair market value. A house may be readily accepted in exchange for goods and services, but often not at its fair market value. Plus, how many people would want a house's worth of apples or shoes? A similar situation holds for cars, furniture, bulldozers, and many other items.

In contrast, all of the items in M_{1A}, M_{1B}, and M_2 are liquid. One dollar will always buy goods and services whose price is $1. Nevertheless, when economists speak of the money supply, they usually mean M_{1A} or M_{1B}. They exclude time and savings deposits because these deposits generally must be withdrawn before they are spendable.

The nature of money will become clearer in the next section, which discusses the functions of money.

FUNCTIONS OF MONEY

Economists generally agree that money has four basic **functions,** or uses. These functions are (1) medium of exchange, (2) standard of value, or unit of account, (3) standard of deferred payment, and (4) store of wealth.

MEDIUM OF EXCHANGE

One of the primary functions of money is to serve as a medium of exchange. For something to be a medium of exchange people must be willing to accept a sufficient quantity of it in payment for goods and services. For example, if we wish to use ripe tomatoes grown in our backyards as money, we may have trouble exchanging even a large quantity of them for a pair of shoes. Shoe store owners may not wish to attempt trading all those tomatoes for other items they desire. Or suppose we offer a department store manager a pig in exchange for a small television set. Unless the manager is terribly eager for pork, we will probably be unsuccessful in making a deal.

In the past, before monetary systems were highly developed, people often did exchange goods and services. For example, they might trade pigs or grain for cloth, sugar, or other items. This kind of system is called a barter system. It can function well in a society with a limited number of available goods and services, but in a complex economy such as that currently existing in the United States it would be cumbersome. Problems occur because of what economists call a "lack of double coincidence of wants." In other words the department store manager may want car repairs rather than a pig. A shoe store owner may want a piece of jewelry instead of a pile of tomatoes.

The use of money enables us to avoid some of these difficulties. We can sell our pig or our tomatoes to people who want them and receive money in return, which we can then exchange for the items we desire, assuming the price is right. The department store manager or shoe store owner can also exchange our money for the items they desire. In this way money makes the exchange of goods and services easier and reduces the cost, at least in time and effort, of carrying out a transaction.

STANDARD OF VALUE

Money is also useful in that it serves as a *standard of value*, or unit of account. In the United States the prices and values of all goods and services are stated in terms of dollars; once we know the dollar prices of any two items, we also know their relative values. For example, if we can sell ten pounds of tomatoes for $3 and a pair of shoes costs $30, then we know that a pair of shoes is worth ten times as much as ten pounds of tomatoes. If we know we can sell a pig for $210, then we know that the pig is worth seven pairs of shoes or, perhaps, one $210 television set. This fact still does not mean, of course, that we can directly exchange the pig for seven pairs of shoes or a television set.

Obviously, it would be much more difficult to keep track of the relative values of goods and services if the value of each good had to be stated in terms of every other good or service. The price of one television set, for example, might be stated as one pig, seven pairs of shoes, seventy ten-pound bags of tomatoes, half a cow, or sixty hours of work as a department store clerk, and so on. A uniform unit of value is a far less complicated way of pricing goods and services.

STANDARD OF DEFERRED PAYMENT

The function of money as a standard of deferred payment is closely related to its use as a standard of value. It would be awkward for someone obligated to make a payment to another person at a future date to state the obligation in terms of pigs or tomatoes or shoes or hours of work. It would also often be difficult for the one to whom the payment is owed to predict the combination of goods and services that would be desired in payment of the debt at some future time. The dilemma is easily resolved by stating the obligation in terms of a payment in monetary units (dollars in the United States) at the future date. Unfortunately for the lender, though, inflation may have reduced the value of the monetary unit in terms of goods and services by the time the payment date arrives.

STORE OF WEALTH

Finally, money is a way in which wealth can be stored. It is often easier to store wealth in the form of money than in the form of goods and services such as pigs, tomatoes, or hours of work. In fact, storing wealth in some of these forms for a long period of time may be impossible. (Pigs will die; tomatoes will rot.) Of course, wealth can also be stored in the form of time and savings deposits, stocks and bonds, houses, cars, and life insurance policies, or a variety of other ways. However, all of these types of wealth are less liquid or readily spendable than money.

At this point, the discussion of the nature of money and its four basic functions should have put to rest any doubts about the usefulness of money. However, we still have to consider where money comes from and the role of banks in creating it—the subject of the following three sections of the chapter.

THE BANKING SYSTEM AND OTHER FINANCIAL INTERMEDIARIES

◆

Although the discussion in this chapter (and in Chapter 11) focuses primarily on banks, other firms perform similar functions. These firms, including banks, are called financial intermediaries.

Financial intermediaries are firms that take funds received from depositors or other sources and lend them to third parties.

Such institutions serve as intermediaries between those who have excess funds on hand and those who currently have insufficient funds for investment, consumption spending, or other purposes. In this way they put to use funds that might otherwise be idle.

Some examples of financial intermediaries, in addition to banks, are savings and loan associations, credit unions, insurance companies, and investment banks. In the past, savings and loan associations used the deposits of savers primarily for mortgage loans and for purchasing marketable securities. Now, because of the Depository Institutions Deregulation and Monetary Control Act of 1980 (discussed more fully in Chapter 11), they are beginning to make a wider variety of loans and to perform many of the same functions as banks. Credit unions have used the deposits of their members to make loans of various types to other members who desired them and who were considered good credit risks. These institutions are also becoming more similar to banks. Insurance companies use funds from insurance premiums to purchase securities issued by government and private businesses. Finally, investment bankers market the newly issued stocks and bonds of other companies.

In the United States commercial banks have traditionally been the only financial institutions with the authority to create demand deposits. However, some credit unions have been allowing their members to open "draft accounts," which are similar to checking accounts at commercial banks. The Depository Institutions Deregulation and Monetary Control Act of 1980 established the legality of these accounts as well as of similar types of accounts at mutual savings banks and savings and loans.[5]

As we saw at the beginning of the chapter, demand deposits or similar accounts make up the largest portion of the money supply. Thus, when the government wishes to affect the economy by increasing or decreasing the money supply, it frequently does so by increasing or decreasing the volume of demand deposits that commercial banks or other financial institutions can create. How the govern-

237

---

5. See "Senate Clears Bill to Expand Scope of Fed's Power," *Wall Street Journal*, March 31, 1980, p. 4.

ment controls the money supply will be examined more carefully in Chapter 11. The remainder of this chapter will show how banks are able to create new money in the form of demand deposits and how bank reserves serve as a limit on the ability of private banks to engage in money creation. Although the discussion will center on commercial banks, a similar analysis is now applicable to credit unions, savings and loans, and mutual savings banks.

TYPES OF BANKS

There are two main types of private banks in the United States—state banks and national banks. *State banks* are chartered by state authorities and are not required to be members of the Federal Reserve System (known as the Fed and discussed in detail in Chapter 11). *National banks* are chartered by the Comptroller of the Currency and must be members of the Federal Reserve System.

All member banks of the Federal Reserve System must have their deposits insured by the Federal Deposit Insurance Corporation (FDIC), a federal agency created in 1933 for the purpose of insuring deposits at commercial banks. However, many nonmember banks also insure their deposits with the FDIC. During 1981 the FDIC insured each bank account up to a total of $100,000.[6]

On June 30, 1978, there were 9,765 state banks insured with the FDIC and 4,616 national banks in the United States, for a total of 14,381 insured banks. Only 317 banks were not insured. Thus only about 2 percent of U.S. banks, with less than 0.5 percent of total bank deposits, were not members of the FDIC. Approximately 39.1 percent of the insured banks, or 5,619 of them, were members of the Federal Reserve System. However, these member banks held 59.3 percent of the total assets of all banks, so they are of greater importance than their number alone would indicate.[7]

The next two sections of the chapter will examine a simplified bank balance sheet and discuss how banks can expand their demand deposits, thereby creating money. A more detailed discussion of the banking system and its history will appear in Chapter 11.

BANK BALANCE SHEETS

Basically, a *balance sheet□* is an accounting concept that gives a summary, at a point in time, of the financial status of some economic entity—an individual, a business firm, or a public agency. It states the value of all of the *assets* (things such as property, money, or claims against others) owned by the entity, all of the claims that outsiders have against it, and ownership interests. Claims by outsiders, called *liabilities,* are primarily amounts owed to others. The difference between the assets and liabilities of a given economic entity is called the *net worth* of that entity:

$$\text{Assets} - \text{Liabilities} = \text{Net worth.}$$

Net worth reflects the ownership claims of whoever has property rights to the entity. Thus the net worth of a business reflects the value of its owners' or shareholders' claims on its assets, while the liabilities reflect the value of outsiders' claims on its assets. The section of a balance sheet listing net worth is frequently referred to as the *capital accounts section.*

---

6. The level of federal insurance was increased from $40,000 to $100,000 as a result of a bill passed in early 1980. See "A New Charter for U.S. Banking," *Newsweek,* March 17, 1980, p. 82.

7. "Table 1.25: "Commercial Bank Assets and Liabilities," *Federal Reserve Bulletin* 65 (May 1979): A17.

It follows that

Assets = Liabilities + Capital accounts,

or that all assets are claimed either by outsiders or by owners. In a balance sheet, assets are frequently listed on the left-hand side of the page, and liabilities and capital accounts appear on the right-hand side. *Each side of the sheet sums to the same amount*, since capital accounts are a residual, or what is left over after liabilities are subtracted from assets. That is why the sheet "balances." A balance sheet set out in this style is often called a *T account*, because it is shaped like a "T":

Assets	Liabilities and Capital Accounts
. . . . .	. . . .
. . . . .	. . . .
. . . . .	. . . .
	Total liabilities and capital
Total assets _____	accounts _____

In Table 10–1 a consolidated balance sheet for all U.S. commercial banks is presented.

The statement is simplified, showing only major types of bank assets and liabilities. The balance sheet for an individual bank would be similar to that for all banks except for the dollar amounts and the division of assets and liabilities into more categories. Table 10–2 shows what percentages the various accounts are of the total assets or total liabilities and capital accounts, respectively.

From Table 10–2 we can see that on March 25, 1981, demand deposits made up 23 percent of bank liabilities and capital accounts, while savings and time deposits made up 52.7 percent. Thus total deposit liabilities were 75.7 percent of the banks' total liabilities and capital accounts. Most of the banks' assets, 56.0 percent, were loans. Securities (mostly bonds) made up 21.9 percent of bank assets, cash assets made up 11.1 percent, and other assets made up 11.0 percent. We can conclude from Tables 10–1 and 10–2 that banks make most of their income from loans and securities and obtain most of their funds from deposits.

The next section explains how demand deposits and, therefore, the money supply are increased when a bank makes loans.

TABLE 10–1
Consolidated Balance Sheet for
Commercial Banks,
March 25, 1981
(in Billions of Dollars)

Assets			Liabilities and Capital Accounts		
Currency and coin	$17.8		Demand deposits	$345.4	
Deposits with federal					
reserve	31.7		Savings deposits	220.6	
Cash items in process			Time deposits	570.7	
of collection	63.3		Other liabilities	244.4	
Other cash assets	53.6		Total liabilities		1,381.1
Total cash assets		$ 166.4	Capital accounts		120.0
Total securities held					
(book value)		329.0			
Loans		840.8			
Fixed assets—buildings,					
furniture, real estate					
Other assets		164.9			
			Total liabilities and capital		
Total assets		$1,501.1	accounts		$1,501.1

Source: "Table 1.25: Assets and Liabilities of Commercial Banks," *Federal Reserve Bulletin* 67 (April 1981): A17.

TABLE 10–2
Consolidated Balance Sheet for
Commercial Banks,
March 25, 1981
(in Percentages)

Assets		Liabilities and Capital Accounts	
Currency and coin	1.2%	Demand deposits	23.0%
Deposits with Federal		Savings deposits	14.7
Reserve	2.1	Time deposits	38.0
Cash items in process		Other liabilities	16.3
of collection	4.2	Total Liabilities	92.0%
Other cash assets	3.6	Capital accounts	8.0
Total cash assets	11.1%		
Total securities held	21.9		
Loans	56.0		
Other assets	11.0		
		Total liabilities and capital	
Total assets	100.0%	accounts	100.0%

Source: Based on "Table 1.25: Assets and Liabilities of Commercial Banks," *Federal Reserve Bulletin* 67 (April 1981): A17.

BANKS AND THE CREATION OF MONEY

Commercial banks can and do create money. Later in this section the procedure whereby banks create money will be explained. Although the explanation will be couched in terms of banks, it now applies to such financial institutions as credit unions and savings and loan associations as well.

THE GOLDSMITHS

The process of money creation described below had its roots in the practices of goldsmiths hundreds of years ago. Besides creating gold jewelry and other gold items, goldsmiths stored gold coins and other gold items for wealthy people, charging a fee for this service.

After a while, it became clear to the goldsmiths that they always had on hand a substantial amount of gold coins stored for other people. The rich folk did not all show up on the same day to demand their gold. Moreover, while some people were wanting their gold coins returned, others were bringing in new gold coins for safekeeping. When this fact sunk in, the goldsmiths realized that they had a wonderful opportunity for making a profit.

Since a substantial amount of the gold was always on hand, why not lend some of it to others and, of course, charge them interest for the use of it? As long as the goldsmiths kept large enough reserves of the gold coins to supply those who might want their gold returned on any given day, the remainder could be loaned out at interest. Thus the goldsmiths began to keep only a fraction of the gold coins deposited with them as reserves.

In this manner the forerunner of our modern system of fractional reserve banking was created. In a fractional reserve banking system, banks hold reserves equal to only a fraction of their deposits. As we will see in Chapter 11, the size of this fraction is regulated in the United States by federal and state authorities.

*Under a **fractional reserve system** financial intermediaries maintain reserves equal to only a portion of their deposits.*

BANK LOANS AND DEMAND DEPOSITS

Let's begin our discussion of how banks create money by using a simplified balance sheet, or T account, for the First National Bank of Luckenbach, Texas. In order to highlight the process by which banks affect the supply of money, the balance sheet will show only those changes in asset or liability items that occur during the course of the discussion.

Initially, suppose that Sally Doe, a rancher, has come into the bank with $1,000 in currency and has asked the bank to accept the $1,000 in exchange for increasing her checking (demand deposit) account balance by $1,000.[8] The changes in the bank's balance sheet at this point are shown in Table 10–3. Demand deposit liabilities have increased by $1,000, as has the cash in the bank's vault (known as vault cash).

The money supply, however, has not increased at this point. Money in the form of cash held by the nonbank public has been reduced by an amount equal to the increase in money in the form of demand deposits.

> Economists call a deposit that represents new reserves brought into the banking system a **primary deposit.** They call additional deposits created on the basis of these new reserves **derivative deposits.**

In the real world the First National Bank of Luckenbach would likely transfer part or all of the $1,000 cash to a Federal Reserve bank in exchange for a credit to its reserve account with the Federal Reserve. The effect on the balance sheet of the Luckenbach Bank of a transfer of $1,000 of vault cash to the Federal Reserve is shown in Table 10–4.

Now assume that John Smith enters the bank and requests a $900 loan so that he can buy a piece of equipment for his restaurant. If the bank grants the loan and credits his check-

---

8. A bank may also obtain excess reserves in other ways. (See Chapter 11.)

TABLE 10–3
Effect of Sally Doe's Deposit

First National Bank of Luckenbach

Assets	Liabilities and Capital Accounts
Cash + $1,000	Demand deposits + $1,000

ing account with $900, the net changes in the bank's balance sheet as a result of these three transactions are summarized in Table 10–5.

At this point, something significant has happened; the bank has created money. It created the money when it made the $900 loan to Smith, because demand deposits increased by $900 and there was no offsetting decrease in the money supply. (Recall that no money was created when Doe deposited her cash because one type of money, currency held by the nonbank public, was exchanged for another type of money, a demand deposit.)

THE RESERVE REQUIREMENT QUALIFICATION

If there were no restrictions, the bank could, in theory, continue to create money as long as there was a demand for its loans. However, there are rules, established by law, which prevent them from doing so.

> **Reserve requirements** are rules that banks maintain reserves equal to a certain percentage of their deposit liabilities.

The requirements about the percentage of each type of deposit that must be covered by reserves are set by the Board of Governors of the Federal Reserve System within guidelines established by Congress. (These reserve requirements will be discussed more thoroughly in Chapter 11.)

For purposes of this discussion we will assume that the reserve requirement for all banks is that they maintain an amount equal to at least 10 percent of their demand deposits

228

TABLE 10–4

Transfer of Vault Cash to the Federal Reserve

First National Bank of Luckenbach

Assets		Liabilities and Capital Accounts
Vault cash	− $1,000	
Reserves at Federal Reserve	+ $1,000	

TABLE 10–5

Effects of John Smith's Loan and Sally Doe's Deposit

First National Bank of Luckenbach

Assets		Liabilities and Capital Accounts
Reserves at Federal Reserve	+ $1,000	Demand deposits + $1,900
Loans	+ $900	

as reserves in the form of vault cash or deposits with a Federal Reserve bank. Thus, since the First National Bank of Luckenbach has reserves equal to $1,000, it could theoretically create $9,000 worth of loans and still meet its reserve requirement.

The **required reserves** of a financial institution are equal to the reserve requirement multiplied by the dollar amount of the institution's deposit liabilities.

The **excess reserves** of a financial institution are equal to total reserves minus required reserves.

We can calculate the loans that the First National Bank of Luckenbach can create as a result of the original $1,000 demand deposit and the corresponding $1,000 increase in reserves as follows. If the reserve requirement is 0.10, the total amount of deposits, D, that the $1,000 in reserves can support must be a number such that

$$0.1 \times D = \$1,000.$$

Solving this equation for D, we find that

$$D = \frac{\$1,000}{0.1} = \$10,000.$$

Therefore, $10,000 represents the total amount of demand deposits that can be supported by the $1,000 in new reserves. However, a $1,000 demand deposit liability was created when Sally Doe deposited her money at the First National Bank of Luckenbach.

Thus the bank can theoretically make $10,000 − $1,000 = $9,000 worth of new loans.

We can reach this answer by another method. When Doe deposits her $1,000, thereby increasing both the demand deposit liabilities of the bank and its reserves by $1,000, the reserves that the bank is required to hold increase by $100:

$$\text{Change in required reserves}$$
$$= 0.1 \times \text{Change in demand deposits}$$
$$\$100 = 0.1 \times \$1,000.$$

The change in the bank's excess reserves as a result of Doe's deposit is therefore:

$$\text{Change in excess reserves} = \$1,000 - \$100$$
$$= \$900.$$

(New reserves of $1,000 were created by Doe's deposit, but the bank is required to hold an additional $100 of reserves as a result of this deposit.)

The bank can theoretically use the $900 in excess reserves to create $9,000 of new loans and, consequently, new demand deposits. We know that the new excess reserves must be equal to one-tenth of the new demand deposits created by the loans:

$$0.1 \times \text{Change in demand deposits}$$
$$= \text{Change in excess reserves}$$
$$= \$900.$$

Solving for the change in demand deposits, we find:

$$\text{Change in demand deposits} = \frac{\$900}{0.1}$$
$$= \$9,000,$$

the amount of new loans that can be created. This answer, of course, is the same as the one we found before.

We are now in a position to state a general rule for the relationship between a change in excess reserves and the new loans that can theoretically be created:

$$r_D \times \text{Change in demand deposits} = \text{Change in excess reserves} \quad (10-1)$$

$$\text{Change in demand deposits} = \frac{\text{Change in excess reserves}}{r_D},$$

where r_d is the reserve requirement on demand deposits.

We have shown that the First National Bank of Luckenbach could, in theory, create $9,000 of loans as a result of the $900 in excess reserves. However, the bank will probably not do so at this point. Why not?

THE ROLE OF OTHER BANKS

One reason why the bank may not make further loans at this time is that while Sally Doe may choose to store her wealth in the form of a demand deposit at the bank rather than as cash in her mattress, John Smith's loan and corresponding demand deposit were created so he could purchase a piece of equipment.

Let's assume that Smith buys the equipment from Bill Bailey's restaurant supply company, paying for it with a $900 check drawn on his account at the First National Bank of Luckenbach. Bailey will probably take the check written by Smith to his own bank, Citizens' National Bank. That bank will credit Bailey's demand deposit account and present the check to the First National Bank of Luckenbach for collection. If the banks are in the same small town, one bank may present checks directly to the other for payment. Otherwise, the checks will be presented for payment through a local clearinghouse or the Federal Reserve System□. In any case, the

TABLE 10–6
Effect of John Smith's Payment to Bill Bailey

First National Bank of Luckenbach

Assets	Liabilities and Capital Accounts
Reserves at Federal Reserve −$900	Demand deposits −$900

Citizen's National Bank

Assets	Liabilities and Capital Accounts
Reserves at Federal Reserve +$900	Demand deposits +$900

resulting effect on the balance sheets of the two banks will likely be as shown in Table 10–6.

After Smith's check clears, the First National Bank of Luckenbach is left with a $100 net increase in reserves, a $900 increase in loans, and a $1,000 increase in demand deposits as a result of the transactions involving both Doe and Smith. These changes are summarized in Table 10–7.

At this point the First National Bank of Luckenbach is fully "loaned up"; its reserves of $100 are just sufficient to meet the 10 percent reserve requirement for the $1,000 deposit. Since demand deposits created as a result of bank loans are frequently withdrawn soon after the loan is made, one rule-of-thumb is that *banks should lend only an amount equal to their excess reserves.*

The First National Bank of Luckenbach kept to the rule when it made the $900 loan to John Smith. Then, when Smith spent the proceeds

TABLE 10–7
Summary of the Net Effects of the Transactions of Sally Doe and John Smith

First National Bank of Luckenbach

Assets	Liabilities and Capital Accounts
Reserves at Federal Reserve +$100 Loans +$900	Demand deposits +$1,000

of the loan, the bank's reserves exactly matched the amount required for Doe's deposit.

We can now observe how Citizens' National Bank is able to continue the money creation process. Suppose that Tom Dooley wishes to spend $810 on a new video recorder from Susan Anthony's TV Store. Dooley goes to Citizens' National Bank and obtains a loan of $810. The effect of this loan on the balance sheet of Citizens' National Bank is shown in Table 10−8.

New money in the amount of $810 has been created. At the same time Citizens' National Bank has also followed the policy of lending only its excess reserves. (The bank was required to hold $90 of reserves as a result of John Smith's deposit, since $0.1 \times \$900 = \$90$. The change in the bank's excess reserves, therefore, is equal to $\$900 - \$90 = \$810$.)

Summarizing the net results of all of these transactions, beginning with Sally Doe's deposit at the First National Bank of Luckenbach, we find that the money supply has increased by $\$900 + \$810 = \$1,710$. (Doe's original deposit of $1,000 does not represent an increase in the money supply. Money in the form of cash held by the nonbank public was reduced by an amount equal to the increase in money in the form of demand deposits.) The net changes in the balance sheets of the two banks are shown in Table 10−9.

After Tom Dooley gives Susan Anthony's TV Store an $810 check for the video recorder, the store will probably take the check to its bank, People's National Bank of Luckenbach, so the proceeds can be deposited in its account. The net effects of Dooley's payment on the balance sheets of Citizens' National Bank and People's National Bank of Luckenbach are shown in Table 10−10. At this point People's National Bank has excess reserves equal to $\$810 - 0.1\,(\$810) = \$729$ and could loan someone that amount. The money supply would correspondingly be increased by $729.

THE MAXIMUM MONEY SUPPLY EFFECT

How long can this process continue? So far, the money supply has increased by $\$900 + \$810 + \$729 = \$2,439$ as a result of the excess reserves created by Sally Doe's deposit.

TABLE 10−8
Effect of Tom Dooley's Loan

Citizen's National Bank

Assets		Liabilities and Capital Accounts	
Loans	+$810	Demand Deposits	+$810

TABLE 10−9
Summary of the Effects of the Transactions Involving Sally Doe, John Smith, Bill Bailey, and Tom Dooley

First National Bank of Luckenbach

Assets		Liabilities and Capital Accounts	
Reserves at Federal Reserve	+$100	Demand Deposits	+$1,000
Loans	+$900		

Citizens' National Bank

Assets		Liabilities and Capital Accounts	
Reserves at Federal Reserve	+$900	Demand Deposits	+$1,710
Loans	+$810		

TABLE 10−10
Effects of Tom Dooley's Payment

Citizens' National Bank

Assets		Liabilities and Capital Accounts	
Reserves at Federal Reserve	−$810	Demand deposits	−$810

People's National Bank of Luckenbach

Assets		Liabilities and Capital Accounts	
Reserves at Federal Reserve	+$810	Demand deposits	+$810

TABLE 10–11
Creation of Money from Sally Doe's Deposit

Bank	(1) New Reserves	(2) Required Reserves	(3) Excess Reserves (1) − (2)	(4) New Loans	(5) New Money Created
Luckenbach	$1,000	$100	$900	$900	$ 900
Citizens'	900	90	810	810	810
People's	810	81	729	729	729
Other banks					6,561
Total					$9,000

Theoretically, in our simple case, the money supply could increase by:

Change in excess reserves

$$\times \frac{1}{\text{Reserve requirement}} = \$900 \times \frac{1}{0.1}$$

$$= \$900 \times \frac{1}{1/10}$$

$$= \$900 \times \frac{10}{1}$$

$$= \$9,000.$$

This figure is the maximum amount by which the money supply could increase (and the maximum amount of derivative deposits that could be created) as a result of Sally Doe's original deposit. We can easily demonstrate that $9,000 is the correct number because $900 was the amount of excess reserves from Sally Doe's deposit and $9,000 × the reserve requirement = $9,000 × 0.1 = $900. We can therefore state a general rule for determining the maximum amount by which the money supply can increase, as follows:

Change in money supply =

$$\text{Change in excess reserves} \times \frac{1}{r_D},$$

where r_D is the reserve requirement on demand deposits.

> The term 1/reserve requirement is called the **deposit expansion multiplier** because it indicates the maximum amount by which demand deposits and, therefore, the money supply can increase as a result of a given increase in excess reserves.

The deposit expansion multiplier indicates that a specific increase in excess reserves may result in a much larger increase in the money supply. We know that the general rule given above is correct because:

Change in money supply × r_D = Change in excess reserves.

Dividing by r_D, we obtain the rule stated above.[9]

Of course, as we saw in the example, many banks will likely take part in the money creation process, even though the primary deposit bringing the excess reserves into the banking system was at only one bank. This dispersal of the money creation function occurs because firms and individuals usually spend the demand deposits created by loans, which often results in a withdrawal of funds from one bank and a deposit in some other bank. If the funds are redeposited in the original bank, that bank can carry on the money generating process. Table 10–11 summarizes the effect on the money supply of Sally Doe's original deposit, assuming that the money supply is expanded by the maximum possible amount.

MONEY CREATION IN THE REAL WORLD

As we might expect, the money creation process in the real world is not quite so simple as the one in our model. Some of the new money

---

9. Note the similarity between this equation and Equation 10–1 above.

created by loans is not redeposited as demand deposits. Some amounts of it are held as cash by the nonbank public. Other amounts are redeposited in time or savings accounts. Finally, because banks are uncertain about how much of their deposits will be withdrawn during any particular time period, they often maintain some excess reserves, called *precautionary reserves*. All these factors tend to result in a smaller increase in the money supply. Nevertheless, while the money supply creation formula in the real world is a little more complicated than that of our model, the basic process whereby banks increase the money supply is the same.[10]

The money supply may also be increased if the government prints money and gives it to the general nonbank public in exchange for goods and services. If this money is then deposited in banks, a much larger increase in the money supply may eventually be created.

Finally, and perhaps most importantly, the potential for banks to create new money in the form of demand deposits based on excess reserves can be increased or decreased by various means that the Federal Reserve System employs to affect private banks' reserves. The Fed's management of the money supply under the U.S. fractional reserve banking system will be thoroughly examined in Chapter 11.

SUMMARY

1. This chapter discussed the nature and functions of money. Money is anything that is generally accepted as payment for goods and services. In the United States economists used to consider the money supply to consist of cash and demand deposits held by the nonbank public. The supply of money as defined in these terms is labeled M_{1A}. A broader definition of money, M_{1B}, includes all of the items in M_{1A} plus NOW accounts, credit union

---

10. We can derive a mathematical formula that will reflect more closely what happens in the real world. First:

$$\Delta E = r_D(\Delta D) + r_T(\Delta T) + \Delta C + \Delta P, \quad (1)$$

where:

ΔE = the original change in excess reserves,
ΔD = the change in demand deposits,
ΔT = the change in time deposits,
ΔC = the change in cash held by the nonbank public,
ΔP = the change in precautionary reserves held by banks,
r_D = the reserve requirement for demand deposits, and
r_T = the reserve requirement for time deposits.

The equation merely says that when a new equilibrium is eventually reached, the original change in excess reserves must be equal to the sum of the possible uses of those reserves. To obtain a formula telling us what the eventual change in the money supply will be, we have to make some assumptions about the fraction of the newly created demand deposits that end up as time deposits, cash held by the nonbank public, and precautionary balances. Let us assume that

$$\Delta T = t(\Delta D),$$
$$\Delta C = c(\Delta D), \text{ and}$$
$$\Delta P = p(\Delta D),$$

where t is the fraction of newly created demand deposits that ends up as time deposits, c is the fraction of newly created demand deposits that ends up as cash held by the

nonbank public, and p is the fraction of newly created demand deposits that ends up as precautionary balances.

If we substitute these values for ΔT, ΔC, and ΔP in Equation 1 above, we obtain

$$\Delta E = r_D(\Delta D) + r_T(t\Delta D) + c\Delta D + p\Delta D. \quad (2)$$

Factoring out ΔD, we find that

$$\Delta E = \Delta D(r_D + r_T \times t + c + p). \quad (3)$$

Thus the resulting change in demand deposits is

$$\Delta D = \Delta E \left(\frac{1}{r_D + r_T \times t + c + p} \right)$$

For example, if ΔE = \$900, r_D = 0.1, r_T = 0.05, t = 0.1, c = 0.1, and p = 0.045, then

$$\Delta D = \$900 \left(\frac{1}{0.1 + 0.005 + 0.1 + 0.045} \right)$$

$$= \$900 \left(\frac{1}{0.25} \right)$$

$$= 900 \left(\frac{1}{1/4} \right)$$

$$= \$900 \left(\frac{4}{1} \right)$$

$$= \$3,600, \text{ and}$$

$$\Delta C = 0.1(D)$$

$$= \$360.$$

Therefore, the increase in the money supply, ΔM_s, is $\Delta D + \Delta C = \$3,960.$

share draft accounts, and demand deposits at mutual savings banks. The four commonly accepted functions of money are (1) a medium of exchange, (2) a standard of value, (3) a standard of deferred payment, and (4) a store of wealth.

2. Until January 1, 1981, banks were unique among private financial institutions in the United States in that they alone had the legal authority to create money, in the form of demand deposits (checking accounts). However, credit unions can now issue share draft accounts, and other financial institutions can now offer similar account services.

3. There are two general types of banks—national banks and state banks. All national banks must be members of the Federal Reserve System. State banks may be members. All member banks must have their deposits insured by the Federal Deposit Insurance Corporation.

4. Most of banks' liabilities consist of demand and time deposits. The majority of bank assets consist of loans and securities.

5. Banks increase the money supply by making loans and creating corresponding demand deposits. Banks are limited, however, by reserve requirements on their deposits. In the simple model the maximum increase in the money supply is given by the change in excess reserves resulting from a primary deposit at a bank × 1/reserve requirement.

6. In the real world not all newly created money is held in the form of demand deposits. Some is held as cash by the nonbank public, some is redeposited in savings accounts, and some is held by banks that wish to keep more than the required amount of reserves as a precautionary measure. Nevertheless, even in the real world, the process whereby banks create money is basically the same as depicted by the simple model.

IMPORTANT TERMS AND CONCEPTS

Money	Primary deposit
M_1, M_{1A}, M_{1B}, and	Derivative deposit
M_2	Reserve requirements
Functions of money	Required reserves
Barter system	Excess reserves
Financial	Deposit expansion
intermediaries	multiplier
Fractional reserve system	

QUESTIONS AND PROBLEMS

1. What characteristics must something have to be considered money?

2. What is the traditional definition of *money* used by most U.S. economists? What is the difference between M_{1A} and M_{1B}?

3. What is the formula for the simple model that indicates the maximum amount that banks can expand the money supply given an increase in excess reserves in the banking system resulting from a primary deposit?

4. What are the four functions of money? Explain them.

5. According to the simple model, if excess reserves increase by $10,000 and the reserve requirement is 0.25, what is the maximum amount by which banks can increase the money supply?

6. Given a reserve requirement of 0.20, what will be the maximum effect on the money supply if excess reserves decrease by $5,000?

7. Bank liabilities consist primarily of what items? The majority of bank assets are made up of what two things?

8. What is a primary deposit? What is a derivative deposit?

9. Why does a bank frequently make loans equal in amount only to its excess reserves?

10. Suppose that a primary deposit of $30,000 is brought into the banking system. If the reserve requirement is 0.10, what is the maximum amount by which the banking system as a whole can increase the money supply by creating derivative deposits through loans? What rule will govern the dollar amount of loans that an individual bank can make?

HAS THE FED
LOST HOLD OF THE
MONEY LEVERS?

In speech after speech since last October, Federal Reserve Board Chairman Paul A. Volcker has repeatedly promised to bring down the rate of growth in the money supply and thus, in time, to bring inflation under control. That this approach has not yet worked is evident from the latest numbers on the rate of inflation and from the chaos in the bond and other financial markets. But two questions are being raised now among some economic analysts: Can the Fed even define the money supply? And if so, does it know the right levers to bring it under control?

A $5 billion bulge in at least two methods of calculating the money supply in the last week of January and the first week of February is the primary reason the question comes up. There is so far no authoritative explanation of the bulge, which was concentrated in commercial bank demand deposits. According to one theory, it could have been a technical blip caused by higher-than-expected tax refunds that would have shifted funds from U.S. Treasury accounts, which are not counted in the money supply, to private accounts. Faulty seasonal adjustments may also have been a factor, some optimists believe.

SPECULATIVE BEHAVIOR?

A more pessimistic appraisal is that the money bulge was caused by surging loan demand, perhaps connected with speculative inventory behavior. If so, the surge was at least initially accommodated by the Fed, which in the week ended Feb. 22 pumped up bank reserves by nearly $2 billion to support deposit growth of two weeks earlier. (Under the lagged reserve requirements in effect since 1968, banks have two weeks to come up with reserves to back deposits. The Fed has indicated that it is considering changing this system, which economists insist makes monetary control more difficult.)

The two-week money bulge brought the growth rate of the monetary aggregates a bit above the range that the Fed has announced as its 1980 target. But most economists still believe that

Source: Lewis Beman, "Has the Fed Lost Hold of the Money Levers?" *Business Week*, March 10, 1980, p. 38.

the Fed has subsequently tightened up enough to come in under the wire. Recently, they note, the Fed's open market desk has been selling securities—which pulls reserves out of the banking system—when the interest rate on federal funds, which the banks lend each other overnight, has been as low as 14%. They speculate that the upper end of the intervention range—the point at which the rate signals the need for more reserves—has been boosted to nearly 17%, which would indicate a considerable tightening of money supply control since January.

UNLUCKY TIMING

One of the problems is that in the midst of a developing crisis, the Fed on Feb. 7 changed its definition of what constitutes the money supply. The change itself was necessary and long anticipated. The growth of negotiated order of withdrawal (NOW) accounts at savings banks and of automatic transfer services (ATS) at commercial banks blurred the distinction between savings and checking accounts and rendered obsolete the old concepts of M_1 and M_2.

But the Fed was unlucky in the timing, which came as the underlying data began to behave erratically, and which introduced a rather extraneous element into a situation that would have been confusing on its own account.

Now economists have a whole new family of Ms to worry about. There is the new M_{1A}, which includes domestically owned demand deposits in commercial banks, and M_{1B}, which adds in NOW and ATS accounts. There is an amended M_2, which includes not only savings accounts and bank-issued repurchase agreements (RPs) but also money market funds; a changed M_3, which sweeps up all other RPs and large time deposits; and a totally new measure named L, which adds in U.S.-owned Eurodollars, commercial paper, bankers' acceptances, and some Treasury obligations. No one knows how the various money measures really relate to the Fed's control procedure.

ECONOMY'S STRENGTH

Economists do know, however, that the Fed cannot afford much slippage because of the growing signs that the economy is much stronger than expected. "The Fed has to be on the safe side since there are widespread doubts about the economic slowdown and a clear conflict between the announced monetary goals and the trend of fiscal policy," says Jerry Jordan, chief economist of Pittsburgh National Bank. Like most economists, he expects interest rates to get even higher before an eventually weakening economy brings some relief.

There are, however, nagging doubts that even a tightening monetary policy will actually do the job of slowing the economy. "The Fed has tightened up another notch, but I doubt if the conventional management of the money supply is enough," says Henry Kaufman, chief economist for Salomon Bros.

QUESTIONS

1. How is M_{1B} different from M_{1A}?
2. How many measures of the money supply are now used by the Federal Reserve?
3. Why does the Fed consider the old definition of the money supply (M_1) to be obsolete?
4. How have the new definitions of the money supply added to the confusion regarding the Fed's monetary policy?

CHAPTER 11

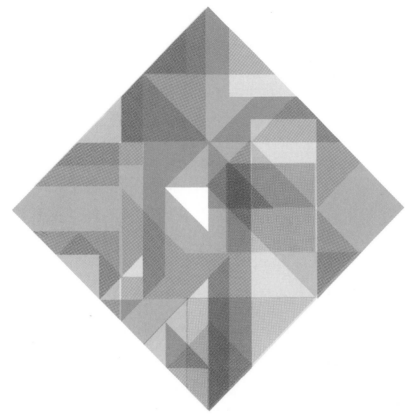

MONETARY POLICY
AND THE
FEDERAL RESERVE

THE
POWER OF THE
FED

A lot of business people, bankers, and stockbrokers malign the Federal Reserve System, known popularly as the "Fed." They think it is meddlesome and that it often pursues unpredictable monetary policy choices that cause instability in the economy. Even members of Congress frequently attack the Fed's actions, and academic and business economists often criticize its policy moves.

Why is the Fed such a source of controversy? First, because it is one of the most independent of government agencies, Congress, the other branches of government, and lobbyists seem unable to affect its policies in a significant way. Second, since the Fed has major responsibility for controlling the U.S. money supply and, ultimately, interest rates for loans made by private financial institutions (banks, savings and loan associations, and credit unions), its power over the fate of the U.S. economy is substantial.

A lot of people were upset with the Fed in late 1980, for example, when, in an effort to curb inflation by limiting spending, it slowed the growth of the money supply and allowed interest rates to rise to well over 20 percent on an annual basis. As Newsweek put it:

After a year of stop-and-go money management, ballooning inflationary expectations have forced the Fed into the thankless task of tightening the credit noose and propelling interest rates to breathtaking levels. . . . distortions were showing up in every nook and cranny of the U.S. economy. The nation was almost certainly faced with a return to recession, and corporate balance sheets were so weakened that a wave of bankruptcies among small and medium-size companies seemed inevitable.[1]

Despite this gloomy picture, Donald T. Regan, President Reagan's choice for Treasury secretary, said that tight money "is the price we have to pay for the inflation this country finds itself in. It's the only game in town."[2]

We might ask, "But what if it was the Fed's earlier policies that caused the inflation for which we subsequently had to 'pay the price'?" Economist Milton Friedman and other experts have argued that this is indeed the case.[3] What does this matter to the average person? Plenty! At 1975 interest rates of about 8 percent per year, the principal and interest payments on a $65,000 house came to about $429 a month. In late 1980, depending on state laws regulating mortgage loans, principal and interest payments for a $65,000 house ran from $600 to $750 per month.[4]

In this chapter the Fed and the tools it uses to exercise its power over the money supply and interest rates are described. The issues surrounding appropriate management of monetary policy are dealt with more directly in Chapters 12 and 13.

1. "The Fed Takes on the Economy," *Newsweek.* December 22, 1980, p. 65.
2. Ibid.
3. Milton Friedman, "The Fed and Inflation," *Newsweek,* December 29, 1980, p. 57.
4. "Home Buyers to Face Higher Costs and Risk as Banks Offer New Types of Mortgage Plans," *Wall Street Journal,* August 18, 1980, p. 26.

C H A P T E R 11

MONETARY POLICY
AND THE
FEDERAL RESERVE

WHAT THIS CHAPTER IS ABOUT

Commercial banks and other financial institutions do not operate in a vacuum. They must attempt to meet the legitimate credit and deposit needs of their customers, cope with their competition, and satisfy their stockholders. In addition, they must comply with the requirements of one or more regulatory agencies. The requirements depend on whether the institution is a member of the Federal Reserve System or the Federal Deposit Insurance Corporation, the type of organization it is, and the source of its charter.

The discussion in this chapter will focus mainly on the role of the Federal Reserve System and the commercial banking system in determining the supply of money. Since the Monetary Control Act of 1980 (discussed later in this chapter) legalized Negotiable Order of Withdrawal (NOW) and other similar accounts at other thrift institutions (as well as banks), these institutions can also affect the money supply. (In Chapter 10 NOW accounts and share draft accounts at credit unions were shown to be included in the new, more broadly defined, money supply, M_{1B}.) However, the largest portion of the money supply is still held in the form of currency and demand deposits at commercial banks. Nevertheless, we shall point out many instances where the Monetary Control Act affects the operations of other financial institutions as well as those of commercial banks and, consequently, the money supply as well.

As indicated in Chapter 10, commercial banks may receive either a national charter from the Comptroller of the Currency or a state charter from the appropriate state agency. All national banks are required to become members of the Federal Reserve System, and all members of the Federal Reserve System are required to become members of the Federal Deposit Insurance Corporation (FDIC). Thus all national banks are regulated by three agencies: the Comptroller of the Currency, the Federal Reserve, and the FDIC.

State banks are regulated by the state that gives them their charter. State banks that are members of the Federal Reserve System are also regulated by the Fed and the FDIC. Under the Monetary Control Act of 1980, nonmember state banks must also comply with some Fed regulations. In addition, even if they are not members of the Federal Reserve System but only have their deposits insured by the FDIC, they must fulfill the requirements of the latter agency.

As noted in Chapter 10, on June 30, 1978, only 39.1 percent of the commercial banks chartered in the United States were members of the Federal Reserve System. However, these banks owned 59.3 percent of the total assets of all commercial banks, so their relative importance is greater than that indicated only by their number. Over 97.8 percent of all commercial banks had their deposits insured by the FDIC.

Most countries rely on a government controlled central bank to help oversee their commercial banks, institute national monetary policy, and control the supply of money and certain monetary markets. In Europe the Bank of England, the Banque de France, and the Deutsche Bundesbank (West Germany) are some of the principal central banks. The U.S. counterpart of these banks is the Federal Reserve System, a network of "bankers' banks" controlled by a central authority.

In this chapter the structure of the Federal Reserve System and the tools whereby the Fed regulates the supply of money are examined. First, however, the reasons underlying the establishment of the Federal Reserve System are discussed.

HISTORY OF THE U.S. BANKING SYSTEM

◆

The history of attempts by the United States to establish a stable monetary and banking system is filled with trial, error, and conflict. The highlights of this struggle are summarized here, beginning with the First Bank of the United States.

FIRST BANK OF THE UNITED STATES

Before the Federal Reserve Act of 1913 was passed, the only attempts by the United States to create some sort of central bank were connected with the First Bank of the United States and the Second Bank of the United States. The **First Bank of the United States** was given a twenty-year charter by the federal government in 1791. The bank's capital stock was $10 million, $2 million of which was owned by the federal government. The remainder was subscribed to (owned) by private sources. The bank's main office was in Philadelphia, but branches were established in other major U.S. cities.

At the time the First Bank of the United States was established, private banks commonly printed and issued their own currency, known as *bank notes*. Although these notes were accepted as money, the degree of public confidence in them and in some of the banks was variable. The First Bank performed all the usual functions of an ordinary commercial bank during its brief history: making loans, buying securities, issuing deposits and bank notes, and transferring funds from one part of the country to another. In addition, it served as a depository for federal government funds, loaned money to the government, and transferred government funds. Finally, it performed some of the functions of a central bank; it regulated lending and the issuing of bank notes by state banks.

The charter of the First Bank was not renewed in 1811 for several reasons. These reasons included (1) concern over the power of the federal government and the effect of the First Bank on state banks, (2) concern about paper money in general, and (3) concern that a significant portion of the First Bank's stock was owned by foreigners. Early citizens were suspicious of the federal government and of banks and debt in general.

SECOND BANK OF THE UNITED STATES

In 1816, the **Second Bank of the United States** received a twenty-year charter from the federal government. Its capital stock was also owned by the federal government, by private individuals and groups, and by states. In a fashion similar to that of the First Bank, the Second Bank performed both central and commercial banking functions. In 1836 the charter of the Second Bank was not renewed—for many of the same reasons that the First Bank was disbanded. In addition, Andrew Jackson, who was president at the time, did not believe in paper money and thought that the Second Bank had become too powerful. Jackson's campaign against the bank and its president, Nicholas Biddle, contributed greatly to the bank's demise.

The National Banking Act of 1864 established a system through which private banks could receive a charter from the federal government. However, no further attempts at establishing a central bank were made until the Federal Reserve System was authorized in 1913.

THE FEDERAL RESERVE ACT

The banking system, which consisted of many small commercial banks before the Federal Reserve System was established, was criticized for not having a centralized banking authority that could provide "elasticity" to the money supply.

Elasticity of the money supply refers to flexibility in the money supply. During periods when bank customers became anxious and desired to hold more cash, there was no way to ensure an orderly increase of the quantity of hard currency or paper money in the economy.

Because of this lack of elasticity, at times banks could not pay cash on demand to all depositors who requested it. Serious bank panics occurred in 1873, 1884, 1893, and 1907. Under such circumstances many banks stopped payments and frantically called in loans, and some went out of business. Moreover, during boom times there was no way to reduce the money supply to limit inflation and overexpansion. Reserve requirements were inflexible; they remained the same during boom or bust.

By the early 1900s it had become abundantly clear to both bankers and public officials that the U.S. banking system badly needed reorganization. After the panic of 1907 a commission was authorized to study the banking system and recommend a solution to the problem. As a result, on December 23, 1913, the Glass-Owen bill (the Federal Reserve Act) was passed.

The **Federal Reserve Act of 1913** established the Federal Reserve System.

STRUCTURE OF THE FEDERAL RESERVE SYSTEM

◆

The main structure of the Federal Reserve System consists of twelve Federal Reserve banks, the Board of Governors, the Federal Open Market Committee, and the member banks.

THE FEDERAL RESERVE BANKS

The continental United States, Alaska, and Hawaii are divided into twelve Federal Reserve Districts, as shown in Figure 11–1. There is one Federal Reserve bank in each district, and the twenty-five branches of the twelve banks are spread unevenly among the districts. The twelve Federal Reserve banks are listed below:

- Federal Reserve Bank of New York
- Federal Reserve Bank of Philadelphia
- Federal Reserve Bank of Boston
- Federal Reserve Bank of Richmond
- Federal Reserve Bank of Minneapolis
- Federal Reserve Bank of Cleveland
- Federal Reserve Bank of Atlanta
- Federal Reserve Bank of Chicago
- Federal Reserve Bank of St. Louis
- Federal Reserve Bank of Kansas City
- Federal Reserve Bank of Dallas
- Federal Reserve Bank of San Francisco

The Federal Reserve banks are owned by the member banks. By law, each member bank can be required to subscribe to Federal Reserve stock in an amount equal to 6 percent of its own paid-in capital and surplus. So far, such a large subscription has not been necessary, and each bank has been required to pay to its Federal Reserve bank an amount equal to only 3 percent of its paid-in capital and surplus. Annual dividends to stockholders cannot exceed 6 percent of the paid-in capital. Recently, any Fed earnings in excess of dividends to stockholders have been paid to the Treasury.

Each Federal Reserve bank has a nine-member board of directors, of whom three are called Class A directors, three Class B directors, and three Class C directors. The Class A directors represent the member banks and are chosen by them. The Class B directors represent industry, commerce, and agriculture within the district but are still chosen by the member banks. The Class C directors are chosen by the Board of Governors of the Federal Reserve System (to be discussed next). The Class C directors are supposed to represent the general public, and they cannot be connected with the operation of any bank.

BOARD OF GOVERNORS

The **Board of Governors of the Federal Reserve System** consists of seven members, each appointed by the president of the United States with the advice and consent of the Senate. The members serve staggered fourteen-year terms, with one term ending every two years. The president designates one member as chairman and one as vice-chairman. No more than one member of the Board of Governors can be selected from any Federal Reserve district, and the president must make sure that industry, commerce, agriculture, and financial institutions are all duly represented.

The Board of Governors has the power to supervise the Federal Reserve banks, approve the appointment of their presidents and first vice-presidents, remove any of their officers or directors, examine their accounts, require

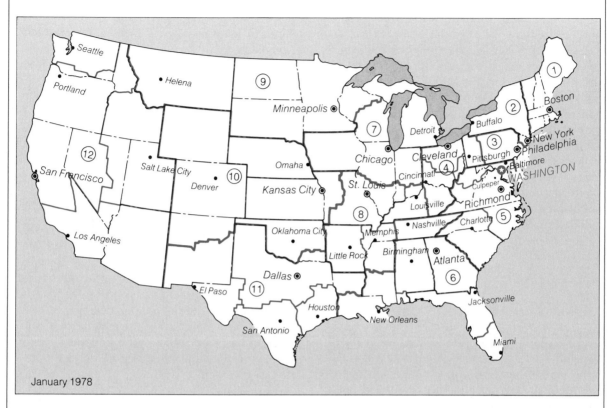

January 1978

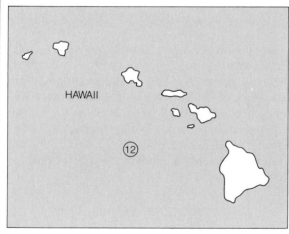

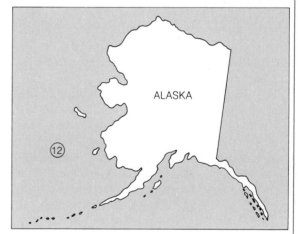

LEGEND

▬▬▬	Boundaries of Federal Reserve Districts	◉	Federal Reserve Bank Cities
——	Boundaries of Federal Reserve Branch Territories	•	Federal Reserve Branch Cities
✪	Board of Governors of the Federal Reserve System	·	Federal Reserve Bank Facility

FIGURE 11–1   The Federal Reserve System: Boundaries of Federal Reserve Districts and Their Branch Territories

Source: *Federal Reserve Bulletin.*

reports by them, and oversee their issuance and retirement of Federal Reserve notes. Within legal limits set by Congress the Board of Governors can determine the types of loans the Federal Reserve banks and commercial banks can make. Also within limits the board can set the reserve requirements for commercial banks and other depository institutions, including mutual savings banks, savings and loan associations, and credit unions. Furthermore, it has the power to regulate loans on securities and to approve or disapprove discount rates established by the Federal Reserve banks. Finally, the board makes up a majority of the Federal Open Market Committee, described next.

FEDERAL OPEN MARKET COMMITTEE

The Federal Open Market Committee (FOMC) determines the amounts of government securities and other obligations that Federal Reserve banks buy or sell. As we will see later, this is the tool most frequently used by the Federal Reserve System to control the money supply. The committee also controls Federal Reserve purchases of foreign currencies in the international money markets (to be discussed in Chapter 30).

The Federal Open Market Committee has twelve members, seven of whom make up the Board of Governors of the Federal Reserve System. The other five must be either a president or a vice-president of one of the Federal Reserve banks. Furthermore, one of these five members must be from the Federal Reserve Bank of New York, because New York City is at the center of open market activity in the United States.

The remaining four positions on the FOMC are distributed as follows.

■ One representative is from the Federal Reserve banks of Boston, Philadelphia, and Richmond;

■ One representative is from the Reserve banks of Atlanta, Dallas, and St. Louis;

■ one representative is from the Reserve banks of Minneapolis, Kansas City, and San Francisco; and

■ One representative is from the Reserve banks of Cleveland and Chicago.

Within these constraints, the members are elected by the boards of directors of the Reserve banks, each board having one vote.

The FOMC meets at least once every three weeks to determine the goals of its open market policy and to prescribe in a general way the actions to be taken. Purchases and sales are carried out by the manager of the open market account, who is a vice-president of the Federal Reserve Bank of New York. The FOMC members are usually in daily contact by telephone so they can determine precisely which open market transactions are to be made on a particular day. Although the Federal Reserve Bank of New York makes the actual open market purchases and sales, each Federal Reserve bank is responsible for a transaction in proportion to its assets.

FEDERAL ADVISORY COUNCIL

The Federal Advisory Council consists of one representative from each of the twelve Federal Reserve districts. These representatives, who are selected by the board of directors of the Federal Reserve bank in each district, are usually prominent bankers in their district. However, the Federal Advisory Council has no power to ensure that its advice is followed.

MEMBER BANKS

To become a member of the Federal Reserve System a commercial bank must first satisfy the Board of Governors that it has sufficient capital. The minimum capital required is established by the board after it considers the nature and quantity of the bank's assets and liabilities and the population of the city in which the bank is located.

Moreover, to become a member a bank must agree to abide by all of the rules and regulations of the Federal Reserve System. In addition to maintaining the required reserves, each member bank must agree to pay all checks drawn on it and submitted for payment through the Reserve System at par value. Other regulations prevent interlocking (common) bank officers, directors, and employees among member banks and limit the types of assets the banks can acquire.

Before 1981, in return for membership, a commercial bank could use Federal Reserve clearing and wire transfer facilities, obtain short-term loans from its Federal Reserve bank, obtain currency as needed, and take advantage of the information services provided by the system. Many of the services (not loans) were provided free of charge. However, nonmember banks could also obtain many of these services through correspondent banking relationships without meeting the other requirements of membership. Consequently, by the spring of 1980 a substantial number of banks had chosen to leave the Federal Reserve System, thereby reducing government control over the money supply.

This problem should be alleviated, at least to some extent, by the **Depository Institutions Deregulation and Monetary Control Act of 1980,** signed into law on March 31, 1980. This law provides for a uniform **reserve requirement** for all banks and other depository institutions, including mutual savings banks, savings and loan associations, and credit unions. It further requires that the Federal Reserve charge all depository institutions alike for its services. To offset these charges, the Fed has proposed paying an "earnings credit" on clearing balances (accounts the financial institutions must keep so that checks can be paid). The credit is similar to an interest payment, except that it can be used only as a credit against the service charges levied by the Federal Reserve. Starting January 1, 1981, these charges are gradually being phased in. The controversy that has surrounded the rights and responsibilities of member versus nonmember

banks is examined further in the For Discussion article at the end of this chapter.

The major monetary policy tools of the Federal Reserve System are described in the next section.

MONETARY POLICY TOOLS

The Federal Reserve has at its disposal three primary, or major, monetary policy tools: member bank reserve requirements, open market operations, and the discount rate. Other policy instruments, sometimes called "minor" or "qualitative" tools, include the margin requirement on securities, other selective credit controls, and moral suasion. The Federal Reserve can also influence the total amount of bank loans by using the major monetary policy tools to affect the Federal funds rate.

RESERVE REQUIREMENTS

As noted earlier, the Board of Governors of the Federal Reserve System is responsible for determining the reserve requirements of depository institutions within broad limits set by Congress. Before 1980 the Board of Governors was empowered to set the reserve requirements only for member banks. However, the Depository Institutions Deregulation and Monetary Control Act of 1980 made all depository institutions subject to the same reserve requirements. The requirements under the old system, which were in effect in 1980, are shown in Table 11–1. A comparison between the old reserve requirements for member banks and the new requirements for all depository institutions is shown in Table 11–2. The statutory limits for the new reserve requirements are generally lower under the new law.

The ability to change the reserve requirements is a powerful monetary policy tool. For

TABLE 11–1   Member Bank Reserve Requirements, November 30, 1980

Type of Deposit and Deposit Interval (in Millions of Dollars)	Reserve Requirement (Percent)	Effective Date
Net demand		
0–2	7	12/30/76
2–10	9 1/2	12/30/76
10–100	11 3/4	12/30/76
100–400	12 3/4	12/30/76
Over 400	16 1/4	12/30/76
Savings and time		
Savings	3	3/16/67
Time:		
0–5, by Maturity:		
30–179 days	3	3/16/67
180 days to 4 years	2 1/2	1/08/76
Over 4 years	1	10/30/75
Over 5, by Maturity		
30–179 days	6	12/12/74
180 days to 4 years	2 1/2	1/08/76
Over 4 years or more	1	10/30/75

Source: "Table 1.15: Depository Institutions Reserve Requirements," *Federal Reserve Bulletin* 66 (December 1980): A8.

example, using the simple deposit expansion model developed in Chapter 10, we can show that if bank reserves are $40 billion, increasing the reserve requirement from 10 percent to 12 percent can result in a $67 billion, or 16.75 percent, decrease in the money supply. Where r_D is 10 percent,

$$\text{Possible deposits} = \text{Reserves} \times \frac{1}{r_D}$$

$$= \$40 \text{ billion} \times \frac{1}{0.10}$$

$$= \$400 \text{ billion}.$$

Where r_D is 12 percent,

$$\text{Possible deposits} = \text{Reserves} \times \frac{1}{r_D}$$

$$= \$40 \text{ billion} \times \frac{1}{0.12}$$

$$= \$333.33 \text{ billion}.$$

This result assumes, of course, that banks initially had no excess reserves. The opposite effect on the money supply would be made possible if the reserve requirement were decreased instead of increased.

Because changing the reserve requirement can have such a large effect, it is used only when the Board of Governors wishes to have a major impact on member bank reserves. A glance at the dates on which the old reserve requirements were put into effect (Table 11–1) shows that the board has not deemed it desirable to adjust the reserve requirements very often. This monetary policy instrument is also the least favored by depository institutions, because the necessary adjustments in their asset portfolios as a result of an increase in the reserve requirements can often be quite troublesome.

OPEN MARKET OPERATIONS

Open market operations *consist of buying and selling securities on the open market. The term open market refers to the market for highly liquid, predominantly short-term securities, especially securities of the U.S. government.*

Open market operations are the method used most frequently by the Federal Reserve to adjust the money supply. The Federal Reserve banks, commerical banks, other depository institutions, and the general public are participants in the open market. The actual buying and selling operations in this market are carried out primarily by a network of government securities dealers, who are concentrated in New York City. As indicated earlier, the Federal Open Market Committee is responsible for determining the kinds and amounts of open market transactions the Federal Reserve will carry out during any given day.

The direct effect of Federal Reserve purchases or sales on the money supply is likely to depend on whether the other party to the transaction is a depository institution or the general public. However, the total effect may be the same in either case. For example, suppose the Federal Reserve purchases $10,000 worth of government securities from the First

TABLE 11–2 Comparison of Old and New Reserve Requirement Structures

Old Requirements for Member Banks			Type of Deposit or Account		New Requirements for All Depository Institutions[1]	
Statutory Range	Actual (as of 8/31/80)				Initial (under Act)	Statutory Range[2]
(Percent)					(Percent)	
			Transaction Accounts[3]			
7 to 22[4]	7	$ 0–2 mil.				
	9.5	2–10				
	11.75	10–100	Net demand			
	12.75	100–400		$0–25 mil.[5]	3	3
	16.25	Over 400				
	3		Savings (NOWs, ATS, etc.)	Over $25 mil.[5]	12	8 to 14
			Nontransaction Accounts			
	3		Other savings	Personal	0	0
				Nonpersonal	3	0 to 9
3 to 10		With original maturity of[6]				
	3	30–179 days $0–5 mil.	Time deposits	Personal	0	0
	6	Over $5 mil.				
	2.5	180 days to 4 years		Nonpersonal[7]	3	0 to 9
	1	Over 4 years				

[1]Under the act, the new requirements are phased in according to various schedules for member and nonmember institutions.

[2]Under extraordinary circumstances, the board can impose a requirement outside statutory ranges on any type of depository institution liability.

[3]The board can impose a supplementary requirement of up to 4 percent on transaction accounts.

[4]Statutory range for reserve city banks was 10 to 22 percent; for other member banks it was 7 to 14 percent.

[5]The $25 million tranche is to be adjusted each year by 80 percent of the change in total transaction accounts at all depository institutions.

[6]A minimum 3 percent reserve was required, on average, against time and savings deposits.

[7]The board can vary requirements on nonpersonal time deposits by maturity.

Source: *Economic Perspectives, Federal Reserve Bank of Chicago* (September–October 1980): 8. The new requirements are to be phased in gradually, over the period ending September 3, 1987.

National Bank of Luckenbach, Texas. The Fed will probably pay for the securities by increasing the First National Bank of Luckenbach's deposits with its Federal Reserve bank by $10,000.

The immediate results of this transaction are shown in Table 11–3. There are no direct effects on the supply of money as a result of this transaction. However, because member bank deposits at a Federal Reserve bank can be counted as reserves, the excess reserves of the First National Bank of Luckenbach are increased by $10,000. If the reserve requirement is 10 percent, using our simple deposit expansion model we find that the maximum increase in the money supply that can indirectly result from the securities purchase is

$$\Delta D = \$10,000 \times \frac{1}{0.1}$$
$$= \$100,000.$$

Thus, through its effect on member bank reserves, a purchase of government securities by the Federal Reserve may indirectly result in a much larger increase in the money supply.

A similar total result will likely occur if the

TABLE 11-3

Effects of Federal Reserve Purchase of Securities from First National Bank of Luckenbach

Federal Reserve

Assets		Liabilities and Capital Accounts	
Government securities	+$10,000	Member bank deposits	+$10,000

First National Bank of Luckenbach

Assets		Liabilities and Capital Accounts
Deposits at Federal Reserve	+$10,000	
Government securities	−$10,000	

TABLE 11-4

Effects of Federal Reserve Purchase of Securities from Travis Lamar Doe

Federal Reserve

Assets		Liabilities and Capital Accounts	
Government securities	+$10,000	Member bank deposits	+$10,000

First National Bank of Luckenbach

Assets		Liabilities and Capital Accounts
Reserves at Federal reserve	+$10,000	Demand deposits +$10,000

Travis Lamar Doe

Assets		Liabilities and Capital Accounts
Government securities	−$10,000	
Checking account, First National Bank of Luckenbach	+$10,000	

Fed purchases $10,000 worth of securities from the general public. Suppose, for example, that the Fed buys $10,000 of government securities from an individual, Travis Lamar Doe. Probably, Doe will take the check given to him in payment to his bank, the First National Bank of Luckenbach, for deposit. The results of these transactions are shown in Table 11−4.

If Doe either accepts cash as payment or deposits the money in his checking account (demand deposit), the money supply will increase by $10,000, directly as a result of the purchase by the Federal Reserve. If Doe decides to hold the payment as cash, the $10,000 increase will also be the total effect on the money supply.

However, if Doe decides to deposit the payment in his checking account at the bank, the bank will then have an increase in excess reserves. In this case, if the reserve requirement is 0.1, the bank will be required to hold 0.1 × $10,000 = $1,000 as reserves against Doe's deposit. Therefore, the bank's excess reserves will increase by $10,000 − $1,000 = $9,000. The banking system can then further increase the money supply by an amount equal to

$$\Delta D = \Delta E \left(\frac{1}{r_D}\right)$$

$$= \$9,000 \times \frac{1}{0.1} = \$90,000.$$

Thus the money supply will increase by $10,000 as a direct result of the Federal Reserve purchase and may increase by an additional $90,000 as an indirect result. The total maximum increase in the money supply will be $100,000, the same amount as in the previous example.

Of course, Doe might deposit the payment in his savings account at a commercial bank. In this case the money supply will not increase as a direct result of the purchase by the Fed. However, the banking system can still expand the money supply. The result will depend on the reserve requirement for time deposits and on the amount by which cash holdings, demand deposits, and time deposits are increased as a result of the newly made bank loans.

It is also possible that the banking system will not wish to create any additional loans on the basis of the new reserves. In this case it is possible for the Federal Reserve purchase of securities to have no effect on the supply of money. Nevertheless, such a result is unlikely, except, possibly, during a deep depression.

Naturally, the opposite effects will probably occur if the Federal Reserve sells securities, resulting in a decrease in the money supply. If the depository institutions have no excess reserves, a Federal Reserve purchase of securities will very likely force these institutions to reduce their outstanding loans, thereby causing the money supply to drop.

Open market operations are carried out by the Federal Reserve on a daily basis. They are the most frequently used monetary policy tool, partly because of their flexibility. The system can determine each day whether securities will be bought or sold and in what amounts. The Fed can also affect long- and short-term interest rates differently, depending on the types of government securities it buys or sells.

Of the Fed's three major policy tools, open market transactions are clearly the most important and have the most significant day-to-day effects. Yet, ironically, the news media generally pay a good deal more attention to the discount rate and the reserve ratio when reporting changes in government monetary policy. Probably the oversight occurs because the significance of the Fed's open market activities is not widely understood.

THE DISCOUNT RATE

The **discount rate** is the interest rate that a Federal Reserve bank charges a depository institution when it gives the institution a loan.[1]

Although each Federal Reserve bank can set its own discount rate, the Board of Governors has the right to approve or disapprove of the rates.

However, the Federal Reserve expects financial institutions to request loans only under special circumstances, such as a large, unexpected withdrawal of deposits. In fact, if a Federal Reserve bank decides that an institution is attempting to rely too heavily on borrowing from it, the Fed may refuse outright to grant the institution a loan.

Because the Federal Reserve discourages depository institutions from borrowing large amounts or even frequent small amounts, the effect of a change in the discount rate is not as great as it would be if the central bank were willing to make loans on request. Nevertheless, raising or lowering the discount rate may have some direct effect on loan requests by financial institutions.

In addition, especially in the past, changes in the discount rate seemed to have "announcement effects." Many people believed that if a Federal Reserve bank raised the discount rate, it was an indication that the government was attempting to restrict credit. On the other hand, if the discount rate was lowered, such an event was usually taken to be a sign that the Federal Reserve wished to increase the money supply. However, the Federal Reserve banks have changed the discount rate far more frequently in the last few years in response to changes in market interest rates than they have in the past. For example, in 1979 they changed the discount rate three times, whereas in 1980 they changed it seven times. As a result, the announcement effect of such changes may be diminished. Nevertheless, the significance of the discount rate as a policy tool may still rest primarily on the indirect effects of a change in its level on people's expectations.

---

1. A Federal Reserve bank can loan money to a member bank in one of two ways. First, it can discount short-term, self-liquidating commercial loans made by a bank (hence the term *discount rate*). In this case the Federal Reserve assumes ownership of the note and credits the commercial bank reserve account by an amount equal to the discounted value of the note. The Federal Reserve can also make a loan (called an *advance*) to a member bank. The interest rate on the advance can be 0.5 percent or more above the discount rate, depending on the collateral for the loan.

OTHER POLICY TOOLS

Several other policy tools, including margin requirements on security purchases, other selective credit controls, and moral suasion, either are used or have been used by the Federal Reserve. As noted earlier, these tools are sometimes called minor or qualitative tools. They are called *minor* because they are not used as frequently as the major tools and because they are of less importance in affecting the money supply. They are sometimes called *qualitative* because they tend to affect the type of credit rather than the total amount of credit issued. Each of the minor policy tools is discussed here.

Margin Requirements on Securities In 1934, as a result of stock market speculation in the 1920s and the crash in 1929, Congress gave the Board of Governors the power to regulate the margin requirement on securities purchases.

*The **margin requirement** is the percent of the current market price of securities that must be used as a down payment.*

Therefore, the margin requirement regulates the maximum amount that can be borrowed to finance securities purchases. This rule applies on loans where a security listed on a national exchange is used as collateral for the loan and the loan is for the purpose of purchasing or holding securities.[2] During June 1981 the margin requirement was 50 percent.[3]

The margin requirement undoubtedly has some effect on the demand for securities. However, it is possible for investors to avoid the intent of it to some extent by borrowing money with other assets as collateral and then using these funds to purchase securities.

Moral Suasion At times the Federal Reserve has attempted to achieve its policy goals by publicly urging banks or the general public to do one thing or another. For example, Fed officials might chide bankers for expanding loans rapidly during an inflationary period or for being too conservative about lending during a recession. The effectiveness of this approach is questionable.

Selective Credit Controls During World War II selective consumer credit controls were instituted under Regulation W of the Federal Reserve, which went into effect September 1, 1941. It regulated consumer credit for items other than housing by specifying the minimum down payments and the maximum maturity of installment loans and the length of time charge accounts could run. Regulation W was suspended on May 7, 1952.

During the Korean War selective credit controls were placed on financing for new residential construction under Regulation X. That regulation was introduced in October 1950 and suspended two years later.

Although Regulations W and X were abandoned, there is growing sentiment for reinstating them. The Credit Control Act of 1969 already authorizes such actions to be taken at the request of the president.[4]

In March 1980 President Carter took a step in this direction by placing tighter restrictions on credit card issuers. Under the new rules, all credit card issuers except those with less than $2 million of credit outstanding had to deposit 15 percent of any new credit granted in a noninterest-bearing account with the Federal Reserve.[5] These rules were suspended in the summer of 1980 after interest rates rose dramatically and the economy appeared to be in a recession.

---

2. Government securities and certain others are exempted.

3. "Table 1.36: Stock Market—Selected Statistics," *Federal Reserve Bulletin* 67 (June, 1981): A26.

4. "The Likelihood of Selective Credit Controls," *Business Week*, March 19, 1979, pp. 64–65.

5. "Credit-Card Firms Are Likely to Initiate or Lift Yearly Fees, Set Steeper Payments," *Wall Street Journal*, March 17, 1980, p. 2.

Regulation Q   Formerly, through Regulation Q, the Federal Reserve established the maximum rates that commercial banks were permitted to pay on their time and saving deposit liabilities. Savings and loan associations were faced with similar restrictions. These interest rate ceilings had an effect on commercial bank operations only when interest yields that investors could earn on investments with little or no risk outside the banking system were higher than the maximum rates that banks were allowed to pay.

This type of situation occurred in early 1980, when banks were restricted to paying under 6 percent on passbook savings accounts while the *prime rate* (the rate charged by banks on loans to their best customers) was 20 percent. Faced with such alternatives, many people and businesses invested their money outside the system of depository institutions. Their action reduced their deposits in such institutions and consequently reduced the ability of the institutions to make loans.

*The process whereby individuals and businesses reduce their deposits at commercial banks and other depository institutions in order to invest directly in other assets is known as **disintermediation**.*

The Depository Institutions Deregulation and Monetary Control Act of 1980 provided for the phasing out of Regulation Q by 1986.[6] The implementation of this part of the act was delegated to the Depository Institutions Deregulation Committee, which consists of the heads of the major federal financial agencies.

FEDERAL FUNDS RATE

The Federal Reserve has also recognized that the federal funds rate is an important variable

6. See "Major Changes Due under Banking Bill," *San Antonio Express*, March 31, 1980, p. 10A; and "Fed Lists Fees It Plans to Charge Banks for Certain Services Starting Next Year," *Wall Street Journal*, August 29, 1980, p. 5.

affecting banks' decisions to extend credit. Consequently, the funds rate has become one of the target variables that the Fed tries to influence through its actions.

*The **federal funds rate** is the rate that commercial banks charge each other when they loan their excess reserves, usually on a one-day basis.*

Although the Federal Reserve does not directly set the federal funds rate, it can influence its level through open market operations and other policy tools.

The federal funds rate has increased in importance in recent years, as interest rates have risen and financial institutions have more aggressively tried to maximize their profit. Moreover, because there are no prohibitions on borrowing or lending of federal funds, the federal funds rate has a significant effect on bank credit policies.

THE IMPACT OF THE MONETARY CONTROL ACT OF 1980

The Depository Institutions Deregulation and Monetary Control Act of 1980 mandated major changes in the U.S. financial system. As indicated earlier, the act made all depository institutions, including commercial banks, mutual savings banks, savings and loan associations, and credit unions, subject to the same reserve requirements. Furthermore, it stated that all these institutions must be given equal access to the services of the Federal Reserve System and that the Fed must charge a fee for the services that covered the direct and indirect costs of offering them. In addition, it mandated that the Regulation Q ceilings on deposit accounts be phased out. As indicated in Chapter 10, the act also authorized NOW accounts, share draft accounts, and certain other interest-bearing accounts that can be used like checking accounts at financial institutions. (Previously, no interest could be paid on demand deposit accounts.) Finally, it relaxed the restrictions on the types of loans that financial institutions could make.

The initial impact of this act has been an increase in competition among the depository institutions. It has increased the costs of financial institutions by allowing higher interest rates on deposits and by requiring that the Federal Reserve charge fees for its services. As a result, the depository institutions have had to charge higher fees for their services; and loan rates and check service charges have risen. Increased competition among these institutions, however, may moderate the fee increases. It remains to be seen whether, under the new act, the Federal Reserve will be able to control the growth of the money supply more or less effectively than it has in the past.

4. The Board of Governors is also responsible for approving the discount rate set by each Reserve bank. The discount rate is the interest rate that Reserve banks charge depository institutions for loans. However, since the Fed discourages frequent borrowing from it by such institutions, the effectiveness of the discount rate as a policy tool is reduced.

5. The Federal Open Market Committee is responsible for determining purchases and sales of government securities by the Federal Reserve System. Open market operations are the most frequently used monetary policy tool. The tool is flexible; policy adjustments with regard to both scale and nature are easily made on a daily basis.

6. Other monetary policy tools of the Federal Reserve System include margin requirements on securities, other selective credit controls, and moral suasion. Actions that the Fed can take to affect the federal funds rate may also significantly affect the money supply.

SUMMARY

1. This chapter examined the Federal Reserve System. It also offered a brief history of the banking system in the United States before the Federal Reserve System was established, in 1914. (The Federal Reserve Act was passed in December 1913.)

2. The Federal Reserve System consists of the twelve Federal Reserve banks, the Board of Governors, the Federal Open Market Committee, the Federal Advisory Council, and the member banks. The seven members of the Board of Governors are appointed by the president to staggered, fourteen-year terms. The Federal Open Market Committee is made up of the Board of Governors plus five representatives of the Federal Reserve banks. The Federal Advisory Council contains one representative from each of the Reserve banks. However, it serves only in an advisory capacity.

3. The Board of Governors is responsible for specifying many of the requirements that depository institutions, including commercial banks, savings and loan associations, mutual savings banks, and credit unions, must meet. One of its tasks is setting the reserve requirements on deposits at such institutions. The ability to change the reserve requirement is a powerful monetary tool that is used infrequently.

IMPORTANT TERMS AND CONCEPTS

First Bank of the
   United States
Second Bank of the
   United States
Elasticity of the
   money supply
Federal Reserve Act
   of 1913
Board of Governors of
   the Federal Reserve
   System
Federal Open Market
   Committee
Federal Advisory
   Council

Depository
   Institutions
Deregulation and
   Monetary Control
   Act of 1980
Reserve requirement
Open market
   operations
Discount rate
Margin requirement
Disintermediation
Federal funds rate
Selective credit
   controls

QUESTIONS AND PROBLEMS

1. Why was the Federal Reserve System formed?

2. What were the two central banks in the United States before 1913? Why were they disbanded?

3. What are the primary institutions that form the structure of the Federal Reserve System?

4. What are the responsibilities of the Federal Open Market Committee?

5. How are the members of the Board of Governors selected? What are their duties?

6. Explain how a change in the reserve requirement can affect the supply of money. Is this policy tool used frequently? Explain.

7. What is the discount rate? Discuss the use of the discount rate as a monetary policy tool.

8. Explain how open market operations may be used to alter the money supply. Is this way of changing the money supply an important monetary policy tool? Explain.

9. What is the Federal Funds rate? How is it used to affect the supply of money?

10. What are margin requirements on securities? What is their purpose?

11. Assume that the Federal Reserve System buys $30 million worth of government bonds from commercial banks. What is the resulting increase in commercial bank reserves? If the reserve requirement is 0.25, what is the maximum possible increase in the money supply that can occur as a result of this action?

FEDERAL RESERVE FRETS ABOUT INCREASING LOSS OF ITS MEMBER BANKS

Two years ago, a Boston bank-holding company called BayBanks Inc. found a way to add 9% to its earnings in a single move: It pulled five of its 11 banks out of the Federal Reserve System.

In New York, Citicorp, the holding company for Citibank, doesn't have any plans to do the same, but if it did, says Chairman Walter B. Wriston, the bank would save about $100 million a year in gross pretax profits.

The reason for BayBanks' savings and Citibank's wistful thoughts of possible savings is the demands that the Federal Reserve,

Source: Mitchell C. Lynch, "Federal Reserve Frets about Increasing Loss of Its Member Banks," *Wall Street Journal*, April 9, 1979, pp. 1, 14.

the nation's central bank, makes on its 5,624 member banks. In return for such services as loans and check processing, the Fed requires its members to set aside various percentages of all their accounts as reserves on which they don't earn interest.

Because this money isn't invested, Fed membership costs a typical bank 9% of its pretax profit, it's estimated by Frank E. Morris, president of the Federal Reserve Bank of Boston, one of the 12 regional banks that make up the Fed system. For commercial banks with deposits of more than $100 million, the cost rises to about 12%, he says. Reserves, he says, are "a franchise tax, a penalty on those who belong."

"MATTER OF ECONOMICS"

That's why BayBanks hasn't been alone in pulling out of the Fed. In the past six years, 337 banks have withdrawn—152 of these within the past two years. And the departing banks are getting bigger. In the past two years, 25 of the banks had deposits of $100 million or more, compared with only five of that size in 1975.

The five banks pulled out by BayBanks had deposits totaling $1.25 billion and constituted the biggest single withdrawal from the Fed in history. "The Fed was tying up too much of our money," says William M. Crozier, president of BayBanks. "Our decision was a matter of economics."

Such decisions are creating a dilemma for the Fed. A top priority in its fight against inflation is to control spending by taking money out of circulation. This it can do by raising its members' reserve requirements. But if it puts new demands on the reserves, it fears that more banks will pull out. The effect, says a Fed insider, "is like raising subway fares.". . .

In the days of low, 4% interest rates, the banks were content to accept the trade-off of reserves for Fed services and loan availability. But now that banks can earn 12% or more on their funds, they are looking anxiously at their reserves tied up by the Fed.

WHO GETS THE MOST

A problem for member banks is that there is no specific value attached to the various services offered by the Fed. Mr. Wriston of Citicorp says the company hasn't found any way to accurately measure their value. Even the regional Fed banks can't agree because, it appears, the return on the services varies across the country. A study by the Federal Reserve Bank of St. Louis shows that large banks get proportionately greater benefits than do small banks from Fed membership. By translating the Fed's services into an interest-rate return on the idle reserves, the study asserts that banks with deposits up to $100 million get a 1% return and banks with deposits up to $1.5 billion get a 1.7% return.

But a study by the Federal Reserve Bank of New York shows the opposite. The study asserts

that banks with deposits under $100 million get a 0.93% return, and the biggest banks, with deposits over $2 billion, get a mere 0.3%. . . .

Commercial banks' desire to see their reserves earning interest has been increased by rising competition from thrift institutions. Six years ago, thrift institutions in New England were authorized to start offering NOW—or negotiated order of withdrawal—accounts. These not only enabled the thrift institutions for the first time to offer checking accounts but also enabled them to pay interest on the checking-account deposits. NOW accounts are spreading across the country, and commercial bankers are clearly worried by the competition.

One new Fed study shows what has happened to commercial-bank profits in the six New England states as a result of the increased competition. Between 1970 and 1978, commercial banks' profit margins have fallen by 50%, compared with a 25% drop in the rest of the U.S. . .

"LEGISLATED INEQUITY"

In February, Fed Chairman Miller bluntly told the Senate Banking Committee that Fed members are "at a competitive disadvantage relative to other depository institutions." He called the current reserve system "legislated inequity" and said, "It is no wonder that member banks continue to withdraw." . . .

Mr. Miller worries that as more banks pull out, the Fed's leverage is weakened. "Fewer banks within the Federal Reserve mean that

fewer institutions can be influenced by changes in the reserve requirements," he says.

BRAKE ON SPENDING

By controlling the reserve requiremens of its members, the Fed is able to control the amount of demand deposits, or "quick-spending money," that the banks have on hand. This reduces the amount of money in circulation, which allows the Fed to put the brakes on spending and, theoretically, to slow the economy and inflation.

Last November [1978], for example, the Fed raised the reserve requirements, which had the effect of pulling $3 billion out of circulation. Because of this and other anti-inflation measures, such as raising the discount rate, the dollar shot up on foreign-exchange markets, the price of gold plunged and the stock market had a record one-day rise.

But some critics contend that reserves have little influence on the money supply, and they note that the Fed rarely adjusts the reserve requirements. George J. Benston, a professor at the graduate school of management at the University of Rochester, says that the Fed manages the money supply by manipulating interest rates and that "membership in the Fed isn't relevant" when the central bank does this.

Fed authorities say that the reserve requirements and interest rates go hand in hand. To reduce the money supply, the Fed, in effect, reduces the amount of reserves. In the simplest case, it does this mainly by selling

Treasury securities directly to banks, which pay for the securities by drawing on their reserve accounts at the Fed. Because they have reduced their reserves, the banks also have to reduce their deposits. They do this by cutting back on new loans, which are recorded as deposits.

To keep a close watch on this operation, the Fed monitors the federal-funds market. Federal funds are the excess reserves that banks lend or borrow, usually on a day-to-day basis. By reducing reserves, the Fed increases the fed-funds rate, or the interest rate the banks pay to borrow reserves from one another. An increase in that rate strongly influences other short-term interest rates.

But in order for the Fed to know which money-supply lever to pull, it must monitor its member banks. As membership declines, "We lose precision and predictability," says Mr. Morris of the Boston Fed.

QUESTIONS

1. According to this article, why were banks leaving the Federal Reserve System?

2. Why was the Federal Reserve concerned about the situation?

3. Why did the Fed face a dilemma at the time this article was written?

4. What are NOW accounts? How do they affect the position of banks?

5. What did the studies show about the past benefits to banks of Fed membership?

6. Do you agree with the solution offered by the Depository Institutions Deregulation and Monetary Control Act of 1980, which provided for uniform reserve requirements for all banks and required that the Federal Reserve charge member and nonmember banks for its services? (This law also legalized NOW accounts and draft accounts at credit unions.) Would you favor another solution? Explain.

CHAPTER 12

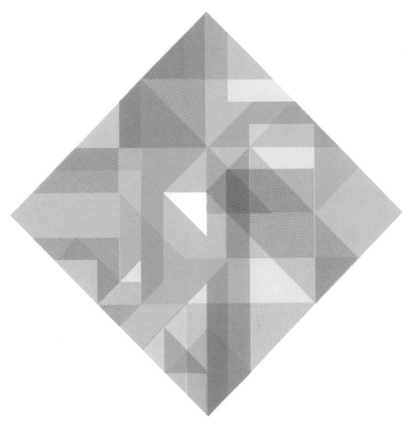

AN
INTEGRATION
OF MONETARY
AND FISCAL
POLICY

MONETARY
POLICY,
THEN
AND NOW

Economists are fond of discussing the great monetary debacles of history, because these events illustrate vividly what can happen when a country's monetary policy goes completely haywire. Some well-known cases are cited here:

1. In 1775 the Second Continental Congress of the United States decided to issue currency to finance the Revolutionary War. The notes were to be redeemable in silver or gold. However, the government issued so much of this currency that such redemption became impossible. After the war the notes depreciated markedly, giving rise to the expression "not worth a Continental."

2. In Germany, following World War I, a government known as the Weimar Republic tried to cope with a generally depressed postwar economy by printing vast amounts of currency and raising workers' wages. By 1923 Germans found it cheaper to fuel home heating and cooking fires with their virtually worthless paper Marks than to attempt to buy coal or firewood with the currency.

3. The year 1931 was a bad one for the U.S. economy. The depression had already begun, and business and bank failures were rampant. Still, starting around September, the Federal Reserve allowed credit conditions to tighten. With this further decrease in the money supply and the subsequent collapse of the international monetary system, the stage was set for a worsening of the worldwide depression and deflation in 1932 and 1933.

4. Israel's inflation rate in 1980 was well over 100 percent. Needless to say, "not worth a Shekel" was becoming a popular phrase all over the country. Israel's problem is attributed to government creation of too much money. The inflation was leading to worker strikes and a great deal of consternation among political leaders.

Enough of glaring examples! They all tell the same story: If a government creates too much money, the purchasing power of the money will fall. If it creates too little money, deflation or unemployment or both may occur.

Apparently, the chief cause of history's monetary crises has been mismanagement by government authorities. What can we say, however, about periods of inflation and unemployment that are troublesome but clearly not at crisis level? Can we expect monetary or perhaps fiscal fine tuning by the government to eliminate undesirable fluctuations altogether? What policy changes should we expect government to make under various sets of economic circumstances?

This chapter examines how monetary and fiscal policy are integrated in economic theory. As will be shown, today's economists do not agree on the relative potency of the two types of policies or on their consequences.

C H A P T E R 12

AN
INTEGRATION
OF MONETARY
AND FISCAL
POLICY

WHAT THIS CHAPTER IS ABOUT

THE DEMAND FOR MONEY
Transactions Demand
Precautionary Demand
Speculative Demand
THE INVESTMENT–INTEREST RATE
   CONNECTION
THE EFFECTS OF MONETARY POLICY
THE LIQUIDITY TRAP
CLASSICAL MONETARY THEORY
MONETARISM
THE MONETARY EFFECTS OF FISCAL POLICY

In the last two chapters we discovered how banks and the Federal Reserve System affect the supply of money. Now it is time to examine how the money supply affects the economic variables about which we are all concerned—inflation, employment, and national product.

Two quite different theories about the effectiveness of monetary policy exist. One theory, the monetarist view, has its roots in the classical economic philosophy that excess supply and unemployment cannot be serious problems for a significant period of time as long as market forces are allowed to operate freely. The opposing point of view is held by "Keynesian" economists, who believe that the instability of the private sector's demand for goods and services and the slowness of wages and prices to adjust to decreases in demand require the use of economic policies by the government to ensure a noninflationary but full-employment □ level of output.

In the first part of the chapter the Keynesian point of view as it is probably held by most economists is discussed. Then the classical and monetarist theories are explained and compared with the Keynesian position.

A KEYNESIAN VIEW OF HOW MONETARY POLICY WORKS— AND SOMETIMES DOES NOT
◆

Economists who generally agree with the Keynesian argument believe that government intervention in the economy is often necessary to keep inflation under control and maintain full employment. (The use of fiscal policy, □ ignoring the role of money, was examined in Chapter 7.)

In this chapter we will see how the demand for money by the private sector and the factors influencing business investment play crucial roles in determining the effectiveness of both monetary and fiscal policy. The demand for money will be considered first.

THE DEMAND FOR MONEY

According to Keynes, people and businesses have three reasons for holding money—the transactions motive, the precautionary motive, and the speculative motive. Of the three,

the transactions motive is the least controversial among economists.

Transactions Demand

*The **transactions demand for money** reflects the fact that businesses and individuals need to hold money in some form (demand or similar deposits or currency and coin) to pay for their day-to-day purchases and make other necessary payments.*

Businesses and individuals need to keep some money on hand because their cash inflows usually are not timed to occur exactly when cash is needed to make payments. For example, many people are paid on the last day of each month, and they maintain cash balances in order to pay the bills falling due throughout the next month.

Of course, some of the cash could be put into savings accounts, where it would earn interest, and transferred to checking accounts as needed. However, this course of action would involve a significant amount of time, and some banks require savings deposits to be held with the bank for a minimum number of days before interest will be paid.

Businesses with much larger cash holdings have more opportunities to purchase interest-bearing assets, such as Treasury bills and notes, for brief periods of time. Individuals often cannot meet the minimum investment requirements for purchasing these assets. Also, transactions costs, such as brokerage fees, are relatively large for small sums of money.

Nevertheless, even in these days of credit card purchases, both businesses and individuals need to keep some money balances in order to facilitate their transactions. Moreover, the dollar volume of purchases of newly produced goods and services usually rises as the level of income increases, so economists frequently assume that the transactions demand for money is proportional to the level of income (measured in dollars in the United

States). We can express this assumption as

$$M_T = k_1 Y, \qquad (12-1)$$

where:

M_T = the transactions demand for money,
k_1 = some constant, and
Y = net national product □ in dollars.

Precautionary Demand

The *precautionary demand for money* arises because people believe that they must keep some cash balances on hand to meet unforeseen needs.

The precautionary motive for holding cash balances is based on the possibility of unexpected catastrophes occurring—the family car breaking down, illness striking, or a storm damaging personal property, for example. Economists usually assume that the amount of precautionary balances held varies with the level of income: The higher the level of income, the higher the quantity demanded of precautionary balances. One justification for this assumption is that the higher the level of income, the more property and the more expensive the property individuals and businesses will likely hold that may be damaged.

Speculative Demand

Keynes argued that the *speculative demand for money* exists because people desire to hold part of their wealth in the form of money for investment reasons.

As interest rates change, the prices of previously issued bonds with fixed dollar amounts of interest also change. This process occurs in the following way. Suppose that a firm issues a $1,000 face value bond paying a stated annual interest premium of 10 percent of face value, or $100. If the bond has no maturity

date (such a bond is called a **perpetual bond** or a **consol**), its market value is given by

$$P_B = \frac{R}{i},$$

where:

P_B = the market value or current price of the bond,
R = the annual interest payment in dollars, and
i = the current market rate of interest.[1]

If the market rate of interest is 10 percent when the bond is initially issued, then the

---

1. We can derive this formula as follows. The current, or present, value of a stream of returns of equal dollar amounts received over t periods is given by

$$PV = \frac{R}{(1 + i)} + \frac{R}{(1 + i)^2} + \frac{R}{(1 + i)^3} + \ldots + \frac{R}{(1 + i)^t}, \quad (1)$$

where:

PV = the present value of the returns,
R = the dollar return received each period, and
i = the current market rate of interest.

We can sum the right-hand side of Equation 1 as follows. First we multiply both sides of the equation by $(1 + i)$ to obtain

$$PV(1 + i) = R + \frac{R}{(1 + i)} + \frac{R}{(1 + i)^2} + \ldots + \frac{R}{(1 + i)^{t-1}}. \quad (2)$$

Subtracting Equation 1 from Equation 2, we get

$$PV(1 + i) - PV = R - \frac{R}{(1 + i)^t}, \text{ or} \qquad (3)$$

$$iPV = R - \frac{R}{(1 + i)^t}.$$

As t approaches infinity, $\frac{R}{(1 + i)^t}$ approaches zero. Thus, for a consol, which has no maturity date,

$$iPV = R$$
$$PV = \frac{R}{i}.$$

If we assume that the market price of the bond reflects its current value, we then obtain

$$P_B = \frac{R}{i}.$$

firm can sell the bond at face value (less brokerage fees), because

$$P_B = \frac{\$100}{0.10}$$
$$= \$1,000.$$

If the market rate of interest later falls to 5 percent, the value of the bond will double, because the dollar interest payment is fixed at $100:

$$P_B = \frac{\$100}{0.05}$$
$$= \$2,000.$$

If the holders of such bonds now wish to sell them, they should be able to find willing buyers at a price of $2,000. Buyers will be willing to pay up to $2,000 for the bonds because a $1,000 bond paying 10 percent now affords the same dollar return as a $2,000 bond bearing the 5 percent current market rate of interest: $1,000 \times 0.10 = $100 = $2,000 \times 0.05 = $100.

Of course, the market price of the bond will fall if the market rate of interest rises. For example, if i increases to 12 percent, the market price of the bond will fall to $833.33, because

$$P_B = \frac{\$100}{0.12}$$
$$= \$833.33.$$

In this case, bondholders who purchased the bonds at a price of $1,000 will incur a loss if they sell them. If they do not sell their bonds, they still earn interest at a rate equal to only 10 percent of the money they have invested, rather than 12 percent.[2]

Under these circumstances, investors may be better off if they hold their funds in the form of money until interest rates rise, and then purchase bonds. Thus the demand for speculative balances is greater when interest rates are expected to rise in the near future than when they are expected to fall.

2. The market prices of bonds with shorter periods to maturity vary in the same direction as those of consols. However, *ceteris paribus*, the dollar amount does not vary as widely.

If all people had the same expectations about the future level of interest rates, they would all want to put their wealth in bonds if they expected interest rates to remain the same or to fall. They would all want to hold their wealth in money if they expected interest rates to rise. They would either hold all of their financial assets in the form of money or the speculative demand for money would be zero.

People do not all have the same expectations about the future levels of interest rates. Still, it is generally true, other things equal, that more people expect interest rates to fall in the future when the rates are currently high, by historical standards, than when the rates are currently low. Conversely, when interest rates are low by historical standards, more people expect them to rise than expect them to fall even lower. On this basis we can expect people to demand a smaller amount of speculative balances when interest rates are high than when interest rates are low. Therefore, the quantity demanded of speculative money balances varies inversely with the interest rate. The nature of the speculative demand for money will be discussed in more detail later in this chapter.

Keynes stated that the demand for money is a function of interest rates as well as income.[3] In figure 12–1, a simple example of the money market in equilibrium is shown. The supply of money, represented by M_0, is assumed to be constant no matter what the rate of interest. The demand for money, given by M_D, is greater the lower the interest rate. One other factor that affects the demand for money, national income, is not represented in this graph. Consequently, M_D applies for only a constant level of income, $Y = Y_0$.

If income increases, the demand for money shifts upward, because people demand a greater amount of money for transactions purposes. In Figure 12–1 the equilibrium □ rate of interest is at i_0, where the quantity demanded of money is equal to M_0.

3. John Maynard Keynes, *The General Theory* (New York: Harcourt, Brace, World, 1964), Chapter 15.

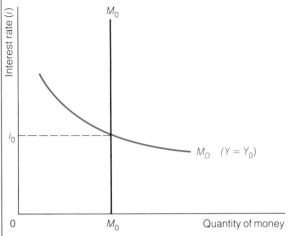

FIGURE 12–1 Equilibrium in the Money Market

The supply of money, M_0 is assumed to be constant no matter what the rate of interest. The demand for money is represented by M_D. The quantity demanded of money will be greater the lower the interest rate. The quantity demanded of money will also be greater the greater the level of national income. In this case, the level of national income is assumed to be constant at Y_0. Equilibrium in the money market occurs at i_0, where the quantity demanded of money is equal to M_0.

In the next few sections of this chapter we will discuss the link between the interest rate and investment in capital goods and equipment. We will then look at the connection between the money supply, investment, and net national product.

THE INVESTMENT–INTEREST RATE CONNECTION

The type of investment to be discussed here is investment □ in physical assets. Presumably, firms invest in plant, equipment, and inventories in order to make a profit. One way of expressing the amount of that profit is as a rate of return.[4]

For example, if a firm invests $1,000 in an asset, incurs no additional expense, and sells

the asset one year later for $1,100, we can say that the firm made a profit of $100 or a 10 percent annual rate of return: $100/$1,000 = 10 percent. Businesses generally call this rate of return the *internal rate of return*. Economists, following Keynes, often call it the marginal efficiency of investment (MEI).[5]

> The **marginal efficiency of investment** is the rate of return, or profit, expressed in percentage terms, on an investment.

According to Keynes, if a firm makes decisions that lead to profit maximization, then the interest rate, the marginal efficiency of investment, and the level of the firm's investment in physical assets are all interrelated in the following manner. If a firm is to invest in new physical assets (buildings, equipment, and other property), it must obtain financing. One alternative is for the firm to borrow the money, which will cause it to incur an added expense—interest. The amount of this expense will depend on the interest rate.

Another alternative is for the firm to use its own internally generated funds. In this case the firm does not incur an explicit interest expense. However, it does incur an opportunity cost, □ because it could have placed the funds in a savings account or have purchased other interest-earning assets, such as marketable securities. Consequently, a firm should not consider the use of even its own funds to be "free," since by investing them in plant and equipment the opportunity to earn interest from their use elsewhere is given up.

Under these circumstances the profit-maximizing firm will invest in physical assets until the marginal efficiency of investment is equal to the market rate of interest. It will invest up to this point because when the MEI is greater than the market rate of interest, the firm is earning a rate of return greater than the cost of borrowing the money, or the opportunity cost

9

---

4. Profit maximization is discussed in Chapter 19.

5. Actually, Keynes used the term *marginal efficiency of capital*. See Keynes, *General Theory*, Chapter 11.

of funds. If the MEI is less than the market rate of interest, the firm will earn less by investing in physical assets than the cost of borrowing the necessary money or the interest it could earn on its own funds elsewhere. If the MEI is equal to the market rate of interest, the firm will earn a rate of return on the investment that is just equal to the cost of funds for the investment.

In general, the lower the market rate of interest, the more funds firms are willing to invest in physical assets, and vice versa. This relationship holds because the marginal efficiency of investment tends to decline as the amount of investment expenditures by businesses increases, at least in the short run. For one thing, investment projects have unequal rates of return. As firms invest in more and more capital projects, after some point they will find that the remaining projects have lower rates of return than the initial ones did.

For example, suppose a firm is considering the four investment projects listed here with their respective rates of return:

Project	Rate of Return
A	30%
B	25
C	15
D	10

If the interest rate is below 10 percent, all four projects will increase the firm's profit. If the interest rate is 20 percent, only projects A and B will be profitable. If the interest rate is above 30 percent, none of the projects will be profitable.

In addition, the productive capacity of firms may increase up to the point where the prices of the goods produced by the firms decrease enough that the rate of return on new equipment purchased falls. Figure 12–2 illustrates a possible investment–interest rate relationship for a firm.

In the next section, we will see why Keynesian economists believe that the interest rate, money market, investment, and net national product are interrelated.

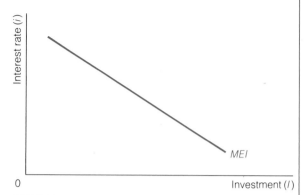

FIGURE 12–2 The Relationship between Investment and the Market Rate of Interest

In general, the internal rate of return on investment projects, or the marginal efficiency of investment *(MEI)* declines as firms invest greater dollar amounts in plant and equipment or other capital items.

THE EFFECTS OF MONETARY POLICY

Keynesian economists believe that an increase in the supply of money □ will usually result in the following scenario. Once the increase in the money supply occurs, firms and individuals will be holding more money than they wish to hold. Consequently, they will attempt to reduce their money balances by purchasing bonds or other interest-earning assets. The increase in the demand for such assets will cause their price to rise and the current market rate of interest to fall. (Recall that these two variables move in opposite directions.)

The decrease in the market rate of interest will have two direct effects. First, the quantity demanded of speculative money balances will increase. Second, firms will desire to increase their level of investment in plant, equipment, and inventories. As explained in Chapter 6, an increase in investment will have a multiplied effect on national income.[6] The increase

---

6. In the simple model, the investment and government expenditures multiplier was given by

$$\frac{1}{1 - b},$$

where b is the marginal propensity to consume. However, because of the effects of the demand and supply of money, the full mulitplier effect may not occur.

in national income will then result in an increase in the quantity demanded of transactions and precautionary money balances. This process will continue until the quantity supplied and the quantity demanded of money are equal.

Thus Keynesian economists believe that changes in the supply of money will affect the level of aggregate demand by affecting the market rate of interest and, consequently, the level of investment in real assets such as plant and equipment. If an increase in the quantity of money results in people holding greater money balances than they desire, these people will try to buy bonds, which will result in an increase in the price of bonds and a decrease in the market rate of interest. The decrease in the interest rate will make more investment projects profitable, which will result in an increase in investment and a multiple increase in the equilibrium level of income.□

A simplified version of this process is illustrated in Figure 12–3. In panel (a) the demand for money, M_{D1}, is drawn as a function of the interest rate, given the level of national income $Y = Y_1$. M_{D1} is downward sloping because larger speculative money balances are demanded at lower interest rates than at higher interest rates. (If the level of income changes, the quantity demanded of transactions and precautionary balances will change, shifting M_{D1}. For example, if the level of income increases, the quantity demanded of transactions and precautionary balances will increase, thereby causing the demand for money curve to shift upward.) If the money supply initially is M_1, the interest rate will be i_1, the level of investment will be I_1, and the equilibrium level of income will be Y_1—found where $I_1 = S_1$ in panel (c) (assuming that there are no government expenditures or taxes).

Suppose the money supply is increased to M_2. Because the quantity of money available is greater than the quantity supplied, people will attempt to buy bonds, thereby increasing the price of bonds and decreasing the interest rate. The decrease in the interest rate will

cause investment and, consequently, income to increase.

At this point, a small complication arises. The increase in income will cause the quantity demanded of transactions and precautionary balances to increase, which will shift the demand for money curve outward, say to M_{D2}. Eventually, a new equilibrium will be reached at an interest rate such as i_2 and a level of income such as Y_2, where the quantity of money supplied is equal to the quantity of money demanded and investment is equal to saving.

THE LIQUIDITY TRAP

Keynes believed that under certain circumstances an increase in the money supply would have no effect on the interest rate and, consequently, no effect on investment or national income. This situation would occur when the interest rate was so low that people would be willing to hold any new money that was created by the Federal Reserve System as speculative balances rather than using it to purchase bonds. In this case *an increase in the money supply would have no impact on the rate of interest or national income and would be totally ineffective.*

In general, Keynes believed that this phenomenon might occur when interest rates were low by historical standards, so that individuals and firms would be wary of buying bonds (expecting interest rates to rise in the future). Keynes also believed that these circumstances could exist during a serious depression, especially one that occurred along with a bank panic, such as happened in the 1930s. Today we would expect such a situation to be extremely rare.

*An economy is said to be in a **liquidity trap** when the interest rate falls so low that individuals and businesses wish to hold any new money created in the banking system as speculative balances.*

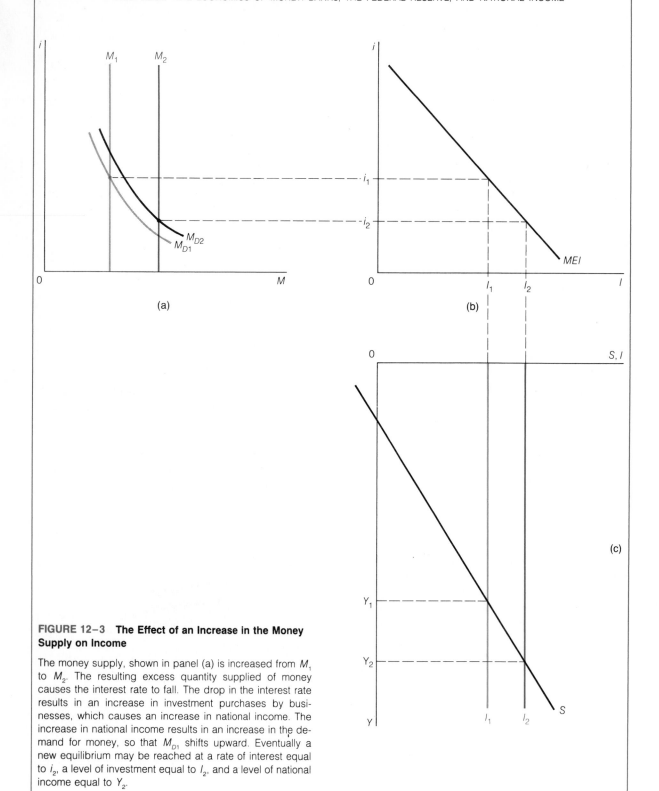

FIGURE 12–3   The Effect of an Increase in the Money Supply on Income

The money supply, shown in panel (a) is increased from M_1 to M_2. The resulting excess quantity supplied of money causes the interest rate to fall. The drop in the interest rate results in an increase in investment purchases by businesses, which causes an increase in national income. The increase in national income results in an increase in the demand for money, so that M_{D1} shifts upward. Eventually a new equilibrium may be reached at a rate of interest equal to i_2, a level of investment equal to I_2, and a level of national income equal to Y_2.

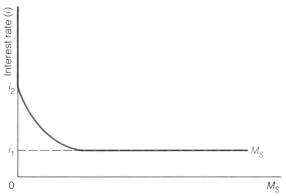

FIGURE 12-4 The Speculative Demand for Money

The quantity demanded of speculative money balances increases as the interest rate falls. At i_1, no one believes that the interest rate will fall any lower, and the liquidity trap is reached.

Figure 12–4 is a graph of the speculative demand for money, M_S, with three distinct regions. At interest rates above i_2, the quantity demanded of speculative money balances is zero because most people believe that the interest rate will either fall or remain constant in the near future. The liquidity trap is reached at i_1. Between i_2 and i_1, the quantity demanded of speculative money balances increases as the interest rate falls. This response occurs because as the interest rate reaches lower and lower levels, more and more people expect it to rise in the near future.

Although monetary policy is totally ineffective in the liquidity trap, fiscal policy (changing government expenditures or taxes) is still effective. For this reason, Keynes was somewhat biased in favor of the use of fiscal policy during a depression.

In the next two sections, classical monetary theory and one of its modern offsprings, monetarism, are discussed. An explanation of why Keynesian economists disagree with these views is also given. Then the effects of fiscal policy on the money supply are briefly considered. Finally, in Special Topic D, a synthesis of the Keynesian and classical positions is examined.

CLASSICAL MONETARY THEORY

As explained in Chapter 7, classical economists □ in general believed that unemployment □ would never be a serious problem—at least not for substantial periods of time. According to Say's law, □ supply implies its own demand. Thus a lack of aggregate demand □ would not be a long-run problem.

If, as Mill suggested, an excess quantity of some goods could be supplied only while others were being demanded in quantities greater than those supplied, the situation would be only temporary. The relative prices of these items would adjust, bringing the markets back into equilibrium.

According to classical economists the same process would occur in the labor market. If unemployment existed, the unemployed workers would offer to work at lower wage rates. Accordingly, wage rates would fall, and the quantity of labor employed would increase. The reverse process would occur if more workers were demanded than were supplied at the going wage rate.

Under these assumptions the money supply would serve merely as a medium of exchange and determine the general level of prices. Neoclassical economists summarized this role of the money supply in the following "equation of exchange":

$$MV = P \times Q,$$

where:

M = the quantity of money,
V = the velocity of money, or how many times the supply of money turns over or changes hands,
P = a general price index, and
Q = gross national product in real terms.[7]

---

7. This version of the equation of exchange is similar to that used by Irving Fisher. See his *Purchasing Power of Money*, 2d ed. (New York: Macmillan, 1913), especially Chapters 1–8. (Reprinted by A. M. Kelley, 1971.) For a slightly different version of this equation see Alfred Marshall, *Money, Credit, and Commerce* (1923), Book 1, Chapter 4.

The **equation of exchange** states that the quantity of money in the economy times the velocity of money is equal to gross national product in real terms multiplied by a general index of prices of newly produced goods and services.

The concept of the *velocity of money* can be explained in the following way. Suppose that the market value of newly produced goods and services in the country (equal to $P \times Q$) were $1 million and the supply of money were $200,000. Each $1 of money would have to change hands five times for all of the $1 million of new goods and services to be purchased. Thus the velocity of money would be five.

Because we are referring to the velocity of money in terms of national product and income, we can call the concept the *income velocity of money*.

The **income velocity of money** is the average number of times the money supply of an economy changes hands during a year in the process of purchasing the country's gross national product. It is equal to GNP at current prices divided by the quantity of money.

As shown in Table 12–1, during the last sixty years the income velocity of money in the United States has varied between 2.1 and 6.8, although it has been gradually increasing over time.

Nevertheless, classical economists believed that the velocity of money was constant or nearly constant in the short run. They thought that it was determined by the structure of the financial system, the vertical integration of businesses, and other factors that do not change rapidly.

Furthermore, these economists also believed that national product would remain constant at the full employment level. In this situation the quantity of money and the general level of prices would vary directly and by the same proportion. If the quantity of money

TABLE 12–1 Gross National Product, the Money Supply, and the Velocity of Money, 1916–1980 (in Billions of Dollars)

Year	(1) Gross National Product[1]	(2) Average Money Supply[2]	(3) Velocity of Money (1)/(2)
1916	$ 48.3	$ 20.8	2.3
1920	91.5	34.8	2.6
1925	93.1	42.0	2.2
1929	103.4	26.6	3.9
1930	90.4	25.8	3.5
1933	55.8	19.9	2.8
1935	72.2	25.9	2.8
1940	100.0	39.6	2.5
1945	212.3	99.2	2.1
1950	286.2	114.1	2.5
1955	399.3	135.2	3.0
1960	506.0	144.2	3.5
1965	688.1	171.4	4.0
1970	992.7	215.3	4.6
1971	1,077.6	229.2	4.7
1972	1,185.9	250.5	4.7
1973	1,326.4	264.1	5.0
1974	1,434.2	275.3	5.2
1975	1,549.2	287.9	5.4
1976	1,718.0	305.0	5.6
1977	1,918.0	328.4	5.8
1978	2,156.1	351.6	6.1
1979	2,413.9	369.7	6.5
1980	2,627.4	385.4	6.8

[1]Sources: Series FI, U.S. Department of Commerce, Bureau of the Census, *Historical Statistics of the United States, Colonial Times to 1970* (Washington, D.C.: Government Printing Office, 1975), p. 224; end "Table B–1: Gross National Product, 1929–80," *Economic Report of the President* (Washington, D.C.: Government Printing Office, 1981), p. 233.

[2]Sources: Series X 410–419 (Money Stock—Currency, Deposits, Bank Vault Cash, and Gold: 1867 to 1970), U.S. Department of Commerce, Bureau of the Census, *Historical Statistics of the United States, Colonial Times to 1970* (Washington, D.C.: Government Printing Office, 1970), p. 992; and "Table B–59: Money Stock Measures and Liquid Assets, 1959–80," *Economic Report of the President* (Washington, D.C.: Government Printing Office, 1981), p. 301.

doubled, the general level of prices would double; if the quantity of money were cut in half, the general level of prices would fall by half.

We saw in Chapters 6 and 7 why Keynes argued that an equilibrium in the market for goods and services could occur at a level of income that was less than the full employment level. We will see shortly why Keynes anticipated problems connected with a more sophisticated version of classical theory.

WICKSELL: A FURTHER DEVELOPMENT OF CLASSICAL THEORY

Around 1900 a Swedish economist named Knut Wicksell recognized that the link between the supply of money, the price level, and national income might not be as clear-cut as the classical economists thought.[8] Wicksell believed that the aggregate quantity demanded of goods and services might be different from the aggregate quantity supplied at full employment but that they could be equated through changes in the interest rate.

This process would occur in the following way. Wicksell believed that the amount saved out of current income was determined by the interest rate. As the interest rate rose, people saved more because the reward for saving was greater. He also believed that the higher the interest rate, the smaller would be the corresponding investment in plant and equipment. (Reasons for this phenomenon were given earlier in this chapter.)

Wicksell thought that a change in the money supply in the appropriate direction would result in a change in the interest rate. The change in the interest rate would tend to equate saving and investment, bringing the economy to a full employment level of income.

Figure 12–5 is a graph of saving and investment functions that are compatible with Wicksell's theory. If the interest rate is initially above the equilibrium rate, say at i_0, the amount that savers want to save is greater than the amount that investors want to invest ($S_0 > I_0$). If we assume that there are no govern-

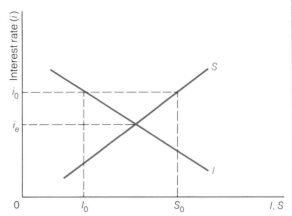

FIGURE 12–5 Wicksell's Saving and Investment Functions

If the interest rate is at i_0, the amount which savers want to save is greater than the amount which investors want to invest. An increase in the money supply would cause the interest rate to fall to i_e, where saving and investment are equal.

ment expenditures, aggregate quantity demanded will be less than aggregate quantity supplied. If, by increasing the amount of bank loans, the interest rate can be made to fall to i_e, the amount that savers want to save and that investors want to invest will be made equal.

Wicksell believed that a similar process could occur without any government intervention to increase the money supply. The interest rate would adjust as follows. As a result of the excess aggregate quantity supplied, prices would begin to fall and the money supply in real terms (equal to M/P) would automatically increase. This increase would tend to lower interest rates—or at least real interest rates—with the same effect on national income as stated before. However, Wicksell acknowledged that the monetary authorities could speed up the process by increasing the money supply and, consequently, the amount of bank credit.

The *nominal rate of interest* is the percentage rate of return received on loans, without any adjustment for the general rate of inflation or deflation. The *real rate of interest* is the

---

8. Wicksell's ideas are only briefly summarized in a simplified form here. For more information, see Knut Wicksell, *Lectures on Political Economy*, vol.II, *Money* (London: Routledge and Kegan Paul, 1956), pp. 142–212; and Knut Wicksell, "Influence of the Rate of Interest on Prices," *Economic Journal* 17 (June 1907): especially 213–216.

percentage rate of return adjusted for the general rate of inflation or deflation. For example, if a person loaned money at a 14 percent nominal rate of interest for one year and the rate of inflation during that year was 10 percent, the real rate of interest would be given by 1.14/1.10 or 3.6 percent.

As Keynes pointed out (see Chapters 6 and 7), decisions by individuals to save and decisions by firms to invest in plant and equipment are made independently of each other, and they are primarily determined by two different variables. Consumption and therefore saving are functions of the level of personal income. Investment, on the other hand, is a function of the interest rate. Thus no mechanism exists in the private sector to automatically equate saving and investment. Moreover, although monetary policy may be used to affect the interest rate and, consequently, the level of investment, it is completely ineffective in the liquidity trap.

MONETARISM

Monetarism is one modern-day version of classical monetary theory. A leading proponent is Milton Friedman, a winner of the Nobel Prize in economics.[9] Although many economists who state that they are monetarists have somewhat differing ideas regarding monetary policy, their views are similar to the position summarized here.

Monetarists believe that the relationship between current consumption and income is unstable. In other words, the marginal propensi-

9. See Milton Friedman, "A Monetary and Fiscal Framework for Economic Stability" *American Economic Review* 38 (June 1948): 245–264; Friedman, "Statement on Monetary Theory and Policy," in *Employment, Growth, and Price Levels,* Hearings before the Joint Economic Committee, 86th Congress, First Session, May 25–28, 1958, pp. 605–612; and Friedman, "The Quantity Theory of Money—A Restatement," Friedman, *Studies in the Quantity Theory of Money,* ed. Milton Friedman (Chicago: University of Chicago Press, 1956), pp. 3–21.

ty to consume □ varies a great deal from year to year—so much so that we cannot predict the effect of a change in government expenditures because we cannot predict the value of the multiplier □ during any given period.

Monetarists view the relationship between the quantity of money and national income as more stable, because, like the classical economists, they believe that the velocity of money is nearly constant in the short run. Thus, to the extent that they are willing to use either fiscal or monetary policy, they favor monetary policy.

However, some monetarists, like classical economists, believe that if left to itself, an economy will always eventually work its way back to full employment through flexible wages and prices. They see government policies such as minimum wage rates and licensing requirements as only hindering this process.

In addition, some monetarists believe that government fiscal and monetary policies often tend to destabilize the economy by increasing inflation or unemployment. These problems occur partly because lags between the point at which the policies are implemented and the point at which their impacts are felt on the economy make the proper timing of such policies difficult. Besides questioning the need for and the success of government intervention, monetarists believe that the politics of getting reelected tends to bias government officials toward using fiscal and monetary policies that will result in inflation.

The monetarist point of view is summarized as follows:

The major impact of monetary actions is believed by monetarists to be on long-run movements in nominal economic variables such as nominal GNP, the general price level, and market interest rates. Long-run movements in real economic variables such as output and unemployment are considered to be little influenced, if at all, by monetary actions. Trend movements in real variables are essentially determined by growth in such factors as the labor force, natural resources, capital stock, and technology.

In the short run, however, actions of the central bank which change the trend rate of monetary expansion or produce pronounced variations around a given trend rate exert an impact on both real and nominal variables. . . . For example, an acceleration in the rate of monetary expansion at a time of a high level of resource utilization will have little short-run influence on output but a quick influence on the price level. On the other hand, a reduction in the rate of monetary expansion will result in slower growth in real output in the short run. . . .

In the short run, fiscal actions are believed by monetarists to exert some but little lasting influence on nominal GNP expansion and, therefore, have little affect [sic] on short-run movements of output and employment. It is argued that Government expenditures financed by taxes or borrowing from the public tend to crowd out over a fairly short period of time an equal amount of private expenditures, either by interest rate and price changes or by credit rationing.[10]

Friedman recommends that the monetary authorities merely increase the money supply by a small percentage each year to accommodate growth in the economy:

In order to attain a reasonably stable price level over the long pull, we must adopt measures that will lead to a growth in the stock of money at a fairly steady rate roughly equal to or slightly higher than the average rate of growth of output.[11]

Keynesian economists criticize the monetarist philosophy in the following way. First, while they admit that an economy might get itself back to full employment in the long run, they argue that often the amount of time required is intolerably long, partly because money wage rates and prices tend to be rigid in a downward direction.

Furthermore, these economists contend that it is precisely because of the instability of private sector spending that government intervention in the economy is required. Also, just because GNP and the supply of money are fairly closely correlated does not mean that changes in the supply of money *cause* the changes in GNP. The changes in GNP could cause the changes in the money supply. Finally, Keynesian economists point out that monetary policy is completely ineffective in the liquidity trap.

In the next section the possible monetary effects of fiscal policy are explained. We will see that the way deficit spending is financed or a budget surplus is handled can affect the money supply.

In Special Topic D following this chapter, Keynesian and neoclassical theories about monetary and fiscal policies are summarized through the use of IS-LM curves. These curves make it easy to graphically show how the market for goods and services interacts with the money market to determine the level of income.

THE MONETARY EFFECTS OF FISCAL POLICY

◆

Whenever the federal government's spending or taxing policies result in a budget surplus or deficit □, fiscal policy may affect the money supply as well as aggregate demand. For example, if fiscal policy results in a budget deficit of $5 billion and the government finances this deficit by creating $5 billion worth of new money, $5 billion of new potential bank reserves will be injected into the economy. The government might create the initial amount of new money in one of two ways: by selling bonds to the Fed and receiving in return an increase in its demand deposit (called the Treasury account) at the Fed or by simply printing new currency.

In the first case, when the government purchases goods and services, it will write checks

10. Leonall C. Anderson, "A Monetarist View of Demand Management: The United States Experience," *Federal Reserve Bank of St. Louis Review* 53 (September 1971): 4–5.

11. Friedman, "Statement on Monetary Theory and Policy," reprinted in Warren L. Smith and Ronald L. Teigen, eds., *Readings in Money, National Income, and Stabilization Policy* (Homewood, Ill.: Richard D. Irwin, 1965), pp. 84–85.

175

on the Treasury account in payment for them. The sellers of the goods will in turn take these checks to their banks to be cashed and will usually deposit the proceeds in checking accounts. This entire process results in an increase in commercial bank reserves, which will enable banks to expand the money supply even further.

For example, suppose the government finances the purchase of a $100,000 piece of defense equipment by selling bonds to the Federal Reserve. The results of this sale are shown in Table 12–2. In the next step the Treasury issues a check for $100,000, which the seller of the machine then takes to his or her commercial bank for collection, depositing the proceeds in a checking account. The commercial bank sends the check to the Fed for collection. The Fed deducts $100,000 from the Treasury account and adds $100,000 to the commercial bank's reserve account. (See Table 12–3.)

If the reserve requirement on demand deposits is 10 percent, the commercial bank now has $90,000 of new excess reserves □, which it can lend and thereby create additional new money. (The bank's required reserves also increase by 0.10 × $100,000 = $10,000, so its new excess reserves are $100,000 − $10,000 = $90,000.)

In reality, the government usually does not sell new bonds to the Federal Reserve. In fact, by law the Fed cannot hold more than $5 billion of government securities purchased directly from the Treasury, partly because Congress feared that the government would rely too much on this alternative, increasing the money supply and causing inflation. However, the Fed can help the Treasury accom-

plish the same end by purchasing from the general public the same dollar amount of securities as the Treasury wishes to sell. The Treasury can then more easily sell the new bonds to the general public.

The second theoretical method of financing a deficit, printing money, is not currently used by the United States government. All paper currency now being printed is a liability of a Federal Reserve bank. The amount of currency in circulation is now determined by the desire of the general public to hold money in that form.

However, in the past, and especially in other countries, governments have printed money in order to finance spending. In this case, the newly printed money could be given in exchange for goods and services, thereby increasing the money supply. If the sellers deposited this money in their commercial banks, bank reserves would increase and an even greater increase in the money supply would be facilitated.

Therefore, if the federal government were to finance a deficit by either of the two methods, the resulting increase in the money supply could cause inflationary pressures. The reverse effect could occur if the government had a budget surplus that resulted in a reduction in bank reserves.

On the other hand, a budget deficit may

TABLE 12–3
Results When Seller of Equipment
Deposits the Government Check

Federal Reserve

Assets	Liabilities and Capital Accounts
	Treasury account − $100,000
	Commercial bank reserves + $100,000

Commercial Bank

Assets	Liabilities and Capital Accounts
Reserves at Fed + $100,000	Demand deposits + $100,000

TABLE 12–2
Result of Government Sale of Bonds to

Federal Reserve

Assets	Liabilities and Capital Accounts
Government bonds + $100,000	Treasury account + $100,000

have no effect on the money supply if it is financed by selling bonds to the general public with no intervention by the Federal Reserve. The money that the Treasury withdraws from the private sector when it sells the bonds will be returned later in exchange for goods and services. If the government retires bonds held by the public, as a result of a budget surplus, there may also be no net effect on the money supply.

However, even though government expenditures do not affect the money supply, they may affect private sector spending in another way (besides through the multiplier effect). As government expenditures cause incomes to rise, people demand more transactions money balances.

The increased quantity demanded of transactions balances causes more people to sell bonds, which results in a decrease in the price of bonds and an increase in the interest rate. The increase in the interest rate results in a decrease in private investment spending.

The term **crowding out** □ is used to refer to this phenomenon: Government spending results in an increase in interest rates, which causes private investment spending □ to fall. Thus government spending crowds out private investment spending. Of course, the rise in the interest rate may not occur if the Federal Reserve increases the money supply. (It also may not occur if the economy is in a deep depression and the liquidity trap phenomenon is present.)

Therefore, government policy makers should consider how the manner in which a budget deficit is financed or the disposal of the funds brougnt in by a surplus will affect the money supply and, indirectly, aggregate demand. Otherwise, the total effect on aggregate demand may be significantly greater than policy makers would predict as a direct result of the fiscal policies.

SUMMARY

1. This chapter discussed how changes in the money supply affect the level of aggregate demand.

The effectiveness of monetary policy depends on the nature of the demand for money.

2. Three general motives that individuals and businesses have for holding money are the transactions motive, the precautionary motive, and the speculative motive. Money is held for transactions and precautionary purposes because cash inflows and outflows seldom coincide exactly. Speculative money balances are held because interest rates are expected to fall in the near future. In the liquidity trap, everyone expects interest rates to rise in the future, so any additional money injected into the economy is held as speculative balances. In this case, monetary policy is completely ineffective.

3. Keynesian economists believe that changes in the supply of money will affect the level of aggregate demand by affecting the market rate of interest and, consequently, the level of investment in real assets, such as plant, equipment, and inventories. The profit-maximizing firm will invest in real assets up to the point where the marginal efficiency of investment or the rate of return on investment is equal to the market rate of interest.

4. If an increase in the quantity of money results in people holding greater money balances than they desire, they will try to buy bonds, which will result in an increase in the price of bonds and a decrease in the market rate of interest. The decrease in the interest rate will make more investment projects profitable, which will result in an increase in investment and a multiple increase in the equilibrium level of income. However, monetary policy is completely ineffective in the liquidity trap, because people are willing to hold as speculative balances any additional money injected into the economy.

5. Classical and neoclassical economists thought the supply of money affected only the general level of prices in an economy. Believing in Say's law, these theorists thought that the economy would remain at full employment except for very short periods of time. Money would be held only for transactions purposes according to the "equation of exchange":

$$MV = P \times Q,$$

where M is the supply of money, V the velocity of money, P the general price level, and Q the net national product in real terms. Because neoclassical economists considered V and Q to be constant in the short run, they assumed that the supply of money and the general price level were directly related. An increase in *M* would result in a proportional increase in *P*. (An increase in the quantity demanded of speculative balances would mean a decrease in velocity.)

6. Wicksell believed that the connection between the money supply and the general price level was not as simple as other classical economists thought it was. However, he thought that the aggregate quantity demanded and the aggregate quantity supplied could be made equal through the interest rate, which would equate saving and investment.

7. Monetarism, a modern-day version of classical monetary theory, considers fiscal policy to be totally ineffective or to have adverse effects. Many monetarists prefer that the government not try to affect the economy through either monetary or fiscal policy. They believe the government should merely increase the money supply by a constant rate each year to accommodate growth. However, they generally would choose monetary policy over fiscal policy if the government insisted on doing something.

8. Keynesian economists answer the monetarists by arguing that while the economy may reach full employment by itself in the long run, the long run may be an intolerably long period of time. They also point out that monetary policy may be ineffective at times.

9. How the government handles the financial aspects of fiscal policies may affect the money supply and, indirectly, the level of aggregate demand.

IMPORTANT TERMS AND CONCEPTS

Transactions demand for money
Precautionary demand for money
Speculative demand for money
Marginal efficiency of investment
Liquidity trap
Equation of exchange
Income velocity of money
Monetarism
Crowding out

QUESTIONS AND PROBLEMS

1. According to Keynes, what are the three reasons that people hold money? Explain.

2. What is the marginal efficiency of investment?

3. Why do changes in the market rate of interest affect the level of investment?

4. What is monetarism?

5. Explain the concept of the income velocity of money.

6. What is the liquidity trap?

7. What did classical economists believe would be the effect of a change in the money supply? Explain.

8. Why do Keynesians think that a change in the supply of money may affect aggregate demand? Explain.

9. What is meant by "the monetary effects of fiscal policy"?

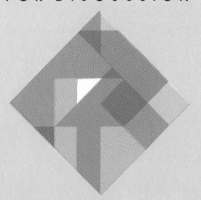

THE
LAST DAYS
OF THE
BOOM

Where do we stand? On the verge of a slump? Or is the economy overheated, with even worse inflation still ahead?

There is no one view concerning all this. But I find the present lack of consensus remarkable. It requires close study.

Begin with the knowable facts. Last year ended with a bang, not a whimper. Real GNP grew at almost a 7 per cent annual rate at the year-end. Most experts had been expecting more like a 2 per cent rate.

The new year brought snow. No big deal in that. And no surprise that the first-quarter real GNP

Source: Paul A. Samuelson, "The Last Days of the Boom," *Newsweek,* April 30, 1979, p. 58. Condensed from Newsweek. Copyright, 1979, by Newsweek, Inc. All Rights Reserved. Reprinted by Permission.

growth looked weak. In recent weeks, though, the pace seems to have quickened. From autos to machine tools, the word comes that sales are strong. And I speak not of oil and food alone. Firms find they can pass along all cost increases to the buyer.

Congressmen and voters act surprised. That shows how little thought they gave to what their own acts would do to push up prices. Payroll taxes were raised for 1979. So was the minimum wage. Since the Fed has in recent years created enough money for us to spend, and since we are learning how to turn over each unit of our money faster, the flame of cost rises meets with enough tinder to keep a pretty hot fire going.

MADE IN WASHINGTON

Why then do most economists see a recession just ahead? Some argue from strength to weakness. Things are just too good to last, they guess. Consumers have spent for so long, have gone so deeply into debt, that they surely will have to pull in their belts.

Firms now scramble for inventory. As each supplier becomes slow in filling orders, companies turn to other sources, engaging in multiple ordering that imparts a false sense of strength in over-all demand. The rosy hue on entrepreneurial cheeks is the flush of fever, not of sustainable good health.

I monitor some three dozen forecasters, those bank and research teams with past records worth watching. Most of them, I find, see considerable natural strength in the private American economy despite the fact that our present expansion is now a veritable Grandma Moses in age, if not a Methuselah.

The reason they expect a U.S. recession before Election Day 1980 lies mostly in their confidence that the government--the Administration, Congress and the Federal Reserve--will act to cool off the accelerating inflation now at work.

Loudest in singing this tune are the monetarists. What sex is to the single-minded Freudian, the money supply is to the monetarists. Why waste time with 36 experts and 57 sets of statistics when it is the drumbeat of Federal Reserve money creation that alone calls the tune?

If only Freud could deliver the goods he promises. My colleague Robert Solow has termed monetarism an advertising campaign still in search of its product. I must spend much of my time studying the many forces that alter the velocity of circulation of our money supply because sad experience has shown that predictions based solely on the money aggregates suffer needlessly large errors.

Money does matter. The fact that its growth has slowed down markedly since last fall is one of many factors to weigh. But how much weight? At this time there are several different schools of monetarists. Amen to that. There is more to learn from their disagreements than from their *simpliste* formulas.

Fed chairman G. William Miller is not a monetarist. Still, to explain why he has been as slow as he has been in putting on the credit brakes to fight inflation, one must take into account his perception--a correct one--that vocal monetarists will be blaming him for the next recession if it comes in the wake of a declining growth rate for the money supply.

Those who believe that a recession is too high a price to pay for a crusade against inflation are grateful to the monetarists. Like the sight of the piano soloist crossing hands at dramatic crescendos, we face the spectacle of Carter's Keynesian advisers putting pressure on the Fed to tighten up further on credit and money, at the same time that conservative monetarists and full-employment advocates are both opposing those moves.

ELECTION TIMING

Mr. Carter has a special problem—that of getting re-elected. Time is getting short for him to tuck in a mild recession, thereby damping down inflation, and be back in a vigorous recovery during the half year before November 1980.

I know the government has the powers to create a recession—a growth recession or a full-fledged one. I suspect it will find itself increasingly with the will to use those powers. So it is my guess that the natural vigor of the private economy will yield in the end.

Though that needn't be fatal to his cause, it won't be good for Candidate Carter. It will be good for the Republicans—and not bad for Teddy Kennedy.

QUESTIONS

1. In this article, why did Samuelson say that Congress was responsible for rising prices?
2. According to Samuelson, what has happened to the velocity of money? Why does he spend so much time studying it?
3. Does Samuelson believe that money "matters"? Explain.
4. When this article was written, what were President Carter's "Keynesian" advisers advising?
5. Why did Samuelson believe that a recession was likely before November 1980? Was he correct?

IS-LM
ANALYSIS:
AN EXPANSION
OF KEYNES

Keynesian and neoclassical views of monetary and fiscal policy can be summarized through the use of what economists call IS-LM curves. (Neoclassical theories are a modern version of the classical monetary theories.) Before such a summary can be developed, the concepts of IS and LM curves must first be explained.

IS CURVE

An **IS** (short for investment = saving, or $I = S$) **curve** indicates the combinations of net national product and the interest rate that would result in a level of aggregate demand equal to the aggregate quantity supplied in the market for goods and services. We graphically derive the IS curve as shown in Figure D–1.

Panel (a) is a graph with interest rates on the vertical axis and net national product on the horizontal axis. The IS curve is plotted in this panel. The investment demand is drawn as a function of the interest rate in panel (b). The

purpose of panel (c) is to ensure that saving equals investment through the use of a 45-degree line. Panel (d) is a graph of the saving function, $S = -C_0 + (1 - b)Y$, where b is the marginal propensity to consume.

We derive an IS curve in a simple model without government expenditures or taxes as follows.[1] We pick an interest rate such as i_0 in panel (a). We draw a dashed horizontal line until it intersects the investment demand curve, and then we draw a vertical line upward until it intersects the $S = I$ line in panel (c). This point establishes the amount of saving needed for $S_0 = I_0$. Finally, we extend a horizontal line to panel (d) to determine the value of net national product, Y_0, needed to generate a saving of S_0, and we draw a dashed line downward until it intersects with the

---

1. To accommodate taxes and government expenditures in the model we would add the level of government expenditures to investment in panel (b) and graph $S + T$ in panel (d). The axes of panel (c) would then be labeled $I + G$ and $S + T$.

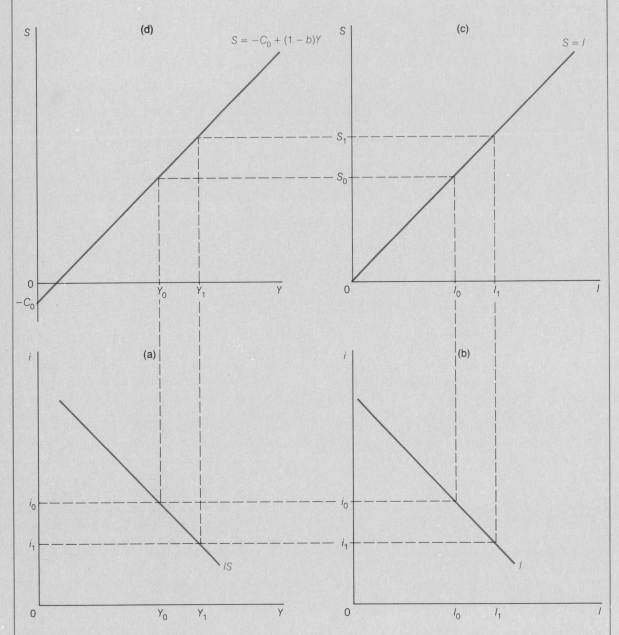

FIGURE D–1 Derivation of the IS Curve

The IS curve can be derived in the following way. First pick an interest rate such as i_0 in panel (a). Draw a horizontal dotted line from i_0 until the investment schedule (I) in panel (b) is reached (at I_0). Then draw a vertical dotted line until the $S = I$ line in panel (c) is reached. Third, draw a horizontal line through S_0 until the saving function is reached, at Y_0. Finally, draw a vertical line downward through Y_0 until it intersects with the horizontal line from i_0. The point formed by the intersection of the two lines is one point on the IS curve. Another point can be found by picking another interest rate and performing the same procedure.

original line drawn from i_0 in panel (a). We have now determined one point on the IS curve. By beginning with other interest rates, such as i_1, we can determine other points on the IS curve.

Note that the IS curve is downward sloping so that *the lower the interest rate, the higher the equilibrium level of income*. This relationship occurs because investment is greater at lower rates of interest, which increases the aggregate quantity demanded.

LM CURVE

◆

The **LM** (short for $L = M$) **curve** shows the combinations of the interest rate and net national product that will equate the quantities of money demanded and supplied. The letter L represents the demand for money, or liquidity, and the letter M represents the supply of money.

Figure D–2 shows an LM curve. As with the IS curve, various interest rates are placed on the vertical axis, and net national product appears on the horizontal axis. Given a linear transactions demand for money, the shape of the LM curve reflects the shape of the speculative demand for money function.

In panel (b), a speculative demand for money □ curve with three distinct regions is sketched. Above interest rate level i_1, no speculative money balances are demanded, because the interest rate is so high that people do not expect it to rise further. Between interest rates i_1 and i_3, as the interest rate falls, greater speculative money balances are demanded. At i_3, the interest rate is so low that people are willing to hold any additional money injected into the economy as speculative balances, since they expect the interest rate to rise in the future. At this point, the liquidity trap is reached.

Panel (c) ensures that the total quantity of money demanded is equal to the supply of money. The quantity of money demanded for

transactions purposes is measured on the vertical axis; the speculative balances are measured on the horizontal axis. The line drawn from m_0 on each axis indicates that the total quantity of money supplied is m_0, and it is drawn so that whatever portion of the money supplied is not demanded for speculative balances will be reflected on the transactions demand for money (M_T) axis.

In Panel (d) the transactions demand for money □ is sketched, with M_T on the vertical axis and net national product on the horizontal axis. Because both the transactions demand and the precautionary demand for money □ are functions of net national product, these two reasons for holding money are combined under the general heading of "transactions demand for money."[2]

To derive the LM curve we use the same procedure as for the IS curve. We pick an interest rate such as i_2 in panel (a) and draw a horizontal line from it into panel (b) to the M_S curve, which indicates that M_{S2} of speculative balances are demanded at an interest rate equal to i_2. Next, we extend a vertical line upward until it intersects with the $m_0 m_0$ line in panel (c). This point will determine M_{T2}, the quantity of transactions money balances necessary for equilibrium in the money market. Now, by drawing a horizontal line over to the M_T curve in panel (d) we can determine the level of net national product required for M_{T2} to be demanded. Finally, by extending a line down through Y_2 into panel (a), we find the point on the LM curve where the horizontal line from i_2 and the vertical line from Y_2 intersect.

By beginning this process with an interest rate equal to i_1, we can determine the starting point of the vertical portion of the LM curve. By beginning with i_3, we can determine the initial point of the horizontal section.

---

2. *Earlier in this chapter, we learned that the transactions demand for money was equal to* $k_1 Y$ *and that the precautionary demand for money was also a function of income. Here both demands for money are combined into one function,* $M_T = kY$.

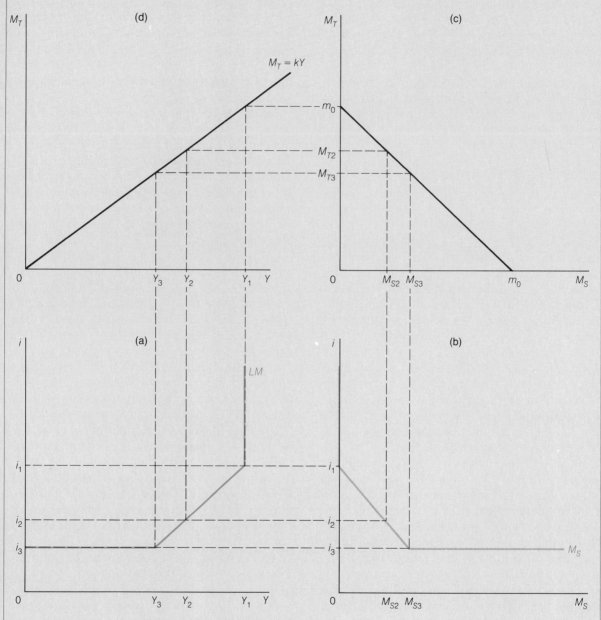

FIGURE D–2 Derivation of the LM Curve

The LM curve can be derived in the following way. First pick an interest rate, such as i_2, in panel (a). Draw a horizontal line from i_2 until it intersects the M_S curve in panel (b) at M_{S2}. Second, draw a vertical line from M_{S2} until it intersects with the money supply (M_0) line in panel (c), at M_{T2}. Now, draw a horizontal line through M_{T2} until it intersects the M_T line in panel (d) at Y_2. Finally, draw a vertical line downward through Y_2 until it intersects the horizontal line from i_2. This national income and interest rate combination (Y_2, i_2) represents one point on the LM curve. Other points on the LM curve could be found in a similar fashion by beginning at interests rates such as i_1 and i_3.

PRODUCT AND MONEY MARKET EQUILIBRIUM

◆

In Figure D–3 an IS curve intersects an LM curve. The figure thus shows the rate of interest and level of net national product that will result in an equilibrium simultaneously in the money market and in the market for goods and services. In this case, the equilibrium position is in the intermediate region of the LM curve, although it could occur in either of the other two regions.

The regions of the LM curve are labeled in accordance with the corresponding regions of the speculative demand for money. We call the vertical region "neoclassical" because no speculative money balances are being held, a situation in accordance with neoclassical theory.

IS-LM ANALYSIS AND FISCAL POLICY

◆

When the government changes the level of government expenditures or taxes, it causes a shift in the IS curve by a horizontal distance equal to the change in government expenditures times the government expenditure multiplier or the change in taxes times the tax multiplier. However, the effect on the equilibrium level of income depends on which region of the LM curve the IS curve intersects.

Figure D–4 shows the effect of an increase in government expenditures or a decrease in taxes in each of the three regions of the LM curve. In each case, IS_i is the initial IS curve and IS_i' is the IS curve after the fiscal policy is instituted. The horizontal distance of the shift in each region is the same.

In the liquidity trap region of the LM curve the equilibrium level of income increases by the full amount of the horizontal shift. In this

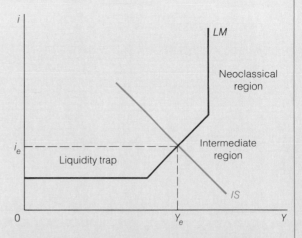

FIGURE D–3 **Equilibrium in the Product and Money Markets**

The national income and interest rate combination that occurs where the IS curve intersects the LM curve will result in equilibrium in both the money and the product markets. In this case, equilibrium occurs when national income is Y_e and the interest rate is i_e.

situation we say that fiscal policy is fully effective.

In the intermediate region the equilibrium level of income rises but not by the full amount of the horizontal shift in the IS curve. The reason that the full multiplier effect is not obtained here is that when income begins to rise as a result of the fiscal policy, more transactions balances are demanded. People try to obtain additional money balances by selling bonds, which lowers the price of bonds and raises the market rate of interest.

The increase in the rate of interest has two effects. First, it reduces the amount of speculative money balances demanded, which leaves more money available for transactions balances. Second, it reduces investment in real assets, which results in a smaller net effect on aggregate quantity demanded and on the equilibrium level of income. This process continues until both the product market and the money market are in equilibrium, at Y_1' in the intermediate region.

In the neoclassical region of the LM curve, fiscal policy is totally ineffective, because the equilibrium level of income does not change.

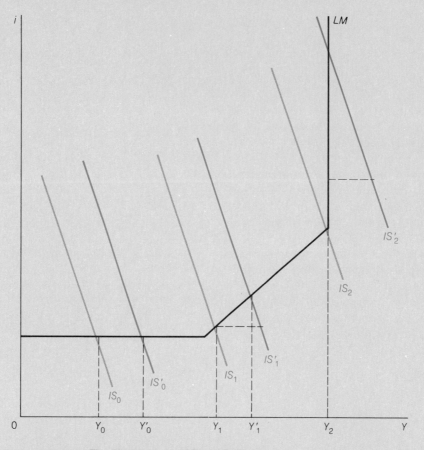

FIGURE D–4   The Effectiveness of Fiscal Policy

This graph illustrates the point that fiscal policy is fully effective in the liquidity trap region, partially effective in the intermediate region, and totally ineffective in the neoclassical region. Note the amount of the shift of the IS curve relative to the size of the change in national income in each region.

This result occurs because there are no speculative money balances that can be reduced to obtain more transactions money balances as the level of income begins to rise. Thus, as people sell bonds, bond prices fall and interest rates rise, but the only effect of the interest rate change now is to reduce investment. This process continues until investment is reduced by an amount sufficient to exactly offset the effect of the fiscal policy action. In this case we get the result that the monetarists expect from fiscal policy: Government spending merely results in a crowding out of private spending.

Thus we find that fiscal policy is most effec-tive in the liquidity trap region and least effec-tive in the neoclassical region. In the next sec-tion we will see that monetary policy is most effective in the neoclassical region.

IS-LM ANALYSIS
AND
MONETARY POLICY

Figure D–5 shows the effect of an increase in the money supply on the LM curve. As the money supply is increased, the LM curve

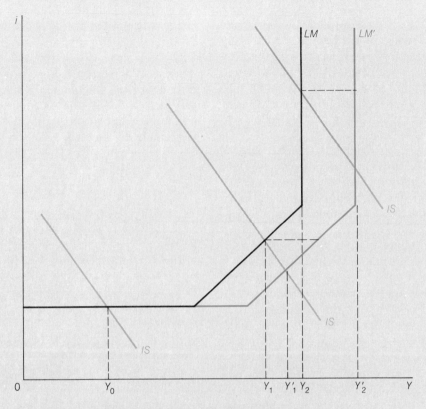

FIGURE D–5 **The Effectiveness of Monetary Policy**

This graph illustrates the point that monetary policy is totally ineffective in the liquidity trap region, partially effective in the intermediate region, and fully effective in the neoclassical region. Note the amount of the shift of the LM curve relative to the size of the change in national income in each region.

shifts from *LM* to *LM'*.[3] In the liquidity trap region the increase in the supply of money has no effect on the equilibrium level of income, which remains constant at Y_0. Thus in the liquidity trap region monetary policy is totally ineffective.

In the intermediate region the equilibrium level of income increases from Y_1 to Y_1', but the increase is not as large as the horizontal shift in the LM curve. As the money supply is increased, people have greater money balances than they desire, so they attempt to buy bonds. This action raises the price of bonds, which lowers the market rate of interest.

The decrease in the market rate of interest has two effects in this region. First, investment expenditures increase, which increases income and, consequently, the quantity demanded of transactions money balances. Second, the quantity demanded of speculative money balances increases. This process continues until the quantity of money demanded is once again equal to the quantity supplied.

In the neoclassical region, monetary policy is totally effective. The equilibrium level of income increases from Y_2 to Y_2', the full amount of the horizontal shift in the LM curve. In this case, as the quantity of money supplied is increased and people bid up the price of bonds, causing the interest rate to fall, there is only one effect. Investment ex-

---

3. If $M_T = kY$, then the horizontal shift must be equal to $\Delta Y = (1/k)\Delta M$.

penditures rise, increasing income and the quantity demanded of transactions balances. Since a decrease in the interest rate in this region will not induce people to hold greater speculative money balances, income must increase enough so that all the additional money generated by the monetary policy is demanded as transactions balances.

To summarize, fiscal policy is most effective in the liquidity trap region of the LM curve and is totally ineffective in the neoclassical region. On the other hand, monetary policy is most effective in the neoclassical region and is totally ineffective in the liquidity trap region. Both monetary and fiscal policy are partially effective in the intermediate region.

Which type of policy should the government use? The answer to this question obviously depends in part on whether the economy is in the liquidity trap, the intermediate, or the neoclassical region of the LM curve. If the economy is in the intermediate region, the choice between fiscal and monetary policy will likely depend on other goals and values of the policy makers. If monetary policy is used, the total effect on aggregate demand

will be generated through changes in private sector investment spending. If fiscal policy is used, changes in government spending or taxes will affect both aggregate demand and the size of the federal budget surplus or deficit. In either case the distribution of income and the composition of the national product will likely be affected.

QUESTIONS

1. What does the IS curve represent? The LM curve?

2. How are the liquidity trap, intermediate, and neoclassical regions of the LM curve different? Explain.

3. Explain what happens when the government uses fiscal policy.

4. In what region of the LM curve is fiscal policy most effective? Least effective? Explain.

5. Explain how a change in the money supply affects the LM curve.

6. In what region of the LM curve is monetary policy most effective? Least effective? Explain.

ECONOMIC ORIGINS III

THE PATH TO MODERN MACROECONOMICS

Adam Smith and his nineteenth century followers, the classical economists, wrote a great deal about individual behavior, prices, and markets, but their main concern was economic progress and the policies that would foster it. Oddly enough, their prescription turned out to be one of as little policy as possible. Government, they said, frequently does more harm than good. People know what they want, and left to their own devices they will maximize social well-being by maximizing individual well-being. Laissez-faire was their rule; free markets and free will would ensure the best possible performance of the economy.

Starkly absent from the work of the classical economists is any enduring analysis of the problem of unemployment. The economists recognized voluntary unemployment, which was simply the choice not to work at the market equilibrium wage rate. They also recognized seasonal unemployment as characteristic of certain kinds of work, but they argued that the market wage rate for such jobs would take into account idleness and uncertainty of employment. Any kind of unemployment that today would be viewed as cycli-

cal (caused by business cycles) was viewed by the classical economists as temporary. John Stuart Mill's *Principles of Political Economy* does not contain the word *unemployment* in its index. Even the giant of the neoclassical school, Alfred Marshall, made only brief references to unemployment in his turn-of-the-century masterwork, *Principles of Economics* (1890).[1]

Underlying the classical and neoclassical views on unemployment was **Say's law,** which was seriously questioned only by Malthus. As indicated in Part II, Say's law stated that there could never be a deficiency of aggregate demand—that production in and of itself would create sufficient demand for all output. Furthermore, since people produced output for either their own consumption or to exchange for other goods and services, not working implied that one's wants were already satisfied. Everyone who wanted to work, or was willing and able to work,

---

1. The neoclassical school in Great Britain begins with the work of Marshall, who attributed value, or price, to the interaction of supply and demand.

271

Jean B. Say

Karl Marx

would be employed. The neoclassical economists argued that labor unions could fix wages high enough to cause unemployment in a specific trade or industry but that this was a market imperfection that would eventually just shift workers from one employment to another. Still, a number of nineteenth and early twentieth century economists continued to argue the case for a general glut, or oversupply, of goods. They became known as underconsumptionists.

The Underconsumptionists did not constitute a school of economic thought or offer a consistent explanation for a deficiency of aggregate demand. The fact of such deficiency was the only thing they held in common. In short, they must be viewed as a group of individuals, many of whom were not contemporaries and did not communicate with one another, whose views conflicted with Say's law. The underconsumptionists, by and large, were inferior to the classical and neoclassical economists as theoreticians, but they may have been more adept than the latter at seeing what was going on around them. Between 1814 and 1901, there were ten identifiable recessions in Britain and seven in the United States. While all this

went on, economists in the classical tradition stood by Say's law. Even as late as 1920, Marshall, in his eighth edition of *Principles,* rather offhandedly acknowledged that recessions do occur, but he attributed them almost exclusively to a lack of confidence. A revival begins "as soon as traders think that prices will not continue to fall."[2]

Besides Malthus, only three of the underconsumptionists merit discussion here. They are **Jean Simonde de Sismondi** (1773–1842), **Karl Marx** (1818–1883), and **John Hobson** (1858–1940). Sismondi, who was born in Switzerland, traveled extensively in England and became a critic of the classical school. He believed that competition gave rise to a rivalry between large firms and small and between capitalists and workers. Large firms would reduce their costs by investing in labor-saving machinery. In the process, small firms would be eliminated and workers would be displaced. Production would outrun the ability of consumers to purchase output, and the result would

---

2. Alfred Marshall, *Principles of Economics,* 8th ed. (London: Macmillian, 1920), p. 592.

be a depression. Sismondi's argument was repeated in dramatic tones by Marx, who wrote:

The enormous power, inherent in the factory system, of expanding by jumps, and the dependence of that system on the markets of the world, necessarily begets feverish production, followed by over-filling of the markets, whereupon contraction of the markets brings on the crippling of production.[3]

In Sismondi's view, depressions and their effects could be mitigated by social changes that would provide income security for workers. In fact, he proposed a guaranteed annual wage as well as benefit plans for sick and aged workers. Marx, on the other hand, saw revolution as the inevitable outcome of increasingly severe depressions.[4] Neither Marx nor Sismondi recognized the possibility that increases in investment might generate sufficient aggregate demand to keep the economy at full employment.

John Hobson, a contemporary of John Maynard Keynes, was a prolific writer whose hastily compiled works often reaped severe criticism. His underconsumption theory was developed in two books, *The Physiology of Industry* (1889, with A. F. Mummery), and *The Industrial System* (1904). Hobson, like other underconsumptionists, argued that capitalist expansion could result in a tendency for producton to outrun aggregate demand. However, he embellished the argument considerably by explaining more thoroughly why oversaving might take place. A wage lag, he said, was at the bottom of the problem, because capitalists, with superior bargaining power, would turn the distribution of income in their favor as expansion occurred. Thus, what Keynes later labeled the marginal propensity to consume would fall, and consumption would drop. Hobson described a subsequent severe drop in output and employment, in which he anticipated the modern-day discussions of both the multiplier and the acceleration thesis. However, Hobson's theory was never developed in terms satisfactory to mainstream economists before the 1930s, and these economists viewed him as a heretic.

Monetary and Business Cycle Theories advanced in the late nineteenth and early twentieth centuries along lines that attempted to explain fluctuations in economic activity and employment. The classical economists had argued that "money is a veil" and has no effect on production or employment. All increases in the quantity of money would result only in increases in the price level, according to their version of the quantity theory of money. In fact, this view was expressed by David Hume in the eighteenth century, and it remained popular into the twentieth century. In 1911 **Irving Fisher,** an American economist and statistician, reformulated it in mathematical terms.

Fisher's "equation of exchange" states that $MV = PT$, where M is the stock of money in circulation, V is velocity of circulation, or how many times money changes hands, P is the aggregate price level, and T is an index of the volume of transactions. For Fisher, V and T were independent of the money supply, so changes in M led to proportional changes in P. In England the Cambridge school of neoclassical economists, led by Alfred Marshall, used a slightly different formulation of the quantity theory, known as the Cambridge equation.

Irving Fisher

3. Karl Marx, *Capital*, trans. Samuel Moore and Edward Aveling (1867, 1885–1894; New York: Modern Library, 1906), p. 495.
4. Marx's ideas on the decline of capitalism are discussed in Chapters 15 and 32 of this text.

Neither Fisher's equation nor the Cambridge version gave any role to the interest rate, which in classical and neoclassical theory was believed to be determined by productivity and thrift. Although some early economists recognized that a lowering of the interest rate below the "natural rate" (the rate determined by productivity and thrift) would lead to an increase in investment, they used this fact to argue that the interest rate would return to its natural level and largely ignored the effect of increased investment on output.

Swedish economist **Knut Wicksell** (1851–1926) is noted for having argued, in 1901, that a fall in the interest rate would inevitably lead to an increase in aggregate demand and output. However, he did not depart radically from classical monetary theory; in his model an increase in bank lending eventually causes prices to rise. It remained for **John Maynard Keynes** (1883–1946) to explain the money supply–interest rate–investment links that constitute such an important part of modern views on aggregate demand. However, two of Keynes's contemporaries, Ralph Hawtrey and Dennis H. Robertson, would contribute to the development of such a line of reasoning.

Hawtrey and Robertson were friends of Keynes, and both of them read and criticized drafts of his *General Theory*. Robertson, who published books on business fluctuations and monetary economics in 1915, 1922, and 1926, described a precarious equilibrium level of the money supply that would be consistent with both saving and investment plans. Since this level was difficult to maintain, business cycles would occur. Hawtrey, writing in 1926, attributed the expansion phase of cycles to inventory investment caused by low interest rates (monetary expansion) and the contraction phase to a drop in bank lending caused by a cash lag. The cash lag would occur as wage earners, who have a preference for ready cash, drained banks of reserves during the late stages of an expansion. Thus both Robertson and Hawtrey ad-

John Maynard Keynes

vanced arguments that would stimulate Keynes's ideas on the role of the money supply in economic fluctuations.

Keynesian theory has occupied center stage in macroeconomics since the publication of *The General Theory,* in 1936. Keynes, who was a literary buff, intellectual, and journalist as well as an economist, predicted in a 1935 letter to the famous writer George Bernard Shaw that his book would "largely revolutionise . . . the way the world thinks about economic problems."[5] He was right. Economics is now in an epoch that can be called only by the name post-Keynesian.

---

5. As quoted in Ben B. Seligman, *Main Currents in Modern Economics,* vol. 3 (Chicago: Quadrangle Books, 1971), p. 730.

PART FIVE

THE
ECONOMICS OF
STAGFLATION,
BUSINESS CYCLES,
AND GROWTH

C H A P T E R   13

GOVERNMENT
POLICY
AND THE
INFLATIONARY
RECESSION

UNEMPLOYMENT AND THE "GREAT INFLATION"

Senior citizens often tell us about the Great Depression of the 1930s—breadlines, shantytowns, and "Brother, can you spare a dime?" What we have had in the 1970s and the early 1980s is beginning to be known as the Great Inflation. How will it be characterized in years to come? Gas lines, condo booms, and "Brother, can you spare a food stamp?"

When did the Great Inflation start? Some people say it was as early as 1965, even though prices were increasing at only about 2 percent per year and the Kennedy tax cuts together with the beginning of the Vietnam War had apparently created an economic boom. The unemployment rate dropped below 4 percent in 1966, and from then until the recession of 1970, the inflation rate crept upward, but not alarmingly. Then, in 1973 and 1974, in the face of relatively high levels of unemployment (4.9 percent and 5.6 percent, respectively), the inflation rate rose first to 6.2 percent and then to 11 percent. From then on, both persistently high unemployment, in the 6 to 8.5 percent range, and consistent inflation of 6.5 to over 12 percent per year have been a fact of American life.[1]

Data for most of the twentieth century show that the U.S. economy conformed fairly well to the Keynesian notion that either unemployment or inflation would be the principal economic problem, but only recently have both problems appeared at the same time. Lately, the inflation scare has attracted more attention than has unemployment. The reason is that people are insulated from

---

1. Data are from U.S. Department of Commerce, Bureau of the Census, *Statistical Abstract of the United States*, (Washington, D.C.: Government Printing Office, 1980), various pages.

the rigors of unemployment much more now than they were in the past.

For example, in mid 1980, more than 185,000 U.S. auto industry workers were laid off, but many of them received supplemental unemployment benefits (SUBs) while off work because of a system set up between the major auto firms and the United Auto Workers union. Many auto workers were eligible to receive SUBs for up to a year at 90 percent of their normal take-home pay.[2] Thus, while they were producing nothing, they had income to spend on the output of other workers. This phenomenon, of course, contributed to the inflation that accompanied the unemployment.

Other features of the modern U.S. economy (federal unemployment benefits, welfare, a changing work force, and adjustments related to international trade) also tend to lessen labor's fear of unemployment while possibly aggravating inflation. Factors such as the energy crisis and crop failures make matters worse. All these things suggest that the United States may either have to live with higher rates of inflation and unemployment than it had during the 1950s and 1960s or develop new policies to get inflation and unemployment down to lower levels. In this chapter such alternatives are discussed in detail.

2. "Ford Will Close Every U.S. Plant But One Next Week," *Wall Street Journal*, July 3, 1980, p. 3.

C H A P T E R 13

GOVERNMENT POLICY AND THE INFLATIONARY RECESSION

WHAT THIS CHAPTER IS ABOUT

CONVENTIONAL POLICY CONFLICTS
DEMAND-PULL VERSUS COST-PUSH
 INFLATION
INFLATION-UNEMPLOYMENT TRADE-OFF
Phillips Curve
Types of Unemployment
Accelerationist Hypothesis
Distribution of Unemployment
SOME INTERNATIONAL DIMENSIONS OF
 INFLATION
Inflation and Energy
Inflation and International Trade

POSSIBLE SOLUTIONS TO INFLATIONARY
 RECESSIONS
Monetary and Fiscal Policies
Wage and Price Guideposts
Wage and Price Controls
Labor Policies
SUPPLY-SIDE ECONOMICS

In the last few chapters we have seen how monetary and fiscal policy can affect the levels of national income and employment. An increase in the money supply, an increase in government spending, or a decrease in taxes can diminish the impact of a recession or depression by increasing aggregate demand. Conversely, a decrease in the money supply, a decrease in government spending, or an increase in taxes can reduce aggregate demand, thereby diminishing inflationary forces.

CONFLICTS OF CONVENTIONAL POLICY

◆

In theory, monetary and fiscal policy prescriptions are pretty clear-cut. They are able to handle recessions and fight inflations. Unfortunately, the real world complicates this pleasant scenario with an unexpected puzzle. What can be done with an **inflationary recession**—inflation and falling GNP, or at least unemployment, at the same time? Such a problem has haunted us since the early 1970s.

An inflationary recession presents a real conundrum for economic policy makers, because the policies that fight inflation tend to worsen recessions, and vice versa. In fact, until the 1950s, most economists did not expect inflation and significant amounts of unemployment to occur together for very long periods of time. They thought unemployment was an indication of an insufficient aggregate quantity demanded at a full employment level of income. They believed inflation to be an indication of excess demand. Thus they viewed the two problems as mutually exclusive and therefore manageable.

In the remainder of the chapter some economic explanations of how it is possible to have both inflation and recession will be discussed, and some possible solutions to the problem will be presented.

DEMAND-PULL VERSUS COST-PUSH INFLATION

◆

As explained in Chapter 12, classical and neoclassical economists thought that price in-

creases would occur in direct proportion to increases in the money supply or as a result of excess demand. Modern-day monetarists hold similar views. Keynesian economists believe that the causes of inflation are more complex.

Until recently, most economists of all schools of thought believed that inflation occurred when the aggregate quantity demanded was greater than the aggregate quantity supplied.

*Price increases resulting from excess demand are called **demand-pull inflation**.*

In recent years, however, many economists have argued that inflation can be caused even during periods of unemployment by an increase in wage rates or other business costs that encourage firms to raise prices. For example, Abba Lerner states: "Prices may rise because of pressures by sellers who insist on raising their prices even though they may find it not especially easy to sell. We would then have not a buyer-induced inflation but a seller-induced inflation."[1]

How could wage rates increase in the presence of unemployment? The usual argument is that strong unions demanding wage rate increases makes this phenomenon possible. Moreover, it is asserted that many large corporations set prices in accordance with a certain markup on costs, rather than following profit-maximizing decision rules that take both cost and demand into account in determining the optimal price.[2]

---

1. Abba P. Lerner, "Inflationary Depression and the Regulation of Administered Prices," *The Relationship of Prices to Economic Stability and Growth, Compendium of Papers Submitted by Panelists Appearing before the Joint Economic Committee,* 85th Congress, Second Session (Washington, D.C.: Government Printing Office, 1958), pp. 257–268; reprinted in M. G. Mueller, ed., *Readings in Macroeconomics* (New York: Holt, Rinehart and Winston, 1966), p. 362.

2. Profit-maximizing decision rules are discussed in detail in Chapter 19.

Price increases occurring as a result of rising costs, including higher markups, are termed **cost-push inflation,** or **seller's inflation.**

Nevertheless, cost-push inflation is not the only factor responsible for inflation and unemployment occurring together. Another aspect of the problem is considered in the next section.

THE INFLATION-UNEMPLOYMENT TRADE-OFF

Since the late 1950s much of the writing of economists has been concerned with the possibility of a wage rate growth or inflation-unemployment trade-off. In other words, lower levels of unemployment can be achieved only by incurring higher rates of inflation.

The term **Phillips curve,** in honor of A. W. Phillips, who did pioneering work in this area, is frequently used to denote wage rate growth (or inflation)–unemployment trade-off relationships.

THE PHILLIPS CURVE

In 1958 an article published in *Economica* made significant inroads in the economic thought of the time. It was written by a British economist, A. W. Phillips. In this article Phillips cited evidence in support of a wage rate growth–unemployment trade-off. He found that in Great Britain, especially during the years 1861–1913, a relatively stable nonlinear relationship appeared to exist between unemployment rates and wage rate growth, as shown in Figure 13–1.[3]

3. A. W. Phillips, "The Relation between Unemployment and the Rate of Change of Money Wage Rates in the United Kingdom, 1861–1957," *Economica* New Series 25 (November 1958): 283–299.

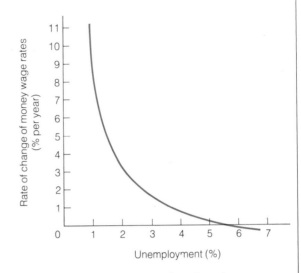

FIGURE 13–1 Phillips' Wage Rate Growth–Unemployment Trade-off for Great Britain, 1861–1913

In Phillips' relationship, the rate of wage rate growth was lower the higher the level of unemployment. However, the percent growth in wage rates did not reach zero until unemployment was above 5 percent.

Why was this idea so earthshaking? According to commonly accepted notions of the day, unemployment was an indication of an excess quantity supplied of labor and wage rates should fall, or at least not rise, when unemployment was present.

Actually, Keynes believed that because of wage rate rigidity in a downward direction, money wage rates would not fall very rapidly, if at all, in the short run. This downward rigidity is the result of two factors—union contracts and money illusion on the part of workers.

Money illusion refers to the situation where workers behave as if their money wage rate matters more than their real wage rate.

The real wage rate is the money wage rate adjusted for price changes. Recall how real GNP □ is derived from money GNP. According to the Keynesian argument, even when prices fall, workers are reluctant to accept lower money wage rates. This behavior is rational to some extent, because many of the workers'

obligations are stated in terms of the previously higher money prices. Examples are mortgage payments and other loan obligations incurred before the price decrease.

However, contrary to the generally accepted view, Phillips' data seemed to indicate that wage rate growth would not be zero until the unemployment rate reached 5.5 percent. Phillips thought that if labor productivity increased by 2 percent a year, prices would remain stable at an unemployment rate of about 2.5 percent. Since the publication of Phillips's research, other economists have found evidence of Phillips curves for various countries, including the United States.[4] (Some of these relationships are couched in terms of inflation-unemployment trade-offs rather than wage rate growth–unemployment trade-offs. The connection between wage rate growth and inflation is that when wage rates grow faster than labor productivity, inflation will likely occur. Thus, the more rapidly wage rates grow, the greater inflation.)

Economists were disturbed by the prospect of having to accept some unemployment in order to maintain a stable price level. They were consoled, though, by evidence which seemed to indicate that the wage rate growth–unemployment trade-off was relatively stable, so at least they had a predictable set of choices from which to pick.

THE LABOR FORCE AND UNEMPLOYMENT

Before proceeding any further, we should examine the official U.S. government definitions of *labor force* and *unemployment*. Each

month the Bureau of the Census conducts its Current Population Survey of a sample of U.S. households to gather information about the employment and earnings of people in the labor force. It also uses business payroll records for this purpose. The **civilian labor force** consists of people who are classified as employed or unemployed according to the following definitions.

Employed persons are (1) all civilians who, during the survey week, did a minimum of an hour's work for pay or profit or who worked fifteen hours or more as unpaid workers in a family enterprise, and (2) all persons who were not working but who had jobs or businesses from which they were temporarily absent for noneconomic reasons such as illness, bad weather, vacation, or a labor-management dispute.

Unemployed persons are (1) all civilians who had no employment during the survey week, who had made specific efforts to find a job (such as by applying directly to an employer or to a public employment service or by checking with friends) within the previous four weeks, and who were available for work during the survey week; and (2) persons laid off from a job or waiting to report to a new job within thirty days.[5]

The **total labor force** consists of the civilian labor force and all the people in the armed forces.

As can be seen from these definitions, the categories of employed and unemployed persons are broadly defined. It takes very little paid work to make one "employed," and it takes relatively little job search effort to make one "unemployed" rather than "not a member of the labor force."

4. See, for example, the following, Bent Hansen, "Excess Demand, Unemployment, and Wages," *Quarterly Journal of Economics* 84 (February 1970): 1–23; Richard G. Lipsey, "The Relation between Unemployment and the Rate of Change of Money Wage Rates in the United Kingdom, 1862–1957: A Further Analysis," *Economica* 27 (February 1960): 1–31; and G. L. Perry, *Unemployment, Money Wage Rates and Inflation* (Cambridge, Mass.: M.I.T. Press, 1966).

5. U.S. Department of Commerce, Bureau of the Census, *Statistical Abstract of the United States*, 1978 (Washington, D.C.: Government Printing Office, 1978), p. 396.

TYPES OF UNEMPLOYMENT

Economists, not the federal government, have divided unemployed workers into three general categories: the frictionally unemployed, the structurally unemployed, and the cyclically unemployed. We will examine each of these types of unemployment in turn.[6] As we shall explain, an understanding of the various types of unemployment may shed some light on the inflation-unemployment phenomenon.

Frictional Unemployment According to one definition, **frictional unemployment** refers to

workers who are unemployed due to "standard" market adjustments. . . . Standard market adjustments refer to those situations in which workers enter the job market with little experience, quit jobs voluntarily to look for better ones, or are released from employment due to employer-employee dissatisfaction, strikes, seasonal factors, or business failures unrelated to changes in aggregate or relative demand.

. . . If he [the worker] had complete information on all alternative employment opportunities, he could take the best job situation, but the absence of such information requires costly search and/or relocation. Strikes, bad weather conditions, a jump in the number of random business failures, increased random worker entry, and worsening overall employer-employee relations lead to higher frictional unemployment and a higher normal rate of unemployment.[7]

Frictional unemployment is generally seen as temporary in nature and a result of inadequate information regarding job opportunities. Policy makers therefore are not generally as concerned about it as they are about other types of unemployment. Frictional unemployment is not thought to be caused by inadequate aggregate demand.

Structural Unemployment Structural unemployment is also not generally considered to be caused by inadequate aggregate demand.

> *Structural unemployment occurs when unemployed workers do not have the skills or other attributes required for the available jobs.*

Such unemployment is a persistent problem. In this case, the solution appears to lie in training of the unemployed rather than in general macroeconomic policies geared toward aggregate demand. In practice, however, it is often difficult to distinguish fully between structural unemployment and cyclical unemployment, discussed in the next section.

The increased participation in the labor force of women and minority workers as a result of the Civil Rights Act of 1964 has resulted in an unusually rapid growth in the number of people looking for work. Because women and minorities tend to have fewer job skills and less education (this situation is slowly changing), their entrance into the labor market has increased the level of structural unemployment. Recent increases in the rate of immigration of residents from other countries to the United States has also been a factor in the current problem. Many economists believe that the minimum wage law has further aggravated the situation for these people and for the young, another group with high unemployment rates. These matters are discussed more fully in Chapter 25.

Cyclical Unemployment The unemployment that policy makers have in mind when they talk about monetary and fiscal policies is cyclical unemployment.

> *Cyclical unemployment is caused by a deficiency of aggregate demand. Thus it can be reduced through macroeconomic policies designed to increase the general level of aggregate demand.*

---

6. For a more thorough discussion of the various types of unemployment, see Gordon F. Bloom and Herbert R. Northrup, *Economics of Labor Relations*, 5th ed. (Homewood, Ill.: Richard D. Irwin, 1965), pp. 432–452.

7. Roger N. Spencer, "High Employment without Inflation: On the Attainment of Admirable Goals," *Federal Reserve Bank of St. Louis Monthly Review*, Vol. 52 (September, 1971), pp. 17–18.

In practice, it is difficult to completely separate the unemployed into the three categories, because even frictional and structural unemployment may be reduced to some extent in a booming economy. However, determining the primary nature of the existing unemployment is crucial to the formation of appropriate national macroeconomic policies, as we will now see.

AN OUTDATED PHILLIPS CURVE?

In recent years there has been some evidence that the Phillips curve relationships may be shifting, at least in the United States, so that a higher inflation rate is associated with a given unemployment rate.[8] Various explanations have been advanced to explain this shift.

The Accelerationist Hypothesis In general, monetarists argue that a stable Phillips curve is an illusion. According to Milton Friedman, the following process will occur when policy makers try to reduce the unemployment rate below the "natural" rate:

Let us assume that the monetary authority tries to peg the "market" rate of unemployment at a level below the "natural" rate. For definiteness, suppose that it takes 3 per cent as the target rate and the "natural" rate is higher than 3 per cent. Suppose also that we start out at a time when prices have been stable and when unemployment is higher than 3 per cent. Accordingly, the authority increases the rate of monetary growth. This will be expansionary. By making nominal cash balances higher than people desire, it will tend initially to lower interest rates and in this and other ways stimulate spending. Income and spending will start to rise.

To begin with, much or most of the rise in income will take the form of an increase in output and employment rather than in prices. People have been expecting prices to be stable, and prices and wages have been set for some time in the future on

that basis. It takes time for people to adjust to a new state of demand. Producers will tend to react to the initial expansion in aggregate demand by increasing output, employees by working longer hours, and the unemployed, by taking jobs now offered at former nominal wages. This much is pretty standard doctrine.

But it describes only the initial effects. Because selling prices of products typically respond to an unanticipated rise in nominal demand faster than prices of factors of production, real wages received have gone down—though real wages anticipated by employees went up, since employees implicitly evaluated the wages offered at the earlier price level. Indeed, the simultaneous fall ex post in real wages to employers and rise ex ante in real wages to employees is what enabled employment to increase. But the decline ex post in real wages will soon come to affect anticipations. Employees will start to reckon on rising prices of the things they buy and to demand higher nominal wages for the future. "Market" unemployment is below the "natural" level. There is an excess demand for labor so real wages will tend to rise toward their initial level.

Even though the higher rate of monetary growth continues, the rise in real wages will reverse the decline in unemployment, and then lead to a rise, which will tend to return unemployment to its former level. In order to keep unemployment at its target level of 3 per cent, the monetary authority would have to raise monetary growth still more. As in the interest rate case, the "market" rate can be kept below the "natural" rate only by inflation. And, as in the interest rate case, too, only by acclerating inflation.[9]

According to the **accelerationist hypothesis** as presented by Friedman, perceived inflation, or wage rate growth, and unemployment trade-offs are merely short-run phenomena. As government authorities attempt to reduce and keep unemployment below the natural rate, workers will demand greater wage rate increases.

Although inflation can fool workers with regard to their real wage (the wage rate adjusted for price changes), eventually the workers

8. See Lila Flory, "Stability of the Phillips Curve and the Accelerationist Hypothesis: Recent Microeconomic Evidence," *Quarterly Review of Economics and Business* 14 (Autumn 1974): 35–45.

9. Milton Friedman, "The Role of Monetary Policy," *American Economic Review* 58 (March 1968): pp. 9–10.

will take past inflation into account when they make their wage rate demands. As a result, the short-run Phillips curve will shift upward, as shown in Figure 13–2. In this case, the long-run Phillips curve is a vertical line at the natural rate of unemployment. Friedman's explanation hinges on his assumption that government policy makers are attempting to reduce unemployment below the natural rate. But what is the "natural" rate of unemployment?

*The **natural rate of unemployment** is the rate of unemployment that is consistent with a minimal level of frictional unemployment. Essentially, then, when the economy is at the natural rate of unemployment, it is at full employment.*

Put in this context, Friedman's argument is that if the government attempts to increase employment *above full employment*, we can expect accelerating (ever-increasing rates of) inflation to be the inevitable result. That such a result would occur from that type of policy is not surprising. What is difficult to comprehend is why policy makers would attempt such a thing in the first place. Their goal is

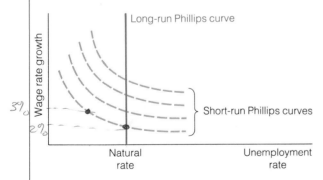

FIGURE 13–2 The Accelerationist View of the Phillips Curve

According to the accelerationist view of the Phillips curve, the short run Phillips curve shifts upward as people expect more inflation to occur. As a result, the long-run Phillips curve is a vertical line at the natural rate of unemployment. Presumably, it would be impossible to reduce unemployment below that rate in the long run.

presumably to keep the economy at or close to full employment, but *not above it*.

Rational Expectations Hypothesis The rational expectations hypothesis goes even further than the accelerationist argument does.

*The **rational expectations hypothesis** states that people take current· information about government economic policies and other economic variables as well as events in the recent past into account when formulating their expectations about future events.*

Economists who adhere to the rational expectations point of view accept the notion that people take past events into account when they develop expectations about future events. For example, people may base their expectations of future rates of inflation on past rates of inflation. The **adaptive theory of expectations** states that people's expectations of future events are formulated by their observing and projecting foward the events of the recent past.

The rational expectations hypothesis is broader than the adaptive expectations hypothesis. It asserts that while people do consider events of the recent past when forming their expectations about the future, they also take into account current information about government monetary and fiscal policies and other factors affecting economic variables. According to proponents of the rational expectations hypothesis, people have more nearly accurate expectations about the future course of such phenomena as inflation when they take the additional data into account than when they merely project past events into the future. Thus, if the government attempted to keep employment above the full employment level through monetary and fiscal policies that would result in accelerating inflation, workers would quickly comprehend what was happening and would adjust their inflationary expectations and therefore their money wage demands accordingly.

As a result, monetary and fiscal policies would not even temporarily increase employment, because workers would not be fooled about the real wage. (An exception to this rule could occur if the government instituted some totally unexpected policies.) Thus proponents of the rational expectations philosophy believe, as do most monetarists, that discretionary monetary and fiscal policies are worthless, or even worse. They argue that inflation can be eliminated with a policy of steady growth in the money supply at a prescribed rate (perhaps 3 or 4 percent per year) to accommodate growth in the economy. They also believe, as do the monetarists, that if involuntary unemployment exists, it will do so for only a short time. Thus it is not a serious problem.

In 1981 rational expectations theorists were saying that President Reagan's proposed tax and government spending reductions would have a quick anti-inflationary impact because workers would expect them to be effective in reducing inflation and would therefore reduce their demands for money wage rate increases. Also, lenders would reduce nominal interest rates to correspond with their new expectations. However, by the early fall of 1981 the interest rate had not fallen as quickly as had been predicted.

As noted earlier, it does not seem reasonable to assume that policy makers have the reduction of unemployment below the full employment level as their goal. (They might, however, misestimate the level of unemployment that corresponds to full employment.) Nevertheless, there is another explanation for the observed changes in the wage rate growth (or inflation)–unemployment trade-off, as presented next.

The Distribution of Unemployment In recent years economists have more greatly appreciated the complexity of the economies of most developed nations. As already explained, in simple Keynesian macroeconomic analysis it was assumed that if unemployment existed, across-the-board measures to increase aggregate demand would correct the problem. On the other hand, if prices were rising, general policies to reduce aggregate demand would

eliminate the inflation. It appears now, however, that the economy frequently cannot be so easily managed. Why not?

We have looked at the various types of unemployment and their significance. As we can guess from that discussion, it is possible for some types of labor to be experiencing 10 or 12 percent or even higher levels of unemployment while others are experiencing only a 2 or 3 percent level of unemployment.

For example, in 1976 the unemployment rate for nonfarm male laborers aged twenty to twenty-four years was 13.2 percent, and the rate for private household workers of the same age group was 18.7 percent. In contrast, the unemployment rate for professional and technical workers of all ages averaged 2.6 percent. For those forty-five years of age and older the unemployment rate was 1.9 percent. For male craft and kindred workers the unemployment rate was 6.8 percent. The corresponding unemployment rates for females were usually slightly higher. The overall unemployment rate was 7.7 percent.[10]

Why is the **distribution of unemployment** so important? For one thing, because of the way it affects wage rate growth. Suppose, for example, that all types of labor experienced equal unemployment rates of 7.7 percent. We would expect very little upward pressure on wage rates. On the other hand, suppose the economy were in a situation where the unemployment rate for some types of labor was around 2 percent and for other types was around 18 percent. In this case we would expect a great deal of pressure for wage rate increases from those types of labor experiencing little unemployment.

However, would there likely be corresponding wage rate decreases for the types of labor experiencing large amounts of unemployment? The answer is no. As discussed earlier, money

10. U.S. Department of Labor, Bureau of Labor Statistics, "Table 59: Unemployment Rates and Percent Distribution of the Unemployed, by Age, Sex, and Major Occupational Group, 1967–76," *Handbook of Labor Statistics: 1977* (Washington, D.C.: Government Printing Office, 1977), p. 124.

wage rates tend to be rigid, or at least "sticky," in a downward direction. Thus, even if the average unemployment rate is 7.7 percent, *because of the manner in which it is distributed, the economy will likely experience wage rate increases.* An increase in the level of structural unemployment could certainly result in this phenomenon; indeed, as discussed earlier, there is reason to believe such an increase has occurred in recent years.

Some economic research supports the hypothesis that shifts in the Phillips curve have occurred as a result of changes in the distribution of unemployment.[11] However, these studies do not include data from the late 1970s, when additional factors may have become significant.

A similar phenomenon could occur with regard to prices, since prices also frequently are sticky in a downward direction. Consequently, if there is an excess quantity demanded of some items and an excess quantity supplied of others, the net effect is likely to be upward pressure on prices. Furthermore, since the contracts of many union members and many government employees specify cost-of-living wage increases, an increase in prices results in an automatic increase in wage rates, which causes still further price increases, and the cycle continues.

In recent years, price increases of products made from petroleum and natural gas have greatly affected the U.S. rate of inflation. This point is discussed briefly in the next section.

SOME INTERNATIONAL DIMENSIONS OF INFLATION
◆

During the recent period of inflationary recession, U.S. policy makers became painfully aware of the connection between domestic inflation and certain events occurring in the international economy. Specifically, there have been important changes in the relative prices of manufactured goods and raw materials, including crude oil. Commodity price increases have raised the production costs of most U.S. firms, and the firms in turn have been forced to raise the prices of their final products. Thus, as discussed below, the competitive position of U.S. output in the international marketplace has been affected.

ENERGY AND INFLATION

The inflation problem in the United States has been made worse by periodic shortages in key commodities such as wheat, beef, lumber, and fuels. In late December 1978 price increases by the Organization of Petroleum Exporting Countries (OPEC) were expected to add between 0.2 and 0.7 of a percent to the rate of inflation during 1979, as measured by the consumer price index.[12] These estimates were probably low. Other economists have estimated that increases in petroleum prices from March 1973 to January 1974 were responsible for approximately a 3 percent rise in the wholesale price index during this period.[13]

The U.S. economy will probably continue to have inflation generated by price increases in petroleum and other energy related products for some time to come, unless suitable substitute products are developed. During this period the inflation-unemployment problem will be a particularly difficult one.

INFLATION AND INTERNATIONAL TRADE

When inflation occurs in the United States, it makes U.S. goods and services more expensive to residents of other countries too, as long as

---

11. See G. C. Archibald, "The Phillips Curve and the Distribution of Unemployment," *American Economic Review* 59 (May 1969): 124–134; and Flory, "Stability of the Philips Curve and the Accelerationist Hypothesis."

12. "OPEC Cracks the Whip," *Newsweek*, January 1, 1979, p. 16.

13. William Nordhaus and John Shoven, "Inflation 1973: The Year of Infamy," *Challenge* 17 (May–June 1974): 22.

the prices of products in other countries rise by a smaller proportion. Such price increases result in a reduction of U.S. exports, which further aggravates inflation and unemployment. The U.S. balance of trade is also adversely affected. All of these matters will be discussed more extensively in Part Nine.

IS THERE
A SOLUTION?

◆

In this section of the chapter we will look at possible solutions to the problem of an inflationary recession.

*Economists frequently use the term **stagflation** to refer to an inflationary recession.*

Economists do not agree on the best approach to fight stagflation, but we will examine several policy suggestions.

MONETARY AND FISCAL POLICIES

Although monetary and fiscal policies can be used to combat either inflation or unemployment, when both are present simultaneously we have a conflict. General measures to reduce inflation by decreasing aggregate demand tend to increase unemployment, and vice versa.

Of course, policy makers may decide which of the two problems is worse and try to alleviate it. In the fall of 1979 it appeared that the Federal Reserve considered unemployment the lesser of the two evils; consequently, it instituted restrictive monetary policies in an attempt to reduce inflation. Unfortunately, unemployment increased as a result. The Fed repeated this approach in 1980 and 1981.

WAGE AND PRICE GUIDEPOSTS

In the 1962 *Economic Report of the President*, President Kennedy set forth certain standards, or guidelines, for wage rate and price increases that he believed would be compatible with the public interest.

***Wage and price guideposts** or **guidelines** are largely voluntary policies which establish certain standards for wage rate and price increases.*

These policies, along with wage and price controls (discussed in the next section of the chapter), are called **incomes policies,** because they attempt to restrict changes in income of labor and other productive inputs, including profit.

President Kennedy's wage guidelines stated that the appropriate annual percentage increase in total employee compensation per man-hour was equal to the annual increase in overall trend output per man-hour. In other words, increases in employee compensation for a particular firm were to be based on the overall average growth rate of labor productivity over a period of years. This trend rate of growth of productivity in manufacturing was estimated to be 3.1 percent from 1954 to 1960.[14]

The price guidepost specified that when the productivity of an industry was growing less rapidly than the national trend, the firms in the industry could raise prices to make up for the increased labor cost. When the productivity of an industry was growing more rapidly than the national trend, the firms in the industry were to lower prices to reflect labor cost decreases.[15]

These guidelines were supposed to result in general, or overall, price stability. Certain exceptions to the wage guidelines were allowed where certain types of labor were in short supply and where wages were unusually high or low compared to the average wage rate for similar work. Exceptions to the general guidelines for price changes were also provided for

---

14. *Economic Report of the President* (Washington, D.C.: Government Printing Office, 1962), pp. 186–189.

15. Ibid., p. 189.

in cases where the rate of return was above or below average in an industry or where changes in costs other than labor were substantial.[16]

The effectiveness of these guidelines is questionable. Between 1962 and 1965 the consumer price index rose only 1 to 2 percent a year. However, in 1966, at least partly as a result of pressures placed on the economy by the Vietnam War, prices began to rise at a faster rate.[17] To what extent price growth was moderated in the first half of the 1960s as a result of the guidelines rather than of lack of pressure from excess demand is a matter of debate.

More recently, at the end of 1978, President Carter announced wage and price guideposts. Again there has been disagreement on their effectiveness. As with President Kennedy's plan, the effectiveness of such largely voluntary guidelines depends on how they affect the demands of labor and business. The main weapon of the president is the power of persuasion, or jawboning, as it is frequently labeled.

In the next section we will look at wage and price controls, which can have a greater short-run impact because they contain stronger penalty provisions. However, many economists believe that they also cause problems.

WAGE AND PRICE CONTROLS

Wage and price controls are mandatory ceilings established for wage and price increases.

These controls have been imposed only three times during the last forty years: during World War II, in 1951, and on August 15, 1971 (by President Nixon). The imposition of controls requires special authorization by Congress.

---

16. Ibid.

17. "Table B–49: Consumer Price Indexes by Expenditure Classes, 1929–78." *Economic Report of the President* (Washington, D.C.: Government Printing Office, 1979), p. 239.

Effectiveness Because they are mandatory, wage and price controls tend to be more effective than voluntary guidelines during the period in which they are imposed. During the ninety-day wage-price freeze imposed by President Nixon and during the other periods of wage and price controls, provisions were made for court injunctions and fines for noncompliance.[18]

To some extent the imposition of wage and price controls worsens shortages of specific commodities and promotes the establishment of black (or illegal) markets. For example, if the legal price of gasoline is fixed at 50 cents a gallon, a gas station may be willing to supply smaller quantities of gasoline at that price than people are willing and able to buy. Those who do obtain the gasoline at that price may attempt to resell it at much higher prices to those who are willing to pay much more than 50 cents a gallon for it.

Nevertheless, while they were in force, wage and price controls did restrict price increases as measured by the official price indexes. However, many economists believe that after the controls were removed, prices and wages rose more rapidly than they would have if the controls had not been imposed; the wages and prices made up for increases that could not occur under the controls.

Allocative Efficiency Wage and price controls are also criticized on the basis of allocative efficiency. According to this argument the prices of all goods and services, including labor, must be able to move freely so that resources will be enticed into the production of goods or services for which shortages exist. The opposing view is that in a world of strong unions and big business, price increases are not necessarily an indication of excess demand. In a cost-push inflation, wage and price controls may not adversely affect allocation of resources.

---

18. See "Nixon Orders a Wage-Price Freeze," *New York Times*, August 16, 1971, p. 14.

Freedom of Choice The final argument against wage and price controls involves the question of individual freedom. People's positions on this issue are based on value judgments about where individual rights end and responsibility to society begins. Of course, this issue arises whenever controls or restrictions involving unions or business are discussed.

TAX-BASED INCOMES POLICIES

Near the end of the last decade, some proposals were advanced for a federal tax-based incomes policy (TIP). The proposals varied widely. However, in general, under such policies the federal government would annually set guidelines for wage rate increases. The guidelines would take into consideration both the growth rate of productivity and the rate of inflation, but they would be less than the rate of inflation. Firms and employees approving wage rate increases above the guidelines would incur income tax penalties. Those approving wage rate increases below the standard set by the guidelines would be given income tax reductions. (Some proposals would use either the penalty or the reward incentives, not both.)

Those in favor of TIP argue that it would let the market system work and yet reduce inflation because it would result in lower wage rate increases. Those who criticize it argue that the approach assumes that inflation is of the cost-push type, caused by wage rate increases. Actually, they contend, inflation may be caused by something else, such as excessive government spending or monetary growth. These critics further contend that TIP would result in market inefficiencies and inequities as firms tried to adhere to the guidelines.

INDEXATION

Indexation policies fall in the realm of "If you can't lick them, join them." Such policies recognize inflation as a fact of life and therefore would make widespread use of escalator clauses.

> *Escalator clauses* are clauses in long-term contracts that provide for automatic adjustment for inflation.

For example, union labor contracts now typically have escalator clauses. Social security payments and federal retirement benefits have also been indexed. Mortgage loan contracts in Mexico City have escalator clauses that adjust the rate of interest according to the rate of inflation.

Under most proposals the federal income tax schedule would be indexed to remove the phenomenon of "bracket creep," which is a result of the progressive tax system coupled with inflation. Bracket creep occurs in the following manner. Suppose a person earns $20,000 in one year and pays federal income taxes equal to 20 percent of the $20,000, or $4,000. Now suppose that at the beginning of the next year the individual receives a 10 percent raise, for a new salary of $22,000 a year. If the inflation rate during the last year was also 10 percent, the person is no better off than before in real income terms ($22,000 can now buy only as much in terms of goods and services as $20,000 could at the beginning of last year).

Nevertheless, this person will probably have to pay proportionally more income tax because the federal income tax structure is progressive and the person will be in a higher marginal tax bracket. Indeed, the individual might now be in a sufficiently high marginal tax bracket that 21 percent of income must be paid to the federal government as income tax. As a result, the person's real disposable income would actually fall. Under indexation proposals the federal income tax rate schedules would be adjusted for inflation so that this type of situation would not occur.

Thus we can define *indexation policies* in the following way.

Indexation policies *are policies (usually applied on a widespread scale) that use escalator clauses to adjust wage rates and long-term contracts for inflation. They would also adjust the tax system and government benefit programs for inflation.*

Those in favor of indexation policies argue that they promote equity among the participants in the economy in the presence of inflation. They also argue that indexation eliminates some degree of uncertainty on the part of workers, pensioners, and creditors about the real values of their future incomes and that it therefore promotes economic stability and growth. (Debtors, though, would be less well off with indexation.)

Those against indexation argue that it would institutionalize inflation—make it officially an acceptable part of the economic system. Moreover, we do not as yet have a perfect measure of the burden or incidence of inflation for individuals or businesses. For example, suppose the consumer price index increases by 1 percent as a result of increases in housing and mortgage costs. Will such an increase affect equally the young family getting ready to purchase its first home and the family of retired persons who already own their own home? Finally, the U.S. Treasury has not been thrilled by the prospect of the likely decreases in tax revenues that would occur as a result of indexation. (However, those who support the theories of supply-side economists, discussed later in this chapter, would consider such a concern to be unfounded.) Nevertheless, the Economic Recovery Tax Act of 1981 □ provided for the indexation of federal individual income taxes beginning in 1985.

MANPOWER POLICIES

Another proposed solution to the inflationary recession dilemma is to use government manpower training programs to combat unemployment. By retraining structurally unemployed workers in areas where there is a shortage of labor, both inflation and unemployment may be reduced. Several laws affecting the federal government's manpower policies are discussed here.

Area Redevelopment Act In 1961 Congress passed the **Area Redevelopment Act.** Funds used to train workers under this act are limited to areas with substantial and persistent unemployment. The training period can extend a maximum of sixteen weeks.

Manpower Development and Training Act of 1962 The expenditure of federal funds for both institutional and on-the-job training is provided for in the **Manpower Development Training Act** of 1962. Special attention was to be given to updating and improving the skills of the unemployed, youth, and individuals from farm families. Unlike the programs under the Area Redevelopment Act, these programs can last as long as fifty-two weeks. This act also requires the submission of an annual report, the *Manpower Report of the President*, which details current labor force developments and manpower programs.

Economic Opportunity Act of 1964 Frequently called the Anti-Poverty Act, the **Economic Opportunity Act** of 1964 established the Job Corps. The Job Corps was intended to increase the employability of youths aged sixteen to twenty-one through education, vocational training, and on-the-job training. The act also authorizes grants for community action programs and programs to alleviate poverty in rural areas. In addition, it created the Office of Economic Opportunity.

Civil Rights Act of 1964 The purpose of the **Civil Rights Act** of 1964 is not to reduce overall unemployment. Rather, it is to prohibit discrimination in employment because of race, religion, sex, or ethnic background.

Comprehensive Employment and Training Act of 1973 Decentralization of most of the federal manpower programs is the purpose of the **Comprehensive Employment and Training Act** of 1973 (CETA). The act provides for grants to state and local sponsors of such programs.[19]

All of these programs have been criticized for sloppy management practices. Some of the local sponsors of CETA programs have even been accused of fraud. However, many unemployed, handicapped, and disadvantaged people have found employment as a result of CETA's efforts.[20] Nevertheless, in 1981 the Reagan administration requested that funds for employment of workers under the CETA program in the public sector be eliminated.

SUPPLY-SIDE ECONOMICS

Recently, a version of economic thought called **supply-side economics** has become popular. Although economists who subscribe to the general point of view advanced by supply-siders are not in complete agreement, their arguments can be summarized as follows.

These economists contend that, particularly during an inflationary recession but at other times as well, governmental authorities should concentrate on policies designed to stimulate an increase in the productive capacity of the country. As productive capacity increases, inflationary pressures will diminish and growth will increase.

The views of classical and Keynesian economists with respect to aggregate supply and aggregate demand are illustrated in Figure 13–

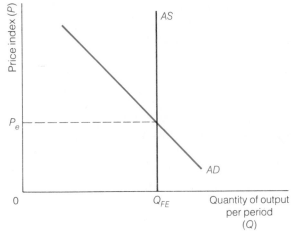

(a) Classical View

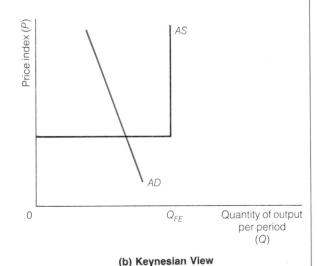

(b) Keynesian View

FIGURE 13–3   Two Views of Aggregate Demand and Aggregate Supply

The classical view, shown in panel (a), holds that the aggregate supply (AS) curve is a vertical line at the full employment level of output (Q_{FE}) in the short run. The intersection of the aggregate supply and aggregate demand (AD) curves determines only the general equilibrium level of prices in the economy. The Keynesian view is shown in panel (b). As a result of rigid wages and prices, the aggregate supply curve is a horizontal line until the full employment level of output is reached, after which it becomes vertical. In this case, the intersection of the aggregate supply and aggregate demand curves determines the level of output and employment as well as the general level of prices.

19. For a more thorough summary of the provisions of these acts see Gordon F. Bloom and Herbert R. Northrup, *Economics of Labor Relations*, 5th ed., pp. 428–432, 456; and F. Ray Marshall, Allan M. Cartter, and Allan G. King, *Labor Economics*, 3d ed. (Homewood, Ill.: Richard D. Irwin, 1976), pp. 564–574.

20. See "Why CETA is in Trouble," *Business Week*, October 2, 1978, pp. 124, 126; and "CETA: Jobs and Rip-offs," *Newsweek*, April 24, 1978, pp. 83–84.

3. (See also Chapter 6 for their views.) As shown in panel (a), classical economists believed that the aggregate quantity supplied was fixed at the full employment level of output, Q_{FE}, in the short run. In this case, aggregate demand could affect only the equilibrium price level. As discussed in Chapter 12, modern-day monetarists share a similar view. Of course, classical economists assumed that prices and wage rates were completely flexible in both an upward and a downward direction.

On the other hand, Keynesian economists believe that wage rate and price rigidities in a downward direction result in an aggregate supply curve such as that shown in panel (b). The supply curve is horizontal until the full employment level of output is reached, at which point it becomes vertical.

Economists who emphasize the importance of aggregate supply during an inflationary period are assuming that the economy is at or close to the full employment level of output and that there is excess aggregate demand equal to $Q^* - Q_{FE}$ at price P^* in Figure 13–4. (We have used the Keynesian graph, since

that has been our primary reference point in this book. These results would apply with the classical-monetarist approach too.)

Supply-side economists correctly point out that viewing aggregate supply as being fixed is rather shortsighted. In the not-so-very-long run, technological changes, growth in the supply of labor, and investment in plant and equipment (above replacement amounts) increase the productive capacity of the economy. Of course, aggregate demand may be increasing as well.

However, the point that these economists make is that the government has the power to institute policies to encourage the expansion of aggregate supply. If the economy is at full employment, policies that result in an increase in aggregate supply will reduce the pressure for price increases. The effects of such policies are demonstrated in Figure 13–5, where the aggregate supply curve has shifted from AS_1 to AS_2. The full employment level of output has increased from Q_{FE1} to Q_{FE2}.

Thus supply-side economists argue that policies designed to encourage private saving and business investment are needed. Such policies

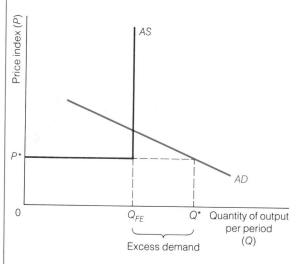

FIGURE13–4 Excess Aggregate Demand

If the general level of prices is so low (P^*) that the aggregate quantity demanded of goods and services is greater than the aggregate quantity supplied (excess demand is present), there will be pressure for prices to rise (inflation to occur).

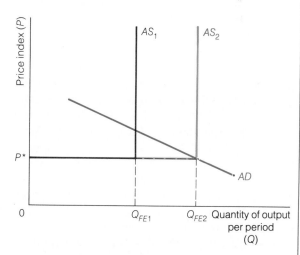

FIGURE 13–5 An Increase in Aggregate Supply

An increase in aggregate supply from AS_1 to AS_2 would eliminate the excess demand shown in Figure 13–4 and, correspondingly, reduce the inflationary pressure.

include reductions in income tax rates, particularly on corporate earnings and interest income, and investment tax credits. In fact, in the spring of 1981 President Reagan proposed an across-the-board cut in personal income tax rates of 25 percent to take effect over a three-year-period. The Reagan administration also promoted tax incentives for business investment in plant and equipment and tax breaks for income from such sources as savings accounts, bonds, stocks, and other types of financial investments. Many of these proposals were later enacted into law by Congress in the Economic Recovery Tax Act of 1981. □

In the past, Keynesian economists have emphasized that a decrease in the tax rate increases disposable income. □ This tends to lead to an increase in consumption spending, thereby increasing any inflationary pressures that might be present. Supply-side economists, however, attach more significance to another possible effect of the tax cut. They argue that the reduction of personal income tax rates will be perceived as a wage rate increase by individuals. The effect of such an after-tax wage increase, they argue, will be to increase the quantity of labor supplied and the productivity of labor. While the more traditional Keynesian economists certainly admit the possibility of the latter effect, they doubt that it will be as significant as supply-siders claim.

In 1974 an economist at the University of Southern California, Arthur B. Laffer, began promoting the notion that an income tax rate reduction could lead to an increase in total tax revenues. To illustrate his idea, Laffer employed the now-famous **Laffer curve,** shown in Figure 13–6. The income tax rate is depicted along the horizontal axis. As shown there, it can range from 0 percent to 100 percent. At a tax rate of 0 percent, the income tax will be $0. At the other extreme, with a tax rate of 100 percent, the government would take away every bit of people's income in taxes. However, tax revenues would be $0, because no one would be willing to work if a person could keep none of the income received.

The total tax dollars taken in by the government are shown along the vertical axis. According to Laffer, as the government first imposes an income tax, the total tax revenues received will rise—initially from $0. For a time, as the tax rates are increased, the total revenues received by the government will also increase. After some point, however, a further increase in the tax rates will lead to a decrease in the total tax revenues received by the government. This point is shown as T^* in Figure 13–6. Laffer argues that total tax revenues will decrease after T^* because the disincentives for people to work and earn income will be so great as to overpower the effect of the higher tax rates.

The greatest controversy regarding the Laffer curve is centered on the position of T^* Many economists argue that T^* is a tax rate higher than any in the United States. However, Laffer and other supply-side economists contend that U.S. tax rates may well be above T^*. The significance of their argument is that a reduction in tax rates could result in an increase in total tax revenues.

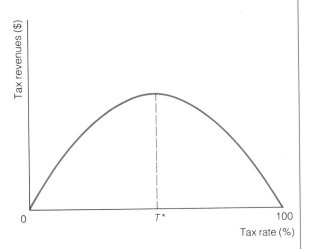

FIGURE 13–6   The Laffer Curve

The Laffer curve shows a hypothetical relationship between total tax revenues and the tax rate. According to Laffer, the total tax revenue received will reach its maximum at a tax rate smaller than 100%. This point is labelled T^* in the graph.

The facts of the matter are not clear. On the one hand, tax incentives that raise workers' after-tax wage rates may encourage them to work harder. On the other hand, people could, after a tax reduction, achieve the same standard of living by working fewer hours than before. Moreover, for many people the workweek, in terms of number of hours at work, is pretty much set by the employer. According to some 1979 estimates by the Congressional Budget Office, the total number of hours worked might increase by 1 to 3 percent for each 10 percent rise in after-tax wages. However, estimates indicate that the effect on aggregate demand would be substantially larger than the effect on aggregate supply, perhaps even five to ten times as large.[21]

Tax incentives to spur business investment in plant and equipment may be more effective than personal income tax reductions in increasing the long-term growth rate of labor productivity in the economy. However, it is not clear what will happen to saving if tax rates on interest and dividend income are cut. After such a reduction, individuals can keep a greater percentage of their interest and dividend income. However, they will need smaller amounts invested in assets with these types of earnings to have the same level of income from them as before.

There are also those who question the supply-side argument that an increase in labor productivity will automatically reduce inflation. The available evidence from Japan, the United States, France, Canada, the United Kingdom, and West Germany does not clearly indicate that this relationship holds.[22] One reason why an increase in productivity may not automatically result in a decrease in inflation is that workers may demand greater wage

increases to reflect their increased efficiency.

In spite of the uncertainties associated with supply-side economics, Israel began trying some policies consistent with the supply-side approach in January 1981. At that time the finance minister, Yoram Aridor, implemented a new program of radical tax cuts, loan subsidies, and savings incentives designed to reduce the inflationary expectations of the Israeli people and to encourage them to work and save more. The initial results seemed positive. In February increased economic activity resulted in an increase in government tax revenues of 10 percent, despite the cut in tax rates. However, although some prices had fallen in the first few months of the new program, on balance inflationary pressures may have grown worse. In February prices rose by 5.5 percent, and it appeared that the April price increases would average about 10 percent.[23]

Thus, by fall of 1981, the relative impact of tax rates on the supply of labor, labor productivity, consumption spending, and inflation were still unclear. Some additional evidence on this subject is presented in the For Discussion article at the end of this chapter.

THE ECONOMIC RECOVERY TAX ACT OF 1981

On August 4, 1981, part of the program proposed by the supply-side economists was passed by Congress in the form of the Economic Recovery Tax Act of 1981. This act provided for a 5 percent reduction in individual income taxes on *earned* income (wages and salaries) beginning on October 1, 1981; an additional 10 percent reduction on July 1, 1982; and a further 10 percent reduction on July 1, 1983. In addition, the top individual tax rate on "unearned" income (for example, interest and dividend income) was reduced from 70 to

21. See Lyle E. Gramley, "Supply-Side Economics: Its Role in Curing Inflation," *Federal Reserve Bank of Dallas Voice*, November 1980, p. 2.

22. Ibid., p. 4. Also see Thomas M. Supel, "Supply-Side Tax Cuts: Will They Reduce Inflation?" *Federal Reserve Bank of Minneapolis Quarterly Review*, Fall 1980, pp. 10–11.

23. See "Israel's Supply-Sider," *Newsweek*, April 6, 1981, p. 70.

50 percent beginning January 1, 1982. The act also reduced the top tax rate on long-term capital gains for individuals from 28 to 20 percent.

In addition, the act provided for an "all savers" certificate, which permits an individual to exclude up to $1,000 of interest income ($2,000 for couples filing joint returns) from one-year certificates issued by qualifying financial institutions after September 30, 1981, and before January 1, 1983. The yield on these certificates must equal 70 percent of the yield on the most recently issued (before a given all savers certificate is issued) 52-week Treasury bills. Once issued, however, the yield on a specific all savers certificate is fixed. Financial institutions must invest 75 percent of the proceeds of these certificates (or 75 percent of their net increase in deposits, whichever is smaller) in the housing and agricultural industries.

The act also allowed a business firm to depreciate (for tax purposes) its plant and equipment more rapidly than in the past. Generally speaking, equipment can now be depreciated on either a 3 or 5 year basis. Buildings generally can be written off in 15 years. Under the previous law, the minimum period over which new equipment could be written off varied from 2 to 40 years, depending on the type of equipment. Before the new act was passed, new buildings were to be depreciated over periods ranging up to 60 years.

Finally, the act also provided for the indexation of individual income tax rates to reflect increases in the cost-of-living in the previous year as measured by the consumer price index.[24] This feature of the new law represented the first time that indexation was a part of federal income tax laws.

---

24. There were a variety of other tax changes provided for in this law. Some of these were also designed to increase aggregate supply, while others (such as the reduction of the marriage penalty) seemed to be primarily designed to promote some notion of equity. Only the major provisions of the act were discussed here.

The purposes of these changes in the income tax laws were

1. to encourage individuals to work more (through the tax reductions on earned income),
2. to encourage individuals to save more (through the reduction in the maximum tax on unearned income and the all savers certificates),
3. to encourage businesses to invest in more plant and equipment (through the provisions for more rapid depreciation), and
4. to increase the availability of loans to the housing and agricultural industries (through funds generated by the all savers certificates).

Economists who believed in the supply side point of view thought, therefore, that aggregate supply would increase as a result of the Economic Recovery Tax Act of 1981. However, the corresponding emphasis of the Reagan administration on government spending cuts indicated that those officials, at least, did *not* believe that the reduction in tax rates would lead to a sufficiently large increase in aggregate supply that the total tax revenue taken in would actually increase (or even remain the same), as Laffer hypothesized.

WHERE
DO WE STAND?

In Chapter 8 the Employment Act of 1946 was explained. □ This act states that it is the responsibility of the government to promote maximum employment, production, and purchasing power. In 1978 the **Full Employment and Balanced Growth Act,** better known as the **Humphrey-Hawkins Act,** was passed.

This act makes the opportunity for employment at fair rates of compensation for all those willing and able to work a national goal. It also recognizes reasonable price stability as a national goal, and it explicitly states the need

179

for improved government policies to deal with inflation. The act emphasizes the role of public and private capital formation in achieving the national goals. Finally, it specifies that a balanced federal budget is a government policy objective, as long as it is consistent with the other goals.

The Humphrey-Hawkins Act requires that the president each year set annual numerical goals for the next five years in the areas of employment and unemployment, real income, productivity, level of production, and prices. The president is also to take account of these goals in the budget, recommending levels of outlays and receipts that are compatible with them.

To improve coordination of monetary and fiscal policies, the act requires the Federal Reserve Board to report to Congress twice a year on its monetary policy goals and plans. Congress will then consider the proposed policies of the president and the Federal Reserve Board together.

The Humphrey-Hawkins Act specifies an initial goal of 4 percent unemployment for workers sixteen to nineteen years of age and 3 percent for workers aged twenty and over; the goal is supposed to be reached in 1983. The act also makes the achievement of a 3 percent increase in the consumer price index a goal for

"Gosh, how I envy you the future, son. Almost my whole life has been lived in a Keynesian context."

Drawing by Donald Reilly; © 1981 The New Yorker Magazine, Inc

1983. However, it authorizes no new programs to achieve these goals.[25] Furthermore, given the policies of the Reagan administration, the practical significance of the Humphrey-Hawkins Act is open to question.

What should be done? We suggest that policies, such as manpower programs, which are directed at specific and serious structural problems continue to be implemented. A way may be found to diminish the inefficiency and waste connected with them in the past. If it can be demonstrated that serious cost-push inflation is being caused by unions or big business, an incomes policy of some sort might be desirable. However, wage and price guidelines and controls have met with questionable success in the past. In cases of overall excess demand or excess supply, general monetary and fiscal policies should still prove useful. Finally, at the end of 1981, the effects of the Economic Recovery Tax Act of 1981 on aggregate supply and employment were yet to be determined.

SUMMARY

1. This chapter examined a real government policy puzzle—how to cope with simultaneous unemployment and inflation. In such a situation, conventional macroeconomic policies directed toward changing the level of aggregate demand present conflicts. If inflation is reduced, unemployment is increased, and vice versa.

2. Traditional demand-pull inflation reflects excess aggregate demand; cost-push inflation can occur in the absence of demand pressures, perhaps because of unions and big business.

3. The notion of the Phillips curve wage rate growth–unemployment trade-off upset economists who believed that wage rates would not rise at all while unemployment was positive. However, there are at least three types of unemployment—frictional, structural, and cyclical—and each has dif-

25. For further discussion of this act, see the *Economic Report of the President* (Washington, D.C.: Government Printing Office, 1979), pp. 106–108.

ferent effects on wage rate growth. Only cyclical unemployment is primarily the result of insufficient aggregate demand.

4. Economists who adhere to the accelerationist hypothesis believe that the long-run Phillips curve is a vertical line at the natural rate of unemployment and that attempts to keep unemployment below the natural rate will result in accelerating inflation. However, the natural rate of unemployment seems to be the unemployment rate that is consistent with a minimal frictional level of unemployment. Thus, for all practical purposes the natural rate of unemployment corresponds to full employment. Presumably policy makers are not interested in more-than-full employment.

5. Changes in the distribution of unemployment may explain recent shifts in the Phillips curve. The distribution of unemployment is particularly significant because of the downward rigidity of money wage rates. Rising energy prices are another structural factor that may have contributed to a worsening inflation-unemployment trade-off in recent years.

6. Proposed solutions to the policy dilemma posed by stagflation include wage and price guideposts and controls and manpower policies. Wage and price guideposts are voluntary, and their effectiveness is questionable. Wage and price controls are mandatory, but they have been criticized because their long-run effects are unclear, they may disrupt economic allocation of resources, and they restrict individual freedom.

7. Manpower programs have been accused of waste, but they have helped some unemployed people find jobs. A structural approach to solving the inflation-unemployment problem would be appropriate. The ideas of supply-side economists also should not be ignored.

IMPORTANT TERMS AND CONCEPTS

Inflationary recession (Stagflation)
Demand-pull inflation
Cost-push (sellers') inflation
Phillips curve
Money illusion
Civilian labor force
Wage and price guideposts (guidelines)
Wage and price controls
Incomes policies
Tax-based incomes policies
Escalator clauses
Indexation
Employed persons
Unemployed persons
Frictional unemployment
Structural unemployment
Cyclical unemployment
Accelerationist hypothesis
Natural rate of unemployment
Rational expectations hypothesis
Adaptive theory of expectations
Distribution of unemployment
Area Redevelopment Act (1961)
Manpower Development and Training Act (1962)
Economic Opportunity Act (1964)
Civil Rights Act (1964)
Comprehensive Employment and Training Act (1973)
Supply-side economics
Laffer curve
Full Employment and Balanced Growth Act (Humphrey-Hawkins Act) (1978)
Economic Recovery Tax Act (1981)

QUESTIONS AND PROBLEMS

1. Why do policy conflicts sometimes occur when government authorities try to manage economic activity using conventional macroeconomic policy tools?

2. Explain the difference between demand-pull inflation and cost-push inflation.

3. Define three types of unemployment.

4. What is the Phillips curve?

5. What are wage and price guideposts? Are they effective? Have they been used in the United States? Explain.

6. Explain the accelerationist hypothesis. Why may it be irrelevant?

7. Why is the distribution of unemployment important?

8. What is money illusion?

9. Discuss the advantages and disadvantages of wage and price controls.

10. List the major legislative acts dealing with manpower programs. What are such programs?

11. How can manpower programs alleviate the twin problems of inflation and recession?

12. What is the Humphrey-Hawkins Act?

13. Explain the message of supply-side economists.

MAKING IT WORK: DESPITE CHOPPY WATERS, THE PRESIDENT HOLDS STEADY ON REAGANOMICS

"Can anyone here say that if we can't do it, someone down the road can do it? And if no one does it, what happens to the country? All of us here know the economy would face an eventual collapse. I know it's a hell of a challenge, but ask yourselves: If not us, who? If not now, when?"

With those stern words last week, Ronald Reagan ordered his Cabinet to find new ways of cutting as much as $15 billion out of next year's budget and a stunning $74 billion in 1983 and 1984. And with those demands, the President opened Chapter 2 in the history of

Source: "Making it Work: Despite Choppy Waters, the President Holds Steady on Reaganomics," Time, September 21, 1981, pp. 38–40, 45.

Reaganomics, the Administration's bold plan to alter fundamentally the policy directions of the past half-century and to put the U.S. back on a course of steady, noninflationary growth after years of stagnation and inflation.

When Reagan left Washington in August for a monthlong vacation at his California ranch, he had just wrapped up Chapter 1 and had every reason to feel satisfied, even a bit smug. No President since Franklin D. Roosevelt had done so much so quickly to change the basic path of the American economy. Though critics had confidently predicted that Congress would never go along with his daring "supply-side" strategy of large budget cuts and deep tax reductions, Reagan had

pushed his programs through the House and Senate virtually intact.

But back in the White House last week, the President had to face the sobering reality that his job of overhauling the U.S. economy has barely begun. Even before the program's first tax cut was to go into effect, on Oct. 1, doubts about Reaganomics were proliferating, notably on Wall Street and among Congressmen, aided and abetted by some economists and editorial pundits.

Despite the disquiet—even near panic in some sectors—the economy overall is doing surprisingly well in a number of ways. Near record interest rates have hampered growth, but most experts do not foresee anything like a major drop in the economy.

To the contrary, after a period of sluggishness, industrial production is expected to rebound sharply. TIME's Board of Economists, (The board members: Otto Eckstein, Martin Feldstein, Alan Greenspan, Walter Heller, James McKie, Joseph Pechman, Charles Schultze.) which met last week in New York City, predicted that by the second half of 1982 business would be growing at a robust 4% annual pace. Alice Rivlin, the director of the Congressional Budget Office and a guest participant at the meeting, reported that her office is assuming a 4% annual economic expansion in the years 1983 and 1984. Said she: "We are quite optimistic about the outlook for the economy." . . .

Why, then, the sudden outburst of postsummer anxiety, even before Reaganomics has a chance to show what it can do? Nearsightedness in a word. And a fear that, in the long run, Reagan cannot deliver what he has promised. Or, put another way, a mix of present pain and future lack of faith. A sizable part of the President's problem stems from the fact that the most vigorous critics of Reaganomics are focused on the short run: Congressmen worried about re-election next year, brokers buying and selling stocks minute by minute, businessmen who need loans. . . .

Wall Street's main concern is the bulging federal deficit, which is $55.6 billion this year and rising. Government borrowing weighs heavily on credit markets already strained by brisk demand for business loans, including the huge sums to finance megabuck corporate mergers like that between Du Pont and Conoco. The Administration has predicted that the deficit will shrink to $42.5 billion in 1982, and disappear altogether by 1984. But those targets are fast slipping away. The Congressional Budget Office forecast last week that the deficit would be $65 billion in 1982 and would total an extra $50 billion in 1984. As the Federal Reserve continues to restrict the growth of the money supply in its fight to bring down inflation, such unrelenting credit demand from the Government is bound to keep interest rates high or force them even higher. . . .

The President himself sowed many of the seeds of the current disillusionment by his boundless campaign promises and early, far too rosy economic predictions. Rather than adopting a Churchillian posture and admitting that it would take sacrifice and patience by all Americans to set the economy right, Reagan has steadily underplayed the pain involved. During last year's presidential campaign, he pledged that strong growth, less unemployment, lower inflation and a restoration of American military might were all just over his supply-side horizon.

Once the new Administration was in office, the happy talk continued. When the supply-side Reaganauts were preparing to unveil their economic plan last February, they used imaginative new computer models to project what would happen when their tax cuts took effect. The results were absurdly Pollyannaish. Growth in 1982 was going to surge to 7%, while inflation would fall to 6.5%.

Businessmen and economists immediately scoffed at the idea that the problems of sluggish growth and high inflation could be solved that quickly. Charles Schultze, former chief economic adviser to President Carter, called the Administration numbers "wishful thinking." Murray Weidenbaum, Reagan's top economist, and other officials eventually persuaded the Administration to tone down its projections. Yet even then, Reagan's aides, apparently counting on pure psychology to do the job, steadfastly insisted that high interest rates would fall sharply once Congress passed its proposals for budget cuts and tax reductions. . . .

The credibility problem of Reaganomics is based, in part, on its origins. In a sense, it was born one evening in December 1974, in the Two Continents restaurant in Washington, D.C. Three men were sipping drinks: Arthur Laffer, a young economist with an early-Beatles haircut who was considered a maverick by many of his colleagues; Jude Wanniski, an editorial writer for the *Wall Street Journal;* and Richard Cheney, a White House aide under President Ford.

Laffer argued that the fundamental problem with the American economy was that federal tax rates had got so high that they were beginning to discourage work and investment, and were thus holding down the supply of goods in the economy. Because the demand for goods raced ahead of their supply, inflation had become a chronic problem.

If tax rates were slashed, Laffer said, the result would be a boom in work, saving and investment. The "supply side" of the economy would be so stimulated that before long the Government would gain more revenue than it lost through cutting taxes. To illustrate his point, as legend now has it, Laffer sketched a crude diagram on a cocktail napkin on the table.* It showed that if taxes went too high, the Government would take in less revenue because people would be working less. That first Laffer curve landed in a wastebasket, but it was destined to become one of the most controversial concepts in recent economic theory.

Wanniski became Laffer's most avid apostle and spread the gospel of tax cutting with all the fervor of a circuit-riding preacher. An important early convert was Jack Kemp, a New York Congressman and former quarterback with the Buffalo Bills. In 1977 Kemp, together with Senator William Roth Jr. of Delaware, introduced a bill to Congress to reduce personal income taxes by almost 33% over three years.

Although the plan was defeated in Congress, the Kemp-Roth bill gained a loyal supporter: Ronald Reagan. As the 1980 presidential campaign began, the tax-cut proposal was the centerpiece of his economic policy. But when

Reagan wrapped up the Republican nomination, the G.O.P.'s main-stream economists flocked to his fold, and the influence of Laffer, Wanniski and Kemp waned as old-line conservatives began having an impact. Among the most prominent: Alan Greenspan, Gerald Ford's chief economic adviser; George Shultz, Treasury Secretary under Richard Nixon; and Arthur Burns, former Federal Reserve Board chairman. Some of those non-Administration advisers met with Reagan last week to discuss the new budget cuts.

The traditional economists gradually began to shift Reagan's program away from the original supply-side doctrine. Laffer assumed that large tax cuts would not be inflationary because they would stimulate enough business to compensate for the lost revenues by significantly increasing the Government's total tax take. But Reagan's more conservative advisers convinced him that tax cuts—and the inevitable, initially huge budget deficits—would fuel inflation unless accompanied by measures to restrain demand. Thus Reaganomics now includes not only a supply-side tax reduction but also calls for less Government spending and strict control over the growth of money. . . .

As the critics pointed out, Reagan's big tax reductions were bound to swell the size of the deficit, at least in the short run. But the Federal Reserve, which controls the growth of money, has not let credit grow faster to pay for

those deficits, so the Government's borrowing demands are pushing up interest rates. The result is the current staggering levels, which threaten to choke off the private investment boom that the tax cut is supposed to bring about. Says Oklahoma Democrat Jim Jones, chairman of the House Budget Committee: "My fear is that the program now put in place by the Administration is the equivalent of stepping hard on the gas at the same time as you slam on the brakes. The result will sound spectacular—until either the brakes fail or the engine blows. It is a gamble of titanic proportions."

*Actually, the cocktail napkin's role in the story may be apocryphal. Laffer cannot remember drawing on it, and Cheney also does not recall it. Other supply-siders say that Wanniski dreamed up the story to add some pizazz to a dry subject. But Laffer now draws the curve on napins and autographs them for admirers.

QUESTIONS

1. What is the connection between the Reagan tax cuts and the Laffer curve?

2. Given Laffer's prediction about the supply-side effects of the tax cuts, why was there so much concern in late 1981 that federal budget cuts had not been sufficient?

3. What kind of monetary policy was the Fed pursuing in the latter half of 1981? Why did the chairman of the House Budget Committee characterize Reagan's program as "stepping hard on the gas at the same time as you slam on the breaks"?

CHAPTER 14

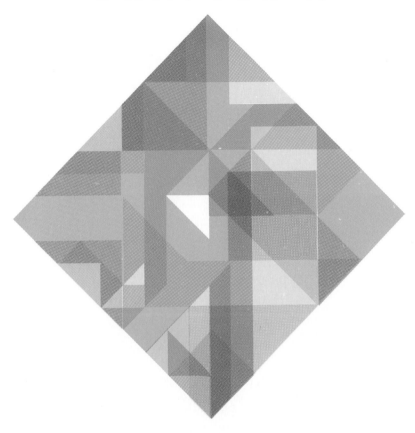

BUSINESS
CYCLES
AND
FORECASTING

WHEN
BUSINESS
GOES
BUST

A recession, according to Mr. Webster, is "a temporary falling off of business activity during a period when such activity has been generally increasing." Now that so many economic forecasters are talking about the possibility of a recession . . . , this may be an appropriate moment to take a closer look at precisely what a recession entails. How long is temporary? How steep is the falling off?

Since 1854, there have been 28 recessions. They have lasted, on the average, 19 months. Of these, 23 have occurred in peacetime, averaging 20 months each. The post–World War II average works out to 11 months. The longest recession began in October 1873 and persisted 65 months. The shortest began in August 1918 and lasted only seven months. The longest postwar recession, which started in November 1973, ran 16 months. One postwar recession, in 1957–58, lasted just eight months.

Slow economic growth has preceded many recessions. Price-adjusted GNP increased at a rate of less than 2% annually in the quarter before the onset of the last slump. But Geoffrey Moore, NBER director of business-cycle research, warns: "A forecaster would be naive to assume that a recession will necessarily develop later rather than sooner simply because economic growth happens to be strong."

Source: Excerpted from Alfred L. Malabre, Jr., "The Outlook: Review of Current Trends in Business and Finance," *Wall Street Journal*, February 5, 1979, p. 1.

It will come as no surprise that corporate profits normally take a steep drop when recessions set in. Or that the jobless rate climbs swiftly. But it may come as a surprise that per-capita personal income, after taxes and adjusted for inflation, was slightly higher just after each of the last three recessions than just before them. Or—notwithstanding the notion that people will work harder when times are bad—that labor-force productivity usually stagnates during recessions.

No one can say for sure that a recession will in fact soon set in. But if one does develop, the record makes clear that its precise nature is unpredictable and it will likely contain some large surprises.

Of course, between periods of recession, we have had both some relatively tranquil times and some out-and-out economic booms. In this chapter, both the history of notable ups and downs in U.S. economic activity and the long struggle of economists to explain and forecast such changes are considered.

C H A P T E R 14

BUSINESS
CYCLES
AND
FORECASTING

WHAT THIS CHAPTER IS ABOUT

THE NATURE OF BUSINESS CYCLES
Definition
Stages
Length
CAUSES OF BUSINESS CYCLES
External Factors
Internal Factors
Money Supply
Lack of Competition
The Acceleration Principle
FORECASTING ECONOMIC ACTIVITY
Economic Indicators
Econometric Models
Forecasting Errors

"Forecasters are sharply divided on the future course of the U.S. economy. Worse yet, they are even in disagreement as to what is occurring at the moment." *Business Week*, May 28, 1979, p. 39.

In this chapter we discuss business cycles and forecasting. As indicated in the quote, these aspects of the economic environment usually are topics of much interest, but they are also frequently a source of frustration and puzzlement to the general public and economists alike. We will begin by considering the nature of business cycles, and later we will examine the track record of forecasters in United States.

THE NATURE OF
BUSINESS CYCLES

In this section, what economists mean when they speak of a business cycle is analyzed. The lengths of various types of business cycles are described, and the findings of some early research on the existence of cycles are surveyed.

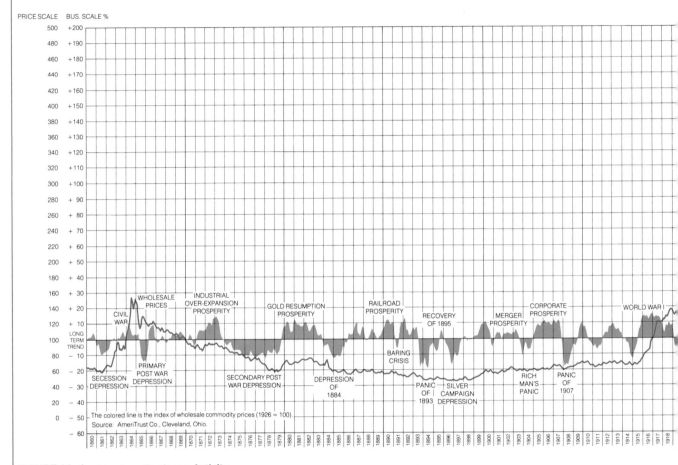

**FIGURE 14–1 American Business Activity
from 1860 to Today**

Business cycles are depicted in this graph as deviations from the long-term trend in a comprehensive index of business activity. The black line is an index of wholesale commodity prices (1926 = 100). (Courtesy of Ameritrust Company, Cleveland.)

DEFINITION OF A BUSINESS CYCLE

Business cycle is a general term that refers to fluctuations in the level of economic activity in a nation.

> More precisely, **business cycles** are repetitive patterns of economic activity characterized by alternating periods of expansion and contraction. Usually this term is applied to variations in aggregate economic variables such as income, output, employment, and prices.

Figure 14–1 depicts these fluctuations for the United States. The solid, jagged figures represent the percent deviation from the long-term trend rate of business activity. The black line represents the behavior of wholesale commodity prices.

Business cycles are depicted as being deviations from a long-term trend, or average value, for a composite, or comprehensive, index of business activity. In this case the values of ten aggregate economic variables were used in computing the index of business activity. In an attempt to determine if the level of economic activity is above, below, or at an average level, economists use deviations from long-term trend rates of growth for variables such as GNP and long-term average levels for variables such as the unemployment rate.

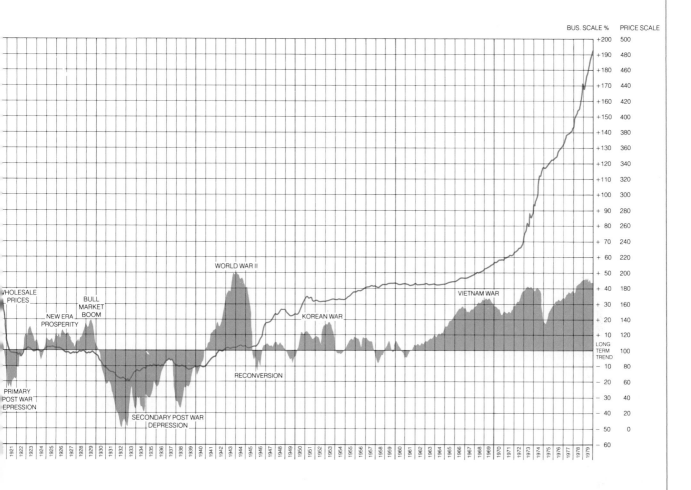

STAGES OF A BUSINESS CYCLE

Typically, economists speak of the business cycle as being divided into four phases—a trough, an expansionary period, a peak, and a contractionary period, followed once again by a trough, as shown in Figure 14–2. During an **expansionary period,** aggregate real income and output are rising and unemployment is falling. The **peak** marks the point where real income and output reach their greatest positive deviation from the long-term trend. During a **contractionary period** real income and output are falling and unemployment is rising. The **trough** is reached when real income and output attain their greatest negative deviation from the long-term trend.

As shown in Figure 14–1, business cycles are not uniform in size or even in length. Consequently, many economists now refer to them as **business fluctuations** instead. In Figure 14–2 the percent deviation from the long-term trend rate of growth of GNP is used as an indication of the position of the economy in the business cycle. A more comprehensive index, such as that used in Figure 14–1, would probably give a better picture of the overall level of economic activity in a country.

LENGTH OF A BUSINESS CYCLE

The average length of a business cycle depends on what is counted as a cycle. Economists have pointed out the existence of cyclical patterns in business activity that have

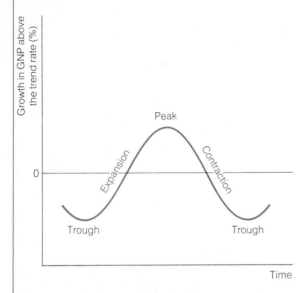

FIGURE 14–2 The Four Stages of a Business Cycle

The four phases of a business cycle are shown in this graph. The trough represents the point where real output and employment reach their greatest negative deviation from the long-term trend. During an expansionary period aggregate output and real income are rising and unemployment is falling. The peak occurs where real income and output reach their greatest positive deviation from the long term trend. During a contractionary period, real income and output are falling (at least relative to their long-run trend rates), and unemployment is rising.

ranged from several years to more than fifty years in length.

Short Cycles Some economists speak of a very short cycle, often called the **minor cycle,** which has averaged forty-four months in duration since 1854, the beginning date of the records of the National Bureau of Economic Research (NBER).[1] Other economists speak of a longer cycle, often called the **major cycle,** which averages more than eight years in length.

According to economist Alvin Hansen,

business cycles in the United States before World War II followed certain patterns:

The American experience indicates that the *major* (emphasis added) business cycle has had an average duration of a little over eight years. Thus, from 1795 to 1937 there were seventeen cycles of an average duration of 8.35 years. . . .

Since one to two minor peaks regularly occur between the major peaks, it is clear that the *minor* (emphasis added) cycle is something less than half the duration of the major cycle. In the one hundred and thirty-year period 1807 to 1937 there were thirty-seven minor cycles with an average duration of 3.51 years. . . .

The major cycles vary in length from a minimum of six years to a maximum of twelve years, though with rare exceptions they fall within the range of seven to ten years. . . . The minor cycles have a range from a minimum of two years to a maximum of six years, though they usually fall within the range of three to four years.[2]

By referring to Figure 14–1, we can observe the cycles described by Hansen. However, the performance of the U.S. economy in the post–World War II period has been such that the times when the level of business activity has fallen below the long-term trend are relatively few and far between.

Kuznets Cycles Cycles of even longer duration (between fifteen and twenty-five years) are often called **Kuznets cycles,** after Simon Kuznets, an economist who described them in 1930.[3] Kuznets observed long, wave-like movements in production and price series for individual commodities after the removal of long-term secular trends. Later, another economist, Arthur Burns demonstrated that similar cycles existed in aggregate economic data for the United States.[4]

1. Michael K. Evans, *Macroeconomic Activity: Theory, Forecasting and Control* (New York: Harper & Row, 1969), p. 4.

2. Alvin H. Hansen, *Fiscal Policy and Business Cycles* (New York: Norton, 1941), pp. 18–19.

3. See Simon Kuznets, *Secular Movements in Production and Prices* (Boston: Houghton Mifflin, Riverside Press, 1930), Chapters 3–4.

4. Arthur F. Burns, *Production Trends in the United States since 1870* New York: National Bureau of Economic Research, 1934), Chapter 5.

Such cycles, or waves, seem to reflect patterns in building construction and to be related to changes in rates of population growth, immigration, and growth of the money supply.[5] According to Hansen:

It appears that the building cycle averages somewhere between seventeen and eighteen years in length, or almost twice the length of the major business cycle.[6]

American experience indicates that with a high degree of regularity every other major business boom coincides roughly with a boom in building construction, while the succeeding major cycle recovery is forced to buck up against a building slump.[7]

Thus, the depressions which have fallen in the interval of the construction downswing are typically deep and long. And the succeeding recovery is held back and retarded by the unfavorable depressional influence from the slump in the building industry.[8]

Kondratieff Cycles N. D. Kondratieff published a paper in 1935 in which he suggested the existence of very long cycles of fifty to sixty years duration.[9] Although some economists have attached great importance to Kondratieff cycles in their interpretation of the history of business cycles, interest in these cycles by other economists has diminished.[10] Evidence to support the existence of the cycles in real variables, such as production, has not been substantial.

---

5. See Moses Abramovitz, "The Nature and Significance of Kuznets Cycles," *Economic Development and Cultural Change* 9 (April 1961): 225–248.

6. Hansen, *Fiscal Policy and Business Cycles*, p. 20.

7. Ibid., p. 23.

8. Ibid., p. 24.

9. N. D. Kondratieff, "The Long Waves in Economic Life," *Review of Economic Statistics* 17 (November 1935): 105–115.

10. J. A. Schumpeter, "The Analysis of Economic Change," *Review of Economic Statistics* 17 (May 1935): 1–10.

CAUSES OF BUSINESS CYCLES

The causes of business cycles seem to be quite diverse, and even economists do not always agree about why a particular fluctuation in the level of economic activity occurred when and how it did.

Economists sometimes separate their proposed causes of business cycles into two groups: forces outside the economic system and forces within the economic system. Although the same classification system is used here, in practice it is difficult to separate the effects of external and internal factors, because internal forces magnify the effects of external ones.

EXTERNAL FACTORS

One of the most famous (but not the most credible) of the business cycle theories was the sunspot theory advanced by British economist William Stanley Jevons in 1878. According to Jevons, sunspots occurred at regular intervals. They affected the weather and, consequently, agricultural production, which then affected the economy as a whole. However, the correlation that Jevons perceived did not last, and the sunspot theory was discredited.

External factors that are more likely to have an impact on production and employment are wars, politics, technological innovations, changes in the attitudes of consumers and investors and changes in the rate of population growth and immigration.

Wars The effects of wars on production seem evident from a study of Figure 14–1. Production boomed during World War I, World War II, the Korean War, and the later stages of the Vietnam War. Although wars are an effective means of promoting an upturn in the economy, they are an unpleasant one. Moreover, the use of economic facilities to produce defense goods rather than capital equipment does not as effectively increase the productive capacity of an economy and therefore does not promote long-term economic growth.

Political Cycles Many people believe that incumbent government officials frequently manipulate the economy for their own short-term gain. An analysis of some of the earlier chapters of this book would indicate how such tactics are possible through fiscal and monetary policies.

Edward Tufte, a political scientist, studied electoral and economic time-series data for twenty-seven countries classified as democracies in 1969. He concluded: "The fundamental point of the aggregate evidence is that 70 percent of the countries showed some signs of a political business cycle."[11]

With respect to the United States, Tufte stated that with the exception of the Eisenhower years, the electoral-economic cycle from 1948 to 1978 has exhibited the following pattern:

A two-year cycle in the growth of real disposable income per capita, with accelerations in even-numbered years and decelerations in odd-numbered years.

A four-year presidential cycle in the unemployment rate, with downturns in unemployment in the months before the presidential election and upturns in the unemployment rate usually beginning from twelve to eighteen months after the election.[12]

Changes in Attitudes In the case of changes in consumer and investor attitudes with respect to the business cycle, we often have a which-came-first situation. However, using the concept of the multiplier, □ we know that a given change in investment or consumption expenditures can eventually have a much larger effect on national income. The most volatile type of investment spending is inventory investment, and the existence of the very

short (four-year) business cycle has often been attributed to changes in this variable.

Expenditures for consumer durables (appliances, televisions, and automobiles, for example) vary more widely than do expenditures for nondurable goods and services. This relationship is to be expected, since most people consider such items as food, clothing, and health care to be necessities and durable goods to be big expenditure items whose purchase can be postponed, at least for a while.

International Factors Immigration and other international factors also affect the economic situation in the United States. In fact, the large influx of immigrants from Indochina in the 1970s and Cuba and Haiti in 1980, along with the continuing arrival of Mexican citizens seeking work in this country, has caused concern about the short-run and long-run impacts on the U.S. economy.[13] Moreover, the foreign trade policies of other countries can also have a significant impact. Consider, for example, the effects of OPEC during the 1970s. (The foreign trade policies of other countries are discussed in Chapter 31.)

INTERNAL FACTORS

It is difficult to determine a set of purely internal forces that stimulate business cycles. One rather naive theory of business cycles was that machines tend to have eight- to ten-year lives and that, consequently, every eight to ten years a big wave of replacement investment will occur. However, the authors of this theory failed to consider that different machines are purchased in different years and that many machines have shorter or longer lives than the average. A more realistic scenario of the role of investment, the acceleration principle, is discussed below. Changes in the money supply and a lack of competition may also cause or at least add to the severity of the business cycle.

11. Edward R. Tufte, *Political Control of the Economy* (Princeton, N.J.: Princeton University Press, 1978), p. 11.

12. Ibid., p. 27.

13. See "The Economic Consequences of a New Wave," *Business Week*, June 23, 1980, pp. 80–86.

Money Supply As explained in Chapter 12, changes in the money supply may have an effect on the level of economic activity. Increases in the money supply tend to cause increases in national income, whereas decreases in the money supply tend to cause decreases in national income. Fluctuations in the money supply can be caused by either external or internal forces.

Lack of Competition The structure of the economy is often blamed for the severity of the recession part of the business cycle. Economists who hold this view contend that, as a result of big business and unions, a lack of competition prevents prices and wage rates from responding quickly to a fall in demand.

The Acceleration Principle The acceleration principle deals with the relationship between net investment, the stock of capital goods, and the level of income.

> More specifically, the **acceleration principle** indicates that net investment will take place only when aggregate demand is increasing.

The acceleration principle is based on the fact that capital stock—plant and equipment—is durable. If the current capital stock is sufficient to supply the current level of aggregate demand, no net investment is required to maintain that level of output. Only worn-out machines need be replaced, which means that net investment is zero. (Chapter 5 indicated that net investment □ is investment expenditures over and above expenditures to replace old machines.) However, if aggregate demand increases and the current level of capital stock is being used at capacity, then net investment will be required.

> The ratio of the net investment required to the change in aggregate demand is called the **accelerator**.
>
> $$\text{Accelerator} = \frac{\text{net investment}}{\text{change in aggregate demand}}.$$

The acceleration principle works in the following manner. Suppose that, over time, plant and equipment and GNP tend to maintain a fairly constant relationship to each other, say $1 worth of capital equipment to every $2 worth of output.[14] Suppose also that the economy has reached a position where GNP is $40 million and the stock of capital equipment is $20 million and that this level of GNP and capital equipment has been maintained for some time. Furthermore, for purposes of explanation, assume that the $20 million worth of capital equipment represents 1,000 machines, each with a life of ten years and each worth $20,000. Over time, the replacement pattern has reached an equilibrium, or steady-state, situation where one hundred machines are replaced each and every year, so that the level of gross investment and the level of capital stock remain constant. The level of gross investment is thus equal to 100 machines × $20,000 or $2 million a year.

Now assume that there is an exogenous (not because of an increase in income) increase in consumption expenditures of $20 million, so that aggregate demand is increased by 50 percent, to $60 million. As inventories are drawn down, businesses will wish to purchase more capital equipment to facilitate higher levels of production. In fact, if the same capital-output ratio is maintained, businesses will wish to increase their capital stock by 50 percent, to $30 million. However, this increase entails a 500 percent increase in gross investment:

$10 million net investment
  + $2 million replacement investment
       = $12 million gross investment.

Therefore,

$$\frac{\$12 \text{ million gross investment}}{\$2 \text{ million}} = 6.0$$

Thus the level of gross investment is six times as great, or five times greater than before.

14. The ratio of capital to output for the United States has actually averaged around 2.5. See Simon Kuznets, *Capital in the American Economy* (Princeton, N.J.: Princeton University Press for NBER, 1961), pp. 80–81.

(Gross investment☐ is equal to net investment plus replacement investment, as shown in Chapter 5.) In this case the accelerator is equal to

$$\frac{\text{net investment}}{\text{change in aggregate demand}} = \frac{\$10 \text{ million}}{\$20 \text{ million}} = \frac{1}{2}.$$

If, in the next year, through a combination of multiplier effects and exogenous factors, demand increases once again by 50 percent, to $90 million, businesses will once again wish to increase their stock of capital equipment by 50 percent, to $45 million. In this case gross investment will increase by only 42 percent over the level of the preceding year—adding $15 million of net investment to $2 million of replacement investment, we get

$$\frac{\$17 \text{ million gross investment}}{\$12 \text{ million}} = 1.42.$$

Suppose that in the third year the economic situation is such that aggregate demand increases by only 20 percent, to $108 million. In this case, businesses will also wish to increase their capital stock by 20 percent, or $9 million. However, it follows that gross investment will actually decrease from $17 million to $11 million. Such a decrease, through the multiplier effect, will likely cause GNP to fall by an even greater amount.

We can draw several conclusions from this example. First, an increase in GNP from an equilibrium state will tend to have a magnified effect on gross investment. Second, if gross investment is to continue to increase in terms of absolute dollars, the *rate of growth* of GNP must not fall; if it does fall, gross investment may actually fall. Third, if the rate of growth of gross investment is to remain constant, the rate of growth of GNP must continually increase, or accelerate. The acceleration principle gets its name from this last relationship and from the fact that an increase in sales from

a steady-state equilibrium position will have a magnified effect on gross investment.

The effects of these increases in GNP on gross investment are summarized in Figure 14–3. As can be seen from the figure, if, after year 3, aggregate demand falls once again to $40 billion, gross investment will fall to $0 for several years, until the machines that were one year old in year 3 wear out. At that time there will be a large increase in gross investment, and the multiplier and acceleration principles will once more begin to work.

Once these principles are working to expand investment and aggregate demand, how can the expansion come to a halt? As discussed earlier, even the effect of the multiplier coupled with exogenous increases in demand may be insufficient to keep aggregate demand growing at a pace fast enough to maintain the level of gross investment. In addition, a rapidly growing economy will most likely eventually reach a full employment ceiling, an output maximum that occurs because of a limited supply of labor or of other resources.

The interaction of the acceleration principle and the multiplier can cause just as dramatic fluctuations in income in a downward direction once aggregate demand fails to increase at the required rate. However, once gross investment is down to $0, a lower limit, or trough, may be reached. Eventually, enough of the capital stock will wear out that gross investment will once more take place, and the upward part of the cycle will begin again.

Although the acceleration principle is discussed here with respect to investment in machines, it is equally applicable to investment in inventories and buildings. However, its effects are somewhat modified because of lags between investment plans and actual investment in capital equipment and buildings. Thus the workings of the acceleration principle and its interaction with the multiplier are much more complex than our simple example has shown. Today, the acceleration principle is an important part of growth theory, due to some pioneering research on the subject by Paul Samuelson, a Nobel Prize winner in eco-

Year 0
GNP: $40 Million   Gross Investment: $2 Million

| 10 YRS OLD | 9 YRS OLD | 8 YRS OLD | 7 YRS OLD | 6 YRS OLD | 5 YRS OLD | 4 YRS OLD | 3 YRS OLD | 2 YRS OLD | 1 YR OLD |

Capital stock of 100 machines ($2 million worth)

Gross investment of 100 machines ($2 million worth)

Replaced

Year 1
GNP: $60 Million   Gross Investment: $12 Million

| 10 YRS OLD | 9 YRS OLD | 8 YRS OLD | 7 YRS OLD | 6 YRS OLD | 5 YRS OLD | 4 YRS OLD | 3 YRS OLD | 2 YRS OLD | 1 YR OLD |

Year 2
GNP: $90 Million   Gross Investment: $17 Million

| 10 YRS OLD | 9 YRS OLD | 8 YRS OLD | 7 YRS OLD | 6 YRS OLD | 5 YRS OLD | 4 YRS OLD | 3 YRS OLD | 2 YRS OLD | 1 YR OLD | 1 YR OLD | 1 YR OLD | 1 YR OLD | 1 YR OLD | 1 YR OLD |

Year 3
GNP: $108 Million   Gross Investment: $11 Million

| 10 YRS OLD | 9 YRS OLD | 8 YRS OLD | 7 YRS OLD | 6 YRS OLD | 5 YRS OLD | 4 YRS OLD | 3 YRS OLD | 2 YRS OLD | 2 YRS OLD | 2 YRS OLD | 2 YRS OLD | 2 YRS OLD | 2 YRS OLD | 1 YR OLD | 1 YR OLD | 1 YR OLD | 1 YR OLD | 1 YR OLD | 1 YR OLD | 1 YR OLD | 1 YR OLD | 1 YR OLD |

FIGURE 14–3 Effect of an Increase in GNP on Gross Investment

The machines have an expected life span of 10 years. Also the ratio of capital stock to output is $1 of capital stock for every $2 of output. In year 0, GNP is $40 million, and gross investment is $2 million, to replace the 100 worn-out machines. In year 1, GNP increases to $60 million, so gross investment increases to $12 million. As before, $2 million is required to replace the worn-out machines. However, an additional $10 million of net investment is required for capacity to produce the $20 million increase in GNP. A similar analysis holds for Year 2, when GNP increases by $30 million. In Year 3, GNP does not increase by as much as in Year 2, and gross investment falls.

nomics, and other contemporary economists.[15]

Keynesian economists would argue that, at least theoretically, business cycles could be greatly reduced in severity or even eliminated if proper monetary and fiscal policies were instituted. Monetarists□ believe that discretionary policies□ either are ineffective or, worse, make fluctuations in economic variables even more pronounced. They believe the economy will do well enough if it is left alone and if a steady rate of monetary growth just sufficient to accommodate economic growth is maintained.

Obviously, business cycles have not yet been eliminated. Why not? For one thing, politics sometimes gets in the way of the monetary and fiscal policies that Keynesian economists would consider appropriate—for

example, when a tax increase or a decrease in government spending might be helpful in reducing excess aggregate demand. Second, policy makers may not know the impacts of their policies precisely enough to fine-tune the economy so that a pattern of price stability, steady growth of output, and full employment is maintained. Finally, policy makers have a difficult time accurately forecasting the future course of the economy with or without government intervention. This last problem is discussed next.

FORECASTING
ECONOMIC
ACTIVITY
◆

---

15. See Paul A. Samuelson, "Interactions between the Multiplier Analysis and the Principle of Acceleration," *Review of Economics and Statistics* 21 (May 1939): 75–78.

Most business firms and government agencies and many consumers are interested in the values that certain economic variables will take on in the future. Businesses want to know future input prices and future demand for the product or service they sell or are considering selling. The federal government wants to know the future levels of unemployment, prices, and gross national product if the level of government involvement in the economy does not change. It also wants to know what effects policy decisions made now will have on the future values of these variables.

State and local governments and consumers are concerned about the future levels of interest rates, prices, and unemployment, at least to the extent that such policies are relevant to them. State and local governments also want to know what effects various tax and spending policies will have on the economies of their areas.

Much of the economic forecasting by small businesses and consumers is done in a relatively informal manner. However, the forecasting by larger businesses and government agencies is far more sophisticated. Moreover, some firms, such as Chase Econometrics and Data Resources, Inc., even make forecasting the values of various economic variables their main business.

The importance of economic forecasting is underscored by the fact that Lawrence R. Klein of the Wharton School at the University of Pennsylvania received the 1980 Nobel Prize in economics for his pioneering work in the development of econometric models.

Econometric models use systems of equations and statistical techniques to forecast the value of economic variables such as national income, employment, and prices.

Although Klein's original model had only twenty equations, at the time he received the Nobel Prize his Wharton model had grown to more than a thousand equations. Econometric models are discussed more thoroughly later in the chapter.

ECONOMIC INDICATORS

In making its forecasts, the federal government uses the values of a group of variables called economic indicators.

Economic indicators are key variables used to predict changes in economic activity. Changes in the value of such variables are thought to indicate changes in the values of other important economic variables.

Indicator variables are divided into three sets: leading, coincident, and lagging, as shown in Table 14–1.

Leading indicators are economic variables whose values typically rise or fall before a corresponding rise or fall in the values of other economic variables that people are trying to forecast, such as GNP. As shown in Table 14–1, the leading indicators include the average workweek and layoff rate in manufacturing, the value of manfacturers' new orders for consumer goods, and the net change in inventories on hand and on order, among others.

Coincident indicators are economic variables whose values seem to rise or fall simultaneously with GNP. They include employees on nonagricultural payrolls, an index of industrial production, personal income less transfer payments (1972 dollars), and manufacturing and trade sales (1972 dollars).

Lagging indicators are economic variables whose values typically rise or fall after corresponding rises or falls in GNP. Lagging indicators include an index of labor cost, manufacturing and trade inventories (1972 dollars), average duration of unemployment, and the average prime rate charged by banks, among others.

The *composite values* for each of the three sets of indicators are an index of the values of the indicators in each set as a group. Unfortunately, as we can see by examining the growth rates of GNP at the top of the chart, the changes in these variables do not always occur in the same time relationship to GNP. If we

TABLE 14-1 Indexes of Cyclical Indicators and Rate of Growth of Real GNP

	1970	1971	1972	1973	1974	1975	1976	1977	1978	1979
Rate of Growth of Real GNP	−.2	3.4	5.7	5.8	−.6	−1.1	5.4	5.5	4.8	3.2
LEADING INDICATORS										
Composite index, 1967 = 100	**104.4**	**113.7**	**124.9**	**131.8**	**122.1**	**114.8**	**128.8**	**136.4**	**141.8**	**140.1**
Indexes:										
Net business formation, 1967 = 100	107.1	109.5	115.5	115.5	111.2	108.8	117.2	126.5	132.9	131.7
Building permits.[1] 1967 = 100	118.1	167.4	192.2	157.1	92.2	80.9	111.8	144.9	145.4	123.8
Common stock prices.[2] 1941−43 = 100	83.2	98.3	109.2	107.4	82.8	86.2	102.0	98.2	96.0	103.0
Percent—										
Layoff rate, manufacturing	1.8	1.6	1.1	.9	1.5	2.1	1.3	1.1	.9	1.1
Change in sensitive prices[3][4]	.4	.3	.8	1.9	2.5	.1	1.2	.7	1.2	2.1
Change in total liquid assets[4]	.5	.8	1.0	1.0	.8	.8	.9	1.0	1.0	1.0
Vendor companies reporting slower deliveries	51	48	63	88	66	30	54	55	64	63
Avg. workweek, manufacturing[5] (hours)	39.8	39.9	40.5	40.7	40.0	39.5	40.1	40.3	40.4	40.2
Net change in inventories (1972 dols.)[4][6] (bil. dol.)	(Z)	3	11	25	6	−19	6	13	19	11
Plant and equip. contracts and orders (1972 dols.) (bil. dol.)	106	111	124	150	150	115	129	145	163	175
New orders, manufacturing, consumer goods and materials (1972 dols) (bil. dol.)	328	344	388	433	395	342	391	420	446	438
Money supply (M2) (1972 dols.) (bil. dol.)	647	696	758	785	751	753	806	855	864	846
COINCIDENT INDICATORS										
Composite index, 1967 = 100	**108.8**	**109.4**	**118.1**	**127.4**	**125.3**	**115.5**	**123.7**	**131.3**	**140.1**	**145.2**
Industrial production index, 1967 = 100	107.8	109.6	119.7	129.8	129.3	117.8	130.5	138.2	146.1	152.2
Employees, nonagric, payrolls (mil.)	70.9	71.2	73.7	76.8	78.3	76.9	79.4	82.5	86.7	89.9
Personal income less transfer payments (1972 dols.) (bil. dol.)	780	792	838	885	867	852	894	942	996	1,024
Sales, mfg and trade (1972 dols.) (bil. dol.)	1,380	1,442	1,559	1,677	1,662	1,558	1,671	1,772	1,876	1,918
LAGGING INDICATORS										
Composite index, 1967 = 100	**115.5**	**107.2**	**107.0**	**122.9**	**138.9**	**126.5**	**119.8**	**125.4**	**143.1**	**166.4**
Index of labor cost,[7] 1967 = 100	112.3	113.1	113.2	117.1	127.3	143.0	145.1	154.3	164.1	175.4
Percent—										
Ratio, consumer installment debt to personal income	12.8	12.9	13.1	13.6	13.3	12.7	13.0	13.8	14.3	15.0
Average prime rate charged by banks	7.9	5.7	5.2	8.0	10.8	7.9	6.8	6.8	9.1	12.7
Average unemployment duration (wks.)	8.6	11.3	12.0	10.0	9.8	14.2	15.8	14.3	11.9	10.8
Inventories, mfg. and trade (1972 dols.) (bil. dol.)	197	202	208	220	227	217	225	237	250	257
Commercial and industrial loans outstanding (bil. dol.)	85	84	80	97	116	118	109	113	126	147

Z Less than $500,000,000. [1]New private housing units authorized. [2]Standard and Poor, 500 stocks. [3]Producer price index, crude materials. [4]Weighted 4-term moving average placed at the terminal month of the span. [5]Production workers. [6]Changes in book value. [7]Cost per unit of output in manufacturing.

Source: U.S. Bureau of Economic Analysis, *Business Conditions Digest,* monthly.

knew, for example, that the layoff rate in manufacturing always decreased two months before an increase in the growth rate of GNP, the job of forecasting would be made far easier.

At best, indicators are helpful in forecasting turning points in the economy—peaks and troughs. By themselves, they are not very useful for predicting the actual future values of other economic variables.

ECONOMETRIC MODELS

The firms and government agencies that attempt to forecast the future values of aggregate economic variables such as gross national product, unemployment, interest rates, and the rate of inflation more precisely than can be done with indicators alone use a system of equations not very different in nature from the simple ones that we used to determine the equilibrium level of national income and to express the demand for money. The primary difference is that the forecasters have many more equations that describe the behavior of the economy in a far more detailed fashion than do the simple ones.

Through the use of the statistical technique of regression analysis and historical data, econometricians can estimate economic functions that seem to "best fit" the way the world behaves. In many cases, they find that economic behavior is more accurately described through the use of lagged variables, which allow for the fact that consumers and firms do not immediately adjust their consumption and investment spending when new levels of income or sales are reached.

For example, through such statistical tools an econometrician might find that the "best fit" consumption function was

$$C_t = 5,000 + 0.9Y_{t-1} + 0.5\Delta Y_t,$$

where:

C_t = the level of consumption in time period t in billions of dollars,

Y_{t-1} = the level of personal disposable income in the previous period in billions of dollars, and

ΔY_t = the change in income in period t, which is equal to $Y_t - Y_{t-1}$, in billions of dollars.

In this case, Y_{t-1} is said to be a *lagged variable*, because current consumption expenditures depend on consumer income one period earlier. We can also see that 0.5, the coefficient of ΔY_t, is less than 0.9, the coefficient of Y_{t-1}. This relationship indicates that consumer do not at once adjust their consumption spending to new levels of income.

In a similar manner, econometricians can estimate functions that describe the behavior of businesses with respect to investment spending on plant and equipment, inventory investment, the rate of residential construction, taxes, and other economic variables. Then, by using these relationships, economists can predict future levels of GNP,

prices, unemployment, interest rates, and other economic variables.

ACCURACY OF FORECASTS

Like weather forecasters, economic forecasters are not always correct (and not always in agreement either). Table 14–2 summarizes the percentage errors of five forecasting organizations over the period 1970–1974. To be fair,

TABLE 14–2 Average Error of Forecasts for Five Forecasters: 1970–1974 (in Percentage Points)

Forecaster	Rate of Increase of Real GNP	Rate of Inflation	Unemployment Rate
	Forecasts of One Quarter Ahead		
ASA-NBER Survey	1.8	1.7	0.1
Bureau of Economic Analysis	1.6	1.4	0.1
Chase Econometrics	1.5	1.4	0.2
Data Resources, Inc.	2.0	1.8	0.2
Wharton	1.8	1.1	0.2
	Forecasts of Two Quarters Ahead		
ASA-NBER Survey	1.4	1.7	0.2
Bureau of Economic Analysis	1.4	1.5	0.2
Chase Econometrics	1.5	1.8	0.3
Data Resources, Inc.	1.6	1.8	0.2
Wharton	1.3	1.6	0.3
	Forecasts of Three Quarters Ahead		
ASA-NBER Survey	1.2	1.7	0.3
Bureau of Economic Analysis	1.5	1.7	0.2
Chase Econometrics	1.2	1.8	0.3
Data Resources, Inc.	1.3	1.7	0.2
Wharton	1.2	1.8	0.3
	Forecasts of One Year Ahead		
ASA-NBER Survey	1.3	1.7	0.3
Bureau of Economic Analysis	1.5	1.7	0.3
Chase Econometrics	1.2	1.6	0.3
Data Resources, Inc.	1.2	1.7	0.3
Wharton	1.0	1.8	0.4

Source: Stephen McNees, "How Accurate Are Economic Forecasts?" *New England Economic Review* (Federal Reserve Bank of Boston) November–December 1974, pp. 2–19.

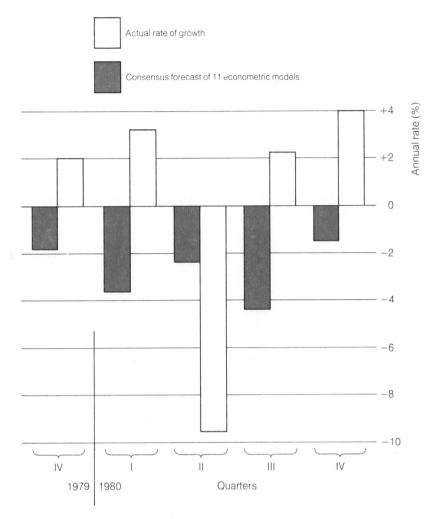

□ Actual rate of growth

■ Consensus forecast of 11 econometric models

FIGURE 14–4 Actual vs. Forecast Growth of Real GNP, 1979–80

This graph shows the relationship between the actual growth rate of GNP and the consensus forecast of eleven econometric models from the fourth quarter of 1979 through the fourth quarter of 1980. Note that the forecasters made their greatest error in the second quarter of 1980, when they greatly underestimated the drop in the rate of growth of GNP.

Source: Based on U.S. Department of Commerce reports.

we should remind ourselves that the economic climate during a period covered by a forecast can change dramatically because of newly instituted monetary and fiscal policies. Moreover, in spite of forecasting errors, many businesses are willing to spend over $10,000 a year for forecasts. In fact, one of the major economic forecasting firms, Data Resources,

Inc., had revenues in 1978 of $31.5 million.[16]

Recently, both economists and the businesses purchasing econometric forecasts have sometimes been unhappy with the accuracy of the forecasters' results. For example, in late

16. See "The Bonanza in Econometrics," *Newsweek*, July 30, 1979, p. 60.

1979 the majority of the forecasts called for a moderate recession during 1980, with real GNP declining less than 2 percent. Even as late as March of 1980, a survey conducted by the American Statistical Association indicated that respondents expected real GNP to decline by only 0.7 percent in the second quarter and 0.2 percent in the third. In April, three of the leading econometric forecasting companies (Data Resources, Chase Econometric Associates, and Wharton Econometric Forecasting Associates) still expected GNP to decline by less than 3 percent.[17] However, *Business Week* noted:

> But when the recession did bite, it was not the paper tiger that had been forecast generally. The economy is well on its way to at least its second worst recession since the 1930s, and quite possibly even the worst. Real GNP plummeted at an annual rate of 8.5% in the second quarter, according to preliminary Commerce Dept. estimates. The unemployment rate shot up 1.6 points in April and May, to 7.8%, on its way to much higher ground.[18]

Figure 14–4 illustrates the difference between the consensus forecast of eleven econometric models regarding growth in real GNP and the actual performance of real GNP during the same period. Needless to say, the forecasters lost face in 1980. They did almost as badly in predicting the 1974 economic downturn. An MIT economist explained at that time, "One advantage the physicist has over the economist is that the velocity of light has not changed over the past thousands of years, while what was in the 1950's and 1960's a good wage and price equation is no longer so."[19]

A basic problem of forecasters is that they have difficulty incorporating into time-tested models the changes in economic structure and in people's expectations. More importantly,

they can only guess what policy changes the executive branch, Congress, the Fed, and international agencies may make over their forecast period. Thus a forecast can be completely turned around by changes over which forecasters have neither control nor predictive power.

The econometric models are still helpful, however, in indicating the results of potential changes in economic policies and events—for example, a tax decrease or an increase in petroleum prices. Such information can be useful to both government and business decision makers. Finally, it seems that, like weather forecasts, people would prefer to have the imperfect information from economic forecasts rather than no information at all.

SUMMARY

1. This chapter concentrated on business cycles and forecasting. The term *business cycle* refers to fluctuations in the level of economic activity in a country. These fluctuations are often discussed in terms of deviations from indexes of long-term trend levels of business activity.

2. Economists typically speak of business cycles as being divided into four phases—a trough, an expansionary period, a peak, and a contractionary period. However, the cycles are not uniform in terms of either their severity or the length of time involved in one cycle. For this reason, some economists prefer to speak of business fluctuations rather than cycles.

3. Economists have observed different sets of business cycles of varying lengths. Minor cycles have had an average duration of forty-four months each in the United States. Major cycles have averaged more than eight years in length. Kuznets cycles, which vary between fifteen and twenty-five years in length, are thought to be related to the construction industry, changes in the rate of population growth, and immigration. Kondratieff suggested the existence of very long cycles of fifty to sixty years. However, little evidence has been found to support the existence of these cycles in real economic variables, such as production.

4. The factors that are thought to contribute to the existence of business cycles are generally separated

17. "1980, the Year the Forecasters Really Blew It," *Business Week*, July 14, 1980, p. 88.

18. Ibid.

19. "Theory Deserts the Forecasters," *Business Week*, June 29, 1974, p. 53.

into two groups—those external to the economic system of a country and those internal to it. In practice, this distinction is often difficult to make.

5. External factors include wars, political cycles, changes in attitude, and international factors. Internal factors include changes in the money supply, lack of competition, and the acceleration principle.

6. The acceleration principle refers to the relationship between changes in sales and gross investment. Specifically, an increase in sales from a steady-state equilibrium position will have a magnified effect on gross investment. Moreover, if the rate of growth of gross investment is to remain constant, the rate of growth of GNP must continue to increase, or accelerate. Of course, this relationship will also operate when sales are falling.

7. Businesses, consumers, and governments are interested in forecasts of the values of economic variables such as interest rates, prices, GNP, and unemployment. In making its forecasts, the federal government uses indicator variables. These variables are divided into three sets: leading, coincident, and lagging indicators. These variables are most useful in forecasting turning points in business cycles.

8. Econometric models employ more sophisticated forecasting techniques. However, even such forecasts are sometimes in error. Still, many people seem to prefer having these forecasts rather than no information at all.

IMPORTANT TERMS AND CONCEPTS

Business cycles	Kondratieff cycles
Expansionary period	Acceleration
Peak	principle
Contractionary period	Accelerator
Trough	Economic indicators
Business fluctuations	Leading indicators
Minor cycles	Coincident indicators
Major cycles	Lagging indicators
Kuznets cycles	Econometric models

QUESTIONS AND PROBLEMS

1. What is meant by the term *business cycle*?

2. Why do we have business cycles? Explain.

3. What external factors are often cited as causes of business cycles? Briefly explain each one.

4. What are the economic indicator variables? How are they used?

5. What is the acceleration principle? Explain by giving an example.

ECONOMIC INDICATORS: TURTLES, BUTTERFLIES, MONKS AND WAITERS

If economic indicators like the length of the average workweek and the percentage of companies reporting slower deliveries leave you cold, try Arkansas Turtles, white Christmases in Boston and last January's Super Bowl.

These and other signals may or may not be as accurate as the standard indicators, but they all have their advocates—or advocate.

The Super Bowl indicator is the brainchild of Leonard Koppett, a sportswriter in Palo Alto, Calif., for the Peninsula Times-Tribune and the Sporting News. It goes back to 1967 and 1968, when the National

Source: "Economic Indicators: Turtles, Butterflies, Monks and Waiters," *Wall Street Journal*, August 27, 1979, pp. 1, 16.

Football League team, the Green Bay Packers, won the first and second Super Bowl games; each time, the stock market was up the following December from the December before. In 1969, the American Football League team, the New York Jets, won the third Super Bowl game; this time the stock market was down the following December.

This pattern has held true almost every year, even after the two leagues merged. If an old NFL team wins the Super Bowl game in January, the market is up the following December; if a former AFL team wins, the market goes down. Last January, two old NFL teams met in the Super Bowl, so an upward trend was predictable even before the game was played.

EXPLANATION IS ELUSIVE

"I've been racking my imagination," Mr. Koppett says, "but I haven't been able to find a reason" why the indicator works. Anyway, he says he doesn't take it very seriously. "All this comes from trying to write a column every week," he says.

The turtles make more sense. Leland Duvall, a business columnist for the *Arkansas Gazette* in Little Rock, says that because the economy in his largely agricultural state depends on the weather, farmers watch the movement of turtles each spring.

"They tell me that if the turtles crossing the road are moving away from the creeks, we'll have a wet, prosperous growing season," Mr. Duvall explains, "but if the turtles are heading for the creeks, we'll be heading for a drought." So far this year, the turtles have been crawling away from the creeks, and Arkansas farmers are looking forward to bumper harvests.

Then there is the BSI—the Boston Snow Index, contrived by David L. Upshaw, a vice president in the research department of Drexel Burnham Lambert, Inc., a New York–based securities firm. "If there is snow on the ground in Boston on Christmas Day, that is a bullish sign for the year to come," Mr. Upshaw says. "It could have snowed the day before or the week before; it doesn't matter, just so there is snow on the ground.

Snow has been on the ground in Boston on 11 Christmas days since 1950, Mr. Upshaw says, and in eight of those cases stock prices rose the following year. The average increases in those 11 years was nearly 10%. Alas, there was no snow on the ground in Boston last Christmas.

Even though the BSI is based on data going back three decades, Mr. Upshaw, like Mr. Koppett, isn't very serious about his index. He calls it "a spoof of forecasters and their indicators, including my own."

MOPS AND BROOMS

Some unusual indicators aren't really odd; they just aren't standard indicators, but they make some sense when you think about them. Mop and broom sales, for example, have unfailingly called turns in consumer spending patterns for the last 10 years, according to Daniel E. Hogan, chairman and chief executive of Standex International Corp. of Salem, N.H.

Standex can track these sales because its National Metal Industries subsidiary in Springfield, Mass., is the sole independent supplier of hardware for the nation's 300-odd mop and broom makers. Its product line includes the metal attachments that hold broom bristles on the handle and the squeegees that go on some mops. When National Metal's sales fall off, consumer spending slips proportionately a little later. When sales pick up, national consumer buying does, too.

It seems that mops and brooms are a deferrable purchase. Homemakers will buy them when they have money to throw around but will put off their purchase when times are tight.

About five months ago, Mr. Hogan says, mop and broom hardware sales dropped, correctly forecasting the second quarter consumer-spending slump. But lately, sales have rebounded strongly, making Mr. Hogan skeptical about the depth of the widely heralded recession.

Similarly, American Greetings Co. of Cleveland, whose cards are sold mostly in drugstores, says it has noticed a relationship between the economy's health and the sales of its higher-priced greeting cards, those costing $1 to $5.

"The experience of our industry has shown that an increase in the sale of higher-priced greeting cards usually signals the beginning of a recession," says Richard H. Connor, senior vice president of marketing. "The increase continues all through the recession."

How come? Mr. Connor can explain it: "The conventional

wisdom has it that in times of financial distress, the consumer who ordinarily buys a gift and an inexpensive card will eliminate the gift and compensate for it by sending a more lavish card."

American Greetings' sales of the higher-priced cards were up sharply in the final quarter ended May 31.

An indicator that is "damn near 100% reliable" is the volume of newspapers' classified advertising, says Marvin C. Veal Jr., president of the Association of Newspaper Classified Advertising Managers, a trade group. "In the past," Mr. Veal says, "if you graphed the gross national product and revenues of classified advertising across the nation, you'd find the same peaks and valleys." In some regions, however, he says, classified's peaks and valleys trail the GNP's by two or three months.

The trade group distributes a monthly newsletter that reports gains and losses in classified volume, based on data from about 100 newspapers. "Right now, results are really kind of hard to figure," Mr. Veal says, "because in the past two months there's been only a minimal softening in classified advertising for employment and for automobiles and merchandise for sale." He says that the number of ads fell first and "now linage is beginning to drop very slightly in certain parts of the country," particularly in the Northeast.

Allan Hyman, marketing director of Best Resumes Services in Pittsburgh, is pretty sure where the economy is heading. "Looks like things are going to get pretty bad pretty fast," he says. Best, a job-search consulting firm, typically derives about 75% of its business from people looking for a better job and about 25% from people who are unemployed. During the recession in 1974, this ratio stood at 50–50. Recently it has slipped from 75–25 to about 65–35.

Getting back to less-economic economic indicators:

• "New England farmers know that if the monarch butterfly heads for Mexico in August or early September, there's going to be a harsh winter," says an official of a fast-growing investment advisory firm in New York. A harsh winter, of course, can hurt the region's economy by disrupting deliveries and causing fuel shortages. So far, so good: The monarch butterfly hasn't yet taken off.
• Kenneth Goldstein, associate economist for the Conference Board, the business research organization, suggests that surliness of waiters is a countercyclical business indicator. When times are bad, waiters are on their best behavior, Mr. Goldstein says, but they get surlier as things start to look up. A Bostonian says that a waiter at an expensive restaurant recently "did everything but shine my shoes"— indicating worsening conditions.
• John B. Olson, an industrial analyst for the Colorado State Commerce and Development Commission, has noticed that "the use of the term 'back burner' multiplies" before a recession hits. "I'd say right now that the back burner is getting pretty crowded," he says, as companies delay more projects.
• "The number of people going into monastic and religious vocations is an inverse indicator," says an executive at Pittsburgh National Bank. He himself was a member of a cloistered order, the Christian Brothers, but he defected in 1968 at the peak of a decade-long economic expansion in the U.S. Such defections, he says, increase with opportunities outside the church, while in bad times the chances of "three squares a day and a good education" draws people into ecclesiastical orders.

"From what I understand from my contacts (in the Christian Brothers)," the executive says, "we must still be in a boom period because religious vocations are at an all-time low."

QUESTIONS

No questions on this article.

CHAPTER 15

ECONOMIC GROWTH

ECONOMIC GROWTH:
FOR BETTER
OR
FOR WORSE?

Economist Michael Boskin recently got his turn in Newsweek's "My Turn" column. Boskin's main task was to raise some questions about U.S. statistics on poverty, federal spending, and growth. One of his revelations was perhaps more surprising than the others. He noted:

We are constantly reminded of the "stubborn problem" of poverty in the United States. Despite the expenditure of hundreds of billions of dollars annually, the official government statistics reveal that about 10 per cent of the U.S. population still lives below the poverty line. Or do they? Back in 1962, when the official poverty index was developed and when about 22 per cent of Americans fell below the poverty line, only *money* income was counted in the index. While the index is adjusted for inflation, family size and location, it excludes the value of in-kind transfer payments, such as food stamps and subsidized housing and medical care. These programs, which were either very small or nonexistent when the poverty index was first developed, now account for a substantial fraction of the income of low-income Americans, and yet they are still not counted. Even conservative estimates of the cash-equivalent value of these programs result in a startling discovery: only about 3 per cent of Americans live below the poverty line.[1]

Boskin is convinced that despite imperfections, our government's attention to the problem has enabled us to "virtually eliminate poverty." He also discussed our GNP:

The United States still has one of the world's highest average standards of living, but our recent growth performance has been simply abysmal, and the usual measures dramatically understate the decline. From 1948 to 1973 inflation-adjusted GNP per capita grew at an average annual rate of 2.4 per cent. At such rates, lifetime incomes double between generations. Since 1973 real GNP per capita has grown at slightly less than half that figure. The 1970s were a period of marked expansion of employment due to the entry into the labor market of the "baby boom" generation and many more married women. Thus, our GNP growth slowed despite a huge influx of new workers. GNP per employed worker grew at only .1 per cent per year, compared with approximately 3 per cent in Japan, Germany and France.[2]

Some of the slack in GNP growth, Boskin noted, is probably a reflection of the expansion of the "underground economy." Furthermore, we still are not sure how to account for improvements in the quality of life, such as pollution abatement.

During the 1960s and 1970s many activists, both inside and outside of economics, questioned whether the United States ought to continue to grow at all. The question still has some validity. After all, if poverty is just about eliminated and our standard of living is among the world's highest, what else do we want?

The answer has to be "more and better." Some people will always be willing to thumb their noses at materialism, but there is plenty of evidence that most of us would like to get bigger and bigger hunks of it. Later in this chapter we will look at some potentially disastrous results of unlimited growth. However, in this chapter we will concentrate on measuring growth, explaining how it can and does take place, and pointing out the kinds of problems even moderate growth can cause.

1. Michael J. Boskin, "Prisoners of Bad Statistics," *Newsweek*, January 26, 1981, p. 15. Condensed from Newsweek. Copyright, 1981, by Newsweek, Inc. All Rights Reserved. Reprinted by Permission.
2. Ibid.

WHAT THIS CHAPTER IS ABOUT

THE MEANING OF GROWTH
GROWTH AND PRODUCTION POSSIBILITIES
THREE CLASSICAL ECONOMIC VIEWS OF
  GROWTH
TWENTIETH CENTURY GROWTH THEORY
ECONOMIC GROWTH IN THE UNITED STATES
PROBLEMS ASSOCIATED WITH GROWTH

In this chapter we will direct our attention to a topic that has attracted the attention of economists throughout modern history—economic growth. Historically, economic growth almost always has been considered a desirable goal. However, as we will see later, in recent years many people have begun to question this attitude.

Among the many dimensions of economic growth are (1) the necessity of growth for increasing the standard of living, (2) its role in facilitating or inhibiting the maintenance of full employment, and (3) its long-term effect on the quality of life. The first two facets of growth are discussed in this chapter, while the last is examined in Chapter 35.

THE MEANING OF GROWTH

The **economic growth** of a country can be defined in various ways—as an increase in gross national product, in real GNP, or in per cap-

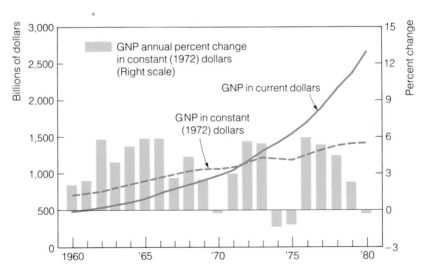

FIGURE 15–1 Gross National Product (GNP) in Current and Constant (1972) Dollars: 1960 to 1980

Both GNP in current dollars and real GNP (in 1972 prices) have continued to grow for most of the last two decades. GNP in current dollars is depicted by the solid black line, whereas real GNP is depicted by the dashed line. The rectangles depict the growth rate of real GNP, which is measured on the right vertical axis.

Source: Chart prepared by U.S. Bureau of the Census.

ita GNP, for example. Figure 15–1 shows current GNP, real GNP in 1972 dollars, and the rate of growth of real GNP in the United States from 1960 to 1980.

The rate of growth of real GNP reflects, at least to some extent, the growth in the productive capacity of a country. (As indicated in Chapter 7, actual GNP and potential, or full employment, GNP □ are not necessarily equal.) In situations that require a measure of the total productive capacity, this measure of growth is the relevant one. For example, the rate of growth of real GNP might be an important factor in measuring the ability of a nation to increase its commitment to a mutual defense force, such as the North Atlantic Treaty Organization (NATO).

However, the measure of growth that seems to best reflect the increase in the well-being of the people of a country is the **rate of growth of real per capita GNP.**

The levels of per capita GNP in the United States in constant (1958) dollars from 1869 to 1980 are shown in Table 15–1. As indicated in this table, real per capita GNP has grown from $531 in the 1870s to $4,389 in 1980, a substantial increase.

The growth rates of real total and per capita GNP from 1974 to 1979 for the United States and other selected countries are shown in Table 15–2. As can be seen from this table, the United States is neither the fastest nor the slowest growing country in this group. Some of the reasons cited for economic growth in the United States being slower than it might be are a short-term outlook on the part of corporate managers, insufficient tax incentives for saving and investment, contradictory government regulatory policies, government economic policy measures that promote uncertainty and make long-range planning difficult, and, to some extent, the behavior of labor unions.[1] Some of these topics have already

been discussed, and others are examined later in this book.

GROWTH AND PRODUCTION POSSIBILITIES

We can examine the meaning of economic growth through the use of a production possibilities curve. □ In Chapter 1 a **production possibilities curve** was used to depict the maximum quantities of two goods or types of goods that can be produced when all of the resources of a country are fully and efficiently utilized.

TABLE 15–1 GNP and Per Capita GNP, 1869–1980 (in 1958 Prices)

Year	Gross National Product (in Billions of Dollars)	Per Capita GNP (in Dollars)
1869–1878[a]	$ 23.1	$ 531
1879–1888[a]	42.4	774
1890	52.7	836
1900	76.9	1,011
1910	120.1	1,229
1920	140.0	1,315
1930	183.5	1,490
1935	169.5	1,331
1940	227.2	1,720
1950	355.3	2,342
1960	487.7	2,699
1970	722.5	3,555
1975	807.9	4,009
1980	977.8	4,389

Sources: Series F1–5, U.S. Department of Commerce, Bureau of the Census, "Gross National Product, Total and Per Capita, in Current and 1958 Prices: 1869–1970," *Historical Statistics of the United States, Colonial Times to 1970* (Washington, D.C.: Government Printing Office, 1975), p. 224; "Table 715: Gross National Product in Current and Constant (1972) Dollars: 1950 to 1978," and "Table 719: Per Capita Income and Product for Selected Items: 1950 to 1978," U.S. Department of Commerce, Bureau of the Census, *Statistical Abstract of the United States, 1979* (Washington, D.C.: Government Printing Office, 1979), pp. 437–438; "Table B–3: Implicit Price Deflators for Gross National Product, 1929–79," *Economic Report of the President* (Washington, D.C.: Government Printing Office, 1980), p. 207; "Table B–2: Gross National Product in 1972 Dollars, 1929–80," and "Table B–26: Population by Age Group, 1929–80," *Economic Report of the President* (Washington, D.C.: Government Printing Office, 1981), pp. 234, 263.

---

1. See "The Reindustrialization of America," *Business Week*, June 30, 1980, pp. 56–84.

TABLE 15–2 Annual Growth Rates of Real GNP and Real Per Capita GNP for Selected Countries, 1974–1979

Country	Growth Rate of Real GNP	Growth Rate of Real Per Capita GNP
United States	3.3%	2.4%
Austria	2.7	2.8
France	2.8	2.4
West Germany	2.8	3.0
Greece	5.1	4.1
Italy	2.1	1.5
Portugal	2.7	1.1
Spain	2.0	0.9
Switzerland	− 1.1	− 0.7
Turkey	5.3	2.7
United Kingdom	1.6	1.6
Australia	2.9	1.7
Canada	3.1	2.0
Japan	5.1	4.0

Source: U.S. Department of Commerce, Bureau of the Census, "Table 1585: Organization for Economic Cooperation and Development (OECD)—Gross National Product, 1975 to 1979, and Change, 1974–1979 and 1978–1979," *Statistical Abstract of the United States, 1980* (Washington, D.C.: Government Printing Office, 1980), p. 910.

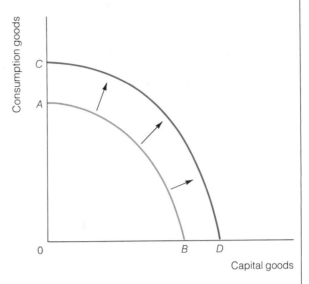

FIGURE 15–2 Growth Shifts the Production Possibilities Curve

The curved lines *AB* and *CD*, respectively, represent two production possibilities curves for a nation. Suppose the production possibilities curve is initially *AB*. If growth takes place so that the production possibilities curve shifts to *CD*, the country can produce more capital goods or consumption goods or both than before.

Figure 15–2 shows a production possibilities curve for capital goods and consumption goods. Initially, a country can produce any single combination of capital goods and consumer goods denoted by the production possibilities curve *AB*. (Of course, the country could produce a combination of capital goods and consumer goods inside *AB*, but these combinations would not entail a full and efficient utilization of the country's resources.)

If growth takes place, the production possibilities curve will shift outward, perhaps to *CD*. In this case the country can produce more of both capital goods and consumption goods.

Of course, the combination of consumption goods and capital goods produced this year will affect the growth of the country and its production possibilities curve next year. For example, if only consumption goods are produced this year, growth may not take place. In fact, if no capital goods are produced, the productive capacity of the country will likely decrease, as plants and equipment now in use wear out. On the other hand, the greater the proportion of capital goods relative to consumption goods produced, the greater is the potential for growth. Clearly, then, the way an economy grows in the future depends on choices made in the present. Choosing to consume at high levels now may make it impossible to do so in the future.

How should the choices that affect economic growth be made? Will they be made automatically in a capitalistic, free enterprise system? What are the possible outcomes of capitalistic growth? Economists have long struggled with the answers to these and other growth related questions. In the next two sections of this chapter, some of their thoughts on these issues are summarized. These sections will begin with Adam Smith in 1776 and end with some twentieth century contributors to economic thought.

THREE CLASSICAL ECONOMIC VIEWS OF GROWTH

◆

The question of economic growth was an important topic of discussion for the classical economists. For one thing, they lived in eighteenth and nineteenth century Europe, where the industrial revolution was just beginning to take hold. For another, some of them were beginning to question the results of long-term population growth. Finally, they were beginning to realize that available land and natural resources were limited.

In this section we will look at the views of three classical economists—Adam Smith, Thomas Malthus, and Karl Marx—with respect to economic growth. Although other classical economists discussed such growth, the ideas of these three will illustrate the range of classical economic thought on the subject.

ADAM SMITH

Earlier in this book we examined Adam Smith's view of how the "invisible hand" □ of self-interest would promote the division of labor, increased production, and economic progress in general. In fact, Smith recognized that much economic growth could be obtained through specialization of labor and application of new technology as well as through international trade.

Nevertheless, Smith saw that economic development would be limited without an increase in capital equipment:

The annual produce of the land and labour of any nation can be increased in its value by no other means, but by increasing either the number of its productive labourers, or the productive powers of those labourers who had before been employed. The number of its productive labourers, it is evident, can never be much increased, but in consequence of an increase of capital, or of the funds destined for maintaining them. The productive powers of the same number of labourers cannot be increased, but in consequence either of some addition and improvement to those machines . . . which facilitate . . . labour; or of a more proper division and distribution of employment. In either case an additional capital is almost always required.[2]

With regard to the progress of economic growth, Smith said:

According to the natural course of things, therefore, the greater part of the capital of every growing society is, first, directed to agriculture, afterwards to manufactures, and last of all to foreign commerce.[3]

However, Smith also recognized that in the case of many European countries the natural order was inverted. He argued that this pattern of growth was the result of manners and customs promoted by the countries' original forms of government.

Smith's outlook for long-run growth was fairly optimistic. He believed that gains in output through the means discussed here could continue to be made for the foreseeable future. He thought that the real wage rate would tend to rise and fall on the basis of the rate of population growth relative to the rate of technological advance and investment in capital equipment. However, his outlook on the long-term prospects of labor was not nearly as gloomy as that of Thomas Malthus, who is discussed next.

THOMAS MALTHUS

Thomas Malthus, writing in the nineteenth century, took a dim view of the long-term economic prospects of civilization. He began his analysis with two seemingly uncontroversial

---

2. Adam Smith, *An Inquiry into the Nature and Causes of the Wealth of Nations* (1776; New York: Random House, 1937), p. 326.

3. Ibid., p. 360.

assumptions: "that food is necessary to the existence of man" and "that the passion between the sexes is necessary and will remain nearly in its present state."[4]

Malthus then made two further assertions that are definitely open to question. First he argued that population would increase geometrically (by a constant multiple) unless its growth were inhibited in some way. Then he argued that food and other items necessary for subsistence could increase only arithmetically (by the addition of a constant). For example, suppose population grew at a rate of 10 percent a year. If the population stood initially at 100 people, it would increase according to the following schedule, so that in sixty years there would be 30,448 people:

Year	Population
0	100
1	110
2	121
.	.
.	.
.	.
8	214
.	.
.	.
.	.
20	673
.	.
.	.
.	.
60	30,448

On the other hand, if the initial quantity of food and other necessities available per year was 1,000 tons and this figure grew at the arithmetic rate of 100 tons per year, in sixty years the yearly quantity supplied of these items would be only 7,000 tons, as shown in the following table:

Year	Tons of Necessities Available
0	1,000
1	1,100
2	1,200
.	.
.	.
.	.,
8	1,800
.	.
.	.
.	.
20	3,000
.	.
.	.
.	.
60	7,000

If such trends were to continue, the growth in population would eventually mean that an insufficient supply of food would be available to support the world's inhabitants at even a subsistence level. No matter what the geometric rate of population growth (above zero) and no matter what the arithmetic constant by which the supply of food increased, this gloomy result would be inevitable. Depending on the numbers, it would merely occur at different times.

According to Malthus, the means of supplying the necessities of life would not grow as quickly as the population because the quantity of natural resources, commonly grouped under the term *land*, was fixed. When increasing numbers of workers were combined with fixed amounts of land, eventually the last worker added would increase total production by a smaller amount than the next-to-last worker added. This phenomenon is an example of the principle of diminishing returns. □

The **principle of diminishing returns** states that when equal increments (amounts) of one variable input are added to the productive process, all other inputs held constant, after some point the addition to total product accounted for by the last unit of input added will begin to fall.

---

4. Thomas Robert Malthus, *On Population* (1798; New York: Random House, 1960), p. 8.

For example, suppose a farmer has a large field of wheat that needs to be harvested, one self-propelled combine, and two trucks to haul the wheat. With no units of labor, total output will be zero, because someone must operate the machinery.

If one worker is added, total output produced (bushels of wheat harvested) per day will certainly increase dramatically. If a second worker is added, the resulting increase in total product (output) per day may be even greater than that from the first worker, since the two workers can specialize—one running the combine and the other driving the truck. However, if the farmer continues to add more workers to the production process, keeping acres of wheat and equipment fixed, after some point (at least after the third or fourth person), the increase in total output per day occurring as a result of adding one more worker will begin to drop.

Malthus had a similar situation in mind when he spoke of the means of subsistence increasing only according to an arithmetic progression. He visualized greater and greater numbers of workers being added to a fixed quantity of land. It is apparent that he also considered the use of capital goods and employment in manufacturing industries when he reached this conclusion: "Dr. Adam Smith defines the wealth of a nation to consist in the annual produce of its land and labour. This definitely includes manufactured produce, as well as the produce of the land."[5]

However, Malthus went on to say that if all of the additional capital were used in the production of manufactured goods, the demand for labor and the wage rate might increase, but the available food supply would not. Consequently, both the money wage rate and the price of food (provisions) would rise. Moreover, even if some of the capital were used in agriculture, a positive impact on the food supply would be slow in coming, if it came at all.

Malthus thought that the population of the earth would double itself every twenty-five years if left unchecked:

A thousand million are just as easily doubled every twenty-five years by the power of population as a thousand. But the food to support the increase from the greater number will by no means be obtained with the same facility.

. . . taking the whole earth . . . and, supposing the present population equal to a thousand millions, the human species would increase as the numbers 1, 2, 4, 8, 16, 32, 64, 128, 256, and subsistence as 1, 2, 3, 4, 5, 6, 7, 8, 9. In two centuries the population would be to the means of subsistence as 256 to 9; in three centuries 4096 to 13, and in two thousand years the difference would be almost incalculable.

In this supposition no limits whatever are placed to the produce of the earth. It may increase for ever and be greater than any assignable quantity; yet still the power of population being in every period so much superior, the increase of the human species can only be kept down to the level of the means of subsistence by the constant operation of the strong law of necessity.[6]

Thus Malthus thought the population would grow until the means of subsistence could no longer support it. At this point misery (starvation, disease) and vice (murder, wars) would come into play and reduce the population. Malthus also believed that moral restraints (such as marrying later) would have a preventive effect but that they would not be sufficient. It is from Malthus, then, that economics inherited the reputation of being "the dismal science."

Karl Marx, the last classical economic thinker to be discussed here, also thought that laborers would generally be miserable. However, his view of the long-term result of economic growth through a capitalistic system was quite different from that of Malthus.

KARL MARX

Marx did much of his writing around the middle of the nineteenth century. He believed,

---

5. Ibid., p. 110.

6. Ibid., pp. 154–157.

like Malthus, that wage rates would be driven to approximately the subsistence level. However, Marx did not couch his argument in quite the same terms as did Malthus.

Malthus was concerned with population growth outrunning the growth of food and other necessities of life. Marx thought that the growth of capitalistic systems, requiring the use of more and more machinery, would create a reserve army of the unemployed.

> The **reserve army of the unemployed** would be former workers who had been replaced by machines.

Other workers would be forced to work as servants for the wealthy (Smith's unproductive labor).

As a result of this process the wage rate would be kept low. Moreover, Marx argued that as more capital equipment was used, the profit rate would also fall. In order to prevent this lowering of the profit rate, the capitalists would have to keep developing new technology and incorporating it into new and better capital equipment. However, such innovations would eventually result in even more people becoming unemployed.

Marx thought that business cycles □ occurred because of the fundamental contradiction of capitalism—production for profit rather than use. He visualized business cycles as having the following stages. During boom periods the demand for labor would increase, depleting the reserve army. As a result, wage rates would rise, profits would fall, and investment would therefore decrease. The decline in investment would reduce aggregate demand and mark the beginning of the downturn. As the downturn progressed, the reserve army would grow and wage rates would fall.

Marx believed that in the long run capitalism as an economic system was doomed:

The transformation of the individualised and scattered means of production into socially concentrated ones, of the pigmy property of the many into the huge property of the few, the expropriation of the great mass of people from the soil, from the means of subsistence, and from the means of labour, . . . forms the prelude to the history of capital. . . .

As soon as this process of transformation has sufficiently decomposed the old society from top to bottom, as soon as the labourers are turned into proletarians, their means of labour into capital, as soon as the capitalist mode of production stands on its own feet, then the further socialisation of labour and further transformation of the land and other means of production into socially exploited . . . takes a new form. That which is now to be expropriated is no longer the labourer working for himself, but the capitalist exploiting many labourers. This expropriation is accomplished by the action of the immanent laws of capitalistic production itself, by the centralisation of capital. One capitalist always kills many. . . . Along with the constantly diminishing number of the magnates of capital, who usurp and monopolise all advantages of this process of transformation, grows the mass of misery, oppression, slavery, degradation, exploitation; but with this too grows the revolt of the working class, a class always increasing in numbers, and disciplined, united, organised by the very mechanism of the process of capitalist production itself. . . . Centralisation of the means of production and socialisation of labour at last reach a point where they become incompatible with their capitalist integument. This integument is burst asunder. The knell of capitalist private property sounds. The expropriators are expropriated.

. . . This does not re-establish private property for the producer, but gives him individual property based on the acquisitions of the capitalist era: i.e., on co-operation and possession in common of the land and of the means of production.[7]

The downfall of capitalism that Marx foretold has not been realized. Indeed, the industrialized countries of the West have managed to avoid both socioeconomic collapse and the dilemma of overpopulation that so haunted Malthus. Still, today there is renewed interest in both lines of argument because of a slow-down in the growth of productivity in the leading countries, alarm over the depletion of certain natural resources, and rather persis-

---

7. Karl Marx, *Capital: A Critique of Political Economy* (New York: Random House, 1906), pp. 835–837.

tent growth of population in the less developed countries.

The last issue is examined in detail in Chapter 32. Our task now is to consider a post-Keynesian growth theory that has been constructed with modern capitalist economies, such as that of the United States, in mind. Then, we will survey twentieth century U.S. economic growth and address the question of the slackening productivity in the United States.

A TWENTIETH CENTURY GROWTH THEORY[8]

◆

Until this chapter, the problem of business cycles has been analyzed from a narrow perspective—without considering the impact of investment and growth in the labor force on the capacity to produce output at full employment. If net investment (investment above replacement) occurs, the full employment level of output will increase as a result.

Sir Roy Harrod and Evsey Domar, as well as other twentieth century economists, have constructed models that incorporate growth of productive capacity and population into the determination of a full employment level of income. A simplified version of these models, using especially the work of Domar, will be presented here.

A DOMAR-TYPE GROWTH MODEL

To simplify matters, let us assume that government expenditures, taxes, and net exports are zero. From Chapter 6 we know that an equilibrium level of national income □ will occur where the aggregate quantity demanded is equal to the aggregate quantity supplied. Equilibrium also implies that the level of saving,

S, is equal to the amount of net planned investment, □ I: or S = I.

Furthermore, if we assume that, given current production technology, the desired ratio of capital equipment to output stays constant, then we can express the capital-output ratio, K/Y, as the constant k.

> The **capital-output ratio,** k, is the desired ratio of capital to output for the economy.

In this case, an amount of net investment equal to I will result in an increase in productive capacity, Y_s, of

$$\Delta Y_s = I \times \frac{1}{k} =$$
$$= I \times \text{Ratio of output to capital equipment.}$$
$$(15-1)$$

If this change in productive capacity is to be fully utilized, aggregate demand must rise in the next period by an amount equal to ΔY_s, so that

$$\Delta Y_s = \Delta C + \Delta I, \qquad (15-2)$$

where ΔC is equal to the change in consumption expenditures. As stated in Chapter 6, ΔC must be equal to $b\Delta Y$, where b is the marginal propensity to consume. □ Substituting $b\Delta Y$ for ΔC in Equation 15–2, we obtain

$$\Delta Y_s = b\Delta Y_s + \Delta I. \qquad (15-3)$$

Now, subtracting $b\Delta Y_s$ from both sides of Equation 15–3, we find

$$\Delta Y_s - b\Delta Y_s = \Delta I.$$

Moreover,

$$(1 - b)\,\Delta Y_s = \Delta I,$$

or

$$\Delta Y_s = \frac{\Delta I}{1 - b}. \qquad (15-4)$$

From Equations 15–1 and 15–4 we know, therefore, that

$$\Delta Y_s = \frac{\Delta I}{1 - b} = I \times \frac{1}{k}. \qquad (15-5)$$

---

8. This section can be eliminated with little loss of continuity.

333

If we divide the two right-hand terms of Equation 15–5 by I, we get

$$\frac{\Delta I}{(1 - b)\, I} = \frac{1}{k}.$$

Finally, if we multiply both sides of this equation by $(1 - b)$, we obtain the rate of growth of investment, $\Delta I/I$, which is required to maintain a sufficiently high level of aggregate demand to utilize the productive capacity of the new capital equipment:

$$\frac{\Delta I}{I} = \frac{(1 - b)}{k} = \frac{s}{k},$$

where s is the marginal propensity to save. □ In our model, income must also grow at the same rate as investment in order for growth with equilibrium levels of income to occur over time. Thus an equilibrium rate of growth will occur when

$$\frac{\Delta Y}{Y} = \frac{\Delta I}{I} = \frac{s}{k}.$$

THE WARRANTED RATE OF GROWTH

Harrod called this equilibrium rate of growth the warranted rate of growth.

The **warranted rate of growth** is the rate of growth that will bring forth sufficient aggregate demand to maintain full capacity use of the capital stock.

This rate of growth may be difficult for a country to attain. In fact, if the actual rate of growth, G_a, is less than the warranted rate, G_w, business firms will have unsold goods and will therefore reduce investment expenditures and production, which will further accentuate the problem. On the other hand, if businesses invest too much, so that $G_a > G_w$, aggregate quantity demanded will be greater than aggregate quantity supplied. It will appear to businesses that they have invested too little. Consequently, they will increase their capital

goods expenditures, thereby raising the level of excess aggregate demand.

Harrod also speaks of the natural rate of growth.

The **natural rate of growth** is the maximum possible sustained rate at which an economy can grow, considering both labor force growth and growth of productive capacity.

If the warranted rate of growth, G_w, is greater than the natural rate of growth, G_n, long-run stagnation involving unemployment will result, because the full capacity rate of growth will be above the full employment ceiling. In this case, the actual rate of growth must be less than G_w. Therefore, planned investment will be less than planned saving, and a tendency toward unemployment and excess capacity will result. If G_w is less than G_n, unemployment will still tend to exist. Thus the Harrod and Domar models have been called "knife-edge" models because they have no built-in economic stabilizers that tend to bring an economy back to a full employment equilibrium rate of growth once it has strayed from it.

In the picture painted by Harrod and Domar the prospects for long-term economic growth are rather precarious. The two economists indicate that government fiscal or monetary policies will be necessary to return an economy to a path of full employment growth once it has deviated from such a course. Other modern-day economists, such as Milton Friedman and Edmund Phelps, and economists of the neoclassical school place more faith in the ability of the market to adjust saving rates and the capital-output ratio if left to itself. In this way an economy can return to a full employment equilibrium rate of growth without government intervention.

The U.S. experience in the twentieth century has involved both periods of relatively little government manipulation of economic aggregates and periods in which government has intervened vigorously to pursue stability and employment objectives. This variation in the extent of government intervention occurred because government policy has been oriented more toward unemployment and inflation than toward growth. Recent research into the sources of U.S. economic growth suggests that technological change and the skill and training of the labor force figure importantly in the nation's long-term economic success. These findings are reviewed in the following section.

ECONOMIC GROWTH IN THE UNITED STATES

Throughout most of its history the story of economic development in the United States

has been one of success. In this section the history of growth in the United States will be examined and then related to the concerns of some economists about the present situation.

THE HISTORICAL RECORD

During the twentieth century real gross national product has grown at an average annual compound rate of about 3.25 percent. Real GNP per capita has grown at an average annual compound rate of slightly less than 2 percent.

In Figure 15–3 the growth in real GNP, the real capital stock, and the labor force since 1925 is depicted. In this graph index numbers are used. The value that each of the three items had in 1925 is assigned an index number of 100; thus all of the variables start at 100.

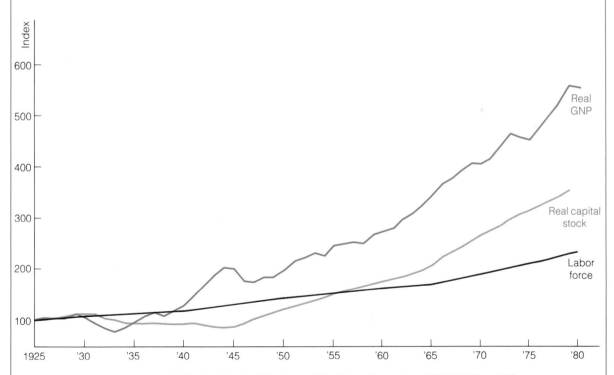

FIGURE 15–3 Growth in Real GNP, Real Capital Stock, and the Labor Force since 1925 (1925 = 100)

Real GNP, the capital stock, and the labor force have all grown since 1925. Real GNP has grown most rapidly, and it is now over five times as large as it was in 1925. The capital stock is over three times as large as it was in 1925, whereas the labor force is only somewhat over twice as large.

The index numbers work in the following way. If an economic variable, such as GNP in 1944, reaches an index number of 200, the variable has grown so that it is 200/100, or twice its size in 1925. If one of the variables drops to an index number of 80, as real capital stock does in 1940, that variable is 80/100, or 0.8 of its size in 1925.

As shown in Figure 15–3, real GNP has increased to more than five times its size since 1925. The labor force has doubled in size, but the quantity of capital assets—plant and equipment—has more than tripled. In this case economists say that *capital deepening* has occurred.

Capital deepening occurs when the stock of capital increases relative to the quantity of labor.

As noted earlier, in spite of population growth, real GNP per person has continued to increase in the United States. Unquestionably, the growth of real capital stock has had some role in increasing labor productivity.

According to economist Edward F. Denison, the increase in the labor force accounted for 28 percent of the growth in potential business output from 1929 to 1948, but it accounted for only 15 percent of the growth between 1948 and 1973. Increased education per worker accounted for 19 percent of the growth in the former period but for only 13.5 percent in the latter. More capital accounted for only 2.9 percent of the growth from 1929 to 1948, but it accounted for 14.6 percent from 1948 to 1973. The biggest single factor was advances in knowledge, or technological advances, which accounted for 23.9 percent of the growth of potential GNP in the earlier period and 37.2 percent from 1948 to 1973.[9] These results and the effects of other factors are summarized in Table 15–3.

In Figure 15–4, the growth in output per labor-hour and the growth of the real hourly wage rate since 1925 are depicted. Index numbers are used as they were in Figure 15–3. As shown in Figure 15–4, output per labor-hour has more than doubled since 1925. Although it has not grown as much as labor productivity, the real wage rate has also risen during most of this period.

9. Edward F. Denison, *Accounting for Slower Economic Growth: The United States in the 1970s* (Washington, D.C.: Brookings Institution, 1979), p. 96.

TABLE 15–3 Contribution of Various Factors to Growth Rate of Potential Output of Nonresidential Businesses

Source of Growth	Percentage Points of Growth in Potential Output		Percent of Growth Rate	
	1929–48	1948–73	1929–48	1948–73
All sources	2.43	3.84	100.0	100.0
More work done	0.68	0.58	28.0	15.1
Increased education per worker	0.47	0.52	19.3	13.5
More capital	0.07	0.56	2.9	14.6
Advances in knowledge	0.58	1.43	23.9	37.2
Improved resource allocation	0.37	0.39	15.2	10.2
Changes in legal and human environment	0.00	−0.05	0.0	−1.3
Economies of large-scale production	0.27	0.42	11.1	10.9
Miscellaneous factors	−0.01	−0.01	−0.4	−0.3

Source: Edward F. Denison, *Accounting for Slower Economic Growth: The United States in the 1970s* (Washington, D.C.: Brookings Institution, 1979), p. 96.

THE RECENT SLOWDOWN
OF PRODUCTIVITY GROWTH

Since 1973, Denison and others have noticed a drop in the growth of output per unit of input in the United States. Denison suggests that some of the factors contributing to this decline in productivity growth may be inflation, government regulation, soaring energy prices, and high taxes. Other suggested factors that Denison considers of less importance over this particular period are a slowdown in the advancement of knowledge, the incorporation of new knowledge into production, and changing attitudes on the part of the people. Nevertheless, Denison argues that much more research into the productivity issue is needed.[10]

U.S. growth has been impressive, despite the recent lag in the rate of increase of productivity. However, growth in the United States, as elsewhere, has generated some economic problems that are difficult to separate from the growth process itself. These problems are touched on briefly in the next section. Some of them are discussed in more detail in later chapters.

_____

10. Ibid., Chapter 9.

PROBLEMS ASSOCIATED WITH GROWTH

Even though economists consider growth of the productive capacity of an economy to be generally desirable, rapid economic growth may have some disadvantages.

RESOURCES AND THE ENVIRONMENT

Rapid growth entails an ever-increasing demand for resources. In fact, it may be accompanied by the depletion of natural resources on a worldwide scale. The recent alarm over the depletion of energy resources such as oil and gas has called attention to this issue. In addition, the growth of all kinds of production brings with it a problem of waste management. The danger that the environment will be increasingly damaged by careless exploitation of resources and mishandling of pollutants and toxic materials has become very real. (See Chapter 35.)

The price system can play an important role in rearranging our activities in ways that will

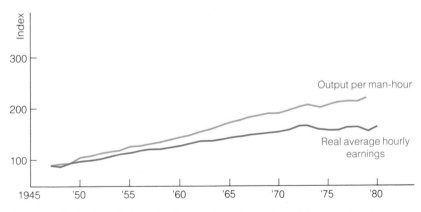

FIGURE 15–4 Growth in Output per Labor-Hour and Real Average Hourly Earnings since 1945 (1945 = 100)

Over the last thirty years, output per man-hour has grown more rapidly than real average hourly earnings. Output per man-hour is over twice as large as it was in 1947, whereas real average hourly earnings are less than twice as large.

Source: _Economic Report of the President_ and _Statistical Abstract of the United States,_ various years.

both prolong and spread economic growth. For example, as nonrenewable resources become more scarce, their prices will rise relative to other resources. These increases should lead to substitution effects □ that will both conserve scarce resources and improve the technology applicable to those that are more abundant or renewable. It is even possible that such price increases will reduce waste and eliminate certain kinds of pollution.

However, it may be risky to depend entirely on the price system to deal with the questions of allocating nonrenewable resources over the long run and protecting the physical environment. What is there in the markets of today that will provide us an incentive to conserve fuel for the automobile drivers of tomorrow? In fact, if the future looks dim, people might decide to take a devil-may-care attitude and use up scarce resources to have a great fling today! Likewise, we can easily choose to let some of the costs of environmental decay be shifted to our neighbors or our posterity. It is doubtful, then, that we can get along without any planning in matters of resource depletion and environmental protection.

INCOME DISTRIBUTION

Although economic growth makes possible the production of more goods and services for a country as a whole, the benefits of growth are frequently not distributed equally among the individual citizens. To economists, inequality of the individual rewards from growth is not all bad. In fact, it is through such inequality that the market system sends its signals regarding what should be produced, how it should be produced, by whom it should be produced, and which occupations have the greatest number of vacancies.

However, if the disparity in incomes and the standard of living among individuals becomes too great, resentment and social unrest result. The problems of poverty and income distribution are discussed at greater length in Chapter 34.

Growth is important for those who desire a rising standard of living. The problem is how to promote and manage growth so that all of society will benefit. *Business Week* summarizes this situation as follows:

Stated plainly, all social groups in the U.S. today must come to understand that their common interest in returning the country to a path of strong economic growth overrides other conflicting interests. The adversary relationships of the past were tolerable because they centered mostly on how to distribute an expanding output of goods and services. Taking growth for granted is no longer possible.

If the country tries to pretend otherwise, further economic decline and social disruption are inevitable as various groups struggle for more and more of less and less. Continuing economic decline means that no group in society will achieve its aspirations.[11]

THE LIMITS TO GROWTH

The title of this section, "The Limits to Growth" is the same as that of a controversial book on world development published in 1972. The book, produced by an MIT research team headed by Donella H. Meadows and Dennis L. Meadows, was the final report of a project commissioned by The Club of Rome and financed by the Volkswagen Foundation. The Club of Rome is an elite group of business people, professionals and academicians who have organized an "invisible college" to " . . . foster understanding of the varied but interdependent components—economic, political, natural, and social—that make up the global system in which we all live; to bring that new understanding to the attention of policy-makers and the public worldwide; and in this way to promote new policy initiatives and action."[12]

In *The Limits to Growth* (LTG), a model of the world is formulated using a computer-based technique known as systems analysis.

11. "Creating a New Sense of Teamwork," *Business Week*, June 30, 1980, p. 86.

12. Donella H. Meadows, *et. al.*, *The Limits to Growth*, New York: Universe Books, 1972, p. 9.

The LTG model is not an economic model; it is an engineering model. It relies much less on data analysis than on intuitive assertions of the model builders. The "standard run" of the LTG world model assumes that population, production, and pollution will grow at exponential rates but that natural resources are absolutely fixed in supply. (Recall that Malthus also expected population to eventually outrun resources.) With such assumptions, it is not surprising that LTG predicts a world-wide social and economic collapse will eventually occur. The surprise is *how soon* the collapse is scheduled to take place.

Under the most pessimistic assumptions, LTG predicts collapse well before the year 2100. The collapse occurs because of depletion of nonrenewable resources; population continues to rise for awhile as per capita income plummets, but . . . "Population finally decreases when the death rate is driven upward because of lack of food and health services."[13] Worse yet, a doubling of the natural resources base produces almost the same collapse, but the cause is pollution!

In this case the primary force that stops growth is a sudden increase in the level of pollution, caused by an overloading of the natural absorptive capacity of the environment. The death rate rises abruptly from pollution and from lack of food.[14]

Gloom and Doom! But did the authors of LTG see any way out for mankind? Indeed they did. In fact, they found that the world model would predict an equilibrium, steady-state level of population, production, and pollution, attained early in the twenty-first century, if the following policies would have been instituted in 1975:

1. Population is controlled so that the birth rate is equal to the death rate.
2. Natural resource consumption per unit of output is reduced to one-fourth of its 1970 level.

3. Pollution per unit of output is reduced to one-fourth its 1970 level.

The LTG authors cautioned that putting off the above policies until the year 2000 would lead to serious food and resources shortages before the year 2100.

Of course, 1975 has come and gone, and the year 2000 is not very far off. We are nowhere near the policies prescribed by LTG, although population growth has slowed dramatically in the industrialized countries. What has happened is that The Club of Rome, as well as other international organizations, scholars, interest groups and government agencies have continued to build models and study the problem of alternative futures. Most of the recent studies are more optimistic than LTG, but most still recognize the notion of a limit to industrialization and to the carrying capacity of planet earth.

In general, economists have been quite critical of the Club of Rome models, especially the LTG model which was completed first and attracted the most attention. Their criticism hinges on the structure of the model and on many of its key assumptions regarding fixed supplies of land and resources, constant productivity, and pollution increases. One economist alleged in 1977 that the Club of Rome " . . . showed a deplorable lack of understanding of how the economic system works and what role prices play."[15]

ECONOMISTS AND THE STATIONARY STATE

In general, economists have rejected the disastrous predictions of LTG and other similar studies but have agreed that exhaustion of certain resources and population increases do point in the direction of an eventual leveling off of growth. This premise leads directly to the notion of a *stationary state.*

13. *Ibid.,* p. 125

14. *Ibid.,* p. 126

15. Herbert G. Grubel, "The Case Against the New International Economic Order," *Weltwirtschaftliches Archiv.,* Band 113, No. 2 (1977), p. 301.

*The **stationary state** is present in an economic system when real output and population remain about the same size and, as one economist has put it, the rule of "more is better" is replaced by that of "enough is best."*[16]

The stationary state notion has a long history in economics. David Ricardo□ predicted a no-growth, stationary state that would occur as increases in population drove profits to zero and allocated all factor payments to labor and rent. Ricardo's stationary state was one in which most of the population lived at a subsistence level, with no hope for improvement. His disciple, John Stuart Mill,□ envisioned a stationary state where, "while no one is poor, no one desires to be richer."[17] Even John Maynard Keynes□ believed that capitalist growth could eventually solve the economic problem of scarcity and that mankind would have to seek other outlets for its creative energy, but he cautioned:

" . . . beware! The time for all this is not yet. For at least another hundred years we must pretend to ourselves and to everyone that fair is foul and foul is fair; for foul is useful and fair is not. Avarice and usury and precaution must be our gods for a little longer still."[18]

Throughout modern history, intellectual contemplation of the future has frequently led to the conclusion that some sort of steady state economy must eventually emerge. This has happened because the alternatives to such a result seem always to be disasters of one sort or another. Certainly, there is a strong presumption that growth must eventually level off or at least change in form. In fact, much of the current debate has to do with how soon

this metamorphosis will happen and the extent of the changes in government and society it will require.

SUMMARY

1. The economic growth of a country can be defined in various ways—as an increase in gross national product, in real GNP, or in real per capita GNP, for example. In this chapter, real per capita GNP was emphasized.

2. While real per capita GNP in the United States has grown substantially since the 1870s, its current growth rate is not particularly outstanding compared to that of other countries with market economies. Among the reasons cited for this situation are insufficient tax incentives for saving and investment, government regulatory policies, and government economic policies that promote uncertainty.

3. Growth can be represented by an outward shift in the production possibilities curve. This curve shows various possible combinations of two goods or types of goods that a country can produce if its resources are fully and efficiently employed.

4. Adam Smith had a basically optimistic view of a country's prospects for long-term economic growth. He emphasized the gains in production that could be achieved through specialization and division of labor, innovation, and capital equipment.

5. Thomas Malthus argued that the earth's population was bound to eventually exceed the means of supporting it because natural resources were limited. Periodically the natural checks of misery and vice would be forced into action.

6. Karl Marx believed that the process of industrialization would create a reserve army of the unemployed. However, he also believed that as the number of exploited and unemployed workers grew, capitalism would eventually bring about its own downfall.

7. According to Sir Roy Harrod, the warranted rate of growth is the rate of growth at which full capacity utilization of capital stock will be maintained. The natural rate of growth is the maximum rate of growth that can be maintained indefinitely, given the rate of growth in the labor force. The Harrod and Domar growth models are called knife-edge models because they do not include any automatic

16. Herman E. Daly, *Steady-State Economics* (San Francisco: W. H. Freeman and Company, 1977), p. 2.

17. John Stuart Mill, *Principles of Political Economy with Some of Their Applications to Social Philosophy* (London: Longmans, Green, 1929), p. 749.

18. John Maynard Keynes, "Economic Possibilities for Our Grandchildren," in *Essays in Persuasion* (New York: W. W. Norton and Company, 1963), p. 372.

adjustment mechanisms to return an economy to a full employment growth path once it has left it.

8. Since 1925, real gross national product has grown at an average annual compound rate of approximately 3.25 percent, while real per capita GNP has grown at a rate slightly less than 2 percent. As a result, GNP has increased to more than five times its value in 1925. During the same period, the size of the labor force has doubled and capital stock has tripled. Since the quantity of capital stock has increased relative to the labor force, capital deepening has taken place.

9. Several problems may be associated with economic growth. They include a scarcity of energy and other resources, the difficulty of maintaining environmental quality, and an inequitable distribution of income.

10. In the 1970s, research sponsored by the Club of Rome predicted that without strict controls on population, natural resource utilization, and population, a world social and economic collapse would occur before the year 2100. Economists were highly critical of this research, and follow-up studies forecast a less gloomy future. However, there is still a widely held view that it will be necessary for society to evolve toward some sort of no-growth stationary state.

IMPORTANT TERMS AND CONCEPTS

Economic growth
Rate of growth of real
  per capita GNP
Production
  possibilities curve
Principle of
  diminishing returns

Reserve army of the
  unemployed
Capital-output ratio
Warranted rate of
  growth
Natural rate of growth
Capital deepening

QUESTIONS AND PROBLEMS

1. Explain two ways of defining *economic growth*. What is the usefulness of each?

2. Why was Adam Smith optimistic regarding the prospects for economic growth?

3. Why was Malthus pessimistic about the long-range future of the population?

4. Explain Marx's view of the manner in which economic growth would take place. How did this way of thinking affect his predictions about the future of capitalism?

5. Why are economic growth models like those of Harrod and Domar called knife-edge models? What factors might make them more stable?

6. Explain the principle of diminishing returns, using your own example.

7. What is the Club of Rome? How did the work sponsored by this group affect thinking about the growth process? Why were the Club of Rome studies and models criticized by economists?

WHY CAN'T WE HAVE IT BOTH WAYS?

A few weeks ago a major publication ran an essay deploring the nation's unwillingness to come to grips with the real and serious energy crisis now upon us. The essay complained that U.S. citizens refuse to think through the issues and set priorities. "They want energy without risks. . . . Americans historically have believed they can have it both ways."

The same might be said regarding what our society expects from technology today. Episodes ranging from a failed nuclear plant to a falling space satellite have reminded us that we are still trying

Source: John W. Hanley, "Why Can't We Have It Both Ways?" *Business Week*, September 10, 1979, p. 16.

to cope with what Dr. Carl Sagan calls the age of "technological adolescence." Like a teenager wondering what he really wants from life, our society wonders what it really wants from technology.

Most Americans are anything but anxious to renounce their hard-won affluence. Witness the current agenda of socioeconomic goals—full employment, equal opportunities, a decent life for all Americans, and so forth—that depend on further economic progress and the national wealth it creates.

Nevertheless, our tastes for economic and technological progress are being tempered by increasing concerns for quality of life. The American people genuinely want cleaner natural and

urban environments, safer and more humanized jobs, improved disease prevention and treatment, workable solutions to world food and energy problems, and continued reduction of the risks associated with modern technologies.

INCONSISTENT ATTITUDES

It's not surprising, then, that public attitudes toward technology are rife with inconsistency and ambiguity. Americans want economic progress and quality of life.

Can we have it both ways? Some in our society say no—hardly surprising in itself—but I'm fascinated by all the different ways they arrive at that conclusion. There are those who follow a moral imperative, believing that this greedy society must be forced to return to more primitive life-styles with less dependence on technology. At the opposite end of the spectrum are those who grouse that weighing anything against economic growth is somehow un-American. In between are the fatalists who knew all along it was too good to last.

None of them, however, has much sense of history. Because wanting it both ways—wanting to break away from some previously unavoidable trade-off—has been the driving force of human progress throughout history.

We hear it said today that we are running out of certain raw-material and energy resources necessary for growth. But when in human history has this not been the case—at least for the most readily recoverable and usable reserves of some resources? Human ingenuity has been the key to extending supplies by improving exploration and processing, by conservation, by recycling, and by substitution. For example, today's oil-supply crisis is not the first this world has seen. In the last century, people were already worrying that whales were being killed faster than they could reproduce. How would the world light its lamps and lubricate its machines without whale oil? The answer was that rising demand and innovative minds brought forth replacement products based on petroleum.

Furthermore, we are only beginning to realize the potential of an intellectual/technological explosion that R. Buckminster Fuller refers to as "doing more with less." He points out that a 200-ton jetliner can outperform the annual passenger-carrying capacity of the 85,000-ton Queen Elizabeth. Likewise, a quarter-ton communications satellite can outperform 150,000 tons of transoceanic cable. The point is that a single intellectual leap translated into new technology can create an entirely new dimension for economic expansion, pushing the physical limits of growth back beyond the horizon again.

UPGRADING

On the quality-of-life side of the equation, we hear that the earth is running out of capacity to absorb the pollution byproducts of growth. Again, however, history is ignored. Look at the considerable progress we've already made in cleaning up the environment by applying our intelligence and technological abilities.

According to the Environmental Protection Agency's latest report, the quality of the nation's air improved significantly from 1972 to 1977. The levels of sulfur dioxide, carbon monoxide, and particulate matter declined. Ozone levels at least held steady despite a 30% increase in motor-vehicle traffic.

We've also been pleasantly surprised to see how quickly polluted waterways can recover once appropriate steps are taken. Around the nation, fish are returning to rivers where no aquatic life could survive a decade ago.

Americans want industrial products and jobs without having to worry about industrial wastes bubbling up in the backyard. I, for one, see nothing unreasonable about that, provided that we are willing to approach the situation rationally and not hysterically.

The same applies to other environmental problems, as well as energy and economic problems. We do have to learn to live with less energy while developing alternative sources. We do have to be more aware of the environmental consequences of our technology while recognizing that a vain quest for a totally risk-free society can only squander scarce economic resources.

These problems are real, and I don't intend to understate their seriousness. Nevertheless, I can't help thinking. If wanting it both ways brought us this far, why should we lose faith in human ingenuity now?

QUESTIONS

1. How is this article related to Denison's analysis of U.S. growth as discussed in this chapter?
2. Does the author of this article think that most Americans want more growth? Why?
3. What sorts of growth-related problems does the author of the article explicitly recognize? Name some that he fails to mention.

PART SIX

THE
ECONOMICS OF
CONSUMER
AND BUSINESS
BEHAVIOR

CHAPTER 16

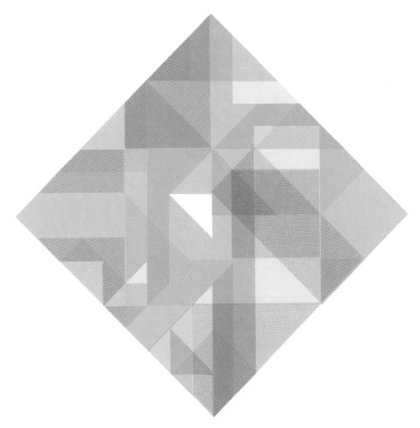

THE
ECONOMICS OF
CONSUMER
CHOICE

This chapter can be omitted without loss of continuity.

PERSPECTIVE

ON
BUDGETS
AND
SPENDING

In mid 1980 the following blurb appeared on the front page of the Wall Street Journal:

Apartment dwellers waste energy when gas and electricity are on master meters and the landlord pays the bills. But a survey by Angeles Real Estate Co., a California developer, shows energy use in apartments drops 45% when each unit has its own meters and the tenant is the one who pays.[1]

It should come as no surprise that people use more electricity and gas when the effect of increased consumption on their budgets is zero than when the effect is to chew up the budget. Once they are given the choice of spending on utility bills or on other things (clothes, trips, meals out), they decide to use less electricity or gas.

Virtually all consumers have three things in common: (1) they know, more or less, what they want; (2) they have limited budgets; and (3) they are faced with prices over which they have little or no control. Thus they are engaged in a day-by-day process of choosing how to spend their limited budgets.

In a real sense, all goods and services are substitutes for one another. We can choose between buying more air conditioning or buying more ice cream, between buying a camera or buying a stereo. The process of dividing up our expenditures (known as budget allocation) depends on what we like, how much money we have, and the prices attached to the alternative things we wish to buy.

Of course, some people can get along on very little, both materially and spiritually, but they are a minority in our part of the

---

1. "What's News," *Wall Street Journal*, May 1, 1980, p. 1.

world. In the United States we have been accustomed for so long to almost universal plenty that even in the 1850s, when Henry David Thoreau, the renowned writer and philosopher, decided to live the life of a hermit at Walden Pond, he observed:

I learned from my two years' experience that it would cost incredibly little trouble to obtain one's necessary food, even in this latitude; that a man may use as simple a diet as the animals, and yet retain health and strength.[2]

Yet men have come to such a pass that they frequently starve, not for want of necessaries, but for want of luxuries. . . . Most of the luxuries, and many of the so-called comforts of life, are not only not indispensable, but positive hindrances to the elevation of mankind.[3]

Unlike Thoreau, most of us will probably go on making those hard choices about the kind of spending that will "hinder our elevation." Economists have long recognized this and have noted that it is the very basis of the law of demand. It is to their analysis of consumer behavior that this chapter and Special Topic E are dedicated.

2. Henry David Thoreau, *Walden* (1854; New York: Doric Books, 1950), p. 13.
3. Ibid., p. 55.

C H A P T E R 16

◆

THE ECONOMICS OF CONSUMER CHOICE

WHAT THIS CHAPTER IS ABOUT

TOTAL, AVERAGE, AND MARGINAL VALUES
A THEORY OF CONSUMER BEHAVIOR
Utility Function
Diminishing Marginal Utility
Utility Maximization
THE DEMAND CURVE AND THE
  LAW OF DEMAND
Deriving the Demand Curve
Substitution Effect
Income Effect
Giffen Good
CRITIQUE OF THE THEORY
  OF CONSUMER CHOICE

In Part Six we are concerned primarily with the economic theory of how consumers and firms behave in response to economic incentives. Throughout this chapter and in later ones, we shall use many terms containing the words *total*, *average*, and *marginal*. Because these terms are always related to each other in certain ways, it will be helpful for us to understand the nature of the interrelationships— the topic of the following section.

TOTAL, AVERAGE, AND MARGINAL VALUES

◆

*A term with the word **total** in it refers to the entire amount of something.*

For example, the *total cost* of a firm is the sum of a firm's costs over a particular time period. The *total revenue* of a firm is the sum of the revenues or dollar sales of a firm over a certain time period. *Total utility* is the entire amount of satisfaction, or utility, obtained by a consumer over a specific time period.

Usually, total revenue, total cost, total utility, and all other total functions depend on the value of an independent variable. For example, the total cost for a firm is a function of the quantity of output produced. The total revenue for a firm is a function of the quantity of goods or services sold. The total utility of a consumer is a function of the quantity of goods and services consumed.

> An **average** value or function is always found by dividing the corresponsing total value by the amount of the independent variable on which it depends.

Thus an *average* term refers to an amount per unit of something. Accordingly, *average cost* is equal to total cost divided by the quantity of output produced, and *average revenue* is equal to total revenue divided by quantity sold.

> A **marginal** value or function is the rate of change of the corresponding total function with respect to changes in the independent variable.

In this book, we will find the value of marginal □ terms by dividing a change in the related total term by the change in the corresponding independent variable. Thus *marginal cost* is equal to the change in total cost divided by the change in quantity produced, *marginal revenue* is equal to the change in total revenue divided by the change in quantity sold, and the *marginal utility* of a good or service is given by the change in total utility divided by the change in the quantity of the good or service consumed.

The relationships between total, average,

and marginal quantities extend to noneconomic variables as well. Figure 16–1 shows Minneapolis–St. Paul's normal total accumulated rainfall to date by month for a year. (The first month is January, the second month is February, and so on.) This information is presented again in Table 16–1, along with average rainfall and marginal rainfall.

The average rainfall per month to date is found by dividing the total rainfall by the number of months that have passed. For example, at the end of May (fifth month), the average rainfall per month up to that date is equal to 8.66 inches/5 months = 1.73 inches per month. By November (eleventh month) this value has risen to 2.28 inches per month.

The rainfall occurring during any particular month is the marginal rainfall. Its value can be calculated by dividing the change in total rainfall by the change in the number of months, in this case 1. (In Table 16–1 the phrase *change in* is denoted by the Greek letter *delta* [Δ].) Thus the marginal rainfall for June is equal to

$$\frac{12.60 \text{ inches} - 8.66 \text{ inches}}{1} = 3.94 \text{ inches}$$

Later in this chapter and elsewhere in the book we will examine total, average, and

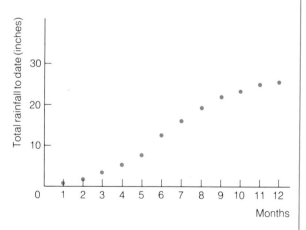

FIGURE 16–1 Normal Total Rainfall for Minneapolis–St. Paul

Each dot indicates the cumulative total rainfall up to and including the indicated month.

TABLE 16–1 Normal Rainfall for Minneapolis–St. Paul,

Number of Months (N)	Total Rainfall to Date in Inches (R)	Average Rainfall per Month to Date (R/N)	Marginal Rainfall (ΔR/ΔN)
			0.73
1 (January)	0.73	0.73	
			0.84
2	1.57	0.79	
			1.68
3	3.25	1.08	
			2.04
4	5.29	1.32	
			3.37
5	8.66	1.73	
			3.94
6	12.60	2.10	
			3.69
7	16.29	2.33	
			3.05
8	19.34	2.42	
			2.73
9	22.07	2.45	
			1.78
10	23.85	2.39	
			1.20
11	25.05	2.28	
			0.89
12	25.94	2.16	

Source: U.S. Department of Commerce, Bureau of the Census, "Table 376: Normal Monthly Rainfall and Annual Precipitation—Selected Cities," *Statitistical Abstract of the United States, 1979* (Washington, D.C.: Government Printing Office, 1979), p. 221.

marginal concepts in much greater detail. In the next few sections our attention will be directed to the neoclassical theory of consumer behavior and demand, the main subjects of this chapter.

BEHIND
THE
DEMAND CURVE
◆

Business firms find it important to have information about the factors that affect the quantity demanded □ of their products. For exam-

ple, in the spring of 1980 Chrysler Corp. was desperately trying to find the key to greater sales, and automobile manufacturers in general were ruefully wishing that they had more gasoline-efficient cars to sell.[1] At the same time, the airlines were puzzling over how to cope with rising fuel costs and still maintain satisfactory plane loads.[2] Coupons and sweepstakes games were tried. Politicians and others involved with social policy making also like to know what motivates people.

Economists have developed a "theory of consumer behavior" that offers an explanation of how individuals make choices. Although we will concentrate on choices involving the purchase of goods and services in this chapter, the theory can be extended to choices in many types of decision-making situations.

Total and Marginal Utility Economists assume that consumers buy goods and services because such items give them satisfaction or utility. **Utility** is the general term economists use to denote the satisfaction, pleasure, or benefits received by consumers from their consumption of goods or services or from other activities, such as sleeping, jogging, or playing tennis.

Total utility is the total amount of want satisfaction obtained by a given consumer.

The *marginal utility* of a particular good or service is the additional utility or satisfaction a consumer receives from one more unit of the good or service.

Marginal utility can be computed as the change in total utility divided by the change in the quantity purchased of a good or service.

---

1. See "Chrysler's Big Bet on the Free Lunch," *Newsweek*, February 4, 1980, pp. 65, 67; and "U.S. Autos: Losing a Big Segment of the Market—Forever?" *Business Week*, March 24, 1980, pp. 78–88.

2. See "Only a Modest Takeoff for Domestic Air Fares," *Business Week*, June 2, 1980, p. 29.

Of course, the utility that someone receives from a particular good or service is a subjective phenomenon. One person may get a great deal of utility from disco music, whereas someone else may hate it. To the latter person, the music causes *disutility*, or negative utility (discomfort or dissatisfaction).

Diminishing Marginal Utility

Economists have noted that over any specific period of time the additional utility received from another unit of a good or service tends to decrease after some point as more and more units of the good are consumed. For example, during a one-week period, one steak may give a great deal of utility to a consumer. However, unless the consumer really loves steak, the marginal utility of the fifteenth steak will likely be much less than that of the first steak.

This phenomenon is called the principle of diminishing marginal utility.

The ***principle of diminishing marginal utility*** *states that as more and more units of a particular good or service are consumed during a specific time period, after some point the marginal utility associated with one more unit of the item will tend to decrease.*

Continuing with the example of steaks, we can further examine the principle of diminishing marginal utility by looking at a consumer's total utility schedule for steaks and deriving both total and marginal utility curves from this schedule. One caution is necessary, however. Clearly, how much a consumer desires steak depends on how much of other things the consumer has (or has eaten). Thus we cannot examine the consumer's preference for steak unless we make a *ceteris paribus* □ (other things remaining the same) assumption—specifically, that the consumer does not change consumption of any other good while we are looking at the total utility data for steak.

Table 16–2 shows a total utility schedule

TABLE 16–2   Total and Marginal Utility of Steak for Gerry

Quantity of Steak Consmed Per Week (Q_s)	Total Utility from Steak Consumption (TU_s)	Marginal Utility of Steak Consumption: $MU_s = \dfrac{\text{Change in } TU_s}{\text{Change in } Q_s}$
0	0	
		80
1	80	
		75
2	155	
		70
3	225	
		60
4	285	
		50
5	335	
		40
6	375	
		20
7	395	
		5
8	400	
		−5
9	395	
		−10
10	385	

Steaks consumed per time period, other things equal.

for consumption of steak by a hypothetical consumer named Gerry. Marginal utility values also appear in the table. They are calculated as

$$MU_s = \frac{Change\ in\ total\ utility}{Change\ in\ quantity\ of\ steak}.$$

The computation is analogous to that of marginal rainfall in Table 16–1. Whereas rainfall was measured in inches, in what follows both total and marginal utility will be measured in *utils*, a hypothetical unit of account for satisfaction. In Gerry's case the marginal utility of an additional steak falls as steak consumption increases. This is in keeping with the principle of diminishing marginal utility. Of course, it is conceivable that Gerry might like her second steak better than her first one, but, surely, as steak consumption continues, ceteris paribus, the marginal utility of an additional steak will fall.

In Figure 16–2 Gerry's total and marginal

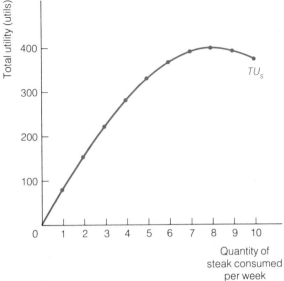

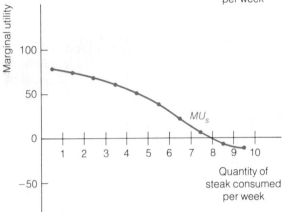

FIGURE 16–2   Total and Marginal Utility Curves for Consumption of Steak by Gerry

The total utility of steaks rises until eight steaks are consumed. Thus the marginal utility of each of the first eight steaks is positive. After this point, total utility falls as more and more steaks are consumed, and marginal utility is negative.

utility curves for steak are plotted from the data in Table 16–2. Total utility rises as long as marginal utility is positive. However, total utility rises ever more slowly as more and more steaks are consumed.

Finally, when Gerry is completely saturated with steaks, the consumption of one more will reduce satisfaction (perhaps even cause pain), and Gerry's total utility will begin to fall. Of course, it is hard to argue that Gerry would ever consume an additional steak if she knows it will make her sick, but stranger things have happened! Nonetheless, economists usually assume that a consumer will not willingly choose to consume something that reduces total utility.

UTILITY MAXIMIZATION CONDITION

Consumers are faced with budget constraints; their purchases are limited by wealth and income. Thus they must make choices about which goods and services to buy. Economists generally assume that consumers make these choices in a way that maximizes their total utility. In other words, consumers make decisions that make their total satisfaction as great as it can possibly be, given their limited budgets.

When a consumer's total utility is maximized, it must be true that the last dollar spent on each good consumed yields the same addition to total utility. In this situation, no good is more appealing than any other, per additional dollar spent; therefore, the consumer will have no reason to switch dollars of expenditure from one good to another.

How can we express the marginal utility of one dollar's worth of a good or service? The answer is that we can divide the marginal utility per unit of the good by the number of dollars that the consumer must spend to get it. For example, if Gerry must spend $10 to get a steak that yields a marginal utility of 70 utils, then the marginal utility per $1 spent on that steak is 70 utils/$10 = 7 utils per $1.

The general expression for the marginal utility of a dollar's worth of any good or service is

$$\frac{\text{Marginal utility}}{\text{Price}} \text{ or } \frac{MU}{P}.$$

We can state the condition for maximizing utility from a given consumer budget and given prices of goods and services, as shown here.

For a consumer to maximize utility *the marginal utility of a good divided by its price must be equal for all goods:*

$$\frac{MU_1}{P_1} = \frac{MU_2}{P_2} = \frac{MU_3}{P_3} = \cdots \frac{MU_n}{P_n},$$

where the subscripts 1, 2, 3, . . . , n refer to goods 1, 2, 3, . . . , n, respectively.

For example, suppose that for a particular consumer the marginal utility of a pair of shoes is 60 utils and the price of the shoes is $20. In addition, assume that the marginal utility of a video disc is 75 utils and its price is $25. Then:

$$\frac{MU_s}{P_s} = \frac{60 \text{ utils}}{\$20} = \frac{MU_d}{P_d} = \frac{75 \text{ utils}}{\$25}$$
$$= 3 \text{ utils per } \$1,$$

where:

MU_s = the marginal utility of a pair of shoes,

P_s = the price of a pair of shoes,

MU_d = the marginal utility of a video disc, and

P_d = the price of a video disc.

For either the shoes or the video disc, the marginal utility received per dollar of expenditure is equal, and the consumer is maximizing utility.

Suppose that the marginal utility of another pair of shoes is 80 utils and that the marginal utility of another video disc is 50 utils, with P_s and P_d the same as before. Now:

$$\frac{MU_s}{P_s} = \frac{80 \text{ utils}}{\$20} = 4 \text{ utils per } \$1,$$

which is greater than

$$\frac{MU_d}{P_d} = \frac{50 \text{ utils}}{\$25} = 2 \text{ utils per } \$1.$$

In this situation, the consumer should reallo-

cate expenditures so that less is spent on video discs and more is spent on shoes.

As a consumer begins to switch some spending from one good to another, we will expect the marginal utility of the first good to increase and the marginal utility of the second good to decrease. Thus if a consumer switches spending from good B to good A, we will expect the marginal utility of good A to decrease and the marginal utility of good B to increase. The marginal utility of A will fall because of the principle of diminishing marginal utility: As the consumer obtains more and more of good A, the additional satisfaction received from another unit of good A will fall. Likewise, as the consumer decreases spending on good B (and therefore has less of good B), the marginal utility of good B will rise. We would expect that eventually the marginal utility received per additional dollar of expenditure will become equal for the two goods.

Table 16–3 gives a more detailed description of the utility of video discs and shoes for the consumer in this example. Suppose that the consumer is spending a total of $295 per year on eleven video discs and one pair of shoes. In this case the marginal utility of the eleventh video disc is 50 utils, and the marginal utility of the first pair of shoes is 80 utils. If we assume that the price of a pair of shoes is still $20 and that of a video disc is $25, then

$$\frac{MU_s}{P_s} = \frac{80 \text{ utils}}{\$20} = 4 \text{ utils per } \$1.$$

Also,

$$\frac{MU_d}{P_d} = \frac{50 \text{ utils}}{\$25} = 2 \text{ utils per } \$1.$$

In this situation, the consumer should begin switching spending from video discs to shoes.

When the consumer spends the $295 by purchasing six pairs of shoes and seven video discs,

$$\frac{MU_s}{P_s} = \frac{60 \text{ utils}}{\$20} = \frac{MU_d}{P_d} = \frac{75 \text{ utils}}{\$25}$$
$$= 3 \text{ utils per } \$1.$$

TABLE 16-3 Total and Marginal Utility of Shoes and Video Discs for a Consumer

Number of Video Discs Purchased per Year (Q_d)	Total Utility of Discs (TU_d)	Marginal Utility of Discs $\left(MU_d = \dfrac{\text{Change in } TU_d}{\text{Change in } Q_d} \right)$	Pairs of Shoes Purchased per Year (Q_s)	Total Utility of Shoes (TU_s)	Marginal Utility of Shoes $\left(MU_s = \dfrac{\text{Change in } TU_s}{\text{Change in } Q_s} \right)$
0	0		0	0	
		110			80
1	110		1	80	
		105			78
2	215		2	158	
		95			75
3	310		3	233	
		90			70
4	400		4	303	
		85			65
5	485		5	368	
		80			60
6	565		6	428	
		75			55
7	640		7	483	
		70			50
8	710		8	533	
		65			45
9	775		9	578	
		60			40
10	835		10	618	
		50			30
11	885		11	648	
		40			20
12	925		12	668	

At this point, the consumer will maximize utility—at least with regard to spending on shoes and video discs. Note that the marginal utility of a pair of shoes has fallen from 80 to 60 utils, whereas the marginal utility of a video disc has risen from 50 to 75 utils.

It is evident from Table 16–3 that the consumer has increased total satisfaction by switching some spending from video discs to shoes. When one pair of shoes and eleven video discs are purchased, total utility is equal to 80 utils (from shoes) + 885 utils (from video discs) = 965 utils. When six pairs of shoes and seven video discs are purchased, total utility is equal to 428 utils (shoes) + 640 utils (video discs) = 1,068 utils.

THE DEMAND CURVE

The combination of the utility maximizing rule discussed in the previous section and the information on a consumer's preferences, budget, and prices will enable us to derive a consumer's demand curve □ for a product.

> The **demand curve** for a product is a graphical representation of the relationship between the quantity demanded and the price charged for each unit of the product.

(The relationships among the demand curve, demand function, and quantity demanded were all discussed in detail in Chapter 3.)

The relationship between price and quantity demanded of a good usually obeys the law of demand.□

The **law of demand** states that, other things equal, the amount of a product that consumers are willing and able to purchase during some period of time varies inversely with the price of that product.

Assuming that consumers wish to maximize their utility, we will now examine how the consumer's demand curve for a product can be derived and why the law of demand usually holds. Later, we will examine the relationship between a consumer's demand curve for a product and the market demand curve. In Chapter 17 we will examine the relationship between a firm's demand curve and its revenue. The relationship between a firm's demand curve and the market demand curve will be dealt with in later chapters.

DERIVING THE DEMAND CURVE

It is possible to derive a consumer's demand curve from information about the individual's tastes and preferences and income or budget and from the prices of goods and services. It is also necessary to use the rule for utility maximization:

$$\frac{MU_1}{P_1} = \frac{MU_2}{P_2} = \frac{MU_3}{P_3} \ldots = \frac{MU_n}{P_n}.$$

For example, in Table 16–4 data on the marginal utilities of apples and oranges and the corresponding quantities of each fruit for a consumer are presented. If we assume that the consumer has $2.40 to spend on apples and oranges, that the price of an apple, P_a, is $.20, and that the price of an organge, P_o, is $.40, the consumer will maximize satisfaction

TABLE 16–4 Marginal Utility of Apples and Oranges

Quantity of Apples per Week	Marginal Utility of One More Apple (in Utils)	Quantity of Oranges per Week	Marginal Utility of One More Orange (in Utils)
0		0	
	40		100
1		1	
	35		85
2		2	
	30		60
3		3	
	25		50
4		4	
	20		48
5		5	
	15		45
6		6	
	10		40
7		7	

To simplify matters, in this table the assumption is that the marginal utility of another orange is independent of the number of apples purchased, and vice versa. However, this assumption may not be realistic.

with respect to apples and oranges by purchasing four apples and four oranges. At this point:

$$\frac{MU_a}{P_a} = \frac{25 \text{ utils}}{\$.20} = \frac{MU_o}{P_o} = \frac{50 \text{ utils}}{\$.40}$$
$$= 125 \text{ utils per } \$1.$$

Moreover, ($.20 × 4 apples) + ($.40 × 4 oranges) = $.80 + $1.60 = $2.40, the consumer's weekly budget for apples and oranges.

Thus we have a point on the consumer's weekly demand curve for apples (when the price of oranges is $.40), we have a point on the consumer's demand curve for oranges (when the price of apples is $.20), and we have a weekly budget constraint of $2.40. We can derive another point on the demand curve for oranges as follows.

First, we assume that the price of an apple remains constant at $.20, while the price of an orange falls to $.30. In this situation the maximum level of satisfaction will be obtained by purchasing three apples and six oranges. At this point (see Table 16–4),

$$\frac{MU_a}{P_a} = \frac{30 \text{ utils}}{\$.20} = \frac{MU_o}{P_o} = \frac{45 \text{ utils}}{\$.30}$$
$$= 150 \text{ utils per } \$1.$$

Moreover, ($.20 \times 3$ apples) + ($.30 \times 6$ oranges) = $.60 + $1.80 = $2.40, the consumer's budget for apples and oranges.

This consumer's weekly demand curve for oranges, given a price of $.20 per apple and a budget constraint of $2.40, would be as shown in Figure 16–3 if it were a straight line.[3] At $P_o = \$.40$, the consumer is at point A on the demand curve, purchasing four oranges per week. When the price falls to $.30, there is a movement to point B, where the consumer buys six oranges per week. Of course, this demand curve will shift if either the price of apples or the consumer's budget changed. (These matters will be discussed more fully in a later section of this chapter.)

INDIVISIBILITY OF GOODS

In explaining how a consumer behaves to maximize satisfaction, economists frequently

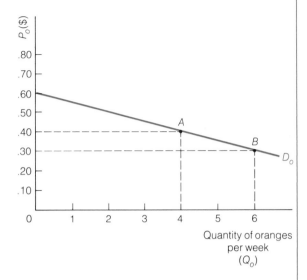

FIGURE 16–3 The Demand Curve for Oranges

When the price of oranges is $.40, the consumer will purchase 4 oranges per week (point A). When the price of oranges drops to $.30, the consumer purchases 6 oranges per week (point B). Thus, we have two points on the consumer's demand curve for oranges, D_o.

---

3. We can find the equation for this demand curve as follows. The equation for any straight line $Y = aX + b$ is given by

$$\frac{Y - Y_1}{X - X_1} = \frac{Y_2 - Y_1}{X_2 - X_1}.$$

Let $.40 be equal to Y_1 and $.30 be equal to Y_2. Then four oranges will be equal to X_1, and six oranges will be equal to X_2. We can substitute these values in the above equation to obtain

$$\frac{Y - 0.40}{X - 4} = \frac{0.30 - 0.40}{6 - 4}$$
$$= \frac{-0.10}{2}$$
$$= -0.05.$$

Multiplying both sides of this equation by $(X - 4)$, we obtain

$$Y - 0.40 = -0.05X + 0.20$$
$$Y = -0.05X + 0.60.$$

Since Y is price and X is quantity demanded in this case, we can substitute P for Y and Q for X to get the equation

$$P = -0.05Q + 0.60.$$

assume that goods and services are infinitely divisible (come in infinitely small units). In the real world, however, goods and services are not all infinitely divisible. Refrigerators, stereos, and automobiles, for example, come in a limited number of sizes. Thus a consumer may be able to only approximately meet the utility-maximizing condition that

$$\frac{MU_1}{P_1} = \frac{MU_2}{P_2} = \ldots = \frac{MU_n}{P_n}.$$

LAW OF DEMAND

Most of us accept without question the notion that the demand curve for a product is downward sloping (has a negative slope), □ which indicates that consumers buy less of a good at high prices than at low prices. In Chapters 1 and 3 this inverse relationship was called the law of demand.

Figure 16–4 shows a supermarket's daily demand curve for ground beef. At a price of

21

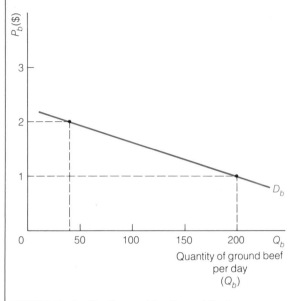

FIGURE 16–4   The Demand for Ground Beef

Demand curve D_b illustrates the law of demand, which states that other things remaining the same, consumers will purchase smaller quantities of a good at high prices than at lower prices. At a price of $2.00 per pound, consumers will purchase only 40 pounds of ground beef per day. At a price of $1.00 per pound, consumers purchase 200 pounds of ground beef per day.

$2 per pound, consumers purchase only 40 pounds of ground beef per day. At a price of $1 per pound, consumers purchase 200 pounds per day, 160 pounds more than at a price of $2.

Why are most demand curves negatively sloped? You can probably explain in your own words why you buy a larger quantity of a good after its price has fallen. The reasons are reviewed here, along with the names given them by economists.

Effect of Diminishing Marginal Utility   The meaning of *diminishing marginal utility* was discussed in a previous section of the chapter. As also indicated earlier, a consumer purchases goods and services until the person's budget is exhausted and the following condition holds for all goods:

$$\frac{MU_1}{P_1} = \frac{MU_2}{P_2} = \frac{MU_3}{P_3} = \cdots = \frac{MU_n}{P_n}.$$

Once a consumer has reached such an equilibrium position, the presence of diminishing marginal utility means that spending cannot be reallocated among goods in a way that maintains the same level of satisfaction unless the price of one of the goods changes. Thus a consumer will buy more of a product only if its price falls (or the prices of other goods and services rise), assuming that the budget does not change.

Substitution Effect   When the price of a good or service changes, its price relative to the prices of other goods and services also changes. Consequently, when the price of a product falls, the product becomes not only absolutely cheaper than before but also cheaper relative to other goods and services. Thus, when T-bone steak is on sale, it becomes cheaper relative to other meats than before.

If consumers are initially in equilibrium with

$$\frac{MU_1}{P_1} = \frac{MU_2}{P_2} = \cdots = \frac{MU_T}{P_T},$$

where the subscript T stands for T-bone steak, a decrease in the price of this steak, P_T, will make $\frac{MU_T}{P_T}$ greater than the corresponding ratio for other commodities. In this situation consumers will tend to substitute T-bone steak for other types of meat. For example, they might buy one more pound of steak and one less pound of hamburger.

> The **substitution effect** of a price change refers to the tendency of consumers, in response to a fall in the price of a good or service, to substitute purchases of the good whose price has fallen for purchases of other goods and services.

The good does not have to be actually cheaper than the other goods; it simply has to be cheaper relative to them than it was before.

For example, suppose T-bone steak is $3

per pound and ground beef is $1.29 per pound. Then suppose the price of T-bone steak falls to $1.79 per pound, while the price of hamburger remains at $1.29. At least some consumers will substitute some T-bone steak for part of the hamburger in their diet, even though T-bone steak is still more expensive than hamburger. The opposite reaction will occur if the price of T-bone steak rises while the price of hamburger remains constant.

Income Effect One additional thing happens when the price of a product changes: Consumers' real incomes □ change as well. As discussed in Chapters 5 and 13, consumers' real income is the quantity of goods and services consumers can purchase.

For example, suppose someone has an income of $1,000 per month and pays $350 a month rent on an apartment. If the rental rate falls, say to $300 per month, the consumer will experience an increase in real income. The individual can pay the rent on the apartment and have $50 more to spend than was available before. In this situation, if the consumer believes the price decrease will be relatively permanent, he or she may rent a slightly larger apartment than before as well as spending some of the $50 on other goods and services.

The **income effect** of a price change reflects the fact that a change in the price of a good causes a change in the real incomes of consumers who purchase it, thereby causing them to alter their purchases of the good or service.

Usually an increase in real income results in an increase in a consumer's purchases of a good. An increase in price usually has the opposite effect. In this case, the good has a positive income effect.

A good is a **normal good** if it has a positive income effect—that is, if consumers buy more of it as their real incomes rise and less as their real incomes fall.

Sometimes an increase in real income causes a consumer to buy less of a good. In this case, the good has a *negative* income effect.

An **inferior good** is a good with a negative income effect.

One example of an inferior good is ground beef mixed with ground soybeans. As incomes rise, consumers tend to buy less of this product and more of other meat products.

Giffen Good In some cases an inferior good has a negative income effect so large that it more than offsets the substitution effect of a price change. In this rare situation the demand curve for such a good or service will be upward sloping: As the price of this good rises, consumers will buy more of it.

A **Giffen good** is a good with a positively sloped demand curve.

Sir Robert Giffen, a British statistician, observed in the nineteenth century in Ireland that during a potato famine and in spite of rising potato prices, people actually bought more potatoes. How could this phenomenon occur? Potatoes were an important food in the diet of the Irish. However, they were an inferior good; as real incomes rose, the Irish tended to purchase more meat and other food in place of some potatoes.

When the price of potatoes rose, consumers experienced a sudden drop in their real incomes, because many of them still spent substantial sums on potatoes. They could now afford fewer of the "extras," such as meat, than before. Therefore, they had to eat more potatoes, and the Giffen effect was observed.

The Giffen effect does not occur very frequently in the United States, and throughout the remainder of this book the market demand curve for a good or service is assumed to be negatively sloped.[4] However, as we will see in Chapter 17, the demand curve for the product of a single firm may have a slope that for all practical purposes, is zero. In this case, the demand curve is a horizontal line.

DERIVATION OF A MARKET DEMAND CURVE

Logically, if the demand curve of each individual consumer of a specific product slopes downward to the right, then the market demand curve for that product will also have a negative slope. This relationship occurs because everyone in the market will take more of the product when its price falls. The market demand curve is simply an aggregate composed of the demand curves of all the individuals who are willing and able to buy the product at all possible prices.

We can formulate a simple example to show how individuals' demand curves are summed to obtain the market demand curve for a product. Suppose we return to the demand curve for oranges, assuming that the orange market consists of only two consumers, Raoul and Tricia. Figure 16–5 shows the market demand curve for oranges and the demand curves of Raoul and Tricia. At the various prices of oranges shown, Tricia is either more willing or more able than Raoul to buy oranges.

The market demand curve for oranges in this two-consumer example is obtained by adding the quantities consumed by the two parties at each possible price. For example, at a price of $.50 per orange, Raoul's demand curve shows that he will purchase three oranges per week, while Tricia's indicates that she will purchase four oranges per week. Each person will be at point A on his or her respective demand curve. We obtain point A′ on the market demand curve for oranges by adding up the amounts that Raoul and Tricia will con-

sume when the price of an orange is $.50. Thus the quantity demanded in the market at P_O = $.50 is (3 + 4) = 7 oranges per week.

If the price falls to $.25 per orange, Raoul and Tricia will adjust to point B on their respective demand curves, and the quantity demanded in the market will be that indicated by point B′, or fourteen oranges per week. Since we are summing quantities that will be purchased at each of the possible prices, this aggregation process is known as horizontal summation.

*The **market demand curve** for a good or service is the horizontal sum of the individual demand curves of consumers of that good or service.*

MARKET VERSUS FIRM DEMAND CURVES

A business firm's demand curve for its product generally will not be the same as the market demand curve for that product. In fact, for the curves to be the same, the firm would have to be the only firm selling the product: that is, it would have to be a monopoly.□

Most firms are not monopolies. They do, however, face demand curves that have one basic characteristic of the demand curves in this chapter. That characteristic is the inverse relationship between price per unit of product and quantity demanded by consumers. In other words, most firms face a demand curve with a negative (downward to the right) slope. Thus they can increase the quantity sold of their product by lowering its price, and they have to decide which price and quantity combination is best from the standpoint of profit.

At this point, only the issue of the firm's demand curve and its relation to profit is being raised. Demand provides only a part of the data necessary for profit analysis, specifically the information necessary to estimate sales revenue. However, firms must have both revenue information and cost information in or-

---

4. Thorsten Veblen, a twentieth century economist, also cited a snob effect as one reason people might buy more of a product at a high price than a low price. The extent of this phenomenon, though, is also limited.

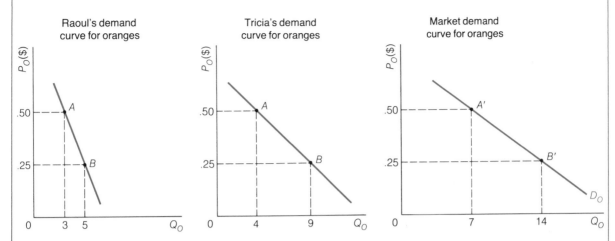

FIGURE 16–5 Summation of Individual Demand Curves for Oranges

The market demand curve for oranges can be derived in the following way. At a price of $.50 per orange, Raoul will purchase 3 oranges per week, while Tricia will purchase 4. If Raoul and Tricia are the only customers in the market, the total quantity demanded of oranges at a price of $.50 will be 3 plus 4, or seven oranges. A similar analysis applies for a price of $.25.

der to accurately assess profit possibilities. In the chapters that follow, we will first explore the relationship between demand and revenue and then move on to cost and profit.

A CRITIQUE OF THE THEORY OF CONSUMER CHOICE

The neoclassical theory of consumer choice discussed in this chapter was developed by neoclassical economists of the nineteenth century. The theory relies on the principle of consumer sovereignty.

Consumer sovereignty *means that consumers determine what is produced through the demand for products that they exhibit in the marketplace.*

If consumer sovereignty is present, consumers are the primary determinants of what will be produced by businesses. Firms producing products that consumers do not wish to buy will have excess inventories of unsold goods,

and their profits will suffer. For example, if U.S. firms produce large cars when consumers want small cars, dissatisfaction with the product will be vividly demonstrated by consumers' purchases of small cars from foreign producers.

Some economists, particularly John Kenneth Galbraith of Harvard University, have argued that consumer sovereignty is really not as strong as neoclassical theory would have us believe. Galbraith stated that our current sophisticated technology, with its requirements for specialized labor and capital, forces producers to anticipate consumer needs months or even years ahead of time. Because the firms must plan to satisfy such needs or wants so long before the goods are actually sold, Galbraith contended that modern businesses must make sure that an adequate demand for their products will exist when these goods are eventually made available to the consumer. According to Galbraith, these businesses control the demand for their products through advertising and sales organizations. In *The New Industrial State*, he states,

Since General Motors produces some half of all the automobiles, its designs do not reflect the current mode, but are the current mode. The proper shape of an automobile, for most people, will be what the automobile majors decree the current shape to be.[5]

In *The Affluent Society*, he similarly argues:

Were it so that a man on arising each morning was assailed by demons which instilled in him a passion sometimes for silk shirts, sometimes for chamber pots, and sometimes for orange squash, there would be every reason to applaud the effort to find the goods, however odd, that quenched this flame. But should it be that his passion was the result of his first having cultivated the demons, . . . there would be question as to how rational was his solution. . . . he might wonder if the solution lay with more goods or fewer demons.

So it is that if production creates the wants it seeks to satisfy, or if the wants emerge *pari passu* (lockstep) with the production, then the urgency of the wants can no longer be used to defend the urgency of the production. Production only fills a void that it has itself created.[6]

Thus Galbraith asserts that wants are dependent on what is produced. Such a view is the reverse of the neoclassical idea that wants determine production.

Dependency effect *is a term used to refer to the idea that production creates wants—that wants are dependent on what is produced.*

Modern economists certainly would agree with Galbraith that advertising and other marketing tactics can affect consumer wants and desires. For one thing, advertising informs consumers about what products are available. Moreoever, it may also play a role in shaping consumers' tastes and preferences.

However, as even Galbraith admits, this control by firms over the demand for their products is by no means perfect. The Edsel, introduced by Ford Motor Company in the 1950s, is only one glaring example of businesses' lack of control over consumer demand. As Friedrich von Hayek, a Nobel prize winner in economics, puts it:

Professor Galbraith's argument could be easily employed, without any change of the essential terms, to demonstrate the worthlessness of literature or any form of art. Surely an individual's want for literature is not original with himself in the sense that he would experience it if the literature were not produced. Does this then mean that the production of literature cannot be defended as satisfying a want because it is only the production which provokes the demand?[7]

Moreover, consumers must make their spending choices under the constraint of limited budgets. They cannot purchase unlimited quantities of all goods or of even one good.

At any rate, it is possible to expand the neoclassical theory of consumer behavior to take into account the effect of advertising on consumers' wants. The model can also be enlarged to include the effects of other consumers' purchases on the tastes of an individual. These effects are often called *demonstration effects*. However, such theoretical refinements will affect few of the principles developed in the remainder of this book, and a more thorough discussion of them is appropriately left for advanced texts in economics. In Chapter 17 we will turn to the relationship between consumer demand and the sales revenue of business firms.

5. John Kenneth Galbraith, *The New Industrial State* (Boston: Houghton Mifflin, 1967), p. 30.

6. John Kenneth Galbraith, *The Affluent Society* (New York: New American Library of World Literature, 1958), pp. 124–125.

7. Friedrich von Hayek, "The *Non Sequitur* of the Dependence Effect," *Southern Economic Journal* Vol. 27 (April 1961): 346–347.

SUMMARY

1. The main topic of this chapter was an economic theory of how consumers make choices. This theory forms the basis of demand analysis in economics. Economists assume that consumers make choices so as to maximize their individual utility or satisfaction within the limits presented by each person's budget.

2. For consumers to maximize utility, the marginal utility received from an additional dollar expenditure on all goods must be equal. Marginal utility is the additional satisfaction received from one more unit of a good or service. Of course, consumers must also stay within their budgets.

3. We can derive a consumer's demand curve for a good or service by finding several equilibrium positions. A demand curve is a graphical depiction of the relationship between the quantity demanded of a good or service and its price. The law of demand implies that demand curves are downward sloping; that is, people buy less of a good or service at higher prices than at lower prices.

4. Three factors may interact to support the law of demand: diminishing marginal utility, the substitution effect, and the income effect. The principle of diminishing marginal utility states that as more and more units of a particular good or service are consumed during a specific time period, the marginal utility associated with one more unit of the item will begin to decrease after some point. The substitution effect is the tendency of consumers, in response to a fall in the price of a good or service, to substitute purchases of the good whose price has fallen for purchases of other goods and services. The opposite purchasing behavior occurs after a price increase.

5. The income effect refers to the fact that changes in the prices of goods and services change consumers' real incomes, thereby causing consumers to change their purchasing patterns. A normal good is a good that people buy more of as their incomes rise, and vice versa. An inferior good is a good that people buy less of as their incomes rise, and vice versa. A Giffen good is an inferior good or service with an income effect so large that it results in an upward-sloping demand curve.

6. The market demand curve for a product can be derived from consumer demand curves. The relationship between the market demand curve for a product and the demand curve of an individual firm is more complex.

7. Galbraith has challenged the neoclassical notion of consumer sovereignty—that consumers determine what is produced through the demand for products that they express in the marketplace. Instead, he argued that the dependency effect was present—that consumer wants are dependent on what is produced. Nevertheless, there is evidence to indicate that producer control over the demand for the firm's product is by no means absolute.

IMPORTANT TERMS AND CONCEPTS

Total	Law of demand
Average	Substitution effect
Marginal	Income effect
Utility	Normal good
Total utility	Inferior good
Marginal utility	Giffen good
Principle of	Market demand curve
diminishing	Consumer sovereignty
marginal utility	Dependency effect
Utility Maximization	
Demand curve	

QUESTIONS AND PROBLEMS

1. Explain the law of demand.

2. Define *utility* and *marginal utility*.

3. What conditions must be met for a consumer to maximize utility?

4. Discuss the assumptions made in the theory of consumer behavior. Are they realistic? Explain.

5. What is the difference between a normal good and an inferior good?

6. What is the substitution effect? Give an example.

7. Briefly explain how the market demand curve for a product can be derived from consumer demand curves.

8. The table below gives a consumer's marginal utility values for ground beef and hot dogs. The price of ground beef is $1 per pound, and the price of hot dogs is $2 per pound. If the consumer has $14 per week to spend on these two items combined, what combination of hot dogs and hamburger should be purchased per week to maximize utility? (Assume that the quantity purchased of ground beef does not affect the marginal utility of hot dogs, and vice versa.)

Quantity (in Pounds)	Marginal Utility	
	Ground Beef	Hot Dogs
0		
	100	230
1		
	95	200
2		
	90	180
3		
	80	120
4		
	70	90
5		
	60	60
6		
	45	50
7		

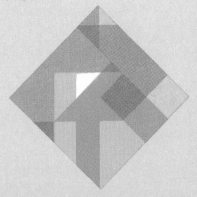

FOREIGN-CAR IMPORTERS SCRAMBLE TO ADJUST TO A SURGE IN DEMAND

TORRANCE, Calif.-For Chuck King, the man in charge of selling Datsuns in this country, last winter started on a dismal note. Sales of his Japanese-built cars were sluggish, prices had climbed alarmingly and Datsun dealers were saddled with a huge supply of leftover models.

From his office here in the striking glass and concrete headquarters of Nissan U.S.A., the second-largest importer of vehicles in the U.S., Mr. King saw only tough times ahead. Like most in the auto industry, he expected total sales of imported cars to drop 10% or more this year as Detroit

Source: Andy Pasztor, "Foreign-Car Importers Scramble to Adjust to a Surge in Demand," *Wall Street Journal*, June 11, 1979, pp. 1, 12.

rolled out more and more small models of its own.

Now all that has changed. Mr. King has a new headache. Instead of struggling to help his dealers unload excess cars, he is fending off their urgent demands for more of them. Datsuns are selling so fast he can't keep showrooms supplied.

The same story is heard almost everywhere imported cars are sold. After faltering for several months, foreign cars took off in early March as the disruption of Iran's oil production and rising gasoline prices coincided with a strengthening of the dollar. Since then, lines at filling stations and fears of gasoline rationing have only accelerated the demand. "The public is shopping for gas

mileage," Mr. King says; the trend "seems to be picking up momentum every day."

WAITING LISTS

Sales of Japanese models are especially hot, running 75% higher in some parts of the country than projected at the start of the year. Import dealers are pleading for extra allocations and offering to buy cars from each other at premium prices. Importers, meanwhile, grimly predict they will be short of many popular models by July or August, and waiting lists already are forming at dealerships for the most-economical foreign subcompacts.

Mr. King says Nissan U.S.A. revised its national advertising a few months ago "to highlight the fuel efficiency" of its cars in comparison with Detroit's newest models.

Nissan also asked its parent company in Japan to step up shipments of its smallest, lowest-priced models to the U.S. Likewise, Toyota Motor Sales U.S.A., the nation's No. 1 importer, is trying to get more of its most-popular, lowest-priced sedans from Japan, and fewer speciality models. (Because of factory schedules, it may be fall before they arrive, says Norman Lean, senior vice president of Toyota U.S.A.)

For both companies, the renewed emphasis on the high-volume, lower-profit end of the market is a turnabout. Just a few months ago, they and other importers figured their chances of competing with Detroit in ordinary small sedans had become slim,

and they were switching their efforts to various higher-priced sporty cars, luxury models and "specialty" vehicles such as four-wheel-drive minitrucks. The idea was to compete by stressing reliability and some sophisticated features that weren't readily available on small domestic vehicles.

Importers were turned from this strategy not only by new demand from mileage-conscious buyers but also by currency fluctuations. By last fall, the sinking dollar had forced prices of many standard, bread-and-butter imported cars up as much as 25% in a year's time. But the dollar now is trading at its highest level in nearly a year against the yen, and for the past eight months Japanese car companies haven't raised prices. Meantime, Detroit has been raising prices steadily.

QUESTIONS

1. Given what this article says about gasoline prices and the effect of the strengthening of the dollar (fall in the price of imports from Japan), what would you predict about the allocation of consumers' incomes between imported cars and gasoline? What about the allocation of incomes between imported and U.S.-made cars?

2. Is the marginal utility of an imported car to a typical consumer independent of the price of gasoline? Explain.

3. Express the situation described in the first question as a change in the ratios of marginal utilities to prices for the two goods, gasoline and imported cars.

A GEOMETRICAL EXPLANATION OF CONSUMER THEORY

The theory of consumer behavior developed in Chapter 16 can be restated graphically using indifference curves. The indifference curve approach reaches basically the same conclusions about consumer choice and demand that were drawn in the chapter, but it uses somewhat less restrictive assumptions and a different technique of analysis. The concept of indifference curves is briefly introduced in the following pages. This topic is usually covered in much greater depth in intermediate-level courses.

The standard assumptions of the indifference curve approach to consumer behavior analysis are:

1. Consumers behave in a rational manner; that is, they try to maximize their satisfaction—to obtain the greatest level of satisfaction they possibly can.
2. Consumers are able to rank items and combinations of items. In other words, consumers can tell whether they prefer one set of items to another or whether they like both sets equally well. In the latter case, we say that a consumer is indifferent between the two sets of items.
3. Consumers are consistent in their rankings. For example, a consumer who prefers coffee to tea but prefers tea to milk must also prefer coffee to milk.
4. Consumers have budget constraints. Each consumer has only a finite amount of wealth or income with which to purchase goods and services.
5. A consumer always prefers more to less of a good in the relevant range of choice.

Given these assumptions, we will now explore how the preferences of an individual consumer can be described with a set of indifference curves.

INDIFFERENCE CURVES

We can derive the same basic principles developed in Chapter 16 through the use of an *indifference map*, as shown in Figure E–1. Each of the curves in the figure is called an indifference curve. An *indifference curve* shows various combinations of two goods (X and Y in this case), that a consumer likes equally well, or is indifferent toward.

Thus each indifference curve represents a different level of utility, or satisfaction. Moreover, as we go from the lower left-hand corner to the upper right-hand corner, each successive indifference curve represents a higher level of utility, as denoted by $U = 1$, $U = 2$, $U = 3$, and $U = 4$. Successive indifference curves must represent higher levels of utility because of our assumption that consumers always prefer more of a good to less. Higher indifference curves have more of both goods than do lower ones; thus higher curves must represent higher levels of satisfaction.

Moreover, indifference curves cannot intersect, because that would imply that one combination of goods gives the consumer two different levels of utility, which is impossible. Of course, a complete indifference map for a

consumer would have many more indifference curves than are shown in Figure E--1—one for each possible level of utility.

MARGINAL RATE OF SUBSTITUTION

In Figure E–2 a single indifference curve for a consumer is drawn. It shows various combinations of pizzas and steaks that will make the consumer equally happy (yield the same utility). For example, ten pizzas and one steak are equally as satisfying to this consumer as six pizzas and two steaks or as one pizza and twelve steaks. These and other combinations of steak and pizza on this indifference curve are listed in Table E–1.

The indifference curve has a curvilinear shape and is convex (bowed) toward the origin of the graph. An indifference curve will have

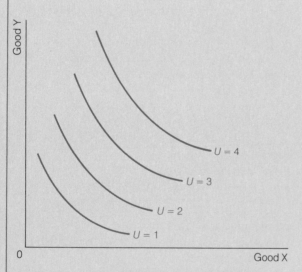

FIGURE E–1   An Indifference Map for a Consumer

Each individual indifference curve indicates various combinations of Good X and Good Y that would make a particular consumer equally satisfied. As one moves from the lower-left hand corner to the upper right-hand corner, each successive indifference curve represents a higher level of utility.

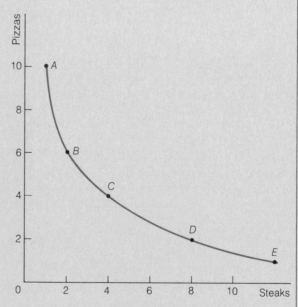

FIGURE E–2   An Indifference Curve for Pizzas and Steaks

This indifference curve indicates that a given consumer would be equally happy with 10 pizzas and 1 steak (Point A), 6 pizzas and 2 steaks (Point B), 4 pizzas and 4 steaks (Point C), 2 pizzas and 8 steaks (Point D), or 1 pizza and 12 steaks (point E).

TABLE E–1 Combinations of Pizza and Steak That the Consumer Is Indifferent Toward

Pizzas (P)	Steaks (S)	Marginal Rate of Substitution $\left(-1 \times \frac{\Delta P}{\Delta S}\right)$
10	1	
		4
6	2	
		1
4	4	
		0.5
2	8	
		0.25
1	12	

this general shape as long as the two goods are substitutes, but not perfect substitutes, as will now be explained.[1]

The slope of an indifference curve indicates the rate at which a consumer can substitute one good for another while maintaining the same level of utility, or satisfaction. This trade-off rate is known as the **marginal rate of substitution** (MRS). For example, between points *A* and *B* in Figure E–2 the consumer is willing to trade four pizzas for one steak, so the marginal rate of substitution is equal to 4/1. The marginal rate of substitution is equal to −1 times the change in pizzas divided by the change in steaks:

$$MRS = -1 \times \frac{\text{Change in pizzas}}{\text{Change in steaks}}.$$

We must multiply the $\frac{\text{change in pizzas}}{\text{change in steaks}}$ by −1 because as we move down the indifference curve (exchange pizzas for steaks), the change in pizzas is negative while the change in

steaks is positive. Thus the change in pizzas divided by the change in steaks is negative, and we wish to express the marginal rate of substitution as a positive number. The marginal rate of substitution is also equal to the ratio of the marginal utility of the good on the horizontal axis to the marginal utility of the good on the vertical axis:

$$MRS = \frac{MU_{\text{steaks}}}{MU_{\text{pizzas}}}$$

in Figure E–2.[2]

In the case of imperfect substitutes, the marginal rate of substitution decreases as more of one good is given up for another good (as we move down the indifference curve). In Figure E–2 the marginal rate of substitution decreases as more and more pizzas are given up for steaks. For example, the MRS between points *B* and *C* is equal to 2/2 = 1, and the marginal rate of substitution between points *C* and *D* is equal to 2/4 = 0.5. As more and more pizzas are given up in exchange for steaks, the marginal utility, or benefit, from another steak falls relative to the marginal utility of another pizza. The consumer becomes hungrier for pizza relative to steak than he or she was previously.

THE BUDGET CONSTRAINT

The position that will maximize the consumer's satisfaction subject to a given budget is as follows. In Figure E–3 are three indifference curves, I_1, I_2, and I_3, for goods X and Y. There is also a **budget constraint line**, X_0Y_0, which represents all the combinations of goods X and Y that can be bought with a given budget, B_0, *with no money left over. The equation for the budget line must be*

$$(P_x \times X) + (P_y \times Y) = B_0, \qquad (E–1)$$

---

1. The indifference curves will never be bowed outward, because that shape would imply that it takes more of both goods to keep the consumer equally happy. This situation violates the assumption that more of a good is always preferred to less. If the two goods were perfect substitutes, however, the indifference curve would be a straight line, indicating the consumer's willingness to trade one good for the other at a constant rate. However, the case of goods that are imperfect substitutes is the typical situation.

2. Although the ratio of these marginal utilities must be equal to the marginal rate of substitution, the values for each individual marginal utility are not presented here.

where:

P_x = the price of good X,

X = the quantity purchased of good X,

P_y = the price of good Y,

Y = the quantity purchased of good Y, and

B_0 = *the dollar amount of the budget.*

Equation E–1 merely states that the amount spent on good X plus the amount spent on good Y must be equal to the total amount of the budget.

We can get this equation into a form in which it can be easily graphed in Figure E–3 as follows. First, we subtract $(P_x \times X)$ from both sides of Equation E–1 to obtain

$$P_y \times Y = -P_x \times X + B_0.$$

Next, we divide both sides of this equation by P_y, so that it is now in the graphable form of

$$Y = -\frac{P_x}{P_y} \times X + \frac{B_0}{P_y}. \qquad (E-2)$$

Points Y_0 and X_0 on the budget line can be found by dividing the total amount the consumer has to spend, B_0, by P_x and P_y, respectively.

Thus $Y_0 = B_0/P_y$, and $X_0 = B_0/P_x$. It must therefore be true that if a consumer spends the entire budget on good Y, the number of units of good Y that can be purchased is equal to the total amount of the budget divided by the price of good Y. Thus, if a consumer has $24 a week to spend on entertainment, and if the price of seeing one movie is $4, then the person can attend $24/$4 = 6 movies per week if the entire budget is spent on movies. On the other hand, if the entire budget is spent on record albums that cost $8 each, $24/$8 or 3 record albums can be purchased.

Since Equation E–2 is in the form of an equation for a straight line, $Y = aX + b$ (where a is the slope), the slope of the budget constraint must be $-P_x/P_y$. This makes sense when we reflect on the fact that the slope of the budget line represents the rate at which the consumer can substitute good X for good Y and still spend only B_0 dollars. Thus, if a unit of good X costs $5 and a unit of good Y costs $10, the two goods can be substituted at the rate of one unit of Y for two units of X, or $-1/2 = -5/10$. Again, the negative sign indicates that some of one good must be given up in exchange for the other good.

CONSUMER EQUILIBRIUM

The consumer will maximize satisfaction by purchasing Y_1 of good Y and X_1 of good X, denoted by point A on I_2 in Figure E–3. This combination of goods X and Y will give the consumer the highest level of satisfaction that can be obtained without violating the budget constraint. (Any point on I_1 represents a lower level of satisfaction, whereas no point on I_3 can be obtained with the current budget.)

At point A in Figure E–3 the slope of the indifference curve I_2 and the slope of the budget line are equal. Since the slope of the indifference curve is equal to $-MU_x/MU_y$ and the slope of the budget line is equal to $-P_x/P_y$, at the point that maximizes the satisfaction of the consumer,

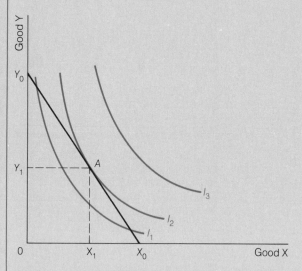

FIGURE E–3 The Equilibrium Position of a Consumer

A consumer will maximize his or her utility by consuming the combination of goods indicated by the point *(A)* where the budget line Y_0X_0 is tangent to an indifference curve, I_2.

$$-\frac{MU_x}{MU_y} = -\frac{P_x}{P_y}.$$

If we divide both sides of this equation by -1, it becomes

$$\frac{MU_x}{MU_y} = \frac{P_x}{P_y}.$$

If we multiply both sides of the equation by MU_y, we get

$$MU_x = P_x \times \frac{MU_y}{P_y}.$$

Dividing both sides by P_x, we obtain

$$\frac{MU_x}{P_x} = \frac{MU_y}{P_y},$$

the rule for consumer equilibrium discussed in Chapter 16. Thus the graphical approach gives the same results as the approach explained in the chapter.

CHANGE IN INCOME

We can show the effect of an increase in income by shifting the budget line outward from X_0Y_0 to X_2Y_2 in Figure E–4. The slope of the budget line remains the same, indicating that the price of good X relative to the price of good Y has not changed.

As a result of the increased budget the consumer will maximize satisfaction by moving from point A to point B and increasing the quantities purchased of both goods. In this case, both good X and good Y are normal goods.

SUBSTITUTION EFFECT

We can demonstrate the effect of a decrease in the price of good X as shown in Figure E–5. Line Y_0X_0 is the original budget constraint, and the consumer is initially in equilibrium at

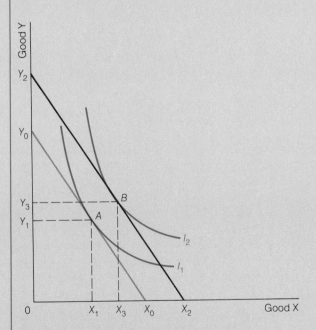

FIGURE E–4   The Effect of a Change in Income

Line Y_0X_0 represents the consumer's original budget line. After an increase in income, the budget line shifts outward to Y_2X_2. The consumer increases purchases of good Y from Y_1 to Y_3 and purchases of good X from X_1 to X_3.

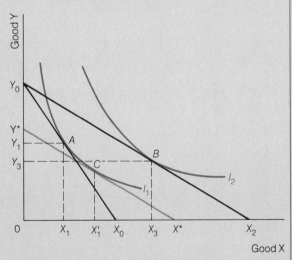

FIGURE E–5   An Illustration of the Substitution Effect

The initial budget line is Y_0X_0, and the consumer purchases Y_1 of Good Y and X_1 of Good X. After a decrease in the price of Good X, the new budget line becomes Y_0X_2. The consumer will now purchase Y_3 of Good Y and X_3 of Good X. We can isolate the substitution effect by drawing a line parallel to the new budget line which is tangent to the original indifference curve, I_1. The substitution effect on the consumer's purchases is then given by $(X_1' - X_1)$.

point A. If the price of good X, P_x, falls, the consumer can purchase a larger quantity of good X than before by spending the entire budget on good X. Thus the X-axis intercept of the budget line will shift from X_0 to a point like X_2. However, the Y-axis intercept will not change, because the price of good Y has not changed and Y_0 is still the maximum amount of good Y that can be purchased.

After the fall in P_x, the consumer will maximize satisfaction by moving from point A to point B. As noted in Chapter 16, the effect of a change in the price of a good can be separated into two parts—the substitution effect and the income effect. We can separate these two effects graphically as follows.

First, we draw a line such as X^*Y^* in Figure E–5 parallel to the new budget line, X_2Y_0, but tangent to the original indifference

curve, I_1. By moving the new budget line back to X^*Y^*, we show the effect of the change in the relative prices of the two goods while keeping the consumer at the same level of satisfaction as before. This approach represents one meaning of the phrase "keeping real income constant."

The movement, then, from point A to point C on I, represents the substitution effect. Thus the substitution effect caused this consumer to increase purchases of good X by $(X'_1 - X_1)$ units. The income effect, consequently, is represented by the movement from point C to point B, or an increase in consumption of good X equal to $(X_3 - X'_1)$.

This special topic has presented only a brief summary of the theory of consumer choice. More advanced texts can be consulted for detailed explanations.[3]

3. See, for example, Richard A. Bilas, *Microeconomic Theory*, 2d ed. (New York: McGraw-Hill, 1971), Chapter 4; David R. Kamerschen and Lloyd M. Valentine, *Intermediate Microeconomic Theory* (Cincinnati: South-Western Publishing, 1977), Chapter 5; and Edwin Mansfield, *Microeconomics*, (New York: W. W. Norton, 1979), Chapter 3.

CHAPTER 17

ELASTICITY
AND
REVENUE

WHAT
PRICE
REVENUE?

Milwaukee, May 15, 1980:

The owner of a small-size real estate brokerage opens the morning mail to find an advertisement from Xerox offering a model 550 compact copier for $1,495.

Across town, an independent insurance agent receives the same ad, but the copier is priced at $995.

At still another location, a dentist receives the ad, and the price is quoted as $1,195.

What is going on here? Is Xerox trying to dupe some of its customers into paying more than others? No. What we are seeing is a firm venturing into a new market and conducting a pricing experiment in order to see what its total sales revenue is likely to be at various prices. With such data, it can then establish a uniform price that will yield a sales quantity consistent with the firm's overall objective in regard to profit.

From Chapter 3 and the discussion of the law of demand, we know that a change in the selling price of a product will affect the quantity of the product that purchasers will buy. In general, reductions in price will increase the quantity demanded and therefore the quantity that firms can expect to sell. However, sales revenue depends on how much is sold at each price; for any specific price, it is equal to the price multiplied by the number of units sold. For example, if I can sell ten apples for $.25 each, my sales revenue will be $.25 × 10 = $2.50.

What did Xerox find out from its pricing experiment? Early on, few buyers were interested in the copying machine at the lowest price, $995. However, there was considerably more buyer interest at the $1,195 price than at the $1,495 price. Xerox stated it was planning to repeat the experiment at $1,295. In other words, the initial data suggested that the best strategy might be to price the copier somewhere between $1,195 and $1,495.[1]

The apparent buyer rejection of the machine at the $995 price violates the law of demand. This kind of buyer behavior, well recognized in economics, is sometimes called the "snob effect." Buyers may reject a product because it is not expensive enough, so that they think it cannot possibly be any good. However, goods that are characterized by such buyer behavior at low prices generally obey the law of demand at higher prices. This phenomenon may explain why Xerox found that the $1,495 price was too high. Other factors that may have contributed to Xerox's result are buyer uncertainty about the product and the possibility that the people surveyed were not representative of actual buyers of the product.

In this chapter we will closely examine the relationship between buyers' demand for a product and the sales revenue that is generated at various possible prices. This is an important prelude to analyzing profit, the subject of Chapter 19.

1. "Marketing," *Wall Street Journal*, July 31, 1980, p. 19.

C H A P T E R 17

ELASTICITY
AND
REVENUE

WHAT THIS CHAPTER IS ABOUT

In Chapter 16 we explored the foundations of the demand curve in the theory of consumer choice. In this chapter we will analyze the relationship between a firm's demand curve and its revenue. Although demand is only one element in a firm's profit picture, by ignoring it or misunderstanding its significance, a firm risks serious harm to its business. On the other hand, by using its knowledge of the demand for its product wisely, the firm may do much to ensure its success.

THE
DEMAND CURVE
AND REVENUE

Basically, we can obtain the demand curve for a firm's product by adding up the quantities of the good or service that all consumers would be willing to buy at some specific price and repeating this process for other prices. Of course, we must assume that the prices of other goods and services and the prices charged by competing firms for the same good or service are held constant. However, we will not examine the relationship between a firm's demand curve and the market demand curve for a product until a later chapter. In this section of Chapter 17 we will see how a firm can calculate what its total revenue, or total dollar sales, will be at various prices from information supplied by the demand curve for its product.

> The **total revenue** that a firm receives from the sale of a particular good or service is equal to the price of the product multiplied by the quantity sold. That is, TR = P × Q, where TR is total revenue, P is price, and Q is quantity sold.

In Figure 17–1 the weekly demand curve for a retail store that sells television video recorders is plotted. As can be seen from this graph, the firm will sell ten video recorders per week at a price of $1,200 each. However, if the price falls to $1,000, the firm will sell fifteen per week. At a price of $1,200, the total revenue of the firm will be equal to $1,200, × 10 = $12,000. At a price of $1,000, the firm's total revenue will be $1,000 × 15 = $15,000. Other corresponding values for price, quantity demanded, and total revenue for this firm are shown in Table 17–1.

> **Average revenue** is equal to revenue per unit sold. It is found by dividing total revenue by quantity sold. In other words,
>
> $$AR = \frac{TR}{Q},$$
>
> where AR is average revenue, TR is total revenue, and Q is quantity sold.

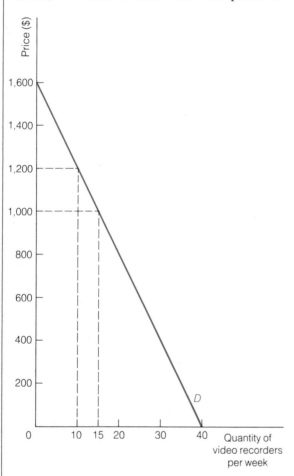

FIGURE 17–1   The Demand for Television Video Recorders

The weekly demand for video recorders sold by a particular firm is depicted by demand curve D. For example, at a price of $1,200 each, 10 video recorders will be purchased per week. At a price of $1,000, 15 video recorders will be purchased per week.

If the firm sells each unit of its product at the same price, price and average revenue are equal: $AR = \frac{TR}{Q} = \frac{P \times Q}{Q} = P.$

TABLE 17–1 Demand, Total Revenue, and Marginal Revenue for a Firm Selling Video Recorders

Price (Average Revenue) (P)	Quantity Demanded per Week (Q)	Total Revenue (TR = P × Q)	Marginal Revenue ($MR = \dfrac{\text{change in } TR}{\text{change in } Q}$)
$1,600	0	$ 0	
			$1,400
1,400	5	7,000	
			1,000
1,200	10	12,000	
			600
1,000	15	15,000	
			200
800	20	16,000	
			-200
600	25	15,000	
			-600
400	30	12,000	
			-1,000
200	35	7,000	
			-1,400
0	40	0	

Marginal revenue *is the rate of change of total revenue with respect to a change in quantity sold. Marginal revenue between two levels of output can be found by dividing the change in total revenue between the two levels of quantity sold by the change in quantity:*

$$MR = \frac{\text{change in TR}}{\text{change in Q}} = \frac{TR_2 - TR_1}{Q_2 - Q_1},$$

where MR is marginal revenue, TR$_1$ and TR$_2$ are the first and second levels of total revenue, and Q$_1$ and Q$_2$ are the first and second levels of quantity sold.

For example, at a price of $1,200, the firm can sell ten video recorders, which will result in a total revenue of $12,000. Thus TR$_1$ is $12,000, and Q$_1$ is 10. If the price falls to $1,000, the quantity sold will increase to fifteen units, and total revenue will increase to $15,000. In this case TR$_2$ will be $15,000, and Q$_2$ will be 15. Marginal revenue between ten and fifteen units of output, therefore, will be equal to

$$\frac{\$15,000 \ - \$12,000}{15 \ - \ 10} = \frac{\$3,000}{5} = \$600.$$

The significance of this number is that the sale of the eleventh through the fifteenth units will bring the firm an *average* of $600 per unit in additional revenue. Note that we said each unit adds an *average* of $600 in revenue. If we had more detailed demand data, we would find that with a down-sloping but straight-line demand curve the marginal revenue of the eleventh unit would be greater than the marginal revenue of the fifteenth unit. Thus the value for marginal revenue found above is really an approximation of marginal revenue, sometimes called *arc marginal revenue*. Nevertheless, we will continue to use this method of calculating marginal revenue.[1]

How is it possible that the marginal revenue generated by the sale of the eleventh through the fifteenth video recorders is less than their price? The answer is that we have assumed that in order to sell these units, the firm must lower the price on all units from $1,200 to $1,000.

1. The exact value of marginal revenue at a specific point can be found by taking the derivative of total revenue with respect to quantity sold. An explanation of this technique appears in more advanced texts.

In some cases it is possible for a firm to charge different customers varying prices for its product. For example, through hard bargaining, a person may be able to purchase a new car at a price lower than what others pay for the same model. Many theaters charge different prices for matinee shows than for evening shows. Airlines have "super saver" fares and regular fares.

When a firm charges different prices for the same product, economists say that *price discrimination* exists. However, in many cases, at least at a given point in time, a firm charges all customers the same price for its product, and we shall assume that this is the case here. We will discuss price discrimination in Special Topic I (which follows Chapter 21).

In the video recorder example, the firm has gained additional revenue equal to $1,000 times the five additional units sold, or $5,000. However, it must also sell the first ten units at a price of $1,000 each rather than $1,200. Thus the firm loses $1,200 minus $1,000, or $200, on each of the first ten units, for a total of $2,000. Consequently, the net increase in total revenue is only equal to $5,000 minus $2,000, or $3,000, and $3,000 divided by the additional five units is only $600 per unit. These calculations are summarized below:

Revenue gain from sale
of 5 additional units =
$\quad\quad$ $1,000 \times 5 =$ $\quad\quad\quad\quad$ \$5,000
Revenue loss because of lower price
on first 10 units =
$\quad\quad$ $200 \times 10 =$ $\quad\quad\quad\quad\quad$ 2,000
Net increase in total revenue = $\quad\quad$ \$3,000

Marginal revenue =
$\dfrac{\text{change in } TR}{\text{change in } Q} = \dfrac{\$3,000}{5} =$ $\quad\quad$ \$600.

If the firm could sell all the units it wanted to at the going market price (that is, if the demand curve were horizontal), marginal revenue and price would be equal. This special case is considered later in this chapter and in Chapter 20.

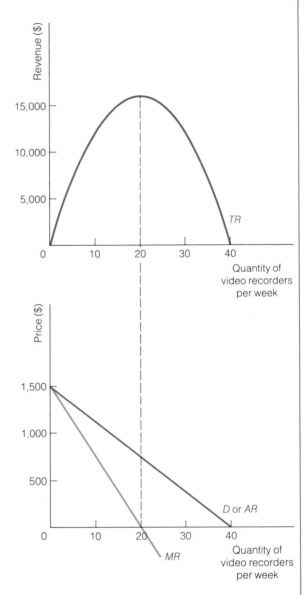

FIGURE 17–2 The Relationships among Total Revenue, Average Revenue, and Marginal Revenue from the Sale of Video Recorders

The relationships among total revenue, average revenue, and marginal revenue are indicated in these graphs. Total revenue (TR) rises until a sales level of 20 video recorders per week is reached, at which point it reaches a maximum. Marginal revenue (MR) is positive up to a sales level of 20 video recorders. After that point, total revenue decreases, and marginal revenue is negative. Note that marginal revenue is less than average revenue.

The relationships among total revenue, average revenue, and marginal revenue from the sale of video recorders are shown in Figure 17–2. Because average revenue is equal to price, the demand curve and the average revenue curve are the same thing. Since arc marginal revenue represents "average" marginal revenue for some change in quantity sold, marginal revenue has been plotted at the midpoint of each output interval. Also, for each level of output, marginal revenue is less than price.

Furthermore, marginal revenue is equal to zero when total revenue reaches its maximum, or highest, level, and marginal revenue is negative when total revenue is falling. This relationship follows from the fact that marginal revenue represents the addition to total revenue from selling another unit of output.

SHIFTS IN THE DEMAND CURVE

◆

As discussed in Chapters 3 and 4, shifts in the demand curve for a good or service are likely to occur from time to time. When a demand curve is drawn, it is assumed that only one variable affecting the quantity demanded □ of the good changes—the price of the good itself.

However, other variables also usually affect the demand for a good. For example, we expect a change in income to change the quantity demanded of a product at all prices. Thus, if consumers achieve an increase in real income, we expect the demand curve for video recorders shown in Figures 17–1 and 17–2 to shift outward, perhaps as shown in Figure 17–3, from D_1 to D_2. In other words, there is an increase in demand □ from D_1 to D_2. The opposite effect will result if consumers experience a decrease in real income.

We also expect the demand curve for a product to shift because of changes in the prices of related goods and services. These goods and services may be of two types—substitutes and complements.

> Two goods or services are **substitutes** if one can be used in place of the other.

Ground beef and ground pork are substitute goods. Ford cars and General Motors cars are substitutes. Coffee and tea are substitutes.

> Two goods are **complements** if having one increases the satisfaction received from having the other.

Examples of complementary goods are automobiles and gasoline, doughnuts and coffee, and video recorders and the movie tapes for them.

If the price of a substitute good rises, we expect the demand for a particular product to increase, and vice versa for a decrease in the price of a substitute good. Thus, if the price of

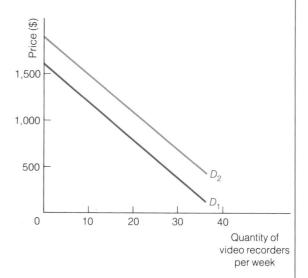

FIGURE 17–3 Increase in the Demand Curve for Video Recorders after an Increase in Real Income

The initial demand curve is D_1. After consumers receive an increase in income, the demand curve shifts to D_2. Demand curve D_2 indicates that consumers will now purchase a larger quantity of video recorders at any given price than with demand curve D_1.

General Motors cars rises, we would expect the demand for Fords to increase, which will cause the demand curve for Fords to shift outward. If the price of brand Y video recorders falls, we would expect the demand for brand X video recorders to decrease. In this case, the demand curve for brand X video recorders will shift inward, from D_1 to D_2 in Figure 17–4.

On the other hand, if the price of a complementary good rises, we would expect the demand for a product to fall, and vice versa for a price decrease. Thus, as the price of gasoline rises, the demand curve for gas guzzling cars shifts inward. If the price of movie tapes for television video recorders falls, the demand curve for brand X video recorders will shift outward, as in Figure 17–5, from D_1 to D_2. The reverse will occur as the result of an increase in the price of movie tapes.

Many other factors, including a change in price expectations (consumers expecting prices to rise or fall in the near future), advertising, or credit availability, can cause the demand curve for a product to shift. You may wish to analyze the effects of some of these other factors on your own, and to draw some graphs to depict what will happen in each case.

ELASTICITY: MEASURING THE RESPONSIVENESS OF QUANTITY DEMANDED

◆

So far, we have seen that a number of variables determine the quantity of a particular good or service that consumers are willing to buy. That businesses are interested in these

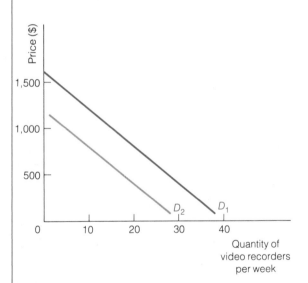

FIGURE 17–4   Decrease in the Demand Curve for Video Recorders after a Decrease in the Price of a Substitute Product

D_1 again represents the original demand curve for video recorders for a firm. After a decrease in the price of a substitute product, the demand curve shifts downward, to D_2. Demand curve D_2 indicates that consumers will purchase a smaller quantity of video recorders from this firm at any given price than with demand curve D_1.

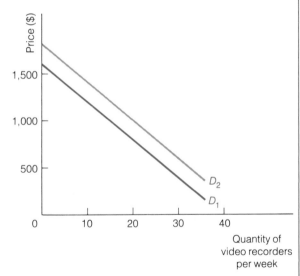

FIGURE 17–5   Increase in Demand for Video Recorders after a Decrease in the Price of Movie Tapes

D_1 is the original demand curve for video recorders for a firm. After a decrease in the price of a complementary good (movie tapes) the demand curve shifts outward to D_2. Demand curve D_2 indicates that a larger quantity of video recorders will be purchased at any given price than with demand curve D_1.

factors is illustrated by the following quote from *Business Week*:

> Scissored between soaring costs and sluggish demand at home and under intense competitive pressure from abroad, U.S. companies are overhauling ancient formulas for setting prices . . . [2]

Business Week reported in 1977 that many U.S. firms were adjusting pricing policies, apparently to improve the firms' profits. For example, Ford Motor Company and General Motors Corporation were charging less for subcompact cars on the West Coast than in the rest of the United States, in an unprecedented effort to meet Japanese competition. Challenging the steel industry's traditional price leaders, Armco Steel announced planned price cuts on four of its products. Moreover, airlines were cutting prices to meet the competition resulting from a decrease in government regulation. Even companies with famous brand names like Zenith, RCA, Singer, and Sony were being forced to cope with a "new world of fierce price competition."[3]

Business Week concluded:

> The upshot is little short of a revolution in pricing practices that will have ramifications for capital spending, the inflation rate, industrial concentration, and the application of existing antitrust laws. Above all, though, an ability to adapt to the new pricing environment will characterize those companies that succeed in competing over the next decade.[4]

One measure of the degree to which the quantity purchased will respond to a change in any single variable is called its **elasticity** with respect to that variable. For example, the measure of the responsiveness of the quantity demanded of a good relative to a change in its price is called the price elasticity of demand for the good. In general, the elasticity of de-

---

2. "Flexible Pricing: Industry's New Strategy to Hold Market Share Changes the Rules for Economic Decision-Making," *Business Week*, December 12, 1977, p. 78.

3. *Ibid.*

4. *Ibid.*

mand for a good with respect to a change in some variable, X, is given by the ratio

$$\frac{\text{Percent change in quantity demanded}}{\text{Percent change in X}}.$$

However, to really understand elasticity, we must get more specific information.

PRICE ELASTICITY OF DEMAND

Price elasticity of demand is the ratio of the percentage change in the quantity demanded of a good or service to the percentage change in its price. Thus, for any good,

$$E_p = \frac{\text{Percent change in quantity demanded}}{\text{Percent change in price}},$$

where E_p is the price elasticity of demand for the good.

For example, suppose that a 10 percent decrease in the price of automobiles will result in a 20 percent increase in the quantity of cars purchased. In this case, we say that the price elasticity of demand, E_p, is equal to 20 percent$/-10$ percent $= -2$. As long as the good obeys the law of demand, □ the price elasticity of demand will be a negative number. This result occurs because quantity demanded will change in the direction opposite to the change in price.

Economists divide the possible values for the price elasticity of demand into three general categories. When the percent changes in price, P, and quantity demanded, Q, are identical except for sign, we get the price elasticity of demand $E_p = -1$. Of course, if for a given percent change in P the change in Q turns out to be a smaller percentage, E_p will be a negative number with an absolute value less than 1.

The *absolute value* of a number is the value that it would have if it were a positive number. Therefore, the absolute value of -2 is 2, and we write this statement as $|-2| = 2$, where the parallel lines denote absolute value.

52

(The absolute value of $+2$ is also 2.) Thus, if the price falls by 20 percent and the quantity demanded increases by 10 percent, we will have $E_p = +10/-20 = -0.5$, and the absolute value of -0.5 is equal to 0.5, which is less than 1.

Finally, if the percentage change in quantity demanded is greater than the percentage change in price, the elasticity coefficient will be negative but will have an absolute value greater than 1. For example, if the price falls by 10 percent and the quantity demanded increases by 30 percent, we have $E_p = +30/-10 = -3$. The $|-3|$ is 3, which is greater than 1.

Classification of Price Elasticity of Demand
The three examples just given illustrate the three general categories of price elasticity of demand, each of which is defined in terms of the absolute value of E_p.

*If $|E_p|$ is less than 1, the percentage change in quantity demanded is less than the percentage change in price (in absolute value terms), and we say that the demand for a good is **inelastic** with respect to its price.*

*If $|E_p|$ is equal to 1, the quantity demanded of a good and its price change by the same percentage (in absolute value), and we say that the demand for the good is **unitary elastic** with respect to its price.*

*If $|E_p|$ is greater than 1, which means that the quantity demanded of a good changes by a larger percentage than the percent change in price (in absolute value terms), we say that the demand for a good is **elastic** with respect to its price.*

This classification system is easy to remember. In common usage we say that something that is very flexible or responsive to a tug or pull (like a rubber band) is *elastic*. Likewise, we say that the demand for a good is elastic if quantity demanded is very responsive to a change in price. Similarly, if something is not very flexible or responsive (like an iron rod), we say it is *inelastic*. If the demand for a good is inelastic with respect to price, then quantity demanded is not very much affected by a change in price. Finally, the term *unitary elastic* comes from the word *unit*, meaning "one."

More precisely, as already indicated, we say that demand is elastic with respect to price if the quantity demanded changes by a larger percentage (in absolute value) than the percentage change in price. Demand is inelastic with respect to price if the quantity demanded changes by a smaller percentage than the percentage change in price. When demand exhibits unitary price elasticity of demand, quantity demanded and the price change by equal percentages. Thus the economist's criterion for classifying the responsiveness of quantity demanded to the price change is whether the percentage change in quantity demanded of a good is greater than, equal to, or less than the percentage change in its price. The three elasticity situations just described are summarized in Table 17-2.

Calculation of Price Elasticity of Demand Figure 17-6 shows a demand curve for movie tickets. At a price of $4 per ticket, 200 tickets will be purchased each day; at a price of $3 per ticket, 300 tickets will be purchased each day. We will now calculate the price elasticity of demand for movie tickets between a price of $4 and a price of $3.

We have seen already that

$$E_p = \frac{\text{Percent change in quantity demanded}}{\text{Percent change in price}}.$$

This definitional equation implies that the

TABLE 17-2   Classification of Price Elasticity of Demand

Value of E_p	Type of Price Elasticity
$|E_p|$ greater than 1	Elastic
$|E_p|$ = 1	Unitary elastic
$|E_p|$ less than 1	Inelastic

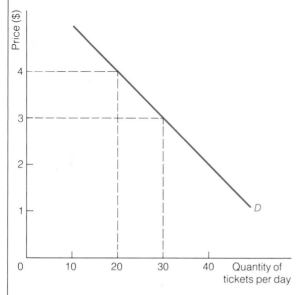

FIGURE 17–6 The Demand for Movie Tickets

The daily demand for movie tickets is given by demand curve, *D*. For example, at a price of $4.00 per ticket, 200 tickets would be purchased per day. At a price of $3.00, 300 tickets would be purchased per day.

price elasticity of demand can be computed by finding

$$E_p = \frac{\text{Change in } Q/Q}{\text{Change in } P/P} = \frac{\text{Change in } Q}{\text{Change in } P} \times \frac{P}{Q},$$

where the change in $Q = Q_2 - Q_1$ and the change in $P = P_2 - P_1$.[5]

In this example, as price falls from $4 to $3, $P_2 - P_1 = -1$, and $Q_2 - Q_1 = +100$. However, we run into a problem with P and Q. Which price and quantity demanded should we use? Should we use $P = 4 and $Q = 200$ or $P = 3 and $Q = 300$? Or some other

___

5. We might write the percent change in Q divided by the percent change in P as

$$E_p = \frac{\Delta Q/Q \ (100\%)}{\Delta P/P \ (100\%)}$$

$$= \frac{\Delta Q/Q}{\Delta P/P}.$$

To simplify this fraction, we can invert the denominator and multiply it by the numerator. Thus:

$$E_p = \frac{\Delta Q}{Q} \times \frac{P}{\Delta P} = \frac{\Delta Q}{\Delta P} \times \frac{P}{Q}.$$

combination? You can verify for yourself that the value of E_p will be different depending on which combination of P and Q is used.

The solution to this problem most economists accept is to use the average of the two prices and the average of the two quantities. To use this method, $\frac{P_1 + P_2}{2}$ is substituted for P and $\frac{Q_1 + Q_2}{2}$ for Q in the equation above. Therefore, the formula for calculating the price elasticity of demand becomes

$$E_p = \frac{\text{Change in } Q}{\text{Change in } P} \times \frac{P_1 + P_2}{Q_1 + Q_2}$$

$$= \frac{Q_2 - Q_1}{P_2 - P_1} \times \frac{P_1 + P_2}{Q_1 + Q_2},$$

because the 2 in the numerator and the 2 in the denominator cancel. This formula is known as an **arc elasticity formula,** because it gives the elasticity between two points along an arc on the demand curve.

For the ticket example,

$$E_p = \frac{Q_2 - Q_1}{P_2 - P_1} \times \frac{P_1 + P_2}{Q_1 + Q_2}$$

$$= \frac{300 - 200}{3 - 4} \times \frac{4 + 3}{200 + 300}$$

$$= \frac{100}{-1} \times \frac{7}{500}$$

$$= \frac{7}{-5}$$

$$= -1.4.$$

Therefore, between the prices of $4 and $3, the price elasticity of demand for movie tickets is equal to -1.4. The absolute value of -1.4 is greater than 1, so the demand for movie tickets is elastic with respect to price over this range. (We would get the same answer if we said that P_1 were $3, P_2 were $4, Q_1 were 300, and Q_2 were 200 as would be the case if the price *increased* from $3 to $4.)

A value of -1.4 for E_p means that over the price interval from $3 to $4, a 1 percent change in price will result in approximately a 1.4 percent change in quantity demanded in the opposite direction. We say "approximately" because −1.4 is the average value of E_p over this price range (since it is an arc price elasticity). In contrast, *point price elasticity values* can be computed for each point of the demand curve. If we were to compute the point elasticity of demand for movie tickets, we would find that it varied over the interval from $3 to $4. However, a discussion of this technique is left to more advanced books.[6]

Importance of Price Elasticity of Demand Through the use of elasticity, we have examined three degrees of responsiveness of quantity demanded of a good or service to a change in its price, but we have yet to see why any of this discussion matters. In Figure 17−7 the monthly demand curve, D_x, for brand X color television sets is shown. At point A on D_x, the price, P_x, is equal to $500 and the quantity demanded is equal to fifty sets per month. At point B, P_x is equal to $400 and quantity demanded has risen to a hundred sets per month.

We can compute the price elasticity of demand between points A and B as follows:

$$E_p = \frac{50}{-100} \times \frac{500 + 400}{50 + 100} = -3,$$

which means that over the range of prices from $500 to $400 a 1 percent change in price will result in approximately a 3 percent change in quantity demanded in the opposite direction. The significance of this value for E_p lies in the fact that something important happens to the amount spent on, or the total revenue received from, the sale of brand X color television sets when the price is lowered from $500 to $400.

When P_x is equal to $500, consumers purchase fifty television sets per month, and total revenue is equal to $500 × 50 = $25,000.

6. See, for example, James L. Pappas and Eugene F. Brigham. *Managerial Economics*, 3d ed. (Hinsdale, Ill.: Dryden Press, 1979), Chapter 4; Arthur A. Thompson, *Economics of the Firm*, 2d ed. (Englewood Cliffs, N.J.: Prentice-Hall, 1977), Chapter 5; and Dale B. Truett and Lila J. Truett, *Managerial Economics* (Cincinnati: South-Western Publishing, 1980), Chapter 2.

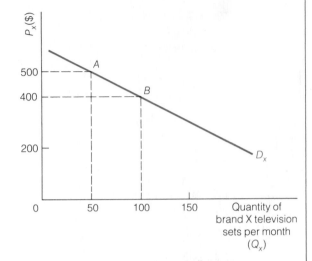

FIGURE 17−7 The Demand for Brand X Color Televisions

Demand curve D_x depicts the monthly demand for brand X color television sets for a store. For example, at a price of $500 per set, 50 television sets would be purchased per month. At a price of $400 per set, a hundred television sets would be purchased per month.

When the price is lowered to $400, the quantity sold rises to a hundred sets per month and total revenue rises to $40,000, a $15,000 increase.

This information is important to the sellers of brand X color televisions, because it indicates that lowering the price from $500 to $400 will increase total monthly sales by $15,000. Obviously, under such circumstances the sellers have a strong incentive to reduce the price below $500, provided that the cost of increasing the number of units sold does not exceed the revenue gain that will result. (This point will be discussed further in Chapter 19.)

In Figure 17−8 the weekly demand curve for gasoline in a small town is shown. In general, the price elasticity of demand for gasoline is less than that for color television sets. For example, at a price of $1 per gallon, customers will purchase 12,000 gallons of gasoline per week. If the price is raised to $1.50 per gallon, consumers will purchase 10,000 gallons each week.

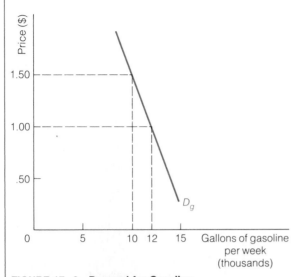

FIGURE 17-8   Demand for Gasoline

Demand curve D_G depicts the weekly demand curve for gasoline in a small town. At a price of $1.00 per gallon, consumers will purchase 12,000 gallons of gasoline per week. If the price increases to $1.50 per gallon, consumers will purchase only 10,000 gallons per week. By computing the price elasticity of demand between these two points, we find that the demand for gasoline is inelastic over this price range.

We can compute the price elasticity of demand for gasoline over the price range of $1 to $1.50 as follows:

$$E_p = \frac{-2,000}{0.50} \times \frac{2.50}{22,000} = \frac{-5}{11} = -0.45.$$

Because the $|E_p|$ is equal to 0.45, which is less than 1, the price elasticity of demand for gasoline over this price range is inelastic. The quantity demanded of gasoline is relatively unresponsive to a change in its price; a 1 percent change in price will result in only a 0.45 percent change in quantity demanded.

At a price of $1 per gallon, total revenue from gasoline sales is equal to $1 × 12,000 = $12,000. If price is raised to $1.50, total revenue rises to $1.50 × 10,000 = $15,000. The fact that total revenue increases when the price is increased in this situation is not a coincidence; nor was the increase in total revenue from a price decrease in the previous example, as we will see in the next section.

Relationship Between E_p and Total Revenue   When the elasticity of demand with respect to price is elastic, a decrease in price will increase total revenue. Total revenue increases because the increase in quantity demanded is so great that it more than offsets the decrease in price. (When demand is elastic, the percentage change in quantity demanded is greater than the percentage change in price.) The opposite effect occurs when demand is elastic and the price is raised; the increase in price is more than offset by the decrease in quantity demanded, and total revenue falls.

On the other hand, if demand is inelastic with respect to price, a decrease in price will result in a lower total revenue, because the increase in quantity demanded will not be large enough to offset the effect of the lower price on revenue. (If demand is inelastic, the percentage change in quantity demanded will be less than the percentage change in price.) Accordingly, if demand is inelastic and price is increased, total revenue will also increase, because the resulting reduction in quantity sold will not be large enough to offset the effect of a higher price.

In the special case where demand is unitary elastic with respect to price, a change in price will have no effect on total revenue. This result occurs because if $|E_p|$ is equal to 1, a certain percentage change in price produces an equal (in absolute value) percentage and exactly offsetting change in quantity demanded. These relationships are summarized in Table 17-3.

With a straight-line, downward-sloping demand curve the price elasticity of demand

TABLE 17-3   Relationship between E_p, Price Changes, and Total Revenue

Price Elasticity of Demand	Price Change	Change in Total Revenue
Elastic	Increase	Decrease
	Decrease	Increase
Inelastic	Increase	Increase
	Decrease	Decrease
Unitary Elastic	Increase	No change
	Decrease	No change

ranges from elastic to unitary elastic to inelastic. This result holds even though the
slope of the demand curve, which is equal to
$\dfrac{\text{change in } P}{\text{change in } Q}$, or $\dfrac{\Delta P}{\Delta Q}$, is constant.

The result is demonstrated in Table 17–4,
which reproduces the demand schedule□ for
a firm selling television video recorders (Table
17–1). In addition, the elasticity of demand is
computed between each set of prices. We can
see from this table that as long as a decrease in
price results in an increase in total revenue
(marginal revenue is positive), demand is
elastic with respect to price. When a decrease
in price results in a decrease in total revenue
(marginal revenue is negative), demand is inelastic with respect to price.

As noted earlier, the elasticities computed
here are called arc elasticities because they are
computed over some range of the demand
curve. In more advanced analysis the price
elasticity of demand would be computed at
the exact point where marginal revenue is
equal to zero, and E_p would be equal to -1
(demand is unitary elastic with respect to

price). These relationships are summarized in
Figure 17–9, which verifies what has been
said about the relationship between the price
elasticity of demand and total and marginal
revenue.

The relationship between total revenue and
the price elasticity of demand is important to
firms. For example, a firm operating in the region where demand is elastic with respect to
price knows that it can raise its total revenue
by lowering prices. Although they must also
consider any resulting increase in costs, companies such as movie theaters, ice skating
rinks, and airlines with excess capacity and
low variable costs are likely to benefit by reducing prices when demand is elastic. As discussed in Chapter 4, the airlines did reduce
fares in the mid 1970s, and their profits rose
dramatically.

On the other hand, if demand is inelastic
with respect to price, a firm can increase its
total revenue by raising its price. Since total
cost is unlikely to increase in this case (quantity sold will either drop or remain the same),
total profit will almost certainly increase as

TABLE 17–4 Price Elasticity of Demand, Total Revenue, and Marginal Revenue of Video Recorders

Price (P)	Quantity Demanded (Q)	Total Revenue (TR = P × Q)	Marginal Revenue (MR = change in TR / change in Q)	E_p
$1,600	0	$ 0		
			$1,400	−15
1,400	5	7,000		
			1,000	−4.3
1,200	10	12,000		
			600	−2.2
1,000	15	15,000		
			200	−1.3
800	20	16,000		
			−200	−0.8
600	25	15,000		
			−600	−0.4
400	30	12,000		
			−1,000	−0.2
200	35	7,000		
			−1,400	−0.1
0	40	0		

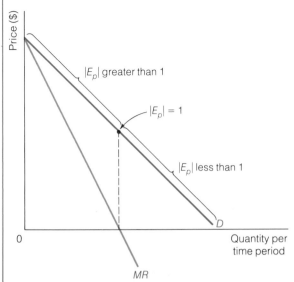

FIGURE 17–9 The Demand Curve, Marginal Revenue, and Price Elasticity of Demand

When marginal revenue is positive, a decrease in price will increase total revenue. Thus, demand is elastic with respect to price. If marginal revenue is zero, a change in price will not affect revenue, and demand is unitary elastic. If marginal revenue is less than zero, a decrease in price will decrease total revenue. In this case, demand is inelastic.

the result of a price increase. The White Mountain Apache in Arizona increased the fee for an elk-hunting permit on their land from $35 to $3,000 and cut the number of permits issued annually from 450 to 32. They realized that total revenue would be greater at the higher price ($96,000 as opposed to $15,750) and that less damage would be done to the environment.[7] Oil companies have also learned to raise price when demand is inelastic.

In fact, there is no reason why a firm would freely choose to operate in the inelastic region of the demand curve for its product. As noted earlier, marginal revenue is negative in this region. In this case, the firm decreases its total revenue by producing and selling another unit of product. Consequently, the firm will wish to raise price and reduce quantity sold until it

is no longer operating in the inelastic portion of the demand curve.

Some Special Demand Cases Figure 17–10 shows some demand curves that are special cases with respect to price elasticity. In panel (a) the vertical demand curve has a price elasticity of 0. The value for E_p is equal to 0 because no change in quantity demanded occurs when price is changed. A demand curve such as this one is said to be **perfectly inelastic.**

The demand for certain goods may well be perfectly inelastic over some price range, particularly if the goods are insignificant in people's total budgets. Take pencils, for example. If pencils priced at 5 cents each rise in price to 6 cents each, it is possible that no change will occur in the quantity of them purchased over a specific time period (unless the price of a competing brand remains at 5 cents).

The absolute value of the price elasticity coefficient for the demand curve in panel (b) of Figure 17–10 is equal to infinity, since the firm can sell as large a quantity as it wishes at the current market price, P_0, but cannot sell even one unit at a higher price.[8] This behavior reflects the ultimate in responsiveness of quantity demanded to changes in price. Correspondingly, a horizontal demand curve like that in panel (b) is called a **perfectly elastic** demand curve. Such demand curves are present in perfect competition, a market structure discussed in Chapter 20.

Finally, panel (c) of Figure 17–10 shows a demand curve that has unitary elasticity at every point. Such a curve will always have the

7. Bill Hess, "White Mountain Apache: Seeking the Best of Two Worlds," *National Geographic*, February 1980, p. 279.

8. Because E_p is equal to

$$\frac{\Delta Q}{\Delta P} \times \frac{P_1 + P_2}{Q_1 + Q_2}$$

and $\Delta P/\Delta Q$ is equal to the slope of the demand curve,

$$E_p = \frac{1}{\text{Demand curve slope}} \times \frac{P_1 + P_2}{Q_1 + Q_2}.$$

Because the slope of the demand curve in panel (b) is 0,

$$|E_p| = \left|\frac{1}{0}\right| \frac{P_1 + P_2}{Q_1 + Q_2} = \infty.$$

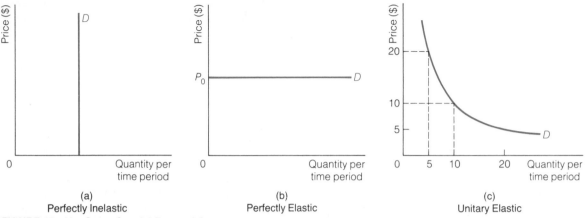

FIGURE 17-10   Some Special Demand Curves

If demand is perfectly inelastic with respect to price, quantity demanded does not vary with price. The demand curve is, therefore, a vertical line as in panel a. If demand is perfectly elastic, a firm can sell any quantity that it wishes to at the going market price. In this case, the demand curve is a horizontal line (panel b). If demand is unitary elastic, the demand curve can be graphed as a rectangular hyperbola (panel c).

shape, called a rectangular hyperbola, shown in panel (c). In addition, the total revenue associated with a unitary elastic demand curve will be constant at every price, because any change in price is exactly offset by an equal (in absolute value) percentage change in quantity demanded. In our example, total revenue is equal to $100.

Determinants of the Price Elasticity of Demand   The price elasticity of the demand for a good is affected by many factors, including how necessary or important consumers view the good to be, what percent of the consumers' budgets is spent on the good, the availability of substitute goods, and the time span over which consumers' adjustments to a price change are being observed. If a good is viewed as a necessity, its price elasticity of demand will tend to be relatively low. A person who has been bitten by a rabid animal will view preventive rabies shots as essential for continued life. Therefore, as long as the person has the available funds, he or she will probably be willing to pay many different prices for exactly the required number of shots.

The percentage of budgets spent on a particular item will also affect consumers' reactions to price increases. If consumers spend a relatively small portion of their incomes on a good or service, the price elasticity of demand for that product, other things remaining the same, will again tend to be relatively low. For example, table salt tends to have a low price elasticity of demand. Consumers' expenditures on table salt are not as a rule a significant part of their budgets. On the other hand, the price elasticity of demand for housing is larger.

The availability of substitutes is also an important factor in determining the price elasticity of demand. For example, as long as there is no readily available substitute for gasoline as a source of energy for motor vehicles, the price elasticity of demand for gasoline will be relatively low. However, because there are many substitutes available for a particular brand of gasoline, the price elasticity of demand for that brand will be highly elastic (assuming that the prices of competing brands do not change).

Finally, the time span over which the adjustment process is observed will affect the price elasticity of demand for a good or service. For example, in the short run many people may believe that they have few possibilities for reducing their purchases of gasoline.

Over a longer period of time they may learn to use public transportation, to develop more economical driving habits, and to purchase more fuel-efficient cars, so that the price elasticity of demand increases as the period under consideration lengthens. Also, given more time, industry will develop more ways for consumers to reduce gasoline fuel consump-

tion, such as by producing electric cars and even more fuel-efficient gasoline-operated cars.

Some Estimates of Price Elasticity of Demand Table 17–5 gives estimates by various economists of the price elasticity of demand for selected products. These goods and services are grouped into two categories—those with a price elasticity of demand (in absolute value) greater than 1 and those with a price elasticity of demand less than 1. Items in the first category tend to be considered less necessary in nature than items in the second category. Also both long-run and short-run elasticities of demand for certain products are reported. As we would expect, the elasticities of demand are smaller in the short run than in the long run. In the long run consumers find that they have an increased number of alternatives available.

TABLE 17–5 Estimated Elasticities of Demand for Selected Products (in Absolute Value)

Product	Elasticity
Elasticity Greater than 1.0	
Fresh tomatoes	4.6
Medical care and hospitalization insurance, long run	3.6
Interest on personal debt, long run	2.7
Intercity railway, long run	2.7
Foriegn travel by U.S. residents, short run	4.1
Airline travel, long run	2.4
Peaches	1.5
Shoe cleaning and repairs, short run	1.1
Shoe cleaning and repairs, long run	1.5
Automobiles	0.8–1.5
Nondurable toys, long run	1.7
Radio and television receivers, records, short run	1.2
Radio and television receivers, records, long run	1.3
Elasticity Less than 1.0[a]	
Citrus fruit	
Eggs	
Milk	
White potatoes	
Margarine	
Kitchen and other household appliances	
Physicians	
Gasoline and oil, short run	
Gasoline and oil, long run	
Legal services	
Interest on personal debt, short run	

[a]Specific elasticity figures not available.

Source: Dean A. Worcester, Jr., "On Monopoly Welfare Losses: Comment," *American Economic Review* 65 (December 1975): 1016. (Worcester made the point in this article that the elasticity of demand for the products of individual firms is generally much larger than that for the market as a whole. He further argued that low demand elasticities are evidence that firms are not exercising monopoly power very successfully. The effect of market structure on firm pricing policies is discussed more fully in chapters 20–22.)

ELASTICITY
OF
SUPPLY

We can also use the concept of elasticity to indicate the responsiveness of the quantity supplied □ of a product to changes in the product's price.

The ***elasticity of supply*** *of a product is the percentage change in the quantity supplied of the good or service divided by the percentage change in its price, other things remaining the same.*

The formula for computing the price elasticity of supply is

$$E_s = \frac{Q_{s2} - Q_{s1}}{P_2 - P_1} \times \frac{P_1 + P_2}{Q_{s1} + Q_{s2}},$$

where Q_s *is the quantity supplied of a good,* P *is the price of the good, and* E_s *is the elasticity of supply with respect to price.*

In general, we would expect the elasticity of supply to be positive; that is, producers would be willing to supply more at higher prices than at lower prices. Moreover, we would expect the elasticity of supply to be greater over longer periods than over shorter periods of time. Over longer periods of time firms have a greater ability to alter their plant capacity and, therefore, the quantity supplied of a product.

In general, a supply curve passing through any given point (combination of price and quantity sold) is more elastic *at that point* the less steep is its slope. In Figure 17–11, at point A, supply curve S_1 is more elastic than supply curve S_2, but both S_2 and S_1 are more elastic than S_3. When supply is totally inelastic, the supply curve is vertical ($E_s = 0$). In this case, the quantity supplied will not change at all in response to a change in the price of a product. At the other extreme, as the supply curve approaches a horizontal line, its elasticity approaches infinity. In this case suppliers will be willing to supply any

quantity at the going market price. Of course, supply curves need not be straight lines. Straight lines are used in Figure 17–11 just for purposes of illustration.

The importance of time as a determinant of supply elasticity can be illustrated using a simple example from the petroleum industry. When an increase in the price of crude oil first occurs, the quantity supplied of crude oil does not change dramatically (supply is not very elastic), because additional oil can come only from existing wells and stocks on hand. However, as time goes on, the higher price causes producers to step up exploration and drill more wells. Thus the long-run supply curve for oil is more elastic than the short-run supply curve. This relationship is illustrated in Figure 17–12, where S_s represents the short-run supply curve for oil and S_L the long-run supply curve. If the price of crude oil rises from P_1 to P_2, the industry's short-run response will be to increase the quantity supplied to Q_2. However, if the price remains at P_2, over the long run the quantity supplied

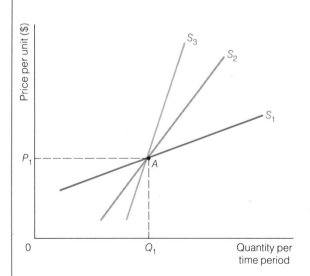

FIGURE 17–11   Three Supply Curves with Different Elasticities at Point A

At point A, S_1 is more elastic than S_2, and S_2 is more elastic than S_3. A change in price from P_1 would have a greater effect on quantity supplied if the supply curve is S_1 rather than S_3.

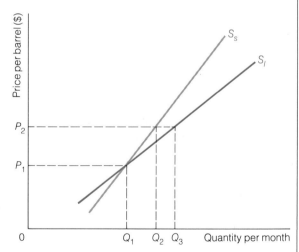

FIGURE 17–12   Comparison of Short-run and Long-run Supply Curves for Crude Oil

The short-run supply curve for crude oil is given by S_s, whereas the long-run supply curve for crude oil is given by S_L. Initially, the price per barrel of crude oil is P_1, and the quantity supplied is Q_1. After the price rises to P_2, the quantity supplied will increase in the short run to Q_2. In the long run, it will increase to Q_3.

will be Q_3, because S_L is more elastic than S_s.

Although time is an important determinant of the elasticity of supply for most goods and services, other factors may affect the responsiveness of quantity supplied to price changes. For example, the substitutability of factors of production from one use to another will determine how easy it is for producers to adjust quantity supplied. In addition, if a good can be stored easily, it may be feasible for producers to respond quickly to price changes by drawing down or increasing inventories. A fourth factor that affects the elasticity of supply is the manner in which costs vary with the level of output. Finally, the expectations producers have about future prices may affect how much they are willing to respond to a price change that takes place today. In Chapter 33 we will examine in some detail how the elasticity of supply of agricultural products affects their prices and, consequently, farm incomes.

SUMMARY

1. This chapter examined the relationship between the demand curve for a firm's product and the revenue of the firm. It began with definitions of total, average, and marginal revenue.

2. Total revenue refers to the total sales (in dollars) of a firm during some particular period of time. Total revenue associated with any level of quantity sold can be found by multiplying price by quantity sold. These price-quantity combinations can be found directly from the demand curve. Average revenue is revenue per unit sold, and it is equal to total revenue divided by the quantity sold. As long as the same price is charged for all units, average revenue and price are equal. In this case the average revenue curve and the firm's demand curve are the same thing. Marginal revenue is the increase in total revenue from selling one more unit of the product, and it is equal to the change in total revenue divided by the change in quantity sold.

3. Since the quantity demanded of a firm's product depends on several factors, it is useful for a firm to know the responsiveness of quantity demanded to changes in these variables. This information is given by the elasticity of demand with respect to the variables.

4. Price elasticity of demand measures the percent change in quantity demanded relative to the percent change in the price of a good. If $|E_p|$ is greater than 1, demand is elastic with respect to price. If $|E_p|$ is less than 1, demand is inelastic with respect to price. If $|E_p|$ is equal to 1, demand is unitary elastic with respect to price. In the elastic case a decrease in price will increase total revenue, and vice versa. In the inelastic case a decrease in price will decrease total revenue, and vice versa. If demand is unitary elastic with respect to price, a change in price will have no effect on total revenue.

5. Information about the value of the price elasticity of demand is vitally important to the profit-maximizing firm when it is determining its optimal pricing and production strategies.

6. The elasticity of supply is a measure of the responsiveness of the quantity supplied of a product to a change in its price. The elasticity of supply is equal to the percentage change in quantity supplied divided by the percentage change in price. Factors that affect it include the time span involved, subsitutability of inputs, possibilities for storing the product, the way costs vary with the level of output, and the price expectations of producers.

IMPORTANT TERMS AND CONCEPTS

Total revenue	Price elasticity of
Average revenue	demand
Marginal revenue	Inelastic demand
Substitute goods	Unitary elastic
Complementary goods	demand
Elasticity	Elastic demand
	Elasticity of supply

QUESTIONS AND PROBLEMS

1. Define *total revenue, average revenue,* and *marginal revenue.* How are price and average revenue related? Make up some examples.

2. Define *price elasticity of demand.* How is the elasticity of demand with respect to price classified?

3. How are price elasticity of demand, total revenue, and marginal revenue related?

4. Give an example of a good that might have a perfectly inelastic demand curve over some price range. Also give an example of a good that might have an infinitely elastic demand curve. Explain your answers.

5. Complete the following table, which gives revenue data for a bicycle manufacturer. Over what range of prices is demand elastic with respect to price? Over what range is it inelastic?

Price	Quantity	Total Revenue	Marginal Revenue
$200	0		
190	1000		
180	2000		
170	3000		
160	4000		
150	5000		
140	6000		
130	7000		
120	8000		
110	9000		
100	10,000		
90	11,000		

6. Complete the following table of revenue data for a manufacturer of toy astronauts. What additional data will the firm need before it can determine the most profitable price?

Quantity	Price	Total Revenue	Marginal Revenue
0	$100	$	$
100	90		
200		16,000	
300			50
400		24,000	
500		25,000	
600	40		

7. (Note: This problem will require some algebra.) Keen Jeans, Inc., a manufacturer of jeans, is currently selling 10,000 pairs of jeans per month at a price of $20 each. The firm is considering increasing its sales by lowering the price to $15. The marketing department has estimated the price elasticity of demand to be − 2. What will be the new quantity of jeans sold per month and the effect on the firm's total revenue if it lowers the price to $15? Is the elasticity of demand with respect to price elastic or inelastic? How do you know?

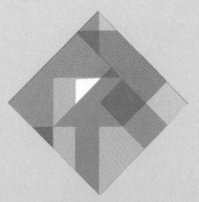

WHY IBM
REVERSED ITSELF
ON
COMPUTER PRICING

When International Business Machines Corp. introduced its powerful 4300 series of mainframe computers a year ago, it knocked the computer industry on its ear. It set prices so low that it appeared that competitors would be hard-put to match the new price/performance standards. Indeed, at least one maker of plug-compatible computers—copycat machines that sell for less than IBM's but run on IBM software—was forced out of the market, and others were badly crippled. Long accustomed to operating under the protection of IBM's price umbrella, the industry, it seemed, was in for

Source: Robin Grossman, "Why IBM Reversed Itself on Computer Pricing," *Business Week,* January 28, 1980, p. 84.

a new era of aggressive and perhaps profitless competition and, eventually, further consolidation.

So the industry was stunned again on Dec. 28 when IBM unfolded its umbrella again, raising prices by 5% to 7% on most of its data processing and word processing products. "IBM has taken a step backward on its march to offer price/performance improvements," observes L. Duane Kirkpatrick, head of the technology group at Dean Witter Reynolds Inc. in San Francisco. While the price boosts undoubtedly reflect increasing costs of doing business, as IBM claims, IBM-watchers say that the post-Christmas reversal is also a clear admission by the company that its original pricing for the 4300 series

was too low—a mistake that IBM is now trying to rectify.

PROFITABILITY

Only the industry's customers are likely to lose by IBM's reversal. The Armonk giant has a lot to gain. No one expects the higher prices to reduce demand for the 4300 series, so profitability—badly needed to underwrite the company's ambitious manufacturing and leasing programs—will only be enhanced. "By the stroke of a pen, IBM has just increased revenue by $1 billion," figures S.S. "Tim" Tyler, a senior consultant at Input, a Palo Alto (Calif.) market research firm.

The episode, though, reflects a deep-seated business problem that, because of IBM's preeminence, must inevitably affect the future pace of product introductions. IBM has a huge customer base, and thus a huge potential for hurting itself each time it announces a new product. The giant walks a fine line between introducing attractively priced machines and milking its installed base.

After the medium-scale 4300 series was announced, for example, users of IBM's top-of-the-line 303X series of mainframes anticipated that the company's impending H series, to replace the 303X line, would echo the aggressive price/performance of the 4300. Expecting that the H series could appear as early as the end of 1979, they stopped buying the 303X machines, fearing that they would decline sharply in value.

As a result, just as IBM was trying to encourage customers to buy instead of lease to improve its cash flow, its 303X customers began to insist on leasing to protect themselves. This cost IBM doubly: Besides losing the purchase revenues, it had to finance a larger lease and rental base than it had planned for. While the company refuses to discuss the matter, "in retrospect, IBM wishes it had not priced so aggressively," says William R. Becklean, an analyst with Bache Halsey Stuart Shields Inc. in Boston. Becklean believes that the 4300 pricing boomerang was largely responsible for the 18% decline in IBM's third-quarter earnings last year. (Earnings for the year were off 3%.)

Those profit declines came at a bad time: when IBM needed money to expand production capacity for the 4300 series and to fund its lease base for the forthcoming H series. In October the company went outside for money for the first time, floating $1 billion in bonds. And in December it announced a $300 million loan from Saudi Arabia. The profit declines also worried IBM stockholders who have come to expect constant improvements in revenues and return on investment. "IBM needs growth to keep its stock at a premium multiple," says Kirkpatrick of Dean Witter.

NOT AS DRAMATIC

Most industry observers expect to see IBM back on the growth track soon. "IBM has never had a profitability or cash flow problem before," notes H. Glen Haney, vice-president for worldwide marketing at Sperry Corp.'s Univac Div. "They'll work at this until they fix it." The yearend price increases may do the trick. They conspicuously excepted the purchase prices, though not the lease and rental rates, of the 303X series. And IBM customers, say the company's competitors, now will not expect the price/performance improvements of the H series to be as dramatic as those originally announced for the 4300 series. Thus they will step up their purchases of the 303X computers.

Meanwhile, by its price action, IBM has breathed new life into some troubled competitors. The chief beneficiaries are the plug-compatible manufacturers, but other full-line computer makers, such as Honeywell, Sperry, and Burroughs, may also be able to let out their pricing belts a notch. J. Roy Henry, executive vice-president for marketing at Burroughs Corp., is still analyzing the IBM move, but he says, "If it gives us room to raise our prices, we will do that." With the price umbrella up, observes Stephen T. McClellan, an analyst with Salomon Bros., "the industry can get under it comfortably and profitably again."

But IBM's competitors would do well not to make themselves too comfortable. By its aggressive pricing a year ago, the industry leader has shown that it intends to hold on to, if not raise, its massive share of the information processing market. Industry experts believe that if competition gets too tough in 1981 or 1982, particularly from the Japanese, IBM will not hesitate to slash its prices again.

QUESTIONS

1. Does the article indicate that the elasticity of demand with respect to price is elastic or inelastic for IBM's 4300 series? Explain.
2. What evidence is cited in the article to indicate that expectations as well as current prices affect the quantity demanded of computers?
3. How have IBM's pricing policies affected the profitability of its competitors? What elasticity of demand concept is relevant here? (Question 3 is to be answered if Special Topic F., which appears after Chapter 17, is assigned.)

INCOME AND CROSS ELASTICITY OF DEMAND

Certain variables other than the price of a good affect the quantity of it that consumers purchase. In this special topic we will examine the impact of consumer income and the prices of related goods on the demand for a particular good or service.

INCOME ELASTICITY OF DEMAND

Firms often want to know the elasticity of demand for their product with respect to changes in the level of consumers' incomes. In other words, they want to know how quantity demanded responds to a change in consumers' incomes, while other factors affecting quantity demanded remain constant.

> The **income elasticity of demand** for a good is the percent change in quantity demanded divided by the percent change in income.

Following the pattern of the price elasticity formula, the formula for computing the arc income elasticity of demand is given by

$$E_y = \frac{Q_2 - Q_1}{Y_2 - Y_1} \times \frac{Y_1 + Y_2}{Q_1 + Q_2},$$

where E_y is the income elasticity of demand, Q is the quantity demanded of a good, and Y is a measure of consumers' incomes.

For example, suppose that at a price of $1,200 and an average annual household income of $15,000, people will purchase ten television video recorders from a particular store per month. If the average annual income rises to $40,000, prices remaining constant, people will purchase twenty video recorders per month. In this case the income elasticity of demand between the income levels of $15,000 and $20,000 is given by

$$E_y = \frac{10}{\$5,000} \times \frac{\$15,000 + \$20,000}{10 + 20} = 2.3.$$

Over this income range, a 1 percent increase in income will yield approximately a 2.3 percent increase in quantity demanded of video recorders.

In this case the income elasticity of demand is positive. Goods with a positive income elasticity of demand also have a positive income effect and are therefore *normal goods*, because an E_y greater than 0 means that people buy more of these goods as their (real) incomes rise and less as their real incomes fall.

Superior goods *are normal goods with an income elasticity of demand greater than 1.*

As discussed in Chapter 16, inferior goods have negative income elasticities of demand, because people buy less of them as their incomes rise, and vice versa.

It is important for the firm to know the income elasticity of demand for its product for two reasons. First, the income elasticity of demand gives the firm vital information regarding the long-range prospects for growth in the sales of its product as the economy grows. Second, it gives the firm some insight into how to plan its production during the ups and downs of business cycles.

For example, if the income elasticity of demand is low, as it is for many agricultural products, a recession or a boom period will have little effect on the quantity demanded of a product. On the other hand, if the income elasticity of demand is high, as it is for automobiles, changes in income over the course of the business cycle will have a significant impact on the quantity sold.

CROSS PRICE ELASTICITY OF DEMAND

Although the elasticity of demand can be measured with respect to many variables, the last such concept to be discussed here is the cross price elasticity of demand. The cross price elasticity of demand is a measure of the responsiveness of the quantity demanded of one good to changes in the price of another good.

The **cross price elasticity of demand** *of good X with respect to changes in the price of good Y is defined as the percentage change in quantity demanded of good X divided by the percentage change in the price of good Y. The formula for computing the arc cross price elasticity is*

$$E_{xy} = \frac{Q_{x2} - Q_{x1}}{P_{y2} - P_{y1}} \times \frac{P_{y1} + P_{y2}}{Q_{x1} + Q_{x2}}.$$

We can illustrate the usefulness of this concept as follows. Suppose, given the current level of annual average household income, a Ford dealer can sell a hundred LTD's per month at a price of $8,000 each if the price of a Chevrolet Caprice is $9,000. If the price of the Caprice falls to $8,500, the Ford dealer can sell only seventy-five Ford LTD's, because some people will switch to Chevrolet Caprices. The cross price elasticity of demand for LTD's with respect to the price of Caprices can be computed as

$$E_{xy} = \frac{-25}{-\$500} \times \frac{\$9,000 + \$8,500}{100 + 75} = 5.$$

This value of E_{xy} indicates that over this price range for Caprices and given a price of $8,000 for LTD's the firm will experience approximately a 5 percent loss in the quantity sold of LTD's for every percent decrease in the price of Caprices.

In this case the cross price elasticity of demand is positive, as will always be the case when two goods are substitutes. The elasticity coefficient is positive when two goods are substitutes because a change in the price of one results in a change in the same direction of the quantity demanded of the other good. Thus a decrease in the price of Caprices results in a decrease in the quantity demanded of LTD's.

The cross price elasticity of demand for complementary goods is negative, because a change in the price of one will result in a change in the opposite direction in the quantity demanded of the other. For example, suppose that the Ford dealership can sell a hundred LTD's per month as long as the price of an LTD is $8,000, the price of a Chevrolet Caprice is $9,000, and the price of gasoline is $.50 a gallon. If the price of gasoline rises to $1 a gallon, other prices remaining constant, the quantity demanded of LTD's will drop, to say sixty per month. We can compute

$$E_{xy} = \frac{-40}{0.50} \times \frac{0.50 + 1.00}{100 + 60} = -0.75.$$

A value of -0.75 indicates that a 1 percent increase in the price of gasoline will result in a 0.75 percent decrease in the quantity demanded of LTDs.

If two goods, X and Y, are not related, E_{xy} will be 0. In this case a decrease in the price of one will have no effect on the quantity demanded of the other.

Information about cross price elasticities of demand is important to a firm for several reasons. First, the values of the cross price elasticities between the quantity demanded of a firm's product and the prices of similar products of other firms will give the firm an inkling as to how it should respond to price changes by its competitors. Moreover, information about the cross price elasticity of demand enables a firm to predict the impact of price changes of complementary goods on sales of its product.

Second, many firms produce or sell several products that are themselves related. For example, Procter & Gamble would find it useful to know how a sale price on one of its dishwashing detergents would affect the quantity sold of one of its other brands of dishwashing detergents. Eastman Kodak might find it useful to know how a decrease in the price of cameras would affect sales of film.

Finally, evidence that two products have a positive cross price elasticity and, therefore, are substitutes can help a firm defend itself against a charge of "monopolizing." This concept was used in an antitrust case involving E. I. du Pont de Nemours and Company in 1956.

In this case du Pont, which made cellophane wrapping paper, was accused by the U.S. government of having a monopoly in the market for cellophane. During the period covered by the suit, the early 1900s, du Pont produced approximately 75 percent of the cellophane sold in the United States. The company successfully argued that the relevant market with regard to the monopolization charge was the market for flexible packaging materials, which included, for example, waxed paper and aluminum foil, rather than the market for cellophane alone. Sales of cellophane accounted for only 20 percent of the total sales of this larger market. Du Pont supported its argument by showing that there were positive cross price elasticities of demand between the price of cellophane and the quantities purchased of other flexible wrappings, which indicated that these goods were substitutes.[1] Thus, du Pont established to the court's satisfaction that it did not have a monopoly on flexible wrappings.

QUESTIONS

(Note: These questions will require some algebra.)

1. Dare Devil Dirt Bikes, Inc., was pleased with its sales prospects until its competitor, Thunderbolt Bikes, lowered its price from $800 to $700. The price of a Dare Devil bike is currently $850. Before Thunderbolt lowered its price, Dare Devil sold 4,000 bikes a month. The estimated cross price elasticity of demand between the price of Thunderbolt bikes and the quantity demanded of Dare Devil bikes is 1 over the relevant range. Find the effect of the price reduction on Dare Devil's total revenue. Are these bikes substitutes or complements? Explain.

---

1. See United States v. E. I. DuPont De Nemours & Co., 351 U.S. 377 (1956).

2. Conrad Jewelry is considering raising the price of its solitaire diamond necklaces as a result of a surcharge that the DeBeers diamond mining company has placed on diamonds. At the present time Conrad Jewelry is selling 50 diamond necklaces per month at an average price of $300 per necklace. It estimates that the price elasticity of demand for its necklaces over the relevant range is −3.

a. What will be the decrease in quantity demanded of diamond necklaces if Conrad Jewelry raises the average price of its necklaces to $400?

b. Is the price elasticity of demand for diamond necklaces elastic or inelastic? How do you know?

c. Because diamond necklaces are a luxury good, the income elasticity of demand for Conrad Jewelry's necklaces is high: $E_y = 5$. Economists estimate that the average annual family income will rise from $14,000 to $16,000 during the next year. How will this increase in income affect the quantity sold by Conrad Jewelry if it has already raised the price to $400? (Use as Q_1 the new quantity you found in part a.)

C H A P T E R 18

PRODUCTION
AND
COST

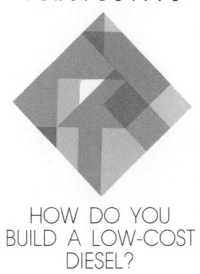

HOW DO YOU
BUILD A LOW-COST
DIESEL?

General Motors is a firm with awesome productive capabilities. Its annual output (some $58 billion in 1980) is greater than the gross national product of many countries. But, just like any other business firm, GM has to worry about the costs of production. In the period 1977–80, when GM introduced diesel engines in its "downsized" full-size and intermediate cars, the costs of its diesel strategy skyrocketed.

An August 1980 Wall Street Journal headline reads: "GM Shoulders Huge Repair Costs for Its Trouble-Ridden Diesel Cars."[1] In an effort to produce a V–8 diesel engine quickly and with a minimum of new investment or change in its production process, GM chose to convert its Oldsmobile gasoline-fueled engines to diesel rather than build a new diesel engine. The initial results were disastrous and saddled the company with all sorts of unanticipated costs. Not only did GM have to absorb the costs of lawsuits filed by dissatisfied customers, it also had to pick up a lot of repair bills and to improve its production technology for the engines.

The Journal noted that GM had to change the way it makes such crucial parts as camshafts and crankshafts and had to employ extra assembly-line workers to hand-tighten critical bolts and belts. In addition, because oil leaks were a major problem, sample cars

1. Leonard M. Apcar, "GM Shoulders Huge Repair Costs for Its Trouble-Ridden Diesel Cars," The Wall Street Journal, August 21, 1980, p. 25.

had to be driven from the assembly lines and parked, engines running, over sheets of clean white paper. This proved to be an expensive and time-consuming process.

Of course, GM has survived its mistake with the Olds diesel, but the cost increases caused by its strategy must have cut into profits. Indeed, a smaller firm might have been destroyed by the unanticipated costs that the engine imposed on GM.

A basic element in the issue of costs is production technology, or what economists call the production function for a particular good or service. For example, the production function for a given type of V–8 diesel engine is a statement of the combinations of resources that can be used to produce various possible quantities of the engines. GM chose one of several resource combinations for its diesel engine, and its management may well regret the choice. Another main element of cost is the prices of resources that a firm must employ to produce output. In this chapter we will examine both production and cost and will identify strategies for keeping cost as low as possible for any quantity of output produced by a business firm.

C H A P T E R 18

◆

PRODUCTION AND COST

WHAT THIS CHAPTER IS ABOUT

PRODUCTION FUNCTION
LEAST COST COMBINATION OF INPUTS
LONG-RUN COSTS
Long-run Total Costs
Long-run Average Costs
Long-run Marginal Costs
PRODUCT CURVES OF A VARIABLE INPUT
Total Product
Average Product
Marginal Product
Law of Diminishing Marginal Productivity
SHORT-RUN COSTS
Short-run Fixed Costs
Short-run Variable Costs
ECONOMIES AND DISECONOMIES OF SCALE
ECONOMIC COST vs. ACCOUNTING COST
PRIVATE COST vs. SOCIAL COST

In the last chapter we examined the first of two basic factors that determine the profitability of a firm—the demand for its product. In this chapter we will consider the second of these factors—the cost of production. Since cost and production are, in a sense, inseparable concepts for a firm, we will deal with production as well. Broadly speaking, efficient production is a goal that all firms must try to achieve if they are to maximize their profits. Even a retail store goes through a sort of production process when it readies and makes available its goods for sale.

Many firms have difficulty managing the cost aspect of their operations, and poor cost management has a negative effect on profits. For example, in early 1981, there were widespread reports that Chrysler Motor Corp. was on the verge of bankruptcy. It had just recorded a $235 million loss for the fourth quarter of 1980, and its 1980 losses exceeded

$1.7 billion.[1] Chrysler's problems involved both high costs and declining sales, and the two factors were related. Many costs of automobile manufacturing are fixed; therefore, because of its low sales volume, Chrysler's cost per unit sold was high compared with that of General Motors.

For another example, a 1978 law that deregulated the airlines to a large extent left the various airline companies scrambling to find markets that would be profitable in the face of increased competition. A 70 percent increase in fuel costs in the first ten months of 1979 made their task more difficult. Many major airlines cut routes and laid off a significant number of employees.[2] The air traffic controllers strike in the fall of 1981 added to the airlines' woes.

Even the government has trouble controlling costs. In the fall of 1979 Amtrak, the passenger train service run and subsidized by the federal government, was forced to eliminate six routes covering five thousand miles in a move to reduce costs. Because of the high government subsidies required to keep Amtrak in business so far, it has a most uncertain future.[3]

THE ECONOMIST'S
VIEW OF COST

Before we look into the relationship between production and cost, we need to examine the items that an economist considers to be costs. As we will see, an accountant's view of cost is somewhat different from an economist's view of cost.

EXPLICIT COSTS

An accountant concentrates on explicit, or accounting, costs.

> *Explicit costs* are the costs for items for which the firm has made a specific payment in the past or for which it is obligated to do so in the future.

Thus explicit costs are based on historical costs. Accountants are concerned with these costs because they are required in firms' formal income statements.[4]□ Explicit costs are based on facts and are therefore considered to be objective.

IMPLICIT, OR OPPORTUNITY, COSTS

Explicit costs alone do not form an adequate basis for decision making. Implicit, or opportunity, costs□ are also relevant.

> *Opportunity costs* represent opportunities that a firm gives up by using a resource in one way rather than another.

For example, suppose the owners of a firm have invested $20,000 of their own funds in the business. They could have earned interest on this money if they had merely left it in an insured savings account. Furthermore, they spend time running the business. Surely, they

---

1. See "Corporate Scoreboard," *Business Week,* March 16, 1981, p. 70. For more information on Chrysler's problems, see "Can Chrysler Be Saved?" *Newsweek,* August 13, 1979, pp. 52–61; and "Chrysler Incurred a Record Deficit in Third Quarter," *Wall Street Journal,* October 31, 1979, p. 2.

2. "Fasten Seat Belts," *Newsweek,* November 5, 1979, pp. 89–90.

3. "Amtrak Avoids Major Surgery," *Newsweek,* September 10, 1979, p. 60; and "Even a Gas Crunch Can't Save Amtrak," *Newsweek,* May 21, 1979, p. 75.

4. The accounting profession is now facing up to the problems involved with calculating depreciation and certain other expenses using historical cost figures. See "The Profit Illusion," *Business Week,* March 19, 1979, pp. 108–112; and "Inflation Accounting," *Business Week,* October 15, 1979, pp. 68–74.

could have earned wages in some other line of work if they had chosen to do so. Opportunity costs are therefore defined as the return from using these resources in their best (most profitable) alternative uses. Since such values usually must be estimated, they are sometimes considered to be less objective than explicit cost figures.

According to economists, however, the **economic cost** of a firm includes both explicit and implicit costs. A firm cannot make profit-maximizing decisions if it considers owner-supplied resources to be free. They are not free because they can be used in a profitable manner elsewhere. Economic cost, then, is equal to accounting, or explicit, costs plus opportunity, or implicit, costs.

ACCOUNTING INCOME
VERSUS ECONOMIC PROFIT

Accounting net income is equal to the total revenues of a firm less its total accounting costs.

*Economic profit is equal to accounting income less opportunity costs, including a **normal** or **average return,** considering the riskiness of the enterprise to the owners of the business.*

Economists argue that a **normal profit** (return) is necessary to keep a firm in business. Otherwise, the owners would invest their resources elsewhere.

Consequently, when a firm's economic profit is zero, it is earning a normal or average return for that type of business. A firm that earns a positive economic profit is earning an above normal return.

PRIVATE COSTS VERSUS SOCIAL COSTS

*The **private costs** of a firm are those costs which it incurs, both explicit and implicit.*

However, the firm may also impose costs on society that it does not have to bear itself. For example, a steel mill may pollute the air surrounding the plant. Other firms may pollute the ground or water with harmful chemicals. Large trucks may do more damage to the roadways than they pay for in taxes.

Social costs are the private costs of the resources that the firm uses plus any additional costs imposed on society by the firm's operation.

The concept of social cost will discussed more thoroughly in chapters 27 and 28.

INPUTS AND THE
PRODUCTION
FUNCTION
◆

We will begin our analysis of the individual firm by examining the relationship between inputs, or factors of production,□ and output. This relationship is expressed through the production function.

13

INPUTS

*An **input** or **factor of production,** is a resource that a firm uses to produce a good or service.*

Examples of inputs are labor, fuel, raw materials, land, machinery, and managerial skills. Chapter 1 noted that economists typically classify inputs as being in one of the following four general categories: land (including raw materials), labor, capital, and entrepreneurship. Most business firms require some of each of these types of inputs to produce goods or services. For example, an automobile manufacturer must have raw materials and land for its factories, buildings and machinery (capital), workers, managers, and investor-owners. Likewise, a retail florist must have a location, flowers and other raw materials, store personnel, refrigerators, managers, and the owner's entrepreneurial skills.

PRODUCTION FUNCTION

The **production function** for a firm specifies the technological relationship between the amounts of various inputs the firm can use and the resulting maximum level of output it can produce.

The maximum level of output is what is relevant here, because all inputs are assumed to be used with technological efficiency. In other words, no inputs are idle or otherwise wasted. The production function can be viewed as a specific recipe for producing a particular kind of output. A recipe for carrot cake is a production function, but it is much less complicated than the production function for a car or a color TV.

In mathematical notation, a general production function with capital and labor as inputs would look like:

$$Q = f(K, L),$$

where:

Q is quantity of output,
K is number of units of capital,
and L is the number of units of labor.

In this context, as in national income analysis, *capital* refers to a firm's plant and equipment, not financial capital. A production function can have many more inputs. However, our examination will be limited to two, because the relevant economic principles can be derived more easily in this simple case.

The mathematical expression above states that the quantity of output for a firm,□ industry,□ or country depends on the amounts of capital and labor used. The exact nature of this relationship depends on the current state of technology. When advances in technology occur, the production function changes. In this section of the book we will be concerned with the output of a firm or business.

LONG RUN VERSUS SHORT RUN

In studying the economics of production we will find it useful to understand the two basic planning periods for a business firm—the long run and the short run.

The **long run** is a period of time sufficiently long to allow the firm to change the physical amounts of all resources in its production.

We can think of the long run as a period of time long enough to build a new plant or to get rid of an old one as well as to vary the amounts used of other resources, such as labor, fuel, or raw materials.

The **short run** is a time period so short that at least one of the inputs of a firm is fixed.

In other words, the firm is unable to vary all its inputs in this span of time. For example, we can think of the short run as a period of time in which the firm's plant size is fixed, even though the amounts of labor, fuel, and raw materials can be increased or decreased. Then, we can examine how output changes as more and more variable inputs are used in the plant.

The long run is not a particular length of calendar time that we can specify for all businesses, because it varies from firm to firm. For example, the long run for an automobile manufacturer, which must invest in the construction of large plants in order to increase its size of operations, is a far longer span of time than the long run for a sidewalk hot dog vendor or a retail florist.

Analysis of production and cost over the long run is somewhat more difficult than

31

404

short-run analysis, and many of the principles needed to understand cost and profit strategies can be developed in the context of the short run. For these reasons, the analysis of production and cost in the long run is placed in the special topic at the end of this chapter.

PRODUCTION
AND COST IN
THE SHORT RUN
◆

In this section of the chapter we will examine the simple case of a firm with two inputs, capital and labor. However, we will assume that only the amount of labor can be varied during the short run. The amount of capital is fixed.

PRODUCT CURVES
OF A VARIABLE INPUT

If the quantity of one input, such as capital, is fixed, many input combinations of the production function are no longer relevant for the time period under consideration. Only the combinations that correspond to employing different amounts of the variable input (for example, labor) and the fixed amount of capital describe the firm's production possibilities in the short run.

Total Product of an Input In order to describe the relationship of variable input use to output in the short run, we derive a total product curve for the variable input.

The **total product of an input** indicates the maximum level of output that can be produced using different amounts of the input and a fixed amount of all other inputs.

From everyday life we would expect, other things equal, that the total product of the var-

iable input will be greater the greater the quantity of fixed inputs with which it is combined. Workers in an automobile manufacturing plant are more productive with an assembly line than without one. Figure 18–1 shows two total product of labor curves, one with capital fixed at 5 units and one with capital fixed at 10 units. As we would expect, the total product of labor (TP_L) is higher for a given quantity of labor when it is combined with the larger amount of capital equipment. (Think how much more wood you can cut with a chain saw than with an ax.) Of course, a firm would have only one relevant total product curve in the short run, and it would depend on the quantity of fixed inputs available.

Average and Marginal Product of an Input As we will see later, the total product of an input is not the only significant short-run productivity variable. A firm that is analyzing its short-run cost structure must also be aware of how the average and marginal products of its variable input change as usage of the input rises.

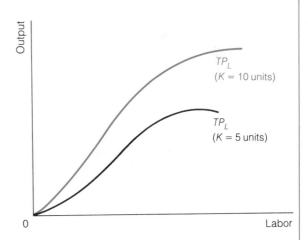

FIGURE 18–1 Two Total Product of Labor Curves

The total product of labor (TP_L) varies with the quantity of labor utilized. Moreover, in general, the total product of labor will be greater for a given amount of labor the greater the amount of capital which it has to work with. Note that TP_L when $K = 10$ units is above TP_L when $K = 5$ units.

The **average product of an input** represents output per unit of the input. It is found by dividing the total product of the input by the quantity of the input in use.

Thus, when labor is the variable input, the average product of labor, AP_L, is equal to TP_L/L.

The **marginal product of an input** is the addition to output or total product obtained from adding one more unit of the input, keeping the amounts of all other inputs fixed.

Marginal product is equal to the change in total product divided by the change in quantity of output. For example, the marginal product of labor, MP_L, is equal to the change in the total product of labor divided by the change in the quantity of output.

Table 18–1 gives the values for total product of labor, average product of labor, and marginal product of labor per week for Celex, Inc., a firm that sells Acapulco vacation packages over the telephone. The firm has a given plant size (office and number of phones), and its only variable input is labor (telephone solicitors). For the short-run time period we are studying, the amount of capital equipment available to Celex, Inc., is totally fixed.

The total product column in Table 18–1 shows how output (number of units of Acapulco vacation packages sold) varies as Celex increases the amount of labor it hires to do the selling. Total product refers to the number of packages sold per week. Average product is the weekly output per worker. Marginal product is the increase in output attributable to employing an additional worker. The quantity of labor column shows the number of workers hired; one unit of labor is one person working a forty-hour week.

Law of Diminishing Marginal Productivity
Table 18–1 shows that as Celex increases the amount of labor employed, the MP_L increases until it reaches a maximum (between the second and third units of labor) and then begins to fall (with the fourth unit of labor). These numbers illustrate what economists call the law of diminishing marginal productivity, or the **law of diminishing returns to a variable input.**

TABLE 18–1   Total Product, Average Product, and Marginal Product of Labor per Week for Celex, Inc.

Quantity of Labor (L)	Total Product of Labor (TP_L)	Average Product of Labor ($AP_L = \dfrac{TP_L}{L}$)	Marginal Product of Labor ($MP_L = \dfrac{\text{change in } TP_L}{\text{change in } L}$)
0	0	Undefined	
			10
1	10	10	
			14
2	24	12	
			18
3	42	14	
			14
4	56	14	
			9
5	65	13	
			7
6	72	12	
			5
7	77	11	
			3
8	80	10	
			1
9	81	9	
			0
10	81	8.1	

The **law of diminishing marginal productivity** *states that if equal amounts of one variable input are added, while all other inputs are kept fixed, total product may increase, but after some point the additions to total product will begin to decrease.*

In other words, if all other inputs are kept fixed, the marginal product of the variable input will, after some point, begin to fall. This happens because the amount of the fixed input available for the variable input or inputs to work with does not change. In the case of Celex, the physical facilities of the firm are limited; as more and more solicitors are hired, they crowd the facilities and add, successively, less and less to total output. Table 18–1 shows that diminishing returns to labor set in after three units of labor are employed.

Figure 18–2 we have plotted total product, average product, and marginal product of labor curves corresponding to the data given in Table 18–1. The MP_L is equal to the AP_L when the AP_L is at a maximum. This relationship is no coincidence. Whenever an average value— whether revenue, cost, or product of an input—is at a maximum or minimum, the corresponding marginal value will be equal to it. Why is this so?

Any time a marginal value is greater than the average, it will cause the average to rise. For example, if the average height of people in a room is 5 feet, 7 inches, and a 7-foot-tall person walks in, the average height of the people in the room will rise. Similarly, if the marginal value is lower than the average, the average will fall. Thus, if a 5-foot-tall person walked into the room, the average height would fall.

An average value at a maximum or minimum is, technically speaking, not changing at that point. For an average value to be constant, the marginal value must be equal to it at the relevant point. Suppose another person walked into the room discussed above. If the average height of 5 feet, 7 inches were to be maintained, the new person would have to be exactly 5 feet, 7 inches tall.

It is also true that the marginal product of labor is equal to zero when the total product of labor is at a maximum. If MP_L were positive, TP_L would be increasing. In other words, the addition of another unit of labor would increase total output. If MP_L were negative, TP_L would be decreasing. Thus MP_L

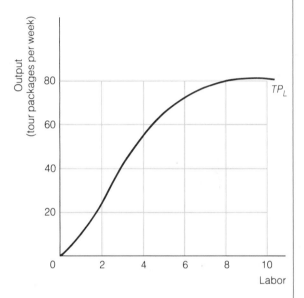

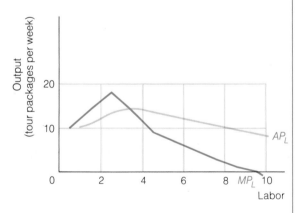

FIGURE 18–2   Total, Average, and Marginal Product Curves for Celex, Inc.

The total product *(TP_L)*, average product *(AP_L)*, and marginal product of labor *(MP_L)* for Celex, Inc. are shown in this figure. Note that when the total product of labor is at a maximum (at 9 units of labor), marginal product is equal to zero. The marginal product of labor curve intersects the average product of labor curve at its maximum point.

must be zero when TP_L is at its maximum level.

Suppose someone asked you the following question: "Is it true or false that the productivity of a variable input affects the short-run costs of a business?" What would you answer? The correct answer, as you may have reasoned, is "true." Given the price of an input, the less productive the input, the greater will be the cost per unit of the resulting output.

For example, suppose Celex hires a new telephone solicitor for $420 a week. If the new person increases output by ten vacation packages per week, the cost per additional package sold will be less than if the new person increases output by only seven packages per week ($42 versus $60).

In the next section of the chapter we will explore in more detail the relationship between the productivity of a variable input and the short-run cost of production.

SHORT-RUN COSTS

A firm's short-run costs are governed by the amount of its fixed inputs. For example, the cheapest way for a firm to produce fifty units of output per week might be to employ four machines and twenty workers. However, if the firm has only two machines, the fifty-unit level of output might be obtained by substituting labor for the two missing machines, but only at a higher cost. In the long run, the firm would want to obtain two more machines if it expected to produce fifty units of output per week regularly. In the short run, however, by definition, it could not increase the number of machines and would therefore have a higher total cost for a fifty-unit level of output.

Because at least one input is fixed in the short run, two types of short-run costs must be defined. This task is undertaken in the following section.

Fixed Cost Versus Variable Cost There are two components of short-run cost—fixed cost and variable cost.

Fixed costs are costs that do not vary with the level of output in the short run.

They are the costs to the firm of having fixed inputs such as plant and equipment. The firm bears these costs in the short run even if it produces no output. Examples of fixed costs are mortgage interest, property taxes, and depreciation.

Variable costs are costs that increase or decrease as the level of output increases or decreases.

Examples of variable costs are expenditures for labor, fuel, raw materials, and component parts.

Short-run Variable Cost Concepts Three short-run variable cost concepts are used in economics: short-run total variable cost (TVC), short-run average variable cost (AVC), and short-run marginal cost (SMC).

Short-run total variable cost is all of the costs of the firm that vary with the level of the firm's output in the short run.

Short-run average variable cost is the variable cost per unit of output produced. Thus,

$$AVC = \frac{total\ variable\ cost}{quantity\ of\ output}.$$

Short-run marginal cost is the addition to total variable cost from producing one more unit of output. Thus,

$$SMC = \frac{change\ in\ total\ variable\ cost}{change\ in\ quantity\ of\ output}.$$

We have already seen that in the short run the productivity of the variable inputs affects the short-run variable costs. We can now demonstrate the nature of this relationship. First, it is important to understand that total variable cost is inversely related to (varies in an opposite direction from) the productivity of a variable input.

Variable Cost and Productivity   Suppose, for example, that 5 workers can produce 10 units of output per hour. If the cost of 1 worker is $5 per hour and labor is the only variable input, the total variable cost of the 10 units of output will be $25. If the 5 workers can produce 20 units of output per hour, the total variable cost associated with the 20 units will be $25. Thus the total variable cost associated with 10 units of output will now be smaller.

A similar relationship exists between average variable cost and the average product of the variable input. Consider the situation where 5 workers produce 10 units of output per hour. In this case the average product of labor = 10/5 = 2 units per hour. How is this figure related to average variable cost? If each worker, on the average, produces 2 units of output per hour and costs $5 per hour, then

$$AVC = \frac{\$5 \text{ per hour}}{2 \text{ units of output per hour}}$$

$$= \$2.50 \text{ per unit of output.}$$

Therefore, when labor is the variable input, the average variable cost is equal to the price of labor divided by the average product of labor, or P_L/AP_L.

If the 5 workers could produce 20 units per hour, then the average product of labor would equal 20/5 = 4 units per hour. Average variable cost would then equal

$$\frac{P_L}{AP_L} = \frac{\$5 \text{ per hour}}{4 \text{ units of output per hour}}$$

$$= \$1.25 \text{ per unit of output.}$$

Consequently, we can see that if the *average product* of labor *doubles*, *average variable cost is cut in half*.

The marginal product of an input affects short-run marginal cost in much the same fashion. Suppose that the marginal product of the 10th worker were 1 unit of output per hour. If the worker costs $5 per hour, the marginal cost of the unit produced is equal to

$$\frac{P_L}{MP_L} = \frac{\$5 \text{ per hour}}{1 \text{ unit of output per hour}}$$

$$= \$5 \text{ per unit of output.}$$

In the same fashion, we could show that if the marginal product of the 10th worker were to increase to 2 units of output per hour, marginal cost would fall to $2.50 per unit of output. Therefore, we can say that when the *mar-*

TABLE 18–2   **Total Variable Cost, Average Variable Cost, and Marginal Cost for Celex, Inc.**

Quantity of Labor (L)	Quantity of Output (Q or TP$_L$)	Total Variable Cost (TVC)	Average Variable Cost (AVC = $\frac{TVC}{Q}$)	Marginal Cost (SMC = $\frac{\text{change in } TVC}{\text{change in } Q}$)
0	0	$ 0	Undefined	
				$ 42.00
1	10	420	$42.00	
				30.00
2	24	840	35.00	
				23.33
3	42	1,260	30.00	
				30.00
4	56	1,680	30.00	
				46.67
5	65	2,100	32.31	
				60.00
6	72	2,520	35.00	
				84.00
7	77	2,940	38.18	
				140.00
8	80	3,360	42.00	
				420.00
9	81	3,780	46.67	
				∞
10	81	4,200	51.85	

ginal product of the variable input *increases,* the *marginal cost falls.*

Table 18–2 shows the values for Celex's total variable cost, average variable cost, and short-run marginal cost corresponding to the total product of labor, average product of labor, and marginal product of labor figures in Table 18–1. The price of a unit of labor is assumed to be $420 per week. We can find average variable cost either by dividing total variable cost by quantity of output or by dividing price of labor by average product of labor. We can find marginal cost either by dividing the change in total variable cost by the change in quantity of output or by dividing the price of labor by the marginal product of labor.

In Figure 18–3 Celex's total variable cost, average variable cost, and marginal cost curves are graphed. Note how the shapes of these curves are related to the shapes of the total, average, and marginal product curves in Figure 18–2. The diagram of average variable cost and short-run marginal cost resembles the diagram of the average product of labor and the marginal product of labor, except that it is inverted or "flipped over." This relationship is no accident since, as we have just shown, these cost concepts are inversely related to productivity.

Fixed Cost in the Short Run In the short run, the firm will usually have both variable and fixed costs. In the previous section, we stated that our telephone soliciting firm had its stock of capital (building and equipment) fixed at some level. Suppose it has 15 telephone lines that cost $100 each per week and pays office rent, managerial salaries, and overhead equal to $1,500 per week. Celex's total fixed costs per week will be 15 ($100) + $1,500 = $3,000.

The **total fixed cost** of a firm is the sum of all of the firm's costs which do not vary with the level of output in the short run.

As stated above, many firms have interest and depreciation expense, property taxes, and li-

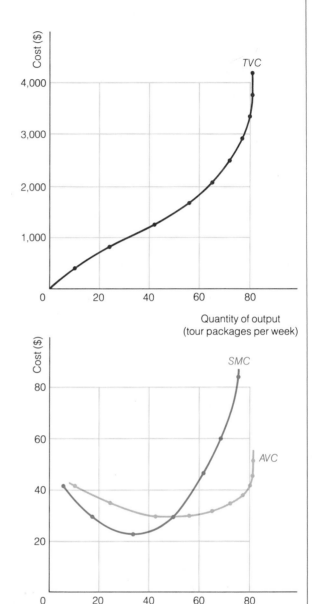

FIGURE 18–3   Total Variable Cost, Average Variable Cost, and Marginal Cost for Celex, Inc.

The total variable cost (TVC), average variable cost (AVC), and short-run marginal cost (SMC) curves for Celex are shown in this graph. Note that the short-run marginal cost curve intersects the average variable cost curve at its minimum point.

cense fees that would fall into this category.

In order to be able to price its product competitively, a firm must also be concerned about its average fixed cost.

A firm's **average fixed cost,** AFC, is fixed cost per unit of output. Average fixed cost is equal to $\dfrac{total\ fixed\ cost}{quantity\ of\ output}$.

However, because marginal cost refers to the change in total *variable* cost from producing another unit of output, there is no similar term applicable to fixed cost. Fixed costs do not change.

Short-run Total Cost and Average Cost   The two remaining short-run cost terms that need to be defined are short-run total cost (STC) and short-run average cost (SAC).

Short-run total cost is the sum of all of a firm's short-run costs. Since costs must be either fixed or variable, STC is equal to total fixed cost plus total variable cost.

Short-run average cost is the short-run total cost per unit of output. SAC is equal to short-run total cost divided by quantity of output. It is also equal to average fixed cost plus average variable cost.

Short-run marginal cost was defined earlier in the chapter. Because fixed cost does not change, short-run marginal cost could be found either as the change in total cost divided by the change in quantity of output or by the change in total variable cost divided by the change in quantity of output.

Values for all the short-run costs for Celex, Inc., are computed in Table 18–3. The figures are consistent with the data in Tables 18–1 and 18–2.

In Figures 18–4 and 18–5 all of the short-run cost curves for Celex are sketched. As expected from the discussion of the average and marginal product curves, SMC intersects AVC and SAC at their respective minimum points. AFC does not have a minimum, but it keeps getting smaller and smaller. AFC always decreases as the level of output increases because a given amount of total fixed costs is spread over a greater number of units of output. Thus, at 10 units of output, average fixed cost is equal to $3,000/10 = $300. At 24 units of output, AFC = $3,000/24 = $125.

Short-run Costs Versus Long-run Costs   As already indicated, costs generally are higher for a firm in the short run than in the long run. Figure 18–6 illustrates this point. Panel (a) shows three short-run average cost curves corresponding to three plant sizes. SAC_3 is for the

TABLE 18–3   Short-run Costs for Celex, Inc.

Q (Tour Packages Per Week)	TFC	TVC	STC	$AFC = \dfrac{TFC}{Q}$	$AVC = \dfrac{TVC}{Q}$	$SAC = \dfrac{STC}{Q}$	$SMC = \dfrac{change\ in\ STC}{change\ in\ Q}$
0	$3,000	$ 0	$3,000	Undefined	Undefined	Undefined	
10	3,000	420	3,420	$300.00	$42.00	$342.00	$ 42.00
24	3,000	840	3,840	125.00	35.00	160.00	30.00
42	3,000	1,260	4,260	71.43	30.00	101.43	23.33
56	3,000	1,680	4,680	53.57	30.00	83.57	30.00
65	3,000	2,100	5,100	46.15	32.31	78.46	$ 46.67
72	3,000	2,520	5,520	41.67	35.00	76.67	60.00
77	3,000	2,940	5,940	38.96	38.18	77.14	84.00
80	3,000	3,360	6,360	37.50	42.00	79.50	140.00
81	3,000	3,780	6,780	37.04	46.67	83.71	420.00

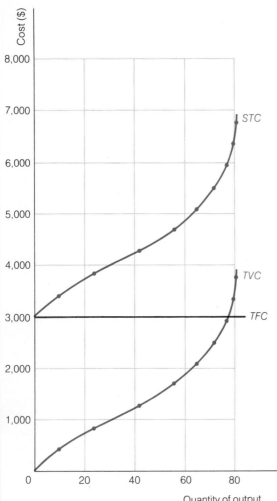

FIGURE 18–4   Short-run Total Variable Cost, Total Fixed Cost, and Total Cost Curves for Celex, Inc.

The short-run total cost (STC), total fixed cost (TFC), and total variable cost (TVC) curves for Celex appear here. Note that TFC is graphed as a horizontal line, indicating that it is a constant dollar amount for all levels of output. Short-run total cost is equal to TFC plus TVC.

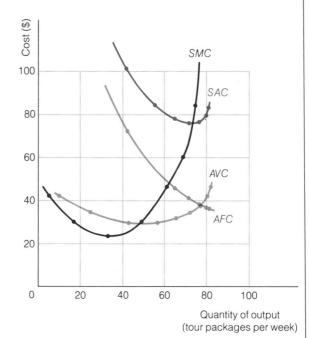

FIGURE 18–5   Average Fixed Cost, Average Variable Cost, Marginal Cost, and Short-run Average Cost Curves for Celex, Inc.

Short-run average cost (SAC), average variable cost (AVC), average fixed cost (AFC), and short-run marginal cost (SMC) for Celex, Inc., appear in this graph. Note that average fixed cost gets smaller as the level of output increases. Also note that short-run average cost is equal to AFC plus AVC. Finally, note that the short-run marginal cost curve intersects the AVC and SAC curves at their respective minimum points.

largest plant,☐ which can produce greater outputs (Q) than can the plant sizes associated with either SAC_1 or SAC_2.

If these three were the only possible plant sizes that could be built in the long run, we could plot a curve depicting **long-run average cost** (LAC) by determining the least possible average cost for each output on the Q axis. Outputs between 0 and Q_1 would be produced at least cost in plant SAC_1. Outputs between Q_1 and Q_2 would be produced at least cost in plant SAC_2, and outputs greater than Q_2 would be produced at least cost in plant SAC_3. The bold, scalloped line in panel (a) is the LAC curve.

However, many plant sizes are usually at least technologically possible. In fact, if an infinite number of plant sizes are feasible, we can derive the LAC curve as shown in panel (b) of the figure. One point on each SAC curve is also a point on the LAC curve. At all other points, SAC is greater than LAC.

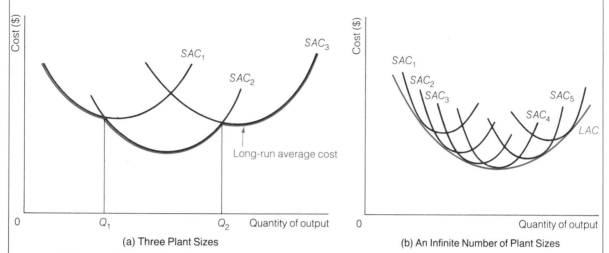

(a) Three Plant Sizes   (b) An Infinite Number of Plant Sizes

FIGURE 18–6   The Relationship between Long-run Average Cost and Short-run Average Cost

In panel (a) the long-run average cost curve is shown for a firm with three possible plant sizes. The SAC_1, SAC_2, and SAC_3 curves are the short-run average cost curves for each respective plant size, from the smallest to the largest. The long-run average cost curve is formed from those points which represent the cheapest per unit cost, given that any of the three plant sizes is available. In panel (b), the long-run average cost curve (LAC) is drawn for a firm with an infinite number of plant sizes available.

ECONOMIES AND DISECONOMIES OF SCALE

In panel (b) of Figure 18–6, the LAC curve is U-shaped to reflect the existence of economies and diseconomies of scale.

> **Economies of scale** *are characteristics of long-run production that cause average cost to decrease as plant size is increased. When economies of scale predominate, the LAC curve slopes downward.*

> **Diseconomies of scale** *are characteristics of long-run production that cause average cost to increase as plant size is increased. When diseconomies of scale predominate, the LAC curve slopes upward.*

Figure 18–7 indicates the regions of economies and diseconomies of scale on a long-run average cost curve.

Economies of scale can arise when machines that have twice the productive capacity of smaller machines do not cost twice as much to buy or operate. Some economies of scale are realized by large firms that can take advantage of specialization of labor and management.

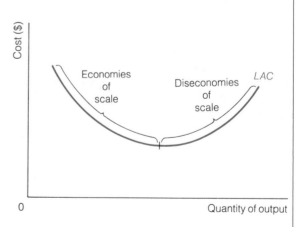

FIGURE 18–7   Economies and Diseconomies of Scale

Economies of scale are present when long-run average cost (LAC) is decreasing. Diseconomies of scale are present when long-run average cost is increasing.

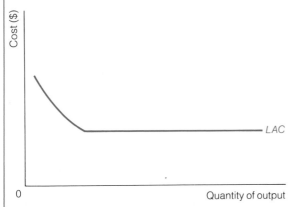

FIGURE 18-8   A Possible Long-run Average Cost Curve for a Firm without Diseconomies of Scale

The firm with the long-run average cost curve (LAC) in this graph would not experience diseconomies of scale. Economies of scale would be present when the *LAC* curve is downward-sloping. After the *LAC* curve becomes horizontal, all possible economies of scale have been exhausted.

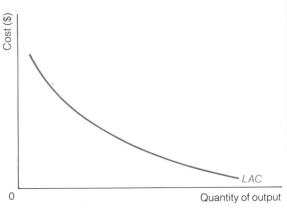

FIGURE 18-9   A Possible Long-run Average Cost Curve for a Public Utility

A public utility usually finds that economies of scale are present over a large range of possible outputs. This fact is depicted by the downward-sloping long-run average cost (LAC) curve in this graph.

Economists often cite bureaucratic red tape as the reason for diseconomies of scale. However, many large manufacturers, such as General Motors, avoid diseconomies of scale by organizing their management efficiently. The long-run average cost curves of such firms are similar in shape to the curve in Figure 18-8.

Some companies, such as public utilities and telephone companies, have large ranges of output over which economies of scale are present. For example, once a set of telephone lines or cables is installed in a town, the marginal cost of servicing an additional customer is relatively small. In this case, the long-run average cost curve looks like the one in Figure 18-9.

SUMMARY

1. This chapter has dealt with the relationship between production and cost for a firm. The production function gives the relationship between different amounts of resources used and the maximum resulting level of output.

2. In the short run, not all of a firm's resources are variable. For example, often its plant and equipment are fixed. In this case, the firm's variable costs depend on the prductivity of the firm's variable inputs. The *total product of a variable input* represents the total amount of output that can be obtained with different amounts of the variable input and a fixed amount of all other inputs. The *average product of an input* is the output per unit of the input. Thus the average product of labor is equal to the total product of labor divided by the quantity of labor.

3. The *marginal product of an input* is the addition to total output that can be obtained from adding one more unit of an input, holding all other inputs fixed. For example, the marginal product of labor is equal to the change in total product of labor divided by the change in quantity of labor.

4. The *law of diminishing marginal productivity* (diminishing returns) states that if equal amounts of a variable input are added, all other inputs fixed, total product may increase, but after some point the additions to total product, or the marginal product, will begin to fall.

5. In the short run the firm's variable cost and the productivity of the variable inputs are inversely related. In other words, higher productivity on the part of the variable inputs, other things equal, means lower variable costs.

6. The short-run total variable cost of a firm is all the costs of the firm that vary with the level of output in the short run. Average variable cost is variable cost per unit of output, and it is equal to total variable cost divided by quantity of output. Short-run marginal cost is equal to the change in total variable cost divided by the change in quantity of output, which is equal to the change in short-run total cost divided by the change in quantity of output. It can be viewed also as the addition to total variable cost (or short-run total cost) from producing another unit of output.

7. Since some of the firm's inputs are fixed in the short run, some of the firm's costs are also fixed. The firm's total fixed cost is equal to the sum of the costs that do not vary with the level of output in the short run. Average fixed cost is equal to the fixed cost per unit of output, or total fixed cost divided by quantity of output.

8. The short-run total cost of a firm is equal to the total fixed cost plus the total variable cost. *Short-run average cost* is total cost per unit of output, and it is equal to the short-run total cost divided by quantity of output, which is equal to average fixed cost plus average variable cost.

9. The long-run average cost (LAC) curve shows the lowest possible per unit cost of producing each quantity of output, assuming all inputs in the production function are variable. The downward-sloping portion of the curve indicates economies of scale; the upward-sloping portion indicates diseconomies of scale.

10. An economist's view of cost is somewhat different from an accountant's view. An accountant considers only explicit costs, whereas an economist considers explicit plus implicit costs. Implicit, or opportunity, costs are costs that a firm incurs by using its resources in one way, thereby giving up the opportunity to use them in some other way. To an economist, therefore, a normal rate of return represents a cost. Correspondingly, an economic profit represents profit above an average or normal return.

11. The private costs of a firm are all the costs, explicit and implicit, that it incurs. Social cost includes the private costs of a firm plus any additional costs imposed on society through the firm's operation.

IMPORTANT TERMS AND CONCEPTS

Explicit cost	Marginal product of
Implicit, or	an input
opportunity, cost	Law of diminishing
Economic cost	marginal
Accounting net	productivity
income	Fixed costs
Economic profit	Variable costs
Private costs	Short-run total
Social costs	variable cost
Input, or factor of	Short-run average
production	variable cost
Production function	Short-run marginal
Long run	cost
Short run	Total fixed cost
Total product of a	Average fixed cost
variable input	Short-run total cost
Average product of a	Short-run average
variable input	cost
	Economies of scale
	Diseconomies of scale

QUESTIONS AND PROBLEMS

1. What is a production function?

2. Explain the difference between the long run and the short run for a firm.

3. What are fixed costs? Variable costs? Give an example of each.

4. Why does marginal cost always equal average cost when average cost is at a minimum?

5. Define *total product of labor, average product of labor,* and *marginal product of labor.*

6. What is the law of diminishing marginal productivity?

7. What is the difference between economic cost and accounting cost?

8. What are opportunity costs? Give an example.

9. Which of the following are likely to be explicit costs? Which are likely to be opportunity costs?
a. Raw materials cost
b. Cost of component parts
c. Interest on money invested in a firm by its owner
d. Interest on a mortgage
e. Salary to an owner-manager
f. Wages paid to workers

10. Why may the social cost of a product be different from its private cost?

11. The table below gives production data for an automobile assembly plant.

Quantity of Labor per Hour	Quantity of Cars per Hour	Average Product of Labor	Marginal Product of Labor
0	0	Undefined	
100	2		
120	4		
130	6		
135	8		
140	10		
150	12		
170	14		

a. On the basis of the data in the table, calculate AP_L and MP_L.

b. If $P_L = \$15$ per hour, what is the marginal cost of each of the first 100 cars (ignoring the obvious increase in material and component parts costs)?

12. Complete the table below, which gives monthly cost data for a motorbike manufacturer.

Quantity of Output	Total Variable Cost	Average Variable Cost	Total Fixed Cost	Average Fixed Cost	Total Cost	Average Cost	Marginal Cost
0	$ 0	Undefined	$	Undefined	$120,000	Undefined	$
1,000	150,000	$		$		$	
2,000	290,000						
3,000	420,000						
4,000	540,000						
5,000	640,000						
6,000	720,000						
7,000	795,000						
8,000	875,000						
9,000	975,000						
10,000	1,095,000						

MOVABLE FEASTS: CENTRAL KITCHENS HELP RESTAURANT FIRMS KEEP FOOD COST DOWN

At the Joshua Tree restaurant in Jenkintown, Pa., schoolteacher Mary Ann Coe is celebrating her birthday with her husband. The couple sits at a discreetly lighted table surrounded by stained-glass windows, darkwood paneling and hanging copper pots. "It's an elegant place," says Mrs. Coe.

Nor is she disappointed in the meal: beef ribs, baked potato and mushrooms. The meat is "tender and juicy," she says. But if Mrs. Coe wanted to compliment the chef, she couldn't. There isn't a chef.

The food had been trucked, fresh, frozen and vacuum-packed, from a huge commissary 165 miles away in Beaver Heights, Md. Here,

Excerpted from Daniel Machalaba, "Movable Feasts: Huge Central Kitchens Help Restaurant Firms Keep Food Cost Down," *Wall Street Journal*, July 13, 1978, pp. 1, 8.

Marriott Corp., the owner of the chain of nine Joshua Tree restaurants, every week turns out vast amounts of food, including 10,000 pounds of chili, 14,400 layer cakes and 10,000 gallons of soup. All of this is shipped in 94 trucks to Marriott's 240 Eastern U.S. dinner restaurants, coffee shops and fast-food units, stretching from Syracuse, N.Y., to Miami.

By one estimate, about a fourth of U.S. restaurant chains are now using central kitchens to service their far-flung units, including Howard Johnson, Hardee's and Dutch Pantry, a subsidiary of CPC Inc. According to the National Restaurant Association, commissaries have helped the chains increase their share of U.S. restaurant revenues to 24% from 10% a decade ago.

"A Lot for the Money"

Corporate restauranteurs claim that the success of their commissaries lies in their ability to cater to the fast growing American habit of regularly dining out by delivering a product of medium, yet consistent, quality at reasonable prices. "People want the food to look and taste good and be a lot for the money. But they don't care if their steaks and lobster were once frozen," says Frederick Rufe, the former head of Marriott's dinner restaurants.

Others aren't so sure. Some restaurant companies contend that the economics of operating huge central kitchens are doubtful. Others say that the commissaries produce bland, unexciting food. "It's not food designed for fine dining but for the mass market," says Vance Christian, a professor at Cornell University's School of Hotel Administration.

Part of the corporate appeal of commissaries is the cost saving from buying and cooking food in bulk. With the commissary chefs trimming the meat, making the sauces, cooking the soups and baking the cakes, restaurants can get by with microwave ovens and largely untrained, lowerpaid help. Even the smaller commissaries that are limited to grinding hamburger and cutting and freezing meat for the coffee-shop chains such as Denny's and Sambo's are viewed as big cost savers.

"Because we have experts at the commissary, we can have kids pushing buttons in our restaurant," says Robert Jackson, a Marriott vice president. As a result Marriott's 19 dinner restaurants, with names like Phineas Ribs and Franklin Stove, have been able to insulate themselves against the high turnover of restaurant workers, estimated to be running at 35% a year by Thomas Haas, an editor of Restaurant News.

The money that is saved on restaurant kitchens, with mixers and pressure steamers, is lavished on elaborate decor. The Joshua Tree in Jenkintown, for example, cost about $1 million.

"If all the food had to be prepared at the restaurant, there would be greater waste and higher labor costs," says William Nelson, president of Dutch Pantry, whose 82 restaurants are serviced by a commissary in Hummelswharf, Pa. Also, he says, "It takes a lot less energy to make 4,000 meat loaves at once in a commissary than to make 50 in each of over 80 restaurants." Without a

commissary, he estimates that Dutch Pantry's food costs would rise by 5% to 10%.

Even so, there are a good many people in the restaurant industry who believe that the multimillion-dollar investment necessary for a commissary doesn't make economic sense. They also cite the high costs of shipping food. "The freight costs would be prohibitive because our restaurants are so scattered," says James Mitchell, an executive of the Victoria Station chain, which relies on outside suppliers. . . .

The quality of the food produced by commissaries also is widely criticized. "Bland average-type food," is the way it is described by James Meyer, a restaurant analyst at the Philadelphia investment firm of Janney Montgomery Scott. Win Schuler's, an eight-restaurant chain in Michigan, once roasted and froze meat at a commissary. Now each restaurant cooks its own. . . .

On the other hand, Marriott's Mr. Jackson points out that if a restaurant prepares food from fresh ingredients there is a sporting chance of turning out a poor meal. Although he agrees that "you lose at least 3% to 5% in flavor when you freeze food," the chance of serving a bad meal "is much less with prepared, frozen foods." And he says, "customers remember a bad meal.". . .

But a recent experience that Marriott had with its Roy Rogers hamburgers illustrated one of the disadvantages of mass-producing food. Customers began complaining last summer that they were finding pieces of bone and gristle in their hamburgers. The

company traced the problem back to the hamburger grinder in the Fairfield Farm meat room. Now the grinder nozzle has to be cleaned twice as often as before, at an extra labor cost of $7,500 a year. "It doesn't take many of these decisions to raise hamburger prices," says Mr. Schwartz.

As another example, Marriott recently tried to trim labor costs by installing a 30-foot-long machine to assemble and frost layer cakes. But the machine applies the frosting so unevenly that a woman has to touch up each cake with a spatula. . . .

Marriott has found that for some items, mass-production at the commissary is a losing proposition. Recently it stopped making ice cream partly because it couldn't stop deterioration during shipping, and the volume didn't justify the investment in special trucks. It also stopped making hamburger rolls. "When you're making 600 items in one building, you can't always be as efficient as a processor specializing in one thing," says Mr. Jackson. But for much else, the Marriott commissary is a model of efficiency. . . .

QUESTIONS

1. How do central kitchens or commissaries reduce costs for a restaurant?
2. What costs are increased by using a central kitchen?
3. What cost concept does this article illustrate?
4. What criticisms are leveled at centrally prepared food?
5. Give one example of a food product for which mass production is not cost efficient.

SPECIAL TOPIC G

PRODUCTION
AND COST
IN THE LONG RUN

To analyze the long run, we will begin with the case of a firm that has a two-input production function using only labor and capital. In Chapter 18 the *long run* was defined as a period of time sufficiently long for a firm to change the amounts used of all inputs in its production function.

Table G–1 shows the production relationship between quantity of output and the quantities of labor and capital for a ditch digging company, Digger, Inc. Output is stated in terms of cubic feet of trench dug per hour,

and capital and labor are given in terms of units used per hour. As shown in the table, using 6 units of capital and 1 unit of labor, 24 cubic feet of trench can be dug per hour. The same quantity of output per hour can be obtained with 6 units of labor and 1 unit of capital or with 3 units of capital and 2 of labor. The table also indicates that there is a fourth way of digging 24 cubic feet of trench per hour. Can you find it?

Of course, a production function may indicate the relationship between the amounts of

TABLE G–1 Production Function for Digger, Inc.

Units of Capital per Hour	Cubic Feet of Trench Dug per Hour					
6	24	35	42	48	54	60
5	22	32	39	45	50	54
4	20	28	35	40	45	48
3	17	24	30	35	39	42
2	14	20	24	28	32	35
1	10	14	17	20	22	24
0	1	2	3	4	5	6
	Units of Labor per Hour					

any number of inputs and quantity of output. However, we will generally consider the case of only two inputs here in order to keep the examples simple. Nevertheless, all the economic decision rules developed here can easily be extended to situations in which the firm employs three or more variable inputs.

LEAST COST COMBINATION OF INPUTS

If a firm wishes to maximize its profit, it must keep its costs as low as possible, given its level of output. In the language of economists, the firm must use a least cost combination of inputs.

A **least cost combination of inputs** is a combination of inputs that will enable the firm to produce a particular level of output for the lowest possible cost.

It can also be seen as a combination of inputs that will enable a firm to produce the greatest amount of output possible for a given dollar cost. A firm cannot maximize profit if its costs are greater than they need be for a particular level of output.

Marginal Product of an Input Before we can examine the condition that must be fulfilled for the firm to have a least cost combination of inputs, we must define a few more terms, the first being the marginal product of an input.

The **marginal product of an input** is the addition to output or total product resulting from the use of one more unit of the input during some particular time period (an hour, a week, or a month, for example), while all other inputs are kept fixed.

Thus, for example, the marginal product of labor, MP_L, is equal to the change in the quantity of output (ΔQ) divided by the change in the quantity of labor (ΔL).

Price of an Input

The **price of an input** is the cost to the firm of using one more unit of that input for some particular time period, assuming that the input price stays the same.

For example, the price of labor per hour, P_L, is the cost to a firm of using one more unit of labor per hour. It includes the hourly wage rate plus any fringe benefits costs prorated on an hourly basis. The corresponding price of capital, P_K, is the cost per hour of another unit of capital, such as one more square foot of warehouse space or one more machine. For example, the price per hour of a bulldozer includes depreciation, fuel costs, and perhaps interest on the debt incurred to buy the machine. All of these cost items are computed on an hourly basis.

A Decision Rule

For a firm to have a least cost combination of two inputs, say labor and capital, it is necessary that the following condition hold:

$$\frac{MP_L}{P_L} = \frac{MP_K}{P_K}.$$

The **least cost combination of inputs decision rule** states that a firm will have a least cost combination of inputs only when the output obtained per additional dollar spent on labor is equal to the output obtained per additional dollar spent on capital.

Consider an example where these two ratios are not equal. Suppose $MP_L = 10$ units of output per hour, $P_L = \$5$ per hour, $MP_K = 60$ units of output per hour, and $P_K = \$20$ per hour. Then,

$$\frac{MP_L}{P_L} = \frac{10 \text{ units of output per hour}}{\$5 \text{ per hour}}$$

$$= 2 \text{ additional units of output per additional \$1 spent on labor.}$$

However,

$$\frac{MP_K}{P_K} = \frac{60 \text{ units of output per hour}}{\$20 \text{ per hour}}$$

$$= 3 \text{ additional units of output}$$
$$\text{per additional \$1 spent on capital.}$$

At this point, we could substitute 1 unit of capital for 4 units of labor and get more output for the same amount of money:

Add 1 unit of capital
Change in output = +60 units per hour
Change in cost = +\$20 per hour

Subtract 4 units of labor
Change in output = −40 units per hour
Change in cost = −\$20 per hour

Net change in output from substituting capital for labor = 20 units per hour.
Net change in cost from substituting capital for labor = \$0 per hour.

We could not have made such a profitable substitution of inputs if MP_K were equal to 40 additional units of output per hour, so that

$$\frac{MP_L}{P_L} = \frac{MP_K}{P_K}.$$

In this case, the 1 additional unit of capital would have added only 40 units of output per hour. The net effect after substituting 1 unit of capital for 4 units of labor would be no change in output and no change in cost.

Does a situation where MP_L/P_L is less than MP_K/P_K mean that a firm should use all capital and no labor? No. As long as the two inputs are not perfect substitutes, MP_K will decrease and MP_L will increase as more and more capital is used relative to labor. Think back to the example of General Motors and its assembly lines. *Someone* must operate those machines!

Since inputs such as labor and capital are generally not perfect substitutes, we would expect the marginal product of labor to decrease as the number of workers increases, while the quantity of capital is fixed. Economists call this the law of diminishing marginal productivity (discussed in Chapter 18). For ex-

ample, from Table G–1 we can see that if the quantity of capital is fixed at 3 units, the marginal product of the third worker is

$$\frac{\Delta Q}{\Delta L} = \frac{30 - 24}{1}$$
$$= 6 \text{ cubic feet of trench per hour.}$$

However, the marginal product of the fifth worker is only 4 cubic feet of trench per hour. The marginal product of an additional worker decreases because he or she must share the 3 units of capital, so that each person has less time to work at a machine.

Consequently, as we begin to substitute capital for labor in the example where $MP_K = 60$ and $MP_L = 10$, the ratios of MP_K/P_K and MP_L/P_L usually begin to get closer together and eventually become equal. At this point the firm has obtained a least cost combination of inputs. In the example above, this point occurs where $MP_L = 12$ units per hour and $MP_K = 48$ units per hour.

From Table G–1 we can obtain another example of a least cost combination of inputs. The table shows four methods of digging 35 cubic feet of trench per hour. These methods are summarized in Table G–2.

Given that the price of capital, P_K, is \$5 per hour, and the price of labor, P_L, is \$4 per hour, the cost to the firm per hour of using each of the four methods is as shown in Table G–3. Method 3, using 3 units of capital and 4 units of labor per hour, is clearly the cheapest way to dig the trenches.

TABLE G–2 Four Methods of Digging 35 Cubic Feet of Trench per Hour

Method	Units of Capital per Hour (K)	Units of Labor per Hour (L)	Output per Hour
1	6	2	35 cubic feet
2	4	3	35
3	3	4	35
4	2	6	35

TABLE G–3   Total Cost of Digging 35 Feet of Trench for Four Methods

Method	Units of Capital per Hour (K)	Units of Labor per Hour (L)	Total Cost per Hour (P_K = $5, P_L = $4)
1	6	2	$30 + $8 = $38
2	4	3	$20 + $12 = $32
3	3	4	$15 + $16 = $31
4	2	6	$10 + $24 = $34

We can demonstrate that the use of our least cost combination of inputs rule, $MP_L/P_L = MP_K/P_K$, would also cause us to choose method 3. In Table G–4, MP_L, MP_K, MP_K/P_K, and MP_L/P_L are calculated for each of the four methods. For method 3,

$$\frac{MP_K}{P_K} = \frac{5 \text{ cubic feet}}{\$5} = \frac{MP_L}{P_L} = \frac{4 \text{ cubic feet}}{\$4}$$

= 1 additional cubic foot of trench dug per additional $1 expenditure by the firm.

As emphasized above, method 3 represents the cheapest combination of inputs given this particular set of input prices: P_K = $5 and P_L = $4. (It can also be verified that method 2 would give a least cost combination of inputs if P_K were $4 and P_L were $5.)

A different least cost combination of inputs will exist for each possible level of a firm's output. It is from such input combinations that we can derive the relationship between cost and output for the firm in the long run. The long-run costs for a firm will be analyzed in the next section.

LONG-RUN COSTS

We have already seen that production and cost are inseparable. This point should be made clear as we examine how a firm's long-run total cost schedule is obtained.

Long-run Total Cost   The long-run total cost curve for a firm is obtained by finding the least cost combination of inputs for each possible level of output. As already discussed, the least cost combination of inputs for a particular level of output is the input combination that will enable the firm to produce that level of output at lowest cost.

Moreover, a least cost combination of two inputs, say capital and labor, must satisfy the condition that $MP_K/P_K = MP_L/P_L$. In other words, the change in output obtained per additional $1 expenditure on an input must be equal for all inputs. A firm will have a different least cost combination of inputs for each possible level of output. It is from such input combinations that we can obtain the relationship between long-run total cost and output.

Suppose, for example, that a firm has the sets of least cost input combinations shown in Table G–5. Each of these combinations represents the cheapest possible way of producing a particular level of output. It the price of capital is $50 per hour and the price of labor is $10 per hour, we can compute total cost for the firm at each of the given levels of output as shown in the table.

Given this information, we can sketch the firm's long-run total cost curve, as shown in Figure G–1.

TABLE G–4   Computations Using the Least Cost Combination of Inputs Rule for the Four Methods of Trench Digging

Method	MP_K	MP_L	MP_K/P_K	MP_L/P_L
1	2	7	2/5 = 0.4	7/4 = 1.75
2	4	5	4/5 = 0.8	5/4 = 1.25
3	5	4	5/5 = 1.0	4/4 = 1.00
4	7	2	7/5 = 1.4	2/4 = 0.50

TABLE G–5 Computing A Firm's Long-Run Total Cost Schedule

Quantity of Output per Hour	Quantities of Labor and Capital per Hour	Total Cost per Hour (P_K = $50, P_L = $10)
Q = 100	K = 3, L = 15	$ 300
Q = 200	K = 4, L = 25	450
Q = 300	K = 6, L = 33	630
Q = 400	K = 12, L = 40	1,000
Q = 500	K = 20, L = 75	1,750

Long-run total cost indicates the relationship between the total cost of a firm and its level of output when all inputs are variable, so that the firm can produce each level of output with the optimal (least cost) combination of inputs.

Average and Marginal Cost Although any firm is certainly concerned about the level of its total costs, two other measures of cost are relevant to its decisions.

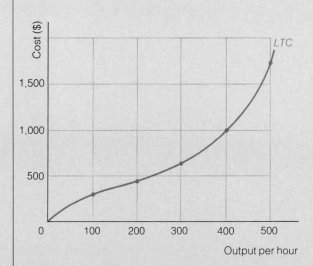

FIGURE G–1 The Long-run Total Cost Curve for a Firm

This long-run total cost curve is obtained by plotting the total cost per hour for each value of Q that appears in Table G–5. It shows the least total cost of each possible level of output.

Average cost, or cost per unit of output, is found by dividing total cost by quantity of output. Thus long-run average cost (LAC) is equal to long-run total cost divided by quantity of output.

Marginal cost is the increase in total cost from producing another unit of output. Thus long-run marginal cost (LMC) is equal to the change in long-run total cost divided by the change in quantity of output.

Values for LAC and LMC corresponding to the values for total cost given in Table G–5 are shown in Table G–6. The corresponding LAC and LMC curves are graphed in Figure G–2.

In Table G–6 the lines for marginal cost are placed between the lines corresponding to two levels of output. This is done because marginal cost represents the change in cost from producing one more unit of output between those two levels of output. For the same reason, the marginal cost curve is graphed so that each long-run marginal cost value is plotted at the midpoint of the corresponding output interval. As explained in Chapter 18, it is not a coincidence that the LMC curve passes through the minimum point of the LAC curve in Figure G–2.

Although a profit-maximizing firm will always try to use a least cost combination of inputs, it may not always be able to do so. Many firms cannot quickly change their plant size or amount of equipment. For example, it may

TABLE G–6 Relationships among Long-run Total Cost, Average Cost, and Marginal Cost

Units of Output (Q)	Long-run Total Cost (LTC)	Long-run Average Cost $\left(\dfrac{LTC}{Q}\right)$	Long-run Marginal Cost $\left(\dfrac{\Delta LTC}{\Delta Q}\right)$
0	$ 0	Undefined	
			$3.00
100	300	$3.00	
			1.50
200	450	2.25	
			1.80
300	630	2.10	
			3.70
400	1,000	2.50	
			7.50
500	1,750	3.50	

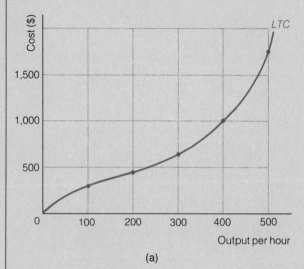

(a)

take months or even years from the time certain pieces of equipment are ordered until the time they are installed and ready for use.

IMPORTANT TERMS AND CONCEPTS

Least cost
  combination of
  inputs
Marginal product of
  an input
Price of an input

Least cost
  combination of
  inputs decision rule
Long-run total cost
  curve
Average cost
Marginal cost

QUESTIONS AND PROBLEMS

1. What is a least cost combination of inputs?

2. What condition must be fulfilled for a firm to have a least cost combination of inputs? Give an example to show why this rule must hold.

3. If $MP_L = 8$, $MP_K = 25$, $P_L = \$4$, and $P_K = \$5$, is a firm using a least cost combination of inputs? Explain.

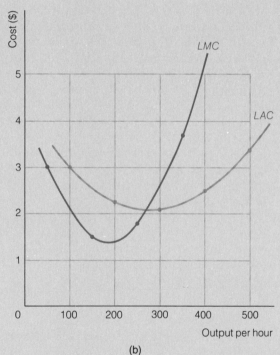

(b)

FIGURE G–2 Relationships among Long-run Total Cost, Average Cost, and Marginal Cost Curves

This set of cost curves is plotted from the data of Table G–6. *LAC* is obtained by dividing *LTC* by *Q*. *LMC* is the ratio of the change in *LTC* to that in *Q* and is plotted at the middle *Q* value for each 100-unit change in *Q*.

CHAPTER 19

PROFIT
MAXIMIZATION

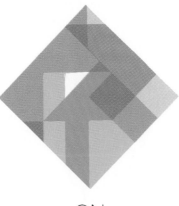

ON
HAVING TO MAKE
A PROFIT

"If you are going to stay in business, you have to make a profit. It's as simple as that!" So say the captains of industry to the media, to the government, and to everyone else. But is the situation really that simple?

Surely a firm does not have to make a profit all the time; indeed, as the newspapers regularly tell us, many firms do report losses. Further, if a firm is going to make a profit, we might ask such questions as: How much profit should it make? Should it accept less profit now in order to get more profit later? Is it only profit that motivates business managers when they make their decisions? If firms choose to sacrifice some profit, how much should they sacrifice and for what purpose? Finally, if a firm's managers wish to maximize profit, what strategy should they follow to do it?

Henry Ford II once told an assembly of business people:

There is no such thing as planning for a minimal return less than the best you can imagine—not if you want to survive in a competitive market. It's like asking a professional football team to win by only one point—a sure formula for losing. There's only one way to compete successfully—all-out. If believing this makes you a greedy capitalist lusting after bloated profits, then I plead guilty. The worst sin I can commit as a businessman is to fail to seek maximum long-term profitability by all decent and lawful means. To do so is to subvert economic reason.

Ford expressed the view that profit maximization ought to be the central objective of a business firm—in fact, that it is the moral obligation of managers. Many corporate executives view profit maximization as an obligation to shareholders (the firm's owners), but Ford's statement was stronger. He implied that by seeking to maximize profits, the manager serves society.

How can business profits serve society? Suppose investors always seek the most profitable use of their resources. If two industries are equally risky but one is more profitable than the other, investors will be attracted to the more profitable one. Thus a larger share of productive resources will be allocated to it. In fact, resources may even be transferred from the less profitable industry to the more profitable one. Output of the more profitable industry will expand; the supply of whatever it produces will increase. Profit therefore serves a resource allocation function. It plays a role in determining both the amount of productive resources used in a specific industry and the quantity of goods or services produced by that industry.

In Chapters 19 through 22 we will examine the resource allocation role of profit under various kinds of market environments. It will become evident that the extent to which profit serves this function depends on the characteristics of a given industry or market. Chapter 19 will measure and analyze profit at the level of the individual business firm. To best serve their firms, managers need to know how to identify profit and what effect various strategies will have on it. Also, anyone who lives and votes in a country characterized by a private enterprise system needs to know something about the nature and function of profit in order to evaluate public policies that affect business.

C H A P T E R 19

PROFIT
MAXIMIZATION

WHAT THIS CHAPTER IS ABOUT

MEANING OF PROFIT MAXIMIZATION
DECISION RULES FOR MAXIMUM PROFIT
BREAKEVEN ANALYSIS
INCREMENTAL PROFIT ANALYSIS

The last few years have been marked by the decline of several well-known firms. In October 1975 W. T. Grant Company, the seven-

teenth largest retailer in the United States, filed for bankruptcy. As recently as 1972 its profits were $38 million out of revenues of $1.6 billion.[1] Food Fair, Inc. (at one time the eighth largest supermarket chain in the United States), Robert Hall, and Abercrombie and Fitch are other well-known firms that have

---

1. "Investigating the Collapse of W.T. Grant," *Business Week*, July 19, 1976, p. 60.

filed for bankruptcy in recent years.[2] Obviously, survival itself is a tricky business for many firms. In fact, statistics from the Small Business Administration indicate that 50 percent of all new firms fail within two years, and only 20 percent survive five years.[3]

The following section of the chapter will describe the decision rules a firm must follow if it wishes to maximize its total profit. The discussion will begin with an explanation of profit maximization as the goal of a firm. Later parts of the chapter will consider breakeven analysis, a simple decision tool frequently used by business managers, and incremental profit analysis, a decision-making technique that helps firms determine whether to accept special orders or to undertake new projects.

THE GOAL OF THE FIRM

◆

In economics we generally assume that the primary goal of any firm is to maximize its total profit. In other words, the firm wishes to make the greatest profit it possibly can in legal ways. As indicated in Chapter 18, economists define *economic profit* differently from accounting net income.□

403

| **Economic profit** is total revenue minus total cost, including all opportunity costs.

Because a normal return is included in opportunity costs, when economic profit is greater than zero, the firm is earning an unusually high return.

---

2. See "Abercrombie's Last Sale Starts Thursday," *Wall Street Journal*, November 15, 1977, p. 11; "Death of a Salesman," *Newsweek*, August 15, 1977, p. 64; and "Food Fair's Path to Chapter XI," *Business Week*, November 20, 1978, pp. 62–68.

3. Geoffrey Leavenworth, "Small Business: Still a Gamble," *Texas Business and Texas Parade*, June 1979, pp. 65–68.

*As the term is used in economics, **total profit** refers to the total economic profit of a firm.* ▌

Some economists have suggested that firms may have other goals, such as maximizing sales, obtaining the respect of society, or merely making a satisfactory return. For example, they have noted that managers of corporations usually are not owners of the firms they control. The owners are shareholders, and shareholders seldom interfere with managerial decisions.

In such a setting, economists argued, managers might not try to maximize profit, because it might be rational from their point of view to sacrifice some profit to achieve such objectives as growth of the firm or an increase in the firm's share of the market. Managers' salaries may depend more on the latter goals than on maximization of profit, provided that the firm's profit is at a satisfactory level. Such behavior on the part of business firms is known as *satisficing behavior*.

However, more and more businesses are now emphasizing profit and profit maximization. For example, in the spring of 1978, Texaco announced that in the future it would concentrate more on profit than on sales volume.[4] In 1977 W. H. Krome George, chairman of Alcoa, underscored his belief that the firm could earn 14 percent on its invested capital. In previous years that rate of return seldom rose above 8 percent and more frequently was below 6 percent.[5] Frank Berger, head of Seagram Distillers Company, has remarked, "We've set up mathematical models to show the best return on different levels of investment, and we've studied how each brand reacts to price changes."[6] Moreover, even satisficing behav-

---

4. James Tanner, "Texaco Is Pruning Marketing Activities, Putting Emphasis on Profit, Not Volume," *Wall Street Journal*, March 16, 1978, p. 9.

5. "Doing It by the Numbers," *Forbes*, February 15, 1977, p. 71.

6. "Seagram Antes $40 Million," *Business Week*, August 22, 1977, p. 68.

ior in the short run may lead to profit-maximizing behavior in the long run.

Consequently, the decision rules we will examine in this chapter are based on the assumption that the foremost goal of the firm is profit maximization. Moreover, even if a firm's managers do not wish to maximize profit, by understanding the decision rules that would enable them to do so they can estimate the amount of profit they are giving up in order to pursue other goals.

APPROACHES TO PROFIT MAXIMIZATION

◆

Of all the possible quantities of output a firm can produce over some time period, which quantity will maximize its profit? This is the basic question of profit analysis. To approach the question logically, we must realize that both cost and sales revenues will increase as the quantity of output produced and sold is increased (assuming that demand is elastic).□ Suppose that for a one-unit increase in quantity sold, cost increases less than revenue. What will happen? Clearly, if the addition to revenue exceeds the addition to cost, there will be an increase in profit.

AN EXAMPLE OF PROFIT MAXIMIZATION

To construct an example of profit maximization, suppose that you are running a firm that recycles scrap silver and that competition has stabilized the market price of silver at $12 per ounce. Your firm will have to take the $12 price as given. Furthermore, its objective will be to maximize profit.

You will be willing to increase your monthly output of silver as long as the cost of producing an additional ounce is less than $12. If you can produce an ounce of silver for $10 and sell

it for $12, that ounce will add $2 to total profit for the month.

Probably your recycling operation will be subject to diminishing returns (law of diminishing marginal productivity).□   That is, as you increase the number of ounces of silver produced per month, the marginal cost□ of additional ounces produced will rise. This may happen because of plant congestion or because your firm will have to employ successively lower grades of scrap in order to further increase output. Thus you may find that beyond a certain monthly output, an additional ounce will cost $11, instead of the $10 it cost at a somewhat lower monthly output. Will you be willing to increase your output if an additional ounce costs $11 instead of $10 to produce? If the price that you can obtain for the silver remains at $12, the answer is certainly yes. You will still add $1 to total profit when an ounce of silver produced for $11 is sold for $12.

What if the cost of producing an additional ounce of silver rises to $11.99 as you continue to increase your monthly output? Can you still add to total profit by producing and selling it? The answer is still yes. You will add $12 − $11.99 = $.01. Not very exciting, but an addition to profit nonetheless. When will you stop increasing the monthly output? When the last ounce produced costs $12. Here, the addition to total profit is zero. Assuming that the cost of any additional ounces would be $12.01 or more, you would not wish to expand output further, because these ounces would add more to cost than to revenue. They would actually reduce profit rather than add to it.

GENERAL RULE FOR PROFIT MAXIMIZATION

From this example we can now state a general rule for profit maximization. For simplicity, let us assume that the firm is in the short-run, and its goal is to maximize its total profit. Total profit ($T\pi$) is the difference between total revenue□ from sales (TR) and total cost□ (TC). Thus we can say that the firm's $T\pi = TR -$

TC. Total revenue is equal to price times quantity sold, just as it was in Chapter 17. Short-run total cost—the total economic costs of the firm—is used here just as it was in the production and cost analysis of Chapter 18.

Assuming demand is elastic,□ we normally expect both total revenue and total cost to increase as the firm increases its output per time period. From the analysis in Chapter 17, we know that the change in revenue that occurs when output (quantity sold) increases is called *marginal revenue*□ (MR). From Chapter 18 we know that the change in cost that occurs when output increases is *marginal cost* (MC). Thus, drawing from our example of the silver recycling firm, we know that profit will increase when output is expanded as long as marginal revenue exceeds marginal cost (*MR is greater than MC*).

If marginal revenue is greater than marginal cost but marginal cost is increasing as output rises, the firm should continue to expand output until the marginal cost of one more unit just equals the marginal revenue obtained from selling it. This is exactly what we saw in the case of the silver recycling firm. There, the firm's market price of $12 was marginal revenue, and we found that the best rate of output per month would be the one where marginal cost also equaled $12. Thus the rule for profit maximization is to expand output until marginal cost equals marginal revenue (*MC = MR*).

The **profit-maximizing decision rule** states that the firm will increase its output per time period (month, quarter, year) up to the point where the marginal cost of an additional unit of product is equal to the marginal revenue from selling it.

There are two important qualifications to the profit-maximizing rule. The first is that the firm must be at a point where, for greater outputs, marginal cost will begin to exceed marginal revenue. This ensures that profit will not rise at outputs greater than the output where

marginal cost equals marginal revenue. The second qualification has to do with loss minimization rather than profit maximization. If, because of the nature of its costs and sales revenue, the best the firm can do in the short run is to minimize its loss (there is no output where profit is zero or greater), it will have to consider two options. One is to produce at the output where marginal cost equals marginal revenue. The other is to shut down temporarily and produce zero output. If its loss would be less when shut down than when operating, the firm should shut down and reject the notion of operating where marginal cost equals marginal revenue. The shutdown condition for the firm will be examined more thoroughly later in this chapter.

In the next section we will graphically analyze the profit-maximizing rule under the assumption that instead of facing a fixed market price (as in the case of the silver recycler), the firm must choose the price and quantity that will maximize its profit. Most firms in modern capitalistic economies face situations of this sort.

GRAPHICAL AND NUMERICAL EXAMPLES OF PROFIT MAXIMIZATION

In Figure 19–1 total revenue (TR), total cost (TC), and total profit (Tπ) curves for a firm are sketched. The firm is assumed to have a downward-sloping demand curve□ for its product and must therefore determine which of the possible combinations of price and quantity sold will maximize its profit. (All firms that are not perfectly competitive face a decision problem similar to the one posed here. The special case of a perfectly competitive firm is discussed in Chapter 20.) As Figure 19–1 shows (and as is true by definition), total profit is greatest where the difference between total revenue and total cost is the greatest positive value (or the smallest negative value, if the firm must incur a loss).

Panel (b) of Figure 19–1 shows that total profit is maximized where marginal revenue

(MR) is equal to marginal cost (MC). At the same output, Q^*, marginal profit (Mπ) is 0 in panel (c) of the figure.

> ***Marginal profit*** *is the additional profit the firm can obtain from selling one more unit of output.*

Correspondingly, marginal profit is also equal to the additional revenue received from selling one more unit of output minus its cost, or *marginal profit equals marginal revenue minus marginal cost (Mπ = MR − MC).*

Thus a zero marginal profit means marginal revenue equals marginal cost; that is, the additional revenue received from selling another unit is exactly offset by the additional cost incurred. Therefore, to maximize total profit, a firm should continue to increase the quantity sold of its product until no more profit can be gained from sales of additional units.

For example, at quantity Q_1, the vertical distance between total revenue and total cost is not as great as at Q^*. The slope of the total revenue curve is greater than the slope of the total cost curve at Q_1, which means that marginal revenue is greater than marginal cost. If marginal revenue is greater than marginal cost, it follows that marginal profit is positive, because one more unit of output will add more to revenue than to cost. Thus the firm can increase its profit by increasing its level of output.

On the other hand, at Q_2 the slope of the total revenue curve is less than the slope of the total cost curve, and marginal revenue is, therefore, less than marginal cost. In this case, marginal profit is negative, because the production of an additional unit adds more to cost than to revenue. *When marginal profit is negative, the firm can increase its profit by reducing its level of output.* Thus an alternative statement of the profit-maximizing decision rule is that a firm will maximize profit by producing where marginal profit is zero (marginal revenue equals marginal cost) and marginal profit for higher levels of output is negative.

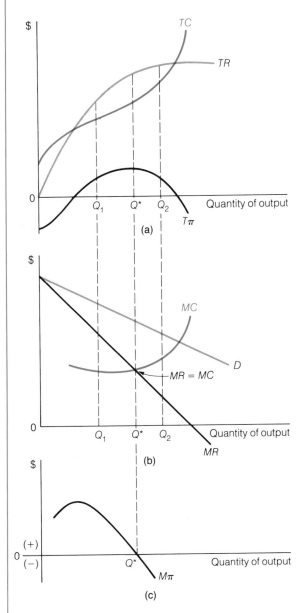

FIGURE 19–1   Profit-Maximizing Position for a Firm

Total revenue (TR), total cost (TC), and total profit (Tπ) curves are shown for a firm in panel (a). Note that total profit is greatest where the vertical distance between total revenue and total cost is the greatest. The firm's demand (D), marginal revenue (MR), and marginal cost (MC) curves are shown in panel (b). You can see that marginal revenue is equal to marginal cost at the level of output where total profit is at a maximum. Marginal profit (Mπ) is shown in panel (c). Marginal profit is zero when total profit is at its maximum level.

| The **profit-maximizing rule** can be restated to say that the firm will increase output up to the point where marginal profit equals zero and is thereafter negative.

Table 19–1 shows corresponding values of various revenue, cost, and profit concepts for a hypothetical firm. Total profit for this firm is maximized where marginal revenue is equal to marginal cost, at an output level of 4 or 5 units and a corresponding price of $70 or $60, respectively. Higher or lower outputs than these would result in lower profit. For example, if the firm were to produce only 3 units of output, it would forego $15 of potential profit, since the marginal profit of the fourth unit is $15. On the other hand, if the firm were to produce 6 units of output, total profit would be $25 less than is possible, since the marginal profit of the sixth unit is a negative $25. Note, however, that the total profit for the firm will be the same whether or not the firm sells the fifth unit, for which marginal profit is zero.

If a firm wishes to maximize total profit, it will *not* attempt to maximize the difference between price and cost per unit of output. In other words, it will not try to maximize profit per unit sold.

Average profit is profit per unit sold. It is equal to total profit divided by quantity of output. |

As we can see from Table 19–1, average profit $(A\pi)$ is not at its greatest level when total profit is maximized. We have already observed that total profit is maximized at a quantity of output equal to four or five units. However, average profit is at its maximum at an output level of two or three units where average profit is $30.

Extremely high per unit profit may sound like a reasonable goal for a firm to pursue, but from our data we see that it is not. For example, suppose a Cadillac dealer tried to sell cars for the maximum per unit profit by charging $100,000 for a certain model that cost the

TABLE 19–1 Relationships among Revenue, Cost, and Profit

Output (Q)	Price (P)	Total Revenue (TR)	Marginal Revenue (MR)	Marginal Cost (MC)	Marginal Profit $(M\pi = MR - MC)$	Total Cost (TC)	Total Profit $(T\pi = TR - TC)$	Average Cost $\left(AC = \dfrac{TC}{Q}\right)$	Average Profit $(A\pi = T\pi/Q)$
0	$120	$ 0				$ 30	– $ 30	—	—
			$100	$50	$ 50				
1	100	100				80	20	$80.00	$20.00
			80	40	40				
2	90	180				120	60	60.00	30.00
			60	30	30				
3	80	240				150	90	50.00	30.00
			40	25	15				
4	70	280				175	105	43.75	26.25
			20	20	0				
5	60	300				195	105	39.00	21.00
			0	25	– 25				
6	50	300				220	80	36.67	13.33
			– 20	40	– 60				
7	40	280				260	20	37.14	2.86
			– 40	50	– 90				
8	30	240				310	– 70	38.75	– 8.75
			– 60	60	– 120				
9	20	180				370	– 190	41.11	– 21.11

firm $15,000. The firm might sell only two cars at the $100,000 price, reaping the whopping profit of $85,000 per car, for a total profit of $170,000. Suppose that during the same time period the dealer had set the price for the model at $20,000 and had sold 100 cars at $5,000 profit per car. The firm certainly would have been better off, since $5,000 times 100 cars yields a total profit of $500,000.

As noted earlier, we are assuming the firm is interested in maximizing total profit rather than average profit where the two are maximized at different points. In other words, total profit, not profit per unit of output sold, is most important to the firm.

We have already stated that total profit is equal to total revenue minus total cost. It is also equal to average profit multiplied by the quantity of output produced since, as stated above, average profit is equal to total profit divided by quantity of output. Thus,

$$A\pi = \frac{T\pi}{Q}, \quad \text{and} \quad T\pi = A\pi \times Q.$$

Average profit is also equal to average revenue minus the average cost of a unit of output. This relationship must hold because average revenue represents the revenue received per unit sold and average cost is the cost, on the average, of each unit. The difference between average revenue and average cost, therefore, must be equal to profit per unit sold or average profit. As stated in Chapter 17, if a firm sells all units at the same price, price and average revenue are equal. Thus, average profit is also equal to price minus average cost $(A\pi = P - AC)$.

The profit-maximizing level of output and the corresponding total profit for a firm with a downward-sloping demand curve are depicted in panel (a) of Figure 19–2. The profit-maximizing price and level of output are P^* and Q^*, respectively (where $MR = MC$). The corresponding average cost is AC^*. Total profit for the firm will be given by $(P^* - AC^*) \times Q^*$, the area of rectangle P^*EFAC^* in Figure 19–2a.

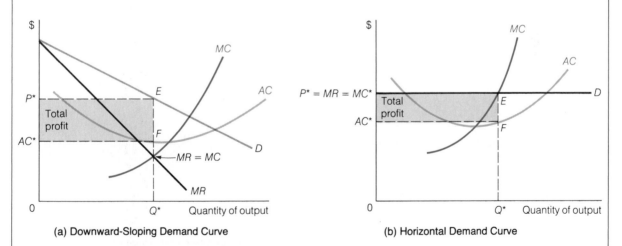

(a) Downward-Sloping Demand Curve (b) Horizontal Demand Curve

FIGURE 19–2 Profit-Maximizing Position and Total Profit for a Firm

Panel (a) shows a downward-sloping demand curve for a firm's product. The firm will maximize profit by producing Q^* units of output, where $MR = MC$, and charging a price of P^*. Total profit is equal to $(P^* - AC^*) \times Q^*$, the area of rectangle P^*EFAC^*. A horizontal demand curve for a firm's product is shown in panel (b). In this case price and marginal revenue are equal, and the firm will maximize profit by producing where $P = MR = MC$, at Q^*. Total profit is once again equal to $(P^* - AC^*) \times Q^*$, the area of rectangle P^*EFAC^*.

THE FIRM'S
SHUTDOWN POINT

◆

Over the long run, we assume that a firm will go out of business if it cannot make a normal return,◻ taking into consideration the riskiness of its endeavor. A firm may also find that to minimize its losses it should close its doors in the short run, even though it will still incur some fixed costs.

The crucial decision variable is the difference between price and average variable cost◻ (P − AVC). If the selling price is less than average variable cost, the loss-minimizing firm will close down, at least temporarily. If it continues operations, the firm's loss will include a sum not only equal to its fixed costs but also including part of its variable costs.

*Thus the firm's **shutdown point** is reached when, at the level of output where marginal revenue is equal to marginal cost, price is also equal to average variable cost.*

Panel (a) in Figure 19–3 shows the shutdown point for a firm with a horizontal demand curve, and panel (b) shows the shutdown point for a firm with a downward-sloping demand curve. The selling price of the product is constant in the former case.

In panel (b) the profit-maximizing level of output and corresponding total profit are depicted for a firm with a horizontal demand curve. Since price remains the same no matter how many units of output are sold, price is equal to marginal revenue. This case occurs in an industry characterized by perfect competition, to be discussed in Chapter 20. In this case, a firm will maximize profit by producing where $P^* = MR = MC$, at Q^*. Total profit is once again equal to the area of rectangle P^*EFAC^*. As we shall see in Chapter 20, economic profit can exist only in the short run in a perfectly competitive industry.

For example, suppose a farmer is trying to decide whether to plant a given parcel of land. The farmer believes that wheat will be the most profitable crop but that revenues will not be great enough this year to completely cover costs. The farmer expects to receive $2.50 per bushel of wheat, but average total costs per bushel are equal to $3. If average variable costs are $2 per bushel, the loss-minimizing farmer

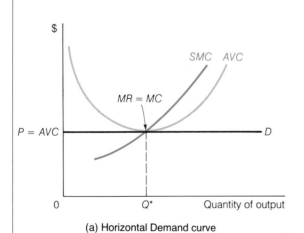

(a) Horizontal Demand curve

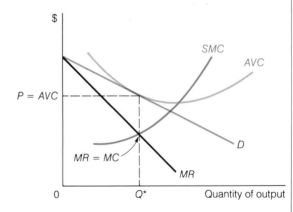

(b) Downward-Sloping Demand Curve

FIGURE 19–3   The Shutdown Point for a Firm

In panel (a) the firm has a horizontal demand curve. In this case, price (P) and marginal revenue (MR) are equal. The shutdown point for such a firm occurs where price = marginal revenue = short-run marginal cost (SMC) = average variable cost (AVC). In panel (b), the firm has a downward sloping demand curve. In this case, marginal revenue is less than price, and the shut-down point occurs where the average variable cost curve is tangent to the demand curve.

will go ahead and plant the wheat. Why? Because the revenue received will still cover all the variable costs and some of the fixed costs of the output. In this case the farmer will minimize the farm's losses by planting wheat.

Tables 19–2 and 19–3 are based on this example. These two tables and Table 19–4 are simplified versions of what is known in accounting as an income statement.□ An *income statement* shows the revenue (sales), cost, and profit (net income or loss) of a firm for some specified time period. Accounting income statements frequently overlook opportunity costs.□ However, in this case we will assume that all of the farmer's opportunity costs have been included in the cost data. (Detailed accounting statements for two real firms are discussed in the special topic that appears at the end of this chapter.)

In Table 19–2 Poverty Acres Farm is as-

TABLE 19–2 Income Statement: Poverty Acres Farm for the Year Ended December 31, 198_

Sales	$ 00.00
Less cost of goods sold	00.00
Gross profit	00.00
Less fixed costs	15,000.00
Net income (loss) before tax	$<15,000.00>

TABLE 19–3 Income Statement: Poverty Acres Farm for the Year Ended December 31, 198_

Sales (15,000 bushels at $2.50)	$37,500
Less variable cost of goods sold (15,000 bushels at $2.00)	30,000
Gross profit	7,500
Less fixed costs	15,000
Net income (loss) before tax	$<7,500>

TABLE 19–4 Income Statement: Poverty Acres Farm for the Year Ended December 31, 198_

Sales (15,000 bushels at $1.80)	$27,000
Less variable cost of goods sold (15,000 bushels at $2.00)	30,000
Gross profit	<3,000>
Less fixed costs	15,000
Net income (loss) before tax	$<18,000>

sumed to have $15,000 of fixed costs. If nothing at all is planted, the loss for the year will be $15,000. In Table 19–3 Poverty Acres Farm is assumed to sell 15,000 bushels of wheat at $2.50 per bushel. With average variable costs of $2 per bushel, the net loss drops to $7,500.

In Table 19–4 Poverty Acres Farm is presented as worse off by planting a crop. The farm is assumed to sell 15,000 bushels of wheat at $1.80 per bushel, while average variable costs remain at $2 per bushel. In this case the firm loses not only an amount equal to the fixed costs of $15,000 but an additional $3,000 as well. Therefore, we can conclude that *when price is less than average variable cost, the loss-minimizing firm will not produce at all.*

BREAKEVEN ANALYSIS

Many businesses use a simple form of profit analysis, called breakeven analysis, to aid them in making certain pricing and investment decisions.

> The **breakeven quantity** of output is the level of output where the firm breaks even—where total profit is zero.

When a firm uses breakeven analysis, it frequently assumes that price and average variable cost associated with a particular plant are constant over the relevant range of output levels and, normally, that price is greater than average variable cost. It also assumes that total fixed cost is some definite amount.

The result of these assumptions is shown in Figure 19–4. The firm's total revenue curve is a straight line out from the origin (a ray), and its total cost curve is also a straight line. However, the total cost curve begins at the level of total fixed cost on the vertical axis and rises at a slower rate than does total revenue. Once the breakeven quantity is reached (Tπ = 0), greater output produces greater profit.

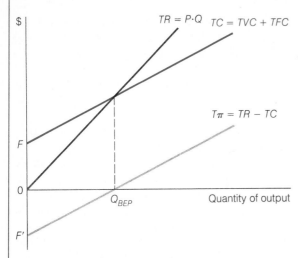

FIGURE 19–4 Total Revenue, Total Cost, and the Breakeven Point

A firm's total revenue (TR), total cost (TC), and total profit (Tπ) curves are shown in this graph. Price and average variable cost are assumed to be constant. Total profit is $-F$, since the amount of total fixed cost is $F, when output is zero. The firm breaks even where total revenue is equal to total cost (total profit is zero), at Q_{BEP}.

The formula for the breakeven point quantity, Q_{BEP}, is

$$Q_{BEP} = \frac{\text{Total fixed cost}}{\text{Price} - \text{Average variable cost}}.[7]$$

---

7. We can derive the formula for the breakeven quantity (Q_{BEP}) as follows. When the firm is at its breakeven point,

$$TR = TC$$
$$= TVC + TFC,$$

where TR is total revenue, TC is total cost, TVC is total variable cost, and TFC is total fixed cost. Subtracting TVC from both sides of the equation we obtain

$$TR - TVC = TFC.$$

We can write total revenue as price times quantity and total variable cost as average variable cost times quantity. Therefore,

$$P{\cdot}Q - AVC{\cdot}Q = TFC.$$

After we factor out Q, the equation becomes

$$Q(P - AVC) = TFC.$$

Dividing by $(P - AVC)$ we arrive at the breakeven point formula:

$$Q_{BEP} = \frac{TFC}{P - AVC}. \qquad (1)$$

The term Price − Average variable cost is called the **contribution margin per unit,** because it indicates how much the sale of another unit will contribute to covering fixed costs or adding to profit.

The breakeven formula tells the firm what quantity of output (number of units) it must sell to break even.[8] Given the price of its product and its total costs, this level of output will be the quantity that just yields a normal profit. Of course, if it is possible to sell more than the breakeven quantity, profit will be greater than normal.

For example, suppose a restaurant has total fixed costs of $5,000 per month. If the average price of its meals is $6 and its average variable cost is $2, the firm's breakeven point quantity is

$$Q_{BEP} = \frac{5,000}{6 - 2}$$
$$= \frac{5,000}{4}$$
$$= 1,250 \text{ meals per month.}$$

For a 30-day month, the restaurant must sell 1,250/30, or approximately 42 meals per day to break even.

Firms often use breakeven analysis in deter-

---

8. We can transform the equation to show the total dollar sales required for the firm to break even by multiplying both sides of Equation 1 by price:

$$P{\cdot}Q_{BEP} = \frac{P{\cdot}TFC}{P - AVC}$$
$$= \frac{TFC}{\dfrac{P - AVC}{P}}$$
$$= \frac{TFC}{1 - \dfrac{AVC}{P}}.$$

Thus the breakeven point dollar sales or total revenue for a particular price, P, is given by

$$TR_{BEP} = \frac{TFC}{1 - \dfrac{AVC}{P}}. \qquad (2)$$

The term $1 - (AVC/P)$ is called the *contribution margin ratio,* because it is the ratio of the contribution margin per unit to price.

mining the effect on breakeven quantity if the company were to change certain factors, such as plant capacity (and, consequently, fixed costs and perhaps variable costs) or price. However, firms should be aware of the fact that while the unit contribution margin is important in determining breakeven point quantity, actual sales volume is also a crucial factor in determining whether a firm ever breaks even. Thus profit-maximizing firms are aware of how quantity sold will vary for different prices. *A high contribution margin per unit but no sales will not enable a firm to break even.* These firms will also be aware of the level of output where the range of constant average variable cost ends and marginal cost begins to rise.

Breakeven analysis is a simple and handy tool that can be used to determine the sales required to break even under a given set of circumstances. However, a single breakeven computation will not tell the firm the profit-maximizing price to charge. At least several breakeven computations are required to discover which price will actually maximize profit. As the additional data are compiled, the decision-making process gets closer to the traditional profit-maximization analysis described at the beginning of this chapter.

INCREMENTAL PROFIT ANALYSIS

This chapter will end with an examination of one more decision tool, incremental profit analysis. Suppose a firm is trying to decide whether to accept a special order for its product or to undertake a new project. In this case, the firm will compare the additional, or incremental, revenue to be obtained with the additional, or incremental, cost to be incurred.

Incremental profit is the additional profit that would be obtained from a new undertaking; it is equal to incremental revenue minus incremental cost.

If the incremental profit is greater than zero, the project should be accepted. If it is zero or negative, the project should be rejected.

Consider the case of an airline trying to decide whether to add a daily round-trip, late-night flight from New York to Los Angeles.[9] The company has a plane available for the flight, and there are no other flights for which this particular plane could be used during this time period. The incremental revenue from this flight is expected to be an average of 100 passengers times a $75 fare, or $7,500. The incremental costs per trip are estimated to be the following:

Wages and salaries	$2,500
Fuel	500
Plane maintenance	1,000
Total	$4,000
Less cost saved on hangar rental	100
Net incremental cost	$3,900

Thus the estimated incremental profit per round-trip flight is:

Incremental revenue	$7,500
Less incremental cost (net)	3,900
Equals incremental profit	$3,600

Under these circumstances, the airline should add the flight. We do not take into account any of the airline's fixed costs, because they are not relevant to this type of decision. Only the incremental cost and incremental revenue are relevant. Of course, the firm must be careful to account for all the incremental costs, including any opportunity costs associated with the new undertaking.

9. Two airlines, Continental and United, have used this type of analysis. See "Behind the Superboom at United Airlines," *Business Week*, October 23, 1978, pp. 137, 140; and "Airline Takes the Marginal Route," *Business Week*, April 20, 1963, pp. 111–114.

SUMMARY

1. In this chapter we have discussed the goals of a firm, assuming that the primary goal is maximizing total profit. The profit-maximizing rule for the firm is to produce up to the point where marginal revenue equals marginal cost or marginal profit is zero.

2. If the selling price is less than average variable costs, the firm will shut down, at least in the short run, until a more profitable situation emerges. Under these circumstances, the greatest loss the firm will incur is from its fixed costs.

3. Breakeven analysis is a simple decision tool that many businesses use. The formula allows a firm to determine the quantity of output it must sell to break even, given a particular price, level of average variable cost, and total fixed cost. This level of output is given by

$$Q_{BEP} = \frac{TFC}{P - AVC}.$$

The amount of dollar sales required to break even is given by

$$TR_{BEP} = \frac{TFC}{1 - \frac{AVC}{P}}.$$

4. Incremental profit analysis is a decision technique that a firm can use when it is trying to determine whether to accept a special order, undertake a new project, or perform any other similar activity. If the incremental profit is expected to be positive, the new activity will be undertaken. If the incremental profit is expected to be negative, the new project will be rejected.

IMPORTANT TERMS AND CONCEPTS

Economic profit	Shutdown point
Total profit	Breakeven quantity
Profit-maximizing	Contribution margin
decision rule	per unit
Marginal profit	Incremental profit
Average profit	

QUESTIONS AND PROBLEMS

1. What is profit maximization?

2. What other goals might a firm have?

3. State and explain the decision rule a firm should follow to maximize profit.

4. Under what circumstances should a firm shut its doors in the short run?

5. Explain breakeven analysis, including the assumptions made about fixed cost, variable cost, and price.

6. What is incremental profit analysis? Give an example of how this decision tool can be used.

7. Find the monthly breakeven quantity for a firm if it has fixed costs per month of $12,000, an average variable cost of $6 for the proposed good, and a price of $10 for the good.

8. Find the annual breakeven dollar sales for a firm with $240,000 in fixed costs per year, a price of $50 for the proposed good, and average variable costs of $25 for the good.

9. A hotel has an offer from a national organization to hold a convention there if the organization can be guaranteed 100 rooms per night for three nights at a price of $30 per room per night. The usual price of these rooms is $50. However, this is a slack season, and the hotel believes that without the convention it will have at least 100 rooms vacant every night for these three nights. The average variable cost per room per night is $20. Should the hotel accept the offer? Explain.

10. Because of a bumper crop of tomatoes this year, the price a tomato grower will receive per bushel is $2. The tomatoes are ripe and ready to pick, and the grower must make the decision of whether to pick them or let them rot in the fields. The average total costs per bushel are $5, and the average variable costs per bushel (including planting, cultivating, spraying, and picking) are $2.50. However, the average variable cost of picking the tomatoes is just $.50 per bushel. What should the tomato grower do? Why?

11. Complete the table on the next page and find the profit-maximizing price and level of output.

Q	P	TR	MR	MC	Mπ	TC	Tπ
0	$10,000	$ 0				$ 2,000	
1	9,000	9,000				10,000	
2	8,000	16,000				15,000	
3	7,000	21,000				17,000	
4	6,000	24,000				20,000	
5	5,000	25,000				24,000	
6	4,000	24,000				29,000	
7	3,000	21,000				34,000	

SMALLER FAST-FOOD CHAINS FEEL THE BRUNT OF BIG-THREE COMPANIES' "BURGER WAR"

McDonald's, Burger King and Wendy's are heating up their hamburger war, but it's the smaller fast-food chains that are getting burned.

Smarting from the heightened competition among the fast-food giants, several smaller chains are closing stores, scuttling expansion plans and looking for new ways to cut the mustard against their bigger rivals.

Steak 'n Shake Inc., a regional chain based in Indianapolis, last year closed all 17 of its stores in Chicago and Houston, ending a two-year effort to crack those

Source: Paul Ingrassia and Laurie Cohen, "Smaller Fast-Food Chains Feel the Brunt of Big-Three Companies' 'Burger War,'" *Wall Street Journal*, February 20, 1979, p. 38.

markets. More recently the company dropped its car-hop service, calling it a casualty of the drive-through windows being opened by the big chains.

Long John Silver's, a fast-fish chain and the major unit of Louisville-based Jerrico Inc., has pulled out of Boston and has abandoned plans to expand into new markets. Now the chain is starting to remodel its existing restaurants, trying to make their atmosphere less plastic.

Ralston Purina is sharply slowing the growth of its Jack in the Box chain following a recent earnings slump. The company is trying to boost sales in existing stores by adding pancakes, French toast and scrambled eggs to its breakfast menu, and is working on

new marketing and remodeling programs.

A GLOOMY YEAR

Restaurant chains always seem to be working themselves into and out of trouble, but the list of problem-plagued companies in the $21 billion-a-year fast-food industry is especially long right now. It includes General Foods Corp.'s Burger Chef, PepsiCo Inc.'s Pizza Hut and Orange-co Inc.'s Arthur Treacher's Fish & Chips. Heublein Inc.'s long-troubled Kentucky Fried Chicken is showing new life under new management, but the chain still isn't the high flyer it once was.

"McDonald's, Burger King and Wendy's are fighting a rough battle, but they're hurting all the other fast-food chains more than they're hurting each other," says William F. Maguire, vice president of Blyth Eastman Dillon & Co., an investment firm.

McDonald's spent about $200 million on advertising and promotion last year and will probably spend more this year, based on its customary formula of about 4.4% of sales for promotion. Burger King, a unit of Pillsbury Co., will spend about $50 million in the fiscal year ending May 31. And Wendy's which spent $30 million in 1978, plans to spend $45 million to $50 million this year (1979). In contrast, Long John Silver's, with less than a fourth as many units as McDonald's, will spend only about $18 million in its fiscal year ending in June 1979.

The top three hamburger chains, though, aren't escaping the fighting unscathed. All three have had nearly flat sales, at best, in recent months—not counting price increases and the opening of new stores. Rising prices are keeping would-be customers at home, to the distress of large and small restaurant chains alike.

The price of hamburger is up more than 40 percent from a year ago (1978), and the federally prescribed minimum wage jumped to $2.90 January 1, from $2.65 in 1978 and $2.30 in 1977. The upshot is one price rise after another at most chains. A Wendy's double hamburger, for example, costs about $1.49 today, compared with $1.25 a year ago. At the same time, inflation has gnawed away at consumers' disposable income, curbing their seemingly ever-growing appetite for eating out.

"The prices at these fast-food places are getting out of hand," says Richard Lasek of Hinsdale, Illinois, a Chicago suburb. "I used to take my kids to Burger King or McDonald's three or four times a month, but now we've stopped going."

Deborah Milano, who works in Chicago's Loop, says the people in her office are bringing their lunch more often these days, instead of going out for a hamburger.

Meanwhile, the larger chains are pushing ahead with more new stores. McDonald's, which already has more than 5,000 stores world-wide, plans to add another 450 to 500 in 1979. Wendy's, with 1,400 stores, expects to add another 500 by year end, and Burger King is adding 350 new stores in the current fiscal year, bringing its total to about 2,500 units.

Steak 'n Shake says that within the last two years, an average of 14 new restaurants has opened within one mile of each of its 135 stores. "I don't think the whole country is saturated, but certain areas might be," says Thomas R. Delph, a Steak 'n Shake vice president.

SOME "WORRISOME" PATTERNS

Thomas R. Postek, an analyst with William Blair & Co., also voices concern. "With a recession in prospect, the fast-food chains might have expanded too rapidly," he says. "I can't say the country is now saturated with fast-food places, but the sluggish customer-traffic patterns are worrisome." The chance that a gasoline crunch will keep Americans off the highways is another bad omen, he adds.

Fred L. Turner, chairman and chief executive of McDonald's, concedes that "the coming year will be a trying time for us." But he adds that "it will hit our smaller competitors even harder. I don't see a quick shakeout, but some companies just won't be around for the long haul."

The fast-foods fight has been going on in earnest for about a year, but the first rumblings began to be heard in early 1977. That's when Pillsbury Co., fearful of losing its position as the No. 2 hamburger chain to fast-growing Wendy's, raided McDonald's, taking its No. 3 executive—Donald N. Smith. Under Mr. Smith, Burger King has launched its Magic Burger King character to compete with Ronald McDonald, enlarged its hamburger to two ounces (McDonald's standard hamburger is 1.6 ounces), added beef fat to its French fries for a meatier taste, and started Operation Grand Slam to remodel its stores for a more-appetizing look.

More recently, Burger King has pushed personal appearances by the Magic Burger King character; 20 Kings travel from store to store to perform magic tricks and pull in more customers. McDonald's has responded with a variety of promotions, including free sundaes and other giveaways for youngsters. Wendy's drive-through pickup windows for a while gave that aggressive company an advantage over its two larger rivals, but now McDonald's and Burger King have started adding drive-through windows of their own.

AN UNWISE EXPERIMENT

As if the intense competition wasn't making enough trouble for the smaller fast-food companies, some of them were cooking up their own problems. Long John Silver's, for example, cut its fish portions and wound up cutting Jerrico's profits 17% in the fiscal year ended last June. Now the company is bringing back larger portions. It's handing out little pirate chests filled with rings, toys and other knicknacks to kids and planning to air TV commercials on network prime time, as well as remodeling many of its stores.

Steak 'n Shake's mistake was trying to get too big too fast, and at a time when its costs and competition both were escalating. Now the company is paying. Partly because of the recent store closings, net income dropped to $1.7 million in the September 30 fiscal year, down from $2.8 million a year earlier. So the company is doing some rethinking and rearranging. Table service, long a Steak 'n Shake hallmark, is all but eliminated in four experimental stores in Louisville, Indianapolis, St. Louis and Atlanta. Customers will fetch their own food and drinks, and waitresses will just pour coffee and water. The move will cut the number of waitresses to two from six. Another test store to be opened in Tampa this month will have a drive-through window and no table service at all.

After opening more than 80 stores in each of the two preceding years, Jack in the Box opened only 48 stores last year and plans only 52 for 1979. Ralston Purina, the chain's parent, says the unit's earnings dropped an undisclosed amount in fiscal 1978. And industry analysts don't see much improvement this year. They cite strong competition from McDonald's and Burger King in the chain's Southern California market.

Burger Chef, long an also-ran and still a money loser for General Foods, is trying to copy Burger King's effort to copy McDonald's. Like Burger King, Burger Chef has raided McDonald's for new leadership; its president, Terrance Collins, is a former McDonald's regional executive.

What's more, Burger Chef also has started to remodel its restaurants. Garish colors are giving way to earth tones of brown, yellow and orange, and the stores are getting carpeting, chandeliers and wall hangings. As an added twist the company is testing limited table service; customers place their orders at a counter and the food is brought to their tables.

A similar move from bright colors to earth tones is starting at Arthur Treacher's, which lost money for Orange-co in the fiscal year ended last August. The company, which blames the loss largely on higher food costs, is making menu changes to bring in new customers.

Pizza Hut also is changing its menu to change its fortunes. A new menu item is "Super Style" pizza, with more cheese, more toppings and more of a profit margin than the chain's regular pizzas.

Whether all these changes will solve the various chains' problems remains to be seen, but fast-food recoveries aren't unheard of. The Arby's roast-beef-sandwich chain, for example, went bankrupt in the fast-food shakeout of the early Seventies, but now the company is prospering as part of Royal Crown Cos.

Arby's says its pretax operating income last year was about $6 million, compared with $4.7 million in 1977. A major reason for the chain's recovery is the addition of indoor seating and of new items like a barbecue sandwich. Now the company is planning to start advertising on network television this spring.

QUESTIONS

1. Why are the smaller fast-food chains hit especially hard by the "burger war"?
2. What problems are the larger firms having as they attempt to maximize their profits?
3. What suggestions would you give to both sizes of firms to help them maximize profit?

SAMPLE FIRM
FINANCIAL STATEMENTS

The example of Poverty Acres Farm in Chapter 19 introduced the concept of a simplified income statement. Economists and financial analysts frequently have to deal with the financial statements of firms in order to answer questions about profit or other economic variables. Because of this, and because many introductory-level economics students go on to complete degrees in business administration, it is useful to follow our discussion of profit with a brief review of some standard accounting statements. The statements that follow are for two real companies, Eaton Corporation, Crown Zellerbach, and Knight-Ridder Newspapers, Inc.[1] Although they are lengthy, the discussion should make them understandable.

The set of financial statements for each company is accompanied by an extensive set of footnotes which more fully explain how the items in the statements are calculated. We have omitted these footnotes in the interest of brevity. However, an investor who is interested in these companies would be well-advised to obtain the entire reports and to read them carefully.

Businesses use three basic financial statements: the balance sheet, the income statement, and the statement of changes in financial position. The purpose of the **balance sheet** is to report the financial position of a business as of a specific date, normally the end of the firm's business year (which may not be December 31), although sometimes more frequently. The **income statement** describes the results (profit or loss) of the firm's operations for some particular time period. Again, all firms must compile an income statement at least at the end of each business year. The

---

1. Eaton Corporation produces technology—intensive products for industry. Crown Zellerbach is a forest products and paper company. Knight-Ridder is in newspapers and broadcasting.

statement of changes in financial position explains the changes in the firm's financial resources, usually concentrating on working capital, that have occurred during the reporting period.[2]

A fourth statement, the *statement of changes in owners' equity*—or, for a corporation, the *statement of retained earnings*—is often prepared as well. Its purpose is to more fully explain any changes in owners' equity (the value of the owners', or shareholders', interest in the firm) that have taken place during the reporting period. Such changes may occur not only because of income received or losses incurred but also because of adjustments to the results reported for prior periods or because of dividend payments, for example.

The sample financial statements presented here are *consolidated statements*. When a corporation owns a majority of another corporation's stock, thereby controlling the affairs of the second corporation, the first corporation is said to be the *parent company* and the second corporation the *subsidiary company*. The parent company name appears at the top of each of the following consolidated financial statements.

Since the parent company and its subsidiary companies are all separate legal entities, separate financial statements may be prepared for each of them. However, investors may find it useful for the parent company to prepare a set of financial statements, called *consolidated financial statements*, which treats the parent and subsidiary companies as one business entity.

The balance sheet may be prepared in *report form*, with assets listed first, then liabilities, followed by owners' equity. The sample consolidated balance sheet of Crown Zellerbach and its subsidiaries is in this form. The balance sheet may also be prepared in *account form*, with assets listed on the left-hand side and liabilities and owners' equity reported on the right-hand side. The sample consolidated balance sheet of Eaton Corporation and its subsidiaries is in this form.

In either case, within the asset section, current assets are listed first. *Current assets* are assets that can be expected to be converted into cash within a normal operating cycle of the firm or one year, whichever is longer. The *normal operating cycle* of a business is the length of time required to convert cash into inventories, inventories into receivables, and receivables back into cash. These items usually include cash, securities that the firm expects to hold for a brief period of time, receivables, inventories, and prepaid expenses.[3]

Except for marketable securities and inventories, these items are usually reported at their estimated realizable values. Marketable equity securities (stocks) are reported at the lower of their aggregate cost or market value. Inventories may be reported on a cost basis or at the lower of cost or market value. All assets are usually listed in order of their *liquidity*, or how easily they can be converted into cash without disrupting the normal operations of the firm.

The noncurrent assets are listed next. Property, plant, and equipment are still listed on the basis of their historical cost, although the Securities and Exchange Commission now requires the top thousand U.S. corporations to file supplementary statements indicating the current value or replacement value of these assets.

In the liabilities and owners' equity section, liabilities are listed first. In the liabilities section, current liabilities are listed first. *Current liabilities* are the obligations that the firm has accrued as a result of its normal operating cycle or that represent debts that must be paid within one year. Current liabilities are followed by long-term liabilities.

---

2. *Working capital* is defined as current assets minus current liabilities. Current assets and current liabilities are defined in the discussion of the balance sheet.

---

3. The prepaid expenses included are those that represent prepayments of expenses, such as insurance, that would otherwise require cash payments by the firm during the current operating cycle.

BALANCE SHEETS
CROWN ZELLERBACH AND SUBSIDIARIES

December 31,	(In millions of dollars)	
	1980	1979
Assets		
Current Assets		
Cash	$ 3.6	$ 9.7
Short-term investments, at cost (approximates market)	54.4	82.3
Trade accounts receivable, net of allowances for losses (1980: $6.8; 1979: $5.5)	270.9	248.1
Other receivables	51.1	32.8
Inventories	433.7	396.6
Prepaid expenses	44.5	46.8
Total current assets	858.2	816.3
Properties, at cost		
Buildings, machinery and equipment	2,076.1	1,881.1
Less allowances for depreciation	902.5	855.6
	1,173.6	1,025.5
Land, timberlands and logging facilities, net of amortization and cost of timber harvested	256.2	230.6
Oil and gas properties (on successful efforts basis), net of depletion and amortization	8.8	8.5
Total properties	1,438.6	1,264.6
Other Assets		
Investments in 50 percent owned affiliates	14.7	53.0
Other investments (at cost) and receivables	38.3	5.3
Deferred charges	22.9	21.4
Total other assets	75.9	79.7
	$2,372.7	$2,160.6
Liabilities and Shareholders' Equity		
Current Liabilities		
Commercial paper notes payable	$ 84.0	$ 39.9
Notes payable, banks	17.6	—
Notes payable, other	10.9	2.4
Accounts payable, trade	148.4	137.6
Accounts payable, other	38.9	36.5
Accrued federal, state and foreign income taxes	2.6	50.7
Accrued payrolls	70.1	63.9
Other accrued liabilities	66.7	58.1
Long-term debt, installments due within one year	33.1	25.0
Total current liabilities	472.3	414.1
Other Liabilities		
Long-term debt	486.1	545.2
Deferred income taxes	161.1	118.8
Other	20.2	16.7
Total other liabilities	667.4	680.7
Minority Interest in Canadian Subsidiary	44.0	35.2
Shareholders' Equity		
$4.625 Cumulative convertible preferred stock	125.0	—
Common stock, outstanding 1980: 25,588,710 shares; 1979: 25,422,792 shares	127.9	127.1
Other capital	67.4	65.7
Income retained in the business	868.7	837.8
Total shareholders' equity	1,189.0	1,030.6
	$2,372.7	$2,160.6

Consolidated Balance Sheets
Eaton Corporation and Subsidiaries

December 31	1980	1979
Assets	(Thousands of Dollars)	
Current Assets		
Cash	$ 13,865	$ 25,685
Short-term securities—at cost (approximates market)	7,503	4,308
Accounts receivable, less allowance of $13.6 million in 1980 ($9.4 million in 1979)	493,971	516,595
Inventories	718,885	782,753
Other current assets	46,017	48,319
Total Current Assets	1,280,241	1,377,660
Other Assets		
Investments in and advances to finance subsidiaries	46,126	40,724
Investments in associate companies	33,433	25,800
Excess of cost over net assets of businesses acquired, less amortization of $4.0 million in 1980 ($2.5 million in 1979)	55,234	55,239
Other intangible assets, less amortization of $14.1 million in 1980 ($9.6 million in 1979)	39,813	44,763
Other assets	27,079	36,060
	201,685	202,586
Property, Plant and Equipment—on the basis of cost		
Land	32,544	33,059
Buildings	317,067	304,044
Machinery and equipment	920,211	844,599
	1,269,822	1,181,702
Less allowances for depreciation and amortization	449,288	401,603
	820,534	780,099
	$2,302,460	$2,360,345

In the shareholders' equity section of a corporate balance sheet there are two basic types of equity: paid-in capital and retained earnings. Basically, *paid-in capital* represents equity originating from stockholder investments in the firm. It is frequently divided into two sections: capital stock and capital in excess of par or stated value. The latter amount represents sums that stockholders paid to the company for stock that were over and above its par or stated value. *Retained earnings* represents equity originating from the income of the firm.

In the case of a proprietorship, only one capital account is used. In a partnership, each partner has a separate capital account.

Income statements may also be prepared in two formats, the single-step form or the multiple-step form. In the *single-step* form, illustrated by the sample Statement of Consolidated Income for Eaton Corporation and its subsidiaries, all of the revenue items are grouped together and all of the cost items are grouped together. Income before taxes is then found by subtracting total cost from total rev-

Consolidated Balance Sheets
Eaton Corporation and Subsidiaries

December 31	1980	1979
Liabilities and Shareholders' Equity	(Thousands of Dollars)	
Current Liabilities		
Short-term debt	$ 67,135	$ 88,939
Trade payables	188,260	200,141
Payrolls and other accruals	253,588	254,236
Income and other taxes	83,834	109,108
Current portion of long-term debt	14,583	18,146
Total Current Liabilities	607,400	670,570
Long-Term Debt—less current portion	516,952	607,843
Other Long-Term Liabilities	77,911	71,666
Deferred Income Taxes	95,090	79,636
Shareholders' Equity		
4³/₄% Cumulative Convertible Preferred Shares	1,244	1,450
Serial Preferred Shares (aggregate liquidation value of $15.1 million at December 31, 1980)	189	223
Common Shares (26,724,738 and 26,115,508 shares outstanding at December 31, 1980 and 1979, respectively)	13,362	13,058
Capital in excess of par value	109,898	103,381
Retained earnings	880,414	812,518
	1,005,107	930,630
	$2,302,460	$2,360,345

enue.[4] Net income is found by subtracting income taxes from income before taxes.

In a corporate income statement, the earnings per share of common stock are then reported. The net income per share on a diluted basis indicates the amount to which income per share would be reduced if all persons holding rights to convert bonds or preferred stock into common stock did so. (Holders of preferred stock are usually entitled to a specific return on their shares, if the corporation has sufficient earnings, before any dividends are paid to common stockholders. Holders of preferred stock often do not have voting rights at stockholders' meetings.)

The sample Consolidated Statement of Income for Knight-Ridder Newspapers, Inc. and its subsidiaries is in multiple-step form. Usually, although not in this case, revenue from sales and cost of goods sold is isolated first, and the *gross profit on sales* is computed.

---

4. Extraordinary revenue and expense items are kept separate. This matter is discussed later.

Statements of Consolidated Income
Eaton Corporation and Subsidiaries

Year Ended December 31	1980	1979	1978
	(Thousands of Dollars)		
Net sales	$3,176,466	$3,359,914	$2,790,521
Interest income	5,546	8,052	10,445
Excess of insurance settlement over book value	25,360	-0-	-0-
Other income—net	37,172	26,353	14,255
	3,244,544	3,394,319	2,815,221
Costs and expenses:			
Cost of products sold	2,392,355	2,487,770	2,067,228
Selling and administrative expenses	482,753	453,300	357,962
Research and development expenses	74,328	67,582	47,202
Interest expense	89,179	86,925	67,202
Exchange loss—net	3,897	3,935	15,957
	3,042,512	3,099,512	2,555,551
Income Before Income Taxes and Extraordinary Credit	202,032	294,807	259,670
Income taxes	86,248	141,543	140,378
Income Before Extraordinary Credit	115,784	153,264	119,292
Extraordinary credit	-0-	-0-	11,584
Net Income	$115,784	$153,264	$130,876
Per Common Share:			
Net Income:			
Primary:			
Income before extraordinary credit	$4.35	$5.86	$4.55
Extraordinary credit	-0-	-0-	.45
Net income	$4.35	$5.86	$5.00
Fully diluted:			
Income before extraordinary credit	$4.18	$5.56	$4.33
Extraordinary credit	-0-	-0-	.42
Net income	$4.18	$5.56	$4.75
Dividends	$1.72	$1.61	$1.50
Average number of Common Shares outstanding	26,377,422	25,925,648	25,842,855

Next, other operating expenses, basically selling and administrative expenses, are subtracted from gross profit to arrive at *operating income*. Then, other revenue and expense items, such as interest income and expense, are computed, and a figure for income before income tax is finally obtained. In the sample multiple-step statement, income taxes are subtracted earlier than they normally would be.

In both the single-step form and the multiple-step form, the effects of extraordinary gains or losses, occurring not as a result of the usual line of operations of the firm, are reported in the last step. This approach is taken because such items are believed to present a

Consolidated Statement of Income
(In thousands of dollars, except per share data)
Knight-Ridder Newspapers, Inc.

	Year Ended December 31	
	1979	1978
Operating Revenue		
Newspaper advertising		
Retail	$391,436	$361,553
General	99,751	85,362
Classified	243,805	215,261
Total	734,992	662,176
Cash discounts	(4,912)	(6,365)
Net advertising	730,080	655,811
Circulation	186,859	173,590
Broadcasting	26,759	19,615
Other	36,221	29,859
Total Operating Revenue	979,919	878,875
Operating Costs		
Labor and employee benefits	379,368	343,145
Newsprint, ink and supplements	237,622	214,121
Other operating costs	179,589	156,777
Depreciation and amortization	26,327	21,821
Total Operating Costs	822,906	735,864
Operating Income	157,013	143,011
Other Income (EXPENSE)		
Interest income	5,332	3,585
Interest expense, principally on long-term debt	(4,440)	(3,147)
Other, net	1,834	2,864
Total	2,726	3,302
Income before income taxes	159,739	146,313
Income taxes	71,379	69,557
Net Income	$ 88,360	$ 76,756
Net Income per Common and Common Equivalent Share	$ 2.69	$ 2.34

false picture of the results that can be expected from a firm's continued operation. The sample income statement for Eaton Corporation has an extraordinary credit in 1978.

Although a sample of the statement of changes in financial position for Eaton Corporation and its subsidiaries appears at the end of this special topic, it will not be explained in any more detail here. Students who wish to obtain further information regarding statements of retained earnings or statements of changes in financial position should consult the following references.

SELECTED REFERENCES

Meigs, Walter B.; Mosich, A. N.; and Johnson, Charles E. *Accounting: The Basis for Business Decisions.* 3d ed. New York: McGraw-Hill, 1972.

Meigs, Walter B.; Mosich, A.N.; Johnson, Charles E.; and Keller, Thomas F. *Intermediate Accounting.* 3d ed. New York: McGraw-Hill, 1974.

Simons, Harry. *Intermediate Accounting: A Comprehensive Volume.* 6th ed. Revised by Jay M. Smith Jr., and K. Fred Skausen. Cincinnati, Ohio: South-Western Publishing, 1977.

Statements of Consolidated Changes in Financial Position
Eaton Corporation and Subsidiaries

Year Ended December 31	1980	1979	1978
	(Thousands of Dollars)		
Source of Working Capital			
Income before extraordinary credit	$115,784	$153,264	$119,292
Items included not affecting working capital:			
Depreciation and amortization	89,521	86,247	64,620
Amortization and write-off intangible assets	6,601	7,128	15,427
Noncurrent deferred income taxes and certain other liabilities	24,984	22,539	23,561
Earnings of finance subsidiaries and associate companies	(13,777)	(8,648)	(5,921)
Exchange (gain) loss on noncurrent accounts—net	(2,491)	5,437	18,813
Provided From Operations Exclusive of Extraordinary Credit	220,622	265,967	235,792
Extraordinary credit	-0-	-0-	11,584
Provided From Operations	220,622	265,967	247,376
Long-term borrowings	147,868	257,111	277,865
Disposals of property, plant and equipment	9,975	5,511	6,999
Sale of Common Shares under stock option plans	6,345	3,933	4,793
Net noncurrent assets of businesses sold	1,935	7,402	11,950
Issuance of Common Shares in acquisitions of businesses	12	2,650	3,350
Other—net	9,723	(18,483)	(5,198)
	396,480	524,091	547,135
Use of Working Capital			
Prepayments and current maturities of long-term debt and other long-term liabilities	240,588	361,958	87,834
Expenditures for property, plant and equipment	141,273	135,200	99,491
Cash dividends	46,435	43,083	40,365
Acquisitions of businesses, less working capital acquired	2,433	11,706	179,277
Purchase of shares for treasury	-0-	10,751	10,527
	430,729	562,698	417,494
(Decrease) Increase in Working Capital	$(34,249)	$(38,607)	129,641
Changes in Components of Working Capital			
Current asset increase (decrease):			
Cash	$(11,820)	$(10,044)	$(696)
Short-term securities	3,195	(89,430)	(7,387)
Accounts receivable	(22,624)	(36,785)	254,527
Inventories	(63,868)	63,174	197,055
Other current assets	(2,302)	4,089	26,268
Current liability (increase) decrease:			
Short-term debt	21,804	(1,462)	(9,838)
Trade payables	11,881	(32,792)	(69,780)
Payrolls and other accruals	648	(55,451)	(92,104)
Income and other taxes	25,274	(28,473)	(15,169)
Current portion of long-term debt	3,563	148,567	(153,235)
(Decrease) Increase in Working Capital	$(34,249)	$(38,607)	$129,641

PART SEVEN

THE
ECONOMICS OF
PRODUCT
AND
INPUT MARKETS

C H A P T E R   20

PERFECTLY
COMPETITIVE
MARKETS

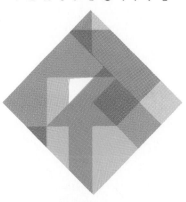

COMPETITION AND THE FREE MARKET IDEOLOGY

"I don't meet competition, I crush it!" This statement, attributed to Charles Revson, of Revlon cosmetics, seems to capture the popular meaning of the word competition. *In everyday language,* competition *means rivalry between individuals or groups. Boxers compete with their rivals; so do football teams, political parties, and many business firms.*

In the language of economics, competition has a very different meaning, especially when it is modified by the adjective perfect. *A perfectly competitive market is a market with such a large number of buyers and sellers that no single buyer or seller can have an effect on the market price. All market participants take the going price of a product as given and adjust their purchases and sales in accordance with that price. The combined effect of their separate decisions is what determines market price. Thus there are no moves to crush one's competition, because the competitors in the market are all equally powerless.*

The essence of the perfectly competitive model is freedom—the freedom of buyers and sellers to decide how much of a given product they will purchase or supply. It includes the freedom of inves-

tors to place their resources in the industries that they find the most attractive in terms of profit. There is no government interference in a perfectly competitive market, and there are no large and powerful firms. Such a market is the essence of the laissez-faire ideal governed by Adam Smith's "invisible hand"; it is the epitome of the notion of the free market.

Many economists advocate free markets as the best solution to a society's problems of production and distribution. Milton Friedman, co-author of the bestseller Free to Choose and winner of a Nobel Prize in economics, is perhaps the most well-known economist staunchly supporting the free market ideal. Being for free markets goes hand-in-hand with being against government intervention in economic activities, but it seldom goes hand-in-hand with limiting private economic power.

The perfectly competitive market is the model of the free market that is almost always implicitly assumed to exist by economists who compare the virtues of competition with the vice of government intervention. But do many markets conform to the perfectly competitive model? Certainly, Revson's does not, or he would know that "crushing" his competition is impossible. (Revlon operates in a market characterized by oligopoly—fewness of firms—a subject discussed in Chapter 22.) Yet Friedman would say that the model of perfect competition is a close approximation of many markets: "But as I have studied economic activities in the United States, I have become increasingly impressed with how wide is the range of problems for which it is appropriate to treat the economy as if it were competitive."[1]

The reactions of other economists to Friedman's statement range from total agreement to violent opposition. However, one thing all economists have in common is a knowledge of how the ideal market of perfect competition is supposed to work. Whether one becomes a critic or a champion of the free market, understanding economists' arguments about it requires familiarity with the perfectly competitive model, the subject of this chapter.

---

1. Milton Friedman, *Capitalism and Freedom* (Chicago: University of Chicago Press, 1962), p. 120.

WHAT THIS CHAPTER IS ABOUT

In this chapter and the next two chapters we will direct our attention to how firms react within different types of market structures.□ As we will see, the constraints imposed by the type of industry structure in which a firm exists affect the firm's profit-maximizing opportunities and, consequently, its behavior.

Economists have separated all the possible market structures into four broad types: perfect competition, monopolistic competition, oligopoly, and monopoly. Our discussion will begin with perfect competition, a market structure that many economists consider "ideal," in that it promotes economic efficiency in several ways. As we will see later, it is the standard by which the performance of all other industry structures is measured.

CHARACTERISTICS
OF PERFECT
COMPETITION

The characteristics of a **perfectly competitive industry** are:

1. There are many firms in the industry, and the market for the product has a large number of independently acting buyers and sellers.
2. The products of all firms are identical (homogeneous).
3. Because of items 1 and 2, each firm accepts the price for its product as given by the interaction of the market demand for and supply of the product.
4. There is free movement of resources into and out of the industry, including free entry and exit of firms in the long run.
5. Buyers and sellers have perfect knowledge of existing market conditions.

Each of these points will be discussed here.

A perfectly competitive industry is characterized, first of all, by many firms producing identical products. Because no firm's product has any distinguishing characteristics to make people prefer it over the product of any other firm in the industry, and because each firm is quite small relative to the entire market, all the firms accept the selling price as a given. In other words, a perfectly competitive firm accepts the equilibrium price determined by the industry supply of and demand for its product. It considers its primary decision variable to be the level of output it will produce. This type of firm is called a price taker.

The firm accepts the market price for two reasons. First, if it were to try to charge a price higher than the market price, it would not have any customers. Why? Because a large number of other firms will sell at the market price, and buyers will purchase from these firms. Second, it has no need to charge a price lower than the market price, because a large number of buyers (more than it can possibly supply) are willing to buy the product at the going market price.

When a firm can sell all that it wishes to at the going market price, price or average revenue◻ is constant. In this case, price is equal to marginal revenue,◻ because the sale of additional units does not require a lowering of price. Thus the additional revenue or marginal revenue received from selling one more unit of output is just equal to its price. For example, if a farmer can sell as many bushels of wheat as desired at a price of $4 per bushel, then the additional revenue received from selling one more bushel of wheat will be $4.

Since price is constant, the demand curve ◻ for a perfectly competitive firm's product is a horizontal line at the going market price, as shown in panel (a) of Figure 20–1. Panel (b) shows how the equilibrium price◻ is deter-mined by the industry supply and demand curves. The horizontal axis of the industry graph uses a scale of thousands of units to in-dicate that the total industry output is much larger than the output of a single firm.

Moreover, in a perfectly competitive indus-try, over the long run all the factors of produc-tion,◻ including entire firms, can freely move into or out of the industry. There are no bar-riers to entry or exit and no artificial limita-tions on the movement of resources. Finally, each firm is assumed to be fully informed of the current market price and of its own cost structure.

One industry that approximates perfect competition is farming. Imagine, for example, a small midwestern farm. The farm owner must accept whatever price is determined by the market demand for and supply of wheat, corn, beef, or whatever. Moreover, one farm's wheat, corn, or beef looks very much like another's, so there is no reason for con-sumers to prefer the produce of any particular farm. Finally, although entry into farming is becoming increasingly difficult, it is still pos-sible to purchase and profitably operate a farm (at least some of the time).

Although farming approximates perfect com-petition, it is not a true example of a perfectly competitive industry. The reason is that farm-

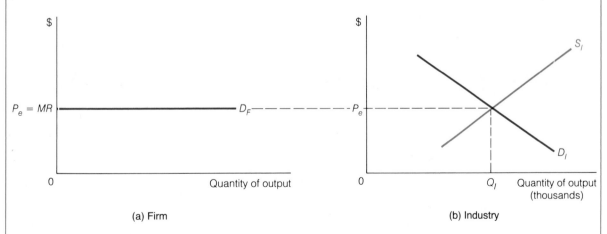

(a) Firm   (b) Industry

FIGURE 20–1   **The Demand Curve for a Perfectly Competitive Firm**

The market price is determined by the industry supply and demand for a product (panel b). The individual firm demand curve is then a horizontal line at the equilibrium market price, P_e, since the firm takes the price as given.

ers do not always act independently in the marketplace; instead they react to government policies such as acreage allotments and subsidies. Indeed, in the United States, the federal government purchases a good deal of farm output and is a major factor on the buyer's side of the market. (See Chapter 33 for more on this subject.)

PROFIT-MAXIMIZING
DECISION RULES

◆

As discussed in Chapter 18, a firm operates in two time frames. It must make short-run◻ decisions constrained by fixed plant sizes or other fixed inputs. In the long run,◻ however, it may adjust the amounts of all its inputs according to what it believes will be their optimal levels. Thus a firm makes its short-run profit-maximizing◻ decisions on the basis of its short-run costs. When it can change the quantities of all its inputs, its long-run costs become relevant. We will now examine the decision rules a purely competitive firm should follow to maximize profit in both the short run and the long run.

MAXIMIZING PROFIT IN THE SHORT RUN

We saw in Chapter 19 that a firm will maximize profit (or minimize losses) in the short run by producing its goods or services up to the point where marginal revenue◻ is equal to short-run marginal cost,◻ as long as price is greater than or equal to short run average variable cost. If price is less than average variable cost, the firm should shut down, because its revenues will not cover even its variable production costs,◻ much less its variable and fixed costs.◻

The same short-run profit-maximizing rule holds for the perfectly competitive firm. However, because price is equal to marginal revenue in this case, the perfectly competitive firm will maximize profit or minimize losses in the short run by producing its goods or services at the point where price equals marginal revenue equals short-run marginal cost, as long as price is greater than or equal to average variable cost◻ (see Figure 20–2). Recall that the firm's economic profit in the short run, if any, will be equal to $(P^* - SAC^*) \times Q^*$, where Q^* is the profit-maximizing level of output and P^* and SAC^* are the corresponding values of price and short-run

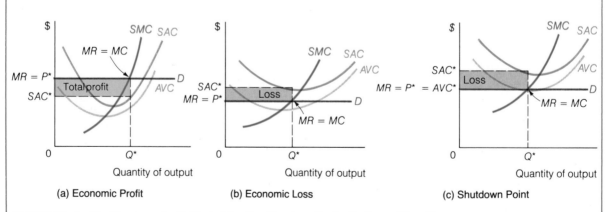

FIGURE 20–2 **The Short-run Profit-Maximizing Position for a Perfectly Competitive Firm**

The perfectly competitive firm will maximize profit (or minimize its loss) in the short run by producing where price (P) is equal to short-run marginal cost (SMC), as long as price is greater than or equal to average variable cost (AVC). If price is greater than short-run average cost (SAC), an economic profit will be made (panel a). If price is less than short-run average cost, an economic loss will be incurred (panel b). The shut-down point is reached where price is equal to minimum average variable cost (panel c).

average cost.□ In panel (a) of Figure 20–2, price is greater than short-run average cost at the profit-maximizing level of output, and the firm is making an economic profit. In panel (b), P^* is less than SAC^*, and the firm is minimizing its short-run losses. In panel (c), $P^* = AVC^*$, and the firm is at the shutdown point. If the price falls any lower, the firm will cease operations, at least temporarily.

The short-run supply curve for a perfectly competitive firm can now be obtained. First, however, note that if the going market price rises or falls, the new profit-maximizing level of output will be given by the level of output where price is once again equal to short-run marginal cost, assuming that price is greater than or equal to average variable cost.

Because the firm's short-run marginal cost curve indicates the profit-maximizing (or loss-minimizing) quantity of output at each possible price greater than or equal to average variable cost, it also represents the firm's short-run supply curve. The only exception to this rule is that at prices below minimum average variable cost (where SMC intersects AVC), the firm will shut down and produce nothing. Figure 20–3 shows the short-run supply curve for a perfectly competitive firm.

> The **short-run supply curve** of the perfectly competitive firm is its short-run marginal cost curve, where short-run marginal cost is greater than average variable cost.

For example, Table 20–1 gives revenue and cost data for Golden Ears Farm, which grows corn. If Golden Ears expects the price of corn to be $3 per bushel, it will maximize profit by producing corn where price (equal to marginal revenue) equals marginal cost, or at 20,000 bushels of corn. This point is illustrated in Figure 20–4. (The farm will also have the same total profit at 15,000 bushels of corn, because the marginal profit of the 15,001st through the 20,000th bushel is zero.)

If the market price increases to $4, the firm will maximize profit by producing where $P = MC = \$4$, or 25,000 bushels of corn. If the

market price falls to $2, the firm will produce the level of output where $P = MC = \$2$, provided that MC exceeds the price at higher levels of output. In Table 20–1 marginal cost is $2 for production of two different outputs, 5,000 bushels and 15,000 bushels. However, it falls to $1 from 5,000 to 10,000 bushels, so that marginal profit (now $2 − \$1$) is positive at the $2 price. Thus the firm will increase output to 15,000 bushels. Beyond this level, marginal cost exceeds $2, so more output will not be produced.

Finally, if the price falls to $1 per bushel, the firm will not produce at all, because price will be less than average variable cost. In this case the firm cannot even cover the variable costs of production, because the average variable cost in the table never falls below $1.50.

The **industry supply curve** is obtained by horizontally summing the supply curves of the individual firms. This type of summation simply involves adding together the quantities that each firm is willing to supply at each price.

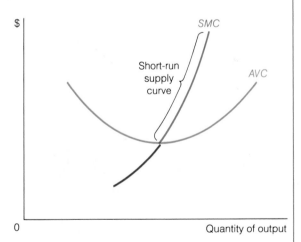

FIGURE 20–3 The Perfectly Competitive Firm's Short-run Supply Curve

The perfectly competitive firm maximizes profit (or minimizes its loss) in the short run by producing where price (P) is equal to short-run marginal cost (SMC), as long as price is greater than or equal to average variable cost (AVC). Thus, the firm's short-run supply curve is given by the short-run marginal cost curve above the point where it intersects the average variable cost curve.

TABLE 20-1 Revenue and Cost Data for Golden Ears Farm

Bushels of Corn (Q)	Price (P)	Total Revenue (TR)	Marginal Revenue $\left(MR = \dfrac{\text{change in } TR}{\text{change in } Q}\right)$	Marginal Cost $\left(SMC = \dfrac{\text{change in } TC}{\text{change in } Q}\right)$	Marginal Profit $(M_\pi = MR - MC)$	Total Cost (TC)	Total Variable Cost (TVC)	Average Variable Cost $(AVC = TVC/Q)$	Total Profit $(T\pi = TR - TC)$
	$3	$ 0				$ 5,000	$	Not defined	$ -5,000
			$3	$2	$1				
5,000	3	15,000				15,000	10,000	$2.00	0
			3	1	2				
10,000	3	30,000				20,000	15,000	1.50	10,000
			3	2	1				
15,00C	3	45,000				30,000	25,000	1.67	15,000
			3	3	0				
20,000	3	60,000				45,000	40,000	2.00	15,000
			3	4	-1				
25,000	3	75,000				65,000	60,000	2.40	10,000
			3	5	-2				
30,000	3	90,000				90,000	85,000	2.83	0

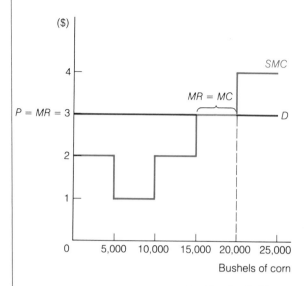

FIGURE 20-4 **Profit-Maximizing Position for Golden Ears Farm**

The demand curve is a horizontal line at $3, since price is constant and equal to $3. Golden Ears Farm will maximize profit by producing where price (equal to marginal revenue) equals short-run marginal cost (SMC), or 20,000 bushels of corn.

TABLE 20-2 **Derivation of Industry Supply Schedule for Corn**

Golden Ears Farm		Industry	
Price	Quantity Supplied (Bushels of Corn)	Price	Quantity Supplied (Bushels of Corn)
$0	0	$0	0
2	15,000	2	15,000,000
3	20,000	3	20,000,000
4	25,000	4	25,000,000
5	30,000	· 5	30,000,000

will maximize its profit by producing its goods or services up to the point where price (equal to marginal revenue) is equal to long-run marginal cost,□ as long as price is greater than or equal to long-run average cost.□ As discussed in Chapter 19, if a profit-maximizing firm cannot earn at least a normal profit□ (where $P = LAC$) in the long run, it will go out of business in its current line of production and its owner's resources will be shifted to activities that yield at least a normal profit. However, it is not possible for a perfectly competitive firm to earn an above normal or economic profit over a period of time sufficiently long to enable other firms to enter the industry. We will soon see why.

The **short-run supply curve of a perfectly competitive industry** is the horizontal sum of the firms' short-run supply curves.

For example, assume that Golden Ears Farm is only one of a thousand identical farms that grow corn. It follows that the industry output will be 1,000 times greater than the quantity supplied by Golden Ears Farm at each possible price. Thus the industry supply schedule can be derived by multiplying the quantity supplied by Golden Ears Farm at each price by 1,000, as shown in Table 20-2.

MAXIMIZING PROFIT IN THE LONG RUN

In the long run a firm is able to vary all its factors of production, so that it should be able to achieve a least cost combination of inputs. □ (The firm is assumed to be able to predict its optimal level of output correctly in the long run.)

In this case, the perfectly competitive firm

LONG-RUN
INDUSTRY EQUILIBRIUM

Figure 20-5 shows a perfectly competitive firm operating with the optimal size plant for a level of output corresponding to Q^*, maximizing profit by producing where $P = LMC$, and earning an economic profit. However, such a situation cannot be maintained indefinitely, because these higher than normal profits will attract new firms into the industry.[1]

---

1. The prices of factors of production are assumed to remain constant as industry output expands. This assumption is relaxed in the next section.

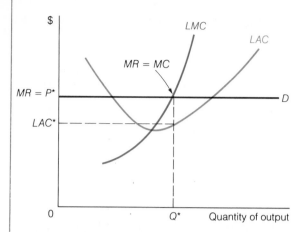

FIGURE 20–5   A Temporary Profit-Maximizing Position for a Perfectly Competitive Firm

The perfectly competitive firm will attempt to produce in the long run where price is equal to long-run marginal cost (LMC), as long as price is greater than or equal to long-run average cost (LAC). However, if price is greater than long-run average cost, an economic profit will be made, and this situation will encourage new firms to enter the industry.

The entry of new firms will cause the industry short-run supply curve to shift downward, which will result in a lower price. This pro-

cess will continue until all firms are earning only a normal profit.

The beginning and end of this process are shown in Figure 20–6. At P_1, established by the industry demand and supply curves, D and S_1, the firm is earning an economic profit. After the entry of new firms, the short-run industry supply curve shifts to S_2, the equilibrium price is P_e, and the firm is earning a normal profit. At this point there is no particular incentive for new firms to enter the industry.

Figure 20–7 shows the position of the perfectly competitive firm when the industry is in long-run equilibrium once more. In this situation the firm will always be producing where $P = MR = LMC = $ minimum LAC. Price must be equal to long-run marginal cost for the firm to be in its long-run profit-maximizing position. Moreover, price must be equal to long-run average cost for the firm to earn a normal profit. The only point where both of these conditions can hold is where long-run marginal cost is equal to long-run average cost, at minimum LAC.

Figure 20–8 shows the reverse process. Perhaps as the result of a recent decrease in de-

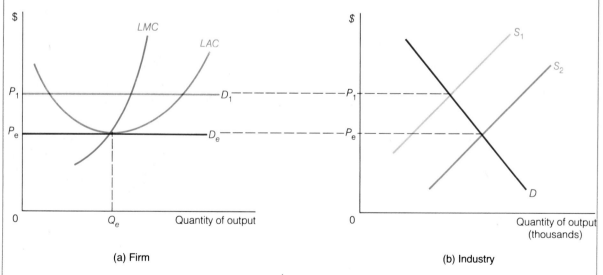

(a) Firm

(b) Industry

FIGURE 20–6   Entry of New Firms Eliminating Economic Profits in a Perfectly Competitive Industry

The presence of economic profit encourages new firms to enter the industry. As a result, the industry supply curve shifts downward from S_1 to S_2 (panel b), and the equilibrium price falls from P_1 to P_e.

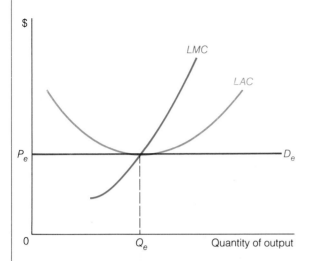

$

LMC

LAC

P_e ——————————————— D_e

0   Q_e Quantity of output

FIGURE 20-7   The Position of the Perfectly Competitive Firm in Long-run Industry Equilibrium

When a perfectly competitive industry is in equilibrium, a firm will produce where price (P) is equal to long-run marginal cost (LMC) and minimum long-run average cost (LAC). At this point, the firm maximizes profit since price is equal to long-run marginal cost. Also, since price is equal to long-run average cost, no economic profits or losses exist so there is no incentive for firms to enter or leave the industry.

mand for the product, the market price is initially established by the intersection of D and S_1, at P_1, which is below the minimum LAC. At this point, because firms are earning less than normal profits, they will begin to leave the industry, causing the industry supply curve to shift leftward. Eventually, the long-run industry equilibrium will be restored at the intersection of D and S_2, at P_e.

LONG-RUN INDUSTRY SUPPLY CURVE

The shape of the long-run supply curve for a perfectly competitive industry depends on how input prices behave as the industry output expands.

*If input prices remain constant as industry output increases, the industry is called a **constant cost industry**.*

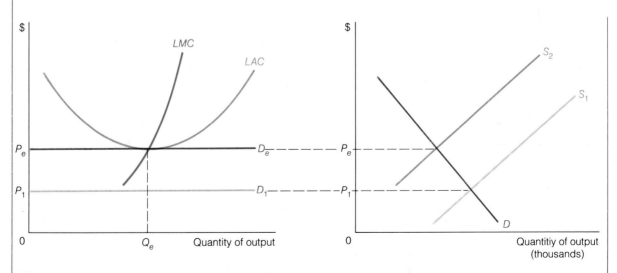

FIGURE 20-8   Exit of Firms Making Possible a Normal Return in a Perfectly Competitive Industry

At price P_1, price is less than long-run average cost (LAC), so firms are incurring economic losses. As a result, some firms leave the industry, and the industry supply curve shifts upward from S_1 to S_2. A new price of P_e is established. Industry equilibrium will occur at price P_e, since firms will receive a normal profit, but no economic profit.

*If input prices rise as industry output increases, the industry is called an **increasing cost industry.***

*If input prices fall as industry output rises, the industry is called a **decreasing cost industry.***

Each of these cases will be discussed here.

CONSTANT COST INDUSTRY

In a constant cost industry, input prices do not change as the industry output expands or contracts. In this case, the long-run average cost curve for an individual firm does not shift as industry output rises. Consequently, the long-run industry equilibrium will always occur at the same price, P_e, which is equal to minimum LAC, as shown in Figure 20–7.

If the industry demand curve shifts outward, initially causing price to rise above P_e, firms will be earning an economic profit. □ The existence of above normal profits will entice new firms to enter the industry. This process, illustrated in Figure 20–9, will continue until the price is once again driven down to P_e. In the figure, D_1 is the original industry demand curve, and S_1 is the original industry short-run supply curve. P_e is the equilibrium price.

Suppose now that demand increases to D_2, resulting in a price rise to P_2. The price increase allows firms currently in the industry to earn an economic profit. The presence of economic profit tempts new firms to enter the industry until the short-run supply curve shifts outward to S_2, which intersects D_2 at P_e. At this point the industry is producing a larger total quantity at the original price, P_e. Thus the industry long-run supply curve is a horizontal line, S_L, at price P_e.

INCREASING COST INDUSTRY

In an increasing cost industry, input prices rise as industry output increases. Input prices

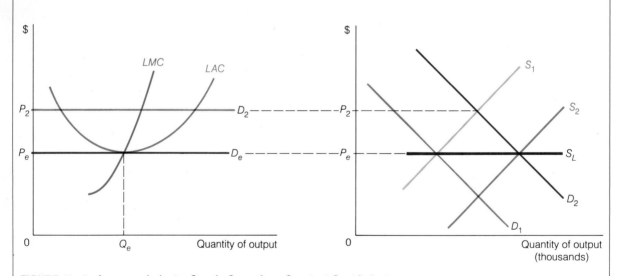

FIGURE 20–9   Long-run Industry Supply Curve for a Constant Cost Industry

The long-run supply curve (S_L) is a horizontal line for a constant cost, perfectly competitive industry. This point can be shown as follows. Suppose industry demand increases from D_1 to D_2. Initially, the price will increase from P_e to P_2. However, at a price of P_2, firms can obtain an economic profit. As a result, new firms will enter the industry, causing the industry short-run supply curve to shift from S_1 to S_2. An equilibrium position will be reached when price is once again equal to P_e, since firms will receive a normal profit, but no economic profit.

rise because as industry output expands, firms compete for inputs, thereby bidding up their prices. The rising input prices cause the long-run average cost curve for each firm to shift upward. This phenomenon happens periodically in the construction industry when a prolonged increase in building activity causes the price of inputs such as concrete to rise.

Remember that the LAC curve shows how cost per unit of output changes as the level of output changes for an individual firm. Its shape reflects economies and diseconomies of scale, ▫ but input prices are assumed to remain constant.

However, when an entire industry is expanding, the demand for these inputs is greatly increased. In an increasing cost industry, a rise in input prices will result, causing an upward shift in the LAC curve for each

firm. In this case the new equilibrium price will be higher.

Figure 20–10 illustrates this process. At price P_1, a firm and its industry are in a long-run equilibrium determined by the intersection of the industry demand and short-run supply curves, D_1 and S_1. If industry demand rises to D_2, the price will rise initially to P', so that the firms in the industry will be making an economic profit.

However, two things will then happen. First, the presence of economic profit will cause new firms to enter the industry and the short-run supply curve to shift outward. Second, as industry output expands, the prices of inputs will rise, causing the LAC curve for each firm to shift upward.

The new equilibrium will occur at a point such as P_2 in Figure 20–10, where a new

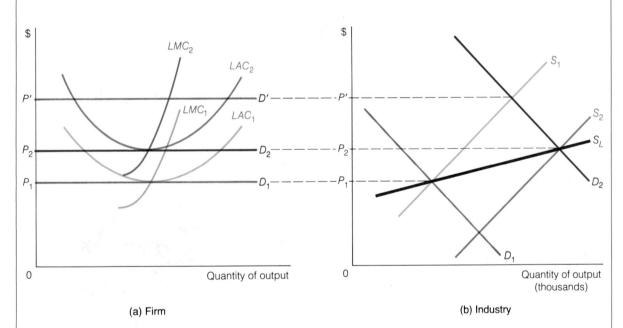

(a) Firm

(b) Industry

FIGURE 20–10 **Long-run Industry Supply Curve for an Increasing Cost Industry**

The long-run supply curve (S_L) for an increasing cost industry is upward sloping. This point can be shown as follows. The original firm demand curve, long-run marginal cost curve, and long-run average cost curve are D_1, LMC_1, and LAC_1, respectively. If industry demand shifts to D_2, the price will increase initially to P'. However, at this price economic profits exist, so that new firms are enticed to enter the industry. As a result of the entry of new firms, the short-run industry supply curve shifts downward to S_2. Simultaneously, the expansion of industry output results in rising input prices. Consequently, firm cost curves shift upward to LMC_2 and LAC_2. Eventually, a new equilibrium could be reached at a price such as P_2, where once again no economic profits or losses exist. Note that the new equilibrium price, P_2, is higher than the initial equilibrium price, P_1.

short-run industry supply curve, S_2, inter-sects D_2 at P_2, which is equal to minimum long-run average cost on a new, higher LAC curve. In this case the long-run industry sup-ply curve, S_L, slopes upward. Consequently, *in an increasing cost industry, a greater level of output will be supplied only at higher prices.*

DECREASING COST INDUSTRY

Input prices fall in a decreasing cost industry as industry output expands. This drop fre-quently occurs as a result of economies of scale in the industries that produce the in-puts, such as component parts. Although not perfectly competitive, the electronics industry is an example of a decreasing cost industry. Typically, the price of newly developed in-puts such as microcircuits or chips falls dra-matically once these parts become available in mass quantities. Decreases in input prices are one reason that in the recent past the prices of such products as calculators and digital watches have fallen markedly.

In this situation the long-run average cost curve shifts downward for a firm as industry output increases. In this case, firms are will-ing to supply larger quantities at a lower price, and the long-run industry supply curve is downward sloping. This result is the oppo-site of that obtained for an increasing cost in-dustry.

We frequently observe this phenomenon in relatively new industries, such as those of color televisions, calculators, digital watches, and video recorders. As industry output rises, prices of component parts fall; the firms in the industry are therefore willing to supply a larger quantity at a lower price.

PERFECT COMPETITION: WHY THE IDEAL?

The beginning of this chapter noted that econ-omists generally view perfect competition as an ideal market structure. Why is this so? Be-cause in long-run industry equilibrium, the perfectly competitive firm produces where price equals long-run marginal cost equals long-run average cost, which represents an optimal, or best, allocation of productive re-sources.

What is an optimal allocation of resources? To economists it is an allocation that will maximize society's welfare given the amount of productive resources available at any point in time. Resources are optimally allocated when the benefit society receives from the last unit produced of a given product is identical to the benefit that would be forgone (lost) if more resources were switched from other products to the given product.

*The social benefit added by the last unit of a good or service produced is called its **marginal social benefit.***

*The cost to society of using resources to pro-duce an additional unit of this product, rather than something else, is called its **marginal social cost.***

To maximize social welfare, a society should produce each good or service up to the point where its marginal social benefit (MSB) is equal to its marginal social cost (MSC). Only then will resources be optimally allocated.

It has been argued that perfect competition automatically accomplishes this goal. How-ever, the argument is not without its qualifi-cations, as indicated here.

P = LMC

We have already seen that freedom of entry as-sures that over the long run $P = LMC = LAC$ for each firm in a perfectly competitive indus-try. If we assume for the moment that the price of a product represents its marginal social ben-efit, we can argue that the result under perfect competition is $MSB = LMC$. If we also assume that the marginal cost of the product to the firm represents its marginal social cost, we then have *MSB = MSC* as an automatic result of perfect competition. Consequently, because a perfectly competitive firm produces its goods or services up to the point where price is equal to long-run marginal cost, it also produces them where *MSB = MSC*. Such a situation represents an optimal allocation of resources, because production of this item could not be altered to achieve a positive net benefit to society.

Of course, this result depends on the equality of price with MSB and the equality of LMC with MSC. These two assumptions will be qualified in a later section of this chapter.

P = MINIMUM LAC

The perfectly competitive firm in long-run industry equilibrium is producing a level of output that is consistent with minimum long-run average cost. In other words, the output of the industry is being produced in the cheapest possible way. Moreover, since *P* = minimum *LAC*, consumers are paying the lowest possible price consistent with a normal profit for the firms.

SOME QUALIFICATIONS

We must qualify, to some extent, the image of the perfectly competitive industry as the ideal market structure. These qualifications center around the questions of economies of scale, the distribution of income, and externalities.

ECONOMIES OF SCALE

If the technology associated with the production of some item makes possible large economies of scale, □ it may not be possible for an industry to be perfectly competitive and for its firms to be producing at minimum LAC. Only a few firms producing at minimum LAC may supply enough output to satisfy the total quantity demanded in the market. The automobile industry is an example. Long-run average cost is said to decrease markedly in automobile assembly plants with production capacities of up to about 250,000 cars per year. If there were many small auto manufacturers instead of just a few large ones, each firm would likely have assembly plants producing fewer than 250,000 cars per year, and production costs would be higher. Consumers would not benefit from the cost reductions provided by economies of scale. (Chapter 18 noted that Chrysler's cost per car tends to be higher than that of General Motors because Chrysler produces lower levels of output and therefore cannot take full advantage of economies of scale.) The same argument applies in certain other industries, such as steel and electric power generation.

DISTRIBUTION OF INCOME

Furthermore, a perfectly competitive market structure allocates resources efficiently only for a particular distribution of income. The preferences expressed in the market are made possible because of the incomes of the participants. If the distribution of income were changed, the preferences might also change.

What is the best distribution of income? That depends on one's point of view, which often depends on one's relative income level. Someone in an upper income bracket is probably satisfied with the status quo. Someone in a lower income bracket may not be so content. At any rate, economists have no objective answer to the question of what represents the optimal distribution of income.

EXTERNALITIES

Externalities come in the form of either social benefits or social costs.

An **external social benefit** is a benefit obtained by some person or group of people other than the ones who purchased the product or service in question.

For example, if an exclusive golf course were built across from our house, it would probably increase the value of our property as well as that of our neighbors. The increase in value represents an external social benefit of the golf course.

On the other hand, if one of our neighbors were to turn the property next door into a commercial junkyard, property values in our neighborhood would probably decline substantially. This decline represents an external social cost.

An **external social cost** is a cost borne by those not directly connected with producing, selling, or purchasing a particular good or service.

If external benefits or costs are connected with the production, sale, or use of some good or service, then we can no longer assume that its price represents its marginal social benefit or that its marginal cost represents its marginal social cost. Consequently, in this situation we also cannot say that a perfectly competitive market structure results in an optimal allocation of resources from a social point of view.

DOES PERFECT COMPETITION EXIST?

◆

It is doubtful that any large industry in the United States meets all the requirements for perfect competition. Certain sectors of agriculture, particularly the small family farm, probably come closest.

Why, then, do we bother to study perfect competition? First of all, it does seem to help explain what happens in certain cases, such as agriculture. Second, many economists consider perfect competition to be the ideal industry structure. Therefore, it can be used as a standard by which to measure the performance of other market structures. It can also be used to obtain guidelines for establishing price ceilings and other government regulations for more concentrated industries (industries with fewer firms).

SUMMARY

1. This chapter has examined perfect competition, the first of four general market structures to be discussed in this book. Perfect competition is characterized by many firms producing identical products. Consequently, each firm accepts the market price of its product as a given. Moreover, in a perfectly competitive market, resources are mobile and firms can move freely into or out of the industry.

2. The profit-maximizing decision rules that a perfectly competitive firm should follow vary slightly between the long run and the short run. In the short run the perfectly competitive firm will maximize profit by producing where $P = MR = SMC$, as long as price is greater than or equal to average variable cost. Consequently, the firm's short-run supply curve is given by its SMC curve above minimum average variable cost. In the long run the perfectly competitive firm maximizes profit by producing where $P = MR = LMC$, as long as price is greater than or equal to long-run average cost. The firm's long-run supply curve is its LMC curve above minimum long-run average cost.

3. However, if the firms in a perfectly competitive market are earning an economic profit, new firms will enter the industry, thereby driving the price down. If the firms are earning less than a normal profit, some of them will leave the industry, which will result in a price increase. Thus, for industry equilibrium to exist, each firm must be earning a normal profit. At this level, each will be producing goods or services up to the point where $P = MR = LMC = $ Minimum LAC.

4. The shape of the long-run industry supply curve for a perfectly competitive industry depends on whether it is a constant cost, increasing cost, or decreasing cost industry. In a constant cost industry the long-run supply curve is a horizontal line at the price equal to minimum long-run average cost for the firm.

5. In an increasing cost industry an expansion of the output of the industry causes input prices to rise, which results in an upward shift in each firm's long-run average cost curve. In this case the long-run industry supply curve is upward sloping.

6. In a decreasing cost industry an expansion in industry output results in falling input prices, and the firms' LAC curves shift downward. In this situation the industry's long-run supply curve is downward sloping.

7. Economists consider the perfectly competitive industry to be the ideal market structure for two reasons. First, each firm maximizes its profit by producing where $P = MC$. Given certain assumptions, this point is where marginal social benefit is equal to marginal social cost. Moreover, when the industry is in long-run equilibrium, each firm produces where $P = $ Minimum LAC. At this point each firm is earning only a normal return, and the output of the industry is being produced as cheaply as is possible.

8. There are some qualifications to this evaluation of a perfectly competitive industry. First, the above conditions may not hold in the presence of externalities or economies of scale. Second, a perfectly competitive industry gives an optimal allocation of resources only on the basis of a particular distribution of income.

9. Not too many industries in the United States are perfectly competitive. Farming is probably one of the closest approximations to perfect competition, though. It is still important to understand how a perfectly competitive industry structure works, because this structure is frequently regarded as a standard by which all other types of markets are measured.

IMPORTANT TERMS AND CONCEPTS

Perfectly competitive industry
Price taker
Short-run supply curve
Industry supply curve
Constant cost industry
Increasing cost industry
Decreasing cost industry
Marginal social benefit
Marginal social cost
External social benefit
External social cost

QUESTIONS AND PROBLEMS

1. Give an example of an industry that is perfectly competitive, or at least approximately so.

2. Draw a graph to show the short-run profit-maximizing position of a perfectly competitive firm, and explain it.

3. What is the long-run profit-maximizing position of a perfectly competitive firm?

4. Draw a graph to show the position of a perfectly competitive firm when its industry is in long-run equilibrium, and explain it.

5. What are the characteristics of a perfectly competitive industry?

6. Why do many economists consider perfect competition the ideal market structure? What qualifications to this view should be considered?

7. Why is it important to understand how firms behave in a perfectly competitive market structure?

8. What is the perfectly competitive firm's short-run supply curve?

9. Describe the long-run industry supply curve for a perfectly competitive industry in each of the cases below:
  a. Increasing costs
  b. Decreasing costs
  c. Constant costs
Why is the long-run industry supply curve different in each of these three situations?

10. Why is marginal revenue equal to price for a perfectly competitive firm?

11. The following table gives demand and cost data for a perfectly competitive firm, a small wheat farm. Complete the table and find the profit-maximizing level of output.

Bushels of Wheat	Price per Bushel	Total Revenue	Marginal Revenue	Marginal Cost	Total Cost
0	$4				$10.000
1,000	4				13,000
2,000	4				15,000
3,000	4				16,000
4,000	4				17,000
5,000	4				18,000
6,000	4				20,000
7,000	4				23,000
8,000	4				27,000
9,000	4				32,000
10,000	4				38,000

THOSE
BEEFY PRICES

With a T-bone selling for $17.95 at some Manhattan steakhouses, an aide to New York Mayor Ed Koch proposed that consumers go "beefless" every Wednesday. The gambit drew an angry response from beef-state pols, with Gov. Tom Judge of Montana hinting at a tourist boycott of New York. Koch quickly proposed a truce: he invited Judge to New York, and last week the two men had a steak dinner—on Wednesday. "I'm not advocating a beef boycott," swore Koch. "I assure you I eat beef Monday through Sunday and love it." "That," mooed a Judge aide happily, "is the end of that."

Not quite. Even as Koch and Judge were chewing over the politics of beef, the Labor

Department was calculating its consumer price index for March—and it was enough to give anyone indigestion. For the month, the CPI rose a full 1 per cent, completing a first quarter in which retail prices soared at an annual rate of 13 per cent. And once again, the price of beef was a key culprit, jumping 3.6 per cent in March alone.

A LONG WAIT

Over the last six months, the average retail price of choice beef has increased from $1.88 to a record $2.30 a pound, sparking increasing consumption of other protein products and scattered attempts to buck the trend with consumer boycotts of beef. But as Administration officials from Agriculture Secretary Bob Bergland to anti-inflation czar Alfred Kahn pointed out last week,

there is little that can be done: while the rate of increase may moderate in the months ahead, it will probably be a couple of years before housewives can confront a pound of hamburger in a supermarket without flinching.

The price surge really isn't anybody's fault. Both cattlemen and consumers are dependent on the beef cycle, a delicate, twelve-year pattern that largely determines the price paid at both the ranch and the butcher shop. Prices reach their highest point at the beginning and end of the cycle when the size of the nation's cattle herd is unusually low. Under ideal conditions, ranchers begin to increase the size of their herds to take advantage of high prices—and over a period of six years or so, that growth tends to drive retail prices back down to reasonable levels.

A DISASTER

The last beef cycle began in 1967, when the cattle herd stood at a low 109 million head, but it was disturbed by two unforeseen events. First, just as ranchers were increasing their herds in the early '70s, Richard Nixon engineered the massive Soviet grain deal, which reduced supplies and dramatically pushed up the price of domestic feed grains. Two successive summers of drought drove grain prices even higher; in one six-month period in 1974, for example, the price of feed corn doubled—and the ranchers, who by then had increased the national herd to 132 million head, were taking a terrible beating. "It cost $200 to produce a calf and you could only get $100 for it," remembers Tommy Beall, an economist with the National Cattlemen's Association. "It was like throwing away a $100 bill every time you went to market."

Consumers, of course, were delighted; choice beef was selling at retail for an average of $1.46 a pound in 1974. But the hard-pressed ranchers began what Beall described as "the biggest liquidation in the history of the cattle business," and by early 1979, the herd was down to 111 million head. With the number of steers in feedlots similarly down, the daily beef slaughter fell—and at the meat counter, retail prices began to climb.

Given current price levels, ranchers like Myron Zumbach, who is raising 1,600 head of cattle near Coggon, Iowa, are now in no hurry to flood the market. Back in 1974 and '75, Zumbach's cattle fetched only $32 a hundred weight at the packing plant; now they're selling for $76. He hopes to make enough profit this year to pay off part of the $1 million in debts he accumulated over the past five lean years. Zumbach also has little sympathy for the angry consumers. "Why weren't they eating beef five times a day back in '74?" he asks. "They don't understand that we have to make a profit now to stay in business. If we don't, there won't be meatless Wednesdays, there'll be meatless weeks."

A SHIFT

In fact, Zumbach needn't worry. The New Jersey Legislature last week passed a resolution calling for beefless Wednesdays and there were other scattered efforts at retail boycotts, but they were not having much effect—and demand will probably remain strong at least through the summer barbecue season. Still, some grocery-trade experts say that beef sales have slipped somewhat in recent weeks and supermarket chains report a definite shift to chicken, pork and fish.

That shift was accelerated by campaigns such as the one conducted by Stop & Shop Supermarket, a grocery chain in New England. "Don't beef, switch!" Stop & Shop urged in newspapers ads. "Switch to chicken. Switch to pork, switch to fish, cheese, eggs, rice, nuts, pasta . . ." Stop & Shop also introduced a hamburger alternate composed of 75 per cent beef and 25 per cent soy protein and water that meat sales manager Marty Donohoe said is "starting to show signs of being a big seller." In Atlanta, Betty Jones, shopping at Food Giant, sighed: "I've eaten so much chicken lately I feel that I'm going to fly away." And in southern California, the New Zealand Lamb Co. took advantage of the high price of beef by mounting a campaign to sell imported lamb—at retail prices as much as 52 cents per pound below the cost of American-produced lamb chops.

In Washington, meanwhile, Agriculture Secretary Bergland said, "We're over the hump on meat supplies." But the immutable law of the beef cycle suggests that while prices may stop rising at double-digit rates, there seems to be little hope that beeflation will end any time soon. Most agriculture economists do not expect beef supplies to return to the level of the mid-'70s until 1982 at the earliest. Until then, a growing population with a powerful appetite for beef will serve to keep beef prices high.

QUESTIONS

1. Why was the price of beef relatively high during the spring of 1979?
2. What is the "beef cycle"?
3. Why was the quantity of beef supplied in 1979 low?
4. How were consumers and supermarkets reacting to the higher beef prices?
5. Does this article suggest that cattlemen are "price takers," as the term is explained in this chapter? Explain.

CHAPTER 21

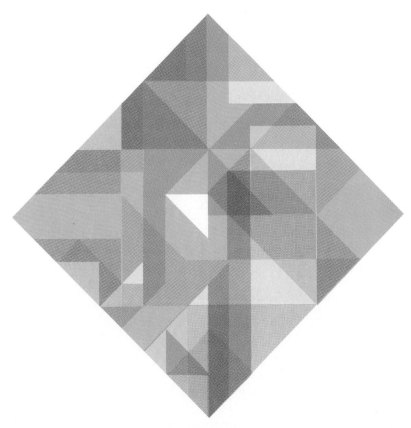

MONOPOLY:
THE CASE
OF A
SINGLE SELLER

THE
IATA
BLUES

IATA is not an opera, a Japanese baseball team, or a rock group. It stands for International Air Transport Association, and it is (or was) a cartel of international airlines. (A cartel is a group of firms that band together to act as a monopoly—to agree on such issues as prices and the division of markets among cartel members. The usual result of cartel activities is the restriction of output or service and an increase in prices paid by consumers.)

IATA was set up in 1945 and had almost exclusive say-so on international (especially European and trans-Atlantic) air fares until the late 1970s. Under U.S. law, the Civil Aeronautics Board (CAB) must approve the rates set by U.S. carriers in agreements with IATA. As a practical matter, this requirement had no relevance until recent years. The CAB's refusal to approve a 1963 international fare hike provides a vivid example of how effective a cartel IATA was. The reaction of other IATA member countries was to threaten to seize the aircraft of U.S. companies that failed to raise rates and dared to land in such countries. Needless to say, the CAB backed down.[1]

1. See H. H. Liebhafsky, *American Government and Business* (New York: Wiley, 1971), pp. 466–467.

Discount air fares (discussed in Chapter 4) were the downfall of IATA, but they proved a bonanza to consumers, hoteliers, tour organizers, and even some of the airlines. In fact, in the summer of 1978, many travelers were happy to camp out in the rain in London to await a discount return seat to the United States on Freddie Laker's Skytrain. Shivering and sometimes soaked to the skin, Yankee tourists still shouted "God bless Freddie Laker!" when the TV newspeople came by to film the event.

IATA is one monopoly we can probably do without. This chapter will also examine some monopolies that we have to live with. However, it discusses some methods for regulating them as well.

C H A P T E R 21

MONOPOLY:
THE CASE
OF A
SINGLE SELLER

WHAT THIS CHAPTER IS ABOUT

CHARACTERISTICS OF MONOPOLY
One Seller
Barriers to Entry
PROFIT MAXIMIZATION IN THE SHORT RUN
LONG-RUN PROSPECTS
MONOPOLIES AND SOCIAL WELFARE
Underproduction
Economic Profit
Economies of Scale
REGULATED MONOPOLIES

Monopoly and perfect competition □ represent opposite ends of the spectrum of market structures. Strictly defined, **monopoly** is the case of a single seller of some given product. A monopolistic industry consists of only one firm, and the market demand curve is the demand curve of the firm. Monopolies are common in public utilities, because typically only one firm supplies a given type of service (natural gas, electricity, or telephone service, for example) within a prescribed geographical area. Such monopolies are the result of government franchises that grant the monopoly firms exclusive selling rights.

The government allows public utility monopolies to exist because the firms have large economies of scale. □ (Can you imagine ten companies, each with its own power lines, selling electricity in a town?) Such firms— firms with large economies of scale—are called natural monopolies. Because monopoly firms can conceivably earn greater than normal profits over the long run and because their profit-maximizing price and level of output are not likely to be consistent with efficient allocation of economic resources, public utilities in the United States and other countries are either regulated or owned by the government.

Outside the public utilities field, monopolies are rare in the United States. One reason is that the federal antitrust laws □ generally prohibit monopolization. Nonetheless, large, multi-product firms frequently are able to have near monopolies on specific products because patents, trademarks, or other restrictions keep rival firms from supplying exactly the same products. Where a restrictive device

456

413

593

475

makes it impossible to produce a close substitute for a given product, a monopoly or near monopoly in that product exists.

In the first section of this chapter the characteristics of monopoly are described, and some examples of real-world firms that have monopolies or near monopolies in certain products are provided. Then the conditions for profit maximization of the monopoly firm in both the short run and the long run are examined, and their implications for social welfare are discussed. Finally, the chapter shows how regulation is employed in the public utilities field to improve the economic performance of monopoly firms from a social point of view. The special topic following the chapter examines price discrimination, a device frequently used by monopolies and other firms to increase profits.

CHARACTERISTICS OF MONOPOLY

A **pure monopoly** is an industry consisting of only one firm.

ONE FIRM IN THE INDUSTRY

Because a pure monopoly is an industry with only one firm, there are no close substitutes for the product of this firm. The market demand for its product constitutes the only constraint on the price charged by a profit-maximizing monopoly firm. Although the firm can charge any price it wishes, we shall see later that if its goal is to maximize profit, it must consider both the demand for its product and its costs when it sets price.

It is the case for virtually all products that market demand is not completely inelastic with respect to all prices. For example, even though most of us consider basic telephone service almost a necessity, at some price, say $200 per month, many of us would do with-

out phones. Furthermore, substitutes of some sort exist for most products of monopolies. We can write letters rather than use the telephone, for example.

Even if there are no substitutes for a firm's product, the product can be priced so high that people cannot afford to purchase it. For example, if the services of a kidney machine cost $1 million a year, very few people with kidney diseases would be on kidney machines.

BARRIERS TO ENTRY

A monopoly firm maintains its position in the market through **barriers to entry,** things which prevent other firms from entering the industry. These barriers may include large amounts of financial capital required to enter the market, consumer loyalty, or the exclusive control of vital patents, franchises, raw materials, or locations.

Financial Capital In many industries, starting a new business requires a huge amount of financial capital. This requirement is at least partly the result of economies of scale in production. (Chapter 18 noted that the presence of economies of scale means that the long-run average cost of a firm is falling.) In an industry characterized by substantial economies of scale, large firms can produce at lower cost per unit than small firms. Thus small firms may have difficulty competing with large firms. Examples of industries requiring large amounts of capital are the automobile, steel, and aluminum industries, although none of these industries is a monopoly.

Consumer Loyalty New firms may find it difficult to successfully enter an industry whose consumers are loyal to products of particular firms. For example, consider Corning, Inc. One of the firm's products for which there is no exact substitute is its Corningware cooking and baking dishes. Most cooks are familiar with the claim that these dishes can go directly from the freezer to the oven or stovetop and have found it to be true. The microwave oven has further increased the usefulness of the dishes.

A new firm might have difficulty entering this market, because Corningware is widely respected and has many satisfied customers. Furthermore, many households have begun to accumulate sets of Corningware dishes in particular styles or patterns.

Patents, Franchises, Raw Materials, and Locations A firm can also maintain a monopoly position by exercising control over crucial patents, franchises, raw materials, or locations. For example, Eli Lilly was the first commercial producer of insulin and still controls at least 75 percent of the market for that drug. Although its patent will eventually expire, Lilly has three new patented drugs which are expected to substantially increase its earnings. In 1976 Smith Kline, another drug company, began marketing Tagamet, a patented anti-ulcer drug. This product helped the company increase its sales by 60 percent and its net income by more than 100 percent in two years.[1]

One must have a franchise or license to sell many name-brand products. McDonald's hamburgers and GM cars are just two examples. The diamond industry is an example of the importance of control over raw materials. The De Beers Company owns nearly all of the world's diamond mines.

Control over location is also important. The company with a hamburger stand next to a local high school has a distinct advantage over the company whose stand is two miles away.

REGULATED MONOPOLIES

As a result of federal antitrust laws, most of the monopolies in the United States are now regulated monopolies. The prices of their products and certain other aspects of their

business are controlled by various levels of government. These monopolies are usually allowed to exist because of their substantial economies of scale. Among them are local utility companies, Bell Telephone, and locally franchised cable TV companies.

DEMAND AND MARGINAL REVENUE

Chapter 20 indicated that the perfectly competitive firm is a price taker—that it accepts the market price as given by the industry supply and demand. The pure monopoly firm is a price maker; it determines the level of output and corresponding price that will maximize its profit.

The perfectly competitive firm faces a horizontal demand curve. It can sell as many units of output as it wishes to at the going market price; therefore, price and marginal revenue are equal.

The demand curve for a monopoly firm's product is the demand curve for the industry. Usually, the market demand curve for a product is downward sloping, which indicates that consumers are willing to purchase larger quantities at lower prices and smaller quantities at higher prices. Likewise, the market demand curve for the product of a purely competitive industry is normally downward-sloping.

As discussed in Chapter 17, if the demand curve for a firm's product is downward-sloping, marginal revenue □ is less than price. The reason is that to sell more units of output, a firm must lower its price. If the firm must charge the same price to all customers, it must also sell at a lower price output that it could have sold at a higher price if it had been content to sell a smaller quantity of it. Thus, as market price is lowered, the revenue generated by the sale of additional units is offset to some extent by the effect of the lower price on other units.

1. "Eli Lilly: New Life in the Drug Industry," *Business Week*, October 29, 1979, pp. 134–145.

The emphasis here is that the demand curve faced by a pure monopoly is downward-sloping, which results in marginal revenue being less than price. Figure 21–1 shows the demand and marginal revenue curves for a monopoly, Ambrosia, Inc., which makes an exclusive health tonic.

If the monopoly were to set the price of its tonic at $30 a pint bottle, it could sell 50 bottles per week, for a total revenue of $1,500. However, if the firm charged only $20 per bottle, it could sell 150 bottles per week, for a total revenue of $3,000. Marginal revenue between 50 and 150 units of output is equal to

$$\frac{\text{Change in total revenue}}{\text{Change in quantity of output}}$$

$$= \frac{\$1,500}{100} = \$15 \text{ per bottle,}$$

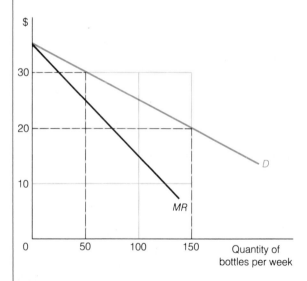

$$D$$

$$MR$$

FIGURE 21–1 Demand and Marginal Revenue Curves for a Monopoly (Ambrosia, Inc.)

The demand curve *(D)* for a monopoly firm is usually downward-sloping, since it is the market demand curve for the product in question. As a result, the marginal revenue curve *(MR)* is also downward-sloping, and marginal revenue is less than price. At a price of $30, Ambrosia can sell 50 bottles of tonic per week. If it lowers the price to $20 a bottle, the firm can sell 150 bottles per week. However, marginal revenue between 50 and 150 bottles of tonic is only equal to change in total revenue divided by change in quantity sold or $15.

which is less than either the higher or lower of the two prices. We can quickly calculate why this is so.

Revenue from the sale of an additional 100 bottles:

$$\$20 \times 100 \text{ bottles} = \$2,000$$

Lost revenue from the sale of the first 50 bottles at a lower price:

$$(\$20 - \$30) \times 50 \text{ bottles} = \underline{- \quad 500}$$

$$\text{Net increase in revenue} = \underline{\$1,500}$$

$$MR = \frac{\text{Change in total revenue}}{\text{Change in quantity of output}} =$$

$$\frac{\$1,500}{100} = \$15 \text{ per bottle.}$$

Since this value of marginal revenue represents average marginal revenue between 50 and 150 units of output, we plot it at the midpoint of the interval, where $Q = 100$.

PROFIT MAXIMIZATION IN THE SHORT RUN

As is the case for any firm, the pure monopoly maximizes profit (or minimizes losses) □ in the short run by producing its goods or services at the point where marginal revenue is equal to short-run marginal cost, □ as long as price is at least sufficient to cover average variable cost. The profit-maximizing price and output for a monopoly is sketched in Figure 21–2. A profit-maximizing monopoly will usually not charge the highest price at which there is some quantity demanded of its product. Instead the firm will increase its total profit by lowering its price and selling more units of its product until the marginal revenue brought in by another unit is just equal to its marginal cost.

For example, Table 21–1 gives revenue and

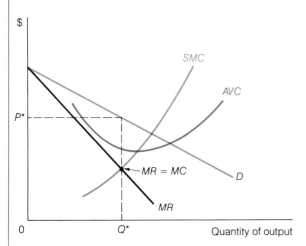

FIGURE 21–2   Short-run Profit-Maximizing Price and Output for a Monopoly

A monopoly firm will maximize profit in the short run by producing where marginal revenue (MR) is equal to short run marginal cost (SMC), as long as price (P) is greater than or equal to average variable cost (AVC). This point occurs at Q*, and the firm will charge a price of P*.

cost data for Ambrosia, Inc., the manufacturer of the exclusive health tonic. As shown in the table, Ambrosia will maximize its profit by producing 125 bottles of its tonic per week and charging a price of $22.50 per bottle. The

marginal revenue between 100 and 125 units of output is $12.50 per bottle, and the marginal cost is $8. Thus, between 100 and 125 units of output the marginal profit is $4.50 per bottle. Between 125 and 150 units of output, the marginal revenue is $7.50 and the marginal cost is $10, which makes the marginal profit −$2.50. Because marginal profit is negative beyond 125 bottles, the firm should not produce more than 125 bottles. Production of 125 bottles per week is the closest that the firm can come to producing where MR equals MC, without producing where MR is less than MC, so that marginal profit is negative. With a production rate of 125 bottles per week, Ambrosia is making a weekly economic (above normal) profit of $1,862.50.

Although in the short run many monopolies earn an economic profit, □ it is possible for a monopoly to earn only a normal or less than normal profit. □ These possibilities are shown in Figure 21–3, where economic profit is equal to $(P^* - SAC^*) \times Q^*$.

In the case of a monopoly, price is greater than marginal cost at the profit-maximizing level of output. For perfect competition, $P = MC$. The significance of this point will be discussed later in the chapter.

TABLE 21–1   Weekly Revenue and Cost Data for Ambrosia, Inc.

Number of Bottles (Q)	Price (P)	Total Revenue (TR)	Marginal Revenue $(MR = \frac{change\ in\ TR}{change\ in\ Q})$	Marginal Cost $(SMC = \frac{change\ in\ TC}{change\ in\ Q})$	Marginal Profit $M\pi = (MR - SMC)$	Total Variable Cost (TVC)	Total Cost (STC)	Total Profit $(T\pi = TR - TC)$
0	$35.00	0				$ 0	$ 100	$ −100.00
			$32.50	$10	$22.50			
25	32.50	812.50				250	350	462.50
			27.50	6	21.50			
50	30.00	1,500.00				400	500	1,000.00
			22.50	4	18.50			
75	27.50	2,062.50				500	600	1,462.50
			17.50	6	11.50			
100	25.00	2,500.00				650	750	1,750.00
			12.50	8	4.50			
125	22.50	2,612.50				850	950	1,862.50
			7.50	10	−2.50			
150	20.00	3,000.00				1,100	1,200	1,800.00
			2.50	15	−12.50			
175	17.50	3,062.50				1,475	1,575	1,487.50
			−2.50	20	−22.50			
200	15.00	3,000.00				1,975	2,075	925.00

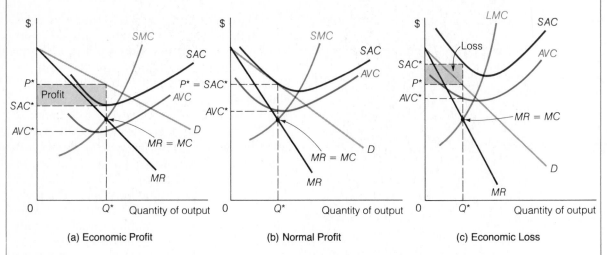

FIGURE 21–3   Three Short-run Profit Possibilities for a Monopoly

As shown in Figure 21–2, a monopoly will maximize profit (or minimize its loss) in the short run by producing where marginal revenue *(MR)* is equal to short-run marginal cost *(SMC)*, as long as price *(P)* is greater than or equal to average variable cost *(AVC)*. In panels (a), (b), and (c) these conditions are met when the firm produces Q^* units of output and charges a price of P^*. However, in the short run a monopoly firm may receive an economic profit, only a normal profit, or incur an economic loss. The firm is receiving an economic profit in panel (a), since price (P^*) is greater than short-run average cost (SAC^*). In panel (b), the firm is receiving only a normal profit, since $P^* = SAC^*$. In panel (c), the firm is incurring an economic loss, since P^* is less than SAC^*.

PROSPECTS FOR THE LONG RUN

◆

In the long run the pure monopoly will maximize profit by producing where marginal revenue is equal to long-run marginal cost. This rule assumes, of course, that the monopoly has been able to predict its profit-maximizing level of output well enough so that it is using a least cost combination of inputs.□

The rule that marginal revenue equals long-run marginal cost also assumes that the firm is earning at least a normal return (price is greater than or equal to long-run average cost). If it is not earning a normal return, the firm will leave this industry. Figure 21–4 shows the long-run profit-maximizing position for a monopoly. In panel (a) the firm is earning an economic profit. In panel (b) it is earning a normal return.

MONOPOLIES AND SOCIAL WELFARE

◆

Chapter 20 indicated that a perfectly competitive market results in an optimal allocation of resources for two reasons. First, each firm maximizes profit by producing its goods or services at the point where the marginal social benefit □ of its product is equal to its marginal social cost □ (where price is equal to marginal cost). Second, when the industry is in long-run equilibrium, each perfectly competitive firm is earning only a normal profit and producing at minimum long-run average cost.

UNDERPRODUCTION

In contrast to a perfectly competitive firm, a monopoly maximizes profit by producing where marginal revenue is equal to marginal

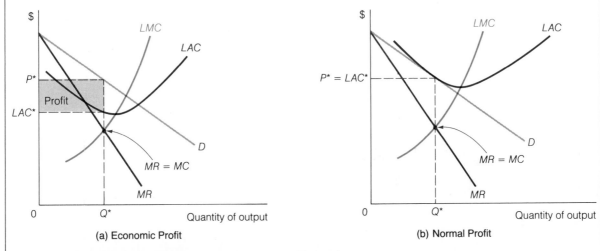

FIGURE 21–4   Long-run Profit-Maximizing Position for a Monopoly

In the long run, a monopoly firm will maximize profit by producing where marginal revenue *(MR)* is equal to long-run marginal cost *(LMC)*, as long as price *(P)* is greater than or equal to long-run average cost *(LAC)*. In both panels (a) and (b), the firm will produce at *Q** and charge a price equal to *P**. In panel (a), the firm is receiving an economic profit since *P** is greater than *LAC**. In panel (b), the firm is receiving only a normal profit, since *P** is equal to *LAC**.

cost but price is greater than marginal cost. This relationship holds true in both the short run and the long run. Figure 21–5 illustrates the difference between the short-run equilibrium for a perfectly competitive industry and that for a monopoly with identical costs.

From Chapter 20 we know that the short-run industry supply curve under perfect competition is the horizontal sum of the short-run marginal cost curves of the individual firms in the industry. At every point on the short-run industry supply curve, each firm is producing at a point where price equals short-run marginal cost. This position is consistent with profit maximization because, for the perfectly competitive firm, price is equal to marginal revenue. In Figure 21–5 the perfectly competitive market equilibrium occurs at point E_c, where the industry supply curve intersects the market demand curve. The perfectly competitive price is P_c, and output is Q_2.

Suppose all the perfectly competitive sellers of Figure 21–5 are organized into a monopoly. (Such an organization is known as a *cartel.*) Since $S_I = MC$, the monopoly equilibrium condition *(MR = MC)* will be satisfied at point

E_m. However, this point yields a profit-maximizing price of P and a quantity of Q_1. Thus the monopoly price will be higher than the perfectly competitive price, and less than the perfectly competitive quantity of the product will be produced.

If we calculate the total revenue reduction associated with the drop in output $(Q_2 - Q_1)$ by summing up the *MR*'s of all units between Q_2 and Q_1, we find it is equal to area $Q_1 E_m Z Q_2$. Summing up the *MC*'s of the same units gets us an area equal to $Q_1 E_m E_c Q_2$. Since the latter area includes the above area plus triangle $E_m E_c Z$, costs have fallen more than revenues, and profit is therefore greater for the monopoly than it was for the perfectly competitive firms.

Because monopolies produce where *MR = MC* with price greater than marginal cost, a problem arises from a social point of view. Society would benefit from increased production up to the point where *P = MC*, but the monopoly does not supply this much output. If we assume, as in Chapter 20, that price is equal to marginal social benefit and the firm's marginal cost is equal to marginal social cost,

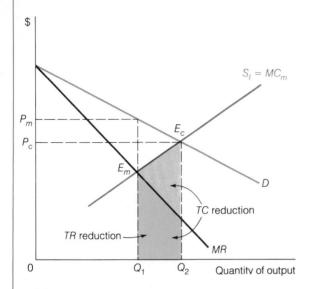

FIGURE 21–5 A Comparison of Short-run Equilibrium for a Perfectly Competitive Industry with That for a Monopoly

In this graph, we compare the short run equilibrium position of a perfectly competitive industry with that for a monopoly with identical costs. The perfectly competitive industry supply curve is S_I, which we shall also assume is the marginal cost curve for the monopoly firm (MC_m). The industry demand curve is D in either case. If the industry is perfectly competitive, the equilbrium price will be P_c, the price at the point where the industry supply and demand curves intersect, and the equilibrium quantity sold will be Q_2. However, if a monopoly is now organized, this firm will maximize its profit by producing where marginal revenue (MR) is equal to MC_m, at Q_1, and charging a price of P_m. We can see that this point will be more profitable for the monopoly firm than Q_2, since the reduction in total cost by reducing output to Q_1 is given by the area of $Q_1Q_2E_cE_m$. However, the reduction in total revenue is equal to only the area of $Q_1Q_2ZE_m$. Thus, total costs will fall by more than total revenue if the monopoly firm cuts output from Q_2 to Q_1.

then the monopoly firm stops production where the marginal social benefit of another unit of its good or service is greater than the marginal social cost. But the welfare of society would increase if the firm were to continue production until $MSB = MSC$. Thus, from a social point of view, a monopoly produces too little output at too high a price. In Figure 21–6, P_m is the monopoly price, and Q_m is the monopoly output; P_s^* is the socially optimal price, and Q_s^* is the socially optimal out-

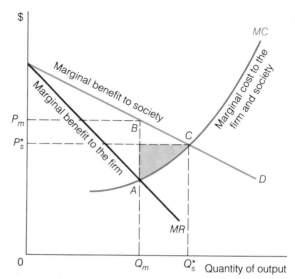

FIGURE 21–6 Monopoly Output and Price Compared with Socially Optimal Output and Price

As explained earlier in this chapter, a monopoly firm will maximize profit by producing where marginal revenue (MR) is equal to marginal cost (MC), at Q_m^* and charging a price equal to P_m. If the price which people are willing and able to pay for a good represents its marginal benefit to society, while the marginal cost to the firm represents the marginal cost of the good to society, then social welfare would be maximized if the firm were to produce where the price of the product is equal to its marginal cost, or where $P_s^* = MC$, at Q_s^*. By producing only Q_m units of output, the monopoly firm forces society to give up the net social benefit (equal to $P - MC$) received from each unit of output between Q_m and Q_s^*, shown as the shaded area in the graph.

put. If the output of the monopoly firm is increased to Q_s^* and the price is lowered to P_s^*, the welfare of society will increase in an amount equal to the area inside triangle ABC.

ECONOMIC PROFIT

Because of barriers to entry, a monopoly firm may earn economic profit in the long run. There are no pressures exerted by the entry of new firms causing the price to fall so that price is equal to long-run average cost.

Some economists contend that the presence and possibility of economic profit are not altogether bad for society. They argue that economic profit generally encourages product research and development. However, economists by no means agree on this issue, and the statistical evidence is unclear.

ECONOMIES OF SCALE

A monopoly firm may be able to produce the output of an industry more cheaply than could perfectly competitive firms if substantial economies of scale are present. For example, it would be quite costly for a city to have ten water companies, each with a different set of water mains running underground. The same can be said for companies that provide natural gas, electricity, many forms of public transportation, and certain other products and services. These companies and public utilities in general are examples of natural monopolies.

A **natural monopoly** exists where economies of scale are so large that if two or more firms were to be involved in the production of the industry output, unit cost would be higher than for a monopoly.

In these cases, one firm is usually granted an exclusive franchise to service the market, but its price is regulated by some government body. Price regulation of monopolies is discussed in a later section.

PRICE
DISCRIMINATION

Monopoly firms sometimes employ price discrimination to increase their profits.

A firm practices **price discrimination** when it charges more than one price for identical units of its product.

Price discrimination involves either selling the good or service at different prices to different buyers or charging a single buyer one price for a given amount of the product and a different (usually lower) price for additional units of the same product. It is practiced not only by monopolies but also by other firms that have some control over the price of their product (monopolistically competitive and oligopoly firms, discussed in Chapter 22). For example, electric utility firms (monopolies) practice price discrimination when they discriminate by type of buyer, charging different rates for residential, commercial, and industrial uses of kilowatt hours of electricity. The phone company sets its rates so that businesses pay more for local service than do individuals. Moreover, long distance telephone rates are higher during the daytime than during the night. Railroads charge a different rate for shipping coal than for shipping other commodities. Even automobile dealers practice price discrimination when they attempt to get each buyer to pay the maximum amount possible for a given model of car.

Why is price discrimination profitable? Suppose that Blue Star Mercedes Benz is the only Mercedes Benz dealer in town and that its weekly demand and revenue data for sales of full-size, four-door sedans are those given in Table 21–2. Suppose too that the cars come fully equipped from the factory and cost the dealer $30,000 each. If Blue Star sets its price at $35,000 and charges all customers the same price, its total revenue for a week will be

TABLE 21–2 Hypothetical Demand and Revenue Data for Sales of Mercedes Benz Sedans

Number of Cars Sold per Week (Q)	Price per Car (P)	Total Revenue without Discrimination (P × Q)	Total Revenue with Discrimination (Sum of Individual Prices)
0	$60,000	$ 0	$ 0
1	55,000	55,000	55,000
2	50,000	100,000	105,000
3	45,000	135,000	150,000
4	40,000	160,000	190,000
5	35,000	175,000	225,000

$35,000 × 5 = $175,000. However, according to the demand data, four of the five purchasers of the cars would have been willing and able to pay more than $35,000. In fact, one person would pay $55,000, and three others would pay $50,000, $45,000, and $40,000. Clearly, if the firm charges each buyer what he or she is willing and able to pay, the firm's total revenue will increase.

The last column in Table 21–1 shows the result if each buyer pays the maximum "willing and able" price for a car. If Blue Star gets each of the five buyers to pay the maximum, total revenue for the five cars sold will be $50,000 more than it will be with a uniform price of $35,000 per car. Because the firm pays the factory the same price ($30,000) for each car, Blue Star's profits will certainly be higher if it practices price discrimination than if it does not.

Of course, it is difficult to predict accurately the maximum price each buyer will be willing and able to pay for a given product. However, car salespeople do their best to approximate this result when they haggle over price with each individual buyer.

Other firms may have less trouble identifying which buyers will pay more and which will not. For example, it is easy for an electric utility to tell who is a residential consumer and who is an industrial consumer. In addition, many businesses can easily discriminate between wholesale and retail buyers of their products.

Two conditions must be met for price discrimination to be profitable for a firm. First, different buyers must have different price elasticities of demand □ for the product. That is, some buyers must be willing and able to pay more than others for the product. Second, the firm must be able to keep the different buyers segregated, so that those who buy at a low price cannot resell to those who are willing and able to pay a higher price. Price discrimination is examined in more detail in the special topic that follows this chapter. A graphical analysis of a case involving two separate markets is also presented there.

REGULATED MONOPOLIES

Figure 21–7 shows the unit cost curves and the market demand curve for a natural monopoly. The long-run average cost curve reaches its minimum point at a level of output outside the demand curve.

If the monopoly is allowed to determine its profit-maximizing price and level of output with no restrictions, it will produce where $MR = LMC$, at a level of output equal to Q_{ur} and a price of P_{ur} (with ur standing for "unregulated"). At this point the firm will earn an economic profit equal to $(P_{ur} - LAC_{ur}) × Q_{ur}$.

A REGULATORY DILEMMA

If a government body steps in now to regulate the price of the monopoly, it will be presented with a dilemma. If it sets $P = LMC$, where the long-run marginal cost curve cuts the demand curve, so that marginal social benefit is equal to marginal social cost, the firm will be earning less than a normal profit, because price will be less than long-run average cost.

FAIR-RETURN PRICING

Recognizing this problem, regulatory agencies frequently take a different approach. They allow the firm to make a normal profit—but only a normal profit—by setting a ceiling price equal to the price level, P_r (with r standing for "regulated"), where the long-run average cost curve intersects the demand curve, as shown in Figure 21–7.

In this situation the firm chooses to produce at Q_r, because that is as close as it can come to equating MR and LMC. Until an output level of Q_r is reached, marginal revenue under the ceiling price is constant and equal to P_r. However, at levels of output greater than Q_r the firm's original demand and marginal reve-

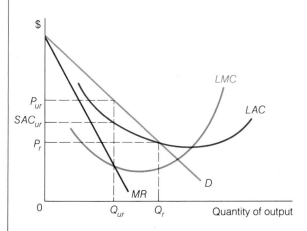

FIGURE 21–7   A Regulated Monopoly

An unregulated monoply firm would maximize profit in the long run by producing where marginal revenue *(MR)* is equal to long-run marginal cost *(LMC)*, at Q_{ur} units of output, and charging a price equal to P_{ur}. At this point, the firm will be receiving an economic profit of $(P_{ur} - LAC_{ur}) \times Q_{ur}$, where LAC_{ur} is the long-run average cost of production at Q_{ur}. If a regulated price or price ceiling of P_r is now established, the firm will maximize profit by producing Q_r units of output and charging a price equal to P_r. This point will result in profit maximization after the ceiling price is imposed since P_r is equal to marginal revenue until a horizontal line from P_r intersects the original demand curve, *D*. After that point, the original demand and marginal revenue curves apply, since people are not willing to buy additional units of the product at a price of P_r. Thus, after Q_r marginal revenue will be less than long-run marginal cost. Since the ceiling price, P_r, is equal to the long-run average cost at Q_r, the firm will only receive a normal profit after the ceiling price is imposed.

nue curves become relevant once again. The reason P_r does not represent marginal revenue at higher levels of output is that the monopoly must set a lower price if it wishes to sell that large a quantity. Consequently, the best that a monopoly can do in this situation is to produce where P_r = LAC, at Q_r, and earn a normal return.

Fair-return pricing *is a type of price regulation that allows a firm to charge a price sufficiently high to make a normal return but no economic profit.*

Two problems exist with the fair-return approach to regulating the price a monopoly can charge. First, the government must generally rely on the firms themselves to supply accurate cost data and to produce each level of output at the lowest possible cost. Second, government officials, customers, and firm owners often have widely different notions of what constitutes a fair return. This point is vividly illustrated each time a company petitions a regulatory agency for a rate increase.

SUMMARY

1. This chapter examined the market structure that is generally regarded as the opposite of perfect competition—monopoly. A *pure monopoly* is characterized by an industry consisting of only one firm. There are no close substitutes for the product of this firm, and the only limitation on the price it can set is the market demand for its good or service.

2. In addition, *barriers to entry* prevent other firms from entering the market. These barriers may include large financial capital requirements, consumer loyalty, and exclusive control of vital patents, franchises, raw materials, or locations.

3. Because the demand curve for a monopoly firm is the market demand curve and because consumers as a group generally wish to purchase larger quantities of a good or service at lower prices, the demand curve for a monopoly firm is usually downward sloping. In this case, marginal revenue is less than price.

4. The monopoly firm maximizes profit in the short run by producing its good or service at the point where marginal revenue is equal to short-run marginal cost, as long as price is greater than or equal to average variable cost. If price is less than average variable cost, the firm should shut down. Consequently, a monopoly firm that wishes to maximize its profit must determine its price and level of output according to the decision rules of Chapter 19. The optimal price is usually not the highest price at which some people will buy the product.

5. The firm maximizes profit in the long run by producing its good or service at the point where marginal revenue is equal to long-run marginal cost, as long as the firm is earning at least a normal return. In the long run the firm should be able to use a least cost combination of inputs, so that its costs are represented by the long-run curves. If it cannot earn at least a normal profit, it should shut down.

6. From a social point of view, monopoly firms underproduce because their profit-maximizing level of output is at a point where marginal social benefit is still greater than marginal social cost. Moreover, barriers to entry make it possible for a monopoly to earn an economic profit in the long run. Thus, under monopoly, consumers may be forced to pay a higher price for a smaller quantity of output than under perfect competition. However, a monopoly may be able to take advantage of economies of scale that a perfectly competitive firm cannot achieve. The presence or possibility of economic profit may also stimulate product research and development.

7. The government frequently allows natural monopolies to exist but regulates the prices they can charge. The price ceiling is often set so that price is equal to long-run average cost, which allows the firm to earn a normal profit. This type of policy is called *fair-return pricing*.

IMPORTANT TERMS AND CONCEPTS

Monopoly	Natural monopolies
Barriers to entry	Fair-return pricing
Regulated monopolies	Price discrimination
Price maker	

QUESTIONS AND PROBLEMS

1. What are the characteristics of a monopoly?

2. Explain what barriers to entry are. Give some examples.

3. Explain how a price ceiling will affect the profit-maximizing price and output of a monopoly. Draw a graph to illustrate your answer.

4. How does the demand curve for the product of a pure monopoly differ from the demand curve for the product of a purely competitive firm? Why does it differ? Of what importance is this difference?

5. Will a monopoly firm always charge the highest price that any customers are willing to pay? Explain.

6. What is fair-return pricing?

7. Why do government regulators of monopoly firms face a dilemma when they try to set a ceiling price?

8. What is the short-run profit-maximizing decision rule for a monopoly? Draw a graph to illustrate your answer.

9. Why do economists argue that a monopoly underproduces from a social point of view?

10. What is a natural monopoly?

11. Of what significance, from a social point of view, is the fact that a monopoly may earn an economic profit in the long run?

12. What is the long-run profit-maximizing decision rule for a monopoly? Draw a graph to illustrate your answer.

13. The table below gives demand and cost data for a monopoly. Complete the table and determine the price and level of output that will maximize the firm's profit.

14. Is it possible for a pure monopoly to incur a loss? Explain.

Quantity of Output	Price	Total Revenue	Marginal Revenue	Marginal Cost	Total Variable Cost	Marginal Profit
0	$800	$ 0	$	$	$ 0	
5,000	750				2,500,000	
10,000	700				4,500,000	
15,000	650				6,000,000	
20,000	600				6,500,000	
25,000	550				7,000,000	
30,000	500				7,500,000	
35,000	450				8,000,000	
40,000	400				8,500,000	
45,000	350				9,500,000	

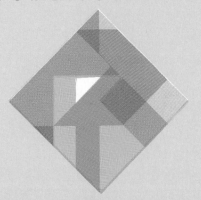

DE BEERS'
SQUEEZE ON
GEM SPECULATORS

This week the 300 diamond dealers and cutters who filed into the London "sight" room of the Central Selling Organization (CSO) found the rough stones marked up on average of 10%. The increase was the fourth surcharge in recent months on rough diamond prices by De Beers Consolidated Mines Ltd., the South African-based producer that controls the CSO, marketer of 85% of the world's rough diamonds.

The latest increase, which followed surcharges of 40%, 25%, and 15% since March, is viewed as the final move in a classic squeeze on speculators who have

Source: "De Beers' Squeeze on Gem Speculators," *Business Week*, July 24, 1978, pp. 61–62.

been raking off huge profits on rough diamonds by charging premiums of up to 100% in reselling through secondary markets. For De Beers Chairman Harry F. Oppenheimer, cutting out speculator premiums was critical to quash a growing threat to his carefully constructed CSO monopoly. Diamond producers felt that more of the profits from a booming gem market should have accrued to them rather than to traders in major cutting centers, notably Tel Aviv.

INCREASED UNCERTAINTY

This spring, Oppenheimer moved decisively against speculators, striking at their confidence and their credit. He hit dealers and

manufacturers with a huge 40% surcharge on the CSO's 2,000 different prices, telling them that a surcharge would continue as long as the CSO deemed necessary. The proceeds of the surcharge were passed directly to producers. The CSO unsettled dealers further by sharply reducing allocations of stones to each client. "Uncertainty was increased because the speculators did not know whether the stocks were being held back, or whether they really weren't there," says London diamond broker William Nagel.

With speculators reeling from the surcharges, an earlier CSO-instigated credit squeeze began to bite. CSO representatives called on banks in New York and Tel Aviv, arguing that speculation, fueled by bank credit, threatened industry stability. (Oppenheimer himself is a director of Barclay's Bank International in London.) In March, the New York banks responded, reducing credit to New York cutters, who buy 33% of Israel's diamond exports. Israeli banks catering to the diamond trade lowered credit from 80% to 70% of a diamond's value on news of the first surcharge.

The CSO's monthly reduction is interpreted in London as evidence that De Beers feels it has reined in the speculators. In Tel Aviv, Raymond Darwish, head of the diamond section at Israel Discount Bank, agrees. "The situation has improved; there is no speculation at the moment," he says. He adds that the banks will be sticking to their reduced credit policy.

OVERKILL?

While Oppenheimer and De Beers have tamed the speculators, they have paid a price. The market for polished gems has been disrupted by the turbulence in the rough market, and sales of polished gems are off their earlier highs.

There may also have been a degree of overkill in the CSO squeeze. According to Moshe Shnitzer, president of the International Federation of Diamond Bourses in Tel Aviv, the Israeli diamond industry has been hit hard, with almost all producers losing money since the surcharges and tighter credit were invoked.

The CSO has nevertheless successfully balanced the surcharges with reduced supplies to generate a 13% increase in income for the first half of the year. This week it announced a rise of $138 million in sales, to $1.2 billion. Still unknown, however, is the strategy's impact on the profits of De Beers. Recently, rough diamonds have been the most important contributor to profits for Oppenheimer's South African-based gold, metals, and industrial empire. De Beers last year earned $728.5 million on sales of $1.1 billion.

But at least one U.S. brokerage house, Merrill Lynch, is betting that De Beers's profit drive will continue unabated. Its bullish report on the company, forecasting a 1978 dividend of 70¢ (1977: 60¢), last month propelled the share price from $3 to $5. Says the report's author, Merrill Lynch analyst David J. Fitzpatrick: "Even at $4.75, 70¢ is a yield of 15%, and that's almost double the prime rate."

Note: The prime rate was above 20% in the summer of 1981. As a result of a world economic slowdown and rising interest rates, the price of a top grade investment stone had fallen by as much as 17% in three months. See "De Beers Reduces Diamond Supply Due to Price Slide," *Wall Street Journal*, February 17, 1981, p. 2; and "De Beers: Riding Out a Slump That May Curb Its Expansion Plans," *Business Week*, June 1, 1981 pp. 104–105.

QUESTIONS

1. What percent of the world market for rough diamonds does De Beers Consolidated Mines, Ltd., control?

2. What is the CSO?

3. Why did De Beers impose the surcharges on the sales to diamond dealers? How did De Beers correspondingly adjust the quantity of diamonds supplied?

4. Would it be possible for De Beers to raise the price "too high" from the standpoint of maximizing its own profit? Explain.

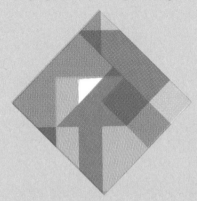

A FURTHER ANALYSIS
OF PRICE
DISCRIMINATION

As indicated in Chapter 21, a firm in a monopolistic or other highly concentrated industry can frequently increase its profits by charging different prices to different customers or groups of customers for the same product. This practice is known as *price discrimination*. Another version of price discrimination involves charging various consumers prices for similar products that do not reflect the differentials in production or transportation costs incurred in selling to them. Common examples of price discrimination include charging lower prices for matinee showings of movies than for night showings, special discount fares offered by airlines, and seasonal and convention room rates charged by hotels.

Certain forms of price discrimination are forbidden by federal antitrust laws. Section 2 of the Clayton Act as amended by the Robinson-Patman Act□ of 1936 states

that it shall be unlawful for any person engaged in commerce, . . . to discriminate in price between different purchasers of commodities of like grade and quality, . . . where such commodities are sold for use, consumption, or resale within the United States or any Territory thereof or the District of Columbia . . ., where the effect of such discrimination may be substantially to lessen competition or tend to create a monopoly in any line of commerce.[1]

The amended act goes on to state, however:

Nothing herein contained shall prevent differentials which make only due allowance for differences in the cost of manufacture, sale, or delivery resulting from the differing methods or quantities in which such commodities are to such purchasers sold or delivered.[2]

The Robinson-Patman Act expressly allows price changes in response to changes in the market or marketability of goods, including

---

1. Seventy-fourth Congress, Session 2, "Antitrust Act of 1914, Amendment," *The Statutes at Large of the United States of America*, vol. 49 (Washington, D.C.: Government Printing Office, 1936), p. 1526. Also see Sixty-third Congress, Session 2, *The Statutes at Large of The United States of America: 1913–1915*, vol. 38, pt. I (Washington, D.C.: Government Printing Office, 1915), p. 730.

2. Seventy-fourth Congress, Session 2, "Antitrust Act of 1914, Amendment," p. 1526.

changed prices for goods about to deteriorate or become obsolete, for distress sales, or for closing out a particular line of goods. It also permits price discrimination in "good faith" to meet competition. At the same time, the act makes the giving or receiving of any illegal price differential a criminal offense.[3]

Aside from the question of legality, however, two purely economic conditions must be met if price discrimination is to be profitable for the firm:

1. Different buyers or groups of buyers must have different price elasticities of demand.
2. The seller must be able to segregate or separate the different buyers according to their elasticities of demand.

These two conditions state that for price discrimination to be profitable, some buyers

must be willing to pay a higher price for the commodity than others are paying. Moreover, the seller must be able to segregate the buyers who are willing to pay more. If the seller cannot keep the buyers willing to pay higher prices separated from those who are not willing, then even the former will purchase the commodity at a lower price. (Most of us want to purchase commodities as cheaply as possible, even though we are willing to pay more if necessary.) Furthermore, it must be impossible for some buyers to purchase the commodity at the lower price and then sell it to others at the higher price.

Given that price discrimination is legal and economically profitable and that the marginal cost of output is the same for all markets, *a firm will maximize its profit by producing its good or service up to the point where the marginal revenue for each set of customers is equal to the firm's marginal cost.* This profit-

---

3. Ibid.

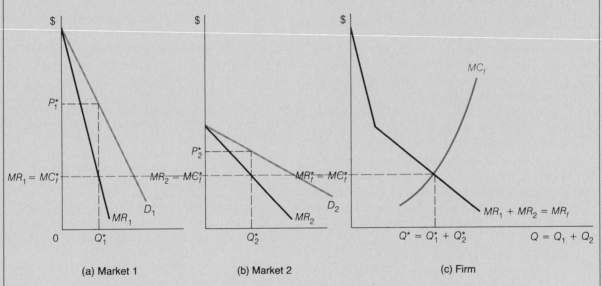

(a) Market 1　　　　　　　(b) Market 2　　　　　　　(c) Firm

FIGURE I–1 Profit-Maximizing Prices for Two Markets with Price Discrimination

The firm depicted here sells its product in two markets, Market 1 and Market 2. D_1 and MR_1 are, respectively, the demand and marginal revenue curves for Market 1. D_2 and MR_2 are, respectively, the demand and marginal revenue curves for Market 2. The firm's aggregate marginal revenue curve, MR_f, is obtained by horizontally summing MR_1 and MR_2. The firm will maximize profit by producing where MR_f is equal to the marginal cost to the firm of producing another unit of output, MC_f. This point occurs at Q^*. The firm will divide up this output between the two markets by selling output in each respective market until the marginal revenue in each market is equal to MC_f^*. Thus, the firm will sell Q_1^* units of output in Market 1, since MR_1 = MC_f^* at that point, and charge a price equal to P_1^*. Correspondingly, the firm will sell Q_2^* units of output and charge a price equal to P_2^* in Market 2.

maximizing decision rule is illustrated in Figure I–1, which shows a firm with two markets or groups of customers. The demand and marginal revenue curves applicable for customers in market 1 are shown in panel (a). The curves for customers in market 2 are shown in panel (b).

In panel (c) an aggregate marginal revenue curve, MR_f, is sketched for the firm. This curve is obtained by adding the relevant quantities from market 1 and market 2 that correspond to a given dollar level of marginal revenue. The procedure is called *horizontal summation*, because quantities, which are on the horizontal axis, are summed (rather than dollars, which are on the vertical axis). Panel (c) also shows the firm's marginal cost curve, MC_f. The firm's profit-maximizing level of total output is Q^*, where $MR_f = MC_f$.

Because the marginal cost of producing another unit of output is identical for either market, it does not matter from a cost standpoint in which market the output is sold. The market does matter a great deal, however, with regard to the revenue obtained.

The optimal total quantity, Q^*, should be allocated between market 1 and market 2 so that $MR_1 = MR_2 = MR_f^* = MC_f^*$. In this way the firm will maximize the revenue obtained from Q^* units of output. P_1 and P_2 are determined from the demand curves of each respective market. In general, the higher price will be charged in the market with the less elastic demand for the product.

Some forms of price discrimination may be beneficial to society. For example, reduced evening rates for telephone service may reduce the daytime congestion on the telephone lines. It also may allow more people to make calls. Doctors argue in a similar fashion when they defend the practice of charging wealthy customers or those with health insurance higher rates than those who are relatively poor and do not have insurance. If these businesses had to charge the same price to all customers, they might be unable to earn even a normal profit by charging the lower prices.

QUESTIONS

1. Explain how a firm practicing price discrimination and selling its product in two markets will set price if it wishes to maximize profit.

2. What are some examples of price discrimination in addition to those mentioned in the text?

3. Can you think of another situation in which price discrimination might be beneficial to both the firm and the consumer?

CHAPTER 22

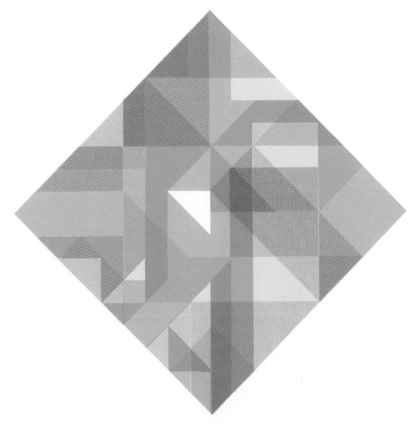

MONOPOLISTIC
COMPETITION
AND
OLIGOPOLY

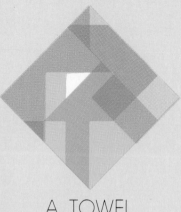

A TOWEL
FOR
ALL SEASONS?

Here is something that everyone needs: a paper towel that is so strong you can run it through an automatic washer and it will come out in one piece! Just think, if you could save all those towels and stick them back together again, you could make an almost new roll of towels (provided, of course, that you also saved the cardboard roll they came on). Better yet, in case of a prison break or a hotel fire, they could be tied together and used to lower people from a building's upper stories.

Who is making this product, and why? The who is American Can Company, which, despite its name, also produces some best-selling brands of ordinary paper towels. The why is to see whether it can profitably corner a specialty segment of the paper towel market—a segment largely ignored by rival manufacturers.

The paper towel and tissue industry in the United States is highly concentrated. To economists, this means that a small number of firms produce a large share of the total industry output. We can count them easily on one hand: (1) Kimberly Clark, (2) Scott Paper, (3) Procter & Gamble, (4) Georgia Pacific, and (5) Crown Zellerbach. Anyone wanting to play wet towel with these firms has two choices: getting together with someone else to act like a monopoly (illegal in the United States) or playing a hard and fast game of introducing new products and fighting for market share.

The consensus in the industry is that American Can's new towel, called Bolt, is likely to be of higher quality than consumers

494

desire.[1] *If this prognosis is accurate, the towel will probably just wipe itself right out of the market. Such is life in markets where firms are few in number, and each must consider the actions of its rivals when trying to increase its market share. These firms form an oligopoly, one of the two types of market structures to be discussed in this chapter.*

1. "What Happens If the Product Offers More than Users Need?" *Wall Street Journal,* September 25, 1980, p. 31.

C H A P T E R 22

MONOPOLISTIC COMPETITION AND OLIGOPOLY

WHAT THIS CHAPTER IS ABOUT

MONOPOLISTIC COMPETITION
Characteristics
Profit-Maximizing Behavior
Long-run Prospects and Social Welfare
OLIGOPOLY
Cartels
Price Leadership
Kinked Demand Curves
Effect on Social Welfare

In 1979 headlines such as the following became commonplace: "More Oil Firms Post Big Gains in 1st Period Net," "Exxon Registers Doubling of Net for 3rd Quarter," "Mobil Corp. Posts Record 130% Rise in 3rd Period Net," and "An Embarrassment of Riches: A Look at Big Oil's Big Profits in 3rd Period."[1]

1. "More Oil Firms Post Big Gains in 1st Period Net," *Wall Street Journal,* April 25, 1979, p. 18; "Exxon Registers Doubling of Net for 3rd Quarter," *Wall Street Journal,* October 23, 1979, p. 3; "Mobil Corp. Posts Record 130% Rise in 3rd Period Net," *Wall Street Journal,* October 25, 1979, p. 6; and "An Embarrassment of Riches: A Look at Big Oil's Big Profits in 3rd Period," *Wall Street Journal,* October 25, 1979, p. 6.

Did the nature of the oil market have something to do with these profits? An explanation of oligopolistic market structures, discussed later in this chapter, may help us understand why it probably did.

In the last two chapters we examined perfect competition and monopoly. These two market structures represent the two extreme ends of the spectrum of possible product market situations.

Perfect competition,□ with many firms in an industry producing identical products and having no control over price, is usually considered the ideal market structure. When the industry is in long-run equilibrium, perfectly competitive firms make only a normal profit.□ In the absence of externalities,□ they produce their goods or services at the point where marginal social benefit is equal to marginal social cost□ and where long-run average cost□ is at a minimum.

A monopoly,□ on the other hand, is an industry that consists of one firm whose price is limited only by the market demand for its product. Barriers to entry prevent other firms from entering the industry. From a social point of view, a monopoly underproduces and overcharges.

Few, if any, firms in the United States completely satisfy the requirements for either perfect competition or monopoly. This chapter will consider two other market structures, *monopolistic competition* and *oligopoly*. These structures make up most of the "real world" in the United States. Monopolistic competition will be examined first.

MONOPOLISTIC COMPETITION: WHERE IMAGE COUNTS

◆

Monopolistic competition is similar in many ways to perfect competition. One result of this similarity is that when the industry is in long-run equilibrium, a monopolistically competitive firm, like its perfectly competitive counterpart, earns only a normal profit. We will soon see why.

CHARACTERISTICS OF MONOPOLISTIC COMPETITION

A **monopolistically competitive industry** has the following three characteristics.

1. There are many firms in the industry.
2. The firms produce slightly differentiated products.
3. Barriers to entry are relatively small or non-existent, and factors of production are mobile.

Differentiated products are goods and services whose perceived or actual attributes vary enough so that consumers can distinguish the products from each other.

For example, through advertising, a consumer may perceive one laundry detergent to be different from another even though the two detergents are actually identical. On the other hand, two laundry detergents may be differentiated by their relative effectiveness in removing dirt. Products can be differentiated in many ways, including style, color, location, taste, and quality.

Although there are many firms in any monopolistically competitive industry, the fact that the firms produce slightly differentiated products allows each firm to have some control over the price it charges for its product. Some people are willing to pay more for the product of one firm than for similar products of other firms. For example, some people may be willing to pay more for a haircut at Command Performance than a haircut at BJ's Barbershop. Their reasons may be that they believe the hair stylists at Command Performance do a better job than those at BJ's barbershop, Command Performance may simply be closer to their homes or places of work, they may not have to wait at Command Performance, or they may see Command Performance as being a more prestigious establishment.

The degree of control each firm has over price depends on the extent to which the firm's product is differentiated from similar products of other firms. The demand for each firm's product is highly but not perfectly, elastic◻ with respect to price. Because demand is not perfectly elastic, marginal revenue◻ is less than price, as was the case for a monopoly. Price must be lowered if a larger quantity is to be sold.

382
377

PROFIT MAXIMIZATION IN THE SHORT RUN

The demand curve for the product of a monopolistically competitive firm is generally much less steeply sloped (more elastic) than the demand curve for the product of a monopoly. This situation occurs because a large number of firms operate in a monopolistically competitive market and no single firm can expect to charge a price significantly higher than that charged by others. Furthermore, the firm can probably sell all its potential output at a price only slightly below that charged by others. Such circumstances result in a relatively flat, though downward sloping, demand curve. However, in all other respects the graphical representation of the short-run profit-maximizing position for a monopolistically competitive firm (as shown in Figure 22–1) resembles the representation for a monopoly. The firm produces a level of output equal to Q^*, where marginal revenue is equal to short-run marginal cost, and charges a price equal to P^*.

All firms, regardless of their industry structure, will maximize profit in the short run by producing the level of output where marginal revenue is equal to short-run marginal cost,□ as long as price is at least sufficiently high to cover average variable cost (as long as SMC rises above MR at higher levels of output). For all industry structures except perfect competi-

tion, price is greater than marginal revenue and marginal cost at the profit-maximizing level of output. Of course, a firm may earn an economic profit,□ normal profit, or economic loss in the short run.

PROFIT MAXIMIZING IN THE LONG RUN

In the long run the monopolistically competitive firm will maximize profit by producing the level of output where marginal revenue is equal to long-run marginal cost, as long as price is at least as great as long-run average cost. If price is less than long-run average cost, the firm should leave the industry. Of course, we are assuming here that the firm can vary its factors of production□ so that it has a combination of inputs that will enable it to produce its output at the lowest possible cost.

Figure 22–2 shows a monopolistically competitive firm operating with an optimal size plant for its level of output and maximizing

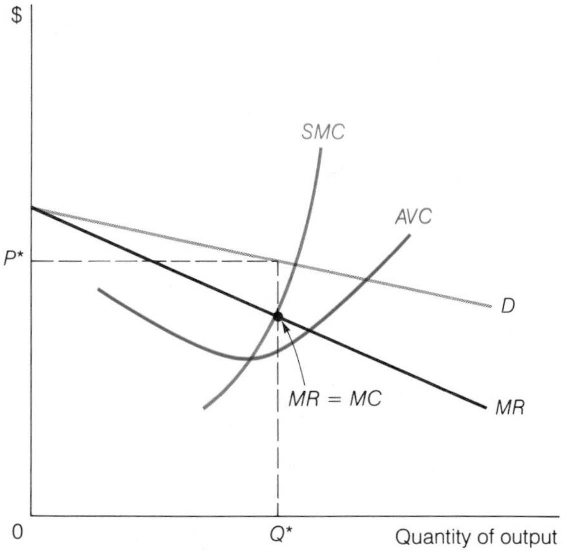

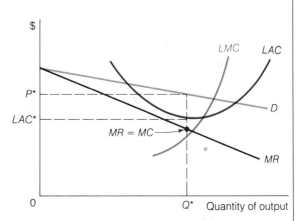

FIGURE 22–1   The Profit-Maximizing Position of the Monopolistically Competitive Firm in the Short Run

As in the case of any other firm, a monopolistically competitive firm will maximize its profits (or minimize its losses) in the short run where marginal revenue (MR) is equal to short-run marginal cost (SMC), at Q^*, as long as price (P^*) is at least sufficient to cover average variable costs (AVC). In this diagram, the firm has greater than normal profit.

FIGURE 22–2   The Profit-Maximizing Position of the Monopolistically Competitive Firm with Temporarily Greater than Normal Profit

In the long run, the monopolistically competitive firm will maximize profit by producing where marginal revenue (MR) is equal to long marginal cost (LMC), as long as the firm is receiving at least a normal profit—price (P) is greater than or equal to long-run average cost (LAC). In this case, the firm is receiving a greater than normal profit, so that other firms will have an incentive to enter the industry.

profit. In this case the firm is earning an economic profit, because price is greater than or
equal to average cost. However, because of the
absence of barriers to entry into the industry,
the situation is not stable.

LONG-RUN INDUSTRY EQUILIBRIUM

When firms in a monopolistically competitive
industry are earning an economic profit, other
firms are attracted to the industry. The entry of
new firms results in a smaller market share for
each firm. In this case the demand curves of
firms already in the industry shift downward.

The monopolistically competitive industry
will reach a long-run equilibrium position
when each firm is in a situation similar to that
shown in Figure 22–3. Price is equal to long-
run average cost at the profit-maximizing level
of output, so that each firm is earning only a
normal profit.

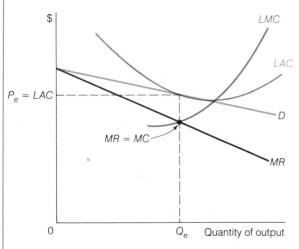

**FIGURE 22–3 The Position of the Monopolistically
Competitive Firm in Long-run Industry Equilibrium**

The monopolistically competitive firm will maximize its profit
in the long run by producing where marginal revenue *(MR)*
is equal to long-run marginal cost *(LMC)*, as long as it is
receiving at least normal profit. When, in addition, price *(P)*
is equal to long-run average cost *(LAC)*, the firm is receiving only a normal profit and there is no incentive for firms to
enter or leave the industry.

MONOPOLISTIC COMPETITION AND THE "REAL" WORLD

Small, independent retail firms are often monopolistically competitive firms, particularly
in larger metropolitan areas. Typical businesses of this sort are clothing boutiques, garages, hair styling salons, restaurants, and
taverns. The merchandise of these firms may
be differentiated by brand name, service, location, quality, style, taste, atmosphere, or
other attributes.

Advertising Because product differentiation
is crucial for a monopolistically competitive
firm to have any control over price, firms in
this type of industry often attempt to achieve
their differentiation through advertising. Advertising can also be used as a means of in-
forming the public about the availability of the
firm's product. Thus it may increase demand
for the product (shift the demand curve outward). If advertising increases the firm's revenue more than its costs, the firm will find it
profitable to advertise.

Examples of advertising by monopolistically
competitive firms abound. The "Weekender"
section of the May 29, 1981, *San Antonio Express-News* contained advertisements for 16
restaurants, and this was not a very big week
for such ads. More than 150 advertisements by
restaurants (as opposed to mere listings of
these establishments) appeared in the yellow
pages of the 1981 San Antonio telephone di-
rectory.

Some economists argue that an extensive
use of advertising is a waste of resources from
a social point of view because, in general, it
serves no useful social purpose. They admit,
however, that some advertising is beneficial to
society in that it gives consumers information.
In practice, of course, it is difficult to determine the point where socially "good" advertising ends and "bad" advertising begins.

**Monopolistic Competition and Social Wel-
fare** As is the case in perfect competition,
monopolistically competitive firms earn only

a normal profit when the industry is in long-run equilibrium. However, because each firm's demand curve is sloped downward, the firm produces a level of output smaller than that at which long-run average cost is at a minimum. Moreover, because price is greater than marginal revenue and marginal cost, the firm's profit-maximizing level of output occurs where marginal social benefit is greater than marginal social cost (see Figure 22–3).

Thus, from a social point of view, monopolistically competitive firms produce too little and charge too much. Nevertheless, if their demand curves are highly elastic, the prices and output of monopolistically competitive firms may not be very different from those of perfectly competitive firms. Moreover, in a monopolistically competitive industry, society does obtain the advantages of differentiated products. In a world where people have different tastes, this variety may be of significant benefit.

OLIGOPOLY: LAND OF THE GIANTS

◆

We now turn to **oligopoly,** the fourth and last type of market structure. Oligopoly more closely resembles monopoly than does either perfect competition or monopolistic competition.

CHARACTERISTICS OF OLIGOPOLY

We can describe an **oligopolistic industry** as follows:

1. There are only a few firms in the industry.
2. The firms recognize their mutual interdependence.
3. There are substantial barriers to entry into the industry.
4. The firms may produce either identical or differentiated products.

As we have indicated above, there are sufficiently few firms in an oligopolistic industry that they recognize their mutual interdependence. Although there is no precise definition of *fewness* with regard to an oligopoly, an oligopolistic industry must be concentrated enough for each firm to recognize that the demand for its product is significantly affected by its rivals' prices and levels of output.

> **Mutual interdependence** *refers to a situation where the market share of one firm is significantly affected by the actions of one or more of its rival firms.*

Even though the word *competition* is not part of the name for this market structure, oligopolistic firms frequently have a sense of competition or rivalry that is not present in any other type of industry.

Several kinds of barriers to entry □ are common in oligopolistic industries. First, economies of scale □ can serve as a barrier to new firms, because existing firms may have large, low-cost plants that can be duplicated only by massive, and sometimes high-risk, investment. For example, there have been only two new entrants in the world automobile industry in recent years. The first, Bricklin, occurred in Canada and was supported by substantial government investment. It failed nonetheless. The second, DeLorean, was launched with the backing of the government of Northern Ireland. DeLorean only began marketing cars in 1981, so by the fall of 1981 the success of that venture was still not determined.

Another important kind of barrier to entry is a technological or cost advantage secured by a patent or exclusive access to resources. Finally, existing firms may attempt to discourage entry through a number of restrictive practices. For example, they may expand their plant facilities in advance of anticipated increases in demand, making it clear to potential entrants that plenty of low-cost productive capacity already belongs to the established firms. Existing firms also may make huge out-

| 476 |
| 413 |

lays on advertising that, if matched by new firms, would substantially raise their cost of entry.

Advertising may be accompanied by product proliferation. Recently, U.S. manufacturers of breakfast cereals have attracted the attention of antitrust specialists. The reason is that the firms pursue a strategy of producing many types of cereals. It is argued that this practice cuts up the market into such small segments that no new firm will find it profitable to enter with only one or a few brands or types of products.

As indicated, barriers to entry prevent new firms from entering an industry easily and therefore keep the industry highly concentrated.

A **concentrated industry** has a large percentage of its output produced by a few firms.

Table 22–1 indicates the level of concentration in some oligopolistic manufacturing industries.

The firms in an oligopolistic industry may produce either identical or differentiated products. Firms in the steel and aluminum industries produce virtually identical products, whereas firms in the automobile and computer industries are characterized by differentiated products. In certain oligopolistic industries with differentiated products, firms typically spend a great deal of money on advertising and product development, each hoping to convince consumers that its product is superior to that of its rivals. (The paper towel industry is a case in point.) Each firm tries to increase the demand for its product and thereby increase its market share through differentiation and advertising. However, all these efforts may simply cancel each other out. This result can lead to higher costs and higher prices, with detrimental effects on both consumers and firms.

Because oligopolistic firms are so interdependent, it is impossible for one firm to determine the demand curve for its product without making some assumptions about the

TABLE 22–1   Percentage of Output Produced by the Four Largest Firms in Selected Manufacturing Industries

Industry	Percent of Output Produced by the Four Largest Firms
Primary lead	93
Motor vehicles	93
Flat glass	92
Cereal breakfast foods	90
Chewing gum	87
Cigarettes	84
Gypsum products	80
Primary aluminum	79
Calculators and accounting machines	73
Primary copper	72
Aircraft	66
Beet sugar	66
Metal cans	66
Soap and detergents	62
Blast furnaces and steel mills	45

[a]Measured by share of value of shipments.

Source: U.S. Department of Commerce, Bureau of the Census, "Table 5: Share of Value of Shipments Accounted for by the 4, 8, 20, and 50 Largest Companies in Each Manufacturing Industry: 1972 and Earlier Years," *1972 Census of Manufactures*, vol. 1 (Washington, D.C.: Government Printing Office, 1976), pp. SR 2–6 to SR 2–49.

behavior of its rivals. For example, the firm needs to know how its rivals will respond to price increases or decreases. Will they follow with similar price changes, or will they keep their prices constant? Also, how will rival firms react to changes in the firm's advertising expenditures? Because oligopolistic firms are so conscious of the actions of their rivals (with good reason), the behavior patterns of firms in an oligopolistic industry may be quite complex unless the firms cooperate. Three theories of how oligopolistic firms behave are discussed next.

CARTEL

In a **cartel,** the firms in an oligopoly formally agree on a price to charge and on the market share for each firm. Thus they behave very much like a monopoly.

This type of industry structure violates the antitrust laws □ of the United States, but it is legal in many other countries.

With a cartel, the firms in an oligopoly can maximize their joint profit. In fact, citizens of the United States and Japan greatly regret the success of the cartel known as the Organization of Petroleum Exporting Countries (OPEC). Moreover, as indicated at the beginning of this chapter, OPEC actions have helped U.S. oil companies implement price increases that have led to record profits. In the late 1970s, cartels in such industries as steel, synthetic fibers, and shipbuilding were being established by the European Common Market countries in an effort to increase profits.[2]

If the firms in a cartel wish to maximize the profit of the group as a whole, they should determine their price and respective levels of output as shown in Figure 22–4. First, the industry output and the price to be charged are determined by the point where industry or total market marginal revenue is equal to industry marginal cost, Q_I^*.

2. "The Common Market's Rush into Cartels," *Business Week*, March 27, 1978, pp. 107–108.

The industry marginal cost is obtained by horizontally summing the marginal cost curves of the firms. Horizontal summation means that quantities of output for each firm corresponding to a given level of marginal cost are summed, as shown in Table 22–2 for a two-firm cartel.

Once the price and the industry output are established for a cartel, the share of the market assigned to each firm must be determined. If the total profit of the group is to be maximized, each firm should produce where its marginal cost is equal to the industry marginal revenue and marginal cost at the optimal point, as shown in Figure 22–4. Thus Firm A will produce Q_A^* and Firm B Q_B^*.

As long as the firms in a cartel cooperate in this manner, the total profit of the group is maximized. However, one or more firms often become greedy and attempt to capture a larger market share for themselves. To do so they may secretly lower their price slightly below the established cartel price. Such actions are usually quickly discovered, and the remaining firms retaliate with deeper price cuts. Cartels often break up as a result.

Gentlemen's agreements are a less formal

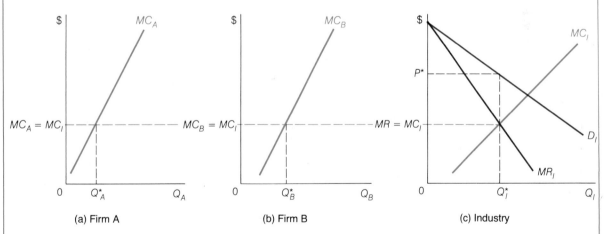

FIGURE 22–4 Determination of Price and Output in a Cartel

Firm A and Firm B have formed a cartel in this industry. The marginal cost curves of A and B *(MC_A and MC_B)* are horizontally summed to derive the marginal cost curve for the industry, *MC_I*. The cartel will maximize profit by restricting industry output to the level where the marginal cost for the industry is equal to the marginal revenue for the industry *(MR_I)*, at *Q_I**. Each firm will produce at that level of output where its respective marginal cost is equal to the industry marginal cost. The cartel will establish a price of *P**, which corresponds to an industry output level of *Q_I**.

TABLE 22–2   Horizontal Summation of Firms' Marginal Costs

Firm A		Firm B		Industry	
Q_A	MC_A	Q_B	MC_B	Q_I	MC_I
0		0		0	
	$ 3		$ 3		$ 3
1		1		2	
	5		5		$ 5
2		2		4	
	8		8		8
3		3		6	
	10		10		10
4		4		8	
	12		12		12
5		5		10	
	15		15		15
6		6		12	
	18		18		18
7		7		14	

way for oligopoly firms to set prices and establish market shares. They often take the form of informal verbal agreements on the golf course or in other, similar meeting places. These agreements also violate federal antitrust laws.

PRICE LEADERSHIP AND THE DOMINANT FIRM

The ***dominant firm explanation of price leadership*** *assumes that there is one large firm and other, smaller firms in the industry. The large firm sets the price, and the smaller firms accept it as a given and produce where price is equal to marginal cost—like purely competitive firms.*

An oligopolistic industry characterized by the dominant firm version of price leadership is shown in Figure 22–5. The dominant firm is

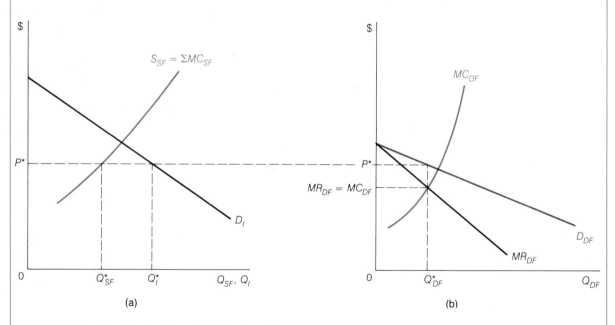

(a)   (b)

FIGURE 22–5   Price Leadership and the Dominant Firm

The demand curve for the industry, D_I, and the supply curve for the small firms, S_{SF}, are shown in panel (a). The dominant firm derives its demand curve by subtracting the quantity supplied by the small firms from the total quantity demanded in the industry at each price. The dominant firm produces where its marginal revenue (MR_{DF}) is equal to its marginal cost (MC_{DF}), at Q_{DF}^*. Correspondingly, the firm sets price at P^*. The small firms produce where price equals their joint marginal cost, given by S_{SF}, at Q_{SF}^*. The quantities $Q_{SF}^* + Q_{DF}^* = Q_I^*$, the total quantity produced in the industry.

the price setter, and it follows the procedure outlined here.

First, the dominant firm estimates the industry demand curve, D_I, and the joint supply curve □ of the smaller firms, S_{SF}. As in the case of perfect competition, the supply curve for the smaller firms is found by horizontally summing their marginal cost curves (excluding the portion that falls below minimum average variable cost).

The dominant firm then determines its demand curve, D_{DF}, as the difference between the industry demand curve and the supply curve of the smaller firms, as shown in panel (b) of Figure 21–5. At each possible price, the quantity demanded of the dominant firm's product will be equal to the total industry quantity demanded less the quantity supplied by the smaller firms.

Once the dominant firm has determined its demand curve, it can then find its marginal revenue curve, MR_{DF}. The dominant firm will maximize its profit by producing its product up to the point where its marginal revenue is equal to its marginal cost, Q_{DF}^*, and by setting its price at P^*.

The smaller firms will then accept P^* as a given and will produce their products up to the point where price is equal to marginal cost, Q_{SF}^* units of output. The total output of the industry is Q_I^*, which is equal to $Q_{SF}^* + Q_{DF}^*$.

Why doesn't the dominant firm attempt to expand its market share more aggressively? One reason is that if the firm, for example, were to temporarily set price so low that the small firms would be driven out of business, it would probably be accused of predatory pricing—a violation of the antitrust laws.

In the United States, industries characterized by some form of price leadership include the automobile industry, where General Motors is the recognized price leader; the steel industry, where U.S. Steel is frequently the price leader; the aluminum industry, with Alcoa as the price leader; and the tobacco industry, with R.J. Reynolds as the price leader. Thus we are used to headlines such as "Ford Motor Says Price Rise to Trail GM's, But Keeps Rival in Dark on Overall Boost" and "U.S. Steel Pricing Likely to Prompt Industry Boosts."[3]

However, in the latter part of the 1970s the Justice Department expressed concern that by announcing proposed price increases to the media, companies might be engaging in improper price signaling. This view has at least restrained the price announcements by Alcoa, and overt price leadership may be a thing of the past.[4]

Kinked Demand Curve Theory A third explanation of the behavior of firms in an oligopolistic industry was developed by economist Paul Sweezy, who theorized that, over time, a common market price tends to be established in an oligopolistic industry. Sweezy contended that if one firm in the industry raises its price above the going market price, the other firms will not follow with similar price increases. Consequently, the firm that raises its price will experience a large drop in the quantity demanded of its product.

On the other hand, if one firm lowers its price below the established market price, all the other firms in the industry will counter with similar price cuts. Consequently, the demand for the firm's product will be much less elastic with respect to price in this region than it will for a price rise.

3. See, for example, "Ford Indicates '78 Model Price Boosts Will Be Close to 5.7% Announced by GM," *Wall Street Journal*, September 2, 1977, p. 3; "Ford Motor Says Price Rise to Trail GM's, But Keeps Rival in Dark on Overall Boost," *Wall Street Journal*, September 9, 1976, p. 2; "U.S. Steel Pricing Likely to Prompt Industry Boosts," *Wall Street Journal*, August 16, 1976, p. 3; "Kaiser to Raise Aluminum Sheet Price about 8%," *Wall Street Journal*, September 8, 1977, p. 2; and "Cigarette Prices Go Up," *Business Week*, August 29, 1977, p. 34.

4. "Alcoa Omits Price-Boost Announcement, Heeds Complaints on Media 'Signaling,'" *Wall Street Journal*, September 6, 1977, p. 2; and "Antitrust Officials Plan Investigations into Pricing in Concentrated Industries," *Wall Street Journal*, May 13, 1977, p. 3.

> A **kinked demand curve** exists for some oligopoly firms that believe rivals will follow a price decrease but not a price increase.

In Figure 22–6 the established market price is P_M. The corresponding level of output for the firm is Q_M. At a level of output less than Q_M the upper portion of demand curve D_1 will be the relevant demand curve for the firm, since D_1 will be the firm's demand curve if no other firms change price in response to a price change by the first firm. At prices lower than P_M the relevant demand curve for the firm will

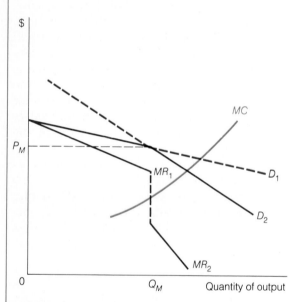

FIGURE 22–6 Profit Maximization with a Kinked Demand Curve

D_1 is the demand curve that would apply if other firms in the industry did *not* follow a single firm when it changed price. On the other hand, demand curve D_2 applies when all other firms *will* follow a price change made by one firm. P_M is the going market price. Since the kinked demand curve theory states that firms will not follow a price increase above P_M, but will follow a price decrease below P_M, demand curve D_1 applies at prices above P_M, whereas D_2 applies at lower prices. As a result, the demand curve for the firm has a kink in it at P_M and Q_M. Also, the marginal revenue curve is discontinuous (has a "gap") at Q_M. As long as its marginal cost curve passes through the gap in the marginal revenue curve, the firm will maximize profit by producing Q_M units of output and charging a price equal to P_M.

be demand curve D_2. That curve is the relevant demand curve for the firm if all other firms change their prices in response to a price change by this firm.

In this situation the firm's marginal revenue curve will have a gap, or point of discontinuity, at Q_M. MR_1 is the marginal revenue curve that corresponds to D_1. MR_2 is the marginal revenue curve that corresponds to D_2.

As long as the firm's marginal cost curve passes through the gap in the marginal revenue curve at Q_M, the firm will maximize profit by charging P_M and producing Q_M units of output, as shown in Figure 22–6. However, if the firm's marginal cost curve were to intersect MR_1 at a level of output less than Q_M, the firm would maximize its profit by raising its price and producing a lower level of output. If the marginal cost curve were to intersect MR_2 at a level of output greater than Q_M, the firm would maximize its profit by lowering its price and producing a level of output greater than Q_M.

In most cases the firm's marginal cost curve will pass through the gap at Q_M, and the profit-maximizing price will be P_M. In fact, Sweezy offered this explanation of why a firm in an oligopoly might continue to charge the same price and produce the same level of output after its marginal cost of production had risen or fallen.

The kinked demand curve theory has seemed to apply sometimes to firms like local gasoline stations. However, in the inflationary setting of the 1970s and early 1980s such firms have tended to raise prices in response to cost increases, particularly when the cost increases affect all the firms in the industry.

OLIGOPOLY AND SOCIAL WELFARE

In general, other things equal, *firms in an oligopoly tend to charge higher prices and produce a smaller total industry output than do firms in perfectly or monopolistically competitive industries.* However, some economists and many business people argue that there are advantages to an oligopolistic market structure. We will examine these points here.

High Prices and Underproduction Since price is greater than marginal revenue and marginal cost at the profit-maximizing level of output, the oligopolistic firm produces where the marginal social benefit □ of another unit of the product is greater than its marginal social cost.□ In social welfare terms this situation represents underproduction and inefficient allocation of resources.

Economic Profit Moreover, barriers to entry prevent other firms from entering the market, so that firms in an oligopoly are able to earn an economic profit in the long run. Thus, in an oligopoly, barriers to entry allow firms to charge higher prices than would be the case in perfect or monopolistic competition.

Advertising As in monopolistic competition, oligopolistic firms also attempt to achieve product differentiation through advertising. In fact, in the fall of 1979 many firms were willing to spend $75,000 for each thirty-second, prime-time commercial on the ABC television network.[5] The arguments for and against advertising as it relates to social welfare are the same for oligopoly firms as for firms in monopolistically competitive industries. Nevertheless, several points can be cited in favor of an oligopolistic market structure.

Economies of Scale Some economists and many firm managers in oligopolistic industries contend that the presence of significant economies of scale □ in these industries is a primary factor in encouraging the merger of competing firms until an oligopoly results. Thus they argue that larger firms can produce at lower unit costs than can smaller firms.

The federal government indicated in 1978 that this argument had some merit, at least in the steel industry, by allowing LTV Corpora-

tion to merge its Jones and Laughlin Steel Corporation to Lykes Corporation's Youngstown Sheet and Tube Co.[6] In an antitrust case involving cereal companies, Kellogg asserted that its high profits were the result not of monopoly behavior but of economies of scale and other cost efficiencies.[7] General Motors and the oil companies have made similar arguments.

Progressive Oligopolies John Kenneth Galbraith, □ a well-known economist, has argued that corporations need to be large in order to be able to incur the risks and the product research and development expenses and to do the planning necessary for profitability in the latter part of the twentieth century. Galbraith states:

The size of General Motors is in the service not of monopoly or the economies of scale but of planning. And for this planning—control of supply, control of demand, provision of capital, minimization of risk—there is no clear upper limit to the desirable size.[8]

The evidence does not clearly indicate, however, that large firms are necessarily the most progressive in terms of either the production technology they utilize or the products they develop. For example, in the fall of 1979 U.S. Steel, the largest steel producer in the United States, announced the permanent shutdown of thirteen steel manufacturing plants. One of the reasons for U.S. Steel's problems was its use in many plants of outmoded facilities, such as open-hearth furnaces.[9]

---

5. "A Rush to Lock up Scarce TV Ad Time" *Business Week*, July 9, 1979, p. 23.

6. "Antitrust: A Soft Line on a Steel Merger," *Business Week*, July 3, 1978, p. 30.

7. "Kellogg: Still the Cereal People," *Business Week*, November 26, 1979, p. 86.

8. John Kenneth Galbraith, "The Corporation," *The New Industrial State* (Boston: Houghton Mifflin, 1967), p. 76.

9. See "What Biting the Bullet Means to Big Steel," *Business Week*, December 10, 1979, pp. 32–33; and "Blues for Big Steel," *Newsweek*, December 10, 1979, pp. 92–97.

In fact, companies relatively new to the steel industry were the ones that implemented the newest technology. Kaiser obtained the first U.S. patent for the basic oxygen furnace (BOF), and McLouth installed the first BOF plant in the United States. McClouth was also the first mass-producer of steel to install a working continuous casting machine.[10]

Moreover, Datapoint Corporation, a small producer of computers and other data-processing equipment and related products, introduced on November 22, 1979, what it called an Integrated Electronic Office. According to *Business Week*:

This single system combines data processing functions with the electronic counterpart of the typewriter, mailroom, and filing cabinet. And by making all of those office functions available from a single terminal, the small but fast-growing San Antonio computer maker is leapfrogging a pack of 100 or more companies that is zeroing in on the office automation market—a list that includes such heavyweights as International Business Machines, American Telephone and Telegraph, Xerox, and Exxon.[11]

Thus bigness does not always imply progressiveness.

Countervailing Power   In the 1950s Galbraith argued that countervailing power would prevent large corporations from earning monopoly profits.

By **countervailing power**, *Galbraith was referring to situations in which a large firm has to deal with other large firms, unions, or other entities, all of which have sufficient power on the other side of the market to counteract the power of the first firm.*

In other words, big buyers can offset the power of big sellers, and vice versa. Galbraith

offered examples such as the Big Four automobile producers buying steel from big steel producers or tires from large tire manufacturers. Moreover, the presence of unions such as the United Auto Workers (UAW) limits the ability of large corporations to take advantage of labor.[12]

However, the existence of countervailing power does not necessarily mean that the best interests of consumers will be served. For example, it may be easier at some point for the automobile manufacturers to pass on high costs to consumers than to battle their steel suppliers or the UAW.[13]

Consequently, the effect of an oligopolistic market structure on the welfare of society is at best mixed. Perhaps bigness does in some cases result in lower unit costs. However, it may also be a primary factor in permitting economic profit to exist in the long run.

THE FOUR MARKET STRUCTURES IN REVIEW

Table 22–3 summarizes the four general types of market structures and their characteristics. Under perfect competition many firms offer identical products. Each firm accepts the market price as a given. Firms maximize profit by producing their commodities at the point

10. Leonard W. Weiss, "Oligopoly-Steel," *Case Studies in American Industry* (New York: Wiley, 1967), p. 197.

11. "Datapoint Leapfrogs into the Office," *Business Week*, December 10, 1979, p. 93.

12. See John Kenneth Galbraith, *American Capitalism: The Concept of Countervailing Power* (Boston: Houghton Mifflin, 1956), especially Chapter 9. Galbraith later modified this view and emphasized the need for planning on the part of the corporation. According to Galbraith, planning requires that the firm be able to control the demand for its product and its cost. See, for example, John Kenneth Galbraith, *Economics and the Public Purpose* (Boston: Houghton Mifflin, 1973), especially Chapters 9, 10, and 13.

13. See, for example, "A Year for Union Collisions with the Guidelines," *Business Week*, January 8, 1979, pp. 70–71.

TABLE 22–3 The Four Types of Market Structures and Their Characteristics

Type of Market Structure	Number of Producers	Product Differentiation	Degree of Control Over Price	Relationship Between Price and Marginal Cost	Barriers to Entry.	Economic Profit in Long Run Industry Equilibrium
Perfect Competition	Many	None	None	P = MC	None	None
Monopolistic Competition	Many	Some (perceived, whether or not actual)	Some	P > MC	None or very limited	None
Oligopoly	Few	May or may not have differentiated products	Some	P > MC	Substantial	Possible
Monopoly	One	No close substitute for this product	Limited only by market demand	P > MC	No entry possible	Possible

where price is equal to marginal cost, so that under the assumptions discussed in Chapter 20 the marginal social benefit of another unit of the commodity is equal to its marginal social cost. There are no barriers to entry, and there is no economic profit in the long run.

Many firms operate in monopolistically competitive industries, and each firm maintains some control over price as a result of a limited amount of product differentiation. Price is greater than marginal cost (marginal social benefit is greater than marginal social cost) at the profit-maximizing level of output. In this case, there is underproduction from the viewpoint of society as a whole. However, no economic profits are generated in long-run industry equilibrium because there are no (or very limited) barriers to entry into the industry.

Oligopoly is characterized by having only a few firms in the industry, with each firm clearly recognizing its mutual interdependence with the other firms. These firms have some control over price and may or may not have differentiated products. At the profit-maximizing level of output, price is greater than marginal cost. Economic profits may exist in the long run because of substantial barriers to entry.

In a monopoly there is only one firm in the industry, and its control over price is limited only by the market demand for its product. Again, price is greater than marginal cost. No entry into the industry is possible. Consequently the firm may make an economic profit in the long run.

SUMMARY

1. This chapter has examined the two types of industry structures that are most pervasive in the real world: monopolistic competition and oligopoly.

2. A monopolistically competitive industry generally has the following characteristics: (a) there are many firms in the industry, (b) the firms produce slightly differentiated products, and (c) barriers to entry are relatively small or nonexistent and factors of production are mobile. Because of product differentiation the monopolistically competitive firm has some control over the price of its product. Consequently, its demand curve is downward sloping, and its marginal revenue is less than its price.

3. As is true for all firms, in the short run the monopolistically competitive firm maximizes its profit by producing the level of output where marginal revenue is equal to short-run marginal cost, as long as price is at least equal to average variable cost. In the long run the firm maximizes profit by producing

where marginal revenue is equal to long-run marginal cost, as long as price is greater than or equal to long-run average cost.

4. A monopolistically competitive industry will not be in a long-run equilibrium position until each firm is producing at a level of output where marginal revenue is equal to long-run marginal cost and price is equal to long-run average cost, so that each firm is earning only a normal profit. If the firms in a monopolistically competitive industry are earning a greater than normal profit, new firms will enter the industry, which will result in a smaller market share for each firm. The reverse process will occur if the firms are earning less than a normal profit.

5. To increase the control they have over price, monopolistically competitive firms frequently advertise. Advertising increases the profit of a firm as long as it increases the firm's revenues more than its costs.

6. An oligopolistic market structure may produce results similar to those of a monopoly if the firms in the industry cooperate. An oligopolistic industry can be characterized as follows: (a) there are only a few firms in the industry, (b) the firms may produce either identical or differentiated products, (c) the firms recognize their mutual interdependence, and (d) there are substantial barriers to entry into the industry.

7. Since the firms in an oligopolistic industry are so interdependent, the behavior of one firm that will maximize its profits depends on the actions taken by the other firms. Three theories regarding the behavior of firms in an oligopoly are the cartel theory, the dominant firm (or price leadership) theory, and the kinked demand curve theory.

8. In a cartel, the firms formally set prices and industry output. If group profits are to be maximized, the cartel members will set prices and levels of output for the industry as is done in a monopoly, where industry marginal revenue is equal to industry marginal cost. If the profit of the whole group is to be maximized, each firm must produce the level of output where its marginal cost of production is just equal to industry marginal revenue and marginal cost at the optimal point. Cartels are illegal in the United States. Moreover, gentlemen's agreements, a less formal manner in which firms set prices or market shares, are also illegal.

9. The dominant firm, or price leadership, theory assumes that one dominant firm in the industry is the price leader. The remaining firms accept the price set by the dominant firm as given and produce where price is equal to marginal cost, as in perfect competition.

10. The kinked demand curve theory is based on three assumptions. The first assumption is that a standard industry price has been established. The second assumption is that if one of the firms raises its price, no other firms will follow with a price increase; however, if one firm lowers its price, all firms will follow suit. The third assumption is that firms wish to maximize their profit in these circumstances. The second assumption implies that the demand curve has a kink at the going market price and that the marginal revenue curve has a gap at the corresponding level of output. As long as the firm's marginal cost curve passes through the gap in the marginal revenue curve, the firm will maximize profit by charging the going market price and producing the corresponding level of output.

11. The kinked demand curve theory has been offered as an explanation of why a firm in an oligopoly does not always change its price in response to a change in its marginal cost curve. Nevertheless, when the costs of all the firms in the industry rise, all the firms tend to raise prices together.

12. From a social point of view, an oligopolistic industry structure frequently results in a higher price and a lower total industry output than would be the case in a perfectly competitive industry. Moreover, barriers to entry allow oligopolistic firms to make an economic profit in the long run.

13. In some cases, large firms may be able to produce at lower unit cost because of economies of scale. However, bigness and progressiveness in terms of production technology or of product development do not always go together. Also, the presence of countervailing power does not necessarily benefit the consumer.

IMPORTANT TERMS AND CONCEPTS

Monopolistic competition	Concentrated industry
Differentiated products	Cartel
Oligopoly	Gentlemen's agreements
Mutual interdependence	Price leadership
	Kinked demand curve
	Countervailing power

QUESTIONS AND PROBLEMS

1. Describe a monopolistically competitive industry. Give an example.

2. Draw graphs showing the short-run profit-maximizing position of a monopolistically competitive firm and its position when the industry is in long-run equilibrium.

3. How does a monopolistically competitive industry structure affect the welfare of society?

4. Why are oligopolistic firms said to be more competitive than firms in perfectly competitive or monopolistically competitive industries?

5. Briefly describe the dominant firm, or price leadership, theory of how oligopolistic firms establish price and level of output. Use graphs in your explanation.

6. How does the kinked demand curve theory attempt to explain the stability of prices in an oligopolistic industry?

7. What is countervailing power? Give an example.

8. What are gentlemen's agreements? Why are they not openly used by more oligopolistic firms?

9. Compare the effects of an oligopolistic industry and a monopolistically competitive industry on social welfare.

10. Discuss the following statement: The bigger the firm, the more progressive it is in developing new technologies and new products.

11. Discuss the following statement: A cartel and a monopoly are the same thing.

ECONOMICS
101
FOR OPEC

The scene was painfully familiar. The result was not. After a decade of mercilessly driving up prices and creating economic chaos in rich and poor nations alike, the thirteen OPEC oil ministers who met in Geneva last week faced sobering new reality: a world market awash in surplus oil. Following two days of closed-door meetings, the once-militant oil ministers emerged in a glare of television lights to announce a freeze in prices for the rest of the year. "The lesson we are learning is that we are compelled to respond to market forces," said Indonesian oil minister Dr. Soebroto.

OPEC's new lesson in market economics is a partial victory for Saudi Arabia, the cartel's largest producer. In recent months the Saudis have pumped 10.3 million barrels a day—2 million barrels more than normal—and flooded the market with lower-priced crude oil in an attempt to stabilize prices. At the same time, demand has been plunging as major industrial powers conserve oil. U.S. oil consumption was down 5.2 per cent in the first quarter, for example, and U.S. imports declined 18 per cent. Nonetheless, OPEC hard-liners went to Geneva hoping to force another round of price hikes, a production cutback or both.

Throughout the conference, Saudi Arabia's oil minister, Sheik Ahmad Zaki Yamani, refused to give in to pressure from the other members to cut production. The Saudis—who produce nearly half of OPEC's output—also refused to raise their price of $32 a barrel, $9 a barrel below the highest OPEC prices. Faced with Saudi intransigence, the other OPEC members finally agreed to hold the line on prices, but in retaliation they voted unanimously to cut production by 10 per cent, beginning this week, in an attempt to shrink the oil glut.

For all their bravado, some

OPEC members will have trouble sacrificing oil income to meet that goal. Indonesia, for instance, has a huge population and an ambitious economic-development plan to support with its oil revenues. "We can use every cent we earn from our oil," says Soebroto. "The price freeze and production cut will certainly hurt us." But Soebroto vows to support the decision, if only to keep the cartel's power from eroding further.

RIFT

In fact, though no one expects OPEC to disintegrate anytime soon, the price freeze of 1981 signals a major change in the cartel. Barring an unexpected disruption in supply or a drastic policy reversal by Saudi Arabia, the oil cartel can no longer set prices by fiat alone. Last week several major oil companies threatened to terminate supply contracts unless producing countries cut prices. What's more, there's a growing split between OPEC members like Saudi Arabia, which has vast reserves that will last well into the next century, and those countries that are rapidly depleting their oil. "The OPEC of the end of the '80s is going to be a very different place from what it was at the beginning," said Humberto Calderón-Berti, Venezuela's energy minister. "By the end of the 1980s some OPEC countries won't be exporter countries anymore, but importing oil for their own use."

In the meantime, OPEC's price freeze is good news for American motorists; the crude-oil oversupply should keep gasoline prices flat in the near future. And if the glut persists much longer, some wags suggest, OPEC oil ministers may even have to resort to Detroit's old marketing trick: rebates.

QUESTIONS

1. What did the Indonesian oil minister mean when he said that OPEC would have to respond to "market forces"?
2. Why is Saudi Arabia such an important member of the OPEC cartel?
3. Why do cartel "hard liners" want to raise prices? What do they seem to be assuming about the elasticity of demand for crude oil?

THE EFFECTS OF
TAXES
ON THE FIRM

Often a tax levied on specific products or businesses seems to be a popular way of attacking certain problems or of attempting to achieve certain ends. Sometimes the goal is merely to tax the sales of an undesirable or luxury product. In other cases the goal is to tax monopoly profits, raise revenue, or a combination of the two. In the spring of 1980, for example, Congress passed a law that provided for a windfall profits tax on the profits of the oil companies. These profits were considered "excessive" because of the large increases in the price of oil during the 1970s.

This appendix will analyze the effects of three basic types of taxes—a per unit sales tax, a lump sum profits tax, and a percent of profits tax—on price, quantity sold, and profit.

SALES TAX

Figure J–1 shows a daily demand curve, D_C, for a firm that sells cigarettes. The firm is assumed to operate in an imperfectly competitive market. If no tax is charged, MC is the firm's marginal cost curve, $1 is the profit-maximizing price, and 150 packs of cigarettes per day is the quantity.

If a sales tax of $.15 per pack of cigarettes sold is levied on the firm, the firm's marginal cost curve will shift upward by $.15, to $MC + T$. The new profit-maximizing price is approximately $1.05, and the new level of output is about 135 packs per day. In this case the consumer pays $.05 more per pack of cigarettes than before the tax was imposed. The firm receives $1.05 − $.15 = $.90 per pack, $.10 less than it received before the tax. Thus in terms of the prices paid by the consumer and received by the firm, the consumer pays $.05/$.15 = 1/3 of the tax, whereas the firm pays $.10/$.15 = 2/3 of the tax. In this case the demand for cigarettes is relatively elastic.□

In Figure J–2 the demand curve for cigarettes is relatively inelastic. Here, a $.15 tax results in an increase of $.10 in the profit-maximizing price. In this situation the consumer pays $.10 more than before, and the producer receives $1.10 − $.15 = $.95, or $.05 less

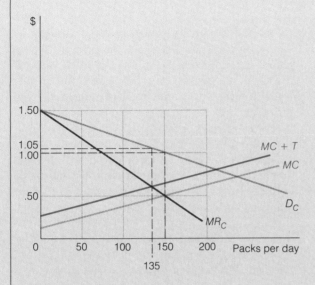

FIGURE J–1   The Effect of a Per Unit Sales Tax When Demand Is Relatively Elastic

The firm's marginal cost curve before the tax is imposed is given by *MC*. The firm's demand and marginal revenue curves are D_c and MR_c, respectively. Before the tax is imposed, the firm will maximize profit by producing where $MR_c = MC$, at an output level of 150 packs per day, and charging a price equal to $1.00 a pack. After the sales tax of $.15 per pack is imposed, the relevant marginal cost curve for the firm becomes *MC* + *T*, where *T* is the amount of the tax (equal to $.15). Now, the firm will maximize profit by producing where $MR_c = MC + T$, at a level of output equal to 135 packs per day, and charging a price of $1.05 per pack.

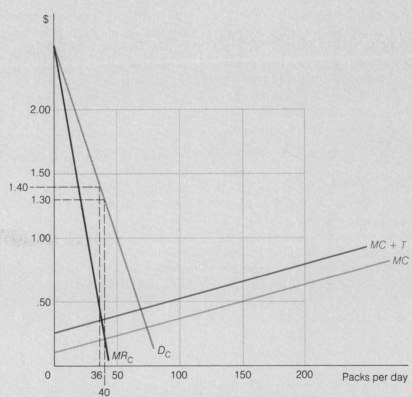

FIGURE J–2   The Effect of a Per Unit Sales Tax When Demand Is Relatively Inelastic

As in Figure J–1, the firm's marginal cost curve before the tax is imposed is *MC*. Also, the firm's marginal revenue and demand curves are given by MR_c and D_c, respectively. Initially, before the tax is imposed, the firm will maximize its profit by producing 40 packs a day and charging a price of $1.30 per pack. After the $.15 tax is imposed, the firm will maximize profit by producing 36 packs per day and charging a price of $1.40 per pack.

513

than before. Consequently, the consumer pays $.10/$.15 = 2/3 of the tax, whereas the producer pays $.05/$.15 = 1/3 of the tax.

These two examples illustrate an important economic principle: *The more elastic demand is with respect to price, the smaller is the portion of a per unit sales tax that will be borne by the consumer* (assuming that firms charge a profit-maximizing price). This relationship would also hold if the tax were levied as a percent of the sales price.

LUMP SUM TAX

A lump sum tax—a tax of a fixed dollar amount—is merely an addition to the fixed cost □ of a firm. Two examples of such a tax are property taxes and license fees.

Since a lump sum tax affects only a firm's fixed cost, and not its marginal cost, the imposition of such a tax will leave the profit-maximizing price and output level of the firm unchanged, as long as the tax does not prevent the firm from earning a normal rate of return. Thus a lump sum tax is borne entirely by the firm if economic profit is present in an amount sufficient to cover the tax.

However, in a purely competitive industry with no economic profit present in the long-run, the tax burden will be borne by consumers. This occurs because in the face of less than normal profit, firms will leave the industry until the price rises enough to result in a normal profit once again for the remaining firms.

Percentage Profit Tax A percentage profit tax is what its name implies, a tax computed as some percent of a firm's accounting profit. Because it depends only on the firm's total profit, such a tax will not affect the profit-maximizing price and level of output for the firm, as long as the firm still earns a normal profit after paying it.

We can conclude that a per unit sales tax generally alters the profit-maximizing price and level of output for a firm, whereas a lump sum tax or a percentage profit tax does not, as long as the firm can still earn a normal rate of return. It does not automatically follow, however, that the welfare of society will be enhanced by levying either of the latter two types of taxes on firms earning economic profit. The net effect on the social welfare will depend on both the efficiency with which the tax is collected and the uses to which the funds are put.

QUESTIONS

1. What are the differences among a sales tax, a lump sum tax, and a percentage profit tax?

2. Will the imposition of any of these taxes alter the profit-maximizing price and level of output for a firm?

3. Illustrate graphically the effect of a sales tax on gasoline.

4. What would be the effect of a percentage profit tax on oil producers?

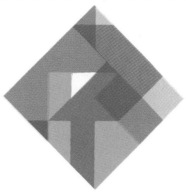

THE PATH TO
MODERN
MICROECONOMICS

As noted in "Economic Origins II," classical economists generally argued that the force of competition, operating in free markets, would serve to answer most of the important economic questions facing a society. They discussed at length both the workings of competitive markets and the concepts of supply and demand. However, their analyses usually focused on the macroeconomic question of how a market system operates, not on the microeconomic question of how supply and demand determine the market price of a specific good or service. Certainly, the economists discussed the latter topic at length, but their verbal models were frequently imprecise and they did not draw supply and demand curves. Finally, they presented only skeletal theories of consumer behavior, production, and profit maximization. In the heyday of British classical economics, the elements of modern microeconomics were being developed in France.

Augustin Cournot (1801–1877) and **Jules Dupuit** (1804–1866) were French contemporaries of John Stuart Mill who contributed significantly to economic theory but who were not viewed as economists during their lifetimes. Cournot, a mathematician and statistician, was educated in Paris and taught briefly at the University of Lyons. He spent most of his life in public service, as a school superintendent or government bureaucrat. His major work in economics, *Researches into the Mathematical Principles of the Theory of Wealth* (1838), contains most of his important contributions to the discipline, including the law of demand.

Cournot stated that, other things equal, quantity demanded is a function of price, and he was the first to draw a demand curve expressing this relation. In addition, he analyzed monopoly and a special case of two-firm oligopoly (duopoly) using a mathematical approach. In this analysis he concisely stated the profit-maximizing condition for a single firm (marginal revenue = marginal cost) and recognized that some firms must take into account the reactions of their rivals.

Dupuit, an engineer who specialized in public works projects, also drew demand curves. Both Cournot and Dupuit viewed quantity demanded as a function of price and therefore put quantity on the vertical axis of their diagrams. Dupuit related quantity demanded to the satisfaction, or utility, that consumers obtained from purchasing a good, and his demand curve was more properly a marginal utility curve. The concepts of diminishing marginal utility and price discrimination are found in Dupuit's discussion of the economics of public works, and he is today regarded as the earliest practitioner of public sector microeconomics.[1] Neither Cournot nor Dupuit was widely read by economists of the time (indeed, the two men did not know of each other's work), which may explain to a degree why the next steps in the development of modern microeconomics did not take place in France.

Marginal Utility Theory, which was understood by Dupuit, has its roots in the utilitarian philosophy of **Jeremy Bentham** (1748–1832). Bentham, who participated in the upbringing of John Stuart Mill, believed that rational persons were motivated by sensations of pleasure and pain. If left to their own devices, individuals would maximize their own personal well-being. This behavior would be consistent with maximum social welfare, because (much like the theory of Adam Smith) moral and institutional sanctions would temper personal actions. Bentham ac-

1. See Chapter 28 of this text for a discussion of public sector microeconomics.

Bentham's "bones."

tually tried to do some calculations of pleasure and pain (a "felicific calculus"), but his efforts were frustrated by his ignorance of the marginal approach to decision making.[2]

William Stanley Jevons (1835–1882), an English economist who studied under the followers of Mill, and Karl Menger (1840–1921), an Austrian lawyer and journalist, both published books on the theory of marginal utility in 1871. Jevon's approach was mathematical and graphical, while Menger's relied on lengthy discussion of tabular examples. Jevons assumed that the marginal utility of a good or service would fall as the quantity of it consumed by an individual increased. Thus, although total utility would rise as a consumer took more and more of a good, the additional utility derived from one more unit of consumption would fall. Jevons argued that an individual who possessed a stock of some commodity, X, and could trade it for some other commodity, Y, would choose between the two goods by giving up X and taking Y until the marginal utility of the last unit of X retained was equal to that of the last unit of Y taken, or $MU_X = MU_Y$. (A unit of X is the amount of X that can be exchanged for a unit of Y.) From this discussion stems the well-known equimarginal principle:

$$\frac{MU_X}{P_X} = \frac{MU_Y}{P_Y}$$

which states that $1 worth of each good will have the same marginal utility.

Although Jevons correctly formulated the theory of maximization of consumer satisfaction, his work was not well received by his English colleagues. There were several reasons for this reaction. First, his book, *The Theory of Political Economy,* was mathematically difficult and not well written. Second, he was an introvert and, by all reports, an awful teacher. Finally, he overstated his case by arguing that he had found the only true theory of value, the theory of final degree of utility. As Jevons himself put it:

Cost of production determines supply.
Supply determines final degree of utility.
Final degree of utility determines value.[3]

2. Bentham was an eccentric. When he died, he left his estate to the University of London on the condition that his remains be present at future board meetings. "Bentham's bones," appropriately attired, were placed in a cabinet for the purpose of fulfilling his request.
3. William Stanley Jevons, *Theory of Political Economy* (1871; New York: Kelley and Macmillan, 1957), p. 179.

William Stanley Jevons

Thus Jevons substituted an excessive emphasis on utility for the classical economists' excessive emphasis on cost of production.

Menger's book, unlike that of Jevons, was well received in his native Austria. Its success won him an appointment in economics at the University of Vienna. Nonetheless, Menger had to fight for acceptance of his views, because German economics was dominated by a historical school that liked neither his emphasis on the role of individual behavior nor his deductive theorizing. His argument for the equimarginal principle parallels that of Jevons, but Menger also developed a theory of input prices that imputes factor values from the value of final goods. This approach was not only conceptually difficult but it also reflected the same overemphasis on utility that flawed the work of Jevons.

In 1874 a French-born economist who taught at the University of Lausanne in Switzerland, **Leon Walras,** published a highly mathematical treatise, *Elements of Pure Political Economy,* that also contained the marginal utility theory of consumer behavior. Walras, who was familiar with Cournot's work, did not know about the theories of Jevons and Menger. Walras was probably the best technician of the three, and his book went much further in integrating the theory of consumer behavior and a similar theory of production into a mathematical model of an economy with *n* markets. In Walras's view, any change in the price of

a good sets off changes in the prices of related goods and factors of production, so that equilibrium can be discussed only in terms of the system as a whole. His method, known as **general equilibrium analysis,** is one of the most elegant and appealing approaches in economics, as well as one of the most difficult.

Although Walras is revered by modern economists, his work was not widely accepted in his time. This fact certainly could not be attributed to lack of zeal on his part, since, over a period of about fifty years, he corresponded with virtually all of the world's major economists. Walras was so enamored of his own work that he actively lobbied for a Nobel Peace Prize for his contributions to solving the world's social and economic problems. However, most of the world was far more disposed to follow the path laid out by **Alfred Marshall** (1842–1924), whose work Walras spitefully criticized at every turn.[4]

Marshallian Economics and the Neoclassical School are virtually synonymous with one another. It was Marshall who successfully synthesized the classical analysis of production and supply with a marginal utility–based theory of demand. He picked up the loose ends left by the classical economists and the marginal utility theorists and defined an equilibrium market price based on the interaction of demand and supply. As he put it: "We might as reasonably dispute whether it is the upper or the under blade of a pair of scissors that cuts a piece of paper, as whether value is governed by utility or cost of production."[5]

Marshall came to economics from mathematics. In fact, if his father's will had prevailed, he would have become a clergyman. However, he rejected a scholarship in religion at Oxford and chose to study mathematics at Cambridge. There, in 1867, he decided to change his field to economics. While at Cambridge, he married Mary Paley, one of his former students. In 1877 they moved to a new university in Bristol, where they both taught economics and collaborated on writings.

4. Vilfredo Pareto (1848–1923) was the most important follower of Walras. Pareto used indifference curves to show that an optimum exchange between two traders occurs when neither one of them can gain without hurting the other. Such a situation is today called "Pareto optimal."

5. Alfred Marshall, *Principles of Economics,* 8th ed. (London: Macmillan, 1920), p. 290.

Alfred Marshall

In 1884 the Marshalls returned to Cambridge, where they spent the rest of their lives. Alfred Marshall produced over eighty articles and books on economics during his long career. His partial equilibrium approach and marginalist way of thinking influenced virtually all twentieth century economists. In fact, John Maynard Keynes and many other well-known economists of the mid twentieth century were Marshall's students.

As noted, in formulating economic propositions Marshall preferred to use a partial equilibrium approach. In **partial equilibrium analysis** a key variable affecting a specific outcome, such as market price, is changed in isolation from other possible important variables under the assumption that the latter are held constant, or do not change. This assumption, known as the "other things equal," or *ceteris paribus,* assumption, allowed Marshall to describe both consumer adjustments to changes in product prices or incomes and producer adjustments to changes in demand or costs.

Marshall emphasized the importance of analyzing the effects of small changes in consumption and production and argued that the incremental, or marginalist, approach to economic decison making pro-

vided the most fruitful method for developing economic principles. Although he often used examples from everyday life in his writing, Marshall relied heavily on deductive reasoning to make theoretical points. His ability to create abstract concepts for purposes of developing general propositions greatly strengthed his work. For example, he frequently used the notion of a representative firm in his discussion of production, cost, and supply. The representative firm was a useful fiction that allowed him to reach broad conclusions about producers' reactions to changes in important economic variables.

Marshall realized that time played an important role in the decision process of firms, and his definitions of the *short run* and *long run* are still used in microeconomics today. The modern concepts of elasticity of demand and elasticity of supply are thoroughly developed in Marshall's work, and he greatly refined the link between marginal utility theory and the market demand curve for a good or service. Marshall drew intersecting supply and demand curves and described the equilibrium quantity as the quantity that would equate the demand price with the supply price. He derived his demand curve through the use of marginal utility theory, and he based his supply curve on verbally stated laws of production.[6] Marshall also made significant contributions to the theory of monopoly, the theory of international trade, and monetary theory.

Marshall's followers have included many well-known economists in Great Britain and the United States. In addition to Keynes, who turned the neoclassical world upside down by using Marshall's partial equilibrium approach within a new framework of macroeconomic analysis, the Marshallians count among their number those who refined and extended microeconomics to its present-day form.

The modern graphical depiction of total product, marginal product, and average product of an input is attributable to an Amercian neoclassical economist, **Frank H. Knight** (1885–1972). Knight's student, **Jacob Viner** (1892–1970), is the source of the graphical analysis of perfect competition. Knight and Viner can be viewed as founders of the "Chicago school"

6. The notion that price adjusts in response to an inequality of quantity demanded and quantity supplied, which is found in most modern textbooks, is Walras's version of equilibrium, not Marshall's.

Milton Friedman

Thorstein Veblen

of free market economics, typified today by Nobel Prize winner **Milton Friedman.**

The microeconomic analyses of monopolistic competition and oligopoly that appear in today's economics texts were developed originally by **Edward Chamberlin** (an American) and **Joan Robinson** (a student of Marshall and a colleague of Keynes). The indifference curve approach to the neoclassical theory of consumer behavior was expanded by **J. R. Hicks** (England) and **Paul Samuelson** (United States), both recipients of the Nobel Prize in economics.

Neoclassical microeconomic theory is the basis for the analysis of public sector economic decision analysis and has played an important role in modern theories of international trade and development. Today, most economists know and understand the theory very well, but not all of them accept it or agree with its premises. The path to modern microeconomics continues with the analyses presented in Chapters 16 through 28 of this text. However, the historical discussion is incomplete without reference to those who dissented from the mainstream.

Thorstein Veblen (1857–1929) and **John Kenneth Galbraith** (b. 1908), both Americans, have been the best-known critics of the neoclassical school. Veblen, in his *Theory of the Leisure Class* (1899), argued that the market system wasted society's resources because the rich engaged in "conspicuous consumption"—an excessive tendency toward leisure or spending on frivolous products or services for the purpose of demonstrating their superiority to others. In *The Theory of Business Enterprise* Veblen argued that technology, or the "machine process," was inherently efficient but that business maneuvering in response to the profit motive often hampered its productivity. For example, he argued that the formation of U.S. Steel Corporation served no purpose from a technological or industrial point of view but only profited the financiers who put the maneuver together (J. P. Morgan and Co.). The financiers received $65 million for their efforts. According to Veblen, businesses' pursuit of profits often causes unemployment, price inflation, delays in innovation, and decreases in productivity.[7]

7. For some modern evidence on this point, see J. Patrick Wright, *On a Clear Day You Can See General Motors* (New York: Avon Books, 1979). This book is an autobiographical exposé of the corporation by John Z. DeLorean, who served as general manager of both the Chevrolet and Pontiac divisions but quit GM to found De-Lorean Motor Car Company in Northern Ireland.

Like Marx, Veblen predicted that capitalism was doomed, but for different reasons. He argued that there would be a conflict between the growth of technology and the conservatism of the leisure class and that the conflict would lead either to the rise of scientists, engineers, and skilled workers to positions of authority in a socialistic state or to a society dominated by a military-industrial state.[8] In Veblen's view, production, consumption, and growth are all processes characterized by evolutionary change. Thus, in journal articles, Veblen frequently attacked neoclassical economics for its emphasis on static equilibrium conditions, its ever-present conception of the selfish nature of rational people, and its failure to shift its focus from individual to social norms of behavior.

Galbraith, the leading critic of capitalism in the late twentieth century, also rejects the notion that the market will efficiently allocate resources. In fact, he rejects the hypothesis of profit maximization by firms, arguing that firms are guided by a "technostructure" that does not view the interest of owners (shareholders) as its primary concern. Consumers, on the other hand, are subject to manipulation of their tastes and preferences, a phenomenon largely ignored in the conventional wisdom of neoclassical economics. Wants increasingly become satisfied by the process that creates them—the introduction of new goods. The dependence of wants on production, advertising, social change, or salesmanship is what Galbraith calls the **dependence effect**.

The dependence effect leads consumers to overvalue private output and undervalue public goods. Thus, according to Galbraith, too few public goods will be produced unless someone intervenes to cor-

John Kenneth Galbraith

rect the social imbalance inherent in the system. Neither the consumers nor the technostructure can answer the social imbalance problem. In Galbraith's system that problem is left in the hands of the intellectuals and the government. Galbraith's major works, *The Affluent Society* (1958) and *The New Industrial State* (1967), spell out the foregoing arguments in an interesting and provocative fashion. His critics have rightly questioned some of his assumptions and have complained about his failure to define a plan of action for coping with social imbalance, but the fact remains that he has raised questions of importance for both economic analysis and government policy.

---

8. Although Veblen's argument may seem a bit farfetched today, the experiences of Germany, Japan, and Italy before World War II seem to fit his case.

CHAPTER 23

THE
MARKET FOR
PRODUCTIVE
RESOURCES

RESOURCE
SUBSTITUTION
IN THE
SOUTHWEST

The southwestern United States (especially south-central Texas) is notorious as a low-wage labor market. Studies have shown that migration of Mexican nationals, both legal and illegal, has resulted to some extent in an increase in the supply of unskilled and semi-skilled labor, which has depressed wages. This appears to be particularly true in the nonunion sector of the construction industry. Here, the companies really do not care whether a worker is an alien or a U.S. citizen, as long as the job gets done. The result is that the same wages are paid to citizens and aliens.

The low wages for unskilled labor have led to the kind of factor substitution indicated by the economic theory of production. The authors experienced a real-life example of this phenomenon when they were building an addition to their home. Two slab contractors submitted bids for the foundation work. Because a multi-level patio had to be removed, the job involved the demolition of a considerable amount of old concrete.

The first contractor bid $2,900, attributing his relatively high price per square foot to the need to rent an air hammer to break up the old concrete. The second contractor bid only $1,875 and said nothing about how he would demolish the patio. Both contractors were reputable, and neither of them employed alien workers. Naturally, we took the lower bid.

Much to our surprise, every bit of the concrete breaking was done by hand with enormous sledge hammers. Although we do not attribute the large difference in the two bids entirely to the substitution of labor for capital, we do believe that the second contractor had made the correct economic choice given the state of the local market for unskilled labor.

This chapter will examine markets for productive resources and show how the profit-maximizing firm decides how much of each type of resource to hire. As in the study of product markets, we will find that market structure has a significant effect on the amount of a resource hired and the price paid for its services.

C H A P T E R   23

THE
MARKET FOR
PRODUCTIVE
RESOURCES

WHAT THIS CHAPTER IS ABOUT

DERIVED DEMAND
MARGINAL REVENUE PRODUCT OF AN INPUT
PROFIT-MAXIMIZING RULES FOR
  EMPLOYMENT OF INPUTS
One Variable Input
More than One Variable Input
Output Rule versus Input Rule
DEMAND CURVE FOR AN INPUT
TYPES OF INPUT MARKETS
Monopsony
Oligopsony
Monopsonistic Competition
Perfect Competition
INPUT MARKET EQUILIBRIUM
Perfect Competition
Imperfect Competition
Bilateral Monopoly

Chapters 19 through 22 dealt with decision rules for finding the profit-maximizing level of output for a business firm. The present chapter reconciles output decisions with profit-maximizing rules for input use. The chapter begins with an examination of the firm's employment of a single variable input or factor of production and relates the use of the input to the revenue of the firm. By comparing input cost with the revenue an input generates, we can develop a rule for determining how much of the input to employ. The chapter also examines input market structure and the determination of the equilibrium price and quantity of an input for various types of market conditions.

By the end of the chapter, we should be able to answer questions such as: How many assembly line employees will a computer manufacturer hire, assuming that plant and equipment are fixed? Where does the concept of least cost combination of inputs enter into the picture?

As we will see shortly, the firm's demand for inputs or factors of production is a *derived demand*. That is, it is directly related to, or *derived from*, the demand for the final product or output of the firm. In other words, the demand for productive *inputs* by a firm stems from the demand for its *output*.

PROFIT-MAXIMIZING RULES FOR EMPLOYMENT OF INPUTS

◆

In general, a firm will continue to employ additional units of a productive factor until the last unit employed just pays for itself. We will examine the implications of this seemingly simple principle next.

ONE VARIABLE INPUT

In the short run, certain of the firm's inputs are fixed. A new assembly line may take months or even years to design and install, for example. In many cases a firm may have only one variable input, typically labor, in the short run. This section of the chapter explains how the profit-maximizing firm determines the quantity of a single variable input to employ.

The profit-maximizing decision rule for employing one variable input, given that other inputs are fixed, is similar to the corresponding rule for output. A firm maximizes its profit by producing the level of output where the marginal revenue obtained from one more unit of the product is just equal to its marginal cost, or $MR = MC$.

Likewise, *the firm will maximize profit with respect to a variable input by employing the input up to the point where the marginal revenue resulting from the use of one more unit of the input is just equal to its marginal cost.* This statement is another way of expressing the rule that additional units of an input should be employed until the last one just pays for itself.

Marginal Revenue Product Economists have a special name for the marginal revenue gen-

erated by one more unit of a variable input— the marginal revenue product of the input.

> The **marginal revenue product of an input** is *the additional revenue generated for the firm by using another unit of that input, assuming the amounts used of all other inputs do not change.*

The chapter 18 analysis of production and cost noted that the amount of output produced by an increase in the use of just one input is called the **marginal product of the input.** □ Thus, if L is a measure of the amount of labor a firm is using, the marginal product of labor is defined as:

$$MP_L = \frac{\text{Change in output}}{\text{Change in labor}}.$$

What an additional unit of labor is worth to the firm depends on the amount of revenue the labor generates. For example, suppose a firm hires an additional worker who increases production by 5 units of output per day. If the firm can sell any number of units of output for $10 each, the additional worker will generate an increase of $50 per day in the firm's revenue. The amount of revenue obtained per unit of new output is **marginal revenue:** □

$$MR = \frac{\text{Change in revenue}}{\text{Change in output}}.$$

In our example, marginal revenue equals $50/5 = $10. Because all units of output are sold for the same price, marginal revenue is constant and equal to $10. Of course, this is what happens if the product market faced by the firm is perfectly competitive.□

The additional worker who generates $50 per day in new revenue for the firm (by producing 5 units of output that sell for $10 each) is worth up to $50 per day to the firm. That is, $50 is the maximum the firm is willing to pay for the additional worker, because at that amount the firm just breaks even on the added output produced. The $50 is equal to the marginal revenue product of the worker, a mea-

406

377

456

sure of the revenue the firm gets from the worker's marginal product. The marginal revenue product (MRP) of any input is equal to the input's marginal product multiplied by the marginal revenue obtained from additional output *(MR)*. Thus, for labor,

$$MRP_L = \text{Marginal product of labor} \times \text{marginal revenue of output.}$$

If the marginal revenue product of an input is its contribution to the revenue of the firm, we can determine why it must be calculated this way. Take a hair styling salon, for example. Suppose the employment of one more hair stylist will enable the firm to handle an average of 20 more appointments per day. In this case the marginal product of one more hair stylist is 20 appointments per day. However, in order to determine the significance of these appointments with respect to the firm's revenue and profit, we must put a monetary value on them.

Let us assume that the marginal revenue associated with 1 more appointment is $11. Thus the monetary value of the additional 20 appointments per day is $11 × 20 = $220 per day. This sum is the amount of additional revenue that one more hair stylist will bring into the firm per day. Using the terminology of economics we can state that $220 is the marginal revenue product per day of one more hair stylist *at this point*.

Law of Diminishing Marginal Productivity
The words *at this point* are emphasized because (as explained in Chapter 18) if equal increments of one variable input are added, with all other inputs fixed, after some point the marginal product of the variable input will begin to decrease, at least in most cases. This relationship is called the law of diminishing marginal productivity □ or the law of diminishing returns.

Consequently, if a hair styling salon continues to add hair stylists while keeping the number of sinks, chairs, and dryers fixed, after some point the marginal product of one more hair stylist will begin to fall because the styl-

ists will have to wait their turn to use the facilities. Customers will probably become irritated, and some will refuse to wait.

Deriving MRP_L: A Numerical Example   To derive the marginal revenue product of labor, we will use a hypothetical example of a firm in the business of picking coffee beans, Colombia Pickers Co. We will assume that the market for the service of bean picking is perfectly competitive and that many plantation owners will pay $5 per sack of beans picked. The price of a unit of output (a sack of beans picked) is therefore equal to $5. With the price given and constant, $5 is the marginal revenue of Colombia Pickers. The plantations supply the empty sacks, and Colombia's workers simply fill them up and close them. Colombia has a fixed amount of capital goods and other inputs and can increase its bean-picking output solely through the hiring of additional labor.

Marginal Revenue Product Schedule   Table 23–1 is a schedule of labor use, total output, marginal product of labor, marginal revenue, and marginal revenue product. As more workers are hired, output increases, but the marginal product of additional workers falls from the second worker onward. This happens because Colombia Pickers has only a certain amount of other inputs (trucks, bagging machines) to work with. Of course, the marginal revenue product of labor, which is $MP_L \times MR$, or $MP_L \times \$5$, also falls as more workers are hired.

Marginal Revenue Product Curve   A curve showing how MRP_L varies as the number of workers hired is increased can be plotted from the data in Table 23–1. Figure 23–1 shows such a curve, the *marginal revenue product curve for labor*. MRP_L falls as labor used is increased beyond two workers per day, because MP_L falls while *MR* is constant.

Because MRP_L measures the contribution of one more worker to the revenue of the firm, and because it falls as labor use is increased,

TABLE 23–1 Derivation of Marginal Revenue Product of Labor for Colombia Pickers Co., a Firm That Picks Coffee Beans

Number of Workers Hired (L)	Quantity of Beans Picked (Sacks per day; Total Product) (Q)	Marginal Product of Labor $\left(\dfrac{\text{change in } Q}{\text{change in } L}\right)$	Marginal Revenue (Equal to Price per Sack Picked) ($P = MR = \$5$)	Marginal Revenue Product of Labor (MRP_L)
0	0			
		10	$5	$ 50
1	10			
		20	5	100
2	30			
		15	5	75
3	45			
		10	5	50
4	55			
		9	5	45
5	64			
		6	5	30
6	70			
		4	5	20
7	74			
		2	5	10
8	76			

it will become less and less attractive to Colombia Pickers to hire an additional worker as the number of workers hired is increased. We will assume that the market for laborers who can pick beans is perfectly competitive and that Colombia can get as many workers as it wants for a market wage of $25 per day. Will it pay $25 for a worker who only adds $20 to the firm's total revenue? No! A worker who costs the firm $25 but brings in only $20 is not worth hiring. From this proposition, a general rule for the hiring of a variable input can be developed. This development is undertaken in the next two sections of the chapter.

Marginal Cost of an Input Suppose that Columbia Pickers does face a given market price of $25 for a day's labor by a bean-picking worker. To the firm, $25 is the marginal cost of using an additional worker. This cost, called the marginal factor cost (MFC) of labor, is also the change in total cost that occurs when one more worker is hired. Thus we can say that

$$MFC_L = \frac{\text{Change in total cost}}{\text{Change in quantity of labor}}.$$

Marginal factor cost is the cost to the firm of hiring an additional unit of some given input.

In choosing how much labor to hire, Colombia Pickers will compare the marginal factor cost of labor with the marginal revenue product of labor. With the price of each worker (P_L) being $25 per day, the firm knows that $P_L = MFC_L = \$25$. When an additional worker is hired, revenue must increase by at least $25 if the firm is to cover the cost of the worker.

Input Use Rule Table 23–2 compares the marginal revenue product of labor with the $25 per day marginal factor cost of labor. If Colombia wishes to maximize profit, □ it will continue to employ workers as long as the marginal revenue product of labor exceeds the marginal factor cost of labor. This occurs in Table 23–2 up through the sixth worker. Be-

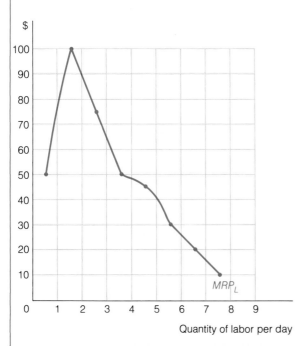

FIGURE 23–1 **A Marginal Revenue Product Curve for Labor Used in Picking Coffee Beans**

MRP_L is the marginal revenue product of labor curve for labor used in picking coffee beans. It is found by multiplying the marginal product of labor (in sacks of beans per day) by the marginal revenue received from another sack of beans.

TABLE 23–2 **Comparison of MRP_L with MFC_L for Colombia Pickers Co.**

Number of Workers Hired (Q_L)	Marginal Revenue Product of Labor (MRP_L)	Marginal Factor Cost of Labor (MFC_L)
0		
	$ 50	$25
1		
	100	25
2		
	75	25
3		
	50	25
4		
	45	25
5		
	30	25
6		
	20	25
7		
	10	25
8		

yond six workers per day, additional laborers add more to total cost than they do to total revenue, or MFC_L is greater than MRP_L. Thus the firm will hire no more than six workers.

Any time the marginal revenue product of labor exceeds the marginal factor cost of labor, the firm will hire more workers, because an additional worker will contribute more to revenue than to cost. Therefore, the rule for hiring the profit-maximizing number of workers is to stop hiring where the marginal revenue product of labor is equal to the marginal factor cost of labor.

As noted earlier, the profit-maximizing decision rule with respect to output is quite similar—continue to produce output until the marginal revenue brought in by the last unit produced is equal to the marginal cost of that unit of output. The corresponding decision rule with respect to inputs is: Continue to employ the input until the additional revenue brought in by the input (its marginal revenue product) is equal to the marginal factor cost of the input. In either case, what matters is the relationship between incremental or additional revenue and incremental cost. With the *output* rule the incremental revenue and cost of another unit of *output* is spotlighted. With the *input* rule the focus is on the incremental revenue and incremental cost of the *input*.

> The **input use rule** states that a profit-maximizing firm will hire additional units of a single variable input up to the level where the marginal revenue product equals the marginal factor cost for the resource or input in question.

The profit-maximizing quantity of workers for Colombia Pickers is shown in Figure 23–2. As already indicated, Colombia will maximize profit by employing six pickers, because at this point the marginal revenue product of another worker is just equal to the worker's marginal factor cost.

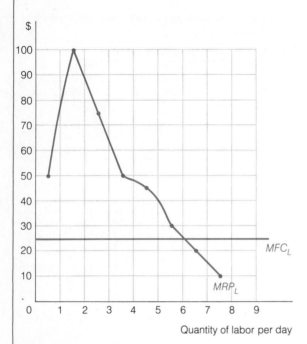

FIGURE 23–2 Profit-Maximizing Quantity of Labor Used in Picking Coffee Beans

The marginal revenue product of labor curve for coffee bean pickers is once again given by MRP_L. The marginal factor cost of labor is equal to $25 and is given by MFC_L. Colombia Pickers Co. will maximize profit by employing pickers until the marginal revenue product of labor is equal to the marginal factor cost of labor. Thus, the firm will employ six pickers.

PROFIT MAXIMIZATION:
THE OUTPUT RULE
VERSUS THE INPUT RULE

If a firm hiring labor maximizes profit where the marginal revenue product of labor is equal to the marginal factor cost of labor, the input use rule must be consistent with the general rule for the profit-maximizing level of output developed in Chapters 19 through 22—that marginal revenue equals marginal cost, or $MR = MC$. We can easily show that this is so.

First, we must note that for any input, say A, the marginal factor cost of input A divided by its marginal product equals the marginal cost of another unit of output. Consider the ex-

ample of Colombia Pickers. If a worker whose daily wage is $25 adds 10 sacks of output to the bean-picking production, the marginal cost of one sack of beans is

$$\frac{\text{Marginal factor cost of worker}}{\text{Number of sacks picked by worker}}$$

$$= \frac{\$25}{10} = \$2.50 \text{ per sack.}$$

Now we can reconsider the input use rule—that the marginal revenue product of labor is equal to the marginal factor cost of labor. Since the marginal revenue product of labor is equal to the marginal product of labor multiplied by marginal revenue, the input use rule can be rewritten as

Marginal product of labor $\times$ Marginal revenue
= Marginal factor cost of labor.

Dividing both sides of the expression by the marginal product of labor yields

$$\text{Marginal revenue} = \frac{\text{Marginal factor cost of labor}}{\text{Marginal product of labor}}.$$

However, the term on the right is the same as marginal cost, so marginal revenue is actually equal to marginal cost. What we have shown is that with one variable input (labor), a firm that hires up to the point where the marginal revenue product of labor is equal to the marginal factor cost of labor will also be automatically at the output level where marginal revenue is equal to marginal cost. At this point, of course, the firm will maximize its profit.

Even in the short run, most firms have more than one variable input. For example, many production processes require that the use of additional labor be accompanied by some expenditure on components (parts or raw materials) or other inputs necessary to get any change in output at all. Frequently, the components have a marginal product of zero if additional labor is not hired to use them. In the following section a new concept, net marginal revenue, is used to devise a practical method for determining the profit-maximizing level of input use when components costs must be considered.

COMPONENTS COSTS AND PROFIT-MAXIMIZING INPUT USE[1]

In applied economics, it is customary to define the *marginal revenue product* of a firm's primary variable input as the marginal product of the input multiplied by net marginal revenue (NMR).

Net marginal revenue is *marginal revenue minus the cost of certain components, or parts.*

Often, when we speak of increasing a primary factor of production such as capital or labor, we also implicitly assume that any necessary parts or raw materials for making the product will increase as well. Even Houdini could not produce a television set from thin air! However, in the real world, once the design and makeup of a good is determined, a given set of raw materials and parts will be used for each unit of output produced. At this point, because each additional unit of output requires a certain package of raw materials and parts, no decision need be made regarding these inputs. If additional output is desired, then corresponding additional amounts of the inputs must be used.

For example, once the design and materials for a new Ford Escort are set for a particular year or production run, Ford does not reevaluate how much of the materials to use for each additional car produced. It does not ask how many engines, transmissions, or steering wheels to use each time another car is assembled, and it does not change the basic materials used in the car bodies each time another automobile is produced. Thus, while raw materials and part inputs are variable, the firm frequently considers the amounts of these in-

puts used *per unit of output* to be given in the short run.[2] We will therefore concentrate on the profit-maximizing rule for using other types of variable inputs, such as labor.

Nevertheless, when the contribution of these other factors of production to the revenue of a firm is estimated, the cost of additional materials or parts must be accounted for in some way. As we will see, computing net marginal revenue is a convenient means of doing so.

Returning to the coffee bean example, let us suppose that Colombia Pickers must supply the sacks used to hold the beans and that the sacks cost the firm $1 each. If Colombia hires an additional worker who adds 10 sacks of beans to total output, marginal revenue will still be $5 per sack (the amount charged the plantation), but the return to the firm from hiring the worker is reduced by the cost of the sack—a components cost. Thus the net marginal revenue from an additional sack of beans picked is

Net marginal revenue = Marginal revenue
 − Marginal cost of components
$$= \$5 - \$1$$
$$= \$4.$$

The effective marginal revenue product of the additional worker is now equal to net marginal revenue multiplied by the worker's marginal product:

$$MRP_L = NMR_L \times MP_L.$$

---

1. This section can be omitted without loss of continuity.

2. Of course, at various points in time a firm must make basic decisions regarding the design and composition of its product. At those times the firm compares the relative costs of two substitutable materials or parts and their respective effects on the price at which the product can be sold. For example, suppose Fred's Drive-In can use either all ground beef or a mixture of ground beef and soybeans in its hamburgers. If the firm uses only ground beef, its cost per hamburger will be $.50. However, if the firm uses a mixture of ground beef and soybeans, its cost per hamburger will be only $.20. If the all-beef hamburgers can be sold for over $.30 more than the beef and soybean hamburgers, Fred's will use only ground beef. However, if people are willing to pay less than a $.30 premium for an all-beef burger, Fred's will use the beef and soybean mixture.

For the worker who added 10 sacks to total output:

$$MRP_L = \$4 \times 10$$
$$= \$40.$$

This figure is $10 less than MRP_L would have been if Colombia did not have to buy the sacks.

Is the net marginal revenue concept legitimate? After all, it is customary to define MP_L as the change in output when only labor is increased by one unit. It is true that we blur the exact definition of MP_L when we allow the number of sacks to increase, but what is the marginal product of workers without sacks? Clearly workers and sacks are a composite input. No output can be achieved without some of both. The ultimate test of the net marginal revenue approach is whether it helps us identify the profit-maximizing level of output use, and we will see that it does.

Table 23–3 is a schedule of the data neces-

sary to adjust the information from Table 23–1 in a way that takes into account the component cost of sacks. If the MRP_L column in Table 23–1 is compared with the MRP_L column in Table 23–3, it becomes clear that MRP_L falls when the components cost of sacks is deducted from MR. This does affect the firm's profit-maximizing level of output. In fact, if Colombia can hire additional workers for $25 per day, it will choose to hire only five instead of the original six. The marginal revenue product of a sixth worker is now only $24, not enough to justify increasing employment to six workers ($24 is less than $25, the marginal factor cost of labor).

Is this approach consistent with profit maximization? The answer is yes. To maximize profit we need to increase output as long as marginal revenue is greater than marginal cost. For Colombia, marginal revenue is $5 and marginal cost is $(P_L/MP_L + \$1)$, where the $1 is the marginal factor cost of one sack. When

TABLE 23–3   Derivation of Marginal Revenue Product of Labor from Data on Net Marginal Revenue for Colombia Pickers Co.

Number of Workers Hired (L)	Quantity of Beans Picked (Sacks per day; Total Product) (Q)	Marginal Product of Labor $\left(\dfrac{\text{change in } Q}{\text{change in } L}\right)$	Net Marginal Revenue (MR minus Components Cost)	Marginal Revenue Product of Labor (MRP_L)
0	0			
		10	$4	$40
1	10			
		20	4	80
2	30			
		15	4	60
3	45			
		10	4	40
4	55			
		9	4	36
5	64			
		6	4	24
6	70			
		4	4	16
7	74			
		2	4	8
8	76			

the fifth worker is hired, we have

$$\text{Marginal cost} = \frac{P_L}{MP_L} + \$1$$

$$= \frac{\$25}{9} + \$1$$

$$= \$3.78.$$

This amount is less than the marginal revenue of \$5, so it pays to hire the fifth worker. However, if a sixth worker is hired,

$$\text{Marginal cost} = \frac{P_L}{MP_L} + \$1$$

$$= \frac{\$25}{6} + \$1$$

$$= \$5.17.$$

The marginal cost of \$5.17 exceeds marginal revenue, which is still only \$5, so the sixth worker will not be hired.

In this section we developed two ways for handling the matter of components costs. First, we showed that it is appropriate to subtract components cost per unit of output from marginal revenue when defining the profit-maximizing level of input use ($MRP = MFC$ rule). Second, we showed that it is appropriate to include components cost in the marginal cost of output when considering the profit-maximizing output level ($MR = MC$ rule).

MULTIPLE INPUTS AND THE LEAST COST RULE

Generally, a firm will have two or more variable inputs that are, to some degree, substitutes for one another. This is especially common over comparatively long periods of time, when firms have opportunities to add to their stock of capital equipment or build new plants. However, even in the short run, choices between substitutable inputs are frequently made. For example, a fencing contractor may have to choose between renting a jackhammer and hiring additional laborers to put in an especially long fence. A delivery service that leases vehicles may have to choose between gasoline- and diesel-powered trucks or use some combination of the two during certain periods of the year. Even in cattle feeding, firms must choose between various substitutable inputs. In fact, computer programs have been devised to identify the lowest cost combination of feed grains given the market prices of corn, soybeans, and other feedstuffs. With or without a computer, the logic of finding a least or lowest cost combination of inputs □ is easy to understand, as we will see next.

420

Least Cost Combination of Inputs

A ***least cost combination of inputs*** is the combination of inputs that will enable a firm to produce a given level of output at the lowest possible cost.

To identify that combination, it is necessary to consider the effect of increases in each input on the quantity of output produced and to relate this effect to the amount that a unit of the input costs the firm. The effect on total output of an increase in the use of an input has already been identified in this chapter and in Chapter 18. It is the marginal product of the input. The cost of a unit of some particular input is what we have called input price. Thus, what the firm must examine for each variable input is the relationship between marginal product and input price.

Specifically, the least cost combination of inputs can be identified by comparing the additional output received per dollar spent on each alternative input. The additional output per additional \$1 spent is equal to the marginal product of a given input divided by the price of that input. For example, if a firm spends \$40 per day for a machine that increases output by 200 units per day, the marginal product per \$1 spent on the machine will be 200 units/\$40 = 50 units per \$1. The fraction 200/40 is the marginal product of the machine divided by its price. In general, the marginal product of an input divided by its price tells us the additional output received per \$1 spent on the input.

A firm will have no reason to substitute one input for another if the additional output per $1 spent on each input is the same. For a firm that uses only two inputs, labor and capital, such a condition will exist if

Marginal product of capital
––––––––––––––––––––––––––––
        Price of capital

$$= \frac{\text{Marginal product of labor}}{\text{Price of labor}}, \text{ or}$$

$$\frac{MP_K}{P_K} = \frac{MP_L}{P_L}.$$

When this relationship holds, the firm can gain nothing from switching its expenditure on inputs from capital to labor or vice versa, since $1 spent on either input yields the same change in output.

> A *least cost combination* of inputs is obtained when the marginal product per $1 spent on any one input is equal to the marginal product per $1 spent on any other.

To illustrate the least cost input combination, let us consider a fencing contractor. Suppose that due to area economic growth the contractor wishes to expand output by as much as 1,200 feet of fence installed per day. Suppose further that, given the amount of labor and equipment the firm currently employs, the marginal product of an additional jackhammer is 120 feet of fence installed per day while that of an additional worker is 60 feet of fence per day. If the jackhammer can be rented for $60 per day and the price of a worker is $40 per day, which will the contractor use?

Let us look at the additional output received per $1 spent on each input. For the jackhammer (K), we have

$$\frac{MP_K}{P_K} = \frac{120 \text{ feet}}{\$60}$$

$$= 2 \text{ feet of fence installed per \$1 spent.}$$

For the additional worker (L), we have

$$\frac{MP_L}{P_L} = \frac{60 \text{ feet}}{\$40}$$

$$= 1.5 \text{ feet of fence installed per \$1 spent.}$$

Clearly, the contractor will get more fence installed per $1 spent on additional inputs by using another jackhammer rather than another worker. In fact, as long as the additional output obtained per $1 spent on labor is less than the additional output obtained per $1 spent on capital, the contractor will maximize profit by using more jackhammers rather than more workers.

Of course, common sense tells us that the contractor cannot go on using jackhammer after jackhammer without hiring some workers to run the jackhammers and to put up posts and fencing. Economics tells us this is so because the marginal product of jackhammers will fall as more of them are employed, while the availability of jackhammers will increase the marginal product of an additional worker. Thus we can expect the marginal product of labor to rise and the marginal product of capital to fall as the contractor begins to use more and more jackhammers. For any level of output the firm will have just the right amount of jackhammers and workers when

Marginal product of labor
––––––––––––––––––––––––––
       Price of labor

$$= \frac{\text{Marginal product of capital}}{\text{Price of capital}},$$

because no gain can be received from substituting one for the other.

In this example we have assumed that input prices are constant and, consequently, that the price of an input represents its marginal factor cost to the firm. A more general way of stating the least cost combination of inputs condition for capital and labor is:

$$\frac{\text{Marginal product of labor}}{\text{Marginal factor cost of labor}}$$
$$= \frac{\text{Marginal product of capital}}{\text{Marginal factor cost of capital}}, \text{ or}$$

$$\frac{MP_L}{MFC_L} = \frac{MP_K}{MFC_K}. \qquad (23-1)$$

Profit Maximization At this point we have only the rule for determining the cheapest way of producing a particular level of output. How do we determine which level of output is the most profitable?

One way is to compute the long-run total cost schedule for the firm from the various least cost input combinations and then to find the profit-maximizing level of output where marginal revenue is equal to marginal cost. A second way is to make sure that the profit-maximizing decision rule for employing one variable input (given at the beginning of this chapter) is satisfied for all inputs. In the case where labor and capital are the two variable inputs, profit will be maximized when

$$MRP_L = MFC_L \qquad (23-2)$$

and

$$MRP_K = MFC_K. \qquad (23-3)$$

If there are more than two inputs, the marginal revenue product of each input must be equal to its marginal factor cost.

Dividing Equation 23–2 by MFC_L and Equation 23–3 by MFC_K, we can obtain an alternative way of stating the profit-maximizing condition:

$$\frac{MRP_L}{MFC_L} = 1,$$

and

$$\frac{MRP_K}{MFC_K} = 1.$$

Thus, if profit is to be maximized, not only must

$$\frac{MRP_L}{MFC_L} = \frac{MRP_K}{MFC_K},$$

which is required by the rule for least cost input combinations,[3] but both ratios must equal 1:

$$\frac{MRP_L}{MFC_L} = 1 = \frac{MRP_K}{MFC_K}.$$

The two ratios must equal 1 because of the profit-maximization requirement that an input should be used until the revenue generated by one more unit of the input is just equal to its marginal factor cost.[4]

One word of caution, however. As the firm alters the combinations of two inputs, their entire marginal product schedules may be altered. For example, the marginal product schedule of steel workers will differ according to the number of blast furnaces a steel mill is

---

3. We can easily prove that

$$\frac{MRP_L}{MFC_L} = \frac{MRP_K}{MFC_K}$$

for a least cost combination of inputs as follows. The least cost combination of inputs rule as given in Equation 23–1 is that

$$\frac{MP_L}{MFC_L} = \frac{MP_K}{MFC_K}.$$

We know that $MRP_L = MR \times MP_L$ and that $MRP_K = MR \times MP_K$. The marginal revenue per unit of output, MR, is the same regardless of whether we are discussing labor or capital. Thus, if we multiply both sides of the above equation by MR, we obtain

$$\frac{MR \times MP_L}{MFC_L} = \frac{MR \times MP_K}{MFC_K},$$

or

$$\frac{MRP_L}{MFC_L} = \frac{MRP_K}{MFC_K}.$$

4. This rule can be generalized for any number of inputs:

$$\frac{MRP_1}{MFC_1} = \frac{MRP_2}{MFC_2} = \ldots = \frac{MRP_n}{MFC_n}.$$

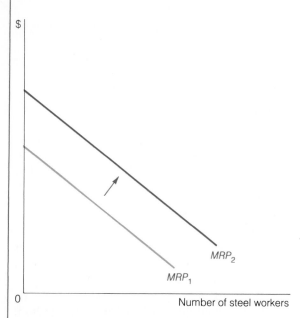

FIGURE 23-3   Shift in the Marginal Revenue Product Curve of Steel Workers Resulting from an Increase in the Number of Blast Furnaces Used

The original marginal revenue product curve for steel workers is MRP_1. However, after the firm utilizes more blast furnaces, workers become more productive. As a result, the marginal revenue product curve for steel workers shifts outward to MRP_2.

using. In Figure 23-3 the marginal revenue product curve of steel workers shifts from MRP_1 to MRP_2 after an increase in the number of blast furnaces being used. The fact that marginal revenue product curves may shift does not change the nature of the analysis at all; it merely indicates that the firm must be aware of the effects of changes in input combinations on productivity.

INPUT DEMAND,
PRODUCT
MARKETS, AND
INPUT PRICES

◆

In the two preceding sections we generally assumed that the prices of both the variable in-

puts and the output were given (constant). The firm simply determined how to maximize profit from the given data. This section concentrates on the question of how input prices are determined. The pricing of inputs is one of the most complex issues in microeconomics, because any analysis of it must take into account the structure of the firm's product market as well as the input or factor markets from which the firm purchases productive resources.

TYPES OF MARKET STRUCTURES

Because the purchasers of a particular factor of production often have a significant amount of market power, the structure of the market for the input is frequently defined in terms of the buyer's side of the market. As with the market for a final product, many types of market structures are possible. As we will see shortly, the structure of the input market affects the equilibrium price of an input and the quantity employed of an input.

At one extreme is monopsony.

> A **monopsony** is a market with only one buyer.

(The term *monopoly* □ refers to a market with only one seller.)

At the other extreme the market for an input may be perfectly competitive from the standpoint of the buyers.

> A **perfectly competitive market** from the demand, or buyers', side means that no buyer acting alone has enough market power to be able to affect the market price of the product or input.

In between these two extremes are two other types of market structures—oligopsony and monopsonistic competition.

Oligopsony *is the case where there are a few buyers or a few dominant buyers.*

 (*Oligopoly* □ is the term used for the corresponding situation on the seller's side of a market.)

Monopsonistic competition *is the term used to describe a market with a relatively large number of buyers, each of which has some control over the price of the item it is purchasing.*

 (*Monopolistic competition* □ is the name given to a similar situation on the seller's side of the market.) The market for nuclear engineers is an example of an oligopsony. The markets for computer programmers and garage mechanics are probably characterized by monopsonistic competition.

The various types of buyer and seller market structures are summarized in Table 23–4. However, any combination of these market structures is possible. For example, the market for beef cattle can be considered purely competitive on the seller's side of the market but oligopsonistic on the buyer's side. Near the Kansas hometown of one of the authors are many ranchers who produce beef cattle. Each ranch supplies so few cattle relative to the total market that it has virtually no control over the price of beef. On the other hand, there are relatively few buyers (meatpacking plants) for the fattened cattle. Consequently, the buyers do have some control over the price of cattle.

Some markets may be purely competitive from the standpoint of both buyer and seller. The market for unskilled farm labor is an ex-ample. On the other hand, there may be only one buyer and one seller of a particular item. The term *bilateral monopoly* is used to denote this situation. Many other combinations of market structures exist as well.

In the next few sections of this chapter we will examine the process by which the equilibrium price and quantity of a factor of production are determined. We will analyze several situations, considering the structures of both the market for the final product and the input market.

IMPORTANCE OF MARKET STRUCTURES

To appreciate the dual nature of the market structure, we should think about the input use rule for a single variable input. The firm's measure of the worth of an additional unit of some given input is marginal revenue product (MRP). The cost of the input to the firm is marginal factor cost (MFC). The firm will maximize profit where $MRP = MFC$. Marginal revenue product is equal to marginal product times marginal revenue. Marginal revenue, however, depends on the demand for the output of the firm. This is why product market structure is important to the firm's input use decision. We cannot calculate marginal revenue product without knowing marginal revenue, and marginal revenue depends on the demand curve for the firm's output.

The other side of the input use rule is, of course, marginal factor cost. To the firm, marginal factor cost depends on the market for the input in question. If the market is perfectly competitive, MFC is a constant; if not, the firm knows that the quantity supplied of a given input increases only as higher and higher prices are paid for the input. In the latter case, as we will eventually see, MFC will not be a constant but will rise as more units of an input are used. Our first step in describing input price determination is to define the firm and market demand curves for a given input.

TABLE 23–4 Possible Market Structures

Demand Side	Supply Side
Perfect competition	Perfect competition
Monopsonistic competition	Monopolistic competition
Oligopsony	Oligopoly
Monopsony	Monopoly

INPUT DEMAND
CURVE OF THE FIRM

With a fixed input price, the profit-maximizing decision rule for an input, say input A, becomes: Employ the input until the marginal revenue product of A equals the price of A. Because the marginal revenue product curve in this situation indicates how many units of the input will be employed by the firm at each possible price, that curve is also the firm's demand curve for the input.[5]

> The **firm's demand curve for an input** indicates how many units of the input will be employed by the firm at each possible price. It is the marginal revenue product curve of the input when the price of an input is given.

For example, in Figure 23–4 a marginal revenue product per hour curve for unskilled laborers for Lundrus Manufacturing is sketched. If the wage rate is fixed at $4 per hour, the firm will maximize profit by hiring workers until $MRP_L = \$4$, at $L = 20$. If the wage rate is $3 per hour, the firm will maximize profit by employing 30 workers. Thus, from the standpoint of the individual firm, as long as the price of an input is given, the firm's demand curve for the input will be its marginal revenue product curve.

MARKET DEMAND CURVE

> The **market demand curve for an input** indicates the total quantity demanded of the input by all firms at each possible price.

The market demand curve for an input can be estimated by summing the quantities of the in-

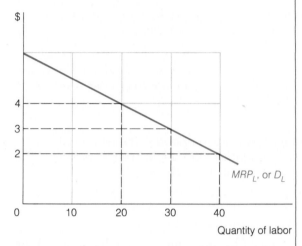

FIGURE 23–4 Demand Curve for Unskilled Labor for Lundrus Manufacturing

Since Lundrus Manufacturing cannot by its actions alone affect the wage rate for unskilled labor, the company will maximize profit by employing unskilled workers up to the point where their wage rate is equal to their marginal revenue product (MRP_L). Thus, if the wage rate is $4.00 per hour, the firm will employ 20 unskilled laborers. If the wage rate is $3.00 per hour, the firm will employ 30 workers. Thus, the marginal revenue product curve of unskilled workers is also the firm's demand curve, D_L, for that type of labor.

put demanded by each firm at each possible price for the input.[6]

EFFECT OF PRODUCT MARKET
STRUCTURE ON MARGINAL
REVENUE PRODUCT

In what follows we will assume that the firm must buy inputs under perfect competition, so that input prices are given. In the preceding section we noted that with a given input price the demand curve of the firm for a variable input is the MRP curve for that input.

As far as the firm's product market is concerned, we must consider two possibilities.

---

5. Technically speaking, there is no unique relationship between the price of an input and the quantity demanded of it if the individual firm does not consider the input price to be given. In this case a demand curve as such for the input does not exist.

6. The market demand curve for an input can be estimated in this manner (but not derived exactly), because the expansion of output by similar firms as they employ additional amounts of an input may cause the marginal revenue associated with a given level of output for an individual firm to fall.

The product market is either perfectly competitive or less than perfectly competitive. The label *less than perfectly competitive* is used to denote monopolistic, monopolistically competitive, and oligopolistic market structures. Under perfect competition □ the product demand curve faced by a selling firm is a horizontal line, and price is equal to marginal revenue. For all other product market structures the firm's demand curve slopes downward to the right and marginal revenue is less than price. Perfect competition is dealt with next. It is followed with a discussion of less than perfect competition.

INPUT PRICING WHEN FACTOR MARKETS ARE PERFECTLY COMPETITIVE

◆

In this section of the chapter, we will consider the determination of the price of an input when the market for that input is perfectly competitive. We will also examine how the quantity employed of an input is determined by firms that wish to maximize their profit. Although the factor market is assumed to be perfectly competitive, the product market may be either perfectly competitive or imperfectly competitive. We will consider the case of a perfectly competitive product market first.

PERFECTLY COMPETITIVE INPUT AND OUTPUT MARKETS

The first case we will examine is one where the markets for both the input and the final product are perfectly competitive. In this case there must be many sellers of an identical final product so that the individual sellers have no influence over the product price. Correspondingly, there must be many buyers and sellers in the market for the input or factor of produc-

tion so that no buyer or seller of the input has any influence over its price. This case is the same as the Colombia Pickers example, but now the market equilibrium price is related in more detail to the firm's marginal factor cost.

Market Equilibrium   In a perfectly competitive market the equilibrium price and quantity of a factor of production are determined by the total market supply of and demand for the input, as shown in Figure 23–5. The equilibrium price is P_e, and the equilibrium quantity is Q_e. At a higher price, such as P_1, the sellers of the input would wish to supply a larger quantity, Q_{s1}, than buyers would wish to purchase, Q_{d1}. If there were no artificial constraints on the market, such as a minimum

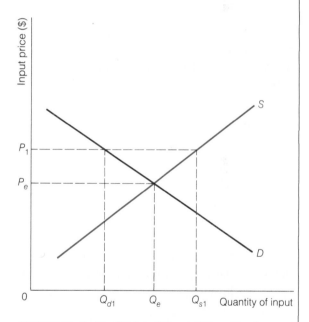

FIGURE 23–5   Equilibrium Price and Quantity of an Input in a Perfectly Competitive Input Market

The equilibrium price and quantity employed of an input in a perfectly competitive input market are given by the intersection of the market supply and demand curves, at P_e and Q_e. At a higher price, such as P_1, the quantity supplied of the input (Q_{s1}) will be greater than the quantity demanded (Q_{d1}). At a lower price, the quantity demanded of the input will be greater than the quantity supplied. Only at a price equal to P_e and a quantity of Q_e will the quantity demanded of the input be equal to the quantity supplied.

wage rate, the price would tend to drop to P_e. The reverse would occur if the price were to fall below P_e.

Firm Level   In this case the individual firm perceives that it can purchase as much of the input as it wishes to at a price equal to P_e, so that the supply curve of the input from the standpoint of the firm is a horizontal line at P_e. We have already seen that a firm's demand curve for the input is determined by the marginal revenue product curve of the input.

We have also seen that the marginal revenue product of an input is obtained by multiplying the marginal product of the input by the marginal revenue obtained from selling one more unit of the final product. If the seller of the final product is a perfectly competitive firm, the price of the final product is constant and is equal to its marginal revenue. In this case the marginal revenue product of an input, say input A, is equal to the price of the final product (MR) times the marginal product of input A:

$$MRP_A = MR \times MP_A = P \times MP_A = VMP_A,$$

where:

MRP_A = the marginal revenue product of input A,

MR = the marginal revenue per unit of the final product,

MP_A = the marginal product of input A,

P = the price of the final product, and

VMP_A = the value of the marginal product of input A.

Value of the Marginal Product   At this point, we can introduce a new term, the *value of the marginal product* of input A, or VMP_A, which is equal to $P \times MP_A$.

The **value of the marginal product of an input** is the value of an input's marginal product at the going market price for the final product.

If a farm hires a laborer to pick corn and this person increases the amount of corn picked per day by 200 bushels, the laborer's marginal product is 200 bushels per day. If the corn can be sold for $2.50 per bushel, the value of the marginal product of the laborer is $2.50 × 200 = $500 per day.

As already indicated, in the case of a perfectly competitive market for the final product, the price and marginal revenue of the final product are equal, so that the marginal revenue product of an input is equal to the value of the marginal product of an input. The significance of this equality between VMP and MRP is that the firm's measure of the worth of the marginal product of the input (MRP) is the same as society's measure of the worth of the marginal product (VMP). The latter assumes, of course, that market price is a measure of marginal social value or benefit.□ When $VMP = MRP = MFC$ = price of the input, the input is paid just what the addition to output produced by the last unit of input is worth.

Panel (a) of Figure 23–6 shows the equilibrium price of input A as determined by the market. The horizontal axis gives quantity in thousands of units. Because the total quantity of input A employed is far greater than the quantity for a single firm, the horizontal axis in panel (b) gives quantity in single units. The firm takes the market price, P_A^*, as given and operates at Q_{Af}^*, where the value of the marginal product of A is equal to P_A^*. Because under perfect competition the value of the marginal product equals the marginal revenue product and the input price equals the marginal factor cost, the firm is at the profit-maximizing level of input use. As explained earlier in the chapter, this point occurs where marginal revenue product equals marginal factor cost, or $MRP_A = MFC_A$.

Returning to the farm laborer example, Table 23–5 shows the number of workers employed by a farm to help pick corn, the corresponding marginal product, and the value of the marginal product of another laborer. If the equilibrium wage rate is $36 per day, the farm

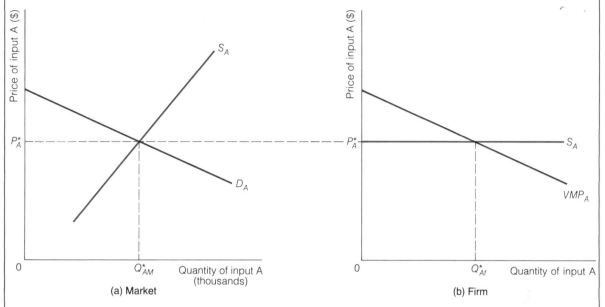

FIGURE 23–6   Equilibrium Price and Quantity of Input A with Perfectly Competitive Input and Output Markets

The equilibrium price (P_A^*) of an input, input A, and the total market quantity employed (Q_{AM}^*) are determined by the market supply and demand curves for the input (S_A and D_A, respectively) in panel (a). An individual firm accepts the price of input A, P_A^*, as a given. It will employ the input up to the point where the value of the marginal product of input A (VMP_A) is equal to P_A^*, or Q_{Af}^* units of input A, in panel (b).

TABLE 23–5   Revenue and Productivity Data for Farm Labor

Number of Workers (L)	Number of Bushels of Corn (Q)	Marginal Product of Worker ($MP_L = \dfrac{\text{change in } Q}{\text{change in } L}$)	Price per Bushel of Corn (P)	Marginal Revenue Product and Value of the Marginal Product ($MRP_L = VMP_L = P \times MP_L$)
0	0		$2.50	
		1,000		$2,500
1	1,000		2.50	
		500		1,250
2	1,500		2.50	
		200		500
3	1,700		2.50	
		100		250
4	1,800		2.50	
		50		125
5	1,850		2.50	
		30		75
6	1,880		2.50	
		16		40
7	1,896		2.50	
		6		15
8	1,902		2.50	

will employ seven workers. It will not hire an eighth worker, because the value of the marginal product of labor is less than $36 for the eighth worker.

IMPERFECTLY COMPETITIVE OUTPUT MARKET BUT PERFECTLY COMPETITIVE INPUT MARKET

Suppose the market for the final product is imperfectly competitive whereas the market for a factor of production is perfectly competitive. One example of this type of situation is the market for unskilled laborers who are not represented by unions. How will the analysis be different from that of a case of perfectly competitive input and output markets?

The equilibrium price of the input will still be determined by the market demand for and supply of the input. However, in this case the firm's demand curve for an input, say input A, is given by MRP_A but not by VMP_A. The reason MRP_A is no longer equal to VMP_A is that in an imperfectly competitive market for

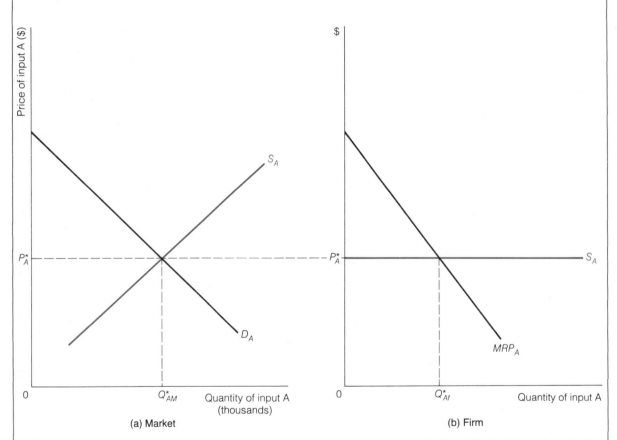

(a) Market

(b) Firm

FIGURE 23–7 Equilibrium Price and Quantity of Input A with a Perfectly Competitive Input Market But an Imperfectly

As in Figure 23–6, the equilibrium price (P_A^*) of an input, Input A, and the total market quantity employed (Q_{AM}^*) are determined by the market supply and demand curves for the input (S_A and D_A, respectively). In an imperfectly competitive output market, the marginal revenue received from selling another unit of the output will be less than its price. In this case, the marginal revenue product of the input will be less than the value of the marginal product of the input. The firm considers P_A^* to be given. Thus, it will maximize profit by employing Input A up to the point where P_A^* is equal to the marginal revenue product of Input A (MRP_A), at Q_{Af}^*.

the final product the firm has some control over the price of the final product. In this case the demand curve for the firm's product is downward sloping and (as discussed in Chapter 21) marginal revenue is less than price. In fact, most firms face this type of demand curve for their product.

Consequently, the marginal revenue product of an input is less than the value of its marginal product in most situations. Moreover, because the marginal revenue product of an input represents the additional revenue brought into the firm from one more unit of the input, it is the appropriate decision variable for the profit-maximizing firm to consider.

As shown in panel (a) of Figure 23–7, the equilibrium price of input A is determined by the intersection of the market supply and demand curves for input A. Again, from the standpoint of an individual firm the supply curve of input A is a horizontal line at P_A^*, as shown in panel (b). The firm can purchase as much of input A as it desires at the going market price. It will use input A until MRP_A is equal to P_A^*, at Q_{Af}^*.

Table 23–6 presents revenue and productivity data for Little Venice Restaurant, a firm that faces a less than perfectly competitive product market. The final product market is that for Italian food. The input under consideration is waiters and waitresses. If the cost of a waiter or waitress is $5.95 per hour, in order to maximize profit, Little Venice will hire 10 waiters or waitresses. More table help will not be hired, since beyond this point the marginal revenue product of labor is less than $3.[7]

Because Little Venice Restaurant sells in an imperfectly competitive product market, it will not maximize profit where factor price is equal to the value of the marginal product. When 10 waiters and waitresses are employed, the marginal revenue product of labor is approximately equal to the price of labor ($6 is approximately equal to $5.95). However, at $L = 10$ employees and $Q = 84$ meals per hour, the *value of the marginal product of labor* (equal to the price of a meal multiplied by the marginal product of labor) is equal to $7 \times 1 = 7$. Since $7 is greater than the wage

_____

7. In this example the components cost of food is ignored for the sake of simplicity. It could be taken into account by using net marginal revenue instead of marginal revenue in Table 23–5.

TABLE 23–6 Revenue and Productivity Data for Little Venice Restaurant

Number of Waiters, Waitresses (L)	Number of Meals per Hour (Q)	Marginal Product of Labor per Hour $\left(MP_L = \dfrac{\text{change in } Q}{\text{change in } L}\right)$	Average Price per Meal (P)	Total Revenue (TR)	Marginal Revenue $\left(MR = \dfrac{\text{change in } TR}{\text{change in } Q}\right)$	Marginal Revenue Product of Labor $(MRP_L = MP_L \times MR)$
0	0		$10.00	$ 0		
		20			$9.00	$180.00
2	40		9.00	360.00		
		10			6.00	960.00
4	60		8.00	480.00		
		6			5.00	30.00
6	72		7.50	540.00		
		4			4.50	18.00
8	80		7.20	576.00		
		2			3.00	6.00
10	84		7.00	588.00		
		1			2.70	2.70
12	86		6.90	593.40		
		0			0.00	0.00
14	86		6.90	593.40		

rate of $5.95, the firm is producing where the market value of the marginal product of the input is greater than the price of the input. In other words, the marginal social benefit of another unit of output is greater than its marginal social cost.

If the product market were perfectly competitive, output would increase until the value of the marginal product of labor was equal to the input price. Assuming that all firms in the industry increased their output, input price might also rise. However, the main point is that additional resources would be allocated to the production of Italian restaurant meals if the product market were perfectly competitive.

INPUT PRICING
WHEN FACTOR
MARKETS
ARE NOT
PERFECTLY
COMPETITIVE
◆

In this section we will assume that *input* markets are **imperfectly competitive.** What this means is that a firm buying a given input knows that the input supply curve slopes upward and to the right. Thus it is clear to the firm that the price it pays per unit of the input depends directly on the quantity of the input it is buying. Three major types of input market structures that fall into this category are monopsony, oligopsony, and monopsonistic competition.□

LESS THAN PERFECTLY COMPETITIVE OUTPUT AND INPUT MARKETS

In one situation the markets for both the output and the inputs of a firm are imperfectly competitive. That situation is one in which the seller of the final product has some control over both the selling price of the product and the price of the input. Although there are many possible degrees of less than perfect competition in the market for a factor of production, the analysis is the same for all of them unless the seller of the input has some monopoly power. We will assume for now that the input supplier has no monopoly power.

Upward-Sloping Input Supply Curve When the buyer has some control over the price of the input, the supply curve of its input is no longer horizontal. Instead it has a positive slope; larger quantities of the input are supplied at higher prices than at lower prices.

If the firm must pay a higher price for all units of the input when it desires to purchase a larger quantity, the marginal factor cost of one more unit of the input is greater than its price. For example, consider a firm that employs two computer programmers at an annual wage of $20,000 each but will have to pay $25,000 for a third programmer.

If the firm employs the third programmer at a wage of $25,000, is $25,000 the marginal factor cost of that person? Probably not. The reason is that the other two programmers will likely learn that the third person is being paid $5,000 more per year and will demand equal pay. As a result, the marginal factor cost of the third programmer will be $25,000 plus $5,000 for each of the other two programmers, for a total of $35,000.

Profit-Maximizing Quantity of Input In the case of an imperfectly competitive market for the input and the final product, the price a profit-maximizing firm will pay for a factor of production is determined as shown in Figure 23–8. The firm will use the input, input A, until MRP_A is equal to MFC_A, at Q_A^*. The firm will pay only P_A^* for each unit of input A, because P_A^* is the price at which the suppliers of input A are willing to supply Q_A^*. In this case, P_A is less than the marginal factor cost of input A.

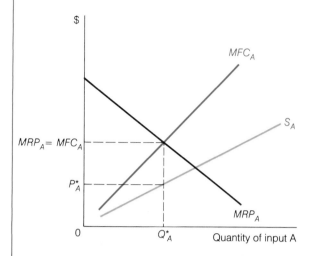

FIGURE 23–8 Equilibrium Price and Quantity of Input A for a Firm with Imperfectly Competitive Input and Output Markets

When an input market is imperfectly competitive, the firm no longer can consider the price of the input to be given. It faces an upward-sloping supply curve for the input, S_A for input A in this graph. In this case, the marginal factor cost of the input (MFC_A) will rise as more and more units of input A are utilized, and the marginal factor cost of the input will be greater than its price. The firm will maximize profit by employing input A up to the point where the marginal revenue product of input A (MRP_A) is equal to the marginal factor cost of input A, at Q_A^*. The firm will pay a price of P_A^* for each unit of the input.

BILATERAL MONOPOLY[8]

The last input market structure case we will consider is that of bilateral monopoly.

> **Bilateral monopoly** is a situation where there are only one seller and one buyer of a particular input or product.

Consequently, there is a monopoly on the supply side of the market and a monopsony on the demand side.

One example of a bilateral monopoly is the market for certain items manufactured for na-

_____
8. This section can be eliminated without loss of continuity.

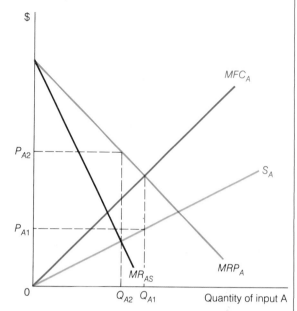

FIGURE 23–9 Bilateral Monopoly

As in Figure 23–8, the _buyer_ of input A will maximize its profit by employing the input up to the point where the marginal revenue product of input A (MRP_A) is equal to the marginal factor cost of input A (MFC_A), at Q_{A1} and P_{A1}. The _seller_ of input A will maximize profit by selling input A up to the point where the marginal revenue to the seller from selling another unit of input A (MR_{AS}), intersects the supply curve for input A (S_A), at Q_{A2} and P_{A2}. Since the seller maximizes profit by selling Q_{A2} units at a price equal to P_{A2}, and the buyer maximizes profit by purchasing Q_{A1} units at a price of P_{A1}, a conflict exists between the wishes of the buyer and those of the seller. The end result is likely to depend on the outcome of bargaining between the buyer and the seller.

tional defense. The U.S. government is the only approved buyer, and only one firm can make the item, usually as specified by a government contract. Another market closely resembling a bilateral monopoly is that for production workers in the automobile industry. The Big Four auto manufacturers are nearly a monopsony on the buying side, and the United Auto Workers union is a virtual monopoly on the selling side. (This situation is discussed in more detail in Chapter 25.)

The bilateral monopoly model assumes that both the seller of an input, say input A, and the buyer of the input wish to maximize their profits. On the demand side the *buyer* will maximize profit if it employs the input up to the point where $MRP_A = MFC_A$, at Q_{A1} and P_{A1} in Figure 23–9.

On the supply side the *seller* of the input will maximize profit by selling Q_{A2} units of the input at a price of P_{A2}. This quantity is at the point where the marginal revenue to the seller from selling another unit of input A, MR_{AS}, intersects the supply curve for input A, S_A. In other words, the seller of input A will maximize profit by supplying the input up to the point where the marginal revenue received from selling another unit of A is equal to the marginal cost of producing A, which is represented by the supply curve of input A, S_A.[9]

The seller of the input will try to charge a price of P_{A2}, the maximum amount a buyer without any monopsony power will be willing to pay for Q_{A2}. P_{A2} is obtained from MRP_A, which, in the absence of monopsony power, is the demand curve for input A.

Because the seller maximizes profit by selling Q_{A2} units at a price equal to P_{A2} and the buyer maximizes profit by purchasing Q_{A1} units at a price of P_{A1}, a conflict exists between the wishes of the buyer and the wishes of the seller. The end result is likely to depend on the outcome of bargaining between the buyer and the seller.

SUMMARY

1. This chapter discussed profit-maximizing decision rules for the employment of productive resources. The demand for factors of production is a derived demand. A firm wishes to purchase the services of inputs in order to meet the demand for some final product. Thus the firm's demand for inputs is directly related to the public's demand for the output of the firm.

2. In the short run a firm may have only one variable input. In this case the firm will employ the input until the additional revenue brought into the firm by another unit of input is equal to its marginal cost. The additional revenue brought in by another unit of an input is its marginal revenue product.

3. The marginal revenue product of an input is equal to the marginal revenue per unit of output multiplied by the marginal product of the input. Marginal revenue is equal to the change in total revenue divided by the change in output as the firm's rate of production is increased. Marginal product is the incremental physical output produced by one more unit of the input. If the firm has components costs, net marginal revenue may be used in place of marginal revenue to derive the marginal revenue product of an input.

4. If a firm has more than one variable input, for example capital and labor, the firm will maximize profit by employing capital and labor until

$$\frac{MRP_K}{MFC_K} = 1 = \frac{MRP_L}{MFC_L}.$$

A least cost combination of inputs requires that

$$\frac{MRP_K}{MFC_K} = \frac{MRP_L}{MFC_L}.$$

However, profit maximization requires the additional condition that both of these ratios equal 1, because the marginal revenue product of an input must be equal to its marginal cost.

5. The profit-maximizing decision rules for output and for inputs are consistent. If the marginal revenue products of all variable inputs are equal to their respective marginal costs, then the marginal revenue associated with another unit of output is also equal to its marginal cost.

6. A firm's demand curve for an input is given by the marginal revenue product curve of the input. The market demand curve for an input can be estimated by summing the quantities demanded of the input by individual firms at each price of the input.

7. Because the buyer of a productive resource frequently has some market power, economists often

---

9. The curve giving the marginal cost of producing an item is its supply curve as long as the item is produced in a purely competitive market on the supply side. Technically speaking, there is no unique supply curve for the item in other cases.

classify markets for productive resources according to the structure of the demand side. *Monopsony* is a situation in which there is one buyer. *Oligopsony* denotes a market with several or several dominant buyers. In *monopsonistic competition* there are many buyers, but each buyer has some control over price. In *perfect competition* the buyer has no control over price.

8. The behavior of a profit-maximizing firm regarding its employment of productive resources varies according to the structure of the input market and the structure of the market for the final product. If the input market is perfectly competitive, the equilibrium price is determined by the market demand for and supply of the input.

9. If the market for the final product is also purely competitive on the supply side, a firm will maximize profit by employing an input up to the point where the value of its marginal product is equal to its price. (When the market for an input is perfectly competitive, the price of the input is equal to its marginal factor cost.) The value of the marginal product of an input is equal to the price of the final product multiplied by the marginal product of the input. In this case the price of the final product is constant, so marginal revenue is equal to price; for input A, $VMP_A = MRP_A$. In all other cases the marginal revenue of the final product is less than price, so that MRP_A is less than VMP_A. In such cases MRP_A is the appropriate profit-maximizing decision variable for the firm.

10. If an input market is characterized by imperfect competition, the buyer is faced with an upward-sloping supply curve for the input. In this case the marginal cost of another unit of the input is greater than its price. The buyer, however, will still maximize profit by employing the input up to the point where its marginal revenue product is equal to its marginal cost.

11. *Bilateral monopoly* is the term used to describe a market with one buyer and one seller. The profit-maximizing position of the seller occurs where the marginal revenue to the seller from selling another unit of the input is equal to the marginal cost of supplying it. The optimal point for the buyer is where $MRP_A = MFC_A$ for input A. Under these circumstances the profit-maximizing quantities and prices of the input for the buyer are usually different than those for the seller. Ultimately, the price and quantity employed of the input will likely be the result of a bargaining process.

IMPORTANT TERMS AND CONCEPTS

Marginal revenue
  product of an input
Marginal product of
  an input
Marginal revenue
Marginal factor cost
Input use rule
Net marginal revenue
Least cost
  combination of
  inputs
Monopsony
Perfectly competitive
  market

Oligopsony
Monopsonistic
  competition
Firm's demand curve
  for an input
Market demand cruve
  for an input
Value of the marginal
  product of an input
Bilateral monopoly

QUESTIONS AND PROBLEMS

1. What is the profit-maximizing decision rule for the employment of one variable input? More than one variable input?

2. Define the following terms: *value of the marginal product, marginal revenue product,* and *marginal product.*

3. What are the four classifications of markets according to the structure of the demand side? Explain each one.

4. How does the profit-maximizing decision rule for employment of more than one variable input differ from the condition that must be satisifed for a least cost combination of inputs?

5. Draw a graph and explain how the equilibrium price and quantity of an input are determined in a perfectly competitive input market.

6. How does the profit-maximizing firm determine the optimal quantity to purchase and the optimal price to pay for a productive resource when the input market is imperfectly competitive? Draw a graph to illustrate your answer.

7. What is a bilateral monopoly? How are price and quantity determined in a market characterized by bilateral monopoly? Give an example.

8. What is derived demand with respect to an input? How is a firm's demand curve for a productive factor determined?

9. Given the following information for a firm that manufactures product X:

Quantity of Labor (L)	Total Output (Q_x)	Price of Product (P_x)	Total Revenue (TR)	Marginal Product of Labor (MP_L)	Marginal Revenue (MR)	Marginal Revenue Product of Labor (MRP_L)
0	0	$15	$ 0			
10	200	15				
20	400	15	6,000			
30	700	15	10,500			
40	900	15	13,500			
50	1,000	15	15,000			
60	1,075	15	16,125			
70	1,125	15	16,875			

a) Complete the table. (Attribute all MR to labor.)
b) Assuming labor is the only variable input, what *condition* determines the quantity of labor taken by the firm, and how is this consistent with profit maximization?
c) If labor is the only variable input, how much labor will the firm employ, based on the above data, assuming perfect competition in the labor market and a wage of $140 per unit of labor hired?

10. Complete the following table, giving productivity and revenue data for a small manufacturer of pruning shears. The materials cost for one pair of shears is $.50. After completing the table, explain how many workers the firm will employ if the wage rate is $3.10 per hour and why the firm will choose that number.

Quantity of Labor (L)	Quantity of shears Manufactured per Hour (Q)	Price per Pair of Shears (P)	Total Revenue (TR)	Marginal Revenue (MR)	Net Marginal Revenue (NMR)	Marginal Product of Labor (MP_L)	Marginal Revenue Product of Labor (MRP_L)
0	0	$8.00	$				
1	20	7.00		$	$		
2	32	6.25					
3	40	5.80					
4	44	5.50					
5	46	5.35					
6	47	5.25					

A
BARGAIN AT
$600,000?

Baseball teams use a lot of gimmicks to get people to the ballpark, especially when they're not winning; there are bat days, helmet days, jacket days, beer nights and exploding scoreboards all over the place, anything to get people to the ballpark because people spend money at the ballpark. The best surefire gimmick is a big bat in the hands of a player like Pete Rose. After a summer of headlines, Pete Rose

Source: Excerpted from "A Bargain at $600,000?" *Weekend*, December 2, 1978. Courtesy of National Broadcasting Company, Inc.

became a free agent. If his Cincinnati Reds wouldn't make him the highest paid player in baseball, he figured some other team would. Well, the New York Mets bid five hundred thousand dollars a year, and the Phillie's it's said offered six hundred thousand dollars. Everybody said that's a lot of money. . . . but, during the last 12 days of his 44 game hitting streak Pete Rose spent nine days on the road in four cities, Philadelphia, Montreal, New York, and Atlanta: The attendance at those nine road games was 125 thousand above average. Now the average fan spends four dollars for a ticket and

let's say another four bucks for a program, a hot dog, a beer, and some peanuts and crackerjacks, a total of eight bucks conservative. In just nine days, Pete Rose lured 125 thousand extra fans into four ballparks, one million dollars worth of extra business in just nine days. At Shea Stadium alone 42 thousand extra fans showed up to watch Pete Rose in 3 games. . . . that was about 350 thousand dollars worth of extra business for the Met's, who may have needed it but didn't deserve it. When the season ended, the only thing extra Pete Rose had to show for his hitting streak, that we know about, was a thank you note . . . . not from the Met's but from 110 vendors who sell beer and hot dogs at Shea Stadium.

QUESTIONS

1. Explain why employing Pete Rose for $600,000 or even $800,000 a year may be a bargain.

2. What was Pete Rose's marginal product per game for the nine road games (for the host teams)? What was marginal revenue per person?

3. Do you think *Weekend's* calculation of Pete Rose's marginal revenue product for the host teams is correct? Explain.

4. How would the calculations of attendance at road games be useful to the Cincinnati Reds or any other team that might consider making Rose an offer?

C H A P T E R 24

RETURNS
TO
PRODUCTIVE
RESOURCES

SOME EXPLANATIONS FOR MALE-FEMALE INCOME DIFFERENTIALS

Labor, an important resource in most production processes, is generally recognized to come in two sexes, male and female. Recent laws relating to job discrimination and the fact that women have become an increasingly large proportion of the labor force have called attention to differences in earnings between men and women in the same or similar lines of work.

In general, studies show that women receive lower salaries or wages than do men who perform similar tasks. However, recent evidence indicates that such differentials can be explained in part by variations in occupational choices and experience levels. In other words, although most female workers are in low-paying clerical jobs, even women in nontraditional jobs receive less pay than their male counterparts for reasons that may not be related to discrimination.

For example, a study released in 1980 reported that in 1978 female M.D.s in private practice had an average net income of about $40,000, whereas male M.D.s had an average of $67,450. The study also indicated, however, that female physicians preferred to work in the lower-paying specialties, such as pediatrics and psychiatry, instead of in the more lucrative fields, such as surgery. Another finding of the research was that female doctors saw an average of forty fewer patients per week than male doctors did. The study attributed this finding in part to female doctors' devoting a *larger share of their time to family duties, so tradition probably still contributed somewhat to the earnings differential.[1]*

Another study released in 1980 noted that women are more likely to interrupt their careers than are men. (Obviously, child rearing is one of the causes.) The study found that interruptions of three or four years are common and that they lead to a drop in real wages when the women return to the workforce. One author of the study suggested that women who drop out of the workforce suffer an erosion of skills that hampers their future progress. Some earlier research involving the same author showed that women who do not interrupt their careers also earn less than their male counterparts, but the differentials are not so great.[2]

Obviously, the question of earnings differentials can have many dimensions, including specialization and skills as well as discrimination. In this chapter we will examine not only wage diffferentials but also returns to other factors of production, such as property and entrepreneurship. Labor market structure and the effects of unions will be covered more thoroughly in Chapter 25.

1. "The Earnings Gap between Female and Male Physicians Stays Wide," *Wall Street Journal*, March 18, 1980, p. 1.
2. "New Reasons Women Earn Less than Men," *Business Week*, October 20, 1980, p. 21.

C H A P T E R 24

◆

RETURNS
TO
PRODUCTIVE
RESOURCES

WHAT THIS CHAPTER IS ABOUT

WAGES
WAGE RATE DIFFERENTIALS
Skills or Education
Geographical Immobility
Institutional Restrictions
RENT
Henry George and the Single Tax
Quasi-rents
INTEREST
PROFIT
Entrepreneurship

The focus of this chapter is on the types of returns to factors of production.□ Economists frequently separate these returns into four classifications: wages, rent, interest, and profit. These classifications reflect the functions in the process of production of those who receive the income.

*The distribution of income according to the activity performed by its recipients is called the **functional distribution of income.***

As we will see later, it is often difficult to precisely divide income received by productive resources into four distinct categories. However, we can do so well enough to capture the nature of these relationships. Accord-

13

ing to the gross national product accounts, compensation of employees accounted for approximately 75 percent of national income☐ in 1980. Of the remaining 25 percent, rent was approximately 1.5 percent, interest was 8.5 percent, and profits were 15 percent.[1]

WAGES

◆

Wages *are the payment that labor receives in return for its services.*

In terms of the GNP accounts, wages in an economic sense are approximated by the category compensation of employees.☐ Viewed in this manner, they make up three-fourths of national income.

However, according to economists, this amount is an understatement. The portion of proprietors' income☐ that represents a return to the proprietor for labor services such as management, sales, and janitorial work actually constitutes wages as well. For an individual we can estimate the share of proprietors' income that represents wages using the standard of **opportunity cost**: what the person could earn in wages if he or she were employed by another firm to supply those services.

In 1980 compensation of employees totaled $1,596.5 billion. Proprietors' income was only $130.6 billion. If we were to estimate wages as economists use the term by finding the sum of compensation of employees plus one-half of proprietors' income, we could probably obtain a ballpark figure. In this case the estimate of wages would be $1,596.5 billion + 1/2 ($130.6 billion) = $1,596.5 + $65.3 billion = $1,661.8 billion.[2]

---

1. From data supplied in "Table B–19: National Income by Type of Income, 1929–80," *Economic Report of the President* (Washington, D.C.: Government Printing Office, 1981), pp. 254–255.

2. Ibid., p. 254.

WAGE RATE DIFFERENTIALS

Table 24–1 shows the average hourly earnings of production, or nonsupervisory, workers for April 1981. Petroleum and coal products workers were the highest paid, with average hourly earnings of $11.40. Workers in the apparel and the leather products industries were the lowest paid, with average hourly earnings less than half those of petroleum and coal products workers.

TABLE 24–1 Average Hourly Earnings of Production, or Nonsupervisory, Workers, April 1981

Industry	Average Hourly Earnings
Total private	$ 7.13
Mining	9.70
Construction	10.43
Lumber and wood products	6.83
Furniture and fixtures	5.78
Stone, clay, and glass products	8.11
Primary metal industries	10.76
Fabricated metal products	8.05
Machinery, except electrical	8.67
Electric and electronic equipment	7.51
Transportation equipment	10.14
Instruments and related products	7.25
Food and kindred products	7.37
Tobacco manufactures	8.90
Textile mill products	5.36
Apparel	4.96
Paper	8.37
Printing and publishing	8.04
Chemicals	8.94
Petroleum and coal products	11.40
Rubber and plastics products	7.15
Leather and leather products	4.93
Transportation and public utilities	9.54
Wholesale trade	7.47
Retail trade	5.22
Finance, insurance, and real estate	6.20
Services	6.30

Source: U.S. Department of Labor, Bureau of Labor Statistics, "Table C–2: Gross Hours and Earnings of Production or Nonsupervisory Workers on Private Nonagricultural Payrolls by Industry", *Employment and Earnings*, vol. 28 (Washington, D.C.: Government Printing Office, July, 1981), pp. 124–139.

Even the hourly earnings of petroleum and coal products workers, however, are peanuts compared to wages paid other types of labor. For example, Henry Ford II earned $992,000 as chairman of Ford Motor Company in 1977.[3] Moreover, world champion boxers such as Muhammad Ali or Leon Spinks can collect a $3.75 million purse in a single night.[4] (Of course, much time and expense is necessary to prepare for a fight.)

Why do wage differentials occur, and why are they so large? In the first place, the demand for labor, like that for any other input, is a derived demand. That is, the demand for an input is directly related to the demand for the product it produces.

In the second place, the productivity of an input affects the demand for it, and the pro-

ductivity of different types of workers varies. For example, as we will see, some workers have greater skill or training than others do. Finally, the supply of and demand for an input are important in the determination of its price. There are few Muhammad Ali's around.

Many specific factors, including varying requirements for skills and education, geographical immobility, institutional restrictions, discriminatory practices, and different market structures, promote wage differentials. Each of these factors is discussed here.

SKILL OR EDUCATIONAL REQUIREMENTS

Generally speaking, economic theory suggests that employees who perform jobs that require more skills or education will be paid more than employees who perform jobs that require fewer skills or less education. At least to some extent, the higher wages paid in these jobs re-

---

3. "Annual Survey of Executive Compensation," *Business Week*, May 15, 1978, pp. 66–67.

4. "Young Again at 36," *Time*, September 25, 1978, p. 103.

TABLE 24–2   Average Annual Earnings Related to Age and Education, 1970

(a) Males

Age (Years)	Education			
	Elementary (0 to 8 Years)	High School (4 Years)	College	
			(4 Years)	(5 Years or More)
25–34	$5,981	$8,268	$10,677	$10,995
35–54	6,826	9,862	15,856	18,482
55–64	6,540	9,521	15,915	19,246

(b) Females

Age (Years)	Education			
	Elementary (0 to 8 Years)	High School (4 Years)	College	
			(4 Years)	(5 Years or More)
25–34	$2,854	$3,935	$5,812	$6,731
35–54	3,149	4,327	6,306	8,473
55–64	3,232	4,728	7,137	9,237

Source: U.S. Department of Commerce, Bureau of the Census, "Table 1: Earnings and Occupation of Total and White Males 25 to 64 Years Old in the Experienced Civilian Labor Force with Earnings in 1969, by Work Experience in 1969, Years of School Completed and Age: 1970" and "Table 7: Earnings and Occupation of Total and White Females 25 to 64 Years Old in the Experienced Civilian Labor Force with Earnings in 1969, by Work Experience in 1969, Years of School Completed, and Age: 1970," *1970 Census of Population Subject Reports: Earnings by Occupation and Education* (Washington, D.C.: Government Printing Office, 1973), pp. 1, 242.

flect a return on an investment—an investment in human capital.

Human capital is created when people invest in training or education. Through this investment they become eligible for jobs for which they otherwise would lack the appropriate credentials. In general, as shown by Table 24–2, a greater investment in human capital results in higher earnings. Presumably, increased skill or knowledge makes labor more productive and therefore worth more to employers.

However, as with other investments, there is always the possibility that an investment in human capital may not be profitable. For example, a plumber may go back to school in order to become a high school teacher and find that earnings of high school teachers are lower than those of plumbers. The relationship between the market demand for and supply of the input should not be disregarded.

GEOGRAPHICAL IMMOBILITY

Many workers settle in a particular geographical location and are reluctant to or cannot move to another area. This reluctance or inability to change locations is called **geographical immobility.**

For workers who do have mobility, economic theory suggests that when wage rates are higher in one area than in another, workers will move from the low-wage area to the high-wage area. Immigration by citizens of Mexico into the United States is one example of this phenomenon. Their response will decrease the supply of labor in the low-wage area

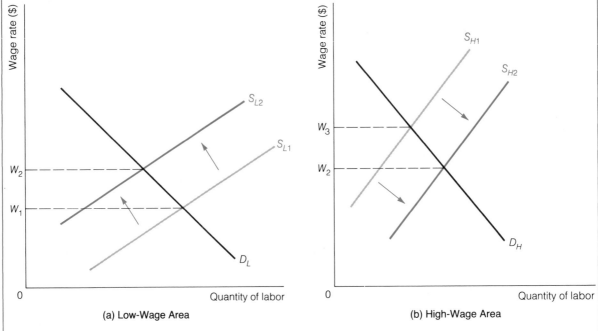

FIGURE 24–1 Movement of Labor from a Low-Wage to a High-Wage Area

In panel (a), the low-wage area, the initial supply of labor and demand for labor curves are given by S_{L1} and D_L, respectively, and the initial wage rate is W_1. In panel (b), the initial supply of labor and demand for labor curves are given by S_{H1} and D_H, respectively, and the wage rate is W_3. After workers from the low-wage area move to the high wage area, the supply of labor in the low wage area decreases to S_{L2}. Likewise, the supply of labor in the high-wage market increases to S_{H2}. The equilibrium wage rate in both markets now becomes W_2.

and increase the supply of labor in the high-wage area. As a result, wage rates will tend to rise in the low-wage area and fall in the high-wage area.

In Figure 24−1, S_{L1} represents the original supply of labor curve in the low-wage area, and S_{H1} represents the original supply of labor curve in the high-wage area. After workers move from the low-wage to the high-wage location, the supply of labor curves are S_{L2} and S_{H2}, respectively, and the wage rates in the two markets are equal.

Of course, worker migration does not always result in equal wage rates in all areas, even within the same country. The average hourly earnings by state of production workers on manufacturing payrolls is presented in Table 24−3. Average hourly earnings are highest in Alaska, at $10.31. They are lowest in Mississippi and North Carolina, at $5.97 and $5.79, respectively.

Why don't more workers leave Mississippi and North Carolina and move to Alaska? Some workers refuse to move because they prefer their present location. Perhaps they dislike cold weather or do not wish to leave friends and relatives. Economists would say that they get **psychic income** from staying in their present location. Thus the satisfaction, or utility□ (see Chapter 16), they receive from their money wage plus their living environment is equal to or exceeds what they would get from having a higher wage in a less desirable location.

Moving costs may also be an important consideration. Furthermore, wage rate differentials among areas may to some extent reflect differences in workers' average levels of education or training.

Finally, the differentials in real wage rates between areas may not be as great as the money wage rates. The **real wage rate** for an area is computed by dividing the money wage rate by a cost of living index for the area. The real wage rate is an adjustment to the money wage rate to reflect buying power in terms of goods and services.

Although comparable price indexes are not

TABLE 24−3 Average Hourly Earnings of Production Workers by State, April 1981

State	Average Hourly Earnings
Alabama	$ 7.01
Alaska	10.31
Arizona	7.85
Arkansas	6.15
California	8.34
Colorado	8.12
Connecticut	7.55
Delaware	8.53
District of Columbia	8.79
Florida	6.44
Georgia	6.28
Hawaii	7.49
Idaho	7.99
Illinois	8.80
Indiana	9.31
Iowa	9.42
Kansas	7.77
Kentucky	7.79
Louisiana	8.44
Maine	6.48
Maryland	8.25
Massachusetts	6.89
Michigan	10.23
Minnesota	8.30
Mississippi	5.97
Missouri	7.78
Montana	9.08
Nebraska	7.85
Nevada	8.34
New Hampshire	6.21
New Jersey	7.90
New Mexico	6.33
New York	7.73
North Carolina	5.79
North Dakota	7.04
Ohio	9.44
Oklahoma	8.20
Oregon	9.30
Pennsylvania	8.22
Rhode Island	6.00
South Carolina	6.07
South Dakota	6.94
Tennessee	6.59
Texas	7.78
Utah	7.62
Vermont	6.60
Virginia	6.67
Washington	10.29
West Virginia	8.80
Wisconsin	8.65
Wyoming	7.95

Source: U.S. Department of Labor, Bureau of Labor Statistics, "Table C–13: Gross Hours and Earnings of Production Workers on Manufacturing Payrolls by State and Selected Areas," *Employment and Earnings*, vol. 28 (Washington, D.C.: Government Printing Office, July 1981), pp. 149−153.

available for the following cities, the 1980 cost of living for a family of four on an intermediate-level budget was $21,131 in Atlanta, Georgia, and $24,028 in Milwaukee, Wisconsin. During September 1979 the average hourly wage rate for production workers in Atlanta was $7.50; the average in Milwaukee was $9.47. However, wage rate differentials do not entirely reflect differences in cost of living. The comparable figures for Honolulu, Hawaii, are $28,488 and $7.39.[5] Other factors are therefore important, too.

INSTITUTIONAL RESTRICTIONS

Institutional restrictions are factors such as licensing requirements and membership limitations by craft unions that prevent workers from freely entering certain job markets. Only a limited number of students are accepted by medical schools, law schools, and other professional schools. In at least some states, one must have a license to be a beautician, a taxi driver, or a dirt and gravel hauler, for instance.

By limiting the supply of labor for a specific occupation, such restrictions help cause and maintain wage rate differentials. In fact, for that very reason, some economists wish that entry into their own profession were more restricted!

DISCRIMINATION

Discrimination is a special type of institutional restriction. It can take the form of outright refusal to hire certain categories of work-

ers, such as blacks and women. It can also take the form of paying workers unequal pay for equal work.

As with other types of institutional restrictions, discrimination restricts the supply of labor for certain occupations, which results in higher wage rates for those jobs than would otherwise be the case. Discrimination and the Civil Rights Act of 1964 are discussed in greater detail in Chapter 25.

Market Structures If labor has monopoly power, as with a union, or if a firm has monopsony power, the market wage rate may be affected. These matters are discussed in detail in Chapter 25.

RENT

> **Rent** is a payment for a factor of production that is fixed in terms of the quantity supplied.[6]

Under a strict interpretation of this definition, few payments to inputs would constitute rents. Land or other natural resources are often cited as the prime examples of fixed inputs. Correspondingly, the return attributable to the ownership of land or natural resources has traditionally been called rent.

HENRY GEORGE AND THE SINGLE TAX

Henry George, a nineteenth century economist, argued that because the supply of land was fixed, a tax levied on land would not affect the supply of land or the productivity of

---

5. U.S. Department of Labor, Bureau of Labor Statistics, *Autumn 1980 Urban Family Budgets and Comparative Indexes for Selected Urban Areas*, (Washington, D.C.: Bureau of Labor Statistics, April 22, 1981); and U.S. Department of Labor, Bureau of Labor Statistics, "Table C–13: Gross Hours and Earnings of Production Workers on Manufacturing Payrolls by State and Selected Areas," *Employment and Earnings*, vol. 28 (Washington, D.C.: Government Printing Office, July 1981, pp. 149–153.

6. A broader definition of *rent* is payment to a factor of production greater than is necessary to secure its services. Any payment to a completely fixed productive resource fits into this category. If the quantity supplied of an input is fixed, no payment at all is necessary to obtain its services.

the economy. According to George, as the population of the world increased, landowners would earn higher and higher returns through no productive effort on their part but merely because, relatively speaking, land was becoming more scarce. Thus a tax on land would also be an equitable way for the government to raise revenue.[7]

George viewed the situation regarding land as shown in Figure 24–2, where the supply of land is represented by a vertical line, S_L. According to George as the demand for land increased, so would rents. He believed that a government could raise all the funds it needed through a single tax—a tax on land.

However, George failed to recognize that even land is not fixed in terms of usage. It may be used to support a skyscraper, a freeway, a parking lot, a house, or a field of corn, for example. It may also be improved; swamps

---

7. Henry George, *Progress and Poverty* (New York: Robert Schalkenbach Foundation, 1971), especially Book 3, Chapter 2, and Book 8, Chapter 3.

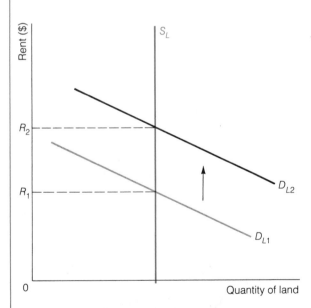

FIGURE 24–2 The Supply and Demand for Land

The supply of land is fixed and given by S_L. Originally, the demand for labor curve is D_{L1} and the rent is R_1. If the demand for land rises to D_{L2}, the rent will rise to R_2.

may be drained and sidewalks and sewer systems installed.

Moreover, as a population increases and an economy grows, the prices of many things besides land often increase. On the other hand, the price of land in certain locations has increased far more than that in other locations. Is a particular investor to be denied a return for making an astute decision regarding which plot of land to buy?

Finally, on what basis is the tax to be figured—number of acres, valuation, or some other basis? Certainly, the returns to various types of land are not equal, but if land is taxed on anything but a per acre basis the taxes will affect the uses to which the land is put. For example, some land in the middle of metropolitan areas has cattle grazing on it because the property tax rate for farmland is less than the rate for other types of land.

IS JOHNNY CARSON'S SALARY A RENT?

Returns to various types of performers are sometimes called rent. For example, there is only one Willie Nelson, Walter Cronkite, and Johnny Carson. However, even these people can decide to work fewer hours in their chosen fields or change jobs if they are dissatisfied with their pay. Thus it is questionable what fraction of their earnings, if any, represents rent.

QUASI-RENTS

If we use the strict economic definition of rent, we will be hard pressed to find even one concrete instance of rental income. For example, rent paid for the use of an apartment or office space does not really constitute payment to a fixed factor of production, at least in the long run. An apartment complex may be converted into an office building or torn down entirely. Also, apartments or office buildings may be built on unoccupied land. Thus even land is not fixed in usage.

A more practical definition of rent *is the return to productive factors, excluding labor,
that in the short run are fixed. Such returns
are sometimes called **quasi-rents.***

This definition is more representative of rental
income as defined in the GNP accounts. As
noted in Chapter 5, *rental income* □ as measured in the GNP accounts includes income
received from the rental of real property (land
and buildings), imputed or estimated rental
returns to owner-occupants of houses, and
royalties received by individuals from patents, copyrights, and right to natural resources. According to the GNP accounts, the
1980 rental income of persons was $31.9 bil-
lion.[8]

INTEREST

*Interest has traditionally been defined as the
return to real capital—buildings and machines, for example.*

Interest can be approximated by the payment
made for the privilege of using financial capital. Through the use of borrowed funds, businesses are able to obtain the services of plants
and equipment more quickly than they could
otherwise. The opportunity cost of owner-supplied funds should also be considered. Individuals are able to obtain the return from
owning their own homes or the pleasure
of enjoying consumption goods earlier than
would be possible if they could not obtain
loans.

INTEREST RATES

Interest is usually stated in terms of a specific
annual percentage of the amount of the loan,
such as 12 percent of $5,000. As explained in

8. "Table B–19," *Economic Report of the President,*
p. 255.

Chapter 12, the general level of interest rates
depends on the demand for and supply of
money and the market for goods and services.

VARIATIONS IN INTEREST RATES

At any point in time, interest rates vary from
one loan to another primarily because of different degrees of risk, or uncertainty. The uncertainty may be of two types: uncertainty regarding the debtor and uncertainty as to the
future opportunity costs of making the loan.
The latter type is related to the length to maturity of a loan.

Default Risk   The risk of default is the uncertainty regarding the eventual repayment of the
borrowed funds and payment of the interest.
For example, a loan to the federal government
is generally considered to be risk-free. In June
1981 the market interest rate on one-year U.S.
Treasury bills was 13.22 percent. At the same
time the prime rate—the interest rate on short-
term loans that banks charge their best corporate customers—was 20.03 percent.[9] The
interest rates charged less reliable debtors is
often substantially higher. Moreover, in the
case of interest rate ceilings, some financial
institutions merely refuse loans to certain prospective borrowers.

Length to Maturity

The **length to maturity** of a loan is the length
of time before the loan must be repaid.

Other things equal, loans for longer time periods have higher interest rates than do loans
for shorter periods.

One major reason for this differential is that
lenders must accept more risk when they
make loans with longer maturities. First, a
lender usually must commit the money at a

9. See "Table 1.33: Prime Rate Charged by Banks," and
"Table 1.35: Interest Rates: Money and Capital Markets,"
Federal Reserve Bulletin 67 (July 1981): A24–A28.

specified rate; and the farther into the future the maturity date of the loan, the more difficult it is for the lender to forecast the opportunity cost □ of the funds at the future date. Imagine the dismay of a bank that made a thirty-year real estate loan at 5 percent interest during the 1960s, when the going rate on a similar loan in 1981 was over 16 percent.

Second, the longer the length of a loan, the more difficult it is for the lender to predict the ability of the debtor to repay it. A business that is flourishing at the time the loan is made may be bankrupt ten or twenty years later. The Penn Central railroad is a good example of how a once well-established firm can be forced into bankruptcy.

In 1980 net interest payments as recorded in the GNP accounts totaled $179.8 billion.[10] As explained in Chapter 5, this figure represents the net interest payments of U.S. businesses plus net interest received from abroad. It does not include estimated opportunity costs of funds supplied by owners of firms to their businesses; nor does it include interest payments on the federal debt.

PROFIT

Profit is the fourth type of return to productive resources.

*Although economists do not agree on its exact nature, most would say that **profit** is the return to an input called entrepreneurship.*

However, pinning down what is meant by entrepreneurship is no simple task.

ENTREPRENEURSHIP

One workable definition of entrepreneurship is the following one.

10. "Table B–19, *Economic Report of the President,* p. 255.

Entrepreneurship is the input that, using its knowhow and innovative ability and accepting the related risks, combines the other three inputs (labor, land or other natural resources, and capital) for the purpose of making a return over and above the returns to these inputs. This extra return is profit.

DEFINITION OF PROFIT

Chapter 18 pointed out that accounting profit or net income, normal profit, and economic profit were three different things. *Accounting profit* is equal to the total revenue of a firm minus its explicit costs. *Economic profit* is equal to the total revenue of a firm minus its explicit and implicit, or opportunity, costs. *Normal profit* is considered one of the implicit costs. Where does plain profit, or the extra return to entrepreneurship, fit in?

In our use of the term, *profit* is the sum of normal profit□ and economic profit,□ if any. Economic profit is easily described. What is meant by normal profit, however, is less clear; therefore we will examine the term through the use of an example.

It is the expectation of at least a normal profit that entices an investor to purchase stock in a firm (rather than bonds) and thus to accept the risks and responsibilities of ownership of the firm. More precisely, a normal profit is the minimum expected return differential over the bond interest return that is sufficient to get the investor to purchase an ownership share in the firm rather than the firm's bonds. Of course, an owner may hope to earn more than the minimum differential, but this additional increment is economic profit.

Ownership Risks Why is there a need for payment to entrepreneurship? The discussion above hinted at one reason—to get people to accept the risks and responsibilities of firm ownership. A firm's owners are responsible for seeing to it that the revenue of the firm is at least sufficient to pay returns to the other three productive resources. The owners get the remaining revenue, if there is any. If a firm goes bankrupt, the owners are last in line when it comes time to divide up the firm's assets. In the case of a sole proprietorship or partnership, each owner is personally liable for any funds due the other productive resources. Thus an entrepreneur accepts more risk than other inputs do.

Innovation The expectation of profit encourages innovation and productive efficiency. By developing a new or better product, an entrepreneur may even be able to earn an economic profit, at least for a short time. Such decisions, expertise, and foresight are not expected of bondholders.

According to the GNP accounts, corporate profits were $181.7 billion in 1980 and proprietors' income was $130.6 billion, for a total of $312.3 billion.[11] Of course, not all of this amount represents profit in the sense that it has been defined here, because the opportunity costs of owner-supplied labor, land and buildings, and financial capital must be subtracted. The exact figure for profit is hard to estimate given our limited data, but it is significantly smaller than the figure given by the GNP accounts.

ECONOMIC PROFIT

Up to this point we have been examining normal profit, or the return to entrepreneurship. Earlier in this chapter and in previous chapters, we identified economic profit as a return over and above normal profit.

Economic profit does not exist in the long run in perfectly competitive□ and monopolistically competitive□ industry structures. However, it may exist in the long run for industries that are oligopolistic□ or are pure monopolies.□ Here, economic profit is a return to monopoly power, which enables the firms in an industry to limit the total quantity supplied of a product. It occurs as the result of

---

11. Ibid., pp. 254–255.

an artificial, or contrived, scarcity of a product and therefore is similar to a rent. However, this type of scarcity is brought about not by natural forces but by the actions of the firms in the industry.

In the short run, economic profit may exist in all types of industry structures. In industries without barriers to entry, it is an incentive for economic resources to enter the industries. Thus it serves a socially useful purpose.

SUMMARY

1. This chapter discussed the four types of returns to productive resources: wages, rent, interest, and profit.

2. *Wages* are the return to labor for its services. Wage rates vary widely and for many reasons. Several specific factors that promote wage rate differentials are differences in skill or education, geographical immobility, institutional restrictions, discrimination, and different market structures.

3. Strictly speaking, *rent* is a payment for a factor of production that is fixed in terms of quantity supplied. Economists frequently consider land or other natural resources to be prime examples of inputs that earn rent. In fact, Henry George argued in the late nineteenth century that because land was fixed in terms of quantity supplied, a government could raise sufficient revenue through a single tax on land without disrupting the economy. George thought that such a tax was justified because he believed rent to be unearned income.

4. However, even land can be altered. A more practical definition of *rent* might be the return to productive factors, excluding labor, that in the short run are fixed. Such payments are sometimes called *quasi-rents*.

5. The payment made for the privilege of using capital is called *interest*; it is usually stated as a specific annual percentage of the principal, or the amount of the loan. The general level of interest rates depends on the demand for and the supply of money and the market for goods and services.

6. At any point in time, interest rates vary from loan to loan, primarily because of different degrees of risk, or uncertainty. These risks include the risk

of default (nonpayment of the loan or the interest) and the risk of underestimating the future opportunity cost of funds.

7. *Profit* is the return to entrepreneurship. *Entrepreneurship* is the input that, using its knowhow, combines the other three inputs for the purpose of making a return over and above the returns to these inputs. In other words, profit is the return for the risks of ownership. It also is a reward for innovation and productive efficiency. The exact dollar amount of profit is difficult to estimate, however, because of the implicit costs of owner-supplied labor, financial capital, and land and buildings.

IMPORTANT TERMS AND CONCEPTS

Functional
  distribution
  of income
Wages
Opportunity cost
Human capital
Geographical
  immobility
Real wage rate

Rent
Quasi-rents
Interest
Length to maturity
Profit
Entrepreneurship

QUESTIONS AND PROBLEMS

1. Define the following terms as they have been used in this chapter: wages, rent, interest, and profit.

2. Why did Henry George believe that a tax system consisting of a single tax on land was appropriate?

3. How are accounting profit, normal profit, economic profit, and profit (as we have used the term in this chapter) related?

4. What is entrepreneurship? Give an example.

5. Give several reasons for the existence of wage rate differentials.

6. What factors affect the general level of interest rates? Why do interest rates differ from loan to loan?

AS RENT CONTROL SPREADS ACROSS COUNTRY, ITS FRIENDS AND FOES WATCH LOS ANGELES

Los Angeles—The way economist Chapman Findlay looks at it, this city's adoption of rent control has given his profession "one of the largest experimental laboratories ever constructed."

The laboratory is the Los Angeles housing market. The experiment: to see whether rent control can be imposed on a metropolis without causing some of the problems blamed on rent regulation in New York City. The problems there have included a dearth of new rental-apartment construction and a wholesale decline in the value and upkeep of rental property.

Source: G. Christian Hill, "As Rent Control Spreads across Country, Its Friends and Foes Watch Los Angeles," *Wall Street Journal,* February 1, 1980, p. 34.

Supporters here say that the Los Angeles way protects tenants while providing a "just and reasonable return" to landlords. "Rent control doesn't have to be like New York's," says Joel Wachs, the city councilman who led the campaign for rent control in Los Angeles. "Most tenants and landlords are happy with it" here.

Maybe so, but interviews with more than 50 landlords, tenants, builders, investors and lenders suggest otherwise. None seem really enthusiastic about it. Many, in fact, believe that in several ways it is the worst of all possible rent-control plans.

Whereas the great majority of New York renters have some degree of protection, nearly half of Los Angeles renters aren't covered, and many of the

unprotected are being hit with huge rent increases. The program also appears to be worsening the city's already critical rental-housing shortage by driving off big builders and their money sources. They fear that the moderate program will be toughened this year.

SPECULATION CURBED

On the other hand, Los Angeles-style rent control has benefited most of the tenants it does cover, keeping their rent increases at an authorized 7% annually, or about half the inflation rate. It also appears to have broken the back of feverish speculation in apartment-house purchases. That speculation had greatly contributed to surging rents.

Whether or not this city's rent

control actually works is of more than academic interest. Similar plans are spreading throughout California and to other parts of the country. About 50% of this state's 10 million tenants now are covered. The National Rental Housing Council, a landlord group, estimates that, all told, nearly 100 cities outside the New York-New Jersey area, the traditional bastion of rent control have adopted some kind of rent regulation. Other plans, the group says, are being proposed in many more cities in 30 states.

Some economists believe that the condition fostering the spread of rent control—a nationwide rental-housing shortage that allows landlords to charge whatever the market will bear—is here to stay. As a result, "rent control will spread everywhere," predicts George Sternlieb, director of Rutgers University's Urban Land Policy Center.

Both tenant groups and landlords have formed national organizations for and against rent control. The two camps are looking to Los Angeles for ammunition because this city was the first major one to adopt a form of rent control since New York did. Two months ago, Baltimore voters also approved a rent-control measure.

ADOPTED AFTER FREEZE

The Los Angeles City Council, responding to tenant pressure, adopted rent control last March after earlier freezing rents at May 1978 levels. Tenants had been angered by speculators who bought apartment houses from less savvy, or less greedy,

landlords and then raised rents. The tenants had been angered, too, by the refusal of most landlords to share tax savings from Proposition 13, the state measure that cut property taxes 57%.

The rent-control law is a compromise between pro-landlord and pro-tenant councilmen. The city attorney has no power to prosecute landlords who violate the law. Seeking to avoid a large and expensive bureaucracy of rent-control administrators such as New York's, the city council left enforcement of the law entirely to tenants, through civil action. The average apartment house here has only 15 to 20 apartments, a circumstance that may make it tough for tenants to throw their weight around in litigation. . . .

PROVISIONS FOR TENANTS

Before rent control, tenants in many parts of the city had been experiencing yearly rent increases of 15% to 20% or more. The shortage of rental housing not only allowed all landlords to jack up rents; it also enabled speculators to buy properties with low rents and resell the buildings in a few months at higher prices after the rent had been raised. Many investors were paying so much for apartment houses and incurring such high mortgage payments that their cash flow was negative at first, but they gambled that, as leases expired, they could raise rents sharply because of the housing shortage.

The 7% cap on rent increases has almost ended speculation in buildings with low turnover, because it limits their rate of

appreciation. "Speculation is practically nonexistent today," says broker H. Bruce Hanes. Mr. Hanes calculates that the value of the average building he handles has risen only 8% in the last year, compared with 20% annual rises since 1976. Other real-estate people report no increases, or even slight declines, in property values. No one, they say, is buying apartment houses with negative cash flows anymore.

NO PINCH FOR SOME

Yet most investors who bought rental property here several years ago, and had healthy cash flows before controls were adopted, say they haven't been pinched by the rent freeze or controls, and other investors continue to buy in Los Angeles. In a typical case, the cash flow of a 14-unit apartment house in West Los Angeles bought 10 years ago increased to $2,308 a month in 1979 from $1,417 a month in 1978. The apartment house's manager, Wagner-Jacobson Co., says it raised income by cutting operating expenses and increasing the rents on vacated apartments. . . .

Meanwhile, many tenants paying low rent have more incentive than ever to stay put, and many are doing just that. (Apartment managers estimate that only one-third of the city's rental units are being vacated in this first year of rent control, compared with one-half annually before controls.) In these cases, it is the landlords who are suffering. Apartment brokers say that at least 20% of the city's apartment houses were bought in the last two years by landlords—

not all of them speculators—who figured to reverse negative cash flows by raising rents. But the May 1978 freeze caught them with their rents down.

"HURT VERY BADLY"

Many of these landlords are experiencing widening losses, or are struggling to avoid losses, because their tenants aren't moving and their operating expenses are climbing.

"We've been hurt very badly," says Nestor Maheras, who along with some partners bought a 50-unit apartment house in January 1978. He says the property was losing just a little money at first, now, he says, it is losing $2,000 a month thanks to rent control and thanks to operating costs that include payments for an expensive new boiler whose cost can be passed on—if it can be passed on—only gradually and after long administrative hearings.

Landlords are trying to improve their finances by cutting maintenance expenses. As a result, tenants often find themselves living in shabbier apartments. "We're doing nothing for renters now," says the manager who supervises 1,500 units here. "We're better off if a good tenant gets disgusted and moves." Suppliers who sell carpet, furniture and other items to landlords report that their business is off 30% to 70% since 1978. . . .

Even though the rent-control plan here is riddled with loopholes, the big apartment builders, lenders and investors who fear a toughened measure say they are boycotting Los Angeles, causing the supply of much-needed new apartments to dry up. But their fear appears unjustified. A city-council procedure vote this week on extending the present ordinance to July ended in a tie, with two rent-control advocates absent. Sources close to the council expect the law to survive, but they doubt that it will be measurably toughened.

QUESTIONS

1. How is the concept of fixed inputs related to the policy of rent control?

2. Does the experience of California after the passage of Proposition 13 support some of Henry George's beliefs regarding the single tax? Explain.

3. What definition of *rent* corresponds to the use of the term in this article?

4. What have been the advantages, if any, of rent control? The disadvantages?

5. Considering the results of rent control, what do you think would be the effects of a single tax on land?

C H A P T E R 25

UNIONS,
COLLECTIVE BARGAINING,
AND THE
MINIMUM WAGE:
LABOR DEMANDS
A LARGER SHARE

WHEN LABOR
DECIDES
TO BACK OFF

A lot of managers these days are fond of remembering when a COLA was something you drank. Now they cringe when they hear the word, because in the language of labor negotiations it is the abbreviation for "cost-of-living adjustment." According to a Wall Street Journal article, "It's hard to estimate the size of union contracts these days, because so many of them have cost-of-living adjustments."[1] Often, such adjustments are tied to government price indexes and can be determined only after prices have changed.

To organized labor COLA seemed like a good idea for inflationary times; however, it failed to recognize the connection between productivity and the value of workers to the firm. That is, in a given firm or industry, COLA results in an overly large wage bill if worker productivity and the firm's prices do not keep up with the general rate of inflation. Furthermore, many workers in the economy are not covered by COLA, and the onset of a recession brings them lower incomes even if the recession is an inflationary one. The result is a great deal of distortion in product and resource markets.

During the inflationary recession of 1980–81 (which some economists called a recession and some did not), it was frequently the industries with COLA protection for workers that got into the deepest trouble. Prices in these industries increased, but workers in other economic sectors could not afford to buy the high-priced output. The result was that labor in several major industries (steel, autos, and rubber, for example) had to back down—in some cases not only on cost-of-living adjustments but also on hourly wages.

1. "More Employees Accept Cuts in Pay to Help Their Companies Survive," *Wall Street Journal*, October 22, 1980, p. 1.

A few examples from 1980 are:

1. The United Steelworkers agreed to defer a COLA of 30 to 32 cents an hour destined to help finance pension increases. The union also dropped several other demands.[2]

2. A 13 percent cut in wages and benefits was approved by five thousand members of the United Rubber Workers at Uniroyal, Inc.[3]

3. General Motors reduced the pay of most salaried employees by about 5 percent by cutting company contributions to a savings plan.[4]

In an economy characterized by huge firms and powerful labor organizations, bargaining is a complex and important process, whether its result is to bring pay increases or to defer them. One thing is clear, though; labor will consent to wage reductions when job security is a serious issue. Better to be employed at a falling real wage than not to be employed at all.

In this chapter the primary topics of discussion are the development of the U.S. labor movement and the application of microeconomic theory to the question of wage determination. The latter topic will help explain what labor is worth to the firm and why there is room for bargaining and negotiations between big firms and big unions.

2. "Labor Cools It with Big Steel," *Business Week*, April 28, 1980, p. 26.
3. "Unions Bend with the Recession," *Business Week*, September 8, 1980, p. 110.
4. "More Employees Accept Cuts in Pay," p. 25.

CHAPTER 25

UNIONS, COLLECTIVE BARGAINING, AND THE MINIMUM WAGE: LABOR DEMANDS A LARGER SHARE

WHAT THIS CHAPTER IS ABOUT

HISTORY OF THE U.S. LABOR MOVEMENT
American Federation of Labor
Congress of Industrial Organizations
Public Employee Unions
Injunctions, Yellow-dog Contracts, Blacklists, Lockouts
LAWS AFFECTING UNIONS
Clayton Act
Norris-LaGuardia Act

Wagner Act
Taft-Hartley Act
Landrum-Griffin Act
Civil Rights Act
UNIONS, WAGE RATES, AND EMPLOYMENT
Perfect Competition
Imperfect Competition
Bilateral Monopoly
Union Effectiveness
MINIMUM WAGE

In this chapter we will examine several aspects of the U.S. labor scene, including the movement toward labor organizations, laws affecting unions, the effects of unions on wage rates and employment, and the minimum wage. Many of these issues have been surrounded by controversy. Consequently, it is often difficult to determine what the facts are, let alone what constitutes justice for both employer and employee.

THE U.S. LABOR MOVEMENT

◆

We will first briefly summarize the history of attempts by labor in the United States to organize for the purpose of raising wages and improving working conditions.[1] Labor unions have had a difficult and stormy existence, the result of both external forces and internal strife.

Externally, unions have been criticized for interfering with the right of firm owners to conduct their businesses as they see fit and, therefore, with the right of free enterprise. Internally, unions have disagreed considerably about both membership issues and union goals. These matters will be discussed next.

STATUS BEFORE 1881

Before 1881, the U.S. labor movement was relatively disorganized. This lack of organization was partly the result of the treatment given unions by the courts. Frequently, union attempts to raise wage rates and improve work-

ing conditions were held to be criminal conspiracies in restraint of trade, a ruling based on English common law.[2] Moreover, the courts readily issued injunctions preventing union strikes, boycotts, and picketing.

Employers also used a number of other tactics to discourage unions. For example, union members were often fired and blacklisted.

Discriminatory discharge is the practice of firing union members.

Such policies obviously made it difficult for union members to find jobs. **Yellow-dog contracts,** contracts under which workers agreed not to join unions, were often made a condition of employment. The lockout was also an effective management technique.

A *lockout* occurs when an employer shuts down the firm until its employees agree to work in accordance with the terms offered.

Other means used to control the growth of unions were more pleasant. Sometimes a company would offer fringe benefits to workers in an attempt to convince them that management would take as good or better care of them than would a union.

Paternalism refers to actions by management designed to convince workers that the company would do more for them than a union would.

Another way of coping with the workers' desire to organize was to form a company union.

Company unions are unions organized on an individual business firm basis and controlled by management.

---

1. For a more thorough summary, see Gordon F. Bloom and Herbert R. Northrup, *Economics of Labor Relations,* 5th ed. Homewood, Ill.: Richard D. Irwin, 1965), Chapter 2; and F. Ray Marshall, Allan M. Cartter, and Allan D. King, *Labor Economics: Wages, Employment, and Trade Unionism,* 3d ed. (Homewood, Ill.: Richard D. Irwin, 1976), Chapters 4 and 5.

2. English common law is a set of rules developed in the courts through custom and usage. The British introduced this body of law to North America during the colonial period.

In spite of all of these difficulties, unions persisted.

City-wide Unions   As early as 1790, certain craftsmen in larger cities such as Boston, New York, and Philadelphia formed local unions to seek higher wages and better working conditions. As a result of what they considered poor treatment by the courts and, in some cases, denial of the right to vote, these groups formed city-wide organizations called *workingmen's parties*. These parties had the general goal of promoting the rights of workers. However, they often went so far as to advocate socialism or utopianism and therefore to reject capitalism and the ownership of private property.

Although these notions were certainly not popular among business people, workingmen's parties frequently held the balance of power between the Federalists and the Democrats in the larger cities. (The Federalists and the Democrats were the two main political parties of the time.)

The depression that began in 1837 dealt a severe blow to these unions. Although many attempts were made at national organization during the 1840s, 1850s, and 1860s, the most important national federation of labor established during this period was the Noble Order of the Knights of Labor.

Knights of Labor   In 1869 the Knights of Labor was formed by a U.S. garment worker, Uriah Smith Stevens, and some of his fellow workers as a secret organization. In the late 1870s they abandoned secrecy in an attempt to gain general respectability. The Knights of Labor is noteworthy because it was one of the first organizations of workers in the United States to permit membership by both craft (trade) unions and by groups organized on an industrial or mixed basis. Only lawyers, bankers, gamblers, liquor dealers, and Pinkerton detectives were excluded.

The Knights of Labor viewed the ideal society as one based on cooperative industrial and agricultural enterprises owned and operated by their workers. They tried to achieve their goals by working for producer cooperatives and political reform. In 1878, at the first general assembly of representatives from local organizations, the Knights of Labor adopted a platform calling for an eight-hour workday, abolition of convict labor, prohibition of the employment of children under fourteen years of age, equal opportunities and wages for women, and establishment of a federal Bureau of Labor Statistics.

After 1886 the Knights of Labor declined rapidly, partly because of losses in several strikes and partly because of the looseness of the union's organization and the resulting instability of its membership. Also, the Knights of Labor was dealt a severe blow when it lost many of its craft unions to the American Federation of Labor.

AMERICAN FEDERATION OF LABOR

The American Federation of Labor (AFL), under the leadership of Samuel Gompers and Adolph Strasser of the Cigarmakers' International Union, was organized in 1881 as the Federation of Organized Trades and Labor Unions. In 1886 the organization adopted the name American Federation of Labor. The AFL was a voluntary organization of national craft unions, each of which was autonomous and each of which had exclusive jurisdiction in its trade.

Except for one year (1894–95), Samuel Gompers served as the AFL president until his death, in 1924. Gompers believed that to be successful, a national federation of unions would have to organize on a craft union basis, to concentrate on short-run economic objectives, and to maintain political neutrality.

Trade Union Membership   Gompers contended that an effective and permanent national labor organization could be formed only on the basis of autonomous trade unions, one union for each craft. Otherwise, the organization would lack the cohesion and drive necessary for it to have a significant impact. Because of this philosophy, the AFL did not organize workers in some of the nation's largest industries, and the Congress of Industrial Organizations (discussed later in the chapter) arose to fill the vacuum.

Short-run Economic Goals Gompers further asserted that the only way in which unions could gain general acceptability by the public was by embracing the notions of capitalism and free enterprise. Although at that time many unions were promoting socialistic principles, Gompers believed they were doomed to failure. He insisted that the AFL concentrate on such short-run economic goals as higher pay, shorter hours, and better working conditions.

Nonintervention by Government Although Gompers realized that the passage of laws relating to minimum wages and collective bargaining might be of help to unions, he feared government control. Thus he argued that labor should maintain complete neutrality with regard to political parties. Nevertheless, he favored the use of political pressure groups and the rewarding of labor's friends and the punishing of its enemies at the polls, regardless of political party membership.

Whether or not these philosophies were in the best interest of the labor movement, the AFL has remained a significant force to this day (although now as part of the combined AFL-CIO). The formation of the CIO will be discussed as soon as the history of one more national federation of unions, the Industrial Workers of the World, is recounted.

INDUSTRIAL WORKERS OF THE WORLD

The socialists had always been dissatisfied with Gompers's willingness to work within the free enterprise system and to negotiate with employers. Many unskilled and semi-skilled workers were also unhappy because they were excluded from the AFL. Moreover, the needs of workers in frontier industries, such as metal mining and logging, were largely ignored. In 1897 the metal miners' union, the Western Federation of Miners, dissociated itself from the AFL.

In 1905 the Western Federation of Miners, the Socialist Trade and Labor Alliance, and other dissident groups formed the Industrial Workers of the World (IWW). Its members were known as "Wobblies." The basic philosophy of the IWW was that workers should control management. The IWW's preamble stated that the trade unions were unable to cope with the increasing power of employers and that these unions aided employers in promoting the belief that employers and workers had common interests. The Wobblies favored the use of industry-wide or economy-wide strikes to achieve their goals.

The direct action tactics of some of the unskilled and frontier workers offended the theoretical socialists, who had withdrawn from the organization by 1908. By 1912 the IWW consisted largely of lumberjacks from the Northwest and the South, migratory workers from the wheat fields of the Midwest, textile workers, miners, and longshoremen.

The IWW did gain some fame as a champion of free speech and the underdog. Moreover, in certain situations its organizers did succeed in obtaining better wages, hours, and working conditions. However, because of its socialistic philosophy and as a result of several violent strikes and demonstrations, the IWW came under vigorous attack from both business and government. It was attacked most strongly by the federal government for not supporting the participation of the United States in World War I. Partly as a result of this criticism and partly because of its philosophy of direct action and suspicion of well-organized and well-financed labor unions, the IWW was never able to build a strong and stable organization. However, it still exists as a small organization headquartered in Chicago.

CONGRESS OF INDUSTRIAL ORGANIZATIONS

As we will see later, during the 1930s the American public began to adopt a more favorable attitude toward labor unions. Moreover, the upsurge in mass production industries increased the pressure for unionism along industrial lines.

The AFL made a few exceptions to its trade union philosophy. For example, the United Mine Workers, the International Ladies' Garment Workers', the Amalgamated Clothing Workers of America, and the Brewery Workers unions were successfully formed and affiliated with the AFL.

During the 1935 AFL convention, however, John L. Lewis and other leaders of industrial unions formed the Committee for Industrial Organization. Their goal was to organize non-union workers, particularly industrial workers. Their main area of controversy with the AFL concerned the jurisdiction of craft unions over workers in their trades in the various industries. In 1938 the Committee was formally expelled from the AFL, and the Congress of Industrial Organizations (CIO) was formed.

The CIO proceeded to successfully organize the steel, rubber, automobile, and meat packing industries, among others. As its strength grew, opposition from the AFL weakened.

AFL-CIO

In 1952 the presidents of both the CIO and the AFL died. Walter Reuther, president of the United Auto Workers, became president of the CIO. George Meany, a former official of the Plumber's Union, became president of the AFL. The two presidents began negotiations, and in 1955 the American Federation of Labor and Congress of Industrial Organizations (AFL-CIO) was formed, with George Meany as president. Meany remained head of the AFL-CIO until fall 1979, when he retired.

As a result of the merger, two basic philosophies of the AFL were abandoned. One was

that trade unions had exclusive jurisdiction over all workers of a particular craft. The AFL-CIO agreed that the jurisdictions exercised by AFL and CIO unions at the time of the merger would be preserved.

The second issue involved the autonomy of national unions. The original AFL principle was modified to state that if national unions wished to remain affiliated with the AFL-CIO, they must abide by a code of ethics. In 1957 the International Brotherhood of Teamsters was expelled for failing to abide by this rule.

Over the last several years, union membership as a percent of total nonagricultural employees has declined. In 1955, when the AFL-CIO was formed, union members accounted for 33.2 percent of the nonagricultural employees. In 1978 the figure had declined to 23.6 percent.[3]

Part of the reason for the decrease may be the recent rapid growth of employment in the service industries. In addition, imports have reduced job growth in certain industries, such as shoes and electronics. Moreover, the public image of unions has also worsened in recent years.[4]

PUBLIC EMPLOYEE UNIONS

A dramatic exception to the relative decline in union membership in recent years has been the growth of public employee unions. In 1960 just 10 percent of all government employees belonged to unions. In 1978 almost 50 percent of these employees belonged to unions.[5]

3. U.S. Department of Commerce, Bureau of the Census, Table No:714: Labor Union and Employee Association Membership:1950–1978," *Statistical Abstract of the United States: 1980* (Washington, D.C.: Government Printing Office, 1980), p. 429.

4. See "Why Do Unions Flop?" *Wall Street Journal*, September 12, 1978, p. 1; "Embattled Unions Strike Back at Management," *Business Week*, December 4, 1978, pp. 54–69; and "Labor's Creaking House," *Newsweek*, December 12, 1977, pp. 83–87.

5. "The Public Strikes Back," *Newsweek*, September 18, 1978, p. 71.

At the federal level, the issuance of Federal Order 10988 by President John F. Kennedy marked the first recognition by the federal government that its employees were entitled to join unions and bargain collectively. This order was later superseded by the Civil Service Reform Act of 1978.

However, as wage rates have risen and public employee unions have shown an increasing willingness to strike, there has also been increasing opposition from the general public. The upsurge in resentment toward taxes (such as that embodied in California's Proposition 13 which limited property tax rates) that occurred in the late 1970s has not helped their cause either. The decision by the Federal Labor Relations Authority in the fall of 1981 to decertify the Professional Air Traffic Controllers Organization (PATCO) because of an illegal strike further highlighted the problems of public employee unions. Thus, at this writing, the future of public employee unions is uncertain.[6]

MAJOR LAWS
AFFECTING LABOR
UNIONS
◆

As indicated at the beginning of the chapter, the courts have often made union life quite difficult. In this section we will examine the development of laws affecting labor in the United States. The examination will show a trend toward better definition of the rights of workers and their organizations but also a deepening of lawmakers' concerns about excessive union power and the honesty of union leaders.

As already noted, English common law was used to fight unions on the ground of criminal conspiracy. Another "conspiracy" attack on unions came through the **Sherman Antitrust Act (1890).**☐ This act was probably not intended to apply to unions, but it was used against them as well as against big business. The AFL began a campaign to get labor excluded from the Sherman Act, and the result was the Clayton Act.☐

THE CLAYTON ACT

One of the objectives of the **Clayton Act (1914)** was to exclude labor from the antitrust laws. Section 6 states:

That the labor of a human being is not a commodity or article of commerce. Nothing contained in the anti-trust laws shall be construed to forbid the existence and operation of labor, agricultural, or horticultural organizations, instituted for the purposes of mutual help, and not having capital stock or conducted for profit, or to forbid or restrain individual members of such organizations from lawfully carrying out the legitimate objects thereof; nor shall such organizations, or the members thereof, be held or construed to be illegal combinations or conspiracies in restraint of trade under the anti-trust laws.[7]

Section 20 provides that restraining orders or injunctions are not to be used against labor unions unless "necessary to prevent irreparable damage to a property right."[8]

As it turned out, the Clayton Act did little to improve the plight of unions. The courts held that unions per se were legal but that it was up to the courts to decide which of their actions were lawful. In the 1930s, however, public opinion turned more in favor of unions, as evidenced by the two laws discussed next.

---

6. Ibid., pp. 71–73. Also see "A Backlash to the Tax Revolt," *Business Week*, July 31, 1978, pp. 69–70; and "U.S. Decertifies Air Controllers Union for Strike," *Wall Street Journal*, October 23, 1981, p. 4. The Federal Labor Relations Authority performs similar functions with regard to federal employer-employee relations as does the National Labor Relations Board in the private sector.

7. "Antitrust Act, 1914," *The Statutes at Large of the United States of America: 1913–1915*, vol. 38, pt. 1 (Washington, D.C.: Government Printing Office, 1915), p. 731.

8. Ibid., p. 738.

THE NORRIS-LAGUARDIA ACT

The **Norris-LaGuardia Act** did much to remove two legal barriers against union activity. First, the act made yellow-dog contracts unenforceable.

A **yellow-dog contract** *was a contract between an employee and his employer in which the employee agreed not to join a union.*

The contracts were not used to harass employees—they could be fired anyway—so much as to prosecute union organizers for encouraging employees to break their contracts.

Second, the act made it much more difficult for employers to obtain injunctions against unions.

An **injunction** *is a court order directing that some action not be carried out, on the ground that the people or organizations affected by the action will suffer irreparable harm as a result of it.*

In the past, employers had found it relatively easy to obtain injunctions prohibiting strikes or other union activities. Now that power was limited.[9]

THE WAGNER ACT

The **Wagner Act (1935),** more formally known as the National Labor Relations Act, is often called labor's Magna Carta. Section 7 gives employees the following rights:

1. To join or assist labor organizations.
2. To bargain collectively through their duly elected representatives.

Perhaps of greater significance, Section 8 forbids certain "unfair labor practices" on the part of employers, among them:

1. Interfering with the exercise of rights granted employees in Section 7.
2. Dominating or interfering with the formation or administration of any labor organization or contributing financial or other support to it.
3. Discriminating against union members in regard to hiring, promotions, and tenure of employment (firing).

The purpose of item 2 was to outlaw company unions. Frequently, firms had helped organize unions, which were then dominated by the company and therefore less effective in achieving the goals of their employees.

The National Labor Relations Board (NLRB) was established by the Wagner Act to conduct representative elections, in which the workers could vote on what union, if any, they wanted to represent them. The NLRB was also given the responsibility of investigating unfair labor practices and the power to issue cease and desist orders to employers that were enforceable in the federal courts.[10]

The Wagner Act did a great deal toward stimulating union growth during the 1930s. However, in the 1940s and 1950s public opinion once more turned against the unions.

THE TAFT-HARTLEY ACT

The **Taft-Hartley Act (1947),** officially the Labor-Management Relations Act, is a complex piece of legislation that amends the Wagner Act. It contains provisions that prohibit unfair union practices, regulate union administration, specify collective bargaining procedures and certain terms of bargaining agreements, and prescribe remedies for strikes deemed injurious to the national health and safety.

___

9. "Injunctions in Labor Disputes," *The United States Statutes at Large: 1931–33,* vol. 47, pt. 1 (Washington, D.C.: Government Printing Office, 1933), pp. 70–73.

10. See "National Labor Relations Act," *United States Statutes at Large: 1935–36,* vol. 49, pt. 1 (Washington D.C.: Government Printing Office, 1936), pp. 449–457, especially pp. 452–453.

Unfair Union Practices Until it was amended by the Taft-Hartley Act, Section 8 of the Wagner Act contained no restrictions against unfair labor practices by unions. The Taft-Hartley Act, however, prohibits secondary strikes and boycotts, jurisdictional strikes, and strikes to compel an employer to bargain with one union when another is certified.

Secondary boycotts or strikes are boycotts or strikes called against a third party, which uses or is in some way involved with the products of an employer against whom the union has a direct strike for higher wages or other matters.

In other words, a secondary boycott or strike involves a third party who is not directly concerned with the immediate labor-management dispute.

Jurisdictional strikes are strikes for the purpose of forcing an employer to assign particular work to employees in one union rather than to employees who are members of another union.

The Taft-Hartley Act also makes it illegal for a union to coerce an employee to join it except where the union's collective bargaining agreement provides for a union shop.

Union shop agreements stipulate that employees must join the union within thirty days if the union is the duly certified bargaining agent.

Closed shops require that a person must already be a member of the union before he or she can be hired.

Closed shops are outlawed by the Taft-Hartley Act. Furthermore, states also have the right, under Section 14 (b), to pass **right-to-work laws**, which prohibit union shops and therefore require open shops.

Open shops do not require employees to be union members.

In 1980, nineteen states had right-to-work laws in force.[11]

The Taft-Hartley Act also makes it an unfair labor practice for a union to refuse to bargain collectively with an employer. Finally, it prohibits featherbedding.

Featherbedding is causing or trying to cause an employer to pay for services that are not to be performed.

Actually, this provision has been interpreted so narrowly that many "make-work" rules are still allowed to exist.

Union Administration The Taft-Hartley Act requires unions to make detailed annual financial reports to the Secretary of Labor and to file copies of their constitutions and bylaws. Moreover, it prohibits union contributions or expenditures in connection with any election to federal public office. However, the unions are able to get around this restriction in most states by soliciting voluntary donations from members. The Committee on Political Education (COPE), formed by the AFL-CIO, is one organization that operates in this manner.

Bargaining Agreements Besides declaring closed shop agreements illegal, the Taft-Hartley Act insists that where union welfare funds are maintained by employer contributions, the collective bargaining agreement must provide that these funds be held in trust and administered jointly by representatives of the union and management. It also prohibits compulsory checkoffs except where individual employees sign authorizations.

---

11. U.S. Department of Commerce, Bureau of the Census, *Statistical Abstract of the United States, 1980* (Washington, D.C.: Government Printing Office, 1980), p. 429.

*A **checkoff** is a situation where union dues are deducted from an employee's pay by the employer and turned over to the union.*

Furthermore, labor and management must give the other party sixty days' notice of their desire to terminate or change an existing bargaining contract.

National Emergency Strikes If employees engage in a strike that is considered to endanger the national health and safety, the president can ask the attorney general to obtain an injunction against the strike. During the next sixty days the parties are to attempt to settle their differences through the auspices of the Conciliation Service of the federal government. A board of inquiry is also to be appointed to study the matter. During the sixty-first through the eightieth days the NLRB is required to poll the workers to determine if they will accept the employer's last offer and to present the results to the attorney general. If the employees reject the offer, the president then submits a report to Congress. After the eighty days, the union can strike.[12]

By 1980 the national emergency provisions of the Taft-Hartley Act had been invoked thirty-five times, and injunctions had been issued in thirty cases. In four cases the president did not ask for an injunction. In one case a federal district court judge refused to grant an injunction on the ground that the strike did not endanger the national health or safety. In six cases strikes were begun or resumed after the injunction expired.[13]

Some people believe that the Taft-Hartley Act, by prescribing a rigid procedure that the president must follow, makes it less likely that the parties to the dispute will resolve their differences.[14] Such a result can occur if one of the parties believes it can gain more from the government than from the other party. This position was apparently held by the union in the steel strike of 1952 and by the steel firms during the strike of 1959–60. However, other observers believe that the act is adequately serving the purpose it was intended to serve in these circumstances.

THE LANDRUM-GRIFFIN ACT

The **Landrum Griffin Act (1959)**, formally the Labor-Management Reporting and Disclosure Act, places additional restrictions on unions and mangement. It regulates the term of office of union officials, the removal of such officials, and election procedures. For example, it prevents Communists and persons convicted of certain felonies from holding union office (The Communist Party ban was later ruled unconstitutional by the Supreme Court.)

Furthermore, it requires regularly scheduled elections of officers, with secret ballots, and the bonding of union officials responsible for union funds. Each union must file an annual report with the secretary of labor that states the salary and allowances given every union employee who is paid more than $10,000 a year.

The act also requires employers to file annual reports with the secretary of labor that disclose payments or loans to unions or employees of unions. This reporting requirement covers direct and indirect payments and loans of anything of value over $250. The purpose of this section of the act is to limit "sweetheart" contracts (agreements detrimental to union

---

12. For the complete text of the law, see "Labor-Management Relations Act, 1947," *The United States Statutes at Large: 1947,"* vol. 61, pt. 1 *(Washington, D.C.: Government Printing Office, 1948),* pp. 136–162.

13. Arthur A. Sloane and Fred Witney, *Labor Relations,* 4th ed. (Englewood Cliffs, N.J.: Prentice-Hall, 1981), p. 120.

14. See "Injunction Is the Wrong Way to Settle Problems," *U.S. News & World Report,* October 19, 1959, p. 74; and George W. Taylor, "The Adequacy of Taft-Hartley in Public Emergency Disputes," *Annals of the American Academy of Political and Social Science* 333 (January 1961): 78.

members) between union officials and employers.[15]

The law that we will consider next affects not only unions and employers but many non-union sectors of society as well. It is included in the discussion of laws affecting unions because it is a landmark piece of legislation concerning labor in the U.S.

THE CIVIL RIGHTS ACT

Title VII of the **Civil Rights Act (1964)** prohibits discrimination in hiring, firing, or promotions on the basis of race, color, religion, sex, or national origin. The law applies to employers, labor organizations, employer services, and apprenticeship programs serving at least twenty-five people. The Equal Employment Opportunity Commission (EEOC) is charged with seeing that the provisions of the law are carried out.[16]

In 1972 amendments to the act extended the law to organizatons of fifteen or more people and gave the EEOC the power to go to court to seek relief on the part of those who had suffered discrimination. This provision made the Civil Rights Act far more effective, since previously the attorney general had had to file such suits.

It is difficult to measure the impact of the Civil Rights Act except in specific cases. Nevertheless, we can gain some idea of its effects by examining Table 25–1. This table gives the labor force participation rates for various types of workers from 1964 to 1979. These rates are the percent of the total number of particular types of worker who are in the labor force, whether employed or unemployed.

From the table we see that the labor force participation rates of males of all races have fallen between 1964 and 1979. However, the participation rates of white females have increased dramatically, from 37.5 percent in 1964 to 49.9 percent in 1979.

Of course, factors other than the Civil Rights Act may have influenced these figures. Some of them may be changes in welfare benefits, more women who are heads of households, and a rate of inflation that makes two incomes necessary to maintain a family's standard of living. Still, the labor force participation rates of both married and single women have risen substantially during this period.[17]

Furthermore, the impact of the Civil Rights Act on blacks should be measured not only by changes in the percent of participation in the labor force but also by changes in the types of jobs held. For example, in 1967, 6.2 percent of black male workers and 9.1 percent of black female workers were professional and technical workers. In 1976, these figures were 9.6 percent and 14.2 percent, respectively.[18]

In the future we will have to determine how to enforce the spirit of the Civil Rights Act without discriminating against the formerly favored groups, particularly white males. This issue was raised in 1978 in the *Bakke* decision by the Supreme Court. Bakke was a white male who was refused admission to a medical school because of the school's quota system for minority students. The Supreme Court declared that Bakke should be allowed to attend the medical school. It further ruled that while it was legal for a school to set goals for increasing the number of minority students, it was

15. See "Labor-Management Reporting and Disclosure Act of 1959," *The United States Statutes at Large: 1959*, vol. 73 (Washington, D.C.: Government Printing Office, 1959), pp. 519–546.

16. "Civil Rights Act of 1964," *The United States Statutes at Large: 1964*, vol. 78 (Washington, D.C.: Government Printing Office, 1965), pp. 241–268, especially pp. 253–266.

17. U.S. Department of Labor, Bureau of Labor Statistics, "Table 5: Civilian Labor Force Participation Rates, by Marital Status, Age, and Sex, 1967–76," *Handbook of Labor Statistics: 1977* (Washington, D.C.: Government Printing Office, 1977), p. 33.

18. U.S. Department of Labor, Bureau of Labor Statistics, "Table 18: Employed Persons, by Occupational Group, Race, and Sex, 1967–76," *Handbook of Labor Statistics: 1977* (Washington, D.C.: Government Printing Office, 1977), pp. 58–61.

TABLE 25-1 Labor Force Participation Rates by Sex and Race, 1964–1979

Type of Worker	Year				
	1964	1968	1972	1976	1979
All males	81.0%	80.1%	79.0%	77.5%	77.1%
White males	81.1%	80.4%	79.6%	78.4%	78.0%
Black and other males except white	80.0%	77.6%	73.7%	70.7%	70.7%
All females	38.7%	41.6%	43.9%	47.3%	50.3%
White females	37.5%	40.7%	43.2%	46.9%	49.9%
Black and other females except white	48.5%	49.3%	48.7%	50.2%	53.1%

Sources: U.S. Department of Labor, Bureau of Labor Statistics, "Table 4: Civilian Labor Force Participation Rates for Persons 16 Years and Over, by Sex, Color, and Age, 1947–74," *Handbook of Labor Statistics, 1975 Reference Edition* (Washington, D.C.: Government Printing Office, 1975), pp. 34–38; and U.S. Department of Labor, Bureau of Labor Statistics, "Table 4: Civilian Labor Force Participation Rates for Persons 16 Years and Over, by Sex, Race, and Age, 1967–76, "*Handbook of Labor Statistics, 1977* (Washington, D.C.: Government Printing Office, 1977), pp. 29–32; and U.S. Department of Commerce, Bureau of the Census, Table No. 653: "Labor Force and Participation Rates, By Race, Sex, and Age: 1960 to 1979," *Statistical Abstract of the United States: 1980* (Washington, D.C.: Government Printing Office, 1980), p. 394.

not legal to use a strict quota system for doing so.[19]

In 1979 a similar issue was once again before the Supreme Court, this time in a case involving a lab technician, Brian Weber. Weber had filed a reverse-discrimination suit against Kaiser Aluminum and Chemical Corporation when two blacks with less seniority than he had were picked ahead of him for a job training program. In this case, however, the court ruled that the Kaiser program did not violate the law even though it did include a type of quota system.[20] Obviously, determining what is a fair affirmative action (minority employment) program is not easy.

UNIONS
AND
WAGE THEORY

In this section we will examine what a union can expect to accomplish in terms of wage rates and employment in various industry

19. See "Bakke: Spelling Out the Rules," *Newsweek*, October 22, 1979, p. 83.

20. "Weber: 'Now I Know It's Over,' " *Newsweek*, October 22, 1979, p. 24.

structures. As we will see, what a union may obtain in a setting of imperfect competition□ is quite different from what it may gain when it is trying to take control of a perfectly competitive□ labor market.

PERFECTLY COMPETITIVE MARKETS FOR LABOR

If the market for the services of a particular type of labor is perfectly competitive, all firms will pay the going wage rate for this type of labor and the individual workers will not believe that they can control the wage rate. In this situation the equilibrium wage rate is determined by the total market demand for and supply of that type of labor.[21] The equilibrium quantity of labor and the wage rate in a perfectly competitive labor market is shown at (L_e, W_e) in Figure 25–1.

If a union is now formed, it may find it possible to raise the wage rate above the market

21. Chapter 23 showed that a firm's demand curve for a particular type of labor, given a constant wage rate, is indicated by the marginal revenue product curve for that type of labor. The market demand curve for that type of labor can be obtained by summing individual firm marginal revenue product of labor curves, after adjusting for price changes in the final products of the firms as the levels of output of their industries change.

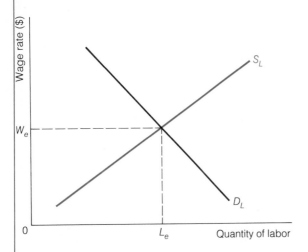

FIGURE 25–1   Equilibrium in a Perfectly Competitive Labor Market

In a perfectly competitive labor market the equilibrium wage rate and quantity of labor employed are determined by the intersection of the market supply (S_L) and demand (D_L) curves for that type of labor. In this graph, the equilibrium wage rate and quantity of labor are W_e and L_e, respectively.

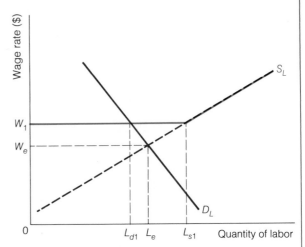

FIGURE 25–2   Effect of a Union in a Perfectly Competitive Labor Market

As in Figure 25–1, the equilibrium wage rate and quantity of labor employed in a perfectly competitive labor market would be W_e and L_e. If a union is now established which bargains for a wage rate equal to L_1, *the quantity of labor demanded will fall to L_{d1}.* However, the quantity supplied of labor will rise to L_{s1}. As a result, more workers will wish to work than employers will want to hire, so that $L_{s1} - L_{d1}$ workers want to work but cannot find jobs.

equilibrium rate, to W_1, as shown in Figure 25–2. A negotiated wage rate of W_1 changes the effective supply of labor curve to $W_1 S_L$. The portion of S_L below W_1 becomes irrelevant. However, the wage increase will not be cost-free for all workers. More workers will wish to work at the new, higher wage rate, but fewer will be able to. At a wage rate equal to W_1, L_{d1} workers are demanded by firms, but L_{s1} wish to work. Thus $L_{s1} - L_{d1}$ workers wish to work but cannot find jobs. Moreover, $L_e - L_{d1}$ workers who were formerly employed are now out of work. Employment has decreased as a result of the wage hike.

What happens now will depend on the loyalty that workers, especially the unemployed ones, have toward the union. It will also depend on the percentage of union members who are unemployed and on the other types of jobs available. The unemployed workers may try to break the control of the union by offering to work at lower wage rates, or they may attempt to find jobs elsewhere.

IMPERFECTLY COMPETITIVE LABOR MARKETS

If we drop the assumption that firms accept the wage rate as given, the constraints placed on unions change substantially. Before we go any further, however, let us review the situation where a union does not exist.

In Chapter 23, where the theory of resource pricing was presented, we saw that a firm will wish to employ workers up to the point where the marginal revenue product of labor□ (MRP_L) is just equal to the marginal factor cost of labor (MFC_L).□ In a perfectly competitive labor market the wage rate is constant and equal to the MFC_L. In an imperfectly competitive labor market□ the MFC_L is greater than the wage rate, because the supply of labor curve for the firm is upward sloping. In this case the firm must pay a higher wage to all its workers if it wishes to employ more of them.

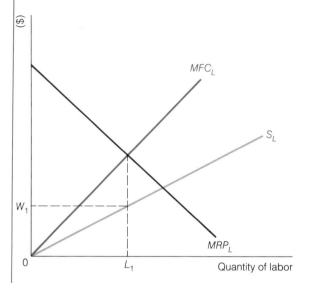

FIGURE 25-3 Profit-Maximizing Position of a Firm in an Imperfectly Competitive Labor Market

In an imperfectly competitive labor market firms will maximize profit by employing workers up to the point where the marginal revenue product of labor (MRP_L) is equal to the marginal factor cost of labor (MFC_L). In this graph the firm will employ L_1 units of labor and pay them a wage rate equal to W_1.

Figure 25-3 shows the profit-maximizing quantity of labor, L_1, and the wage rate, W_1, for a firm in an imperfectly competitive labor market. The profit-maximizing quantity of labor is determined by the intersection of the MFC_L and MRP_L curves, at L_1 in the figure. The corresponding profit-maximizing wage rate, W_1, is given by the supply of labor curve at the point corresponding to L_1.

In this case it is possible for a union to increase both the wage rate and the level of employment. For example, suppose that through bargaining the union is able to obtain wage rate W_2 for its members, as shown in Figure 25-4. The effective supply of labor curve is now a horizontal line up to L_2. The new MFC_L curve coincides with the effective supply curve of labor up to L_2, because the wage rate is constant at W_2 for quantities of labor up to L_2. Because no more than L_2 workers wish to work unless the wage rate is raised above W_2,

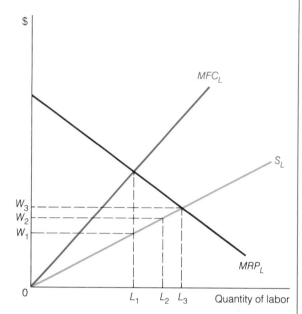

FIGURE 25-4 Effect of a Union in an Imperfectly Competitive Labor Market

As in Figure 25-3, before a union is established the profit-maximizing quantity of labor for the firm to employ would be L_1 and the wage rate would be W_1. If a union is now organized, and it bargains the wage rate up to W_2, the profit-maximizing quantity of labor to employ becomes L_2. This is so because W_2 becomes the firm's marginal factor cost curve up to L_2. After L_2, the firm's original marginal factor cost of labor (MFC_L) and supply of labor curves once again become relevant, since no more than L_2 workers are willing to work for a wage rate equal to W_2. By bargaining for a higher wage rate, a union can thus bring about both an increase in the wage rate and increased employment up to a wage rage equal to W_3.

the former MFC_L and S_L curves apply beyond this point.

The profit-maximizing quantity of labor is now L_2, and the wage rate is W_2. The profit maximizing quantity of labor is now L_2 because at that quantity the firm comes as close as it can to equating MRP_L and MFC_L. Until L_2 the marginal factor cost of labor is now constant and equal to W_2, the negotiated wage rate. However, beyond L_2 the original curve applies, because no more than L_2 workers wish to work at a wage equal to W_2. As can be seen in Figure 25-4, at L_2, the MFC_L equals, W_2, and MFC_L is less than MRP_L. However at quantities of labor greater than L_2, because the original MFC_L curve applies, MFC_L will be greater than MRP_L. Thus, for quantities of labor above L_2, the pre-union MFC_L and S_L curves apply, and MFC_L is greater than MRP_L. Therefore, the profit-maximizing quantity of labor will be L_2 in this situation.

The amazing result of the formation of a union in this case is that both the wage rate and the level of employment have increased, from W_1 to W_2 and L_1 to L_2, respectively. As expected, however, there is a limit to this happy (from the viewpoint of labor) scenario. If the wage rate is raised above W_3, where the marginal revenue product of labor curve intersects the supply of labor curve, the quantity of labor employed will be smaller than L_3, the maximum level of employment consistent with labor market equilibrium (in the sense that the quantity of labor demanded equals the quantity supplied).

BILATERAL MONOPOLY

Some economists believe that the market for certain types of workers is characterized by bilateral monopoly.

Bilateral monopoly is a situation where, for all practical purposes, there is one seller of an input and one buyer of an input.

In some respects the Big Four domestic automobile producers and the United Auto Workers are an example of this type of market.

As applied to the labor market, the firms purchasing the labor are presumed to act as monopsonists□ and the union as a monopoly. □This situation is depicted in Figure 25–5. The supply of labor curve, S_L, now represents the quantity of labor that will be supplied if laborers believe that they have to accept the wage rate offered by management. The MFC_L curve still represents the marginal cost of labor to management. The marginal revenue of the union (MR_u) curve represents the marginal rev-

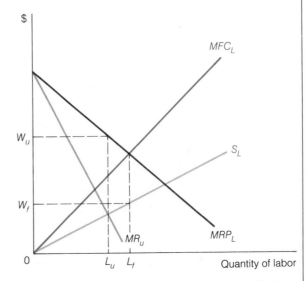

FIGURE 25–5 Bilateral Monopoly in the Labor Market

The supply of labor curve, S_L, represents the quantity of labor that would be supplied if laborers felt they had to accept the wage rate offered by management. The marginal factor cost of labor curve is MFC_L. The marginal revenue to the union members from offering their services is MR_u. The marginal revenue product of labor curve is MRP_L. The firm which employs the labor would maximize profit by hiring workers up to the point where the marginal factor cost of labor is equal to the marginal revenue product of labor, at L_f, paying a wage rate of W_f. If the union behaves as a monopoly firm, it will consider the optimal quantity of employment to be where MR_u intersects S_L, at L_u, with a wage rate of W_u. The wage rate eventually agreed on will depend on the relative bargaining strength of the union and management. The level of employment will be determined where the resulting MFC_L is equal to the MRP_L.

enue accruing to the workers from offering their services.

If the union behaves as a monopoly, its optimal quantity of employment will occur where MR_u intersects S_L, at L_u, with a wage rate of W_u. This position is equivalent to that of a monopoly firm determining the price of and quantity of its product to offer for sale.

The monopsonistic firm will find its profit-maximizing position where $MFC_L = MRP_L$. Thus its optimal wage rate and quantity of labor are W_f and L_f, respectively. How is the disparity between the positions of union and management resolved? The answer is through collective bargaining, but the final position is not fixed. The wage rate eventually agreed on will depend on the relative strengths of union and management. The level of employment will be at the point where the resulting MFC_L is equal to the MRP_L.

Some economists argue that the bilateral monopoly model is not appropriate for explaining the behavior of labor unions. They contend that the goal of a union is the maximization of its members' well-being, not the maximization of profit.

As already indicated, higher wage rates frequently imply higher levels of unemployment. Thus a union is faced with the problem of determining which wage rate–unemployment combination is best for its members.

EFFECTIVENESS OF UNIONS

The effects of labor unions on the U.S. economy are not completely clear. However, we will briefly examine union goals with respect to wage rates, the demand for union labor, and the supply of union labor.

Wage Rates   Economists do not agree on the effectiveness of unions in raising wage rates. At best the evidence on the subject is inconclusive. Economist Clark Kerr states:

The conclusion from this record is that trade unionism in the United States to date has had no important effect on labor's share. . . . There is no evidence of any significant permanent effect through normal collective bargaining, except possibly in highly unionized metropolitan areas. . . . There may have been some slow secular shift toward labor over the half century since 1900, but most of it occurred before 1929 (thus before the rise of the modern trade union movement), and in nonmanufacturing sectors.[22]

_____

22. Clark Kerr, "Labor's Income Share and the Labor Movement," in _New Concepts in Wage Determination_, ed. G. W. Taylor and F. Pierson (New York: McGraw-Hill, 1957), p. 287.

Evidence published in the fall of 1979 suggests that union members fared better than nonunion workers under the wage-price guidelines imposed by President Carter.[23] Nevertheless, the long-run effects of the guidelines have yet to be determined.

Demand for Union Labor   Some unions have attempted to increase the demand for union labor by working to restrict imports and promoting union shops and the purchase of products with union labels. Often they also insist on make-work rules. In these ways they hope to ease the effects of higher wage rates on employment.

Supply of Union Labor   Unions also frequently attempt to reduce the supply of labor. Their tactics include apprenticeship programs, limits on union membership, restriction of the number of hours in a workweek, increases in the number of paid holidays, and the favoring of strict immigration laws.

Figure 25–6 illustrates the effects of union activities to increase the demand for union labor and decrease its supply. In panel (a) the demand for labor increases while the supply remains constant. As a result, both the wage rate and the quantity of labor employed increase. In panel (b) the supply of labor decreases while the demand for labor remains constant. In this situation the wage rate increases but the quantity of labor employed decreases. Panel (c) shows one example of the effects of both a decrease in supply and an increase in demand. In this case both the wage rate and the quantity of labor employed increase. While the wage rate will increase in all such situations, the net effect on the quantity of labor employed will depend on the relative size of the shifts in the demand and supply curves.

The next section compares the effects of a minimum wage with the effects of unions.

_____

23. "How the Guidelines Disrupted Wage Patterns," _Business Week_, August 6, 1979, p. 12.

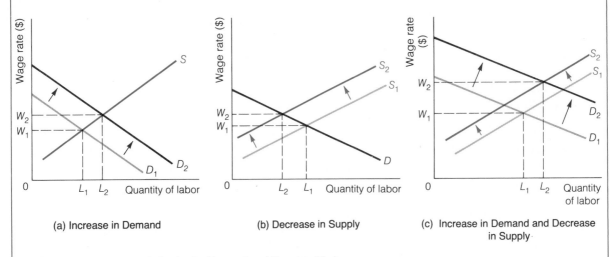

(a) Increase in Demand

(b) Decrease in Supply

(c) Increase in Demand and Decrease in Supply

FIGURE 25–6   Effects of Shifts in the Demand and Supply of Labor

In panel (a), a union increases the wage rate by increasing the demand for its labor. The supply of labor curve is S. Initially, the demand for labor curve is D_1, and the wage rate is W_1. After an increase in the demand for labor, the demand curve shifts to D_2, and the wage rate rises to W_2.

In panel (b), a union increases the wage rate by decreasing the supply of labor. The demand curve for labor is D. The original supply of labor curve is S_1, and the initial wage rate is W_1. After a decrease in the supply of labor, the supply curve shifts to S_2, and the wage rate rises to W_2.

In panel (c), both an increase in the demand for labor (from D_1 to D_2) and a decrease in the supply of labor (from S_1 to S_2) have occurred. The wage rate rises from W_1 to W_2.

THE MINIMUM WAGE: BOON OR BOONDOGGLE?

In 1938 the Fair Labor Standards Act, which provided for a minimum wage of 25 cents an hour for all covered workers, was passed.[24]

A **minimum wage** sets a lower limit on the wage rate of covered workers.

Since 1938 the minimum wage rate has been raised periodically. It reached $3.35 an hour on January 1, 1981.[25]

24. "Fair Labor Standards Act of 1938," *United States Statutes at Large: 1938*, vol. 52 (Washington, D.C.: Government Printing Office, 1938), pp. 1060–1069, especially p. 1062.

25. "Minimum Wage Bill Is Passed by House and Is Sent to Carter," *Wall Street Journal*, October 21, 1977, p. 4.

The theoretical effects of a minimum wage on employment are the same as those of a higher wage bargained for by unions. Panel (a) of Figure 25–7 shows a perfectly competitive labor market with an equilibrium wage rate, W_e. At this point the quantity of labor supplied, given by S_L, is equal to the quantity demanded of labor, given by D_L. If the government now imposes a minimum wage rate of W_m that is higher than W_e, the quantity of labor employed will fall from L_e to L_m, and $L_2 - L_m$ workers will be unemployed.

Panel (b) depicts an imperfectly competitive labor market. The initial wage rate is W_1, and the initial quantity of labor employed is L_1, because labor is employed up to the point where the marginal factor cost of labor is equal to the marginal revenue product of labor. If a minimum wage rate equal to W_2 is now imposed, the quantity of labor employed will increase to L_2. As happened in the case of unions, the supply of labor curve and the MFC_L curve now become a horizontal line at

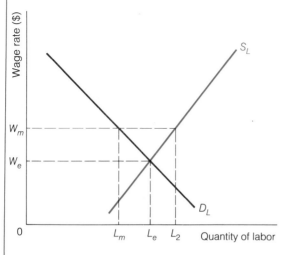

(a) Perfectly Competitive Market

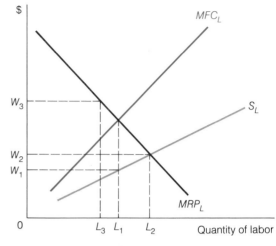

(b) Imperfectly Competitive Market

FIGURE 25–7 Effects of a Minimum Wage

In panel (a), D_L and S_L are the demand for labor and supply of labor curves, respectively, in a perfectly competitive labor market. The equilibrium wage rate is W_e and the quantity of labor employed is L_e. If a minimum wage rate of W_m is now established, firms will hire L_m workers. However, L_2 workers will offer their services, so that a quantity of labor equal to L_2-L_m workers will be unemployed.

In panel (b), S_L is the supply of labor curve in an imperfectly competitive labor market. Initially, a firm will maximize profit by employing workers up to the point where the marginal revenue product of labor (MRP_L) is equal to the marginal factor cost of labor (MFC_L), at L_1, and pay a wage rate equal to W_1. If a minimum wage rate of W_2 is now established, the firm's marginal factor cost of labor becomes W_2 up to the point where a horizontal line through W_2 intersects S_L. After that point, the original S_L and MFC_L curves apply. In this case, the firm will maximize profit by employing L_2 units of labor and paying a wage rate equal to W_2. In this case, the imposition of a minimum wage rate has resulted in both an increase in the wage rate and an increase in employment. However, if the minimum wage rate were set at W_3, the level of employment would fall below the original level of employment to L_3.

W_2 until the line intersects with the old S_L curve. In this example, the point is where the horizontal line at W_2 intersects S_L and MRP_L at L_2. Thus, at L_2 a firm is coming as close as it can to equating the marginal factor cost of labor to the marginal revenue product of labor. However, if a minimum wage rate higher than W_2 were imposed, such as W_3, the quantity of labor employed would be less than L_2. Moreover, the new quantity of labor employed might even be less than L_1, as is true for L_3 in panel (b).

Thus an imperfectly competitive labor market represents the only case in which the imposition of a minimum wage rate may not have an adverse effect on employment. However, even in this situation, employment will

fall if the minimum wage rate is established at a sufficiently high level.

As in the case of unions, economists do not agree on the effects of the minimum wage on employment. However, many of them believe that it has a negative impact on employment opportunities for teenagers.[26]

It seems clear that if a minimum wage does

26. See "A Higher Minimum Wage Hurts Teenagers," *Business Week*, August 22, 1977, p. 14; "Rise in Minimum Wage Spurs Some Firms to Cut Work Hours and Hiring of Youths," *Wall Street Journal*, August 15, 1978, p. 40; Steven P. Zell, "The Minimum Wage and Youth Unemployment," *Economic Review* (Federal Reserve Bank of Kansas City), January 1978, pp. 3–16; and "Minimal Impact? The Minimum Wage's Effects on Employment Are Subtle," *Wall Street Journal*, January 16, 1979, p. 1.

cause some people to be unable to find work, its effects are not totally desirable. Thus, while such a wage may be politically popular, it is not likely to make all bottom-rung workers better off.

SUMMARY

1. This chapter has discussed how workers' wages can be raised by union bargaining and by minimum wage laws. In either case, one possible result is a trade-off between the wage rate and the quantity of employment. In other words, one effect of higher wages may be higher rates of unemployment.

2. The U.S. labor movement did not really get started until the American Federation of Labor was formed, in 1881. City-wide unions and the Knights of Labor, two earlier attempts to organize labor, met with limited success. The AFL was organized on a trade union basis, so that unskilled workers were excluded.

3. In 1938 the Congress of Industrial Organizations was formed. Its goal was to organize workers along industry lines rather than according to trade or craft. Finally, in 1955, the American Federation of Labor and the Congress of Industrial Organizations merged, to form the AFL-CIO. This organization still exists as the major federation of labor unions.

4. Various techniques, including injunctions, yellow-dog contracts, lockouts, blacklists, and company unions, have been used to discourage union membership. In the 1800s the courts often held that labor union leaders were engaged in criminal conspiracies. The Clayton Act of 1914 gave workers the right to join unions, but the courts still frequently issued injunctions prohibiting strikes.

5. In the 1930s the attitude of the U.S. public changed. The Norris-LaGuardia Act (1932) made injunctions harder for firms to obtain and made yellow-dog contracts unenforceable.

6. The Wagner Act (1935) was known as labor's Magna Carta. It emphasized workers' right to join unions and outlawed several unfair labor practices on the part of employers. It also established the National Labor Relations Board, one of whose responsibilities is to conduct elections to determine which union, if any, should represent a particular group of workers.

7. Public opinion turned against the unions once more in the 1940s. In 1947 the Taft-Hartley Act was passed. This act was significant because, for the first time, unfair union practices, such as secondary boycotts and jurisdictional strikes, were prohibited. The act regulated certain aspects of union administration, and it specified collective bargaining procedures and certain terms of bargaining agreements. It also gave the president the right to obtain temporary injunctions against strikes that were expected to cause a national emergency, outlawed closed shops, and provided for the passage of right-to-work laws by the states.

8. The Landrum-Griffin Act (1959) placed certain restrictions on union elections and officers and required that certain reports be submitted by unions to the secretary of Labor. It also required employers to file reports disclosing loans or payments to employees of unions.

9. The Civil Rights Act (1964) was another landmark piece of labor legislation. Title VII of this act forbade discrimination in hiring, firing, and promotion on the basis of race, color, religion, sex, and national origin. It also formed the Equal Employment Opportunity Commission and gave it the responsibility of seeing that the provisions of the Civil Rights Act were carried out.

10. The effects of the union movement are not clear. In a perfectly competitive labor market unions cannot raise wage rates without causing unemployment. However, in an imperfectly competitive labor market it is possible for unions to raise wage rates and increase employment. Nevertheless, the preponderance of the evidence to date does not show that unions have been clearly able to increase labor's share of the national income.

11. In recent years the percentage of the U.S. nonagricultural work force has declined. However, membership in public employee unions has risen rapidly in the last decade.

12. The Fair Labor Standards Act (1938) implemented the notion of a minimum wage. Originally $.25, the wage rose to $3.35 in 1981. The effect of the minimum wage on employment is not obvious, although some evidence supports the hypothesis that teenage unemployment has increased as a result of it.

IMPORTANT TERMS AND CONCEPTS

Discriminatory
  discharge
Yellow-dog contract
Lockout
Paternalism
Company unions
Knights of Labor
American Federation
  of Labor
Industrial Workers of
  the World
Congress of Industrial
  Organizations
AFL-CIO
Sherman Anti-Trust
  Act (1980)
Clayton Act (1914)
Norris-LaGuardia Act
  (1932)

Wagner Act (1935)
Injunction
Taft-Hartley Act
  (1947)
Secondary boycotts or
  strikes
Jurisdictional strikes
Union shop
Closed shop
Right-to-work laws
Open shop
Featherbedding
Checkoff
Landrum-Griffin Act
  (1959)
Civil Rights Act
  (1964)
Bilateral monopoly
Minimum wage

QUESTIONS AND PROBLEMS

1. Why is the Wagner Act called labor's Magna Carta?

2. Why was the Taft-Hartley Act a unique law dealing with labor unions? When was it passed?

3. When was the American Federation of Labor formed? What basic principles made up the philosophy of this organization? Who was one of its founders and its president for many years?

4. Why and when was the Congress of Industrial Organizations formed?

5. What is the Fair Labor Standards Act?

6. Explain what lockouts, yellow-dog contracts, paternalism, and blacklisting are.

7. Why was the Norris-LaGuardia Act significant? When was it passed?

8. Draw a graph and describe a situation in which a union may achieve both a higher wage rate and an increase in employment.

9. What are secondary boycotts and jurisdictional strikes? Are they legal? Explain.

10. What does the bilateral monopoly model state about the equilibrium wage rate and level of employment? Why has this model been criticized?

11. What was the purpose of Title VII of the Civil Rights Act (1964)?

12. How effective have labor unions been in increasing labor's share of the national income?

UAW FEARS AUTOMATION AGAIN

Despite near-record employment in the auto industry, a recent proliferation of labor-saving devices in auto plants has rekindled workers' fears that automation will wipe out large numbers of jobs. And these fears could have significant impact on this summer's auto negotiations.

Bargainers for the United Auto Workers are likely to come under increasing pressure from rank and filers to win big concessions from General Motors, Ford Motor, and Chrysler on job security issues, such as demands for a four-day week and a cost-of-living increase for pensions. These demands have already become popular slogans and are advertised on UAW windbreaker jackets. UAW leaders do not expect to win a four-day week this year, although they have been planning for some time to

Source: "UAW Fears Automation Again," *Business Week;* March 26, 1979, pp. 94–95.

approach that goal by further reducing the work year. Pension escalation has also been a long-time goal of UAW bargainers.

THE LATEST WORRIES

But these demands have gained increasing rank-and-file support as a means of offsetting job losses arising from automation and computerization. The tougher such demands are, the harder it will be for the UAW to bargain within the 7% guideline—if it is still intact— and still win a hefty wage increase as a hedge against inflation (BW— Mar. 5). Moreover, the auto companies will argue that they face keen competition from foreign auto makers whose plants are already automated.

Rank-and-file worries about the potential job loss from the latest wave of technology emerged at the union's skilled trades conference in February. Tougher

terms were demanded for retraining workers, providing special stewards to monitor technical change, and giving earlier notice of automation plans. In theory, UAW contracts already require prior notice of technological changes. But those clauses "don't work very well," admits UAW Vice-President Irving Bluestone, director of the union's GM department. Instead, Bluestone says he has been sending union staffers into the plants to scout new labor-saving machines.

Ever since the first Model T rolled off the assembly line at Henry Ford's Highland Park (Mich.) plant in 1913, the auto companies have been spending huge sums of money to replace workers with machines. The pace of change quickened after World War II, when the word "automation" was coined to refer to new materials handling machines. By 1955, UAW Research Director Nat Weinberg was warning *Saturday Review* readers about a "second industrial revolution" that would leave labor "on the hook." But despite ominous forecasts about the loss of production jobs, concern waned as automation's progress either failed to meet its promise or was overshadowed by a booming economy.

Indeed, the UAW has historically recognized the inevitability of technological change. Rather than negotiate restrictive work rules, it has bargained for more of the productivity pie. The result: Big Three auto workers have some of the highest wages and benefits in U.S. industry (GM's average straight-time hourly labor cost is now more than $14.50).

A DOUBLING OF OUTPUT

But the auto work force is not rising in direct proportion to the boost in production of cars and trucks. Units built per production worker have risen from 12.8 in 1955 to 17.7 last year. Productivity as measured by the Bureau of Labor Statistics has been growing at a relatively fast rate in autos, averaging 3.9% per year from 1972 to 1977, compared with 1.7% in all manufacturing industries.

However, the displacement of jobs by machines and computers has been masked by a doubling of U.S. car-truck output since 1961, heavy overtime scheduling, and a tacit understanding between union and management that the loss would occur no faster than attrition. "The companies have played it very intelligently," says retired UAW staffer Anthony W. Connole.

"They've introduced [technology] gradually with no immediate layoffs. As a result, I don't believe the local union leadership understands the impact."

Now that equilibrium is threatened. The industry's $80 billion crash program to meet 1985 mileage and emission standards— by retooling for smaller cars—is bringing with it a massive overhaul of productive capacity. Old machines are being replaced with faster, more automated systems. Computers are sprouting in an array of applications on the plant floor. Engineers are seeking ways to employ a new breed of robots that have already proved they can take over the nasty work of welding and painting. New materials and improved car design are greatly simplifying assembly.

"The rate of productivity growth will be much faster now," says LeRoy H. Lindgren, director of new product planning for Rath & Strong Inc., a Lexington (Mass.) consulting firm. "The new small cars will have to be much more automated for the companies to maintain their profitability." Lindgren adds: "I'm sure their goal is a 30% reduction in manhours per car. They can't cost-justify such major investment without that kind of improvement."

THE UAW'S METHODS

Industry officials, sensitive to the job loss issue, insist that improved productivity from these changes will enable U.S. companies to regain the 18% market share held by imports and revive the export market for U.S. cars and trucks. They argue that this will mean

more, not fewer, jobs. "But I'm not as optimistic as the industry," says the UAW's Bluestone. "My feeling is there will be slow growth for a period of time, then a leveling of sales while productivity continues to zoom at an accelerating rate. Meeting the attrition rate doesn't answer the problem. We've got to do better than that."

The UAW has used two principal methods in trying to slow the shrinkage in the auto work force, thus putting new workers on the job and insulating older ones from unemployment. Since the early 1960s, the union has demanded— and won—financial incentives for older workers to retire at ever earlier ages, thereby opening up jobs. The UAW won "30-and-out," or retirement with 30 years of service regardless of age, in 1970, and 70% of eligible auto workers retire early under this rule.

The union has also tried to spread the work by negotiating more and more paid time off the job. Under a new benefit won in 1976, auto workers get seven "personal paid holidays" (PPH) this year in addition to 13 regular holidays. This has "created" 11,000 jobs at GM alone, Bluestone says. He adds that, counting all days off for holidays and vacations, the work year is equivalent to 52 work weeks of $4\frac{1}{2}$ days each.

The UAW will try to win more PPH days in bargaining this year, with the idea of reducing the length of the work year to the point where a four-day week becomes an actuality. The cost of achieving that goal in 1979 would be prohibitive, given the UAW's other bargaining priorities. But UAW

President Douglas A. Fraser says that the four-day week is "absolutely inevitable. The only open question is how fast we're going to get there."

COSTS OF ROBOTS

A survey last year by the Society of Manufacturing Engineers (SME) found that 80% of key industrial managers expect the 32-hour week to be standard by 1990. "The union sees this coming down the road, and they're setting the stage for it," says Donald N. Smith, director of industrial development at the University of Michigan's Institute of Science & Technology. "Eventually, in the 1980s there will be a long strike over the four-day week, and my bet is, they'll get it."

Some of the new robot technology is almost irresistibly affordable. A "Unimate" robot welder, for instance, which costs $45,000, can pay for itself in less than 15 months by replacing two $28,000-a-year welders. Over its eight-year life, the cost to buy and operate the machine, including its depreciation, runs about $4.80 an hour, says Joseph F. Engelberger, president of Unimation Inc., of Danbury, Conn. This month GM will install a Unimation PUMA (programmable universal machine for assembly) at its Delco Electronics Div. at Kokomo, Ind., to handle car radio speaker parts on an assembly line. Functioning much like a human arm, the PUMA arms are designed to substitute for assembly line workers, roughly on a one-for-one basis. GM says it is buying 10 PUMAS this year and 100 in 1980 at an eventual volume of about $21,000 apiece. "They'll go

all out and get rid of material handlers," says Rath & Strong's Lindgren. "You can't stop GM from automating. That's what they're good at."

GM already has more than 150 robots of various kinds working in its plants, and GM documents show there are plans for 330 more applications. Ford is even further ahead, with 236 robot applications at the end of 1978, up from 150 a year before, with plans to increase that number at the rate of 50% a year. Even Chrysler, strapped for funds to finance its downsizing program, has put more than 100 robots in new plants at Newark, Del., and St. Louis.

INABILITY TO COPE

The SME survey predicts that 20% of the direct labor in automobile final assembly will be replaced by programmable automation by 1985 and 50% by 1995. By 1988, half of the direct labor in small component assembly will be replaced. Inspection work will be even more automated.

Robert T. Lund, a senior research associate at the Massachusetts Institute of Technology Center for Policy Alternatives, wrote a report on automation for GM last year. He hypothesized a "substantial permanent sector of unemployment" because of the inability of industry and government to cope with the social effects of changing technology. But Lund thinks that the old automation scare prevents people from thinking seriously about today's situation. "Perhaps we've heard 'wolf' cried too frequently in

the past, when we were really in an evolutionary stage," Lund says. "We may still be in an evolutionary stage, but the capability to move ahead rapidly is now here."

Computerized and robotized plants, Lund says, will divide workers into very highly skilled and very low-skilled categories, wiping out the intermediate skill range vital for a sense of upward mobility. "It's scary," says Adam G. Ulbin, a UAW skilled trades committeeman at GM's Willow Run (Mich.) assembly plant. "It may mean more skilled jobs, but we're not getting the training. When one of these machines breaks down, they call in the vendor."

Note: The problems of the U.S. auto manufacturers in the early 1980s have increased their incentives to install robots. See "GM's Ambitious Plans to Employ Robots," *Business Week,* March 16, 1981, p. 31.

QUESTIONS

1. What tactics has the UAW used in an attempt to reduce unemployment among its members?
2. Why is automation such a threat at the present time?
3. Considering the requirements for a least cost combination of inputs, what do you think will likely be the long-run employment implications of the UAW obtaining higher wage rates?
4. How is your answer to Question 3 supported by the issue of the $45,000 robots?
5. Why do auto industry officials argue that the increased labor productivity resulting from automation creates more jobs?

PART EIGHT

THE
ECONOMICS OF
GOVERNMENT-BUSINESS
RELATIONSHIPS

CHAPTER 26

ANTITRUST
AND
MONOPOLY

NOTHING
FINER THAN
A
CUISINART

Food processors became the "hot item" Christmas gifts for 1978–1980 as consumers became more aware of what the products could do. Consumer Reports *tested these machines in 1977 and again in 1978.*[1] *Both times they found the French original, Cuisinart, to be one of the top-rated processors. However, in 1978 they reported that the Sunbeam model 1411 was virtually the equal of the Cuisinart.*

There was, however, one important difference between the two processors that *Consumer Reports* missed. Cuisinarts could not be purchased at a discount. In 1978 the processor came in two models, one with a suggested list price of $140 and the other with a suggested price of $200. Typically, Cuisinarts were carried only by fancy department stores and specialty shops, and they seldom were put on sale. At the same time the Sunbeam model 1411 was readily available at catalogue showroom and discount stores, and although its suggested list price was $140, these stores generally sold it in the $85 to $95 price range. Moreover, as late as 1981, these sorts of stores did not have Cuisinarts available at any price.[2]

In December 1980 a federal judge imposed a fine of $250,000 on Cuisinart Incorporated after the company pleaded no contest to the

---

1. "Food Processors: Does the Cuisinart Still Beat Its Rivals?" *Consumer Reports*, September 1978, pages 495–501.
2. The 1981 catalogues of Best Products, O. G. Wilson, Service Merchandise, and Unity Buying Service contained many brands of food processors, but none offered the Cuisinart.

charge that it conspired with retailers to fix the final selling price of its food processors. Under the antitrust laws of the United States, it is illegal for a manufacturer or wholesaler to dictate resale prices to its customers. The antitrust complaint charged that Cuisinart not only suggested the prices at which its machines should be sold but also threatened to cut off or reduce shipments to dealers who tried to sell them at less than the suggested prices.[3] If you want to buy one of the Cuisinarts now, you may find them in a more tolerable price range, thanks to Uncle Sam's action.

Price fixing is just one of a number of business activities prohibited by U.S. antitrust laws. In this chapter we will survey the antitrust laws and their intent and will consider some of the issues involving the interpretation of the laws and their economic effects.

3. "Cuisinart Is Fined on Felony Charges in Antitrust Case," *Wall Street Journal*, December 22, 1980, p. 4.

C H A P T E R 26

ANTITRUST
AND
MONOPOLY

WHAT THIS CHAPTER IS ABOUT

THE ANTITRUST LAWS
Sherman Act
Clayton Act
Federal Trade Commission Act
Robinson-Patman Act
Celler-Kefauver Act
THE COURTS AND THE ANTITRUST LAWS
Monopolies versus Monopolizing
Mergers
Price Fixing
ENFORCEMENT OF ANTITRUST LAWS
PATENTS, TRADEMARKS, AND COPYRIGHTS
CURRENT ISSUES IN ANTITRUST

The laws affecting government-business relationships can be separated into three categories: criminal law, the law of torts, and contract law.

Criminal law deals with acts that are viewed as offenses against a federal, state, or local government.

The **law of torts** is concerned with injuries sustained by private parties as a result of nonperformance of a duty created by law.

Contract law pertains to the establishment of contractual obligations and to wrongful acts in breach of contract.

In this chapter we will consider only one set of laws affecting business activities—the antitrust laws.

The **antitrust laws** are laws affecting any business practices and agreements that intensify monopoly power or otherwise restrict trade.

It is possible for antitrust violations to involve all three major categories of business law. They may constitute crimes or torts, or they may involve the breaking of contracts. Most violations, however, are civil offenses, or torts.

THE ANTITRUST LAWS

◆

Antitrust cases are in the news frequently these days. In the late 1970s and early 1980s the *Wall Street Journal* carried the following headlines: "Paper Companies Get Heavy Fines for Price-Fixing," "Stiff Penalties for Price-Fixing Levied by Court" (on electrical companies), "Pan Am, Lufthansa, TWA Fined for Fixing Some Excursion Fares," "U.S. Charges 8 Potash Makers with Conspiracy," "Antitrust Investigation Could Reshape Makers of Off-shore-Oil Gear," and "Paving Firms Accused of Rigging Road Bids on Southeast Projects."[1] And these headlines are only a small sample! In the next few sections of the chapter we will examine the laws whose violations or alleged violations got these companies into such predicaments.

The basis for U.S. antitrust laws can be found in English common law. Before 1600 some English towns restricted commercial activity by strangers in order to protect local businesses. Sometimes the English courts overruled these restrictions. In one case, known as the *Case of Monopolies*, the plaintiff sought to prevent the defendant from importing playing cards into England, on the ground that Queen Elizabeth had given the plaintiff the exclusive right to import such cards. The court declared that the monopoly□ was void because it was "contrary to the common law." (**Common law** is law that is developed by custom and usage and is subsequently enforced by the courts.) Monopoly was considered to restrict competition, deprive others of a business, and result in higher prices and poorer quality. In 1623 the English parliament passed the **Statute of Monopolies,** which voided all monopolies except for patents for inventors and new manufacturers, certain monopolies held by towns and guilds, and parliamentary grants.[2]

By the second half of the nineteenth century the political climate in the United States was ripe for the passage of an antitrust law. Farmers were enraged by what they considered unreasonable price discrimination□ by railroads, grain elevators, manufacturers of farm machinery, and eastern financiers. Moreover, although many new firms were created during the industrial expansion of this period, a significant number of these businesses subsequently disappeared as a result of mergers that were not always voluntary. Practices such as predatory (cutthroat) pricing and price fixing as well as outright fraud were thought to be common practices.

Chapter 21 showed the disadvantages of monopoly over perfect competition□ from the point of view of economic efficiency. At least to some extent, this consideration formed the basis for the antitrust laws of the United States. However, other factors were also important.

During congressional debates over his antitrust bill in 1890, Senator Sherman argued that large businesses should be eliminated be-

---

1. "Paper Companies Get Heavy Fines for Price-Fixing," *Wall Street Journal*, September 21, 1978, p. 2; "Stiff Penalties for Price-Fixing Levied by Court," *Wall Street Journal*, February 6, 1978, p. 8; "Pan Am, Lufthansa, TWA Fined for Fixing Some Excursion Fares," *Wall Street Journal*, October 25, 1977, p. 30; "U.S. Charges 8 Potash Makers with Conspiracy," *Wall Street Journal*, June 30, 1976, p. 8, "Antitrust Investigation Could Reshape Makers of Offshore-Oil Gear," *Wall Street Journal*, July 7, 1978, pp. 1, 23; and "Paving Firms Accused of Rigging Road Bids on Southeast Projects," *Wall Street Journal*, May 29, 1981, p. 1.

2. See Phillip Areeda, *Antitrust Analysis: Problems, Text, Cases,* 3rd ed. (Boston: Little, Brown, 1981), pp. 44–46.

cause individuals were helpless in their presence. This point of view was reflected in an 1897 Supreme Court decision, which held:

[Large businesses] may even temporarily, or perhaps permanently, reduce the price of the article traded in or manufactured, by reducing the expense inseparable from the running of many different companies for the same purpose. Trade or commerce under those circumstances may nevertheless be badly and unfortunately restrained by driving out of business the small dealers and worthy men whose lives have been spent therein and who might be unable to readjust themselves to their altered surroundings. Mere reduction in the price of the commodity dealt in might be dearly paid for by the ruin of such a class.[3]

In the next section we will examine the major federal antitrust laws: the Sherman Antitrust Act, the Clayton Act, the Federal Trade Commission Act, the Robinson-Patman Act, and the Celler-Kefauver Act. State antitrust laws also exist, but most enforcement activities in the area of antitrust are concentrated at the federal level.[4]

THE SHERMAN ANTITRUST ACT

The **Sherman Antitrust Act,** passed in 1890, represented the first attempt by the U.S. government to regulate restrictive trade practices. The most famous parts of this law are in Sections 1 and 2. Section 1 stated:

Every contract, combination in the form of trust or otherwise, or conspiracy, in restraint of trade or commerce among the several States, or with foreign nations, is hereby declared to be illegal.[5]

Section 2 continued:

Every person who shall monopolize, or attempt to monopolize or combine or conspire with any other person or persons, to monopolize any part of the trade or commerce among the several States, or with foreign nations, shall be deemed guilty of a misdemeanor.[6]

Thus the Sherman Act made monopolizing and other acts in restraint of trade illegal. Either the federal government or parties injured by such acts could bring suit against those allegedly committing them. Persons convicted of such acts were subject to fines and imprisonment. Moreover, any property connected with an illegal contract or conspiracy and transported interstate or to a foreign country could be confiscated by the federal government. Finally, any person or firm sustaining damages as a result of a violation of this act was entitled to compensation from those responsible for the injury equal to three times the damages incurred.[7]

Because of the general nature of its wording, the Sherman Act was relatively ineffective at first in controlling practices in restraint of trade. It simply did not clarify the specific acts that were to be considered illegal. Moreover, no single agency was charged with enforcing the law until 1903, when the antitrust division was established in the U.S. Department of Justice.

THE CLAYTON ACT

In 1914 the **Clayton Act** was passed in an attempt to clarify the antitrust policies of the federal government. This act specified four particular types of practices that were in restraint of trade: (1) price discrimination, (2) exclusive and tying contracts, (3) intercorporate stockholdings, and (4) interlocking directorates.

---

3. *United States v. Trans-Missouri Freight Association,* 166 U.S. 323 (1897).

4. However, see "Antitrust Enforcement Stepped up by States; Budgets, Staffs Grow," *Wall Street Journal,* October 4, 1976, pp. 1, 12.

5. *The Statutes at Large of the United States of America,* vol. 26 (Washington, D.C.: Government Printing Office, 1891), p. 209.

6. Ibid.

7. Ibid., Sections 3–7, pp. 209–210.

Price Discrimination

Price discrimination is the practice of charging different buyers different prices for the same product or service.

Section 2 of the Clayton Act declared:

That it shall be unlawful for any person engaged in commerce, in the course of such commerce, either directly or indirectly, to discriminate in price between different purchasers of commodities, which commodities are sold for use, consumption, or resale within the United States or any Territory thereof or the District of Columbia . . . , where the effect of such discrimination may be to substantially lessen competition or tend to create a monopoly in any line of commerce: *Provided,* that nothing herein contained shall prevent discrimination in price between purchasers of commodities on account of differences in the grade, quality, or quantity of the commodity sold, or that makes only due allowance for difference in. the cost of selling or transportation or discrimination in price in the same or different communities made in good faith to meet competition.[8]

However, sellers were permitted to charge different prices according to whether the buyers were wholesalers or retailers.

Price discrimination was discussed in some detail in Special Topic I, which follows Chapter 21. An example of legal price discrimination is charging different admission fees for matinee and evening showings of movies. In this case the two showings are deemed to be sufficiently different commodities that the prohibition against price discrimination is not violated.

Proof of illegal price discrimination is often difficult to come by and is usually centered around the effects on a seller's or a buyer's competitors. However, such discrimination has been found to exist in a number of cases. For example, in a 1957 case involving Maryland Baking Company and the Federal Trade Commission, the court found that Maryland had practiced illegal price discrimination. The company had cut the price of its ice cream cone in a limited area where a small competitor had its only operation, and evidence indicated that the purpose of the price cut was to drive the competitor out of business. Illegal price discrimination was also found to have occurred in a 1959 case involving Atlas Building Products Company and Diamond Block and Gravel Company. Atlas sold building blocks in El Paso, Texas, and in nearby Las Cruces, New Mexico. Atlas, which was competing with Diamond in the Las Cruces area, lowered its prices in that area. The court held that the price cuts were predatory in nature and that Atlas's prices in Las Cruces were at too low a level to allow Diamond to operate profitably.[9]

Exclusive and Tying Contracts Exclusive and tying contracts are contracts including an agreement that the purchaser or the lessee of a commodity will not buy from or deal with firms that are competitors of the selling firm.

> **Exclusive dealing** means that a firm buying or leasing the goods of one firm agrees not to deal with competing suppliers.
>
> Under a **tying agreement** a firm agrees that the goods sold or leased will be used only with other goods of the seller or lessor.

Section 3 of the Clayton Act makes such contracts and practices illegal:

It shall be unlawful for any person engaged in commerce, in the course of such commerce, to lease or make a sale or contract for sale of goods . . . , or fix a price charged therefor, or discount from, or rebate upon, such price, on the condition, agreement, or understanding that the lessee or purchaser thereof shall not use or deal in the goods . . . of a competitor or competitors of the lessor or seller,

---

8. "Antitrust Act of 1914," *The Statutes at Large of the United States of America,* vol. 38, pt. 1 (Washington, D.C.: Government Printing Office, 1915), p. 730.

9. See Areeda, *Antitrust Analysis,* 3rd ed., Chapter 7, for a discussion of these and other cases involving price discrimination.

. . . where the effect may be to substantially lessen competition or tend to create a monopoly.[10]

For example, in a 1936 case involving International Business Machines and the U.S. government, the courts held that IBM had violated the prohibition against tying contracts by requiring that lessees of its tabulating machines use only tabulating cards manufactured by IBM.[11]

Interlocking Stockholdings

Interlocking stockholdings is the ownership by one corporation of the stock of a competing corporation.

Section 7 of the Clayton Act forbade a corporation engaged in commerce to acquire the stock of another corporation engaged in commerce where the effect would be to "substantially lessen competition . . . or tend to create a monopoly."[12] thus the purpose of this section was to prevent interlocking stockholdings if such holdings would result in monopolizing behavior.

Interlocking Directorates

An *interlocking directorate* occurs when one person serves on the boards of directors of two companies.

Section 8 of the Clayton Act stated that (with a few exceptions) a person who was a director, officer, or employee of any member bank of the Federal Reserve System could not also be at the same time a director, officer, or employee of any other bank, banking association, savings bank, or trust company. In addition, this section made it illegal for any person to be concurrently a director in two or

more corporations if one of them had capital, surplus, and undivided profits amounting to $1 million or more, so that the elimination of competition between them would constitute a violation of the antitrust laws. Consequently, this section declared that an interlocking directorate was unacceptable if one of the companies was above a particular size and if such a situation would tend to lessen competition.[13]

THE FEDERAL TRADE COMMISSION ACT

The **Federal Trade Commission Act (1914)** established the Federal Trade Commission (FTC), which was to consist of five members appointed for seven-year terms by the president, with the advice and consent of the Senate. The act empowered and directed the FTC to act to prevent any "unfair methods of competition."[14] However, jurisdiction over banks has been given to the Federal Reserve System and jurisdiction over interstate carriers to the Interstate Commerce Commission. (The responsibilities of the FTC with respect to the enforcement of the antitrust laws is dealt with in more detail later in the chapter.)

Section 5 of the Federal Trade Commission Act broadly prohibited "unfair methods of competition." Because the meaning of this section was unclear, the **Wheeler-Lea Act** was passed in 1938. This act amended Section 5 of the Federal Trade Commission Act to prohibit unfair *and deceptive* acts or practices.[15] Previously, false advertising had not been held to be unfair because all competing firms could use it. The possibility that consumers could be misled was irrelevant.

---

10. "Antitrust Act of 1914," p. 731.

11. See Areeda, *Antitrust Analysis*, 3rd ed., Chapter 5, p. 776. Also see "International Business Machines Corp. v. United States," 298 U.S. 131 (1936).

12. "Antitrust Act of 1914," p. 731.

13. Ibid, p. 732.

14. "Federal Trade Commission Act," *The Statutes at Large of the United States of America*, vol. 38, pt. 1 (Washington, D.C.: Government Printing Office, 1915), pp. 717–724, especially pp. 719–721.

15. "Federal Trade Commission Act, Amendments," *United States Statutes at Large*, vol. 52 (Washington, D.C.: Government Printing Office, 1938), pp. 111–117, especially p. 111.

THE ROBINSON-PATMAN ACT

The **Robinson-Patman Act (1936)** strengthened Section 2 of the Clayton Act, which prohibited certain forms of price discrimination. One development that prompted this law was the interaction between wholesalers and large retailers or chain stores. Since World War I, chain stores had been growing rapidly and had been able to obtain discounts in the form of "brokerage fees" on items purchased from wholesalers.

The Robinson-Patman Act made it illegal for a firm to pay a brokerage fee unless it was for the services of an independent, third-party broker. The act also made it illegal for firms to give special terms or services to some customers that were not available to all customers. Moreover, it was declared unlawful for any person engaged in commerce to knowingly induce or receive a price differential prohibited by this law.[16]

THE CELLER-KEFAUVER ACT

The purpose of the **Celler-Kefauver Act (1950)** was to close a loophole in Section 7 of the Clayton Act. The original Section 7 outlawed the aquisition of the stock of one corporation by another corporation when the effect would be to lessen competition. However, it did not prevent a corporation from buying the assets of another firm and thereby effectively merging with it. The Celler-Kefauver Act amended this section so that it applied to mergers consummated by purchasing either the stock or the assets of another company.[17]

The Celler-Kefauver Act also extended the Clayton Act in another respect. The original

law applied only to **Horizontal mergers**— mergers of two companies that produce and sell similar products. (An example of a horizontal merger is the merger of two supermarkets.) The Celler-Kefauver Act applied to vertical and conglomerate mergers as well as horizontal mergers. A **vertical merger** is a merger of two firms where one firm produces an input used by the other firm in the production of its output. (The merger of a steel company and a machinery company is a vertical merger.) A **conglomerate merger** is a merger of two firms that produce unrelated products. (The merger of a restaurant chain with a shoe manufacturer is an example of this type of merger.)

> A **horizontal merger** is a merger of two firms which produce the same product.
>
> A **vertical merger** is a merger of two firms in which one firm produces a product used by the second firm as an intermediate good or component part in the production of its product.
>
> A **conglomerate merger** is a merger between two firms which produce unrelated products.

The Celler-Kefauver Act made illegal only those mergers that would have the effect of substantially lessening competition or tending to create a monopoly. However, as we will see in the next section, the federal government has interpreted this qualification quite broadly.

ENFORCEMENT OF ANTITRUST LAWS

◆

Most of the antitrust cases brought to court are civil in nature, not criminal. In general, violations of the Clayton Act and the Robinson-Patman Act are not crimes. However, violations of Sections 1 and 2 of the Sherman Act

---

16. "Antitrust Act of 1914, Amendment," *The Statutes at Large of the United States of America*, vol. 49 (Washington, D.C.: Government Printing Office, 1936), pp. 1526–1528.

17. *United States Statutes at Large*, vol. 64, pt. 1 (Washington, D.C.: Government Printing Office, 1952), pp. 1125–1128.

and Section 3 of the Robinson-Patman Act (which also restricts price discrimination) are criminal offenses.

The reluctance on the part of the government to make such violations crimes seems to stem from the fact that many of the antitrust laws are purposely vague and the interpretations of them by the courts do change. Thus a court might hold that a firm had violated an antitrust law when the firm itself thought that it was obeying the law. Under such circumstances it seems unreasonable to charge a firm with a criminal offense.

CRIMINAL PENALTIES

When criminal prosecution is initiated, it is done so by the antitrust division of the Department of Justice or by a United States attorney under the direction of the attorney general. The Department of Justice has typically limited prosecution to cases where the offense is clear, such as price fixing, or where the defendant has acted with the specific intent to restrain trade or has engaged in other obviously illegal acts, such as predatory practices, that the defendant knows are illegal. The government may also initiate a criminal prosecution if the defendant has previously been convicted of an antitrust offense.

In cases where convictions on criminal offenses are obtained, companies are subject to fines up to $1 million. Individuals who are responsible for or who participated in a criminal violation can be personally fined up to $100,000 and imprisoned up to three years.

CIVIL PENALTIES

Under the Sherman and Clayton acts the government is authorized to initiate civil cases to prevent antitrust violations. The courts have considerable leeway as to the remedies they can impose in such cases. Among them are decrees forbidding certain acts or forcing a defendant to dispose of certain assets or to take other actions in order to restore competitive conditions.

Consent Decrees   Many civil antitrust cases brought by the Department of Justice are settled by consent decrees.

> ***Consent decrees*** *are statements of certain provisions agreed to by both the government and the defendant.*

These settlements may occur at any point after a case is brought to court, although usually they are agreed upon before a decision has actually been reached by a court.

Role of the Federal Trade Commission   The responsibility of enforcing the Federal Trade Commission Act ban against "unfair methods of competition and deceptive trade practices" rests with the Federal Trade Commission. It shares the responsibility of enforcing the Clayton Act with the Department of Justice. Most FTC complaints are settled before the formal hearing stage is reached.

One method of resolving an issue is for the party under investigation to submit an affidavit called an *assurance of voluntary compliance*, which promises that a questioned practice will be discontinued. A second method is for the FTC and the party under investigation to negotiate a cease and desist order.

> *In a **cease and desist order** the investigated party, without admitting any guilt, agrees to refrain from certain activities.*

Such an order has the same standing as a regular FTC final order.

In cases where a cease and desist order is not made available by the FTC or where negotiations fail, a formal hearing is held by an administrative law judge. To facilitate this process the FTC has established certain standards, called *Trade Regulation Rules*, that interpret the prohibition against unfair methods of competition with regard to specific business practices. The findings of the administrative law judge are subject to review by the FTC, and commission findings and orders can be reviewed by a federal court of appeals. Failure to comply with an FTC final order (unless it is under judicial review) subjects a party to a civil penalty of $5,000 per day in violation.

Treble Damages   Under both the Sherman Act and the Clayton Act, any private party "injured in his business or property by reason of anything forbidden in the antitrust laws . . . , shall recover three fold the damages by him sustained, and the cost of suit, including a reasonable attorney's fee."[18] The awarding of **treble damages** serves two purposes. It compensates an injured party, and it gives firms a significant incentive to obey the antitrust laws.

As we will see in the next section, even with all the refinements in the antitrust laws, many times the exact meaning of their provisions is in doubt. The process by which the laws take on meaning through court interpretations is illustrated by a few noteworthy cases.

THE COURTS AND THE ANTITRUST LAWS

◆

In this section we will examine three issues that have been prominent in court cases involving the antitrust laws—monopolizing behavior, mergers, and price fixing. Especially with regard to the first two items, the position of the courts has not been consistent.

MONOPOLIES VERSUS MONOPOLIZING

One troublesome issue that has marked the history of antitrust cases in the United States has been the relationship between monopolies

and **monopolizing behavior.** Section 2 of the Sherman Act specifically prohibits monopolizing behavior; but the status of a monopoly, apart from monopolizing acts, is less clear.

*One group of people, sometimes called **structuralists,** adhere to the philosophy that large size (relative to the entire market) alone will always result in the undesirable effects of a monopoly—high price, low output, and an economic profit.*

A second view holds that large size by itself does not necessarily result in monopolizing behavior. In fact, several large firms in an industry may be quite competitive and may therefore keep prices low. Furthermore, these firms may have lower costs per unit than would smaller firms because of economies of scale.

*People who consider size alone to be insufficient evidence of monopolizing behavior are called **behavioralists.***

The courts have supported both points of view. In a 1920 case involving United States Steel the Supreme Court ruled that size alone was not a sufficient indication of monopolizing behavior.[19] This decision was based on the "rule of reason."

*The **rule of reason** holds that size alone is not illegal as long as a firm acts within reasonable limits and does not abuse its position.*

In a 1911 case involving Standard Oil, Chief Justice Douglass White expressed the idea of the rule of reason as follows:

Although the statute [Sherman Act] . . . makes it certain that its purpose was to prevent undue restraints of every kind or nature, nevertheless by the

---

18. "Antitrust Act of 1914," p. 731.

19. *United States v. United States Steel Corp.,* 251 U.S. 417 (1920).

omission of any direct prohibition against monopoly in the concrete it indicates a consciousness that the freedom of the individual right to contract when not unduly or improperly exercised was the most efficient means for the prevention of monopoly.[20]

However, Justice White went on to conclude that there was prima facie (sufficient) evidence of the abuse of power by Standard Oil.

Correspondingly, in a case heard the same year involving American Tobacco Co., the court stated:

We say these conclusions are inevitable, not because of the vast amount of property aggregated by the combination, not because alone of the many corporations which the proof shows were united by resort to one device or another. Again, not alone because of the domination and control over the tobacco trade which actually exists, but because we think the conclusion of wrongful purpose and illegal combination is overwhelmingly established by the following considerations.[21]

The attitude represented by the rule of reason was modified in a 1945 case involving Alcoa Aluminum. The famous appeals court opinion in this case was written by Judge Learned Hand, who said:

Having proved that "Alcoa" had a monopoly of the domestic ingot market, the plaintiff had gone far enough; *if it was an excuse, that "Alcoa" had not abused its power, it lay upon "Alcoa" to prove that it had not. But the whole issue is irrelevant anyway, for it is no excuse for "monopolizing" a market that the monopoly has not been used to extract from the consumer more than a "fair" profit.* The Act has wider purposes. Indeed, even though we disregarded all but economic considerations, it would by no means follow that such concentration of producing power is to be desired, when it has not been used extortionately. . . . True, it might have been thought adequate to condemn only those monopolies which could not show that they had exercised the highest possible ingenuity, had adopted every possible economy, had anticipated every conceivable improvement, stimulated every possi-

ble demand. No doubt, that would be one way of dealing with the matter, although it would imply constant scrutiny and constant supervision, such as courts are unable to provide. *Be that as it may, that was not the way that Congress chose; it did not condone "good trusts" and condemn "bad" ones; it forbad all.*[22] (Emphasis added.)

According to Judge Hand, (1) it does not matter whether a monopoly position was gained through merger or through reinvestment of earnings; (2) size alone constitutes an offense, because it is impossible to separate the power to abuse from the actual abuse of power; and (3) Alcoa's market share of 90 percent "is enough to constitute a monopoly; it is doubtful whether 60 or 64 percent would be enough, and certainly 33 percent is not."[23]

This position of the courts was reaffirmed in the 1948 case *United States v. Griffith*, when Justice William O. Douglas wrote: "So it is that monopoly power, whether lawfully or unlawfully acquired, may itself constitute an evil and stand condemned under [Section] 2 even though it remains unexercised."[24]

Thus the monopoly issue centers around the question of market power. Usually, as the concentration of an industry increases, the market power of firms in the industry also increases. Whether market power in and of itself is a violation of the Sherman Act has been a highly controversial question. The current trend of court opinions seems to indicate that the answer to the question is yes.

MERGERS

Since the passage of the Celler-Kefauver Act in 1950, the Department of Justice and the Federal Trade Commission have frequently challenged horizontal and vertical mergers. These agencies have been less vigorous in their at-

---

20. *Standard Oil v. United States*, 221 U.S. 62 (1911).

21. *United States v. American Tobacco Co.*, 221 U.S. 182 (1911).

22. *United States v. Aluminum Company of America*, 148 F.2d 416 (2d cir., 1945).

23. Ibid.

24. *United States v. Griffith*, 334 U.S. 100 (1948).

tacks on conglomerate mergers because of uncertainty regarding their effect on competition.

One noteworthy case involving a vertical merger is the 1962 case of *Brown Shoe Co. v. United States,* in which Brown Shoe Co. wanted to merge with Kinney Shoe Co.[25] Brown Shoe was primarily a manufacturer of shoes, and Kinney Shoe was mainly a retailer. Both firms had relatively small market shares. Brown had approximately 4 percent, and Kinney had 0.5 percent of the wholesale market. In addition, Kinney had a 1.2 percent share of the retail market.

Nevertheless, the Justice Department contended that competition would be lessened in both the wholesale and retail markets for shoes as a result of the merger. The district court found a definite trend among shoe manufacturers to purchase retail stores. Moreover, once such a purchase was made, the parent manufacturing company tended to supply an increasing percentage of the needs of its retail stores. The court also found a definite trend toward a decrease in the number of shoe manufacturers. Furthermore, it determined that Brown Shoe Co. had participated in these trends. The court therefore denied the merger of Brown and Kinney. The Supreme Court affirmed the decision of the district court.

Since 1950 the Justice Department has usually challenged any horizontal merger in which the acquiring firm and the acquired firm each have 5 percent or more of the market for the product. If the market for the product is highly concentrated, the figure falls to 4 percent or even lower.[26] The typical cutoff points for questioning vertical mergers are 10 percent for the acquiring company and 6 percent for the acquired company.[27]

The Justice Department has indicated its willingness to consider the special economic situation of an industry by its approval of the merger of Jones & Laughlin Steel Corporation and Youngstown Sheet & Tube Company. After the merger the new firm became the fourth largest steel company in the United States.[28] The merger was allowed because both companies lost money in 1977, and it was predicted that one or both would go out of business if they had to remain separate. After the merger, the new business was expected to have both lower operating costs and lower freight costs. As a result of this decision, some observers are expecting economic considerations to play an increasingly important role in the Justice Department's position on mergers. In addition, in 1981 the Reagan administration indicated an intention to rewrite the Department of Justice's guidelines on mergers to reflect this new attitude.

PRICE FIXING

In general, the courts have considered price fixing by firms to be a per se (intrinsic) violation of Section 1 of the Sherman Act.

> ***Price fixing*** *is a practice whereby a group of firms get together and agree to set the price of a final or intermediate product at a specific level.*

Proof that the price fixing occurred is sufficient for a conviction. Firms accused of price fixing have argued that it has beneficial effects, such as preventing cutthroat competition, reducing uncertainty, preserving firms and employment, and preventing the deterioration of quality.

The courts have usually found these justifications to be without merit. In a 1927 case, *United States v. Trenton Potteries Co.,* Justice Harlen Fiske Stone stated,

The aim and result of every price-fixing agreement, if effective, is the elimination of one form of competition. The power to fix prices, whether reason-

---

25. *Brown Shoe Co. v. United States,* 370 U.S. 294 (1962).

26. 1 Trade Regulation Reporter #4510 (1974).

27. Ibid.

28. "Antitrust: A Soft Line on a Steel Merger," *Business Week,* July 3, 1978, p. 30.

ably exercised or not, involves power to control the market and to fix arbitrary and unreasonable prices. The reasonable price fixed today may through some economic and business changes become the unreasonable price of tomorrow. Once established, it may be maintained because of the absence of competition secured by the agreement for a price reasonable when fixed. Agreements which create such potential power may well be held to be in themselves unreasonable or unlawful restraints, without the necessity of minute inquiry whether a particular price is reasonable or unreasonable as fixed.[29]

This position was affirmed by the Supreme Court in the 1940 *Socony-Vacuum Oil Co.* case:

Ruinous competition, financial disaster, evils of price cutting and the like appear throughout our history as ostensible justifications for price-fixing. If the so-called competitive abuses were to be appraised here, the reasonableness of prices would necessarily become an issue in every price-fixing case. In that event the Sherman Act would soon be emasculated.[30]

Agreements among competing firms to divide product or geographical markets have also generally been treated in the same manner as price-fixing agreements.

In recent years, however, the courts seem to have relaxed slightly their position on price fixing. In a 1978 decision a federal court held that in order to obtain a conviction on criminal price-fixing charges the government must prove both that the price-fixing activities actually took place and that the defendants intended to restrict competition.[31] This requirement can make a significant difference in cases where there has been no apparent secret agreement to set prices but only some sort of information exchange. Such a situation is discussed with respect to price leadership later in the chapter.

---

29. *United States v. Trenton Potteries Co.*, 273 U.S. 392 (1927).

30. *United States v. Socony-Vacuum Oil Co.*, 310 U.S. 150 (1940).

31. "A Subtle Easing of the Price-Fixing Rules," *Business Week*, December 24, 1979, p. 90.

PATENTS, COPYRIGHTS, AND TRADEMARKS

Congress has allowed some restriction of competition by providing for patents, copyrights, and trademarks. According to the Patent Act (1952) a formula, method, or device can be patented if it meets the following three criteria:

1. *Newness*—previously unknown to the public.
2. *Usefulness*—representing a substantial advance in technology.
3. *Unobviousness*—not obvious to anyone knowledgeable in the relevant area.[32]

> A **patent** gives an inventor an exclusive right to a formula, method, or device for a specific period of time—seventeen years in the United States.

A patent gives an inventor the authority to manufacture, transfer, exclude others from using, or withhold from use the item covered by the patent. The purpose of patents, of course, is to encourage innovation and technological advance. However, if one dominant firm in an industry owns many patents, the courts may consider such a concentration to violate the antitrust laws. In such a case the courts may provide for compulsory licensing of the patents to other firms.

Federal law also provides for copyrights.

> A **copyright** gives an author or firm the exclusive right to possess, make, publish, and sell copies of a production.

A copyright can be obtained for lists of addresses, books, maps, musical compositions,

---

32. Title 35, U.S. Code, *United States Statutes at Large*, vol. 66 (Washington, D.C.: Government Printing Office, 1953), pp. 792–817, especially p. 797.

motion pictures, and sound recordings. However, the work must be an original expression of an idea. Effective January 1, 1978, copyrights are issued for the life of the author plus fifty years after the author's death.

A **trademark** *is a distinctive word, name, symbol, device, or combination thereof used by a manufacturer to distinguish its goods from those of other firms.*

According to federal law a trademark can be registered for twenty years. A trademark must be distinctive to be registered.

CURRENT ISSUES IN ANTITRUST

◆

In this section we will examine some of the current controversial issues in the area of antitrust. The issues range from the impact of price leadership and brand proliferation to questions of bigness and economic efficiency and lengthiness of antitrust proceedings.

PRICE LEADERSHIP

The Department of Justice is currently investigating price practices in such concentrated industries as steel and aluminum. One of the practices coming under close scrutiny is price leadership.[33]□ How such an investigation can be reconciled with the recent easing of the price-fixing rules is not yet clear.

BRAND PROLIFERATION

In 1972, the Federal Trade Commission charged that Kellogg, General Mills, and General Foods discouraged new firms from entering the breakfast cereal market by developing many different varieties of breakfast cereals.[34] The FTC argued that the proliferation of brands of cereals by the major companies was extensive enough to convince outsiders that entry into this market would not be economically attractive.

Specifically, the FTC charged the Big Three cereal companies with having a shared monopoly. As a remedy, it proposed a system of licensing trademarks that would make it possible for new or smaller companies to easily imitate the leading brands. However, in the fall of 1981, FTC Administrative Judge Alvin L. Berman ruled that the FTC had not been able to prove its charges. Nevertheless, Judge Berman did not rule on whether the antitrust laws made a shared monopoly illegal.

FULL DISCLOSURE

In 1973 the Federal Power Commission declared that the electric utilities must make public once a month the prices they pay for fuel, the names of their suppliers, and the lengths of their contracts.[35] The original purpose of the full disclosure rule was to make it easier for individuals and consumer groups to intervene more effectively in rate hearings.

Recently, however, the Justice Department and the Federal Trade Commission have challenged this issue on antitrust grounds. In particular, these agencies are concerned that full disclosure will promote and facilitate price fixing. How to keep the need for information from encouraging anticompetitive behavior is a complex problem.

---

33. "Antitrust Officials Plan Investigations into Pricing in Concentrated Industries," *Wall Street Journal*, May 13, 1977, p. 3.

34. "Too Many Cereals for the FTC," *Business Week*, March 20, 1978, pp. 166, 171; "Kellogg: Still the Cereal People," *Business Week*, November 26, 1979, pp. 80–93; and "Cheerio to an Old Antitrust Case," *Newsweek*, September 21, 1981, p. 90.

35. "Full Disclosure That May Be Too Full," *Business Week*, August 8, 1977, pp. 28, 30.

502

ADVERTISING BY PROFESSIONALS

Many professionals, such as doctors, lawyers, and certified public accountants, have traditionally been prohibited from advertising their services by professional codes of ethics. In a 1977 case the Supreme Court declared such rules unconstitutional.[36] The position of those who favor a ban on advertising by professionals is that advertising will encourage some people to offer cut-rate services at cut-rate prices. Nevertheless, the courts have ruled that both free speech and consumers will be helped by such advertising. The results remain to be seen.

TELEVISION NETWORKS

In December 1974 the Justice Department filed suit against ABC, CBS, and NBC, charging that the three networks monopolized prime-time television with programs they had produced or in which they had a substantial interest.[37] By summer 1980 settlements had been reached with all three networks. The consent decrees◻ prohibit the networks from forcing independent producers to give up rights to their works in exchange for access to a network. In addition, they limit the amount of entertainment programming each network can produce for itself over the next ten years.[38] The effect of these settlements on network programming is yet to be determined.

FARM COOPERATIVES

At the present time, farm cooperatives are excluded from the antitrust laws. However, as we will see in Chapter 33, these organizations are becoming increasingly powerful in the market for farm products on the selling side and in the market for farm inputs, such as machinery, on the buying side. Some economists have argued that their market power approaches that of a cartel and that they should therefore be subject to the antitrust laws.[39]

TERRITORIAL RESTRICTIONS

In 1978 the Federal Trade Commission ruled that territorial restrictions placed by Coca-Cola and PepsiCo on their bottlers violate the federal antitrust laws by restricting competition.[40] The two companies limit bottlers to sales within specific geographical boundaries, and normally the boundaries for one bottler do not overlap with those of other bottlers of the same product.

An administrative law judge ruled in 1975 that territorial limitations were legitimate because they enhanced competition among bottlers of different brands of soft drinks and because many small bottling companies might fail without them. Thus the outcome of a policy to outlaw such restrictions might actually result in a lessening of competition. The entire commission rejected this argument in issuing its order. However, Coca-Cola and PepsiCo have appealed the ruling.

COMMUNICATIONS INDUSTRY

In early 1980 the Federal Communications Commission issued a ruling that completely deregulated the marketing of terminal communications equipment from dial telephones

---

36. See "Supreme Court Rules Lawyers Can Advertise," *San Antonio Express,* June 28, 1977, p. 1A.

37. "NBC's Plan to Settle U.S. Antitrust Suit on TV Programming Approved by Court," *Wall Street Journal* December 2, 1977, p. 11.

38. "ABC Falls into Line," *Business Week,* September 8, 1980, p. 44.

39. See "The Billion-Dollar Farm Co-ops Nobody Knows," *Business Week,* February 7, 1977, pp. 54–64; and "Thinner Cream for the Dairy Business," *Business Week,* July 31, 1978, pp. 90–91.

40. "Soft-Drink Bottlers Choke on FTC Ruling against Exclusive-Territory Restrictions," *Wall Street Journal.* April 25, 1978, p. 8.

599

to complex electronic devices.[41] At the same time the FCC eliminated restrictions on American Telephone and Telegraph Co. (AT&T) that had kept the company from entering the data processing industry.

In 1956 the Justice Department and AT&T had agreed to a consent decree that attempted to limit AT&T's business to telephone service. However, the dividing line between the communications industry and the data processing industry has become so blurred that the FCC decided the decree was no longer enforceable. This decision is expected to spark many lawsuits before the issues are resolved.

SIZE AND ECONOMIC EFFICIENCY

In 1979 the Justice Department was working on a legislative proposal for limiting corporate mergers. The proposed legislation would ban most mergers of corporations in which the resulting corporation would have more than $2 billion in sales or assets. An exception would be made if the acquired company had sales of less than $100 million.[42] Those in favor of such a law contend that bigness inevitably results in higher prices through such apparently legal price leadership tactics as publication of detailed price lists and press releases.

Those who oppose such broad legislation argue that bigness often promotes economic efficiency through economies of scale. Economist John Kenneth Galbraith, for one, argues that corporations need to be large and diversified in order to cope with the uncertainties of the modern economy and to undertake costly research and development. (This statement does not mean, however, that Galbraith favors monopolization. His views are discussed at greater length in Chapter 22.)

Currently, there is some evidence to support both positions, although the evidence in

support of large size per se is not as clear-cut as its advocates sometimes lead people to believe. These issues are discussed in greater depth in Chapters 21 and 22.

LENGTHINESS OF
THE JUDICIAL PROCESS

Antitrust procedures in the United States have been criticized because they sometimes result in court proceedings that seem never to be resolved. A glaring example of this problem is an antitrust suit brought by the Department of Justice against IBM.[43] The suit was filed in 1969, and there appears to be no end in sight. The Justice Department spent six years preparing for the case, and its prosecution arguments in court lasted three years. After the defense presents its side and a decision is reached, the appeals process will probably be initiated. Consequently, a final resolution of the case may not be reached until the mid 1980s or even later.

Besides the cost of such proceedings to both sides, an additional economic problem is created because such lengthy hearings may encourage firms to interpret the antitrust laws loosely under the assumption that even if a suit is initiated, a final verdict will take so long that significant benefits may be obtained in the meantime. Moreover, the firm might win the case. Unfortunately, an easy solution to this problem—one that protects the rights of the defendant and allows for the collection of necessary factual material at reasonable cost—seems remote at the present time.

SUMMARY

1. This chapter discussed the major antitrust laws of the United States. These laws have their foundations in English common law and in economic theory, which indicates that monopolies may

---

41. "The FTC Turns Ma Bell Loose," *Newsweek*, April 21, 1980, pp. 73–74.

42. "How Bad Is Bigness?" *Newsweek*, January 22, 1979, p. 51–52.

43. See "Antitrust: The Methuselah Case," *Newsweek*, January 29, 1979, pp. 66, 69.

charge unnecessarily high prices and produce too little output from a social welfare point of view.

2. The Sherman Antitrust Act (1890) marked the first attempt by the U.S. government to regulate restrictive trade practices. Section 1 banned contracts or combinations in restraint of trade, and Section 2 outlawed monopolizing behavior. The act was vague, however, in indicating the specific acts that were illegal. In an attempt to reduce the inevitable enforcement problems, Congress passed the Clayton Act in 1914.

3. The Clayton Act specifically forbade, under certain circumstances, (1) price discrimination, (2) exclusive and tying contracts, (3) intercorporate stockholdings, and (4) interlocking directorates. *Price discrimination* is the practice of charging different buyers different prices for the same product or service. *Exclusive, or tying, contacts* are contracts that include an agreement that the purchaser of a commodity or a lessee will not buy from or deal with firms that compete with the selling firm. *Interlocking stockholdings* means the ownership by one corporation of the stock of a competing corporation. An *interlocking directorate* is a situation where one person serves on the boards of directors of two companies at the same time.

4. The Federal Trade Commission Act, also passed in 1914, established the Federal Trade Commission. Moreover, Section 5 of this law broadly prohibited "unfair methods of competition." In 1938 the Wheeler-Lea Act was passed. It extended Section 5 of the Federal Trade Commission Act to include a ban against deceptive trade practices.

5. The Robinson-Patman Act, enacted in 1936, strengthened Section 2 of the Clayton Act, which prohibited certain forms of price discrimination. This law was aimed particularly at large retail chain stores that were obtaining discounts in the form of brokerage fees from wholesalers.

6. Finally, the Celler-Kefauver Act (1950) strengthened Section 7 of the Clayton Act by declaring illegal the acquisition of the stock or assets of one corporation by another corporation if the effect was to lessen competition. This act also extended the Clayton Act so that it applied to vertical and conglomerate mergers as well as horizontal mergers.

7. A *horizontal merger* is a merger of two companies selling similar products. A *vertical merger* is the merger of two companies where one produces an input used by the other. A *conglomerate merger* is a merger of two companies with unrelated products.

8. Most of the antitrust cases brought to court are civil rather than criminal in nature. In general, violations of the Clayton Act and the Robinson-Patman Act are not crimes. However, violations of Sections 1 and 2 of the Sherman Act and of Section 3 of the Robinson-Patman Act are criminal offenses. In cases where convictions on criminal offenses are obtained, companies may be subject to fines of up to $1 million. Individuals who are responsible for or who participate in a criminal violation may be personally fined up to $100,000 and imprisoned up to three years.

9. Under the Sherman and Clayton acts the government is authorized to initiate civil cases to prevent antitrust violations. The courts have considerable leeway in the remedies they may impose in such cases. Many civil antitrust cases are settled by consent decrees, which state certain provisions agreed to by both the government and the defendant.

10. The Federal Trade Commission has the responsibility of enforcing the Federal Trade Commission Act ban against unfair methods of competition and deceptive trade practices. It also shares the responsibility of enforcing the Clayton Act with the Department of Justice. In cases brought by the FTC, if a settlement in the form of a cease and desist order is not reached, a formal hearing before an administrative law judge is held. The findings of this judge are subject to review by the FTC, and commission findings and orders may be reviewed by a federal court of appeals. Failure to comply with an FTC final order not under appeal makes a party subject to a civil penalty of $5,000 per day in violation.

11. Under the Sherman Act and the Clayton Act, private parties injured by a violation of these laws can recover three times the damages incurred, plus attorneys' fees. The treble damages provisions provide an incentive to obey the antitrust laws.

12. A major controversial issue throughout the history of antitrust court cases is that of monopoly versus monopolizing. Originally, the courts tended to follow the principle of the "rule of reason," which held that size alone is not illegal as long as a firm does not abuse its position. Judge Learned Hand reversed this trend in 1945 by stating that Congress "did not condone 'good trusts' and condemn 'bad' ones; it forbad all."

13. A second area of controversy historically has centered around mergers. Those in favor of a lenient merger policy believe that mergers tend to promote economic efficiency through economies of scale. Those favoring a strict merger policy believe that mergers lead to high prices and a lessening of competition. Since 1950 the Justice Department has usually challenged any horizontal merger in which the acquiring firm and the acquired firm each have 5 percent or more of the market for the product; 10 and 6 percent market shares, respectively, have been the typical cutoff points for questioning vertical mergers.

14. A third antitrust issue frequently heard in the courts is that of price fixing. In general, the courts have considered price fixing to be a per se violation of Section 1 of the Sherman Act. In recent years, however, the courts have relaxed their position on price fixing slightly.

15. By providing for patents, copyrights, and trademarks, Congress has allowed some restriction of competition.

16. Among several other current areas of controversy in the field of antitrust are price leadership, brand proliferation, full disclosure, advertising by professionals, monopolization, territorial restrictions, size of firms and economic efficiency, and lengthiness of the judicial process. All these issues illustrate the fact that antitrust policies and interpretations of antitrust laws frequently change.

IMPORTANT TERMS AND CONCEPTS

Criminal law	Interlocking
Law of torts	directorate
Contract law	Federal Trade
Antitrust laws	Commission Act
Common law	(1914)
Sherman Antitrust	Wheeler-Lea Act
Act (1890)	(1938)
Clayton Act (1914)	Robinson-Patman Act
Price discrimination	(1936)
Exclusive dealing	Celler-Kefauver Act
Tying agreement	(1950)
Interlocking	Horizontal merger
stockholdings	Vertical merger

Conglomerate merger	Structuralists
Consent decrees	Behavioralists
Cease and desist	Rule of reason
order	Price fixing
Treble damages	Patent
Monopolizing	Copyright
behavior	Trademark

QUESTIONS AND PROBLEMS

1. What are the main provisions of the Sherman Act? In what ways did the Clayton Act make the antitrust laws more specific?

2. What was the purpose of the Federal Trade Commission Act?

3. How did the Robinson-Patman Act extend the Clayton Act?

4. What is the issue in the "monopoly versus monopolizing" controversy? Explain.

5. What has been the attitude of the courts toward price fixing?

6. Discuss the policies of the Department of Justice regarding mergers. What are the provisions in the Celler-Kefauver Act regarding mergers?

7. What are treble damages? How may they be obtained in antitrust cases?

8. Pick one of the current antitrust issues mentioned in this chapter and discuss it thoroughly, using your own ideas as well as those presented in the text.

9. Have the antitrust laws generally been beneficial or harmful to the social welfare? How can these laws be improved? Explain.

UNCLE SAM V. IBM:
WHY?

One of the last actions of the Johnson administration, before leaving office in January 1969, was to file an antitrust complaint against the International Business Machines Corp. alleging monopolization of the general-purpose computer systems market. Now, 10 years later, the case is probably only half way towards completion, including an almost certain appeal to the Supreme Court. If the final verdict goes against IBM, the resulting triple-damage suits could easily run into the next century.

What, it may well be asked, is the point of all this? Is this the law gone wild, or is there some social purpose after all?

Source: Hendrik S. Houthakker, "Uncle Sam v. IBM: Why?" Wall Street Journal, February 5, 1979, p. 14.

Before trying to give an answer to these questions, I should reveal my own part in the case, so that readers may assess my objectivity or lack of it. I was a consultant and prospective witness on the government side from 1971 to 1977, when I had to withdraw because of a disagreement concerning my testimony. Most of my work for the government was directed towards an out-of-court settlement, but I also had some responsibility for the filing of the case in the first place. In early 1968, an antitrust division economist and I (then on the staff of the Council of Economic Advisors) drafted a list of priorities in antitrust enforcement, on which IBM was number one.

After all these years this judgment still appears to be defensible. There can be no serious doubt that IBM's share of the market was and is about 70%, well above the usual standards for monopoly. IBM's own internal statistics, compiled by IBM before the filing of the case, confirm that figure.

POINTS FOR DEBATE

We get on more debatable ground when we ask whether IBM's monopoly was merely the result of "skill, industry and foresight," or also of anticompetitive behavior. The government alleges that IBM engaged in predatory practices in the 1960s against other mainframe manufacturers and in the early 1970s against the manufacturers of peripheral equipment. IBM says that it was merely being competitive.

These legal matters have to be left to the courts. As an economist my concern is less with the legality of IBM's business practices, or even with its market share, than with its effect on the U.S. economy as a whole. From that point of view what matters is IBM's performance: the prices it charges, the output it produces, its contribution to new technology and efficiency generally. In these respects the computer industry's performance has been excellent, and as the dominant firm in the industry IBM must be given its share of the credit.

Along with the other firms, IBM has reduced its prices steadily, its production has grown by leaps and bounds and although IBM is by no means the only innovator in the computer industry, it has probably contributed in accordance with its market share. Of course it could be plausibly argued that the industry performance would have been even better if IBM had not had a monopoly. In fact, the main blot on IBM's performance is its accumulation of huge amounts of cash, which could have been used for new investment. However, in the real world perfection cannot be expected.

Here we encounter a major difficulty with the antitrust laws as currently interpreted. My lawyer friends (admittedly mostly on the government side) tell me that in law there is no such thing as a good monopolist. In other words, the monopolist's performance is irrelevant; all that matters is his market share and whether he got it

by legal means. This view is not without support from specialists in industrial organization, who usually argue from the structure-conduct-performance theory. This theory maintains, in essence, that if you know how many firms there are in an industry and what their market shares are, then you know how they will determine their prices and output, and hence how the industry will perform. It is partly on the basis of this theory, for instance, that the Antitrust Division is so obsessed about mergers regardless of their effect on competition, though populist aversion to bigness is also a factor.

Unfortunately the structure-conduct-performance theory does not agree too well with the facts. My own studies of price-output patterns by industry show that the best overall performance is found in the telephone industry, highly monopolized as it is. The primary metals industry (principally steel) has the worst performance, even though it consists of quite a few firms, none of which is truly dominant. One should not conclude that monopolistic industries necessarily perform better than industries with dispersed market shares, merely that the connection between structure and performance is too weak to be a sufficient basis for antitrust policy.

Where does that leave the IBM case? In a way the question is academic: The legal juggernaut, once set in motion, cannot be easily stopped. One of the few things that could stop it is a settlement, a possibility that must be considered remote. Intensive

discussions of the basis for a settlement were held in 1974 and 1975, but they never reached the stage of negotiation. IBM was willing to contemplate a very large divestiture, but not one that would reduce its share of the market at issue in the trial. The Justice Department was less interested in the size of the divestiture than in the future structure of the general-purpose computer-systems market.

Neither the government nor (presumably) IBM have been sympathetic to an injunctive or regulatory solution. In such a solution IBM would be enjoined from certain practices, for instance, discriminatory pricing or leasing rather than selling. Consistent with its general position on regulation, the Antitrust Division has considered injunctive relief too cumbersome to enforce, whereas IBM, one gathers, considers it too great an interference in its normal operations. In the settlement discussions the matter of injunctive relief never came up.

Ironically, regulation is precisely what has emerged. During the last six or eight years IBM has become considerably more circumspect in its dealings with competitors. Its two most formidable competitors, General Electric and RCA, left the field around 1970. The companies involved deny that their departure was attributable to an abuse of IBM's market power, but the government has evidence to the contrary.

In the early 1970s, IBM also inflicted severe punishment on its competitors in peripheral equipment, such as Telex and Memorex; unlike General Electric and RCA, these smaller companies have not been content to blame their losses on their own mistakes only.

Whatever IBM's responsibility for these developments may have been, more recently it has been on its best behavior. Thus it has shown remarkable forbearance to Amdahl, a company founded by an ex-IBM'er whose products resemble IBM's so closely that they can use the same software. If ever anyone twisted the lion's tail, it is Amdahl, yet it continues to flourish, as does Itel, which has adopted a similar strategy.

By its very length, therefore, the trial may be strengthening competition in the general-purpose systems market. Since both parties, and also the judge, have often deplored the length of the trial, they can hardly take credit for this unintended benefit. To be sure, these protestations cannot be taken at face value. IBM's tactics have generally been those of delay, as is natural in a firm that earns $8 million per day. The government's desire for a speedy resolution may be sincere, but the Antitrust Division is not organized for fast action.

Consequently, the trial is likely to go on and on, and the future of the industry is left in uncertainty. The all-important subject of relief will only be discussed when and if IBM has been found to have violated the antitrust laws. Even this preliminary determination is probably at least four years away.

WHAT OF THE FUTURE?

Let me nevertheless end with some thoughts on the future. It is widely recognized that IBM's tremendous resources in marketing, management and technology could be usefully deployed in related industries where it is not now operating, particularly communications. This would bring it into competition with AT&T, a firm whose potential is also not fully realized; in Bell Labs and Western Electric it has the capability to be an effective competitor in computers. Instead of pursuing separate monopoly actions against IBM and AT&T, the Justice Department should encourage them to compete with each other, thus realizing the benefits of the different technologies developed by these firms. A further integration of computer and communications technology is in any case inevitable.

As to the antitrust laws, the experience with IBM has led the administration and congressional leaders to consider changes that would shorten lawsuits by reducing the burden of proof on the Justice Department. This proposal raises the danger of even greater reliance on structural characteristics in the choice of antitrust targets. It would be more productive to introduce into the law criteria of economic performance, such as average increases and output, disposition of profits and attitude toward competitors. This would make antitrust policy a more effective tool of long-term economic policy.

QUESTIONS

1. What are the legal issues in the IBM case, according to this article?
2. What are the economic issues?
3. Why does Houthakker suggest that IBM is not a "bad" monopoly?
4. What suggestions does Houthakker have for improving the antitrust laws? Are they practical? Explain.

C H A P T E R 27

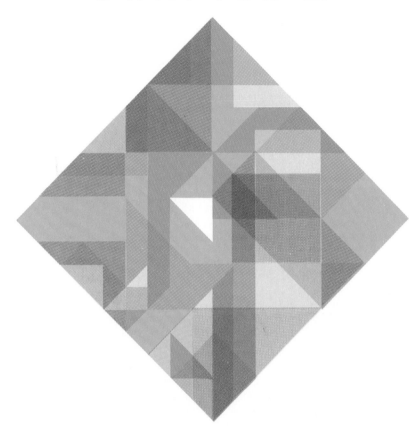

REGULATION
AND
EXTERNALITIES

CUB SCOUTS, GOOD WILL, AND THE POSTAL SERVICE

A lot of nonprofit civic organizations may someday list the members of Cub Scout Den #5 of Coram, New York, as unsung heroes in a judicial battle that attempted to put a 1934 government regulation back in its proper place. It seems that the Cubs hand-delivered their den's 1980 Christmas greetings to friends and supporters by placing them, without postage stamps, in the recipients' mailboxes. The Postal Service threatened to charge the Cub Scouts $38.25 in postage due and to fine them up to $76,500 for illegal use of mailboxes. Fortunately for the Scouts, the postmaster general intervened and settled for sending them a letter of reprimand.

Since 1934 it has been illegal to use private citizens' mailboxes for mailable material without postage. Thus the Cub Scouts were clearly in the wrong. However, a group of nonprofit organizations recently succeeded in getting a U.S. district court judge to rule that the postal regulation constitutes a cost to free expression that outweighs the potential loss of revenues to the Postal Service or losses the public might incur from mail fraud. The judge also stated that it is not financially feasible for many civic groups to pay postage for the distribution of fliers and other information.

Where did all of this lead? By 1981, the controversy found its way to the Supreme Court. Now, all of us buy our own mailboxes; they are not furnished by the government or its Postal Service. If the mailbox is a convenient way for us to receive nonpostal material, maybe we would rather have it be used that way. Nonethe-

less, in June 1981, the court decided that mailboxes would remain the exclusive domain of the postal service.

The so-called "mailbox rule" is one of the less pressing issues in the field of government regulation—a field that covers pollution control, job safety standards, transportation safety and fares, the pricing of public utilities, and many other economic questions that affect society. In this chapter we will survey the nature, extent, and problems of government regulation.

Source: This story is based on an editorial, "Mailbox Order," *Wall Street Journal*, January 14, 1981, p. 24.

C H A P T E R 27

REGULATION
AND
EXTERNALITIES

WHAT THIS CHAPTER IS ABOUT

THE CASE FOR REGULATION
Monopoly Power
Externalities and Social Benefits and Costs
THE GOAL OF REGULATION
REGULATORY COMMISSIONS
REGULATORY PROBLEMS
HOW MUCH REGULATION?

In this chapter we will continue to examine the relationship between government and private enterprise, concentrating on the regulation of business by government. This topic is not without controversy. In fact, there is no shortage of people who argue that we should do away with government regulation of business entirely. Others prefer to increase it.

This chapter deals with the goal of government regulation of business, explains the economic justification for intervention, and cites some of the problems that have occurred as a result of such intervention. As we will see, the regulatory picture is not completely clear.

THE CASE FOR REGULATION

Two economic justifications are frequently given for government regulation of business— monopoly power□ and the presence of externalities.□ In both cases a market free of government intervention may not achieve a socially optimal allocation of scarce resources.

36
38

MONOPOLY POWER

One of the major objectives of government regulation is the control of monopoly power. This type of regulation has occurred in the public utility, trucking, airline, railroad, and other similar industries. The regulation of prices charged by natural monopolies□ was discussed in Chapter 21. The theory behind such regulation will be reviewed here.

483

Natural Monopolies A fundamental goal of the federal antitrust laws is to promote competition among firms. In some industries, however, perfect competition◻ would result in higher unit costs of production. In these industries, large economies of scale◻ are present so that the long-run average cost curve of a firm is downward sloping. In other words, the unit cost of production falls as output expands.

A **natural monopoly** exists when economies of scale are so large that the cheapest (least costly) way for the industry output to be obtained is to have it produced by one firm. In this case the market demand curve intersects the long-run average cost curve◻ for a firm at a point where it is still falling, as shown in Figure 27–1. If the firm were not regulated, it would choose to produce where marginal revenue is equal to marginal cost, at Q^*_{ur}, and would charge a price equal to P^*_{ur}. Economic profit equal to

$$(P^*_{ur} - LAC^*_{ur}) \times Q^*_{ur}$$

would then be obtained.

Fair-Return Pricing In exchange for allowing the existence of natural monopolies, governments usually demand the right to regulate their prices. As explained in Chapter 21, government agencies frequently attempt to follow the principle of *fair-return pricing*◻—establishing a ceiling price at the point where the firm will earn a normal or average profit,◻ but nothing more. At such a point price is equal to average cost.

In Figure 27–2 the regulated price and corresponding level of output are P^*_r and Q^*_r, respectively. The ceiling price is set where the long-run average cost curve intersects the demand curve, so that the $P = LAC$ (normal profit) objective is met.

Under these circumstances the firm's marginal revenue◻ is equal to the ceiling price, P^*_r, until Q^*_r is reached. Beyond that point the firm would have to lower its price to sell a larger quantity, and the firm's original mar-

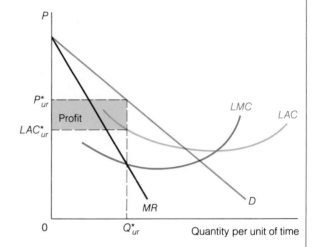

FIGURE 27–1 An Unregulated Natural Monopoly

An unregulated monopoly will maximize profit in the long run by producing where long-run marginal cost (LMC) is equal to marginal revenue (MR), as long as the firm is earning at least a normal profit—price is at least as great as long-run average cost (LAC). In this case, the firm will charge a price equal to P^*_{ur} and receive an economic profit equal to $(P^*_{ur} - LAC^*_{ur}) \times Q^*_{ur}$.

ginal revenue curve would apply. Consequently, with the imposition of the ceiling price, the firm will maximize profit◻ by producing a level of output equal to Q^*_r. At this level it will come as close as possible to equating marginal revenue and marginal cost. Theoretically, as a result of the price ceiling, society is able to obtain a higher level of output at a lower cost, and economic profits are zero.

In the case of a natural monopoly, government authorities frequently do not attempt to achieve an efficient allocation of resources as dictated by the price-equals-marginal-cost guideline. This point occurs where the demand curve intersects the marginal cost curve. As shown in Figure 27–2, in the case of natural monopolies, marginal cost◻ is usually below average cost here. Such a pricing policy would force the firm to take an economic loss or to go out of business, because price would be less than average cost. However, a regulatory agency sometimes follows a marginal cost pricing policy for certain incremental units

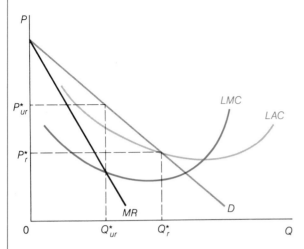

FIGURE 27–2   Price Regulation of a Monopoly

The unregulated price and quantity produced are equal to P^*_{ur} and Q^*_{ur}, respectively. If a ceiling price is now established, at P^*_r, so that only a normal profit is received (price is equal to long-run average cost or LAC), a firm will increase the quantity produced to Q^*_r. Given the ceiling price of P^*_r, The firm will maximize profit at Q^*_r, since the firm's marginal revenue from another unit of output is equal to P^*_r until a horizontal line from P^*_r intersects the demand curve, D. After that point, the original demand and marginal revenue (MR) curves once again become applicable.

produced, such as for late-night telephone service.

EXTERNALITIES

Another primary reason for government intervention in the market for goods and services is the presence of externalities.

A good or service has an **externality** associated with it if it has a benefit or cost that accrues to people not engaged in a market transaction involving the good.

(External benefits and costs are sometimes called third-party benefits and costs.)

For example, if an exclusive golf course were built on vacant land next to a residential area, the nearby homeowners would probably receive an external benefit in the form of an increase in the property value of their houses. On the other hand, the building of a slaughterhouse in the neighborhood would probably impose some external costs on nearby homeowners. However, the addition of the new firm might also yield external benefits in the form of increased employment and business activity.

Social Benefits and Costs   When externalities are associated with a product or service, the market transactions involving it may not totally reflect its social benefits□ or social costs.□ For example, if the owners of a golf course do not purchase the land surrounding the course, they will not receive any benefit from the increase in the value of nearby property once the course is built. On the other hand, if the owners of a factory are not forced to clean up any pollutants discharged by the firm, the firm has imposed a cost on society that the firm itself does not have to bear.

The **social benefit** of a product or service is the benefit received by those who purchase the product or service plus any external benefit associated with it.

The **social cost** of a product or service is equal to the private cost, both explicit and implicit, incurred by the firm that produces it plus any external costs imposed on society.

Socially Optimal Production   Chapter 20 indicated that when a purely competitive firm produces at the point where the price of the good or service is equal to the firm's marginal cost of production, it is using resources in a socially optimal manner—in a way that will maximize the well-being of society. Producing at such a level is an optimal allocation of resources because at this point marginal social benefit is equal to marginal social cost. However, this proposition is true only when no externalities are connected with the good.

If external benefits are connected with a

good, such as a golf course, then the price paid by the users of the good does not reflect all the benefits of the product received by society. For example, the users of the golf course would certainly not wish to pay a golf fee that reflected the increase in surrounding property values—unless the users also owned the nearby property.

Likewise, if external costs are connected with a good or service, the firm's private cost of producing or selling the commodity does not reflect the entire social cost of it. Thus, if private firms do not pay to eliminate the pollution they generate, the private costs of these firms understate the true social cost of producing the commodity.

If the price of a good does not reflect its marginal social benefit and if the marginal cost of a good does not reflect its marginal social cost, then producing the good up to the point where price is equal to marginal cost will no longer assure a socially optimal allocation of resources. Such a situation is one in which a case can be made for government intervention in the market.

WORKABLE REGULATION

◆

To make economic sense, government regulation must achieve a better allocation of the resources of society with respect to the regulated industries than the industries would have accomplished by themselves. Furthermore, this regulation must be done in such a manner that its social cost is not greater than the social benefits it generates.

As mentioned earlier, the goal of government regulation of business is to promote an allocation of resources that will maximize the well-being of society. In order to achieve this goal, the production of all goods and services must continue until their marginal social benefit is equal to their marginal social cost.

One way the government attempts to achieve a close approximation to this goal is by regulating the prices charged by monopoly, or near-monopoly, firms. A second way it works toward this goal is by passing laws to internalize external costs. In other words, the government tries to make the firm's marginal cost of production equal to the marginal social cost of the firm's output.

Specifying the exact nature of these regulations and enforcing them often become the tasks of regulatory commissions. The fact that many regulatory commissions have existed for more than thirty years may be an indication that people generally believe that these bodies are accomplishing their goals or, at the least, that society is better off with the commissions than without them. Nevertheless, some recognizable problems have arisen out of the policies of the commissions. In the next section of the chapter we will examine the nature and scope of the regulatory agencies, along with some of the problems surrounding their operations.

THE REGULATORY COMMISSIONS

The federal regulatory commissions were created by acts of Congress. In general, they have both quasi-legislative and quasi-judicial powers. These bodies have quasi-legislative powers in that they can specify certain rules and regulations within broad legislative guidelines established by Congress. They also have quasi-judicial powers in that they are frequently authorized to hold hearings to determine whether their rules and regulations are being followed in specific cases and to set fines or other penalties. The courts, however, can overturn commission decisions thought to be unjust or unconstitutional. (Regulatory commissions also exist at the local and state levels, where they frequently deal with licensing, regulation of intrastate public utilities, and state and local health and safety matters.) Although the initials of the federal regulatory commissions cover nearly the entire alphabet, we will examine only a few of the more well-known ones here.[1]

The Civil Aeronautics Board The Civil Aeronautics Authority was created by the **Civil Aeronautics Authority Act (1938).** It consisted of five members, appointed by the president with the advice and consent of the Senate for six-year staggered terms. The Air Safety Board was also established within the Authority. In 1940 the Air Safety Board and the Civil Aeronautics Authority were combined into the Civil Aeronautics Board (CAB) which is responsible for awarding air routes, setting rates, and handling some functions pertaining to safety and accident prevention.

The **Airline Deregulation Act (1978)** drastically changed the nature and scope of the Civil Aeronautics Board. Previously, the board had considered its primary responsibility to be keeping all certified airlines profitable. However, the 1978 act provides for the removal of government protection of the airlines. In fact, the CAB will lose its route and fare control powers completely by 1983 and will later be abolished.[2]

The Environmental Protection Agency Created in 1970, the Environmental Protection Agency (EPA) is charged with establishing and enforcing environmental standards for air, water, solid wastes, pesticides, radiation, and noise. The standards set by the EPA or, in some cases, the EPA together with the states, have the force of law.

The Federal Communications Commission Created by the **Federal Communications Act (1934)**, the Federal Communications Commission (FCC) is composed of seven members, appointed by the president with the advice and consent of the Senate, for seven-year staggered terms. The commission has regulatory power over telephone and telegraph communication, which was formerly held by the Interstate Commerce Commission. The FCC also has the power to license and regulate radio and television stations.

In early 1980, in a dramatic illustration of its authority, the Federal Communications Commission revoked the license of a Boston television station owned by RKO, Inc., charging the company with misconduct so serious that it could not be trusted as a broadcaster. RKO and its parent company, General Tire and Rubber, have appealed the decision in the courts. If it stands, RKO could lose $400 million.[3]

The Federal Power Commission The Federal Power Commission (FPC) in its present form was created by the **Water Power Act (1930).** It consists of five members, who serve five-year staggered terms. The FPC regulates the interstate sale of natural gas, authorizes natural gas imports, regulates the rates of public utilities selling electricity wholesale in interstate commerce, issues licenses for construction and operation of hydroelectric projects on lands and waters subject to federal jurisdiction, and regulates the merger of public utilities producing electricity.

The Federal Trade Commission Created by the **Federal Trade Commission Act (1914),** the Federal Trade Commission (FTC) consists of five members appointed by the president, with the advice and consent of the Senate, to serve seven-year staggered terms. The FTC enforces the provisions of the Clayton Act□ that define and prohibit certain unlawful trade actions. When it finds such violations, it has the power to issue cease and desist orders□ subject

---

1. Three additional sources for information on the federal regulatory agencies are Robert E. Cushman, *The Independent Regulatory Commissions* (New York: Octagon Books, 1972); H. H. Liebhafsky, *American Government and Business* (New York: Wiley, 1971); and William Ruder and Raymond Nathan, *The Businessman's Guide to Washington* (New York: Macmillan, 1975).

2. "Carter Signs Airline-Deregulation Law, CAB Will Grant Routes More Generously," *Wall Street Journal*, October 25, 1978, pp. 2, 13.

3. "The FCC's Toughest Crackdown," *Newsweek*, February 4, 1980., p. 65.

to peer review. It also has the power to investigate business misconduct at the direction of the president or Congress and to gather information on business practices.

In 1975 the **Magnuson-Moss Act** gave the Federal Trade Commission broad powers to establish rules restricting unfair business practices in entire industries. In the late 1970s and early 1980s, however, the FTC has been criticized for being overzealous. The issue of advertising on children's television programs is a case in point. The FTC wanted to regulate television commercials for snacks and presweetened cereals during children's prime viewing hours. It argued that parents have little control over the breakfast foods their children eat and that the ads influenced the youngsters to eat foods that were not as healthy for them as were other foods.[4] The FTC dropped its probe of such commercials in the fall of 1981.

The Food and Drug Administration Primarily responsible for enforcing the **Food, Drug, and Cosmetic Act (1938)** and its subsequent amendments, the Food and Drug Administration (FDA) regulates the purity, safety, and labeling of foods, drugs, cosmetics, and therapeutic devices that are shipped in interstate commerce or imported. A 1958 amendment to the act extended the power of the FDA to the realm of packaging materials.

The Interstate Commerce Commission The Interstate Commerce Commission (ICC) was established by the Interstate Commerce Act (1887). Through this act and through later legislation, it has regulatory power, including the power to establish rates, over the railroads, interstate trucking, and domestic water carriers. The commission consists of eleven members who serve staggered seven-year terms.

In the early 1980s the primary issue before the ICC is the deregulation of the trucking and the railroad industries. This process began with the Railroad Revitalization and Regulatory Reform Act (1976), which promised $1.6 billion in federal aid to the railroads until regulatory reforms were developed that would make them more profitable.[5]

The National Highway Traffic Safety Administration The National Highway Traffic Safety Administration (NHTSA) was created by the Highway Safety Act of 1970. The NHTSA imposes more than thirty motor vehicle safety performance standards for parts such as tires, brakes, and seat belts. It also sponsors research and publishes information relating to motor vehicle safety and costs. (A forerunner of the NHTSA, the National Highway Safety Agency, was established in 1966. However, this agency was abolished when the NHTSA was established.)

The Occupational Safety and Health Administration The **Occupational Safety and Health Act (1970)** is administered by the Occupational Safety and Health Administration (OSHA). The act was the most comprehensive legislation ever enacted to protect U.S. workers from on-the-job health and safety hazards.

OSHA is responsible for developing and setting standards in all aspects of occupational safety and health and for encouraging compliance through education and training programs. It is also charged with inspecting workplaces to ensure employer cooperation. Disputes over employer compliance are heard by the Occupational Safety and Health Review Commission, an independent agency.

The Securities and Exchange Commission Established by the **Securities Exchange Act (1934),** the Securities and Exchange Commission (SEC) is responsible for overseeing nearly all interstate sales of securities to the public. It also regulates the national securities exchanges, such as the New York Stock Ex-

---

4. "Regulating the FTC," *Newsweek*, October 15, 1979, pp. 104, 107.

5. "What Rate Freedom Will Mean to the Railrods," *Business Week*, May 14, 1979, pp. 55–56.

change. Companies whose securities are listed on an exchange must provide periodic reports to the SEC. The commission consists of five members who serve five-year staggered terms.

PERVERSE INCENTIVES AND REGULATORY FAILURES

The policy and rate decisions made by the regulatory commissions have been criticized by the public and by the regulated businesses. Some of these criticisms are caused by the commissions' conflicting public policies.

For example, in many cases regulations increase the costs of doing business and, consequently, promote inflation. In other instances they place undue hardship on small firms, thereby raising the possibility of a reduction in the competitiveness of an industry. Several of these problem areas are considered here.

Trucking Industry In the late 1970s the Interstate Commerce Commission came under fire for its regulation of interstate trucking. Independent truckers argued that the rates they were allowed to charge the regulated carriers for subcontracts had fallen behind costs because of inflation. They also argued that they were discriminated against in regard to obtaining certificates of authority, without which they could not haul loads across state lines. They also found other rules unreasonable. For example, one regulation allowed independents to haul unshelled peanuts, but not roasted ones, across state lines.

According to *Newsweek*, in 1978, "even the ICC agrees that perhaps a third of the 80,-000 independent interstate truckers now on the road (out of 250,000 to 275,000 heavy-duty, long-haul trucks in service) may go out of business before the end of this year."[6]

The **Motor Carrier Act**, signed on July 1, 1980, addressed many of these problems. It provided for easier entry into the trucking in-

dustry, and it gave motor carriers greater freedom in setting their rates. Moreover, it declared that:

Not later than 180 days after the date of enactment of this subsection the [Interstate Commerce] Commission shall—

(A) eliminate gateway restrictions and circuitous route limitations imposed upon motor common carriers of property; and
(B) implement by regulation, procedures to process expeditiously applications of individual motor carriers of property seeking removal of restrictions in order to—

(i) reasonably broaden the categories of property authorized by the carrier's certificate or permit;
(ii) authorize transportation or service to intermediate points on the carrier's routes;
(iii) provide round-trip authority where only one-way authority exists;
(iv) eliminate unreasonable or excessively narrow territorial limitations; or
(v) eliminate any other unreasonable restriction that the Commission deems to be wasteful of fuel, inefficient, or contrary to the public interest.[7]

Railroads and Coal The Interstate Commerce Commission has also been criticized for allowing the railroads huge rate increases for hauling coal after public utilities converted to the usage of coal from oil or natural gas. In one case, City Public Service Board, a public utility in San Antonio, was given an estimate in 1973 by Burlington Northern Railroad of a transportation cost of $7.90 per ton for hauling coal from Wyoming. A rate of $10.93 was authorized by the ICC in October 1976. By December 1978 the allowable rate had risen to $12.42. In that month the railroad was granted a rate increase to $17.01. By July of 1979 the rate had risen to $18.43, with further increases imminent.[8]

6. "The Joy of Truckin'," *Newsweek*, February 20, 1978, p. 68.

7. "Motor Carrier Act of 1980," *United States Statutes at Large*, vol. 94 (Washington, D.C.: Government Printing Office, 1981), pp. 796–797.

8. "Rail Rates Slow a Shift to Coal," *Business Week*, July 23, 1979, pp. 171–172.

According to John M. Sullivan, Federal Railroad Administrator, these rate increases are necessary to enable the railroads to earn a reasonable return. However, the coal rate increases are much greater than the rate increases granted railroads for transporting other products. Moreover, the railroad involved in this dispute allegedly has spent more time and money than any other railroad in fighting the building of coal slurry pipelines.[9] The Department of Energy, which is promoting conversion to coal, has backed San Antonio in appealing the ICC's decisions.

In the fall of 1980 Congress passed a railroad deregulation bill, the **Rail Act (1980).** This act states that railroads are free to set their own prices, as long as they do not exceed their variable costs□ by 160 percent. In 1984 this limit will rise to 180 percent. However, the bill also contains a provision directed specifically at the coal-hauling problems of San Antonio. The long-run impact of this measure remains to be seen.[10]

Petroleum Industry   The two-tier pricing system set up for domestic crude oil in the mid 1970s resulted in some "disappearing" oil. The system set the price of crude oil from wells established before May 1973 ("old oil") at around $5 per barrel, while "new oil" could be sold for as much as $12 a barrel. The system was set up to encourage oil companies to develop new wells while moderating the effects of these price incentives on the consumer.

The result? According to one estimate, almost 40 million barrels of low-cost oil disappeared, presumably to emerge later as new oil at the higher price.[11] Moreover, in March 1979, five oil resellers and two oil companies were indicted on charges of obtaining as much as $4 million in illegal profits by selling old oil as new oil. One person pleaded guilty in connection with the charges.[12]

In spring 1981 President Reagan removed the price controls on domestically produced crude oil. Partly as a result of the increased quantities of oil supplied and partly because of a decline in consumption—both factors the effects of higher prices for energy products—it appeared in early summer 1981 that an oil glut (a surplus of oil) had developed.

Motor Vehicle Regulation: Chrysler's Downfall?   According to Chrysler Corporation, a large part of the trouble in which the company found itself in 1979 was the direct result of government regulations. The company has argued that because it must spread the cost of meeting fuel-economy and emissions-control standards over fewer cars than can General Motors, it has to bear an unfair burden. Chrysler says that it costs the company $640 per car to comply with these standards, while the cost per car for GM is only $340.[13] Moreover, Chrysler estimated that it would have to spend $1 billion "extra" in 1979 and 1980 to comply with government regulations.[14]

The question thus becomes: Are cars with greater fuel economy and lower emissions standards to be obtained at a cost of reducing the competitiveness in the auto industry? Furthermore, the cost of complying with government regulation is reflected in new car prices, which fuel inflation. In fact, one estimate is that the cost of production per car increased by $800 from 1970 to 1976 as a result of safety and emission controls. In 1976 it was also estimated that the combined fuel economy and

---

9. Ibid.

10. See "Rail Bill Approved; On to Carter," *San Antonio Express*, October 2, 1980, p. 3–A; and "Rail Act Cited as Costly Legislation for Texas Utilities," *San Antonio Express*, October 3, 1980, p. 9–A.

11. "'Lost' Regulated Oil Is Back at Twice the Price," *San Antonio Express-News*, June 26, 1977, p. 10–A.

12. "Oil: The Two-Tier Scam," *Newsweek*, March 19, 1979, p. 82.

13. "Can Chrysler Be Saved?" *Newsweek*, August 13, 1979, p. 53.

14. "Is Chrysler the Prototype?" *Business Week*, August 20, 1979, p. 103.

emission standards could add an additional $300 to the cost of producing a car by 1980.[15]

HUD and Adobe   For centuries, Indians in the Southwest have been building houses out of soil and water. Historically, these adobe homes have been prized for their durability and fuel efficiency. In fact, some adobe houses have reportedly been standing for seven hundred years.[16]

Nevertheless, the Department of Housing and Urban Development required that additional insulation be placed in adobe houses. Government officials also specified that waterproof additives be placed in the adobe. In addition, HUD officials are upset that there is no standard adobe brick. And to top it off, federal contractors are obliged by law to pay prevailing wages on government jobs. This requirement causes problems because the government has classified adobe workers as masons or bricklayers, which are considered skilled laborers. However, builders argue that the main requirement for adobe workers is that they be strong rather than skilled.[17]

The upshot of all these regulations is that government financed adobe housing is almost prohibitively expensive. Astrid Trauth of HUD's Office of Indian Programs comments:

It's very difficult for me to understand why the Indians have ancient Pueblo structures that are comfortable in the winter and summer, yet the federal government can't do it. . . . I don't think anybody is the bad guy. Adobe is just a traditional building material that has run up against a modern, technological standards-oriented society.[18]

In the next section we will examine the issue of how much government regulation of business is useful to society.

15. "Detroit Must Retool Its Old Success Formula," *Business Week*, March 8, 1976, p. 76.

16. "Adobe Is Adorable, But Today's Pueblos Can't Build with It," *Wall Street Journal*, February 4, 1980, pp. 1, 25.

17. Ibid.

18. Ibid., p. 25.

HOW MUCH REGULATION?

It is difficult to calculate the entire cost, including the cost to both business and government, of government regulation. Murray L. Weidenbaum, chairman of the Council of Economic Advisors in the Reagan administration, stated that the annual expenditures of "major regulatory agencies shot up from $2 billion in fiscal 1974 to $3.8 billion in fiscal 1978."[19] Weidenbaum estimated that the total annual cost of government regulation was around $103 billion in 1979. However, this figure was not obtained in a precise manner; Weidenbaum merely multiplied the total budget figure for all the regulatory agencies by twenty.[20]

During the late 1970s and early 1980s both President Carter and President Reagan and Congress were pushing the regulatory agencies to be more conscious of the relative costs and benefits of their rules and regulations and, in fact, to justify new regulations by indicating that their benefits would be greater than their costs. Perhaps as a result of such pressure, the Occupational Safety and Health Administration has repealed 1,100 of its more than 10,000 rules.[21]

According to the general economic decision rule regarding the production of goods and services so as to maximize social welfare, government regulation should be used until the marginal social benefit of further regulation is just equal to its marginal social cost. While theoretically this principle is sound, translating it into dollars and cents is frequently difficult. The problem of estimating long-term social benefits is particularly acute. For example, what is the value of one more year

19. "Government Intervention," *Business Week*, April 4, 1977, p. 47.

20. "What Price Regulation?" *Newsweek*, March 19, 1979, p. 82.

21. "The Regulation Mess," *Newsweek*, June 12, 1978, p. 86.

of life? We can speak of the earning power of an individual, but few would argue that this sum adequately measures the value of a life.

Nevertheless, regulatory agencies are attempting more frequently to estimate the benefits and costs associated with their proposed rules. In 1978 the Carter administration established the Regulatory Analysis Review Group for the purpose of analyzing the cost of regulation. In addition, the Business Roundtable, an organization of chief executives of major corporations, in 1979 completed a study that represented a pioneering effort to apply rigorous auditing standards to cost estimates of government regulation borne by forty-eight manufacturing companies. However, even the authors of this study admitted that many indirect costs, such as loss of productivity, construction delays, and misallocation of resources, were omitted.[22]

As inflation continues to persist, we expect more and more pressure to be exerted on agencies to justify their regulations in accordance with the economic decision rule stated above. Perhaps such an accounting has been long overdue.

SUMMARY

1. This chapter examined the case for government regulation of business. Two general justifications are frequently cited for government intervention in the marketplace: monopoly power and the existence of externalities.

2. A natural monopoly exists in an industry when economies of scale are present in such magnitudes that the lowest per unit production cost is obtained when one firm produces the entire industry output. The government usually regulates natural monopolies through the use of fair-return pricing. A fair-return price allows a firm to make a normal return but no more. This price occurs where the demand curve for a product intersects the firm's average cost curve, so that price is equal to average cost.

3. A good or service has an externality associated with it if it has a benefit or cost that accrues to people who do not engage in market transactions involving the good. If externalities are present, there is likely to be a divergence between social benefits and costs and private benefits and costs.

4. The social benefit of product or service includes the benefits received by those who purchase it plus any external benefits associated with it. Likewise, the social cost of a product or service is equal to the private cost, both explicit and implicit, incurred by the firm that produces it plus any external costs that are imposed on society.

5. The level of production of any good that will maximize the well-being of society is where the marginal social benefit of the good is equal to its marginal social cost. However, when externalities are present, there is no guarantee that the private sector will produce that level of output, even if a firm is producing where the price of a good is equal to the firm's marginal cost associated with it. In such circumstances, government intervention in a free enterprise system may increase social welfare.

6. To make economic sense, government regulation must achieve a better allocation of the resources of society than private enterprise would have achieved by itself. Furthermore, this regulation must be done in such a manner that its cost is not greater than the benefits it generates.

7. Governments attempt to achieve a socially optimal level of output through regulation of private industry in two basic ways. In the case of a natural monopoly, a ceiling price is established for the product. When external costs are present, an attempt is made through laws to internalize the external costs and thereby make private costs and social costs equal.

8. Specifying the exact nature of regulations and enforcing them often becomes the task of one or more federal regulatory commissions. However, many regulatory agencies exist at the state and local levels of government as well.

9. Regulators are being increasingly pressured to justify their rules in terms of benefits and costs.

---

22. "A Start at Auditing the Cost of Regulation," *Business Week*, March 26, 1979, pp. 30, 34.

IMPORTANT TERMS AND CONCEPTS

Civil Aeronautics
  Board
Environmental
  Protection Agency
Federal
  Communications
  Commission
Federal Power
  Commission
Federal Trade
  Commission
Food and Drug
  Administration
Interstate Commerce
  Commission
National Highway
  Traffic Safety
  Administration
Occupational Safety
  and Health
  Administration

Securities and
  Exchange
  Commission
Natural Monopoly
Externality
Social Benefit
Social Cost
Airline Deregulation
  Act of 1978
Motor Carrier Act of
  1980
Rail Act of 1980

QUESTIONS AND PROBLEMS

1. What economic justifications are given for government regulation? Explain how government intervention in the market may increase social welfare.

2. Why may social benefits and costs differ from private benefits and costs? Explain.

3. How is the ceiling price set, at least theoretically, for a regulated monopoly?

4. Describe the duties of these regulatory commissions:
   a. Environmental Protection Agency
   b. Federal Trade Commission
   c. Food and Drug Administration
   d. Interstate Commerce Commission
   e. Occupational Safety and Health Administration

5. What is the economic principle that determines the optimal level of production (from a social welfare standpoint) of any product or service? Explain why following this decision rule would maximize social welfare with respect to the production of a good.

6. Why may policy conflicts and other problems develop as a result of government regulation? Give an example.

7. How far should government regulation extend? For example, is it the proper role of government to insist that cars have seat belts or to outlaw the sale of food containing saccharin? Defend your position.

8. Does it make economic sense to ask regulators to calculate the benefits and costs of proposed regulations? Are there any possible pitfalls connected with this approach? Explain.

9. Define *natural monopoly* and *externality*.

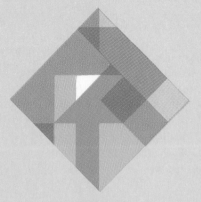

WHY WE NEED A REGULATORY BUDGET

Statutes establishing regulatory programs generally represent ad hoc decisions made in response to particular social, economic, or policy concerns. The regulations mandated by such statutes constitute separate regulatory programs, administered by different departments, bureaus, and agencies—120 by the latest tally.

The obvious flaw in this pattern is the absence of an overview. There is no government-wide mechanism for assessing the cumulative impact of regulation, for setting regulatory priorities, and making difficult trade-offs. The inevitable results, particularly with

Source: Juanita M. Kreps, "Why We Need a Regulatory Budget," *Business Week*, July 31, 1978, p. 14.

the relative autonomy of independent agencies, are lack of overall management and coordination, lack of any systematic evaluation of total costs and benefits, and lack of information about a type of government action that may well have macroeconomic consequences.

Better understanding and effective management of the sprawling regulatory process are plainly needed. An important first step was President Carter's executive order on improving regulatory practices.

SOMEONE ALWAYS PAYS.

To build on this momentum, it will also be important to develop better

understanding of the total benefits and costs. The suggestion that businesses internalize more of the "social costs" of their operations implies to some that costs are absorbed, not paid. But these costs are obviously paid—by all of us. Accordingly, for each federal regulation it is essential to ask: What does it cost? What benefits are we buying? Do these costs and benefits accurately reflect our priorities? Is there a way to achieve the same benefits at lower cost?

Typically, the dollar expenditures that regulations force businesses to make are some multiple of the budgets of the regulatory agencies. Perhaps even more significant are the hidden costs reflected in higher consumer prices, job dislocation, etc. In part, because costs are difficult to measure, we seldom have a good idea of their magnitude.

We are also poorly informed about benefits. Many involve health or safety. Others advance important policy objectives. But typically, we make no systematic attempt to assess benefits in part because most are not readily translatable into dollars. With overextended resources and demanding agendas, most agencies have little time for evaluating the efficacy of their regulatory programs. This lack of information on benefits increases the difficulty of making rational choices and setting priorities among a multitude of social goals. How, for example, do we allocate resources when facing multiple objectives—preventing a pension plan from failing, reducing a long-term cancer risk, preventing discriminatory hiring?

If we are to make rational management, regulatory, and legislative decisions, we must improve our understanding of approximate costs and benefits. If that is to be more than a spasmodic endeavor, we must create an institutional mechanism to force systematic analysis. As a start, we at the Commerce Dept. are seeking to develop a framework for assessing the costs of regulations, individually and collectively, and for comparing the results with alternative kinds of public expenditure. We are trying to devise a "regulatory budget."

A regulatory budget would analyze all federal regulatory activities and their costs. As a specific example, take effluent guidelines for point-source pollution. The budget for this program would contain:

• A compilation of the direct outlays of the regulatory agency administering the requirement. Taken from the appropriate federal budgetary line items, this cost assessment would include expenditures for administration, evaluation, and enforcement.
• An estimate of the associated indirect federal costs. If, for instance, federal grants under the Local Public Works program were used for a construction project designed to achieve compliance with an effluent guideline, the costs of such grants would be encompassed in the budget.
• Compliance costs for the private sector. These costs, which would be organized by industry and by regulatory areas, would cover capital expenditures, related overhead, reporting, and other associated business costs. The budget would then present the total of these three types of costs.

A regulatory budget would not be the complete answer. It would not cover indirect private sector costs, such as opportunity costs, diminished technological innovation, decreased international competitiveness, unemployment, etc. Notwithstanding their obvious importance, it would not attempt to measure benefits or assess how they offset or reduce costs.

THE REWARDS.

Such a budget will take time to develop. And we must assure that the regulatory budget itself is cost-effective. The case for the budget would be less than compelling if it were to cost more than the savings it effects.

Nonetheless, a regulatory budget could have impressive payoffs. It could provide an overview of the direct federal and private costs by regulatory objective, show the allocation of regulatory costs by regulatory objective, and estimate the costs of regulation by sectors of the economy. A regulatory budget would create a permanent mechansim through which public decision-makers could analyze the costs, both individual and cumulative, of federal regulation. Such analysis would facilitate better evaluation of regulatory programs and the setting of regulatory priorities.

QUESTIONS

1. According to Kreps, what are some of the current problems connected with government regulatory programs?
2. Explain what Kreps means when she says: "The suggestion that businesses internalize more of the 'social costs' of their operations implies to some that costs are absorbed, not paid. But these costs are obviously paid—by all of us."
3. What problems are encountered in attempts to measure the benefits of regulatory measures?
4. What items does Kreps propose to include in a regulatory budget?
5. What does Kreps mean when she states that a regulatory budget must be cost-effective?

C H A P T E R 28

PUBLIC
SECTOR
MICROECONOMICS

PERSPECTIVE

AIR
POLLUTION
CONTROL COSTS
AND BENEFITS

JOHNNY: *Boy, the smog was thick in Los Angeles today.
I hope no one had a cardiac arrest waiting in
line to get tickets to the show. It was sure
smoggy out there!*

AUDIENCE (in   *How smoggy was it?*
fractured unison):

JOHNNY: *It was so smoggy, that I saw a robin wearing a
miner's hat with a light on top just to make
sure he wouldn't lose his worm.*

*Smog, it turns out, is both a joke and a real public problem. In
Miami, several years ago, air pollution from automobile and bus
exhaust became so dangerous on the lower ramp of the International Airport that people with heart or lung ailments were advised
not to leave the air terminal from that ramp. Their luggage had to
be carried to an upper ramp, where they could exit safely. At considerable expense, the airport authorities have since improved the
situation markedly by adding ventilating equipment.*

*Of course, in recent years government at all levels has taken
steps to reduce environmental pollution. The measures have generally involved the expenditure of both public and private funds.
Often, the private firms that have had to install pollution control
equipment have complained bitterly about the cost of such equipment and about the effect of cost increases on the prices that con-*

630

sumers must pay for goods and services. In some cases, these complaints are justified.

A White House study released in 1979 estimated that in the preceding year about $13.1 billion had been spent by both the public and private sectors on air pollution control. The savings in damages that would have occurred without the pollution control expenditures were estimated to be about $22 billion. Thus, from a social point of view, public and private investments in clean air appear to have been a bargain; their benefits far exceeded their cost.[1]

Of course, from the discussion in Chapter 27, it is clear that an economic activity such as pollution control involves external costs and benefits. Such externalities make both cost and benefit calculations somewhat difficult. Still, there are reasonable economic criteria for making the calculations and for choosing from among various public investment alternatives. This chapter surveys the procedures that relate to microeconomic decision making in the public sector.

1. "Economic Benefits of Air Pollution Curbs Exceed Compliance Cost, Council Asserts," *Wall Street Journal*, January 26, 1979, p. 16.

CHAPTER 28

PUBLIC
SECTOR
MICROECONOMICS

WHAT THIS CHAPTER IS ABOUT

PUBLIC GOODS VERSUS PRIVATE GOODS
NEED FOR GOVERNMENT INVOLVEMENT
OPTIMAL PUBLIC GOOD OUTPUT
Social Welfare Maximization
Mutually Exclusive Projects
Budget Constraints
PROBLEMS AND PITFALLS
Estimating Social Benefits and Costs
Social Rate of Discount
Cost of Cost-Benefit Studies
PUBLIC CHOICE AND THE FUTURE

In this chapter we will examine the microeconomic aspects of decisions involving public goods. By *microeconomic decisions* we mean answers to questions such as: What public goods should be produced? How much of a particular public good should be produced? For whom should public goods and services, such as fire and police protection, be provided?

Specifically, government bodies must reach decisions on issues such as: How much money should be spent on building and maintaining public roads this year? Should funds be allocated for a new mass transit system? Would a city, county, or other government body benefit by increasing the number of police officers or fire fighters? How should tax receipts be allocated among various projects such as national defense, elimination of poverty, and job training programs? The economic way of making such decisions is the focus of this chapter.

In contrast, *macroeconomic decisions* involve answers to questions such as: Should the general level of government spending or taxes be altered to promote full employment without inflation? Is the federal budget deficit too large? Thus macroeconomic public sector decisions are concerned with the overall size of government budgets and the corresponding levels of taxes and budget deficits.

PUBLIC GOODS VERSUS PRIVATE GOODS

◆

We examined the problem of externalities☐ in Chapter 27.

617

*A **public good** is a product or service whose benefits cannot be limited to those who directly pay for it.*

External benefits are benefits that accrue to parties who do not engage in a specific market transaction to obtain the good or service with which they are connected. For example, all citizens of the United States receive the benefits of federal government expenditures on national defense, whether or not they pay any taxes. Similarly, all ship navigators who can see the light of a lighthouse receive its benefits whether or not they pay a fee for its services.

*A **pure public good** is a product or service all of whose benefits have the property that they are nondivisible (cannot be broken up into individual units) and nonexclusive (impossible to limit to individuals who have paid for the good).*

Besides national defense, examples of pure or nearly pure public goods are clean air and police-type protection. (Although one firm or family may hire a security guard, the presence of the guard probably discourages crime at nearby locations as well.)

*the **Mixed public goods** are goods with the property that some of their benefits are private, or exclusive, in nature, while others are public, or nonexclusive.*

For example, public transportation systems charge a fee to riders, who receive the private benefits of transportation. However, drivers of private vehicles receive the public benfits of reduced air pollution and congestion and a decrease in the demand for gasoline.

National parks are also mixed public goods. Those who use the park facilities are charged fees and receive the corresponding private benefits of park use. However, those who live near the national parks also receive public benefits, such as the preservation of natural beauty and an increased volume of tourist related business in the area. Postal service, golf courses, free radio and television, and education are other examples of mixed public goods. The cases of golf courses, education, and radio and television show that mixed public goods are frequently produced by the private sector. Nevertheless, many public goods are produced by the public sector—for the reason given in the following section of the chapter.

NEED FOR GOVERNMENT INVOLVEMENT

◆

Often governments or other associations produce public goods because they are the only groups that can finance such endeavors. Those who receive private benefits from such public goods as schools, parks, and hospitals are often unwilling or unable to pay the full cost of supplying them. In the case of pure public goods, such as national defense, whose benefits are indivisible and nonexclusive, the only means of financing them is through general taxes, or government debt, or through gifts. The reason such projects usually cannot be financed by the private sector is that their nonexclusive nature means that people will be able to receive their benefits whether or not they pay for them. In that situation many people will choose not to pay.

OPTIMAL PUBLIC GOOD OUTPUT

◆

Because the production of public goods requires the use of scarce resources that could otherwise be employed by the private sector, it is important to have a standard that can be used to determine whether the production of a specific public good will result in a net gain in social welfare.

SOCIAL WELFARE MAXIMIZATION

If its goal is to maximize social welfare, how does a government decide which public goods and how much of them to produce? An understanding of the principles set forth earlier in the microeconomic sections of this book may make the answer obvious.

The following decision rules will result in the maximum social welfare.

To maximize social welfare a government will undertake the production of any public good whose social benefit is greater than its social cost. Moreover, any public good will be produced up to the point where the marginal social benefit of the good is equal to its marginal social cost.

At the point where the marginal social benefit is equal to the marginal social cost, as shown

in Figure 28–1 at Q_A^*, the net social benefit (social benefit minus social cost) will be maximized as far as the output of this good is concerned.

If the benefits associated with any public good are greater than its costs, then it is also

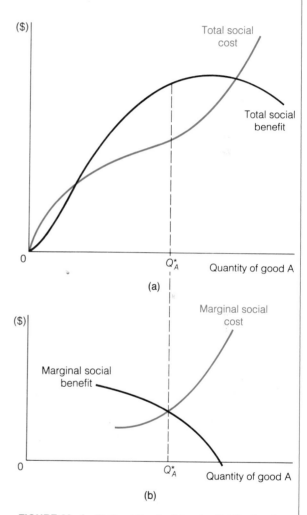

FIGURE 28–1 Optimal Production of a Public Good

Social welfare will be maximized if a good such as Good A is produced up to the point where the total social benefit received from the good (TSB) minus the total social cost from producing the good (TSC) is the greatest amount possible. This point occurs at Q_A^*, where the marginal social benefit of another unit of the good (MSB) is equal to its marginal social cost (MSC).

true that the ratio of the benefits of the project to its costs are greater than 1, or

$$\frac{B}{C} > 1,$$

where:

   B is the benefit associated with the project, and

   C is the cost of the project.

> The ratio of the benefits to the costs of a project is called the **benefit-cost ratio.**

The decision rule given here is sometimes stated as follows: Any public project is acceptable as long as its benefit-cost ratio is greater than 1. However, regardless of how it is phrased, the meaning of the decision rule remains the same.

PRIVATE AND SOCIAL BENEFITS AND COSTS

> The **social benefit** of a public or mixed public good is the sum of the private benefits, if any, plus the external, or third-party, benefits of the good.

For example, the social benefits associated with public education include the private benefits to those receiving the education plus the external benefits to the nation itself of an educated citizenry.

> The **social cost** of a pure or mixed public good includes the costs, if any, recorded by the private sector plus the additional external cost of resources used up, borne by the general public.

In the case of education, private costs are any fees paid by the students. External costs are the remaining cost in terms of resources no longer available for the production of other outputs.

OPTIMAL PRODUCTION OF TWO GOODS

It follows from the decision rule stated here that if two public goods, A and B, are being considered, *each product should be produced up to the point where its marginal social benefit□ is equal to its marginal social cost,□ or* where

$$MSB_A = MSC_A,$$

and

$$MSB_B = MSC_B.$$

Dividing both sides of the first equation by MSC_A and of the second equation by MSC_B, we obtain

$$\frac{MSB_A}{MSC_A} = 1,$$

and

$$\frac{MSB_B}{MSC_B} = 1,$$

or

$$\frac{MSB_A}{MSC_A} = \frac{MSB_B}{MSC_B} = 1 \qquad (28-1)$$

Equation 28–1 states that for social welfare to be maximized, the additional benefit received for an additional dollar's worth of social cost must be equal for both goods and equal to $1. For example, suppose that one more unit of good A will cost $500 and will yield $500 worth of social benfits, whereas one more unit of good B will cost $1,000 and will yield $1,000 worth of additional social benefits. In this case,

$$\frac{\$500}{\$500} = \frac{\$1,000}{\$1,000} = 1,$$

and Equation 28–1 is satisfied.

   It is easy to demonstrate that if Equation 28–1 is not satisfied, society can alter the production of the two goods in a way that will increase social welfare. Suppose, for example, that $MSC_A = \$500$, but $MSB_A = \$600$. Also assume that $MSC_B = \$1,000$, but that $MSB_B = \$900$. Thus:

$$\frac{MSB_A}{MSC_A} = \frac{\$600}{\$500} = 1.20,$$

which is greater than

$$\frac{MSB_B}{MSC_B} = \frac{\$900}{\$1,000} = 0.90.$$

For good A society is receiving $1.20 worth of benefits for each additional $1 of expenditure, but for good B society is receiving only $.90 worth of benefits for an additional $1 of expenditure.

Two things are wrong with this situation. First, because MSB_A is greater than MSC_A, society will receive a net benefit if more of good A is produced. Correspondingly, because MSB_B is less than MSC_B, production of good B is at a point where the marginal benefit to society of good B is not large enough to cover its marginal cost.

In this situation the social welfare of society will be increased if scarce resources are reallocated so that one less unit of good B and two more units of good A are produced. The total cost to society will be unchanged, but total social benefits will be increased by $300. These results are summarized below.

Addition to social benefit from two more units of A	$1,200
Reduction in social benefit from one less unit of B	− 900
Net increase in social benefit	$ 300
Addition to social cost from two more units of A	$1,000
Reduction in social cost from one less unit of B	− 1,000
Net change in social cost	0

As shown, at this point social welfare is increased by producing more of good A and less of good B. However, it is reasonable to assume that the marginal social benefit of a good will fall as its production increases. Thus, as the process of substituting resources from the production of good B to good A continues, the marginal social benefit of good A will decrease and the marginal social benefit of good B will

increase. If the marginal social cost of each good remains constant, the optimal point, where something like

$$\frac{MSB_A}{MSC_A} = \frac{\$500}{\$500} = \frac{MSB_B}{MSC_B} = \frac{\$1,000}{\$1,000} = 1$$

occurs, should eventually be reached.

THE TIME VALUE OF MONEY

Because many public projects involve benefits received and, possibly, costs incurred over many years, it is important that we recognize how the *present*, or *current*, *value* (the value today) of benefits received and costs incurred depends on their timing. Economists refer to the relationship between the time at which a cash flow is received and its present value as the **time value of money.**

The present value of $1,000 received today is not the same as the present value of $1,000 received one year from now. Why not? The $1,000 received today can be invested for the year—even in a savings account—and can therefore earn a return during that year. If the $1,000 is placed in a savings account paying 6 percent interest, in one year the owner of the account will receive $1,000 × 0.06, or $60 interest. Thus, at the end of one year, the total amount in the savings account will be $1,060. No one would trade $1,000 received today for $1,000 received one year from today under this circumstance. The value today of $1,000 received now is greater than the value of $1,000 received one year from now because we can invest the $1,000 received today and earn interest during the coming year.

*The **present value** of a future payment or series of payments represents the amount received today that is equivalent in value to the future payment or payments.*

In the next few sections of this chapter we will examine the concept of present value in greater detail.

DISCOUNT RATES AND DISCOUNTING

We use a discount rate and discounting to determine the dollar amount of a payment that, if it were received today, would be equivalent in value to a payment or series of payments to be received at future dates. As indicated, the equivalent current dollar value of a series of future payments is its present value. However, before we examine the process of finding present values, we will look into one other concept—future value.

Future Value

The **future value** of a sum of money held today is the amount that would be accumulated at some future date if we invested that sum of money in a particular way.

As we saw earlier, if today we put $1,000 in a savings account that pays interest at an annual rate of 6 percent, one year from now we will have an amount equal to $1,000 + $1,000 (0.06) = $1,000 (1.06) = $1,060. If we leave the entire $1,060 in the account for another year, at the end of the second year we will have $1,000 (1.06) (1.06) = $1,060 (1.06) = $1,123.60. If we leave the money in the account for a third year, at the end of that period of time we will have $1,000 (1.06) (1.06) (1.06) = $1,123.60 (1.06) = approximately $1,191.02.

We can summarize these results in the following way:

Original Sum of Money	Interest Rate	Time Period Invested	Future Value
$1,000	6%	1 years	$1,000 (1.06) = $1,060.00
$1,000	6	2 years	$1,000 (1.06)^2 = $1,123.60
$1,000	6	3 years	$1,000 (1.06)^3 = $1,191.02

In general, we can say that *the future value after* t *time periods of some amount invested now at interest rate* i *is equal to*

$$FV = P_0 (1 + i)^t, \qquad (28-2)$$

where:

FV = future value,
P_0 = the principal, or beginning amount, at time period 0,
i = the interest rate, and
t = the number of time periods.

This formula reflects the process of *compounding*.

Compounding is the practice of paying interest on both the original amount invested and any accumulated interest.

Simple interest is interest paid only on the original amount invested.

Discount Rate The discussion of future values should be a further indication that $1,000 received today is worth more than $1,000 received three years from now. Why? Because if we put the $1,000 received today in a savings account paying 6 percent interest compounded annually, then in three years we will have $1,191.02 in the account. On the other hand, the $1,000 payment received at the end of the three years will still be worth only $1,000.

We have just compared the future value (in three years) of $1,000 received today and $1,000 received three years from now, through the use of compounding. Similarly, we can compare their present values through the use of *discounting*, as follows.

Earlier we saw that the future value of $1,000 received today and invested at 6 percent interest for three years was given by

$$FV = \$1,191.02 = \$1,000 (1.06)^3.$$

We can also turn this statement around and ask: What is the present value of $1,191.02 received three years from now if the going rate of interest is 6 percent? Although we already know that the answer to this question is $1,000, we can explicitly solve for it in the above equation by dividing $1,191.02 by $(1.06)^3$:

$$\frac{\$1,191.02}{(1.06)^3} = \frac{\$1,191.02}{1.19102} = \$1,000.$$

The general formula for future value was given earlier as

$$FV = P_0 (1 + i)^t.$$

By the same token, the general formula for present value implied by this formula is

$$PV = P_0 = \frac{FV}{(1 + i)^t}, \qquad (28-3)$$

where:

PV = present value,
FV = a sum of money received after t time periods, and
i = the discount rate.

The **discount rate** is the rate of interest used to compute present values; the process of computing present values is called **discounting.**

Using the present value and future value formulas, we can compare on an equivalent basis two sums of money received at two different periods.

We have seen that the future value of $1,000 received now and invested at 6 percent interest for three years is $1,191.02. We have also seen that the future value (in three years) of a $1,000 payment received three years from now is $1,000.

However, by using the present value formula we can also compare the present values of $1,000 received now and of $1,000 received three years from now. The present value of $1,000 received now is

$$PV = \frac{\$1,000}{(1.06)^0} = \frac{\$1,000}{1} = \$1,000.$$

The present value of $1,000 received three years from now is

$$PV = \frac{\$1,000}{(1.06)^3} = \frac{\$1,000}{1.19102} = \$839.62.$$

Therefore, by comparing either their future values or their present values, we find that $1,000 received today is worth more than $1,000 received three years from now.

As long as we compare the values of two money payments on an equivalent basis, it does not matter whether we use present values or future values as our basis for comparison. However, most business and public sector decisions involving such comparisons are made on the basis of present values.

INTEREST FACTORS

To make the computation of future values and present values easier, tables are available in which the relevant interest factors, or the terms involving the interest rate, are given, frequently to four decimal places (see the appendix to this book).

The **future value interest factor** at a rate of interest equal to i for t time periods, or FVIF (i%, t), is equal to $(1 + i)^t$.

For example, FVIF (6%, 3) is equal to $(1.06)^3$, or approximately 1.1910.

The **present value interest factor** at an interest rate equal to i for t time periods, or PVIF (i%, t) is equal to

$$\frac{1}{(1 + i)^t}$$

Thus

$$PVIF\ (6\%, 3) = \frac{1}{(1.06)^3} = \frac{1}{1.1910} = 0.8396,$$

Note that

$$PVIF\ (i\%, t) = \frac{1}{FVIF\ (i\%, t)}.$$

We can use computed interest factors in the following way. The future value of a sum of money, P_0, invested today at i percent rate of interest for t time periods is equal to $P_0 \times$ FVIF $(i\%, t)$. For example, by using Table A at the end of this book, we can see that the future value of $1,000 invested today at 6 percent interest for three years is given by $1,000 $\times$ FVIF $(6\%, 3) = \$1,000 \times 1.1910 =$ approximately $1,191. The present value of $1,000 received three years from now discounted at a rate of 6 percent is equal to $1,000 $\times$ PVIF $(6\%, 3) = \$1,000 \times 0.8936 =$ approximately $893.60.

In the next section of this chapter we will see how the time value of money is an important factor in the analysis of the costs and benefits of a public project.

PUBLIC DECISION ANALYSIS
◆

Cost-benefit analysis is the term usually applied to the decision-making process for the production of public goods. In this type of analysis the costs and benefits of a project are calculated and compared. The project is economically acceptable only if its benefits are greater than or equal to its costs.

The term *cost-benefit analysis* reflects the fact that optimal decisions involving public goods require a careful analysis of social benefits and costs. As we will see in the following example, this analysis is merely an extension of capital budgeting theory to the realm of public sector microeconomic decisions.

Public projects run the gamut from schools to hospitals to the Concorde supersonic jet to the "Great Pyramid" of Bedford, Indiana.[1]

---

1. See " 'And on Your Right Is the Great Pyramid of Bedford, Indiana,' " *Wall Street Journal*, January 2, 1980, p. 1; and "Closed Assembly Lines for Concorde Signal Halt in Supersonic Era," *Wall Street Journal* January 16, 1980, pp. 1, 15.

(This pyramid is to be ten stories high, made of limestone blocks, in a limestone commemorative park. Bedford calls itself the "limestone capital of the world.") A subway project will be used as our example of the decision-making process for public goods.

SUBWAY PROJECT

Suppose that a city plans to build a subway system. It estimates the cost associated with the subway to be $50 million at the end of the first year (for construction) and $2 million annually thereafter for operation and maintenance of the system. It estimates the benefit to be $10 million per year, beginning at the end of the second year after the project is undertaken. With normal maintenance and use, the subway system should last twenty years.

Any public project will result in a net addition to social welfare if its benefit exceeds its cost. In other words, a project should be accepted as long as its net benefit (equal to the incremental benefit less its incremental cost) is positive.

As for any other long-term investment, to properly estimate the net benefit of a public project we must compare the present values of its benefits and costs. The present values are particularly important in this situation because the benefits and costs are not spread evenly throughout the twenty-year period. (No benefit is received in the first year, but $50 million of cost is incurred.) Furthermore, we know that $100 received today is worth more than $100 received next year, because a year's interest can be earned on the $100 received today. In other words, we must find the present value of future benefits and costs so that we can compare them in terms of equivalent dollar values.

If we assume that the appropriate discount rate is 10 percent, the estimated benefits and costs of the project can be computed in present value terms as shown in Tables 28–1 and 28–2. The net benefit in present value terms is

TABLE 28-1   Computation of Present Value of Benefits of Subway System

Year	Benefit (Dollar Value)	×	Present Value Factor[a]	=	Present Value of Benefit
1	$ 0		.9091		$ 0
2	10,000,000		.8264		8,264,000
3	10,000,000		.7513		7,513,000
4	10,000,000		.6830		6,830,000
5	10,000,000		.6209		6,209,000
6	10,000,000		.5645		5,645,000
7	10,000,000		.5132		5,132,000
8	10,000,000		.4665		4,665,000
9	10,000,000		.4241		4,241,000
10	10,000,000		.3855		3,855,000
11	10,000,000		.3505		3,505,000
12	10,000,000		.3186		3,186,000
13	10,000,000		.2897		2,897,000
14	10,000,000		.2633		2,633,000
15	10,000,000		.2394		2,394,000
16	10,000,000		.2176		2,176,000
17	10,000,000		.1978		1,978,000
18	10,000,000		.1799		1,799,000
19	10,000,000		.1635		1,635,000
20	10,000,000		.1486		1,486,000
Total present value of benefits					$76,043,000

[a]Taken from the present value interest factor table (Table B) in the appendix to this book, using a discount rate of 10 percent.

TABLE 28-2   Computation of Present Value of Costs of Subway System

Year	Cost (Dollar Value)	×	Present Value Factor[a]	=	Present Value of Cost
1	$50,000,000		.9091		$45,455,000
2	2,000,000		.8264		1,652,800
3	2,000,000		.7513		1,502,600
4	2,000,000		.6830		1,366,000
5	2,000,000		.6209		1,241,800
6	2,000,000		.5645		1,129,000
7	2,000,000		.5132		1,026,400
8	2,000,000		.4665		933,000
9	2,000,000		.4241		848,200
10	2,000,000		.3855		771,000
11	2,000,000		.3505		701,000
12	2,000,000		.3186		637,200
13	2,000,000		.2897		579,400
14	2,000,000		.2633		526,600
15	2,000,000		.2394		478,800
16	2,000,000		.2176		435,200
17	2,000,000		.1978		395,600
18	2,000,000		.1799		359,800
19	2,000,000		.1635		327,000
20	2,000,000		.1486		297,200
Total present value of costs					$60,663,600

[a]Taken from the present value interest factor table (Table B) in the appendix to this book, using a discount rate of 10 percent.

equal to $76,043,000 − $60,663,600 = $15,379,400. Because the incremental benefits of the subway system exceed its incremental costs, the project should be undertaken. As noted earlier, any public project is acceptable from a social welfare standpoint as long as its net benefit is positive.

OPTIMAL SUBWAY SIZE

Obviously, subway systems can be built to service greater or smaller areas. How is their optimal size determined?

According to the decision rule given earlier in this chapter, *additional segments of the subway system should be built until the marginal social benefit of another segment is just equal to its marginal social cost*. This rule is similar to the profit-maximizing rule□ for firms: Continue to produce a particular product until the marginal revenue generated by another unit is just equal to its marginal cost.

Suppose the subway system as proposed consists of five segments: a central city loop, a north branch, a south branch, an east branch, and a west branch. Suppose also that the construction and operating costs of each of the five segments are equal. In this case the cost of one segment is equal to

$$\frac{\text{Total social cost}}{5} = \frac{\$60,663,600}{5}$$
$$= \$12,132,720.$$

The incremental benefit of the central city loop is estimated to be $3 million per year, while the incremental benefit associated with each of the four branches is estimated to be $1.75 million per year. One can easily verify that $3 million + (4 × $1.75 million) = $10 million, the total annual social benefit of the subway system.

We can calculate the marginal social benefit and net marginal benefit associated with each segment of the subway as shown in Tables 28–3 and 28–4. In Table 28–3 the present value of the benefits for each segment is calculated by multiplying the fraction of the yearly benefits accounted for by each segment by the present value of the benefits of the total system.

As shown in Table 28–4, the net benefit associated with each of the five subway segments is positive, because the marginal social benefit of each segment is greater than its marginal social cost. Consequently, all five segments should be built.

Suppose, however, that the city is also considering the construction of a sixth segment of the subway—an outer loop to connect all the branch lines. The present value of the benefits of this segment is estimated to be $16.5 million, whereas the present value of the associated costs is estimated to be $18 million. In this case the marginal social benefit of the outer loop is less than its marginal social cost, so this segment should not be built. In other words, the net benefit of the sixth segment is actually a net cost of −$1.5 million.

MUTUALLY EXCLUSIVE PROJECTS

If more than one public project can accomplish the same goal, the projects may be mutually exclusive.

> Two projects are **mutually exclusive** if the acceptance of one makes the other one unacceptable, usually because it has become redundant.

For example, suppose that the goal of city planners is to facilitate the transportation of people to and from the central city area and that this goal can be accomplished by any of the following three methods: (a) improving the city bus system, (b) building more express-

TABLE 28–3   Calculation of the Present Value of Benefits of the Subway System Segments

Segment	Yearly Benefit	Present Value of Total Benefit
Central city	$3,000,000	$\frac{\$3,000,000}{\$10,000,000}$ × $76,043,000 = $22,812,900
North branch	$1,750,000	$\frac{\$1,750,000}{\$10,000,000}$ × $76,043,000 = $13,307,525
South branch	$1,750,000	$\frac{\$1,750,000}{\$10,000,000}$ × $76,043,000 = $13,307,525
East branch	$1,750,000	$\frac{\$1,750,000}{\$10,000,000}$ × $76,043,000 = $13,307,525
West branch	$1,750,000	$\frac{\$1,750,000}{\$10,000,000}$ × $76,043,000 = $13,307,525
Present value of benefits of the total system		$76,043,000

TABLE 28–4 Calculation of the Net Benefits of the Subway System Segments

Segment	Present Value of Benefits	Present Value of Costs	Net Benefit (Present Value)
Central city	$22,812,900	$12,132,720	$10,680,180
North branch	13,307,525	12,132,720	1,174,805
South branch	13,307,525	12,132,720	1,174,805
East branch	13,307,525	12,132,720	1,174,805
West branch	13,307,525	12,132,720	1,174,805
Net benefits of total system (present value)			$15,379,400

TABLE 28–5 Ways to Improve Central City Transportation

Project	Net Benefit (Present Value)
Improve city bus system	$12,500,000
Build more expressways	10,000,000
Build subway system	15,379,400

ways, and (c) building the subway system proposed here. Because any one of these projects will accomplish the desired goal by itself, the projects are mutually exclusive. If one of them is undertaken, the other two will become redundant.

How should the city choose among the three projects? Table 28–5 lists these projects along with their net benefit in present value terms. As for private investment decisions, if the social welfare of the city is to be maximized, the project with the highest net benefit should be selected. In this case the proposed subway system has the highest net benefit, so it should be selected. However, this example has not explicitly indicated the total cost of each of the three projects. It assumes that none of the three projects has a price tag outside the range of feasibility for the city.

In the next section we will consider the impact of budget limitations on social project analysis.

BUDGET CONSTRAINTS

In the real world, governments do not have unlimited funds to spend on public goods, no matter how worthwhile they are or, in economic terminology, no matter what their net benefits are. In this situation *social welfare will be maximized if officials select the group of projects that yields the highest total net so-* cial benefit and still satisfies the budget constraint. This rule is the same decision rule that firms use when they are faced with a limited capital budget.

For example, Table 28–6 gives the net benefit (present value of benefits minus present value of costs) and initial cost for eight projects under consideration by a city. Suppose that the city is faced with a $70 million budget constraint and therefore cannot undertake all these projects. How should it choose among them, assuming that they do not come in any smaller versions? (In other words, these are the smallest sizes for which these projects are viable. To some extent this assumption is an oversimplification, but often a minimum size is indeed required for a certain public project to be functional.)

Table 28–7 shows the three possible combinations of the eight projects that will satisfy the $70 million budget constraint. The first combination of projects will bring the largest total net benefit. Thus the subway and drainage projects should be undertaken.

TABLE 28–6 Possible Capital Projects for a City

Project	Net Benefit	Initial Cost
Subway project	$15,379,400	$50,000,000
Urban renewal	6,000,000	25,000,000
Drainage project	8,000,000	20,000,000
Street improvement project	3,500,000	10,000,000
Auditorium	2,000,000	8,000,000
New school	1,800,000	4,000,000
Additional parks	400,000	2,000,000
New recreational equipment	250,000	1,000,000

TABLE 28–7 Combinations of Projects That Meet the Budget Constraint

Combination	Net Benefit	Initial Cost
#1		
Subway project	$15,379,400	$50,000,000
Drainage project	8,000,000	20,000,000
Total	$23,379,400	$70,000,000
#2		
Subway project	$15,379,400	$50,000,000
Street improvement project	3,500,000	10,000,000
Auditorium	2,000,000	8,000,000
Additional parks	400,000	2,000,000
Total	$21,279,400	$70,000,000
#3		
Urban renewal	$ 6,000,000	$25,000,000
Drainage project	8,000,000	20,000,000
Street improvement project	3,500,000	10,000,000
Auditorium	2,000,000	8,000,000
New school	1,800,000	4,000,000
Additional parks	400,000	2,000,000
New recreational equipment	250,000	1,000,000
Total	$21,950,000	$70,000,000

PROBLEMS AND PITFALLS

Of course, some problems may be encountered in the decision-making process involving public goods. We will deal explicitly with three of them in this section: obtaining accurate estimtes of social benefits and costs, determining the appropriate discount rate to use when evaluating public projects, and evaluating the expense of cost-benefit studies. (Politics often is a fourth troublesome factor, but we will leave its consideration to political scientists.)

ESTIMATING SOCIAL BENEFITS AND COSTS

As should be evident from the subway example, an accurate estimate of the social benefits and costs associated with a public project is essential for economic decision making. These benefits and costs are often both direct and indirect.

> **Direct benefits** are the benefits obtained by the users of a project.
>
> **Direct costs** are the costs directly connected with a project.
>
> **Indirect benefits and costs** are external, or third-party, benefits and costs.

Direct benefits and costs may be either explicit (in the form of a payment) or implicit (in the form of an opportunity cost◻). Indirect benefits and costs are frequently implicit, but not necessarily so.

For the subway, direct and explicit benefits would consist primarily of the gasoline and other car expenses saved by the subway riders. Direct and explicit costs would include the payments for construction and operation of the system.

Implicit benefits and costs, both direct and indirect, are generally more difficult to estimate because they involve opportunity costs or intangibles. Chapter 18 noted that the opportunity cost of a resource is given by its value in its next best alternative use.

The direct but implicit benefits of the subway project would include the value of commuting time saved by the subway riders. In addition, some riders might be able to save time by reading the newspaper or office reports while on the subway. Direct but implicit costs would include the value of any city owned resources used in the subway project but not explicitly charged to it. For example, the subway might run through some land already owned by the city. Some workers already on the city payroll might spend time on the project, but a proportionate share of their wages and salaries might not be reflected in the explicit payments for the subway's costs. Therefore, the opportunity costs of such resources represent an implicit cost of the project.

Indirect and implicit benefits would include a reduction in commuting time for nonusers of the system, due to the reduction in traffic congestion, and a reduction in noise and air pollution. The central city might receive a further indirect benefit—an increase in business activity as people found it easier to travel downtown.

Indirect costs would include the inconvenience imposed on people during the construction period and any reduction in downtown business activity as a result of the construction. These types of costs for the subway system are summarized in Table 28–8.

Because the estimates of the benefits and costs of a project are crucial to the decision-making process, it is important from the standpoint of social welfare that they be calculated as accurately as possible. The greatest weight should be given to the benefits and costs that are the most easily quantified—ex-

plicit benefits and costs and the more tangible implicit benefits and costs. Intangibles should perhaps be merely mentioned, or at least any attempts to quantify them should be given less weight. Some of the difficulties of estimating the costs and benefits associated with a public project are illustrated in the reading at the end of this chapter.

SOCIAL RATE OF DISCOUNT

There is some disagreement among economists and public officials concerning the appropriate discount rate for projects involving public goods.

> *The discount rate used for evaluating public goods projects is called the **social rate of discount.***

As we will see, this rate is also a crucial factor in the evaluation of public projects.

For example, we saw that with a social rate of discount of 10 percent, the subway project had a net benefit in present value terms of $15,379,400. However, the same calculations done with a discount rate of 16 percent will yield a net benefit of −$2,571,400. Thus if 16 percent is the appropriate discount rate, the project should be rejected.

A 1967 study of the budgeting practices of the federal government discovered that thirteen government agencies used no discount rate at all (which implies a 0% rate of discount) in project analysis. The ten agencies that did use discount rates in evaluating projects employed rates ranging from 0 to 12 percent![2] In recent years, however, the federal

---

TABLE 28–8 Direct and Indirect Benefits and Costs of the Subway System

Benefits

Direct
Explicit: Saving in gasoline and other motor vehicle expenses by subway riders
Implicit: Value of time saved by subway riders

Indirect
Time saved by nonusers
Reduction in noise and air pollution
Increase in downtown business activity

Costs

Direct
Explicit: Payments for construction and operating expenses
Implicit: Opportunity cost of city-owned land and other resources

Indirect
Inconvenience and loss of time during construction
Reduction in downtown business activity during construction

---

2. See Elmer B. Staats, "Survey of Use by Federal Agencies of the Discount Technique in Evaluating Future Programs," in *Program Budgeting and Benefit-Cost Analysis*, ed. Harley H. Hinricks and Graeme M. Taylor (Pacific Palisades, Calif.: Goodyear Publishing, 1969), pp. 212–228.

Office of Management and Budget has disapproved of evaluating public programs with a discount rate of less than 10 percent.[3]

Some economists argue that the appropriate social rate of discount is the rate at which the relevant government body (city, county, state, or federal) can borrow money. However, some government bond yields (such as those for municipal bonds) are tax free. Moreover, these bonds are frequently considered to be less risky for the investor than are many private sector bonds. As a result, the cost of borrowing for a government agency is often less than for a private sector firm with a project of comparable risk.

The effect of the nontaxable feature can be illustrated as follows. Suppose a private sector firm is able to borrow money at a 14 percent rate of interest. If the people who loan the money are in the 40 percent marginal tax bracket, then their after-tax yield is only 14 percent $(1 - 0.40) = 8.4$ percent. Thus these people should be willing to loan money at a tax-free rate of 8.4 percent, a substantially lower yield than 14 percent.

However, the best estimate of the appropriate social rate of discount may be the discount rate that reflects the cost of funds for a project of similar length and riskiness in the private sector. Public projects do take resources from the private sector, and the fact that a government body may be able to borrow money more cheaply than a private firm because of the tax laws seems irrelevant when one is attempting to value these resources. Therefore, it seems reasonable to argue that the private sector cost of funds reflects the opportunity cost of funds used by the public sector for a similar project.

Interest rate data can be obtained from such sources as the *Wall Street Journal* and the *Federal Reserve Bulletin*. The relative riskiness of bond issues is rated by Moody's and Standard & Poor's investment services.

COST OF COST-BENEFIT STUDIES

The information needed to do a careful cost-benefit analysis of a proposed project may be expensive to obtain. One example of this problem occurred during the administration of President Lyndon Johnson when the Bureau of the Budget (now the Office of Management and Budget) implemented an approach to public project analysis known as the Planning, Programming, and Budgeting System (PPBS). Under this system, federal agencies were to annually review all their programs, using the cost-benefit method to rank their projects internally. Then, the Bureau of the Budget would make recommendations to the executive branch about how funds should be allocated to the agencies.

PPBS proved useful in the internal project evaluation process of the agencies. However, it failed as a system because it generated more information, in terms of sheer volume, than the Budget office could analyze. In fact, in 1969 an additional 1,145 people were needed in twenty-one agencies just to conduct the PPBS analysis.[4] Moreover, Congress frequently ignored the information gathered by the PPBS in making decisions.

The experience with PPBS suggests that while cost-benefit analysis can prove workable and useful, the cost of obtaining information should not be ignored. Furthermore, the ability and willingness of the final decision makers to use such studies should be taken into consideration.

PUBLIC CHOICE AND THE FUTURE

As we become increasingly aware of the scarcity of our resources, whether oil, natural gas,

3. Steven H. Hanke and Richard A. Walker, "Benefit-Cost Analysis Reconsidered: An Evaluation of the Mid-State Project," *Water Resources Research* 10 (October 1974): 901.

4. U.S. Congress, Joint Economic Committee, *Analysis and Evaluation of Public Expenditures: The PPB System*, vol. 2 (Washington, D.C.: Government Printing Office, 1969), p. 636.

gold or other minerals, labor, or simply clean air and water, the importance of making economic choices in both the public and private sectors becomes more and more apparent. Without doubt, when used properly, cost-benefit analysis is a highly useful tool in the decision-making process. Although gathering the required information is usually not costless, public officials can adopt a policy of seeking further information until the cost of additional data is deemed greater than any benefits they would likely yield.

Despite the problems connected with this approach, cost-benefit analysis is the only systematic way we have of analyzing public projects in an economic manner. Policy makers should therefore use it carefully, attempting to avoid its shortcomings and placing sensible limits on its expenditures.

SUMMARY

1. This chapter discussed economic decision rules for public sector microeconomic decisions. These choices involve such questions as: What public goods should be produced? and How much of a particular public good should be produced? In contrast, macroeconomic decisions are concerned with the general levels of public expenditure, taxes, and debt.

2. Public goods are goods whose benefits cannot be limited to those who directly pay for the goods. A pure public good is a good or service all of whose benefits have the property that they are nondivisible and nonexclusive. Mixed public goods are goods with the property that some of their benefits or costs are private, or exclusive, in nature, while others are public, or nonexclusive.

3. Because of the nonexclusive nature of public goods, many of them are produced by the government. People can obtain the benefits of such goods without paying for them; therefore, they are often reluctant to pay voluntarily. In other cases, people are unable to pay for their share of the cost of public goods, such as education.

4. Cost-benefit analysis is the decision-making process for the production of public goods. The term itself reflects the fact that optimal decisions involving public goods require a careful analysis of social benefits and costs.

5. In general, the production of any public good whose benefit is greater than its cost will increase the social welfare. In other words, a public good should be produced as long as its net benefit is positive, as long as its benefit-cost ratio is greater than 1. Moreover, a public good should be produced up to the point where the marginal social benefit of another unit of the good is equal to its marginal social cost.

6. The social benefit of a good is the sum of the private and external benefits of the good. Similarly, the social cost of a good is the sum of the costs recorded by the private sector plus the additional external cost of resources used up, which is borne by the general public.

7. Two projects are mutually exclusive if the acceptance of one makes the other one unacceptable, usually because it has become redundant. In the case of mutually exclusive projects, the social welfare will be maximized if the project with the highest net benefit is selected.

8. Government agencies usually face another limitation on their production of public goods—a budget constraint. The social welfare will be maximized if officials select the group of projects that yields the highest total net social benefit and still satisfies the budget constraint.

9. Certain problems may be encountered in the decision-making process for public goods. The areas of potential trouble are obtaining accurate estimates of the social benefits and costs associated with a public project, determining the appropriate discount rate to use when evaluating public projects, and evaluating the expense of cost-benefit studies. Although an accurate estimate of the relevant social benefits and costs is crucial for making decisions that will maximize the social welfare, the cost of obtaining such information must also be considered. Public officials can adopt a policy of seeking additional information until the cost of more data is estimated to be greater than any likely benefits from obtaining it. With regard to the discount rate, it seems reasonable to conclude that the best estimate of the appropriate social rate of discount is the discount rate that will reflect the opportunity cost of funds for a project of similar length and riskiness in the private sector.

10. As the general public becomes increasingly aware of the fact that resources are limited, the need for making economic choices in both the public and private sectors becomes apparent. Although there are some potential pitfalls connected with it, cost-benefit analysis is the only systematic way we have of analyzing public projects in an economic manner. Policy makers should use it carefully.

IMPORTANT TERMS AND CONCEPTS

Public good	Cost-benefit analysis
Pure public good	Mutually exclusive
Mixed public good	projects
Benefit-cost ratio	Direct benefits
Social benefit	Direct costs
Social cost	Indirect benefits and
Present value	costs
Future value	Social rate of
Compounding	discount
Simple interest	
Discount rate	
Discounting	

QUESTIONS AND PROBLEMS

1. Explain the difference between a pure public good and a pure private good.

2. Suppose that two public goods, good X and good Y, are being produced. If the marginal social benefit of good X is $10, the marginal social cost of good X is $20, the marginal social benefit of good Y is $40, and the marginal social cost of good Y is $30, is an optimal combination of the two goods being produced? Explain. If not, explain how resources could be reallocated to increase social welfare.

3. What are the social benefit and the social cost of a good? Give an example.

4. A midwestern city needs to increase the capacity of its elementary school system. It has two mutually exclusive alternatives—remodeling an exist-

ing building or building a new school. The two alternatives along with their net benefits and initial costs are shown below:

Project	Net Benefit	Initial Cost
Remodeling	$350,000	$2,000,000
Building new school	625,000	4,000,000

Assuming that there is no budget constraint for the school district, which alternative should it choose? Explain.

5. The federal government is planning to build a dam as part of a flood control project. The initial cost of the dam is estimated to be $70 million, payable at the end of the first year of construction. The annual cost for the maintenance and operation of the dam is expected to be $500,000, beginning at the end of the second year. The annual benefits of the dam are estimated to be $12 million per year, beginning at the end of the second year. The dam is expected to last twenty years, and the appropriate social rate of discount is 10 percent. Should the project be accepted? Explain.

6. How would your answer to Question 5 change if the social rate of discount were 16 percent?

7. What is the decision rule for accepting or rejecting a public project? Give an example.

8. What possible problems may be encountered with cost-benefit analysis? Explain.

9. What is the decision rule for determining how much of a public good to produce? Give an example.

10. A state government is considering the following public projects:

Project	Net Benefits	Initial Cost
Build new highways	$2,500,000	$20,000,000
Build a new state office building	800,000	10,000,000
Develop a new state park	1,600,000	5,000,000
Repave existing state highways	500,000	5,000,000
Expand a state university	1,400,000	5,000,000

The state has a budget constraint of $25 million for public projects this year. Which of the listed projects should it accept? Explain.

11. Using an example, explain the difference between direct and indirect benefits and the difference between direct and indirect costs of a public project.

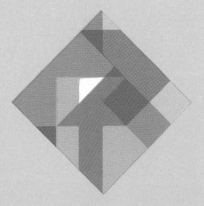

THE BIG
TENN-TOM:
BENEFIT
OR BOONDOGGLE?

This week President Carter included $143 million in his proposed fiscal 1979 budget to pay for this year's work on the huge Tennessee-Tombigbee Waterway. When completed at a cost of at least $1.6 billion in 1987, the project, the costliest single public works project under way in the country, will link two river systems—the Tennessee and Tombigbee—and provide access to the Gulf of Mexico at Mobile, Ala.

Its promoters, mostly the Corps of Engineers and local politicians and business interests, say that Tenn-Tom, as it is called locally,

Source: "The Big Tenn-Tom: Benefit or Boondoggle?" *Business Week,* February 6, 1978, pp. 94–98.

will induce major economic growth in the mostly rural area surrounding it—80,000 sq. mi. in eastern Tennessee, eastern Mississippi, and western Kentucky and Alabama. But to its detractors, mainly three railroads that now serve the area and numerous environmental groups, it is the country's major public works boondoggle and its most conspicuous example of how federal funds promote favored sections of the country at the expense of others.

Tenn-Tom headed President Carter's "hit list" last year of public works to be scuttled. But it was saved with the political clout of such powerful senators as John C. Stennis and James O. Eastland of Mississippi, John J. Sparkman of

Alabama, and Howard Baker of Tennessee. Because $477 million has already been spent on Tenn-Tom, its supporters believe its completion now is inevitable.

ROSY PREDICTIONS

Completion, say supporters, will herald an economic bonanza for the area. They forecast that by the year 2000 it will generate over 100,000 new jobs and nearly $3 billion in personal income and private investment, and add 270,000 new residents. And the project, for which the federal government is paying 90% of the costs, will be self-sustaining, according to studies done for the Corps of Engineers.

Darkening this rosy picture are

serious questions whether the economic benefits justify the enormous disruption that building the waterway is causing. Moreover, the arithmetic used by the Corps of Engineers is suspect.

The railroads fighting the project also argue that waterways in general put them in a competitive hole because they are used free by the barge industry. Spearheading the railroads' fight is the Louisville & Nashville RR.; it is supported by the St. Louis-San Francisco Ry. and Illinois Central Gulf RR.

One way the L&N is trying to stop Tenn-Tom is through a federal district court suit filed in Washington. Joining the L&N with a companion suit are environmentalists.

"It is nothing but a huge earthmoving project," charges G. Randall Grace, director of the Tombigbee River Council of Starkville, Miss., one of the environmental groups, including the Environmental Defense Fund Inc., that is opposing the project. As planned, the 232-mi. waterway would provide shippers with straight shot by barge into the 16,000-mi. inland waterway system of mid-America. It would give the coal mines of eastern Tennessee and western Kentucky shorter access to the Gulf of Mexico. Coal shipped to the Gulf from there now must either use more expensive rail service or go down the Mississippi River, 600 mi. farther west by water.

FIGURING COSTS

The project's opponents charge that since construction started in

1972 the $1.6 billion estimated cost has risen more than fourfold from $386 million. Even more seriously, they claim that Tenn-Tom makes no economic sense, and that the Corps of Engineers used outdated data in determining its economic viability. The corps says its research shows that for every dollar spent on Tenn-Tom it will, in effect, "earn" $1.20; in other words, its benefit-cost ratio is $1.20/$1. The corps adds that this ratio is based not only on the $1.6 billion construction cost but $250 million more that will be needed to operate and maintain the facility during its 50-year lifespan.

When the corps figures costs, though, it must factor in the federal interest rate as if the tax money were borrowed funds. The corps used an interest rate of only 3¼%. "That is just ludicrous," says Paul Roberts, a Washington-based economist who has done several studies, including one on Tenn-Tom. "The benefit-cost ratio is less than $1."

The corps is forced to agree with Roberts that if a more realistic interest rate, such as the current 6⅝%, were used it would give a minus ratio of 64¢/$1. But the corps says that it had to use the lower rate because Congress required that when it passed the Water Resources Development Act of 1974.

BENEFITS

Undoubtedly, if Tenn-Tom were proposed today it would not be approved. "It's certainly true that you don't go out and borrow money at 3¼% today," conceded Colonel Charlie L. Blalock, district

engineer for the corps' Mobile office. "With a new project, if the benefit-cost ratio is below $1 we don't normally recommend that we start it."

Glover Wilkins, the administrator of the Tennessee-Tombigbee Waterway Development Authority, is also critical of how the corps figures its benefit-cost ratio, but maintains that its method is far too conservative.

The corps, for example, cannot take into account "induced" benefits that the project may cause, such as the kind of industrial development Wilkins believes will occur. Wilkins says: "If we were to use induced developmental benefits you could use a 10% or 12% interest rate and we'd still be above [break even]."

To support that contention, he cites a 1976 study done by the Washington-based economic research firm of Hammer, Siler, George Associates for the Appalachian Regional Commission. The study projects that through 2000 Tenn-Tom wll generate 134,600 new jobs and $1.4 billion in personal income.

SO WHAT?

The opponents of Tenn-Tom, such as environmentalist Randall Grace, however, like to cite the same study to back their claim that the region, as part of the fast-growing Sunbelt, is going to prosper with or without the project. For instance, the study says that, without the project, personal income will increase by at least $32 billion and about 1 million new jobs will be created. "So [Tenn-Tom] is going to account for about 12% or 13% of the jobs," shrugs Grace.

The need may be debatable because many of the 165 counties in the Tenn-Tom region have unemployment rates below the national average of 6.4%. "What this area suffers from more than unemployment," Wilkins explains, "is per capita income. We don't need any more pants factories." Per capita income in the region is about 75% of the national average.

MAKING THEM PAY.

That cuts no ice with the railroads. They are pressuring Congress to make the barge industry start paying to use waterways. "If Congress would impose an adequate use charge on commercial users of waterways, we would have no basis to oppose construction and operations of waterways," says Prime F. Osborn, president and chief executive of the L&N. "Adequate" to Osborn and

other railroad men means that the federal government should recoup the entire cost of constructing and operating waterways.

For the moment, however, the railroads are willing to settle for little more than half of that. They are supporting a proposal by Senator Pete V. Domenici (R-N. M.) that would require the government to recover all operating costs and half of construction expenditures. That, too, would be too steep for the waterways industry, says Wilkins. Rather, he favors a bill already passed by the House that would impose on commercial waterways users a fee of 4¢ per gal. of fuel beginning in October, and then 6¢ per gal. two years later. "then we could see if we needed to adjust it," he says.

But the Association of American Railroads claims that the fee of 6¢ would recover no more than 10% of costs and would still give barges unfair advantage. To that, chafes Wilkins, "Nobody has ever

asked for recovery of all the land grants they [the railroads] got" in the 1800s to lay their track.

QUESTIONS

1. What are the alleged benefits of the Tenn-Tom project?
2. Why has the project been criticized?
3. What data does the Corps of Engineers have to indicate that the project is an acceptable one according to the decision rule that the net benefit must be positive? Explain.
4. What was the social rate of discount used in the analysis of the Tenn-Tom project? How did this rate affect the Corps's conclusion regarding the acceptability of the project?
5. What indirect benefits may be associated with the project? What indirect costs?

THE CRISIS
OF
THE CITIES

Although the finances of most U.S. cities seem to be in good shape, the finances of some are not. In the second half of the 1970s the monetary woes of some of the major cities could be hidden from public view no longer.

For example, in 1975 New York City was rescued from almost certain default on loans by the establishment of the state-backed Municipal Assistance Corporation. The purpose of MAC was to convert $3 billion of the city's short-term debt to long-term debt.[1] In December 1978 Cleveland became the first major U.S. city since the depression to formally default on a loan.[2] In late 1979 and early 1980 the news media were filled with reports of turmoil in Chicago; city transit drivers and firefighters went on strike, and taxi drivers threatened to do the same. Teachers in Chicago city schools stayed home because the schools could not meet their payrolls.[3] During the same period Kansas City was without firefighters for a short time.[4] Moreover, these cities have not been alone in their troubles.

What has happened in the cities? For one thing, inflation has made public workers demand more substantial increases in wages. Also, such workers are becoming less reluctant to form unions and to strike in an attempt to achieve their demands. Inflation has also caused other city costs to increase. As evidenced by the passage of Proposition 13 (which put a ceiling on property tax rates) in California, taxpayers are becoming frustrated with the need for more and more tax revenues. Finally, citizens are demanding that the cities expand their services in some areas while maintaining the same level of services in other areas.

1. "Explosive Problems That New York Still Faces," Business Week, June 14, 1976, pp. 82–84.

2. "Capsized Cleveland Gets Ready to Pick a New Navigator," Wall Street Journal, September 28, 1979, pp. 1, 26.

3. "Chicago's Jangle Bells," Newsweek, December 31, 1979, pp. 36–37.

4. "A City without Firemen," Newsweek, January 7, 1980, p. 31.

Tables K–1, K–2, and K–3 present data regarding revenues, expenditures, and outstanding debt for U.S. cities from 1960 to 1978. Over this period, revenues increased from $14.9 billion to $80.1 billion, expenditures increased from $15.2 billion to $77.3 billion, and outstanding debt increased from $23.2 billion to $78.2 billion.

Over the same period, the percent of city revenues received from state and federal government sources more than doubled, from 15.5 percent to 32.2 percent. Most other sources of city revenues, including taxes, fell in relative terms. (The percent of total revenue accounted for by these items declined.) In absolute dollar terms, however, city taxes rose, and taxpayers were unhappy.

From Table K–2 we can see that in relative or percentage terms the only areas of increased expenditures are for police protection, public welfare, interest, and miscellaneous expenditures. Expenditures in most of the other areas have declined. Herein lies another source of public discontent.

Nevertheless, the picture is not altogether gloomy. The debt of cities relative to their revenue has actually fallen for the nation as a whole. The Center for Municipal and Metropolitan Research conducted a survey of city financial statements for 1977 and found that the financial situation of twenty-seven large cities had made a "dramatic recovery" in recent years.[5]

Moreover, with funds from a combination of public and private sources, large revitalization projects are either being seriously considered or are already underway in many large cities, including New York City, Boston, Baltimore, Portland (Oregon), Atlanta, and Chicago.[6] Many urban projects have received partial funding through federal Urban-Development Action grants initiated by the Carter administration. Although some critics claim that such grants simply provide windfall profits for private developers, they were a political success and show certain tangible results.[7]

5. "A Partial Recovery by the Cities," *Business Week*, January 22, 1979, pp. 94, 96.

6. See "A Rush to Redo the Waterfront," *Business Week*, February 11, 1980, pp. 108–111; "A Born-Again Times Square," *Business Week*, November 12, 1979, pp. 79–80; and "More Action in Action Grants," *Business Week*, November 5, 1979, pp. 172–180.

7. "More Action in Action Grants."

TABLE K–1   Sources of Revenue for Cities, 1960–1978

Source of Revenue	Year					
	1960		1970		1978	
	Millions of Dollars	Percent	Millions of Dollars	Percent	Millions of Dollars	Percent
General revenue	**11,647**	**78.1**	**26,621**	**81.4**	**65,486**	**81.7**
Intergovernmental	2,321	15.5	7,906	24.2	25,833	32.2
Taxes	7,109	47.7	13,647	41.7	27,830	34.7
Property	5,197	34.8	9,127	27.9	16,293	20.3
Sales	1,217	8.2	2,422	7.4	6,508	8.1
Licenses	695	4.7	2,098	6.4	5,029	6.7
Miscellaneous	2,217	14.9	5,068	15.5	11,824	14.8
Utility and liquor store	**2,861**	**19.2**	**5,168**	**15.8**	**12,501**	**15.6**
Insurance trust	**407**	**2.7**	**915**	**2.8**	**2,136**	**2.7**
Total	**14,915**	**100.0**	**32,704**	**100.0**	**80,125**	**100.0**

Source: U.S. Department of Commerce, Bureau of the Census, "Table 513: City Governments—Summary of Finances: 1960 to 1978, *Statistical Abstract of the United States, 1980* (Washington, D.C.: Government Printing Office, 1980), p. 312.

TABLE K-2   Expenditures by Cities, 1960–1978

Type of Expenditure	Year					
	1960		1970		1978	
	Millions of Dollars	Percent	Millions of Dollars	Percent	Millions of Dollars	Percent
General expenditure	**11,818**	**77.5**	**27,682**	**81.0**	**60,964**	**78.9**
Police protection	1,275	8.4	2,994	8.8	6,991	9.0
Fire protection	885	5.8	1,762	5.2	3,855	5.0
Highways	1,573	10.3	2,499	7.3	4,740	6.1
Sewerage, etc.	1,332	8.7	2,553	7.5	6,251	8.1
Public welfare	608	4.0	2,215	6.5	4,357	5.6
Education	1,801	11.8	4,548	13.3	7,973	10.3
Libraries	185	1.2	407	1.2	732	1.0
Health care	799	5.2	1,944	5.7	3,618	4.7
Parks and recreation	551	3.6	1,306	3.8	2,798	3.6
Housing and urban renewal	464	3.0	1,154	3.4	2,084	2.7
Airports	189	1.2	435	1.3	772	1.0
Interest	431	2.8	1,098	3.2	2,869	3.7
Other	1,726	11.3	4,767	14.0	13,924	18.1
Utility and liquor store expenditure	**2,975**	**19.5**	**5,489**	**16.1**	**13,912**	**18.0**
Insurance trust expenditure	**458**	**3.0**	**1,002**	**2.9**	**2,408**	**3.1**
Total	**15,251**	**100.0**	**34,173**	**100.0**	**77,283**	**100.0**

Source: U.S. Department of Commerce, Bureau of the Census, *Statistical Abstract of the United States, 1980* (Washington, D.C.: Government Printing Office, 1980), p. 312.

The cities are allowed to spend such grants on land acquisition and public works improvements, such as sewage disposal systems or drainage. They can also lend the grant

TABLE K-3   Revenue, Expenditures, and Outstanding Debt of Cities, 1960–1978 (Dollar Amounts in Millions of Dollars)

Item	Year			
	1960	1965	1970	1976
Revenue	$14,915	$20,318	$32,704	$80,125
Expenditures	$15,251	$20,680	$34,173	$77,283
Outstanding debt, year end	$23,178	$31,862	$43,773	$78,167
Debt as a percent of revenue	155.4	156.8	133.8	97.6

Source: U.S. Department of Commerce, Bureau of the Census, *Statistical Abstract of the United States, 1980* (Washington, D.C.: Government Printing Office, 1980), p. 312.

money at reduced interest rates to private sources for development or for neighborhood revitalization projects. According to *Business Week*, the Department of Housing and Urban Development "boasts that such leveraging averages $6 of private money for every dollar of federal grant. This would mean that the $841 million in action grants approved so far has generated $5.1 billion in private investment."[8] The future of such grants under the Reagan administration was not clear in 1981.

Although the picture has brightened, the crisis of the cities is not yet past. The possibility of recession and the reality of federal aid cutbacks still pose threats to the recovery of the cities.[9] Citizens are going to have to make some hard choices regarding goods and the financing of their production. Whether or not they will do so in an economically sound manner remains to be seen.

8. Ibid., p. 172.

9. See "A Partial Recovery by the Cities."

PART NINE

THE
ECONOMICS OF
INTERNATIONALISM:
TRADE, PAYMENTS,
AND GROWTH

CHAPTER 29

COMPARATIVE
ADVANTAGE
AND
INTERNATIONAL
TRADE

A HEALTHY U.S. TRADE PATTERN FOR THE 1980s?

Because of huge increases in crude oil prices in the 1970s, a lot of people were pessimistic about the ability of the United States to export sufficient goods to cover its thirst for oil and efficient foreign cars to save fuel. As this chapter and the next will show, an inability of U.S. exports to match U.S. imports causes the dollar to lose value in relation to other currencies. The dollar did indeed fare rather poorly during most of the 1970s, although it became stronger in 1980 and 1981.

Fortunately, the U.S. economy has some basic strengths that even massive changes in the international trade climate cannot undermine. First, its agricultural sector is very productive and has long been a supplier of food grains to the the rest of the world. Rising oil prices may cause farmers to lay out more money for fuel, but they are also likely to charge foreigners more for exported grain. Second, the United States is a world leader in technology and manufactured goods, exports that become more attractive as dollars become cheaper in terms of other currencies. Finally, the U.S. economy, because of its mixed capitalistic system and its sophisticated trade policies, is one of the most flexible in the world. If certain export markets deteriorate it is likely that U.S. entrepreneurs will focus on new, more promising, alternatives.[1]

1. For a discussion of the 1980 trade performance of the United States, see "The Shifting Trade Winds," *Newsweek*, November 10, 1980, p. 88.

Adjustments in international trade patterns sometimes take a while to work themselves out. Thus, at the beginning of the oil crisis, the United States ran massive trade deficits (imports greatly exceeded exports) and the dollar's value declined in relation to other important currencies, such as the German mark, French franc, Japanese yen, and Swiss franc. However, in late 1980 and early 1981, the foreign trading partners of the United States were fearing exactly the reverse. Despite strong competition from Japan in the automobile market and in other markets and despite further increases in oil prices, the U.S. dollar was strengthening and the U.S. trade deficit was narrowing. In general, trade analysts expected the United States to do well in the international marketplace during the 1980s.

In this chapter we will examine the rationale for international trade. The two things especially important in determining a nation's trade pattern are its resources and the value of its currency in terms of those of other countries.

C H A P T E R 29
◆
COMPARATIVE ADVANTAGE AND INTERNATIONAL TRADE

WHAT THIS CHAPTER IS ABOUT

In this chapter and in Chapters 30, 31, and 32 we will turn our attention toward the nature, causes, and effects of trade between nations. In a sense, we will take a step beyond conventional micro- and macroeconomics into the realm of world economic relations. However, what we will discover is that many of the tools used to analyze economic problems at the level of the nation, the market, and even the individual firm or consumer can be applied to questions of international economic relations.

The first task of this chapter is to provide some background data on world trade and its importance to different nations and economic groups. The second task is to analyze the forces underlying international trade. To do this we will retrace the steps of the earliest classical economists, Adam Smith□ and David Ricardo,□ who developed the principles of absolute and comparative advantage.

The principle of comparative advantage leads to the conclusion that the existence of different relative prices of goods from nation to nation opens up the prospect for gain from international trade. Although early theories of international trade argued that differences in relative prices were cost-based, modern international trade theory offers other possibilities, among them overlapping patterns of demand and the product life cycle.

The final part of the chapter will take up the question of how the gains from trade are divided among countries. This important question has no simple answer. However, it must be addressed because economists and political leaders in some of the less developed countries have argued that industrialized countries like the United States reap an unwarranted share of the gains from international trade.

THE PATTERN OF
WORLD TRADE

Before we examine the economic principles governing international trade, we should know who trades and what goods are traded in today's world. Both historically and today the principal trading nations are those in Western Europe and, since the nineteenth century, North America. In the twentieth century Japan, Australia, South Africa, and Israel have

joined this group, which is referred to in United Nations (U.N.) jargon as the developed market economies.

For reporting trade statistics the U.N. divides the world into three main groups of countries: the **developed market economies,** the **developing market economies,** and the **centrally planned economies.** Most countries in the communist block fall into the last group: the middle group includes such countries as the Latin American, Caribbean, and African nations (other than South Africa), the Middle Eastern nations (excluding Israel), and much of Asia.

Because one country's *exports* (goods shipped to foreigners) are another country's *imports* (goods received from foreigners), we can determine total world trade by adding up either the value of the exports of all countries or the value of the imports of all countries. However, these two procedures will not give us the same number, because most countries value exports f.o.b. (excluding freight and insurance) and imports c.i.f. (at cost plus insurance and freight). We can come closest to estimating the amount earned from the sale of goods (not of shipping and insurance services) in international trade by counting exports rather than imports. Nonetheless, both figures are useful in describing world trade, as shown in Table 29–1, which pertains only to trade of the market economies.

TABLE 29–1   International Trade of the Market Economies

	1970				1975				1980			
	Exports		Imports		Exports		Imports		Exports		Imports	
Market Economies	Dollar Value (in Millions)	Share (Percent)	Dollar Value (in Millions)	Share (Percent)	Dollar Value (in Millions)	Share (Percent)	Dollar Value (in Millions)	Share (Percent)	Dollar Value (in Millions)	Share (Percent)	Dollar Value (in Millions)	Share (Percent)
Developed market economies	$224,900	80.3	$237,800	80.9	$578,600	73.4	$614,500	76.2	$1,273,000	69.6	$1,425,900	76.7
Developing market economies (including OPEC)	55,100	19.7	56,300	19.1	209,700	26.6	191,600	23.8	555,000	30.4	432,400	23.3
OPEC	17,400	6.2	9,900	3.4	113,300	14.4	54,000	6.8	283,400	15.5	124,500	6.7
All market economies	280,000	100.0	294,100	100.0	787,700	100.0	806,100	100.0	1,828,100	100.0	1,858,300	100.0

Source: United Nations Statistical Office, *United Nations Statistical Yearbook* (New York: United Nations 1977), pp. 466–467; and *United Nations Monthly Bulletin of Statistics*, July, 1981, pp. 106–111.

THE MARKET ECONOMIES

The data in Table 29–1 span a period of time when OPEC (the Organization of Petroleum Exporting Countries) created a dramatic impact on world trade by successfully implementing a cartel□ to raise the price of crude oil. In 1970 OPEC was a loose organization of oil-producing countries, but by the mid 1970s it was the virtual dictator of world oil prices.

Nonetheless, as the table shows, in 1980, 70 percent of both the exports and the imports of the market economies were attributable to the developed group. From 1970 to 1980 the developing economies' share of trade (in relation to all market economies) increased markedly, and most of this increase was attributable to OPEC, which more than doubled its share in both exports and imports. Furthermore, if we compare 1980 data with 1975 data, we see that OPEC's share as an exporter rose only slightly—from 14.4 percent to 15.5 percent of the exports of all market economies. We can conclude that although OPEC has had a dramatic impact on world trade, the bulk of the trade of the market economies still involves the developed market economies dealing with each other.

TRADE AND GROSS NATIONAL PRODUCT

One indicator of the importance of international trade to a particular country is the percentage share of exports in the country's gross national product.□ For example, in 1978 U.S. merchandise exports were $217 billion and U.S. GNP was $2,128 billion. Exports were thus 217/2,627 (100) = 9.3 percent of GNP.[1] This is a substantial proportion of the nation's total output, but in comparison with other countries, particularly the United States' trading partners in Western Europe, it is small relative to GNP. For 1977 the U.S. Department of Commerce reported the following data on exports in relation to GNP:[2]

Country	Exports as Percent of GNP
West Germany	23.4
Italy	19.7
Netherlands	51.2
United Kingdom	22.2
Japan	12.4
Canada	26.1

For countries with exceptional export economies, these ratios are much higher. For example, in 1980 Saudi Arabia's exports (principally oil) accounted for over 80 percent of its GNP.[3]

Countries with a relatively large proportion of exports to GNP are more vulnerable to changes in the international marketplace than are countries that do not depend so heavily on international trade as a generator of income and employment. For example, the Netherlands and Saudi Arabia would likely suffer much worse effects than some other countries if the United States placed an across-the-board surcharge (tax) on imports. In both of these countries a large proportion of total employment depends on exports, and anything that disrupts foreign trade will have a dramatic impact. On the other hand, for larger countries with more diversified economies, changes in the international marketplace, while significant, will have less impact on domestic production and employment.

CHANGING POSITION OF THE UNITED STATES

Immediately after World War II, the United States was the dominant trader in interna-

1. *Economic Report of the President* (Washington, D.C.: Government Printing Office, 1981), pp. 233; and *United Nations Monthly Bulletin of Statistics,* July 1981, p. 107.

2. *United Nations Monthly Bulletin of Statistics,* July 1981, pp. 106–111; and International Monetary Fund, *International Financial Statistics,* August 1981.

3. United Nations Monthly Bulletin of Statistics, July 1981, p. 111; and International Monetary Fund, *International Financial Statistics,* August 1981.

tional markets. For example, in 1948 U.S. exports were 23.5 percent of the trade of all market economies. As Europe progressed through postwar reconstruction, the U.S. share of world exports fell, so that by 1958 it was 18.5 percent of the total for market economies.[4] The U.S. share dropped to 15.4 percent in 1970, and it generally continued to fall during the 1970s, as Table 29–2 shows.

This table also indicates that West Germany and, especially, Japan gained market shares in world exports while the U.S. share was declining. Analysts have attributed this change in the U.S. position vis-a-vis the other industrialized nations to a decline in U.S. productivity and to the tendency of U.S. corporations to invest in manufacturing facilities abroad rather than attempting to export goods produced in the United States. In addition, it is said that many U.S. firms have been content with their domestic mass market and have not geared up to compete in foreign markets.

Another important change in the U.S. position in international trade is that the United States has moved from being a net exporter to being a net importer. In fact, from the end of World War II until 1971, the merchandise exports of the United States exceeded its imports—typically by several billion dollars each year. Since 1971 the United States gen-

erally has been a net importer (has had a trade deficit); and in 1980 imports exceeded exports by almost $39 billion.[5]

> A country has a **trade deficit** when its imports exceed its exports over some specific period of time, such as one year. If exports exceed imports, the country has a **trade surplus.**

To some extent the U.S. trade deficits after 1971 are attributable to increased expenditures for imported crude oil, but the sluggishness of U.S. exports has added to the problem. (Further discussion of this issue will appear in Chapter 30 in the section on the nature of international payments between countries.)

THE CENTRALLY PLANNED ECONOMIES

Thus far the discussion of world trade patterns has focused on the market economies. In such economies a large share of international trade is carried on between and among private business firms and prices are generally established by market forces of supply and demand. In the centrally planned economies, however, virtually all international trade is controlled by agencies of the central government. Trade between the Soviet Union and other members of

---

4. United Nations Statistical Office, *United Nations Statistical Yearbook* (New York: United Nations, 1977), p. 467.

5. *United Nations Monthly Bulletin of Statistics*, July 1981, pp. 106–107.

TABLE 29–2 Developed Market Economies: Shares of Total World Exports (in Percents)

Year	United States	France	West Germany	Italy	Netherlands	United Kingdom	Japan	Canada
1960	18.2	6.0	10.1	3.2	3.6	9.4	3.6	5.1
1970	15.4	6.5	12.2	4.7	4.2	6.9	6.9	6.0
1972	13.3	7.1	12.5	5.0	4.5	6.5	7.6	5.7
1974	12.8	6.0	11.6	3.9	4.3	5.1	7.2	4.5
1976	12.8	6.4	11.4	4.1	4.5	5.2	7.5	4.5
1977	11.9	6.4	11.5	4.4	4.3	5.7	7.9	4.2
1978	12.2	6.7	12.1	4.7	4.2	6.1	8.3	4.1
1979	12.0	6.6	11.5	4.8	4.3	6.1	6.9	3.7
1980	11.9	6.1	10.6	4.3	4.0	6.3	7.1	3.5

Source: U.S. Department of Commerce, International Trade Administration, *International Economic Indicators* (Washington, D.C.: Government Printing Office, December 1976 and December 1979); and United Nations, *Monthly Bulletin of Statistics*, July 1981.

the Eastern bloc, as well as trade with China, is generally carried on by means of bilateral (two-country) agreements covering the specific kinds and quantities of goods to be exchanged.

World market prices are used as a guide in negotiations, but trade between centrally planned economies is in effect a type of **barter** (an exchange of goods for goods, rather than goods for money), in which each party to a transaction attempts to keep export and import values closely balanced. State trading agencies are in charge of such negotiations.

A *state trading agency* is the government unit that carries on virtually all the international trade activities of a centrally planned economy.

In general, state trading agencies also take care of negotiations with private firms and government agencies in the market economies, when trade occurs between a centrally planned economy and some entity outside it.

The period since World War II has been characterized by isolation of the communist bloc nations from the noncommunist world. In addition, relations between the largest communist nations, the Soviet Union and China, have been strained. As a result of these conditions and of the fact that the level of economic development of the centrally planned economies is far below that of the developed market economies, the amount of international trade carried on by the centrally planned group is relatively small. For example, the United Nations reports that in 1980 the total value of the exports of the Soviet Union and its major Eastern European trading partners (Bulgaria, Czechoslovakia, East Germany, Hungary, Poland, and Romania) amounted to $155.1 billion. This amount is less than one-tenth the value of the exports of the market economies ($1,828.1 billion) in the same year.[6]

During the 1970s trade began to open up be-

tween the communist countries and the major industrialized nations of the noncommunist world. The United States has been a leader in this development. By the late 1970s U.S. exports to communist nations were running $2.5 billion to $3.5 billion per year, while the United States typically imported over $1 billion worth of products from them.[7] The future will probably bring further growth in trade between the market economies and the centrally planned economies. However, political considerations are likely to be every bit as important as economic ones in determining how rapidly this trade will expand.

MERCHANDISE TRADE PATTERN

To complete our introduction to the world trade environment, we need a brief survey of the product composition of goods traded internationally and the direction of trade (who sells what to whom). Our focus will be the market economies. To facilitate our examination we can divide products into three main categories: industrial raw materials (including fuels), foodstuffs (including animal feeds and beverages), and manufactures. Because the first two categories consist mainly of products of the land and are traded in an unprocessed or semiprocessed form, they are called primary products.

In today's world a large share of the primary products moving in international trade are produced in the developing market economies. For example, most of the crude oil comes from the developing countries of the Middle East or from Venezuela, Libya, Nigeria, Indonesia, or Mexico. Three developing countries—Columbia, Brazil, and Nigeria—are the main exporters of coffee. Two others—Malaysia and Bolivia—are the leading producers of tin. In addition, several of the less devel-

---

6. Ibid., pp. 106, 107.

7. U.S. Department of Commerce, International Trade Administration, *Trade of the U.S. with Eastern Europe and Asia, 1975–77* (Washington, D.C.: Government Printing Office, September 1978).

oped tropical countries are the principal exporters of such products as sugar, bananas, and cocoa. Countires whose main exports are primary goods are frequently called primary producing countries.

> The **primary producing countries** are a large group of developing countries, each of which is highly specialized in exporting either industrial raw materials or agricultural products (or some combination of the two).

Most of the exports of the primary producing countries are sold to the industrialized countries (developed market economies), and the main buyer in this group is the United States. On the other hand, most manufactured goods traded internationally are exported by the industrialized countries, both to each other and to the primary producing countries. Of course, there are exceptions to this pattern. For example, the United States and Canada export substantial quantities of foodstuffs as well as manufactured products.

During the 1950s and 1960s economists in the primary producing countries frequently argued that the historical trend in international prices benefited the industrialized countries at the expense of the less developed, primary producing countries. They based their belief on data that seemed to show that the prices of manufactured goods tended to increase at a faster rate than the prices of primary products. We will take a closer look at this problem (known as the terms of trade issue) later in the chapter. At this point it is sufficient to note that during the 1960s and 1970s many efforts were made to increase the relative prices of primary products and that some of these efforts (notably OPEC) were successful. In fact, shortages of certain raw commodities have occurred repeatedly in recent years and have caused some alarm in the industrialized countries.

The data of Table 29–3 underscore the fact that while the United States, the European Economic Community, and Japan may be the giants in world trade, they are heavily depen-

TABLE 29–3 Dependence on Selected Imported Industrial Raw Materials, 1975 (Imports as a Percent of Consumption)

	United States	European Community	Japan
Aluminum (ore and metal)	84%	75%	100%
Chromium	91	98	98
Cobalt	98	98	98
Copper	—[a]	98	90
Iron (ore and metal)	29	55	99
Lead	11	85	73
Manganese	98	99	88
Natural rubber	100	100	100
Nickel	72	100	100
Phosphates	—[a]	100	100
Tin	84	93	97
Tungsten	55	100	100
Zinc	61	70	53

[a]Net exporter.

Source: *International Economic Report of the President* (Washington, D.C.: Government Printing Office, 1977), p. 187.

dent on trade to obtain important raw materials for their industrial sectors. Thus the market behavior of the exporters of these primary products will have a significant impact on world trade in the future, especially as those who are less developed struggle to obtain the tools and capital goods necessary to pursue their own industrialization goals. The issue of trade and economic growth will be discussed in a later chapter. In the remainder of the present chapter we will turn our attention to the economic rationale for international trade and its theoretical underpinnings.

WHY NATIONS TRADE

The obvious answer to the question "Why do nations trade?" is that it is possible for the citizens of one nation to buy certain products more cheaply in the international market, or from citizens of other nations, than they can buy them in their own country. The real question, then, is why producers in some countries are able to offer products to foreign buyers at attractive prices.

It takes no great imagination to see why, for example, U.S. consumers might buy a lot of foreign produced bicycles, once it is known that these bicycles are available locally at prices substantially below those of U.S. made bikes of the same quality. The real question is how the foreigners are able to offer their bikes at the lower prices. Over the years, economic theory has provided two main answers to this question: the principle of absolute advantage and the principle of comparative advantage.

ABSOLUTE ADVANTAGE

The principle of absolute advantage is usually attributed to Adam Smith,□ who, in his *Wealth of Nations* (1776) said that a country might possess natural or other resources (climate, minerals, skills, and so on) that simply were not available in some other countries. This would enable the country to produce certain products absolutely cheaper than they could be produced in other countries, when cost is measured in terms of the physical amount of labor or other inputs required to produce a unit of output.

Smith's principle survives today as an explanation of why certain countries export specific commodities. It explains why the Arab nations and Venezuela are the principal exporters of petroleum, why bananas are exported by tropical countries, and why most opals come from either Australia or Mexico. Smith himself put it this way:

The natural advantages which one country has over another in producing particular commodities are sometimes so great that it is acknowledged by all the world to be in vain to struggle with them. By means of glasses, hotbeds, and hotwalls, even good grapes can be raised in Scotland, and very good wine too can be made of them at about thirty times the expense for which at the least equally good can be brought from foreign countries.

Whether the advantages which one country has over another, be natural or acquired, is in this respect of no consequence. As long as one country has those advantages, and the other wants them, it will always be more advantageous of the latter, rather to buy of the former than to make.[8]

Smith pointed out also that there really is no difference in the basis for trade between nations and between persons. Thus a medical doctor who knows nothing about masonry has an obvious reason to trade with a mason if the doctor wishes to have a wall built around his garden.

The **principle of absolute advantage** states that a country's exports will consist of goods that it can produce with fewer resources per unit of output than can its trading partners. Similarly, it will import those goods that its trading partners can produce with fewer resources per unit of output than the country itself would need to produce the same goods. (The principle applies to persons and regions as well as to countries.)

Absolute Advantage and Modern Trade Today, it is widely accepted that the principle of absolute advantage explains the pattern of trade between industrialized countries and certain nonindustrialized countries. In the latter group are the countries called the primary producing countries. As mentioned earlier, the products of this group are basic raw materials for industry or, in some cases, tropical agricultural goods. Examples are tin (Bolivia, Malaysia), copper (Chile), petroleum (Arab nations, Venezuela), bananas (Central American and Caribbean nations), and coffee (Brazil, Colombia, and Nigeria). In each of these cases it is clear that the country or group has an absolute natural advantage over other coun-

8. Adam Smith, *An Inquiry into the Nature and Causes of the Wealth of Nations*, 5th ed. (1789; New York: Modern Library, 1937), pp. 425–426.

tries in the ability to produce the good in question and that the source of this advantage is either geographical (climate) or natural resource-related.

COMPARATIVE ADVANTAGE

The principle of comparative advantage extends the analysis of the basis for trade one step further by showing that two countries can gain from trade, even when one of them has an absolute advantage in the production of all goods. The earliest statement of the principle of comparative advantage is attributed to David Ricardo,□ an English economist who was a follower of Smith. In his *Principles of Political Economy and Taxation* (1817), Ricardo used the example of trade between England and Portugal, in cloth and wine, to illustrate how comparative advantage works. We use a similar illustration here.

Table 29–4 shows the labor requirements for the production of both wine and cloth in England and in Portugal. In terms of labor cost, Portugal has an absolute advantage in both wine and cloth. That is, it takes fewer units of labor to produce *either* product in Portugal then it does in England. Should the English give up on the idea of trade with Portugal?

Let's look at the internal price ratios. In Portugal on the basis of labor cost as a measure of market value, 1 barrel of wine will exchange for 1 bolt of cloth (30 = 30) if there is no trade with England. Wine is relatively cheap in Portugal. However, in England, wine is relatively expensive, since it requires 1.5 times as much labor per unit produced (90/60 = 1.5).

Suppose the Portuguese offer 8/10 of a barrel

of wine for a bolt of cloth. Will the English deal with them? Because the English can get only 60/90 = 2/3 of a barrel of wine for a bolt of cloth at home, they certainly have a basis for trade with the Portuguese.

Identifying a Comparative Advantage The reason the numbers in Table 29–4 result in a basis for trade is that although Portugal has an absolute advantage in both wine and cloth, its absolute advantage is greater in wine (90/30 > 60/30). It can outproduce the English by 3 to 1 in wine but only 2 to 1 in cloth. A greater absolute advantage, such as Portugal has in wine, is called a comparative advantage.

> According to the **principle of comparative advantage,** *a country will export goods that are relatively cheap compared with other goods it can produce in terms of the resource cost per unit of output. Its imports will consist of goods that are relatively expensive to produce at home. (The principle also applies to persons and regions.)*

Compared to Portugal, England is at an absolute disadvantage in both wine and cloth, but it is at a lesser absolute disadvantage in cloth (60/30 < 90/30), where the Portuguese outproduce it only by 2 to 1. A lesser absolute disadvantage is also called a comparative advantage. Thus England has a comparative advantage in cloth production and can gain from trading its cloth for Portuguese wine. We can conclude that either absolute or comparative advantage can provide a basis for trade between countries, because either one will lead to dissimilar relative internal prices (different opportunity costs□ before trade).

CURRENCIES AND COMPARATIVE ADVANTAGE

◆

The above examples were stated in terms of barter (so much of one good for so much of

TABLE 29–4 A Numerical Example of Comparative Advantage

Country	Units of Labor Required to Produce	
	1 Barrel of Wine	1 Bolt of Cloth
England	90	60
Portugal	30	30

TABLE 29-5 Different Relative Internal Prices

Country	Internal Money Price of	
	1 Barrel of Wine	1 Bolt of Cloth
England (pounds)	£ 90	£ 60
Portugal (escudos)	30 escudos	30 escudos

another). Without too much trouble we can put money into the picture. Suppose that instead of using Smith's labor values, we reconstruct Table 29–4, showing internal money prices as our basic data. This is done in Table 29–5, where the numbers now pertain to the prices of wine and cloth in England (where the pound sterling is the currency unit) and in Portugal (where the escudo is the currency unit).

EXCHANGE RATES, PRICES, AND TRADE

In international markets the number of units of one currency that it takes to buy another is known as the rate of exchange, or simply the **exchange rate,** between the two currencies. The rate can be stated in terms of either currency. For example, in August 1981, the exchange rate between U.S. dollars and Mexican pesos was $1 = 24.9 pesos or, alternatively, 1 peso = 1/24.9 = $.0402.

Returning to the example of England and Portugal, in Table 29–5 suppose the exchange rate between pounds and escudos is £1 = 1 escudo. In this situation the Portuguese would not want to buy either wine or cloth from the English, but the English would want to buy both products from the Portuguese. Thus trade would be only one-way if no other goods were involved. The Portuguese would earn a lot of pounds sterling, but they would not want to spend them on English cloth, because it would be too expensive.

The exchange rate, however, is very important. For example, if it were possible to get £ 2.5 for 1 escudo, a two-way trade in cloth and wine would take place between England and Portugal. We can see this easily in Table 29–6, where English prices are converted into escudos (left side of table) and Portuguese prices are converted into pounds sterling (right side of table), using the exchange rate of £ 2.5 = 1 escudo. Now, given the exchange rate of £ 2.5 per escudo, the Portuguese can obtain cloth more cheaply in England (24 escudos per bolt) than at home (30 escudos per bolt), although wine is still too expensive to import from England. At the same exchange rate the English can buy Portuguese wine for £75 per barrel, or £15 less than at home. However, Portuguese cloth is no bargain to the English buyer.

We see now that different relative money prices (30/30 ≠ 90/60), presumably reflecting different relative production costs in the two countries, also lead to two-way trade. We should now ask: Is there anything that would cause a movement in the rate of exchange between pounds sterling and escudos from £1 = 1 escudo toward something like £2.5 = 1 escudo, given the data in Table 29–5? The answer is yes.

If there is a free market for currencies, the Portuguese sellers who build up holdings of pounds from sales of both wine and cloth to the English at the £1 = 1 escudo exchange rate

Table 29-6 Result of an Exchange Rate of £2.5 = 1 Escudo

Country	Money Price of Product in			
	Escudos		Pounds	
	1 Barrel of Wine	1 Bolt of Cloth	1 Barrel of Wine	1 Bolt of Cloth
England	36	24	90	60
Portugal	30	30	75	75

will sell the pounds in that currency market to get escudos or other currencies useful to them. The supply of pounds will increase, for this reason and for another one. The second reason is that the English will also want to sell pounds to get escudos with which to pay for importing cheap Portuguese goods. For any given demand curve□ the increase in the supply of pounds will cause their price in terms of other currencies to fall.

Figure 29–1 illustrates such a situation with respect to the price of pounds in terms of escudos per pound. Here, as the supply curve□ of pounds sterling shifts from S to S′, the number of escudos it takes to buy £1 drops from 1 to 0.40. This is the same thing as saying that 1 escudo will now buy £2.5, or £2.5 = 1 escudo.

THE IMPORTANCE OF
DIFFERENT RELATIVE PRICES

This chapter will not go further into the role of exchange rates and currency markets in establishing the basis for trade between coun-

tries. Such topics are discussed in more detail in Chapter 30. The main objective here is simply to show that different relative money prices can lead to a basis for two-way trade between countries. In fact, we can show that if relative money prices do not differ, the basis for two-way trade disappears. We can prove this fact by going back to Table 29–5 and assuming that the internal prices of Portugal are 1 barrel of wine = 45 escudos and 1 bolt of cloth = 30 escudos. In this case the relative prices are the same in Portugal as in England—45/30 = 90/60. If we try to construct a table like Table 29–6, we will find that no exchange rate between pounds and escudos is compatible with two-way trade, although if pounds sterling become cheap enough the Portuguese will buy both wine and cloth from England. (This situation will require that more than £2 be obtained for 1 escudo.)

EFFECTS OF TRADE ON A COUNTRY'S
PRODUCTION, CONSUMPTION, AND
PRICES

A simple analysis using supply and demand curves can help illustrate how the possibility of trading internationally affects a country's production, consumption, and internal prices. If we assume that the world market for some specific product is perfectly competitive,□ then an equilibrium price□ for that product will be generated by the combined actions of all the buyers and sellers in the market. This means that a large number of countries must be engaged in selling or buying the product. However, no single consumer group (nation) or producer group can by itself affect the price of the product.

Panel (a) of Figure 29–2 shows the domestic demand and supply curves for shoes in the United States. The horizontal line, P_I, is the international market price of shoes. Without international trade, the U.S. price (as well as U.S. production and consumption) will be determined at point E_{US}, where S_{US} and D_{US} in-

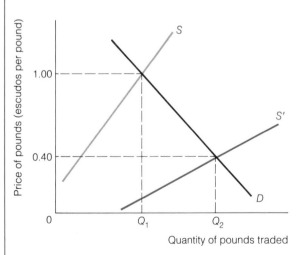

FIGURE 29–1 Fall in the Price of the British Pound Caused by an Increase in Supply

The effect of England's desire to import both wine and cloth from Portugal is to increase the supply of pounds, shifting the supply curve from S to S′. The price of pounds in terms of escudos drops to 0.40 escudos per pound.

tersect. However, with international trade, shoes can be bought or sold in the world market for price P_I. Thus U.S. producers sell the amount of shoes, Q_S, that they are willing and able to produce for price P_I. At P_I, the demand curve shows that there is excess demand for shoes in the United States, because consumers are willing and able to purchase Q_D of them. Therefore, U.S. consumers will buy Q_D of shoes, and the United States will import quantity ($Q_D - Q_S$) of shoes. Trade has caused shoe production in the United States to be less than it would have been at E_{US}, but consumption is greater than at E_{US}. Finally, P_I is less than the price would be at E_{US}.

Panel (b) of Figure 29–2 shows the U.S. demand and supply curves for another product, wheat, which has a world price of P_W. Here, there is an excess U.S. supply of wheat at the world market price, and the United States exports quantity ($Q_S - Q_D$) to other countries. Without trade the United States would both consume and produce at E_{US}. Thus trade results in a higher price and a lower quantity demanded in the United States than would otherwise exist. With trade, U.S. producers grow

more wheat, because they can get P_W for any amount they export.

In both the wheat and shoe examples the U.S. consumer ends up paying the international price for the product, and the same price is received by U.S. producers. The U.S. imports shoes because its internal price of shoes without trade would be higher than the world market price. Similarly, it exports wheat because its internal price of wheat would be lower than the world market price without trade. How much a country gains from trade depends in part on the relationship between the prices it pays for imports and the prices it receives for exports. This is a matter we will take up in a later section.

MODERN VIEWS ON THE DETERMINANTS OF TRADE
◆

Although a country's resources and productiveness are important determinants of its

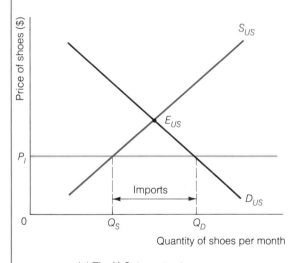

(a) The U.S. imports shoes . . .

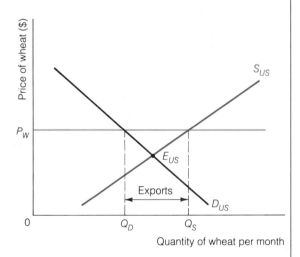

(b) . . . but exports wheat.

FIGURE 29–2 Effects of Trade on U.S. Consumption, Production, and Prices of Shoes

In panel (a), the world price of shoes (P_I) is less than the price that would exist in the U.S. without trade, so the U.S. imports shoes. In panel (b), the world price of wheat (P_W) is greater than the price that would exist in the U.S. without trade, so the U.S. exports wheat.

trade pattern, demand also plays an important role in explaining the international flow of goods and services. In fact, modern economists attribute a substantial part of total world trade to overlapping patterns of preferences and demand in the industrialized nations. These nations have similar production possibilities and in some cases similar resource bases. Yet, as the data at the beginning of the chapter showed, the bulk of world trade in manufactured products takes place among such nations (Europe, the United States, Canada, and Japan).

DEMAND-BASED TRADE: THE LINDER THESIS

A Swedish economist, Staffan Linder, first popularized the argument (known as the **Linder thesis**) that the similarity of demand in the large consumer markets of the industrialized countries opens up more possibilities for comparative advantage to work than can be found among countries with very different levels of development.[9] Thus an electric face scrubber developed in Europe or Japan can be sold easily to consumers in the United States and Canada if it is competitively priced. However, the likelihood of a mass demand for such a product in Peru is much smaller. Even though the Europeans or Japanese would clearly have a comparative advantage over Peru in the production of such a good, it is not likely to account for a significant amount of trade with less developed countries such as Peru.

THE PRODUCT CYCLE: VERNON

Trade among the industrialized countries is also explained in part by the life cycle of new products (known as the **product cycle**). Raymond Vernon of Harvard University has argued that because the industrialized countries

possess mass consumer markets and highly developed technology, most new products are introduced in one or another of them.[10] In fact, the United States is a world leader in such new product development. Once a product has been developed, it is usually marketed first in the country where it was conceived and initially manufactured. Thus the initial stage in the product cycle is marked by both production and consumption of the new product in the country where it was originated.

The introduction of a successful new product is usually followed by its export to foreign markets where consumer tastes are similar to those in the country of origin. Thus international trade begins at this point in the cycle. However, once the product is successful in foreign markets, the manufacturer may seek production facilities in those markets, particularly if it is cheaper to produce the product there than to continue to produce it in the country of origin and ship it to such markets. So production may now take place in both markets. Finally, it may turn out that foreign production is so much cheaper than production in the country of origin that the trade pattern reverses itself. Thus the county that originally exported the product may become an importer of it and may no longer manufacture it.

SOME PRELIMINARY CONCLUSIONS

As the preceding sections have pointed out, the question of the basis for trade between countries is complex. Certainly, each country's resource base—including natural resources, climate, and human resources (the education and skill of its people)—contributes to the structure of its comparative advantage. Both absolute and comparative advantage can account for the differences in domestic, or in-

9. Staffan B. Linder, *An Essay on Trade and Transformation*, New York: Wiley, 1961).

10. Raymond Vernon, "International Investment and International Trade in the Product Cycle," *Quarterly Journal of Economics* Vol. LXXXI, No. 2 (May 1966): 190–207.

ternal, relative prices that constitute a basis for gains from trade. However, it is clear that demand patterns are also important. Indeed, each country's pattern of relative prices depends on both supply and demand. Finally, it can be argued that the life cycle of products may be such that trade patterns inconsistent with comparative advantage do exist, although perhaps only temporarily.

With all these forces interacting, what can we conclude about the basis for trade? Perhaps our paramount conclusion should be that the opportunities for gains from trade, given all the circumstances that can lead to dissimilar relative prices from country to country, seem to be virtually innumerable. In addition, we can say that the pattern of trade is fairly predictable when it is dictated by absolute advantage. (Not too many countries are destined to be exporters of diamonds or copper.) To some extent, the same is true of trade based on comparative advantage, although the structure of comparative advantage in manufactured goods changes as technology is dispersed and refined. Thus some countries, even though their resource bases suggest otherwise, may become exporters of manufactured goods that they have historically imported—once they obtain the production technology for such goods. Finally, given what we know about the influences of demand and the product cycle, we can expect the trade pattern to provide surprises from time to time.

DIVISION OF THE GAINS FROM INTERNATIONAL TRADE

◆

Because international trade occurs among nations and because any nation that chooses to trade does so because it is better off with trade than without, an important question is whether some nations reap more gains from international trade than do others. This ques-

tion has long been a central issue in debates between economists from developing countries and economists from the industrialized nations. The debate has to do with what economists call the terms of trade question.

THE TERMS OF TRADE AND ITS MEASUREMENT

Fundamentally, the *terms of trade* is the relationship between the prices a country pays for its imports and the prices it obtains for its exports. Clearly, if U.S. consumers find that the prices of imported goods have risen, they will have become worse off because of having to pay the higher prices. If U.S. producers find that the prices they sell their exports for have fallen, they too will have become worse off. Thus, either a rise in the prices of imports or a fall in the prices of exports (or both at once) will worsen the terms under which the U.S. deals with other trading nations.

Such a worsening in the relationship between export prices and import prices constitutes a deterioration in the terms of trade of the United States. Conversely, if U.S. export prices rise while import prices fall, the U.S. terms of trade will have improved. To measure changes in the terms of trade, an index consisting of the ratio of export prices to import prices must be constructed. Such an index is described here.

Terms of Trade Index In its simplest and most direct form, a **terms of trade index** is a ratio of the price index□ of a country's exports to a price index of its imports. For any country an export price index can be calculated by selecting a representative group of export goods and determining the weighted average of their prices.[11] A base year is also selected, and usu-

----

11. A weighted average takes into account the amounts of each item traded as well as the prices. Thus, if the price of a good exported in very small quantities doubles, there may not be much of an effect on the export price index.

ally the index number of the base year is 100. For future years the weighted average price for the same group of export goods is calculated, and the index number for each year is expressed as a percent of the original year's number (100). Thus, if 1978 is the base year (index = 100) and in 1981 the weighted average price of the export goods is 50 percent higher than the 1978 price, the index for 1981 will be 150.

A country's import price index can be constructed similarly, using representative import goods rather than export goods as the relevant data. Its terms of trade index is simply its export price index divided by its import price index and multiplied by 100, or

$$P_x/P_m\ (100)\ =\ TOT.$$

A Terms of Trade Example Suppose that from 1978 to 1981 the export price index of Australia rose from 100 to 140 and the import price index rose from 100 to 160. Australia's terms of trade obviously worsened, because the weighted average price of its exports increased by less than the weighted average price of its imports. This is reflected as a decline in its terms of trade index. Using the formula just given, we have

$$TOT_1 = \frac{100}{100} \times 100 = 100,$$

and

$$TOT_2 = \frac{140}{160} \times 100 = 87.5,$$

where TOT_1 is the terms of trade for Australia in 1978 and TOT_2 is the terms of trade in 1981. The index shows that a given amount of Australian exports would buy only 87.5 percent as much in imports in 1981 as it would in 1978. Alternatively, we can say that in 1981 the Australians had to export a larger physical output of their goods to buy the same amount of foreign goods that they imported in 1978.

DETERMINANTS OF THE TERMS OF TRADE

If there were no government interference with international trade and if goods were produced and sold in competitive markets, each country's terms of trade would be determined by the international patterns of supply and demand for its exports and its imports. In the example above, Australia would have only fate to blame for the worsening that occurred in its terms of trade. However, the real world is considerably more complex than the theoretical world of perfect competition. Even though a large number of buyers and sellers do exist for many products in international trade, there is also much interference with the operation of markets, both for the products traded and the factors used to produce them.

Tarrifs on imports (taxes collected by the country receiving the goods) affect the terms of trade. Also, government policies that restrict the quantity of imports or exports (quotas) or subsidize certain producers or consumers can alter the terms of trade. A third determinant of the terms of trade is the degree of monopolization found in the production of internationally traded goods. Cartels of producers may succeed in improving the terms of trade for exporting countries, —petroleum being a case in point. During the 1970s the OPEC cartel succeeded in markedly improving the terms of trade of oil-exporting countries.

TERMS OF TRADE OF THE LESS DEVELOPED COUNTRIES: THE PREBISCH THESIS

Prior to OPEC's success, economists of the primary producing countries frequently used terms of trade arguments to help explain why such countries were not very successful in raising their overall level of economic development during the nineteenth and twentieth centuries. They held that the terms of trade had steadily worsened for producers of primary products for more than a century.

One of these economists, an Argentinian named Raul Prebisch, offered an impressive set of statistics based on British trade data to prove the point.[12] According to Prebisch and others, this phenomenon was caused by (1) the fact that demand for primary products grew more slowly than demand for industrial products as world economic growth took place, and (2) the monopolization of both product and factor markets in the industrialized countries, which allowed the gains in productivity of the primary producers to be appropriated—through higher prices, wages, and profits—by the factors of production□ in the industrialized countries.

When the **Prebisch thesis** was scrutinized by economists in the developed countries, the new data they introduced did not confirm the claim that the terms of trade of primary producing countries had worsened over the long run. However, these data did show that recessions in the industrialized countries greatly affected the primary producing countries, so that the terms of trade of these countries were subject to wide fluctuations.[13]

After 1960 enough attention was paid to the problem of the fluctuating terms of trade of primary producing countries to lead to the development of international policies to promote stability in markets for primary goods. However, the nature of the terms of trade issue changed markedly following the success of OPEC in the 1970s. It became clear that henceforth the primary producing countries would be divided into two groups—those that had

oil and those that did not. For the latter group the future began to look bleak.

SUMMARY

1. This chapter examined developing world trade patterns and some of the fundamental reasons that countries trade with each other. It also showed that the terms of trade determine the relative benefits received by trading partners.

2. The United Nations divides the countries of the world into three major groups: the developed market economies, the developing market economies, and the centrally planned economies. At least partly as a result of OPEC, in the 1970s the developing economies increased their share of world trade among the market economies by approximately 5 percent. With regard to the importance of foreign trade, the ratio of exports to gross national product for the United States is relatively small in comparison with the ratios for other developed economies.

3. The position of the United States in international trade has worsened in the post–World War II period. For example, the share of U.S. exports in the total for all market economies has fallen from 23.5 percent in 1948 to less than 12.0 percent in 1980. The United States has also moved from being a net exporter to being a net importer. Some analysts have attributed these changes to a decline in labor productivity in the United States as compared with the productivity of other countries. Also, U.S. companies have tended to either remain content with the U.S. market or build plants in foreign countries.

4. In the centrally planned economies virtually all international trade is controlled by agencies of the central government, known as state trading agencies. However, the share of international trade accounted for by the exports of the Soviet Union and its major Eastern European satellites is less than one-tenth the share of the market economies.

5. Products shipped in international trade can be divided into three main categories: industrial raw materials (including fuels), foodstuffs (including animal feeds and beverages), and manufactures. Products in the first two categories come mainly from the land and are called primary products. A large share of the primary products are produced by

12. Raul Prebisch, *The Economic Development of Latin America and its Principal Problems* (New York: United Nations Economic Commission for Latin America, 1950), and United Nations Conference on Trade and Development, *Towards a New Trade Policy for Development* (New York: United Nations, 1964).

13. For a summary of views relating to the Prebisch argument, see Franklin R. Root, *International Trade and Investment,* 4th ed. (Cincinnati, Ohio: South-Western Publishing, 1978), pp. 421–428.

the developing market economies and are sold to the developed market economies. Most manufactured goods traded internationally are exported by the developed market economies and sold to each other or to the countries producing primary products.

6. The two main bases for international trade are centered around the principles of absolute advantage and comparative advantage. In 1776 Adam Smith pointed out in *The Wealth of Nations* that a country might have natural or other resources that simply were not available in some other countries. These resources would enable the country to produce certain products absolutely cheaper than they could be produced in other countries, when cost is measured in terms of the physical amount of labor or other inputs required to produce a unit of output. The principle of absolute advantage explains, for example, why the Arab nations export oil and why tropical countries export bananas.

7. The principle of comparative advantage explains how it may be beneficial for two countries to trade when they have different relative internal prices, even when one of them has an absolute advantage in the production of all goods. David Ricardo, a nineteenth century English economist, is given credit for first verbalizing this principle.

8. In the example given in the text, Portugal had an absolute advantage in the production of cloth and wine. However, it had a greater absolute advantage in the production of wine, and England had a smaller absolute disadvantage in the production of cloth. In this case Portugal had a comparative advantage in the production of wine, and England had a comparative advantage in the production of cloth. Given certain internal relative prices in the two countries and certain exchange rates, the people in both countries could be made better off through trade. However, this result does not hold for all exchange rates.

9. Modern economists attribute much of world trade to overlapping patterns of demand in the industrialized nations. However, these countries have similar production possibilities and sometimes similar resource bases. A Swedish economist, Staffan Linder, explained this phenomenon with the argument that the similarity of demand in the large consumer markets of the industrialized countries opens up more possibilities for comparative advantage to work than can be found between countries with very different levels of development.

10. According to Raymond Vernon, a Harvard economist, trade among the industrialized nations is also partly explained by the life cycle of new products. Vernon argued that because the industrialized countries possess mass consumer markets and highly developed technology, most new products are introduced in one or another of them, particularly in the United States. The first stage of the product cycle is marked by both production and consumption of the new product in the country where it was originated. In later stages the product may be exported to other countries, eventually produced there, and perhaps later even exported to the country that originally developed it.

11. The gains from international trade by a specific country depend on the terms of trade. A terms of trade index is the ratio of the price index of a country's exports to the price index of its imports. For each country an export price index can be calculated by selecting a representative group of export products and finding the weighted average of their prices.

12. According to Raul Prebisch and some other economists, the terms of trade have steadily worsened for producers of primary products. They explain that this phenomenon was caused by the fact that the demand for primary products grew more slowly than the demand for industrial products and by monopolization of both product and factor markets in the industrialized countries.

13. Although economists do not generally agree about the issue of worsening terms of trade for primary producing countries, there is evidence that recessions in the industrialized countries have relatively large effects on the primary producing countries. However, the terms of trade issue has changed following the success of OPEC in the 1970s. For primary producing countries that have no oil the future looks bleak.

IMPORTANT TERMS AND CONCEPTS

Developed market economies

Developing market economies

Centrally planned economies

Trade deficit

Trade surplus

Barter

State trading agency

Primary producing countries

Principle of absolute advantage

Principle of comparative advantage

Linder thesis

Product cycle

Terms of trade index

Prebisch thesis

QUESTIONS AND PROBLEMS

1. Which countries account for the bulk of current world trade? Discuss the relative importance of trade to this group of countries and to the other groups with whom they trade.

2. Which are the primary producing countries? What kinds of products do they export and import? What recent development has increased their share of world trade?

3. How is trade carried on among countries in the communist bloc? Relative to the market economies, how large is their volume of trade? How is their trade with market economies arranged?

4. What is the principle of absolute advantage? Briefly explain how it works.

5. What is the principle of comparative advantage? How can you tell when a country has a comparative advantage, vis à vis some other country, in a given product? In the following table, who has a comparative advantage in what? Explain how you know.

Country	Internal Price per Unit of	
	Blue Jeans	Phonograph Records
England	£6	£3
United States	$12	$4

6. In the table in Question 5, what trade pattern should we expect if £1 = $1.80? Will there be two-way trade? Suppose £1 = $2.50. What will happen? Are there any foreign exchange market implications for this latter situation?

7. Although the original theory of comparative advantage was cost-based, new explanations of the basis for trade find other forces underlying world trade patterns. What are these forces, and how do they explain trade?

8. It can truly be said that a country's gains from trade depend in part on its terms of trade. What does this mean? How is it related to the problems of primary producing countries?

9. Given the following set of export and import price data, explain what has happened to the terms of trade index of each country. Calculate the terms of trade.

Country	Export Price Index		Import Price Index	
	1970	1980	1970	1980
Middle Arabia	100	250	100	170
United States	100	180	100	200
Germany	100	160	100	170
Mexico	100	200	100	240

THE U.S.
LAUNCHES AN
EXPORT DRIVE

International money men frequently picture the United States as the most reluctant of major trading nations. After all, only 10 per cent of American manufacturing companies export at all—and most sales abroad are made by a relatively small number of giant corporations. But there are signs the sleeping giant may be stirring. U.S. exports have increased at a surprisingly sharp rate in recent years, and now the government is launching a comprehensive new program it hopes will accelerate the trend by encouraging smaller

Source: David Pauly with Rich Thomas, John J. Lindsay, and Pamela Lynn Abraham, "The U.S. Launches an Export Drive," *Newsweek*, May 26, 1980, p. 73. Copyright 1980, by Newsweek, Inc. All Rights Reserved. Reprinted by Permission.

concerns to play the game, too. "This will be the first time this country has ever had an integrated global marketing system, direct contact, Peoria to Paris," says Herta Seidman, Assistant Commerce Secretary for Trade Development. "Companies are still going to have to make their own final sales—but we can give them much more help and focus than in the past."

A close look at U.S. trade statistics shows that the huge increase in the cost and quantity of imported oil tends to mask a substantial rise in the nation's exports. Overseas sales of made-in-America goods totaled $180 billion in 1979, a fourfold increase in a decade. Manufactured exports now account for nearly 5 per cent

of the country's gross national product, compared with the 3 per cent average that prevailed in the 1950's and 1960. The spurt in sales abroad has continued into 1980. "Export orders are one reason we didn't fall into recession earlier, and they are cushioning the downturn now," maintains Alfred C. Holden, chief economist for the Foreign Credit Insurance Association, a group of 51 companies that insures exporters against nonpayment by foreign buyers.

Italian Ice

The biggest reason for the splurge has been the long decline of the dollar—a factor that has made American business increasingly cost-competitive in world markets. Basic wage costs in the United States still top those in other countries, but higher fringe benefits in Europe, for instance, balance the scales. The U.S. textile and garment industry, once written off as a high-cost loser in world trade, now markets denims, corduroys, towels, spun yarns and even men's shirts in Europe. "We scared the hell out of the competition," says Geza Feketekuty, director of policy planning for the U.S. Special Trade Representative Office. "And this is supposed to be an industry that's obsolete." Conversely, an Italian manufacturer, Indesit, now finds it cheaper to make small refrigerators in New York state than at home—and it exports 40 per cent of its U.S. production to Canada and Latin America.

Still, most smaller and medium-size U.S. companies shy away from the export market, and the new U.S. trade-promotion effort is aimed at nudging them into the fray. This week, the Commerce Department will activate a globe-girdling computer network that will eventually match prospective American exporters with buyers in key importing countries. Commerce is also attempting to develop commercial officers in U.S. embassies into a single cadre of salesmen representing the interests of all American companies. And last week, the Senate Banking Committee passed a bill that would grant antitrust and financing relief to smaller companies bidding for overseas business. "American business participation cannot be encouraged unless some barriers are down," says Illinois Democrat Adlai Stevenson, co-sponsor of the bill.

Trade experts say the companies may need even more cost-cutting incentives if they are to export in a serious way—everything from faster write-offs on plants and equipment and reduced regulation to lower taxes on foreign operations. Whatever breaks Washington ultimately provides, the United States must continue to flog exports if it is to pay its imported-oil bills. At the moment, the experts are encouraged. The record of the last ten years indicates that exporting may be easier than many companies think—and if the government continues to remove barriers and stimulate incentives to trade, it may be easier still in the years ahead.

QUESTIONS

1. How does the value of the dollar in terms of other currencies affect the cost-competitiveness of U.S. products?
2. How does the principle you explained in Question 1 relate to the idea of comparative advantage? What examples are cited in this article?
3. According to the article, what steps are being taken or considered by the U.S. government in order to stimulate exports?

C H A P T E R 30

INTERNATIONAL
PAYMENTS,
INVESTMENT,
AND FOREIGN EXCHANGE

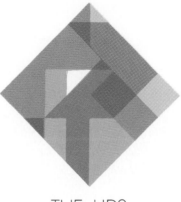

THE UPS
AND DOWNS
OF THE DOLLAR

While the airfare war (see Chapter 4) made getting to Europe relatively easy for many Americans during the late 1970s and 1980, the exchange value of the dollar left food and accommodations far from a bargain. Who wants to pay $1.25 for a Coke or $4.50 for a Big Mac, even if one does get to down them in Paris? The price of European hotel rooms (particularly in first-class hotels) has been a subject best left undiscussed by ordinary folks. Of course, the change in the international value of the dollar also affected other foreign goods. These goods, which had sometimes appeared to be bargains compared with their American counterparts, began to seem very expensive. The reverse happened to U.S. goods in the eyes of foreigners. Indeed, an export boom was created for the United States, particularly in capital goods like earth movers and machine tools, but also in agricultural products and textiles.

What made the dollar decline during the 1970s? The decline was largely a result of the U.S. government's decision to allow the dollar to float in the world's currency markets. This decision actually was made in 1971, prior to the OPEC price increases for crude oil. After the oil price hikes, the dollar moved downward with respect to the most important of the other world currencies—until just recently. For example, the West German mark was valued at $.27 U.S. in 1970. In 1980 the mark cost $.55 U.S., but in mid-1981 it had slipped to $.42. Investment flows and government monetary policy affect the relative values of currencies. So does speculation by professional currency traders. All these forces will be examined in this chapter.

INTERNATIONAL
PAYMENTS,
INVESTMENT,
AND FOREIGN EXCHANGE

WHAT THIS CHAPTER IS ABOUT

In Chapter 29 our primary concerns were the basis for international trade and the nature and division of the gains from trade. We found that trade provides consumers with more goods than they would otherwise have, because countries tend to specialize in and export the goods that they can produce relatively cheaply and tend to obtain from others the goods that are relatively expensive to produce at home.

As we saw in Chapter 29, in the planned economies of the communist bloc, individual countries barter exports for imports. **Bartering** is trading goods for other goods without using money as a medium of exchange. For example, when Rumania obtains cars from Czechoslovakia, it may trade 150,000 barrels of oil for 500 cars. If the Rumanians want 100 more

cars, they will have to come up with another 30,000 barrels of oil or find some other commodity that the Czechs are willing to take for cars. Thus barter requires a careful matching of the commodity demands of the trading partners.

In the market economies of the noncommunist world, imports are bought with money rather than goods, and a system of international financial markets eliminates the need for barter. If country A sells some of its goods to country B but does not purchase B's exports, it can simply take the money earned from sales to B and spend it on goods from country C or country D or any other market oriented country. Thus the international financial system facilitates what is known as the multilateral settlement of claims earned by exporting countries. As we will see in this chapter, the private banking system of the market economies plays an important role in facilitating the transfer of purchasing power from one currency to another.

HOW
TRADE IS
FINANCED

In domestic business transactions, such as those in the United States between supplier firms and customer firms (manufacturers and wholesalers or wholesalers and retailers), much trade is handled on **open account.** This means that sellers ship goods to buyers who pay within thirty, sixty or even ninety days from the date of shipment or receipt of merchandise. In effect, the sellers are providing short-term credit (loans) to the buyers. Such **trade credit** is provided because it attracts customers and because the risk is not very great. (The sellers have access to abundant credit information and a legal system that provides remedies for breach of contract.)

Trade credit is much less common in international business, however, because sellers (exporters) often have only limited information about the creditworthiness of foreign buyers and about the degree to which creditors are protected under foreign law. Foreign buyers, on the other hand, are just like domestic buyers in that they do not want to pay for merchandise until it is received or at least until it is shipped and on its way to them, insured against loss. In addition, foreign buyers are accustomed to paying for goods in the currency of their home country, whereas sellers wish to receive *their* own country's currency in payment. Fortunately, banks can solve these international payments problems.

THE ROLE OF BANKS

Commercial banks facilitate import-export trade by providing credit to cover the period of time between the sale and receipt of merchandise, by guaranteeing that sellers will be paid for their exports, and by translating payments from one currency into another. They play a similar role in foreign investment, making loans, supplying guarantees, and facilitating transactions from one currency to another. We can best understand how banks operate in this sphere by tracing the steps in a typical transaction.

Example of an International Transaction[1]
Suppose that an importer in the United States wishes to purchase goods from an exporter in

---

1. The transaction described here illustrates one of a number of ways in which foreign trade transactions are typically financed. Other financing patterns are common; the purpose of using this one is simply to describe a standard pattern that will illustrate how payment, credit, and risk are handled in the international financial system.

Germany. The German exporter will want to be paid in marks, not dollars. To him, dollars are foreign exchange.

> **Foreign exchange** is the currency of any country other than one's own.

The importer will have dollars, not marks, with which to pay the exporter. The importer wants to be sure that what is paid for is received, and the exporter desires payment for what is shipped. As a result the German exporter will ask the U.S. importer to supply a letter of credit from a U.S. bank.

> A **letter of credit** is a document issued by an importer's bank indicating that the bank will pay an exporter or the exporter's bank a specific amount for a specific shipment of goods.

In our example, this letter will state that the U.S. bank will honor a draft (check) drawn by the German exporter against the importer and presented, with appropriate proof that the goods in question have been shipped (a bill of lading or shipper's receipt), to a specific bank in Germany. Usually, the exact amount to pay the exporter will be specified in the letter of credit—and in the importer's currency.

The German bank that is cooperating with the U.S. bank (called a "correspondent bank") may be asked to confirm the letter of credit irrevocably. This confirmation means that the exporter's claim against the importer has been transferred into a claim against the German bank. The German bank is willing to accept this liability because its correspondent bank in the United States maintains a mark account with it, against which charges for such claims can be drawn. In other words, what happens when the German exporter is finally paid is that the German correspondent bank will debit (subtract from, or reduce) the U.S. bank's mark account by an amount equivalent to the dollars owed the exporter at the time the exporter's draft, now called an acceptance, is paid off.

*An exporter's draft against an importer be-
comes an* **acceptance** *once the exporter's
bank establishes that all conditions necessary
for present or future payment of the draft have
been met.*

For example, suppose a U.S. Mercedes
dealer wishes to purchase two cars valued at
$30,000, or 53,700 marks, each, given an
exchange rate of 1.79 marks per dollar. Table
30–1 shows the changes occurring on the balance sheets□ of the German bank and the U.S.
bank involved in this transaction. The German
exporter has an increase in deposits equal to
107,400 marks. The deposits of the U.S. bank
are reduced by 107,400 marks, and the U.S.
importer's deposits in that bank are also reduced by $60,000, an equivalent amount.

TIME DRAFTS AND
FOREIGN EXCHANGE RISK

In this example, how many marks the exporter receives will depend on the rate of exchange, a concept introduced in Chapter 29.
In 1979 the exchange rate between dollars and
marks was about 1.79 marks to $1, or 1 mark

**TABLE 30–1 Bank Balance Sheet Changes as the
Result of an International Trade Transaction**
(a) German Bank

Assets	Liabilities and Capital Accounts	
	Deposits of German exporter (marks)	+ 107,400
	Deposits of U.S. bank (marks)	– 107,400

(b) United States Bank

Assets		Liabilities and Capital Accounts	
Deposits at German bank	– $60,000[a]	Deposits of U.S. importer	– $60,000

[a]Equal to 107,400 marks.

to $.56. That is, if 1.79 marks = $1, then 1
mark = $1/1.79 = $.559.

The **rate of exchange** *(or exchange rate) between two currencies is the price of a unit of
one of them in terms of the other.*

Often, when a considerable delay is to occur between the time of the sale and the receipt of merchandise by the importer, the importer's letter of credit will state that the
exporter can draw only a time draft against the
importer.

A **time draft** *is an order to pay at some future
date. It is drawn by an exporter against an importer's account.*

With a time draft the importer is likely to have
received the merchandise by the date payment
is made; thus the exporter shoulders the burden of financing the export while it is in transit.

If the German exporter draws a time draft
against the U.S. importer, a specific number of
days (usually thirty, sixty, or ninety) must
pass before the acceptance can be paid by the
accepting bank in Germany. Because of this
delay the exporter runs a **foreign exchange
risk** from the time of sale to the time the acceptance is paid. The risk exists because the
exchange value of the dollar (the number of
marks in a dollar) may fall between the time
the exporter's draft is approved by the German
bank (the time it becomes an acceptance) and
the date payment is due. Thus, if the exporter
quotes the importer a price of $100,000 for a
particular good and at the time of sale the exchange rate is 1.79 marks per dollar, the sale
will be for 179,000 marks. If the exporter then
holds the acceptance to maturity and at that
time faces an exchange rate of 1.75 marks to
the dollar, the proceeds from the sale will be
only 175,000 marks, 4,000 marks less than
originally anticipated. Usually, in order to
avoid this complication, the exporter will im-

mediately sell the acceptance to a bank or broker at a discount.[2]

THE FOREIGN EXCHANGE MARKET AND THE RATE OF EXCHANGE

◆

In the preceding section we noted that a primary concern of exporters is to be paid in their own country's currency. The mechanism through which this was accomplished in our United States–Germany example was the reduction of the United States bank's mark account at the German correspondent bank. If, in general, U.S. banks are losing marks from their accounts in German banks because the United States is importing more from Germany than it is exporting to Germany, the U.S. banks will eventually reach a point where they need to replenish their supplies of marks. In the foreign exchange market this will lead to an increase in the demand for marks or to an increase in the supply of dollars. Because currencies are priced in terms of one another, either increase will have the same result, as Figure 30–1 illustrates.

SUPPLY AND DEMAND IN THE FOREIGN EXCHANGE MARKET

Panel (a) of Figure 30–1 shows an increase in the supply of dollars from S_d to S'_d. The price of the dollar (number of marks per dollar) will fall when the supply of dollars increases, and the market equilibrium will move from E to E'. Panel (b) records the equivalent change in marks.

Because the increase in the supply of dollars is tantamount to an increase in the demand for marks, the price of marks (measured in dollars per mark) rises from $.56 to $.57. The effect of this rise on the exchange rate is the same no matter which diagram is used. At point E the rate of 1.79 marks per $1 translates into $1/1.79 = $.56 per mark, whereas at point E' the rate of 1.75 marks per $1 translates into $1/1.75 = $.57 per mark.

TRADE, INVESTMENT, AND THE EXCHANGE RATE

In our example a loss of mark balances due to an excess of U.S. imports over exports from Germany leads to an increase in the supply of dollars to the foreign exchange market. The result is a fall in the rate of exchange for the dollar, from 1.79 marks per $1 to 1.75 marks per $1. Such a drop in exchange value is called a depreciation of the dollar. The mark, on the other hand, appreciated, because the number of U.S. cents needed to purchase a mark rose from 56 to 57.

*A currency **depreciates** when its price, in terms of another currency, falls. It **appreciates** when its price, in terms of another currency, rises.*

It is evident that an imbalance in the merchandise trade of a country (for example, an excess of imports over exports) can lead to adjustments in the foreign exchange market that will cause that country's currency either to depreciate or to appreciate. Thus trade flows play an important part in determining the rate of exchange for any currency. However, two other kinds of economic activity also are important in determining exchange rates. They are investment and speculation.

---

2. Since the end of World War II the acceptance market has grown tremendously. In mid 1945 about $100 million in U.S. banker acceptances was outstanding. At the end of 1977, over $25 billion was outstanding. See Ralph T. Helfrich, "Trading in Banker Acceptances: A View from the Acceptance Desk of the Federal Reserve Bank of New York," *Monthly Review* (Federal Reserve Bank of New York), February 1976, pp. 51–57.

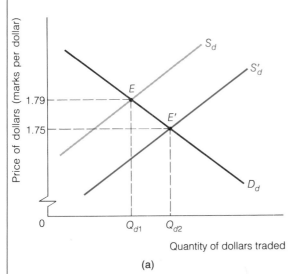
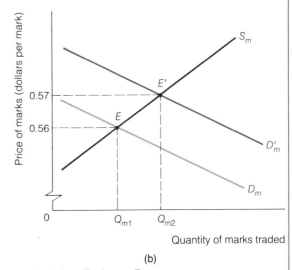

(a)   (b)

FIGURE 30–1   Effect of Increase in Supply of Dollars (Demand for Marks) on Exchange Rate

Panel (a) shows an increase in the supply of dollars from S_d to S'_d. The price of the dollar (in terms of number of marks per dollar) falls, and the market equilibrium moves from E to E'. Panel (b) shows the equivalent change in marks.

Effects of Investment and Speculation Investment activities have impacts on the foreign exchange market that are similar to those generated by trade. For example, if a U.S. firm wants to build a plant in Germany, when it transfers funds from the United States to Germany to do so, it will need to exchange dollars for marks in order to pay its German contractors and employees. Normally, it will not go directly to the foreign exchange market but will instead pay through the banking system. U.S. banks will make the necessary mark payments from their correspondent accounts.

As in our trade example, if investment is not balanced (if U.S. investors are making more investments in Germany than German investors are making in the United States), the result will be an increase in the supply of dollars (demand for marks) in the foreign exchange market and a tendency for the dollar to depreciate. Purchases of foreign stocks or bonds will have a similar effect on currency supply and demand. The main difference between this kind of investment (called **portfolio investment**) and investment in physical assets such as plant and equipment (called **direct**

investment) is that stocks and bonds can be easily liquidated, whereas physical assets cannot.

Speculation also affects exchange rates.

> ***Speculation*** *is simply taking a position in (holding) one currency or another based on a belief that the currency's exchange rate will move upward in the future.*

For example, a U.S. speculator may buy marks at $.56 apiece, hoping to make a profit in dollars if the mark rises to $.59. If the speculator buys $1 million of marks at $.56 and sells them in ninety days for $.59, the person will make a profit of $53,571: $1,000,000/$.56 ($.59) = $1,053,571, from which the initial $1 million is subtracted to arrive at the $53,571 profit.[3] This amount constitutes a

3. We can compute the level of profit as follows. With $1 million we can buy $1,000,000/$.56 = 1,785,714 marks at a price of $.56 each. If the price of marks then rises to $.59 cents each, we can sell the 1,785,714 marks for 1,-785,714 × $.59 = approximately $1,053,571. Total profit is thus $1,053,571 − $1,000,000 = $53,571.

21.4 percent profit on an annual basis.[4] Of course, the willingness of speculators to take a position in a currency depends on their expectations about the future rate of exchange.

EXCHANGE RATE SYSTEMS AND PAYMENTS IMBALANCE

Up to this point the discussion of the foreign exchange market has indicated how imbalances in trade and investment activity, coupled with currency speculation, can lead to pressures for the depreciation or appreciation of a country's currency. How much the exchange value of a currency will change depends fundamentally on two things—the type of international payments system in existence and the government policies of the country experiencing the change.

At the present time the payments system of the principal market economies is a flexible rate system that relies heavily on market forces to establish rates of exchange. The system is fairly new, dating from the early 1970s.

*In a **flexible rate system** rates of exchange are allowed to vary with changes in market conditions.*

In the nineteenth century, the major trading nations adhered to the gold standard. During most of the twentieth century, they have operated under either a modified gold standard or what has become known as the IMF system (named after the International Monetary Fund, an organization formed to oversee the system). Both the gold standard and the IMF system are fixed rate systems.

---

4. The percent return for the ninety-day period is $53,-571/$1,000,000 × 100 percent = approximately 5.36 percent. Because there are approximately four ninety-day periods in one year (360/90 = 4), the annual rate of return is 5.36 percent × 4 = 21.44 percent.

*In a **fixed rate system** the foreign exchange market is characterized by government intervention to keep the rates of exchange between currencies stable.*

The operation of a fixed rate system requires that each government have a stock of international reserves that can be used to intervene in the foreign exchange markets.

*A country's **international reserves** consist of its monetary authorities' holdings of foreign currencies, gold, and certain other assets that can be used to purchase its own currency in the foreign exchange markets.*

Actually, reserves can also be of some use under a flexible rate system, as a later section of this chapter will show.

In the material to follow, we will examine the prospects for returning to an equilibrium position from a situation where a country's trade and investment flows are not in balance. Here, we will consider only variations of the flexible rate system, leaving fixed rate systems to Special Topic L. The main objectives will be to describe the mechanisms through which payments flows tend to adjust automatically under flexible rates and to discuss the steps a country can take unilaterally to cope with a **payments imbalance.** However, we will first see what is meant by the "balance of payments"

BALANCE OF PAYMENTS CONCEPTS

◆

A country's **balance of payments accounts** represent a systematic effort to record the monetary effects of all transactions between its citizens, businesses, and government and those of other countries. Most such transactions arise because of international trade and investment, although some have to do with payment for services or transfers of income (gifts).

A typical set of balance of payments accounts includes (1) a *current account*, covering trade, shipping, service transactions, and gifts; (2) one or more *capital accounts*, covering investments and short-term monetary flows; and (3) an *official reserves account*, covering changes in government holdings of foreign exchange, gold, and other international monetary reserves.[5]

A balance of payments statement for a country is conceptually similar to a statement of changes in financial position□ for a business firm. Thus, every transaction leads to both a credit (plus) entry and a debit (minus) entry in the statement. The entire statement must therefore balance, although the individual accounts (current, capital, official reserves) usually do not balance.

THE BALANCE OF TRADE

For most countries, a large share of total international transactions arises from merchandise trade. A country's exports generate receipts from foreigners, and its imports result in payments to foreigners. The difference between these two payments flows, in any given accounting period, is the country's balance of trade.

> A country's **balance of trade** is the difference between its export earnings and its expenditures on imports over some time period.

If the value of exports (X) exceeds that of imports (M), the trade balance (X − M) is positive. Such a situation is called an *export balance of trade* or a **trade surplus.** When a country's imports exceed its exports, it is said to have an *import balance of trade* or a **trade deficit.**

If there were no flows of investment, gifts, or services between countries, a country with a trade surplus would also have a balance of payments surplus, since it would experience a net flow of payments from foreigners who purchase its excess of exports over imports. However, when investment or *capital flows* are present, the balance of payments is much more difficult to analyze.

CAPITAL FLOWS AND PAYMENTS DEFICITS

Capital flows cloud the balance of payments picture because their effects on the foreign exchange market cannot always be predicted. For example, it is hard to tell whether a foreigner who receives dollars from the sale of a stock or bond to a U.S. citizen will be content to just hold the dollars or whether the foreigner will want to sell them to obtain some other currency. Likewise, it is difficult to predict how long the U.S. investor would hold the stock or bond before selling it and creating a demand for dollars.

Prior to 1977, the U.S. defined a *basic balance* in its balance of payments as the sum of the current account balance and the balance on long term capital (investment in plant and equipment or non-liquid securities). The government's reasoning was that net U.S. long term investment overseas would create an increase in the supply of dollars in foreign hands and leave U.S. citizens with less liquid assets. The result would be downward pressure on the exchange rate of the dollar. In other words, the combined desire of U.S. citizens to import foreign goods and invest in foreign countries would increase the supply of dollars to the foreign exchange market, causing the rate to fall or, at least, causing the government to have to use up its reserves in order to defend the rate.

---

5. For the United States quarterly balance of payments data are published in the U.S. Department of Commerce's monthly *Survey of Current Business.*

Figure 30–2 shows the behavior of the trade balance, the basic balance (to 1976), and the U.S. government's stock of international reserves (principally gold and foreign exchange) from 1960 to 1980. In the Figure, a negative value for the basic balance indicates a payments deficit. Figures for the basic balance after 1976 are not available. Note that before 1971, the deterioration of the trade balance and the basic balance were accompanied by a reduction in U.S. reserves, which were used up as the government tried to keep the exchange value of the dollar from falling. After the advent of flexible rates in 1971, the drain on reserves stopped, since the dollar was allowed to depreciate.

Current Views on Deficits and Reserves The basic balance deficit is still calculated by some international agencies, but it is no longer reported by the U.S. Department of Commerce. The deficit is a difficult concept to define sta-

tistically, because it is hard to say what portion of portfolio investments (bonds, stocks) is really long term. Such investments often are easy to sell internationally, and therefore they may be more like short-term capital (bank deposits and short-term notes) than long-term investment in something like a factory, hotel, or farm. Currently, under the system of flexible exchange rates, concern about balance of payments deficits is focused primarily on a country's official reserves.

PAYMENTS
ADJUSTMENT
WITH A FREELY
FLUCTUATING RATE SYSTEM
◆

In a system of flexible exchange rates, shifts in supply and demand are the major determi-

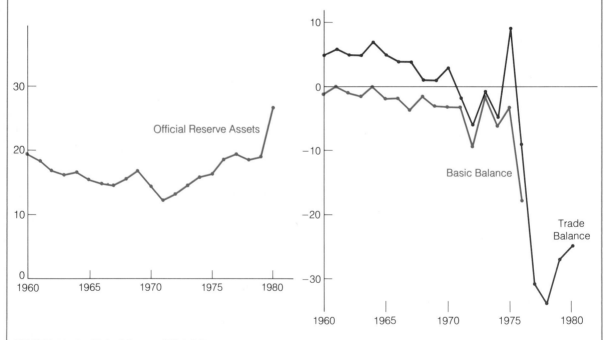

FIGURE 30–2 United States Official Reserves, Merchandise Trade Balance, and Basic Balance, 1960–1980 (billions of dollars)

Source: U.S. Department of Commerce, *Survey of Current Business*, June 1978, pp. 16–17; June 1981, pp. 38–39.

nants of changes in exchange rates. The extreme case of such a system is known as freely fluctuating rates.

> With **freely fluctuating rates** governments do not intervene in the foreign exchange market, and rates are determined by the activities of private banks, traders, and speculators. Such a system is a theoretical ideal that has never existed.

In today's system of flexible rates, government intervention in the exchange market is frequent and sometimes pervasive. Still, governments find it difficult to stem the trend toward depreciation of a given currency once trade and investment flows make depreciation likely. To fully understand this situation, we need to examine the automatic adjustment processes occurring under freely fluctuating rates without government intervention.

FREELY FLUCTUATING RATES: ADJUSTMENT WITHOUT INTERVENTION

In a system of freely fluctuating rates a country experiencing excessive outflows of its currency as the net result of trade, investment, and speculation will undergo a currency depreciation. This situation was illustrated in Figure 30–1. In general, it is argued that the depreciation will be limited, because the very fact of a fall in the currency's exchange value will automatically set in motion forces that will alleviate the country's payments imbalance.

These forces include the following:

1. A rise in the home country price of imports, which will lead to a reduction in purchases from foreign countries.
2. A fall in the foreign currency price of exports, which will lead to increased sales to foreign countries.
3. A possible rise in interest rates that will attract an inflow of foreign investment funds and depress income and imports.

Let us examine each of these forces independently.

Rise in Home Country Price of Imports If the U.S. dollar depreciates with respect to the German mark in the foreign exchange market, U.S. buyers of German goods will have to offer more U.S. currency per mark than they did before. This means that even if the price tags of German goods remain constant in marks, they will increase in dollars.

For example, suppose the dollar depreciates from a level of 1.79 marks per $1 to 1.59 marks per $1. A German car with a price tag of 25,000 marks will cost 25,000/1.79 = $13,966 before the depreciation but 25,000/1.59 = $15,723 afterwards. From the law of demand, we can expect Americans to buy fewer German cars at the new price.

Whether rising prices of imported goods will entirely stem the excessive flow of dollars into the exchange market depends on the responsiveness of U.S. buyers to the price increases. In other words, the U.S. elasticity of demand□ for imports with respect to price will be an important determinant of the effect of rising import prices on the exchange market.

This relationship is illustrated in Figure 30–3. In panel (a) U.S. demand for imports is relatively elastic. From the U.S. point of view the rise in the price of imported goods is a leftward shift of the foreign supply curve, S_F, to S_F', because every foreign exchange–denominated price now corresponds to a higher price in dollars. If U.S. demand is elastic,□ as in panel (a), the amount spent on imports will fall. Total U.S. expenditure at point E will be $P \times Q$, or an amount equal to the area of the shaded rectangle $OPZQ'$ plus rectangle I. After the depreciation of the dollar, imports will fall to Q', while price will rise to P'. Total U.S. expenditure at point E' will be $P' \times Q'$, an amount equal. to the shaded rectangle $OPZQ'$ plus rectangle II. Because rectangle II is smaller than rectangle I, the outflow of dollars to pay for U.S. imports will fall. This should help alleviate the pressure toward depreciation of the dollar.

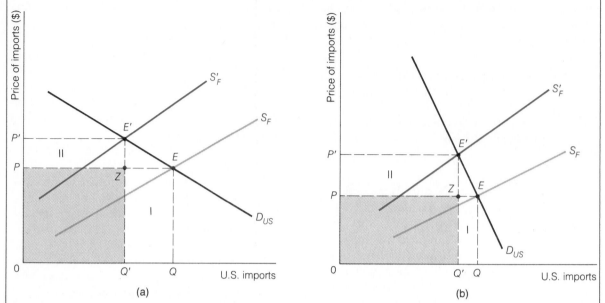

FIGURE 30–3 Effect of Currency Depreciation on Home Country Expenditures for Imports

In panel (a) the U.S. demand for imports is relatively *elastic*. From the U.S. point of view, the rise in the price of imported goods is a leftward shift of the foreign supply curve, S_F, to S_F', because every foreign exchange-denominated price now corresponds to a higher price in dollars. In this case, the amount spent on imports will fall. Total U.S. expenditure at point E will be $P \times Q$, or an amount equal to the area of the shaded rectangle OPZQ' plus rectangle I. After the depreciation of the dollar, imports will fall to Q' while the price rises to P'. Total U.S. expenditure at point E' is $P' \times Q'$, an amount equal to the shaded rectangle OPZQ' plus rectangle II. Since rectangle II is smaller than rectangle I, the outflow of dollars to pay for U.S. imports will fall. In panel (b) the U.S. demand is *inelastic*. In this case, the total U.S. expenditure on imports actually *rises*, even though the quantity of imports falls.

Panel (b) of Figure 30–3 illustrates the same shift in the foreign supply curve with a U.S. demand curve that is inelastic. In this case, the total U.S. expenditure on imports actually rises, even though the quantity of imports falls. This occurs because the quantity change is less than proportional to (of a smaller percentage than) the price increase. Thus the total expenditure on imports at E' is equal to the shaded area plus rectangle II, and rectangle II is clearly larger than rectangle I. The outflow of dollars to pay for imports increases, despite the fall in the quantity of imports. We can conclude that depreciation will reduce the payments outflow for imports only if the demand for imports is elastic. For the United States,

then, depreciation has mixed results, because the demand for many imported consumer goods is elastic but the demand for certain commodities (coffee and crude oil, for example) is very inelastic with respect to price.

Fall in Foreign Currency Price of Exports From the viewpoint of foreigners a depreciation of the U.S. dollar has the effect of lowering the prices of U.S. export goods. At 1.79 marks per $1 a piece of U.S. machinery with a $10,000 price tag costs a German buyer 17,900 marks. If the dollar falls to 1.59 marks, the price to Germans will be only 15,900 marks, a reduction of 2,000 marks. The law of demand□ tells us that the Germans will buy

52

more U.S. goods when their price, in marks, falls.[6]

From the viewpoint of the United States the increased willingness of foreigners to buy exports at every dollar price is seen as a rightward shift of the foreign demand curve, from D_F to D_F' in Figure 30–4. Both the price and the quantity demanded of U.S. exports increase as the equilibrium position moves from E to E'. Total dollar earnings from exports increase from $P \times Q$ to $P' \times Q'$. The only case in which such an increase would not occur is that of perfectly inelastic foreign demand.

In that situation D_F' and D_F would be the same vertical line and equilibrium would stay at E. Such a case is highly unlikely, so we can conclude that depreciation will increase dollar earnings from exports. However, the size of the increase will depend on the foreign elasticity of demand for U.S. exports, which is what underlies the extent of the shift of D_F in the figure. Consequently, because of depreciation, the more elastic world demand for a country's exports, the greater will be the increase in foreign demand for the country's currency.[7]

Rise in Interest Rates The conditions under which a currency depreciates are usually accompanied by substantial inflationary pressure, especially once depreciation has begun to take place. Also, for the country undergoing the depreciation, exports increase while

_____

6. Investment by U.S. citizens in foreign countries will be affected by a depreciation of the dollar in much the same way that imports by U.S. citizens are affected, because the investment may involve the purchase of real assets, such as plant and equipment, in foreign countries. Conversely, investment by foreigners in the United States will be affected in the same way that exports are, because it involves the purchase of such assets in the United States.

7. In the context of this section and the preceding one, if the home country supply elasticity of exports and the foreign supply elasticity are both infinite and if trade is balanced at the time of depreciation, the depreciation will result in an excess of exports over imports for the depreciating country if the sum of the elasticities of demand (home plus foreign) is greater than 1. This situation is known as the Marshall-Lerner condition.

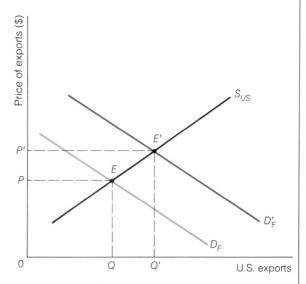

FIGURE 30–4 Effect of Currency Depreciation on Home Country Export Receipts

As a result of the depreciation of the dollar, the demand curve of foreigners for U.S. exports shifts rightward, from D_F to D_F'. Both the price and quantity demanded of U.S. exports increase as the equilibrium position moves from E to E'. Total dollar earnings increase from $P \times Q$ to $P' \times Q'$.

the prices of imported goods rise. The monetary policy needed to combat the internal inflation that is bound to follow is a restrictive one. If a contractionary monetary policy (reducing the money supply or at least slowing its growth) is followed, interest rates should rise. The rise may attract a short-term capital inflow, as foreigners shift their funds into the country to take advantage of the higher rates, thereby helping to reduce the deficit balance.

The interest rate increase described here is not certain to occur, however, because it depends on discretionary government monetary policy, and external and internal economic goals may result in policy conflicts. Moreover, the country in question will likely be undergoing both inflation and depreciation, so that the nominal interest rate level necessary to attain a real increase in interest rates relative to the rest of the world may be very high indeed. If the country also has significant unemployment, the monetary authorities may be unwilling to pursue a contractionary policy. Thus, barring direct controls on trade and investment, in this case only the current account balance can be depended on to help alleviate the deficit and stave off further depreciation of the currency.

EXTERNAL AND INTERNAL GOALS AND POLICY CONFLICTS

As just mentioned, external and internal goals may result in policy conflicts. For example, if a country is faced internally with a recession and externally with a balance of payments deficit, the appropriate policies to deal with the internal problem will often tend to worsen the external problem. In this case the recession can be alleviated by expansionary government fiscal policies, which will increase employment and incomes. However, as incomes rise, the demand for imports will also tend to rise, which will worsen the balance of payments deficit. If expansionary monetary policies are used to combat the recession, interest rates will fall and there will be a capital outflow. This outflow will also worsen the balance of payments deficit. A similar conflict will occur in the presence of inflation at home together with a balance of payments surplus. That is, contractionary fiscal policy will cause imports to fall and will increase the balance of payments surplus. Contractionary monetary policy, on the other hand, will raise interest rates and attract a capital inflow. This inflow

will also increase the balance of payments surplus.

A conflict between government policies to combat internal and external problems will not exist in the situation where a domestic recession is combined with a balance of payments surplus. Expansionary fiscal and monetary policies will tend to alleviate both problems. A conflict also will not exist in the presence of domestic inflation and a balance of payments deficit. Contractionary policies will tend to lessen both problems.

Unfortunately, the combinations that result in policy conflicts occur with frustrating frequency, and therein lies a dilemma for government policy makers. (The relationships discussed here are summarized in Table 30–2.)

RESTRICTIVE TRADE AND INVESTMENT POLICIES

A government faced with continuing balance of payments deficits and, therefore, continuing pressure toward depreciation of its currency can take certain unilateral measures relating to international trade and investment. These measures are mostly restrictive. The most commonly used ones are import restrictions and controls on capital movements. On the import side, increases in tariffs□ (perhaps by means of a surcharge—a method used by President Nixon in 1971) or quantitative restrictions (import quotas and licensing requirements) can reduce the outflow of pay-

710

TABLE 30–2 Possible Relationships between Appropriate Policies to Alleviate External and Internal Problems

External Problem	Internal Problem	Appropriate Policies for External Problem	Appropriate Policies for Internal Problem	Relationship between External and Internal Policies
Deficit	Recession	Contractionary	Expansionary	Conflict
Deficit	Inflation	Contractionary	Contractionary	No conflict
Surplus	Recession	Expansionary	Expansionary	No conflict
Surplus	Inflation	Expansionary	Contractionary	Conflict

ments for goods and services. Investment controls and special taxes on interest or dividends from foreign investment will also reduce the outflow.

Few economists favor these kinds of measures, because they are disrupting to both trade and resource allocation. Presumably, some of the gains from both comparative advantage and efficient allocation of world resources are sacrificed through the use of these restrictive practices. In addition, such policies invite retaliation on the part of trading partners, and the effects of retaliatory restrictions can be substantial, as we will see in Chapter 31.

THE
MANAGED FLOAT:
TODAY'S
INTERNATIONAL
MONETARY SYSTEM
◆

Since the early 1970s the exchange rate system of the major trading nations has been characterized by flexible exchange rates with government intervention in the markets. This system differs from the system of freely fluctuating rates in that the exchange market activities of individual national governments can and do alter the exchange rate adjustments that would occur if the forces of demand and supply were allowed to have their full impact.

Basically, what government monetary authorities do is sell their own currency (increase its supply) in foreign exchange markets when they wish to keep it from appreciating in terms of other currencies and buy their own currency (increase its demand) when they wish to keep it from depreciating. The former action is simple enough, because a government's monetary authorities can presumably create as much of their own money as they wish to. However, in order to buy their own currency in the exchange markets, these authorities must have reserves of other currencies.

*A system of flexible rates characterized by government intervention in the foreign exchange market is called a **managed float**.*

PROBLEMS INHERENT IN THE MANAGED FLOAT

The managed float presents two main problems. First, a country that wants to keep its own currency relatively cheap can easily (perhaps too easily) do so by creating new money and selling it for a low price in the foreign exchange markets. The risk it runs is that this increase in its money supply will generate inflation at home. A government may be willing to take this risk in order to keep exports and employment from falling, which is what will happen if its own currency becomes more expensive (appreciates).

Such actions on the part of a country are not likely to be welcomed by its trading partners when they themselves are running deficits. Japan has repeatedly chosen to increase the supply of yen in the foreign exchange markets at times when U.S. monetary authorities hoped to see the yen appreciate with respect to the dollar. During the late 1970s U.S. officials often criticized Japan because its monetary authorities deliberately kept the yen cheap and generated continuing trade surpluses with the United States. However, in late 1979 Japan finally switched to a "strong yen" policy.

Reserve Problem The second problem with the managed float is that a country that wishes to keep its currency from depreciating must have adequate reserves of foreign currencies with which to buy its own currency when there is an increase in its supply in the foreign exchange markets.

Reserves can be obtained in several ways. A trade surplus (excess of exports over imports) will earn foreign currency reserves. An increase in these reserves will also result from a net inflow of foreign investment. A country that has gold can readily exchange it for foreign currency reserves. Reserves can also be created in the form of special drawing rights (SDRs, a form of international money) at the International Monetary Fund. Finally, a country can borrow reserves or swap them with other countries. In a nutshell, the reserves problem is that countries that may need reserves to forestall depreciation of their currencies are not necessarily and indeed are not likely to be, those that have substantial reserves to draw on.

Special Drawing Rights To some degree, the reserve problem is lessened by the IMF's system of special drawing rights, under which countries with a surplus of reserves must accept a certain amount of SDRs in exchange for their currencies. However, the total amount of SDRs thus far created by the IMF amounts to a relatively small percentage of total world reserves; and the less developed countries, many of which suffer from a chronic lack of reserves, argue that the SDRs have not been fairly allocated. It is generally agreed that SDRs now constitute a true international money. (Indeed, not only do countries freely accept SDRs, but the IMF pays interest on SDR holdings and collects interest from countries that borrow SDRs.) However, the problems of determining how to manage the total supply of this new money and how to allocate additions to it are not yet solved.

U.S. PAYMENTS PROBLEMS AND THE DECISION TO FLOAT

In this section we will examine the international monetary system as it existed immediately after World War II. Then we will look into the forces that led to the establishment of our current system, the managed float, in the 1970s.

Bretton Woods System Near the end of World War II, in 1944, the Allied nations held a conference at Bretton Woods, New Hampshire, to organize a new international

monetary system. They were convinced that such a system was needed to prevent the international financial chaos that existed during the 1930s and the war. The international monetary system of pegged exchange rates that was developed as a result of this conference is sometimes called the **Bretton Woods System.**

From the end of World War II until 1971, the Allied countries, along with Japan and most of the smaller market economies (well over a hundred countries in all), operated under this system of relatively fixed rates of exchange monitored by the IMF. Each country was committed by agreement to maintain its currency within 1 percent of a par value officially recognized by the IMF. Immediately following World War II the dollar was the strongest currency in the world; therefore, most par values were set in terms of so many units of foreign currency per dollar.

Reserves were an absolute necessity under the original IMF system, because countries had to stand ready to buy their own currencies any time market forces threatened a depreciation. The IMF maintained a huge pool of reserves that it would loan to deficit countries for rate stabilization purposes. No country was supposed to change the par value of its currency without IMF permission.

Thus currencies were not allowed to appreciate or depreciate as market forces changed. If a country did change its par value, it would then commit itself to maintaining the new par value at a fixed rate.

> When a country adheres to a fixed exchange rate, a reduction in the par value of its currency is called a **devaluation** and an increase in the par value is called a **revaluation**.

While the IMF fixed rate system operated (1944–1971), there were many cases of devaluation, but few countries ever revalued their currencies upward.

Under the original IMF system there were two main reserve assets, gold and the U.S. dollar. The dollar was pegged to gold (at $35 per ounce), and most other currencies were pegged to the dollar. Gold reserves increased very slowly because of physical and political limits on gold mining activities. Thus the world depended on increasing amounts of dollars for the bulk of its international reserves. However, for other countries to increase their holdings of dollars, the U.S. would have to run balance of payments deficits. This point proved to be a major flaw in the IMF system, although the magnitude of the problem did not become evident until long after the economies of Europe and Japan had recovered from World War II.

U.S. Payments Deficits Although the United States had small basic balance deficits throughout most of the 1950s, from 1958 onward the deficits became large and persistent. The major reserve asset of the United States was gold, and under the IMF system the United States had to use gold or foreign currencies to buy up dollars when foreign countries wanted to reduce their dollar holdings. Total reserve assets of the United States fell from $24.8 billion in 1957 to $14.5 billion in 1970, while the U.S. official gold stocks dropped from $22.9 billion to $11.1 billion (see Table 30–3). However, the merchandise trade balance remained positive (as an export balance or trade surplus) by several billion dollars per year through 1970 (see Table 30–4).

To a large extent the deterioration of the

TABLE 30–4 The U.S. Balance of Trade, 1950 to 1980 (Millions of Dollars)

Year	Merchandise Exports	Merchandise Imports	Balance of Trade
1950	$ 10,203	$ 9,081	$ 1,122
1955	14,424	11,527	2,897
1960	19,650	14,758	4,892
1965	26,461	21,510	4,951
1970	42,469	39,866	2,603
1971	43,319	45,579	−2,260
1972	49,381	55,797	−6,416
1973	71,410	70,499	911
1974	98,306	103,649	−5,343
1975	107,088	98,041	9,047
1976	114,745	124,051	−9,306
1977	120,816	151,689	−30,873
1978	142,052	175,822	−33,770
1979	184,473	211,819	−27,346
1980	223,966	249,308	−25,342

Source: "Table B–98: U.S. International Transactions, 1946–79," *Economic Report of the President* (Washington, D.C.: Government Printing Office, January 1980), p. 316; and *Survey of Current Business*, June, 1981, p. 500.

U.S. reserves position (also called a reduction in U.S. liquidity) during the 1960s appears to have been caused by huge outflows of dollars for foreign investment and economic or military aid to friendly countries. During that time, U.S. corporations invested heavily in production facilities in Europe as well as in other parts of the world. Foreign aid to developing countries did not increase significantly, but in the second half of the decade military

TABLE 30–3 U.S. Reserve Assets, 1957 to 1980 (Millions of Dollars)

Type of Asset	1957	1960	1965	1970	1975	1980
Gold stock	$22,857	$17,804	$13,806	$11,072	$11,599	$11,160
Special drawing rights	a	a	a	851	2,335	2,610
Convertible foreign currencies	a	a	781	629	80	10,134
Reserve position in IMF	1,975	1,555	863	1,935	2,212	1,822
Total	24,832	19,359	15,450	14,487	16,226	26,756

[a]Not applicable or negligible amount.

Source: U.S. Department of Commerce, Bureau of the Census, "Table No. 1494: U.S. Reserve Assets: 1960 to 1979," *Statistical Abstract of the United States, 1979* (Washington, D.C.: Government Printing Office, 1979), p. 849; and *Federal Reserve Bulletin*, February 1969, A73, and July 1981, p. A53.

aid (mostly to Vietnam) did. The United States simply was not realizing enough of a surplus on its goods and services trade to cover the dollar outflows for investment and aid. In addition, the deterioration in the U.S. payments position reduced foreign confidence in the dollar and made foreign governments and individuals less willing to hold dollar denominated assets (bonds, bank accounts, and so on).

The Crises of 1971 and 1973 On August 15, 1971, facing the first U.S. merchandise trade deficit since the 1930s, President Nixon announced that the United States would no longer use its gold to redeem the dollar holdings of foreign central banks and that the dollar would be allowed to float in the foreign exchange markets. After a period of floating, with much intervention by the European and Japanese governments, the United States agreed to devalue the dollar with respect to gold. At the same time, new "central rates," similar to par values, were established between the dollar and other major currencies, and the permissible band of fluctuation about these rates was widened to 2.25 percent. (It had been 1 percent about par.) All these new terms were drafted at a December 1971 meeting at the Smithsonian Institution in Washington and became known as the Smithsonian Agreement.

The Smithsonian Agreement did not last. The United States had a merchandise trade deficit of over $6 billion in 1972, and the dollar was devalued by another 10 percent in February 1973. After early attempts by the Europeans to support the new rate and the development of a joint float of European currencies against the dollar, there followed a period of sharp depreciation of the dollar. By June 1973 the German mark had risen 45.8 percent above its Smithsonian control rate. The Swiss franc had risen by about the same percentage, and other European currencies and the Japanese yen had appreciated by smaller, but still substantial, amounts.

FLOATING ALONG

Since 1973 the major trading nations have had to learn to live with the managed float. The money markets have been chaotic at times, and speculation in gold and silver reached truly historic levels during 1979–80. Furthermore, it is not at all clear that governments have intervened with the right medicine at the right time. What can be said for the current situation is that the managed float has not prevented world trade from growing vigorously since 1973 and that none of the major partici-

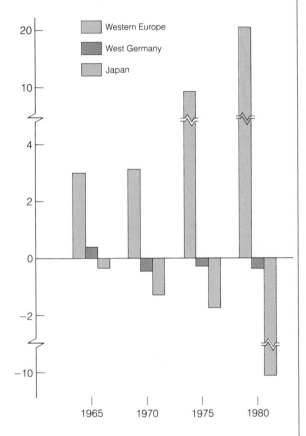

FIGURE 30–5 United States Trade Balance With Western Europe, Germany, and Japan (billions of dollars)

Although the U.S. generally enjoyed a trade surplus with Western Europe from 1965–1980, it had substantial deficits with West Germany and Japan.

Source: U.S. Bureau of the Census, *Statistical Abstract of the United States, 1979*, pp. 862–863; and *Survey of Current Business*, June 1981, p. 50.

pants in the float appears to be anxious to return to a fixed rate system of exchange.

However, the managed float did not bring about quick adjustments in the U.S. trade balance vis-à-vis Germany or Japan, even though exchange rates did move in the appropriate direction (see Figures 30–5 and 30–6). Still, the trade balance with all of Western Europe improved markedly.

To some extent the failure of the U.S. trade balance to adjust completely can be attributed to lagging productivity and high rates of price inflation at home, as well as to U.S. consumers' switching to Japanese and German automobiles as fuel prices increased in the late

1970s. A further complication occurred in late 1979 and early 1980 as U.S. monetary authorities pushed interest rates to record levels in order to both reduce domestic inflation and attract foreign short-term investment. U.S. international reserves swelled (Table 30–3), and the dollar became so strong in the money markets (despite continuing U.S. trade deficits) that its rise began to have an inflationary impact on Europe and Japan. The reason was that oil prices are denominated in dollars, and appreciation of the dollar therefore means higher prices for oil purchased with foreign currency–denominated accounts.

In 1980 and 1981, cooperation between Eu-

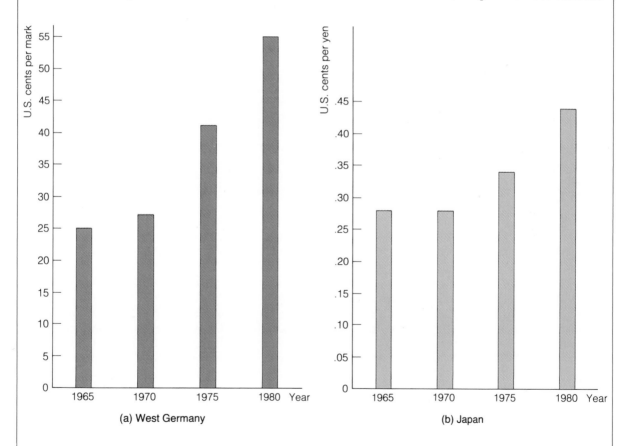

(a) West Germany

(b) Japan

FIGURE 30–6   **The Prices of Foreign Currencies in Terms of U.S. Dollars**

The prices of the mark and the yen in terms of U.S. dollars generally rose from 1970 to 1980. These increases reflect the U.S. government's decision to allow the dollar to float, a move that did improve the competitiveness of U.S. exports.

Source: U.S. Bureau of the Census, *Statistical Abstract of the United States: 1979*, p. 915, and International Monetary Fund, *International Financial Statistics*, August, 1981, pp. 160, 222.

ropean and U.S. monetary authorities was at a low ebb as the Europeans contemplated an "interest rate war" to lessen demand for the dollar. With the dollar appreciating, the U.S. authorities stopped intervening in the exchange markets, but the Europeans continued to do so. Thus, it appeared that the managed float would be around for quite some time.

SUMMARY

1. This chapter summarized the system of international payments as it relates to the market economies. Most international transactions are facilitated through a system of correspondent banks and letters of credit or drafts, called acceptances.

2. If a significant amount of time will elapse during the shipping of exported goods, the importer may issue a time draft, for which the exporter cannot receive payment until a specific time period has passed. However, during this period of time the exporter may run an exchange risk, because the draft is usually stated in terms of the importer's currency.

3. The term *exchange risk* refers to the risk that an exporting firm incurs because the value of the currency of the importing firm's country may decrease in terms of the value of the currency of the exporting firm's country. These relative values are expressed in terms of exchange rates. For example, the exchange rate between the German mark and the U.S. dollar might be 1.79 marks per dollar, or, equivalently, $.56 per mark.

4. The rates of exchange between the currencies of the market economies are determined by the levels of exports and imports among the various countries, by foreign investment, and by the actions of speculators. Without government intervention the value of a country's currency will tend to fall relative to the values of foreign currencies if the imports of the country exceed its exports or if it is a net investor in foreign countries. The currency will tend to appreciate, of course, if exports exceed imports or if foreigners are net investors in the country.

5. A country's balance of payments accounts represent a systematic effort to record the monetary effects of all transactions between the country's citizens or businesses and those of other countries. A typical set of balance of payments accounts in-

cludes (1) a current account, covering trade, shipping, service transactions, and transfer payments; (2) one or more capital accounts, covering investments and short-term monetary flows; and (3) an official reserves account, covering changes in government holdings of foreign exchange, gold, and other international monetary reserves.

6. The difference between the exports and the imports of a country is called the balance of trade. The basic balance of payments is given by the sum of the balance on current account plus that on long-term capital flows.

7. In a freely fluctuating exchange rate system, governments do not intervene in the foreign exchange market and rates are determined by the activities of private banks, traders, and speculators. In such a system, market forces tend to bring about an automatic adjustment in exchange rates in the face of a balance of payments deficit or surplus. However, such a system is a theoretical ideal that has never existed.

8. From 1944 to 1971 international trade among most of the market economies was carried on under a "pegged" exchange rate system, sometimes called the Bretton Woods System. This system was monitored by the International Monetary Fund, and it required each member country to keep the value of its currency stable relative to the currencies of other member countries.

9. The current system of managed floating exchange rates was fabricated by the United States and its Western European allies in response to a number of problems involving the relationship of the dollar to other key currencies, particularly problems caused by nearly continual balance of payments deficits on the part of the United States.

10. A system of managed floating exchange rates is characterized by both floating exchange rates and government intervention in the foreign exchange markets. Problems can arise if a country insists on intervening in a foreign exchange market to keep the value of its currency relatively low in order to promote employment and growth at home at a time when other countries have a deficit balance vis-à-vis that country.

11. Another problem often arises because countries with balance of payments deficits do not have sufficient amounts of international reserves to intervene in the foreign exchange market to support the value of their currencies. To some extent the reserves problem is lessened by the IMF's system of special drawing rights, under which countries with balance of payments surpluses must accept a certain amount of SDRs in exchange for their currencies.

12. Since 1973 the major trading nations have had to learn to live with the managed float. Although they have had mixed experiences with this system, none of the major participant countries appears to be anxious for a change, and the volume of international trade has grown vigorously.

IMPORTANT TERMS AND CONCEPTS

Bartering	Payments imbalance
Open account	Flexible rate system
Trade credit	Fixed rate system
Foreign exchange	Balance of payments
Letter of credit	Balance of trade
Acceptance	Export balance of
Rate of exchange	trade (trade surplus)
Time draft	Basic balance
Foreign exchange risk	Freely fluctuating rates
Currency depreciation	Managed float
and appreciation	International reserves
Portfolio investment	Bretton Woods system
Direct investment	Devaluation and
Speculation	revaluation

QUESTIONS AND PROBLEMS

1. Briefly explain the role of the banking system in facilitating payment for exports and imports.

2. What is foreign exchange risk? What steps can an exporter take in order to avoid such risk?

3. What kinds of activities underlie the demand for a given currency in the foreign exchange markets?

4. Define the following terms: *currency appreciation, currency depreciation,* and *speculation.*

5. Given the following diagram:
   a. What would happen if German demand for U.S. dollars were to increase?
   b. Show your answer to Question 5a on the diagram.
   c. Would the dollar appreciate or depreciate in the circumstances given in Question 5a? Explain.

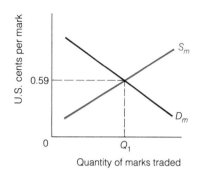

6. What is the difference between a country's balance of trade and its balance of payments? Can a country with a trade surplus have a payments deficit? Explain.

7. If a country has a continuing imbalance in its international payments and is operating under freely fluctuating exchange rates, what is likely to happen? Will the imbalance persist? Explain.

8. What is the relationship of elasticity of demand to the problem of payments adjustment under freely fluctuating exchange rates? Can we generally expect receipts from exports (measured in domestic currency) to increase after a country's currency depreciates? Explain.

9. What is the role of monetary policy in the balance of payments adjustment process under a system of freely fluctuating exchange rates? Why might there be a conflict between domestic and external goals in the implementation of monetary policy?

10. What kinds of unilateral restrictive policies might accompany a government's efforts to correct a payments imbalance?

11. How would you characterize the current international monetary system with regard to:
   a. Exchange rate determination
   b. Government intervention
   c. The issue of reserves

12. Briefly discuss the chain of events that led to the float of the U.S. dollar in 1972. Was the U.S. dollar overvalued in terms of other major currencies prior to the float? Explain.

13. You are about to buy a Volkswagen for $12,525. The dealer places an order for you but notes that your final purchase price will depend on the value of the mark on the date the car is delivered to you. When you place the order, the mark is trading at $.55. If it appreciates by 2 percent when you finally get the car, how much will your purchase price be in dollars?

THE
DOLLAR SHOCK
OF 1981

On a recent trip to Europe, Commerce Secretary Malcolm Baldrige heard honeyed words about President Reagan—and bitter ones about U.S. monetary policy. Soaring interest rates have helped to push up the dollar, weakening almost all European currencies and the Japanese yen and skewing traditional patterns of foreign trade. But Baldrige and other American officials consider the gripes in Europe and Japan to represent a misguided desire for the best of both economic worlds. "When the dollar was weak, they were very worried and just about everyone agreed that the world

needed a strong dollar,' says Baldrige. "Now it's strong and they're still complaining." What can the United States say in response to such complaints? Shrugs Baldrige: "Tough."

For the Europeans and the Japanese it promises to get even tougher. In mid-May the dollar, on a trade-weighted basis, finally returned to the level of December 1971, when Richard Nixon initiated the first of two formal devaluations. Its immediate fortunes in foreign-exchange markets depend as much as anything else on U.S. interest rates and inflation—and even accounting for some moderation in both areas, most experts predict that interest rates will remain high for the foreseeable future. As a result, there is a rising

clamor among foreign leaders for relief. During his recent visit to Washington, West German Chancellor Helmut Schmidt stressed to President Reagan that his country had been badly hurt by high U.S. rates, and just last week Japanese Finance Minister Michio Watanabe added his complaint.

Why the worry? Interest rates that are significantly higher in the United States than in Europe and Japan tend to increase global demand for dollar-denominated assets, weakening foreign currencies in world markets and upsetting central-bank planning. For example, the Bank of France has used an estimated 10 per cent to 25 per cent of its foreign-currency reserves to prop up the French franc—undermined, in part, by the election of Socialist François Mitterrand as President.

'PRESSURES'

The Europeans, and to a lesser extent the Japanese, have been hurt in other ways as well. As the dollar strengthens and their own currencies decline, America's trading partners must pay more for imported commodities, particularly crude oil. And in an effort to maintain some sort of equilibrium, they must raise their own interest rates, adding to both inflationary and recessionary pressures. West Germany has been particularly hard hit in this regard; rising interest rates in the Federal Republic have begun to deter industrial investment, creating additional unemployment and placing a growing burden on the national budget because of higher social-welfare payments.

For Americans the strong dollar is both good news and bad news. The good news is that it holds down the price of imports and competing products made in the United States; at the same time, Americans traveling abroad get a bit more for their money. For example, the British pound is now worth about $2.07. "When I first began a long visit in Britain, the pound was at about $2.40," says Knoxville businessman Jack Patterson. "Since then, things have gotten so good I've decided to furnish my new house with all British furniture. Even with the shipping costs, I've saved."

The bad news for Americans is

that it makes U.S. products less competitive in weakened economies abroad—and as a result, the U.S. trade deficit is beginning to widen. Last week, for instance, the Commerce Department reported that U.S. merchandise exports in April totaled $19.8 billion, 7.5 per cent lower than in March, and the deficit for the month jumped to a staggering $3.5 billion, compared with $451 million a month earlier.

Some experts predict that the trend could continue for the next year or two. In their view, U.S. exports could drop a full 10 per cent from last year's level if the dollar remains strong and foreign economies stay weak. The movement of capital goods and big-ticket items such as airplanes and earth-moving equipment tends to lag eighteen to 24 months behind changes in exchange rates—in part because of the long lead time between orders and delivery. Thus, while exports of these goods may be brisk right now, thanks to the relatively cheap dollar of two years ago, a more expensive dollar could dampen trade by 1983.

More important, many economists are convinced that the United States will face growing competition from its trading partners in the next few years. This will be particularly true of West Germany, which expects to recover from its current recession later this year by stepping up its exports. Japan, of course, reckons to be as aggressive as ever in world markets.

BOTTOM LINE

In an effort to even the odds, the Reagan Administration is working on a package of legislative proposals dealing with trade. They include changes in the Foreign Corrupt Practices Act to make it easier for Americans to compete with freewheeling competitors overseas, the easing of tax liabilities for Americans working overseas and the amendment of antitrust laws to allow the establishment of cooperative export-trading companies. But the bottom line for both the United States and its trading partners is an end to America's inflationary spiral—and a lowering of interest rates to levels that encourage growth in production and trade. Only then will both sides come out winners.

QUESTIONS

1. According to the article, what happened to the exchange rate of the U.S. dollar in 1981? Why? Relate your answer to the demand for and supply of dollars in the foreign exchange markets.
2. Using the concepts developed in this chapter, explain what action the Bank of France would have to take to "prop up the French franc," and explain also how this strategy causes a reduction in the Bank's foreign exchange reserves.
3. Discuss the effects of a stronger dollar on U.S. trade and investment flows.

THE GOLD STANDARD
AND ADJUSTMENT
UNDER
FIXED EXCHANGE RATES

In Chapter 30 the discussion of international payments and the adjustment process focused on flexible exchange rates and the problems of the managed float that have characterized the international monetary system since the early 1970s. Although the chapter described the IMF system and the problems that led to the collapse of its fixed rate approach to international monetary relations, it did not discuss the process of balance of payments adjustment under a fixed rate system. One of the main purposes of this special topic is to describe the adjustment process and its problems under fixed rates. The other main purpose is to describe the international gold standard, another version of the fixed rate system.

To many economists the gold standard is a nineteenth century curiosity that has long since worn out its welcome as a system of international payments. The following statement by Leland B. Yeager, a leading scholar on international monetary relations, puts the gold standard in its proper perspective:

An international gold standard exists when most major countries maintain two-way convertibility between gold and their national monetary units at substantially fixed ratios and leave inward and outward shipments of gold substantially free from interference. This system is a normal state of grace, hallowed by centuries of practice, from which the world has fallen away only in recent decades—or so goes a widely believed myth. In fact, a full-fledged international gold standard held wide sway for at most about 40 years just before World War I.[1]

After World War I there was a partial return to the gold standard, but a true international gold standard was never reestablished. The gold standard is worth studying for three reasons, however:

1. To learn how it was supposed to work.
2. To learn how it actually did work.
3. To gain some insight into the general problem of adjustment under fixed exchange rates.

---

1. Leland B. Yeager, *International Monetary Relations: Theory, History, and Policy* (New York: Harper & Row, 1976), p. 295.

THE GOLD STANDARD MECHANISM

Under the gold standard every participating country agrees to define its monetary unit in terms of a physical amount of pure gold. Thus, if a dollar is defined as 1/20 of an ounce of gold and a British pound is defined as 1/4 of an ounce of gold, there will be an **implicit exchange rate** of £1 = $5. Put another way, it would take $20 but only £4 to buy one ounce of gold. Thus a British pound is worth $5.

Gold standard countries are always committed to redeeming their currencies for the amount of gold in which they are defined. In the example here, the U.S. Treasury would always be willing to take back its dollars in exchange for gold at $20 an ounce, and the British treasury would always sell gold for £4 per ounce. Thus the **par value** of the pound would be fixed at $5. People would not pay more than $5 for £1, because they could obtain gold from the U.S. Treasury at $20 per ounce and exchange it for pounds at the British Treasury at £4 per ounce. Shipping costs would be the only reason for slight deviations from the rate of $5 = £1.

Gold Flows In the normal course of trade and investment transactions, if a currency appreciates to the point where it will be advantageous to buy gold and ship it to the country with the appreciated currency rather than buy the currency in the foreign exchange market, there will be a gold flow to that country. In the nineteenth century the range in which exchange rates could move was very small, because the tie-in with gold made it possible to profit from gold and currency dealings once an exchange rate moved only slighly out of line with its implicit par value.

For example, if the implicit exchange rate is $5 = £1 and in the New York foreign exchange market the pound rises to $5.20 = £1, a U.S. dealer in gold and currencies can make a profit by buying gold from the U.S. Treasury, selling it to the British treasury, and exchanging pounds for dollars in the exchange market. The dealer can buy, say, 50,000 ounces of gold from the U.S. Treasury for 50,000 × $20 = $1,000,000. At the same time the dealer can buy pounds from the British treasury with the 50,000 ounces of gold and get 50,000 × £4 = £200,000. The transaction is completed by selling the pounds in the foreign exchange market for $5.20 = £1. This sale will yield 200,000 × $5.20 = $1,040,000. The U.S. dealer will reap a profit of $40,000 from the three transactions.

This example describes **gold arbitrage.** The net effect of arbitrage activities under the gold standard is to keep foreign exchange rates closely in line with implicit par values. If we consider the example again, the reason for the stabilizing effects of arbitrage will be clear. The dealer, in the final transaction, increased the supply of pounds in the foreign exchange market. Profit from arbitrage was possible because the pound was overpriced in the foreign exchange market. However, if arbitrageurs in general are attempting to profit from such transactions, they will all sell pounds for dollars in the foreign exchange market. This overall increase in the supply of pounds will cause the exchange rate to drop back toward $5 = £1. Thus any deviation from the implicit exchange rate will be very small.

Monetary Policy Monetary policy under the gold standard is exceedingly simple. If a country experiences a gold inflow, the rules of the game call for the monetary authorities to increase the money supply of that country. On the other hand, countries experiencing gold outflows are bound by the rules to decrease their domestic money supplies.

Price Adjustment Under the gold standard it is envisioned that gold flows will be determined by a country's balance of trade. Thus a country with an export balance (exports in excess of imports) will experience a gold inflow.[2]

2. Actually, the historical evidence shows that very little gold ever flowed from deficit to surplus countries under the gold standard. The reason is that deficit countries generally had high enough interest rates to attract foreign investment inflows that would offset their deficits and substitute for the gold flows.

On the other hand, a country with an import balance of trade will experience a gold outflow. Thus the money supply will be increased in the country having a trade surplus and will be decreased in a country having a trade deficit.

With this type of system the main impact of changes in the money supply is said to be on prices. Where the money supply increases, prices will rise as money becomes abundant relative to goods. Where the money supply decreases, prices will fall as money becomes scarce relative to goods.

Adjustment of Trade Flows   Adjustment of a country's trade balance and, consequently, its balance of payments will follow from the changes in prices. The rise in prices of the country with a trade surplus (gold inflow) will cause its exports to fall and its imports to rise, in keeping with the law of demand. The reverse will happen to the country with a trade deficit. Thus the price changes will adjust each country's trade and payments. The **price adjustment mechanism** is summarized in Figure L–1.

INCOME ADJUSTMENT VERSUS PRICE ADJUSTMENTS

In retrospect, economists have found that the gold standard does not function in the manner prescribed by the price adjustment mechanism. In fact, historically, income adjustments appear to have played an important role in the workings of the gold standard. As shown in Chapter 12, the money supply changes called for under gold standard rules can be expected to affect interest rates and therefore domestic investment. The change in investment, because of the multiplier effect, can have a dramatic impact on income and employment.

Consider the case of a country with a trade deficit operating under the gold standard. It will experience a gold outflow and a contrac-

tion of the money supply. Interest rates will rise, and investment will fall. National income and employment will fall. The country's consumers will reduce their imports, because the fall in their incomes will reduce their expenditures on both foreign and domestic goods. Thus the trade deficit will be "cured" by a recession rather than by a fall in prices.

For a country with a trade surplus (export balance), the **income adjustment mechanism** will be just the opposite of that for a country with a deficit. The money supply will expand,

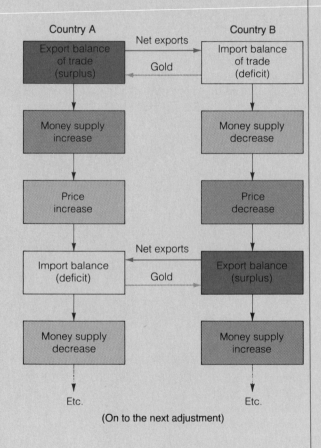

FIGURE L–1   The Price Adjustment Mechanism under the Gold Standard

Country B's trade deficit decreases its money supply and leads to a fall in prices and imports. Country A's trade surplus increases its money supply and leads to an increase in prices and imports. Thus, price changes adjust the trade balance.

investment will increase, income and employment will rise, and consumers will increase their purchases of imports. The income adjustment process is summarized in Figure L–2.

Of course, any price inflation in a country with a trade surplus that is undergoing expansion of economic activity or any price deflation in a country with a trade deficit that is experiencing a recession will reinforce the adjustment process depicted in Figure L–2. In addition, the interest rate changes in the fig-

ure will attract foreign investors to the deficit country (high interest rates will cause them to place short-term funds there) and cause a short-term investment outflow from the surplus country. Both phenomena will relieve the balance of payments difficulties of the deficit country and relax the pressure on its currency (the cause of the gold outflow).

However, evidence from the historical gold standard period shows that although short-term investment flows were important, the price adjustment did not take place. Thus adjustment of the trade balance appears to have been dependent on income changes, as described in Figure L–2.

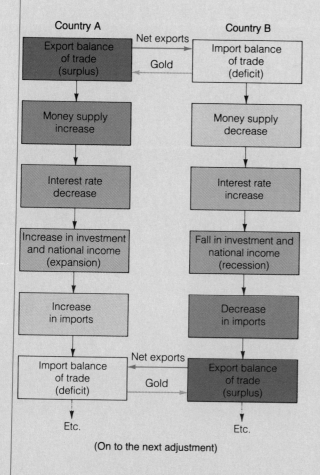

FIGURE L–2 The Income Adjustment Mechanism under the Gold Standard

Country B's trade deficit contracts its money supply and leads to a drop in national income and imports. Country A's trade surplus expands its money supply and leads to an increase in national income and imports. Thus, income changes adjust the trade balance.

FIXED EXCHANGE RATES AND THE INCOME ADJUSTMENT PROCESS

An important corollary to what has been said about the income adjustment process is that the findings apply to fixed exchange rate systems in general, not only to the gold standard. Thus the IMF system of fixed exchange rates that was established after World War II also depended on income adjustments to remedy short-term balance of payments problems.

The IMF did recognize that a fundamental disequilibrium could exist such that exchange rate changes (devaluations for the most part) would be necessary for adjusting the trade and payments of certain countries with persistent deficits or surpluses. However, it generally relied on income adjustments to correct short-term or temporary disequilibriums. In such situations it prevailed on monetary authorities to behave just as they would have under the gold standard. Deficit countries were advised to contract their money supplies and tighten their belts (have a recession). Of course, a country that already had a recession could not be expected to take kindly to the IMF's advice. Thus numerous devaluations took place without the IMF's permission.

Today most economists agree that the IMF's stabilization fund approach to the payments system of 1947–1971 was much too inflexible. The main problem was that changes in the fixed par values of exchange rates were withheld until deficit countries reached a crisis point. The IMF, through its lending of reserves, attempted to help deficit countries, but it still relied on the adjustment of domestic income and, to some extent, prices to remedy balance of payments problems. For deficit countries these changes (monetary contraction, high interest rates, increases in unemployment, and general deflation) were too high a price to pay for a fixed exchange rate. Therefore, we can expect that however the international monetary system is changed in the future, flexible exchange rates are here to stay.

C H A P T E R   31

INTERNATIONAL
COMMERCIAL POLICY,
TARIFFS,
AND
TRADE RESTRICTIONS

WHO
WANTS
FREE
TRADE?

In August 1980 Nobel Prize winning economist Paul A. Samuelson remarked:

The inroads made by Japanese and German automobile companies have converted Detroit executives from card-carrying free traders to lobbyists for protection of their market.[1]

In October of that year chairman-elect of General Motors, Roger B. Smith, in his address to the National Foreign Trade Council in New York, said:

We must work to make world trade as open and liberal as possible even while we help our trading partners advance their legitimate self-interest. Tariffs, quotas, local content laws, and other forms of protectionism present a serious problem. However attractive they may seem on the short-term basis, ultimately they reduce efficiency, shrink markets, and invite retaliation. Instead of helping, they hurt. As a result, the greater the reduction in open and liberal

---

1. "Threat of New Tariffs," *Newsweek*, August 11, 1950, p. 66.

world trade, the less the opportunities to achieve growth in the world's output and in the world's economy.[2]

Smith made this statement in the closing quarter of a year in which GM would post a loss—something it had done on only one other occasion since the 1920s.

In November 1980 the U.S. International Trade Commission (ITC) decided not to limit imports of Japanese cars to the United States, even though the United Auto Workers and Ford Motor Company had done their best to press for such barriers. A Ford executive said:

We sent the wrong signal to Japan. This country has just shown the Japanese that we don't care if they flood our market with their products and put workers out of jobs.[3]

Actually a lot of people were pleased with the ITC's decision. As the Wall Street Journal *noted early in the debate:*

A Detroit economist agrees: "If you take away a half million Japanese cars, does that mean you'll sell that many more Chrysler Imperials? Hell no." He suggests that the total auto market would instead shrink, there wouldn't be any recalls of laid-off auto workers, and the national economy would suffer more . . . .

Some 140,000 people, representing a $2 billion annual payroll, are employed in importing, selling and servicing foreign cars. Some 7,000 local dealerships also depend on foreign cars for part or all of their revenues.[4]

In this chapter the main issue is free trade versus protection. The discussion will show that there are many arguments for protecting domestic industries from foreign competition, but that few of these arguments are supported by economic analysis.

---

2. Roger B. Smith, "World Trade: To Advance Human Welfare," remarks made at the World Trade Dinner, National Foreign Trade Council, New York, New York, October 20, 1980, as reprinted by General Motors.
3. "Car Makers Fear U.S. Decision on Imports May Mean Further Gains by the Japanese," *Wall Street Journal*, November 12, 1980, p. 10.
4. "Car Wars: Protectionism Battle over Imports of Autos May Head for Congress," *Wall Street Journal*, February 15, 1980, pp. 1, 19.

◆

INTERNATIONAL
COMMERCIAL POLICY,
TARIFFS,
AND
TRADE RESTRICTIONS

WHAT THIS CHAPTER IS ABOUT

A nation's international commercial policy consists of its laws and its agreements with other countries that affect the international exchange of goods and services. The idea that a nation can benefit from regulating its foreign trade is probably as old as written history. Ancient writing abounds with tales of kings and despots who extracted tribute and tolls from merchant caravans passing through or selling foreign merchandise in their territories. Of course, such policies served mainly to provide revenue for the rulers; their effects on the general population were seldom analyzed.

When modern nation-states were formed, tariffs, or import duties, continued to be important sources of government revenue. In many countries these taxes were accompanied by export duties collected on shipments of domestic merchandise to foreign purchasers. During the sixteenth through the eighteenth centuries European monarchs regulated trade under a system known as **mercantilism.**□ This system was highly restrictive, designed to encourage exports and discourage imports. The theory was that the nation and its sovereign would be enriched by the inflow of gold that an export balance of trade would provide. A substantial store of gold was important to a nation in the days when kings needed to hire foreign mercenaries to smite their enemies (or rebellious citizens) and needed to buy strategic goods (lumber, tar, and pitch for sailing vessels) from foreign suppliers who would accept no other payment.[1]

Today, countries still use most of the instruments of commercial policy that were developed historically, but they recognize that free international trade can provide substantial benefits to all trading nations by improving the world allocation of resources and economic activity. In this chapter we will first examine the objectives of modern commercial policy and the types of policy instruments that governments have at their disposal. Then we will analyze the economic impacts of the various

27

---

1. The mercantilist system is discussed in Daniel R. Fusfeld, *The Age of the Economist*, 3d ed. (Glenview, Ill.: Scott, Foresman, 1977), Chapter 2.

policy instruments and the evolution of both U.S. and Western bloc trade policy, focusing on the period after World War II.

OBJECTIVES AND INSTRUMENTS OF COMMERCIAL POLICY

◆

Modern government policy makers have long realized that a nation's international trade policy has far-reaching effects on its citizens. As we will soon see, trade restrictions have predictable effects on such variables as domestic prices, production, and the distribution of income. Because of this, governments must develop their commercial policies according to the objectives the policies are meant to serve. In addition, they must identify appropriate policy tools (instruments) to accomplish such objectives. Both problems are addressed here.

POLICY OBJECTIVES

A nation's commercial policy generally has several objectives, among them economic welfare, self-sufficiency, security, and economic growth. All these objectives are both interrelated and subject to problems of definition. However, we can clarify their meanings by examining each one in detail.

Economic Welfare Simply stated, the commercial policy objective of economic welfare means obtaining for a country's citizens the maximum possible gains from trade. It involves recognition by government policy makers that international trade can improve the well-being of consumers; it also involves a conscious effort to take best advantage of the opportunities that trade provides. In a sense, economic welfare is the most important objective of commercial policy, because it deals

with making the most of what international trade has to offer. However, it is also the goal most frequently sacrificed to achieve other objectives.

Self-sufficiency An economy that is entirely self-sufficient is by definition an economy without trade. Such an economy would sacrifice all the potential gains from trade in order to avoid dependence on foreigners for supplies of any product. Clearly, the self-sufficiency objective of modern commercial policy cannot refer to this extreme situation. What it does mean is taking advantage of the nation's own endowment of resources to market for both domestic consumption and export the goods that can be produced at domestic costs that are competitive with international prices. In other words, a modern nation will not rely on other nations for goods that it can produce more cheaply than it can import them in the absence of tariffs or other protection. Sometimes, though, self-sufficiency involves the temporary imposition of a tariff in order to stimulate domestic production.

A second dimension of the self-sufficiency objective is the avoidance of dependence on foreign sources of supply for important raw materials. In many instances this kind of self-sufficiency cannot be achieved, but where substitute materials are available, commercial policy is sometimes used to foster their production.

Security Closely related to self-sufficiency is the objective of security. The security referred to here encompasses both provision for military defense and the safeguarding of citizens' economic well-being. Thus the architects of a modern nation's commercial policy attempt to protect both the lives and the incomes of citizens.

The military security issue seems clear-cut, but it is far-reaching and can conflict dangerously with the overall objective of economic welfare. The problem is that a large number of domestic industries may consider themselves necessary for national defense. After all, soldiers need blankets, so should not the blanket industry be protected from foreign competition?

The income security objective has two important facets. First, because consumers' real incomes depend on the goods and services they can purchase with their money incomes, the income security objective overlaps with the economic welfare objective. That is, to the extent that commercial policy safeguards the gains from trade, it protects consumers' incomes. If that policy becomes too restrictive, trade will decline and incomes will fall. On the other hand, income security requires relatively full employment. Therefore, when changing trade patterns lead to displacement of workers, it may be necessary for commercial policy to include measures that will speed the reallocation of resources. The United States recognizes this problem and provides government aid to workers and industries that suffer because of increased competition from imports. This aid, known as **adjustment assistance,** is viewed as a better alternative than protection of declining industries, because the latter misallocates resources and is detrimental to consumers.

Economic Growth   A country's international commercial policy can significantly affect its economic growth. For example, as just noted, a country that chooses to protect its declining industries will misallocate its domestic resources. To the extent it does so, it may operate inside its production possibilities curve☐ and pay a price in terms of future output.

Developing countries rely heavily on commercial policy to stimulate new industries. Their usual approach is to restrict imports of manufactured goods so that domestic producers can expand operations without foreign competition. Supposedly, when the new industries have grown, economies of scale☐ will make them cost-competitive with their foreign counterparts and the import restrictions can be removed. Historically, however, the results are mixed. The danger is that once industries are protected, they will try to retain that pro-

tection, whether or not it is economically justifiable.

POLICY INSTRUMENTS

The main instruments of commercial policy are: tariffs, nontariff trade barriers, subsidies, and adjustment assistance. Each of these tools is briefly discussed here.

Tariffs   Most tariffs assessed on products traded internationally are import tariffs. They are enacted by national governments and collected by customs officers as goods enter a country.

> An **import tariff** is a tax that a country's government imposes on foreign goods allowed to enter the country for sale to its residents.

The two principal types of import tariffs are specific and ad valorem. A **specific tariff** is a tariff of so much per unit (piece, pound, ton, liter, and so on) of the product imported. An **ad valorem tariff** is a tariff assessed as a percent of the value of the product. Some countries assess both specific and ad valorem tariffs on certain products. For example, leather gloves may be subject to a tariff of $.50 per pair and 10 percent ad valorem. If an exporter charged $5 for a pair of gloves, the total tariff would be $1. Some countries also assess tariffs on exports. Such a policy has two purposes. The first is to generate government revenue, and the second is to discourage, or at least limit, domestic production of a specific product. Export tariffs are common in developing countries but not widely used elsewhere.[2]

Nontariff Trade Barriers   The principal nontariff trade barriers are quotas and licenses.

---

2. The U.S. Constitution prohibits export tariffs, so they are not a policy option for the United States.

An **import quota** is a specific quantitative limit on the amount of some product that importers can bring into a country.

Ostensibly, by international agreement, quotas are not used by the major trading nations to regulate international trade. In other words, a nation wishing to set such a quota must use some other objective, such as domestic stabilization or national defense, to justify it. However, the effect will still be to restrict imports. The United States has maintained quota systems for many products, including textiles, sugar, beef, and petroleum. In addition, it has used export quotas to curtail sales of raw materials to foreign countries when it is experiencing shortages of such materials.

Licensing goes hand-in-hand with quotas, because it provides a way to divide up the quota among importers who wish to bring in the restricted product.

A **license** is a permit to import or export a particular product.

Some countries require import and export licenses for a broad range of products, even when no quota exists. Quotas and licenses are more restrictive than tariffs, because they control the absolute amount of the product imported or exported.

Besides quotas and licenses, nontariff trade barriers include requirements that products be stamped with country-of-origin labels, that liquids be shipped in specific sizes of containers, and that government agencies give preferential treatment to domestic suppliers over foreign suppliers. For example, every tile in a shipment of ceramic floor tiles from Mexico or other countries to the United States must be marked with the name of the country of origin.

Subsidies

Export subsidies are direct payments to producers or exporters who export a particular product.

Export subsidies can be disbursed as so much per unit of product exported. The major trading nations have banned the use of direct export subsidies on manufactured goods, so subsidies are frequently given in an indirect form. For example, a government might offer tax reductions or low-interest loans to exporters of a given product. Whether direct or indirect, subsidies are a form of protection for domestic producers, because they give these producers a price advantage over foreign competition.

Adjustment Assistance Many governments now use adjustment assistance as a commercial policy tool. Usually, the change that has harmed the industry eligible for such assistance occurs because of the removal of trade restrictions that afforded it some degree of protection. Government assistance may include technical advice, aid to workers for retraining or relocation, or loans to help firms reallocate their resources into new activities. The United States has had a program of adjustment assistance since the early 1960s.

ECONOMIC
ANALYSIS
OF
IMPORT
RESTRICTIONS

In a survey course on international economics it is customary to analyze the various commercial policy instruments. For our brief introduction to the topic, however, we will limit our analysis of policy tools to the two most widely used restrictive devices on the import side—tariffs and quotas. To simplify our analysis, we will assume that the imposition of a tariff or quota by a single country will not affect the world market price of the imported good, and we will consider only the microeconomic effects on the importing country.

EFFECTS OF A TARIFF

Figure 31–1 shows domestic demand and supply curves (D_d, S_d) for a single country, along with a world supply curve (S_w) that is horizontal, or perfectly elastic.□ The assumption is that the country in question can buy as much of the product as it wants at the world market price, P_w. Without trade, the domestic price would be P_d.

With free access to the world market, domestic consumers will purchase Q_4 of the product and domestic producers will supply Q_1. The difference, $Q_4 - Q_1$, is imports. The world price, P_w, will now be the price of this product within the country. Also, the quantity supplied by domestic producers will be less than the pretrade quantity at price P_d (point E_d), but the quantity demanded will be greater than the pretrade quantity.

If an import tariff of amount t is imposed on each unit bought from foreigners, the result

for this country can be represented by a shift of the world supply curve to S_w', because any amount of foreign output can now be obtained for price $P_w + t$. The effects of the tariff can be summarized as follows:

1. *Price effect:* The price paid by domestic consumers rises from P_w to $P_w + t$.
2. *Protective effect:* The protection afforded domestic producers increases their output by $Q_2 - Q_1$.
3. *Consumption effect:* The quantity demanded by consumers falls from Q_4 to Q_3 because of the increase in price.
4. *Static welfare effects:* The areas labeled r, a, g, and c represent reductions in consumer welfare associated with the higher price and lower quantity consumed.

The first three effects speak for themselves, but the static welfare effects require further explanation. Before the tariff was imposed, areas r, a, g, and c were all within the triangle formed by the demand curve, the horizontal line P_w, and the vertical axis. This triangle is known as the consumers' surplus.

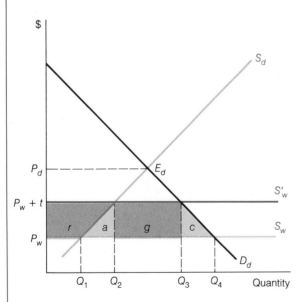

FIGURE 31–1   Effect of a Per Unit Import Tariff on Domestic Consumers and Producers

Initially, the world price is P_w. The imposition of a tariff *(t)*, increases price to $P_w + t$ and reduces imports from $(Q_4 - Q_1)$ to $(Q_3 - Q_2)$. The government collects tariff revenues equal to area *g*, while consumers also lose consumers' surplus equal to areas *r*, *a*, and *c*.

> The **consumers' surplus** is the difference between the amount consumers actually spend on a good (market price times quantity demanded) and the amount they would be willing and able to spend for the same quantity (area under the demand curve). The latter amount could be collected only by charging a different price for each unit sold.

In Figure 31–1 the consumers' surplus represents the amount consumers were willing and able to spend for up to Q_4 units of product but did not have to spend because of the uniform price, P_w. This spending power was available to consumers to allocate on other goods and services. At price $P_w + t$, areas r, a, g, and c were lost from the consumers' surplus. Thus consumers were made worse off.

Where did r, a, g, and c go? First, area g, which is equal to the amount of tariff (t) times the amount of imports $(Q_3 - Q_2)$ went to the government as tariff revenue. Area r was redistributed to domestic producers who increased their output to Q_2. Area a represents the cost of putting additional resources into domestic production of this product (an efficiency loss, because resources were better allocated before the tariff). Finally, area c was simply lost to consumers because of the reduction in quantity demanded from Q_4 to Q_3. Although the redistribution of areas g and r from consumers to producers and the government does not necessarily cause a net loss in national welfare, the misallocation of resources associated with area a and the loss from reduced consumption (area c) certainly do cause it. In any event, consumers are made worse off by the tariff, but domestic producers gain.

EFFECTS OF A QUOTA

Figure 31–2 illustrates the effects of a quota. The amount of the quota is $(Q_3 - Q_2)$, and when only this amount of foreign product can enter, the domestic quantity supplied plus imports will equal the domestic quantity demanded at price P' and quantity Q_3. Thus Figure 31–2 appears to be almost identical to Figure 31–1. The loss in consumers' surplus (shaded area) occurs just as with a tariff. In fact, all but one of the effects are the same. Because the government is not collecting a tariff, it may not get the revenues generated by the difference between the world price. P_w, and the post-quota price, P'.

What happens to area n depends on how the quota system is run. If the government auctions off licenses to importers, it can conceivably collect all of area n. If it does not, importers will obtain area n as **quota profits.** The latter situation assumes, of course, that exporters are unable to raise their price above P_w.

To summarize, tariffs and quotas have similar effects. Both improve the lot of domestic producers, reduce consumer welfare, and result in higher domestic prices and reduced consumption of the product. Tariffs provide

government revenue. Quotas may or may not do so. If the government fails to capture potential quota profits, they will accrue to importers or exporters.

THE PROS AND CONS OF TRADE RESTRICTIONS
◆

Thus far, our analysis has shown that import tariffs and import quotas benefit domestic producers of import-competing goods at the expense of domestic consumers and foreign exporters. **Protectionists** argue for the imposition of tariffs to protect domestic firms and workers from foreign competition. However, not all

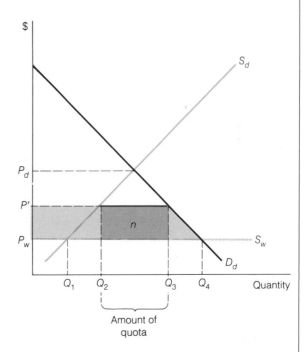

FIGURE 31–2 Effect of an Import Quota on Domestic Consumers and Producers

When the world price is P_w, imposition of a quota equal to $(Q_3 - Q_2)$ will raise price to P'. If the government does not sell licenses, area n will represent the quota profits of exporters and importers.

producers are protectionists. For example, producers who buy raw materials or intermediate goods in both the domestic and the international markets have a vested interest in keeping tariffs low, especially if they also export their final product to the international market. In the United States, certain manufacturers of heavy earth-moving equipment have lobbied against tariffs on imported steel, because they know that tariffs will raise their input costs and make their output higher priced and less able to compete with similar foreign-made goods.

THE CASE FOR FREE TRADE

The case for unrestricted trade is clear. Free trade allows countries to gain from comparative advantage□ and improved efficiency in the allocation of the world's productive resources. Trade restrictions reduce these opportunities and in most cases reduce world welfare. As we have seen, import tariffs benefit domestic producers of import-competing goods (both the businesses and their employees) at the expense of domestic consumers. Thus, if the United States were to impose a high tariff on foreign cars, the U.S. automobile companies would certainly be better off (although their foreign subsidiaries would suffer); so would the members of the United Auto Workers union. However, the rest of us would end up paying higher prices for both domestically produced and foreign cars. Furthermore, the U.S. firms protected by the tariff would have little incentive to develop cars that would effectively compete with the foreign makes in terms of fuel economy and quality.

PROTECTIONIST ARGUMENTS

If trade restrictions benefit special interests at the expense of the consuming public, what arguments are the protectionists able to use in order to get tariffs and quotas enacted? There is no shortage of seemingly reasonable arguments for the need to restrict imports, but few of them will stand up under analysis. The most popular and frequently used protectionist arguments are the national defense argument, the cheap foreign labor argument, the employment argument, and the infant industry argument.

National Defense   We have seen that national security is a generally accepted objective of commercial policy. It would therefore seem reasonable for a country not to rely on foreigners for supplies of arms and ammunition. After all, in the event of a war, they might not wish to or be able to sell it all the needed weapons. But even if a country makes all its own weapons, what about the raw materials that go into their production? Generally, such inputs are used only secondarily in the production of military goods; their primary use is in the production of nonmilitary consumer and capital goods. Thus an attempt to protect domestic producers of these inputs would reduce the gains from trade for the economy at large.

As noted earlier, many industries will use the national defense argument to obtain protection from foreign competition. In the United States the list includes the steel industry, the textile industry, and the chemical industry. However, the lion's share of the output of all these industries is nonmilitary in nature. In addition, it is unlikely that any of these industries would disappear without protection from foreign competition. Such competition might reduce their size, but it would also probably force them to be more efficient. That efficiency can actually improve national defense rather than impair it.

Cheap Foreign Labor   The cheap foreign labor argument asserts that we must protect our workers and businesses from the ruinous competition of countries where laborers are poorly paid. It claims that workers in such countries are exploited and must accept a low standard of living. The implication is that, in order to compete, either our workers have to be similarly paid (which would pauperize them) or our industries must be protected.

The analysis of comparative advantage showed that the gains from trade occur because of differences in the relative costs of production from one country to another. The fact that a country has relatively cheap labor does not mean that it can produce all goods more cheaply than they can be produced in some other country. In fact, countries with cheap labor are those where labor is more abundant than other productive resources. Their comparative advantage lies in the production of goods that require a large amount of labor, in combination with other inputs, per unit of output produced. Comparative advantage will lead to gains from trade when such goods (called *labor-intensive goods*) are produced where labor is abundant and therefore relatively cheap. In labor-scarce countries, other inputs (capital goods and technology) are often relatively abundant. These countries, the United States included, will benefit most greatly from trade by specializing in and exporting goods that are not labor-intensive and by obtaining their labor-intensive products from the labor-abundant countries.

This strategy will not, on the whole, harm U.S. labor. As the analysis of factor markets in Chapter 23 showed, the income of workers depends mainly on their productivity. However, the more capital a worker has to work with, the higher the marginal product□ of the worker. Thus, in the United States, where capital is relatively abundant, workers will be best rewarded when they engage in capital-intensive production, not when they use trade barriers to mimic the low productivity employment of foreign workers. This point can be illustrated with a simple example.

Suppose we take Joe Doe off the drill press assembly line at Rockwell International, train him, and put him to work making Panama hats. Back at Rockwell, drill press production will drop by six presses per day if Joe is not replaced. Meanwhile, because of superior training, Joe can weave twelve Panama hats per day. The United States has thus lost six

drill presses and gained twelve Panama hats. How many hats would the United States likely have gotten by selling six drill presses to Panama? Will Doe earn as much weaving the hats as he did working on the drill press line? End of story.

Employment The employment argument asserts that buying foreign goods means employing foreign workers, whereas buying domestic goods means employing domestic workers. It suggests that employment can be increased by restricting imports, thereby forcing domestic consumers to spend on output produced at home. This argument can best be examined in the light of the Keynesian theory of national income determination, developed in Chapter 6.

It is true that imports represent a diversion of expenditure from a given country's income stream and are therefore a "leakage" out of that stream in much the same way that saving is a leakage. However, one country's imports are another country's exports. Thus they represent an injection into the expenditure stream of the other country.

According to Keynesian theory, what happens in any given country when there is a new or "exogenous" injection of expenditure? The answer is that income increases by a multiple of the amount of the new spending, and there is an induced change in consumption. Some of this consumption expenditure will be directed toward imports, the proportion depending on the size of the ratio $\Delta M/\Delta Y$, where M is imports and Y is income. This fraction is called the marginal propensity to import (MPM).

The **marginal propensity to import** is the fraction of an increase in income that will be spent on imports.

Because exports represent an injection into a country's expenditure stream, any one-period increase in exports will raise Y, and through the marginal propensity to import, imports will also increase.

If a country imposes an import tariff to bolster its employment, imports will fall. But these imports are exports to some other countries. In the exporting countries, incomes will fall by a multiple of the drop in exports. Because of the marginal propensity to import, these countries will reduce their imports from the country that imposed the tariff. Thus its exports will fall, and its citizens' income and employment will be negatively affected. The increase in employment caused by switching the spending of domestic consumers from imports to domestic production will be in part offset by a drop in the exports of the country imposing the tariff. This effect, known as the **foreign repercussion effect** on domestic exports and income, will be negligible unless the country that imposes the tariff is large.

If many countries simultaneously impose import tariffs to bolster employment, they will all lose, because everyone's exports will fall. This is exactly what happened during the Great Depression of the 1930s, when trade came to a virtual standstill. Thus, using import restrictions to stimulate employment is not a good bet, especially for a large country like the United States. First of all, the foreign repercussion effect will limit the amount of increase in economic activity that can be generated at home, and other countries may retaliate with restrictions of their own. In addition, employment in inefficient, import-competing industries will be stimulated, and employment in efficient, export-oriented industries will drop.

Infant Industries   The infant industries argument is related to the economic concepts of economies of scale□ and decreasing cost industries.□ According to proponents of this argument, new industries must be protected from foreign competition until they become large enough to achieve the economies of scale already possessed by their foreign rivals or until domestic supplier industries are large enough to produce inputs at internationally competitive costs. (The latter would provide

inputs to the infant industries at lower and lower prices.)

The infant industry argument has been around for a long time. In fact, it was used by Alexander Hamilton in his *Report on Manufactures*, prepared for the U.S. government in 1791.[3] Today, the argument is frequently voiced by policy makers in the less developed countries.

One problem with the infant industry argument is that the infants are hard to identify. New industries that clamor for protection are not necessarily those that have the potential to become internationally competitive. If the wrong industries are protected, they may grow, but they may never become relatively low cost. What then? Will they ever be willing to give up their protection?

Even if a protected industry becomes large and relatively efficient, chances are that any effort to remove the protective tariff will meet with resistance from both management and labor. The special interests inside the protected industry are clearly better off with the tariff, even though it may not be a good thing for the economy as a whole. We can therefore conclude that the infant industry argument is valid in theory but likely to break down in practice.

TRADE
LIBERALIZATION
AND U.S. POLICY

Trade liberalization *is the removal or reduction of restrictions on international trade.*

There has been a sweeping trend toward trade liberalization among the developed market economies since the end of World War II. In addition, trade between this group and the

3. The *Report* is reprinted in A. H. Cole, ed., *Industrial and Commercial Correspondence of Alexander Hamilton* (New York: Augustus M. Kelley, Publishers, 1968).

centrally planned economies (the Soviet bloc and China) has recently opened up. The United States has been a leader in both developments, even though protectionist sentiment has at times been strong in certain industries and in Congress. Protectionism has long been a significant force in U.S. trade policy, as the next section shows.

HISTORY OF THE U.S. TARIFF

During the two centuries the United States has been a nation, its tariff policy has displayed a cyclical pattern.[4] Tariffs were an important source of government revenue during the early years of nationhood, a time when the infant industry argument was popular, especially in the manufacturing states of the North. The southern states favored low tariffs, because they exported agricultural goods and wanted to import cheap foreign manufactures. The passage of an extremely high tariff in 1828 (the so-called Tariff of Abominations) led to South Carolina's "Ordinance of Nullification," which was an attempt to nullify the tariff at South Carolina ports. Although the Ordinance was unsuccessful, it fueled the states' rights philosophy that finally led to the South's secession from the Union.

Figure 31–3 shows the **average height of tariff** (duties as a percent of dutiable imports) on U.S. imports for the period 1821–1979. The Tariff of Abominations was followed by the Compromise Tariff of 1833, and thereafter the trend for average duties was downward until the Civil War. During the war, Congress imposed excise taxes☐ on U.S. goods in order to raise government revenue and passed a series of tariffs to offset these excises. The reasoning was that foreign producers should not

have an unfair advantage over U.S. producers, whose costs were increased by the excise taxes. After the war, the excise taxes lapsed, but the tariffs remained. In fact, U.S. tariffs remained quite high during the remainder of the nineteenth century and were not substantially reduced until the Wilson administration (Underwood Tariff, 1913).

The aftermath of World War I brought economic chaos to Europe and fostered a new wave of protectionism in the United States. Both industry and agriculture lined up for protection, and they got it in the Fordney-Mc-Cumber Tariff of 1922. In the second half of the 1920s, both European and U.S. tariffs continued to rise.

After the stock market crash of 1929, Congress enacted the Smoot-Hawley Tariff (1930), the highest tariff in U.S. history. This tariff was meant to stimulate employment in the United States. But as exports and employment fell in other countries, these countries also imposed tariffs. The result was a collapse of international trade and a deepening of the depression.

THE ROAD TO LIBERALIZATION

With the world locked in the grips of depression, in 1934 President Roosevelt asked Congress for legislation that would allow him to reduce tariffs through negotiations in which other countries would agree to reduce tariffs in return. The result was the **Reciprocal Trade Agreements Act (1934)**. Under this act, the president could cut tariffs by as much as 50 percent of the Smoot-Hawley rates in return for concessions from other countries. Bilateral trade agreements (between just two countries) would not have to be ratified by the Senate, and concessions granted bilaterally would be automatically extended to other countries that had trade agreements with the United States.

*The principle of extending concessions granted one country to all other countries is known as **most-favored-nation treatment**.*

---

4. For a more complete discussion of the history of U.S. tariffs, see Robert J. Carbaugh, *International Economics* (Cambridge, Mass.: Winthrop Publishers, 1980), Chapter 7; and Franklin R. Root, *International Trade and Investment* (Cincinnati, Ohio: South-Western Publishing, 1978), Chapter 7.

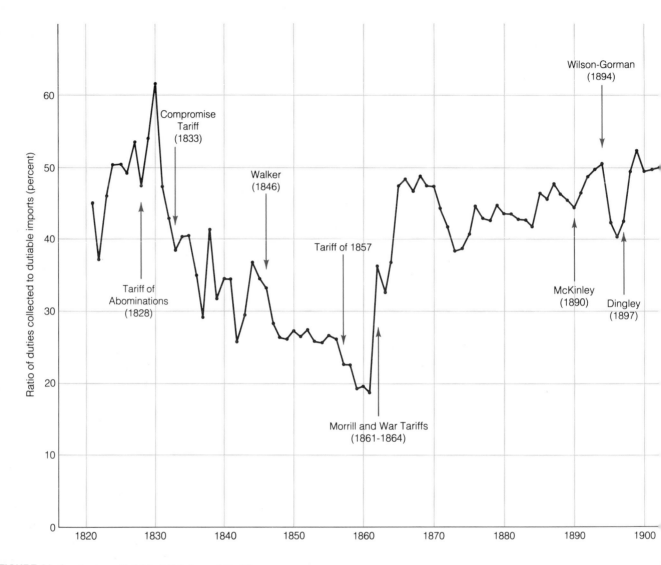

FIGURE 31–3   Average Height of U.S. Import Tariff

Source: U.S. Department of Commerce, Bureau of the Census, *Historical Statistics of the United States: Colonial Times to 1970* (Washington, D.C.: Government Printing Office, 1975), p. 888; and *Statistical Abstract of the United States* (Washington, D.C.: Government Printing Office, various years).

Since the Reciprocal Trade Agreements Act, the United States has generally adhered to the most-favored-nation approach in its dealings with other market economies.

By the 1950s the average height of the U.S. import tariff had fallen to less than 15 percent as the result of reciprocal agreements under the 1934 act and its extensions and of the eroding effect of inflation on specific tariffs.

However, the Cold War years of the 1950s were marked by a rise in protectionist sentiment and restriction of the trade agreements program. While this was happening in the United States, the European countries were successfully putting together a major trading bloc, which became known as the European Economic Community (EEC). It soon became clear that the United States would have to de-

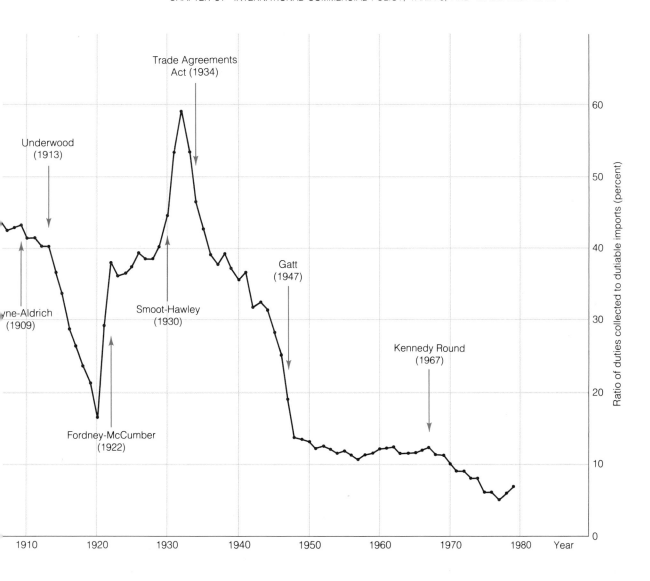

velop a bold trade agreements policy to deal with both the EEC and Japan, which had developed a strong capacity to export while protecting its domestic market.

GATT AND THE TRADE EXPANSION ACT

The **General Agreement on Tariffs and Trade (GATT)** proved to be the primary vehicle for progress in trade liberalization between the United States and its major trading partners during the 1960s and 1970s. GATT was created in 1947 as a provisional agreement on trade policy that was to establish rules and provide a vehicle for negotiations until a projected International Trade Organization (ITO) was established as an affiliate of the United Nations. The ITO was never established, but GATT remains with us today.[5]

GATT's main objectives have been to pro-

5. Miltiades Chacoliades, *Principles of International Economics* (New York: McGraw-Hill, 1981), pp. 248–249.

vide a mechanism for negotiating tariff reductions, to eliminate the use of import quotas, to settle trade disputes among its members, and to help promote the trade of the developing countries. GATT requires that its members extend unconditional most-favored-nation treatment to each other, and its success in reducing tariffs has been commendable. One reason for GATT's success is continuing cooperation from the United States, which has repeatedly passed trade legislation enabling the president to lower tariffs.

Under the Kennedy administration, in 1962, the United States passed the **Trade Expansion Act.** This act empowered the president to lower tariffs by up to 50 percent of the rates prevailing at that time. It also provided for reductions of up to 100 percent in the tariff rates on industrial products where the combined exports of the United States and the European Economic Community accounted for 80 percent or more of free-world trade. It allowed the president to eliminate "nuisance duties" of 5 percent or less, and it contained some special provisions for trade liberalization in tropical products and agriculture.

Because the tariff reductions authorized by the Trade Expansion Act were expected to have some disruptive effects on certain U.S. industries, the act provided for adjustment assistance in the form of government aid to workers and businesses harmed by the reductions. This aid could include loans and retraining programs, as well as technical assistance. Adjustment assistance is in keeping with the economic notion that resources should be allocated (or reallocated) in a way that takes maximum advantage of the gains from international trade. It has remained a feature of U.S. commercial policy.

The Kennedy Round Passage of the Trade Expansion Act led to a lengthy conference of GATT negotiations known as the **Kennedy Round,** which lasted from 1964 to 1967. It was extremely successful in reducing tariffs on manufactured goods, where tariff cuts averaged 35 percent of previous duty levels. More than 60,000 industrial products were subject to tariff reductions.[6] However, little progress was made on liberalizing trade in agricultural products.

THE 1970s: PROTECTIONISM AND THE TOKYO ROUND

The 1970s were years of inflationary recession for the United States. World trade was growing by leaps and bounds, but the U.S. economy was growing slowly and the country's traditional export balance of trade was eroding away. Protectionist sentiment again arose in both industry and labor. In 1971 the Burke-Hartke bill, possibly the most dangerous piece of protectionist legislation in U.S. history, was introduced in Congress.[7] The bill provided for an across-the-board system of quotas on imports into the United States. Fortunately, it failed, and two trade acts with much milder protectionist clauses were passed in 1974 and 1979. Both of these acts compel the president to protect industries when the U.S. International Trade Commission determines that they are being injured by increased imports. The mechanism employed can be a regular protective tariff or a **countervailing duty**—a special tax to offset government subsidization of industry in the exporting country.

With Burke-Hartke out of the way, it was possible for the members of GATT to make significant progress on trade liberalization during the 1970s, despite the disruption of international trade caused by OPEC and the Arab-Israeli conflict. A new round of GATT negotiations took place in Tokyo, with bargaining sessions that lasted from 1974 to 1979. The *Tokyo Round* produced agreements on tropical products, freer trade between Europe and the United States in agricultural goods, and further liberalization of trade in manufactured

---

6. Root, *International Trade and Investment*, p. 182.

7. Irwin Ross, "Labor's Big Push for Protectionism," *Fortune*, March, 1973, pp. 93–97, 170–174.

goods. Tokyo Round concessions went into effect in 1980, and many U.S. firms were optimistic about increased exports of high-technology manufactures. However, it will be some time before the effects of these concessions can be adequately assessed.[8] Meanwhile, we can expect the U.S. International Trade Commission to be kept busy by domestic producers seeking protection under the trade acts of 1974 and 1979.

SUMMARY

1. This chapter examined the objectives of international commercial policy and the instruments used by governments to pursue those objectives. A nation's international commercial policy consists of laws and agreements that regulate export and import trade. Its objectives generally include the promotion of economic welfare, national self-sufficiency, military and economic security, and national economic growth.

2. The policy tools or instruments used to regulate a nation's international trade include tariffs (taxes) on imports and exports, quotas that limit the physical amount of goods imported or exported, subsidies to export industries, and a host of nontariff barriers to trade, such as labeling requirements, restrictions on sizes of containers, and preferential treatment of domestic producers in government purchasing of goods. A recent development in policy instruments is the provision of adjustment assistance in the form of government aid to firms and workers harmed as a result of changes in the competitive environment of trade. As governments have reduced tariffs and liberalized world trade, the need for this new policy tool has become apparent.

3. Import tariffs and quotas, the most widespread types of trade restrictions, have similar economic effects. When the world supply of a given product is assumed to be infinitely elastic, a tariff reduces imports, increases domestic production of the good, reduces domestic consumption of the good, and redistributes income from consumers to producers and government. In addition, national welfare falls, because resources are shifted into import-competing industries and a part of the consumers' surplus is lost.

4. The case for free trade lies in its beneficial effects on resource allocation and world output. Presumably, countries that engage in free international trade will enjoy consumption possibilities not otherwise feasible. Among the arguments for trade restrictions are those relating to national defense, protection from the competition of cheap foreign labor, the preservation or promotion of domestic employment, and the promotion of infant industries. In general, none of these arguments constitutes much of a case for protection of domestic industries, although the defense and infant industries arguments may be applicable in certain special circumstances.

5. The early history of the United States was characterized by protective tariffs that contributed to the strife between the northern and southern states. Tariffs were relaxed prior to the Civil War but were raised during the war and remained high until 1913. In the aftermath of World War I, U.S. tariffs were successively increased, and in 1930 the Smoot-Hawley Tariff was passed. This tariff was the highest in U.S. history and, along with retaliation by other countries, contributed to the collapse of world trade during the Great Depression.

6. In 1934 Congress passed the Reciprocal Trade Agreements Act, which marked the beginning of U.S. leadership in the liberalization of world trade. This act embodied the principle of most-favored-nation treatment in trade negotiations, so that tariff concessions negotiated on a bilateral basis would be extended to other countries. By the end of World War II the average height of the U.S. tariff was a fraction of what it had been in 1932. Still, after the war, trade liberalization continued under the auspices of the General Agreement on Tariffs and Trade. Despite several upsurges of protectionist activities in Congress, GATT has continued to be effective. U.S. trade legislation has led to further reductions in tariffs and other restrictions.

---

8. Chacoliades, *Principles of International Economics*, p. 252.

IMPORTANT TERMS AND CONCEPTS

Mercantilism

Adjustment assistance

Import tariff

Specific tariff

Ad valorem tariff

Import quota

License

Export subsidy

Consumers' surplus

Quota profits

Protectionists

Marginal propensity
  to import

Foreign repercussion
  effect

Trade liberalization

Reciprocal Trade
  Agreements Act
  (1934)

Most-favored-nation
  treatment

General Agreement
  on Tariffs and
  Trade (GATT)

Trade Expansion Act
  (1962)

Kennedy Round

Countervailing duty

Tokyo Round

QUESTIONS AND PROBLEMS

1. What are the objectives of a nation's international commercial policy? Define each objective, and relate it to the issue of free trade versus protection.

2. What are the main instruments used by national governments to foster their commercial policy objectives? Are all of them restrictive in nature? Explain.

3. Use a supply and demand curve diagram to describe the effects of a tariff on an importing country. Indicate who gains from the tariff and who loses, as well as the nature of the gains and losses.

4. Explain how a quota on imports differs from a tariff in terms of its effects on the importing country.

5. Explain why you agree or disagree with this statement: The steel industry is a vital component of our national defense and must be protected from foreign competition no matter what the cost.

6. Analyze this statement in terms of the case for free trade: Opening up the country to imports from places where labor is paid only a fraction of the daily wage of U.S. workers will destroy the U.S. labor force and lower the U.S. standard of living.

7. What was the main policy objective of the Smoot-Hawley Tariff of 1930? Was it achieved? Explain.

8. Underdeveloped countries frequently use the infant industry argument to justify protective tariffs and other forms of import restrictions. Why do they think the argument makes sense? What are the problems encountered in implementing this approach?

9. In the early years of U.S. history, what differences did the northern and southern states have on the tariff issue? What was the South's reaction to the Tariff of Abominations?

10. What is the importance of each of the following in the trend toward trade liberalization that followed the Great Depression and World War II:

  a. The Reciprocal Trade Agreements Act (1934)
  b. The Trade Expansion Act (1962)
  c. GATT

"BUY
AMERICAN"
REVIVAL

Not content with [current protectionist measures], the steel industry has been actively lobbying for import protection on the state level. Fully 27 states have enacted laws that require a preference, in public works procurement, for goods made of American steel. Having twice vetoed earlier "Buy American Steel" bills, Governor Carey of New York has indicated he will probably sign a third, provided the state legislature attaches a three-year "sunset" amendment. Governor Brown of California may soon face a similar decision, for a Buy American bill has passed the

California Assembly and is likely to be approved by the state senate.

We hope they say no. The case against "Buy American" statutes is the same as that against all import barriers. Protection raises prices for consumers, in this case taxpayers who have to pay more for public construction. Like all protection, Buy American preferences encourage domestic steelmakers to remain inefficient and discourage them from making the structural transformations necessary to restore their international competitiveness. Finally, every additional import barrier makes it more likely that foreign nations will retaliate with their own restrictions on trade—a consideration which should weigh heavily on New York and

California, both of whose economies depend on export industries as well as international shipping and banking.

It can be argued, of course, that foreign countries already have protectionist procurement codes. In the recent Tokyo Rounds of Multilateral Trade Negotiations, the world's industrial countries agreed to phase out the buy-domestic preferences of their national government purchasers. However, the Tokyo Rounds did not cover state and local preferences, and in several foreign countries, particularly Canada and West Germany, provincial and state governments operate under restrictive procurement codes.

Alan Wolff, former deputy to the U.S. Special Trade Representative,

Source: " 'Buy American' Revival," *Wall Street Journal*, June 10, 1980, p. 24.

has indeed commented that state Buy American laws might be used as "bargaining chips" in knocking down similar foreign restrictions in the next round of trade negotiations beginning in 1983. However, since no one expects a great deal of further progress on reducing trade barriers during this decade, it could be a long time before those chips are cashed, and Americans will be paying the bill for all that delay.

Moreover, state laws in the U.S. will serve as an invitation for more governmental subdivisions in other countries to put up barriers, so

American export industries will suffer. Finally, even with sunset laws and even under pressure from U.S. trade negotiators, we are not confident these laws will not be perpetually renewed. Once the steel industry becomes accustomed to such crutches, it will fight hard not to have the crutch pulled away. And other industries will see steel as a precedent for their own protectionist demands.

Protectionism is protectionism whether it is at the local, state or federal level. And with growth in economic efficiency already

weakening in the industrial nations, no one can afford these further blows to competition.

QUESTIONS

1. Who benefits from "buy American" laws, and who is hurt by them?

2. What is the likely reaction of other nations to the passage of "buy American" laws in the United States?

3. What do you think of the argument that such laws can be used as "bargaining chips in future trade negotiations"?

C H A P T E R 32

INTERNATIONAL
ECONOMIC
DEVELOPMENT

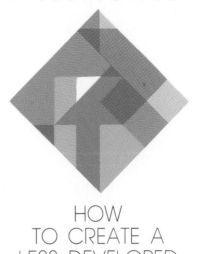

HOW
TO CREATE A
LESS DEVELOPED
COUNTRY

In December 1980, by a vote of 295,891 to 1,642, the descendants of the ancient Xhosa tribe chose to break away from South Africa and form a new republic called Ciskei. From the size of the vote, it is obvious that Ciskei is not a very large country. In fact, its land area is about the size of the state of Delaware. Its people are poor and uneducated, and it is not rich in natural resources. Time magazine describes it as follows:

Its barren, eroded soil supports few crops or even trees. The pastoral people subsist on beans, maize, goats, and a few dairy cattle. A drought last summer was so severe that it took $9.28 million in emergency aid from Pretoria to avert mass starvation. Though the territory is already densely populated, the [South African] government, under a "resettlement" program, sends in truckloads of unwanted blacks from urban areas. Once in Ciskei, many of the new arrivals live in stark tent towns with no schools, shops, or running water.[1]

From this description, it is obvious that Ciskei is not viable as an independent nation. In fact, an international commission recommended in February 1980 that Ciskei not be allowed the option of autonomy from South Africa. However, the territory's native minister, believing, no doubt, that his own self-interest would be

---

1. "Voting for Puppethood", *Time*, December 29, 1980, p. 37.

served by the creation of the republic, campaigned vigorously to get his people to support a vote for independence. He is reported to have said: "We are not just a group of blacks in South Africa. We are a nation. As blacks in South Africa, we have no rights. We are just pigs."[2]

Ciskei is an anomaly—a special case created by white South Africa to disenfranchise black South Africans, or at least to keep from sharing the country's wealth with them. Still, in the recent past, many other new, independent states, both on the African continent and elsewhere, have been created from ex-colonies and ex-territories of wealthy countries far removed from them both geographically and culturally. This could, in fact, be a form of international segregation much more subtle than the apartheid practiced by the South Africans. It may divide the world between the rich and the poor in a way that will make it difficult for the poor ever to catch up. As this chapter will show, the large disparities that now exist between the rich countries and the poor countries cannot easily be ignored or eliminated.

2. Ibid.

C H A P T E R 32

INTERNATIONAL ECONOMIC DEVELOPMENT

WHAT THIS CHAPTER IS ABOUT

CHARACTERISTICS OF LESS DEVELOPED
  COUNTRIES
Per Capita GNP
Income Distribution
Population Growth
Institutional Rigidities
ECONOMIC THEORY AND DEVELOPMENT
  STRATEGY
Institutional and Historical Theories
Stages of Economic Growth
Saving and Capital Formation
Balanced Growth and the "Big Push"
Social Overhead Capital and Growth
Import Substitution and Export Promotion
Foreign Aid and Investment
THE LDCs TODAY: STRATEGY FOR THE 1980s
The Widening Income Gap
International Development Policy for the Future
Internal Policies for Growth

Many of the earlier chapters in this book centered on the U.S. economy and its problems of resource allocation, growth, and stability. Only in the three preceding chapters has the well-being of the rest of the world been considered, and then solely in the context of international trade and its effects. In this chapter the primary concerns will be international economic inequality and how the issues of equity and growth affect economic relations between the developed market economies and the rest of the world. We examined the relationship between trade and economic development at various points in Chapters 29 to 31. There we saw that comparative advantage, the terms of trade, international payments, and commercial policy constitute special problems for countries that consider economic development a primary national goal. Here we will take a closer look at these countries and their economic difficulties, not only as they relate to international trade but also as they relate to overall internal economic growth.

We will begin by identifying the less developed countries and describing their economic characteristics. Then we will survey economic development theory and policy. We will conclude with a description of what the less developed countries can do to help themselves.

THE LESS DEVELOPED COUNTRIES AND THEIR CHARACTERISTICS

◆

In the 1970s it became fashionable among diplomats and scholars to divide the world into three groups: the developed market economies, the centrally planned economies, and everyone else. "Everyone else" is the **Third World**—the countries we have labeled the developing market economies□ along with a few nonaligned states that cannot easily be lumped with either of the other two main groups. Despite the fact that most of the centrally planned economies are at a level of development considerably below that of the developed market economies, they are seldom included in the catch-all categories of Third World or less developed countries (LDCs) because of the pervasive influence of the Soviet Union and China on their economic and political strategies. In general, the countries known as LDCs are politically, even if not economically, independent.

In 1978 the U.S. Bureau of the Census reported that there were 149 countries in the world; it classified 116 of them as less developed.[1] The single outstanding characteristic common to all the LDCs is poverty. Large numbers of citizens in all these countries live at or near the subsistence level, having little more than food, clothing, and primitive shelter to call their own. Thus LDCs are easy to identify if we are walking around in them, but for analytical purposes we need to have a numerical measure of the level of a country's development. Such a measure will enable us to compare the LDCs with the developed countries and with each other.

PER CAPITA GNP

The measure generally employed to compare levels of national economic development is **per capita GNP**. It is obtained by simply dividing a country's GNP by its population:

$$\frac{GNP}{Population} = \text{Per capita GNP}.$$

For the United States, per capita GNP in 1980 was approximately \$11,792.[2] Meanwhile, in more than 60 countries the 1980 per capita GNP was estimated at less than \$750; in many of these countries it was less than \$250.[3]

The idea that someone could live on \$250 per year or less is, no doubt, difficult to comprehend. In fact, such a notion points out two problems with using GNP per capita as a measuring stick for welfare. First, in many LDCs, a good deal of output produced probably is not counted. People who grow food for their own consumption often are not part of the monetary economy, where output is valued and recorded in a way that provides statistical data. Second, the structure of both output and consumption varies greatly from country to country. Peasants in a pre-industrial economy neither produce nor consume such products as canned foods or Big Macs. Thus, whereas

1. U.S. Department of Commerce, Bureau of the Census, *Statistical Abstract of the United States, 1980*, (Washington, D.C.: Government Printing Office, 1980), pp. 897–899.

2. *Economic Report of the President* (Washington, D.C.: Government Printing Office, 1981), pp. 233, 263.

3. Estimate based on 1977 data from *1978 World Bank Atlas* (Washington D.C., 1979), pp. 27–30.

658

subsisting on $250 per year in the United States might appear to be impossible, subsisting on the foreign exchange equivalent of $250 in a place like Burma might be conceivable.

In any event, it is widely agreed that per capita GNP suffices as a rough indicator of level of development, because it correlates fairly well with other indicators, such as life expectancy, literacy, and availability of public services like schools and hospitals. Per capita GNP tells us a good deal about the relative positions of countries, as we will see.

DIVERSITY AMONG THE LDCs

Bangladesh is perhaps the poorest of the LDCs. Its per capita GNP was under $100 in 1980, and the life expectancy of its people is in the forty to fifty years range. Venezuela is also an LDC, but its 1980 per capita GNP was over $3,000, and its people can expect to live to age sixty or more. One does not have to look far in the less developed world to find wide differences in basic data on economic and social development. All these countries are poor in comparison with the United States, but some are much poorer than others. Some have relatively high GNP per capita, but a trip through them would convince you that they do indeed belong in the less developed category. Income distribution is one reason for the discrepancy between GNP per capita and the general standard of living.

Table 32–1 lists selected LDCs and developed countries by level of development and 1980 per capita GNP. The broad range of per capita GNP levels among the less developed countries is perhaps the most striking feature of the table. A number of oil-exporting countries are included to indicate just how high the per capita income figure has gotten for some of them.

Kuwait and the United Arab Emirates are very small countries in term of both population and area. Kuwait has only about 200,000 inhabitants and the United Arab Emirates just about 1 million. They both can develop very

TABLE 32–1 Per Capita GNP by Levels of Development, Selected Countries, 1980

Less Developed Countries

Lowest income (1980 per capita GNP of less than $500):

Afghanistan	$ 195	India	$ 221
Bangladesh	98	Indonesia	420
Burma	177	Pakistan	292
Haiti	285	Uganda	315
		Zaire	285

Middle income (1980 per capita GNP of $500–$1,499):

Colombia	$ 1,195	Nicaragua	$ 731
El Salvador	744	Nigeria	758
Guatemala	1,145	Peru	794
Honduras	584	Philippines	671
Ivory Coast	1,160		

Highest income (1980 per capita GNP of $1,500 or more):

Algeria	$ 1,175	Mexico	$ 1,957
Argentina	2,490	South Korea	1,184
Brazil	2,033	United Arab	
Iran	2,521	Emirates	22,334
Kuwait	18,341	Uruguay	2,310
		Venezuela	3,492

Developed Countries

Low income (1980 per capita GNP of less than $7,500):

Greece	$ 4,571	New Zealand	$ 6,587
Ireland	4,735	Poland	4,262
Israel	4,704	Spain	4,999
Italy	5,929	United Kingdom	7,040

High income (1980 per capita GNP of $7,500 or more):

Austria	$ 9,792	Japan	$10,505
Australia	10,219	Netherlands	11,530
Belgium	12,369	Sweden	13,315
Canada	11,254	United States	11,792
France	11,279	West Germany	13,208

Source: Estimates based on growth rate and GNP data from World Bank, *World Development Report 1981*, pp. 134–135; and additional per capita GNP statistics from the following sources: U.S. Department of Commerce, Bureau of the Census, *Statistical Abstract of the United States, 1980*, p. 907; U.S. President, *Economic Report of the President, 1981*, pp. 233, 263; and Chase Manhattan Bank, *International Finance*, May 11, 1981, p. 4.

quickly if their leaders choose to let them, but they cannot at present be considered developed, despite their high per capita GNP. As a recent report by an international organization put it: "This income can hardly be looked upon as a satisfactory way of measuring development, since the social indicators (literacy, infant mortality, life expectancy) are well below those usually associated with this level of income."[4]

The oil-exporting countries aside, Table 32–1 gives us a reasonable picture of levels of development. Among the LDCs, those with a per capita GNP level of over $1,500 are generally the ones that have achieved some industrialization and diversification of their economies over the past forty or so years. They include several of the larger Latin American countries and Taiwan. The middle-income LDCs consist of a large number of countries that are only slightly industrialized but whose citizens, for the most part, are noticeably better off than those of the very poorest countries. Finally, the lowest-income LDCs tend to have little industrial capacity and high population density. In this group are some very crowded countries of widely divergent size. Bangladesh, for example, has 1,515 inhabitants per square mile of its 55,126 square mile area. Haiti, with only 10,714 square miles of area, has 504 persons per square mile. By comparison, the population density of the United States is 81 persons per square mile; that of Europe is 251 per square mile.[5]

INCOME DISTRIBUTION PROBLEM

Most of the LDCs have severe problems of income distribution. Typically, a small proportion of the population lives in luxury, and a small middle class enjoys a modestly up-to-date existence. The rest of the population lives close to subsistence, with many people either unemployed or underemployed. The underemployed have jobs, but their productivity is

extremely low. Of course, this means the bulk of the population of most LDCs is considerably worse off than the per capita GNP figures suggest.

Many economists have argued that the LDCs are characterized by economic dualism.[6]

> An economy characterized by **economic dualism** is divided into two distinct sectors, one modern and the other traditional.

The modern sector generally centers around the major cities, where all the trappings of industrial society can be found. People in the modern sector live and work much like people in the United States and Europe do.

A step into the traditional sector, however, is like a step backward in time. In that sector, ancient methods of production prevail, and productivity is low. Output consists almost entirely of agricultural goods and handicrafts. Agriculture is not mechanized as it is in the industrialized countries; people and beasts of burden work the fields. Many of the people who live in the countryside are unemployed, because there is not enough agricultural activity to keep everyone occupied. In certain LDCs rural land is concentrated in the hands of wealthy estate owners, and much of it lies fallow.

Typically, the growth of the modern sector in the LDCs has caused the rural unemployed and underemployed to migrate to the cities in search of a better life. Most of these people are illiterate and unskilled. Some better themselves in the cities, but many do not. As a result, major cities in the LDCs have grown to enormous size and contain some of the worst slum areas in the world. Governments that are already strapped for resources find that they must provide urban services and social programs for staggering numbers of urban poor.

---

4. *Interfutures, Facing the Future: Mastering the Probable and Managing the Unpredictable* (Paris: Organization for Economic Co-operation and Development, 1979), p. 217.

5. U.S. Department of Commerce, Bureau of the Census, *Statistical Abstract of the United States, 1979*, pp. 885–886.

6. For a discussion of economic dualism see Benjamin Higgins, *Economic Development: Problems, Principles, and Policies* (New York: W. W. Norton, 1968), pp. 227–241, 732–736.

Growth Rate of Population Generally speaking, the LDCs have population growth rates far in excess of those found in the developed countries. Table 32–2 documents this fact for selected countries. In the LDCs the growth rate of population tends to exceed 2.5 percent per year. This means that the population will double in about twenty-five years. At 1 percent per year, it takes seventy years for the population to double. Recently, most developed countries have had population growth rates below 1 percent per year.

Of course, the rapid growth of population makes it all the more difficult for the governments of the LDCs to manage their economies in ways that will yield real increases in standards of living. Even if they can achieve a relatively high rate of growth in GNP, it does not translate into much of an improvement in per capita GNP. For example, an LDC that has a 6 percent growth rate in GNP and a 3 percent rate of population increase will have an an-

nual increase in per capita GNP of 2.9 percent (1.06/1.03 = 1.029). Thus, as long as the high rates of population growth persist, it will be difficult for the LDCs to make much progress in closing the per capita GNP gap between them and the developed countries.

INSTITUTIONAL RIGIDITIES AND POLITICAL IMPEDIMENTS TO GROWTH

Another characteristic of LDCs is the existence of social or cultural barriers to development, sometimes called *institutional rigidities*.

> A society's **institutional structure** consists of its rules and traditions and the myths or justifications that stand behind them.

For example, feudalism was the prevailing institutional structure in medieval Europe. The basic economic unit was the manor, the estate of a nobleman. The operation of the manor was based on a master-serf relationship in which serfs were brought up to believe that their lot in life was to be serfs. The church admonished them to be content with their role in this world and to look for a better life only in the hereafter. The manor, the home of both the master and the serf, depended for its very existence on each of them playing out his or her assigned roles. The breaking of any of the rules of the system was cause for severe penalties, even death.

Of course, a system with rigid rules and ingrained traditions is not likely to be conducive to change. In many of today's LDCs vestiges of past systems of authority remain, and peasants are bound by tradition to ancient ways of life—the only ways they understand. We have already seen that land is sometimes concentrated in the hands of a small number of wealthy estate owners and that the rural sector is often characterized by widespread underemployment and unemployment as well as by the inefficient use of land. Where the wealthy

TABLE 32–2 Population Growth Rates, Selected Countries, 1970–1979

Selected Countries	Annual Growth Rate of Population (Percent)
Less Developed Countries	
Bangladesh	2.6
Brazil	2.4
Guatemala	2.9
Iran	2.9
Kenya	3.8
Mexico	3.0
Nigeria	3.1
Saudi Arabia	4.5
Developed Countries	
Australia	1.4
Belgium	0.2
France	0.6
West Germany	0.1
Netherlands	0.8
Canada	1.2
Japan	1.2
United States	0.8
Soviet Union	0.9

Source: U.S. Department of Commerce, Bureau of the Census, *Statistical Abstract of the United States*, 1980 (Washington, D.C.: Government Printing Office, 1979), pp. 897–899.

are content with such a system and the poor know of no other, change is painstakingly slow. In numerous LDCs *land reform* has been undertaken to change the system of land ownership, raise agricultural productivity, and improve the lot of rural peasants. These measures have met with some success, but they have also resulted, in some areas, in the atomization of farmland into plots too small to be economically viable.

Where the wealthy control the land, they frequently control the government also. After all, participating in the process of government is a luxury, so who but the wealthy can afford to do so in an LDC? Many LDCs, therefore, are ruled by oligarchies, even though they ostensibly are constitutional democracies. Such oligarchies also constitute rigid institutional structures that can and frequently do inhibit both change and economic growth.

Because of the dire economic plight of the average inhabitants of LDCs and the likelihood that their governments are either despotic (Iran, Nicaragua, and Haiti, for example) or not very effective in improving living conditions (India, Colombia, and Jamaica, for example), political upheavals are not uncommon in these countries.[7] This fact has led some observers to argue that the political instability of less developed countries is a significant cause of their insufficient growth. However, the evidence for their point of view is inconclusive. One thing is certain, though. The LDCs have a long way to go before the material well-being of their citizenry will begin to approach that of the industrialized world. However, the more their people learn about the rest of the world, the more they will look toward their own governments and those of the developed countries for the means to make them prosper. In the next section, we will take a look at what economic theory has had to say about growth strategies for the LDCs.

---

7. For a discussion of the relationship of political stability to growth, see Clarence Zuvekas, Jr., *Economic Development: An Introduction* (New York: St. Martin's Press, 1979), pp. 59–62.

ECONOMIC THEORY AND DEVELOPMENT STRATEGY

◆

As long as there have been economists, they have studied and written about the burning issue of why some countries prosper more than others. In fact, the complete title of Adam Smith's□ pathbreaking eighteenth century study is not just *The Wealth of Nations* but *An Inquiry into the Nature and Causes of the Wealth of Nations*. Smith argued that nations prospered when people worked hard, labor was specialized, and a great deal of reliance was placed on the "invisible hand" (the market) to solve problems of distribution and resource allocation. However, as we saw in Chapter 29, economists and policy makers in many of the LDCs are not content with what the international market has done for them. Moreover, opting for the invisible hand would in many cases be viewed as responding to the urgent problem of development with a do-nothing policy. Finally, there have been a lot of economists since Smith, and they have offered other ideas about the determinants of development, as we will see next.

INSTITUTIONAL AND HISTORICAL THEORIES

In the nineteenth and early twentieth centureis, European economic historians examined the growth of their own economies, and some of them concluded that cultural or institutional variables were of paramount importance in the process of development. One of the nineteenth century historical economists was Karl Marx.[8] Marx believed that societies passed through various stages of economic and social organization as economic growth took place. To him, capitalism was an intermediate stage of development in which the owners of

---

8. Marx's major work is *Capital*, first published in German in 1867.

businesses exploited workers by paying them only a subsistence wage and appropriating the difference between the "real" value of their output and the meager wage they were paid. For Marx, the real value of any product was measured by the amount of labor embodied in it, but the worker who produced the product did not receive a wage sufficient to buy other goods of the same value.

Marx predicted that capitalism would collapse because of severe business cycles and the eventual uprising of a **reserve army of the unemployed.** It would be followed by socialism, and then Marx's ideal, the communist society, would be established and would flourish. Today, it seems obvious that Marx was wrong in his assessment of the effects of capitalism on workers and in his dire predictions about the viability of the capitalist system. Marx's economics has not survived the test of time. However, his communist ideology remains an important force in today's world, and some LDCs (such as Cuba) have adopted it as one route to economic development.

Early twentieth century historical economists had a more positive view of capitalism than did Marx, and they sought to explain its success. In particular, Max Weber, a German, and R. H. Tawney, an Englishman, popularized the view that the "Protestant ethic" explained why some countries grew more rapidly than others.[9] Protestants, they said, were urged by their "calling" to work hard and to become a success at whatever God willed them to do. Profit was not immoral because it gave them the wherewithal to do more good works.

The **Protestant ethic thesis** states that the rapid growth of the capitalist countries occurred because of protestant attitudes toward work and profit.

Although there probably is a grain of truth in this thesis, it is likely that the attitudes toward work and its rewards that spurred the Protestants' economic activities are and have been present in the cultural makeup of many other groups. The work ethic and business acumen of Jews, Chinese, Japanese, and the Parsi of India are legendary, and all of these groups could give the Protestants a reasonably good run for their money under the proper set of circumstances. But what are these circumstances?

Contemporary institutionalist economists, whose work reflects the thinking of earlier historical economists, argue that growth will be more rapid where resources can be readily obtained, where there is easy access to technology, and where the institutional structure is flexible enough to adapt to the changes necessary for employing modern productive processes. All three ingredients are necessary for rapid economic growth. Thus a country with a strong work ethic and a permissive attitude toward change is unlikely to grow rapidly if it is isolated from modern technology or has limited access to economic resources.[10] By and large, these views have been appropriated into the literature of development economics, while economists have searched for explanations of how to get a sustained growth process under way.

THEORY AND POLICY AFTER WORLD WAR II

Economists in the developed countries turned their attention toward the LDCs once the post–World War II reconstruction of Europe and Japan was well on its way to success. There were several reasons for this heightened interest in countries that had earlier played only a small role in the world economy. First, West-

9. Weber's *The Protestant Ethic and the Spirit of Capitalism* was first published in German in 1904–1905. Tawney's *Religion and the Rise of Capitalism* first appeared in 1926.

10. A recent treatment of institutionalist views on development is W. C. Gordon, *Institutional Economics: The Changing System* (Austin: University of Texas Press, 1980).

ern leaders were impressed by the rapid success of the European Recovery Program, a reconstruction plan financed primarily with U.S. aid. If aid worked for Europe, why not for the LDCs?

During the war, the importance of the LDCs as suppliers of raw materials and safe havens for U.S. and European investment was underscored. In addition, many of the LDCs got their first taste of modern prosperity during the war years, as their economies responded to the demands placed on them by the countries that were actually engaged in the fighting. Having experienced a period of rapid growth, they looked to their allies for a way to sustain the process.

Finally, the so-called Cold War between the Western powers and the Soviet Union became a way of life after the close of World War II. One feature of the Cold War was (and still is) efforts on the part of both sides to attract or coerce the LDCs into their spheres of influence. It became clear that countries searching for a key to rapid economic growth might be willing to embrace any ideological position that appeared to be expedient for this end. Thus, to some extent, the U.S. embraced "growthmanship" because its leaders perceived a communist threat in Latin America, Asia, and Africa.

Stages of Economic Growth During the 1950s and 1960s interest in historical theorizing on economic growth was revived, largely because of the popularization of an argument about **stages of economic growth** put together by **W. W. Rostow,** an economic historian who would later become an adviser to President Lyndon B. Johnson. Rostow developed a stage theory very different from that of Marx and called it "a non-communist manifesto."

According to Rostow, countries go through five stages of economic growth:

1. *Traditional society*—rigid institutions, low productivity, reliance on subsistence agriculture.

2. *Preconditions for takeoff*—improved insti-

tutional climate, higher productivity in agriculture, emergence of entrepreneurial class.

3. *Takeoff into sustained growth*—increase in rates of saving and investment, emergence of industrialization and modern attitudes toward growth.

4. *Drive to maturity*—consolidation of industrial growth, with lagging sectors catching up, growth becoming self-sustaining.

5. *High mass consumption*—fruits of economic development shared by all levels of society, high standard of living prevailing.[11]

Of course, what Rostow has described is something very much like the growth process of the United States and Western Europe. His work has been criticized because the conditions found in today's LDCs are markedly different from those that prevailed when the industrial revolution of the nineteenth century heralded the takeoff of Europe and the United States. In the LDCs, dualistic development has often led to the coexistence of a modern industrial sector with a backward agricultural sector. Thus part of the economy appears to be in Rostow's third stage while the rest of it is in the first or second. Sometimes takeoffs occur and then fizzle.

Rostow's takeoff stage is characterized by increased rates of both saving and investment. The emphasis on saving is a common thread in much of the writing on economic development after World War II, because Keynesian theory was, by that time, a standard part of the economics of growth.

Saving and Capital Formation The widespread acceptance by economists of the Keynesian explanation of the level of aggregate economic activity led them to investigate its application to the growth problems of the LDCs. Some of them reasoned that if the

---

11. Rostow first discussed the takeoff in *The Process of Economic Growth* (New York: W. W. Norton, 1952). His later book, *The Stages of Economic Growth: A Non-Communist Manifesto* (Cambridge, England: Cambridge University Press, 1960), drew heavily on *The Process.*

masses consumed virtually all of the gross national product of an LDC, investment would be next to impossible, because no resources would be used to make capital goods or to buy them from abroad. Thus, they argued, the problem was saving. People in the LDCs would have to be forced to save so that capital formation could take place.

Of course, saving in the Keynesian sense is a flow. Thus, in a growing economy it would be possible for output, consumption, saving, and investment all to grow at once. Somewhere in the postwar discussion this point got lost, and during the 1960s it was commonplace to hear economists and policy makers admonish the LDCs to tighten their belts in order to save and invest more.

One way that people can be forced to save is by an inflationary policy that reduces the real value of their incomes and transfers purchasing power to the government. A government can do this by simply creating more money and spending it on production or imports of capital goods. To some extent this notion explains the high rates of inflation experienced by certain LDCs in the postwar years.

Balanced Growth and the "Big Push" Some early postwar theories of development called for a massive effort to increase the stock of capital goods in all sectors of an LDCs economy. The reason for this approach was that many economists believed the large size of modern investment undertakings and the limited market for goods in an LDC made it unlikely that individual private investments in productive activities would, or even could, be undertaken. Their argument was made famous by economist **Paul N. Rosenstein-Rodan**. Using a shoe factory as an example, Rosenstein-Rodan argued that if 20,000 unemployed workers were put to work making shoes, there would be sufficient demand for their output only if they spent all their wages on shoes. However, if they did not choose to do so, they would bid up the prices of basic foodstuffs, while some of the shoes would go unsold. He then proposed that not just 20,000,

but rather a million workers be employed in not one, but a whole series of industries producing goods on which workers would want to spend their wages. He concluded, ". . .what was not true in the case of one shoe factory would become true in the case of a whole system of industries: it would create its own additional market. . . ."[12]

The logic of Rosenstein-Rodan and others led to the conclusion that growth of an LDC would have to be balanced, in the sense that many sectors of its economy (agriculture, industry, and public utilities, for example) would have to grow at once. This **balanced growth** would ensure, first of all, that there would be a market for the output of new productive activities, as in the shoe factory example. In addition, it would make available a wide array of inputs that would be required to sustain the growth of the new activities. In short, balanced growth would bring with it an array of external benefits□ without which development could not occur.

In general, the balanced growth advocates argued that a "big push" was needed to get the economy of an LDC started on the path to self-sustaining growth. It was up to the government of the LDCs, they argued, to increase both the saving rate and the investment rate in order to get the big push under way. The emphasis was on government's role in the mobilization of domestic resources for capital formation, even though, as we will see later, an LDC might be able to speed up the growth process by obtaining external resources through foreign investment or foreign aid.

Social Overhead Capital and Growth Strategy One common feature of the LDCs is a lack of public capital goods such as roads, dams, irrigation projects, schools, and port facilities. These types of goods are known as **social overhead capital (SOC)** or as an eco-

12. Paul N. Rosenstein-Rodan, "Industrialization of Eastern and Southeastern Europe," *Economic Journal*, June–September, 1943, p. 206.

nomic infrastructure. It has been argued that the growth of directly productive activities such as manufacturing is not likely to occur until government has provided the social overhead capital necessary to support investment in such activities. Historically, governments have used various strategies to promote the formation of such capital. In the United States and Canada, for example, private railroad companies were subsidized during the nineteenth century through the mechanism of land grants. In the Soviet Union and some other countries, virtually all SOC has been provided by government.

Social overhead capital is obviously important for the promotion of economic development, but how should scarce resources be divided between investment in it and investment in directly productive activities? Furthermore, should a government invest in directly productive activities such as the manufacture of consumer goods? Economists do not agree on these issues. Those who are strong free market advocates deplore any extension of government activity beyond the provision of basic social overhead capital; they argue that government is not likely to do as good a job of allocating resources in other areas of production as would the market.

A U.S. economist, Albert O. Hirschman, has argued that in some cases growth may be speeded up when investment in directly productive activities precedes investment in social overhead capital.[13] Hirschman's argument is viewed by many economists as a refutation of the balanced growth theories.

Recognizing that a certain threshold level of SOC formation must be reached before investment in certain directly productive activities is possible, Hirschman advocates going ahead with the latter type of investment even if the level of social overhead capital is just barely adequate. His reasoning is that this strategy will create a situation in which the provision of more and better SOC becomes imperative.

13. Albert O. Hirschman, *The Strategy of Economic Development* (New Haven, Conn.: Yale University Press, 1958).

For example, if there is an inadequate road to the site of an important new factory, there will be strong pressure from managers and workers to improve the road. However, building a road where there is not yet a factory (SOC preceding investment in directly productive activities) might not result in strong pressure to get a factory built.

Externalities, Economies of Scale, and Industrialization One reason government is generally viewed as the prime supplier of social overhead capital is that SOC is characterized by widespread externalities□ and economies of scale□ in production. SOC projects are by their very nature large undertakings. Many of them are not profitable enough from a private standpoint to attract capitalistic investment, whether domestic or foreign. Furthermore, if they are undertaken on too small a scale, their costs of operation can be prohibitive.

Once an SOC investment comes to fruition, however, its impact on those who do not pay directly for its output can be dramatic. For example, a hydroelectric plant can provide irrigation for farmers and jobs for factory workers even if they themselves are not the consumers of the power it generates. Such externalities make the social value of an SOC investment project much greater than its private value to purchasers of its output.

Of course, similar arguments about economies of scale and externalities can be made for investment in directly productive activities. For example, the growth of a metal transforming industry would provide externalities that could stimulate investment in a steel industry or a capital goods industry. Also, as an LDC's manufacturing industries grow, economies of scale should lead to reductions in the cost of production. Many LDCs have looked upon industrialization as the key to economic development because of the external benefits and economies of scale it provides.

Import Substitution and Export Promotion Widespread acceptance of the notions that manufacturing is characterized by economies of scale and that individual development is accompanied by substantial external benefits prompted many LDCs to engage in a policy of import substitution during the 1960s.

Import substitution *is a deliberate policy of replacing imports with domestically produced goods.*

<!-- margin note: 713 -->

Basically, this approach by the LDCs involved protectionism□ and promotion of investment in lines of production that would substitute domestic output for imports. A variant of the infant industry argument, import substitution seemed to be a reasonable growth strategy, because there was an obvious internal market for the products and because investments in the final goods stage of production required less capital than investment in basic industry. The strategy was also attractive to LDC policy makers because it seemed to provide some hope of improving a country's balance of payments□ by reducing its import bill.

By the late 1960s and early 1970s economists were in broad agreement that import substitution had about run its course in many of the LDCs. In the future they would have to look for other means to stimulate economic development. Those countries with substantial manufacturing capacity began to look toward increased exports as a source of income and employment. To facilitate this approach they negotiated with the industrialized countries for a system of **trade preferences** that would give their goods a competitive advantage in the international markets. These trade preferences are currently in effect, but they are the subject of much controversy since their benefits have been very unevenly distributed among the less developed countries.

FOREIGN AID AND INVESTMENT

Because LDCs face many difficulties in mobilizing their scarce domestic resources for investment in infrastructure and directly pro-

ductive activities, it would seem that foreign resources might provide a partial answer to the problem of getting the growth process started. Such resources can be obtained

TABLE 32-3 Foreign Aid: Net Disbursements of Official Development Assistance (ODA), 1970–1975

Donors	ODA (in Millions of 1975 Dollars)	Percent of Total Aid
Noncommunist Industrialized Countries		
United States	$28,632	29.7
France	12,416	12.9
Federal Republic of Germany	8,661	9.0
Japan	6,105	6.3
United Kingdom	5,276	5.5
Canada	4,188	4.3
Netherlands	2,900	3.0
Australia	2,616	2.7
Sweden	2,344	2.4
Belgium	1,899	2.0
Italy	1,499	1.6
Denmark	1,000	1.0
Norway	737	0.8
Switzerland	526	0.5
Austria	255	0.3
New Zealand	235	0.2
Finland	211	0.2
Subtotal	$80,243	83.2
OPEC		
Saudi Arabia	$ 3,018	3.1
Kuwait	1,728	1.8
Iran	873	0.9
United Arab Emirates	853	0.9
Iraq	749	0.8
Libyan Arab Republic	655	0.7
Qatar	252	0.3
Venezuela	91	0.1
Algeria	72	0.1
Nigeria	48	0.0
Subtotal	$ 8,365	8.7
Communist		
Soviet Union	$ 5,170	5.4
People's Republic of China	2,259	2.3
Eastern Europe	364	0.4
Subtotal	$ 7,819	8.1
Total	$96.427	100.0

Source: Joris J. C. Voorhoeve, "Trends in Official Development Aid," *Finance and Development* (June 1977): 12.

through borrowing, gifts, or foreign private investment.

Much of the borrowing done by the LDCs represents aid, because the interest rates they obtain from international agencies and foreign governments often are significantly lower than market rates. In addition, they receive some aid in the form of grants from international agencies and governments. The principal agencies that provide financial assistance to the LDCs are the World Bank Group, the United Nations, and various regional banks, such as the Inter-American Development Bank and the Asian Development Bank.

Much of the aid that flows to the LDCs is in the form of loans, grants, and technical assistance from governments of the industrialized noncommunist countries. About 64 percent of such aid is bilateral—arranged directly between the donor country and the LDC recipient. Table 32–3 shows that in absolute terms the United States is the largest source of aid. The noncommunist industrialized countries account for over 80 percent of all aid. And recently OPEC has given more aid (primarily to Islamic countries) than have all of the communist countries combined.

The total amount of aid to the LDCs is not large. In fact, in 1980 the aid given by all the Western industrialized countries amounted to less than $27 billion, and the United States accounted for about $7.1 billion of that total. The GNP of the United States in 1980 was $2,626 billion. Thus U.S. aid was only 0.27 percent of U.S. GNP. Table 32–4 shows the relationship of aid to GNP for a large group of donor countries in 1974–75 and in 1980. In 1970 a target level of 0.7 percent of GNP in development aid was established by a large majority of countries in the United Nations. As Table 32–4 shows, only a few countries have achieved this target.

The effect of aid on the economies of the LDCs is a controversial subject. Some economists have argued that aid does not supplement domestic capital formation but merely displaces it. Others have held that aid is a way of imposing the political will of the donor

TABLE 32–4 Aid Disbursements as a Percentage of GNP: 1980 and 1974–75 (Donors Ranked by Relationship of 1974–75 Foreign Aid to GNP)

Country	Aid as a Percent of GNP	
	1974–75	1980
Qatar	5.43	4.50
United Arab Emirates	4.29	3.96
Saudi Arabia	2.55	2.60
Kuwait	2.49	3.87
Iraq	2.24	2.19
Libyan Arab Republic	1.31	0.92
Iran	0.80	0.03
Sweden	0.78	0.76
Netherlands	0.70	0.99
Norway	0.62	0.82
France	0.60	0.62
Australia	0.58	0.47
Denmark	0.57	0.72
Belgium	0.55	0.48
Canada	0.54	0.42
New Zealand	0.42	0.27
Federal Republic of Germany	0.39	0.43
United Kingdom	0.38	0.34
Algeria	0.25	0.21
United States	0.25	0.27
Japan	0.24	0.32
Austria	0.18	0.22
Finland	0.18	0.22
Switzerland	0.17	0.24
China	0.15	n.a.
Venezuela	0.14	0.23
Italy	0.12	0.15
Nigeria	0.11	0.05
Soviet Union	0.08	n.a.
Eastern European nations	0.02	n.a.

n.a. - not available

Source: Joris J. C. Voorhoeve, "Trends in Official Development Aid," *Finance and Development* (June 1977): 14, and World Bank, *World Development Report 1981*, New York: Oxford University Press, 1981, pp. 164–65.

countries on the governments of the recipients—a form of economic imperialism.[14] The public often has a negative view of aid because

14. For example, see K. B. Griffin and J. L. Enos, "Foreign Assistance: Objectives and Consequences," *Economic Development and Cultural Change* (April 1970): 321; and Teresa Hayter, *Aid as Imperialism* (Middlesex, England: Penguin Books, 1971).

stories of mismanagement and corruption in the LDCs are commonplace in the world press. Still, most economists believe that aid can help the LDCs. Aid has stagnated recently because of the unwillingness of governments in the industrialized countries to increase their committments or, in some cases, to even maintain them at previous levels.

Foreign investment by private firms can result in a transfer of resources to an LDC. However, in development economics, foreign investment is even more controversial than foreign aid. The reason is that foreign investors are capitalists whose private interests in production and profits may not coincide with the social interests of the people or government of an LDC. One group of development economists, known as **dependency theorists,** have argued that foreign investment causes the LDCs to become economic satellites of the industrialized countries.[15] In their view the LDCs have been programmed by the foreign investment process to be suppliers of inputs and profits to the industrial system of the developed countries.

Even though the dependency theorists have voiced some valid complaints, most economists do not take quite so dim a view of foreign investment. Much of the technology at the disposal of the LDCs has been introduced through the foreign investment process. In addition, some of today's LDCs have become expert at negotiating the terms of private investment and insisting that foreign firms adhere to the dictates of national development planning. It is quite possible, then, that the foreign investment of the future will have a positive effect on the growth of the LDCs.

CURRENT STATE
OF DEVELOPMENT THEORY

Since the 1950s and 1960s there has been a decline in theorizing about economic devel-

15. For a discussion of dependency theory, see Richard L. Bath and Dilmus D. James, "Dependency Analysis of Latin America," *Latin American Research Review* (Vol. XI, No. 3, 1976): 3–54.

opment, and the pondering of economists during those two decades never did produce a general theory of the development process. What we are left with is a lot of partial theories that have supplied policy makers with insights about the appropriateness of various strategies in specific development circumstances. Armed with this not altogether satisfactory bag of tools, economists from both the developed and the developing countries continue to advise, debate, and help formulate policy. They have gained from the theorizing and policy experiments of the past, but most have concluded that economic development is an evolutionary process. It can be speeded up under the right set of circumstances, but only rarely does it take place over the span of a generation of human existance. In a recent text on economic development, Clarence Zuvekas, Jr., summarized the current attitude of economists as follows:

Why this declining interest in theorizing? One reason has already been given—the difficulty in finding, and incorporating into our theories and models, institutional or noneconomic phenomena common to more than 100 developing countries. In a different kind of world, economists might have devoted more attention to these knotty theoretical problems. But today's world differs radically from that of the 1940's and 1950's, and this leads us to the second reason for the decline of theorizing: the pressures by the developing countries—many of them newly independent and in control of their destinies for the first time—for immediate development results. What concerns them is not whether they are in Stage 2 or Stage 3 of the growth sequence described by economic historian W. W. Rostow (1971), but rather what specific actions they can take to better feed their growing populations and increase educational opportunities. These are policy questions, and policy must deal with the unique situation of each country; what works in one country will not necessarily work in another. A third reason for the shift away from theorizing is that many economists now have extensive overseas experience as employees of or consultants to international development agencies. As such, they, too, have become concerned with policy, and with the costs and benefits of specific development projects in individual countries. Finally, the increased

availability of statistical data has enticed economists into directing their talents toward empirical
studies of particular issues.[16]

A final cause of the decline in economic development theorizing is the preoccupation of
many economists in the developed countries
with new problems that have emerged in the
1970s and 1980s. Many economists and policy
makers are now devoting their efforts to the
energy crisis, the inflationary recession problem in the industrialized countries, and the
reorganization of the international financial
system. Thus economic development of the
LDCs is a lower priority issue in the industrialized world than it was ten or fifteen years
ago. Nonetheless, it remains a pressing worldwide problem that is nowhere near solution.

THE LDCS TODAY: STRATEGY FOR THE 1980s

◆

Given the emphasis on development strategy,
investment, and foreign aid in the period
since World War II, we should expect to find
that the per capita GNP differential between
the citizens of the LDCs and those of the industrialized countries has narrowed. Unfortunately, except for the oil-exporting LDCs,
such improvement is not what the data show.
This lack of progress was hinted at in an earlier section of the chapter, which showed that
population growth rates in the LDCs frequently make it difficult to achieve significant
increases in per capita GNP.

THE WIDENING INCOME GAP

Table 32–5 provides a comparison of U.S. real
per capita GNP in 1970 and 1980 with that of
selected LDCs. For every country listed (even

---

16. Zuvekas, *Economic Development*, p. 13.

Brazil, which grew very rapidly) the per capita GNP differential with the United States
widened by a substantial number of dollars
over the seven-year period. The table could include many more countries. Even some oil-exporting countries, such as Iraq, were unable
to make any progress toward closing the per
capita GNP gap with the industrialized countries between 1970 and 1980.

These data do not mean that the LDCs have
failed to make any progress. On the contrary,
in many of them people are becoming significantly better off, but they are doing so from a
small base of income. Thus a high rate of
growth in per capita income does not result in
a large absolute amount of income change. If
we take Brazil as an example, a 6.5 percent
increase in its 1980 per capita GNP of $2,033
would amount to $2,033 × 0.065 = $132.15.
Between 1980 and 1981 the United States
would need less than a 1.2 percent increase in
per capita GNP to outdo Brazil in per capita
terms ($11,792 × .012 = $141.50).

Can the LDCs ever catch up? The answer is,
theoretically, yes, but it will take a long time.
How long? Let us assume that from 1980 onward the U.S. real capita income continued to
grow at 2.2 percent per year while that of Brazil grew at 6.5 percent. Here is how the future
would look:

	Per Capita GNP	
Year	United States	Brazil
1990	$14,659	$ 3,816
2000	18,222	7,164
2010	22,652	13,447
2020	28,159	25,242
2030	35,005	47,382

In other words, it would take Brazil about
43 years to catch up with the United States in
terms of per capita GNP. This is not an impossibility, but it would take some doing. Furthermore, some scholars argue that there may
not be enough resources around in forty years
to allow everyone to live the way people have
recently lived in the United States. Nonetheless, we can conclude that when one takes a
long-run view of the growth process, the LDCs
probably can improve their living standards

TABLE 32-5   Per Capita GNP Differentials and Growth Rate, United States and Selected LDCs

| Country | GNP Per Capita[a] | | | | Rate of Growth in Per Capita GNP, 1970-1980 (Percent per Year) |
| | 1970 | | 1980 | | |
	Amount	Differential from United States	Amount	Differential from United States	
United States	$9,440	—	$11,792	—	2.2
Brazil	1,088	$8,352	2,033	$ 9,759	6.5
Burma	158	9,282	177	11,615	1.1
India	180	9,260	221	11,571	2.1
Iraq	1,258	8,182	2,521	9,271	7.2
Mexico	1,304	8,136	1,957	9,835	4.1
Nigeria	473	8,967	758	11,034	4.8
Philippines	434	9,006	671	11,121	4.5
Uganda	389	9,051	315	11,477	-2.1

[a]In dollars of 1980 purchasing power.

Source: U.S. Department of Commerce, Bureau of the Census, *Statistical Abstract of the United States, 1979* (Washington, D.C.: Government Printing Office, 1979), p. 895; U.S. President, *Economic Report of the President, 1981*, p. 237; and Table 32-1, above.

significantly over the next generation or so. It will be a monumental task, however, and they will most likely need a lot of help.

INTERNATIONAL DEVELOPMENT POLICY FOR THE FUTURE

In 1974 the U.N. General Assembly passed a resolution known as the Declaration on the Establishment of a New International Economic Order (NIEO).[17] This document stated that the development of the international economy had been characterized by trade and investment patterns that benefited the industrialized countries but were not designed to promote the economic and political well-being of the less developed countries. The NIEO called on the developed countries to work with the LDCs on a restructuring of the international economic system to reduce inequalities in income between countries for the mutual benefit of all.

The NIEO concept was the result of several

17. The "Declaration on the Establishment of a New International Economic Order" is found in U.N. General Assembly Resolutions 3201 (S–VI) and 3202 (S–VI), May 1, 1974.

long-term and more recent developments in international economic relations. First, the developing countries were becoming more and more successful in presenting a united front in their negotiations with the industrialized countries. The LDCs had formed a Southern Alliance within the United Nations (most of them are in the southern hemisphere) and had sparked discussions with the developed countries that came to be called the **North-South debate.** The main vehicle for this debate was the United Nations Conference on Trade and Development (UNCTAD). UNCTAD began as a conference in 1964 but evolved into a permanent organization. Its conferences, held at four-year intervals, have been characterized by increasingly vocal demands from the LDCs for not only more equitable but even preferential treatment by the industrialized countries in matters involving trade and development.

Second, the success of OPEC showed clearly that there was a realignment of economic and political power in the world of the 1970s. (This success, however, divided the LDCs into two groups—those that had oil and those that did not.)

These events tended to splinter the united front of the LDCs, but they also posed a threat to the economic well-being of the industrialized countries. Thus, to some extent, both groups hoped that the NIEO would provide a way out of some new international dilemmas. However, the NIEO declaration was clearly an LDC position paper that did not enjoy the full support of the industrialized countries. Some of the measures it called for are:

1. Special aid for the least developed LDCs.
2. Regulation of the activities of transnational corporations.
3. Equitable management of international prices of raw materials, intermediate goods, and manufactures.
4. Increased reliance on multilateral, rather than bilateral, aid.
5. Improvements in the transfer of financial resources to the LDCs.
6. Preferential and nonreciprocal treatment of LDCs in trade relations.
7. Improvements in the transfer of technology to the LDCs.
8. Facilitation of the functioning of producer organizations of LDCs.
9. Use of commodity agreements to stabilize trade in new materials.
10. Restrictions on investments in production of synthetic goods that would replace primary goods.

During the 1980s we can expect to see some of the NIEO demands put into effect. In fact, the United States, Europe, and Japan have already instituted programs of trade preferences for the exports of LDCs. These programs, known as the **generalized system of preferences (GSP),** are nonreciprocal. This means that tariff reductions are granted to the exports of LDCs but that the LDCs do not have to relax any of their trade barriers in return for such concessions. So far, the higher-income LDCs have benefited significantly from the GSP, but the poorest countries have not gained much.

At present, the NIEO declaration is viewed as a historical document suggestive of change but lacking in authority. In the next section of the chapter we will consider what steps the LDCs can take on their own to promote national economic growth.

INTERNAL POLICIES FOR GROWTH

International efforts to help the LDCs will have little lasting impact if the governments of the LDCs themselves do not take steps to solve their own countries' internal economic problems. Many of the LDCs certainly need to improve their internal distribution of income. Industrialization requires that there be a strong and growing domestic market for consumer goods. If income is concentrated in the hands of the upper classes, the effective demand for mass consumption goods will be limited. It is likely that income redistribution will require an overhaul of the tax system in most LDCs, so that government revenues will be adequate and the burden of indirect taxes on lower-income consumers will be reduced.

In many LDCs increases in per capita income will be slight unless a reduction occurs in the rate of population growth. Family size generally falls as economic development takes place, but it will probably be necessary to actively promote birth control and family planning in most of the LDCs that currently have excessive population growth rates. Of course, people are an important resource, especially if they possess productive skills. In order to increase the productivity of their people, the LDCs will have to improve their educational systems in a way that emphasizes technical and vocational training for effective labor force participation.

Hand in hand with skills training, the LDCs will need to implement technology policies that identify and encourage the use of appropriate technologies for their respective resource bases and levels of development. To avoid continuing reliance on external sources of foodstuffs, technological advancement in agriculture is a must for many LDCs that have abundant arable land. Programs in agriculture may also require land reforms that will encourage more intensive use of cropland.

Finally, many of the LDCs are at a point in their development where they should review the structure of their protective tariffs and nontariff trade restrictions. During the import substitution phase of development, protection may have permitted the growth of industries that otherwise could not have flourished. However, continued high levels of protection may encourage monopolization of internal markets and discourage efficiency in production and resource allocation. In addition, the developed countries are not likely to extend trade preferences for long if markets in the LDCs remain protected and inaccessible. Successful bargaining between the two groups of countries may not be possible if the LDCs do not relax some of their own trade barriers.

SUMMARY

1. This chapter discussed the diverse characteristics of the less developed countries (LDCs). The measure usually employed to compare levels of national economic development is per capita GNP. The per capita GNP of a country is obtained by dividing the country's GNP by its population.

2. The 1980 per capita GNP of the LDCs ranges from $98 for Bangladesh to $22,334 for the United Arab Emirates. However, in all the LDCs large numbers of people live at or near the subsistence level. In addition, most of the LDCs have problems associated with income distribution, high rates of population growth, and institutional rigidities.

3. In the nineteenth and early twentieth centuries, some European economic historians concluded, after examining their countries' economies, that cultural or institutional variables were of paramount importance in the process of development. Karl Marx, Max Weber, and R. H. Tawney were three prominent economists who held these views. Marx believed that capitalism was an intermediate stage of development in which the owners of businesses exploited workers. He thought that severe business cycles and the eventual uprising of a reserve army of the unemployed would cause its downfall. Weber and Tawney emphasized the importance of the Protestant ethic.

4. After World War II, leaders of the Western world, impressed by the success of the European Recovery Program, turned their attention to the less developed countries. Correspondingly, the attention of economists was also channeled in this direction.

5. W. W. Rostow developed a theory of economic growth that stated that countries go through five stages of economic growth: (1) traditional society, (2) preconditions for takeoff, (3) takeoff into sustained growth, (4) drive to maturity, and (5) high mass consumption. However, some economists believe that this theory better describes the growth process of the United States and Western Europe than the growth process of the less developed countries.

6. The widespread acceptance of the Keynesian theory of national income determination led economists to investigate the relationship between saving and investment in less developed countries. They stated that people in the LDCs would have to be forced to save so that capital formation could occur. However, in a growing economy it is possible for output, consumption, saving, and investment to all grow at once.

7. Proponents of balanced growth and big push theories argued that the growth of an LDC would have to be balanced, in the sense that many sectors of its economy would have to grow at once. Such balanced growth would ensure a market for the output of new productive activities as well as make available a wide array of inputs. These economists argued that a big push was needed to get the economy of an LDC started on the path to self-sustaining growth, and they emphasized the government's role in the mobilization of domestic resources.

8. Other economists emphasized the importance of social overhead capital (SOC) or infrastructure such as roads, dams, irrigation projects, schools, and port facilities. They argued that the growth of directly productive activities such as manufacturing is not likely to occur until government has provided the necessary social overhead capital. However, one economist, Albert Hirschman, argued that sometimes growth may be speeded up when investment in directly productive activities precedes investment in social overhead capital.

9. Widespread acceptance of the idea that manufacturing is characterized by economies of scale and that industrial development is accompanied by substantial external benefits prompted many LDCs to engage in a policy of import substitution during the 1960s. However, by the late 1960s and early 1970s economists were in broad agreement that many of the LDCs would have to look for other means to stimulate economic development.

10. Foreign resources represent another possible

solution to the problems of the LDCs. The principal internationl agencies that provide financial assistance to these countries are the World Bank Group, the United Nations, and various regional banks, such as the Inter-American Development Bank and the Asian Development Bank. The effect of foreign aid and of private foreign investment on the economies of the LDCs is a controversial subject. Furthermore, as a result of stories of mismanagement and corruption, the public often has a negative view of foreign aid. Still, most economists believe that foreign aid and investment can be helpful to the LDCs.

11. In the 1970s and 1980s there has been a decline in theorizing about economic development. Many economists have concluded that economic development is an evolutionary process that can be speeded up under the right circumstances but that in most cases will not occur quickly. Moreoever, economists have been preoccupied with other problems, such as the energy crisis, the inflationary recession, and the reorganization of the international financial system.

12. From 1970 to 1980 the per capita GNP differential between the United States and most of the less developed countries widened. In 1974 the U.N. General Assembly passed a resolution known as the Declaration on the Establishment of a New International Order (NIEO), which stated that the development of the international economy was characterized by trade and investment patterns that benefited the industrialized countries but not the LDCs. The NIEO called for the developed countries and the LDCs to work together to restructure the international economic system.

13. Internally, almost all the less developed countries need to improve their distribution of income and to overhaul their tax systems. They also need to reduce their rate of population growth, develop and implement appropriate technologies, and review the structure of their trade restrictions.

IMPORTANT TERMS AND CONCEPTS

Third World
Per capita GNP
Economic dualism
Institutional structure
Reserve army of the
  unemployed
Social overhead
  capital (SOC)
Import substitution
Trade preferences
Dependency theorists
North-South Debate
Protestant ethic thesis
Stages of economic
  growth
Balanced growth
Generalized system of
  preferences (GSP)

QUESTIONS AND PROBLEMS

1. What is per capita income? How is it helpful in describing levels of economic development? What problems accompany its use as a measure of development?

2. What is economic dualism? Relate the concept of dualism to some of the development theories discussed in this chapter.

3. How do population growth rates in the LDCs compare with those in the developed countries? How long will it take population size to double in the countries where it is growing at comparatively high rates? Contrast this with the countries that have low population growth rates.

4. What institutional problems are common in the LDCs? How do such problems affect economic growth and political stability?

5. Contrast Marx's views on the capitalistic stage of economic development with Rostow's stages of economic growth. Analyze the applicability of these historical views to today's LDCs.

6. Discuss the notions of balanced growth and the big push. Contrast them with Hirschman's argument about the relationship between investments in social overhead capital and investments in directly productive activities.

7. Is the amount of foreign aid received by the LDCs large in relation to the output of the donor countries? Which countries are the principal donors? Why is aid a controversial subject?

8. Why is foreign investment a controversial subject in development economics? Can foreign investment speed up development? Explain.

9. What progress have the LDCs made in closing the per capita income gap during the past few years? Do you think the gap will widen or narrow in the next decade or so? Explain.

10. What is the NIEO? What kinds of changes does it call for?

11. What can the LDCs do to help themselves through internal policies? Be specific about the measures they can take and their desired effects.

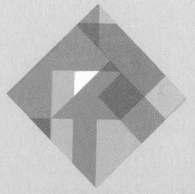

LDC TRADE
BARRIERS
AND ECONOMIC
DEVELOPMENT

. . . The management of a transition from extreme forms of import substitution to a policy of export promotion (defined in this context as providing equal incentives for production for home and foreign markets) is not an easy matter. As already stated, a major obstacle is political: domestic beneficiaries of protective measures resist government efforts to alter their privileges. If a modified principle of reciprocity could be introduced into the multilateral trade negotiations, it could be invoked by newly emerging export interests

Source: Adapted from Isaiah Frank, "Reciprocity and Trade Policy of Developing Countries," *Finance and Development* Vol. 15 (March 1978): 22–23.

in the developing countries and could serve as a focus for counterpressures in support of the government's efforts to moderate the system of protection. Such a modified principle would apply to the higher-income developing countries and would recognize that significant rather than equivalent benefits would be provided.

In addition to facilitating trade liberation by those developing countries which deem it in their own interest to do so, there are two other reasons why the relaxation of the nonreciprocity principle should be seriously considered at least for the more advanced of the developing countries.

The first has to do with trade among developing countries,

which is not of considerable importance. About 22 percent of their total exports, and as much as 30 percent of their exports of manufactures, currently go to other developing countries. But the scope of this trade would be much larger if access to each other's markets were less restricted. Attempts to achieve this through customs unions or other forms of regional economic integration have not been notably successful. One of the main impediments has been disputes over the distribution of costs and benefits among member countries at different stages of development. Reliance on such unstable special arrangements would be less important, however, if developing countries were to moderate their protective systems and move toward convertible currencies and more realistic exchange rates. To the extent that such measures are encouraged by the obligation to grant reciprocal concessions in trade negotiations, an important contribution would be made to facilitating the expansion of trade among developing countries.

A final reason for reintroducing the reciprocity principle stems from the need to differentiate among developing countries. The notion of developing countries' "graduation" from eligibility for special treatment is recognized in the World Bank's criteria for credits from the International Development Association and in the ceilings applied in most schemes for generalized preferences. But no such principle applies to the nonreciprocity rule, although the issue is being discussed in the current multilateral trade negotiations. Brazil's per capita income is more than ten times that of Mali. Should both be treated alike in being relieved of obligations to reciprocate the trade concessions by industrial countries? Italy's per capita income, on the other hand, is only

about three times that of Brazil, yet the former is subject to the full obligations of the GATT while the latter is in practice relatively free of them. This anachronistic situation is becoming untenable in many industrialized countries as an increasing number of middle-income and higher-income developing countries emerge as major exporters of manufactured products. It is understandable, therefore that the industrialized countries are pressing for some degree of reciprocity from developing countries in the multilateral trade negotiations now under way in Geneva.

How persuasive the industrial countries will be in this respect is open to question, however. The developing countries have little interest in most-favored-nation tariff reductions by the industrial countries, since these would narrow the margins of preference under the GSP. Perhaps the main hope for introducing a modified principle of reciprocity would be in conjunction with negotiations on nontariff barriers and particularly on safeguards against market disruption. These two closely related issues are at this juncture

far more critical for the developing countries than the question of tariff reductions.

The developing countries have a major stake in an open world trading system governed by internationally agreed rules of conduct. Without such a system, national governments would be much more prone to yield to the forces of protection, especially from the "low-wage competition" of poorer countries. It is questionable, however, whether an open world trading system can long remain viable without all major beneficiaries of the system sharing the serious responsibility of maintaining it.

QUESTIONS

1. How have earlier policies of import substitution made it difficult now for LDCs to grant reciprocal reductions in trade barriers?
2. What benefits might the LDCs gain by reducing their own tariffs and quantitative barriers against imports?
3. Of what significance is the diversity in levels of development among LDCs to the question of reduction of trade barriers?

PART TEN

CONTINUING
ECONOMIC
PROBLEMS

CHAPTER 33

AGRICULTURE: PROBLEMS AND POLICIES

HOW ARE THEY GOING TO MAKE IT DOWN ON THE FARM?

Farm families' nonfarm income has become an important factor in the land market, enabling many farmers to bid for the dwindling supply of available farmland. These nonfarm earnings have shown steady growth for many years, providing a supplement to net farm income and increasing farmers' ability to invest in real estate and service real estate debt. The situation is especially common for families with farm sales under $10,000; their average off-farm income generally at least equals and often far exceeds their average debt.

By the mid 1960s nonfarm earnings for a farm family equaled the family's net farm income. But today's farm families generally earn more from their sources of off-farm income than from their farming operations. Of each $100 of income received by farm families in 1977, for instance, $61 came from nonfarm sources. On the average, the families' total income from farm and nonfarm sources amounted to little more than $19,000. Of this sum, around $7,400 was net farm income, and the remaining $11,600 was off-farm income.

While nearly all farm families have some off-farm income, such earnings are most important on small farms. The lower the value of a farm's sales, the larger is the share of nonfarm income in total farm family income. Farm families whose farm sales in 1977 totaled $100,000 and over, for example, earned $.20 of every $1 of their total income from nonfarm sources. Those with farm sales of $10,000 to $19,999 had off-farm earnings amounting to $.66 of each $1 of total income. Families with farm sales below $5,000 depended on off-farm income for $.91 of every $1 of total earnings.

The off-farm income supplements to net farm income have contributed to the ability of some farmers, particularly those on small farms or those who farm part time, to compete for and purchase additional farmland. For much of the history of this country, many individuals uninterested in farming have invested in farmland. Such investments have proved to be effective hedges against inflation for more than forty years. Many people also use farmland as a safe long-term investment. Farmland prices, in fact, have outstripped consumer prices throughout the last twenty years. During that period, there has generally been a 2 percent average annual rate of increase in farmland values for every 1 percent average annual rate of gain in the consumer price index.[1]

It appears that some small farmers are as much real estate speculators as they are crop growers. However, the fact remains that the United States is an agricultural giant among nations. The fortunes of its farmers who are primarily in the business of growing and selling crops vary greatly with such factors as market conditions, weather, inflation, and the general economic climate. In this chapter we will examine the farm problem in the United States, concentrating on why and how government intervention has come to be important to the farm sector.

1. Adapted from Sada L. CLarke, "Farm Land . . . an Increasingly Valuable Asset," *Economic Review* (Federal Reserve Bank of Richmond) (March–April 1979): 6–8.

C H A P T E R 33

AGRICULTURE: PROBLEMS AND POLICIES

WHAT THIS CHAPTER IS ABOUT

SHORT-RUN INSTABILITY OF FARM PRICES
LONG-RUN TRENDS IN AGRICULTURE
FIVE APPROACHES TO THE FARM PROBLEM
HISTORY OF FARM PROGRAMS
WHY THE "FARM PROGRAM"
"MIDDLEMEN" PROFITS
THE RISING PRICE OF LAND

In spring 1981 both the consumer who paid $1.49 per pound for ground beef and the farmer (or rancher) who raised the cattle agreed on one thing—that there was a problem in the agriculture industry. From 1967 to 1980 food prices rose at an average annual compound rate of about 7.8 percent.[1] This rate of growth means that retail food prices more than doubled during the thirteen-year period.[2] Still, many farmers claim that they are barely earning a living, and others say they are going broke.

What farmers consider to be the "farm problem" really has two parts. First, the short-run prices for farm products are volatile. They change dramatically in response to relatively small percentage changes in the quantity supplied. This variability, coupled with the possibility of crop failures due to the weather and to insects and disease, means that farm incomes also vary widely from year to year. Second, farmers believe that their long-run prospects for achieving a reasonable return from their investment of funds and labor are not good.

In this chapter we will first examine some of the factors behind the difficulties of the agriculture sector. These factors include the short-run instability of prices and the long-run growth in the supply of and demand for agricultural products in the United States. Second, we will consider various theoretical approaches to helping the farmer. Third, we will look into the agricultural aid programs that the government has actually implemented. Fourth, we will deal with the question of why the government is involved in the agriculture industry. Finally, we will consider two other areas of controversy involving agriculture in the 1970s and early 1980s: middlemen's profits and the purchase of agricultural land by citizens of other countries.

---

1. Based on data from Table B–50: "Consumer Price Indexes, Major Expenditure Classes, 1929–80," *Economic Report of the President, 1981* (Washington, D.C.: Government Printing Office, January 1981), p. 289.

2. This rate of growth is slightly higher than that of prices for all consumer items, which grew at a rate of approximately 7.5 percent for the same period. See Table B–50. "Consumer Price Indexes, Major Expenditure Classes, 1929–80," *Economic Report of the President, 1981* (Washington, D.C.: Government Printing Office, January 1981), p. 289.

SHORT-RUN PRICE INSTABILITY

◆

The producers of agricultural goods face the serious problem of short-run instability of prices; these prices may double or be cut in half within a year.[3] As we will see, the price inelasticity of both the supply of and demand for these products contributes significantly to the problem.

PRICE INELASTICITY OF SUPPLY AND DEMAND

We have already learned about supply, □ demand, □ and the equilibrium price □ for a product. We also know that if demand is inelastic □ with respect to price, a change in price will cause a relatively small change in quantity demanded. The same result also applies to quantity supplied if supply is inelastic □ with respect to price.

Moreover, if demand is price inelastic, a shift in the supply curve will have a relatively large effect on the equilibrium price. Similarly, if supply is price inelastic, a shift in the demand curve will have a relatively large effect on price.

For example, Figure 33–1 illustrates the price changes resulting from a shift in the demand curve when supply is relatively elastic (Panel [a]) and relatively inelastic (Panel [b]). It is obvious that the price change is greater in the second case. Figure 33–2 shows the same results for a change in supply when demand is relatively elastic (Panel [a]) and relatively inelastic (Panel [b]).

Short-run Supply Turning specifically to the case of agriculture, we find that both the supply of and the demand for farm products are highly inelastic with respect to price. Once a

---

3. See "The Uneven Squeeze on the U.S. Farmer," *Business Week*, December 19, 1977, p. 70.

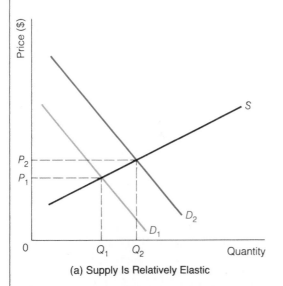

(a) Supply Is Relatively Elastic

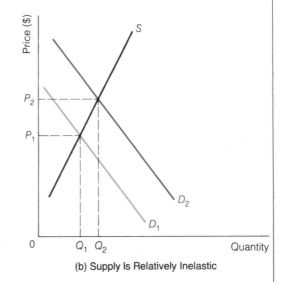

(b) Supply Is Relatively Inelastic

FIGURE 33–1   Effects of a Change in Demand on Price

In both panel (a) and panel (b), the supply curve is S, the initial demand curve is D_1, and the initial price is P_1. After an increase in demand to D_2, the price rises to P_2. However, note that the price rise is greater in panel (b), where supply is relatively inelastic.

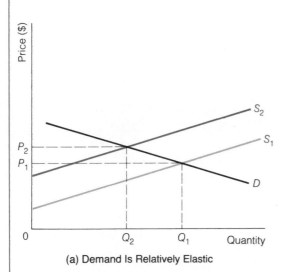

(a) Demand Is Relatively Elastic

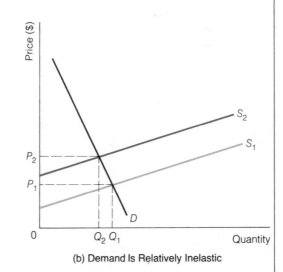

(b) Demand Is Relatively Inelastic

FIGURE 33–2   Effects of a Change in Supply on Price

In both panel (a) and panel (b) the demand curve is D, the initial supply curve is S_1, and the initial equilibrium price is P_1. After a decrease in supply to S_2, price rises to P_2. Note that the price increase is greatest in panel (b), where demand is relatively inelastic.

crop has matured in the fields, the farmer has only three choices (or a combination of them): (1) harvest the crop and sell it at whatever is the going price; (2) harvest it and place it in storage, or (3) plow it under without harvesting it. If the farmer (or rancher) raises hogs, cattle, or chickens and the animals are ready for the slaughterhouse, often there is only one economic alternative—selling the livestock at the going market price. If they are held longer, more cost is incurred and the quality of the meat may deteriorate. If they are destroyed, no revenue is obtained. Because shipping costs are rarely as high as the animals' market value, this approach is not economical.

Furthermore, farmers often plan this year's crop plantings on the basis of last year's prices. In the case of beef cattle, it takes approximately three years from the birth of a heifer (female calf) until her first offspring is ready for slaughter.[4] Thus the supply of farm products is highly inelastic with respect to current prices in the short run. □

Short-run Demand Simultaneously, the demand for agricultural products is highly inelastic with respect to price. We desire to eat only so much food; we also do not like going hungry, even if food is expensive. If the price of one food rises substantially relative to the prices of other, similar foods, consumers may buy less of it and more of the others. But even in this case the changes in buying habits are not dramatic.

For example, in January 1979 the price of lettuce more than doubled, from 39 cents a head to 89 cents or 99 cents. Did our family reduce the amount of lettuce we purchased? A little bit. We were more careful about wasting it and sometimes substituted canned or frozen vegetables for salads. However, the quantity of lettuce purchased by our family probably did not decline by over 30 percent in spite of a more than 100 percent increase in price.

4. Marvin Duncan and C. Edward Harshbarger, "A Primer on Agricultural Policy," *Monthly Review* (Federal Reserve Bank of Kansas City) September–October 1977, p. 6.

Table 33–1 presents estimates of the price elasticity of demand for selected farm products. All the estimates indicate that the demand for selected farm products is inelastic (although the demand for buckwheat is nearly unitary elastic). Because demand is inelastic, an increase in price will increase the total revenue □ of the farmer.

SHIFTS IN SHORT-RUN DEMAND AND SUPPLY CURVES OF FARM PRODUCTS

As we have seen, because of the price inelasticity of both the supply of and the demand for agricultural products, a small shift in either the supply or the demand curve will result in a proportionally large change in the equilibrium price of a commodity. Such shifts often occur. Bad weather or disease may cause the short-run supply curve of a crop to shift. Changes in foreign demand for agricultural exports may cause the demand curve to shift. Thus farm prices are subject to a great deal of short-run instability, as indicated by the changes in the index of farm prices in Table 33–2. The table shows that farm prices jumped dramatically in the 1970s. Price variations are even greater for individual farm products.

TABLE 33–1 Estimates of Price Elasticity of Demand for Selected Agricultural Commodities

Product	Price Elasticity
Barley	0.39
Buckwheat	0.99
Corn	0.49
Cotton	0.12
Hay	0.43
Oats	0.56
Potatoes	0.31
Sugar	0.31
Wheat	0.19

Source: Henry Schultz, *The Theory and Measurement of Demand* (Chicago: University of Chicago Press, 1938), pp. 548–549.

TABLE 33–2 Index of Prices Farmers Received for Their Products; 1929–1980 (1967 = 100)

Year	Price Index
1929	59
1933	28
1939	38
1940	40
1941	49
1942	64
1943	77
1944	79
1945	83
1946	94
1947	110
1948	115
1949	100
1950	103
1951	121
1952	115
1953	102
1954	98
1955	93
1956	92
1957	94
1958	100
1959	96
1960	95
1961	96
1962	98
1963	97
1964	95
1965	98
1966	106
1967	100
1968	102
1969	107
1970	110
1971	113
1972	125
1973	179
1974	192
1975	185
1976	186
1977	183
1978	210
1979	241
1980	245

Source: *Economic Report of the President, 1979* (Washington, D.C.: Government Printing Office, January 1979), p. 290; and *Economic Report of the President, 1981*, (January, 1981), p. 340.

To add to their woes, farmers face not only unstable prices in the short run but also a multitude of other difficulties in the long run. In the next section we will examine this second set of problems.

LONG-RUN TRENDS IN AGRICULTURE

The agriculture industry faces several long-run problems: the lack of mobility of resources, productivity gains that have increased the supply of farm products (causing a rightward shift in the supply curve), and the low income elasticity of demand for their commodities. We will first examine the problem of low mobility of resources.

LONG-RUN PRICE ELASTICITY OF SUPPLY

Over a longer period of time than one growing season, farmers have some flexibility. They can plant different crops, raise different types of livestock, or at least adjust the quantities of each product they supply. However, even over the long run, because of a high proportion of fixed costs, many farmers have few options.

Most of the machinery and land used in the production of farm goods are specialized; they have limited usefulness outside of agriculture. Even farmers themselves, especially older ones, often do not have the skills or education that would help them find jobs in the city. Thus a decision to leave farming can be extremely painful, both economically and emotionally, for a farmer. Table 33–3 presents some estimates of the short-run and long-run price elasticities of supply for various vegetables. As we would expect, the elasticities are greater in the long run than in the short run. Still, for many of the products, even the long-run price elasticity of supply is low. The low

TABLE 33–3 Estimates of the Short-run and Long-run Elasticity of Supply of Vegetables

Product	Price Elasticity	
	Short Run	Long Run
Green lima beans	0.10	1.70
Green snap beans	0.15	∞[a]
Cabbage	0.36	1.20
Carrots	0.14	1.00
Cucumbers	0.29	2.20
Lettuce	0.03	0.16
Onions	0.34	1.00
Green peas	0.31	4.40
Green peppers	0.07	0.26
Tomatoes	0.16	0.90
Watermelons	0.28	0.48
Beets	0.13	1.00
Cantaloupes	0.02	0.04
Cauliflower	0.14	1.10
Celery	0.14	0.95
Eggplant	0.16	0.34
Kale (Virginia only)	0.20	0.23
Spinach	0.20	4.70
Shallots (Louisiana only)	0.12	0.31

[a]Over a limited range of output.

Source: Marc Nerlove and William Addison, "Statistical Estimation of Long-run Elasticities of Supply and Demand," *Journal of Farm Economics* 40 (November 1958): 872.

price elasticites of supply, especially in the short run, mean that the percentage change in quantity supplied occurring as the result of a price change will be relatively low compared with the percentage change in price.

INCREASES IN PRODUCTIVITY

Another long-term problem for farmers is increases in the supply of farm products as a result of increases in productivity in the agriculture industry. From Table 33–4 we can see that farm output per unit of total input has more than doubled in the last fifty years. The increase in farm output per hour of work is even more dramatic; it has increased to over ten times its value in 1929. These developments have caused downward pressure on the prices of agricultural commodities.

TABLE 33–4 Index of Farm Productivity 1929–1980 (1967 = 100)

Year	Farm Output	
	Per Unit of Total Input	Per Hour of Farm Work
1929	52	16
1933	53	16
1939	59	19
1940	60	20
1941	62	21
1942	68	24
1943	66	24
1944	67	24
1945	68	26
1946	71	27
1947	68	28
1948	74	31
1949	71	32
1950	71	34
1951	71	35
1952	74	38
1953	75	39
1954	76	42
1955	78	44
1956	80	47
1957	80	51
1958	87	57
1959	87	59
1960	90	65
1961	91	67
1962	92	71
1963	96	77
1964	95	81
1965	100	89
1966	97	92
1967	100	100
1968	102	106
1969	103	110
1970	102	115
1971	110	128
1972	110	136
1973	111	130
1974	105	136
1975	115	152
1976	115	162
1977	114	173
1978	116	183
1979	119	184
1980	115	189

Source: *Economic Report of the President, 1979* (Washington, D.C.: Government Printing Office, January 1979), p. 289; and *Economic Report of the President, 1981* (January, 1981), p. 338.

TABLE 33–5 Estimates of the Income Elasticity of Demand for Selected Commodities

Product	Income Elasticity
Butter	0.42
Cheese	0.34
Cream	0.56
Eggs	0.37
Fruits and berries	0.70
Flour	−0.36
Margarine	−0.20
Meat	0.35
Milk and cream	0.07
Restaurant consumption	1.48
Tobacco	1.02

Source: H. Wold, *Demand Analysis* (New York: Wiley, 1953), p. 265.

INCOME ELASTICITY OF DEMAND FOR FARM PRODUCTS

A third long-run problem for farmers has stemmed from the low income elasticity of demand□ for farm products (see Table 33–5). As per capita income□ has grown, the demand for farm commodities has not grown at a corresponding rate. In most of the developed countries the demand for agricultural products grows at a rate roughly corresponding to the rate of growth of the population.[5] In the United States in the 1970s this growth in demand was only slightly above zero.[6]

Thus long-range forces as well as short-run instability hurt farm profits. In the next section we will consider several solutions to the problems of the agriculture industry.

---

5. Ibid., p. 5.

6. According to one estimate, the U.S. population increased by 7.5 percent from 1969 to 1977. However, the National Center for Health Statistics reported that at current rates a woman of childbearing age could be expected to have approximately 1.8 children. See "Regional Differences in Per Capita Income Are on the Decline," *Wall Street Journal*, September 22, 1978, p. 31; and "U.S. Birth Rate Declined to Low in 1976, Data Show," *Wall Street Journal*, January 3, 1977, p. 8.

FIVE APPROACHES TO THE FARM PROBLEM

The problems of the agriculture industry can be tackled in a variety of ways, among them:

1. Ignoring the problem and letting market forces equate quantity demanded and quantity supplied.
2. Giving low-income farmers an income subsidy.
3. Implementing a crop restriction program.
4. Creating a price support–loan–crop storage program.
5. Instituting a price subsidy program.

MARKET FORCES

One way to resolve the problem of too low farm prices is to let the market forces work. If farmers cannot make a normal return (or keep from going bankrupt), they will gradually leave the agriculture business. In fact, the total number of people living on farms has declined from 32.4 million in 1933 to 6.1 million in 1980, and the number of people working on farms has declined from 12.8 million in 1929 to 3.8 million in 1980.[7] To the extent that the exodus from farming results in less agricultural production at all prices, the supply curve of farm products will shift leftward and the equilibrium market price will be increased.

However, this effect will be modified if large enterprises purchase the farms and produce crops more cheaply than small farmers can. The effect of farmers leaving the industry is also counteracted by technological change, which has greatly increased farm productivity.

Many policy makers and other people con-

---

7. See "Table B–94: Farm Input Use, Selected Inputs, 1929–1980," *Economic Report of the President, 1981* (Washington, D.C.: Government Printing Office, January 1981), p. 339.

sider the free market approach by itself, insofar as it is effective, to be too harsh. We have seen the problem of the specialized nature of resources used in the production of farm products. Because of such specialization, the decision to leave farming is a difficult one for a farmer to make. Therefore, although market forces to some extent take their toll, the government has instituted policies to soften the effects of such forces.

SUBSIDY FOR LOW-INCOME FARMERS

Another approach to the farm problem is to give **income subsidies** to low-income farmers until they leave their farms. The advantage of such a program is that it offers no incentive to "overproduce". (Price support and price subsidy programs do lead to overproduction.) Moreover, to encourage farmers to leave agriculture, a limit can be placed on the number of years for which they can receive the subsidies, and programs can be instituted to retrain them for other jobs. Most farmers have not been in favor of this type of payment, preferring to "earn" their subsidies. Also, many farmers wish to remain in farming.

CROP RESTRICTION PROGRAMS

Crop restriction programs are a third method of raising farm prices.

Crop restriction programs are programs designed to limit the production of certain agricultural crops.

Through "set-aside", or "soil bank", programs the government can limit the number of acres farmers are allowed to plant in various crops. In this way it can restrict the quantity supplied of farm products and, consequently, cause the establishment of higher equilibrium market prices.

In Figure 33–3 the free market demand

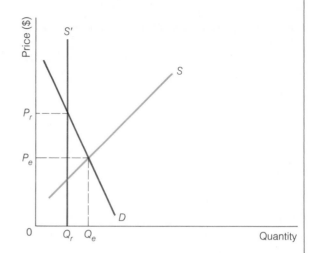

FIGURE 33–3 Effect of a Crop Restriction Program

The initial market supply and demand curves are S and D, respectively. The initial quantity produced is Q_e, and the initial price is P_e. After an effective crop restriction program is instituted, the supply curve becomes S', the quantity supplied is Q_r, and the price is P_r.

curve is D, and the free market supply curve is S. The corresponding free market equilibrium price and quantity are P_e and Q_e. The new supply curve after the government limits farm production is S'. The new equilibrium price is P_r. Because the demand for farm products is inelastic with respect to price, as long as the crop restriction program is effective, farmers can receive greater total revenue by selling smaller quantities at higher prices.

However, the government has had some difficulty in making its crop restriction programs effective. Farmers, of course, try to keep their best acres in crop production, leaving marginal acres idle. Also, they farm the producing acres more intensively than they would have, using more fertilizer and better weed control. To give farmers an incentive to work within these acreage set-aside programs the government has made participation in them mandatory for farmers who wish to participate in other farm programs. It also sometimes gives direct subsidies for leaving farmland idle. These programs will be discussed more thoroughly later in the chapter.

Price Support–Loan–Crop Storage Program

*Under a **price support–loan–crop storage** program the government agrees to support farm prices at a particular level. It does so by giving farmers loans equal to the value of their crops, figured at the support price levels.*

If the market price rises above the support price, the farmer can sell the crop and pay off the loan plus interest. (It is usually mandatory that the farmer pay off the loan if the market price rises to a level that is a specified percent above the support price.) If the market price does not rise above the support price by the end of a certain period of time, either the farmer can keep the crops and pay off the loan and interest or the government will accept the crops as full payment for the debt.

The effects of this type of program are shown in Figure 33–4. The free market equilibrium price and quantity□ are P_e and Q_e. Farmers will supply Q_{s0} of a crop with prices supported at level P_0. However, at price P_0 only Q_{d0} will be demanded in the market. The cost to the government, ignoring interest and storage costs, is given by the support price times the surplus quantity supplied: $P_0 \times (Q_{s0} - Q_{d0})$. In order to reduce the cost of price support programs the government usually makes participation in a crop restriction program a requirement for eligibility in them.

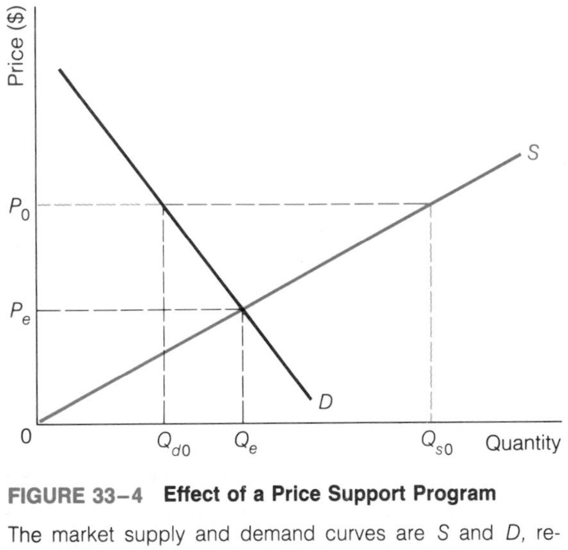

PRICE SUBSIDIES

Price subsidy programs work as illustrated in Figure 33–5.

*Under a **price subsidy program** the government agrees to pay farmers a subsidy equal to the difference between a set support price, P_0, and the market price, P_M, that they receive when their crop is sold.*

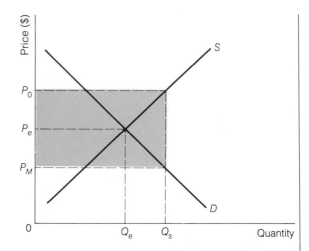

FIGURE 33–5   Effect of a Price Subsidy Program

The market supply and demand curves are S and D, respectively. The initial price is P_e, and the initial quantity sold is Q_e. After a price subsidy program is instituted, the government guarantees farmers a price of P_0 for their crop. Under this type of program, the government tells farmers to sell their crop at the going market price. If the market price is less than the support price, the government will pay them a subsidy equal to the differential. In this case, the farmers produce a quantity equal to Q_s and sell it at a market price of P_M. The government pays the farmers a subsidy equal to $(P_0 - P_M) \times Q_s$.

FIGURE 33–4   Effect of a Price Support Program

The market supply and demand curves are S and D, respectively. The initial price is P_e and quantity sold is Q_e. After the government establishes a support price of P_0, the quantity supplied is Q_{s0}, while the quantity demanded is Q_{d0}. Thus, there will be an excess quantity supplied equal to $(Q_{s0} - Q_{d0})$.

In this case farmers are to sell their whole crop for whatever it will bring in the market. Because they know they will receive P_0 per unit, the quantity they bring to market is Q_s. However, with the given demand curve, D, only P_M per unit will be paid for this quantity in the market. Thus the market price will be P_M. The cost to the government (shaded area) is $(P_O - P_M) \times Q_s$, where Q_s is the quantity sold in the market.

A version of this type of plan, the Benson-Brannan plan, was proposed in the 1950s, during President Eisenhower's administration. However, it was not approved by Congress, in part probably because, ignoring storage and interest costs, it would have been more costly for the government than a price support–loan–crop storage program. (The price subsidy program is more expensive as long as the demand for farm products is inelastic with respect to price.) The target price□ program introduced in 1973 embodies some features of this type of policy.

In the next section we will examine the approaches to the plight of the farmers that the government has actually implemented.

HISTORY
OF
FARM
PROGRAMS
◆

We will divide our history of government intervention in the agriculture industry into four periods: the nineteenth century, 1920 to 1939, 1940 to 1969, and the 1970s and early 1980s.

NINETEENTH CENTURY

Before the twentieth century the federal government programs involving the agriculture industry emphasized increasing production.

The Homestead Act, passed in 1862, enabled farmers to obtain 160 acres of unoccupied public land by living on it for five years and paying a nominal fee. The Morrill Act, passed the same year, provided for an endowment of public lands in each state for colleges to teach subjects related to agriculture and the mechanical arts. Also during this year the Bureau of Agriculture became the Department of Agriculture. Later, laws such as the Hatch Act (1887) and the Smith-Lever Act (1914) provided for county agents and funding for the teaching of agricultural subjects in high school.

1920 TO 1939

After World War I the prices of agricultural products dropped dramatically (see Table 33–2), and the government began formal programs to increase farm incomes. In the first part of this period the Emergency Tariff Act (1921) and the Fordney-McCumber Act (1922) were responsible for increasing and maintaining high tariffs on a wide variety of farm products. The Agricultural Credits Act (1923) enabled farmers to obtain credit for periods ranging from six months to three years.

In 1929 the **Agricultural Marketing Act** was passed. The philosophy behind this act was that through the formation of marketing cooperatives, one for each crop, the problem of surpluses and shortages of agricultural products could be solved and farm prices could be stabilized. The act established the Federal Farm Board to administer the program, and Congress appropriated $500 million to be loaned to cooperatives when crops had to be held off the market. However, the Panic of 1929 soon erupted, farm prices again dropped drastically, and it became apparent that much more than the $500 million would be required to support farm prices at the stated loan levels.

In 1933 the landmark **Agricultural Adjustment Act** was passed. The goal of this act was to enable farmers to achieve parity.

762

Parity refers to a situation where farm prices are high enough that crops have the same purchasing power in terms of other commodities as they did in 1910–1914.[8] The period 1910–1914 is often called the **golden age** of agriculture.

The goal was to be achieved by restricting production of farm products. Farmers who agreed to cut back production were to receive government subsidies funded by a tax on the processors of agricultural products. The Commodity Credit Corporation (CCC) was established by executive order to administer the price supports.

In 1936 most of the Agricultural Adjustment Act was declared unconstitutional. Congress reacted that year by passing the Soil Conservation and Domestic Allotment Act, which provided subsidies to farmers who planted certain crops that would build up the soil and that were not in surplus.

In 1938 Congress passed a second Agricultural Adjustment Act. This act maintained and extended the soil conservation measures of the 1936 act. It gave the Secretary of Agriculture

---

8. The simple *parity ratio* is found by dividing the index of prices received by farmers by the index of prices paid by farmers for commodities, services, interest, taxes, and farm wages. In both cases, 1910–1914 is the base, with the index for both the numerator and the denominator equal to 100 during that period. An adjusted parity ratio is also computed; it includes government payments to farmers. To compute the parity price for an individual commodity, the government now uses the concept of an *adjusted base price*. This price is calculated for a particular product by dividing the average of the prices received by farmers for that commodity for the most recent 120-month period by the average of the index of prices received by farmers for all commodities for the same period. As before, the years 1910–1914 are the base years, and all government support payments are included in the averages. The *parity price* for a product is then equal to its adjusted base price multiplied by the percentage change in the index of farm prices paid by farmers since 1910–1914. For more information on how these prices are calculated see the U.S. Department of Agriculture's *Agricultural Prices*, July 1949, pp. 23–29; January 1950, pp. 49–53; and January 1978, pp. 25–26.

the power to offer subsidies to farmers who restricted crop production. If surpluses still existed, the secretary could establish marketing quotas to regulate the total amount of particular farm products that could be sold during the year and could impose a penalty tax on farmers who exceeded the quota. During periods of surpluses, the Secretary made loans to farmers to help them postpone selling their products. These loans were usually based on crops valued at above the free market price but below 100 percent of parity.

1940 TO 1969

During the 1940s, 1950s, and 1960s laws were passed to provide for price supports for farm products at various levels, but usually less than 100 percent of the parity price. Measures to limit crop production were also passed.

In 1956 Congress established the **soil bank program,** which paid farmers for planting their land to grasses and legumes, such as alfalfa, and then leaving it idle. Other measures were intended to reduce the surplus of agricultural products while aiding the needy. These measures included the food stamp program, the school lunch program, and the **Agricultural Trade Development and Assistance Act (1954)** (Public Law 480). This last law provided for the sale or outright granting of farm products to foreign countries. Payment could be made with a country's own currency.

THE 1970s AND EARLY 1980s

Between 1933 and 1973 the general goal of the federal government's farm program was to support farm prices and restrict production. By 1973, however, greatly increased foreign demand, such as that for wheat by the Soviet Union and for soybeans by Japan, had reduced U.S. grain stocks. The **Agriculture and Consumer Protection Act (1973)** introduced the concept of target prices.

Target prices *are prices the government considers to be fair prices for wheat, feed grains, cotton, and rice.*

If the average price during the first months of the market year for one of these commodities is below the target price, farmers receive a deficiency payment from the government equal to the difference between the target price and the higher of the Commodity Credit Corporation loan rate or the average market price. The quantity of output on which this payment is made is now based on the smaller of a farm's allotment acres or planted acres and the normal output per acre.

From 1973 to 1977 market prices were relatively high and target prices were generally below them. Loan rates were set even lower than target prices.

The 1973 act expired in 1977 and was replaced by the **Food and Agriculture Act (1977).** The new law raised the target prices on corn and wheat and extended the basic support provisions for all commodities until 1981. In addition, the law raised the limit on government payments that a producer could receive for feed grains, wheat, and cotton on a gradual basis from $20,000 per year in 1977 to $50,000 per year in 1980. Disaster payments (payments for crops damaged by natural disasters) no longer counted as part of the total.

The 1977 act replaced the old historical acreage allotments with a normal crop acreage base.

*A farm's **normal crop acreage base** for a given year depends on which designated crops were grown on the farm in the previous year (Designated crops include most crops except hay and pasture.)*

To be eligible for the deficiency payments and the loan program, the planted acreage of all designated crops plus the acreage required to be set aside could not exceed the farm's normal crop acreage base.

The 1977 act also established a national grain reserve program for feed grains and wheat. The purpose of the reserve is to help stabilize prices and to make stocks available in case of emergencies. For the most part these reserves are held by farmers through three- to five-year extended crop loans.[9]

In 1981 farmers were upset by the embargo on grain shipments to the Soviet Union during the winter of 1979–80 and by droughts that damaged the 1980–81 crops. In December 1981, Congress passed an $11–billion, four-year farm bill, extending the life of commodity price support and farmer subsidy programs. It also created a new government loan program for sugar processors. As requested by President Reagan, the bill restrains annual increases in dairy, wheat, and corn price supports and reduces the likelihood that grain farmers will receive income subsidies when prices fall. The previously scheduled level of food stamp spending for fiscal 1982 was also cut by $700 million.

In the next section we will examine several reasons given to justify government aid to agriculture.

WHY THE "FARM PROGRAM"?

◆

Preliminary government estimates indicated that implementing the 1977 Food and Agricul-

9. For additional information on government policies concerning farmers, see Lance E. Davis, Jonathan R. T. Hughes, and Duncan M. McDougall, *American Economic History* (Homewood, Ill.: Richard D. Irwin, 1969); Marvin Duncan and C. Edward Harshbarger, "A Primer on Agricultural Policy," *Monthly Review* (Federal Reserve Bank of Kansas City), (September–October 1977): 3–10; Marvin Duncan and C. Edward Harshbarger, "Solving the Farm Income Dilemma: The New Farm Program and the Outlook for 1978," *Monthly Review* (Federal Reserve Bank of Kansas City), (December 1977): 3–12; Marvin Duncan and C. Edward Harshbarger, "The Agricultural Outlook: Stable Farm Income in 1979?" *Economic Review* (Federal Reserve Bank of Kansas City), (December 1978): 3–12; and Gilbert C. Fite and Jim E. Reese, *An Economic History of the United States* (Boston: Houghton Mifflin, 1973).

ture Act would cost about $11 billion over the four years from 1977 to 1981.[10] Why was Congress willing to spend so much money to aid one industry? Among the reasons usually given are:

1. The farmer has little market power, whereas the firms to which farm products are sold and from which machinery, fertilizer, pesticides, and other necessary inputs are purchased have greater market power.

2. The economic welfare of the nation depends on the well-being of the agriculture sector.

3. Prices received for farm products are highly variable and unpredictable because of their dependence on weather conditions.

We will now examine each of these points in detail.

MARKET POWER OF FARMERS

In the past the farming industry consisted primarily of many small farmers, each with virtually no market power. The banks, farm implement dealers, feed companies, and other

_____

10. Duncan and Harshbarger, "Solving the Farm Income Dilemma," p. 9.

firms from which farmers bought inputs had a great deal more market power. Moreover, the industries to which farmers sold their products, such as the grain elevators and the meat packers, were *concentrated*. (There were fewer individual firms in each industry, which gave a single firm more control over the market.)

In recent years this picture has changed to some degree. As indicated earlier, the number of farmers has fallen since the 1920s. Table 33–6 shows how concentration□ in the farming industry has increased since 1960. Although, thanks to inflation, a farm with $100,000 worth of sales in 1960 would have $200,000 worth of sales if it had the same physical volume of sales in 1977, *the percentage of farms in the highest sales category has increased by more than enough to account for the price differential.*

Farm Co-ops Another factor that is changing the market power of farmers is the rapid growth of farm co-ops. One example of such co-ops is Sunkist Growers, Inc., a California organization of 7,300 small citrus producers. According to the *Wall Street Journal*, Sunkist supplies about 50 percent of the fresh oranges and 80 percent of the fresh lemons in the U.S.

500

TABLE 33–6   **Concentration in Farming, 1960–1980**

Farm Classification (Sales)	Percent of Total U.S. Farm Receipts				Percent of Total Number of U.S. Farms			
	1960	1969	1977	1980	1960	1969	1977	1980
$200,000 and over		21.0	35.6			0.5	2.0	
$100,000–$199,999	59.6[a]	10.0	17.0	65.0[a]	0.6[a]	1.2	4.0	11.6[a]
$40,000–$99,999	20.3	21.9	25.6	35.0[b]	2.3	5.7	12.9	88.4[b]
$20,000–$39,999	10.1	20.5	11.1		5.7	11.0	11.9	
$10,000–$19,999	·4.9	13.2	5.4		12.5	13.3	11.5	
$5,000–$9,999	2.4	6.9	2.7		16.7	13.8	11.2	
$2,500–$4,999	1.3	3.6	1.4		15.6	14.5	11.2	
Less than $2,500	1.4	2.9	1.2		46.6	40.0	35.3	

[a]Farms with sales of $100,000 and over (no higher category available).

[b]Farms with sales of less than $100,000. No further breakdown available. Sources: U.S. Department of Agriculture, Economic Research Service, "Farm Income Trends," *Agricultural Outlook*, AO 25 (Washington, D.C.: Government Printing Office, September 1977), p. 20; U.S. Department of Agriculture, Economic Research Service, "Farm Income Trends," *Agricultural Outlook*, AO 37 (Washington, D.C.: Government Printing Office, October 1978), p. 6; and "Farm Income Update," *Agricultural Outlook*, AO 68 (Washington, D.C.: Government Printing Office, August, 1981), p. 12.

market. The California citrus fruit market operates in the following way:

An agricultural marketing order is passed by the majority of growers in a given region. Some of these will be independent, others will be part of a cooperative. Once passed, it has the force of law and is enforced by the Agriculture Department. A committee of growers is appointed and meets at the beginning of each growing season to sketch out the weekly shipping schedule of the amount of produce to go to the fresh market. From then on, the committee meets every week to adjust the sales quotas. All of the growers get a pro-rata share of the fresh-market business, which is the most profitable. Any grower exceeding the sales quota risks a heavy fine from the Agriculture Department.

. . . Thus the produce not sent to the fresh market must be shipped to processing plants where hundreds of citrus products are prepared. Sunkist's plants, for example, turn out 1,600 products, including juices, concentrates, citrus oils, flavorings and cattle feed.

Being the dominant cooperative in the region, Sunkist can get marketing orders passed and thus can exert a degree of control over the supply of each crop.[11]

Sunkist does not have absolute control over the supply, however, because it is not allowed to have a majority of the votes on the fresh fruit market quota committees.[12]

Table 33–7 summarizes the 1975 revenues and income before taxes of the ten largest farm co-ops. Annual revenues of all farm co-ops more than doubled, from $25 billion to $57 billion, in the first half of the 1970s, giving them more than one-third of the total market (of $165 billion) for the sales of farm products and the machinery and other inputs that farmers buy.[13]

Moreover, power is becoming more concentrated even among the co-ops themselves. In 1975 the sales of the ten largest farm co-ops

---

11. Hal Lancaster, "Giant Sunkist Co-op Beset by Government, Business, and Growers," *Wall Street Journal*, July 24, 1978, pp. 1, 23.

12. Ibid.

13. See "The Billion-Dollar Farm Co-ops Nobody Knows," *Business Week*, February 7, 1977, p. 54.

TABLE 33–7 Revenues and Income of the Ten Largest U.S. Farm Co-ops in 1975

Rank	Co-ops	Millions of Dollars	
		Sales	Income before Taxes
1	Farmland Industries	1,529	196.9
2	Associated Milk Producers	1,478	4.9
3	Agway	1,329	40.7
4	Grain Terminal Association	1,261	32.9
5	Land O'Lakes	1,124	36.4
6	Far-Mar-Co	1,007	5.5
7	Gold Kist	828	25.6
8	Illinois Grain	806	10.5
9	Indiana Farm Bureau Cooperative	697	24.6
10	Farmers Grain Dealers Association of Iowa	652	0.3

Source: "The Billion-Dollar Farm Co-ops Nobody Knows," *Business Week*, February 7, 1977, pp. 54–55.

---

made up 20 percent of the total sales for all co-ops, approximately double the 1960 percentage. In addition, on the marketing side, co-ops have increased their portion of the wholesale dairy market from 65 percent to 80 percent in the last ten years. Furthermore, 37 percent of the cotton crop is sold by co-ops. Farm co-ops are also increasing their food processing activities.[14]

A different aspect of the co-ops' business is buying certain farm inputs in large quantities and then selling them to farmers. Another significant development is the movement of co-ops into the manufacturing of farm supplies.[15]

The rapid growth of the farm co-ops has spawned resentment among other agribusiness firms, because the co-ops get tax breaks and must meet less stringent antitrust standards. Even some co-op members are unhappy, citing administrative costs and lack of results. The federal government is also investigating

---

14. Ibid.

15. Ibid.

Sunkist for possible antitrust violations.[16] Still, farm co-ops represent a sector of the agriculture industry that will likely gain increasing market power in the years to come.

Farmers' Strikes In late 1977 a new farm organization, the American Agriculture Movement, organized a farm strike. Some farmers participated in tractor parades and protest demonstrations in Washington, D.C., and other parts of the country. The government target price for wheat was raised, but there was no significant reduction of farm output as a direct result of the strike.[17]

In early 1979 farmers once more rumbled into Washington with their tractors.[18] The effects of this protest were also not substantial. Even now, getting farmers organized for an effective demonstration remains a difficult task, because the effect of an individual farmer's participation is perceived to be negligible.

AGRICULTURE AND
THE NATIONAL INCOME

It has been estimated that agriculture related industries are responsible for approximately one-sixth of GNP, one-fifth of the nation's employment, and one-fourth of export earnings.[19] The U.S. Department of Agriculture estimated that the cash receipts of farmers in 1980 for farm marketings were $136 billion.[20] If we use the 1980 farm price–retail price

spread for a market basket of food of 37.2 percent, we find that the final market value of farm production in 1980 is approximately $366 billion. The difference between $366 billion and $136 billion ($230 billion) is the cost of "middlemen's" services: processing, packaging, transportation, and distribution.

In 1977 consumers' expenditures for food amounted to approximately $186 billion, of which $57 billion represents the farm value of these products. Nearly half the food marketing costs ($59.8 billion in 1977) were labor costs involving an estimated 6 million workers.[21] Furthermore, the Department of Agriculture has estimated that the $22 billion of farm exports in 1974 were responsible for an additional $21 billion of business activity in related industries, which resulted in 1.2 million jobs.[22] The value of farm exports was over $40 billion in 1980, and it was estimated to be well over $46 billion in 1981.[23]

On the farm input side of the picture the Department of Agriculture reported that farm expenditures for capital goods totaled $7 billion in 1971, creating an additional $8.1 billion of business activity and 640,000 additional jobs.[24] A large amount of additional farm

16. Lancaster, "Giant Sunkist Co-op Beset by Government, Business, and Growers," pp. 1, 23.

17. See "The Tractor Rebellion," *Newsweek*, December 19, 1977, p. 57.

18. See "Farmers Are Heading for Washington Again Following '78 Success," *Wall Street Journal*, January 30, 1979, pp. 1, 31.

19. *A New U.S. Farm Policy for Changing World Food Needs* (New York: Committee for Economic Development, October 1974), p. 29.

20. U.S. Department of Agriculture, Economic Research Service, "Farm Income Update," *Agricultural Outlook*, AO 68 (Washington, D.C.: Government Printing Office, August 1981), p. 9.

21. See Andrew Weiser, Leland Southard, and Terry Crawford, "Marketing Costs for U.S. Farm Foods," *Agricultural Outlook*, U.S. Department of Agriculture, Economic Research Service, AO 38 (Washington, D.C.: Government Printing Office, November 1978), pp. 11–15; and Duncan and Harshbarger, "A Primer on Agricultural Policy," p. 4.

22. U.S. Department of Agriculture, Economic Research Service, "Impacts of Agricultural Trade on Food and Fiber Sectors of the U.S. Economy," *Agricultural Outlook*, AO 4 (Washington, D.C.: Government Printing Office, September 1976), p. 16.

23. See U.S. Department of Agriculture, Economic Research Service, "World Agriculture and Trade," *Agricultural Outlook*, AO 66 (Washington, D.C.: Government Printing Office, August 1981), p. 10.

24. Gerald Schluter and Thomas A. Niles, "Farmers' Capital Expenditures and Their Effects on the U.S. Economy," *Agricultural Outlook*, U.S. Department of Agriculture, Economic Research Service, AO 7 (Washington, D.C.: Government Printing Office, February 1976), p. 17.

spending goes for fertilizer, seed, fuel, labor, and interest.

Thus farming cannot be viewed as an isolated sector of the economy. Farm policies affect not only farmers themselves but also all the related agribusinesses and consumers.

PRICE INSTABILITY AND "ACTS OF GOD"

We have already seen that the price inelasticity of the demand for and supply of agricultural products causes shifts in the demand and supply curves that result in relatively large price changes. Furthermore, shifts in domestic supply curves and foreign demand curves frequently occur as the result of a factor over which farmers have little control—the weather.

Although irrigation is available to farmers in some dry areas and smudge pots can be used by citrus growers to ward off frost, in many cases farmers are still at the mercy of rain, hail, snow, wind, and fluctuating temperatures. Consequently, farmers have difficulty accurately predicting their level of output, the prices they will receive, and their revenues for any given year.

What can we conclude? First, it is obvious that agribusiness affects a large part of the economy. Second, a substantial expenditure of money is connected with federal government farm programs. Third, although certain aspects of farming present unique problems, the distinctions between farming and other industries appear to be blurring. Farmers are gaining market power through co-ops, and the technology available for coping with the weather is improving. Finally, because government programs affect the use of scarce economic resources in both the public sector and the private sector, it is important that citizens carefully consider their impact on the welfare of the nation.

AGRICULTURAL MARKETS AND "MIDDLEMEN" PROFITS

As noted in the previous section, the farm sector supports employment in many agriculture related industries, such as food processing and distribution. However, these "middlemen" industries have come under increasing attack by both farmers and consumers for earning excessive profits.

As shown in Table 33–8, the farmer's share of the retail value of farm products has fallen

TABLE 33–8 Farm Price–Retail Price Spreads for Selected Food Products

Item	(Farm Value ÷ Retail Value) × 100 Percent									
	1970	1971	1972	1973	1974	1975	1976	1977	1978	1980
Market basket[a]	38	37	39	45	42	41	38	38	39	37
Cereal and bakery products	16	16	17	22	25	19	15	13	14	15
Meat products	55	55	58	63	56	60	54	55	58	51
Fruits and vegetables	25	25	25	28	27	27	26	25	32	28
Dairy products	48	47	48	50	49	49	51	50	51	52
Fats and oils	30	32	27	37	47	34	32	36	34	29
Poultry and eggs	54	52	52	64	61	62	61	60	—[b]	—[b]

[a]Average quantities of farm originated foods purchased annually per household in 1960–61 by wage earner and clerical worker families and workers living alone.

[b]Not available.

Source: U.S. Department of Agriculture, *Agricultural Statistics 1978* (Washington, D.C.: Government Printing Office, 1978), pp. 446–447; U.S. Department of Agriculture, Economic Research Service, "Food and Marketing," *Agricultural Outlook*, AO 36 (Washington, D.C.: Government Printing Office, September 1978), p. 5; and U.S. Department of Agriculture, Economic Research Service, *Agricultural Outlook*, AO 68 (Washington, D.C.: Government Printing Office, August 1981), p. 31.

since 1973. In 1970 the farm value of a market basket of farm products was 38 percent of its retail cost. In 1973 the corresponding figure was 45 percent. By 1980 it had dropped to 37 percent. However, the reduction between 1973 and 1980 was not uniform over all farm products; it was greatest for cereal and bakery products, meat products, and fats and oils. In fact, the farm value relative to retail cost for dairy products and fruits and vegetables was greater in 1980 than it was in 1970.

Although the farm price–retail price spread has dropped during recent years, this fact does not necessarily mean that profits of food processing and distributing firms are excessive. Labor costs, which represent nearly half the food marketing costs, rose 10.7 percent in 1977 and were rising at the annual rate of 11.6 percent in 1981, with additional increases in the intervening years. Packaging costs, the second largest component of the marketing bill, were expected to rise 7 percent in 1981 after increasing by 6 percent in both 1976 and 1977 and additional amounts from 1978 to 1980. Energy costs increased 9 percent during 1976 and 20 percent during 1977 and continued to rise in later years. Other food processing and distributing costs have also been soaring.[25]

Of course, similar costs have been increasing for the farmers. However, at least partly because of a lack of market power, farmers have not always been able to raise prices in proportion to their increases in costs. In 1970 the ratio of the index of prices received by farmers to the index of prices paid for production items was 110/108, or about 1.02. In 1980 the ratio was 245/275, or about 0.89, a decrease of nearly 13 percent.[26]

According to a Federal Trade Commission study covering the period from the third quarter of 1972 until the first quarter of 1975, the increases in food prices were caused not by higher profits for meat packers, milk processors, bread bakers, or brewers but by increased costs. The FTC did caution, however, that there were some data deficiencies in its sample.[27]

Thus, at this point we cannot conclude that soaring food prices are attributable to the increased profits of middlemen. In the next section we will examine one rapidly increasing farm cost—the price of land.

THE RISING PRICE OF LAND

Another controversy related to agriculture is that of skyrocketing U.S. land prices related to the purchase of land by residents of other countries. From 1972 to 1980 the prices of farmland rose at an average annual rate of approximately 15 percent.[28]

Because of the rising price of land, explicit production costs vary widely from farm to farm. The turnover rate for farmland is low; therefore, many farmers do not have to pay high explicit costs□ associated with their land.[29] (However, as Chapter 18 noted, the firm manager should base economic decisions on implicit, or opportunity, costs□ as well as on explicit costs.) For example, the average

25. See Weiser, Southard, and Crawford, "Marketing Costs for U.S. Farm Foods," p. 17; and "Food and Marketing," Agricultural Outlook, AO 68 (August 1981), p. 20.

26. See "Table B–95: Indexes of Prices Received and Prices Paid by Farmers and Selected Farm Resource Prices, 1940–1980" Economic Report of the President, 1981 (Washington, D.C.: Government Printing Office, January 1981), p. 340.

27. "FTC Unit Study Finds Food-Price Jumps Were Caused by Higher Costs, Not Profits," Wall Street Journal, August 22, 1975, p. 2.

28. U.S. Department of Agriculture, Economics, Statistics, and Cooperatives Service, "The Land, the Price, and the Marketplace," Farm Index, vol. 17 (Washington D.C.: Government Printing Office, December 1978), p. 7; and U.S. Department of Agriculture, Agricultural Statistics, 1980 (Washington, D.C.: Government Printing Office, 1980), p. 422.

29. "A Bumper Crop of Controversy over Farm Aid," Business Week, April 18, 1977, p. 111.

explicit cost of producing wheat has been estimated at $3 per bushel. Farmers who bought their land and machinery more than five years ago have costs estimated as low as $2 per bushel. For those not so fortunate, the estimated cost per bushel ranges as high as $4.75.[30]

To some extent U.S. land purchases by foreigners have been blamed for the rising land prices. In fact, concern has become so widespread that Congress has passed a law requiring disclosure of foreign farm holdings. Moreover, twenty-nine states now limit farm ownership by citizens of other countries to some extent.[31] Whether additional steps will be taken to limit ownership of U.S. farmland by foreigners remains to be seen.

SUMMARY

1. The problems farmers face are both short run and long run in nature. The short-run problem is centered around the instability of agricultural prices. This instability is magnified by the inelasticity of both demand and supply with respect to price. The long-run problems include productivity increases, which have increased the supply of farm products, low mobility of farm resources, and low income elasticity of demand.

2. Among the solutions to these problems are free market forces, income subsidies, crop restriction, price support–loan–crop storage programs, and price subsidies. Many people believe that allowing free market forces to solve farm problems would cause farmers great hardship. Farmers also do not favor a purely income subsidy approach.

3. Farmers have been willing to support crop restriction policies when they are combined with price support or price subsidy programs. Price support programs are based on the concept of parity prices—prices for farm products that represent the same kind of purchasing power for the farmer as did corresponding farm prices in 1910–1914, the golden age of agriculture. Under price support pro-

grams, if farmers cannot sell their crops at prices equal to or above the support price (which is usually less than 100 percent of the parity price), the government will give the farmers loans for the value of their output according to the support price. If the farmers cannot sell their crops at prices high enough to cover the loans and interest within a certain period of time, the government will accept the crop as full payment for the loan. Variations of this type of program have been used by the federal government since the 1930s.

4. Under price subsidy programs farmers are paid a subsidy equal to the difference between a price set by the government and the market price received when they sell their crops, as long as the market price is the lower price. This type of approach has never been used in the United States, perhaps because it is more expensive (ignoring storage costs) than price support approaches when demand is inelastic.

5. Among the reasons commonly offered to justify the special consideration given by the government to agriculture are: the farmer has little market power, the agriculture sector is crucial to the welfare of the nation, and weather conditions cause farm prices to be highly variable. The growth of farm co-ops, however, is increasing farmers' market power. So far, the effectiveness of farmers' strikes has not been great.

6. Two other issues related to the agriculture industry are middlemen's profits and the rising price of land. While the data indicate that the farm price–retail price spread has widened from 1973 to 1978, there is no conclusive evidence that the profits of food processors and distributors are out of line with the rest of the economy.

7. The rising price of land has caused the explicit cost per unit of agricultural products to vary widely from farm to farm. Purchases of land in the United States by citizens of foreign countries have frequently been blamed for the high price of land. Congress has passed a law requiring disclosure of farms held by foreigners. Twenty-nine states have restrictions on farm ownership by those who are not citizens of the United States.

8. As we all realize, the problems of the agriculture industry are complex. A solution satisfactory to everyone has so far eluded economists and government policymakers. It is unlikely that the difficulties of the farmers and the consumers of farm products will be resolved soon.

30. See "The Uneven Squeeze on the U.S. Farmer," *Business Week*, December 19, 1977, p. 70.

31. "The Buying of America," *Newsweek*, November 27, 1978, p. 88.

IMPORTANT TERMS AND CONCEPTS

Income subsidies

Crop restriction
programs

Price support–loan–
crop storage
program

Price subsidy
program

Agricultural
Marketing Act
(1929)

Agricultural
Adjustment Act
(1933)

Parity

Agricultural
Adjustment Act
(1938)

Soil bank program

Agricultural Trade
Development and
Assistance Act
(1954)

Agriculture and
Consumer
Protection Act
(1973)

Target prices

Food and Agriculture
Act (1977)

Normal crop acreage
base

QUESTIONS AND PROBLEMS

1. Why are agricultural prices characterized by such a large amount of short-run instability?

2. What are the major long-run problems that farmers face?

3. How do crop restriction programs work in theory? In practice?

4. Explain several possible solutions to the farm problem.

5. Explain how a price support–loan–crop storage program works. What are the disadvantages of such programs?

6. What factors are responsible for the lack of mobility of farm resources?

7. What are the advantages of an income subsidy program? Why do farmers dislike this approach?

8. What are the advantages of a price subsidy program?

9. Briefly explain the concept of parity price.

10. What were the Agricultural Adjustment Acts of 1933 and 1938?

11. What are the main provisions of the Food and Agriculture Act of 1977?

12. List and explain the arguments frequently used to justify government aid to agriculture.

13. What are the recent trends with regard to farm co-ops?

14. Why do farmers' strikes tend to be ineffective?

15. How have recent events affected the price of land and farmers' costs?

16. Does the available evidence seem to support the hypothesis of excessive profits for agricultural middlemen? Explain.

FARMING THESE DAYS IS A LOT LIKE RUNNING A SMALL CORPORATION

"Farming is like sitting down to a game of Monopoly," says Steven Sickafoose. "You've got the same weather, the same markets, as the next guy. You've got to play your variables better than he does."

That isn't the way farmers used to talk. But as Mr. Sickafoose, a 33-year-old college economics graduate and hog grower, would be the first to tell you, farmers can't farm the way they used to either.

Mr. Sickafoose and his twin brother, Stanley, cultivate 1,500 acres of the heavy, clay-like soil of northeastern Indiana. Besides

Source: Meg Cox, "Farming These Days Is a Lot Like Running a Small Corporation," *Wall Street Journal,* September 25, 1978, pp. 1, 18.

corn, soybeans, and wheat, they raise 4,000 hogs a year and 33,000 laying hens. Efficient, large-scale operators, they are among the biggest 17 percent of American farmers, a group responsible for 80 percent of U.S. agricultural sales.

Steve and Stan Sickafoose talk of productivity, of the cost of labor, of return on investment. They know exactly how much it costs them to grow a bushel of corn or put a pound on a hog, and they hedge their bets in the futures market. They are educated, incorporated and profitable. And their methods indicate what it takes in skill, capital and equipment to operate a modern family farm. . . .

To Dennis Burch, an agricultural-

loan officer at a bank near the Sickafooses, it appears that "The family has never been stronger.". .

STARTED AS SALESMEN

This strength helped draw the Sickafooses, who grew up on their father's farm, into full-time farming themselves. After graduating from college, both took jobs as salesmen for Central Soya, an agribusiness concern, and Steve managed a local grain elevator. The experience of visiting many farm clients proved valuable: "We saw that agriculture was profitable," says Stan, "and we benefited from mistakes made on other operations."

By 1972 both twins, whose

round faces, rosy cheeks and broad grins give them a vague resemblance to Billy Carter, were farming full time. They quickly set out to get big enough to buy materials and equipment straight from distributors when possible, saving the middleman's margin. Acquiring at least one piece of land between them each year, they built their holdings to about 1,000 acres, plus 500 that are rented. "The growth rate has been tremendous," Steve notes.

The men live on separate farms, owning the biggest pieces of equipment jointly but keeping separate books. Thus, if Stan runs out of corn for his hogs and gets some from Steve, it is a sale of inventory.

A HALF MILLION OF DEBT

With the help of surging land prices, the Sickafooses' combined net worth has swiftly climbed to an estimated $1.6 million. Their debt has mounted too, to more than a half million dollars, but apparently according to plan. Steve recalls one lesson in particular from his off-farm work: "It taught me to be more aggressive and not afraid to spend big money like other businessmen do," he says.

Large-scale operation has done little to shorten the farmer's workday. Six a.m. finds Steve in his big farrowing house, feeding and looking after sows that are about to give birth or recently have.

On one wall is a cartoon poster drawn by his wife, Beth Ann, portraying sows in T-shirts that read "on strike." As hog farmers, the Sickafooses are no better able

to go on strike than the hogs are. "There are always pigs to castrate, shots to give, manure to haul," Steve says.

Though pigs begin life in the farrowing house, at weaning a few weeks later they are moved to a separate building for fattening. There, fed a mixture of corn, soybean meal, vitamins and minerals, the pigs grow to market weight of 220 pounds or so in less than half a year. Despite their well-known preference for mud, these hogs live their entire lives on concrete.

Such a "confinement" operation, as it is called, has its drawbacks. With the animals penned so close together, for one thing, any disease problems are magnified. But the hogs grow rapidly and efficiently, as they can be fed a controlled ration and they don't run their weight off in a pasture as in days past. The Sickafooses calculate they can bring a hog to market on eight to 10 bushels of feed, compared with the 20 bushels it took their father four decades ago.

The Sickafooses are equally systematic in their approach to crops. Steve rattles off a list of chemicals used to grow an acre of corn the way some men recite baseball statistics: two quarts of grass killer, at $5.45 an acre; 13 pounds of insecticide, at $7.28; two pounds of broadleaf-weed herbicide, costing $5.30. This year, because of a problem with Western Corn Beetles, 40 percent of the crop also had to be sprayed with another chemical, at a cost of $6.50 an acre. . . .

The Sickafooses coordinate the size of their corn crop and their

hog production so they don't have to buy extra corn for feed. And they try to grow enough soybeans each year to cover the cost of soybean-meal protein supplement, which must be bought at a local grain elevator. A modest wheat crop provides straw to cover the concrete floors of hog barns.

MARKET OUTLOOK

This year the Sickafooses expect to average about 46 cents a pound for the hogs they will market—far above their break-even price of 32 cents a pound. They should do all right on soybeans, too, with a big crop ready for harvest and a local elevator offering 80 cents a bushel above their break-even figures. After losing several cents a dozen on eggs earlier in the year, they're making a cent or two a dozen now. Steve predicts that "margins should be getting better in the future, with feed costs so low."

As the scale of their operations grows, farmers seem to be becoming increasingly independent and aware of their economic power. "Young farmers today don't have any affiliation," says James Bollenbacker, manager of the Farmer's Co-op grain elevator here. "They say, 'I'll listen to what you say, but I won't belong to you.' They won't do business with me just because their dad did, but only if it will do something for them."

In addition, Steven Sickafoose believes that "young farmers are a lot more bitter than the earlier generation," partly because they have had more and thus expect more from life. They are more likely, for instance, to be well educated and well traveled.

"Our generation goes and goes," says Stan Sickafoose, "We go to the university for short courses; we go to specialists; we go fishing, hunting and water skiing. Our dad stayed at home and visited his neighbors."

For now, Steve and Stan plan to keep on doing better and getting bigger. But, whereas their father, Gale, says he would just as soon die sitting on his tractor, the twins want to enjoy the fruits of their work before they're old. As she cleans up after her 18-month-old son, Steve's wife Beth Ann confides, "When we're 40, we're going to travel all over the world."

QUESTIONS

1. Why does Steven Sickafoose say that "farming is like sitting down to a game of Monopoly"? Do you agree? Explain.

2. What indications do you find in the article that the Sickafooses are using economic principles to help them maximize their profit? Explain.

3. Give an example of where the brothers have achieved an economy of scale.

CHAPTER 34

INCOME
INEQUALITY
AND
POVERTY

THE
POVERTY
THAT
REMAINS

America the beautiful, America the free, America the rich—well, the mostly rich when compared to many other countries. Still, there is poverty around us, and we know it. We see it on the nightly news or when we wander around cities. Some of us see it on our own block or in our own family. It seems as though it will never go away, no matter how hard our government tries to eliminate it. Thomas Paine, the great writer and political philosopher of the American revolution, wrote at the turn of the nineteenth century:

When it shall be said of any country in the world, "My poor are happy; neither ignorance nor distress is to be found among them; my jails are empty of prisoners, my streets of beggars; the aged are not in want, the taxes are not oppressive . . . "—when these things can be said, then may that country boast of its constitution and its government.

Almost two centuries later, Americans are indeed proud of their Constitution and, for the most part, their government. However, although the poor are few, they are not happy. In fact, as the twin problems of inflation and unemployment beleaguer the country, the plight of those who remain poor seems worse. In 1980 Jonathan Kaufman wrote about the effects of inflation on America's poorest families, many of whom were receiving welfare. He noted that welfare benefits have tended to increase much more slowly than the rate of inflation and that the welfare poor were therefore becoming poorer in real terms.

Kaufman told of a Mrs. Willingham, who was struggling to maintain herself and her six-year-old son on a welfare check of $300 per month, $200 of which went for rent. They usually ran out of food before the end of the month and had to count on aid from charity pantries set up by the city of Chicago and private groups to tide them over. Kaufman wrote:

It is the humiliation of being on welfare that bothers Mrs. Willingham the most. Starting next month, after six months of job hunting, she is leaving the welfare rolls for a job in a neighborhood school that pays $3.00 an hour. "I'll be scrubbing floors, taking out garbage, doing whatever they tell me," she says. Leaving welfare will mean losing free medical care for herself and her son. Mrs. Willingham worries about that. But she says, "You lose your self-respect when you go on welfare. I want that back."[1]

This chapter is about the problem of poverty in America. It covers such questions as who the poor are, why they are poor, what government has done for them, and how government efforts to eliminate poverty might be made more effective.

1. Jonathan Kaufman "The Have Nots: Steep Inflation Means Cutbacks in Essentials for Poorest Families," *Wall Street Journal*, March 27, 1980, p. 1.

C H A P T E R 34

INCOME
INEQUALITY
AND
POVERTY

WHAT THIS CHAPTER IS ABOUT

Consider the case of the "colonias," Spanish speaking settlements in rural areas of the Rio Grande Valley in South Texas. Most of them lack paved streets, sewage systems, and pure drinking water; yet they are densely populated. The communities are filled with shanties built of scrap wood and metal on foundations of rocks or bricks. Some families obtain drinking water from irrigation ditches, hauling it home in old fifty-gallon pesticide containers. Diseases such as viral hepatitis, dysentery, and typhoid are abundant, as are stomach parasites.[1]

Then consider the case of a Massachusetts mother and her six children who allegedly received cash payments, food stamps, medical treatment, and other services equal in purchasing power to a $20,000 income.[2] Which situation is more representative of people with incomes below the poverty level? The answer given depends on whom one asks.

Inequality of income and wealth is the source of much social unrest and much perplexity on the part of economists and politicians. Many of the questions that arise in connection with this issue have no obvious answers specific enough to be operational, to make economic sense, and to be politically acceptable. For example: How much, if any, inequality of income is necessary for economic

progress? What is poverty? What is the state's responsibility for alleviating it? Many citizens—even those receiving welfare, agree that the welfare system is a mess. Few, however, agree on how to clean up the mess.

In this chapter we will examine the extent of income inequality in the United States and its sources. We will then look into the major federal and joint federal-state programs. Finally, we will analyze some of the problems connected with the current system and some of the suggestions for its improvement.

INCOME INEQUALITY

◆

Income inequality has been a troublesome issue in the United States, a country founded on the principles of freedom and equal opportunity. The notion that society has some responsibility for economically deprived persons is a popular one. Yet, how far society can go in legislating provisions for equality before

---

1. "Poor Latin Settlements Spread in South Texas Uncurbed, Unserviced," *Wall Street Journal*, May 30, 1979, pp. 1, 14.

2. "The $60 Billion Welfare Failure," *Business Week*, January 17, 1977, p. 49.

TABLE 34–1   Distribution of Aggregate Household Income in the United States, 1979

Household Income Class	Percent of All Households	Average Household Income of This Class	Percent of Aggregate Income Received by Households in This Class	Percent of Families in This and Lower Classes	Percent of Aggregate Income Received by Households In This and Lower Classes
Under $5,000	13.2	$ 2,884	1.9	13.2	1.9
$5,000 to $9,999	16.4	7,403	6.2	29.6	8.1
$10,000 to $14,999	15.9	12,298	10.0	45.5	18.1
$15,000 to $19,999	14.0	17,371	12.4	59.5	30.5
$20,000 to $24,999	12.0	22,315	14.1	71.9	44.6
$25,000 to $34,999	15.6	29,251	23.3	87.5	67.9
$35,000 to $49,999	8.3	40,895	17.3	95.8	85.2
$50,000 to $74,999	3.1	58,779	9.2	98.9	94.4
$75,000 and over	1.1	101,576	5.6	100.0	100.0
All households	100.0	$ 19,620	100.0		

Source: U.S. Department of Commerce, Bureau of the Census, "Table B: Number of Households, Mean Income, and Aggregate Household Income in 1979," *Money Income of Households in the United States: 1979*, Current Population Reports, Series P–60, No. 126 (Washington, D.C.: Government Printing Office, June, 1981), p. 3.

economic efficiency and the rights of others are unduly sacrificed is a matter on which there is little agreement. In this section we will first examine the existence of income inequality; then we will consider why it is present.

PRESENCE OF INEQUALITY

As Table 34–1 indicates, in 1979, in terms of family income, the bottom 45.5 percent of U.S. families received only 18.1 percent of aggregate household income. On the other hand, the top 12.5 percent of U.S. households received 32.1 percent of total household income. Perhaps even more striking, the top 1.1 percent of U.S. families received 5.6 percent of aggregate household income, whereas the bottom 13.2 percent received only 1.9 percent of aggregate income.

We can depict the nature of the inequality of the distribution of income through the use of a Lorenz curve.

A **Lorenz curve** is a graphical depiction of the relationship between the percent of income generated in an economy received by a certain group of people and the percent of all families in that group.

Figure 34–1 graphically illustrates the information presented in Table 34–1. The percent of income is represented along the vertical axis and the percent of families along the horizontal axis. The straight line segment $0X$ represents absolute income equality in the sense that the bottom 20 percent of the families receive 20 percent of the total income, the bottom 40 percent of the families receive 40 percent of the income, and so on.

In contrast, the curved line $0ABCDEFGHX$ is a Lorenz curve that depicts the actual distribution of income in the United States as given by the last two columns of Table 34–1. For example, at point A, the bottom 13.2 percent of the families receive only 1.9 percent of the in-

come. At point B, the bottom 29.6 percent of the families receive 8.1 percent of the income. Likewise, point C indicates that 45.5 percent of the families receive 18.1 percent of the income. A similar explanation holds for points D, E, F, G, and H.

The shaded area in the figure highlights the inequality of the distribution of income. The larger this area, the greater the inequality of income. If there were no income inequality, the Lorenz curve would coincide with straight line $0X$ and the gap would disappear.

Figure 34–2 contains three Lorenz curves for the United States, one each for 1929,

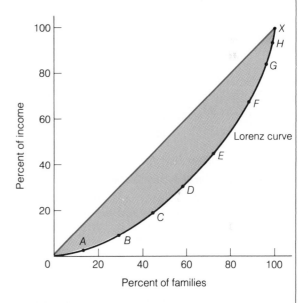

FIGURE 34–1 Distribution of Income in the United States, 1979

The straight line segment $0X$ represents absolute income equality in the sense that the bottom twenty percent of the families receive twenty percent of the income, and so forth. Line segment $0X$ represents absolute income equality because it is a 45° line, equally distant from the horizontal and vertical axes. The curved line $0ABCDEFGHX$ is a Lorenz curve, which depicts the *actual* distribution of income in the United States. For example, at Point A, the bottom 13.2 percent of the families receive only 1.9 percent of the income. The shaded area in this figure highlights the inequality of the distribution of income. The larger this area, the greater the inequality of income.

Source: Department of Commerce, Bureau of the Census.

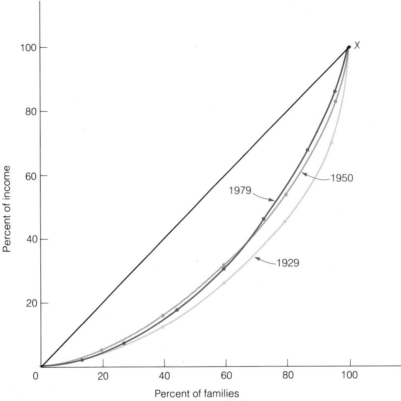

FIGURE 34–2 Comparison of Distribution of Income in the United States, 1929 to 1979

As in Figure 34–1, the line segment 0X represents absolute income equality. Lorenz curves for the United States, one each for 1929, 1950, and 1979, are also shown. As can be seen here, the size of the gap between the relevant Lorenz curve and straight line segment 0X has decreased over the last fifty years. Thus, income inequality has lessened somewhat, although a substantial amount of it is still present.

Source: U.S. Department of Commerce, Bureau of the Census.

1950, and 1979. The figure shows that income inequality has lessened somewhat; the size of the gap between the relevant Lorenz curve and straight line segment 0X has decreased over the last fifty years particularly at higher levels of income. Nevertheless, a substantial amount of income inequality is still present.

REASONS FOR INCOME INEQUALITY

The reasons for income inequality vary widely. Some factors—such as industriousness and, at least partly, education—are un-

der the control of each individual. Other factors—such as inherited wealth, natural abilities, health, discrimination, market power, and luck—are not. Each of these factors is examined next.

Natural Abilities People are born with different talents and abilities. Although each person can choose to develop or not to develop natural abilities, certain activities are easier for some than for others. Most of us would find it impossible to sing as well as Ella Fitzgerald, box as well as Muhammad Ali, or ice skate as well as Eric Heiden. Mathematics is hard for some people; art is difficult for others. People who possess the talents that are in greatest demand and shortest supply will be able to command the highest prices for their services.

Education and Training As Chapter 24 indicated, education and training affect the income earning potential of individuals. In 1964 President Johnson said: "Of families headed by a person with only a grade school education, 37 percent are poor. Of those headed by high school graduates, only 8 percent are poor."[3] To a significant extent, the level of educational achievement is the choice of the individual. However, intellectual abilities and financial considerations place some limitations on the available opportunities.

Health Another factor affecting an individual's earning power is health. Physical disabilities have different impacts on income, depending on the nature of a person's occupation. Obviously, by following rules for proper diet, rest, and exercise, people can increase the likelihood that their bodies will remain healthy.

Nevertheless, partly because of lack of knowledge, health is an area over which people do not have complete control. Also, inherited characteristics seem to play a substantial role in physical and perhaps mental health. Finally, people cannot always avoid natural disasters and accidents that may cause physical and mental harm.

Industriousness One factor, industriousness, is not often listed as affecting income inequality, but it should be included. Many people have become wealthy because they took advantage of available opportunities and even created their own opportunities. Teachers frequently see students with exceptional academic ability who refuse to use it. Other students, with less ability, work hard and excel.

Inherited Wealth The presence of inherited wealth is definitely a factor in promoting income inequality. Although inherited wealth is not the only source of income for the rich, in 1978, 9.4 percent of the income of families in the $50,000 and over income bracket came from dividends, interest, rental, and royalty income. Only 2.4 percent of the income of families in the $3,000 to $4,999 income bracket came from those types of income.[4]

Discrimination A certain degree of income inequality is caused by discrimination on the basis of sex, race, and age. Such discrimination may take the form of lower wage rates or a lack of educational, training, or job opportunities. As we will see later, of the families living in poverty, a larger percentage are nonwhite or headed by women than are white or headed by men. However, as pointed out in Chapter 25, some recent evidence indicates that discrimination with respect to race and sex may be diminishing in importance as far as income inequality is concerned.

Market or Political Power Some individuals, as a result of belonging to a union, through monopoly power, or for other reasons, are able to increase their earnings by exercising market power. Others have powers of persuasion in the political arena. The presence of economic power through either monopoly control or political influence promotes income inequality.

Luck Finally, an element of luck enters into the determination of an individual's income. Sometimes individuals are in the right place at the right time through no conscious effort of their own. Some people make risky business investments and win, but others lose. A favor-

---

3. *Economic Report of the President, 1964* (Washington, D.C.: Government Printing Office, January 1964), p. 15.

4. U.S. Department of Commerce, Bureau of the Census, "Table 758: Money Income of Families—Percent of Families by Type of Income, Mean Income, and Percent of Aggregate Income, by Income Level: 1978," *Statistical Abstract of the United States, 1980* (Washington, D.C.: Government Printing Office, 1980), p. 457.

able outcome is not always the result of a superior ability to analyze the situation.

In the next section we will zero in on one of the most controversial issues connected with income inequality—poverty.

WHO
ARE THE
POOR?

The number of persons below the poverty level for several population classes in the United States is shown for selected years from 1959 to 1979 in Table 34–2. The percentage of people in each population class below the poverty level is also indicated. As is evident from these data, a much higher percentage of the people below the poverty level were in nonwhite households and in households headed by women than in white households or in households headed by men.

Although the percentage of the population living below the poverty level has decreased in all of these classes since 1959, the absolute number of people living in poverty has increased for households headed by women. A probable reason for this pattern is given later in the chapter.

INCOME AND POVERTY DEFINED

*The definition of **income** used to determine whether a person is below the poverty level is before-tax income plus any government cash transfer payments.*□   112

This definition is the one used by the U.S. government and therefore the one used in Table 34–2. The definition of poverty used in the table is a variable one developed by the Social Security Administration.

*According to the Social Security Administration, the **poverty level of income** depends on the number of people in a household, their ages, whether the head of household is a man or a woman, and whether the persons involved live on a farm.*

The poverty standard also varies from year to year as a result of changes in the cost of living.

The average poverty cutoff levels of annual income for a nonfarm family of four are shown in Table 34–3 for the years 1959 through 1978. Mainly as a result of increases in the cost of living, the poverty cutoff level rose from $2,973 in 1959 to $6,662 in 1978.

On the basis of the government's definition of *poverty*, Figure 34–3 shows the aggregate

TABLE 34–2   **Persons below Poverty Level in the United States, 1959 to 1979**

Population Class	1959		1966		1969		1975		1979	
	Number (Millions)	Percent	Number (Millions)	Percent	Number (Millions)	Percent	Number (Millions)	Percent	Number (Millions)	Percent
All classes	39.5	22.4	28.5	14.7	24.1	12.1	25.9	12.3	25.2	11.6
White	28.5	18.1	19.3	11.3	16.7	9.5	17.8	9.7	16.7	8.9
Black and other races	11.0	56.2	8.9	41.8	7.1	32.2	7.5	31.3	7.8	30.9
Male head	29.1	18.7	18.3	10.8	13.7	8.0	13.6	7.8	12.1	6.9
Female head	10.4	50.2	10.3	41.0	10.4	38.4	12.3	34.6	13.1	31.9

Source: U.S. Department of Commerce, Bureau of the Census, "Table 773: Persons below Poverty Level by Family Status, Race, and Sex of Head: 1959 to 1979," *Statistical Abstract of the United States, 1980* (Washington, D.C.: Government Printing Office, 1980), p. 465.

TABLE 34–3 Average Poverty Level Income Cutoffs for Nonfarm Families of Four in the United States, 1959 to 1978

Year	Annual Income
1959	$2,973
1960	3,022
1966	3,317
1970	3,968
1974	5,038
1977	6,191
1978	6,662

Source: U.S. Department of Commerce, Bureau of the Census, "Table 771: Persons below Poverty Level and below 125 percent of Poverty Level: 1959 to 1978," *Statistical Abstract of the United States, 1980* (Washington, D.C.: Government Printing Office, 1980), p. 464.

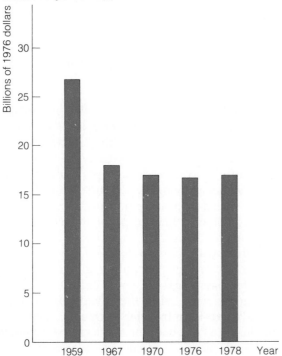

FIGURE 34–3 Income Deficit of Families Below Poverty Level (1976 Dollars)

The bar graphs for the years 1959, 1967, 1970, 1976, and 1978 indicate the income deficit (in billions of 1976 dollars) of families below the poverty level. In other words, in 1978, it would have taken 17 billion dollars of additional income to bring all families up to the poverty level.

Source: U.S. Department of Commerce, Bureau of the Census, Table 759: "Families and Unrelated Individuals Below Poverty Level and Aggregate Income Deficit (1976 Dollars), By Sex and Race of Head: 1959 to 1976," *Statistical Abstract of the United States, 1978* (Washington, D.C.: Government Printing Office, 1978, p. 468; and *Statistical abstract of the United States, 1980*, p. 468.

income deficit for all persons below the poverty level from 1959 to 1978. In other words, it shows the additional dollars (in terms of 1976 purchasing power) required to bring each household up to the poverty level cutoff point. This amount declined from $26.7 billion in 1959 to $17.0 billion in 1978. However, recall that this figure represents the additional money required after government cash transfer payments have been made. It does not necessarily represent an increase in the ability of people to stay above the poverty level through their own efforts. We will return to this point later in the chapter.

METROPOLITAN VERSUS RURAL POOR

Figure 34–4 compares the percentage of population below the poverty level for metropoli-

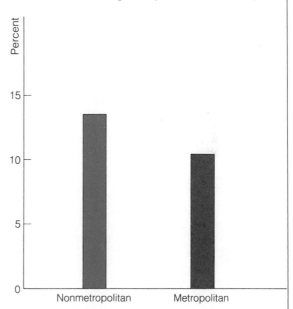

FIGURE 34–4 Percent of Persons Below Poverty Level By Place of Residence: 1978

This graph shows the percentage of people living in metropolitan and nonmetropolitan areas, respectively, who had incomes below the poverty level in 1978.

Source: U.S. Department of Commerce, Bureau of the Census, Table 772: "Persons Below the Poverty Level, By Residence, Race, and Family Status: 1975 and 1978," *Statistical Abstract of the United States, 1980* (Washington, D.C.: U.S. Government Printing Office, 1980), 464.

tan areas with the percentage for nonmetropolitan areas. The percentage of people living in poverty is higher for nonmetropolitan areas (13.5 percent) than for metropolitan areas (10.4 percent).

WORKING
AND NONWORKING POOR

The 1978 employment situation of heads of households with incomes below the poverty cutoff level is depicted in Figure 34–5. Of the

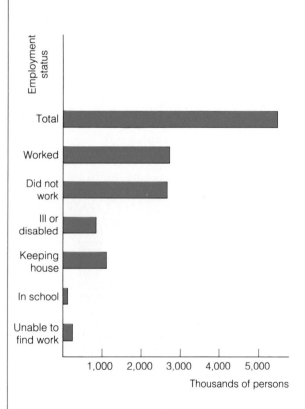

FIGURE 34–5 Employment Status of Family Heads Below The Poverty Level: 1978

This graph shows the employment status of heads of families with incomes below the poverty level in 1978.

Source: U.S. Department of Commerce, Bureau of the Census, Table 781: "Work Experience of Family Heads Below the Poverty Level, By Sex and Race: 1975 and 1978," *Statistical Abstract of the United States, 1980* (Washington, D.C.: Government Printing Office, 1980), p. 469.

5.4 million heads of such households, 2.7 million, or 50 percent, worked at least part of the year. Of the 2.7 million who did not work, approximately 33 percent were disabled, 40 percent were keeping house, 3 percent were in school, and 8 percent were unable to find work.

POVERTY UNDER
ALTERNATE INCOME DEFINITIONS

Obviously, the number of persons with incomes below the poverty level depends partly on what is counted as income. Table 34–4 shows the percentage of families in various population classes that were below the poverty cutoff level of income in 1976. The table uses four income definitions.

If only pretax income before government transfer payments is counted, the percentage of families below the poverty level becomes much higher than under the official definition, particularly for the elderly. (The official definition is pretax income plus government cash transfer payments.) In the case of the elderly, social security payments account for a large portion of the government cash transfer payments.

If the most inclusive definition of income—before-tax income including all government transfer payments—is used, only 8.1 percent of families were below the poverty cutoff point in 1976. (**In-kind transfer payments,** payments in the form of goods or services, are typified by food stamps, Medicaid, Medicare, and public housing.)

Later in this chapter we will consider the relevance of the varying percentages of people with incomes below the poverty cutoff point under alternate definitions of income. In fact, we will see that a reduction of the percentage of people with incomes below the poverty level before any government transfer payments are considered would probably be the most significant indication of a successful war on poverty.

TABLE 34–4 Percent of Families below Poverty Level Using Alternate Definitions of Income, 1976

Income Definition	Percent of Families in Each Class below Poverty Level								
	All Families	Race		Age		Region			
		White	Black and Other	Under 65	65 and Over	Northeast	North-Central	South	West
Income before taxes and before receipt of cash transfers	27.0	24.7	43.8	18.6	59.9	26.4	23.3	30.8	26.2
Income after receipt of cash transfers	13.5	11.4	28.9	12.7	16.7	11.5	10.8	17.8	12.2
Income after receipt of in-kind transfers	8.1	7.1	15.9	8.6	6.1	5.6	5.7	11.9	8.0
Income after taxes and after all transfers	8.3	7.3	16.1	8.9	6.1	5.7	5.9	12.1	8.2

Source: U.S. Department of Commerce, Bureau of the Census, "Table 758: Families below Poverty Level under Alternative Income Definitions," *Statistical Abstract of the United States, 1978* (Washington, D.C.: Government Printing Office, 1978), pp. 468–469.

THE WAR ON POVERTY

In 1964 President Lyndon Johnson announced a "war" on poverty along with a set of proposals for government programs to assist people with incomes below the poverty level.[5] Actually, however, official government efforts to reduce the incidence of poverty had begun much earlier.

One of the landmark efforts in this regard was the **Social Security Act (1935).** This act established the Old-Age, Survivors, Disability, and Health Insurance (OASDHI) program, commonly referred to as the social security program. In addition, the act provided for payments to families with dependent children and aid to the aged, blind, and disabled as supplements to the OASDHI program.

Since 1935, many more federal, state, and local programs have been established to aid the poor. The major income maintenance programs wholly or partly funded under the auspices of the federal government are discussed

_____
5. *Economic Report of the President, 1964*, pp. 14–17.

in the following section and summarized in Table 34–5. As the table shows, most income maintenance programs can be classified either as social insurance programs or as public aid programs. The distinction between the two will be explained later in the chapter.

SOCIAL INSURANCE PROGRAMS

Social insurance programs *are programs financed primarily through payroll taxes on employers or employees.*

Social insurance programs include Old-Age, Survivors, Disability, and Health Insurance (OASDHI), public employee retirement, railroad employee retirement, unemployment insurance, and workers' compensation.

OASDHI As indicated by its name, **Old-Age, Survivors, Disability, and Health Insurance** was established to replace lost earnings due to specific circumstances such as retirement or disability. The program is financed by contributions required by law from employers and employees. In 1981 both employers and em-

TABLE 34–5

Programs	Basis of Eligibility	Source of Funds	Forms of Aid
Social Insurance Programs			
OASDHI	Age, disability, or death of wage Earner; past earnings	Federal payroll tax on employees and employers	Cash
Medicare	Age or disability	Federal payroll tax on employees and employers	Subsidized health insurance
Public Employee Retirement	Age; past earnings	Federal payroll tax on employees and federal government	Cash
Railroad Employee Retirement	Age; past earnings	Federal payroll tax on employees and employers	Cash
Unemployment insurance	Unemployment; past earnings	Federal and state payroll tax on employers	Cash
Workers' compensation	Work connected injury or death; past earnings	Federal or state payroll taxes on employers	Cash
Public Aid Programs			
AFDC	Families with children and absent, disabled or unemployed fathers; income	Federal, state, and local governments	Cash
Medicaid	Eligible for AFDC or SSI or medically indigent	Federal, state, and local governments	Subsidized medical services
Supplemental security programs	Age or disability; income	Federal government	Cash
Food stamps	Income	Federal government	Subsidized purchase of food vouchers

ployees were required to pay a social security tax of 6.65 percent of the first $29,700 of each employee's annual income for a maximum of $1,975. However, both the rate and the amount of wages to which it is applied are scheduled to increase in the future. People with limited amounts of agricultural and domestic employment are excluded, as are self-employed people with annual incomes of less than $400.

Workers achieve eligibility for social security benefits by working in covered jobs for specified periods of time. They receive full benefits if they retire at age sixty-five and partial benefits if they retire at age sixty-two. Also, since 1959 the social security program has been broadened to include benefits for dependents of covered wage earners. In fact, in the early 1970s it was estimated that one out of three social security checks went to persons under sixty-five years of age.[6]

Recently, the financial status of the social security system has caused great concern. The problems, concentrated primarily in three areas, are both short run and long run in nature. First, social security benefit schedules

6. 93rd Congress, Second Session, *Income Security for Americans: Recommendations of the Public Welfare Study*, Report of the Subcommittee on Fiscal Policy of the Joint Economic Committee, Together with Supplementary Views (Washington, D.C.: Government Printing Office, December 4, 1974), p. 34.

have been increased because of the pressures of inflation. Second, relatively high levels of unemployment during the 1970s and early 1980s have reduced payments into the system. Finally, the population growth rate in the United States has decreased. If this trend continues, the ratio of workers to beneficiaries will decline. This decline is cause for concern because to some extent current payments to beneficiaries are financed by current contributions of workers.

In January 1978 Congress passed a law to solve the financial problems of the social security program. Under this law, both the amount of annual wages subject to the social security tax and the tax rate itself were to increase in several steps. However, passage of the law did not completely eliminate the problems connected with the social security program, because middle-income taxpayers were incensed at the larger tax bite. In fact, some argued that the program should be financed at least in part out of general tax revenues. As indicated in Chapter 9, the federal income tax is at least theoretically a progressive tax, □ and it does not have an upper limit with regard to level of income. Moreover, in 1981 there was evidence which indicated that the social security system was still in financial trouble in spite of the scheduled rate increases in the 1978 law. This issue is still being debated in the early 1980s.

Public Employee Retirement Social insurance for federal civilian employees is supplied through the **civil service retirement program.** Benefits for these employees are financed partly by an employee payroll tax and partly by the federal government.

Railroad Employee Retirement Retirement annuities for aged and disabled employees of railroads and for their spouses and survivors are provided by the **Railroad Retirement Act (1935).** In the computation of benefits, wage credits earned as railroad employees plus earnings in employment covered by social security are taken into consideration. These ben-

efits are financed primarily through a payroll tax on employers and employees. The **Railroad Unemployment Insurance Act** (1938) provides unemployment and disability benefits to railroad workers. It is financed by a payroll tax on employers.

Unemployment Insurance The U.S. Employment and Training Administration and the employment security agency of each state administer **unemployment insurance.** The program is financed through state and federal payroll taxes levied on employers. The law requires employers to pay a federal tax of 3.2 percent of the first $8,000 in annual wages paid to each employee. However, a firm is allowed a tax credit of up to 2.7 percent for payments to state unemployment compensation plans.

According to federal law, state unemployment insurance programs must include firms in industry and commerce that have four or more employees during twenty weeks of a year or that pay $1,500 or more in wages during any calendar quarter. Approximately 80 percent of the states cover state and local government employees. In the remainder of the states these employees, along with agricultural employees, railroad employees, employees of nonprofit institutions, family labor, and self-employed workers, are excluded from the program. Legislation enacted in 1974, however, provides special unemployment benefits to workers not otherwise covered if they work in an area with a high unemployment rate.

Workers' Compensation State laws provide **workers' compensation** insurance against work connected injuries and deaths for most employees, with varying exclusions. Federal laws provide for insurance for federal employees, private employees in the District of Columbia, longshoremen, and harbor workers. In addition, the Social Security Administration and the Department of Labor administer a program for coal miners affected with black lung disease.

The benefits received are generally related to

a worker's past earnings. They may or may not be increased by provisions for dependents and as a result of increases in current wage rates.

PUBLIC AID PROGRAMS

Public aid programs differ from social insurance programs in several ways. First, social insurance programs are financed primarily through compulsory contributions by the covered employees or their employers, whereas public aid programs are financed out of general tax revenues. Second, the benefits paid under social insurance programs are generally higher the *higher* the employee's *past* earnings. For public aid programs, on the other hand, the *lower* the beneficiary's current income, the *higher* the benefit payments are. Third, to qualify for public aid programs a person must pass an income test, whereas this requirement usually does not exist or is not applied in such a restrictive fashion for social insurance programs. Thus the social insurance and public aid programs are quite different in nature.

> Under **public aid programs,** transfer payments are financed from general tax revenues, do not depend on an individual's past earnings, and do depend on an individual's current earnings.

The primary federal or combined federal-state public assistance programs are summarized here.

AFDC As mentioned earlier, the Social Security Act established a program giving aid to families with dependent children who were deprived of the support of a parent, particularly the father, because of death, disability, or absence. The number of **Aid to Families with Dependent Children (AFDC)** recipients increased from 1.2 million in 1940 to 10.4 million in 1979.[7]

As with many other combined federal-state public aid programs, the states have a great deal of control over the benefit schedules and other provisions of the AFDC program. We will examine some of the problems resulting from this discretionary power later in the chapter.

Medicaid and Medicare Amendments to the Social Security Act in 1965 established **Medicaid and Medicare.** The purpose of the program was to aid states, if they desired, in providing medical assistance to the aged, the blind, the disabled, people receiving AFDC, and certain other people.

Supplemental Security Income A federal program established in 1974, the **supplemental security income** program is administered by the Social Security Administration. It provides a minimum income for the aged, blind, and disabled under uniform national eligibility requirements and payment standards. States can also supplement the federal payment. Prior to 1974, similar services were provided by the states, assisted by federal grants.

Food Stamps The Food Stamp Act (1964) established the **food stamp** program, which is financed by federal funds and administered by the Department of Agriculture in cooperation with state and local welfare offices.[8] Under this act, low-income persons can obtain food stamps from local welfare agencies. These stamps are used to purchase food items from supermarkets or other grocery stores. Their dollar value of food vouchers received depends on household size and income. House-

7. U.S. Department of Health, Education and Welfare, Social Security Administration, "Table M–32: Public Assistance: Recipients and Average Monthly Payments per Recipient, by Program, 1940–79," *Social Security Bulletin* 42 (November 1979): 56.

8. 88th Congress, "The Food Stamp Act of 1964," *United States Statutes at Large,* vol. 78 (Washington, D.C.: Government Printing Office, 1965), pp. 703–709.

holds in which all persons are receiving other forms of public assistance are automatically eligible for food stamps; monthly income and asset cutoff standards are used for other households.

EXPENDITURES

Federal, state, and local government expenditures for income maintenance programs from 1960 through 1978 are summarized in Table 34–6. The annual growth rate of total expenditures for such programs was quite high—13.5 percent for federal expenditures and 11.0 percent for state and local outlays.

The annual growth rate for public aid expenditures was even greater—18.5 percent at the federal level. The corresponding figure for state and local outlays was 13.6 percent. What these expenditures have purchased in terms of income security for Americans is the topic of the next section.

POVERTY: A PROGRESS REPORT

Given the large expenditures of government (and private) funds for income assistance pro-

TABLE 34–6 Expenditures for Income Maintenance Programs, (in Millions of Dollars)

	1960		1970		1975		1978	
Program	Federal	State and Local	Federal	State and Local	Federal	State and Local	Federal	State and Local
Social insurance	**$14,307**	**$ 4,999**	**$45,246**	**$ 9,446**	**$ 99,748**	**$ 23,199**	**$147,324**	**$27,778**
Old-Age, Survivors, Disability, and Health insurance	11,032	—[a]	36,835	—[a]	78,430	—[a]	117,433	—[a]
(Medicare)	*—[a]*	*—[a]*	*7,149*	*—[a]*	*14,781*	*—[a]*	*25,204*	*—[a]*
Public employee retirement	1,520	1,050	5,517	3,142	13,339	6,780	20,145	9,784
Railroad employee retirement	935	—[a]	1,610	—[a]	3,085	—[a]	4,020	—[a]
Unemployment insurance	474	2,356	1,036	2,783	3,465	10,407	3,770	8,830
Workers' compensation	63	1,245	148	2,803	1,355	5,024	1,749	8,060
Other	284	348	100	718	75	990	207	1,103
Public aid	**2,117**	**1,984**	**9,649**	**6,839**	**27,208**	**13,502**	**40,979**	**18,641**
Public assistance[b]	2,058	1,984	7,594	6,839	14,547	12,212	19,963	17,021
Vendor medical payments (Medicaid)	*200*	*293*	*2,607*	*2,606*	*7,056*	*5,928*	*10,638*	*9,457*
Social services	*—[a]*	*—[a]*	*522*	*191*	*1,963*	*660*	*2,766*	*922*
Supplemental security income	—[a]	—[a]	—[a]	—[a]	4,802	1,290	5,573	1,620
Food stamps	—[a]	—[a]	577	—[a]	4,694	—[a]	5,590	—[a]
Other	59	—[a]	1,477	—[a]	3,166	—[a]	9,853	—[a]
Veterans programs	**5,367**	**112**	**8,952**	**126**	**16,570**	**449**	**19,569**	**174**
Housing	**144**	**33**	**582**	**120**	**2,335**	**632**	**4,887**	**337**
Other social welfare[c]	**417**	**723**	**2,259**	**1,886**	**4,264**	**3,269**	**5,872**	**4,711**
Total	**$22,352**	**$27,851**	**$66,688**	**$18,437**	**$150,125**	**$119,285**	**$218,631**	**$51,641**

[a]Not applicable.

[b]Includes payments under state general assistance programs and, beginning in 1970, work incentive programs.

[c]Includes expenditures for vocational rehabilitation, certain areas of child welfare, institutional care, and miscellaneous expenditures.

Source: U.S. Department of Commerce, Bureau of the Census, "Table 516: Social Welfare Expenditures by Source of Funds and Public Program," *Statistical Abstract of the United States, 1978* (Washington, D.C.: Government Printing Office, 1978), pp. 328–329; and *Statistical Abstract of the United States, 1980*, pp. 332–333.

grams, it is important to question whether progress has been made in reducing the incidence of poverty. As Figure 34–6 shows, the percentage of the total U.S. population below the poverty level has fallen from 22.4 percent in 1959 to 11.4 percent in 1978. The absolute number of persons below the poverty level has also fallen—from 39.5 million in 1959 to 24.5 million in 1978.[9] Certainly these statistics indicate some progress.

In terms of the distribution of personal income, however, the change has not been so dramatic. As shown in Table 34–7, the share cf total income received by the lowest fifth of the population (in terms of income) has increased by only 0.7 percent over the last thirty years. The share of income going to the top 5 percent has fallen by only 1.7 percent over the same period. For better or worse, the degree of income inequality has changed very little.

Moreover, in at least one other respect there has been a lack of progress in reducing poverty. According to data collected by Sheldon Danziger, the percentage of the total U.S. population living in poverty before government cash transfer payments are considered (as they are in the official measure) has remained virtually constant.[10] The significance of this fact is that while the incidence of poverty has been reduced by government programs, people are apparently no better able to keep themselves above the poverty level through their own efforts than they were before the war on poverty. Consequently, although the symptoms of poverty have been alleviated, the causes apparently have not been removed.

One reason for this lack of success may be that many of the poor are unable to work or do not possess the job skills required to earn an

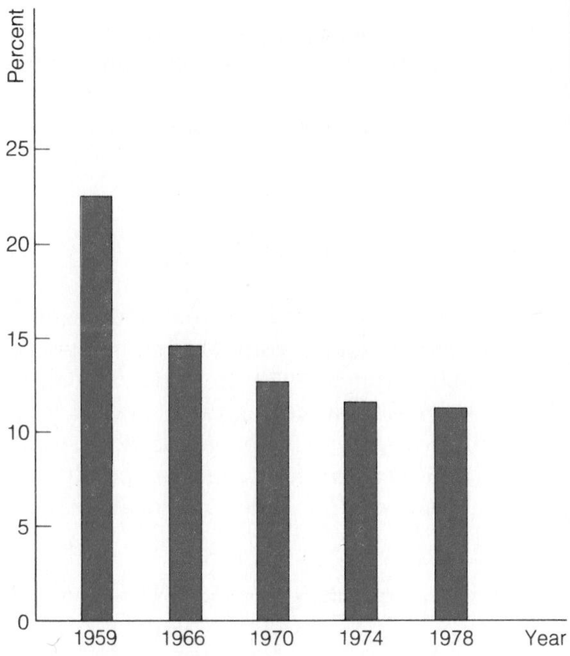

FIGURE 34–6 Percent of Population Below The Poverty Level: 1959–78

This graph shows how the percentage of the United States population with family incomes below the poverty level has decreased over the period from 1959–1978.

Source: U.S. Department of Commerce, Bureau of the Census, Table 771: "Persons Below Poverty Level and Below 125 Percent of Poverty Level: 1959 to 1978," *Statistical Abstract of the United States, 1980* (Washington, D.C.: U.S. Government Printing Office, 1980), p. 464.

income above the poverty level. As indicated in Figure 34–5, 50 percent of the heads of families with incomes below the poverty level already work. In addition, 33 percent were ill or disabled, about 40 percent were keeping house, and 3 percent were going to school. Only about 8 percent were looking for work and not finding it.

Specific problem areas connected with the government public aid programs are discussed in the next section. As we will see, acceptable solutions to these difficulties have so far been elusive.

9. U.S. Department of Commerce, Bureau of the Census, "Table 771: Persons below Poverty Level and below 125 Percent of Poverty Level: 1959 to 1978," *Statistical Abstract of the United States, 1980* (Washington, D.C.: Government Printing Office, 1980), p. 464.

10. Sheldon Danziger, "The War on Poverty Revisited," *Wharton Magazine* (Fall 1979): 63.

TABLE 34–7   Percent of Aggregate Income Received by Each Fifth and Highest 5 Percent of Families, 1950 to 1978

Income Rank	1950	1960	1970	1975	1978
	100.0	100.0	100.0	100.0	100.0
Lowest fifth	4.5	4.8	5.4	5.4	5.2
Second fifth	12.0	12.2	12.2	11.8	11.6
Middle fifth	17.4	17.8	17.6	17.6	17.5
Fourth fifth	23.4	24.0	23.8	24.1	24.1
Highest fifth	42.7	41.3	40.9	41.1	41.5
Top 5 percent	17.3	15.9	15.6	15.5	15.6

Source: U.S. Department of Commerce, Bureau of the Census, "Table 734: Money Income of Families—Percent of Aggregate Income Received by Each Fifth and Highest 5 Percent: 1950 to 1977," *Statistical Abstract of the United States, 1978* (Washington, D.C.: Government Printing Office, 1978), p. 456; and *Statistical Abstract of the United States, 1980*, p. 454.

CRITICISMS OF GOVERNMENT PROGRAMS

The major criticisms of the present government poverty programs are:

1. The programs are administratively too complex, which results in a waste of resources.
2. Work incentives for welfare recipients are weak or totally lacking.
3. Some programs encourage desertion on the part of the father.
4. People with equal needs are not treated equally from state to state.
5. Work incentives for those who support the system through taxes are not maintained.

These criticisms and problems are considered in more detail below.

ADMINISTRATIVE COMPLEXITY

A wide variety of federal, state, and local agencies are responsible for implementing the public aid programs. On the federal level alone, the Departments of Health and Human Services, Labor, Agriculture, and Housing and Urban Development are involved. On the state level the responsibility for welfare programs is shared by various agencies, including state health departments and state welfare agencies. Last, but not least, local government agencies are also involved. According to one source, the existing programs fall under the jurisdiction of 9 federal executive departments, 21 congressional committees, 54 state welfare agencies, and more than 3,000 local welfare offices.[11] Another source estimates that 300,000 workers are required to administer the basic programs.[12]

To add to the administrative complexity, eligibility rules and benefit schedules vary from one type of program to the next. In fact, the complexity of these programs discourages some needy people from applying or causes them to drop out of the application process in frustration.

LACK OF WORK INCENTIVES

Economic efficiency (not to mention social pressure) dictates that if resources are to be used effectively, those who are able to work should do so. In January 1968 Congress enacted a Work Incentive (WIN) program. The purpose of the program was to require people

---

11. David Hsieh, *Fiscal Measures for Poverty Alleviation in the United States* (Geneva, Switzerland: International Labour Organization, 1979), p. 111.

12. "The $60 Billion Welfare Failure, *Business Week*, January 17, 1977, p. 48.

who were receiving AFDC payments, who did not have children under six years of age, and who were able-bodied to participate in training programs or look for work.[13]

Nevertheless, the incentives for aid recipients to enthusiastically search for work are few. From 1969 on, the incentive formula connected with the WIN program is as follows. Each welfare recipient is allowed to keep the first $30 of monthly earnings plus one-third of any additional earnings plus work expenses.[14] Although the percentage of earned wages resulting in a reduction of aid benefits may not be great for any single program, the cumulative reduction over several programs may be very high.

For example, suppose a woman is obtaining AFDC payments of $400 per month, is getting $50 worth of food stamps free, is participating in Medicaid, and is living in public housing. If the woman finds a job that pays $300 a month, her AFDC benefits may be reduced by nearly $200 a month. Moreover, her food stamp and public housing benefits will probably also be reduced. Finally, she may be denied Medicaid benefits. One congressional committee cited the following hypothetical case:

For example, when an AFDC recipient earns extra dollars she can expect a net gain of at least 33 cents per dollar. But if she received other benefits, they, too, will be cut; the food stamp program, taking note of her 33 cent per dollar net cash gain, will raise stamp prices 10 cents per extra dollar (30 percent of the extra net income); public housing will raise rent by 8 cents per extra dollar. Thus the cumulative take-back rate could climb to 85 percent. It does not seem reasonable to expect persons to work for a net gain of only 15 cents per extra dollar, especially at possibly unpleasant work.[15]

Furthermore, the following additional penalty for working mothers was written into the law:

In an attempt to restrain costs and caseloads, Congress withheld the work incentive bonus from non-welfare mothers already at work unless their total net income fell below their State's standard of need, the usual eligibility limit. Thus, if the State standard of need and payment standard were $3,-500 for her family on an annual basis, a woman earning $5,000 and having taxes and work expenses of $900 could not qualify for aid. However, her co-worker with the same wages and work expenses would be eligible for $1,305 in AFDC plus Medicaid if she had become a welfare recipient before taking the job. The new law prohibited the earnings exemption for persons who "deliberately" reduced their earnings or stopped working without good cause, but it was impossible to prevent some working women from taking advantage of the new rules by quitting work, applying for AFDC, and then resuming the job.[16]

In spite of these disincentives to work, the WIN program has met with some success. In 1976 WIN projects placed 230,000 welfare recipients in jobs paying an average of $3.10 an hour, at a time when the minimum wage was $2.30 an hour. Two-thirds of the workers kept their jobs long enough to get off welfare entirely or have their grants reduced.[17]

Another example of success is that of Pratt and Whitney Aircraft in East Hartford, Connecticut. This firm hires 5 to 10 percent of its new employees through WIN. Company officials state that the WIN office does a better job of selecting employees than does the state employment service. Furthermore, 70 percent of the workers hired through WIN stay on the job, a retention rate equal to or better than that for other employees.[18]

Other states, such as New Hampshire and Massachusetts, are running similar employ-

13. See 90th Congress, First Session, "Social Security Amendments of 1967," Title II, Section 204, *United States Statutes at Large*, Vol. 81 (Washington, D.C.: Government Printing Office, 1968), pp. 884–892.

14. See 93rd Congress, Second Session, "Report of the Subcommittee on Fiscal Policy of the Joint Economic Committee," *Income Security for Americans*, p. 37.

15. Ibid., p. 77.

16. Ibid., p. 37.

17. "Efforts to Switch Poor from Welfare to Jobs Make Some Headway," *Wall Street Journal*, November 11, 1977, pp. 1, 14.

18. Ibid., p. 14.

ment and training programs of their own. In 1976 New Hampshire estimated that it saved $107,000 in welfare costs; Massachusetts estimated a savings of $10.5 million.[19]

Family Splitting In addition to the work incentive problem, AFDC regulations encourage families to split up, because AFDC is unavailable to families with an able-bodied employed father. Sometimes the family as a whole may be better off financially if the father leaves. A congressional subcommittee illustrated this possibility as shown in Table 34–8.

In this case, if the father left, the family could pool net wages of $278 plus $437 in welfare benefits for a total monthly income of $715. Also, in many states, families with unemployed fathers present are ineligible for AFDC, another encouragement for fathers to "desert" their families.

Variations in State Benefits Another welfare problem is the wide variation in benefits from state to state. For example, in 1978 a mother with three children living in Mississippi was entitled to $3,071 a year in AFDC payments and food stamp benefits, whereas the same family living in New York would have been entitled to $7,354.[20]

Although differences in the cost of living account for some of the state variations in benefits, they do not account for all of them. As a result, there is an incentive for welfare recipients to move from states that pay relatively low benefits to those that pay relatively high benefits. Such migration, of course, increases the expenditures of states that pay relatively high benefits, such as New York.

Economic Inefficiency If welfare payments result in excessively high marginal income tax rates, people who are not welfare recipients may also reduce the quantity of labor they are

---

TABLE 34–8 **Monthly Family Income**

Working Father at Home (Two-Parent Family, Three Children)		*Father Absent* (Mother, Three Children)	
Net earnings, $2 per hour[a]	$278	AFDC benefit	$300
Food stamp bonus	100	Food stamp bonus	67
Medicaid	0	Medicaid	70
Total	$378		$437

[a]Assuming $35 in bus fare and other expenses plus $20 payroll tax. Based on figures for North Dakota in July 1974.

Source: 93rd Congress, Second Session, *Income Security for Americans*, p. 79.

willing to supply at prevailing wage rates. As a result the economy experiences a further loss of productive output.

The following parable, told by Arthur Okun of the Brookings Institution, illustrates the problem.

If we value less inequality, we'll approve when a dollar is taken in a bucket from the very rich and given to the very poor.

But suppose the bucket of redistributive taxation has a leak in it. Suppose only a fraction—maybe two-thirds—of each dollar the rich lose gets to the poor. *Then redistribution for equity lowers the efficiency determining the size of the total social pie.*[21]

Thus, as a result of economic inefficiency and administrative costs, by redistributing income we may end up with less for everyone.

ALTERNATE POLICIES: IS THERE A BETTER WAY?

One result of the widespread dissatisfaction with the present welfare system is that a variety of proposals for reform have been offered. They range from doing away with government payments entirely to greatly increasing benefits for the poor. Two of the most popular sug-

---

19. Ibid.

20. Sheldon Danziger and Robert Plotnik, "Can Welfare Reform Eliminate Poverty?" *Social Service Review* 53 (June 1979): 246.

21. Arthur M. Okun, *Equality and Efficiency: The Big Tradeoff* (Washington, D.C.: Brookings Institution, 1975).

gestions are to consolidate the present programs into one comprehensive plan and to set up the comprehensive plan on the basis of a negative income tax.

CONSOLIDATION OF PROGRAMS

During the 1976 presidential campaign, Jimmy Carter proposed a simplified welfare system with uniform national benefit standards adjusted for differences in the cost of living and containing strong work incentives. The system was to be financed entirely by the federal government as soon as "feasible." Other people have proposed that in-kind payments be abandoned, arguing that the poor have a right to decide how the money they receive should be spent.

Although a consolidation of welfare programs is generally seen as desirable, in the political climate of the early 1980s it does not seem feasible for the federal government to accept the entire financial burden for these programs. However, if the states continue to bear part of the burden, it is doubtful that they will be able to agree on a uniform benefit schedule. Furthermore, the task of adjusting a uniform benefit scale to reflect differences in the cost of living in the various states would be a monumental task, particularly because intrastate variations in the cost of living may be greater than interstate variations.

Finally, many people believe that in-kind transfer payments should be retained. Their argument is that if a state is giving money to the poor, it has the right to say how it will be spent. Such people are concerned that money that should be spent on food for children might instead be squandered on liquor or fancy cars.

NEGATIVE INCOME TAX

Many economists, from liberal James Tobin to conservative Milton Friedman, have argued that an ideal welfare system would be based on a negative income tax.

*A **negative income tax** would work much like the present federal income tax, except that people with incomes below a certain level would receive payments from the federal government based on their level of income.*

A negative income tax would probably be an integral part of the federal income tax system and would be administered by the Internal Revenue Service.

The ideal welfare system would accomplish three goals. First, it would enable all citizens to obtain a level of income that would allow them to purchase the necessary food, shelter, clothing, and medical supplies for some minimal standard of living. Second, it would maintain work incentives for those able to work. Third, these goals would be accomplished at the lowest possible cost. The achievement of the three goals is a tall order, because the first two conflict to some extent with the third, as we will see.

A negative income tax system established with these three goals in mind might work as shown in Table 34–9. Suppose the government considered $5,000 the minimum level of income necessary for a family of four, so that if such a family had no income the government would pay its members a total of $5,000. If the marginal negative income tax rate were

TABLE 34–9 Earned Income, Government Payments, and Total Income under a Negative Income Tax at a Rate of 50 Percent

Level of Earned Income	Government Payment	Total Income
$ 0	$5,000	$ 5,000
1,000	4,500	5,500
2,000	4,000	6,000
3,000	3,500	6,500
4,000	3,000	7,000
5,000	2,500	7,500
6,000	2,000	8,000
7,000	1,500	8,500
8,000	1,000	9,000
9,000	500	9,500
10,000	0	10,000

set at 50 percent, the government would reduce its payment by $.50 for every $1 of income the family earned.

Under such a system, every family would be guaranteed a minimum level of income, and an incentive to work would be preserved. However, the family would continue to receive government benefits until it earned $10,000, well above the stated minimum level of income necessary for a family of four. Consequently, such a program might well be more expensive than the old plan.

The tax rate could be raised so that the family would be able to keep a smaller fraction of each dollar of earned income. However, the incentive to work would be correspondingly reduced. The cost could also be reduced by lowering the subsidy paid to a family with no income, but a family that had no member able to work might suffer undue hardship.

Beginning in 1970, the Department of Health, Education and Welfare conducted a study in the Seattle and Denver areas that involved 8,500 families and cost $112 million. One set of families (some already on welfare others classified as "working poor") received direct cash assistance with no strings attached for three to five years. Another set of families, called the control group, remained under the current welfare program or made it on their own if they were ineligible for benefits.[22]

The information gained from this study indicated that male heads of households given cash assistance worked an average of 6 percent fewer hours than their counterparts in the control group. Their wives worked 17 percent fewer hours, and female heads of households worked 12 percent fewer hours. Moreover, the men in the study worked 10.6 percent fewer hours when the negative income tax rate was 70 percent but only 6.2 percent fewer hours when the rate was 50 percent. However, few participants in the cash assistance program actually quit their jobs.[23]

The researchers were pleased that the reduction in hours worked was no greater than the percentages found. Furthermore, many of those receiving the cash benefits took the opportunity to get more training or search for better jobs. The study concluded that some type of negative income tax system coupled with mandatory work requirements would be the best solution to the welfare mess. However, it estimated that such a plan could cost as much as $10 billion to $40 billion above current welfare expenditures.[24] Consequently, the financing issue must be resolved before such a plan can be implemented on a national scale.

SUMMARY

1. This chapter wrestled with the problem of income inequality, particularly as it relates to the poor. The reasons for income inequality are many. They include differences in natural abilities, education and training, health, industriousness, inherited wealth, discrimination, market or political power, and luck.

2. The definition of *income* used by the federal government to classify people as either poor or nonpoor is all before-tax earned income plus any cash transfer payments received from government agencies. The definition of *poverty* used by the government is a flexible one developed by the Social Security Administration. It depends on the number of people in a household, their ages, whether the head of the household is a man or a woman, and whether the people involved live on or off a farm. The poverty standard is also adjusted from year to year to account for changes in the cost of living.

3. The percentage of the population below the poverty level has declined since 1959. Data indicate that a much higher percentage of persons living in nonwhite households or in households headed by women are below the poverty level than are those living in white households or in households headed by women.

4. If income before government transfer payments is considered, the percentage of the population with income below the poverty level has not significantly changed in the last twenty years. Thus,

22. "Welfare: A Surprising Test," *Newsweek*, November 27, 1978, pp. 33–34.

23. Ibid.

24. Ibid.

while the symptoms of poverty have been alleviated, the causes of poverty apparently have not been removed.

5. Government sponsored income maintenance programs are of two general types—social insurance and public aid. Public aid programs differ from social insurance programs in three basic ways. First, social insurance programs are financed primarily through compulsory employee or employer contributions, whereas public aid programs are financed out of general tax revenues. Second, the benefits paid under social insurance programs are generally higher the higher the employee's past earnings. For public aid programs, payments are higher the lower the beneficiary's current income. Third, to qualify for a public aid program, a person must pass an income test.

6. The primary federal government sponsored social insurance programs are Old-Age, Survivors, Disability, and Health Insurance, public employee retirement, railroad employee retirement, unemployment insurance, and workers' compensation. Public aid programs sponsored by the federal government include Aid to Families with Dependent Children, Medicaid, supplemental security income, and food stamps.

7. The government sponsored public aid programs have been criticized because of their administrative complexity, lack of work incentives, incentives for fathers to desert their families, and variations in benefits from state to state. Another problem is maintaining economic efficiency when the rich are taxed to give to the poor, because the incentives for the rich to work are decreased. Moreover, the administration may be expensive.

8. Most critics of the present welfare system believe that all the diverse programs now in existence should be consolidated into one program sponsored by the federal government and with uniform benefits nationally. One specific suggestion in this regard is a negative income tax system.

9. Under a negative income tax system each household would be guaranteed a certain minimum income. This minimum would be paid by the government to the household if the members of the household had no other income. If a member of the household became employed, the government would reduce its payment by some fraction of the additional earned income. The size of this fraction, or tax rate, is crucial, because it affects both the incentive to work and the cost of the program to the government.

10. The notion of a negative income tax is not yet generally acceptable because it may involve greater expenditures on the part of the federal government.

IMPORTANT TERMS AND CONCEPTS

Lorenz curve
Income
Poverty level of income
In-kind transfer payments
Social Security Act (1935)
Social insurance programs
Old-Age, Survivors, Disability, and Health Insurance (OASDHI)
Civil service retirement program
Railroad Retirement Act (1935)

Railroad Unemployment Insurance Act (1938)
Unemployment insurance
Workers' compensation
Public aid programs
Aid to Families with Dependent Children (AFDC)
Medicaid and Medicare
Supplemental security income
Food stamps
Negative income tax

QUESTIONS AND PROBLEMS

1. What are the causes of income inequality? What responsibility does the government have to do something about them? What is the responsibility of the individual? Explain.

2. What are social insurance programs? Public aid programs? In what ways do these two types of programs differ?

3. How has the incidence of poverty changed in the last twenty years? Do you think the war on poverty has been successful? Explain.

4. List the primary public aid programs that are entirely or partly funded by the federal government. Describe them briefly.

5. Explain how a negative income tax system would work, and give an example of such a system.

6. Explain the primary criticisms that have been leveled at the current welfare system.

7. What is the point of the parable of the leaky bucket?

CHARITY
BEGINS
AT
HOME

MIKE WALLACE: Remember the good old days when charity began at home and we all felt a responsibility to take care of not only our own family, but to help the family next door, and sometimes those less fortunate folk down the block? Well, believe it or not, we found a town where people still feel that way, feel so strongly that way that they've decided to take on the State of New Jersey on the issue of welfare.

To clarify exactly what we're talking about, the community realizes that aid to old people or the disabled or dependent children is beyond their means. But when it

Source: Transcript of "Sixty Minutes," CBS Television Network, vol. 11, no. 21 (February 4, 1979), pp. 12–22.

comes to that catchall called general assistance, in which New Jersey pays 75 percent and the town 25 percent to folks who have run into hard times, they've told the state, "Thanks, but no thanks. Keep your money. We'll do it our way." Well, what happens when a town tells a state, "Butt out! We'll do it our way"? What happens? Morley Safer went to find out.

MORLEY SAFER: . . . Well, of course, our town is no fictional place. It is Bordentown, New Jersey, about halfway between New York and Philadelphia. And the tale we have to tell is one of those late 20th-century American dramas: What happens when a state with a good idea meets a town with what it thinks is a better idea? And the subject is welfare.

The mayor of Bordentown, with the support of almost everyone here, decided that the most productive form of welfare was something called "workfare"; that is, those able-bodied people who were in need would get assistance and, in return, they'd pay back their benefits by doing work for the city. If you couldn't work, well, you'd still get assistance. Anyway, last summer, the mayor began his program. The state welfare department was furious and said, "You must follow state regulations and state paperwork." "No," said the mayor. "Too much bureaucracy. We won't even accept state welfare funds. We'll pay our own way."

It's fascinating what happens in a town like our town when it decides to stick to its guns. This fellow is the mayor, the man who started the whole thing. His name is Joe Malone. He's young, only 29, but his roots go way back here for four generations, and he feels that Bordentown knows how to look after Bordentown better than the State of New Jersey does.

MAYOR JOE MALONE: I think, basically, it boils down to a small community being able to determine what it feels is in the best interest of its community, and not someone who's off at a distant place making general rules and regulations as to how a small community should be run. Bordentown was told that it should have a full-time director, a full-time caseworker, a waiting room, $500 petty-cash fund. Our present city cash—petty-cash fund is—is approximately $15, and that—that lasts for an entire year. And if we're going to get into that kind of a situation where we need a $500 petty-cash fund for, you know, welfare, we've got a real serious problem here.

SAFER: Next in the cast of characters is G. Thomas Riti. He's the New Jersey State Welfare Director. If you believe the people in Bordentown, he's the bad guy in this story.

Don't you think that, in a certain way, the people who live in a town do, in the end, know really what's best for the town?

G. THOMAS RITI: No, I'm not convinced of that at all. We have a responsibility to see to it that the—the general assistance program

is—is operated in accordance with law. And, you know, what it says is, you know, appoint a local assistance board, have a general assistance director. Okay? And—and, you know, there should be no political involvement in—in that program. And that's what it says.

SAFER: Before workfare, you had about 30 people a month on welfare. When workfare began, you had about three people a month on workfare. What happened to those other, roughly, 27 people? Did they simply not apply for it, or what?

MALONE: I went around and tried to speak to every welfare recipient who was receiving welfare in July. One is in jail. Another one is in a veterans hospital in Philadelphia. And the rest of the people, they either went back to work or were no longer in need of assistance from the city of Bordentown. The figures from last year were approximately $8700, cost; this year's cost for the same period was a thousand dollars. . . .

RITI: You do save money if you pull out of a program, and the people all—all—all of a sudden disappear from the rolls simply because they were ineligible in the first place. The—the problem was, originally, that they were not following the guidelines of the state in the first place. Had they been following those guidelines—okay?—there would have been a lot fewer people on the rolls in the first place.

SAFER: Meet Mrs. Beatrice Busch. She's a secretary in a vending

machine company. She was the welfare director of Bordentown, but she retired when the state threw more paperwork at her than she could handle. She was welfare director for 19 years, and both she and the city thought she did a pretty good job of it. When she retired, the state said she was incompetent.

How come, then, after 19 years of being pretty conscientious, of being known around town, why on earth does the state describe what you were doing as incompetent, in effect?

BEATRICE BUSCH: Well, maybe I wasn't taking care of all the paperwork that they felt that I should. I felt I was bending over backwards, not only in my job, but helping people to get jobs. You know, giving out clothes for welfare. It's a small town, you get to know people very well, and I felt that I was really going over, above and beyond what I was supposed to do. But there were some state requirements that they felt we weren't living up to.

SAFER: Did you tend to go by the book or did you tend to go by your best instincts?

BUSCH: Half and half. Half and half. I think you really have to use, you know, common sense.

MALONE: Miss Busch was loved by this community, and she would go out of her way to do anything for anyone. And if that's being incompetent, then I think maybe someone ought to examine what the word, you know, incompetent is. She was under, basically, their direction for 19 years. If she was doing something that was improper or wasn't right or, you know, wasn't as thorough as they wished, why weren't we told about it?

SAFER: When Mrs. Busch resigned, the mayor took over the job of dispensing general assistance. That, said the state, was illegal. And there were other rules and regulations and ways of doing things that Bordentown was not following. Most important, a new welfare director must be appointed by Bordentown's local assistance board.

There are four more characters you should meet in our town in Bordentown. They're the members of the local assistance board appointed by the mayor years ago to oversee the welfare program. Meet them: Anna Turner, Elsie Valentini, Lillian Reeder and the Reverend Charles Jackson. The board really doesn't exist any more. When Mrs. Busch quit, Mr. Riti told the board that they must appoint a new welfare director quickly and, unless they did, he would bring the full weight of the State of New Jersey down on them and sue them all. They were scared, so they quit.

REV. CHARLES JACKSON: He said in a phone conversation that, if the local assistance board did not appoint a welfare director, that he would begin legal action through the attorney general. . . .

SAFER: Well, why didn't you just go and appoint somebody to take

Mrs. Busch's place and be done with it?

VOICE: Because we didn't have anybody at the time.

REEDER: Right, because we couldn't find anybody that would fill Mrs. Busch's place at the—the money she was getting and the amount of work that she was doing. The—

SAFER: She did a pretty good job of it?

REEDER: She did a wonderful job.

REV. JACKSON: I think the bureaucracy worships paper gods, as opposed to seeing the needs of people.

RITI: The State of New Jersey is clearly in favor of people who rec—who receive welfare, who are able-bodied, to work for their—for that money; and that we do, in fact, have that workfare program. That workfare program is working in New Jersey. But then—so—

SAFER: It's also working in Bordentown.

RITI: But it's the same program, in a sense; the—the difference being that one is operated contrary to law and the other is operated according to law.

MALONE: Our end is to try to insure that the program that we have for our community meets the needs of our residents. I don't think that is the end that—that the state welfare department is—is aiming towards. I think their end is,

"What can we do to insure our jobs, create the bureaucracy, and build an empire?"

RITI: And I don't want to run a program in the city of Bordentown that's different—

SAFER: Even if it's better?

RITI: I don't—I'm not convinced it's better.

SAFER: But even—

RITI: I have said that continually. I'm not convinced it's better—

SAFER: I know you're not.

RITI: —and I know it's not better!

SAFER: But even if it's better, you would still demand uniformity?

RITI: Well, if—if I agreed that it was better, okay, then what I would want is uniformity statewide on a better program. But as of the moment, there is no better program than what we already have. They were telling people, as I understand it, and, as a matter of fact, only one person, they told one person to go wash chairs, and I gather the washing chairs was out in the public square. I mean, you know, what's right is right.

SAFER: In the public square?

RITI: Yeah, I understand there's a little square in Bordentown and they were outside under the trees. At least, that's what I see in the newspaper—you know, pictures of a—of—of a woman actually ending up washing chairs in the public square. You know—And I leave it to you to decide whether or not that's a proper thing to do.

SAFER: You felt that this was humiliating?

RITI: Well, I think—isn't it a matter of human dignity?

MALONE: I can appreciate Mr. Riti's concern. I know he's totally un—uninformed about what's going on. She did not go to a public square. It was a community building. You know, I would like to ask him who does the janitorial work in his own building.

SAFER: Meet Jo Ann Gibbs. She's the woman who agreed to work off her welfare.

JO ANN GIBBS: It wasn't embarrassing for me to work. I don't think it should be embarrassing for anybody to work. I've done it before. I haven't been on welfare all my life.

SAFER: Uh-hmm.

GIBBS: We've needed assistance sometimes, and they've given it to us. And had I not been able to work, I don't think they would have made me. I really don't.

SAFER: Uh-hmm. But they didn't ask you to—to—to do this work out in public where everyone was watching or anything like that?

GIBBS: No. Uh-uh. Right in here, and there's nobody here. There's—I'm usually here alone, really. They're giving me that chance to work it off, which makes

me feel like I'm accomplishing something—

SAFER: Hm-mmm.

GIBBS: —not just going down and begging for the money.

SAFER: Hm-mmm. So it—it did something for your pride?

GIBBS: Mine and my husband's and my whole family's [Laughter]

SAFER: Does Bordentown really look after its own, or is that one of those nice, pleasant small-town myths?

MALONE: We had a situation, oh, I guess it was around the middle part of October. And a family was completely burned out. The house—there was nothing but a shell left. We rallied the community around the—these—this family.

MS. WEST: But everybody pitched in to help me, you know, and my family. And I'm grateful to them for that. I'll never be able to repay them, but I'm grateful to—for the fact that they did help me.

SAFER: Every small town has a place where people stop and talk and meet. It could be a barbershop or a diner. Here in Bordentown, it's a hardware store.

Do you think most of the people are with—with Joe Malone on this?

MAN 1: Yeah, I could probably state that unequivocably.

MAN 2: They got too many political hacks that are doing a job they

don't know how to do. Just that simple. They don't know the people in Bordentown. You get to know these people pretty well around town. I mean, I see them all the time. I—I know who can work and who can't work.

SAFER: Here's a city, a town, that's taken reform into its own hands and has solved its problem to its own satisfaction. Isn't it best to let it be?

RITI: No, it's not. There still has to be uniform rules applied for everybody throughout the state, so that the accident of where you live doesn't result in different kind of treatment.

SAFER: You know, I can't make up my mind whether you're an extreme conservative or an extreme liberal.

MALONE [laughs]: That's a—you know, you're about the tenth person that's asked me that question, and—and I think the best way to answer that is not—is not whether it's a liberal or—or a conservative; I think it's more of a—I think I'm a realist. And I think I try to look at the people, look at their needs, and try to—to assess that and make a judgment from that. Not—not from any particular point of view.

SAFER: Bordentown was ordered by a court to comply with the state regulations. So they've found a new welfare director and they've appointed a new local assistance board, and they are following the letter of the law.

MALONE: In this particular case, the law has been misused. You and I both know that there is quite a bit of difference between what is right and what is legal. And I think this really is the question here: What is right and what is legal? But that is not to say that this battle is over. This thing is going to come to a full trial in a few months, and we fully expect to expose the state for the wasteful, inept bureaucrats that they are.

WALLACE: For the moment, Bordentown is taking care of its needy by giving them regular paying jobs with the town. But Mayor Malone says if the town can't find a person a job, that person will be offered a choice: refer his case to the state employment office, or a chance to work off his assistance under Bordentown's version of workfare. Mr. Riti says they'd better not do that. Offering them a choice, he says, is just as illegal as what Bordentown was doing before.

QUESTIONS

1. Why do the people of Bordentown not want to participate in the New Jersey general assistance program?

2. What is this community's alternative to the state program? Explain how it works.

3. What are the advantages of locally run public aid programs such as "workfare"?

4. Do you think local governments should be able to ignore state requirements for public aid programs? Explain. What are the dangers of allowing local governments such freedom?

C H A P T E R 35

ENVIRONMENTAL
ECONOMICS
AND
ENERGY

PERVERSE
INCENTIVES
AND
NONUNIFORM
POLLUTION LAWS

Have you ever noticed that virtually all national magazine advertising for new cars not only states the EPA estimated mileage but also carries the warning that mileage will be lower on California cars? This is because California emission control laws are stricter than federal laws, something that may cost the California new car buyer three to four miles per gallon in fuel efficiency. Eventually, the U.S. standards may catch up with those for California, or the automobile manufacturers may come up with a technological advance that will eliminate the emissions and gas mileage differentials. In the meantime, however, the difference between California and non-California cars has provided what some economists call a perverse incentive—an incentive to import cars into California illegally.

Anyone driving the freeways of California expects to see a lot of out-of-state license plates. After all, California is a vacationer's paradise, replete with mountains, beaches, amusement parks, redwood forests, the wine country, and San Francisco. However, *many of the out-of-state cars do not belong to out-of-state people. As Newsweek noted:*

One wealthy land developer in Palm Springs drives an $80,000 Rolls-Royce with an Oregon license plate, while a young Beverly Hills playboy cruises the town in a Mercedes-Benz 450SLC identified by a blue-and-white plate from neighboring Nevada. "In our service department," says James Wilson, a Cadillac dealer in the San Fernando Valley, "we see plenty of Nebraska and Oregon plates on cars, but the repair orders show Hollywood addresses. They are totally illegal cars."

The Palm Springs land developer, the Beverly Hills playboy and thousands of other Californians are part of a growing cadre of smog scofflaws—rich people and just plain folk who buy and register their cars out of state to avoid California's supertough auto-emission standards. . . . Given the amount of time Californians spend on the road, the MPG gap is enough incentive to send them shopping across the border. Moreover, sales taxes and annual registration fees are lower in neighboring states. And to cover the higher cost of equipping cars for the California market, automakers now add a special $250 charge.

. . . But some dealers figure that, for now at least, if you can't beat 'em, join 'em. Just last month, one San Francisco dealer collected money from six California customers and took an all-expenses-paid flight to Las Vegas, where he bought them their cars. "I'd lose the business if I didn't do it," he reasoned. "I don't like it, but what can you do? The customer is always right."[1]

California does attempt to police the illegal car situation, but it is a difficult task that has netted the state only $400,000 in fines over three years. Among the winners and losers in this game are new car dealers. The out-of-state dealers are experiencing a boom, while those in California are bitterly complaining that the state law puts them at an unfair disadvantage. Some of them have even taken to doing a bit of illegal importing on their own to avoid losing customers, as the quote indicated.

During the 1970s the public made it clear that a reasonable system of pollution control was needed in the United States. Many laws were passed, and a few were even enforced. The issue is far from dead and will remain a sore spot in dealings between the executive branch and Congress. In this chapter we will combine the examination of environmental issues with that of energy and energy conservation, because the role of the federal government in both areas involves the establishment of programs that take into account the trade-offs among consumption, conservation, and the public well-being.

1. T. Nicholson, with M. Kasindorf, and P. Abramson, "Smog Scofflaws, California Style," *Newsweek*, January 28, 1980, p. 68. Condensed from Newsweek. Copyright 1980, by Newsweek, Inc. All Rights Reserved. Reprinted by Permission.

CHAPTER 35

ENVIRONMENTAL
ECONOMICS
AND
ENERGY

WHAT THIS CHAPTER IS ABOUT

POLLUTION AS AN EXTERNALITY
AN OPTIMAL LEVEL OF POLLUTION?
ENVIRONMENTAL POLICY IN THE UNITED
  STATES
WHERE WE STAND
Water Quality
Air Quality
Solid Waste Recovery
ENVIRONMENTAL POLICIES
Direct Regulation
Subsidies
Effluent Fees
ENERGY: OVER A BARREL?

The headlines screamed warnings: "Fallout Cover-up," "A Nuclear Nightmare," "A Smog Attack in Los Angeles," and "The Oil Spill Is Coming."[1] At the same time, businesses believed they were being overregulated and that, as a result, their costs were soaring.[2]

Without a doubt, the year 1979 was noteworthy in regard to the number of events that dramatically illustrated areas for serious concern about the environment. At 4 a.m. one day in late March, alarm lights flashed on in one of the nuclear reactors on Three Mile Island, outside Harrisburg, Pennsylvania. Before the crisis was over, an estimated 60,000 people

had moved out of the area temporarily.[3] Nearly a year later, tons of radioactive material and a million gallons of radioactive water still remained inside the closed plant. General Public Utilities Corporation, owner of the plant, estimated that the cleanup would take three or four more years and would cost $300 million, if all went well.[4] Soon after, in late April, Senator Edward Kennedy produced documents indicating that in an unrelated earlier incident, the Atomic Energy Commission had knowingly exposed people in a testing area to large amounts of radiation while downplaying the risk.[5]

In June, an oil rig, Ixtoc I, blew out an oil well in the Bay of Campeche off the shore of Mexico. The resulting oil spill damaged the environment and the tourist industry along the Texas Gulf coast.[6] Then, in September, Los Angeles suffered from its worst smog in twenty-four years.[7]

Throughout the year, more information came to light regarding the dangers posed by chemical dumping grounds. During the summer of 1978 residents of the Love Canal section of Niagara Falls, New York, had been forced to evacuate their homes because of chemicals oozing from containers buried there twenty years ago by Hooker Chemicals and Plastic Corporation, a subsidiary of Occiden-

---

1. See "Fallout Cover-up," *Newsweek*, April 30, 1979, p. 32; "A Nuclear Nightmare," *Time*, April 9, 1979, pp. 8–19; "A Smog Attack in Los Angeles," *Newsweek*, September 24, 1979, p. 42; and "Texas: The Oil Spill Is Coming," *Newsweek*, August 13, 1979, p. 24.

2. See, for example, "Ohio Utilities, Coal Industry Battle EPA over Clean-Air Bill and Who Must Pay It," *Wall Street Journal*, February 15, 1979, p. 40; and "Is Chrysler the Prototype?" *Business Week*, August 20, 1979, p. 103.

3. "Cooling Off the Crisis," *Newsweek*, April 16, 1979, p. 38.

4. "A Year after Accident, Three Mile Island Is far from Cleaned Up," *Wall Street Journal*, March 18, 1980, p. 1.

5. "Fallout Cover-Up."

6. "Texas: The Oil Spill Is Coming."

7. "A Smog Attack in Los Angeles."

tal Petroleum. Twenty-three other burial grounds used by Hooker in New York were being investigated in 1979. Outside this state, several other dump sites of Occidental Petroleum and Hooker were showing evidence of toxic discharges.[8]

In February 1979 a report to the Environmental Protection Agency estimated that 32,000 to 50,000 dump sites of hazardous materials may be scattered around the United States. An estimated 1,200 to 2,000 of them may pose significant risks to human health or to the environment, but the Environmental Protection Agency is able to check only 135 sites a year.[9]

In this chapter we will examine the economic aspects of environmental pollution. We will see how economic theory applies in this situation and what the federal environmental protection laws are, and we will analyze several policy alternatives. Finally, we will deal with a closely related problem, the energy crisis.

POLLUTION AS AN EXTERNALITY

◆

Chapter 27 pointed out the problems caused by **externalities.** A good or service has an externality connected with it if it has a benefit or cost that accrues to people not engaged in a market transaction involving it. When externalities are present, it may make economic sense for the government to intervene in the marketplace.

Many environmental problems seem to fit into this category. If a firm is allowed to pollute the air, water, or land without paying for cleaning it up, an external cost□ is connected with its product. Likewise, if motorists foul the air with exhaust fumes or the roadside with litter, they are imposing external costs on society as a whole.

How should society cope with these costs? At first glance, the answer may seem simple: Make the rascals clean up their own messes and be done with it. Unfortunately, there is a catch in this solution. By forcing the "rascals" to clean up the environment, we may end up paying more ourselves for goods and services. Unleaded gasoline is more expensive than regular, and fuel economy equipment and pollution control equipment have already added at least $340 dollars to the price of a car.[10] Pollution control equipment has also resulted in increased costs, followed by increases in prices, in the steel and public utility industries, among others. Moreover, as firms reduce their pollution output levels in response to control measures, unemployment may result, at least temporarily. Are we willing to put our money where our months are?

The problem of external benefits□ arises in the cleanup process. If some people pay to clean up the air by buying automobiles that are less prone to pollute the atmosphere and by purchasing unleaded gasoline, the rest of us also benefit from the cleaner air. If we can get enough other people to reduce harmful exhaust emissions, we might find that the air is tolerable without our having to do anything. Thus, without special incentives, many of us may favor cleaning up the environment—but with the other guy actually doing it.

One further complication arises with respect to environmental policies—how to determine the "optimal" level of pollution. As we will see in the next section, it may not be in society's best interest to completely clean up the environment.

---

8. See "More Love Canals?" *Newsweek*, May 14, 1979, p. 41; and "A Caustic Report on Chemical Dumps," *Newsweek*, October 22, 1979, p. 51.

9. Council on Environmental Quality, *Environmental Quality—1979* (Washington, D.C.: Government Printing Office, 1979), p. 174; and "More Love Canals?"

---

10. "Can Chrysler Be Saved?" *Newsweek*, August 13, 1979, p. 53.

AN OPTIMAL
LEVEL OF
POLLUTION?

◆

In Chapter 28 we saw that to maximize the well-being of society a good or service should be produced until the marginal social benefit□ of another unit of it is equal to its marginal social cost.□ This principle applies not only to goods such as televisions, schools, and dams but also to products such as clean air and water.

Cleaning up the environment is not costless to society as a whole. Resources are used that could have been employed in the production of other things. In order to clean up the environment, society must give up some other products. It therefore makes sense that *pollution should be reduced or abated only to the point where the marginal social benefit of less pollution is equal to its marginal social cost.* If we insist on reducing pollution even when the marginal social benefit is less than the

marginal social cost, society will actually be worse off.

Figure 35–1 shows the marginal social benefit of pollution abatement, MSB_{PA}, and the marginal social cost of pollution abatement, MSC_{PA}. The optimal amount of pollution abatement is at Q^*_{PA}, where $MSB_{PA} = MSC_{PA}$.

In the next section of this chapter we will summarize the major federal laws pertaining to the abatement (reduction) of pollution. Later we will examine the effectiveness of these laws in controlling pollution and the results that could be obtained under alternate policies.

ENVIRONMENTAL
POLICY IN
THE UNITED STATES

◆

The federal laws related to environmental policies generally fall into one or more of the following four categories: laws to control water pollution, laws to control air pollution, laws to control solid waste disposal, and laws designed to improve the quality of the environment. *Solid waste disposal* refers to the disposal of wastes on or in land. Thus water pollution, air pollution, and solid waste disposal cover the three general types of environmental pollution possible. We will examine each of these areas.

WATER POLLUTION

The **Water Pollution Control Act (1956)** marked the first comprehensive attempt by the federal government in recent years to deal with the problem of pollution. This law provided that

the Surgeon General shall, after careful investigation, and in cooperation with other Federal agencies, with state water pollution control agencies and interstate agencies, and with the municipali-

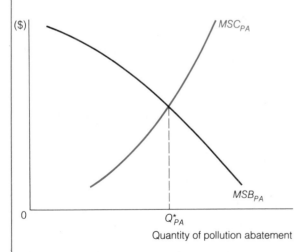

FIGURE 35–1 Optimal Level of Pollution Abatement

The marginal social cost of pollution abatement is shown by MSC_{PA}. The marginal social benefit of pollution abatement is depicted by MSB_{PA}. The welfare of society will be maximized if pollution is abated up to the point where the marginal social benefit of pollution abatement is equal to its marginal social cost, at Q^*_{PA}.

ties and industries involved, prepare or develop comprehensive programs for eliminating or reducing the pollution of interstate waters and tributaries thereof and improving the sanitary condition of surface and underground waters.[11]

The act created a Water Pollution Control Advisory Board, whose purpose was to study water quality in the regulated bodies of water. If such water were found to be polluted, if the pollution were interstate in nature, and if human health or welfare were endangered, the following procedure could be initiated. First, a conference of federal and state officials would be held to recommend specific actions to reduce the pollution. Second, after a specified time period, the federal government could hold public hearings to determine what actions were being taken. Finally, if the actions taken were not satisfactory, the federal government could file suits against the polluters in federal court to force them to take the desired actions.

The law also provided for research grants and for cost sharing in the construction of sewage treatment works to prevent water pollution. During the 1960s the act was amended to make it apply to all navigable waters and to make a finding that water quality was below set standards prima facie (sufficient) evidence that polluters were violating the law.

The 1956 law was strengthened significantly in 1972 with an amendment that made it illegal, after some initial period, to discharge wastes without a permit into a navigable body of water from a point source. The amendment also established guidelines for granting permits. The Environmental Protection Agency (EPA), which is in charge of the permits, must consider available production, waste treatment, and disposal technologies as well as the investment plans of each firm seeking a permit. The act states that it is national policy to eliminate all discharges to such waterways by 1985.[12]

AIR POLLUTION

The first comprehensive federal law to control air pollution was the **Clean Air Act (1963).** In many ways this act was similar to the Water Pollution Control Act. Section 2 states:

The Secretary [of Health, Education and Welfare] shall encourage cooperative activities by the States and local governments for the prevention and control of air pollution; encourage the enactment of improved and, so far as practicable in the light of varying conditions and needs, uniform State and local laws relating to the prevention and control of air polution.[13]

If pollution discharges from sources in one state were believed to be endangering the health and welfare of people in another state, the secretary was empowered to initiate a conference, a hearing, and, if necessary, a court suit in a procedure similar to that specified in the water pollution act. The secretary could also begin this process if requested to do so by state officials of the state in which the discharges were allegedly taking place. Furthermore, the secretary was to encourage the efforts of the motor vehicle and fuel industries to develop pollution control devices and fuels that lessen harmful exhaust emissions.

In 1965 the Clean Air Act was amended to read:

The Secretary shall by regulation, *giving appropriate consideration to technological feasibility and economic costs* [emphasis added], prescribe as soon as practicable standards, applicable to the emission of any kind of substance, from any class

---

11. 84th Congress, "Water Pollution Control Act of 1956," *United States Statutes at Large: 1956*, vol. 70 (Washington, D.C.: Government Printing Office, 1957), p. 498.

12. 92nd Congress, "Water Pollution Control Act Amendments of 1972," *United States Statutes at Large: 1972*, vol. 86 (Washington, D.C.: Government Printing Office, 1957), p. 816.

13. 88th Congress, "Clean Air Act of 1963," *United States Statutes at Large: 1963*, vol. 77 (Washington, D.C.: Government Printing Office, 1964), p. 393.

or classes of new motor vehicles or new motor vehicle engines, which in his judgment cause or contribute to, air pollution which endangers the health or welfare of any persons.[14]

These regulations were to take effect with the 1968 model cars. Increasingly stringent rules were also announced; the 1970 standards were to be twice as restrictive as the 1968 standards.

However, because of limited success in getting states to even set air quality standards, let alone control discharges, amendments to the Clean Air Act were passed in 1970. The amendments made the Environmental Protection Agency responsible for determining two sets of ambient (surrounding) air quality standards—primary and secondary. *Primary standards* were to apply to pollution violations that posed a threat to human health. *Secondary standards* were to be established at levels to protect property and welfare. Primary standards were to be implemented in much shorter time schedules than were secondary standards.

According to these amendments the standards of performance to be set would reflect

the degree of emission limitation achievable through the application of the best system of emission reduction which (taking into account the cost of achieving such reduction) the administrator determines has been adequately demonstrated.[15]

The EPA was also to be responsible for conducting research into the effects of air pollution and into new technologies.

The 1970 amendments took a major step by actually specifying emission standards for mobile sources of air pollution. New cars sold in 1975 were to emit no more than 10 percent of the amount of hydrocarbons and carbon monoxide permitted by the 1970 standards. In

TABLE 35–1 Federal Automobile Emission Standards, 1970 to 1981 (Grams per Mile)

Period	Hydrocarbons	Carbon Monoxide	Nitrogen Oxides
1957–1967 average emissions	8.7	87.0	—[a]
1970–1971 standards	4.1	34.0	—[b]
1972–1974 standards	3.0	29.0	3.0[c]
1975–1979 standards	1.5	15.0	2.0[d]
1980 standards	0.4	7.0	2.0
1981 standards	0.4	3.4	1.0

[a]Data not available.

[b]No standard.

[c]Effective with 1973 model cars.

[d]Effective with 1977 model cars.

Source: U.S. Department of Commerce, Bureau of the Census, "Table 363: Automobile Pollutant Emissions, 1957–1967, and Federal Emission Standards, 1970 to 1981," *Statistical Abstract of the United States, 1979* (Washington, D.C.: Government Printing Office, 1979), p. 213.

1976 automobiles would be required to meet a similar standard for nitrogen oxides. As a result of the oil crises in 1973 and 1979, however, the schedule for the achievement of these standards has been relaxed. As shown in Table 35–1, these standards were scheduled to become effective with the 1981 model cars.

SOLID WASTES

The **Solid Waste Disposal Act (1965)** stated:

The purposes of this Act therefore are—
(1) to initiate and accelerate a national research and development program for new and improved methods of proper and economic solid-waste disposal, including studies directed toward the conservation of natural resources by reducing the amount of waste and unsalvageable materials and by recovery and utilization of potential resources in solid wastes; and
(2) to provide technical and financial assistance to State and local governments and interstate agencies in the planning, development, and conduct of solid-waste disposal programs.[16]

---

14. 89th Congress, "Clean Air Act Amendment of 1965," *United States Statutes at Large: 1965*, vol. 79 (Washington, D.C.: Government Printing Office, 1966), pp. 992–993.

15. 91st Congress, "Clean Air Amendments of 1970," *United States Statutes at Large: 1970–1971*, vol. 84, pt. 2 (Washington, D.C.: Government Printing Office, 1971), p. 1783.

16. 89th Congress, "Clean Air Act Amendment of 1965, Title II: Solid Waste Disposal Act," *United States Statutes at Large: 1965*, vol. 79 (Washington, D.C.: Government Printing Office, 1966), p. 997.

TABLE 35–2 Expenditures in the United States for Pollution Abatement and Control, 1972 to 1979

Type of Expenditure	Expenditure (in Billions of 1972 Dollars)							
	1972	1973	1974	1975	1976	1977	1978	1979
Pollution abatement	**17.5**	**19.8**	**19.9**	**21.4**	**22.5**	**23.0**	**24.1**	**24.4**
Personal consumption	1.6	2.1	2.2	2.7	3.0	3.1	3.0	3.0
Business	11.1	12.6	12.2	12.7	13.3	13.9	14.6	15.0
Government	4.8	5.1	5.5	6.1	6.2	6.0	6.6	6.4
Regulation and monitoring	**0.4**	**0.5**	**0.5**	**0.5**	**0.5**	**0.6**	**0.6**	**0.6**
Research and development	**0.8**	**0.8**	**0.8**	**0.8**	**0.9**	**0.9**	**1.0**	**1.0**
Total expenditures	**18.7**	**21.1**	**21.2**	**22.8**	**24.0**	**24.5**	**25.8**	**26.1**

The Resource Recovery Act (1970) expanded the authority of the federal government in both areas. Moreover, the Resource Conservation and Recovery Act (1976) ordered the EPA to draw up regulations governing the transportation, storage, and disposal of hazardous chemical wastes within eighteen months. However, by October 1979 these regulations were still unwritten. In the meantime, incidents such as Love Canal clearly illustrate the need for further progress in the safe disposal of solid wastes.

GENERAL ENVIRONMENTAL LAWS

The **National Environmental Policy Act (1969)** reiterated the general goal of providing all Americans with "safe, healthful, productive, and esthetically and culturally pleasing surroundings."[17] It also created the Council on Environmental Quality within the Executive Office of the President. The council consists of three members appointed by the president. Each member is required to be "exceptionally well qualified to analyze and interpret environmental trends and information of all

kinds."[18] The council is responsible for submitting to Congress, through the president, an annual report on environmental quality. Later in this chapter we will make extensive use of this data.

WHERE DO WE STAND?

U.S. expenditures, both public and private, for pollution abatement and control from 1972 through 1979 are shown in Table 35–2. The dollar values have been adjusted for inflation so that all figures are in terms of the purchasing power of 1972 dollars. As indicated in the table, expenditures have risen from $18.7 billion in 1972 to $26.1 billion in 1979. The progress made in pollution control in return for these outlays is the topic of the next section.

WATER QUALITY

Government regulators have divided the sources of water pollution into two main categories: point and nonpoint. The distinction between the two is not clear-cut, but the terms are usually defined as follows.

---

17. 91st Congress, "National Environmental Policy Act of 1969," *United States Statutes at Large: 1969*, vol. 83 (Washington, D.C.: Government Printing Office, 1970), p. 852.

---

18. Ibid., p. 854.

Point discharges *are sources of water pollution that "discharge to a waterbody through a discrete pipe or ditch."*[19]

Examples of point discharges are industrial discharges (including large feedlot flows), discharges from municipal sewage treatment plants, and combined sewer (household and storm sewer wastes) discharges.

Nonpoint discharges *are defined by the Environmental Protection Agency to include urban runoff, construction, mining, and agriculture runoffs, irrigation return flow, solid waste disposal, and individual sewage disposal.*

Runoff from urban storm sewers is a major nonpoint source of poor water quality in urban areas. Agricultural activities hold the same distinction for rural areas, although forestry activities can result in severe erosion of soils. Fallout from the air of various chemicals, including lead and phosphorous, can also cause substantial water pollution problems.[20]

According to the 1979 report of the Council on Environmental Quality, there are still many problems with the collection and analysis of water quality data. However, the Council states that available evidence from United States Geological Survey data

suggests that water quality in the United States, while not showing vast improvement since the early 1970's, is at least not getting worse.[21]

There has been little or no overall change in the levels of five major water pollution indicators [fecal coliform bacteria, dissolved oxygen, total phosphorus, total mercury, and total lead] over the 4 water years, 1975 through 1978.[22]

The same situation still appeared to exist in 1980.[23]

The percentage of river basins in various regions of the United States affected by point and nonpoint sources of pollution of various types is shown in Table 35–3. According to the Council on Environmental Quality, some two-thirds of the lakes in the United States may have pollution problems.[24]

AIR QUALITY

The **pollution standard index** *is a system which the federal government uses to classify the overall quality of air in a particular area.*

As shown in Table 35–4, the pollution standard index (PSI) is assigned according to the levels of five major air pollutants: total suspended particulates, sulphur dioxide, carbon monoxide, ozone, and nitrogen dioxide.

According to the 1980 report of the Council on Environmental Quality, combined data from 23 major metropolitan areas indicated that the number of unhealthful days declined by 18 percent between 1974 and 1978. Between 1974 and 1977, the number of very unhealthful days declined by 32 percent. Moreover, data from approximately fifty of the counties with the worst air pollution showed that violations of air quality standards generally either stayed constant or decreased during this period. However, the air in two of the forty-one cities for which reliable data were available (New York and Los Angeles) was still in the unhealthful range for more than one-half of the days of the year. In Kansas City and Houston cities the air pollution appears to have gotten worse.[25]

19. Council on Environmental Quality, *Environmental Quality—1979*, p. 86.

20. Ibid.

21. Ibid., p. 75.

22. Ibid., p. 78.

23. Council on Environmental Quality, *Environmental Quality—1980*, p. 100.

24. Council on Environmental Quality, *Environmental Quality—1979*, p. 89.

25. Ibid., p. 17; and *Environmental Quality—1980*, p. 146.

TABLE 35-3 Percentage of River Basins Affected in Given Regions, by Type of Pollutant

Region and Number of Basins	Bacteria		Oxygen Depletion		Nutrients		Oil and Grease		Suspended Solids		Dissolved Solids		Toxics	
	P	N	P	N	P	N	P	N	P	N	P	N	P	N
Northeast (40)	93	70	93	53	78	63	35	15	70	65	13	10	58	43
Southeast (47)	77	66	89	74	70	57	6	4	26	34	9	4	34	30
Great Lakes (41)	80	51	85	54	71	44	34	20	44	56	27	27	68	44
North Central (35)	89	69	80	66	74	63	0	0	23	80	20	51	60	66
South Central (30)	73	53	87	43	83	63	13	3	30	37	30	70	43	70
Southwest (22)	50	36	36	14	41	45	5	14	14	32	23	68	9	27
Northwest (22)	68	64	55	18	55	55	0	5	23	64	5	14	18	32
Islands (9)	89	89	78	44	56	44	44	0	33	100	11	0	22	44
All basins (246)	78	61	79	51	69	56	16	9	35	54	17	30	44	45

P = Point sources.

N = Nonpoint sources.

Source: U.S. Environmental Protection Agency, *National Water Quality Inventory, 1977 Report to Congress* (Washington, D.C.: Government Printing Office, 1978), pp. 11, 16.

The pollutants causing the greatest problems were carbon monoxide and ozone.[26] In addition, acid rain (rain contaminated by sulphuric acid) is becoming an increasingly serious environmental problem in the eastern half of the United States.[27]

Table 35-5 ranks standard metropolitan statistical areas according to the pollutant standard index described in Table 35-4. As is evident from the data, air quality needs much improvement, especially in eight urban areas.

Table 35-6 indicates that progress has been made in reducing the pollutants emitted by motor vehicles. However, keeping automobile pollution control systems in operation as the cars grow older is a problem. Provisions in national pollution control programs for the inspection and maintenance of these devices are highly controversial.

SOLID WASTE RECOVERY

The growth in municipal solid waste has slowed from an annual rate of 5 percent during the period 1960–1970 to an annual rate of 2 percent during 1970–1978. Total municipal solid waste was estimated to be 154 million tons in 1978, about 1,400 pounds per person.[28]

The two general methods for reuse of solid wastes are the separation of trash into its various components (for example, aluminum,

26. Ibid.

27. Ibid., pp. 70–71.

28. Ibid., p. 256.

TABLE 35-4 **Explanation of Pollutant Standard Index (PSI) Values**

PSI Index Value	Air Quality Level	Total Suspended Particulates[a] (24-Hour) $\mu g/m^3$	Sulphur Dioxide[a] (24-Hour) $\mu g/m^3$	Carbon Monoxide[b] (8-Hour) Mg/m^3	Ozone[a] (1-Hour) $\mu g/m^3$	Nitrogen Dioxide[a] (1-Hour) $\mu g/m^3$	General Health Effect	Specific Health Effects
500	Significant harm	1,000	2,620	57.5	1,200	3,750		
400	Emergency	875	2,100	46.0	1,000	3,000		Premature death of ill and elderly. Healthy people experiencing adverse symptoms that affect normal activity.
300	Warning	625	1,600	34.0	800	2,260	Hazardous	Premature onset of certain diseases in addition to significant aggravation of symptoms and decreased exercise tolerance in healthy persons.
200	Alert	375	800	17.0	400[c]	1,130	Very unhealthful	Significant aggravation of symptoms and decreased exercise tolerance in persons with heart or lung disease, with widespread symptoms in the healthy population.
100	NAAQS[d]	260	365	10.0	240		Unhealthful	Mild aggravation of symptoms in susceptible persons, with irritation symptoms in the healthy population.
50	50% of NAAQS	75[e]	80[e]	5.0	120		Moderate	
0	0	0	0	0	0		Good	

[a]Micrograms of pollutant per cubic meter of air.
[b]Milligrams of pollutant per cubic meter of air.
[c]400 $\mu g/m^3$ was used instead of the ozone alert level of 200 $\mu g/m^3$
[d]National Ambient Air Quality Standards.
[e]Annual primary NAAQS.
Source: U.S. Environmental Protection Agency, "Guidelines for Public Reporting of Daily Air Quality—Pollutant Standard Index."

glass, and paper) for recycling and the burning of trash for its energy yield. At the present time the revenue obtained from recycled materials does not cover all the cost of collecting, sorting, and other types of preparation.[29]

With respect to incineration, the Council on

Environmental Quality has stated that technological difficulties are probably the least important problem with regard to centralized waste recovery systems for the production of energy. However, although such systems emit no radiation or sulphur dioxide, they may give off some potentially hazardous substances. At the present time, public utilities seem reluctant to become involved with

29. Ibid., pp. 270–271.

TABLE 35–5   Ranking Of Standard Metropolitan Statistical Areas (SMSAs) Using the Pollutant Standard Index (PSI) (Based on Data for 1976–1978)

Severity Class and SMSA	Average Number of Unhealthful Days (PSI over 100) per Year	Average Number of Very Unhealthful Days (PSI over 200) per Year	Severity Class and SMSA	Average Number of Unhealthful Days (PSI over 100) per Year	Average Number of Very Unhealthful Days (PSI over 200) per Year
I (More than 150 days of PSI readings over 100)			IV (25–49 days of PSI readings over 100)		
Los Angeles	242	118	Cincinnati	45	2
New York	224	51	Dayton	45	2
Pittsburgh	168	31	Gary-Hammond–East Chicago	36	8
San Bernardino-Riverside-Ontario	167	88	Indianapolis	36	2
II (100–150 days of PSI readings over 100)			Milwaukee	33	6
			Buffalo	31	5
			San Francisco	30	1
Cleveland	145	35	Kansas City	29	6
St. Louis	136	29	Memphis	28	2
Chicago	124	21	Sacramento	28	2
Louisville	119	12	Allentown	27	1
III (50–99 days of PSI readings over 100)			V (0–24 days of PSI readings over 100)		
Washington, D.C.	97	8	Toledo	24	2
Phoenix	84	10	Dallas	22	1
Philadelphia	82	9	Tampa	12	1
Seattle	82	4	Akron	10	0
Salt Lake City	81	18	Norfolk	9	0
Birmingham	75	19	Syracuse	9	1
Portland	75	3	Rochester	6	0
Houston	69	16	Grand Rapids	5	0
Detroit	65	4			
Jersey City	65	4			
Baltimore	60	12			
San Diego	52	6			

[a]Based on only one year of data.

[b]Based on only two years of data.

[c]Not available.

Source: Council on Environmental Quality, "Table 1–2: Ranking of 40 Standard Metropolitan Statistical Areas (SMSAs) Using the PSI, 1976–1978," *Environmental Quality—1980* (Washington, D.C.: Government Printing Office, 1980), p. 154.

TABLE 35–6 **Motor Vehicle Emissions of Pollutants per Vehicle-Mile Traveled, 1970 to 1980 (Estimated Grams per Mile)**

Pollutant	1970	1972	1973	1974	1975	1976	1977	1978	1979	1980
Carbon monoxide	86.9	81.6	80.0	79.0	77.0	74.3	71.4	68.3	65.2	60.6
Hydrocarbons	12.1	10.8	10.3	9.9	9.4	8.9	8.4	7.9	7.3	6.6
Nitrogen oxides	4.7	4.9	4.8	4.7	4.6	4.4	4.1	3.9	3.8	3.6

Source: U.S. Environmental Protection Agency, *Mobile Source Emission Factors*, Final Document (Washington, D.C. Government Printing Office, March 1978).

them.[30] Thus many possibilities in the recovery of solid waste materials remain to be developed.

In the next section we will explore the advantages and disadvantages of three general types of environmental policies.

ENVIRONMENTAL POLICIES

Three general types of government policies often proposed to deal with environmental pollution are direct regulation, subsidies, and effluent fees. We will consider the advantages and disadvantages of each approach.

DIRECT REGULATION

Direct regulation *refers to the passage of laws that prohibit discharges of pollutants above a particular rate.*

In theory, lawmakers would select specific goals for ambient air quality, water quality, and solid waste disposal. Then they would determine the legal standards to set in order to achieve the desired level of pollution abatement.

Unfortunately, this process is not as straightforward as it may seem. Different industries and different firms in the same indus-

try do not have the same opportunities for the use of pollution abatement technology. For example, a firm building a new plant can often employ the latest pollution control equipment at much less cost than can a firm with an older plant. If the regulations are adjusted to consider the wide variations in compliance costs, they can become unmanageably complex.

Another problem with direct regulation is that although everyone is required to hold pollution discharges down to a particular level, there is no economic incentive for anyone to further reduce such discharges, even if the marginal cost of doing so is relatively low. Consequently, it is difficult to formulate pollution abatement laws complex enough to reduce pollution up to the point where the marginal social benefit of further abatement of pollution is equal to its marginal social cost. As we have already seen, social welfare will be maximized when this position is reached.

SUBSIDIES

Another proposal for dealing with pollution is to grant subsidies to those who reduce their discharges of pollutants. These subsidies could take the form of federal income tax credits for the purchase of pollution control equipment.

Although such a policy would be fairly simple to administer, it has several disadvantages. First, a tax credit may be completely ineffective if it is equal to less than the entire cost of the equipment. As long as the purchase of such equipment entails a net cost for firms

---

30. Ibid., pp. 282–289.

or consumers, they have no economic incentive to buy the equipment.

Second, a tax subsidy for the purchase of pollution control equipment gives firms or others no incentive to consider other means of pollution abatement, such as changing the type of fuel used. Such procedures may facilitate the reduction of pollution at a lower cost than that incurred for the purchase and operation of new equipment.

Finally, any kind of subsidy payment for pollution abatement raises the issue of social equity. Who should bear the burden of pollution control—those who produce and purchase the goods and services that cause pollution or taxpayers as a whole?

EFFLUENT FEES

Many economists favor the control of pollution through a system of effluent fee payments.

▌An **effluent fee** is a charge levied on firms or consumers; it is based on their rate of discharge of pollutants.

One advantage of such a system is that firms are free to choose the most cost-effective means of pollution abatement (one that lowers polluting discharges at the lowest cost per unit of reduction achieved). Moreover, if the cost of pollution abatement is greater for some polluters than the payment of the effluent fee, they are free to pay the fee instead. Such a system encourages the reduction of pollution at the least cost to society. It also encourages polluters to develop new means of reducing pollution at lower cost.

Finally, a system of effluent fees places the cost of pollution abatement procedures on those responsible for the pollution. If the fee schedule is set up correctly, firms should adjust their production of goods to closely reflect their marginal social cost, as demonstrated in the next section.

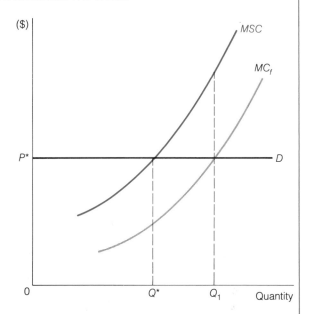

FIGURE 35–2 Profit-Maximizing Quantity and Socially Optimal Quantity of Output for a Polluting Firm

The demand curve for the output of a perfectly competitive firm is D. The marginal cost to the firm of producing the output is MC_f. However, because of pollution costs which the firm does not bear, the marginal cost to society of producing the product is given by MSC. In the absence of governmental intervention, the firm will produce where $P^* = MC_f$, at Q_1 units of output. However, the marginal social cost is greater than price (assumed to be equal to marginal social benefit) at Q_1 units of output. The welfare of society would be maximized by producing Q^* units of output, where P^* is equal to MSC.

GRAPHICAL COMPARISON OF THE POLICIES

Figure 35–2 sketches a perfectly competitive firm's□ demand curve, D, and marginal cost curve,□ MC_f (before government intervention), for a good.[31] It also sketches a marginal social cost curve, MSC,□ that reflects the fact that the production of this good results in polluting discharges with associated costs not borne by the firm.

---

31. Obviously, many firms that cause pollution are not purely competitive. However, the analysis of the effects of pollution control policies is more complex in the case of imperfectly competitive firms, and its discussion is left to a more advanced text.

In the absence of government intervention the firm produces a level of output equal to Q_1, where $P^* = MC_f$. However, if we assume that the price, P^*, represents the marginal social benefit of the good, at Q_1 the marginal social benefit of the good is less than its marginal social cost. Thus too much of the good is produced from a social welfare standpoint.

If a tax subsidy equal to 100 percent of the cost of pollution control equipment is instituted, the firm's marginal cost curve is not altered, because the government and, ultimately, the taxpayers bear the cost of pollution abatement. Pollution may be reduced, but the firm has no incentive to reduce its level of output below Q_1. If the tax subsidy is less than 100 percent of the cost of such equipment, there is no incentive for anything at all to happen.

On the other hand, if an effluent fee system is instituted, the marginal cost curve of the firm rises, perhaps to MC'_f, as shown in Figure 35–3. In this case the firm will reduce its production of the good to Q_2. Ideally, the effluent fee schedule will raise the firm's marginal cost curve so that it will coincide with the marginal social cost curve. In this case, the firm will choose to produce a level of output equal to Q^*, the socially optimum level. (Of course, if many firms in the industry are polluters and experience an increase in their costs as a result of the effluent fee, the industry supply curve will shift upward and the equilibrium price will rise.)

Direct regulation will also tend to raise the marginal cost curve of the firm, because the

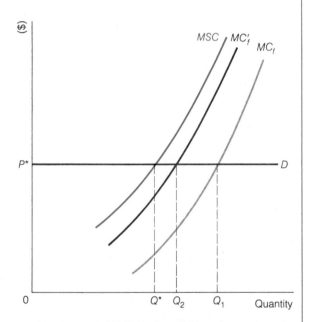

FIGURE 35–3 The Effect of an Effluent Fee

As in Figure 35–2, *D* is the demand curve for the product of a perfectly competitive firm. Also, *MC$_f$* depicts the marginal cost to the firm of producing the product, whereas *MSC* is the marginal cost to society of producing it. In the absence of governmental intervention, the firm will produce Q_1 *units of output, whereas the socially optimal level of output is* Q^*. After an effluent fee system is instituted, the marginal cost curve of the firm rises to *MC$'_f$*. In this case, the firm will reduce its level of output to Q_2. Ideally, the effluent fee schedule would shift the firm's marginal cost curve so that it coincided with *MSC*, and the firm would produce the socially optimal level of output, Q^*.

"So that's where it goes! Well, I'd like to thank you fellows for bringing this to my attention."

Drawing by Stevenson; © 1970 The New Yorker Magazine, Inc.

firm will be legally required to reduce pollution. This policy will tend to have the socially desirable effect of reducing output to conform more closely with the marginal social benefit equals marginal social cost criterion, but it has the disadvantages discussed above—it would be difficult to take into account variations in compliance costs for different firms and there is no incentive for firms to reduce pollution below the required amount.

Direct regulation of very hazardous substances may still be desirable when production of even small amounts of them may result in great danger to health. Also, direct regulation, currently the primary type of government policy employed in pollution control, has resulted in some reduction of environmental pollution. Nevertheless, two economists. Allen Kneese and Charles Schultz, have estimated that a system of effluent fees would cost society 40 to 90 percent less than a direct regulation policy of requiring all firms to reduce polluting discharges by the same fraction.[32].

In the next section we will direct our attention to another, related environmental problem—the production of energy. Air pollution is largely the result of the combustion of fossil fuels, especially wood and coal. Natural gas, the cleanest fuel, is also the most scarce.

ENERGY: OVER A BARREL?

Dramatic increases in the price of foreign crude oil engineered by the Organization of Petroleum Exporting Countries were only one factor in the perceived energy crisis of the 1970s. Warnings were sounded about dwindling supplies of oil and natural gas. The increasing use of nuclear power reflected a reluctance to give up an accustomed life-style of

heavy consumption of energy. On the other hand, environmentalists and incidents such as the Three Mile Island breakdown have warned us that nuclear energy might eventually be our downfall.

THE BASICS: SUPPLY AND DEMAND

In July 1979 *Newsweek*, using data supplied by the Department of Energy, reported that on the basis of current rates of consumption, the United States had enough crude oil left for only 8.7 more years and enough natural gas left for only 10.7 years.[33] These calculations, however, were based on the assumption of no significant additions to reserves. Our supplies of coal are thought to be sufficient for a much longer period of time, but coal presents environmental and safety problems.

As Figure 35–4 indicates, energy consumption in the United States has increased fairly steadily over this century. The most significant exceptions to the pattern occurred during

33. "Why We Must Act Now," *Newsweek*, July 16, 1979, p. 23.

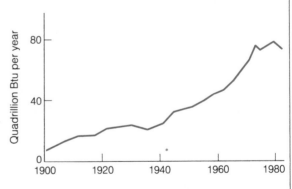

FIGURE 35–4 U.S. Gross Energy Consumption, 1900–1980

This graph depicts the growth of energy consumption in the United States from 1900 to 1980. Energy is measured in terms of quadrillions of Btu's per year on the vertical axis. Energy consumption has increased so that in the late 1970s it is approximately eight times its level in 1900.

Source: U.S. Department of Energy, *Monthly Energy Review*, June 1979 and August 1981.

32. Allen V. Kneese and Charles L. Schultze, *Pollution, Prices, and Public Policy* (Washington, D.C.: Brookings Institution, 1975), pp. 90, 99.

1974 and 1975 and in 1979 and the early 1980s, when energy consumption actually declined. Figure 35–5 depicts the growth in production, imports, and consumption of energy products from 1960 to 1978. It also shows that until 1979, the United States had increasingly relied on imports as a source of energy during the last two decades.

The growth rate of energy *consumption* for the various energy sources from 1950 to 1980 is shown in Table 35–7. The use of nuclear power and hydropower grew most rapidly until 1979, reflecting dwindling supplies and increasing prices of other energy sources. After 1979, the growth rate of nuclear power production was negative, at least partly reflecting the effects of the Three Mile Island incident in 1979. During 1979 and 1980 coal production boomed, as users substituted coal for other types of energy sources. People who are concerned about energy conservation should be encouraged by the decline in the growth rate of energy consumption during the last decade.

As shown in Table 35–8, until 1978–1979 the growth rate of energy *production*, particularly in the last decade, has been far slower than the growth rate of energy consumption. Hence, the current energy dilemma of the 1980s.

The growth rate of energy consumption during 1978 and 1980 by type of user is shown in the following table.

User	Growth Rate (Percent)	
	1978	**1980**
Residential/commercial	3.5	−0.5
Transportation	2.7	−6.7
Industrial	0.3	−4.0

Source: Council on Environmental Quality, *Environmental Quality—1979* (Washington, D.C.: Government Printing Office, 1979), p. 323; and Department of Energy, *Monthly Energy Review*, August, 1981, p. 20.

Residential and commercial users of energy had the highest consumption growth rate, followed fairly closely by transportation users in 1978. However, by 1980 the growth rates of energy consumption by all types of users became negative.

Industry is becoming increasingly efficient in its use of energy, a trend reflected in the fact that the ratio of energy to gross national product declined during the 1970s. In 1980 the ratio was 51,500 Btus per dollar of GNP (after GNP was adjusted for inflation). In 1972 the ratio was about 61,200 Btus per dollar.[34]

In 1979 the Council on Environmental Quality concluded:

With a moderate effort to increase energy productivity, our year 2000 energy consumption need not

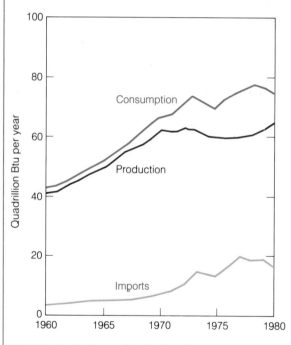

FIGURE 35–5 Energy Production, Consumption, and Imports: 1960 to 1980

This graph depicts the growth of energy consumption, production, and imports since 1960. Note that between 1975 and 1978 energy consumption grew more rapidly than energy production. Imports of energy grew more rapidly than energy production in 1976 and 1977, but declined in 1978. Source: Chart prepared by U.S. Bureau of the Census.

34. Council on Environmental Quality, *Environmental Quality—1979* (Washington, D.C.: Government Printing Office, 1979), p. 323; and Department of Energy, *Monthly Energy Review*, August, 1981, p. 14.

TABLE 35–7 Growth Rate of Energy Consumption by Source of Energy, 1950–1980

Energy Source	Growth Rate of Consumption (Percent)				
	1950–1960	1960–1970	1970–1978	1978–1979	1979–1980
Total consumption	2.8	4.3	2.0	−0.2	−3.5
Petroleum	4.1	4.0	3.1	−2.5	−7.9
Natural gas[a]	7.6	5.8	−1.2	−0.7	−0.8
Coal	−2.4	2.3	1.4	8.9	3.3
Nuclear power	—[b]	37.4	37.0	−7.7	−1.6
Hydropower	1.4	4.9	2.2	−0.3	−1.3
Geothermal and other	—[b]	—[b]	17.0	50.0	28.1

[a]Dry marketed gas.

[b]Not applicable.

Source: U.S. Department of Commerce, Bureau of the Census, "Table 1011: Energy Production and Consumption—Annual Growth Rates by Type of Fuel: 1950–1978," *Statistical Abstract of the United States, 1979* (Washington D.C.: Government Printing Office, 1979), p. 601; *Statistical Abstract of the United States, 1980*, p. 603; and Department of Energy, *Monthly Energy Review*, August, 1981, p. 6.

exceed current use by more than about 25 percent. With a more determined effort, energy consumption need not increase by more than about 10 to 15 percent. At the same time, total real GNP could increase sharply to nearly double today's level. . . .

Second, technology is available to increase U.S. energy productivity in an economical manner. More efficient buildings can save the homeowner several dollars for every dollar judiciously invested in energy-conserving features. By selecting vehicles with more efficient designs, automobile users can economically reduce fuel costs by 50 percent or more. A wide variety of conservation technologies available to industry today can often provide a 30 to 50 percent per year return on investment.[35]

A ROLE FOR GOVERNMENT?

In November 1978 President Carter signed the **National Energy Act** into law. This legislation is really a composite of the following five acts:

1. The *Public Utility Regulatory Policies Act*, which provides methods for encouraging pub-

35. Ibid., pp. 327–328.

TABLE 35–8 Growth Rate of Energy Production by Source of Energy, 1950–1980

Energy Source	Growth Rate of Production (Percent)				
	1950–1960	1960–1970	1970–1978	1978–1979	1979–1980
Total production	1.9	4.1	−0.3	2.6	1.3
Crude oil	2.7	3.2	−1.3	−2.2	0.8
Natural gas liquids	5.9	5.6	−1.3	5.8	−1.0
Natural gas[a]	7.4	5.5	−1.5	−1.6	−1.6
Coal	−2.7	3.1	.1	15.8	6.2
Nuclear power	—[b]	37.4	37.0	−7.7	−1.6
Hydropower	1.3	5.1	1.5	0.0	−1.4
Geothermal and other	—[b]	—[b]	17.0	50.0	28.1

[a]Dry marketed gas.

[b]Not available.

Source: U.S. Department of Commerce, Bureau of the Census, "Table 1011: Energy Production and Consumption—Annual Growth Rates by Type of Fuel: 1950–1978," *Statistical Abstract of the United States, 1979* (Washington, D.C.: Government Printing Office, 1979), p. 601; *Statistical Abstract of the United States, 1980*, p. 603; and Department of Energy, *Monthly Energy Review*, August, 1981, p. 4.

lic utility rate revisions to reflect replacement costs, a program to expedite the production of electricity at small dams, and other measures to improve conservation of energy and efficiency in energy production.

2. The *Energy Tax Act*, which provides for tax credits for energy conservation and for solar energy.

3. The *National Energy Conservation Policy Act*, under which a variety of regulatory, grant, and loan programs were established to promote conservation.

4. The *Natural Gas Policy Act*, which provides for the gradual decontrol of the price of natural gas produced from new wells and also for other measures designed to increase natural gas production.

5. The *Powerplant and Industrial Fuel Use Act*, designed to increase the use of coal.[36]

During his energy message of April 1979 President Carter ordered the gradual decontrol of the price of oil, to occur over a two-year period. He also proposed a windfall profits tax on oil companies, and such a tax was passed by Congress in spring 1980. In later energy messages the president made additional proposals for government intervention in the market for energy.

In this section we will reexamine the general economic rationales for government intervention in the marketplace. We will see that although government may have some economically sound roles to play in the current energy situation, the powerful role of market incentives should not be ignored.

Price Regulation Revisited As pointed out in Chapter 27, the price of natural gas sold in the interstate market has been regulated for many years by the Federal Power Commission. During the 1970s the prices of crude oil and of gasoline were also regulated.

Chapter 21 indicated that regulating the price charged by a monopoly□ may actually re-

sult in an increase in the quantity produced. The same result may be obtained by regulating the price of an imperfectly competitive firm. In Figure 35–6, P_{UR} is the unregulated price and Q_{UR} is the unregulated quantity produced, because the firm will produce at the point where marginal revenue is equal to marginal cost. If a price ceiling is set so that a monopolist can earn a fair return ($P = LAC$), the regulated price will be P_R and the quantity produced will be Q_R, an amount greater than Q_{UR}.

Nevertheless, if the ceiling price is set below P_R, firms will not be able to earn a fair, or average, return. Consequently, they will cut back production and, probably, in the long run will leave the industry altogether. The producers of oil and natural gas have argued that this scenario describes their position under government controls. To some extent, their position may be supported by the fact that Exxon has purchased an electric motor company and Mobil has purchased Montgomery Ward.

In Figure 35–6, if the ceiling price is set at P_1, firms will produce only Q_{s1} units of output in the short run (assuming price is greater than or equal to short-run average variable cost), where P_1 is equal to marginal cost. However, the quantity demanded will be Q_{d1}. Thus a shortage equal to $Q_{d1} - Q_{s1}$ will develop.

The Market versus Rationing As discussed earlier in this chapter, the government has an economically justifiable role if marginal social benefits and costs are not totally reflected in the marketplace. The pollution and congestion aspects of the energy situation can be handled in a way similar to other environmental problems.

Furthermore, government has a role to play in the production of public goods or of mixed public-private goods that offer substantial third-party benefits. Mass transportation and certain kinds of research may fall into this category.

Finally, the government may also argue that monopoly profits should be regulated. How-

---

36. 95th Congress, *United States Statutes at Large: 1978*, vol. 92 (Washington, D.C.: Government Printing Office, 1979), pp. 3117–3349.

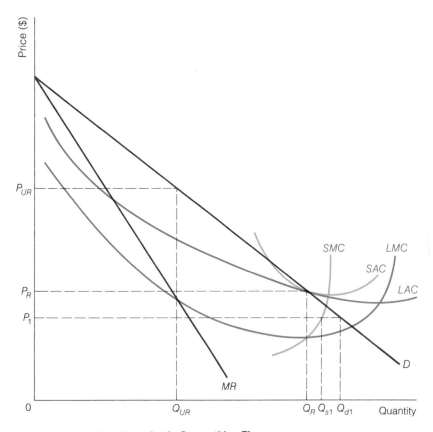

FIGURE 35–6 Price Regulation of an Imperfectly Competitive Firm

An unregulated monopoly with demand curve D, marginal revenue curve MR, long-run marginal cost curve LMC, and long-run average cost curve LAC, would choose to produce Q_{ur} units of output and charge a price equal to P_{ur}. If the government sets a price ceiling equal to P_r, so that the firm can obtain only a normal profit ($P = LAC$, as shown in Figure 21–7 in Chapter 21), the firm will produce Q_r units of output. However, suppose the ceiling price is set at P_1, and the firm has short-run marginal cost and short-run average cost curves corresponding to SMC and SAC, respectively. In this case, firms will produce only Q_{s1} units of output, the point where a horizontal line drawn through P_1 intersects SMC. However, at a price of P_1, the quantity demanded is Q_{d1} units of output. Thus, a shortage equal to $Q_{d1} - Q_{s1}$ will develop. Note also that at P_1, the firm is incurring an economic loss, since P_1 is less than short-run (and long-run) average cost at Q_{s1}. Thus, in the long run, if the ceiling price is not raised to a higher level this firm will leave the industry.

ever, the economic justification for instituting a price ceiling so low that shortages develop is not clear. Those in favor of this type of ceiling usually favor a rationing system to deal with the shortages. The advantage of such a system is that prices are kept low for consumers, particularly for those with low incomes.

The disadvantages of a price ceiling–rationing system are many. First, if suppliers are not allowed to make a fair return, they will prob-

ably eventually leave the industry unless they are given subsidy payments. Second, if a white (legal) market is not allowed to operate, a black (illegal) market usually develops for the rationing coupons. Third, if prices are set without regard to marginal social benefit and marginal social cost, resources are likely to be misallocated. Fourth, the bureaucracy created to administer a rationing program can become quite costly. In fact, Figure 35–7 depicts a

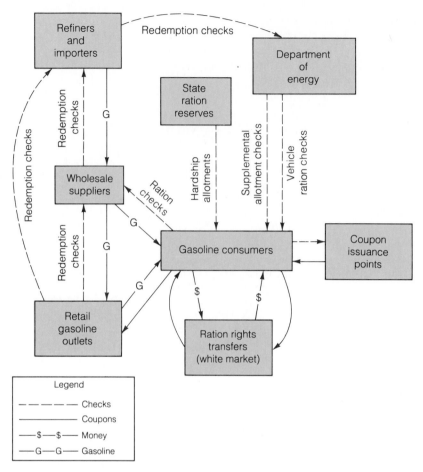

FIGURE 35–7 **"Simplified" Diagram of a Gasoline Rationing System**

Source: Department of Energy.

"simplified" diagram drawn by the Department of Energy to explain how a gasoline rationing system would work.

Market incentives tempered by controls to prevent clearly excessive monopoly profits may yet be the solution to the energy crisis. As a result of rising energy prices, firms and cities have an incentive to develop alternate sources of power. Windmills are once more being used as a source of energy.[37] Small dams

are becoming economically feasible sources of electricity.[38] General Motors and other firms are making progress in the development of an electric car.[39] Currently, much research is also being done on obtaining oil from plants.[40] New techniques of obtaining oil and natural gas

37. See "Welcome to 'The Monster,' " *Newsweek*, July 23, 1979, p. 66.

38. See "Praise for Faint Dams," *Newsweek*, September 17, 1979, pp. 79–80.

39. See "An Electric Car in GM's Future?" *Newsweek*, October 8, 1979, p. 79.

40. See "Science Plants an Oil Crop," *Newsweek*, March 24, 1980, p. 72.

from the ground are also being developed.[41]

The power of the market is clearly illustrated by the fact that the U.S. auto industry was dragging its feet in meeting federal fuel economy standards in spring 1979. By spring 1980, as gasoline prices spiraled upward and consumer tastes changed to small cars, the federal standards became unimportant; the fuel economy standards demanded by the market were even higher![42]

New sources of energy can and will be found as the market provides incentives. In addition, firms and individuals will switch to more energy efficient machines when there are obvious private economic benefits from doing so. When private and social objectives diverge, government intervention in the marketplace may be appropriate. However, recent experience with the energy problem clearly points to the importance of allowing the market to function.

SUMMARY

1. This chapter has discussed the problem of environmental pollution and the related issue of energy consumption and production. When firms or consumers are allowed to emit polluting discharges but are not required to pay for cleaning up the environment, they impose an external social cost on society. In this case, because a firm's marginal cost will understate the actual marginal social cost of producing its good or service, the firm may maximize its profit by producing too much of the good from a social point of view.

2. The reduction of pollution has an external social benefit. People benefit through the actions others take to reduce pollution. In this type of situation there is an incentive to let the other guy do it.

3. Pollution should be abated (reduced) up to the point where the marginal social benefit of further reductions in pollution is equal to their marginal

social cost. An even greater abatement of pollution would only reduce social welfare.

4. Legislation in the United States concerning environmental pollution falls into the following four categories: (1) laws dealing with water pollution, (2) laws dealing with air pollution, (3) laws dealing with solid waste disposal, and (4) general laws pertaining to the environment. The Water Pollution Control Act (1956) marked the federal government's first comprehensive attempt in recent years to deal with the problem of pollution. Since 1956 laws have also been enacted with regard to air pollution and solid waste disposal. These laws have been amended several times, usually becoming more restrictive with regard to the emission of pollutants.

5. Some progress in pollution abatement was made during the 1970s, but there is room for more improvement. Water pollution comes from two general types of sources—point and nonpoint. Point sources discharge into a body of water directly through a pipe or ditch. Nonpoint sources include urban runoff, construction, mining, agriculture, irrigation return flows, solid waste disposal, and individual sewage disposal. According to the Council on Environmental Quality, some two-thirds of the lakes in the United States may have pollution problems.

6. The federal government classifies the overall quality of air in a particular area according to a pollution standard index value that is assigned on the basis of the levels of five major air pollutants: total suspended particulates, sulphur dioxide, carbon monoxide, ozone, and nitrogen dioxide. According to the 1980 report of the Council on Environmental Quality, combined data from forty major metropolitan areas indicated that the number of unhealthful days declined by 18 percent between 1974 and 1978. The number of very unhealthful days declined by 32 percent between 1974 and 1977.

7. During 1978 municipal solid waste totaled about 154 million tons, or about 1,400 pounds per person. More progress can be made in the areas of recycling of solid wastes and of trash incineration for energy.

8. Three policies to promote pollution abatement are direct regulation, subsidies, and effluent fees. Direct regulation refers to the passage of laws prohibiting discharges of pollutants above a particular rate. Although direct regulation has been successful to some extent in reducing pollution in the past, it

---

41. See, for example, "Higher Oil Prices, Deeper Drilling," *Newsweek*, March 31, 1980, p. 60.

42. "U.S. Autos: Losing a Big Segment of the Market— Forever?" *Business Week*, March 24, 1980, pp. 78–80.

has some disadvantages. First of all, the regulations can become unmanageably complex if varying costs of compliance for different firms are taken into account. If they are not, a policy of direct regulation may be quite costly. Second, when all firms are required to keep polluting discharges down to a particular level, there is no economic incentive for further abatement of pollution.

9. A second type of policy is a subsidy to those who purchase pollution abatement equipment. However, if the subsidy is less than the entire cost of such equipment, it may not give businesses any incentive to reduce pollution. Furthermore, businesses have no incentives to consider other methods of pollution abatement, such as changing the type of fuel they use. Finally, the question arises as to whether the burden of pollution abatement should be borne by taxpayers as a whole or by those responsible for the pollution.

10. The third type of policy, that of an effluent fee based on the rate discharge of pollutants, is favored by most economists. Under such a system a firm is free to choose the most cost-effective method of pollution control or to pay the effluent fee if a reduction in pollution can be obtained only at very high cost. If the fee schedules are established correctly, the firm's marginal cost should more closely approximate marginal social cost. An effluent fee also encourages firms to develop new, lower-cost methods of pollution abatement. Nevertheless, direct regulation may be preferred for very hazardous substances.

11. The energy crisis was brought on by a more rapid rate of growth of energy consumption than of energy production and by the policies of OPEC. The government has an economically justifiable role to play in connection with third-party benefits and costs of energy related products and with respect to excessive monopoly profits. However, given sufficient market incentives, producers and consumers will probably find a solution to the energy dilemma.

IMPORTANT TERMS AND CONCEPTS

Externalities
Water Pollution
   Control Act (1956)
Clean Air Act (1963)
Solid Waste Disposal
   Act (1965)
National
   Environmental
   Policy Act (1969)
Point discharges

Nonpoint discharges
Pollution standard
   index (PSI)
Direct regulation
Effluent fee
National Energy Act
   (1978)

QUESTIONS AND PROBLEMS

1. What is meant by an "optimal" level of pollution?

2. Explain why pollution can represent an external cost. In what way does its reduction represent an external benefit?

3. Compare and contrast the policies of direct regulation, subsidies, and effluent fees. Use diagrams to illustrate your answer.

4. Describe and justify the energy program that you would favor if you were president of the United States.

5. How did the energy crisis develop?

THE OLD
MILLSTREAM COST
275 JOBS

So cautioned a blunt staff memo to George McGovern when he was campaigning for the Presidency in New Hampshire, and it was sound advice. For northern New Hampshire is caught in the environmental nutcracker: the new demand to restore its craggy beauty is colliding with the poverty of its troubled, antiquated industry. And nowhere is the clash more dramatic than in Lincoln, a town of 1,300 that lost its only factory to the environmental movement two months ago.

Under several managements, the small pulp and paper mill had

been operating in Lincoln, on the Pemigewasset River, for 66 years—and ironically, it was the first paper mill in New Hampshire to try to meet all the antipollution requirements set by the state legislature in a series of laws beginning in 1959. Under the ownership of Marcal Manufacturing Co., the plant put in $5 million worth of pollution-abatement equipment from 1967 to 1969. But the pulp-cleanup process never worked perfectly, and for weeks at a time untreated waste poured into the river. The mill had labor trouble, too. On the eve of a strike in 1970, Marcal declared bankruptcy and shut down the plant.

The mill lay idle for a year while John Potter and Hammond

Robertson, two former executives for another paper company, negotiated with Marcal and the state pollution commission. They decided to buy the mill, according to Robertson, after the commission "told us that if we operated the facility the way it was designed, with the equipment already there and replacing the steam boilers (another cleanup refinement), we'd have no problem with them or the pollution standards." Reopening the mill as the Franconia Manufacturing Co., Potter and Robertson applied to the Federal Economic Development Administration for a $2.1 million loan to pay for the new boilers. During the shutdown, however, the Pemigewasset had managed to clean itself up; the dark color and stench of the mill's "black liquor" were gone. So, when the mill reopened and pollution resumed, downstream property owners set up a vigorous protest.

The turning point came when the state's aggressive fish and game department set out caged trout in the river near the mill, and most of the fish died. Since the state's new rules somewhat vaguely said that effluent must "not be mimical to fish," further expensive cleanup was indicated. But for many Lincoln residents, who protested that the trout weren't even indigenous to the Pemigewasset, that was the last straw. "My God, I've fished there all my life," exploded one ex-mill employee. When Gov. Walter Peterson visited Lincoln to study the situation, a group of irate citizens presented him with a gallon tank of fish caught in the Pemigewasset.

Others rallied to the mill's support. Sherman Adams, former chief assistant to President Eisenhower and now, at 73, the president of a nearby ski resort and the town's leading citizen, raised the $150,000 in local pledges required as matching funds for the EDA loan. And when the company became strapped for operating funds in February after receiving no word from EDA, its employees voted to take a 20 per cent wage cut.

Nonetheless, Franconia president Potter declared bankruptcy before EDA came to a decision on the loan. "We saw the handwriting on the wall," Robertson says. "Looking back on it, we didn't have a chance." With that, Lincoln lost its only industry, and 275 employees, some of whom had worked for the mill for nearly 40 years, lost their jobs and pensions. Another 500 to 1,000 persons who had supplied the mill were cut off from their major source of business. And the town's already narrow tax base shrank substantially.

The mill might well have closed in any case; the EDA said later that its financial consultant had reported that Franconia would need an outright grant of $5 million to $6 million to stay afloat. But there was no question that the pollution issue had hastened the closing, and the town's hardship was real. "I'm too young to retire and too old to find new work," complains Joseph Mulleavey, 50, a Franconia millwright for twenty years. "I just wish the people against pollution had thought of what it all meant to the people working."

And more than a few townspeople suspect the environmentalists' motives. "They just wanted to get industry out of their way," says Maurice Boyd, 54, a former Franconia supervisor who had worked in the mill for 31 years. "There are a lot of them running all over the place buying up land, planning camps and condominiums. They're the polluters. Wait a couple of years and see how many people are crowding together up here. This was good country, but it won't last now."

With the state pouring emergency funds into Lincoln and urging light industry to move there, the town's prospects for survival are rated good. Still, Sherman Adams, himself an active environmentalist, believes that the government acted rashly: "The mill was culpable, no question about it," he declares. "But I have to say it's been an overreaction. The way things happened here, we might as well say good-by to the paper industry." And he points 50 miles northeast of Lincoln to Berlin, N.H., whose two Brown Co. mills make the Androscoggin River the state's most polluted waterway. The Androscoggin is slated for cleanup in 1974. "That is going to be a heroic battle," Adams warns, "and we're talking about 1,900 jobs, not just a few hundred as was the case here. Their time is coming."

QUESTIONS

1. What is the environmental "nutcracker" referred to in this article?
2. How does the story of the mill illustrate the benefits and costs of pollution abatement?
3. Does this article support the view that the complete elimination of pollution will maximize social welfare? Explain.
4. What do you think should have been done about the mill? Why?

C H A P T E R   36

ALTERNATIVE
ECONOMIC
SYSTEMS

THE UNDERGROUND ECONOMY, RUSSIAN STYLE

Yelizaveta Tyntareva, a lawyer living in Vilnius, Lithuania, a few years ago sold her Zhiguli car for 2,000 rubles (about $3,000). She then used that small amount of venture capital to buy so-called deficit goods, consumer articles like sunglasses and wigs that are almost always in short supply and high demand in Soviet shops. As she bought, Tyntareva also sold. Gradually she built up a stock of everything from gold rings, watches, wigs and jeans to velvet suits, umbrellas and cameras. The business prospered; she acquired a regular clientele among Baltic Sea vacationers, hired four assistants, and even set up a mail-order service. Unfortunately, though, Tyntareva was an economic criminal under tough Soviet "speculation" laws. Early this year she was arrested and sentenced to twelve years in prison. The penalty could have been death.

Tyntareva and her customers were part of the Soviet Union's thriving underground economy. This involves more than just the familiar black marketeers, dealing in Levi's and ballpoint pens, icons and caviar, who greet Western visitors around the main tourist hotels. It is, in fact, a second economy, parallel to the official state-controlled one. In a thriving permanent network, illegal and quasi-legal entrepreneurs, speculators and thieves sell hard-to-get goods and services to workers, peasants and even state officials.

The Soviets call it living na levo—*"on the left."* At its simplest, it is nothing more than passing on to the local butcher tickets for a popular soccer game or concert in return for a good cut of meat; tipping off the plumber about a shipment of shoes that is due to arrive in a shop as payment for fixing a leaking pipe; or holding down a second job as a furniture mover or apartment painter. *Na levo* can and does, however, also extend to smuggling consumer goods in from the West, running a hidden factory, stealing state-owned materials and skipping out from work on a state job to moonlight privately. . . .[It is estimated to account for about 18 percent of all consumer expenditures.]

Despite their illegality, private markets are readily visible in Moscow and other Soviet cities. The gathering place for Moscow apartment hunters is the subway stop on Leningradsky Prospekt. The place to buy women's goods, such as lipstick, lingerie and dresses, is inside the public toilet two blocks from the Bolshoi Theater. On a side street near the Moscow Planetarius, *fartsovsh-chiki* (black marketeers) have set up an underground supermarket, dealing in everything from gin to chewing gum, jeans and Western pop records. One of the hottest selling items in any market is information. Some hustlers charge one or two rubles for "a sentence." The mysterious sentence: a valuable tip-off that an item in short supply will be delivered to a certain shop the following day.

Whole industries have sprung up to service the markets on the left. Printers illicitly run off copies of scarce books, while entire hidden factories make jeans and cosmetics. Truck Drivers Nikolai Butko and Alexander Konovalov developed a very elaborate triangular trade from the Caucasus Mountain city of Krasnodar near the Black Sea. They picked up purloined steel from a state factory, delivered it to government farms in exchange for off-market tomatoes, grapes and peas, and then sold the produce in Siberia, where fresh vegetables were in short supply. . . .

Though Soviet officials are aware of the booming second economy, they generally ignore the dealings of Ivan the Terrible Capitalist. Major violators are sometimes arrested, and officers of the MVD's Administration for Combatting the Embezzlement of Socialist Property and Speculation have infiltrated the black markets. But the Kremlin grudgingly accepts the underground economy because it fills the gaps left in the inefficient Soviet system, eases shortages and makes consumers' lives bearable. Collective-farm managers admit that often the only way to meet their production targets is to buy supplies on the black market. "If they tried to shut down every illegal activity," says one Western diplomat in Moscow, "the economy would come close to collapsing and the party would face serious problems of public disorder.". . .[1]

Marx and Lenin, of course, were leftists, but not the kind described above. The Soviet system today is far from their dreams of

---

1. Excerpted from "Living Conveniently on the Left," *Time*, June 23, 1980, p. 50.

universal communism, and it functions quite differently from the way its present leaders would like it to function. Its recent failure to sustain growth has made the underground economy necessary, but one must wonder who decides which entrepreneurs will go to jail.

In this chapter, we will examine how the Soviet economy is supposed to operate and will briefly survey the economic systems of Yugoslavia, Sweden, and Great Britain as alternatives to both the Soviet system and that of the United States.

CHAPTER 36

ALTERNATIVE ECONOMIC SYSTEMS

WHAT THIS CHAPTER IS ABOUT

THE SOVIET-STYLE PLANNED SOCIALIST
  ECONOMY
Soviet Planning Process
Postwar Plans and Their Implementation
Money and Prices
"Libermanism" and Its Effects
Life in the Soviet Union
MARKET SOCIALISM IN EASTERN EUROPE
The Example of Yugoslavia
The Importance of Yugoslav Experience
WELFARE STATISM IN WESTERN CAPITALISM
The Swedish Welfare State
Britain, France, and West Germany
Planning and Western Mixed Capitalism

Chapter 2 provided a basic introduction to the field of economic systems. There, we saw that the fundamental economic questions of a society—what to produce, how to produce it, how to distribute output, and how to provide for economic growth—can be answered by reliance on three principal modes of organization: tradition, command, and the market. Although societies that arrange their economic activities according to tradition□ still exist, most modern economies can be characterized as relying primarily on command (centralized planning)□, the market, or some combination

of planning and market responses to organize production and distribution and to provide for growth.

The bulk of this book has analyzed a mixed capitalistic economic system□ (the U.S. model). Under these systems, for the most part, the means of production are privately owned, markets are heavily relied on to answer the fundamental economic questions, and government plays an active role in promoting stability and growth, supplying public goods and services, and attempting to combat social ills such as poverty and environmental decay.

In this chapter, we will examine the economic systems of some countries that are significantly different from the United States. We will focus on two main issues for each country—ownership of the means of production and degree of centralization of economic planning. The first issue is that of socialism versus capitalism; the second is that of command versus the market. We will discover that not all socialist economies are planned economies and not all capitalistic economies rely on the market to the same degree as the United States.

One additional issue that is important in the study of economic systems is the extent to which an economy provides income security and social welfare programs (health and housing programs and old age pensions, for example) for its people. The last sections of this chapter will consider the social welfare question in detail.

THE SOVIET-STYLE PLANNED SOCIALIST ECONOMY

◆

It is generally agreed that one characteristic of the Soviet economy since the 1917 Russian revolution has been an extreme system of centralized planning. It is also agreed that the Soviet economy and that of China are among the most socialistic in the world. That is, to a large extent the means of production in these countries are owned and controlled by the state, and private property is limited. Consumers are allowed to own a wide range of nondurable and durable goods, but the ownership of land, buildings, and capital goods is much more restricted. Nonetheless, Soviet peasants can own homes and small plots of land for producing vegetables or other crops, some of which they can sell outside the government systems of distribution.

SOVIET PLANNING PROCESS

After the 1917 revolution, Russia remained in turmoil until 1921–22 because of both civil war and external threats from Germany and Japan. From about 1919 until 1924 (when he died), V. I. Lenin was in virtually complete control of economic planning. During the years of civil war the government confiscated most private property and rapidly nationalized industry and transportation. People who were opposed to the various communist factions, particularly those who were opposed to the majority (the Bolsheviks, headed by Lenin), were persecuted unmercifully. The economy was in chaos. With the blessing of the 10th Congress of the Communist Party in 1921,

Lenin initiated his **New Economic Policy (NEP),** an attempt to restore the economy by reducing taxes, generally relaxing controls over industry and trade, and stimulating small-scale capitalistic production.

Although the NEP was helpful in getting Russia back on its feet economically, it was short-lived because of opposition from the left wing, led by Leon Trotsky, and because of Lenin's failing health. When Lenin died, a struggle for control of the government followed. The man who emerged as Russia's new leader was Josef Stalin, a military bureaucrat (commissar) who had been one of Lenin's early supporters.

The Five-Year Plans   Stalin, who was general secretary of the Communist Party, instituted a purge of both the leftist Trotskyites and some remaining right-wing elements. After 1928 he was in total control of the government and set out to command the economy through a highly centralized system that, for the most part, still exists.

In 1928 the state planning commission, known as **Gosplan**, produced the first national five-year plan. In 1933 it instituted a second five-year plan. Its third plan (1938) was interrupted by World War II. Its fourth, fifth, and sixth five-year plans began, respectively, in 1941, 1946, and 1951. Its seventh plan (1956) was scrapped in favor of a seven-year plan that it put into effect in 1959. From 1966 onward the plans resumed their five-year intervals.[1]

Goals of the Early Plans   In the period since 1928 the Soviet Union has been transformed from the backward, war-torn remains of a feudal society to a powerful military-industrial state. In the process it managed to survive the German invasion of World War II, and thereafter it has dominated almost all of Eastern Europe.

---

1. For a detailed discussion of the various five-year plans, see Jahangir Amuzegar, *Comparative Economics: National Priorities, Policies, and Performance* (New York: Winthrop Publishers, 1981), especially Chapter 11.

The goals of the earliest five-year plans were to reconstruct and expand the industrial sector and to collectivize and mechanize agriculture. The production of consumer goods was held to a bare minimum as resources were allocated in large part to the construction of heavy basic industry (steel mills, power plants, and machinery production) and the expansion of the raw materials and fuels sectors.

The collectivization of agriculture during the early 1930s was met with much resistance by the peasants. Large quantities of agricultural output and livestock were destroyed. Many peasants were killed, and others were transported to work in northern industrial areas or sent to prison camps in Siberia. Disruption of the agricultural sector led to widespread famine during this period.

World War II and Its Aftermath During World War II virtually all industrial production was in military hardware and supplies. The hardships suffered by the Russian people were tremendous. The destruction of productive facilities was so substantial that, after the war, planning again had to focus on reconstruction of factories as well as on expansion of capital goods output and improvement of agricultural productivity. The Soviet Union's continuing fear of the West, its wartime experience with armaments production, its domination of satellite countries in Eastern Europe, and, eventually, its political rift with China all dictated that a large share of both investment and production would continue to be in the defense industries—much to the detriment of consumers. It was not until the seven-year plan began in 1959 that much emphasis was placed on increasing the output of consumer goods.

POSTWAR PLANS AND
THEIR IMPLEMENTATION

The immediate objectives of the postwar five-year plans were reconstruction, military-industrial expansion, and improvement of agri-culture. An underlying theme in most Soviet long-range and mid-range planning has been self-sufficiency, a goal that complements the Soviet Union's strong military posture. Although the country has generally kept its trade with the West at a minimum, it has depended on the West for two major imports—technology and food.[2]

The five-year plans have stated general goals and have identified growth targets for the industry, trade, agriculture, and mining sectors. For example, the tenth five-year plan (1976–1980) called for a target growth of 24 to 28 percent in national income and 35 to 39 percent in industrial output.[3] In a quantitative sense, the five-year plans are not specific at the microeconomic level. However, in order to implement the planning process, Gosplan generates one-year plans that give the specifics of output targets and input requirements for each sector, industry, and enterprise.

An **enterprise** is the Soviet equivalent for what would be a firm in capitalistic economies. However, Soviet enterprises are owned by the state, and enterprise-level managers have little decision-making authority.

Microeconomic Planning With the overall objectives of the five-year plan serving as broad guidelines, the one-year plans get down to the difficult task of coordinating the production goals and resource requirements of all of the state enterprises. Again, Gosplan, the central authority, establishes production targets for the enterprises, based on capacity, past performance, and availability of resources. This is a monumental task, because there are hundreds of thousands of state enterprises.

Various ministries, bureaus, and agencies

---

2. Soviet foreign trade policy is discussed more thoroughly in Alan G. Gruchy, *Comparative Economic Systems* (Boston: Houghton Mifflin, 1966), pp. 758–763.

3. The plan's targets are found in 94th Congress, Second Session, *The Soviet Economy in a New Perspective: A Compendium of Papers Submitted to the Joint Economic Committee*, October 1976, p. 305.

also participate in the planning process. Information flows in both directions between Gosplan and the enterprises. Suggestions from below are allowed, as long as they are consistent with the goals of both the one- and the five-year plans. The planners draw up both production quotas and supply budgets for the enterprises, and making these two key components of the annual plan consistent with each other is one of their most difficult tasks.

Balancing Inputs and Output The key to balancing the output (production quotas) of the annual plan with the available resources is an account known as the **materials balance.** In the early stage of an annual plan this balance usually shows that there are not enough resources to attain the desired production targets. Therefore, the targets of some enterprises must be sacrificed in order to attain other targets. Obviously, the choice will depend on priorities established by both the one- and the five-year plans. The production targets of enterprises with low-priority output are reduced as resources are shifted to higher-priority uses. One U.S. economist has explained the problems faced in adjusting the materials balance as follows:

The process of "balancing" the material balances takes up much time and effort, especially since the adjustment of one balance often calls for numerous adjustments in many others. For example, if the requirements for copper initially exceed its expected availability, the amounts of copper to be allotted to various copper users may be cut back. In this case, the relative priority ratings of the users from the standpoint of national importance are involved. Alternatively, more resources may be shifted into copper production, or additional goods may be earmarked for export in order to purchase more copper abroad. These and other likely adjustments will affect material balances for goods other than copper, which in turn will affect yet others (perhaps also copper again), and so on indefinitely.[4]

Input-output analysis, which was developed by Western economists—particularly Nobel Prize winning economist Wassily Leontief, a Russian-born American—and popularized during the 1950s and 1960s, has been used by Soviet planners to help solve their materials balance problems.

Input-output analysis uses matrix algebra to describe the linkages between various industries in an economy and to determine the input and output levels of each industry that are required for any given level of aggregate output or GNP.

Basically, an input-output model is a table (or matrix) consisting of a set of rows and columns, the rows showing each industry's output and the columns showing each industry's input requirements. The table can cover as many as a thousand industries. The input and output linkages between industries depend on the structure of the model, and the solutions for each industry are obtained simultaneously as the model is solved by an electronic computer.

Input-output analysis has proved useful to Soviet planners at the industry level. However, it is virtually impossible for them to employ the technique for highly detailed annual planning because of the information and computing requirements of a model that would reach down to the enterprise level.[5] Thus annual plans are subject to a good deal of trial-and-error adjustments in targets and resource allocation as bottlenecks occur in the system. Priorities again come into play, and the output of low priority industries is sacrificed to achieve the targets for higher-priority industries. In the Soviet Union this has often meant sacrificing consumer goods to increase the output of armaments, spacecraft, or capital goods.

---

4. Gregory Grossman, *Economic Systems* (Englewood Cliffs, N.J.: Prentice-Hall, 1967), p. 85.

5. Richard L. Carson, *Comparative Economic Systems* (New York: Macmillan, 1973), especially Chapter 8.

MONEY AND PRICES

In the Soviet system there are basically two types of money—*currency*, which is the ruble that the worker receives as wages or salary, and *bank money*, which consists of accounting entries that keep track of the receipts and payments of state-owned enterprises. All of this is handled by the state bank, Gosbank. The enterprise accounts at the Gosbank provide a means for keeping track of how well each enterprise is meeting the targets of the annual plan.

For the system to work, there must be prices, not only for consumer goods but also for the inputs bought by state enterprises from one another. In general, input prices are established by adding up the wage value of the items produced in each enterprise (a sort of value-added approach)□ based on the Marxian labor theory of value) and tacking on a percentage of profit (surplus value) for the enterprise. The latter turns out to be an important source of state revenue.[6]

One notable feature of the Soviet planning process is a general lack of concern for consumer demand. The consumer goods mix that reaches the retail sector where the ordinary person spends hard-earned rubles on life's necessities (perhaps even a few luxuries) is a function of resource availabilities, plant capacities, and, above all, the plan and how well it is working. Thus the Soviet consumer often finds surpluses of goods that few people want and shortages of goods that everyone wants.

In this setting, prices are used as a way of rationing the available supplies of goods to the consumers who want them. Goods that are produced in overabundance are low priced, and goods that are scarce are high priced. In short, prices bring the quantity demanded into line with the relatively fixed short-run output of the producing sector. They do not reflect the costs of production in any systematic way. In fact, the difference between what the enterprise receives for a unit of output and the price tag the consumer finds on that same unit is made up of a **turnover tax.** A high turnover tax is charged on items that are scarce in relation to consumer demand for them, and a low turnover tax is charged on goods that are overproduced in relation to demand.

The retail pricing system based on the turnover tax has three results. First, it affects the quantity demanded in whatever way the government wants to manipulate it. Second, it serves as a major source of government revenue. Third, it is a guide to discrepancies between producer performance and consumer demand and may lead to some realignment of targets in future plans. The last result is tentative because politics, rather than consumer demand, is likely to have the most impact on planning. For example, the existence of a high turnover tax on automobiles probably would not lead to an increase in automobile production if such a move would curtail the production of military tanks.

"LIBERMANISM" AND ITS EFFECTS

The failure of the Soviet planning system to coordinate the linkages between industries (frequent shortages or gluts of capital□ goods or to coordinate consumer goods output with final demand led to a series of modest reforms in the period following 1965. The term **Libermanism** has been attached to these reforms because they were strongly advocated by a Soviet economist named Evsey Liberman. The Liberman reforms constitute more of a step toward decentralization of planning than toward market determination of prices or the allocation of resources. In fact, the principal changes have been to give management more discretion at the enterprise level and to provide a "profit motive" in the form of bonuses to exceptionally successful state enterprises.

Most observers believe that these reforms have not been sufficient to overcome the coor-

---

6. Soviet price policy is discussed more thoroughly in Amuzegar, *Comparative Economics*, pp. 280–282.

dination problems that have plagued Soviet planning.[7] However, greater reliance on enterprise-level planning and incentive programs for managers and workers has met with some significant success in certain Eastern European countries, some of which have higher per-capita incomes then does the Soviet Union itself. In fact, one such country, Yugoslavia, has combined enterprise-level planning with worker initiatives and relatively free markets to form a notably successful example of what is now called market socialism.

Under **market socialism** the means of production are publicly owned, but a system of prices approximating a free market is relied on to organize production and distribution.

The Soviet Union is far from achieving market socialism. However, it is searching for some new answers to its persistent problems in production and distribution.

LIFE IN THE SOVIET UNION

Although the Soviet Union has a population significantly larger than that of the United States, its 1979 GNP was only about 60 percent of the U.S. GNP. That made it second-ranking (the United States is first) in terms of output in the world. However, its per capita GNP ($5,700) was slightly more than half that of the United States.[8] This figure placed it among the low-income, developed countries (see Table 32–1).

To some extent, the per capita GNP figure may overstate the well-being of the average Russian, because a large proportion of the country's annual output consists of armaments and capital goods. In addition, the frequent

shortages of goods can make shopping for clothes and food a traumatic experience. As one Moscow-based U.S. journalist put it:

The stores are always out of something, low on something else, sometimes rationing flour, meat, or butter. As the lines grow longer, the mood grows sour. Someone tries to jump a place. "Get back! Don't think you're special!" protests the chorus.
. . .
The Soviet Union has one of the industrialized world's worst distribution and retail trade systems. Thus, this spring there are no sheets, underwear, or children's shirts. "We have money but nothing to buy," is a refrain of everyday Soviet life.[9]

A complete picture of the economic side of life in the Soviet Union, however, must include the country's adherence to the idea that all citizens should have access to the economic necessities of life. Thus Soviet citizens have free medical and dental care, subsidized housing, low-cost public transportation, and free public education. Despite the problems in the agricultural sector, per capita food consumption is estimated to have doubled between 1951 and 1980. In addition, within the urban-industrial sector, there is labor mobility. In fact, this mobility became something of a problem after the 1965 reforms, because enterprises began bidding against each other for the most talented technicians and workers.

The Russian people have witnessed impressive growth in their country's power and in their own general well-being since World War II. The fruits of this progress have been unevenly distributed between the urban-industrial sector and the agricultural sector, however. In the rural areas the standard of living is much lower than it is in the cities. Furthermore, regional disparities in income and public services are substantial. In recent years, growth has slowed to a crawl; yet the people continue to have rising expectations. All these factors will make the next decade a critical one for the Soviet economy.

---

7. John E. Elliott, *Comparative Economic Systems* (Englewood Cliffs, N.J.: Prentice-Hall, 1973), pp. 505–507.

8. Amuzegar, *Comparative Economics*, pp. 154, 268.

9. "A Fortress State in Transition," *Time*, June 23, 1980, p. 23.

MARKET SOCIALISM
IN EASTERN EUROPE
◆

Soviet domination of formerly capitalistic Eastern European countries since World War II has produced a wide mixture of socialism with centralized and decentralized planning. In addition, the elimination of private property has not been as widespread in Eastern Europe as in the Soviet Union, particularly in the agricultural sector. For example, most of the agricultural output in Poland is produced on family-owned farms. In Yugoslavia, where peasants were herded into collective farms after World War II but allowed to leave them in 1953, about 85 percent of the arable land is now in private hands.[10] Small private businesses are also permitted in Yugoslavia, although there are limits on the number of non-family workers that an entrepreneur can hire.

THE EXAMPLE OF YUGOSLAVIA

Yugoslavia has become the most complete and therefore the most interesting model of market socialism that has developed in the Eastern bloc. Its industrial sector is composed mostly of **socially owned,** rather than state-owned, **enterprises.** Management in these enterprises is elected by the workers, and workers' councils participate in the decision-making process.

Prices, Profits, and Planning The profit motive is important in the operation of Yugoslavia's socially owned enterprises. In fact, workers' earnings are determined in part by the profitability of their enterprise. The enterprise negotiates prices for inputs in the resource market and establishes the price of its output in the product market. Yugoslavia still maintains central planning and produces five-

year plans, but these plans are intended more to indicate to enterprises what the expected output and input linkages will be than to establish specific targets for them.

Structural Problems The Yugoslav system of socially owned enterprises and market-established prices has several notable flaws. First, managers of the large enterprises may realize that they have considerable monopoly power. Thus they may maximize enterprise profit by restricting output, thereby causing prices to go higher than they would in a competitive market. Workers may go along with this strategy, because they participate in the profit. In addition, although the profit incentive may lead to high worker productivity, it discourages increasing the number of workers, because more workers may mean less profit per worker. The same forces may discourage an enterprise from investing in new capacity or spinning off a new enterprise that could eventually become a rival in the market.

Because of the problems inherent in the Yugoslav system of market socialism, the government at times has had to resort to extensive price controls. It also controls workers' earnings in order to keep from developing an overly large disparity in incomes between those who work for very profitable enterprises and those who do not. (Profit, after all, depends in part on the demand side of the market—something over which the worker has no influence.) In addition, it directs the investment process by taxing away a portion of the profits of enterprises and allocating investment funds to lagging sectors or regions. A particular worker group, or "commune," might be chosen to establish a new enterprise with government allocated funds.

Because Yugoslavia is market oriented and because it trades with the West more than other Eastern bloc nations do, the Yugoslav economy does have business cycles.◻ In fact, the phenomenon of stagflation that has plagued the United States, Great Britain, and, more recently, even West Germany, is no stranger to Yugoslavia.

---

10. Amuzegar, *Comparative Economics*, pp. 334–335; and Grossman, *Economic Systems*, p. 100.

TABLE 36–1 Prices and Gross Product in Yugoslavia, 1974–1977 (Product in Billions of Dinars)

	1974	1975	1976	1977	1978
Price index (1970 = 100)	194	245	270	310	336
Gross product:					
Current prices	407	503	593	734	842
1970 prices	210	205	219	237	251
Percent change in real gross product	(2.3)	6.8	8.2	5.8	

Source: *United Nations Monthly Bulletin of Statistics*, October 1979, p. 192, and June 1981, p. 166; and U.S. Department of Commerce, Bureau of the Census, *Statistical Abstract of the United States, 1979* (Washington, D.C.: Government Printing Office, 1979), p. 900, and 1980, p. 907.

In addition to inflationary recession in the urban-industrial sector, Yugoslavia has had to battle social unrest caused by a phenomenon it shares not only with the industrialized nations but also with the less developed countries: unemployment. Yugoslavia's unemployment is aggravated by the migration of unskilled villagers from the backward areas of the country to the modern regions. These people flow into the urban areas more quickly than the socially owned enterprises or capitalistic small businesses can absorb them. Thus the state is engaged in a continuous struggle to provide both employment and social services for the new arrivals to the urban labor force.

Growth The unique structure of Yugoslav market socialism might not have attracted so much worldwide interest if the country had failed to achieve economic growth. However, despite its problems of inflation, unemployment, and business cycles, the country's economy has posted an admirable record of growth. Between 1954 and 1970 Yugoslavia's real GNP grew at a rate of 8.5 to 9.5 percent per year. From 1970 to 1974 the growth rate was about 7.5 percent per year.[11] The growth rates from 1974 to 1978 are shown in Table 36–1. Except for a recession in 1974–75, growth has continued to be impressive. Furthermore, although U.S. foreign aid contrib-

uted importantly to Yugoslavia's successes in the 1950s and 1960s, after 1965 U.S. aid slowed to a trickle; yet, Yugoslavia continued its remarkable growth. Since 1979, however, inflation and balance-of-payments deficits have plagued the economy, and in 1981 the International Monetary Fund approved a loan of $2.5 billion to Yugoslavia to help stabilize its economy and restructure its supply side toward increased exports.[12]

IMPORTANCE OF THE YUGOSLAV EXPERIENCE

Today the Yugoslav experience remains important because other socialist countries have shown interest in similar systems of market orientation and worker incentives.[13] In Poland, workers have made it abundantly clear that they want more voice in economic decision making. In China, as one writer has put it, "the economy is to be reformed along lines already pioneered with a good deal of success in revisionist Eastern Europe."[14] Finally, even in the Western capitalistic countries, including the United States, there have been recent

---

11. Growth rates are based on data from the United Nations and the Organization for Economic Cooperation and Development.

12. "IMF Approves Loan to Yugoslavia of $2.1 Billion," *Wall Street Journal*, February 2, 1981, p. 20.

13. A reform movement in Czechoslovakia was crushed in 1968 by an invasion of Soviet and East European satellite armies.

14. David Bonavia, "China Changes Course," *World Press Review*, December 1980, p. 25.

movements toward and experiments with worker participation in the managerial ‑process. There is good reason to believe that these trends will continue in both the East and the West.

WELFARE STATISM IN WESTERN CAPITALISM

◆

Some features of the socialist economies have developed in the Western capitalistic economies, not because of ideological shifts toward government ownership of industry but because governments have taken the responsibility for maintaining an adequate standard of living for their citizens. These features are basically:

1. Widespread availability of income maintenance, health, and social service programs for citizens.
2. Increased government planning and intervention in the economy.
3. Nationalization of industries, particularly of those that are declining and that might fail under private ownership.

All three of these features are geared toward ensuring that able people will have jobs, that everyone's income will be sufficient to meet basic human needs, that health care and education will be widely available, and that economic fluctuations will not be large. In general, these conditions are found in what have come to be known as welfare states.

In a **welfare state** high priority is placed on the elimination of economic hardships and social ills such as poverty, unemployment, lack of education, inadequate health care, and general personal or family distress.

Virtually all socialist or communist nations are professed welfare states. However, some of them (China is a prime example) have thus far had to settle for the widespread provision of a rather low, but tolerable, standard of living for all citizens.

In the West, welfare statism has become almost synonymous with socialism, even though the countries most representative of the ideals of the welfare state are not those in which most of the means of production are owned by the state. Today, the most advanced forms of the welfare state are found in the Scandinavian countries. Sweden is the largest and richest country in this group, and, until recently, approximately 90 percent of Sweden's industry was owned by firms in the private sector.

THE SWEDISH WELFARE STATE

In the nineteenth century Sweden was a poor country, and large numbers of Swedes emigrated to the United States in search of a better life. The industrial revolution came late in Sweden, and it came at a time when the government was already beginning to establish programs to relieve the economic and social hardships of the poorest classes of citizens. In the first quarter of the present century various political parties, both nonsocialist and socialist, were in favor of improving the welfare system, which consisted mainly of relief for the poor, public health and hospital services, and aid to the unemployed, aged, and infirm.

The social welfare system in Sweden was broadly expanded after the Social Democrats became the leading political party in 1929. One expert on economic systems has described the period between 1929 and World War II in Sweden and other Scandinavian countries as follows:

This new era was marked by a shift from making provision for the harsh consequences of private economic activity to a more preventive approach that attempted to remove the causes of poverty, poor family living conditions, and other types of human distress. The new full-employment policy sought to maintain the incomes of industrial workers, fishermen, and farmers. The coverage of pension schemes, health insurance, and other forms of social insurance was enlarged, social security benefits were increased, and a more vigorous housing program was instituted.[15]

In the period since World War II the Swedish welfare system has become even more comprehensive, and Sweden has been characterized as a land of "cradle to grave" social security.

Elements of the Welfare System The basic ingredients of the social welfare system in Sweden are family assistance and housing programs, unemployment benefits, compulsory health insurance, and old-age pensions. Each of these programs is comprehensive and competently administered. Family assistance includes income supplements (child allowances), maternity benefits, a children's health service, nurseries and day-care centers, free holiday camps, free or subsidized domestic help for mothers or families caring for sick or elderly persons, and a wide range of post-secondary educational benefits, including grants, scholarships, and travel assistance. The family housing program is broad-based and provides adequate housing for single people and pensioners as well as for families. There are building cooperatives, subsidized private contractors, and subsidized rental and purchase-loan plans.

In Sweden the system of unemployment benefits includes not only financial support but also retraining of displaced workers and relocation allowances for workers who must move to accept new jobs. The state will even purchase a worker's house at fair market value in order to facilitate relocation. A public unemployment service plays a large role in matching workers with available jobs.

In the Scandinavian countries the health and old-age insurance programs are usually compulsory. They also require sizable financial contributions by both workers and employers. The national health system in Sweden

is excellent and has never been as controversial as the British system. This is probably because the country has a long history of regulation of the medical profession and state ownership of hospitals. Nevertheless, physicians do have private practices, and patients can choose their own physicians. Old-age pensions in Sweden are not large but are generally considered adequate. Pensioners benefit from special housing and related services that supplement their basic incomes.

Recent Problems and Issues Sweden's welfare state has virtually eliminated poverty and has provided its people with a per capita GNP exceeding that of the United States. The country has had remarkable success in keeping unemployment low—generally at 2 to 3 percent of the labor force. However, it frequently has high rates of inflation, and taxes have reached high levels. (One result of the high taxes is that the Swedes have one of the most nearly equal distributions of income in the world.)

Besides having to put up with inflation and high taxes, Swedes are now seeing their export industries, which have been a mainstay of the economy, disrupted by a loss of international competitiveness. This change is attributable in part to Sweden's higher than average dependence on imported oil. In fact, at the onset of the oil crisis, Sweden's per capita consumption of imported oil was the highest in the world. As the export industries became more troubled, the balance of payments went into deficit. In addition, the government was forced to increase deficit spending to maintain its full employment policy. Of course, the latter also increased inflationary pressure.

In 1976 the Social Democrats were defeated at the polls, and Sweden had its first nonsocialist leadership in forty-four years. To some extent this defeat was attributable to the Social Democrats' pro–nuclear power stance. However, there were other underlying problems as well. For example, some Swedes believe that the bureaucracy had become too cumbersome and that a system designed to gradually turn private factories into worker-owned enter-

15. Gruchy, *Comparative Economic Systems*, pp. 423–424.

prises might accom₁ ʏy ·urther Social Democratic rule. Under this system, known as the **Meidner plan,** 20 percent of a firm's annual profits would be handed over to the trade unions in the form of shares. The unions would eventually become majority shareholders.

Despite the apparent rejection of the Meidner plan and the installation of a somewhat more conservative government, Sweden has had to step up its government participation in industry since 1976. By 1981 all privately owned shipyards were merged into a state-owned enterprise that the Social Democrats had created earlier when they had nationalized one firm. The government recently has given investment subsidies to the specialty steels sector and has partially nationalized basic steel. According to one source, the state and semi-state share of the industrial payroll doubled between 1976 and 1981.[16] Thus, whereas the Sweden of the past was a welfare state based on capitalistic production and government emphasis on macroeconomic and sectoral planning, the Sweden of the future may see much more government involvement at the enterprise level.

BRITAIN, FRANCE, AND WEST GERMANY

The larger, highly industrialized countries of Western Europe—Great Britain, France, and West Germany—all operate under systems of mixed capitalism with substantial social welfare programs. In fact, most of the features of the Scandinavian welfare state are found in these countries. Two of them, France and West Germany, have enjoyed high rates of economic growth and low rates of unemployment since the post–World War II period of reconstruction. Britain, however, has had a poor record of economic performance. Before World War II Britain had a per capita income almost twice that of France or Germany. Today, the situation is almost exactly the reverse.

The British Disease Britain's slump has been so long and its crises so recurrent that its economic decline has come to be known as the **British disease** or the British malaise. The standard of living has actually been falling in the United Kingdom at the same time that it has been rising on the continent, in East Europe, in much of Asia, and in many LDCs. How could this have happened in the land of Adam Smith, Alfred Marshall, and John Maynard Keynes? How could the country with the most celebrated tradition of economic analysis in the world turn in such a poor economic performance?

Conservatives in Britain and elsewhere have attributed the British disease to the welfare state and to socialism in general. The problem with this explanation is that if we look at both the social welfare system and the extent of nationalization of industry, the British economy does not seem to differ markedly from that of France or West Germany, its fast-growing neighbors. We have already seen that cradle to grave social security exists in both of the latter countries.

In France the government owns public utilities (gas, water, electricity, and coal), news and communications media, the largest commercial banks, most of the insurance industry, the largest automobile firm, the French line of ocean shipping, Air France, and part of the petroleum refining industry. In fact, the French government has a complete monopoly on natural gas, coal, and mining. In West Germany the government owns and operates the railroads, most transportation and communications facilities, and the public utilities. In addition, it has substantial investments in shipbuilding, coal, steel, and the aluminum industry. Provincial governments in Germany also own hundreds of enterprises.[17]

These facts suggest that simplistic capitalism versus socialism arguments will not ex-

---

16. Andrew Boyd, "Sweden's New Course," *World Press Review*, February 1981, pp. 31–33.

17. Amuzegar, *Comparative Economics*, p. 151.

plain the British disease. It is necessary to look at how the British economy has been managed and what negative economic and political forces or events have intervened in its postwar history. Several important facts emerge from such an analysis.

First, British politics has been characterized by a continual rift between the Labor Party and the Conservative Party. The Labor Party is supported by a loose confederation of unions, known as the Trade Unions Congress. The Conservatives are supported by the Confederation of British Industry (CBI). There is considerable labor-management strife, which carries over into the political arena. Thus government has swung back and forth from Labor to Conservative over the postwar period.

Neither the Labor nor the Conservative governments have been adept at economic planning, and both have attempted to solve labor problems, internal social strife, and regional problems through income redistribution rather than through policies to increase productivity and output. In addition, labor has resisted changes that could have increased productivity, and investment has been depressed by both labor's attitudes and the redistribution policy that favors consumption. Domestic policy has been highly inflationary during a period in which inflation, until recently, was not found among the country's trading partners. This worsened Britain's export position (toward which the economy is highly geared) at a time when its overseas empire was deteriorating and new competition was increasing from Japan and the LDCs.

The problem with the nationalized industries (transportation and communications, coal, steel, utilities, and part of oil and gas, as well as numerous services) probably has more to do with how they have been managed than with the simple fact of nationalization. In general, they have been the first to give in to labor's demands, and they are characterized by excessive bureaucracy and a ban against diversification of activities. In addition, they have been relatively independent from overall government policy. Thus, they have been able

to disregard the monetary and fiscal efforts of the central government. They are privileged borrowers, and many of them exercise monopoly power in setting rates and prices. Finally, they often benefit from direct government subsidies. In short, it is likely that the British have demanded less efficiency from state-owned enterprises than have the French or the Germans.

The Thatcher Government In 1979 a new Conservative government, led by Prime Minister Margaret Thatcher, promised to cut income taxes, reduce inflation, restore incentives for workers and investors, and relate public spending to the prospects for growth.[18] The new government's program got off to a bad start in 1979 and 1980. Income taxes were cut, but sales and gasoline taxes were sharply increased. Interest rates climbed from about 12 percent to over 20 percent. The rate of inflation was 10.1 percent when Thatcher took office, but it rose to 21.9 percent by May 1980.[19] The nationalized industries continued along their old path of excessive wage increases and government subsidies.

In early 1981 the inflation rate was down to about 12 percent, but unemployment was about 9 percent, the worst it had been since the Great Depression. Many British economists believed the recession would grow deeper, and the Confederation of British Industry simply reported that "things were getting worse more slowly" than in 1980. The CBI announced that it was preparing to draw up a five-year plan for the economy to indicate the direction it should take in order to "help us improve our investment and competitiveness, to modernize, and to develop new products and new markets."[20] Apparently, this

---

18. *The Government's Expenditure Plans* (London: Her Majesty's Stationery Office, 1979).

19. "The British Experiment Shows How Not to Do It," *Business Week*, December 1, 1980, p. 107.

20. "Business Carps over Thatcher Policies, Putting Its Spokesman on a Tightrope," *Wall Street Journal*, February 3, 1981, p. 26.

was something the government had neglected to do.

PLANNING AND WESTERN MIXED CAPITALISM

The failure of Britain to get a grip on its planning process may have contributed substantially to the British disease. In fact, this is one respect in which the British system differs significantly from that of France and, to some extent, that of West Germany. French planning is more comprehensive than that of West Germany, and the French approach has come to be called **indicative planning.** It involves a great deal of cooperation and sharing of information on targets and capabilities among government planners, public and private enterprises, agriculture, and labor. Once a medium-term plan is settled on, each interest group is supposed to adhere to it voluntarily. If things do not go quite according to the plan, the government may choose to use taxes, subsidies, or other policies to elicit the economic response deemed appropriate.

The Western mixed capitalistic nations and even Japan have increased their interest in and reliance on central planning since World War II. Of the highly industrialized countries, only the United States does not have a mechanism for mid-range (five-to-eight-year) planning. In general, the United States has instituted central government planning only through the annual budget-making process and the negotiations between the executive branch and the legislative branch of government.[21] Input from private industry, agriculture, and labor comes primarily through lobbying and the efforts of members of Congress who represent one or another of these constituencies.

The fact that many capitalist-oriented countries have had to increase government ownership of the means of production and to use centralized planning, while the Soviet-type socialist countries have had to increase incentives for profit and to use prices and market signals to allocate resources, has led to what is known as the convergence hypothesis.

The **convergence hypothesis** holds that in their struggle to solve the fundamental economic problems of what, how, and for whom, the capitalist and socialist economies will become progressively more alike.

The convergence hypothesis is quite controversial. Experts in the West point out that the social objectives of a Soviet-type ideology (classless society, little variation in the distribution of income) are incompatible with the capitalist emphasis on personal gain and the profit motive. In the East, especially the Soviet Union, the idea of convergence is anathema. It is viewed as a propaganda device of bourgeois capitalists and is voiced only by dissidents, who are punished for holding such views. Dissident physicist Andrei Sakharov wrote in 1981 from his "internal exile" in Gorki:

My ideal is an open, pluralistic society, with an unconditional observance of the fundamental civil and political rights of man, a society with a mixed economy which would make for scientifically regulated, comprehensive progress. I have voiced the assumption that such a society ought to come about as a result of peaceful convergence of the socialist and capitalist systems. That is the main condition for saving the world from thermonuclear catastrophe.[22]

Today's capitalist and socialist economies may borrow, and even steal, ideas from each other, but how much they will really converge is open to question. Whether they will be saved from destroying each other is equally questionable.

---

21. A mid-range planning system for government agencies, known as the Planning, Programming, and Budgeting System (PPBS), was set up under the administration of President Johnson in the 1960s. Congress paid little attention to it, and it was scrapped during the Nixon administration.

---

22. "Andrei Sakharov's First Year of Internal Exile," *Wall Street Journal,* February 5, 1981, p. 32.

SUMMARY

1. While tradition, command, and the market can all perform the task of organizing the economic system of a society, modern nations generally rely primarily on command, the market, or some combination of planning and market responses to answer fundamental questions of production, distribution, and growth. Modern economies also differ significantly in the degree of state ownership of the means of production (socialism) and in the extent to which they attempt to provide income security, health care, and other social benefits for all their citizens (sometimes also called socialism but perhaps better described as welfare statism).

2. The economy of the Soviet Union, second only to that of the United States in terms of GNP, is characterized by virtually complete state ownership of the means of production and highly centralized planning. Since 1928, when the first five-year plan was instituted under the dictatorship of Josef Stalin, Gosplan, the state planning agency, has controlled production, distribution, and investment. For decades, Soviet planning emphasized the development of heavy industry and the production of capital goods and armaments while sacrificing the production of consumer goods. The agricultural sector was collectivized but only slowly modernized.

3. Soviet planning also includes the setting of annual production quotas for each state enterprise, the establishment of input prices, and the setting of retail prices for consumer goods. The key planning approach is the materials balance, which represents an attempt to coordinate the inputs and outputs of a large number of industries. Input-output analysis, a mathematical tool used by Western planners, has been applied to the materials balance problem. However, the data requirements are too large to use this type of analysis for annual plans covering all state enterprises.

4. Soviet policy on input pricing employs a cost of production approach based on the Marxist labor theory of value. A profit margin supposedly equal to the surplus value of labor is added to the output of each enterprise. Retail prices are established by adding a turnover tax to the price received by final goods producing enterprises. The rate of the turnover tax varies, because it is used to ration consumer goods among buyers. In general, the planning process shows little regard for consumer demand, and the turnover tax not only rations scarce output but also provides a large share of government revenue.

5. The Liberman reforms, instituted in 1965 and later, gave more discretion to the managers of state enterprises and attempted to improve incentives by providing bonuses and additional profit for exceptionally successful enterprises. However, Libermanism did not go far enough to solve many of the Soviet Union's resource allocation problems. Thus even today there are frequent shortages of both inputs and consumer goods. Although the Soviet Union has shown truly impressive growth since World War II, recently its economy has been stagnating and consumers have become increasingly disgruntled with the government's failure to stimulate economic growth.

6. The Soviet satellite countries of Eastern Europe have shown a great deal of interest in market socialism, a system that has reached a high level of refinement in Yugoslavia. Under market socialism in Yugoslavia, workers own socialized enterprises, elect management, and share in profits. Planning is less centralized than in the Soviet Union, and most of the agricultural sector and many small businesses are in private hands. China is experimenting with some revisions along Yugoslavian lines, especially at the enterprise level.

7. The Yugoslav system allows enterprise managers to make pricing decisions, and government planning focuses on investment. However, there have been problems with monopoly pricing and with the enterprises' failure to increase employment because of the built-in incentive to expand both total and per worker profit. The government has had to resort to price and wage controls to counteract the behavior of the enterprises. Yugoslavia trades with the West and recently has been a victim of Western-style combined inflation and unemployment and large balance-of-payments deficits, despite a record of impressive growth.

8. All Eastern bloc countries are professed welfare states, despite their provision of a barely adequate standard of living for some members of society. The notion of a welfare state that provides income security, health care, and a wide range of easily obtained social benefits for all citizens has also evolved in Western mixed capitalism. The so-called welfare state was established earliest in Scandinavia, where Sweden has provided the leading example. Until recently, about 95 percent of Swedish industry was privately owned, even though the government provided income security and such social services as subsidized medical care and housing, child and family allowances, job retraining and moving allowances, day-care centers, and old-age pensions to all residents of the country.

9. The Swedish system has worked, although it has required a high level of income taxation to provide social services to everyone. The result has been a redistribution of income that puts the mass of the country's population at about the same standard of living. Poverty has been virtually eliminated, and the country's per capita GNP has exceeded that of the United States.

10. Sweden has been willing to endure rather high rates of inflation to keep its unemployment rate typically below 3 percent. However, it recently has had economic difficulties stemming from its high per capita consumption of imported oil and a loss of competitiveness in export markets. Thus the government has found it necessary to nationalize some large industries, such as shipbuilding, to keep them from failing. In addition, the government and the electorate have so far rejected a plan that would gradually turn over the assets of private industry to the country's unions.

11. In the period since World War II the welfare state has been firmly established in the mixed capitalist countries of Great Britain, France, and West Germany. France and West Germany have experienced impressive economic growth, but the economy of Britain has been in a long-run decline. It is difficult to attribute the decline of Britain, or the British disease, entirely to the welfare state. The degree of nationalization of industry in Britain is not much different from that in France or West Germany. Britain, however, has had government instability, continual labor-management confrontation in both the nationalized and the private sectors, a deterioration of its international trade position, and a poor record of government planning.

12. Increased reliance of Western mixed capitalist economies on centralized planning and the swing toward incentives and the profit motive in the Eastern bloc have given rise to a convergence hypothesis. This hypothesis states that the two types of economies (Western capitalist and Eastern socialist) will become increasingly similar in structure as each tries new policies to solve persistent economic problems. However, it is argued that the goals of

the two groups of countries, especially with regard to differences in personal income and wealth, are too different for convergence to occur.

IMPORTANT TERMS AND CONCEPTS

New Economic Policy (NEP)
Gosplan
Enterprise
Input-output analysis
Materials balance
Turnover tax
Libermanism
Market socialism
Socially owned enterprises
Welfare state
Meidner plan
British disease
Indicative planning
Convergence hypothesis

QUESTIONS AND PROBLEMS

1. Briefly explain the fundamental economic differences between Soviet-type socialism and Western mixed capitalism. Use examples from the chapter in your answer.

2. Why has the Soviet economy not provided the broad range of consumer goods generally found in countries with similar levels of per capita GNP? To what do you attribute the periodic shortages of specific consumer goods that the country does have the capacity to produce?

3. How are input prices determined under Soviet planning? How are retail prices determined? What are the objectives of government policy in each case?

4. What is the materials balance used in Soviet planning? How is it related to Western economic analysis? Why is it so difficult to make the materials balance approach work?

5. What is Libermanism? Relate Libermanism in the Soviet Union to the Yugoslav economic system and the recent strife in Poland.

6. How is the Yugoslav economy different from that of the Soviet Union? Relate your answer to the concepts of planning, property ownership, and incentives.

7. What have been the principal problems of Yugoslav market socialism, and how are these problems related to (a) the behavior of socially-owned enterprises, and (b) trade with the West?

8. Would you say that Sweden is a socialist economy in the sense that the term is applied to Eastern bloc countries? Explain. Relate Swedish welfare statism to the concept of the welfare state in the East.

9. What has been the extent of welfare statism and nationalization of industry in Britain, France, and West Germany? How has the economic performance of these countries differed since World War II? What has caused the differences in performance?

10. Explain the convergence hypothesis and evaluate it in terms of what you have read in this chapter and what you know about the current world situation.

11. Draw a table with four columns. Use the following headings: United States, European Mixed Capitalism, Market Socialism, and Soviet-Type Socialism. Then, down the columns, compare the four systems with regard to:

a. Extent of central planning
b. Ownership of means of production
c. Establishment of prices
d. Extent of welfare statism

THE MAKING
OF A
MINSK
TRACTOR

The tractors clank down the 200-yd.-long assembly line like gigantic metal insects: 7,500 tractors a month, 90,000 a year, all bearing the trademark Belarus MTZ. Brigades of young laborers clad in work clothes or jeans swarm over each monster, slipping front axles and gear boxes into place, bolting on metal casings, attaching three or four giant wheels.

Finally, after 53 stages of manufacture, the machines lumber off the assembly line; the bright blue ones are destined for the vast farm lands of the Soviet Union, the brilliant red ones for more than 70 nations around the globe. About 3,000 of them have even found their way to the U.S.

The overriding preoccupation in any Soviet factory is fulfilling the five-year plan that has been agreed to in advance by an individual factory and the government. Says Serafim Dedkov, deputy director of the Minsk plant: "We have a five-year plan, a yearly plan and a monthly plan. If we have set the goal of 90,000 tractors in a year, that works out to roughly 330 a day. We have to work rhythmically, turning out the prescribed number every day. If we only make 100 today, we simply can't make 560 tomorrow."

Red and white banners hanging from the walls and rafters exhort the workers to strive for higher productivity. PRECISE RHYTHM, HIGH TEMPO, EXCELLENT QUALITY, says one. The portraits of outstanding workers, only slightly smaller than the pictures of morose Politburo members that adorn buildings before national holidays, line the factory's central avenue. The plant runs on two shifts from 7:40 in the morning until midnight, but the assembly line workers, whose average age is about 30, seem relaxed. At times they even stand around joking. Despite the ever constant exhortations to increase productivity, the Soviets have an easygoing attitude. Minsk employees, for example, are not required to dress in work uniforms on the shop floor.

The plant has what Dedkov calls "a fund for economic

Source: "The Making of a Minsk Tractor," *Time*, June 23, 1980, p. 53.

stimulation." The fund rewards brigades of productive workers with bonuses called the "thirteenth pay" at year's end. Inducements to greater output are also built into the wage system. Most employees of the Minsk factory are paid a piecework rate for each item they produce. The amount is determined by the quality of the work, the number of pieces turned out and whether that exceeds production norms. Dedkov claims that managers are very careful before they raise goals so that a worker does not end up receiving less pay for better work.

Should a worker feel he is not being properly compensated, he can complain to an official of his union called a *profsoyuz*. Unions are almost like state agencies; indeed the former chief of the KGB, Alexander Shelepin, was the official head of the U.S.S.R. trade union movement for many years. "The goals of management and the *profsoyuz* are the same here," says Kazimir Kaspirovich, deputy chairman of the professional union at the factory. "We have no major disagreements with management."

Almost every aspect of a Minsk employee's life is centered around his factory. The tractor plant provides schools for workers and their children, summer camps for kids and vacation cabins for adults. The factory-built "palace of culture" boasts 65 amateur theatrical groups, choirs and dance companies, and there is also a giant sports stadium.

Such extensive services and facilities are maintained at the cost of a smaller paycheck for the Soviet worker than for his American counterpart. The average wage for a 41-hour week at the Minsk plant is 205 rubles ($308) a month. But a full-course lunch in the factory cafeteria costs only 50 or 60 kopecks (75¢ to 90¢), and rent for a factory-subsidized two-room apartment, including heat, electricity, water and telephone, is a scant 12 to 15 rubles ($18 to $23) a month. Medical care is free, and outstanding workers are eligible for factory-sponsored trips to Black Sea and Baltic resorts.

Thus the incentive to keep production at high levels is strong, even away from the shop floor,

and Dedkov insists that at the Minsk factory there are no discussions about whether workers can fulfill the plan. The talk is only about ways to *overfulfill* it. "If we work well, we can build more rest centers, pioneer camps and preventive medical centers," he says. "If we don't, we must cut back. Everyone from the factory director on down works with this in mind."

QUESTIONS

1. What examples of old-line Soviet-style planning are reflected in the production of tractors at Minsk?

2. What is the system of worker incentives like at Minsk? How is it related to the reforms in Soviet planning that began in 1965?

3. How does this article reflect the welfare state aspect of Soviet socialism?

4. Suppose the demand for tractors decreases because of a slump in international trade. How do you think the managers of the Minsk factory would react?

ACKNOWLEDGMENTS (CONTINUED)

p. 393 Reprinted from the January 28, 1980, issue of *Business Week* by special permission, © 1980 by McGraw-Hill, Inc., New York, NY 10020. All rights reserved.

p. 417 Reprinted by permission of *The Wall Street Journal*, © Dow Jones & Company, Inc., 1978. All Rights Reserved.

p. 440 Reprinted by permission of *The Wall Street Journal*, © Dow Jones & Company, Inc., 1979. All Rights Reserved.

p. 471 Copyright, 1979, by Newsweek, Inc. All Rights Reserved. Reprinted by Permission.

p. 487 Reprinted from the July 24, 1978, issue of *Business Week* by special permission, © 1978 by McGraw-Hill, Inc., New York, NY 10020. All rights reserved.

p. 562 Reprinted by permission of *The Wall Street Journal*, © Dow Jones & Company, Inc., 1980. All Rights Reserved.

p. 586 Reprinted from the March 26, 1979, issue of *Business Week* by special permission, © 1979 by McGraw-Hill, Inc., New York, NY 10020. All rights reserved.

p. 609 Reprinted by permission of *The Wall Street Journal*, © Dow Jones & Company, Inc., 1979. All Rights Reserved.

p. 626 Reprinted from the July 31, 1978, issue of *Business Week* by special permission, © 1978 by McGraw-Hill, Inc., New York, NY 10020. All rights reserved.

p. 647 Reprinted from the February 6, 1978, issue of *Business Week* by special permission, © 1978 by McGraw-Hill, Inc., New York, NY 10020. All rights reserved.

p. 723 Reprinted by permission of *The Wall Street Journal*, © Dow Jones & Company, Inc., 1980. All Rights Reserved.

p. 745 Adapted from Isaiah Frank, "Reciprocity and Trade Policy of Developing Countries," *Finance and Development*, March 1978, pp. 22–23. Reprinted courtesy of International Monetary Fund and International Bank for Reconstruction and Development.

p. 770 Reprinted by permission of *The Wall Street Journal*, © Dow Jones & Company, Inc., 1978. All Rights Reserved.

p. 795 From 60 MINUTES, February 4, 1979. © CBS, Inc. 1979.

p. 829 Reprinted by permission from TIME, The Weekly Newsmagazine; Copyright Time, Inc., 1980.

p. 846 Reprinted by permission from TIME, The Weekly Newsmagazine; Copyright Time, Inc., 1980.

A P P E N D I X

INTEREST
FACTOR
TABLES

TABLE A
Future Value Interest Factor (FVIF)
($1 at *I*% for *n* years)
$FVIF = (1 + I)^n$
$FV_n = PV_0 (FVIF \ I\%, n)$

Period n	1%	2%	3%	4%	5%	6%	7%	8%	9%	10%	11%	12%	13%
0	1.000	1.000	1.000	1.000	1.000	1.000	1.000	1.000	1.000	1.000	1.000	1.000	1.000
1	1.010	1.020	1.030	1.040	1.050	1.060	1.070	1.080	1.090	1.100	1.110	1.120	1.130
2	1.020	1.040	1.061	1.082	1.102	1.124	1.145	1.166	1.186	1.210	1.232	1.254	1.277
3	1.030	1.061	1.093	1.125	1.158	1.191	1.225	1.260	1.295	1.331	1.368	1.405	1.443
4	1.041	1.082	1.126	1.170	1.216	1.262	1.311	1.360	1.412	1.464	1.518	1.574	1.630
5	1.051	1.104	1.159	1.217	1.276	1.338	1.403	1.469	1.539	1.611	1.685	1.762	1.842
6	1.062	1.126	1.194	1.265	1.340	1.419	1.501	1.587	1.677	1.772	1.870	1.974	2.082
7	1.072	1.149	1.230	1.316	1.407	1.504	1.606	1.714	1.828	1.949	2.076	2.211	2.353
8	1.083	1.172	1.267	1.369	1.477	1.594	1.718	1.851	1.993	2.144	2.305	2.476	2.658
9	1.094	1.195	1.305	1.423	1.551	1.689	1.838	1.999	2.172	2.358	2.558	2.773	3.004
10	1.105	1.219	1.344	1.480	1.629	1.791	1.967	2.159	2.367	2.594	2.839	3.106	3.395
11	1.116	1.243	1.384	1.539	1.710	1.898	2.105	2.332	2.580	2.853	3.152	3.479	3.836
12	1.127	1.268	1.426	1.601	1.796	2.012	2.252	2.518	2.813	3.138	3.498	3.896	4.335
13	1.138	1.294	1.469	1.665	1.886	2.133	2.410	2.720	3.066	3.452	3.883	4.363	4.898
14	1.149	1.319	1.513	1.732	1.980	2.261	2.579	2.937	3.342	3.797	4.310	4.887	5.535
15	1.161	1.346	1.558	1.801	2.079	2.397	2.759	3.172	3.642	4.177	4.785	5.474	6.254
16	1.173	1.373	1.605	1.873	2.183	2.540	2.952	3.426	3.970	4.595	5.311	6.130	7.067
17	1.184	1.400	1.653	1.948	2.292	2.693	3.159	3.700	4.328	5.054	5.895	6.866	7.986
18	1.196	1.428	1.702	2.026	2.407	2.854	3.380	3.996	4.717	5.560	6.544	7.690	9.024
19	1.208	1.457	1.754	2.107	2.527	3.026	3.617	4.316	5.142	6.116	7.263	8.613	10.197
20	1.220	1.486	1.806	2.191	2.653	3.207	3.870	4.661	5.604	6.728	8.062	9.646	11.523
25	1.282	1.641	2.094	2.666	3.386	4.292	5.427	6.848	8.623	10.835	13.585	17.000	21.231
30	1.348	1.811	2.427	3.243	4.322	5.743	7.612	10.063	13.268	17.449	22.892	29.960	39.116

Period n	14%	15%	16%	17%	18%	19%	20%	24%	28%	32%	36%	40%
0	1.000	1.000	1.000	1.000	1.000	1.000	1.000	1.000	1.000	1.000	1.000	1.000
1	1.140	1.150	1.160	1.170	1.180	1.190	1.200	1.240	1.280	1.320	1.360	1.400
2	1.300	1.322	1.346	1.369	1.392	1.416	1.440	1.538	1.638	1.742	1.850	1.960
3	1.482	1.521	1.561	1.602	1.643	1.685	1.728	1.907	2.067	2.300	2.515	2.744
4	1.689	1.749	1.811	1.874	1.939	2.005	2.074	2.364	2.684	3.036	3.421	3.842
5	1.925	2.011	2.100	2.192	2.288	2.386	2.488	2.932	3.436	4.007	4.653	5.378
6	2.195	2.313	2.436	2.565	2.700	2.840	2.986	3.635	4.398	5.290	6.328	7.530
7	2.502	2.660	2.826	3.001	3.185	3.379	3.583	4.508	5.629	6.983	8.605	10.541
8	2.853	3.059	3.278	3.511	3.759	4.021	4.300	5.590	7.206	9.217	11.703	14.758
9	3.252	3.518	3.803	4.108	4.435	4.785	5.160	6.931	9.223	12.166	15.917	20.661
10	3.707	4.046	4.411	4.807	5.234	5.695	6.192	8.594	11.806	16.060	21.647	28.925
11	4.226	4.652	5.117	5.624	6.176	6.777	7.430	10.657	15.112	21.199	29.439	40.496
12	4.818	5.350	5.926	6.580	7.288	8.064	8.916	13.215	19.343	27.983	40.037	56.694
13	5.492	6.153	6.886	7.699	8.599	9.596	10.699	16.386	24.759	36.937	54.451	79.372
14	6.261	7.076	7.988	9.007	10.147	11.420	12.839	20.319	31.961	48.757	74.053	111.120
15	7.138	8.137	9.266	10.539	11.974	13.590	15.407	25.196	40.565	64.359	100.712	155.568
16	8.137	9.358	10.748	12.330	14.129	16.172	18.488	31.243	51.923	84.954	136.969	217.795
17	9.276	10.761	12.468	14.426	16.672	19.244	22.186	38.741	66.461	112.139	186.278	304.914
18	10.575	12.375	14.463	16.879	19.673	22.901	26.623	48.039	85.071	148.023	253.338	426.879
19	12.056	14.232	16.777	19.748	23.214	27.252	31.948	59.568	108.890	195.391	344.540	597.630
20	13.743	16.367	19.461	23.106	27.393	32.429	38.338	73.864	139.380	257.916	468.574	836.683
25	26.462	32.919	40.874	50.658	62.669	77.388	95.396	216.542	478.905	1033.590	2180.081	4499.880
30	50.950	66.212	85.850	111.065	143.371	184.675	237.376	634.820	1645.504	4142.075	10143.019	24201.432

TABLE B
Present Value Interest Factor (PVIF)
($1 at i% for n years)

$$PVIF = \frac{1}{(1 + i)^n}$$

$$PV_0 = FV_n(PVIF\ i\%,\ n)$$

Period n	1%	2%	3%	4%	5%	6%	7%	8%	9%	10%	11%	12%	13%
0	1.000	1.000	1.000	1.000	1.000	1.000	1.000	1.000	1.000	1.000	1.000	1.000	1.000
1	0.990	0.980	0.971	0.962	0.952	0.943	0.935	0.926	0.917	0.909	0.901	0.893	0.885
2	0.980	0.961	0.943	0.925	0.907	0.890	0.873	0.857	0.842	0.826	0.812	0.797	0.783
3	0.971	0.942	0.915	0.889	0.864	0.840	0.816	0.794	0.772	0.751	0.731	0.712	0.693
4	0.961	0.924	0.889	0.855	0.823	0.792	0.763	0.735	0.708	0.683	0.659	0.636	0.613
5	0.951	0.906	0.863	0.822	0.784	0.747	0.713	0.681	0.650	0.621	0.593	0.567	0.543
6	0.942	0.888	0.838	0.790	0.746	0.705	0.666	0.630	0.596	0.564	0.535	0.507	0.480
7	0.933	0.871	0.813	0.760	0.711	0.665	0.623	0.583	0.547	0.513	0.482	0.452	0.425
8	0.923	0.853	0.789	0.731	0.677	0.627	0.582	0.540	0.502	0.467	0.434	0.404	0.376
9	0.914	0.837	0.766	0.703	0.645	0.592	0.544	0.500	0.460	0.424	0.391	0.361	0.333
10	0.905	0.820	0.744	0.676	0.614	0.558	0.508	0.463	0.422	0.386	0.352	0.322	0.295
11	0.896	0.804	0.722	0.650	0.585	0.527	0.475	0.429	0.388	0.350	0.317	0.287	0.261
12	0.887	0.788	0.701	0.625	0.557	0.497	0.444	0.397	0.356	0.319	0.286	0.257	0.231
13	0.879	0.773	0.681	0.601	0.530	0.469	0.415	0.368	0.326	0.290	0.258	0.229	0.204
14	0.870	0.758	0.661	0.577	0.505	0.442	0.388	0.340	0.299	0.263	0.232	0.205	0.181
15	0.861	0.743	0.642	0.555	0.481	0.417	0.362	0.315	0.275	0.239	0.209	0.183	0.160
16	0.853	0.728	0.623	0.534	0.458	0.394	0.339	0.292	0.252	0.218	0.188	0.163	0.141
17	0.844	0.714	0.605	0.513	0.436	0.371	0.317	0.270	0.231	0.198	0.170	0.146	0.125
18	0.836	0.700	0.587	0.494	0.416	0.350	0.296	0.250	0.212	0.180	0.153	0.130	0.111
19	0.828	0.686	0.570	0.475	0.396	0.331	0.276	0.232	0.194	0.164	0.138	0.116	0.098
20	0.820	0.673	0.554	0.456	0.377	0.312	0.258	0.215	0.178	0.149	0.124	0.104	0.087
25	0.780	0.610	0.478	0.375	0.295	0.233	0.184	0.146	0.116	0.092	0.074	0.059	0.047
30	0.742	0.552	0.412	0.308	0.231	0.174	0.131	0.099	0.075	0.057	0.044	0.033	0.026

Period n	14%	15%	16%	17%	18%	19%	20%	24%	28%	32%	36%	40%
0	1.000	1.000	1.000	1.000	1.000	1.000	1.000	1.000	1.000	1.000	1.000	1.000
1	0.877	0.870	0.862	0.855	0.847	0.840	0.833	0.806	0.781	0.758	0.735	0.714
2	0.769	0.756	0.743	0.731	0.718	0.706	0.694	0.650	0.610	0.574	0.541	0.510
3	0.675	0.658	0.641	0.624	0.609	0.593	0.579	0.524	0.477	0.435	0.398	0.364
4	0.592	0.572	0.552	0.534	0.516	0.499	0.482	0.423	0.373	0.329	0.292	0.260
5	0.519	0.497	0.476	0.456	0.437	0.419	0.402	0.341	0.291	0.250	0.215	0.186
6	0.456	0.432	0.410	0.390	0.370	0.352	0.335	0.275	0.227	0.189	0.158	0.133
7	0.400	0.376	0.354	0.333	0.314	0.296	0.279	0.222	0.178	0.143	0.116	0.095
8	0.351	0.327	0.305	0.285	0.266	0.249	0.233	0.179	0.139	0.108	0.085	0.068
9	0.308	0.284	0.263	0.243	0.226	0.209	0.194	0.144	0.108	0.082	0.063	0.048
10	0.270	0.247	0.227	0.208	0.191	0.176	0.162	0.116	0.085	0.062	0.046	0.035
11	0.237	0.215	0.195	0.178	0.162	0.148	0.135	0.094	0.066	0.047	0.034	0.025
12	0.208	0.187	0.168	0.152	0.137	0.124	0.112	0.076	0.052	0.036	0.025	0.018
13	0.182	0.163	0.145	0.130	0.116	0.104	0.093	0.061	0.040	0.027	0.018	0.013
14	0.160	0.141	0.125	0.111	0.099	0.088	0.078	0.049	0.032	0.021	0.014	0.009
15	0.140	0.123	0.108	0.095	0.084	0.074	0.065	0.040	0.025	0.016	0.010	0.006
16	0.123	0.107	0.093	0.081	0.071	0.062	0.054	0.032	0.019	0.012	0.007	0.005
17	0.108	0.093	0.080	0.069	0.060	0.052	0.045	0.026	0.015	0.009	0.005	0.003
18	0.095	0.081	0.069	0.059	0.051	0.044	0.038	0.021	0.012	0.007	0.004	0.002
19	0.083	0.070	0.060	0.051	0.043	0.037	0.031	0.017	0.009	0.005	0.003	0.002
20	0.073	0.061	0.051	0.043	0.037	0.031	0.026	0.014	0.007	0.004	0.002	0.001
25	0.038	0.030	0.024	0.020	0.016	0.013	0.010	0.005	0.002	0.001	0.000	0.000
30	0.020	0.015	0.012	0.009	0.007	0.005	0.004	0.002	0.001	0.000	0.000	0.000

A N S W E R S

TO ODD-NUMBERED
QUESTIONS AND PROBLEMS

TO THE STUDENT

This list of answers has been prepared to help you use the end-of-chapter questions and problems as a study aid. For questions, as opposed to numerical problems, we have provided only brief or "capsule" answers. These answers are designed to focus on the key concepts that a complete answer would address. In many cases, however, they do *not* constitute a fully-rounded response to the question posed. Thus, it would be entirely appropriate for your instructor to expect you to develop your own answers more fully, using more detailed explanations and citing examples that support what you say.

Chapter 1 Questions and Problems
1. Gather *facts;* search for a *pattern;* construct a generalization or *model.* Facts to be analyzed might include the relationship between quantity of subcompact cars sold and (a) price of subcompact cars, (b) price of larger cars, (c) price of gasoline, (d) consumer incomes, (e) consumer tastes or attitudes toward relative safety of different size cars.
3. Economics can help you understand issues that citizens should be knowledgeable about, such as inflation, unemployment, and poverty, and it can help you understand the personal economic issues of consumption, saving, and investing. Finally, it can be useful in the analysis of business decisions.
5. A production possibilities curve shows the combinations of two goods or services that an economy can produce when, in a technological sense, all its resources are fully and efficiently employed.
7. Positive economics concerns objective economic statements while normative economics concerns subjective statements.
9. (a) The sketch of the curve should be concave toward the origin:

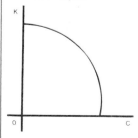

(b) Point U should lie within the curve.
(c) Point I should lie outside the curve.
(d) The principle of increasing cost explains the shape of your curve.

Special Topic A: Working with Graphs
1. Slope = 1. Direct.
3. Nonlinear, because X is squared in the equation.

Chapter 2 Questions and Problems
1. Pure capitalism: private ownership, individual freedom;
   Mixed capitalism: private ownership, individual freedom and some collective decision making and ownership;
   Command economies: centralized planning, collective ownership
3. Answers will vary: adjusting for externalities; improving distribution of income; controlling monopoly power; avoiding worker alienation; improving efficiency of government.
5. Self-interest leads to specialization and a larger aggregate output for society.

Chapter 3 Questions and Problems
1. a. A demand function relates relevant variables to the quantity demanded.
   b. A demand schedule is a table relating price to quantity demanded.
   c. A demand curve is a graphical representation of a demand schedule.
3. The law of demand posits an inverse relation between price and quantity demanded, other things equal; substitution effect, income effect, and diminishing marginal utility.
5. a. price of automobiles, labor, steel and other input prices, technology, number of automakers;
   b. price of oranges, weather conditions, number of orange trees, labor and other input prices, prevalence of fruit flies, prices of other fruits, number of orange growers;
   c. physician's earnings, number of available spaces in medical schools, the inherited qualities necessary to become a doctor;

d. price of t-shirts, price of material, price of other kinds of clothing, number of firms making t-shirts.

7. Demand will increase and the price of steak will rise.

9. a. $35, quantity supplied is equal to quantity demanded.

c. a price of $25 would result in a shortage, thus putting upward pressure on price.

Special Topic B

Problem

a.

P_x	Q_x
800	4096
750	4196
700	4296
650	4396
600	4496
550	4596
500	4696
450	4796
400	4896

b. $Q_x = 5696 - 2P_x$.

d. Increase.

e. Substitutes.

Chapter 4 Questions and Problems

1. Increases in crude oil prices shift the supply curve of gasoline to the left.

3. The attitude was that consumers were not very responsive to changes in fares; because they thought price increases would not strongly affect quantity demanded.

5. Supply will decrease and fares rise.

7. Drastic changes in the price expectations for gold held by speculators and gold investors cause the demand for gold to vary greatly.

9. Engineers suffered because of cutbacks in government spending on research and aerospace programs.

Chapter 5 Questions and Problems

1. GNP is the market value of all final goods and services produced during some time period in a country.

3. GNP measures changes in physical output and changes in prices. Real GNP adjusts GNP for price changes.

5. Real GNP: $398.5, $576.6, $755.3, $1107.5, $1171.1, $1235.0 (all figures in billions of dollars).

7. Yes, through the effects of inflation.

9. Included in 1980's GNP were:

Wages paid to a cook

Increase in business inventories

Rental value of an owner-occupied house

Income of the owner of a jewelry store

11. National income is the sum of the earnings of factors of production. Personal income is actually received by individuals. Subtract corporate profits, net interest, and social insurance contributions from national income. Then add government and business transfer payments, divi-

dends, and personal interest income to get personal income.

13. GNP is greater by $3 billion.

15. Disposable personal income: $413 billion

Personal saving: $50 billion

Chapter 6 Questions and Problems

1. The level of income that makes the aggregate quantity demanded equal to the aggregate quantity supplied is the equilibrium level of income.

3. $APS = \dfrac{Saving}{Disposable\ income}$

$MPS = \dfrac{Change\ in\ saving}{Change\ in\ disposable\ income}$

$APS = 1 - APC$

$MPS = 1 - MPC$

5. The multiplier is the number that multiplies any change in exogenous spending to arrive at the resulting new equilibrium level of income. It is calculated as $\dfrac{1}{1-MPC}$ or $\dfrac{1}{MPS}$.

7. $- $90 billion

9. The equilibrium level of income is $480 billion.

11. If an economy decides to increase its rate of saving, the ultimate effect may be a reduction in its actual saving because its national income may fall. The paradox would not be valid if the increased saving is used to further the productive capacity of the economy.

Inflexible wage rates and prices.

Chapter 7 Questions and Problems

1. Say's Law

3. The balanced budget multiplier indicates that an equal change in taxes and government expenditures will change the equilibrium level of income by the same amount.

5. Taxes reduce spending *and* saving, rather than only spending.

7. $-$400 billion

9. Your graph should show equilibrium at $1600 billion.

Chapter 8 Questions and Problems

1. Annually balanced budget: budget balanced each year;

Cyclically balanced budget: budget balanced over the business cycle;

Functional finance: maintaining full employment and price stability takes priority over balancing the budget.

3. Recessions and booms may not be of equal duration and magnitude.

5. They argue that the government spending is occurring for types of things it should not be. As a result, taxpayers are unhappy, and the beneficiaries of government spending are also not satisfied.

7. The budget that would be in effect if the economy were at full employment.

Chapter 9 Questions and Problems

1. Progressive: income and percentage of income paid in taxes are directly related.

Regressive: income and percentage of income paid in taxes are inversely related.

Proportional: the percentage of income paid in taxes is constant regardless of the amount of income.

3. State and local government outlays: Education and public welfare;

Federal government: Income security and national defense.

5. Ability-to-pay criterion: those with the greatest ability to pay should do so.

Drawbacks: deciding on what will be taxed; effects on incentives to save and invest; difficulties in deciding on the degree of sacrifice.

7. Regressive: sales taxes, value-added taxes, and the social security tax.

Progressive: estate and gift taxes and the federal income tax.

Chapter 10 Questions and Problems

1. The chief characteristics of money are:

  a) its acceptability in exchange, and

  b) its acceptability as payment for debt

3. Change in money supply = Change in excess reserves times 1/reserve requirement.

5. $40,000

7. Liabilities: Time deposits, demand deposits, and savings deposits

Assets: Loans and securities held.

9. It will probably lose the amount of its loans to other banks. If a bank loaned out more than its excess reserves, it might therefore find itself not meeting its reserve requirement.

Chapter 11 Questions and Problems

1. To provide an elastic currency and reorganize the banking system.

3. Twelve Federal Reserve Banks, the Board of Governors, the Federal Open Market Committee, and commercial member banks.

5. Appointed by the U.S. President with the advice and consent of the Senate; duties include overseeing the twelve Federal Reserve banks, and setting policies for them and for commercial member banks.

7. The discount rate is the interest rate that commercial banks pay for loans granted to them by a Federal Reserve bank. It is of less importance to commercial banks that do not request loans from the Fed than to those that do request loans. It may have an effect on the public's expectations about monetary policy.

9. The federal funds rate is the rate on excess reserves that banks loan to each other for short periods of time. It affects bank credit policies.

$30 million; $120 million.

Chapter 12 Questions and Problems

1. Transactions motive: to make payments;

Precautionary motive: to meet unforeseen needs;

Speculative motive: to hold for investment reasons.

3. Because a profit-maximizing firm will invest in physical assets up to the point where the marginal efficiency of investment equals the market interest rate. Increases in the interest rate tend to reduce investment, while lower interest rates tend to increase it.

5. $V = \dfrac{P \times Q}{M}$ = the average number of times the money supply turns over, or changes hands.

7. The classical economists believed the money supply and the price level were directly related. An increase in the money supply would increase prices, while a decrease in the money supply would reduce prices. This relationship can be traced to the equation of exchange and the belief that output would always be at the full-employment level.

9. Budget deficits may be financed by creating additional money, while surpluses may result in a reduction in the money supply. However, these effects may not be manifested if a deficit is financed by selling bonds to the public, and if a surplus results in bonds being retired.

Special Topic D

1. The IS curve represents combinations of net national product and the interest rate that equate the aggregate quantity demanded to aggregate quantity supplied. The LM curve represents combinations of net national product and the interest rate that equate the quantity demanded of money to the quantity supplied of money.

3. The IS curve shifts its position and the equilibrium level of income changes. Increased government spending shifts the IS curve to the right by an amount equal to the change in government spending times the government expenditures multiplier. Decreased government spending has the opposite effect (shifts IS curve to the left). Tax cuts shift the IS curve to the right by an amount equal to the change in taxes times the tax multiplier. Tax increases have the opposite effect.

5. An increase in the money supply will shift the LM curve to the right. A decrease in the money supply will shift the LM curve to the left.

Chapter 13 Questions and Problems

1. Conventional policies are not capable of effectively addressing the simultaneous occurrence of inflation and recession. For example, increased government spending and tax cuts might alleviate unemployment, but they would also tend to aggravate inflation.

3. *Frictional unemployment:* temporary unemployment occuring when new labor force entrants look for their first new job, workers voluntarily quit a job, or when other factors unrelated to inadequate aggregate demand result in unemployment;

Structural unemployment: members of the labor force lack needed skills; a long-run type of unemployment.

Cyclical unemployment: the unemployment that occurs when aggregate demand is insufficient to keep employment at a high level.

5. Wage and price guideposts are a program of government-established permissible wage and price increases. Labor and business are asked to voluntarily comply with the program. The Kennedy-Johnson wage and price guideposts of the 1960's were of questionable effectiveness.

7. Because it can affect the rate of growth in wages. Occupations experiencing low unemployment rates will likely be experiencing significant upward wage pressure, while occupations experiencing high unemployment rates will likely avoid most pressure for wage increases.

9. Advantage: effectiveness in slowing down inflation.

Disadvantages: create black markets, removal of controls results in an explosion of suppressed inflation, resource allocation may be impaired, individual freedom is reduced.

11. By training the unemployed to take jobs where there are labor shortages, unemployment and upward wage pressures are reduced.

13. Government policies can increase the economy's rate of growth and reduce inflationary pressures by encouraging private saving and investment. Such policies include tax rate reductions and investment tax credits.

Chapter 14 Questions and Problems

1. The business cycle refers to the fluctuations in a country's economic activity. Upturns occur from a trough, whereas downturns occur from a peak in activity.

3. The business cycle may be caused by external events or internal ones. Events external to an economic system may include wars, politics, changes in technology, demographic changes, and changes in the attitudes of consumers and investors.

5. The acceleration principle is the theory that for net investment to take place, aggregate demand must be increasing. For example, suppose a firm has been producing 100 units of output a day with 10 machines. Since a machine lasts 5 years, the firm replaces 2 machines each year. As long as the desired level of output is 100 units per day, gross investment is 2 machines a year and net investment is zero. However, if the desired output rises to 110,000 units per day, gross investment will increase to 3 machines and net investment will be 1 machine during the year of increase in desired output. If the *rate of growth* of gross investment is to remain constant, the rate of growth of GNP must continually increase.

Chapter 15 Questions and Problems

1. Growth of real GNP: shows growth in the economy's total productive capacity; Growth of per capita GNP: shows the increase in people's well-being.

3. Population growth would eventually outstrip the food supply until natural or man-made disasters reduced the population, at which point the process would begin again.

5. Knife-edge models lack built-in stabilizers that would tend to put an economy that has deviated from full-employment equilibrium back on track. The inclusion of variable capital-output ratios and savings rates might make them more stable.

7. The Club of Rome is a group of academians and business and professional people dedicated to the study of issues relating to the economic, political and social well-being of countries worldwide. The Club of Rome sponsored *The Limits to Growth*, which predicts worldwide catastrophe by the year 2100. The model has been criticized for its pessimistic assumptions regarding population growth and resource availability in the future and for its failure to consider the effects of price changes on consumption and resource use.

Chapter 16 Questions and Problems

1. The law of demand posits an inverse relationship between price and quantity demanded, all other things equal.

3. $\frac{MU_1}{P_1} = \frac{MU_2}{P_2} = \frac{MU_3}{P_3} = \ldots \frac{MU_n}{P_n}$, and all of the consumer's budget is allocated.

5. Purchases of normal goods are directly related to changes in real income. Purchases of inferior goods are inversely related to changes in real income.

7. Graphically, the market demand curve is the horizontal summation of individual demand curves. The quantities demanded by all consumers must be added together for each possible price.

Chapter 17 Questions and Problems

1. Total revenue: product price times quantity sold;

Average revenue: the ratio of total revenue to quantity sold; revenue per unit sold; product price;

Marginal revenue: the ratio of the change in total revenue to the change in quantity sold.

3. Elastic demand: total revenue will move in the opposite direction to a price change, and marginal revenue is a positive number;

Inelastic demand: total revenue will move in the same direction as a price change, and marginal revenue is negative;

Unitary elastic demand: total revenue will remain unchanged in response to a price change, and marginal revenue will be zero.

5.

Price	Quantity	Total Revenue	Marginal Revenue
$200	0	$ 0	
			190
190	1000	190,000	
			170
180	2000	360,000	
			150
170	3000	510,000	
			130
160	4000	640,000	
			110
150	5000	750,000	
			90
140	6000	840,000	
			70
130	7000	910,000	
			50
120	8000	960,000	
			30
110	9000	990,000	
			10
100	10000	1,000,000	
			−10
90	11000	990,000	

Demand is elastic over the price range of $200 to $100. Between $100 and $90 demand is inelastic.

7.
$$\frac{Q_2 - 10,000}{15 - 20} \cdot \frac{20 + 15}{10,000 + Q_2} = -2$$

$$\frac{35Q_2 - 350,000}{-50,000 - 5Q_2} = -2$$

$$35Q_2 - 350,000 = -2(-50,000 - 5Q_2)$$

$$25Q_2 = 450,000$$

$$Q_2 = 18,000$$

Elastic, since $|E_p| > 1$.

Special Topic F

1. Total revenue when Thunderbolt charged $800 per bike was $3,400,000 ($850 times 4000 bikes). When Thunderbolt lowered its price to $700 Dare Devil's sales fell to 3500 bikes, which would give total revenue of $2,975,000. The bikes are substitutes.

Chapter 18 Questions and Problems

1. The production function shows the relationship between inputs and the maximum output that can be produced.

3. Fixed costs are invariant with the level of output. Variable costs are directly related to the quantity of output.

5. Total product of labor: the maximum amounts of output produced by various amounts of labor and a fixed amount of other inputs;

Average product of labor: the ratio of the total product of labor to the amount of labor;

Marginal product of labor: the ratio of the change in the total product of labor to the change in the amount of labor.

7. Accounting costs are explicit costs. Economic costs include opportunity costs in addition to explicit costs.

9. a. explicit cost
   b. explicit cost
   c. opportunity cost
   d. explicit cost
   e. opportunity cost
   f. explicit cost

11. a.

Quantity of Labor per hour	Quantity of Cars per hour	Average Product of Labor	Marginal Product of Labor
0	0	Undefined	
			0.02
100	2	0.02	
			0.1
120	4	0.033	
			0.2
130	6	0.046	
			0.4
135	8	0.059	
			0.4
140	10	0.071	
			0.2
150	12	0.08	
			0.1
170	14	0.082	

b. $\dfrac{\$15}{0.02} = \$7.50$

Special Topic G

1. The least cost combination of inputs allows a specific output to be produced at the lowest possible cost.

3. $\dfrac{MP_L}{P_L} = \dfrac{8}{4} = 2; \dfrac{MP_K}{P_K} = \dfrac{25}{5} = 5$

Ratios are not equal, therefore this is not a least-cost combination. More output could be obtained by spending more on capital and less on labor.

Chapter 19 Questions and Problems

1. It is a business firm behaving with the goal of making the greatest possible total profit.

3. The firm should increase its production to the point

where the marginal revenue of an additional unit of out-puts equals its marginal cost, as long as P > AVC.

5. The breakeven quantity of product is where total economic profit is zero. Total fixed cost, average variable cost, and price are assumed to be constant.

7. $Q_{BEP} = \dfrac{\$12,000}{\$10 - \$6} = 3000$ units

9. Yes. The price exceeds the average variable cost by $10. The 100 rooms rented will contribute an additional $1000 to covering fixed cost or profit.

11.

Q	P	TR	MR	MC	M	TC	T
0	$10.000	$ 0				$ 2.000	– $2.000
			$ 9000	$8000	$ 1000		
1	9.000	9.000				10.000	– 1.000
			7000	5000	2000		
2	8.000	16.000				15.000	1.000
			5000	2000	3000		
3	7.000	21.000				17.000	4.000
			3000	3000	0		
4	6.000	24.000				20.000	4.000
			1000	4000	– 3000		
5	5.000	25.000				24.000	1.000
			– 1000	5000	– 6000		
6	4.000	24.000				29.000	– 5.000
			– 3000	5000	– 8000		
7	3.000	21.000				34.000	– 13.000

Profit – maximizing price: $7000 or $6000
Profit – maximizing output: 3 or 4

Chapter 20 Questions and Problems

1. Farming

3. Price equals long-run marginal cost. However, when a perfectly competitive industry is in long-run equilibrium, price will also equal long-run average cost, and economic profit will be zero.

5 Characteristics: 1) Many independent buyers and sellers (firms);
2) identical or homogeneous products;
3) firms are price takers; price is given to them by demand and supply of the industry as a whole;
4) free movement of resources;
5) perfect knowledge.

7. Because it serves to explain the behavior of firms in certain industries, such as farming, and because it serves as a benchmark by which to compare the performance of firms in other market structures.

9. a. Increasing costs: upward sloping to the right;
b. Decreasing costs: downward sloping to the right;
c. Constant costs: horizontal.

11.	Bushels of Wheat	Price Per Bushel	Total Revenue	Marginal Revenue	Marginal Cost	Total Cost
	0	$4	$ 0			$10,000
				$4	3	
	1000	4	4000			13,000
				4	2	
	2000	4	8000			15,000
				4	1	
	3000	4	12,000			16,000
				4	1	
	4000	4	16,000			17,000
				4	1	
	5000	4	20,000			18,000
				4	2	
	6000	4	24,000			20,000
				4	3	
	7000	4	28,000			23,000
				4	4	
	8000	4	32,000			27,000
				4	5	
	9000	4	36,000			32,000
				4	6	
	10000	4	40,000			38,000

Profit maximizing quantity: 7,000 or 8,000

Chapter 21 Questions and Problems

1. Characteristics: 1) industry is composed of one firm
2) barriers to the entry of new firms

3. The profit-maximizing price will tend to be lower and the output higher. See Figure 21–7.

5. No. The price that maximizes profit for a monopolist will be where MR = MC. This point usually is not attained at the highest price any customer is willing to pay.

7. A socially optimum ceiling price (P = LMC) may cause a firm to incur economic losses.

9. Because by producing where marginal revenue is equal to marginal cost in order to maximize profit, the price charged will exceed marginal cost. Socially optimum production requires that price equal marginal cost.

11. The monopolist may finance research and development out of economic profits.

13.

Quantity of Output	Price	Total Revenue	Marginal Revenue	Marginal Cost	Total Variable Cost	Marginal Profit
0	$800	$ 0			$ 0	
			750	500		250
5,000	750	3,750,000			2,500,000	
			650	400		250
10,000	700	7,000,000			4,500,000	
			550	300		250
15,000	650	9,750,000			6,000,000	
			450	100		350
20,000	600	12,000,000			6,500,000	
			350	100		250
25,000	550	13,750,000			7,000,000	
			250	100		150
30,000	500	15,000,000			7,500,000	
			150	100		50
35,000	450	15,750,000			8,000,000	
			50	100		50
40,000	400	16,000,000			8,500,000	
			50	200		250
45,000	350	15,750,000			9,500,000	

Profit maximizing price: $450
Profit maximizing output: 35,000 units

Special Topic I

1. Given that the conditions for profitable price discrimination exist, the firm will set its marginal cost equal to the marginal revenue in each segment of the market. See Figure I–1.

3. Price discrimination that affords the firm a profit rather than the loss it would incur if it could not engage in price discrimination would benefit the firm by keeping it in existence and benefit customers by allowing them the opportunity to buy from the firm.

Chapter 22 Questions and Problems

1. Characteristics: 1) Industry is made up of many firms; 2) Products are differentiated; 3) Small or nonexistent barriers to entry. Many types of retail establishments provide an example of monopolistic competition. These include restaurants, laundromats, and boutiques.

3. Advantage: product variety
Disadvantage: a firm's production will be less than the socially optimum output, and its price will be higher than the socially optimum price.

5. This theory is that a dominant firm in an oligopolistic industry sets the price that maximizes its own profit, and that the smaller firms in the industry accept this price as given and produce where their marginal costs equal price. See Figure 22–5.

7. When one large, powerful economic organization conducts business with another large, powerful organization, each can offset the power of the other. An example is when a large automaker buys steel from a large steel producer.

9. Monopolistic competition: Price exceeds marginal cost; no long-run economic profits.
Oligopoly: Price exceeds marginal cost; long-run eco-

nomic profits may exist; unit cost may be lower because of economies of scale.

11. While cartels behave like monopolists in their pricing behavior, they face the additional problems of allocating production among firms and the possibility of breaking up.

Special Topic J

1. Sales tax: shifts a firm's marginal cost curve up by the amount of the tax
Lump sum tax: adds to a firm's fixed costs the amount of the tax
Percentage profit tax: is subtracted from a firm's accounting profit

3. Compare your graph to Figure J–2.

Chapter 23 Questions and Problems

1. Employ the variable input up to the point where its marginal revenue product equals its marginal factor cost. To maximize profit with more than one variable input, the ratios of marginal revenue product to marginal factor cost must be equal for all inputs, and each ratio must equal 1.

3. Perfect competition: no single buyer by itself has the power to affect the market price it pays;
Monopsonistic competition: a large number of buyers, each of which has some control over the price it pays;
Oligopsony: a few buyers or a few dominant buyers;
Monopsony: one buyer in the marketplace.

5. Compare your illustration to Figure 23–5. Equilibrium price and quantity are determined by the market demand for and market supply of the input.

7. Bilateral monopoly exists when there is a monopsony on the demand side facing a monopolist on the supply side of a market. Relative bargaining power of the buyer and the seller will likely determine the price and quantity. An example would be the U.S. automakers on the demand side and the United Auto Workers on the supply side of the labor market.

9. a. The missing figures are:
   i) TR: $3,000
   ii) MP_L: 20, 20, 30, 20, 10, 7.5, 5
   iii) MR: $15, 15, 15, 15, 15, 15, 15
   iv) MRP_L: $300, 300, 450, 300, 150, 112.50, 75

   b. The firm must compare the MRP_L to the MFC_L, employing labor to the point where they are equal. At this point, marginal revenue from another unit of output will be equal to its marginal cost.

   c. 50 workers

Chapter 24 Questions and Problems

1. Wages: payment received by labor in return for its services
Rent: payment to a resource that is fixed in supply
Interest: return to real capital
Profit: return to entrepreneurship

3. Accounting profit: total revenue minus explicit costs
Normal profit: an implicit or opportunity cost representing the minimum return desired by investors
Economic profit: any return over and above normal profit
Profit: the return to entrepreneurship which may include both normal profit and economic profit

5. Differences in human capital (skills, education, health, etc.); geographic differences in wages and the cost of living; the existence of institutional restrictions on the entry into certain occupations; unions; monopsony power on the part of buyers of labor; discrimination.

Chapter 25 Questions and Problems

1. The Wagner Act of 1935 gave workers the right to collective bargaining and set out a number of unfair labor practices for employers.

3. Formed: 1886; Basic founding principles: trade union autonomy, exclusive jurisdiction, focus on economic issues, avoidance of political entanglements; Dominant early figure: Samuel Gompers.

5. The Fair Labor Standards Act (1938) established the first federal minimum wage which was set at $0.25.

7. The Norris-La Guardia Act, passed in 1932, made yellow-dog contracts unenforceable and limited employers' ability to obtain injunctions against certain union activities.

9. Secondary boycott: a union refuses to deal with a third party who has dealings with an employer that the union is striking against.
Jurisdictional strikes: a union calls a strike against an employer in order to force the employer to give its membership particular work that another union claims for itself.
Both are illegal under provisions of the Taft-Hartley Act.

11. Title VII prohibits discrimination in hiring, firing, or promotions on the basis of race, color, religion, sex, or national origin.

Chapter 26 Questions and Problems

1. The main provisions of the Sherman Act are:
    i) "monopolizing" and other acts in restraint of trade were made illegal;
    ii) suits could be filed by the federal government or injured parties against perpetrators of these acts;
    iii) persons convicted of violation of the Sherman Act could be fined or imprisoned;
    iv) property connected to a violation of the act could be confiscated;
    v) triple damages could be assessed by the courts and paid to injured parties.
The Clayton Act specified certain forbidden business practices.

3. The Act prohibited specific forms of price discrimination.

5. Price-fixing is considered a violation of the Sherman Act.

7. Treble means threefold. Parties injured as a result of a violation of the Sherman Act may be awarded damages of three times the dollar amount of the injury.

9. Probably beneficial in their effects on competition. However, they have imposed social costs relating to litigation and enforcement activities.

Chapter 27 Questions and Problems

1. The justifications for government regulation are the existence of monopoly power on the part of business firms and the existence of externalities. Social welfare may be increased if regulation achieves an efficient allocation of resources.

3. $P = LAC$ (normal profit)

5. $P = MC$. The value to society of the last unit of product produced will just equal its cost to society.

7. To the point where the marginal social benefit of further regulation is equal to its marginal social cost.

9. Natural monopoly: production is subject to large economies of scale, so that only one firm can exist if unit costs of production are to be at their lowest possible level.
Externality: a benefit or cost accruing to persons not directly participating in a market transaction.

Chapter 28 Questions and Problems

1. Pure public goods have external benefits that cannot be divided into individual units and that cannot be limited to persons who have paid for the good. Pure private goods lack the latter two characteristics.

3. Social benefits are the sum of private benefits and external benefits. Social costs are the sum of private costs and external costs. The social benefit of education includes the private benefit, such as higher earnings for the individual receiving the education, and the external benefits, such as a lower unemployment rate for the economy.

5. The project should be accepted since its net benefit in present value terms (present value of benefits minus present value of costs) is positive. (PV of benefits is $91.3 million; PV of costs is $67.4 million).

7. If its benefit exceeds its cost, the project should be accepted; if the reverse is true, it should be rejected.

9. Produce to the point where MSB = MSC. This rule could be applied to the decision on whether to build a small, medium, or large dam.

11. Direct benefits: enjoyed by the users of a project;
Indirect Benefits: enjoyed by nonusers of a project; indirect benefits are the external benefits of a project;
Direct costs: costs directly connected with a project;
Indirect Costs: external costs of a project that are imposed on third parties.

Chapter 29 Questions and Problems

1. The principal trading nations are the developed market economies: the countries of North America, Western Europe, Japan, South Africa, and Israel. The developed market economies accounted for 69.6% of market economy exports in 1980, while 30.4% of exports are attributable to the developing market economies. (See Table 29–1.) The amount of international trade done by the centrally planned economies is relatively small.

3. In the centrally planned economies, a state trading agency conducts most trading activities. Most trading is done through bilateral agreements and is a bartering arrangement. International trade conducted by communist nations is relatively small in comparison to that conducted by market economies.

5. The principle of comparative advantage states that although one country may have an absolute advantage over its trading partners in all goods, the country's exports will be those goods that it can produce relatively cheaply, and its imports will be those goods it produces relatively expensively. A comparative advantage for a country can be identified by noting those goods for which it has the greatest absolute advantage or least absolute disadvantage. In the table, England has a comparative advantage in jeans while the U.S. has a comparative advantage in records. England's absolute advantage is greater in jeans than in records ($12/6 > 4/3$).

7. Additional determinants of world trade include:

   i) Demand (The Linder Thesis): developed countries have more possibilities for trade because of similar, higher demands than are found in developing economies for many types of goods;

   ii) Product cycle: most new products are introduced and manufactured in developed countries; after a time, however, they are sold and manufactured in developing countries where it may be possible to produce them more cheaply.

9. Middle Arabia: 147.06

   U.S.: 90

   Germany: 94.12

   Mexico: 83.33

   The terms of trade have improved for Middle Arabia and worsened for the U.S., Germany, and Mexico.

Chapter 30 Questions and Problems

1. Banks in different countries maintain correspondent relations with each other. Corresponding banks maintain accounts with each other that are denominated in the local currency. The bank of an importing firm will issue a letter of credit to an exporting firm, agreeing to pay the exporter's bank a specific amount, usually denominated in the importer's currency, upon shipment of the exports. When the exporter's bank irrevocably confirms the letter of credit, it accepts liability for payment to the exporter, paying the exporter's draft, or acceptance, out of the correspondent bank's account.

3. The more that other countries import from a particular country, the greater the demand for that country's currency, all other things equal. The demand will also be directly related to other countries' investments in the country and to speculation in its currency.

5. a. The supply of marks would increase.

   b. The supply curve in your diagram should shift outward.

   c. The dollar has appreciated. It would take fewer U.S. cents to purchase a mark.

7. The value of the country's currency will adjust so that the imbalance will disappear. If the country is experiencing a deficit, its currency will depreciate, which will make its imports more expensive, its exports cheaper, and may result in higher interest rates. All these effects would tend to reduce the deficit. If the country is experiencing a surplus, its currency will appreciate, which will set in motion effects opposite to those just set out.

9. Tight monetary policy that leads to higher interest rates can cause short-term capital inflows, helping to reduce a payments deficit. Expansionary monetary policy that leads to declining interest rates can cause capital outflows, worsening a payments deficit. There might be a conflict between domestic and international goals if there was a recession, calling for expansionary policy domestically, and a payments deficit, calling for a restrictive policy. Domestic inflation and a payments surplus also result in a conflict.

11. a. Exchange rate determination: flexible exchange rates subject to government intervention, a system referred to as a managed float;

   b. Government intervention: directed toward keeping a country's currency at a desired value and accomplished by a country buying and selling its own currency in foreign exchange markets,

   c. The issue of reserves: a country must maintain adequate reserves of foreign currencies with which to buy its own currency in order to keep its currency from depreciating.

13. $12,775.50. Since $.55 originally bought 1 mark, the $12,525 originally bought 22,772.727 marks (equal to 12,525/.55). When the mark appreciated 2%, it now took $.561 to purchase 1 mark (equal to 1.02 times $.55). You need 22,772.727 marks to buy the VW, and each mark costs you $.561. Therefore, you need $12,775.50 (equal to 22,772.727 times .561).

Chapter 31 Questions and Problems

1. The objectives and their definitions are:

   i) economic welfare—the goal of seeking the maximum gains from trade; maximizing welfare implies that policies of free trade, rather than protectionism, should be pursued;

   ii) self-sufficiency—the twin goals of reducing dependence on foreign suppliers of raw materials and utilizing domestic resources to produce products at home when it is cheaper to do so than to import them; implies limited use of protectionist policies;

iii) security—the goals of providing for an adequate defense and for a prosperous economy; implies protectionism to meet the first goal, free trade to promote prosperity, and perhaps, adjustment assistance to aid industries unable to compete with their foreign competition;

iv) economic growth—this goal may require a policy of protecting new industries; protectionism, however, carries with it the risk of misallocating resources.

3. Compare your diagram to Figure 31–1. Domestic producers gain, and consumers lose from a tariff. Consumers' surplus is reduced and resources are misallocated as a result of a tariff, but domestic producers obtain a higher price and expand their output.

5. Your answer should reflect that steel is used in many nondefense industries and that a reduction in the size of the U.S. industry would not necessarily have strategic consequences.

7. The Smoot-Hawley Tariff Act of 1930 was intended to increase employment in the U.S. by reducing the flow of imports into the country. The actual result was a breakdown in international trade and worsening of the already bad unemployment situation.

9. The South wanted low tariffs and the North wanted high tariffs. This is because the North wanted to protect its infant manufacturing industries, while the South preferred to import its manufactured goods because of their relatively lower cost.

South Carolina passed an "Ordinance of Nullification" in response to the Tariff of Abominations leading to the state's rights movement and the eventual secession of the South from the Union.

Chapter 32 Questions and Problems

1. The ratio of some measure of income (e.g., GNP) to population. It is directly related to several measures of the standard of living in developing countries. Problems include a substantial output that is produced outside the monetary economy, and hence escapes measurement, and variation in production and consumption patterns from country to country that tends to reduce the meaningfulness of comparisons.

3. The LDC's generally have much higher population growth rates. Population will double in 25 years in countries with the highest rates, if those rates are maintained. In countries with the lowest rates it will take over 70 years for population to double.

5. Marx's stages of growth progressed from feudalism to capitalism, then to socialism, which would be followed by communism. Rostow's stages were the traditional society, preconditions for takeoff, the takeoff stage, the drive to maturity, and the final stage, high mass consumption.

In large measure these theories are not applicable to the solution of problems faced by today's LDCs.

7. Aid is typically only a small fraction of the output of donor countries. In absolute terms the U.S., France and Germany are the principal sources of aid (see Table 32–3). In relative terms Qatar, United Arab Emirates, Kuwait, and Saudi Arabia are the most generous sources of aid (see Table 32–4). Aid to LDCs is a controversial subject because of waste, fraud, and mismanagement of aid programs, and because it may create dependency relationships between donors and receivers.

9. In absolute terms the per capita income gap has widened. Because many LDCs are starting from such a small income base, even growth rates significantly higher than those of the industrialized nations may not be sufficient to close the gap over the next several decades.

11. Adopt policies to: I) create a more equal distribution of income; II) improve their tax systems; III) reduce population growth; IV) expand and improve the education and training of the labor force; V) encourage appropriate technological change; VI) secure reforms in the pattern of land ownership; VII) possibly, reduce tariffs and other trade restrictions.

Chapter 33 Questions and Problems

1. Price instability comes about for two reasons:
  1) inelastic demand and supply curves, and
  2) frequent shifts in the supply and demand curves.

3. The government limits the number of acres that can be planted in a particular crop, thus theoretically restricting the supply of a crop. In practice, farmers cultivate these acres more intensively and devote their best land to these crops. Thus, the reduction in acres planted may not have as large an effect on the amount produced as was expected.

5. The federal government agrees to support farm prices above the market level. The method used to accomplish this is to provide nonrecourse loans to farmers of an amount equal to the price-support value of their crops. If the market price should rise above the support level by a specified percentage, farmers must pay off their loans with interest. If the support price remains above the market level, the government will accept farmers' crops in full payment of the loan. Participation in an acreage restriction program is usually required. The disadvantages of such a program include incentives for overproduction and misallocation of resources.

7. The advantage is that there is no incentive to overproduce. Farmers dislike this type of program because it would be provided for only a specified number of years and then stopped, to encourage them to leave farming. Also, many farmers prefer to "earn" their subsidies.

9. Parity price means that farm prices would be sufficient to have the same purchasing power as they did between 1910–1914, the golden age of agriculture. The parity concept was included in the Agricultural Adjustment Act of

1933, much of which was declared unconstitutional in 1936.

11. The major provisions of the Food and Agriculture Act (1977) are:

   i) extended the basic support provisions for all farm commodities to 1981;

   ii) raised target prices on corn and wheat;

   iii) raised the limit on certain government payments to farmers;

   iv) excluded disaster payments from the total;

   v) established normal crop acreage bases;

   vi) provided for a national grain reserve program.

13. Farm co-ops are growing rapidly in number and size. They are becoming more concentrated in terms of market power wielded, and they are increasing the scope of their activities to include processing of agricultural products.

15. The price of U.S. farmland has skyrocketed due in part to purchases by foreigners. This has raised farmers' costs, especially when opportunity costs are considered.

Chapter 34 Questions and Problems

1. The causes are differences in several factors including natural ability, education and training, health, industriousness, inherited wealth, discrimination, market power, and luck. The government is committed to aid persons in poverty through a series of income maintenance programs (see Table 34–5). Individual responsibility is a philosophical question that people might disagree over.

3. The percentage of the population living in poverty has fallen dramatically as has the absolute number of persons living in poverty. By these standards, the war on poverty has been a success. Since the percentage of persons living in poverty before government cash transfer payments has remained virtually constant, the war on poverty could be criticized for treating the symptoms of poverty but not its causes.

5. Persons or families below a certain level of annual earnings would receive payments from the federal government. These payments would be inversely tied to incomes. As an example of such a system, suppose a program considers $6,000 to be the minimum amount necessary to sustain a family of four and that the negative tax rate were 50 percent. The government would pay the family $6,000 if their income was $0. The government would reduce this payment by $.50 for each dollar of income the family earned until at a level of $12,000 the payment would be $0. The HEW study in Seattle and in Denver provides some indication of the effects of such a program.

7. Programs whose purpose is to combat poverty may have as an additional, undesirable effect the reduction in the efficiency with which the economy operates.

Chapter 35 Questions and Problems

1. The optimal level of population will occur at the point where the marginal social benefit of pollution abatement is equal to its marginal social cost.

3. Direct regulation: the discharge of pollutants above a certain level are not legally permitted; there is no incentive to reduce pollution below the specified level; and there is a problem with variations in compliance between firms. See Figure 35–2 and the accompanying discussion in your text.

Subsidies: Federal tax credits for firms buying pollution-control equipment; there is no incentive for firms unless the credits are at least equal to the cost of controlling pollution; there is no incentive to take other actions to reduce pollution; there is an issue of social equity to be considered. See Figure 35–2 and accompanying discussion in your text.

Effluent fees: a charge levied on producers or consumers that is directly related to their rate of discharge of pollutants; firms may choose whatever abatement method they wish, or pay the fee; this policy places the cost of abatement on those responsible. See Figure 35–3.

5. The "energy crisis" developed because the growth in energy consumption outstripped the growth of energy production. OPEC policies which ended the era of cheap energy and government-regulated prices also contributed to the crisis.

Chapter 36 Questions and Problems

1. Soviet-type socialism requires centralized planning that revolves around a five-year plan. Within the five-year plan, annual plans are developed and implemented. The planners must allocate raw materials and supplies to each sector, a trial-and-error process. Prices are set by the state. Consumer prices serve to ration limited supplies of consumer goods. Successful enterprises are eligible for bonuses awarded by the government. While the U.S. is alone among Western economies in foregoing five-to-eight year planning, Western style planning relies largely on market mechanisms.

3. Input prices are the sum of values added at each stage of production plus a surplus value which accrues to the state. Retail prices are set low on overproduced goods and set high on underproduced goods. The objective of this pricing scheme is to ration goods.

5. Libermanism refers to Soviet reforms introduced in 1965 and advocated by Soviet economist Evsey Liberman. These reforms gave enterprise-level management more discretion and provided for a system of bonuses to be awarded to especially successful enterprises. Libermanism is a step in the direction toward the Yugoslav system, which consists of enterprise-level planning and relatively free markets. The unrest in Poland in 1981 has reflected an effort by workers to increase their control over the economy.

7. Economic problems in Yugoslavia are:

   i) the abuse of monopoly power possessed by enterprises,

ii) a system that sometimes discourages enterprises from adding more workers or new lines of business,

iii) the necessity to implement wage and price controls,

iv) the business cycle—including stagflation and unemployment, and

v) balance of payments problems.

9. Welfare statism in Britain, France, and West Germany comes close to matching that of Sweden. All three countries have nationalized a significant number of major industries. Since World War II, the economies of France and West Germany have performed robustly, while the British performance has been anemic. Britain's problems have included labor-management strife, resistance to modernization, poor management, poor government planning, and inflation which tended to reduce British exports.

11.

	United States	European Mixed Capitalism	Market Socialism	Soviet-Type Socialism
Extent of Central Planning	None	Moderate	Moderate	Extensive
Ownership of Means of Production	Privately Owned	Predominantly Privately Owned	Socially Owned	State Owned
Establishment of Prices	Market	Market	Market and State	Predominantly State
Extent of Welfare Statism	Moderate	Extensive	Extensive	Extensive

GLOSSARY

Ability-to-Pay Criterion Holds that those whose ability to pay is greatest should pay the most taxes.

Acceleration Principle An economic principle which implies that net investment will take place only when aggregate demand is increasing.

Accelerator The ratio of net investment required to produce a new level of output to the change in aggregate demand:

$$\text{accelerator} = \frac{\text{net investment required}}{\text{change in aggregate demand}}.$$

Acceptance An exporter's draft against an importer for which the exporter's bank has established that all conditions necessary for present or future payment of the draft have been met.

Accounting Net Income The total revenue of a firm less its total accounting cost.

Aggregate Quantity Demanded The expenditures that all potential purchasers (consumers, business, government, and foreigners) of a country's output are willing and able to make, given a particular level of gross national product.

Aggregate Quantity Supplied The total quantity of goods and services a country produced during a particular year.

Annually Balanced Budget Philosophy The belief that the federal budget should be balanced each year.

Antitrust Laws Laws affecting any business practices and agreements that intensify monopoly power or otherwise restrict trade.

Appreciate A currency appreciates when its price, in terms of another currency, rises.

Automatic Stabilizers Mechanisms that act automatically to increase aggregate demand during recessionary periods and to decrease demand during boom periods. Welfare payments and the progressive income tax are two examples of automatic stabilizers.

Average Fixed Cost Fixed cost per unit of output.

$$\text{AFC} = \frac{\text{total fixed cost}}{\text{quantity of output}}.$$

Average Product of an Input Output per unit of the input. It is found by dividing the total product of the input by the quantity of the input in use.

Average Profit Profit per unit sold. Average profit is equal to total profit divided by quantity of output.

Average Propensity to Consume The fraction of each dollar of income, on the average, that is spent on consumption goods. The average propensity to consume is given by total consumption expenditures divided by disposable income.

Average Propensity to Save The amount saved out of disposable income divided by the total amount of disposable income.

Average Revenue The revenue per unit sold of a product.

$$\text{Average Revenue} = \frac{\text{total revenue}}{\text{quantity sold}}.$$

If all units are sold at the same price, average revenue and price are equal.

Balance of Payments Accounts (for a Country) A record of the monetary effects of all transactions between the country's citizens, businesses, and government and those of foreign countries. Most such transactions arise because of international trade and investment, although some have to do with payment for services or gifts.

Balance of Trade (for a Country) The difference between the country's export earnings and its expenditures on imports over some time period.

Balanced Budget Multiplier Indicates the effect an equal increase (or decrease) in government expenditures and taxes will have on the equilibrium level of income. In the model used in this text, the balanced budget multiplier is equal to 1, indicating that an equal change in government expenditures and taxes will change the equilibrium level of income by the same amount.

Barriers to Entry Factors which prevent other firms from entering an industry.

Behavioralists People who consider size alone to be insufficient evidence of monopolizing behavior.

Benefit-Cost Ratio The ratio of the incremental benefits to the incremental costs of a project.

Benefit Criterion Holds that those who receive the benefits financed by taxes should pay for them.

Bilateral Monopoly A situation where, for all practical purposes, there is one seller of a good or service and one buyer of the good or service.

Budget Constraint Limitation placed on consumer purchases because of the levels of their incomes and wealth.

Business Cycles Repetitive patterns of economic activity characterized by alternating periods of expansion and contraction in the general level of business activity. Usually this term is applied to variations in aggregate economic variables such as income, output, employment, and prices.

Capital Items such as tools, machines, and buildings, used in the productive process.

Capital Consumption Allowance A measure of the productive capacity of capital goods—plant and equipment—used up or destroyed during the current accounting period. It also includes an estimate of the natural resources depleted during that time period.

Capital Deepening A term used to refer to an increase in the stock of capital relative to the quantity of labor.

Capital-Output Ratio (k) The desired ratio of capital goods to output for the economy.

Cartel An organization of the firms in an oligopoly whereby the firms formally agree on a price to charge and on the market share for each firm. In this case the firms behave very much like a monopoly.

Cease and Desist Order An agreement in which the investigated party, without admitting any guilt, agrees to refrain from certain activities.

Change in Demand A shift in the demand curve. A change in demand occurs when some demand function variable other than the product's own price is changed.

Change in Quantity Demanded The change in the amount of a good or service which consumers are willing and able to purchase when a change in the product's price takes place, other things equal.

Change in Quantity Supplied A change in the quantity of a product which producers are willing and able to offer for sale during some time period as a result of a change in the price of the product.

Change in Supply A shift in the supply curve. Occurs when any supply function variable other than the price of the product under consideration changes.

Checkoff The practice by an employer of deducting union dues from an employee's pay and turning them over to the union.

Closed Shop Agreements Agreements that a person must be a member of the union before he or she can be hired.

Command Economic System An economic system whereby all of the what, how, and for whom decisions are made on a collective or group basis. Moreover, there is collective ownership of the factors of production.

Company Unions Unions organized on an individual business firm basis and controlled by management.

Compensation of Employees Wages and salaries, including payments in kind and supplemental benefits, of employees.

Complements Two goods which have the relationship that having one of them increases the satisfaction received from having the other. Complements have a negative cross price elasticity of demand. Coffee and cream are one example of complements.

Compounding The practice of paying interest on both the original amount invested and any accumulated interest.

Concentrated Industry An industry with a large percentage of its output produced by a few firms.

Conglomerate Merger A merger of two firms which produce unrelated products.

Consent Decrees Statements of certain provisions agreed to by both the government and the defendant in cases involving monpolizing or other unfair business practices.

Constant Cost Industry An industry where input prices remain constant as industry output increases.

Consumer Sovereignty The hypothesis that consumers determine what is produced through the demand for products that they exhibit in the marketplace.

Consumers' Surplus The difference between the amount consumers actually spend on a good (market price times the quantity purchased) and the amount they would be willing and able to spend for the same quantity (area under the demand curve). The latter amount could be collected only by charging a different price for each unit sold.

Consumption Expenditures The market value of purchases of goods and services by individuals and nonprofit institutions, and the value of food, clothing, housing, and financial services received by them as income in kind. It includes the rental value of owner-occupied houses, but does not include purchases of dwellings, which are classified as capital goods.

Consumption Function Gives the relationship between consumption and disposable income.

Contract Laws Laws pertaining to the establishment of contractual obligations and to wrongful acts in breach of contract.

Contribution Margin Per Unit Indicates how much the sale of another unit will contribute toward covering fixed cost or adding to profit. The contribution margin per unit sold is equal to price minus average variable cost.

Convergence Hypothesis The belief that in their struggle to solve the fundamental economic problems of *what*, *how*, and *for whom*, the capitalist and socialist economies will become progressively more alike.

Coordinate Plane Two-dimensional space.

Coordinates The numbers that define a point in two-dimensional space.

Copyright Gives an author or firm the exclusive right to possess, make, publish, and sell copies of a production such as books, maps, musical compositions, motion pictures, sound recordings, and maps.

Corporate Income Taxes Taxes levied on the taxable incomes of corporations.

Corporate Profits The before-tax earnings of corporations, excluding nonprofit corporations, that accrue to residents of the United States.

Cost-Benefit Analysis The term used to refer to the decision-making process for the production of public goods. In this type of analysis the costs and benefits of a project are calculated and compared. The project is economically acceptable only if its benefits are greater than or equal to its costs.

Cost-Push or Seller's Inflation General price increases occurring as a result of rising costs, including higher markups.

Countervailing Power A term used by John Kenneth Galbraith to refer to situations in which a large firm has to deal with other large firms, unions, or other entities, all of which have sufficient power on the other side of the market to counteract the market power of the first firm.

Criminal Laws Laws which deal with acts that are viewed as offenses against a federal, state, or local government.

Crop Restriction Programs Programs designed to limit the production of certain agricultural crops.

Cross Price Elasticity of Demand The cross price elasticity of demand for good X with respect to changes in the price of good Y is equal to the percentage change in the quantity demanded of good X divided by the percentage change in the price of good Y.

$$E_{XY} = \frac{\text{percentage change in quantity demanded of } X}{\text{percentage change in price of good } Y}.$$

Crowding Out A phrase used to refer to the possibility that a reduction in private sector expenditures for capital goods may occur as a result of rising interest rates due to public borrowing.

Cyclical Unemployment Unemployment caused by a deficiency of aggregate demand. Thus, cyclical unemployment can be reduced through macroeconomic policies designed to increase the general level of aggregate demand.

Cyclically Balanced Budget Philosophy   The belief that the federal budget need not be balanced every year but should be balanced over the course of the business cycle.

Decreasing Cost Industry   An industry where input prices fall as industry output rises.

Deflationary Gap   Occurs when the actual level of the gross national product is less than the full employment level of gross national product. The deflationary gap is equal to the amount by which the aggregate demand curve would have to shift upward for the equilibrium level of income to coincide with full employment.

Demand   The relationship between the various possible prices of a product and the amounts of it that consumers are willing and able to buy during some period of time, other things remaining the same.

Demand Curve   A graphical representation of a demand schedule. It depicts the relationship between the quantity demanded and the price charged for each unit of a product.

Demand Function   A statement telling how each of a number of relevant variables affects the quantity of a product that consumers will buy during some time period.

Demand-Pull Inflation   General price increases resulting from excess demand.

Demand Schedule   A table showing the relationship between the various possible prices of a good or service and the quantity purchased of that good or service over some period of time.

Dependency Effect   A term used to refer to the idea that production creates wants—that wants are dependent on what is produced.

Deposit Expansion Multiplier   Indicates the maximum amount by which demand deposits and, therefore, the money supply can increase as a result of a given increase in excess reserves. The deposit expansion multiplier is equal to

$$\frac{1}{\text{reserve requirement}}.$$

Depreciate   A currency depreciates when its price, in terms of another currency, falls.

Derivative Deposits   Deposits created on the basis of new excess reserves brought into the banking system by a primary deposit.

Devaluation (of a Currency)   A reduction in the par value of a country's currency in a fixed exchange rate system.

Differentiated Products   Goods and services whose perceived or actual attributes vary enough so that consumers can distinguish the products from each other.

Direct Benefits   Benefits obtained by the users of a project.

Direct Costs   The costs directly connected with a project.

Discount Rate   The interest rate that a Federal Reserve bank charges a depository institution when it gives the institution a loan. In project analysis, the rate of interest used to compute present values. The process of computing present values is called *discounting*.

Direct Regulation   The passage of laws that prohibit or mandate a particular activity. With respect to pollution control, direct regulation refers to the passage of laws that prohibit discharges of pollutants above a particular rate.

Discretionary Fiscal Policies   Deliberate actions which the government takes to reduce fluctuations in the levels of national income and employment and to promote economic growth.

Discriminatory Discharge   The practice of firing union members.

Diseconomies of Scale   Characteristics of long-run production that cause average cost to increase as plant size is increased. When diseconomies of scale predominate, the long-run average cost curve slopes upward.

Disintermediation   The process whereby individuals and businesses reduce their deposits at commercial banks and other depository institutions in order to invest directly in other assets.

Disposable Personal Income   The income paid to individuals which remains after personal income, property, excise, gift, and inheritance taxes are subtracted from personal income. Disposable personal income is equal to personal income less personal taxes.

Dominant Firm Explanation of Price Leadership This theory assumes that there is one large firm and other, smaller firms in an oligopolistic industry. The large firm sets the price, and the smaller firms accept it as a given and produce where price is equal to marginal cost—like perfectly competitive firms.

Econometric Models Economic models which use systems of equations and statistical techniques to forecast the value of economic variables such as national income, employment, and prices.

Economic Dualism A term used to refer to an economy which is divided into two distinct sectors, one modern and the other traditional.

Economic Growth Generally measured by the rate of growth of real per capita GNP.

Economic Indicators Key variables used to predict changes in economic activity. Changes in the value of such variables are thought to indicate changes in the values of other important economic variables. Leading indicators are economic variables whose values typically rise or fall before a corresponding rise or fall in the values of other economic variables that people are trying to forecast, such as GNP. Coincident indicators are economic variables whose values seem to rise or fall simultaneously with GNP. Lagging indicators are economic variables whose values typically rise or fall after corresponding rises or falls in GNP.

Economic Profit Accounting net income less opportunity costs, including a normal or average return, considering the riskiness of the enterprise, to the owners of the business. Total revenue minus total cost, including all opportunity costs.

Economic Theory or Model A generalization, based on a variety of facts, about why or how an economic event occurs.

Economics A science concerned with choosing among alternatives involving scarce resources.

Economies of Scale Characteristics of long-run production that cause average cost to decrease as plant size is increased. When economies of scale predominate, the long-run average cost curve slopes downward.

Effluent Fee A charge levied on firms or consumers based on their rate of discharge of pollutants.

Elastic Price Elasticity of Demand Demand for a product is elastic with respect to its price when the percentage change in quantity demanded is greater than the percentage change in price (in absolute value terms). A decrease in price will cause total revenue to increase, and an increase in price will cause total revenue to decrease.

Elasticity of Supply The percentage change in the quantity supplied of a product divided by the percentage change in its price, other things remaining the same.

$$E_s = \frac{\text{percentage change in quantity supplied}}{\text{percentage change in price}}.$$

Elasticity of the Money Supply: Refers to the flexibility of the money supply. Before the Federal Reserve system was established, the United States monetary system was criticized for its lack of flexibility.

Employed Persons Include (1) all civilians who, during the survey week, did a minimum of an hour's work for pay or profit or who worked fifteen hours or more as unpaid workers in a family enterprise, and (2) all persons who were not working but who had jobs or businesses from which they were temporarily absent for noneconomic reasons such as illness, bad weather, vacation, or a labor-management dispute.

Employment Act of 1946 States that it is the policy and responsibility of the federal government to promote maximum employment, production, and purchasing power.

Enterprise A business firm. In the Soviet Union business firms are owned by the state, and enterprise-level managers have little decision-making authority.

Entrepreneurship Factor of production which denotes the business owner's innovative ability, far-sightedness, and willingness to take risks.

Equation of Exchange States that the quantity of money in the economy times the velocity of money is equal to gross national product in real terms multiplied by a general index of prices of newly produced goods and services.

Equilibrium Level of (National) Income Where the aggregate quantity demanded of newly produced goods and services is equal to the aggregate quantity supplied of these goods and services.

Equilibrium Price and Quantity A price and quantity that will tend to be maintained naturally by market forces. At an equilibrium price, the quantity demanded of a product is equal to the quantity supplied.

Escalator Clauses Clauses in long-term contracts that provide for automatic adjustment for general price increases (inflation).

Estate Taxes Taxes levied on the estate of an individual when he or she dies. The federal government imposes an estate tax. Many states also have inheritance taxes, which they levy on individuals who *receive* bequests of property after the death of another person.

Excess Reserves The excess reserves of a financial institution are equal to total reserves minus required reserves.

Exchange Rate (or **Rate of Exchange**) Between two currencies, the price of a unit of one of them in terms of the other.

Excise Tax A tax levied on the sale of a specific item.

Exclusive Dealing A situation in which a firm buying or leasing the goods of one firm agrees not to deal with competing suppliers.

Explicit Costs Cost of items for which the firm has made a specific payment in the past or for which it is obligated to do so in the future.

Export Subsidies Direct payments to producers or exporters who export a particular product.

External Social Benefit A benefit obtained by some person or group of people other than the ones who purchased the product or service in question.

External Social Cost A cost borne by those not directly connected with producing, selling, or purchasing a particular good or service.

Externality A benefit provided to or cost imposed on third parties as the result of the production or consumption of a good or service. The third parties are not directly involved in either the production or the purchase of the product.

Factor of Production Something that can be used in the production of a commodity or service.

Fair-Return Pricing A type of price regulation that allows a firm to charge a price sufficiently high to make a normal return but no economic profit.

Fallacy of Composition The error in logic that is made when it is assumed that what is true for one person or for part of an economic entity is also necessarily true for society as a whole or for the economic entity as a whole.

Fallacy of Drawing False Conclusions The error in logic that is made when a person observes one thing happening after another and concludes that the first event necessarily caused the second one.

Featherbedding Causing or trying to cause an employer to pay for services that are not to be performed.

Federal Budget The financial plan for the federal government during a particular twelve-month period, called a fiscal year. The federal budget has a *deficit* if expenditures exceed receipts: it has a *surplus* if receipts exceed expenditures.

Federal Funds Rate The rate that commercial banks charge each other when they loan their excess reserves, usually on a one-day basis.

Federal Reserve Act of 1913 Established the Federal Reserve system.

Financial Intermediaries Firms that take funds received from depositors or other sources and lend them to third parties. Banks and savings and loans are two examples.

Firm An individual business organization that produces a good or service.

Fiscal Policy Government policies regarding taxes and government spending.

Fixed Costs Costs that do not vary with the level of output in the short run.

Fixed Exchange Rate System An exchange rate system in which the foreign exchange market is characterized by government intervention to keep the rates of exchange between currencies stable.

Flexible Exchange Rate System An exchange rate system in which exchange rates are allowed to vary with changes in market conditions.

Foreign Exchange The currency of any country other than one's own.

Fractional Reserve System A system whereby financial intermediaries maintain reserves equal to only a portion of their deposits.

Free Enterprise An economic system in which individuals are free to engage in any type of economic activity they wish, as long as they have the means of doing so.

Freely Fluctuating Exchange Rate System An exchange rate system in which governments do not intervene in the foreign exchange market, and rates are determined by the activities of private banks, traders, and speculators. Such a system is a theoretical ideal that has never existed.

Frictional Unemployment Unemployment which is temporary in nature and due to standard market adjustments unrelated to changes in aggregate demand. Frictional unemployment is generally thought to be a result of inadequate information regarding job opportunities and people available to fill the openings.

Full Employment Budget Surplus or Deficit The surplus or deficit that would result from the federal budget if the economy were at full employment.

Functional Distribution of Income The distribution of income according to the activity performed by its recipients.

Functional Finance Philosophy The belief that a balanced budget is of secondary importance to keeping the economy at a full employment but non-inflationary level of income through appropriate spending and taxing policies on the part of the federal government.

Future Value The future value of a sum of money held today is the amount that would be accumulated at some future date if that sum of money were invested in a particular way.

Future Value Interest Factor At a rate of interest equal to i for t time periods, or FVIF $(i\%, t)$, is equal to $(1 + i)^t$. The factor by which an initial amount invested at $i\%$ for t periods should be multiplied to obtain the amount accumulated at the end of period t.

General Equilibrium Analysis A system-wide examination of prices and markets, focusing specifically on the interactions between the system's many product and resource markets.

Giffen Good A good with a positively sloped demand curve. A Giffen good is a good with a negative income effect which is so large that it outweighs the substitution effect.

Gift Tax A tax imposed by the federal government and some state governments on the donor of a gift, not the recipient.

Government Expenditures The expenditures for newly produced goods and services, including government investment expenditures, by all levels of government.

Government Expenditures Multiplier The number by which a change in government expenditures should be multiplied to get the resulting change in the equilibrium level of income. See "multiplier."

Gross National Product (GNP) The market value of all final goods and services produced during some particular time period in a country.

Gross (Private Domestic) Investment All purchases of capital goods, including buildings and equipment, by private businesses and nonprofit institutions. Gross investment is equal to net investment plus the capital consumption allowance. Thus, gross investment is equal to net investment plus purchases of capital goods to replace those used up or destroyed during the current accounting period.

Horizontal Merger A merger of two firms which produce the same type of product.

Humphrey-Hawkins Act of 1978 States that the opportunity for employment at fair wage rates for all those willing and able to work is a national goal. It also recognizes reasonable price stability as a national goal. Finally, it states that a balanced federal budget is a policy objective, as long as it does not interfere with the other goals.

Income Effect The effect of a price change on consumer purchases which reflects the fact that a change in the price of a good causes a change in the real incomes of consumers who purchase it. As a result of this change in their real incomes, consumers alter their purchases of the good or service whose price has changed.

Income Elasticity of Demand The percentage change in quantity demanded of a product divided by the percentage change in income, other things remaining the same.

$$E_y = \frac{\text{percentage change in quantity demanded}}{\text{percentage change in income}}$$

Income Velocity of Money The average number of times the money supply of an economy changes hands during a year in the process of purchasing the country's gross national product. It is equal to GNP valued at current prices divided by the quantity of money.

Increasing Cost Industry An industry where input prices rise as industry output increases.

Incremental Profit The additional profit that would be obtained from a new undertaking. It is equal to incremental revenue minus incremental cost.

Indexation Policies Policies (usually applied on a widespread scale) that use escalator clauses to adjust wage rates and long-term contracts for inflation. They would also adjust the tax system and government benefit programs for inflation.

Indirect Benefits and Costs External, or third-party, benefits and costs.

Industry The seller group that produces a good or service.

Inelastic Price Elasticity of Demand Demand for a product is inelastic with respect to price when the percentage change in quantity demanded is less than the percentage change in price (in absolute value terms). An increase in price will cause total revenue to increase, and a decrease in price will cause total revenue to fall.

Inferior Good A good with a negative income effect. As consumers' real incomes rise, they buy less of such a good. They buy more of it as their real incomes fall.

Inflationary Gap Occurs when aggregate demand is so high that the equilibrium level of gross national product exceeds the full employment level. It is equal to the amount by which the aggregate demand curve would have to shift downward for the equilibrium level of income to coincide with full employment.

Injunction A court order directing that some action not be carried out, on the ground that the people or organizations affected by the action will suffer irreparable harm as a result of it.

Input or Factor of Production A resource that a firm uses to produce a good or service.

Input-Output Analysis A type of economic analysis that uses matrix algebra to describe the linkages between vaious industries in an economy and to de-

termine the input and output levels of each industry that are required for any given level of aggregate output or GNP.

Input Use Rule The decision rule which states that a profit-maximizing firm will employ additional units of a single variable input up to the level where the marginal revenue product equals the marginal factor cost for the resource or input in question.

Institutional Structure (of a Society) The society's rules and traditions and the myths or justifications that stand behind them.

Interest The return to real capital—buildings and machines, for example.

Interlocking Directorate A situation where one person serves on the boards of directors of two companies.

Interlocking Stockholdings The ownership by one corporation of the stock of a competing corporation.

International Reserves (of a Country) The country's monetary authorities' holdings of foreign currencies, gold, and certain other assets that can be used to purchase its own currency in the foreign exchange markets.

Invisible Hand Term used by Adam Smith to denote the fact that in a market economy the price system influences the actions of individual economic units so that it appears that an invisible hand is guiding economic activity in a way that the welfare of society is promoted while individuals are acting in their own self-interest.

Jurisdictional Strikes Strikes for the purpose of forcing an employer to assign particular work to employees in one union rather than to employees who are members of another union.

Kinked Demand Curve The demand curve that exists for oligopoly firms when rivals will follow a price decrease but not a price increase.

Labor: A general term for the services of all human beings except for those of entrepreneurs.

Labor Force The sum of all civilian employed persons, all unemployed persons, and all persons in the armed forces.

Land All types of natural resources.

Law of Demand An economic principle which states that, other things equal, the amount of a product that consumers are willing and able to purchase during some period of time varies inversely with the price of that product.

Law of Diminishing Marginal Productivity (Law of Diminishing Returns) An economic principle which states that if equal amounts of one variable input are added, while all other inputs are kept fixed, total product may increase, but after some point the *additions* to total product will begin to decrease.

Law of Supply An economic principle which states that, other things equal, sellers will increase the quantity of a product which they are willing and able to offer for sale as the price of that product is increased.

Law of Torts Laws concerned with injuries sustained by private parties as a result of nonperformance of a duty created by law.

Least Cost Combination of Inputs A combination of inputs that will enable a firm to produce a particular level of output for the lowest possible cost. A least cost combination of inputs is obtained when the marginal product per \$1 spent on any one input is equal to the marginal product per \$1 spent on any other.

Length to Maturity (of a Loan) The length of time before the loan must be repaid.

Letter of Credit A document issued by an importer's bank indicating that the bank will pay an exporter or the exporter's bank a specific amount for a specific shipment of goods.

License (with respect to international trade) A permit to import or export a particular product.

Liquidity Trap A situation that exists when the interest rate falls so low that individuals and businesses wish to hold any new money created in the banking system as speculative money balances.

Lockout A term used to refer to the practice of an employer of shutting down a firm until its employees agree to work in accordance with the terms offered.

Long Run A period of time sufficiently long to allow the firm to change the physical amounts of all resources used in the production process.

Long-Run Average Cost Cost per unit of output when all inputs are variable so that a least cost combination of inputs can be used. Long-run average cost is equal to long-run total cost divided by quantity of output.

Long-Run Marginal Cost The increase in total cost from producing another unit of output when all inputs are variable, so that a least cost combination of inputs can be used. Long-run marginal cost is equal to the change in long-run total cost divided by the change in quantity of output.

Long-Run Total Cost The relationship between the total cost of a firm and its level of output when all inputs are variable, so that the firm can produce each level of output with the optimal (least cost) combination of inputs.

Lorenz Curve A graphical depiction of the relationship between the percent of total income generated in an economy which is received by a certain group of people and the percent of all families in that group. Basically, a Lorenz Curve is one way of depicting the extent of income inequality in an economy.

Lump Sum Tax A tax that does not depend on income or level of sales. It is a fixed amount per person, household, or business, for example.

Macroeconomics The study of aggregate economic variables such as gross national product, government spending, the level of taxes, inflation, and unemployment.

Managed Float An exchange rate system with flexible rates characterized by government intervention in the foreign exchange market.

Margin Requirement The percent of the current market price of securities that must be used as a down payment.

Marginal Analysis The analysis of the incremental or additional benefits and costs associated with a particular activity.

Marginal Efficiency of Investment The rate of return, expressed in percentage terms, on an investment.

Marginal Factor Cost The cost to the firm of hiring an additional unit of some given input.

Marginal Product of an Input The addition to output or total product obtained from adding one more unit of the input, keeping the amounts of all other inputs fixed.

Marginal Profit The additional profit the firm can obtain from selling one more unit of output.

Marginal Propensity to Consume The fraction of an additional dollar of disposable income which consumers will spend on consumption goods. The marginal propensity to consume is given by the change in consumption expenditures resulting from a change in disposable income divided by the change in income.

Marginal Propensity to Import The fraction of an increase in income that will be spent on imports.

Marginal Propensity to Save The change in saving that occurs as a result of a change in disposable income divided by the change in income. Thus, the marginal propensity to save is equal to

$$\frac{\text{change in saving}}{\text{change in disposable income}}.$$

Marginal Revenue The change in total revenue as a result of selling one more unit of output.

$$\text{Marginal Revenue} = \frac{\text{change in total revenue}}{\text{change in quantity sold}}.$$

Marginal Revenue Product of an Input The additional revenue generated for the firm by using another unit of that input, assuming the amounts used of all other inputs do not change. It is equal to the marginal product of the input multiplied by the marginal revenue of output.

Marginal Social Benefit (of a good or service) The benefit to society added by the last unit of a good or service produced.

Marginal Social Cost (of a good or service) The cost to society of using resources to produce an additional unit of the good or service rather than to produce something else.

Marginal Utility The additional utility or satisfaction received from one more unit of a good or service.

$$\text{Marginal Utility} = \frac{\text{change in total utility}}{\text{change in quantity of a good}}.$$

Market All of the potential buyers and sellers of a particular good or service.

Market Demand Curve The horizontal sum of the demand curves of the individual consumers in the market for a particular product.

Market Socialism An economic system in which the means of production are publicly owned, but a system of prices approximating a free market is relied on to organize production and distribution.

Microeconomics The study of individual economic units—consumers, firms, government agencies, or specific projects, for example.

Minimum Wage A lower limit which is set on the wage rate of covered workers.

Mixed Capitalistic Economic System An economic system that exhibits the characteristics of a free enterprise economy in much of its economic activity. However, it also makes some economic decisions on a collective level, and some of the productive resources or goods typically are owned by a group.

Mixed Public Goods Goods with the property that some of their benefits (or costs) are private, or exclusive, in nature, while others are public, or nonexclusive.

Money Basically, anything that is widely accepted in exchange for goods and services and as payment for debt. Three more specific definitions are listed below.

M_{1A}: Coin, currency, and demand deposits held by the nonbank public.

M_{1B}: M_{1A} plus NOW accounts, credit union share draft accounts, and demand deposits at mutual savings banks.

M_2: M_{1B} plus savings deposits held by the nonbank public, cash invested in money market mutual funds, and certain overnight investments of funds.

Money Illusion In general, a term which refers to the situation where workers behave as if their money wage rate matters more than their real wage rate.

Monopolistic Competition An industry structure in which there are many firms producing slightly differentiated products. Barriers to entry are relatively small or nonexistent.

Monopoly Power The ability of a firm or group of firms to determine market price by restricting the quantity of output produced. It generally results in higher prices than would otherwise exist.

Monopsonistic Competition A market structure characterized by a relatively large number of buyers, each with some control over the price of the item being purchased.

Monopsony A market with only one buyer.

Most-Favored-Nation Treatment The principle of extending concessions granted one country to all other countries.

Multiplier The number by which an increase in investment or other exogenous spending should be multiplied in order to arrive at the change in the equilibrium level of income. In the simple models used in this text, the multiplier is equal to

$$\frac{1}{1 - \text{MPC}},$$

where MPC is the marginal propensity to consume.

Mutual interdependence A term used to refer to a situation where the market share of one firm is significantly affected by the actions of one or more of its rival firms.

Mutually Exclusive Projects Two projects such that the acceptance of one makes the other one unacceptable, usually because it has become redundant.

National Income According to the national income and product accounts, national income is the earnings of factors of production for their services during the current accounting period.

Natural Monopoly An industry where economies of scale are so large that if two or more firms were to be involved in the production of the industry output, unit cost would be higher than for a monopoly.

Natural Rate of Growth According to Sir Roy Harrod, the maximum possible sustained rate at which an economy can grow, considering both labor force growth and growth of productive capacity.

Natural Rate of Unemployment The rate of unemployment that is consistent with a minimal level of frictional unemployment. Essentially, then, when the economy is at the natural rate of unemployment, it is at full employment.

Negative Income Tax A tax system set up so that people with incomes below a certain level would receive payments from the federal government based on their level of income.

Net Exports The purchases of newly produced goods and services in a country by foreigners, less the purchases of new foreign-produced goods by the country's residents. In other words, *net* exports is equal to exports minus imports for a country.

Net Interest (National Income Account Definition) The interest payments minus the interest receipts of domestic business, plus net interest payments received from foreign sources.

Net Investment In the national income and product accounts and in economics, net investment is the net addition to the nation's capital stock—plant and equipment—during a particular accounting period.

Net Marginal Revenue Marginal revenue of another unit of output minus the cost of component parts or raw materials.

Net National Product (NNP) A measure of the final market value of newly produced goods and services in a country, less the value of plant and equipment and natural resources used up during the production process and as a result of "acts of God" and obsolescence.

Normal Good A good or service with a positive income effect. Consumers buy more of such a good when their real incomes rise and less when their real incomes fall.

Normative Economics Economic statements that involve value judgments or subjective conclusions.

Oligopoly An industry structure in which there are only a few firms. These firms recognize their mutual interdependence, and there are substantial barriers to entry into the industry. The firms may produce either identical or differentiated products.

Oligopsony An industry where there are only a few buyers or a few dominant buyers for the product sold.

Open Market Operations The buying and selling of securities by the Federal Reserve on the open market. *Open market* is a term used to refer to the market for highly liquid, predominantly short-term securities, especially securities of the U.S. government.

Open Shops Firms where employees are not required to be union members.

Opportunity Cost The opportunity cost of doing or choosing one thing over the next best alternative is the forgone benefit that the alternative would have provided.

Origin The zero point on a graph.

Paradox of Thrift An apparent contradiction which refers to the fact that while an individual may save more by being thrifty and spending less out of a given level of income, if a nation as a whole decides to save more, national income may fall and total saving may be no greater than before.

Parity A term used to refer to the situation where farm prices are high enough that crops have the same purchasing power in terms of other commodities as they did in 1910–1914. The period 1910–1914 is often called the "golden age" of agriculture.

Partial Equilibrium Analysis A type of economic analysis which focuses attention on a part of an economic system under the assumption that changes in related elements of the system either will not occur or will not be significant.

Patent Gives an inventor an exclusive right to a formula, method, or device for a specific period of time—seventeen years in the United States.

Paternalism A term which refers to actions by management designed to convince workers that the company would do more for them than a union would.

Payroll Taxes Also called employment taxes, these taxes are based on the payrolls of businesses. They include employer, employee, and self-employed taxes for the federal Old-Age, Survivors, and Disability Insurance (OASDI) system; the federal and state unemployment insurance tax on employers; and the railroad retirement tax on employers and employees.

Per Capita GNP The level of a country's GNP divided by the level of its population.

Perfect Competition An industry structure in which there are many small firms producing homogeneous products, and each firm accepts the market price for its product as a "given." From the buyer side of the market, a perfectly competitive market is a market such that no buyer acting alone has enough market power to be able to affect the market price of the product or input being sold.

Personal Income The income that individuals actually receive during the current accounting period, whether or not it is payment for productive services.

Personal Income Taxes Taxes levied on the taxable income of individuals.

Personal Saving The portion of personal disposable income that is not spent.

Phillips Curve A general term used to denote wage rate growth (or inflation)-unemployment trade-off relationships. These relationships were called Phillips curves in honor of A.W. Phillips, who did pioneering work in this area.

Plant A set of production facilities for a firm. For example, General Motors has plants in Detroit, Flint, Mexico City, and elsewhere.

Pollution Standard Index (PSI) A system which the federal government uses to classify the overall quality of air in a particular area. The pollution standard index value is assigned according to the levels of five major air pollutants: total suspended particulates, sulphur dioxide, carbon monoxide, ozone, and nitrogen dioxide.

Positive Economics Objective economic statements that explain that if certain conditions hold, then certain things can be expected to happen.

Precautionary Demand for Money The demand for money which arises because people believe that they must keep some cash balances on hand to meet unforeseen needs.

Present Value The present value of a future payment or series of payments represents the amount received today that is equivalent in value to the future payment or payments.

Present Value Interest Factor At an interest rate equal to i for t time periods, or PVIF $(i\%, t)$ is

$$\text{equal to } \frac{1}{(1 + i)^t}.$$

The present value interest factor is the factor by which an amount to be received in the future should be multiplied to obtain the equivalent value of funds received today.

Price Discrimination The practice of charging more than one price for identical units of a firm's product.

Price Elasticity of Demand The ratio of the percentage change in the quantity demanded of a good or service to the percentage change in its price.

$$E_p = \frac{\text{percent change in quantity demanded}}{\text{percent change in price}}$$

Price Fixing A practice whereby a group of firms get together and agree to set the price of a final or intermediate product at a specific level.

Price Index Gives an indication of the level of prices in a current year relative to the level of prices in some base year. In general, price indexes are computed as follows:

$$\text{Price index} = \frac{\text{Prices}_{\text{current year}}}{\text{Prices}_{\text{base year}}} \times 100.$$

Price Subsidy Program A program whereby the government agrees to pay farmers a subsidy equal to the difference between a set support price, P_o, and the market price, P_M, that they receive when their crop is sold.

Price Support-Loan-Crop Storage Program A program whereby the government agrees to support farm prices at a particular level. It does so by giving farmers loans equal to the value of their crops, figured at the support price levels.

Primary Deposit A deposit that represents new reserves brought into the banking system.

Primary Producing Countries A large group of developing countries, each of which is highly specialized in exporting either industrial raw materials or agricultural products (or some combination of the two).

Principle of Absolute Advantage The economic principle which states that a country's exports will consist of goods that it can produce with fewer resources per unit of output than can its trading partners. Similarly, it will import those goods that its trading partners can produce with fewer resources per unit of output than the country itself would need to produce the same goods. (The principle applies to persons and regions as well as to countries.)

Principle of Comparative Advantage The economic principle which states that a country will export goods that are relatively cheap compared with other goods it can produce in terms of the resource cost per unit of output. Its imports will consist of goods that are relatively expensive to produce at home. (The principle also applies to persons and regions.)

Principle of Diminishing Marginal Utility A principle which states that as more and more units of a particular good or service are consumed during a specific time period, after some point the marginal

utility associated with one more unit of the item will tend to decrease.

Principle of Increasing Cost The economic principle which states that as an economy produces more and more of one good and less of a second good, the amount of the second good that must be given up in exchange for one more unit of the first good will increase.

Private Costs Those costs, both explicit and implicit, which a firm incurs.

Production Function A production function for a firm's product specifies the technological relationship between the amounts of various inputs the firm can use and the resulting maximum level of output it can produce.

Production Possibilities Curve Curve which indicates the various combinations of two goods or services that can be produced by a country or other economic entity when, in a technological sense, all of its resources are fully and efficiently utilized.

Profit The return to owners of business firms for their innovative skills and risk taking. The return to entrepreneurship.

Profit-Maximization Making the greatest profit (legally) possible.

Profit-Maximization Decision Rule The rule that states that a firm will maximize profit by producing where marginal revenue is equal to marginal cost, as long as price is greater than or equal to average variable cost.

Progressive Tax A tax whose rate rises as income increases. Thus those with high incomes pay a greater percentage of their incomes as tax than do those with lower incomes.

Property Taxes Taxes imposed on owners of property.

Proportional Tax A tax for which people pay the same percentage of their incomes regardless of their level of income.

Proprietors' Income The monetary earnings and payments in kind of sole proprietorships, partnerships, and producers' cooperatives from current business operations.

Protestant Ethic Thesis The thesis which states that the rapid growth of the capitalist countries occurred because of protestant attitudes toward work and profit.

Public Aid Programs Programs consisting of transfer payments financed from general tax revenues. These payments do not depend on an individual's past earnings, and do depend on an individual's current earnings.

Public Good A good whose benefits cannot be limited to those who directly pay for it.

Pure Capitalism An economic system based on private ownership and the freedom of individuals to conduct their economic affairs without interference from government bodies or other groups.

Pure Monopoly An industry consisting of only one firm. The market demand for its product constitutes the only constraint on the price charged by the firm.

Pure Public Good A product or service all of whose benefits have the property that they are nondivisible (cannot be broken up into individual units) and nonexclusive (impossible to limit to individuals who have paid for the good).

Quantity Demanded The amount of a good or service that consumers are willing and able to buy at a particular price.

Quantity Supplied The amount of a good or service that producers will make available for sale during a particular period of time at a given price, other things equal.

Quasi-Rent The return to productive factors, excluding labor, that in the short run are fixed.

Quota An *import* quota is a specific quantitative limit on the amount of some product that importers can bring into a country. An *export* quota is a specific quantitative limit on the amount of some product that exporters can ship out of a country.

Rational Expectations Hypothesis The hypothesis that people take current information about government economic policies and other economic variables as well as events in the recent past into account when formulating their expectations about future events.

Real Gross National Product Gross national product valued at the prices prevailing during some base period.

Regressive Tax A tax for which the percentage of income paid out in tax falls as income rises. Therefore, those with low incomes pay a proportionately greater share relative to their level of income than do those with high incomes.

Rent Payment made for the use of land (natural resources.) A payment for a factor of production that is fixed in terms of the quantity supplied.

Rental Income (National Income Account Definition) The monetary earnings from the rental of real property, including the estimated net rental returns to owner-occupied nonfarm dwellings.

Required reserves The required reserves of a financial institution are equal to the reserve requirement multiplied by the dollar amount of the institution's deposit liabilities.

Reserve Army of the Unemployed A term used by Karl Marx to refer to former workers who had been replaced by machines

Reserve Requirements Rules that banks maintain reserves equal to a certain percentage of their deposit liabilities.

Revaluation (of a Currency) An increase in the par value of a country's currency in a fixed exchange rate system.

Roundabout Method of Production A method of production involving the use of capital (machinery, plant). Such a method is called roundabout because the equipment is made before consumer goods are produced.

Rule of Reason A philosophy which holds that size alone is not illegal as long as a firm acts within reasonable limits and does not abuse its position.

Sales Tax A tax imposed on the sale of a large number of commodities.

Saving Function Gives the relationship between saving and disposable income.

Say's Law The economic principle, espoused by Jean-Baptiste Say, that supply implies its own demand. According to Say, no one produces except to consume or sell that which is produced. Moreover, no one sells an item except to buy something else with the proceeds of the sale. Thus, Say did not think that there could be a situation where the aggregate quantity supplied of goods and services would exceed the aggregate quantity demanded.

Secondary Boycotts or Strikes Boycotts or strikes called against a third party, which uses or is in some way involved with the products of an employer against whom the union has a direct strike for higher wages or other matters.

Simple Interest Interest paid only on the original amount invested.

Short Run A time period so short that at least one of the inputs of a firm is fixed.

Short-Run Average Cost Short-run total cost per unit of output. Short-run average cost is equal to short-run total cost divided by quantity of output. It is also equal to average fixed cost plus average variable cost.

Short-Run Average Variable Cost Variable cost per unit of output produced.

$$\text{AVC} = \frac{\text{total variable cost}}{\text{quantity of output}}.$$

Short-Run Marginal Cost The addition to total variable cost from producing one more unit of output.

$$\text{SMC} = \frac{\text{change in total variable cost}}{\text{change in quantity of output}}.$$

Short-Run Total Cost The sum of all of a firm's short-run costs. Since costs must be either fixed or variable, short-run total cost is equal to total fixed cost plus total variable cost.

Short-Run Total Variable Cost The sum of all of the costs of the firm that vary with the level of the firm's output in the short run.

Slope The slope of a line gives the rate of change of the dependent variable (variable measured along the vertical axis) with respect to a change in the independent variable (the variable measured along the horizontal axis). The slope of a straight line is given by

$$\text{Slope} = \frac{\text{change in vertical distance}}{\text{change in horizontal distance}}.$$

Social Benefit The social benefit of a good or service is the benefit its production brings to society as a whole.

Social Cost The social cost of a good or service is the cost that society as a whole incurs as a result of the production of the good or service.

Social Insurance Programs Programs financed primarily through payroll taxes on employers or employees. Payments under such programs usually depend on the recipient's past earnings.

Social Rate of Discount The discount rate used for evaluating public goods projects.

Speculation Taking a position in (holding) a currency or any other item based on the belief that its value will rise in the future.

Speculative Demand for Money According to Keynes, the demand for money which exists because people desire to hold part of their wealth in the form of money for investment reasons.

Stagflation A term used to denote a recession occurring simultaneously with inflation.

State Trading Agency The governmental unit that carries on virtually all the international trade activities of a centrally planned economy.

Stationary State The state of an economic system when real output and population remain about the same size.

Structural Unemployment Unemployment which occurs when unemployed workers do not have the skills or other attributes required for the available jobs.

Structuralists A group of people who adhere to the philosophy that large size (relative to the entire market) alone will always result in the undesirable effects of a monopoly—high price, low output, and an economic profit.

Substitute Goods Goods which can be used in place of one another. For example, coffee and tea are substitute goods. Substitute goods have a positive cross price elasticity of demand.

Substitution Effect The effect of a price change on consumers' purchases of the good whose price has changed because the good is now cheaper or more expensive relative to other goods than it was before the price change. For example, if the price of a good falls, consumers tend to substitute purchases of that good for purchases of other goods and services.

Superior Goods Normal goods with an income elasticity of demand greater than one.

Supply Curve A graphical representation of a supply schedule.

Supply Function Describes the relationship between the quantity of a product supplied and a set of variables that determine it.

Supply Schedule A table that relates the quantity supplied of a good or service during some time period to the various possible prices of that good or service.

Target Prices With respect to agriculture, prices the government considers to be fair prices for wheat, feed grains, cotton, and rice.

Tariff An *import* tariff is a tax that a country's government imposes on foreign goods allowed to enter the country for sale to its residents. An *export* tariff is a tax imposed on goods sold to the residents of foreign countries.

Tax Multiplier The number by which a change in lump sum taxes imposed should be multiplied to get the resulting change in the equilibrium level of income. In the simple model used in this text, the tax multiplier is equal to

$$\frac{-MPC}{1 - MPC}.$$

Terms of Trade Index A ratio of the price index of a country's exports to a price index of its imports.

Time Draft An order to pay at some future date. It is drawn by an exporter against an importer's account.

Total Fixed Cost The sum of all of the firm's costs which do not vary with the level of output in the short run.

Total Product of a Variable Input The maximum level of output that can be produced using different amounts of the variable input and a fixed amount of the other inputs.

Total Profit The total economic profit of a firm. The total profit of a firm is equal to total revenue minus total cost, including all opportunity costs.

Total Revenue The total dollar sales of a particular good or service for a firm. The total revenue received from the sale of a good or service is equal to the price of the product multiplied by the quantity sold.

Total Utility The total amount of want satisfaction obtained by a consumer or society.

Trade Deficit The amount by which a country's imports exceed its exports over some specific period of time.

Trade Liberalization The removal or reduction of restrictions on international trade.

Trademark A distinctive word, name, symbol, device, or combination thereof used by a manufacturer to distinguish its goods from those of other firms. According to federal law, a trademark can be registered for twenty years.

Trade Surplus The amount by which a country's exports exceed its imports.

Traditional Economy An economy where economic matters are largely determined by social or religious customs and traditions.

Transactions Demand For Money The demand for money stemming from the fact that businesses and individuals need to hold money in some form (demand or similar deposits or currency and coin) to pay for their day-to-day purchases and make other necessary payments.

Transfer Payments Payments between economic units for which no productive services are currently received in return.

Tying Agreement An agreement whereby a firm agrees that the goods sold or leased by another firm will be used only with other goods of the seller or lessor.

Unemployed Persons Include (1) all civilians who had no employment during the survey week, who had made specific efforts to find a job (such as by applying directly to an employer or to a public employment service or by checking with friends) within the previous four weeks, and who were available for work during the survey week; and (2) persons laid off from a job or waiting to report to a new job within thirty days.

Union Shop Agreements Agreements which stipulate that employees must join the union within thirty days of being hired if the union is the duly certified bargaining agent.

Unitary Elastic Price Elasticity of Demand Demand for a product is unitary elastic with respect to price if the percentage change in quantity demanded is equal to the percentage change in price (in absolute value). A change in price will not cause a change in total revenue.

Value-Added Tax A tax imposed on the value added to a good at each stage of production.

Value of the Marginal Product of an Input The value of the marginal product of an input is equal to the marginal product of the input multiplied by the price of the output produced.

Variable Costs Costs that increase or decrease as the level of output increases or decreases.

Vertical Merger The merger of two firms where one firm produces a product used by the second firm as an intermediate good or component part in the production of its product.

Wage and Price Controls Mandatory ceilings for wage and price increases established by the federal government.

Wage and Price Guideposts or Guidelines Largely voluntary policies of the federal government which establish certain standards for wage rate and price increases.

Wages and Salaries Payments made for the services of labor.

Warranted Rate of Growth According to Sir Roy Harrod, the rate of growth that will bring forth sufficient aggregate demand to maintain full capacity use of the capital stock.

Welfare State An economic system in which high priority is placed on the elimination of economic hardships and social ills such as poverty, unemployment, lack of education, inadequate health care, and general personal or family distress.

Yellow-Dog Contract A contract between an employee and his employer in which the employee agrees not to join a union.

INDEX

†

Consumer Price Indexes, Major Expenditure Classes, 1950–1981
[1967 = 100]

Year or Month	All Items	Food and Beverages		Housing				Apparel and Upkeep	Trans-portation	Medical Care	Enter-tainment	Other Goods and Services	Energy[4]
		Total[1]	Food	Total[2]	Rent, Residential	Home Ownership	Fuel and Other Utilities[3]						
1950	72.1	....	74.5	72.8	70.4	....	....	79.0	68.2	53.7	....	....	....
1951	77.8	....	82.8	77.2	73.2	....	....	86.1	72.5	56.3	....	....	
1952	79.5	....	84.3	78.7	76.2	....	....	85.3	77.3	59.3	....	....	
1953	80.1	....	83.0	80.8	80.3	75.0	83.0	84.6	79.5	61.4	....	....	
1954	80.5	....	82.8	81.7	83.2	76.3	83.5	84.5	78.3	63.4	....	....	
1955	80.2	....	81.6	82.3	84.3	77.0	85.1	84.1	77.4	64.8	....	....	
1956	81.4	....	82.2	83.6	85.9	78.3	87.3	85.8	78.8	67.2	....	....	
1957	84.3	....	84.9	86.2	87.5	81.7	89.9	87.3	83.3	69.9	....	....	90.1
1958	86.6	....	88.5	87.7	89.1	83.5	91.7	87.5	86.0	73.2	....	....	90.3
1959	87.3	....	87.1	88.6	90.4	84.4	93.8	88.2	89.6	76.4	....	....	91.8
1960	88.7	....	88.0	90.2	91.7	86.3	95.9	89.6	89.6	79.1	....	....	94.2
1961	89.6	....	89.1	90.9	92.9	86.9	97.1	90.4	90.6	81.4	....	....	94.4
1962	90.6	....	89.9	91.7	94.0	87.9	97.3	90.9	92.5	83.5	....	....	94.7
1963	91.7	....	91.2	92.7	95.0	89.0	98.2	91.9	93.0	85.6	....	....	95.0
1964	92.9	....	92.4	93.8	95.9	90.8	98.4	92.7	94.3	87.3	....	....	94.6
1965	94.5	....	94.4	94.9	96.9	92.7	98.3	93.7	95.9	89.5	....	....	96.3
1966	97.2	....	99.1	97.2	98.2	96.3	98.8	96.1	97.2	93.4	....	....	97.8
1967	100.0	100.0	100.0	100.0	100.0	100.0	100.0	100.0	100.0	100.0	100.0	100.0	100.0
1968	104.2	103.6	103.6	104.0	102.4	105.7	101.3	105.4	103.2	106.1	105.7	105.2	101.5
1969	109.8	108.8	108.9	110.4	105.7	116.0	103.6	111.5	107.2	113.4	111.0	110.4	104.2
1970	116.3	114.7	114.9	118.2	110.1	128.5	107.6	116.1	112.7	120.6	116.7	116.8	107.0
1971	121.3	118.3	118.4	123.4	115.2	133.7	115.0	119.8	118.6	128.4	122.9	122.4	111.2
1972	125.3	123.2	123.5	128.1	119.2	140.1	120.1	122.3	119.9	132.5	126.5	127.5	114.3
1973	133.1	139.5	141.4	133.7	124.3	146.7	126.9	126.8	123.8	137.7	130.0	132.5	123.5
1974	147.7	158.7	161.7	148.8	130.6	163.2	150.2	136.2	137.7	150.5	139.8	142.0	159.7
1975	161.2	172.1	175.4	164.5	137.3	181.7	167.8	142.3	150.6	168.6	152.2	153.9	176.6
1976	170.5	177.4	180.8	174.6	144.7	191.7	182.7	147.6	165.5	184.7	159.8	162.7	189.3
1977	181.5	188.0	192.2	186.5	153.5	204.9	202.2	154.2	177.2	202.4	167.7	172.2	207.3
1978	195.4	206.3	211.4	202.8	164.0	227.2	216.0	159.6	185.5	219.4	176.6	183.3	220.4
1979	217.4	228.5	234.5	227.6	176.0	262.4	239.3	166.6	212.0	239.7	188.5	196.7	275.9
1980	244.7	247.5	254.2	260.6	191.2	311.0	272.2	177.9	246.3	264.2	203.3	214.6	347.0
1981 (Oct.)	279.9	270.3	277.6	303.5	213.6	366.7	330.1	191.5	287.2	304.8	225.5	245.2	414.9

[1] Includes alcoholic beverages, not shown separately.

[2] Includes other items, not shown separately. Series beginning 1967 not comparable with series for earlier years.

[3] Fuel oil, coal, and bottled gas; gas (piped) and electricity; and other utilities and public services.

[4] Fuel oil, coal, and bottled gas; gas (piped) and electricity; and gasoline, motor oil, coolant, etc.

Note.—Data beginning 1978 are for all urban consumers; earlier data are for urban wage earners and clerical workers.

Source: Department of Labor, Bureau of Labor Statistics.